Dictionary of
Real People and Places
in Fiction

Editorial staff

Michelle Darraugh
Kerry Munro
Betty Palmer
Emma Waghorn
Julian Zinovieff

Dictionary of
Real People and Places
in Fiction

M.C. Rintoul

LONDON AND NEW YORK

First published in 1993
by Routledge
11 New Fetter Lane, London EC4P 4EE

Simultaneously published in the USA and Canada
by Routledge, Inc.
29 West 35th Street, New York, NY 10001

© 1993 Routledge

Set in Palatino, 600 DPI, by Quorum Technical Services Ltd,
Cheltenham, Gloucestershire
Printed in Great Britain by Clays Ltd, St Ives plc

British Library Cataloguing in Publication Data
A catalogue record for this book is available from the British Library.

Library of Congress Cataloging-in-Publication Data
A catalog record for this book is available on request.

ISBN 0–415–05999–2

Contents

User's Guide

The *Dictionary of Real People and Places in Fiction* might more fully be described as a dictionary of real people, animals, houses, towns, roads, clubs, societies, newspapers, magazines, ships, etc., upon which fictional entities are thought to have been based. The book is divided into four sections: 1 *Authors*, 2 *Real Names*, 3 *Fictional Names*, and 4 *Index of Titles*. It is the second section that forms the core of the book, and the other three sections can be used as access routes to the detailed information it contains.

1 Authors

For each novel or short story included in the *Dictionary*, this section provides a summary of the links between fictional and real names. It is ordered alphabetically first by author and then by the title of the novel or short story. Under each work, an alphabetical list of fictional names is provided, each with its corresponding real name(s).

2 Real Names

This section lists names of real people, places, etc., upon which fictional people, places, etc., are thought to have been based. Biographical information or a brief description is then generally given, followed by the names of the fictional counterparts, which are listed alphabetically. The title, author and year of publication of the work in which the fictional name appears are given, together with the source(s) for the identification and a quotation where relevant. Where a fictional name is a composite of more than one real name, cross-references to other real-name entries are given after the source.

3 Fictional Names

This section provides an alphabetical list of all fictional names included in this book. Each is followed by the title, publication date and author of the work in which the fictional name appears, and the corresponding real name(s). Where a fictional name occurs in works of more than one author, the works are listed chronologically.

4 Index of Titles

This index provides a starting point for accessing the *Dictionary* when the author of a work is not known. It is an alphabetical list of all the novels and short stories covered by the *Dictionary*, together with the names of their authors, and thus leads the reader to the information contained in the *Authors* section.

Alphabetization

Overall, alphabetization is word by word. Surnames beginning with the prefixes 'La' or 'Du' are treated as one word for the purposes of alphabetization. In ordering surnames beginning with 'von' and 'de', these prefixes are generally ignored, unless the people concerned are naturalized in Britain or the United States, e.g. De Angelis. Hyphenated names are treated as two words, Mc is treated as Mac and St as Saint, and apostrophes are ignored.

For both fictional and real names of people, alphabetization is by surname, and then by forename. In entries with forenames, titles are ignored, but those that have titles only are ordered alphabetically by title and appear before those with forenames, and after those that have surnames only. Thus: Smith, Dr Smith, Revd Smith, Mary Smith, Revd Percy Smith, Lord Roger Smith, Vincent Smith.

Throughout the book, street numbers are ignored for the purposes of alphabetization, as are definite and indefinite articles when they appear as the first word.

Typography

Bold face has been used throughout the *Dictionary* for real names that have an entry in the *Real Names* section; in particular, it has been used in that section to indicate cross-references. Small capitals have been used for fictional names that have an entry in the *Fictional Names* section. Throughout the book, real people with identical names are differentiated by superscript numbers, e.g. John Gray[1] and John Gray[2].

Preface

I began to compile this *Dictionary* in 1964, after my husband had died and both my children had left home. The impetus was my reading books by a group of American writers who had lived in Paris in the 1920s, and I found these novels all the more interesting because many of them seemed to be *romans-à-clef*.

I began to collect information about the real-life identities of fictional characters and places, although I never sat down and identified a character myself. Most of the information was gathered from letters and biographies, and some came from sources close to the authors. Some of it, however, was gleaned from personal conversations and other contact with the authors themselves. For example, Angus Wilson, whom I met in the 1930s when we were both working on a British Library catalogue, made inscriptions in my own copies of his novels that identified the real people used as the bases of his characters. His *Old Men at the Zoo* was more or less a direct portrayal of the Library.

This compilation could never have been completed without the cohorts of friends and generous informants who have given me unstinted and invaluable help during the long gestation period of the book. Their names are listed below, but that is a poor acknowledgement of what I owe to them. I must in particular single out Mrs Alida Lessard, of St James, Long Island, who shared with me her wide acquaintance in the twentieth-century American literary world, and Mrs Robert Mathew, whose mother, Lady Young, had an equally wide knowledge (personal or inherited) of an equivalent, though earlier, circle in England. For ungrudging patient encouragement, I am indebted above all to Professor Kathleen Tillotson.

I owe thanks to: Sir Harold Acton; Mrs Anabel Anrep; Sir Thomas Armstrong; Miss Betty Askwith; Mr and Mrs Noel Blakiston; Miss Betty Bostetter; Professor James Boulton; Mr John Byrne; Mr and Mrs John Carswell; Mr and Mrs Richard Chilver, Mrs Louis Henry Cohen; Donald Darling; Dan Davin; Mrs Nicolette Devas-Shephard; Margaret Drabble; Mrs Georgia Dunbar; Mr H.I. Dutton; Mrs Herbert Farjeon; Mrs Denis Farr; Penelope Fitzgerald; Victoria Glendinning; Professor J.E. Gordon; Professor Gordon Haight; Hamish Hamilton; Sir Rupert Hart-Davis; Mr Louis Heydemann, of Tenerife; Norah Hoult; Professor Samuel Hynes; Elizabeth Jenkins; Sir Thomas Kendrick; Dr Joseph Kissane; Brian Lake; Marghanita Laski; James Lees-Milne; Mrs Alida Lessard; William McBrien; Lady Mander; Mrs Robert Mathew; Henry Maxwell; A.T.B. Munby; John Needham; Nigel Nicolson; Mrs Edward Norman-Butler; Mrs Janet Percival; Mr John Potter; Sir Victor Pritchett; John Sandoe; Professor Bernard Sarasin; Mr Saumarez-Smith; Rupert Shepherd; Sheila Smith; Lionel Stevenson; Michael Summerskill; Sir John Summerson; William and Aileen Tatton-Brown; Professor Kathleen Tillotson; L. Wallrich; Alan Watkins; Sir Angus Wilson; the late Lady Winnifrith; Hiram Winterbotham; Armine Wright.

I am also grateful to: the staff of the Buckingham Palace Road branch of Westminster Library; the staff of the Public Library at Purley; the staff of the Dickens House Museum; James Bristow, Assistant Librarian in charge of pictures, Bodleian Library, Oxford; Ruth Kamen, Head of the Information Service, British Architectural Library; Jill Miller, of the Alexander Turnbull Library, National Library of New Zealand, Wellington; Ohio State University Libraries; Miss J.L. Hurn, Registrar, Royal Holloway College; The Secretary, The Savile Club; Sotheby & Co.

I owe a particular debt to the staff of the Reading Room of the British Library, and an even greater one to the London Library, whose lending policy made it possible for me to continue my work during long periods spent abroad. I must also acknowledge my continuing gratitude to four London booksellers: Heywood Hill, Jarndyce, Bertram Rota and John Sandoe.

M.C.R.

1

Authors

A

ACKERLEY, J.R.
Hindoo Holiday (1932)
MAHARAJAH OF CHHOKRAPUR   Maharajah of Chhatarpur

ADAMS, Henry
Democracy (1880)
VICTORIA DARE   Emily Beale
NATHAN GORE   James Russell Lowell
                                          John Lothrop Motley
BARON JACOBI   Grégoire Aristarchi Bey
MADELEINE ADAMS   Henry Adams
                                          Marian Adams
                                          Mrs Bigelow Lawrence
OLD GRANITE   Rutherford Birchard Hayes
SILAS P. RATCLIFFE   James G. Blaine
SYBIL ROSS   Fanny Chapman

Esther (1884)
CATHERINE BROOKE   Elizabeth Cameron
JOHN CARRINGTON   James Lowndes
ESTHER DUDLEY   Marian Adams
WILLIAM DUDLEY   Robert William Hooper
STEPHEN HAZARD   Phillips Brooks
GEORGE STRONG   Clarence King
MR WHARTON   William Sturgis Bigelow
                                          John La Farge
                                          Augustus Saint-Gaudens

ADAMS, Samuel Hopkins
Revelry (1926)
DAN LURCOCK   Harry M. Daugherty
WILLIS MARKHAM   Warren G. Harding

AIKEN, Conrad
'The Orange Moth' (1925)
BUTLER   J.B. Yeats
COOKE   Van Wyck Brooks

'Your Obituary, Well Written' (1928)
REINE WILSON   Katherine Mansfield

AINSWORTH, W. Harrison
The Miser's Daughter (1842)
JOHN SCARVE   John Elwes (or John Meggott)

Rookwood: A Romance (1834)
ROOKWOOD HALL   **Cuckfield Place, Sussex**

ALCOTT, Louisa M.
Jo's Boys (1886)
PLUMFIELD   **Sanborn's School, Concord,**
                                                  Massachusetts

MR TIBER   **Thomas Niles**

Little Men (1871)
PLUMFIELD   **Sanborn's School, Concord,**
                                                  Massachusetts

Little Women (1868) and sequels
FRIEDRICH BHAER   **William Rimmer**
                                                    Reinhold Solger
JOHN BROOKE   **John Bridge Pratt**
MR HYDE   **Henry David Thoreau**
MR LAURENCE   **Colonel Joseph May**
THEODORE LAURENCE ('LAURIE')   **Alfred Whitman**
                                                    Frederick Llewellyn Willis
                                                    Ladislas Wisniewski
MR MARCH   **Bronson Alcott**
MRS MARCH ('MARMEE')   **Abigail Alcott**
AMY MARCH   **May Alcott**
BETH MARCH   **Elizabeth Alcott**
JO MARCH   **Louisa May Alcott**
MEG MARCH   **Anna Alcott**
PLUMFIELD   **Temple School, Boston**

Moods (1865)
ADAM WARWICK   **Henry David Thoreau**

Work (1873)
HEPSEY JOHNSON   **Harriet Tubman**
REVD THOMAS POWER   **Theodore Parker**
DAVID STERLING   **Henry David Thoreau**

ALDINGTON, Richard
All Men are Enemies (1933)
HENRY SCROPE   **Wilfrid Scawen Blunt**

Death of a Hero (1929)
MR SHOBBE   **Ford Madox Ford**

'Now Lies She There', *Soft Answers* (1932)
CONSTANCE TOWNSEND   **Nancy Cunard**

Stepping Heavenward (1931)
JEREMY PRATT CIBBER   **T.S. Eliot**

ALDRICH, T.B.
The Story of a Bad Boy (1870)
TOM BAILEY · **T.B. Aldrich**
RIVERMOUTH · **Portsmouth, New Hampshire**

ALLINGHAM, Margery
Death of a Ghost (1934)
JOHN LAFCADIO · **Augustus John**

More Work for the Undertaker (1948) and others
CHARLES LUKE · **Charles Williams**

ANDERSON, Sherwood
'A Meeting South', *Death in the Woods* (1933)
DAVID · **William Faulkner**

Windy McPherson's Son (1916)
SAM MCPHERSON · **Sherwood Anderson**
WINDY MCPHERSON · **Irwin Anderson**

ANGOFF, Charles
Between Day and Night (1959) and others
HARRY F. BRANDT · **H.L. Mencken**

ANON.
Harold the Exile (1819)
LORD HAROLD AUGUSTUS · **Lord Byron**

Memoirs of an Unfortunate Young Nobleman (1743–7)
JAMES DE ALTAMONT · **James Annesley**

Probation and Other Tales (1832)
MRS SYDNEY HUME · **Mrs Anne Murray Keith**

ARLEN, Michael
The Green Hat (1924)
MR CHERRY-MARVEL · **Harry Melvill**
IRIS MARCH · **Nancy Cunard**
Duff, Lady Twysden
THE LOYALTY CLUB · **The Embassy Club, Soho, London**

Young Men in Love (1927)
REGINALD, 11TH EARL OF MOUNT WYROC · **Lord Castlerosse**

von ARNIM, Elizabeth

See 'Elizabeth'

ATHERTON, Gertrude
'The Bell in the Fog' (1905)
RALPH ORTH · **Henry James**

AUSTEN, Jane
Mansfield Park (1814)

MARY CRAWFORD	Eliza Austen
MANSFIELD PARK	Cottesbrooke Hall, Northamptonshire
	Godmersham Park, Kent
WILLIAM PRICE	Charles John Austen

Persuasion (1818)

CAPTAIN HARVILLE	Sir Francis Austen

B

BAGNOLD, Enid
The Loved and Envied (1951)

RUBY, LADY MACLEAN	Lady Diana Cooper

National Velvet (1935)

MR TAYLOR	McHardy

Serena Blandish (1924)

COUNTESS FLOR DI FOLIO	Catherine, Baroness d'Erlanger

BARING, Maurice
C (1924)

CARYL BRAMSLEY ('C')	Maurice Baring
	Lord Revelstoke
LEILA BUCKNELL	Lady Desborough
	Countess of Lytton

Friday's Business (1932)

STANISLAUS RICHARD DUCROS	J.D. Bourchier

'A Luncheon Party', *Half a Minute's Silence and Other Stories* (1925)

HEREWARD BLENHEIM	Winston Churchill
MONSIEUR FAUBOURG	Paul Bourget
RICHARD GILES	Edmund Gosse
OSMOND HALL	George Bernard Shaw
COUNT SCIARRA	Count Pasolini
SIR HORACE SILVESTER	Sir Edgar Vincent
LADY IRENE SILVESTER	Lady Helen Vincent

BARNES, Djuna
'The Grande Malade' (1962)

MOYDIA AND KATYA	Bronia and Tanya Perlmutter
MONSIEUR X	Raymond Radiguet

The Ladies Almanack (1928)

BOUNDING BESS	Esther Murphy

LADY BUCK-AND-BALK	Radclyffe Hall
EVANGELINE MUSSET	Natalie Clifford Barney
CLITORESSA, DUCHESS OF NATESCOURT	Elisabeth, Duchesse de Clermont-Tonnerre
TILLY TWEED-IN-BLOOD	Una, Lady Troubridge

Nightwood (1936)

MATTHEW O'CONNOR	Daniel A. Mahoney
FELIX VOLKBEIN	Guido Bruno
ROBIN VOTE	Thelma Wood

Ryder (1928)

MATTHEW O'CONNOR	Daniel A. Mahoney

BEACH, J.W.
Glass Mountain (1930)

MAX HARDER	Ernest Hemingway
NORMA HARDER	Hadley Hemingway

BECHER STOWE, Harriet
Uncle Tom's Cabin (1851–2)

UNCLE TOM	Josiah Henson

BEERBOHM, Max
The Happy Hypocrite (1897)

JENNY MERE	Marie Cecilia ('Cissy') Loftus

'James Pethel', *Seven Men* (1919)

JAMES PETHEL	Arthur Hannay

'Maltby and Braxton', *Seven Men* (1919)

STEPHEN BRAXTON	W.B. Yeats
LADY THISBE CROWBOROUGH	Lady Helen Vincent
DUCHESS OF HERTFORDSHIRE	Lady Desborough
KEEB HALL	Taplow Court, Buckinghamshire
LADY RODFITTEN	Lady Londonderry

'Walter Argallo and Felix Ledgett', *A Variety of Things* (1928)

WALTER ARGALLO	Joseph Conrad
FELIX LEDGETT	Alfred Sutro

Zuleika Dobson (1911)

ZULEIKA DOBSON	Constance Collier

BELL, Robert
The Ladder of Gold: An English Story (1850)

RICHARD RAWLINGS	George Hudson

BELLOW, Saul
Humboldt's Gift (1975)

VON HUMBOLDT FLEISCHER	Delmore Schwartz

Seize the Day (1957)
TOMMY WILHELM   **Delmore Schwartz**

BENÉT, William Rose
The Dust Which is God (1941)
LARRY HARRIS   **Sinclair Lewis**
STEVE MANTON   **Tom Mooney**
NORA RAFFERTY   **Theresa Frances Benét**

BENNETT, Arnold
Buried Alive (1908)
PRIAM FARLL   **James Wilson Morrice**

The Card (1911)
COUNTESS OF CHELL   **Duchess of Sutherland**
EDWARD HENRY ('DENRY') MACHIN   **H.K. Hales**

The *Clayhanger* trilogy: *Clayhanger* (1910), *Hilda Lessways* (1911), and
    These Twain (1916)
BLEAKRIDGE   **Cobridge, Burslem, Staffordshire**
THE *CHRONICLE*   **The *Staffordshire Knot***
DARIUS CLAYHANGER   **John Beardmore**
                                                 Enoch Bennett
                                                 Charles Shaw
EDWIN CLAYHANGER   **Edward Harry Beardmore**
                                                 Arnold Bennett
MRS CLARA HAMPS   **Sarah Bennett**
                                                 Frances Bourne
THE HOUSEKEEPER   **Beatrice Collings**
15 LESSWAYS STREET, TURNHILL   **175 Newport Lane, Burslem,**
                                                   Staffordshire
OSMOND ORGREAVE   **Absalom W. Wood**
THE PAGEBOY AT THE ROYAL SUSSEX   **Hardy**
    HOTEL
ROYAL SUSSEX HOTEL   **Royal York Hotel, Brighton**
ST LUKE'S SQUARE   **St John's Square, Burslem,**
                                                   Staffordshire
THE *SIGNAL*   **The *Staffordshire Sentinel***
TRAFALGAR ROAD   **Waterloo Road, Burslem,**
                                                   Staffordshire

Anna of the Five Towns (1902) and others
AXE   **Leek, Staffordshire**
DUCK BANK AND DUCK SQUARE   **Swan Bank and Swan Square**
KNYPE   **Stoke, Staffordshire**
LONGSHAW   **Longton, Staffordshire**
MANEFOLD   **Leek, Staffordshire**
TOFT END   **Sneyd Green, Staffordshire**
TURNHILL   **Tunstall, Staffordshire**

The Imperial Palace (1930)
THE IMPERIAL PALACE   **Savoy Hotel, London**

Lilian (1922)
LORD MACKWORTH   **Lord Castlerosse**

Lord Raingo (1926)
ANDY CLYTH   **David Lloyd George**
TOM HOGARTH   **Winston Churchill**
LORD RAINGO   **Arnold Bennett**
    1st Viscount Rhondda
    Edwin Alfred Rickards

The Man from the North (1898)
MR AKED   **John Eland**
CURPET & SMYTHE   **Le Brasseur & Oakley**
RICHARD LARCH   **Arnold Bennett**
NEW SERJEANT'S INN   **New Court, Lincoln's Inn Fields, London**

THE *TRIFLER*   *Tit-Bits*

The Old Wives' Tale (1908)
BAINES'S   **Longson's**
CYRIL POVEY   **Septimus Bennett**
RICHARD POVEY   **H.K. Hales**
DR STERLING   **Dr John Russell**

The Pretty Lady (1918)
LADY QUEENIE PAULLE   **Lady Diana Cooper**

Riceyman Steps (1923)
T.T. RICEYMAN, BOOKSHOP   **T. James & Co.**
RICEYMAN SQUARE   **Granville Square, London**
RICEYMAN STEPS   **Plum Pudding Steps, Clerkenwell, London**

The Roll Call (1917)
GEORGE CANNON   **Edwin Alfred Rickards**

BENSON, E.F.
The Babe, B.A. (1897)
ARBUTHNOT ('THE BABE')   **Herbert Charles Pollitt**

Dodo (1893)
EDITH STAINES   **Dame Ethel Smyth**
DODO (LADY CHESTERFIELD) VANE   **Margot Asquith**

Queen Lucia (1920) and others
EMMELINE LUCAS ('LUCIA')   **Mary Anderson**
    Sybil, Lady Colefax
MALLARDS   **Lamb House, Rye, East Sussex**
TILLING   **Rye, Sussex**

Robin Linnet (1919)
GEOFFREY BELLINGHAM   **Henry James**
LADY GROTE   **Lady Ripon**
LADY GURTNER   **Lady Leonara Speyer**
SIR HERMANN GURTNER   **Sir Edgar Speyer**
HENRY, LORD THORLEY   **A.J. Balfour**

BENSON, R.H.
The Conventionalists (1908)
ALGY BANNISTER   **Ronald Firbank**

Initiation (1914)
ENID BLESSINGTON   **F.W. Rolfe**

The Sentimentalists (1906)
CHRIS DELL   **F.W. Rolfe**

BERNSTEIN, Aline
Three Blue Suits (1933)
EUGENE LYONS   **Thomas Wolfe**

BLACKMORE, R.D.
The Maid of Sker (1872)
PARSON CHOWNE   **Revd John Froude**

BLAKE, Nicholas
A Question of Proof (1935) and others
NIGEL STRANGEWAYS   **W.H. Auden**

BLESSINGTON, Lady
The Belle of a Season (1840)
MR ERRICE   **Edward Ellice**

Memoirs of a Femme de Chambre (1846)
LADY CALDERSFOOT   **Sydney, Lady Morgan**
           Lady Stepney

The Repealers (1833)
LADY ABBERVILLE   **Lady Charleville**
LORD ABBERVILLE   **Lord Charleville**
LORD ALBANY   **Lord Alvanley**
MR ERRICE   **Edward Ellice**
COUNTESS OF GUERNSEY   **Countess of Jersey**

The Two Friends (1835)
CHARLES, LORD ARLINGTON   **Thomas Slingsby Duncombe**
DESBROW   **Bulwer Lytton**
LADY WALMER   **Jane Digby**

BLUNT, Wilfrid
Of Flowers and a Village (1963)
DELIA LOVELL — Grizel Hartley

BODENHEIM, Maxwell
Ninth Avenue (1926)
BEN HELGIN — Ben Hecht

BOLDREWOOD, Ralph
Robbery Under Arms (1888)
PATRICK — Daniel Morgan

BORDEN, Mary
'To Meet Jesus Christ', *Four O'Clock* (1926)
LOTTIE — Sybil, Lady Colefax

BORROW, George
Lavengro (1851)
THE ANGLO-GERMANIST — William Taylor of Norwich
ISOPEL BERNERS — Elizabeth Jarvis
THE EDITOR OF THE UNIVERSAL REVIEW (OXFORD) — Thomas Busby

John Carey
GALLIPOT JONES — Henry 'Orator' Hunt
THE PAINTER OF THE HEROIC — Benjamin Robert Haydon
PETULENGRO — Ambrose Smith
THE PUBLISHER — Sir Richard Phillips
T—— (THE TEACHER OF ORATORY) — John Thelwall
TAGGART — Benjamin Tabart

The Romany Rye (1857)
THE OLD RADICAL — Sir John Bowring

BOWEN, Elizabeth
The Death of the Heart (1938)
EDDIE — Goronwy Rees

The Last September (1929)
DANIELSTOWN — Bowen's Court, Kildorsey, County Cork, Ireland

BOYLE, Kay
'I Can't Get Drunk' (1933)
DENKA — Robert McAlmon

Monday Night (1938)
WILTSHIRE TOBIN — Harold Stearns

My Next Bride (1934)
ANTONY LISTER — Harry Crosby

BRACKETT, Charles
Entirely Surrounded (1934)

NIGEL FARRADAY	**Noël Coward**
THADDEUS HULBERT	**Alexander Woollcott**

BRADDON, M.E.
Hostages to Fortune (1875)

REVD SLINGSBY EDWARDS	**James Rhys ('Kilsby') Jones**

Lady Audley's Secret (1862)

AUDLEY COURT	**Ingatestone Hall, Essex**

BRINKLEY, William
The Fun House (1961)

VITAL	***Life* magazine**

BRONTË, Anne
Agnes Grey (1847)

MARY ANN BLOOMFIELD	**Mary Ingham**
TOM BLOOMFIELD	**Joshua Ingham**
WELLWOOD HOUSE	**Blake Hall, Mirfield, Yorkshire**
EDWARD WESTON	**William Weightman**

BRONTË, Charlotte
Jane Eyre (1847)

BROCKLEBRIDGE	**Tunstall, Lancashire**
MR BROCKLEHURST	**William Carus-Wilson**
HELEN BURNS	**Maria Brontë**
ALICE FAIRFAX	**Margaret Wooler**
FERNDEAN MANOR	**Wycoller Hall, Lancashire**
GATESHEAD HALL	**Stone Gappe, Yorkshire**
HANNAH	**Tabitha Aykeroyd**
LOWOOD SCHOOL	**Clergy Daughters' School, Cowan Bridge, Lancashire**
LOWTON	**Kirkby Lonsdale, Westmorland**
MORTON	**Hathersage, Derbyshire**
JOHN REED	**John Benson Sidgwick**
DIANA RIVERS	**Emily Brontë**
MARY RIVERS	**Anne Brontë**
ST JOHN EYRE RIVERS	**Henry Martyn**
	Revd Henry Nussey
EDWARD FAIRFAX ROCHESTER	**William Rathbone Greg**
MISS SCATCHERD	**Miss Andrews**
MISS TEMPLE	**Anne Evans**
	Jane Thompson
THORNFIELD HALL	**Norton Conyers, Yorkshire**
	The Rydings, Birstall, Yorkshire

The Professor (1857)

YORKE HUNSDEN	**Joshua Taylor**

MONSIEUR PELET — Joachim-Joseph Lebel

Shirley (1849)
BRIARFIELD — Birstall, Yorkshire
BRIARMAINS — Red House, Gomersal, Yorkshire
JOSEPH DONNE — Revd Joseph Brett Grant
FIELDHEAD — Oakwell Hall, Birstall, Yorkshire
CYRIL HALL — Revd William Margetson Heald
CAROLINE HELSTONE — Anne Brontë
— Ellen Nussey
REVD MATTHEWSON HELSTONE — Revd Hammond Roberson
HOLLOWS MILL — Hunsworth Mill, Yorkshire
SHIRLEY KEELDAR — Emily Brontë
REVD MR MACARTHEY — Arthur Bell Nicholls
PETER AUGUSTUS MALONE — Revd James William Smith
HORTENSE MOORE — Mademoiselle Haussé
ROBERT MOORE — Joseph Taylor
NUNNELLY — Hartshead, Yorkshire
AGNES PRYOR — Margaret Wooler
DAVID SWEETING — Revd James Chesterton Bradley
TARTAR — Keeper
HESTHER YORKE — Ann Taylor
HIRAM YORKE — Joshua Taylor
JESSY YORKE — Martha Taylor
ROSE YORKE — Mary Taylor

Villette (1853)
MADAME MODESTE MARIA BECK — Madame Claire Zoë Héger
BRETTON — Bridlington, Yorkshire
DR JOHN GRAHAM BRETTON — George Smith
MRS LOUISA LUCY BRETTON — Elizabeth Smith
PAUL EMANUEL — Constantin Héger
GINEVRA FANSHAWE — Maria Miller
PAULINA MARY HOME — Julia Gaskell
— Fanny Whipp
THE KING OF LABASSECOEUR — Leopold I, King of the Belgians
LUCY SNOWE — Charlotte Brontë
ZÉLIE DE ST PIERRE — Mademoiselle Blanche
VASHTI — Éliza Rachel
VILLETTE — Brussels

BRONTË, Emily
Wuthering Heights (1847)
REVD JABES BRANDERHAM — Revd Jabez Bunting
HEATHCLIFF — Jack Sharp
— Richard Sutton
PENISTONE CRAG — Ponden Kirk, Yorkshire
THRUSHCROSS GRANGE — Ponden Hall, Yorkshire
WUTHERING HEIGHTS — High Sunderland Hall, Yorkshire
— Top Withins, Yorkshire

BROOKE, Emma
Transition (1895)
PAUL SHERIDAN   **Sidney Webb**

BROOKS, John Nixon
The Big Wheel (1949)
EDWARD MASTERSON   **Henry Luce**
PRESENT DAY   *Time Magazine*

BROUGH, Robert Barnabas
'Calmuck', *Heads and Tails* (1859)
CALMUCK   **Emma Watkins**
MILDMAY STRONG   **Holman Hunt**

BROUGHAM, Lord
Albert Lunel (1844)
CHEVALIER ANDRÉ AGNEAU   **Sir Andrew Agnew**
MONSIEUR BALAYE   **Lord Brougham**
MONSIEUR DE CHAPELEY   **Lord Lyndhurst**
MONSIEUR LA CROASSE   **John Wilson Croker**
EARL OF MORNTON   **Richard, Lord Wellesley**
EMMELINE DE MOULIN   **Eleanor Brougham**
MONSIEUR VELOUR   **Sir John Leach**

BROUGHTON, Rhoda
Belinda (1883)
BELINDA CHURCHILL   **Emilia Francis Pattison**
PROFESSOR JAMES FORTH   **Mark Pattison**

Cometh Up as a Flower (1867)
ELLINOR LE STRANGE   **Rhoda Broughton**

Not Wisely, But Too Well (1867)
KATE CHESTER   **Rhoda Broughton**

BUCHAN, John
Castle Gay (1930)
THOMAS CARLYLE CRAW   **Sir William Robertson Nicoll**
     Lord Rothermere

The Courts of the Morning (1929)
SANDY ARBUTHNOT   **Aubrey Herbert**
     T.E. Lawrence

Greenmantle (1916)
SANDY ARBUTHNOT   **Aubrey Herbert**

A Lodge in the Wilderness (1906)
LADY AMYSFORT   **Lady Desborough**
LORD APPIN   **A.J. Balfour**
     Lord Rosebery
LEWIS ASTBURY   **L.S. Amery**

LADY FLORA BRUME	**Susan Grosvenor**
FRANCIS CAREY	**Cecil Rhodes**
LORD LAUNCESTON	**Alfred, 1st Viscount Milner**
HUGH SOMERVILLE	**John Buchan**

The Thirty-nine Steps (1915) and others
RICHARD HANNAY	**William Edmund, 1st Baron Ironside**

BUECHER, Frederick
The Return of Ansell Gibbs (1958)
HENRY KUYKENDALL	**Walter Rauschenbusch**

BURNETT, Frances Hodgson
Dolly (1877)
GRIFFITH DONNE	**Swan Burnett**

In Connection with the De Willoughby Claim (1899)
DELISLEVILLE	**Knoxville, Tennessee**

Little Lord Fauntleroy (1886)
CEDRIC ERROLL, LORD FAUNTLEROY	**Vivian Burnett**

The Secret Garden (1911)
MISSELTHWAITE MANOR	**Maytham Hall, Rolverden, Kent**

T. Tembaron (1913)
JOSEPH HUTCHINSON	**Ernest Fahnestock**

BURROW, George
Lavengro (1851)
THE EDITOR OF THE UNIVERSAL REVIEW (OXFORD)	**William Gifford**

BURY, Lady Charlotte
The Exclusives (1830)
LORD GASCOIGNE	**Lord Alvanley**
LADY GLENMORE	**Jane Digby**
LORD GLENMORE	**1st Earl of Ellenborough**
COMTESSE LEINSENGEN	**Princess Lieven**
DUKE OF MERCINTON	**Duke of Wellington**
SPENCER NEWCOMB	**Spencer Perceval**
LADY TENDERDEN	**Lady Tankerville**
LADY TILNEY	**Countess of Jersey**

BUSSY, Dorothy
Olivia (1949)
MADEMOISELLE JULIE	**Marie Souvestre**

BUTLER, Samuel
Erewhon (1872)

EREWHON	**Whitcombe Pass, New Zealand**
GIOVANNI GIANNI	**Giovanni Gianni**

The Fair Haven (1873)

JOHN PICKARD OWEN	**Samuel Butler**
MRS OWEN	**Fanny Butler**

The Way of All Flesh (1903)

BATTERSBY	**Langar, Nottinghamshire**
CRAMPSFORD	**Langar, Nottinghamshire**
ELLEN	**Isabella Zanetta**
MRS JUPP	**Mrs Boss**
EDWARD OVERTON	**Samuel Butler**
ALETHEA PONTIFEX	**Eliza Savage**
CHRISTINA PONTIFEX	**Fanny Butler**
ERNEST PONTIFEX	**Samuel Butler**
GEORGE PONTIFEX	**Dr Samuel Butler**
JOHN PONTIFEX	**William Butler**
THEOBALD PONTIFEX	**Thomas Butler**
ROUGHBOROUGH	**Shrewsbury School**
MISS SKINNER	**Miss Kennedy**
DR SAMUEL SKINNER	**Benjamin Hall Kennedy**
TOWNELEY	**Charles Paine Pauli**

BYRON, Robert
The Station (1928)

REINECKER	**Gerald Reitlinger**

C

CAINE, Hall
The Prodigal Son (1904)

OSCAR STEPHENSON	**Dante Gabriel Rossetti**

CANNAN, Gilbert
Mendel (1916)

CALTHROP	**Augustus John**
EDITH CLOWES	**Dorothy Brett**
EDGAR FROITZHEIM	**Sir William Rothenstein**
MENDEL KÜHLER	**Mark Gertler**
JAMES LOGAN	**John Currie**
	D.H. Lawrence
HUMPHREY MITCHELL	**C.R.W. Nevinson**
GRETA MORRISON	**Dora Carrington**
NELLY OLIVER	**Dolly Henry**

(cont.)
TYLNEY TYSOE

Frieda Lawrence
Sir Edward Marsh

Mummery (1916)
LADY BUTCHER
SIR HENRY BUTCHER
ADOLPH GRIFFENBERG
CHARLES MANN

Lady Beerbohm Tree
Sir Herbert Beerbohm Tree
Sir William Rothenstein
Edward Gordon Craig

Pugs and Peacocks (1921)
BIRCH END
T.W. SOPLEY
MELIAN STOKES

Garsington Manor, Oxfordshire
Lytton Strachey
Bertrand Russell

Sembal (1922)
MELIAN STOKES

Bertrand Russell

CARLYLE, Thomas
Sartor Resartus (1833–4)
BLUMINE

Jane Carlyle
Margaret Gordon
Catherine Aurora ('Kitty')
   Kirkpatrick

GRETCHEN CARLYLE
THE DUENNA COUSIN
ENTEPFUHL
ANDREAS FUTTERAL
HINTERSCHLAG
HINTERSCHLAG GYMNASIUM
PHILISTINE
DIOGENES TEUFELSDRÖCKH
TOWGOOD
TOWGOOD ('TOUGHGUT')
GRAF ZÄHDARM
GRÄFIN ZÄHDARM

Margaret Carlyle
Julia Strachey
Ecclefechan, Dumfriesshire
James Carlyle
Annan, Dumfriesshire
Annan Academy
Edward Irving
Thomas Carlyle
Edward Irving
Charles Buller, the Younger
Charles Buller, the Elder
Isabella Buller

CARR, John Dickson
The Mad Hatter Mystery (1933) and others
DR GIDEON FELL

G.K. Chesterton

CARREL, Frederic
The Adventures of John Johns (1897)
JOHN JOHNS

Frank Harris

CARROLL, Lewis
Alice's Adventures in Wonderland (1865)
ALICE
THE DUCHESS

Alice Liddell
Margaret, Duchess of Carinthia
Samuel Wilberforce
THE DUCK
ELSIE

Robinson Duckworth
Louisa Liddell

LACIE	**Alice Liddell**
THE LORY	**Louisa Liddell**
TILLIE	**Edith Liddell**

Sylvie and Bruno (1889)

THE EARL OF AINSLIE	**Lord Salisbury**

Through the Looking-Glass (1872)

ALICE	**Alice Liddell**
LOOKING-GLASS HOUSE	**Hetton Lawn, Gloucestershire**
THE RED QUEEN	**Mary Prickett**
THE ROSE	**Rhoda Liddell**
THE VIOLET	**Violet Liddell**
THE WHITE KNIGHT	**Charles Dodgson (Lewis Carroll)**

CARSTAIRS, Carroll

A Generation Missing (1938)

BENTINCK HOTEL	**Cavendish Hotel, London**
MRS OLIVER	**Rosa Lewis**

CARY, Joyce

The Horse's Mouth (1944)

GULLEY JIMSON	**Augustus John**
	Stanley Spencer
	Dylan Thomas

A House of Children (1941)

PINTO FREEMAN	**Dylan Thomas**

CASPARY, Vera

Laura (1943)

WALDO LYDECKER	**Alexander Woollcott**

CHESTERTON, G.K.

The Innocence of Father Brown (1911) and others

FATHER BROWN	**Monsignor John O'Connor**

The Man Who Knew Too Much (1922)

HORNE FISHER	**Maurice Baring**

The Man Who was Thursday (1908)

SUNDAY	**F.W. Walker**

The Napoleon of Notting Hill (1904)

AUBERON QUINN	**Max Beerbohm**
	G.K. Chesterton

CHEVALIER, Haakon

The Man Who Would Be God (1959)

SEBASTIAN BLOCH	**Robert Oppenheimer**

CHOLMONDELEY, Mary
Prisoners (1906)
WENTWORTH MAINE · A.C. Benson

CHRISTIE, Agatha
Dead Man's Folly (1956)
NASSE HOUSE · Greenway, Devon

Murder in Mesopotamia (1936)
DAVID EMMOTT · Max Mallowan
ERIC LEIDNER · Leonard Woolley
LOUISE LEIDNER · Katharine Woolley

COLLINS, Mortimer
Sweet and Twenty (1875)
CANON TREMAINE · Revd Robert Stephen Hawker

Two Plunges for a Pearl (1872)
OLDGO · John Reilly Newcombe
REGINALD SWYNFEN · Algernon Charles Swinburne

COLLINS, Wilkie
'The Bachelor Bedroom' (1859)
HERR VON MÜFFE · Hans Christian Andersen

The Moonstone (1868)
SERGEANT RICHARD CUFF · Jonathan Whicher
  Adolphus Frederick Williamson
EZRA JENNINGS · Hargrave Jennings

The Woman in White (1860)
ANNE CATHERICK · Caroline Graves
LAURA FAIRLIE · Marquise de Douhault
PROFESSOR PESCA · Gabriele Rossetti

COMPTON-BURNETT, I.
Brothers and Sisters (1929)
MISS PATMORE · Ellen Smith
ANDREW STACE, THE ELDER · Rowland Rees
CHRISTIAN STACE · James Compton-Burnett
ROBIN STACE · Noel Compton-Burnett
SOPHIA STACE · Katharine Compton-Burnett

Dolores (1911)
MISS ADAM · Margaret Hayes Robinson
HERBERT BLACKWOOD · Robert Blackie
MISS BUTLER · Margaret Taylor
DR CASSELL · Dr Molson
SIGISMUND CLAVERHOUSE · Mr Salt
  Thomas Seccombe
MISS CLIFF · Katharine S. Block
MISS DORRINGTON · Marjorie Cunningham

Miss Greenlow	Catherine Frost
Dolores Hutton	Ivy Compton-Burnett
Sophia Hutton	Katharine Compton-Burnett
Perdita Kingsford	Daisy Elizabeth Harvey
Miss Lemaître	Marie Péchinet
Millfield	Dent, Yorkshire
	Great Clacton, Essex
Felicia Murray	Isabel Bremner

Elders and Betters (1944)
Tullia Calderon	Dorothy Kidd

A Family and a Fortune (1939)
Dudley Gaveston	Ivy Compton-Burnett

A Father and His Fate (1957)
Eliza Mowbray	Katharine Compton-Burnett

The Last and the First (1970)
Eliza Heriot	Katharine Compton-Burnett

Men and Wives (1931)
Sir Godfrey Haslam	Robert Blackie

More Women Than Men (1933)
Ruth Giffard	Tertia Compton-Burnett
Maria Rosetti	Marie Péchinet
Jonathan Swift	Samuel Butler

Pastors and Masters (1925)
William Masson	W.H. Macaulay

The Present and the Past (1953)
Fabian Clare	Guy Compton-Burnett
Guy Clare	Noel Compton-Burnett

CONDON, Richard
The Manchurian Candidate (1959)
John Iselin	Joseph McCarthy

CONNOLLY, Cyril
The Rock Pool (1936)
Edgar Naylor	Nigel Richards

CONRAD, Joseph
Almayer's Folly (1895)
Kaspar Almayer	William Charles Olmeijer
Captain Ford	Captain James Craig
Tom Lingard	Captain William Lingard
Pantai River	Berau River, Borneo
Sambir	Berau, Borneo

The Arrow of Gold (1919)
Mrs Blunt	Ellen Blunt

DOMINIC	Dominic Cervoni
PRAX	Frétigny
DON RAFFAEL DE VILLAREL	Don Rafael Tristany

Chance (1914)

DE BARRAL	Frédéric Humbert

'The End of the Tether' (1902)

SOFALA	*SS Vidar*
CAPTAIN ELLIOT	Captain Henry Ellis

'Gaspar Ruiz', *A Set of Six* (1908)

GASPAR RUIZ	Benavides

Heart of Darkness (1902)

THE CENTRAL STATION	Kinshasa, Zaire
THE COMPANY DIRECTOR	G.F.W. Hope
THE COMPANY STATION	Matadi, Congo
ELDORADO EXPLORING EXPEDITION	Katanga Expedition
CAPTAIN FRESLEVEN	Captain Freiesleben
INNER STATION	Stanley Falls, Belgian Congo
MR KURTZ	Major Edmund Musgrave Barttelot
	Arthur Eugene Constant Hodister
	Georges Antoine Klein
	H.M. Stanley
THE MANAGER	Camille Delcommune
THE MANAGER'S UNCLE	Alexandre Delcommune

'The Informer', *A Set of Six* (1908)

THE FRIEND IN PARIS	Ford Madox Ford
YOUNG LADY ANARCHIST	Helen Rossetti Angeli

Lord Jim (1900)

CAPTAIN MONTAGUE BRIERLY	Captain Wallace
GENTLEMAN BROWN	Captain Brownrigg
EGSTRÖM & BLAKE	MacAlister & Co.
CAPTAIN ELLIOT	Captain Henry Ellis
JIM	Sir James Brooke
	William James ('Jim') Lingard
	Augustine Podmore Williams
SS PATNA	*SS Jeddah*
PATUSAN, PATUSAN RIVER	Berau, Borneo
SCHOMBERG'S HOTEL	Hotel du Louvre, Singapore
STEIN	Charles Allen
	Dr Bernstein
	William Lingard
	Mr Mesman
	Alfred Russel Wallace

The Nigger of the 'Narcissus' (1897)

DONKIN	Charles Dutton
SINGLETON	Daniel Sullivan
JAMES WAIT (THE 'NIGGER')	Joseph Barron
	George White

Nostromo (1904)
ANTONIA AVELLANOS	**Antonia Ribera**
DON JOSÉ AVELLANOS	**Pérez Triana, Santiago**
FATHER BERON	**Father Romàn**
CHARLES GOULD	**Robert Cunninghame Graham**
SIR JOHN	**Edward B. Eastwick**
DR MONYGHAM	**George Frederick Masterman**
NOSTROMO	**Dominic Cervoni**
SAN TOMÉ	**San Tomé, Portuguese Guinea**
SULACO	**Valencia, Venezuela**
GIORGIO VIOLA	**Enrico Clerici**
	Giuseppe Garibaldi
	Giovanni ('Leggero') Giuliolo

An Outcast of the Islands (1896)
PETER WILLEMS	**Carel De Veer**
	Alfred Russel Wallace

'An Outpost of Progress', *Tales of Unrest* (1898)
THE MANAGING DIRECTOR	**H.M. Stanley**

The Rescue (1920)
TOM LINGARD	**Sir James Brooke**

The Rover (1923)
JEAN PEYROL	**Dominic Cervoni**

The Secret Agent (1907)
THE ASSISTANT COMMISSIONER	**Sir Robert Anderson**
	Sir Howard Vincent
THE BOMB OUTRAGE	**Greenwich Bomb Outrage**
SIR ETHELRED	**Sir William Harcourt**
CHIEF INSPECTOR HEAT	**William Melville**
MICHAELIS	**Michael Bakunin**
	Edward O'Meara Condon
	Michael Davitt
THE PROFESSOR	**Dr Creaghe**
	Luke Dillon
	'Professor' Mezzeroff
	Johann Most
	Arthur Rossetti
STEVIE	**Martial Bourdin**
ADOLF VERLOC	**Auguste Coulon**
	Adolf P. Krieger
	Henry B. Samuels
WINNIE VERLOC	**Jessie Conrad**
MR VLADIMIR	**General Seliverskov**
KARL YUNDT	**Michael Bakunin**
	Johann Most

'The Secret Sharer', *'Twixt Land and Sea* (1912)
CAPTAIN ARCHBOLD	**Captain Joseph Lucas Clark**

LEGGATT	Sidney Smith
SEPHORA	*Cutty Sark*

The Shadow-Line (1917)

MR BURNS	Charles Born
CAPTAIN ELLIS	Captain Henry Ellis
THE FORMER CAPTAIN	Captain John Snadden
CAPTAIN GILES	Captain Patterson
THE SHIP	*Otago*
THE STEWARD OF THE SAILORS' HOME	C.J. Phillips

Suspense (1925)

LADY LATHAM	Jane, Lady Legard
SIR CHARLES LATHAM	Sir John Legard
DR MARTEL	Dr Marshall
COMTESSE DE MONTERESSO	Adèle, Comtesse de Boigne
COUNT DE MONTERESSO	Benoit, Comte de Boigne
ATTILIO PIESCHI	Dominic Cervoni

Under Western Eyes (1911)

VICTOR HALDIN	G. Sazonov
PETER IVANOVICH	Peter Kropotkin
	Leo Tolstoy
COUNCILLOR MIKULIN	Aleksey Aleksandrovich Lopukhin
MR DE P——	Wenzel von Plehve
KIRYLO SIDOROVITCH RAZUMOV	Sergius Stepniak
GENERAL T.	Dimitri Fedorovich Trepov
FATHER ZOSIM	G.A. Gapon

Victory (1915)

SCHOMBERG'S HOTEL	Hotel du Louvre, Singapore

'Youth' (1902)

JUDEA	*Palestine*
CAPTAIN ELIJAH BEARD	Captain John Beard

CONRAD, Joseph, and FORD, Madox Ford
The Inheritors (1901)

CALLAN	Samuel Rutherford Crockett
EDWARD CHURCHILL	A.J. Balfour
FOX	Lord Northcliffe
CHARLES GURNARD	Joseph Chamberlain
LEA	Edward Garnett
DUC DE MERSCH	Leopold II, King of the Belgians
POLEHAMPTON	T. Fisher Unwin

COOPER, James Fenimore
The Spy (1821)

HARVEY BIRCH	Enoch Crosby

COOPER, Lettice
Black Bethlehem (1947)
ANN DRAKE   Eileen Blair
CHRISTOPHER DRAKE   George Orwell

COOPER, William
Young People (1958)
SWAN   C.P. Snow

CORKE, Helen
Neutral Ground (1933)
ELLIS BROOKE   Helen Corke
DERRICK HAMILTON   D.H. Lawrence
CECILY MORTON   Agnes Mason
HOWARD PHILLIPS   A.W. McLeod

COURNOS, John
Miranda Masters (1926)
ROY CHRISTOPHER   John Gould Fletcher
JOHN GOMBAROV   John Cournos
WINIFRED GWYNNE   Dorothy Yorke
ARNOLD MASTERS   Richard Aldington
MIRANDA MASTERS   Hilda Doolittle
WILFRED RENNELL   Cecil Gray

CRANE, Stephen
The Third Violet (1897)
WILLIAM HAWKER   Stephen Crane

CRAWFORD, Marion
Claudius (1883)
HORACE BELLINGHAM   Samuel Ward

Mr Isaacs (1882)
MR ISAACS   Alexander M. Jacob

CROWLEY, Aleister
The Diary of a Drug Fiend (1922)
OWEN   Augustus John

CUMMINGS, E.E.
The Enormous Room (1922)
B. (OR W.S.B.)   William Slater Brown

D

DANBY, Frank
A Babe in Bohemia (1889)
MORDAUNT RIVERS   **Reginald Shirley Brooks**

DAVIS, Newnham
Jadoo (1898)
MR EMMANUEL   **Alexander M. Jacob**

DEASY, Mary
The Boy Who Made Good (1955)
IVOR KELLY   **F. Scott Fitzgerald**
STELLA KELLY   **Zelda Fitzgerald**

DEFOE, Daniel
The Life and Strange Surprising Adventures of Robinson Crusoe (1719)
ROBINSON CRUSOE   **Alexander Selkirk**

DE VOTO, Bernard
We Accept With Pleasure (1934)
FRANK ARCHER   **Sinclair Lewis**

DICKENS, Charles
American Notes (1842)
DR CROCUS   **Angus Melrose**

Barnaby Rudge (1841)
SIR JOHN CHESTER   **Lord Chesterfield**
DENNIS   **William Calcraft**
GASHFORD   **Robert Watson**
THE MAYPOLE INN   **The King's Head, Chigwell, Essex**

Bleak House (1852–3)
BLEAK HOUSE   **Bleak Hall, St Albans,
     Hertfordshire
     Great Nast Hyde, Hertfordshire**
LAWRENCE BOYTHORN   **Charles Cowden Clarke
     Walter Savage Landor**
INSPECTOR BUCKET   **Charles Frederick Field**
CHESNEY WOLD   **Rockingham Castle,
     Northamptonshire**
THE GRIDLEY CASE   *Cooke v. Fynney* (1844) c.59
HORTENSE   **Maria Manning**
JARNDYCE V. JARNDYCE   *Jennings v. Jennings*
MRS JELLYBY   **Caroline Chisholm**
JO   **George Ruby**
THE LORD CHANCELLOR   **Lord Lyndhurst**
MOONEY   **Looney**

Mrs Rouncewell	Elizabeth Dickens[1]
Harold Skimpole	Leigh Hunt
Esther Summerson	Georgina Hogarth[2]
Mr Tulkinghorn	Edward Blackmore
Mr Turveydrop	John Henry Skelton

The Chimes (1844)

Sir Joseph Bowley	Lord Brougham
Alderman Cute	Sir Peter Laurie
Margaret ('Meg') Veck	Mary Furley

David Copperfield (1849–50)

Blunderstone	Blundeston, Suffolk
Dr Chillip	Dr Charles Morgan
David Copperfield	Charles Dickens
Mr Creakle	William Jones
	Benjamin Rotch
Rosa Dartle	Hannah Brown
Charles Mell	Oliver Goldsmith
	Mr Taylor
Wilkins Micawber	John Dickens
Miss Mowcher	Mrs Jane Seymour Hill
Murdstone & Grinby	Warren's Blacking Warehouse, London
Clara Peggotty	Mary Weller
Salem House	Wellington House Academy, London
Mr Spenlow	Charles Smithson
Dora Spenlow	Maria Beadnell
James Steerforth	George Stroughill
Dr Strong	John Birt
	Richard Valpy
	George Wallace
Dr Strong's School	King's School, Canterbury
	Reading School, Berkshire
Thomas Traddles	Thomas Noon Talfourd
Betsey Trotwood	Mary Pearson Strong
Mick Walker	Bob Fagin
Agnes Wickfield	Georgina Hogarth[2]

Dombey and Son (1846–8)

Dr Blimber	Revd E. Everard
	Joseph Charles King
Cornelia Blimber	Louisa King
Blimber's	Chichester House, Brighton
	Mr King's School, St John's Wood, London
	Wick House, Brighton
Brig Place	Montague Place, London
Captain Cuttle	David Mainland
Mr Dombey	Thomas Chapman

PAUL DOMBEY	Henry Augustus Burnett
COUSIN FEENIX	Chauncey Hare Townshend
SOLOMON GILLS	Mr Norie
MRS PIPCHIN	Elizabeth Roylance
POLLY TOODLE	Mrs Hayes

Edwin Drood (1870)

CLOISTERHAM	Rochester, Kent
THE CROZIER	The Mitre Inn, Chatham, Kent
HELENA LANDLESS	Constance Emily Kent
	Ellen Ternan
NUN'S HOUSE, CLOISTERHAM	Eastgate House, Rochester, Kent
PRINCESS PUFFER	Lascar Sal
MR TOPE	Mr Miles

Great Expectations (1860–1)

MISS HAVISHAM	Margaret Catherine Dick
	Martha Joachim
	The White Woman of Berners Street
ESTELLA PROVIS	Ellen Ternan
SATIS HOUSE	Restoration House, Rochester, Kent
JOHN WEMMICK	John Ruskin

'The Great Winglebury Duel', *Sketches by Boz* (1836)

GREAT WINGLEBURY	Rochester, Kent

Hard Times (1854)

GEORGE BITZER	George Parker Bidder
JOSIAH BOUNDERBY	William Chambers
COKETOWN	Hanley, Staffordshire
COKETOWN STRIKE	Preston Strike
GRADGRIND SCHOOL	Birkbeck Schools
SLACKBRIDGE	Mortimer Grimshaw
SLEARY	John Clarke
THE THIRD GENTLEMAN	Sir Henry Cole

Hunted Down (1870)

JULIUS SLINKTON	Thomas Griffiths Wainewright

Little Dorrit (1855–7)

BAR	Sir Fitzroy Kelly
TITE BARNACLE	Sir James Stephen
THE CIRCUMLOCUTION OFFICE	The Colonial Office
WILLIAM DORRIT	John Dickens
FLORA FINCHING	Maria Beadnell
HENRY GOWAN	W.M. Thackeray
MR MERDLE	George Hudson
	John Sadleir
MONSIEUR RIGAUD	Pierre-François Laçenaire
	Napoleon III, Emperor of France
	Thomas Griffiths Wainewright

'Making a Night of It', *Sketches by Boz* (1836)

THOMAS POTTER	**Charles Potter**
ROBERT SMITHERS	**Charles Dickens**

Martin Chuzzlewit (1843–4)

COLONEL DIVER	**James Watson Webb**
EDEN	**Cairo, Illinois**
SETH PECKSNIFF	**Samuel Carter Hall**
PAUL SWEEDLEPIPE	**William Turner**[1]

'A Message from the Sea' (1860)

CAPTAIN SILAS JONAS JORGAN	**Captain Elisha Ely Morgan**

'Mr Minns and His Cousin', *Sketches by Boz* (1836)

OCTAVIUS BUDDEN (FORMERLY BAGSHAW)	**John Porter Leigh**

'Mrs Joseph Porter', *Sketches by Boz* (1836)

MRS JOSEPH PORTER	**Mrs J.P. Leigh**

The Mudfog Papers (1837–8)

MUDFOG ASSOCIATION FOR THE ADVANCEMENT OF EVERYTHING	**British Association for the Advancement of Science**

'The Nice Little Couple', *Sketches of Young Couples* (1840)

THE BACHELOR FRIEND	**Edward Chapman**
MR CHIRRUP	**William Hall**

Nicholas Nickleby (1838–9)

JOHN BROWDIE	**John and Richard Barnes**
	Thomas Todd
CHEERYBLE BROTHERS	**Daniel and William Grant**
NINETTA CRUMMLES (THE 'INFANT PHENOMENON')	**Jean Margaret Lander**
VINCENT CRUMMLES	**Thomas Donald Davenport**
MISS LA CREEVY	**Rose Emma Drummond**
	Mary Anne Mannin
MRS MICAWBER	**Elizabeth Dickens**[2]
MRS NICKLEBY	**Elizabeth Dickens**[2]
NICHOLAS NICKLEBY	**Henry Burnett**
NEWMAN NOGGS	**Newman Knott**
SMIKE	**George Ashton Taylor**
WACKFORD SQUEERS	**William Shaw**

The Old Curiosity Shop (1840–1)

MRS JINIWIN	**Georgina Hogarth**[1]
DANIEL QUILP	**Charles Dickens**
	Giuseppe Grimaldi
	'Donkey' Prior
MR SLUM	**Alexander Kemp**
DICK SWIVELLER	**Count D'Orsay**
NELL TRENT ('LITTLE NELL')	**Mary Scott Hogarth**

Oliver Twist (1837–8)

FAGIN	**Ikey Solomons**

Mr Fang	Allan Stewart Laing
Rose Maylie	Mary Scott Hogarth

Our Mutual Friend (1864–5)
Mr Podsnap	John Forster
Melvin Twemlow	Chauncey Hare Townshend
Bella Wilfer	Ellen Ternan

The Pickwick Papers (1836–7)
Mrs Bardell	Ann Ellis
Bardell v. Pickwick	*Norton v. Melbourne*
Mr Serjeant Buzfuz	Mr Serjeant Bompas
	Charles Phillips
Eatanswill	Ipswich, Suffolk
	Sudbury, Suffolk
Horatio Fizkin	Sir Fitzroy Kelly
Alfred Jingle	Charles Potter
The Lion	The Swan, West Malling, Kent
Manor Farm, Dingley Dell	Birling Place, Kent
	Cob Tree Manor, Sandling, Kent
Muggleton	Maidstone, Kent
	West Malling, Kent
Nupkins	Allan Stewart Laing
Nupkins's Maid	Mary Weller
Mr Perker	Edward Ellis
Samuel Pickwick	John Foster
	Robert Booth Rawes
Pickwick Club	British Association for the Advancement of Science
Mr Pott	Lord Brougham
Dr Slammer	Dr Matthew Lamert
Count Smorltork	Prince Pückler-Muskau
	Friedrich von Raumer
Augustus Snodgrass	Charles Potter
Mr Justice Stareleigh	Sir Stephen Gaselee
Samuel Weller	Richard Frazier
	Samuel Vale
Tony Weller	Old Chumley
Westgate House	Eastgate House, Rochester, Kent

A Tale of Two Cities (1859)
Sydney Carton	James Gordon Allan
Dr Manette's House	Carlisle House, Soho, London
	1 Greek Street, Soho, London
C.J. Stryver	E.J. James
	Sir Charles Wetherell
Tellson's Bank	Child's Bank, Strand, London

'Tom Tiddler's Ground' (1861)
Tom Mopes	James Lucas

DICKINSON, G. Lowes
A Modern Symposium (1905)

PHILIP AUDUBON	Ferdinand Canning Scott Schiller
GEOFFREY VIVIAN	George Meredith

DICKSON, Carter
The Plague Court Murders (1934) and others

SIR HENRY MERRIVALE	Winston Churchill

DINEEN, Joseph
Ward Eight (1936)

HUGHIE DONNELLY	'Czar' Martin Lomasney

DISRAELI, Benjamin
Coningsby (1844)

DUCHESS OF AGINCOURT	Lady Grenville
DUKE OF AGINCOURT	Lord Grenville, 2nd Duke of Buckingham and Chandos
BEAUMANOIR	Belvoir Castle, Leicestershire
LORD BEAUMANOIR	6th Duke of Rutland
BOOTS AT CHRISTOPHERS HOTEL	Peter Borthwick
GINGERLY BROWN	Brownlow Villiers Layard
SIR CHARLES BUCKHURST	Lord Lamington
MR CASSILIS	George Wombwell
TOM CHUDLEIGH	Augustus Stafford
MADAME COLONNA	Lady Strachan
PRINCESS LUCRETIA COLONNA	Charlotte, Countess Zichy-Ferraris
HARRY CONINGSBY	Lord Lyttelton
	George Smythe
THE DUKE	5th Duke of Rutland
MR EARWIG	Sir George Clerk
LORD ESKDALE	2nd Earl of Lonsdale
LADY EVERINGHAM	Catherine, Countess of Clarendon
LORD EVERINGHAM	7th Earl of Cardigan
	4th Earl of Clarendon
LORD FITZBOOBY	Lord Harrington
	Dudley Ryder
GUY FLOUNCEY	Sir Charles Peter Shakerley
DUCHESSE DE G——T	Ida, Duchesse de Gramont
LADY GAVERSTOCK	Countess of Mexborough
LORD GAVERSTOCK	4th Earl of Mexborough
LUCIAN GAY	Theodore Hook
G.O.A. HEAD	John Arthur Roebuck
MR JUGGINS	Sir Felix Booth
EUSTACE LYLE	Ambrose de Lisle
COUNT M——É	Louis Mathieu, Comte Molé
MR MELTON	James William Bosville Macdonald
MR MILLBANK	Edmund Ashworth
	Mark Philips

OSWALD MILLBANK	William Gladstone
	John Walter
LORD MONMOUTH	3rd Marquess of Hertford
MR ORMSBY	Quentin Dick
	John Irving
SIR BAPTIST PLACID	Sir John Eardley-Wilmot
LORD RAMBROOKE	Lord Rosslyn
NICHOLAS RIGBY	John Wilson Croker
THE RUSSIAN AMBASSADOR	Prince Lieven
THE RUSSIAN AMBASSADRESS	Princess Lieven
ST GENEVIÈVE (SEAT OF EUSTACE LYLE)	Garendon Park, Leicestershire
LADY ST JULIANS	Countess of Jersey
JAWSTER SHARP	John Bright
SIDONIA	Benjamin Disraeli
	Adolph de Rothschild
	Baron James Mayer de Rothschild
	Lionel Nathan de Rothschild
	David Urquhart
LORD HENRY SYDNEY	Lord John Manners
TADPOLE	Alexander Pringle
MR TAPER	Charles Ross
LORD VERE	Lord Edward Howard
	Lord Lyttelton
SIR JOSEPH WALLINGER	Sir William Clay
MR WORDY	Sir Archibald Alison

Contarini Fleming (1832)

BARON FLEMING	Benjamin Israeli
CONTARINI FLEMING	Benjamin Disraeli

Endymion (1880)

COLONEL ALBERT (PRINCE FLORESTAN)	Napoleon III, Emperor of France
AUGUSTUS TREMAINE BERTIE	William Henry Lytton Earle Bulwer
	Richard Monckton Milnes
ENDYMION FERRARS	Sir Charles Wentworth Dilke
WILLIAM PITT FERRARS	Lord Salisbury
COUNT FERROL	Otto von Bismarck
MR GUSHY	Charles Dickens
HURSTLEY	Bradenham, Buckinghamshire
LADY MONTFORT	Selina, Countess of Bradford
	Caroline Norton
	Lady Palmerston
MONTFORT TOURNAMENT	Eglinton Tournament
ADRIAN NEUCHATEL	Lionel Nathan de Rothschild
THE NEUCHATELS	The Rothschilds
NIGEL PENRUDDOCK	Henry Edward Manning
LORD ROEHAMPTON	Lord Palmerston
ST BARBE	Thomas Carlyle
	Abraham Hayward
	W.M. Thackeray
JOB THORNBERRY	John Bright

(cont.)

	Richard Cobden
	Thomas Bayley Potter
Bertie Tremaine	Bulwer Lytton
Vigo	George Hudson
	Henry George Poole
George Waldershare	Lord John Manners
	George Smythe
Sidney Wilton	Sidney Herbert
Zenobia	Countess of Jersey

Henrietta Temple (1837)

Lady Bellair	Lady Corke
Count Alcibiades de Mirabel	Count D'Orsay
Bond Sharpe	William Crockford
Henrietta Temple	Henrietta, Lady Sykes

Lothair (1870)

Mr Ardenne	Evelyn Philip Shirley of Ettington
The Bishop	Samuel Wilberforce
Hugo Bohun	Sir Henry Calcraft
Mr Brancepeth	Christopher Sykes[1]
Brentham	Trentham Park, Staffordshire
Captain Bruges	G.P. Cluseret
Theodora Campion	Jessie Meriton Mario
Lord Carisbrooke	4th Marquis of Bath
Monsignor Catesby	Monsignor Thomas John Capel
Felix Drollin	Alexandre Auguste Ledru-Rollin
Apollonia Giles	Prudentia Penelope Cavendish-Bentinck
Putney Giles	Benjamin Israeli
Cardinal Grandison	Henry Edward Manning
Lothair	Lord Bute
Duchess of Lothair	Louisa Jane Abercorn
Duke of Lothair	James Hamilton Abercorn
The Oxford Professor	Goldwin Smith
Gaston Phoebus	Frederic, Lord Leighton
Mr Pinto	Sir Henry Calcraft
Lady St Jerome	Elizabeth, Lady Herbert
Lord St Jerome	Lord Howard

Sybil (1845)

Sir Vavasour Firebrace	Sir Richard Broun
Lady St Julians	Countess of Jersey
Aubrey St Lys	Frederick William Faber
Wodgate	Willenhall, Staffordshire

Tancred (1847)

Francis Baroni, the Elder	Giovanni Battista Belzoni
Eva Besso	Charlotte de Rothschild
Mr Cassilis	George Wombwell
Harry Coningsby	Lord Lyttelton
Lord Eskdale	2nd Earl of Lonsdale

GUY FLOUNCEY	Sir Charles Peter Shakerley
MR ORMSBY	Quentin Dick
	John Irving
SIDONIA	Baron James Mayer de Rothschild
LORD HENRY SYDNEY	Lord John Manners
MR VAVASOUR	Richard Monckton Milnes

Venetia (1837)

LORD CADURCIS	Lord Byron
MARMION HERBERT	Percy Bysshe Shelley
LADY MONTEAGLE	Lady Caroline Lamb

Vivian Grey (1826–7)

LORD ALHAMBRA	Lord Porchester
MARCHIONESS OF ALMACKS	3rd Marchioness of Londonderry
DUKE OF ALTAMONT	Lord Nugent of Carlanston
ANTILLES	Charles Rose Ellis, 1st Baron Seaford
JULIUS VON ASSLINGEN	Beau Brummell
THE *ATTACK-ALL REVIEW*	The *Quarterly Review*
THE BARONESS	Princess Amelia
BECKENDORFF	Prince Metternich
LORD AMELIUS FITZFUDGE BOROUGHBY	John Fane, 11th Earl of Westmorland
MARQUESS OF CARABAS	1st Marquess of Clanricarde
	Lord Grenville, 2nd Marquess of Chandos
	John Murray[1]
MADAME CAROLINA	Lady Holland
FREDERICK CLEVELAND	J.G. Lockhart
LADY DOUBTFUL	Lady Blessington
VIVACITY DULL	Horace Twiss
MR FITZLOOM	Sir Robert Peel
MR FOAMING FUDGE	Lord Brougham
MR CHARLATAN GAS	George Canning
MARQUESS OF GRANDGOUT	3rd Marquess of Hertford
HARGRAVE GREY	Nathaniel Basevi
HORACE GREY	Isaac D'Israeli
VIVIAN GREY	Benjamin Disraeli
MR STANISLAUS HOAX	Theodore Hook
PRINCE HUNGARY	Prince Paul Anton Esterházy
DUKE OF JUGGERNAUT	12th Duke of Norfolk
MR LIBERAL PRINCIPLES	William Huskisson
LIBERAL SNAKE	John Ramsay McCulloch
MRS FELIX (AMALIA) LORRAINE	Lady Caroline Lamb
LORD LOWERSDALE	1st Earl of Lonsdale
MR MILLION	John Diston Powles
MRS MILLION	Harriot Coutts
THE MISSES OTRANTO	The Misses Berry
LORD PAST CENTURY	Lord Eldon
THE PHILOSOPHER OF THE VILLA PLINIANA	Sir William Gell

The *Praise-All Review*	The *Edinburgh Review*
Lord Prima Donna	Lord William Lennox
The Principal writer for the *Attack-All Review*	Robert Southey
Parthenopex Puff	Samuel Rogers
	William Stewart Rose
Grand Duke of Reisenberg	Charles Augustus, Grand Duke of Saxe-Weimar
The Russian Archduke	Prince Paul Anton Esterházy
Mr Justice St Prose	James Alan Park
Mr Sherborne	Isaac D'Israeli
Count von Sohnspeer	Duke of Wellington
Dr von Spittergen	John Abernethy
Mr Stucco	John Nash
Vivida Vis	John Wilson Croker
Mr Von Chronicle	Jean de Sismondi
Colonel Von Trumpetson	3rd Marquis of Londonderry
Duke of Waterloo	Duke of Wellington
Prince Xtmnpqrtosklw	Prince Gortchakoff

DOOLITTLE, Hilda

See H.D.

DOS PASSOS, John
Adventures of a Young Man (1939)

Elmer Weeks	Earl Browder

Chosen Country (1951)

Eliot Story Bradford	Richard Norton
Elisha Croft	Clarence Seward Darrow
Ben Harrington	Bill Smith
Ezekiel Harrington	W.B. Smith
Lulie Harrington	Katharine Foster Dos Passos
Zeke Harrington	Y.K. Smith
James Knox Polk Pignatelli	John R. Dos Passos
Jay Pignatelli	John Dos Passos
Lydia Rumford (Aunt Lyde)	Mrs J.W. Charles
Judge Joseph Thatcher	William Samson Price
Dr Warner	C.E. Hemingway
George Elbert Warner	Ernest Hemingway

The Great Days (1958)

Roger Thurloe	James Forrestal

Most Likely to Succeed (1954)

Adolph Herman Baum	Otto Kahn
The Craftsman's Theatre	New Playwrights
J.E.D. Morris	John Howard Lawson

Number One (1943)

Homer T. 'Chuck' Crawford	Huey P. Long

U.S.A. (1938)
J. WARD MOOREHOUSE   Ivy Ledbetter Lee
MR PIERCE   William Samson Price

DOUGLAS, Norman
Fountains in the Sand (1912)
PAUL DUFRÉNOIS   Robert Duterme

Looking Back (1933)
MELVILLE L. SMEAD   Axel Munthe

South Wind (1917)
BAZHAKULOFF   Father John of Cronstadt
                                     Rasputin
ERNEST EAMES   John Ellingham Brooks
SIGNOR MALIPIZZO   Signor Capolozzi
MÜHLER (ALIAS RETLOW)   Baron von Veltheim
NEPENTHE   Capri
FREDDY PARKER   Harold Trower
DUCHESS OF SAN MARTINO   Mrs Snow
MADAME STEYNLIN   Clara Grein

DOYLE, Arthur Conan
The Sherlock Holmes stories (1890–1927)
SHERLOCK HOLMES   Joseph Bell
PROFESSOR JAMES MORIARTY   Alfred Wilks Drayson
                                     George Moriarty
                                     James Payn
                                     Adam Worth

The Valley of Fear (1915)
VERMISSA   Pottsville, Pennsylvania

DREISER, Theodore
An American Tragedy (1925)
ROBERTA ('BERT') ALDEN   Grace ('Billy') Brown
BIG BITTERN   Big Moose Lake, New York
BLITZ   South Otselic, New York
CATARAQUI COUNTY   Herkimer County, New York
ASA GRIFFITHS   Asa Conklin
                                     John Paul Dreiser
CLYDE GRIFFITHS   Chester Gillette
ELVIRA GRIFFITHS   Sarah Schönäb Dreiser
ESTA GRIFFITHS   Mary Frances Dreiser
LYCURGUS   Cortland, New York

A Book About Myself (1922)
ALICE KANE   Lois Zahn

The Bulwark (1946)
ETTA BARNES   Anna Tatum
SOLON BARNES   John Paul Dreiser
                                     Mr Tatum

STEWART BARNES   **Marcus Romanus Dreiser**
WILLARD KANE   **Theodore Dreiser**

Dawn (1931)
AMY   **Cecilia Dreiser**
ELEANOR   **Mary Frances Dreiser**
JANET   **Emma Dreiser**
RUTH   **Theresa Dreiser**
WALTER TISDALE   **Austin Brennan**

'Emmanuela', *A Gallery of Women* (1929)
EMMANUELA   **Ann Watkins**
ERNEST SCHEIB   **Fritz Krog**

'Ernestine', *A Gallery of Women* (1929)
ERNESTINE DE JONGH   **Florence Deshon**

'Ernita', *A Gallery of Women* (1929)
ERNITA BARTRAM   **Emma Goldman**

'Esther Norn', *A Gallery of Women* (1929)
DOANE   **Harry Kemp**
J.J.   **Hutchins Hapgood**
ESTHER NORN   **Mary Pyne**

The Financier (1912)
JACOB BORCHARDT   **Daniel Miller Fox**
AILEEN BUTLER   **Mary Adelaide Yerkes**
EDWARD BUTLER   **Edward R. Butler**
FRANK ALGERNON COWPERWOOD   **C.T. Yerkes**
HENRY A. MOLLENHAUER   **James McManes**
LILLIAN SEMPLE   **Susan Guttridge Gamble**
GEORGE W. STENER   **Joseph F. Marcer**

The 'Genius' (1915)
ANGEL BLUE   **Sara Osborne White Dreiser**
EMILY DALE   **Annie Ericsson Cudlipp**
SUZANNE DALE   **Thelma Cudlipp**
EUGENE WITLA   **Theodore Dreiser**
           Everett Shinn
           William Louis Sonntag

'Giff', *A Gallery of Women* (1929)
HONORIA GIFFORD   **Mrs Spafford**

Jennie Gerhardt (1911)
MR GERHARDT   **John Paul Dreiser**
MRS GERHARDT   **Sarah Schönäb Dreiser**
JENNIE GERHARDT   **Cecilia Dreiser**
           Mary Frances Dreiser
SEBASTIAN ('BASS') GERHARDT   **Marcus Romanus Dreiser**
           Paul Dresser
LESTER KANE   **Don Ashley**

'Olive Brand', *A Gallery of Women* (1929)
OLIVE BRAND   Edith Delong Smith
JACK JETHRO   Edward H. Smith

'Rona Murtha', *A Gallery of Women* (1929)
RONA MURTHA   Anna T. Mallon
WINFIELD VLASTO   Arthur Henry

Sister Carrie (1900)
BOB AMES   Elmer Gates
FITZGERALD & MOY   Chapin & Gore, Chicago
GEORGE HURSTWOOD   L.A. Hopkins
CAROLINE MEEBER   Emma Dreiser

The Titan (1914)
TIMOTHY ARNEEL   Philip D. Armour
FRANK ALGERNON COWPERWOOD   C.T. Yerkes
BERENICE FLEMING   Emilie Grigsby
HOSMER HAND   William Collins Whitney
PATRICK KERRIGAN   Michael Kenna
WALDEN LUCAS   Carter H. Harrison
ANSON MERRILL   William L. Elkins
NORMAN SCHRYHART   Peter A.B. Widener
GOVERNOR SWANSON   John Peter Altgeld
MICHAEL TIERNAN   John Coughlin

A Traveler at Forty (1913)
BARFLEUR   Grant Richards

Twelve Men (1919)
CULHANE   William Muldoon
PETER   Peter B. McCord
THE MIGHTY ROURKE   Mike Burke

DU MAURIER, George
Peter Ibbetson (1891)
DUCHESS OF TOWERS   Lady Ida Sitwell

Trilby (1894)
WILLIAM BAGOT ('LITTLE BILLEE')   Thomas Armstrong
                                     Frederick Walker
CHEZ CARREL   Atelier Gleyre, Paris
LORRIMER   Sir Edward Poynter
SANDY MCALLISTER ('THE LAIRD')   Thomas Reynolds Lamont
                                     Sir John Everett Millais
JOE SIBLEY   James McNeill Whistler
TALBOT ('TAFFY') WYNNE   Val Prinsep
                                     Joe Rowley

E

EASTMAN, Max
Venture (1927)
JO HANCOCK   **John Reed**
MARY KITTRIDGE   **Mabel Dodge Luhan**

EDGEWORTH, Maria
The Absentee (1812)
COUNT O'HALLORAN   **Lord Trimleston**

Belinda (1801)
LADY DELACOUR   **Sir Francis Delaval**
CLARENCE HERVEY   **Thomas Day**
MR PERCIVAL   **R.L. Edgeworth**
DR X.   **John Moore**

Castle Rackrent (1800)
THADY M'QUIRK   **John Langan**
LADY RACKRENT   **Elizabeth, Lady Cathcart**
SIR CONNOLLY ('CONDY') RACKRENT   **Paul Elers**
SIR KIT RACKRENT   **Colonel Hugh MacGuire**

'Ennui', *Tales of Fashionable Life* (1809)
LORD Y.   **Lord Charlemont**

'Forester', *Moral Tales for Young People* (1801)
DR CAMPBELL   **Dugald Stewart**
FORESTER   **Lord Ashburton**
                                       Thomas Day

Helen (1834)
GRANVILLE BEAUCLERC   **Francis Edgeworth**
HORACE CHURCHILL   **Samuel Rogers**
GENERAL CLARENDON   **Lestock Wilson**
LADY DAVENANT   **R.L. Edgeworth**
ST LEGER SWIFT   **Mr Waite**

'Madame de Fleury', *Tales of Fashionable Life* (1809)
MADAME DE FLEURY   **Comtesse de Pastoret**
MRS SOMERS   **Mrs Mary Powys**

Ormond (1817)
DR CAMBRAI   **Daniel Augustus Beaufort**
CORNELIUS O'SHANE   **James Corry**
SIR ULICK O'SHANE   **John, Baron de Blaquiere**
                                       Admiral Sir Thomas Pakenham

Patronage (1814)
BUCKHURST FALCONER   **Sydney Smith**
COMMISSIONER FALCONER   **Thomas Lewis O'Beirne**
LADY ANGELICA HEADINGHAM   **Jane, Lady Davy**
                                       Lydia White

LORD CHIEF JUSTICE	Charles Kendal Bushe
LORD OLDBOROUGH	1st Baron Ellenborough
	William Stuart
	Robert Walpole
MR PERCY	R.L. Edgeworth
CAROLINE PERCY	Honora Edgeworth
GODFREY PERCY	Richard Edgeworth
ROSAMOND PERCY	Maria Edgeworth

'Rosanna', *Popular Tales* (1804)

COUNCILLOR MOLYNEUX	R.L. Edgeworth

Vivian (1812)

MISS BATEMAN (THE 'ROSAMUNDA')	Sydney, Lady Morgan

ELIOT, George

Adam Bede (1859)

ADAM BEDE	Robert Evans
SETH BEDE	Samuel Evans
THIAS BEDE	George Evans[1]
	George Evans[2]
BROXTON	Roston, Derbyshire
DONNITHORNE ARMS, HAYSLOPE	Bromley-Davenport Arms, Ellastone, Staffordshire
DONNITHORNE CHASE	Wootton Hall, Ellastone, Staffordshire
EAGLEDALE	Dovedale, Staffordshire
HAYSLOPE	Ellastone, Staffordshire
LOAMSHIRE	Staffordshire
DINAH MORRIS	Elizabeth Evans
NORBOURNE	Norbury, Derbyshire
OAKBOURNE	Ashbourne, Derbyshire
ROSSETER	Rocester, Derbyshire
HETTY SORREL	Mary Voce
STONYSHIRE	Derbyshire

Daniel Deronda (1876)

MIRAH COHEN (NÉE LAPIDOTH)	Hertha Ayrton
	Sally Shilton
MORDECAI COHEN	Cohn (or Kohn)
	Emanuel Deutsch
	Alfred Hyman Louis
DANIEL DERONDA	Sir Edward Bond
	Colonel Albert Goldsmid
	Edmund Gurney
	G.H. Lewes
	Alfred Hyman Louis
HENLEIGH MALLINGER GRANDCOURT	Henry du Pré Labouchère
GWENDOLEN HARLETH	Geraldine Leigh
JULIUS KLESMER	Franz Liszt
	Anton Rubinstein

TOPPING ABBEY	Lacock Abbey, Wiltshire
	Maxstoke Priory, Warwickshire

Felix Holt, the Radical (1866)

FELIX HOLT	Gerald Massey
RUFUS LYON	Francis Franklin
	John Sibree
TREBY MAGNA	Coventry, Warwickshire

'Janet's Repentance', *Scenes of Clerical Life* (1857–8)

MR BUDD	Mr Burton
REVD MR CREWE	Revd Hugh Hughes
JANET DEMPSTER	Nancy Buchanan
ROBERT DEMPSTER	J.W. Buchanan
THOMAS JEROME	Mr Everhard
JONATHAN LAMB	Mr Wheway
BENJAMIN LANDOR	Mr Craddock
MARY AND REBECCA LINNET	The Misses Hill
MR LOWME	Mr Towle
MILBY	Nuneaton, Warwickshire
ORCHARD STREET, MILBY	Church Street, Nuneaton, Warwickshire
PADDIFORD	Stockingford, Warwickshire
MRS PETTIFER	Mrs Robinson
MR PHIPPS	Mr Bull
MR PITTMAN	Mr Greenway
RICHARD PRATT	Mr Bond
HON. AND REVD MR PRENDERGAST	Hon. and Revd Mr Stopford
MRS RAYNOR	Nancy Wallington
THE RED LION	The Bull Hotel, Nuneaton, Warwickshire
MR TOMLINSON	Mr Hinks
REVD EDGAR TRYAN	Revd John Edmund Jones

Middlemarch (1871–2)

MR BROOKE	Charles Holt Bracebridge
CELIA BROOKE	Christiana Clarke
DOROTHEA CASAUBON (NÉE BROOKE)	George Eliot
	Dorothy Wyndlow Pattison
	Emilia Francis Pattison
EDWARD CASAUBON	R.H. Brabant
	Jacob Bryant
	George Eliot
	R.W. Mackay
	Mark Pattison
	Herbert Spencer
CALEB GARTH	Robert Evans
WILL LADISLAW	John Walter Cross
TERTIUS LYDGATE	Sir Thomas Clifford Allbutt
	Edward Clarke
	Charles Benjamin Nankivell
MIDDLEMARCH	Coventry, Warwickshire

The Mill on the Floss (1860)

Lucy Deane	Christiana Clarke
	Bessie Garner
Susan Deane (née Dodson)	Anne Garner
Dorlcote Mill	Arbury Mill, Warwickshire
The Floss	River Trent
Garum Firs	Sole End, Astley, Warwickshire
Jane Glegg (née Dodson)	Mary Everard
Gritty Moss	Christiana Clarke
Sophy Pullett (née Dodson)	Elizabeth Johnson
St Ogg's	Gainsborough, Lincolnshire
Edward Tulliver	Robert Evans
	John Pagden
Maggie Tulliver	George Eliot
Tom Tulliver	Isaac Evans
Philip Wakem	François D'Albert-Durade

'Mr Gilfil's Love Story', *Scenes of Clerical Life* (1857–8)

Lady Assher	Lady Anstruther
Beatrice Assher	Miss Anstruther
Bates (the gardener)	Baines
Lady Cheverel	Hester, Lady Newdigate
Sir Anthony Cheverel	Sir Richard Newdigate
Sir Christopher Cheverel	Sir Roger Newdigate
Cheverel Manor	Arbury Hall, Warwickshire
Revd Maynard Gilfil	Revd Bernard Gilpin Ebdell
Mr Oldinport	Francis Newdigate
Oldinport Arms	Newdegate Arms, Nuneaton, Warwickshire
The Rookery, Cheverel Manor	North Walk, Arbury Hall, Warwickshire
Sarti	Signor Motta
Caterina Sarti	Sally Shilton
Anthony Wybrow	Francis Newdigate
	Charles Parker

Romola (1863)

Romola de Bardi	Barbara Bodichon
Nello	Domenico Burchiello

'The Sad Fortunes of the Revd Amos Barton', *Scenes of Clerical Life* (1857–8)

Revd Mr Baird	Revd Mr Sandford
Amelia ('Milly') Barton	Emma Gwyther
Revd Amos Barton	Revd John Gwyther
Mr Brand	Mr Harris
Edmund Bridmain	Sir John Waldron
Revd Mr Carpe	Revd George Hake
Revd Martin Cleves	Revd John Fisher
Revd Archibald Duke	Revd Mr Hoke
Revd Mr Ely	Revd William Hutchinson King
Mr Farquhar	Henry Richard Harper (or Harpur)
Revd Mr Fellowes	Revd Mr Bellairs

Mr Fitchett	Mr Baker
Revd Maynard Gilfil	Revd Bernard Gilpin Ebdell
Mr Hackit	Robert Evans
Mrs Hackit	Christiana Evans
Knebley	Astley, Warwickshire
Mr Landor	Mr Greenway
Mr Oldinport	Rt. Hon. Charles N. Newdegate
Mrs Patten	Mrs Hutchins
Mr Phipps	Mr Bull
	Mr Craddock
Mr Pilgrim	William Bucknill
Shepperton	Chilvers Coton, Warwickshire
Mr Spratt	Mr Hackett
Tripplegate	Higham on the Hill, Leicestershire
Whittlecombe	Stockingford, Warwickshire
Mrs Woodcock	Mrs Craddock

'ELIZABETH'
Elizabeth and Her German Garden (1898)

Irais	Irene Forbes-Mosse

The Enchanted April (1922)

Castegneto	Portofino, Italy
San Salvatore	The Castello, Portofino, Italy

Vera (1921)

Everard Wemyss	Francis, 2nd Earl Russell
The Willows	Telegraph House, Sussex

EMERSON, Mary S.
Among the Chosen (1884)

Harold	Laurence Oliphant[2]
Father Joseph	Thomas Lake Harris

ENDICOTT, Stephen
Mayor Harding of New York (1931)

George De Angelis	Fiorello Henry La Guardia
Jim White	Alfred Emanuel Smith

F

FARRAR, F.W.
Eric; or Little by Little (1858)

Eric Williams	Cyril Flower, 1st Baron Battersea

FARRELL, James T.
A World I Never Made (1936) and others

Danny O'Neill	James T. Farrell

FAULKNER, J. Meade
The Lost Stradivarius (1895)
VILLA DE ANGELIS   Villa Maya, Posilipo

FAULKNER, William
Mosquitoes (1927)
DAWSON FAIRCHILD   Sherwood Anderson

The Unvanquished (1938)
COLONEL JOHN SARTORIS   William Cuthbert Falkner

The Yoknapatawpha novels: *Sartoris* (1929), *The Sound and the Fury* (1929),
    As I Lay Dying (1930), *Light in August* (1932), and *Absalom, Absalom!*
    (1936)
JEFFERSON   Oxford, Mississippi
YOKNAPATAWPHA COUNTY   Lafayette County, Mississippi

FAY, Theodore S.
Norman Leslie: A Tale of the Present Times (1835)
ANGELO   Horatio Greenough

FIELD, Francis T.
McDonough (1951)
BOSS COYLE   Frank Hague
ED COYLE   Frank Hague Eggers
LENAPE COUNTY   Middlesex County, New Jersey
NEW BOYNTON   New Brunswick, New Jersey
PORT ALBY   Perth Amboy, New Jersey

FIRBANK, Ronald
The Flower Beneath the Foot (1923)
MRS CHILLEYWATER   Victoria Sackville-West
THE ENGLISH AMBASSADRESS   Mary Catherine Nicolson
                                    Flora Roscoe
EDDIE MONTEITH   Evan Morgan

Vainglory (1915)
WINSOME BROOKES   Rupert Brooke
MRS SHAMEFOOT   Lady Angela Forbes

FITZGERALD, F. Scott
'Babylon Revisited' (1935)
MARION PETERS   Rosalind Smith
HONORIA WALES   Frances Scott Fitzgerald

The Beautiful and Damned (1922)
MAURY NOBLE   George Jean Nathan
ANTHONY PATCH   F. Scott Fitzgerald
GLORIA PATCH   Zelda Fitzgerald

'Crazy Sunday' (1935)
MILES CALMAN   Irving Thalberg

JOEL COLES	F. Scott Fitzgerald
	Dwight Taylor
'First Blood' (1930) and others	
JOSEPHINE PERRY	Ginevra King
'The Freshest Boy' (1935)	
TED FAY	Edward Harris Coy
The Great Gatsby (1925)	
JORDAN BAKER	Edith Cummings
JAY GATSBY	F. Scott Fitzgerald
MEYER WOLFSHIEM	Arnold Rothstein
'The Ice Palace' (1921)	
SALLY CARROL	Zelda Fitzgerald
'The Intimate Strangers' (1935)	
CEDRIC KILLIAN	Lefty Flynn
SARA KILLIAN	Nora Flynn
The Last Tycoon (1941)	
CECILIA BRADY	Frances Scott Fitzgerald
	Budd Schulberg
KATHLEEN	Sheila Graham
MINNA STAHR	Zelda Fitzgerald
'Magnetism' (1951)	
HELEN AVERY	Lois Moran
'A Night at the Fair' (1957)	
HUBERT BLAIR	Reuben Warner
RIPLY BUCKNER	Cecil Reed
BASIL DUKE LEE	F. Scott Fitzgerald
'The Rich Boy' (1926)	
ANSON HUNTER	Ludlow Sebring Fowler
'The Scandal Detectives' (1935)	
IMOGENE BISSET	Marie Hersey
Tender is the Night (1934)	
TOMMY BARBAN	Mario Braggiotti
	Thomas Hitchcock
	Edouard Jozan
LUIS CAMPION	Sir Charles Mendl
NICOLE DIVER	Zelda Fitzgerald
	Sara Murphy
RICHARD DIVER	F. Scott Fitzgerald
	Gerald Murphy
ROSEMARY HOYT	Lois Moran
ABE NORTH	F. Scott Fitzgerald
	Ring Lardner
BABY WARREN	Mary Hoyt Wiborg

This Side of Paradise (1920)

ISABELLE BARGÉ	Ginevra King
ROSALIND CONNAGE	Zelda Fitzgerald
MONSIGNOR DARCY	Monsignor Sigourney Fay
THOMAS P. D'INVILLIERS	John Peale Bishop
THORNTON HANCOCK	Henry Adams
BURNE HOLIDAY	Henry Strater
MRS LAWRENCE	Mrs Winthrop Chanler
CLARA PAGE	Cecilia Delihant Taylor

FITZGERALD, Zelda
Save Me the Waltz (1932)

ALABAMA BEGGS	Zelda Fitzgerald
JACQUES CHEVRE-FEUILLE	Edouard Jozan
DAVID KNIGHT	F. Scott Fitzgerald

FLEMING, George
Mirage (1877)

CLAUDE DAVENANT	Oscar Wilde

FORD, Ford Madox
The Good Soldier (1915)

EDWARD ASHBURNHAM	Ford Madox Ford
LEONORA ASHBURNHAM	Elsie Hueffer
FLORENCE DOWELL	Violet Hunt
JOHN DOWELL	Ford Madox Ford

The Marsden Case (1923)

GEORGE HEIMANN	William Ralston
MADAME	Frida Strindberg
THE NIGHTCLUB	The Cave of the Golden Calf, London

The New Humpty-Dumpty (1912)

EMILY, LADY ALDINGTON	Violet Hunt
THE DUKE OF KINTYRE	Arthur Marwood
COUNT SERGIUS MIHAILOVICH MACDONALD	Ford Madox Ford
COUNTESS MACDONALD	Elsie Hueffer
HERBERT PETT	H.G. Wells

Parade's End (1924–8)

GROBY	Busby Hall, Carlton-in-Cleveland, North Yorkshire
CHRISTOPHER TIETJENS	Arthur Marwood
MRS WANNOP	Margaret Hunt
STEPHEN FENWICK WATERHOUSE	C.F. Masterman

The Simple Life Limited (1911)

CYRIL BRANDETSKI	David Soskice
	Sergius Stepniak

OPHELIA BRANSDON	Juliet Soskice
SIMON BRANSDON	Joseph Conrad
GEORGE EVERARD	Frank Harris
HORATIO GUBB	Ford Madox Ford
	J.B. Pinker
	H.G. Wells
MR HANGBIRD	Stephen Crane
EVANGELINE LUSCOMBE	Caroline Marwood
GERALD LUSCOMBE	Arthur Marwood
MR MAJOR	William Harrison Cowlishaw
MR PARMONT	Edward Garnett
MISS STOBHALL	Constance Garnett
	Olive Garnett

See also under CONRAD, Joseph, and FORD, Ford Madox.

FORSTER, E.M.
Howards End (1910)

HOWARDS END	Rooksrest, Stevenage, Hertfordshire
ONITON	Clun, Shropshire
HELEN SCHLEGEL	Virginia Woolf
	The Misses Dickinson
MARGARET SCHLEGEL	Vanessa Bell
	The Misses Dickinson

The Longest Journey (1907)

STEWART ANSELL	A.R. Ainsworth
	H.O. Meredith
CADBURY RINGS	Figsbury Rings, Wiltshire
CADOVER	Acton House, Felton, Northumberland
FREDERICK ('RICKIE') ELLIOT	E.M. Forster
MRS EMILY FAILING	W.H. Forster
	Countess Russell
MR JACKSON	I.F. Smedley
	Nathaniel Wedd
SAWSTON	Tonbridge, Kent
SAWSTON SCHOOL	Tonbridge School, Kent

A Passage to India (1924)

DR AZIZ	Syed Ross Masood
CHANDRAPORE	Bankipore, Patna
NARAYAN GODBOLE	Maharajah of Chhatarpur
KAWA DOL	Kauwãdol, Bihar, India
MARABAR CAVES	Barabar Caves
MAU	Chhatarpur, India
	Dewas, Central India

A Room with a View (1908)

CHARLOTTE BARTLETT	Emily Forster
PENSION BERTOLINI	Pension Simi, Florence
MR EMERSON	Samuel Butler

MRS HONEYCHURCH	Louisa Whichelo
MISS LAVISH	Emily Spender
SUMMER STREET	Holmbury St Mary, Surrey
CECIL VYSE	E.M. Forster

Where Angels Fear to Tread (1905)

SANTA DEODATA	Santa Fina
PHILIP HERRITON	E.J. Dent
	E.M. Forster
MONTERIANO	San Gimignano, Italy
SAWSTON	Tonbridge, Kent

FRANKEL, Ernest
Tongue of Fire (1960)

KANE O'CONNOR	Joseph McCarthy

FRIEDMAN, I.K.
By Bread Alone (1901)

SOPHIA GOLDSTEIN	Emma Goldman
HENRY MARVIN	Henry Clay Frick
MARVIN STEEL MILL	Homestead Steel Mill, Pennsylvania

FRISWELL, Hain
One of Two (1871)

TOM FORSTER	Charles Frederick Field

FROUDE, James Anthony
The Nemesis of Faith (1849)

MARKHAM SUTHERLAND	James Anthony Froude

'The Spirit's Trials', *Shadows of the Clouds* (1847)

DARLING	Dartington, Devon
CANON FOWLER	Robert Hurrell Froude
EDWARD FOWLER	James Anthony Froude
EMMA HARDINGE	Harriet Bush

G

GALSWORTHY, John
'The Doldrums', *Forsytes, Pendyces and Others* (1935)

ARMAND	Joseph Conrad

The Man of Property (1906)

PHILIP BOSINNEY	Edward Garnett
IRENE FORSYTE	Ada Galsworthy
ROBIN HILL	Coombe Warren, Surrey

The Patrician (1911)
CHARLES COURTIER   **H.W. Nevinson**

GALT, John
Lawrie Todd (1830)
LAWRIE TODD   **Grant Thorburn**

The Provost (1822)
THE EARL   **12th Earl of Eglinton**
GUDETOWN   **Irvine, Ayrshire**
JAMES PAWKIE   **Bailie Fullerton**

Sir Andrew Wylie (1822)
LORD SANDYFORD   **Lord Blessington**

GARNETT, David
Beany-Eye (1935)
MRS BUTLER   **Constance Garnett**
JAMES BUTLER   **Edward Garnett**
JOE STARLING   **Bill Hedgecock**

GASKELL, Elizabeth
Cousin Phillis (1864)
EBENEZER HOLMAN   **Samuel Holland**

Cranford (1853)
CRANFORD   **Knutsford, Cheshire**

Mary Barton (1843)
HARRY CARSON   **Thomas Ashton**

My Lady Ludlow (1858)
LADY LUDLOW   **Viscountess Hereford**

North and South (1855)
NICHOLAS HIGGINS   **George Cowell**
MILTON   **Manchester**
MILTON STRIKE   **Preston Strike**

Ruth (1853)
REVD THURSTAN BENSON   **William Turner[2]**
BENSON'S CHAPEL   **Brook Street Unitarian Chapel,**
     Knutsford, Cheshire

Sylvia's Lovers (1863)
MONKSHAVEN   **Whitby, Yorkshire**

GELLHORN, Martha
His Own Man (1961)
LIZ LANGHAM   **Judith Venetia Montagu**

GEORGE, W.L.
Caliban (1920)
RICHARD BULMER   **Lord Northcliffe**

GERHARDI (later Gerhardie), William
Jazz and Jasper (1928)
LORD DE JONES   **Lord Castlerosse**
LORD OTTERCOVE   **Lord Beaverbrook**
VERNON SPROTT   **Arnold Bennett**

Pending Heaven (1930)
MAX FISHER   **Hugh Kingsmill**

GISSING, George
Born in Exile (1892)
MALKIN   **Morley Roberts**
GOODWIN PEAK   **George Gissing**

The Emancipated (1890)
MIRIAM BASKE   **Margaret Gissing**
ROSS MALLARD   **Morley Roberts**

In the Year of the Jubilee (1894)
HUGHIE ROLFE   **Walter Leonard Gissing**

A Life's Morning (1888)
BANBRIGG   **Agbrigg, Yorkshire**
DUNFIELD   **Wakefield, Yorkshire**

New Grub Street (1891)
WHELPDALE   **Morley Roberts**

The Unclassed (1884)
JULIAN CASTI   **Eduard Bertz**
OSMUND WAYMARK   **George Gissing**

The Whirlpool (1897)
HUGHIE ROLFE   **Walter Leonard Gissing**

Workers in the Dawn (1880)
CARRIE MITCHELL   **Nell Gissing**

GLASPELL, Susan
Alison's House (1930)
ALISON STANHOPE   **Emily Dickinson**

GLOVER, Halcott
Both Sides of the Blanket (1945)
JULIAN FIELD   **Leigh Hunt**

GLYN, Elinor
The Career of Katherine Bush (1917)
LADY GARRIBARDINE   **Lady Londonderry**

Halcyone (1912)
ARNOLD CARLYON   **F.H. Bradley**
JOHN DERRINGHAM   **Lord Curzon**
HALCYONE LA SARTHE   **Elinor Glyn**

His Hour (1910)
PRINCESS ARDACHEFF   **Grand Duchess Vladimir of Russia**
PRINCE GRITZKO MILASLAVSKI   **Prince Gregory von Sayn and Wittgenstein**

The Reflections of Ambrosine (1902)
MRS ATHELSTAN   **Mrs Thomas Saunders**
SIR ANTHONY THORNHIRST   **Seymour Wynne Finch**
LADY TILCHESTER   **Frances, Lady Warwick**

Three Weeks (1907)
MADAME ZALENSKA ('THE LADY') **Alexandra Feodorovna, Empress of Russia**

The Visits of Elizabeth (1900)
ELIZABETH   **Lady Angela Forbes**

GODWIN, William
Cloudesley (1830)
BORROMEO   **E.J. Trelawny**
JULIAN CLOUDESLEY   **James Annesley**

St Leon (1799)
MARGUERITE DE ST LEON   **Mary Wollstonecraft**

GRAHAME, Kenneth
The Wind in the Willows (1908)
MR BADGER   **W.E. Henley**
                       5th Duke of Portland
PAN   **F.J. Furnivall**
RAT   **Edward Atkinson**
                       F.J. Furnivall
                       W.E. Henley
MR TOAD   **Alistair Grahame**
TOAD HALL   **Cliveden, Buckinghamshire**
                       Harleyford Manor, Buckinghamshire
                       Mapledurham House, Oxfordshire

GRANT, James L.
Male and Female (1933)
DAVID MARSH   **D.H. Lawrence**

GREEN, Henry
Blindness (1926)
E.V.C.   **Colin Anderson**
BEN GORE   **Robert Byron**

JOHN HAYE   **Henry Green**
NOAT   **Eton College, Berkshire**
NOAT ART SOCIETY **Eton Society of Arts, Eton College,
         Berkshire**

GREENE, Graham
It's a Battlefield (1934)
MRS CAROLINE BURY **Lady Ottoline Morrell**
THE COMMISSIONER **Sir William Graham Greene**
PHILIP SURROGATE **John Middleton Murry**

'The Third Man' (1958)
BENJAMIN DEXTER **E.M. Forster**

H

HALL, Radclyffe
The Well of Loneliness (1928)
ADOLPHE BLANC **Adrien Mirtil**
STEPHEN GORDON **Radclyffe Hall**
MARY LLEWELLYN **Una, Lady Troubridge**
VALÉRIE SEYMOUR **Natalie Clifford Barney**

HAMILTON, Thomas
The Youth and Manhood of Cyril Thornton (1827)
CYRIL THORNTON **Charles O'Hara**

HAMMETT, Dashiel
The Thin Man (1932)
NORA CHARLES   **Lillian Hellmann**

HARDY, Thomas
'Audrey Satchel and the Parson' (1894)
SCRIMPTON   **Frampton, Dorset**
REVD BILLY TOOGOOD **Revd William Butler**

'Barbara of the House of Grebe' (1891)
KNOLLINGWOOD HALL **St Giles House, Wimborne St
         Giles, Dorset**
LORNTON INN   **Horton Inn, Dorset**
LORD UPLANDTOWERS **5th Earl of Shaftesbury**
YEWSHOLT LODGE **Farr House, Dorset**

'A Changed Man' (1913)
CAPTAIN JOHN MAUMBRY **Henry Moule**

Desperate Remedies (1871)
CRESTON   **Preston, Dorset**

KNAPWATER HOUSE	**Kingston Maurward House, Stinsford, Dorset**
EDWARD SPRINGROVE	**Thomas Hardy**
TOLCHURCH	**Tolpuddle, Dorset**

'The Distracted Preacher' (1888)
CHALDON	**East Chaldon (or Chaldon Herring), Dorset**

'The Duchess of Hamptonshire' (1891)
ALWYN HILL	**Revd Caddell Holder**

Far from the Madding Crowd (1874)
WEATHERBURY UPPER FARM	**Druce Farm, Puddletown, Dorset**
	Waterston House, Puddletown, Dorset

'The Fiddler of the Reels' (1894)
MOREFORD	**Moreton, Dorset**

'The First Countess of Wessex' (1891)
BETTY DORNELL	**Elizabeth, Countess of Ilchester**
SUSAN DORNELL	**Susanna Strangways**
THOMAS DORNELL	**Thomas Horner**
ELM-CRANLYNCH	**Corfe Mullen, Dorset**
FALLS-PARK	**Mells, Somerset**
STEPHEN REYNARD (AFTERWARDS EARL OF WESSEX)	**Stephen Fox, 1st Earl of Ilchester**

'The Grave by the Handpost' (1913)
BROAD SIDLINCH	**Sydling St Nicholas, Dorset**
HON. AND REVD MR OLDHAM	**Charles Redlynch Fox-Strangways**

The Hand of Ethelberta (1876)
ETHELBERTA CHICKEREL	**Jemima Hardy**
FLYCHETT	**Lytchett Minster, Dorset**
ROOKINGTON PARK	**Hurn Court, Bournemouth, Dorset**

'The Honourable Laura' (1891)
DOWNSTABLE	**Barnstaple, Devon**

'An Imaginative Woman' (1896)
ELLA MARCHMILL	**Florence Henniker**

'An Indiscretion in the Life of an Heiress' (1878)
FAIRLAND	**Higher Bockhampton, Dorset**
MELPORT	**Weymouth, Dorset**
TOLLAMORE	**Stinsford, Dorset**
TOLLAMORE HOUSE	**Kingston Maurward House, Stinsford, Dorset**

Jude the Obscure (1895)
BEERSHEBA	**Jericho, Oxford**
SUE BRIDEHEAD	**Florence Henniker**
	Tryphena Sparks

CARDINAL COLLEGE, CHRISTMINSTER	**Christ Church, Oxford**
CHIEF STREET, CHRISTMINSTER	**High Street, Oxford**
CHRISTMINSTER	**Oxford**
CRESSCOMBE	**Letcombe Bassett, Oxfordshire**
THE CROZIER HOTEL, CHRISTMINSTER	**The Mitre Hotel, Oxford**
ARABELLA DONN	**Rachel H——**
FENSWORTH	**Letcombe Regis, Oxfordshire**
THE FOURWAYS, CHRISTMINSTER	**Carfax, Oxford**
KENNETBRIDGE	**Newbury, Berkshire**
LEDDENTON	**Gillingham, Dorset**
LUMSDON	**Cumnor, Oxfordshire**
MARYGREEN	**Fawley, Berkshire**
MELCHESTER NORMAL SCHOOL	**Salisbury Training College**
QUARTERSHOT	**Aldershot, Hampshire**
ST SILAS	**St Barnabas, Oxford**
STOKE-BAREHILLS	**Basingstoke, Hampshire**

'The Lady Icenway' (1891)

ICENWAY HOUSE	**Herriard House, Hampshire**

'Lady Mottisfont' (1891)

DEANSLEIGH PARK	**Broadlands, Romsey, Hampshire**
FERNELL HALL	**Embley House, Romsey, Hampshire**

A Laodicean (1881)

MARKTON	**Dunster, Somerset**
JOHN POWER	**Sir Samuel Morton Peto**
STANCY CASTLE	**Dunster Castle, Somerset**
REVD MR WOODWELL	**Revd Mr Perkins**

'Master John Horseleigh, Knight' (1913)

MONTISLOPE HOUSE	**Montacute House, Somerset**
OOZEWOOD	**Ringwood, Hampshire**

The Mayor of Casterbridge (1886)

HIGH-PLACE HALL	**Colliton House, Dorchester, Dorset**
MAI DUN	**Maiden Castle, Dorset**
MIXEN LANE, DURNOVER	**Mill Street, Fordington**
THE THREE MARINERS	**The King of Prussia, Dorchester, Dorset**
THE VIA	**Icening Way, Dorchester, Dorset**

'A Mere Interlude' (1913)

ISLES OF LYONESSE	**Scilly Isles**
PEN-ZEPHYR	**Penzance, Cornwall**
REDRUTIN	**Redruth, Cornwall**
TOR-UPON-SEA	**Torquay, Devon**
TRUFAL	**Truro, Cornwall**

Old Mrs Chundle (1929)

KINGSCREECH	**Kingston, Dorset**

A Pair of Blue Eyes (1873)

BARWITH STRAND	Trebarwith Strand, Cornwall
CAMELTON	Camelford, Cornwall
CASTLE BOTEREL	Boscastle, Cornwall
DUNDAGEL	Tintagel Castle, Cornwall
ENDELSTOW	St Juliot, Cornwall
ENDELSTOW HOUSE	Lanhydrock House, Cornwall
HENRY KNIGHT	Thomas Hardy
	Horace Mosley Moule
ST LAUNCE'S	Launceston, Cornwall
STRATLEIGH	Bude, Cornwall
ELFRIDE SWANCOURT	Emma Hardy

The Return of the Native (1878)

EAST EGDON	Affpuddle, Dorset
MISTOVER KNAP	Troy Town, Dorset
MR YEOBRIGHT	Thomas Hardy, the First

'The Romantic Adventures of a Milkmaid' (1913)

SILVERTHORN	Silverton, Devon
TIVWORTHY	Tiverton, Devon

'Squire Petrick's Lady' (1891)

MILL POOL	Milborne Port, Somerset
TIMOTHY PETRICK, I	Peter Walter[1]
TIMOTHY PETRICK, II	Peter Walter[2]
STAPLEFORD PARK	Stalbridge House, Dorset

Tess of the d'Urbervilles (1891)

BRAMHURST COURT	Moyles Court, Hampshire
ANGEL CLARE	Charles Moule
REVD JAMES CLARE	Revd Henry Moule
TERESA ('TESS') DURBEYFIELD	Agatha Thornycroft
FLOWER-DE-LUCE	Fleur-de-Lis Inn, Cranbourne, Dorset
LEW EVERARD	West Stafford, Dorset
NUTTLEBURY	Hazelbury Bryan, Dorset
STOURCASTLE	Sturminster Newton, Dorset
WELLBRIDGE	Wool, Dorset

The Trumpet Major (1880)

DAMER'S WOOD	Came Wood, Dorset
HAGGARDON	Eggardon Hill, Dorset
OXWELL HALL, OXWELL	Poxwell Manor, Poxwell, Dorset

Under the Greenwood Tree (1872)

CHARMLEY	Charminster, Dorset
MELLSTOCK QUIRE	Stinsford Quire
ROBERT PENNY	Robert Reason

'The Waiting Supper' (1913)

ELSENFORD	Ilsington Farm, Dorset
FROOM-EVERARD HOUSE	Stafford House, Dorset

The Well-Beloved (1897)

EAST QUARRIERS	Easton, Portland, Dorset

Wessex novels and tales (1871–95)

ABBOTSCERNEL	Cerne Abbas, Dorset
ABBOTSEA	Abbotsbury, Dorset
ALDBRICKHAM	Reading, Berkshire
ANGLEBURY	Wareham, Dorset
ATHELHALL	Athelhampton Hall, Dorset
THE BLACKWATER	Frome River
BUDMOUTH	Weymouth, Dorset
CASTERBRIDGE	Dorchester, Dorset
CHALK NEWTON	Maiden Newton, Dorset
CHASEBOROUGH	Cranborne, Dorset
CHENE MANOR	Canford Manor, Dorset
CORVSGATE CASTLE	Corfe Castle, Dorset
DURNOVER	Fordington, Dorset
EGDON HEATH	Puddletown Heath, Dorset
EMMINSTER	Beaminster, Dorset
EVERSHEAD	Evershot, Dorset
EXONBURY	Exeter, Devon
FOUNTALL	Wells, Somerset
THE GREAT FOREST	New Forest, Hampshire
THE GREAT PLAIN	Salisbury Plain
GREENHILL	Woodbury Hill, Dorset
HAVENPOOL	Poole, Dorset
HINTOCK HOUSE	Turnworth House, Dorset
ISLE OF SLINGERS	Isle of Portland
IVELL (OR IVEL)	Yeovil, Somerset
KING'S HINTOCK	Melbury Osmond, Dorset
KING'S HINTOCK COURT	Melbury House, Dorset
KINGSBERE	Bere Regis, Dorset
KNOLLSEA	Swanage, Dorset
LONGPUDDLE	Piddlehinton, Dorset
	Piddletrenthide, Dorset
LOWER MELLSTOCK	Lower Bockhampton, Dorset
LULWIND COVE	Lulworth Cove, Dorset
MARLOTT	Marnhull, Dorset
MELCHESTER	Salisbury, Wiltshire
MELLSTOCK	Stinsford, Dorset
NETHER-MOYNTON	Owermoigne, Dorset
PORT-BREDY	Bridport, Dorset
THE PURE DROP INN, MARLOTT	Crown Inn, Marnhull, Dorset
RINGSWORTH	Ringstead Bay, Dorset
ROY-TOWN	Troy Town, Dorset
SANDBOURNE	Bournemouth, Dorset
SHASTON	Shaftesbury, Dorset
SHERTON ABBAS	Sherborne, Dorset
SHOTTSFORD FORUM	Blandford Forum, Dorset
SOLENTSEA	Southsea, Hampshire

STAGFOOT LANE	Hartfoot Lane, Dorset
STICKLEFORD	Tincleton, Dorset
STREET OF WELLS	Fortune's Well, Portland, Dorset
TONEBOROUGH	Taunton, Somerset
TRANTRIDGE	Pentridge, Dorset
	Tarrant Hinton, Dorset
UPPER MELLSTOCK	Higher Bockhampton, Dorset
WEATHERBURY	Puddletown, Dorset
WEYDON-PRIORS	Weyhill, Hampshire
WINTONCESTER	Winchester, Hampshire
YALBURY WOOD	Yellowham Wood, Dorset

'What the Shepherd Saw' (1913)

MARLBURY DOWNS	Marlborough Downs, Wiltshire
SHAKEFOREST TOWERS	Clatford Hall, Wiltshire

The Woodlanders (1887)

MIDDLETON ABBEY	Milton Abbas, Dorset

HAWTHORNE, Nathaniel
The Blithedale Romance (1852)

BLITHEDALE	Brook Farm, Massachusetts
MILES COVERDALE	Nathaniel Hawthorne
ZENOBIA	Margaret Fuller

Dr Grimshawe's Secret (1883)

MR COLCORD	Bronson Alcott
	George Partridge Bradford
DR ORMSKIRK	Seymour Stocker Kirkup

'The Great Stone Face' (1850)

OLD BLOOD AND THUNDER	Zachary Taylor

The House of the Seven Gables (1851)

THE HOUSE OF THE SEVEN GABLES	Montpelier, Maine
MATHEW MAULE	Sarah Good
COLONEL PYNCHEON	John Hathorne
	Nicholas Noyes
JUDGE PYNCHEON	C.W. Upham
UNCLE VENNER'S 'FARM'	Salem, Massachusetts

The Marble Faun (1860)

VILLA MONTE BENI	Villa Montauto, Florence
MIRIAM SCHAEFFER	Mrs Salomons

The Scarlett Letter (1850)

PEARL	Una Hawthorne

HAY, Cecil
The Club and the Drawing Room (1870)

EGLINTON CONYERS	James Hannay

H.D. (Hilda Doolittle)
Bid Me to Live (1960)

JULIA ASHTON	**Hilda Doolittle**
RAFE ASHTON	**Richard Aldington**
LETT BARNES	**Ezra Pound**
BELLA CARTER	**Dorothy Yorke**
MARY DOWELL	**Amy Lowell**
FREDERICK ('FREDERICO')	**D.H. Lawrence**
ELSE FREDERICK	**Frieda Lawrence**
MORGAN LE FAY	**Brigit Patmore**
IVAN LEFSKY	**John Cournos**
VANE	**Cecil Gray**

HECHT, Ben
Count Bruga (1926)

COUNT BRUGA	**Maxwell Bodenheim**

A Jew in Love (1930)

JO BOSHERE	**Maxwell Bodenheim**

HEMINGWAY, Ernest
Across the River and into the Trees (1950)

RICHARD CANTWELL	**Ernest Hemingway**
	C.T. Lanham
	Charles Sweeny
RENATA	**Adriana Ivancich**

'The Battler', *In Our Time* (1925)

ADOLPH FRANCIS	**Battling Nelson**
	Ad Wolgast

'Big Two-Hearted River', *In Our Time* (1925)

TWO-HEARTED RIVER	**Fox River, Michigan**

'The End of Something', *In Our Time* (1925)

BILL	**Bill Smith**
MARJORIE	**Marjorie Bump**

A Farewell to Arms (1929)

CATHERINE BARKLEY	**Hadley Hemingway**
	Pauline Hemingway
	Elsie Jessup
	Agnes Von Kurowsky
COUNT GREFFI	**Count Giuseppe Greppi**
FREDERIC HENRY	**Ernest Hemingway**
	Edward McKey
RINALDO RINALDI	**Enrico Serena**

'Fathers and Sons', *Winner Take Nothing* (1933)

NICK'S FATHER	**C.E. Hemingway**

'The Fifth Column', *The Fifth Column and the First Forty-nine Stories* (1938)

ANTONIO	**Pepe Quintanilla**

DOROTHY BRIDGES — **Martha Gellhorn**

'Fifty Grand', *Men Without Women* (1927)
JACK BRENNAN — **Jack Britton**
WALCOTT — **Benny Leonard**
Edward Michael Walker

For Whom the Bell Tolls (1940)
GENERAL GOLZ — **Karol Swiercziewski**
ROBERT JORDAN — **Robert Merriman**
KARKOV — **Mihail Koltsov**

The Green Hills of Africa (1935)
DAN — **Ben Fourie**
KANDISKY — **Hans Koritschoner**
KARL — **Charles Thompson**
P.O.M. — **Pauline Hemingway**
JACKSON PHILLIPS — **Philip Percival**

In Our Time (1925)
HENRY ADAMS (THE DOCTOR) — **C.E. Hemingway**
NICK ADAMS — **Ernest Hemingway**

'Indian Camp', *In Our Time* (1925)
UNCLE GEORGE — **George R. Hemingway**

'The Mother of a Queen', *Winner Take Nothing* (1933)
PACO — **Ortiz**

'Mr and Mrs Elliot', *In Our Time* (1925)
CORNELIA ELLIOT — **Olive Cary Smith**
HUBERT ELLIOT — **Chard Powers Smith**

The Old Man and the Sea (1952)
SANTIAGO — **Carlos Gutiérrez**
Eddie Saunders

'The Short Happy Life of Francis Macomber', *The Fifth Column and the First Forty-nine Stories* (1938)
MARGOT MACOMBER — **Jane Mason**
ROBERT WILSON — **Philip Percival**

'The Snows of Kilimanjaro', *The Fifth Column and the First Forty-nine Stories* (1938)
COMPTON — **'Fatty' Pearson**
JULIAN — **F. Scott Fitzgerald**

The Sun Also Rises (1926)
JAKE BARNES — **William Bird**
Ernest Hemingway
MRS BRADDOCKS — **Stella Bowen**
HENRY BRADDOCKS — **Ford Madox Ford**
BRETT, LADY ASHLEY — **Duff, Lady Twysden**
MICHAEL CAMPBELL — **Pat Guthrie**
FRANCES CLYNE — **Kitty Cannell**

ROBERT COHN	**Harold Loeb**
BILL GORTON	**John Dos Passos**
	Bill Smith
	Donald Ogden Stewart
JUANITO MONTOYA	**Juanito Quintana**
ROBERT PRENTISS	**Glenway Wescott**
PEDRO ROMERO	**Cayetano Ordóñez**
HARVEY STONE	**Harold Stearns**
WILSON-HARRIS	**E.E. Dorman-Smith**
'DUKE' ZIZI	**Demetrius Mitzicus**

'Ten Indians', *Men Without Women* (1927)

JOE GARNER	**Joseph Bacon**

'The Three Day Blow' (1925)

BILL	**Bill Smith**

To Have and Have Not (1937)

TOMMY BRADLEY	**George Grant Mason**
FREDDY'S BAR	**Sloppy Joe's**
RICHARD GORDON	**John Dos Passos**
	Edward Fisher
JAMES LAUGHTON	**Jack Coles**
MRS JAMES LAUGHTON	**Mrs Jack Coles**
JOHN MACWALSEY	**Harry H. Burns**
	Arnold Gingrich
EDDY MARSHALL	**Joe Lowe**
HARRY MORGAN	**Joe Russell**
ROBERT ('BEE-LIPS') SIMMONS	**Georgie Brooks**
FREDDY WALLACE	**Joe Russell**

'A Very Short Story', *In Our Time* (1925)

LUZ	**Agnes Von Kurowsky**

'Wine of Wyoming', *Winner Take Nothing* (1933)

FONTAN AND MADAME FONTAN	**Charles and Alice Moncini**

HEMINGWAY, Leicester
The Sound of the Trumpet (1953)

DAN GRANHAM	**Leicester Hemingway**
RANDO GRANHAM	**Ernest Hemingway**

HENRY, Arthur
An Island Cabin (1902)

NANCY	**Anna T. Mallon**
RUTH	**Sara Osborne White Dreiser**
TOM	**Theodore Dreiser**

HERBERT, A.P.
Holy Deadlock (1934)

TIMOTHY BARTER	**E.S.P. Haynes**

The Secret Battle (1919)
HARRY PENROSE   **Edwin Dyett**

HICHENS, Robert
The Green Carnation (1894)
ESMÉ AMARINTH   **Oscar Wilde**
LORD REGINALD HASTINGS   **Lord Alfred Douglas**

HOBBES, John Oliver
Robert Orange (1900)
ROBERT ORANGE   **Benjamin Disraeli**

The School for Saints (1897)
ROBERT ORANGE   **Benjamin Disraeli**

HOGG, T.J.
Memoirs of Prince Alexy Haimatoff (1813)
MONSIEUR GOTHA   **James Lind**
PRINCE ALEXY HAIMATOFF   **T.J. Hogg**
                             Percy Bysshe Shelley

HOOK, Theodore
Gilbert Gurney (1836)
MR HULL   **Thomas Hill**

The Man of Sorrow (1809)
MR MINUS   **Thomas Moore**

HOPKINS, S.H.
Revelry (1926)
SENATOR WELLING   **Robert La Follette**

HOULT, Norah
There Were No Windows (1946)
CLAIRE TEMPLE   **Violet Hunt**

HOWARD, George Bronson
God's Man (1915)
CORNIGAN   **Joseph Corrigan**

'The Parasite' (1912)
MILTON LAZARD   **Wilson Mizner**

HOWELLS, W.D.
A Chance Acquaintance (1874)
MILES ARBUTON   **Thomas Sergeant Perry**

The Coast of Bohemia (1893)
SYNTHESIS OF ART STUDIES   **The Art Students' League**

A Hazard of New Fortunes (1890)
FULKERSON   **Samuel Sidney McClure**

HUGHES, Thomas
The Scouring of the White Horse (1859)
THE SQUIRE   **Edwin Martin Atkins**

Tom Brown's Schooldays (1857)
GEORGE ARTHUR   **W.P. Adam**
                                             August Orlebar
                                             Theodore Walrond
THOMAS BROWN   **Thomas Hughes**
CRAB JONES   **Edmund Smyth**
'SLOGGER' WILLIAMS   **Bulkeley Owen Jones**
THE YOUNG MASTER   **George Edward Lynch Cotton**

HUNT, Mrs Alfred
Thornicroft's Model (1873)
STEPHEN THORNICROFT   **Dante Gabriel Rossetti**

HUNT, Violet
Sooner or Later (1904)
ROBERT ASSHETON   **Oswald Crawfurd**
ROSE NEWALL   **Violet Hunt**

HUNT JACKSON, Helen
Mercy Philbrick's Choice (1876)
MERCY PHILBRICK   **Emily Dickinson**

HURT, Walter
The Scarlet Shadow (1907)
HOOSTMAN   **Walter Vrooman**
DANIEL MELNOTTE   **David Halliday Moffat**
SHOFORTH   **George Shoaf**

HUXLEY, Aldous
After Many a Summer (1939)
VIRGINIA MAUNCIPLE   **Marion Davis**
                                             Paulette Goddard
WILLIAM PROPTER   **Gerald Heard**
JOSEPH PAUL STOYTE   **William Randolph Hearst**

'After the Fireworks' (1930)
MILES FANNING   **François René de Chateaubriand**
PAMELA TARN   **Léontine de Villeneuve**

Antic Hay (1923)
COLEMAN   **Philip Heseltine**
MRS GUMBRIL   **Julia Huxley**
JAMES SHEARWATER   **J.B.S. Haldane**
MYRA VIVEASH   **Nancy Cunard**

HENRY WIMBUSH	**Philip Morrell**

Crome Yellow (1921)

MR BARBECUE SMITH	**Arnold Bennett**
REVD MR BODIHAM	**Revd Mr Horne**
MARY BRACEGIRDLE	**Dora Carrington**
MR CALAMY	**H.H. Asquith**
CROME	**Beckley Park, Oxfordshire**
	Garsington Manor, Oxfordshire
GOMBAULD	**Mark Gertler**
IVOR LOMBARD	**Evan Morgan**
JENNY MULLION	**Dorothy Brett**
MR SCOGAN	**Norman Douglas**
	Bertrand Russell
ANNE WIMBUSH	**Maria Huxley**
HENRY WIMBUSH	**Sir George Sitwell**
PRISCILLA WIMBUSH	**Lady Ottoline Morrell**
	Lady Ida Sitwell

Eyeless in Gaza (1936)

JOHN BEAVIS	**Leonard Huxley**
	Ernest Weekley
MAISIE BEAVIS	**Julia Huxley**
BULSTRODE	**Hillside, Surrey**
BRIAN FOXE	**Noel Trevenen Huxley**
RACHEL FOXE	**Mrs Humphry Ward**
JOSEPH MILLER	**F. Matthias Alexander**
	Gerald Heard
	Theodore Pennell
PURCHAS	**Hugh Richard Sheppard**

'The Farcical History of Richard Greenow' (1920)

MRS CRAVISTER	**Blanche Warre-Cornish**

The Genius and the Goddess (1955)

KATY MAARTENS	**Frieda Lawrence**
HELEN RIVERS	**Maria Huxley**

'The Gioconda Smile' (1922)

HENRY HUTTON	**Harold Greenwood**

'Happily Ever After' (1920)

REVD ROGER PETHERTON	**C.O. Bevan**

Point Counter Point (1928)

JOHN BIDLAKE	**Augustus John**
DENIS BURLAP	**John Middleton Murry**
SUSAN PALEY	**Katherine Mansfield**
ELINOR QUARLES	**Maria Huxley**
PHILIP QUARLES, THE YOUNGER	**Matthew Huxley**
(cont.)	**Geoffrey Mitchison**
MARK RAMPION	**D.H. Lawrence**
MARY RAMPION	**Frieda Lawrence**

SPANDREL	**Charles Baudelaire**
LORD EDWARD TANTAMOUNT	**J.S. Haldane**
LUCY TANTAMOUNT	**Nancy Cunard**
EVERARD WEBLEY	**Sir Oswald Mosley**

Those Barren Leaves (1925)
MRS LILIAN ALDWINKLE	**Lady Ottoline Morrell**
FRANCIS CHELIFER	**John Middleton Murry**
PALAZZO MALASPINA	**Castello di Montegufoni, Italy**

'The Tillotson Banquet' (1924)
LORD BADGERY	**Sir Osbert Sitwell**
WALTER TILLOTSON	**Harry Melvill**

Time Must Have a Stop (1944)
BRUNO RONTINI	**Gerald Heard**

Two or Three Graces (1926)
KINGHAM	**D.H. Lawrence**

'Uncle Spencer', *Little Mexican and Other Stories* (1924)
LONGRES	**St Trond, Belgium**

I

INCHBALD, Elizabeth
A Simple Story (1791)
DORRIFORTH (AFTERWARDS LORD ELMWOOD)	**John Philip Kemble**

IRVING, Washington
'The Legend of Sleepy Hollow', *The Sketch Books of Geoffrey Crayon, Gent* (1820)
ICHABOD CRANE	**Lockie Longlegs**

ISHERWOOD, Christopher
All the Conspirators (1928)
PHILIP LINDSAY	**Hector Wintle**

Down There on a Visit (1962)
AMBROSE	**Francis Turville-Petre**
AUGUSTUS PARR	**Gerald Heard**
PAUL	**Denham Fouts**
RONNY	**Tony Bower**
RUTHIE	**Jean Connolly**

Goodbye to Berlin (1939)
BERNHARD LANDAUER	**Wilfrid Israel**
NATALIA LANDAUER	**Gisa Soloweitschik**

LINA SCHROEDER	**Meta Thurau**
PETER WILKINSON	**William Robson-Scott**

Lions and Shadows (1938)

BARNARD	**John Layard**
CHALMERS	**Edward Upward**
MADAME CHEURET	**Olive Mangeot**
MONSIEUR CHEURET	**André Mangeot**
MR GORSE	**Sir Kenneth Pickthorn**
LEE	**Robert Moody**
PHILIP LINSLEY	**Hector Wintle**
STEPHEN SAVAGE	**Stephen Spender**
HUGH WESTON	**W.H. Auden**

The Memorial (1932)

EDWARD BLAKE	**John Layard**
MARGARET LANWIN	**Olive Mangeot**
MARY SCRIVEN	**Olive Mangeot**

Mr Norris Changes Trains (1935)

ARTHUR NORRIS	**Gerald Hamilton**
LINA SCHROEDER	**Meta Thurau**

Prater Violet (1945)

FRIEDRICH BERGMANN	**Berthold Viertel**
MR CHATSWORTH	**Victor Saville**

Sally Bowles (1937)

SALLY BOWLES	**Jean Ross**

J

JAMES, Henry

The Ambassadors (1903)

MISS BARRACE	**Henrietta Reubell**
JOHN BILHAM	**Jonathan Sturges**
CHADWICK NEWSOME	**Jonathan Sturges**
LEWIS LAMBERT STRETHER	**William Dean Howells**

The American (1876)

BENJAMIN BABCOCK	**William James**

The Aspern Papers (1888)

JEFFREY ASPERN	**Percy Bysshe Shelley**
JULIANA BORDEREAU	**Claire Clairmont**
	Miss Wykoff
TITA ('TINA') BORDEREAU	**Paula ('Pauline') Clairmont**
THE NARRATOR	**Edward Augustus Silsbee**
THE PALAZZINO	**Palazzo Capello, Venice**

MRS PREST	Katherine De Kay Bronson
'The Author of "Beltraffio"' (1884)	
MARK AMBIENT	John Addington Symonds
The Awkward Age (1899)	
NANDA BROOKENHAM	Ethel Sands
MRS BROOKENHAM'S CIRCLE	The Souls
'The Birthplace' (1903)	
MORRIS GEDGE	Joseph Skipsey
The Bostonians (1884)	
MISS BIRDSEYE	Elizabeth Palmer Peabody
OLIVE CHANCELLOR	Katharine Peabody Loring
MARMION	Marion, Cape Cod, Massachusetts
DR MARY PRANCE	Dr Mary Walker
BASIL RANSOM	Lucius Q.C. Lamar
'Broken Wings' (1903)	
MRS HARVEY	Constance Fletcher
'Brooksmith' (1891)	
BROOKSMITH	Miss Past
'The Coxon Fund' (1894)	
FRANK SALTRAM	Samuel Taylor Coleridge
'Crapey Cornelia' (1910)	
MRS WORTHINGHAM	Edith Wharton
'Europe' (1899)	
MRS RIMMLE	Mary Ann Palfrey
The Europeans (1878)	
MR WENTWORTH	Frank Loring
'The Lesson of the Master' (1888)	
SUMMERSOFT	Osterley Park, Middlesex
'A London Life' (1888)	
LADY DAVENANT	Mrs Duncan Stewart
'Mrs Medwin' (1903)	
MAMIE CUTTER	Elizabeth Balch
SCOTT HOMER	Robert Temple
MRS MEDWIN	Lady Grantley
'The Next Time' (1898)	
JANE HIGHMORE	Mary Elizabeth Braddon
	Mrs Humphry Ward
RALPH IMBERT	Henry James
'Nona Vincent' (1891)	
MRS ALSAGER	Florence Bell
VIOLET GREY	Elizabeth Robins

Pandora (1884)	
MRS BONNYCASTLE	Marian Adams
ALFRED BONNYCASTLE	Henry Adams
A Passionate Pilgrim (1875)	
THE RED LION	The Albany, Piccadilly, London
'The Path of Duty' (1884)	
JOSCELIND BERNARDSTONE	Duchess of Sutherland
MARGARET, LADY VANDELEUR	Sibell Mary, Lady Grosvenor
The Portrait of a Lady (1880)	
ISABEL ARCHER	Mary ('Minny') Temple
GILBERT OSMOND	Francis Boott
PANSY OSMOND	Elizabeth Duveneck
RALPH TOUCHETT	Jonathan Sturges
The Princess Casamassima (1886)	
PRINCESS CASAMASSIMA	Principessa di Belgiojoso
	Princess Zoë Sergeievna Obolensky
'The Private Life' (1891)	
LORD MELLIFONT	Frederic, Lord Leighton
CLARE VAWDREY	Robert Browning
The Reverberator (1888)	
FRANCINA DOSSON	May Marcy McClellan
GEORGE FLACK	Julian Hawthorne
THE *REVERBERATOR*	*The World*
Roderick Hudson (1875)	
CHRISTINA LIGHT	Elena Low
SAM SINGLETON	Eugene Benson
The Sense of the Past (1917)	
THE AMERICAN AMBASSADOR	James Russell Lowell
The Spoils of Poynton (1897)	
MRS ADELA GERETH	Harriet Anne Morrell
POYNTON	Black Hall, St Giles, Oxford
WATERBATH	Foxwarren Park, Surrey
The Tragic Muse (1888–9)	
GABRIEL NASH	Herbert Pratt
MADEMOISELLE VOISIN	Jeanne Julia Bartet
'The Velvet Glove' (1910)	
THE PRINCESS ('AMY EVANS')	Edith Wharton
Washington Square (1881)	
CATHERINE SLOPER	Mary Ann Thackeray
MORRIS TOWNSEND	Henry Kemble
The Wings of the Dove (1902)	
MERTON DENSHER	Ford Madox Ford
	Morton Fullerton
	Sir Owen Seaman

PALAZZO LEPORELLI	**Palazzo Barbaro, Venice**
SIR LUKE STRETT	**William Wilberforce Baldwin**
	Sir Andrew Clark
MILLY THEALE	**Alice James**
	Mary ('Minny') Temple

JARRELL, Randall
Pictures from an Institution (1954)

BENTON	**Sarah Lawrence College, New York**
GERTRUDE JOHNSON	**Mary McCarthy**

JENKINS, Elizabeth
Virginia Water (1930)

ATHENE SIMON	**Pernel Strachey**
DEBORAH SIMON	**Marjorie Strachey**
ROGER SIMON	**Lytton Strachey**

The Winters (1932)

KATHY WINTER	**Pernel Strachey**

JOHNSTON, Sir Harry
The Gay-Dombeys (1919)

JOS. CHOSELWIT	**Joseph Chamberlain**
LORD WILTSHIRE	**Lord Salisbury**

JOYCE, James
'Clay', *Dubliners* (1914)

ALPHY DONNELLY	**William Murray**
JOE DONNELLY	**John Murray**[2]

'The Dead', *Dubliners* (1914)

GABRIEL CONROY	**Constantine P. Curran**
	John Joyce
BARTELL D'ARCY	**Barton M'Guckin**
MICHAEL FUREY	**Michael 'Sonny' Bodkin**
FREDDY MALINS	**Freddy Lyons**
MARY JANE	**Mary Ellen Callanan**
MISS JULIA MORKAN	**Mrs Lyons**
MISS KATE MORKAN	**Mrs Callanan**

'An Encounter', *Dubliners* (1914)

FATHER BUTLER	**Father William Henry, SJ**

'Eveline', *Dubliners* (1914)

EVELINE HILL	**Eveline Thornton**

Finnegans Wake (1939)

HUMPHREY CHIMPDEN EARWICKER	**John Joyce**
PROFESSOR JONES	**Wyndham Lewis**
THE ONDT	**Wyndham Lewis**
ANNA LIVIA PLURABELLE	**Nora Joyce**
	Livia Schmitz

SHAUN	Éamon De Valera
	John Ford
	Stanislaus Joyce
SHEM	James Ford
	James Joyce

'Grace', *Dubliners* (1914)

MARTIN CUNNINGHAM	Matthew Kane
TOM KERNAN	Ned Thornton
C.P. McCOY	Charles Chance
JACK POWER	Thomas Devin
FATHER PURDON	Father Bernard Vaughan

'A Little Cloud', *Dubliners* (1914)

IGNATIUS GALLAHER	Fred Gallaher
	Oliver St John Gogarty

'A Mother', *Dubliners* (1914)

O'MADDEN BURKE	O'Leary Curtis

'A Painful Case', *Dubliners* (1914)

JAMES DUFFY	Stanislaus Joyce

A Portrait of the Artist as a Young Man (1916)

JOHN CASEY	John Kelly
UNCLE CHARLES	William O'Connell
CRANLY	John Francis Byrne
DAVIN	George Clancy
DEAN OF STUDIES	Father Joseph Darlington, SJ
SIMON DEDALUS	John Joyce
FATHER DOLAN	Father James Daly, SJ
DONOVAN	Constantine P. Curran
VINCENT HERON	Albrecht Connolly
	Vincent Connolly
VINCENT LYNCH	Vincent Cosgrave
McCANN	Francis Sheehy Skeffington
THE PREACHER AT THE RETREAT	Father James A. Cullen
MRS DANTE RIORDAN	Mrs Hearn Conway
MR TATE	George Stanislaus Dempsey
TEMPLE	John Rudolph Elwood

Stephen Hero (1944)

MAURICE DAEDALUS	Stanislaus Joyce

'Two Gallants', *Dubliners* (1914)

T. LENEHAN	Michael Hart

Ulysses (1922)

ALMIDANO ARTIFONI	Father Charles Ghezzi, SJ
SERGEANT-MAJOR BENNETT	A. Percy Bennett
LEOPOLD BLOOM	Joseph Bloom
	John Francis Byrne
	Charles Chance

(cont.)	Alfred H. Hunter
	Holbrook Jackson
	James Joyce
	John Joyce
	Teodoro Mayer
	Leopoldo Popper
	Ettore Schmitz
MARION ('MOLLY') BLOOM	Mrs Charles Chance
	Mamie Dillon
	Nora Joyce
	Amalia Popper
	Signora Santos
HUGH ('BLAZES') BOYLAN	Blazes Boylan
	Hugh Boyle Kennedy
	Ted Keogh
O'MADDEN BURKE	O'Leary Curtis
PRIVATE CARR	Henry Carr
THE CITIZEN	Michael Cusack
MARTHA CLIFFORD	Marthe Fleischmann
MYLES CRAWFORD	Patrick J. Mead
MARTIN CUNNINGHAM	Matthew Kane
GARRETT DEASY	Francis Irwin
	Henry Blackwood Price
KEVIN EGAN	Joseph Casey
LONG JOHN FANNING	John Clancy
IGNATIUS GALLAHER	Fred Gallaher
RICHIE GOULDING	William Murray
T. LENEHAN	Michael Hart
VINCENT LYNCH	Vincent Cosgrave
C.P. MCCOY	Charles Chance
GERTIE MACDOWELL	Marthe Fleischmann
PROFESSOR MACHUGH	Hugh MacNeill
MISS JULIA MORKAN	Mrs Lyons
BUCK MULLIGAN	Oliver St John Gogarty
LIEUTENANT HARRY MULVEY	Willie Mulvey
W.B. MURPHY	Frank Budgen
JACK POWER	Thomas Devin
MRS DANTE RIORDAN	Mrs Hearn Conway
FLORRY TALBOT	Fleury Crawford
MAJOR TWEEDY	Major Powell

K

KEARY, C.F.
The Journalist (1898)
SOPHUS JONSEN   **Frederick Delius**

KEMBLE, Adelaide
A Week in a French Country-House (1867)
MONSIEUR KIOWSKI   **Frederic, Lord Leighton**

KEMP, Harry
More Miles (1926)
PENTON BAXTER   **Upton Sinclair**
JULIUS 'RED' FLATMAN   **Sinclair Lewis**
HALCYON HALL   **Helicon Home Colony, New Jersey**
JESSIE   **Edith Summers**
JIM   **Allan Updegraff**

KENNEDY, Margaret
The Constant Nymph (1924)
FLORENCE CHURCHILL   **Lucy Kennedy**
CLEEVE COLLEGE   **Cheltenham Ladies' College**
LEWIS DODD   **Henry Lamb**
ALBERT SANGER   **Augustus John**

KEROUAC, Jack
Big Sur (1962)
BEN FAGAN   **Philip Whalen**
IRWIN GARDEN   **Allen Ginsberg**
LORENZO MONSANTO   **Lawrence Ferlinghetti**
CODY POMERAY   **Neal Cassady**
ARTHUR WHANE   **Alan Wilson Watts**

Book of Dreams (1960)
BULL HUBBARD   **William S. Burroughs**
JACK   **Jack Kerouac**
IRVING MINKO   **Allan Bernard Temko**
DANNY RICHMAN   **Lawrence Ferlinghetti**
RAPHAEL URSO   **Gregory Corso**
JAMES WATSON   **John Clellon Holmes**

Desolation Angels (1965)
ALEX AUMS   **Alan Wilson Watts**
DAVID D'ANGELI   **Philip Lamantia**
GEOFFREY DONALD   **Robert Duncan**
BULL HUBBARD   **William S. Burroughs**
HARVEY MARKER   **Norman Mailer**
CODY POMERAY   **Neal Cassady**
MERRILL RANDALL   **James Ingram Merrill**
VARNUM RANDOM   **Randall Jarrell**

RAPHAEL URSO · **Gregory Corso**
JARRY WAGNER · **Gary Snyder**

The Dharma Bums (1958)
REINHOLD CACOETHES · **Kenneth Rexroth**
WARREN COUGHLIN · **Philip Whalen**
FRANCIS DA PAVIA · **Philip Lamantia**
ALVAH GOLDBROOK · **Allen Ginsberg**
CODY POMERAY · **Neal Cassady**
JAPHY RYDER · **Gary Snyder**
RAY SMITH · **Jack Kerouac**

Maggie Cassidy (1959)
MAGGIE CASSIDY · **Mary Carney**
JACK DULUOZ · **Jack Kerouac**

On the Road (1957)
CAMILLE · **Carolyn Cassady**
DODIE CARMODY · **Julie Burroughs**
FRANK CARMODY · **William S. Burroughs**
JANE CARMODY · **Joan Vollmer Burroughs**
RAY CARMODY · **William Burroughs, Junior**
OLD BULL LEE · **William S. Burroughs**
ROLAND MAJOR · **Allan Bernard Temko**
CARLO MARX · **Allen Ginsberg**
DEAN MORIARTY · **Neal Cassady**
SAL PARADISE · **Jack Kerouac**
TOM SAYBROOK · **John Clellon Holmes**

The Subterraneans (1958)
BENNETT FITZPATRICK · **Whit Burnett**
WALT FITZPATRICK · **David Burnett**
YURI GLIGORIC · **Gregory Corso**
ARIAL LAVALINA · **Gore Vidal**
LEROY · **Neal Cassady**
BALLIOL MACJONES · **John Clellon Holmes**
ADAM MOORAD · **Allen Ginsberg**
LARRY O'HARA · **Lawrence Ferlinghetti**
LEO PERCEPIED · **Jack Kerouac**

The Town and the City (1950)
WILL DENNISON · **William S. Burroughs**
MARY GILHOOLEY · **Mary Carney**
LEON LEVINSKY · **Allen Ginsberg**
PETER MARTIN · **Jack Kerouac**

Vanity of Duluoz (1968)
MAGGIE CASSIDY · **Mary Carney**
WILL HUBBARD · **William S. Burroughs**
TOM WILSON · **John Clellon Holmes**

Visions of Cody (1960)
CODY POMERAY · **Neal Cassady**

Visions of Gerard (1963)
ALLEN MINKO   Allan Bernard Temko
DANNY RICHMAN   Lawrence Ferlinghetti

KERR, Robert
His Excellency The Ambassador Extraordinary (1879)
GEORGIUS OLDHOUSEN   William Burges

KING, Francis
A Domestic Animal (1970)
MAURICE RHODES   Duncan Grant

KINGSLEY, Charles
Alton Locke (1850)
THE —— AMBASSADOR   Baron Bunsen
ALTON LOCKE   Thomas Cooper[1]
                                               Walter Cooper
SANDY MACKAYE   Thomas Carlyle
O'FLYNN   Feargus O'Connor

Hypatia (1853)
RAPHAEL ABEN EZRA   Alfred Hyman Louis
BISHOP SYNESIUS   Charles Kingsley

Two Years Ago (1857)
ABERALVA   Clovelly, Devon
STANLAKE   W.H. Hurlbert
TOM THURNALL   George Henry Kingsley
ELSLEY VAVASOUR (JOHN BRIGGS)   Percy Bysshe Shelley
                                               Alfred, Lord Tennyson

The Water Babies (1863)
HARTHOVER PLACE   Malham Tarn House, Yorkshire
TOM   James Seaward

Westward Ho! (1855)
AMYAS LEIGH   Francis Cranmer Penrose
FRANK LEIGH   Charles Blackford Mansfield

Yeast (1848)
THE 'FATHER'   J.H. Newman
ARGEMONE LAVINGTON   Charlotte Froude
                                               Frances Kingsley
                                               Caulia Mansfield
HONORIA LAVINGTON   Anna Gifford
                                               Frances Kingsley
SQUIRE LAVINGTON   Sir John Cope
THE PRIORY   Formosa Place, Cookham, Berkshire
LANCELOT SMITH   Charles Kingsley
TREGARVA   Thomas Carlyle

KINGSLEY, Henry
Oakshott Castle (1873)
LORD OAKSHOTT   **Henry Kingsley**

Silcote of Silcotes (1867)
MISS LEE   **Sarah Maria Kingsley**

KINGSMILL, Hugh
'Disintegration of a Politician', *The Dawn's Delay* (1924)
VICTOR STUBBS   **H.H. Asquith**

'The End of the World', *The Dawn's Delay* (1924)
GLAYDE   **Alec Waugh**
BENJAMIN POLMONT   **Hugh Kingsmill**

The Return of William Shakespeare (1929)
LORD WESTERLEIGH   **Lord Beaverbrook**
LORD YOUNGBROTHER   **Lord Rothermere**

The Will to Love (1919)
BARBARA   **Enid Bagnold**
RODERICK CORY   **Hugh Kingsmill**
CYRIL MEARS   **Hugh Kingsmill**
RALPH PARKER   **Frank Harris**

KIPLING, Rudyard
'Baa, Baa, Black Sheep' (1888)
DOWNE LODGE   **4 Campbell Rd, Havelock Park,
                                         Southsea**
UNCLE HARRY   **Pryse Agar Holloway**
JUDY   **Alice Macdonald Kipling**
PUNCH   **Rudyard Kipling**
AUNTY ROSA   **Sarah Holloway**

'The Bridge Builders' (1898)
FINDLAYSON   **J.R. Bell**
                                       Auckland Geddes
                                       F.T.G. Walton
HITCHCOCK   **L.G. Prickett**

'In the Rukh' (1893)
MULLER   **Ribbentrop**

The Jungle Books (1894–5)
COLD LAIRS   **Chitor, Rajasthan, India**

Kim (1901)
COLONEL CREIGHTON   **A.H. Mason**
KIM (KIMBALL O'HARA)   **Frank A.M. Beatty**
                                       William Rattigan
THE LAMA   **Edward Burne-Jones**
LURGAN SAHIB   **Alexander M. Jacob**
HURREE CHANDER MOOKERJEE   **Sarat Chandra Das**

The Light that Failed (1890)
KAMI — **Charles Gleyre**
MAISIE — **Violet Florence Garrard**

Plain Tales from the Hills (1888)
LUCY HAUKSBEE — **Mrs F.C. Burton**
STRICKLAND — **Mr Christie**[1]
Horace B. Goad

Puck of Pook's Hill (1906)
DAN — **John Kipling**
UNA — **Elsie Kipling**

Rewards and Fairies (1910)
DAN — **John Kipling**
UNA — **Elsie Kipling**

Stalky & Co. (1899)
BEETLE — **Rudyard Kipling**
ARTHUR CORKRAN ('STALKY') — **Lionel Charles Dunsterville**
FOXY — **George Schofield**
REVD JOHN GILLETT — **Revd George Willes**
MR HARTOPP — **Herbert Arthur Evans**
THE HEAD — **Cornell Price**
MR KING — **William Carr Crofts**
F.W. Haslam
MASON — **C.W.L. Beste**
WILLIAM M'TURK — **G.C. Beresford**
MR PROUT — **Matthew Henry Pugh**

'The Tender Achilles' (1932)
SIR JAMES BELTON — **Sir John Bland-Sutton**

L

LAMB, Lady Caroline
Glenarvon (1816)
DUKE OF ALTAMONTE — **6th Duke of Devonshire**
LORD AVONDALE — **Lord Melbourne**
LADY MARGARET BUCHANAN — **Lady Bessborough**
Elizabeth, Duchess of Devonshire
Mrs Maria Kinnaird
WILLIAM BUCHANAN — **Sir Godfrey Webster**
LORD DALLAS — **John William Ward, 1st Earl of Dudley**
DEAD POET — **Samuel Rogers**
CASTLE DELAVAL — **Devonshire House, London**
LADY CALANTHA DELAVAL — **Lady Caroline Lamb**

LORD GLENARVON	**Lord Byron**
HOIAONSKIM	**John Allen**[1]
PRINCESS OF MADAGASCAR	**Lady Holland**
LADY MANDEVILLE	**Lady Oxford**
MENTEITH HOUSE	**Melbourne House, London**
MISS MONMOUTH	**Lady Byron**
LADY AUGUSTA SELWYN	**Lady Collier**
	Countess of Jersey
FRANCES SEYMOUR (AFTERWARDS LADY TRELAWNEY)	**Georgiana, Lady Morpeth**
MRS SEYMOUR	**Lady Bessborough**
	Mrs Maria Kinnaird
	Lady Melbourne
SOPHIA SEYMOUR	**Lady Granville**
LORD TRELAWNEY	**Lord Morpeth**
COUNT VIVIAN	**Lord Byron**

LARDNER, Ring
'The Love Nest' (1926)

LOU GREGG	**E.E. ('Gene') Buck**

LAWRENCE, D.H.
Aaron's Rod (1922)

JAMES ARGYLE	**Norman Douglas**
ALFRED BRICKNELL	**Alfred Woolston Brentnall**
JIM BRICKNELL	**James Robert White**
CLARISS BROWNING	**Brigit Patmore**
ALGY CONSTABLE	**Reginald Turner**
JULIA CUNNINGHAM	**Hilda Doolittle**
ROBERT CUNNINGHAM	**Richard Aldington**
JOSEPHINE FORD	**Dorothy Yorke**
SIR WILLIAM FRANKS	**Sir Walter Becker**
LADY ARTEMIS HOOPER	**Lady Diana Cooper**
RAWDON LILLY	**D.H. Lawrence**
TANNY LILLY	**Frieda Lawrence**
WALTER ROSEN	**Leo Stein**
CYRIL SCOTT	**Cecil Gray**
DR SHERARDY	**Dr Dhunjabhi Mullan Feroze**
AARON SISSON	**Thomas Cooper**[2]
STRUTHERS	**Augustus John**

'The Blind Man' (1922)

ISABEL PERVIN	**Catherine Carswell**

'The Border Line' (1928)

KATHERINE FARQUHAR	**Frieda Lawrence**
PHILIP FARQUHAR	**John Middleton Murry**

'The Captain's Doll' (1923)

ALEXANDER HEPBURN	**Donald Carswell**
	D.H. Lawrence

KAPRUN	**Zell-am-See, Austria**
ANNA-MARIA VON PRIELAU-CAROLATH ('MITCHKA')	**'Nusch' Schreibershofen**
COUNTESS JOHANNA ('HANNELE') ZU RASSENTLOW	**Frieda Lawrence**
HERR REGIERUNGSRAT TREPTE	**Max von Schreibershofen**

'England, My England' (1915)

CROCKHAM	**Greatham, Sussex**
EGBERT	**Perceval Drewett Lucas**
JOYCE	**Sylvia Lucas**
MR MARSHALL	**Wilfrid Meynell**
WINIFRED	**Madeline Lucas**

'The Fox' (1923)

BAILEY FARM	**Grimsbury Farm, Berkshire**
JILL BANFORD	**Cecily Lambert**
	Margaret Radford
HENRY GRENFEL	**Mr Lambert**
NELLIE MARCH	**Violet Monk**

'Glad Ghosts' (1928)

CARLOTTA FELL (AFTERWARDS LADY LATHKILL)	**Dorothy Brett**
	Lady Cynthia Asquith
LUKE, LORD LATHKILL	**Herbert Asquith**
MARK MORIER	**D.H. Lawrence**

'Goose Fair' (1914)

LOIS	**Lois Mee**
WILL SELBY	**Lewis Taylor**

'Jimmy and the Desperate Woman' (1928)

JIMMY FRITH	**John Middleton Murry**

Kangaroo (1923)

JOHN THOMAS BURYAN	**William Henry Hocking**
VICTORIA CALLCOTT	**Mrs A.L. Jenkins**
COO-EE	**Wyewurk, Thirroul, Australia**
BENJAMIN COOLEY	**David Eder**
	S.S. Koteliansky
	Sir John Monash
MR MONSELL	**Robert Mountsier**
MULLUMBIMBY	**Thirroul, New South Wales, Australia**
HATTIE REDBURN	**Dollie Radford**
HARRIET SOMERS	**Frieda Lawrence**
RICHARD LOVAT SOMERS	**D.H. Lawrence**
WILLIE STRUTHERS	**James Holman**
	William Hopkin
JAZ TREWHELLA	**Mr Hawken**

Lady Chatterley's Lover (1928)

CONSTANCE CHATTERLEY	Lady Cynthia Asquith
SIR CLIFFORD CHATTERLEY	Herbert Asquith
	Sir Osbert Sitwell
DUNCAN FORBES	Duncan Grant
MICHAELIS	Michael Arlen
SHIPLEY HALL	Sutton Scarsdale Hall, Derbyshire
TEVERSHALL	Eastwood, Nottinghamshire
WRAGBY HALL	Lamb Close House, Eastwood, Nottinghamshire
	Renishaw Hall, Derbyshire

'The Ladybird' (1923)

LADY BEVERIDGE	Lady Wemyss

'The Last Laugh' (1928)

MISS JAMES	Dorothy Brett
MARCHBANKS	John Middleton Murry

The Lost Girl (1920)

PANCRAZIO CALIFANO	Orazio Cervi
MISS FROST	Miss Fanny Wright
ALVINA HOUGHTON	Florence ('Flossie') Cullen
CLARISS HOUGHTON	Lucy Cullen
JAMES HOUGHTON	George Cullen
KNARBOROUGH	Nottingham
LUMLEY	Langley Mill, Nottinghamshire
MANCHESTER HOUSE	London House, Eastwood, Nottinghamshire
FRANCESCO MARASCA	Francesco Cacopardo
MR MAY	Maurice Magnus
MOON AND STARS INN	Sun Inn, Eastwood, Nottinghamshire
PESCOCALASCIO	Picinisco, Caserta, Italy
MISS PINNEGAR	Miss Pidsley
WOODHOUSE	Eastwood, Nottinghamshire

'Love Among the Haystacks' (1930)

PAULA JABLONOWSKY	Frieda Lawrence

'The Man Who Loved Islands' (1928)

MR CATHCART	Compton Mackenzie
MRS GEE	Faith Compton Mackenzie

'A Modern Lover' (1934)

CYRIL MERSHAM	D.H. Lawrence
MURIEL	Jessie Chambers

'New Eve and Old Adam' (1934)

PAULA MOEST	Frieda Lawrence

'None of That' (1928)

ETHEL CANE	Dora Carrington

'Odour of Chrysanthemums' (1914)
ELIZABETH BATES — Polly Allam

'The Old Adam' (1934)
EDWARD SEVERN — D.H. Lawrence
MR THOMAS — John William Jones
MRS THOMAS — Marie Jones

The Plumed Serpent (1926)
MR BELL — Winfield Scott
DON RAMÓN CARRASCO — John Dibrell
José Vasconcelos
SEÑOR GARCÍA — Miguel Covarrubias
MIRABAL — Luis Quintanilla
SOCRATES TOMÁS MONTES — Plutarco Elias Calles
MRS NORRIS — Zelia Nuttall
ORILLA — El Fuerte
OWEN RHYS — Witter Bynner
HOTEL SAN REMO — Hotel Monte Carlo, Mexico City
SAYULA — Chapala, Mexico
TLACOLULA — Coyoacán, Mexico
BUD VILLIERS — Willard Johnson

'The Primrose Path' (1922)
DANIEL SUTTON — Herbert Beardsall

'The Princess' (1925)
MARY HENRIETTA URQUHART — Dorothy Brett

The Rainbow (1915)
BELDOVER — Eastwood, Nottinghamshire
Quorn, Leicestershire
URSULA BRANGWEN — Louisa Burrows
Frieda Lawrence
WILLIAM BRANGWEN — Alfred Burrows
COSSETHAY — Cossall, Nottinghamshire
MR HARBY — Thomas Beacroft
LYDIA LENSKY (AFTERWARDS BRANGWEN) — Frieda Lawrence
ST PHILIP'S — Eastwood British School,
Nottinghamshire

'Smile' (1928)
MATTHEW — John Middleton Murry
OPHELIA — Katherine Mansfield

Sons and Lovers (1913)
BESTWOOD — Eastwood, Nottinghamshire
THE BOTTOMS — The Breach, Eastwood,
Nottinghamshire
MR BRAITHWAITE — Alfred Woolston Brentnall
CARSON WAITE & CO. — Barber Walker & Co.
GEORGE COPPARD — George Beardsall
CLARA DAWES — Alice Dax

THOMAS JORDAN	John Harrington Haywood
MR LEIVERS	Edmund Chambers
EDGAR LEIVERS	Alan Chambers
MIRIAM LEIVERS	Jessie Chambers
MINTON	Moorgreen, Nottinghamshire
MOON AND STARS INN	Three Tuns Inn, Eastwood, Nottinghamshire
GERTRUDE MOREL	Lydia Lawrence
WALTER MOREL	John Arthur Lawrence
WILLIAM MOREL	William Ernest Lawrence
NUTTALL	Underwood, Nottinghamshire
SELBY	Brinsley Colliery
SPANIEL ROW	Castle Gate, Nottingham
LOUISA LILY DENYS WESTERN	Gypsy Dennis
WILLEY FARM	Haggs Farm, Nottinghamshire
BEATRICE WYLD	Alice Hall

'St Mawr' (1925)

LOUISE CARRINGTON	Elizabeth Humes
MR CARTWRIGHT	Frederick Carter
LAS CHIVAS	Kiowa Ranch, San Cristobal, New Mexico
LAURA RIDLEY	Dorothy Brett
RACHEL WITT	Mrs Humes

'The Thimble' (1917)

LADY HEPBURN	Lady Cynthia Asquith
MR HEPBURN	Herbert Asquith

'Things' (1933)

ERASMUS MELVILLE	Earl Henry Brewster
VALERIE MELVILLE	Achsah Brewster

'The Thorn in the Flesh' (1914)

THE BARON	Friedrich, Baron von Richthofen

Touch and Go (1919)

WILLIE HOUGHTON	William Hopkin
LILLEY CLOSE	Lamb Close House, Eastwood, Nottinghamshire

The Trespasser (1912)

MR ALLPORT	R.H. Aylwin
CECIL BYRNE	D.H. Lawrence
MR HOLIDAY	Ernest Humphreys
LOUISA	Agnes Mason
SIEGMUND MACNAIR	H.B. Macartney
MR MACWHIRTER	A.W. McLeod
OLIVIA	Violet Mary Babbage
HELENA VERDEN	Helen Corke

'Two Blue Birds' (1928)

CAMERON GEE	Compton Mackenzie

The Virgin and the Gipsy (1930)

REVD ARTHUR SAYWELL	**Ernest Weekley**

The White Peacock (1911)

CYRIL BEARDSALL	**D.H. Lawrence**
FRANK BEARDSALL	**John Arthur Lawrence**
LETTIE BEARDSALL	**Ada Lawrence**
EBERWICH	**Eastwood, Nottinghamshire**
ALICE GALL	**Alice Hall**
HIGHCLOSE	**Lamb Close House, Eastwood, Nottinghamshire**
NETHERMERE	**Moorgreen Reservoir, Nottinghamshire**
MR SAXTON	**Edmund Chambers**
EMILY SAXTON	**Jessie Chambers**
GEORGE SAXTON	**Alan Chambers**
	G.H. Neville
STRELLEY MILL	**Felley Mill, Nottinghamshire**
	Haggs Farm, Nottinghamshire
LESLIE TEMPEST	**G.H. Neville**
TEMPEST WARRALL & CO.	**Barber Walker & Co.**

'The Witch à la Mode' (1934)

LAURA BRAITHWAITE	**Laura Macartney**

'The Woman Who Rode Away' (1928)

MRS LEDERMAN	**Mabel Dodge Luhan**

Women in Love (1920)

RUPERT BIRKIN	**D.H. Lawrence**
GUDRUN BRANGWEN	**Katherine Mansfield**
BREADALBY	**Garsington Manor, Oxfordshire**
DR BRINDELL	**Tom Herring Bingham**
CAFÉ POMPADOUR	**Café Royal, London**
DIANA CRICH	**Cicely Barber**
GERALD CRICH	**Thomas Philip Barber**
	John Middleton Murry
	George Henry Neville
THOMAS CRICH	**Thomas Barber**
MINETTE DARRINGTON	**Dora Carrington**
	Minnie Channing
JULIUS HALLIDAY	**Philip Heseltine**
HASAN	**Huseyn Shaheed Suhrawardy**
MAXIM LIBIDNIKOV	**S.S. Koteliansky**
	Maxim Litvinov
LOERKE	**Mark Gertler**
FRÄULEIN MÄRZ	**Juliette Huxley**
SIR JOSHUA MATTHESON	**Bertrand Russell**
ALEXANDER RODDICE	**Philip Morrell**
HERMIONE RODDICE	**Jessie Chambers**
	Lady Ottoline Morrell

SHORTLANDS	**Lamb Close House, Eastwood, Nottinghamshire**
WILLEY WATER	**Moorgreen Reservoir, Nottinghamshire**

LAWRENCE, D.H. and M.L. Skinner
The Boy in the Bush (1924)

JACK GRANT	**Jack Skinner**

LAWRENCE, G.A.
Sans Merci; or Kestrels and Falcons (1866)

CECIL CASTLEMAINE	**James Clay**

LE CARRÉ, John
The Honourable Schoolboy (1977)

WILLIAM CAW	**Richard Hughes**

A Murder of Quality (1962)

SHANE HECHT	**Grizel Hartley**

The Spy Who Came in from the Cold (1963) and others

GEORGE SMILEY	**Sir Maurice Oldfield**

LEE, Holme
Her Title of Honour (1871)

FRANCIS GWYNNE	**Henry Martyn**

LEE, Vernon

'Lady Tal', *Vanitas* (1892)

LADY ATALANTA WALKENSHAW	**Mrs Alice Callander**
JERVASE MARION	**Henry James**

Miss Brown (1884)

ANNE BROWN	**Kate Gurney**
	Jane Morris
COSMO CHOUGH	**Arthur O'Shaughnessy**
WALTER HAMLIN	**Dante Gabriel Rossetti**
MARY LEIGH	**Agnes Frances Mary Robinson**
MRS CLAUDIA MACGREGOR	**Matilda Paget**

'Oke of Okehurst' (1890)

ALICE OKE	**Janey Sevilla Campbell**
OKEHURST	**Godinton, Kent**

LEHMANN, Rosamund
Dusty Answer (1927)

JENNIFER BAIRD	**Grizel Hartley**

LENNOX, Lord William
The Tuft-Hunter (1843)

REGINALD SPARKLE	Theodore Hook

LESLIE, Shane
The Anglo-Catholic (1929)

LOUISA ROSE	Rosa Lewis
SACKVILLE HOTEL	Cavendish Hotel, London

The Cantab (1926)

PROFESSOR BOGGART	John McTaggart Ellis McTaggart
MR BRAZIER	Sir James Frazer
ADOLPHUS BRIGGS	Rupert Brooke
OLIVER BROWNLOW	Oscar Browning
BARON VON BUGLE	Anatole, Baron von Hügel
MONSIGNOR BURNS	Monsignor Barnes
CHERRYUMPTON	Cherry Hinton, Cambridgeshire
	Trumpington, Cambridgeshire
EDGE	E.A. Edghill
BARON FALCO	F.W. Rolfe
FATHER GOODE	E.G. Wood
MR GOW	A.C. Pigou
H.M. HOPINGTON	William Hope-Jones
HENRY JOHNSON	Henry Jackson
MR LOCKSON	Lowes Dickinson
DR MELEAGER	Walter Headlam
THE ORDER OF THE DIVINE BLOOD	Society of the Divine Compassion
PROFESSOR O'RUDGERY	Sir William Ridgeway
THE PROVOST	M.R. James
FATHER ROBERT ROLLE	R.H. Benson
MR SHERRARD	J.T. Sheppard
THE SILVER APPLE	*The Golden Bough*
THE SIMEON SOCIETY	The Walpole Society
DR VERUM	A.W. Verrall

LEVER, Charles
Roland Cashel (1850)

ELIAS HOWE	W.M. Thackeray

LEVERSON, Ada
Bird of Paradise (1914)

LADY KELLYNCH	Mrs George Leverson
	Henrietta Leverson
BERTHA KELLYNCH	Kitty Martineau

The Limit (1911)

HARRY DEFREYNE	Cosmo Gordon-Lennox
FLORA LUSCOMBE	Mabel Beardsley
GILBERT HEREFORD VAUGHAN	W. Somerset Maugham

Love at Second Sight (1916)
SIR TITO LANDI   Sir Paolo Tosti

Love's Shadow (1908) and others
EDITH OTTLEY   Ada Leverson

The Twelfth Hour (1907)
FELICITY, LADY CHETWODE   Kitty Martineau
MARY CROFTON ('AUNT WILLIAM')   Henrietta Leverson

LEWIS, C.S.
That Hideous Strength (1945)
LORD FEVERSTONE   T.D. ('Harry') Weldon

LEWIS, Grace Hegger
Half a Loaf (1931)
SUSAN HALE   Grace Hegger Lewis
TIMOTHY HALE   Sinclair Lewis
SOLON RICHARDSON   Frazier Hunt
ANDREA VENGO   Raffaello Piccoli

LEWIS, Sinclair
Arrowsmith (1925)
MARTIN ARROWSMITH   R.G. Hussey
ANGUS DUER   Henry J. Vanden Berg
MADELINE FOX   Grace Hegger Lewis
ROSCOE GEAKE   R. Bishop Canfield
MAX GOTTLIEB   Jacques Loeb
                               Frederick Novy
RIPPLETON HOLABIRD   Rufus Cole
                               Peyton Rous
JOYCE LANYON   Grace Hegger Lewis
MCGURK INSTITUTE   Rockefeller Institute, New York
FATHER PFAFF   Theodore Adams
ALNUS PICHERBOUGH   William De Kleine
PLAGUE CITY   St Lucia
JOHN A. ROBERTSHAW   Warren P. Lombard
T.J.H. SILVA   T.G. Hinzinger
LEORA TOZER   Rhea E. De Kruif
                               Edith Summers
A. DEWITT TUBBS   Simon Flexner
TERRY WICKETT   T.J. Le Blanc
                               Sinclair Lewis
                               J.H. Northrop

Babbit (1922)
ZENITH   Minneapolis, Minnesota

Cass Timberlane (1945)
JINNY MARSHLAND   Marcella Powers
CASS TIMBERLANE   Sinclair Lewis

Dodsworth (1929)
FRAN DODSWORTH — Grace Hegger Lewis
ROSS IRELAND — Frazier Hunt

Elmer Gantry (1927)
ELMER GANTRY — Revd William L. Stidger
Revd John Roach Straton
MRS EVANS RIDDLE — Elizabeth Towne

It Can't Happen Here (1935)
MRS GIMMITCH — Elizabeth Dilling
DEWEY HAIK — Douglas MacArthur
THE LEAGUE OF FORGOTTEN MEN — Union for Social Justice
BISHOP PAUL PRANG — Father Charles Coughlin
LEE SARASON — Robert E. Clements
BERZELIUS ('BUZZ') WINDRIP — Huey P. Long
Gerald B. Winrod

Kingsblood Royal (1947)
DIANTHA MARL — Margaret Banning

Main Street (1920)
GOPHER PRAIRIE — Sauk Center, Minnesota
CAROL KENNICOTT — Sinclair Lewis
GUY POLLOCK — Charles T. Dorion

The Trail of the Hawk (1915)
CARL ERICSON — Sinclair Lewis
COLONEL HAVILAND — James Walker Benét
JORALEMON — Sauk Center, Minnesota
SAN SPIRITO — Benicia, California
VANZILE MOTOR CORPORATION — Frederick A. Stokes Company
RUTH WINSLOW — Grace Hegger Lewis

LEWIS, Wyndham
The Apes of God (1930)
BETTY BLYTH — Dora Carrington
LADY HARRIET FINNIAN-SHAW — Edith Sitwell
LORD OSMUND FINNIAN-SHAW — Sir Osbert Sitwell
LORD PHOEBUS FINNIAN-SHAW — Sacheverell Sitwell
MATTHEW PLUNKETT — Lytton Strachey
JAMES JULIUS RATNER — James Joyce
THE SIB — Ada Leverson

The Childermass (1928)
PULLMAN ('PULLEY') — James Joyce

The Roaring Queen (1973)
GEOFFREY BELL — Gerald Gould
BABY BUCKTROUT — Nancy Cunard
DONALD BUTTERBOY — Brian Howard
RICHARD DRITTER — Walter Sickert
MRS RHODA HYMAN — Virginia Woolf

Stella Salt	Rebecca West
Samuel Shodbutt	Arnold Bennett
Mrs Maisie Wellesley-Crook	Maud ('Emerald'), Lady Cunard

The Self-Condemned (1954)
| Cedric Furber | Lytton Strachey |

Tarr (1918)
| Guy Butcher | Guy Baker |
| Prism Dirkes | Iris Barry |

LISTER, T.H.
Arlington (1832)
| Henry Beauchamp | Beau Brummell |
| Sir Gerald Denbigh | Count D'Orsay |

Granby (1826)
| Lady Harriet Duncan | Lady Caroline Lamb |
| Mr Trebeck | Beau Brummell |

LLOYD, Charles
Edmund Oliver (1798)
| Edmund Oliver | Samuel Taylor Coleridge |

LOEB, Harold
The Way It Was (1959)
| Lily Lubow | Kitty Cannell |

LONDON, Jack
The Iron Heel (1908)
Ernest Everhard	Eugene Debs
	Jack London
	Ernest Untermann

Martin Eden (1909)
| Russ Brissenden | George Sterling |
| Martin Eden | Jack London |

The Valley of the Moon (1913)
| Mark Hall | George Sterling |

LONGSTREET, Stephen, and LONGSTREET, Ethel
The Politician (1959)
| Paul Hawley Barraclough | Franklin D. Roosevelt |

LOOS, Anita
But Gentlemen Marry Brunettes (1927)
| Joel Crabtree | Franklin P. Adams |

LOWELL, R.T.S.
The Story of the New Priest in Conception Bay (1858)
PETERPORT   **Bay Roberts, Newfoundland**

LUBBOCK, Percy
The Region Cloud (1925)
JOHN CHANNON   **Henry James**

LYALL, Edna
Donovan (1882)
LUKE RAEBURN   **Charles Bradlaugh**

Doreen (1904)
DONAL MOORE   **Michael Davitt**

We Two (1884)
LUKE RAEBURN   **Charles Bradlaugh**

LYTTON, Lady
Cheveley; or The Man of Honour (1839)
LADY DE CLIFFORD   **Rosina Bulwer, Lady Lytton**
LORD DE CLIFFORD   **Bulwer Lytton**
FUZBOZ   **John Forster**

LYTTON, Bulwer
England and the English (1833)
SNEAK   **Charles Molloy Westmacott**

Godolphin (1833)
CONSTANCE, COUNTESS OF ERPINGHAM   **Lady Blessington**
PERCY GODOLPHIN   **Count D'Orsay**
LORD SALTREAM   **John William Ward, 1st Earl of Dudley**

Lucretia (1847)
HONORÉ GABRIEL VARNEY   **Thomas Griffiths Wainewright**

Paul Clifford (1830)
ALLFAIR   **Lord Alvanley**
BACHELOR BILL   **6th Duke of Devonshire**
CUNNING NAT   **John Nash**
FIGHTING ATTIE   **Duke of Wellington**
HARRY FINISH   **Henry de Ros**
GENTLEMAN GEORGE   **George IV**
LONG NED   **1st Earl of Ellenborough**
PETER MACGRAWLER   **The Scots Nation**
MOBBING FRANCIS   **Sir Francis Burdett**
OLD BAGS   **Lord Eldon**
THE SALLOW GENTLEMAN   **William Huskisson**
SCARLET JEM   **Sir James Scarlett**
AUGUSTUS TOMLINSON   **The Whigs**

Pelham (1828)

CLUTTERBUCK	**Richard Warburton Lytton**
LORD GULOSETON	**Lord Mount Edgcumbe**
HENRY PELHAM	**Frederick Villiers**
JOHN RUSSELTON	**Beau Brummell**
THOMAS THORNTON	**John Thurtell**
LORD VINCENT	**Theodore Hook**

M

McALMON, Robert
Post Adolescence (1923)

JIM BOYLE	**William Carlos Williams**
NELLIE BOYLE	**Florence Williams**
REGINALD CRACKYE	**Alfred Kreymborg**
DORA	**Lola Ridge**
O'BRIAN	**Kenneth Burke**
BRANDER OGDEN	**Marsden Hartley**
PETER	**Robert McAlmon**
VERE ST VITUS	**Edna St Vincent Millay**
MARTA WULLUS	**Marianne Moore**

MACAULAY, Rose
Crewe Train (1926)

EVELYN GRESHAM	**Naomi Royde-Smith**

Dangerous Ages (1921)

HILARY	**Grace Macaulay**
NAN	**Rose Macaulay**

Mystery at Geneva (1922)

LORD EDWARD BURNLEY	**A.J. Balfour**

Non-combatants and Others (1916)

ALIX	**Rose Macaulay**
BASIL DOYE	**Rupert Brooke**

The Secret River (1909)

MICHAEL	**Rupert Brooke**

A Tale Told by an Idiot (1923)

AUBREY GARDEN	**Thomas Arnold**
MAURICE GARDEN	**W.T. Arnold**

McCARTHY, Justin, and PRAED, Mrs Campbell
The Rebel Rose (1888)

ROLFE BELLARMINE	**Lord Randolph Churchill**
TOMMY TRESSEL	**Henry du Pré Labouchère**

MacCARTHY, Mary
A Pier and a Band (1918)
M. FITZGERALD   **Desmond MacCarthy**
PERDITA VILLIERS   **Mary MacCarthy**

MacDONALD, George
The Vicar's Daughter (1872)
LADY BERNARD   **Lady Byron**

MACDONELL, A.G.
England, Their England (1933)
WILLIAM HODGE   **Sir J.C. Squire**
CHARLES OSSORY   **Desmond MacCarthy**

MACKENZIE, Compton
Carnival (1912)
JENNY PEARL   **Christine Maude**

Extraordinary Women (1928)
RORY FREEMANTLE   **Radclyffe Hall**
CLÉO GAZAY   **Renata Borgatti**
OLIMPIA LEIGH   **Romaine Brooks**
ROSALBA   **Mimi Franchetti**

The Four Winds of Love: The South Wind (1937)
DAVID RAYNER   **D.H. Lawrence**
HILDEGARDE RAYNER   **Frieda Lawrence**
FREDERICK RODNEY   **Gilbert Cannan**
SUMMERTUNE, ESSEX   **Chesham, Buckinghamshire**

The Monarch of the Glen (1941)
DONALD MacDONALD OF BEN NEVIS   **Sir Donald Walter Cameron of
Lochiel**

Vestal Fire (1927)
ANTHONY BURLINGHAM   **Charles Thornton**
NIGEL DAWSON   **Vernon Andrews**
COUNT MARSAC LÄGERSTROM   **Count Fersen**
EFFIE MACADAM   **Sophie Grahame**
MARTEL   **Gilbert Clavel**
DUNCAN MAXWELL   **Norman Douglas**
MAJOR NATT   **Colonel Bryan Palmes**
MAIMIE PEPWORTH-NORTON   **Saidée Wolcott-Perry**
VIRGINIA PEPWORTH-NORTON   **Kate Wolcott-Perry**
SCUDAMORE   **Thomas Spencer Jerome**
SIRENE   **Capri**

MACNAUGHTAN, Richard
The Preparatory School Murder (1934)
ST ANTHONY'S   **Arnold House, Llanddulas,
Denbighshire**

MALLOCK, W.H.
The New Republic (1877)

LORD ALLEN	13th Earl of Pembroke
DONALD GORDON	Thomas Carlyle
	George MacDonald
LADY GRACE	Emilia Francis Pattison
MR HERBERT	John Ruskin
DR JENKINSON	Benjamin Jowett
OTHO LAURENCE	Laurence Oliphant[2]
ROBERT LESLIE	Charles Hardinge, 1st Baron Hardinge of Penshurst
	W.M. Hardinge
	Sir Leslie Stephen
MR LUKE	Matthew Arnold
MISS MERTON	Baroness von Hügel
MR ROSE	Walter Pater
MR SAUNDERS	W.K. Clifford
DR SEYDON	H.P. Liddon
	E.B. Pusey
MRS SINCLAIR	Mary, Lady Currie
MR STOCKTON	John Tyndall
MR STORKS	T.H. Huxley

The Old Order Changes (1886)

LORD AIDEN	Robert Bulwer, 1st Earl of Lytton
BIRCHESTER	Birmingham
MISS CONSUELO BURTON	Baroness von Hügel
LADY CHISELHURST	Elizabeth, Lady Herbert
JOSIAH FOREMAN	H.M. Hyndman
JAPHET SNAPPER	Joseph Chamberlain
HUMBERT SPENDER	Herbert Spencer

A Romance of the Nineteenth Century (1881)

LORD SURBITON	Bulwer Lytton
	Richard Monckton Milnes

MANNING, Olivia
The Balkan Trilogy (1960–5)

GUY PRINGLE	R.D. Smith

The Levant Trilogy (1977–80)

GUY PRINGLE	R.D. Smith

MANSFIELD, Katherine
'At the Bay' (1921)

LINDA BURNELL	Annie Beauchamp

'The Garden Party' (1922)

MRS SHERIDAN	Annie Beauchamp

'Je ne parle pas français' (1920)

RAOUL DUQUETTE	Francis Carco

'Prelude' (1918)
LINDA BURNELL   **Annie Beauchamp**

'The Stranger' (1922)
MRS HAMMOND   **Annie Beauchamp**

MARRYAT, Florence
Nellie Brooke, A Homely Story (1868)
HILLSTONE   **Winchester, Hampshire**
DR NESBITT   **Samuel Sebastian Wesley**

MARRYAT, Frederick
Midshipman Easy (1836)
THE GOVERNOR   **Sir Thomas Maitland**

Peter Simple (1834)
HMS DIOMÈDE   *HMS Impérieuse*
TERENCE O'BRIEN   **George Vernon Jackson**
CAPTAIN SAVAGE   **Admiral Thomas Cochrane**

MARTINEAU, Harriet
Deerbrook (1839)
DEERBROOK   **Diss, Norfolk**

MASSIE, W.
Sydenham; or Memoirs of a Man of the World (1830)
VINCENT ANSTRUTHER   **George Canning**
RICHARD BEAUMONT   **Beau Brummell**
GEORGE BROUGHTON   **Lord Brougham**
DUKE OF CLAVERTON   **5th Duke of Devonshire**
CLAVERTON HOUSE   **Devonshire House, London**
PAULET   **Count D'Orsay**
WILL SINGLETON   **Richard Brinsley Sheridan**
MARQUIS OF SNOWDON   **George IV**

MAUGHAM, W. Somerset
Ashenden; or The British Agent (1928)
WILLIAM ASHENDEN   **W. Somerset Maugham**

'Behind the Scenes', *Ashenden; or The British Agent* (1928)
WILBUR SCHÄFER   **David Rowland Francis**

Cakes and Ale (1930)
BLACKSTABLE   **Whitstable, Kent**
AMY DRIFFIELD   **Florence Hardy**
EDWARD DRIFFIELD   **Thomas Hardy**
ROSE DRIFFIELD   **Ethelwyn Sylvia Jones**
JASPER GIBBONS   **John Drinkwater**
         Stephen Phillips
LIONEL HILLIER   **Sir Gerald Kelly**
MRS HUDSON   **Mrs Foreman**

ALROY KEAR   Hugh Walpole
'LORD' GEORGE KEMP   George Holden
ALLGOOD NEWTON   Edmund Gosse
BARTON TRAFFORD   Sir Sidney Colvin
MRS BARTON TRAFFORD   Lady Colvin

The Explorer (1908)
ALEC MACKENZIE   H.M. Stanley

'His Excellency', *Ashenden; or The British Agent* (1928)
O'MALLEY   Sir Gerald Kelly
SIR HERBERT WITHERSPOON   Sir George Buchanan

'Love and Russian Literature', *Ashenden; or The British Agent* (1928)
ANASTASIA ALEXANDROVNA LEONIDOV   Alexandra Kropotkin

The Magician (1908)
LE CHIEN NOIR   Le Chat Blanc, Paris
CLAYSON   Paul Bartlett
MARGARET DAUNCEY   Rose Crowley
OLIVER HADDO   Aleister Crowley
O'BRIEN   Roderic O'Conor
WARREN   James Wilson Morrice

The Moon and Sixpence (1919)
DR COUTRAS   Paul Vernié
TIARÉ JOHNSON   Lovina Chapman
AMY STRICKLAND   Sybil, Lady Colefax
CHARLES STRICKLAND   Paul Gauguin
                                    Augustus John
DIRK STROEVE   Claude Emile Schuffenecker
ROSE WATERFORD   Violet Hunt

Mrs Craddock (1902) and others
MISS LEY   Mrs George Steevens

Of Human Bondage (1915)
BLACKSTABLE   Whitstable, Kent
MRS CAREY   Edith Mary Maugham
LOUISE CAREY   Barbara Sophia Maugham
PHILIP CAREY   W. Somerset Maugham
REVD WILLIAM CAREY   Revd Henry Macdonald Maugham
CLUTTON   Roderic O'Conor
J. CRONSHAW   Aleister Crowley
                                    James Wilson Morrice
FLANAGAN   Penrhyn Stanlaws
FOINET   G.-J.-E. Binet
GRIFFITHS   Sir Gerald Kelly
G. ETHERIDGE HAYWARD   John Ellingham Brooks
FREDERICK LAWSON   Sir Gerald Kelly
MICHEL ROLLIN   Raphaël Collin
TERCANBURY   Canterbury

The Painted Veil (1925)
WALTER FANE — Frederic Herbert, 1st Viscount Maugham

The Razor's Edge (1944)
LAURENCE DARRELL — Christopher Isherwood
SHRI GANESHA — Maharshi Venkataraman
SOPHIE MACDONALD — Denham Fouts
ELLIOTT TEMPLETON — Sir Henry ('Chips') Channon
— Henry May

MELVILLE, Herman

'Bartleby the Scrivener', *The Piazza Tales* (1856)
BARTLEBY — Henry David Thoreau

The Confidence Man (1857)
EGBERT — Henry David Thoreau
GONERIL — Fanny Kemble
MARK WINSOME — Ralph Waldo Emerson

Moby Dick (1851)
FATHER MAPPLE — Edward Thompson Taylor

MEREDITH, George

The Adventures of Harry Richmond (1871)
JANET ILCESTER — Janet Ross
AUGUSTUS RICHMOND — John and Charles Allen
— Augustus Urmiston Meredith
— Melchisedek Meredith
SARKELD — Neuwied, Germany

The Amazing Marriage (1895)
CAPTAIN JOHN PETER KIRBY — E.J. Trelawny
GOWER WOODSEER — Robert Louis Stevenson

Beauchamp's Career (1876)
NEVIL BEAUCHAMP — Rear-Admiral Frederick Augustus Maxse
CECILIA HALKETT — Alice Mary Brandreth
EVERARD ROMFREY — Grantley Berkeley
DR SHRAPNEL — Dr Edwin Hearne
BLACKBURN TUCKMAN — Sir William Hardman

Diana of the Crossways (1884)
PERCY DACIER — Sidney Herbert
LORD DANNISBURGH — Lord Melbourne
LADY DUNSTANE — Lucie, Lady Duff-Gordon
ALEXANDER HEPBURN — Sir William Stirling-Maxwell
ARTHUR RHODES — George Meredith
DIANA WARWICK — Caroline Norton
WESTLAKE — A.W. Kinglake
MR WHITMONBY — Samuel Rogers

DORSET WILMERS	**Charles Greville**
HENRY WILMERS	**Henry Greville**

The Egoist (1879)
DR MIDDLETON	**Thomas Love Peacock**
CROSSJAY PATTERNE	**George Hasted Ellis**
SIR WILLOUGHBY PATTERNE	**Ughtred James Kay-Shuttleworth**
VERNON WHITFORD	**Sir Leslie Stephen**

Evan Harrington (1860)
MR AND MRS ANDREW COGGLESBY	**John and Harriet Eustace Hellyer**
MISS ISABELLA CURRENT ('AUNT BEL')	**Louisa Courtenay**
COUNTESS DE SALDAR	**Louise Mitchell Meredith**
EVAN HARRINGTON	**Augustus Urmiston Meredith**
	George Meredith
MELCHISEDEK HARRINGTON	**Melchisedek Meredith**
LADY JOCELYN	**Lucie, Lady Duff-Gordon**
SIR FRANK JOCELYN	**Sir Alexander Duff-Gordon**
ROSE JOCELYN	**Janet Ross**
LYMPORT	**Portsmouth, Hampshire**
MAJOR STRIKE	**Sir Samuel Burdon Ellis**
MRS STRIKE	**Catherine Matilda, Lady Ellis**

The House on the Beach (1877)
MR CRICKLEDON	**Mr Ockenden**
MRS CRICKLEDON	**Mrs Ockenden**
MARTIN TINMAN	**Mr Busby**

Lord Ormont and His Aminta (1894)
LADY CHARLOTTE EGLETT	**Lady Caroline Maxse**
LORD ORMONT	**7th Earl of Cardigan**

One of Our Conquerors (1891)
REVD MR BARMBY	**Augustus Jessop**

The Ordeal of Richard Feverel (1859)
MRS BERRY	**Mrs Ockendon**
HIPPIAS FEVEREL	**Richard Stephen Charnock**
ADRIAN HARLEY	**Maurice Fitzgerald**
BELLA MOUNT	**Mary Ellen Meredith**

Rhoda Fleming (1865)
EDWARD BLANCOVE	**Edward Peacock**
MARGARET LOVELL	**Mary Ellen Meredith**

Sandra Belloni (Emilia in England) (1864)
EMILIA SANDRA BELLONI	**Emilia Macirone**
TRACY RUNNINGBROOK	**Algernon Charles Swinburne**

A Tale of Chloe (1879)
BEAU BEAMISH	**Richard Nash (Beau Nash)**
CHLOE MARTINWARD	**Frances Braddock**
	Christina Rossetti

The Tragic Comedians (1880)

SIGISMUND ALVAN	**Ferdinand Lassalle**
BARONESS LUCIE VON CREFELDT	**Countess Sophie von Hatzfeldt**
PRINCE MARCO	**Count Racowitz**
CLOTILDE VON RÜDIGER	**Helene von Racowitza**

MEREDITH, Isabel
A Girl Among the Anarchists (1903)

AUGUSTIN MYERS	**Martial Bourdin**
JACOB MYERS	**Henry B. Samuels**

MILLER, Warren
The Sleep of Reason (1956)

LARNED AINTREY	**Joseph Alsop**
PROCTER AINTREY	**Stewart Alsop**
R. JOHN BURKE	**Roy M. Cohn**
WEBSTER CALHOUN	**Whittaker Chambers**
G. DUNCAN HARE	**David Schine**
DARTNELL HARNETT	**Dashiel Hammett**
SENATOR MUGONNIGLE	**Joseph McCarthy**

MITFORD, Mary Russell
Belford Regis (1835)

BELFORD REGIS	**Reading, Berkshire**

MITFORD, Nancy
The Blessing (1951)

CHÂTEAU DE BELLANDARGUES	**Château d'Ansouis, Vaucluse**
NANNY	**Laura Dicks**
MRS O'DONOVAN	**Violet Hammersley**
ED SPAIN	**Cyril Connolly**
CHARLES-EDOUARD, MARQUIS DE VALHUBERT	**Gaston Palewski**

Christmas Pudding (1932)

SIR RODERICK ('BOBBY') BOBBIN	**Hamish Erskine**
PAUL FOTHERINGAY	**John Betjeman**

Don't Tell Alfred (1960)

MILDRED JUNGFLEISCH	**Susan Mary Alsop**
LADY LEONE	**Lady Diana Cooper**
NORTHEY MACKINTOSH	**Contessa Cristiana Brandolini**
	Deborah, Duchess of Devonshire
GRACE MARQUISE DE VALHUBERT	**Nancy Mitford**
BASIL WINCHAM	**Oswald Alexander Mosley**

Highland Fling (1931)

ALBERT GATES	**Robert Byron**
	James Lees-Milne
GENERAL MURGATROYD	**Lord Redesdale**

Love in a Cold Climate (1949)
LORD MERLIN	**Lord Berners**
LADY MONTDORE	**Violet Trefusis**
JASSY RADLETT	**Jessica Mitford**
LINDA RADLETT	**Deborah, Duchess of Devonshire**

Pigeon Pie (1940)
LADY BEECH	**Violet Hammersley**
RUDOLPH JOCELYN	**Peter Rodd**
SIR IVOR KING	**Mark Ogilvie-Grant**

The Pursuit of Love (1945)
LADY ALCONLEIGH ('AUNT SADIE')	**Lady Redesdale**
UNCLE MATTHEW	**Lord Redesdale**
LORD MERLIN	**Lord Berners**
ROBERT PARKER	**Donald Darling**
RANDOLPH PINE	**Humphrey Hare**
JASSY RADLETT	**Jessica Mitford**
LINDA RADLETT	**Deborah, Duchess of Devonshire**
FABRICE, DUC DE SAUVETERRE	**Gaston Palewski**
CHRISTIAN TALBOT	**Peter Rodd**
DAVID WARBECK	**Edward Sackville-West**

Wigs on the Green (1935)
JASPER ASPECT	**Basil Murray**
EUGENIA MALMAINS	**Unity Mitford**

MOLESWORTH, Mrs
'Carrots': Just a Little Boy (1878)
FABIAN DESART ('CARROTS')	**Lionel Charles Molesworth**
	Richard Bevil Molesworth
CAPTAIN FRANK DESART	**Richard Molesworth**
SANDYSHORE	**Fleetwood, Lancashire**
SYBIL	**Agnes Venetia Höhler**

A Christmas Child (1880)
NARCISSA	**Mary Josephine Hutton**
TED	**Thomas Grindal Hutton**
THE UNCLE	**William Stanley Jevons**

'Grandmother Dear' (1878)
GRANDMOTHER DEAR	**Agnes Janet Stewart**

Hoodie (1882)
JULIAN ('HOODIE') CARYLL	**Juliet Ainslie**

Lover and Husband (1870)
MALLINGFORD	**Knutsford, Cheshire**

MOORE, George
Confessions of a Young Man (1888) and others
HENRY MARSHALL	**Lewis Weldon Hawkins**

Esther Waters (1894)
JOHN RANDAL ('MR LEOPOLD')   **Joseph Appleby**
WOODVIEW   **Buckingham House, Old**
        Shoreham, Sussex

A Mere Accident (1887)
JOHN NORTON   **Edward Martyn**

A Modern Lover (1883)
LEWIS SEYMOUR   **Lewis Weldon Hawkins**

A Mummer's Wife (1885)
MONTGOMERY   **James Glover**

Muslin (1915)
MR BARTON   **James Browne**
MRS BARTON   **Anna Murphy**

MORDAUNT, Elinor
Gin and Bitters (1931)
LAURENCE HURLE   **W. Somerset Maugham**
MR POLEHUE   **Hugh Walpole**
CYNTHIA STODDARD   **Syrie Maugham**

MORE, Hannah
Coelebs in Search of a Wife (1809)
COELEBS   **John Scandrett Harford**

MORGAN, Lady
Florence Macarthy (1818)
CONWAY TOWNSEND CRAWLEY   **John Wilson Croker**
DE VERE   **Lord Byron**
LORD ROSBRIN   **Lord Blessington**

MORIER, James
The Adventures of Haji Baba of Ispahan (1824)
HAJJI BABA   **Hajji Baba**

MORRISON, Arthur
A Child of the Jago (1896)
EAST END ELEVATION MISSION &   **Toynbee Hall, Whitechapel, London**
   PANSOPHICAL INSTITUTE
THE JAGO   **The Old Nichol**
THE PANJANDRUM OF PHILANTHROPY   **General William Booth**
THE REVD HENRY STURT (FATHER STURT)   **Revd Austin Osborne Jay**

MURRY, J.M.
Still Life (1916)
DUPONT   **Francis Carco**

de NÈVE, Edward
Barred (1932)
HÜBNER
JAN VAN LEEUWEN
STANIA VAN LEEUWEN

Ford Madox Ford
Edward de Nève
Jean Rhys

N

NEWMAN, J.H.
Loss and Gain (1848)
CHARLES REDING

J.H. Newman

NICHOLS, Beverley
Death to Slow Music (1956)
NIGEL FLEET

Noël Coward

Evensong (1932)
MADAME IRELA
BABA LETOILE

Nellie Melba
Toti Dal Monte

NICOLSON, Harold
Some People (1927)
LAMBERT ORME

Ronald Firbank

O

O'CONNOR, Edwin
The Last Hurrah (1956)
FRANCIS SKEFFINGTON

James Michael Curley

O'HARA, John
Appointment in Samarra (1934)
GIBBSVILLE
LANTENENGO STREET, GIBBSVILLE

Pottsville, Pennsylvania
Mahantongo Street, Pottsville,
  Pennsylvania

FOXIE LEBRIX

Papa Turin

BUtterfield 8 (1935)
JAMES MALLOY
GLORIA WANDROUS

John O'Hara
Starr Faithfull

A Family Party (1956) and other stories
LYONS

Lykens, Pennsylvania

A Rage to Live (1949)
FORT PENN — Harrisburg, Pennsylvania

Ten North Frederick (1955)
BOB HOOKER — H.I. Silliman

OLIPHANT, Laurence
Masollam (1886)
REGINALD CLAREVILLE — Laurence Oliphant[2]
DAVID MASOLLAM — Thomas Lake Harris

Piccadilly (1870)
JUGGONATH CHUNDANGO — Coomara Swami
DICKIEFIELD — Fryston Hall, Ferrybridge, Yorkshire
LORD DICKIEFIELD — Richard Monckton Milnes
LORD FRANK VANECOURT — Laurence Oliphant[2]

OLIPHANT, Margaret
Phoebe Junior (1876)
COPPERHEAD — Sir Samuel Morton Peto

Salem Chapel (1873)
ARTHUR VINCENT — Edward Irving

OPIE, Mrs Amelia
Adeline Mowbray; or The Mother and Daughter (1804)
FREDERIC GLENMURRAY — William Godwin
ADELINE MOWBRAY — Mary Wollstonecraft

OPPENHEIMER, James
The Nine-tenths (1911)
UPRISING OF THE THIRTY THOUSAND — Uprising of the Twenty Thousand

ORWELL, George
Burmese Days (1934)
KYAUKTADA — Katha, Upper Burma

Coming up for Air (1939)
LOWER BINFIELD — Henley, Oxfordshire

Keep the Aspidistra Flying (1936)
ANTICHRIST — *The Adelphi*
PHILIP RAVELSTON — Sir Richard Rees

Nineteen Eighty-four (1949)
EMMANUEL GOLDSTEIN — Andrés Nin
MINISTRY OF TRUTH — Broadcasting House, London

OSBOURNE, Lloyd

See under STEVENSON, R.L., and OSBOURNE, Lloyd.

OUIDA
Friendship (1878)

EARL OF ARCHIESTOWN ('LORD ARCHIE')	**Sir Alexander Duff-Gordon**
COUNT D'AVESNES	**Louis Ramé**
ETOILE, COMTESSE D'AVESNES	**Ouida**
SYLVERLEY BELL	**Mr Wells**
LADY CARDIFF	**Lady Walpole**
LADY JOAN CHALLONER	**Janet Ross**
ROBERT CHALLONER	**Henry James Ross**
PRINCE IORIS	**Lotteringhi, Marchese della Stufa**

P

PATER, Walter
'Emerald Uthwart' (1892)

EMERALD UTHWART	**Francis Fortescue Urquhart**

Marius the Epicurean (1885)

MARIUS	**Richard Charles Jackson**

PAULDING, J.K.
The Dutchman's Fireside (1831)

TIMOTHY WEASEL	**Lewis Wetzel (or Weitzel)**

PAYN, James
Lost Sir Massingberd (1864)

MARMADUKE HEATH	**Thomas Pickford**

PEACOCK, Thomas Love
Crotchet Castle (1831)

MR CHAINMAIL	**Sir Edward Strachey**
THE LEARNED FRIEND	**Lord Brougham**
MR MACQUEDY	**John Ramsay McCulloch**
	James Mill
	Robert Mushet
MR RAMSBOTTOM	**John Frank Newton**
RODERICK ROBTHETILL	**James Lloyd**
RUMBLESACK SHANTSEE	**Robert Southey**
MR SKIONAR	**Samuel Taylor Coleridge**
STEAM INTELLECT SOCIETY	**Society for the Diffusion of Useful Knowledge**
MR TOOGOOD	**Robert Owen**
TIMOTHY TOUCHANDGO	**Rowland Stephenson**

MR TRILLO	**Thomas Moore**
WILFUL WONTSEE	**William Wordsworth**

Gryll Grange (1860)
LORD FACING-BOTH-WAYS	**Lord Brougham**
MISS ILEX	**Louisa Courtenay**
LORD MICHIN MALICHO	**John, 1st Earl Russell**
PANTOPRAGMATIC SOCIETY	**Association for the Promotion of Social Science**

Headlong Hall (1816)
MR CRANIUM	**John Gryffydh**
MR ESCOT	**Thomas Love Peacock**
	Percy Bysshe Shelley
MR FOSTER	**Thomas Love Peacock**
	Percy Bysshe Shelley
GEOFFREY GALL	**Francis, Lord Jeffrey**
HEADLONG HALL	**Hafod House, Cardiganshire**
	High Elms, Bracknell, Berkshire
HARRY HEADLONG	**Thomas Johnes**
	W.A. Madocks
MR JENKISON	**T.J. Hogg**
MR MACLAUREL	**Thomas Campbell**
	John Wilson
MARMADUKE MILESTONE	**Humphry Repton**
MR NIGHTSHADE	**Robert Southey**
SIR PATRICK O'PRISM	**Uvedale Price**
MR PANSCOPE	**Samuel Taylor Coleridge**
PHILOMELA POPPYSEED	**Mrs Amelia Opie**

Maid Marian (1822)
HARPITON	**Robert Southey**

Melincourt (1817)
MR ANYSIDE ANTIJACK	**George Canning**
MR DERRYDOWN	**Sir Walter Scott**
MR FAX	**Thomas Malthus**
MR FEATHERNEST	**Robert Southey**
SYLVAN FORESTER	**Lord Monboddo**
	Percy Bysshe Shelley
HUMPHREY HIPPY	**T.J. Hogg**
MR KILLTHEDEAD	**Sir John Barrow**
	John Wilson Croker
ANTHELIA MELINCOURT	**Fanny Falkner**
	Jane Gryffydh
MOLEY MYSTIC	**Samuel Taylor Coleridge**
MR PAPERSTAMP	**William Wordsworth**
MR VAMP	**William Gifford**

Nightmare Abbey (1818)
ASTERIAS	**Pierre Denys de Montfort**
	Sir John Sinclair

MR CYPRESS	Lord Byron
FERDINANDO FLOSKY	Samuel Taylor Coleridge
EMILY GIROUETTE	Harriet Grove
SCYTHROP GLOWRY	Percy Bysshe Shelley
HON. MR LISTLESS	Beau Brummell
	Sir Lumley St George Skeffington
NIGHTMARE ABBEY	Albion House, Marlow, Buckinghamshire
MARIONETTA CELESTINA O'CARROLL	Harriet Shelley
RODERICK SACKBUT	Robert Southey
MR TOOBAD	John Frank Newton
CELINDA ('STELLA') TOOBAD	Claire Clairmont
	Elizabeth Hitchener
	Mary Wollstonecraft Shelley

PLOMER, William
The Case is Altered (1932)

BERYL FERNANDEZ	Sybil Da Costa
PAUL FERNANDEZ	James Achew

The Invaders (1934)

NIGEL EDGE	William Plomer

POE, Edgar Allan
The Mystery of Marie Roget (1842)

PREFECT G.	François Eugène Vidocq
MARIE ROGET	Mary Cecilia Rogers

POLIDORI, J.W.
The Vampyre: A Tale (1819)

LADY MERCER	Lady Caroline Lamb
LORD RUTHVEN	Lord Byron

POOLE, Ernest
The Harbor (1915)

BILLY	Ernest Poole
JIM MARSH	W.D. Haywood

POTTER, Beatrix
The Tailor of Gloucester (1902)

THE TAILOR OF GLOUCESTER	John Samuel Prichard

The Tale of Peter Rabbit (1902) and others

MR MCGREGOR'S GARDEN	Camfield Place, Essendon, Hertfordshire
	Fawe Park, Cumbria

The Tale of the Flopsy Bunnies (1909)

MR MCGREGOR'S GARDEN	Gwaynynog, Denbighshire

POWELL, Anthony
A Dance to the Music of Time (1951–76) (sequence of twelve novels)

ALBERT	**James Gomme**
CASANOVA'S CHINESE RESTAURANT	**Maxim's Chinese Restaurant, Soho, London**
GENERAL CONYERS	**Brigadier-General R.L.A. Pennington**
EDGAR DEACON	**Christopher Millard**
FOPPA	**Pietro Castano**
FOPPA'S RESTAURANT	**Castano's Restaurant, Soho, London**
HUGH MORELAND	**Constant Lambert**
J.G. QUIGGIN	**George Orwell**
CHARLES STRINGHAM	**Hubert Duggan**
PETER TEMPLER	**John Spencer**
XAVIER FRANCIS TRAPNEL	**Julian Maclaren-Ross**
DR TRELAWNEY	**Aleister Crowley**
ALFRED, LORD WARMINSTER	**George Orwell**
KENNETH WIDMERPOOL	**Reginald Manningham-Buller**

The Valley of Bones (1964)

CASTLE MALLOCK	**Gosford Castle, County Armagh, Ireland**

POWYS, John Cowper
Wolf Solent (1929)

GREYLANDS	**Sherborne School, Dorset**

POWYS, Llewellyn
Love and Death (1939)

RANDAL PIXLEY	**Gerald Brenan**
DITTANY STONE	**Gamel Woolsey**

PRAED, Mrs Campbell

See under McCARTHY, Justin, and PRAED, Mrs Campbell.

PREBBLE, John
Brute Streets (1954)

ESMÉE STAINFORTH	**Mrs Van der Elst**

The Mather Story (1953)

JAMES LOVETT	**Sir Alfred Munnings**
LIONEL MATHER	**Stanley Spencer**
THE READER	**Lord Beaverbrook**

PRITCHETT, V.S.
Mr Beluncle (1951)

PHILIP BELUNCLE	**Walter Pritchett**

PUGH, Edwin
The Quick and the Dead (1914)
THEODORE TASKOVER   H.G. Wells

R

RAE, W.F.
The American Duchess (1890–1)
LORD REGINALD WOODSTOCK   **Lord Randolph Churchill**

RAVEN, Simon
Alms for Oblivion (1965–76)
PETER MORRISON   **James Prior**

READE, Charles
It is Never Too Late to Mend (1856)

CARTER	**Hunt**
FRY	**Freer**
DR GULLSON	**James Manby Gully**
MR HAWES	**William Austin**
EDWARD JOSEPHS	**Edward Andrews**
MR LACY	**John George Perry**
NAYLOR	**Taylor**
MR O'CONNOR	**Alexander Maconochie**
MR WOODCOCK	**Mr Luckcock**

Put Yourself in His Place (1870)

GEORGE GROTAIT	**William Broadhead**
HILLSBOROUGH	**Sheffield**

A Terrible Temptation (1871)
RHODA TEMPEST   **Catherine ('Skittles') Walters**

The Wandering Heir (1872)
JAMES ANNESLEY   **James Annesley**

REICHLEY, James
Hail to the Chief (1960)

THEODORE BLAIR	**Robert A. Taft**
THE CHAIRMAN OF THE NATIONAL CONVENTION	**Joseph Martin**
THE GOVERNOR OF NEW YORK	**Thomas Edward Dewey**
LUCAS P. STARBUCK	**Dwight D. Eisenhower**

REVERMORT, J.A.
Cuthbert Learmont (1910)
MARY FOTHERINGHAM   **Lady Ottoline Morrell**

RHYS, Jean
After Leaving Mr Mackenzie (1931)

GEORGE HORSFIELD	Leslie Tilden Smith

Postures (1928)

CAIRN	Ernest Hemingway
H.J. HEIDLER	Ford Madox Ford
LOIS HEIDLER	Stella Bowen
MARYA ZELLI	Jean Rhys

RICHARDSON, Dorothy
Pilgrimage (1915–67)

ANSELM'S INN	Clifford's Inn, London
BABINGTON	Abingdon, Berkshire
MRS BAILEY	Keziah Baker
BANBURY PARK	Finsbury Park, North London
BELMONT CLUB	Arachne Club, London
JAN VON BOHLEN	Ellie Schleussner
BONNYCLIFF	Sandgate, Kent
BENNETT BRODIE	John Arthur Batchelor
FELIX CORRIE	Sir Horace Avory
ROLLO CORRIE	Lady Avory
DIMPLE HILL	Windmill Hill, Sussex
GERALD DUCAYNE	Jack Hale
FLAXMAN'S COURT	Woburn Buildings, Bloomsbury, London
MR AND MRS GREEN	Mr and Mrs Harris
MR GROVE	Frederick Fenton
MR HANCOCK	John Henry Badcock
MR HENDERSON	Charles Richardson
MRS HENDERSON	Mary Miller Richardson
EVE HENDERSON	Alice Mary Richardson
HARRIETT HENDERSON	Jessie Abbott Hale
MIRIAM HENDERSON	Dorothy Richardson
SARAH HENDERSON	Frances Kate Batchelor
SELINA HOLLAND	Miss Moffatt
KENNETT STREET	Kenton Street, Bloomsbury, London
THE LYCURGANS	Fabian Society
MAG	Mabel Heath
MR NOBLE	Alan Odle
OBERLAND	Adelboden, Switzerland
LEYTON ORLY AND FAMILY	Charles Francis Peyton Baly and family
DEBORAH PERNE	Miss Ayre
MR PERRANCE	Francis Cook
LILY PFAFF	Lily Pabst
RICHARD AND RACHEL ROSCORLA	Mr and Miss Penrose
AMABEL SHATOV	Avice Veronica Grad
MICHAEL SHATOV	Benjamin Grad
GEORGE TAYLOR	Charles Daniel

ALMA WILSON   Catherine ('Jane') Wells
HYPO WILSON   H.G. Wells
WORDSWORTH HOUSE   Edgeworth House, Finsbury Park, London

RITCHIE, Lady
Old Kensington (1873)
DOLLY VANBOROUGH   Harriet Thackeray

The Story of Elizabeth (1863)
STEPHEN TOURNEUR   Adolphe Monod

ROBERTS, Morley
The Degradation of Geoffrey Alwith (1895)
WILL CURGENVEN   George Gissing

Maurice Quain (1897)
MAURICE QUAIN   George Gissing

The Private Life of Henry Maitland (1912)
CUMBERLAND MANSIONS (FORMERLY RESIDENCES)   Cornwall Mansions
HAROLD EDGEWORTH   Frederic Harrison
JOHN GLASS   James Payn
MARIAN HILTON   Nell Gissing
J.H. (OR J.C.H.)   Morley Roberts
DR LAKE   Henry Hick
PROFESSOR LITTLE   Joseph Goudge Greenwood
HENRY MAITLAND   George Gissing
MIREFIELDS   Wakefield, Yorkshire
MOORHAMPTON   Manchester
MOORHAMPTON COLLEGE   Owens College, Manchester
G.H. RIVERS   H.G. Wells
EDMUND RODEN   Edward Clodd
SCHMIDT   Eduard Bertz

A Son of Empire (1899)
RICHARD BLUNDELL   Sir Richard Burton

ROBINSON, Emma
The Gold-Worshippers (1851)
MR HUMSON   George Hudson
MRS REDGOLD   Maria Manning

Madeleine Graham (1864)
MADELEINE GRAHAM   Madeleine Smith

ROLFE, F.W.
Hadrian VII (1904)
CARDINAL COURTLEIGH   Cardinal Herbert Alfred Vaughan
MARYVALE   Oscott St Mary's College
CARDINAL OREZZA   Cardinal Oreglia

CARDINAL RAGNA	**Mariano Rampolla**
GEORGE ARTHUR ROSE	**F.W. Rolfe**
ST ANDREW'S COLLEGE	**Scotch College, Rome**

Nicholas Crabbe (1958)

BAINBRIGGE	**Henry Charles Bainbridge**
NEDDY CARNAGE	**E.J. Slaughter**
CAPTAIN THEOPHANES CLAYFOOT	**Arthur Smith Graham**
NICHOLAS CRABBE	**F.W. Rolfe**
ROBERT KEMP	**Sholto Douglas**
DORON OLDCASTLE	**Grant Richards**
KENNETH O'LYMPOS	**Kenneth Grahame**
VERE PERKINS	**Stanhope Perkins**
SLIM SCHELM	**John Lane**
SYDNEY THORAH	**Henry Harland**

The Weird of the Wanderer (1912)

REVD BOBUGO BONSON	**R.H. Benson**

RUTHERFORD, Mark
The Autobiography of Mark Rutherford (1881)

MARK RUTHERFORD	**William Hale White**
THERESA	**George Eliot**
MR WOLLASTON	**John Chapman**

Catharine Furze (1893)

REVD THEOPHILUS CARDEW	**Revd W. Reuben Lewis**

The Revolution in Tanner's Lane (1887)

THOMAS BRADSHAW	**Revd Thomas Binney**
JOHN BROAD	**John Jukes**
ZACHARIAH COLEMAN	**William White**
JAMES HARDEN	**Samuel Hillyard**

S

SACKVILLE-WEST, Victoria
Challenge (1924)

EVE DAVENANT	**Violet Trefusis**
JULIAN DAVENANT	**Victoria Sackville-West**

The Dark Island (1934)

LADY LE BRETON	**Lady Sackville**
SHIRIN LE BRETON	**Gwendolen St Aubyn**
CRISTINA RICH	**Victoria Sackville-West**
STORN	**St Michael's Mount, Cornwall**

The Edwardians (1930)

CHEVRON	**Knole, Kent**

ROMOLA CHEYNE	Alice Keppel
LADY ROEHAMPTON	Sybil, Countess of Westmorland
LADY TEMPLECOMBE	Lady Londonderry
LORD TEMPLECOMBE	Lord Londonderry

Family History (1932)
DAN JARROLD   Benedict Nicolson

Heritage (1919)
RUTH PENNISTAN   Victoria Sackville-West

SANTAYANA, George
The Last Puritan (1935)
JIM DARNLEY   Francis, 2nd Earl Russell

SAPPER (H.C. McNeile)
Bull-dog Drummond (1920) and others
HUGH ('BULL-DOG') DRUMMOND   Gerard Fairlie

SARTON, May
Faithful are the Wounds (1955)
EDWARD CAVAN   F.O. Matthiessen

SASSOON, Siegfried
Memoirs of a Fox-Hunting Man (1928)
DICK TILTWOOD   David Thomas

Memoirs of an Infantry Officer (1930)
DAVID CROMLECH   Robert Graves
THORNTON TYRRELL   Bertrand Russell

SAYERS, Dorothy L.
Murder Must Advertise (1933)
MR INGLEBY   R.A. Bevan
MISS METEYARD   Dorothy L. Sayers
PYM'S PUBLICITY LTD   S.H. Benson Ltd
LORD PETER WIMSEY   Charles Crichton
                              Eric Whelpton

The Unpleasantness at the Bellona Club (1928)
GENERAL ARTHUR FENTIMAN   William Crockford

SCHULBERG, Budd
The Disenchanted (1950)
MANLEY HALLIDAY   F. Scott Fitzgerald

The Harder They Fall (1947)
TORO MOLINA   Primo Carnera

SCOTT, Sir Walter

The Antiquary (1816)

HERMAN DOUSTERSWIVEL	Rudolf Eric Raspe
FAIRPORT	Arbroath, Tayside, Scotland
HECTOR M'INTYRE	George Constable, the Younger
EDIE OCHILTREE	Andrew Gemmells
GRISELDA OLDBUCK	Matilda Constable
JONATHAN OLDBUCK	John Clerk of Eldin
	George Constable, the Elder
	Alexander Gordon
	John Ramsay of Ochtertyre
SIR ARTHUR WARDOUR	Sir John Sinclair
	Sir John Whitefoord

The Black Dwarf (1816)

SIR EDWARD MANLEY	David Ritchie

The Bride of Lammermoor (1819)

LADY ASHTON	Margaret, Lady Stair
LUCY ASHTON	Janet Dalrymple
EDGAR, MASTER OF RAVENSWOOD	Archibald, Lord Rutherford

The Fair Maid of Perth (1828)

CONACHAR, CHIEF OF CLAN QUHELE	Daniel Scott

The Fortunes of Nigel (1822)

CAPTAIN CLUTTERBUCK	Adam Ormiston
	Walter Tait
SIR MUNGO MALAGROWTHER	Charles Kirkpatrick Sharpe

Guy Mannering (1815)

HENRY BERTRAM	James Annesley
	Sir Robert Maxwell
	Henry Routledge
AILIE DINMONT	Catherine Laidlaw
DANDIE DINMONT	James Davidson
	Willie Elliott
	James Laidlaw
	Archibald Park
	James Thorburn
DUDLEY	James Skene
TOD GABBIE ('GABRIEL')	Willie Tod
PROCURATOR FISCAL MACMORLAN	Robert Shortreed
GUY MANNERING	Sir Walter Scott
JULIA MANNERING	Charlotte, Lady Scott
MEG MERRILIES	Margaret Euston
	Jean Gordon
PAUL PLEYDELL	Andrew Crosbie
	Adam Rolland
DOMINIE SAMPSON	James Sanson
	George Thomson

The Heart of Midlothian (1818)
DAVID DEANS   **Patrick Walker**
EFFIE DEANS   **Isobel Walker**
JEANIE DEANS   **Frances, Lady Douglas**
    Helen Walker
MADGE WILDFIRE   **Feckless Fannie**

'The Highland Widow', *Chronicles of the Canongate* (1827)
MARTHA BETHUNE BALIOL   **Anne Murray Keith**

Ivanhoe (1819)
REBECCA   **Rebecca Gratz**

The Lady of the Lake (1810)
ELLEN DOUGLAS   **Lady Hood**

A Legend of Montrose (1819)
DUGALD DALGETTY   **Robert Monro**
    Martin Skene
    Sir James Turner

The Monastery (1820)
CAPTAIN CLUTTERBUCK   **Adam Ormiston**
    Walter Tait

Old Mortality (1816)
OLD MORTALITY   **Robert Paterson**

Peveril of the Peak (1823)
MARTINDALE CASTLE   **Haddon Hall, Derbyshire**

The Pirate (1821)
CAPTAIN CLEMENT CLEVELAND   **John Gow**
NORNA OF THE FITFUL HEAD (ULLA   **Bessie Millie**
    TROIL)

Redgauntlet (1824)
ALAN FAIRFORD   **Sir Walter Scott**
ALEXANDER FAIRFORD (CALLED   **Walter Scott, the Elder**
    SAUNDERS)
FAIRLADIES   **Mereworth Castle, Kent**
JOSHUA GEDDES   **George Waldie**
RACHEL GEDDES   **Ann Waldie**
CRISTAL NIXON   **Tom Purdie**
SIR ARTHUR REDGAUNTLET (DARSIE   **William Clerk**
    LATIMER)   **Charles Kerr**
LILIAS REDGAUNTLET   **Williamina Belsches**
SIR ROBERT REDGAUNTLET   **Sir Robert Grierson**
WILLIE STEENSON (WANDERING WILLIE)   **John Metcalf**
    Williams ap Prichard

Rob Roy (1817)
DIANA VERNON   **Countess Purgstall**

Rokeby (1813)
MATILDA OF ROKEBY   **Williamina Belsches**

St Ronan's Well (1823)
JOSIAH CARGILL   **Alexander Duncan**
                                       George Lawson
MEG DODS   **Marion Ritchie**
LADY PENNEFEATHER   **Mrs Penn**
MR TOUCHWOOD   **Count Platoff**

Tales of a Grandfather (1827–9)
HUGH LITTLEJOHN   **John Hugh Lockhart**

The Talisman (1825)
ROSWAL   **Maida**

Waverley (1814)
BARON BRADWARDINE   **Alexander Forbes**
                                       Laurence Oliphant[1]
                                       Alexander Stuart of Invernahyle
DAVIE GELLATLEY   **John Gray**[1]
                                       David Hinves
FERGUS MACIVOR   **Alexander MacDonell of Glengarry**
COLONEL TALBOT   **Charles Whitefoord**
TULLY-VEOLAN   **Craighall, Perthshire**
                                       Ravelston House, Edinburgh
WAVERLEY   **Alexander Stuart of Invernahyle**

Woodstock (1826)
BEVIS   **Nimrod**
ALICE LEE   **Anne Scott**

SEDGWICK, Anne Douglas
Adrienne Toner (1921)
ADRIENNE TONER   **Mary Alden Childers**

SHAKESPEAR, Olivia
The Journey of High Honour (1895)
CHRISTOPHER BRANDON   **Edward Garnett**

SHAW, Flora
Hector (1883)
MADAME LOUSTANOFF (GRANDMÈRE)   **Léonice du Sualt**

SHAW, George Bernard
Cashel Byron's Profession (1886)
CASHEL BYRON   **Pakenham Thomas Beatty**
                                       Jack Burke
NED SKENE   **Ned Donnelly**

Immaturity (1930)
CYRIL SCOTT   **Cecil Lawson**

An Unsocial Socialist (1887)

CHICHESTER ERSKINE	**Pakenham Thomas Beatty**

SHAW, Irwin
The Young Lions (1948)

AHEARN	**Ernest Hemingway**
LEROY KEANE	**Leicester Hemingway**
LOUISE M'KIMBER	**Mary Hemingway**

SHELLEY, Mary Wollstonecraft
Frankenstein; or The Modern Prometheus (1818)

ALPHONSE FRANKENSTEIN	**William Godwin**
	James Lind
VICTOR FRANKENSTEIN	**Percy Bysshe Shelley**
WALDMAN	**James Lind**

The Last Man (1826)

LORD RAYMOND	**Lord Byron**
ADRIAN, EARL OF WINDSOR	**Percy Bysshe Shelley**

Lodore (1835)

CLORINDA	**Emilia Teresa Viviani**
LODORE	**Lord Byron**
EDWARD VILLIERS	**Percy Bysshe Shelley**

Perkin Warbeck (1830)

HERNAN DE FARO	**E.J. Trelawny**

SHEPPARD, Elizabeth Sara
Charles Auchester (1853)

FLORIMOND ANASTASE	**Hector Berlioz**
ARONACH	**Karl Friedrich Zelter**
CHARLES AUCHESTER	**Charles Horsley**
	Joseph Joachim
CLARA BENETTE	**Jenny Lind**
STARWOOD BURNEY	**Sir William Sterndale Bennett**
JOSEPH CERINTHEA	**Manuel García**
JOSEPHINE CERINTHEA	**Pauline Viardot**
MARIA CERINTHEA	**Fanny Hensel**
	Maria Malibran
LENHART DAVY	**John Pyke Hullah**
MISS LAWRENCE	**Sophia Hutchins**
ST MICHEL	**Sir Michael Costa**
SERAPHAEL	**Felix Mendelssohn**

Rumour (1858)

PORPHYRO	**Napoleon III, Emperor of France**

SHERWOOD, Mary Martha
Caroline Mordaunt; or The Governess (1853)

MRS DELANEY	**Elizabeth Hamilton**

SHIELD, Francis T.
McDonough (1951)
PACKER CITY   **Jersey City, New Jersey**

SHIRER, William L.
Stranger Come Home (1954)
ROBERT A. FLETCHER   **Edward R. Murrow**
SENATOR O'BRIEN   **Joseph McCarthy**
RAYMOND WHITEHEAD   **William L. Shirer**
BERT WOODRUFF   **Walter Winchell**

SINCLAIR, May
Mary Olivier (1919)
RICHARD NICHOLSON   **Richard Aldington**

Tasker Jones: The Real Story (1916)
TASKER JONES   **Arnold Bennett**

SINCLAIR, Upton
Boston (1928)
CORNELIA THORNWELL   **Mrs Burton**

Oil! (1927)
BARNEY BROCKWAY   **Harry M. Daugherty**
J. ARNOLD ROSS   **Harry Ford Sinclair**

SITWELL, Edith
I Live Under a Black Sun (1937)
HENRY DEBINGHAM   **Wyndham Lewis**
JONATHAN HARE   **Pavel Tchelitchew**
LUCY LINDEN   **Edith Sitwell**
ANNA MARTON   **Edith Sitwell**
SIR HENRY ROTHERHAM   **Sir George Sitwell**

SITWELL, Osbert
Donald McDougall (1958)
DONALD MCDOUGALL   **Norman Douglas**

'Gino of the Bookshop' (1958)
GINO   **Giuseppe ('Pino') Orioli**

'The Love-Bird' (1930)
ROBERT MAINWROTH   **Lord Berners**

'The Machine Breaks Down' (1924)
HUGH DEARBORN   **Harry Melvill**

'That Flesh is Heir to . . .' (1930)
MURIEL CHITTY   **Violet Hammersley**

'Triple Fugue' (1924)
PROFESSOR JAMES CRISCROSS   **Edmund Gosse**

MATTHEW DEAN	**Sir Edward Marsh**
DODDERINGHAM OLD HALL	**Garsington Manor, Oxfordshire**
LADY SEPTUAGESIMA GOODLEY	**Lady Ottoline Morrell**

SKENE, Felicia
St Albans; or The Prisoners of Hope (1853)
MR CHESTERFIELD **Revd Thomas Chamberlain**

SKINNER, M.L.

See under LAWRENCE, D.H., and SKINNER, M.L.

SMITH, Haskett
For God and Humanity, a Romance of Mount Carmel (1891)
CYRIL GORDON **Laurence Oliphant**[2]

SMITH, Stevie
The Holiday (1949)
BASIL **George Orwell**

SMOLLETT, Tobias
The Adventures of Peregrine Pickle (1751) (Chapter 98)
MR A. **James Annesley**

SNOW, C.P.
The Masters (1951)
THE COLLEGE **Christ's College, Cambridge**

SPRING, Howard
Fame is the Spur (1940)
HAMER SHAWCROSS **Ramsay Macdonald**

STANHOPE, M. Spencer
Almacks (1826)

ARCHDEACON CARLTON	**Revd Edward John Bury**
LADY MARGARET CARLTON	**Lady Charlotte Bury**
LORD DERWENT	**5th Duke of Portland**
LADY GLENMORE	**Lady Anne Coke**
	Jane Digby
LORD GLENMORE	**Thomas William Coke, 1st Earl of Leicester**
LADY HAUTON	**Countess of Jersey**
EARL OF NORBURY	**3rd Duke of Northumberland**

STEEL, Flora Annie
A Sovereign Remedy (1906)
MR HIRSCH **William Heinemann**

STEIN, Gertrude
Fernhurst (1971) (written 1903–5)

JANET BRUCE	**Mary Gwinn**
FERNHURST	**Bryn Mawr College, Pennsylvania**
NANCY REDFERN	**Gertrude Stein**
PHILIP REDFERN	**Alfred Hodder**
HELEN THORNTON	**Carey Thomas**

'The Good Anna', *Three Lives* (1909)

ANNA	**Lena Lebender**
BRIDGEPOINT	**Baltimore, Maryland**
MISS MATHILDA	**Gertrude Stein**

The Making of Americans (1925)

HANNAH CHARLES	**Carey Thomas**
MR HENRY DEHNING	**Solomon Stein**
MRS HENRY DEHNING	**Pauline Stein**
JULIA DEHNING	**Bird Gans**
CORA DOUNOR	**Mary Gwinn**
GOSSOLS	**East Oakland, California**
DAVID HERSLAND	**Daniel Stein**
FANNY HERSLAND	**Amelia Stein**
MARTHA HERSLAND	**Gertrude Stein**

'Melanctha', *Three Lives* (1909)

JEFFERSON CAMPBELL	**Gertrude Stein**
MELANCTHA HERBERT	**May Bookstaver**

'Miss Furr and Miss Skeene', *Geography and Plays* (1922)

GEORGINA SKEENE	**Miss Squire**

Things As They Are (1950)

ADELE	**Gertrude Stein**
SOPHIE NEATHE	**Mabel Haynes**
HELEN THOMAS	**May Bookstaver**

'Two Women' (1925)

ADA	**Etta Cone**
MARTHA	**Claribel Cone**

STEVENSON, R.L.
The Strange Case of Dr Jekyll and Mr Hyde (1886)

DR HENRY JEKYLL/EDWARD HYDE	**William Brodie**

Treasure Island (1883)

LONG JOHN SILVER	**W.E. Henley**

Weir of Hermiston (1896)

ADAM WEIR (LORD HERMISTON)	**Robert Macqueen, Lord Braxfield**

STEVENSON, R.L., and OSBOURNE, Lloyd
The Wrecker (1892)

JIM PINKERTON	**Samuel Sidney McClure**

The Wrong Box (1889)
MICHAEL FINSBURY   **Charles Baxter**

STONE, Elizabeth
William Langshawe, the Cotton Lord (1842)
HENRY WOLSTENHOLME   **Thomas Ashton**

STRACHEY, J. St Loe
The Great Bread Riots (1890)
THE PRESIDENT OF THE NATIONAL   **Lord Randolph Churchill**
   LABOUR PROTECTION LEAGUE

SUMMERS, Edith
Weeds (1923)
JUDY   **Edith Summers**

SURTEES, R.S.
Mr Facey Romford's Hounds (1865)
COUNTESS OF CAPERINGTON   **Katherine, Countess of Stamford
                                            and Warrington**

Mr Sponge's Sporting Tour (1853)
LORD SCAMPERDALE   **Sir William Chaytor**

T

TABOR, Eliza
Diary of a Novelist (1870)
CANON BURNEY   **Revd Thomas Binney**

The Master of Marton (1864)
CANON BURNEY   **Revd Thomas Binney**

TAYLOR, Bayard
John Godfrey's Fortunes (1864)
BRANDNAGEE   **Fitz-James O'Brien**
SMITHERS   **Walt Whitman**

TAYLOR, Peter
'1939' (1960)
JIM PREWITT   **Robert Lowell**

THACKERAY, W.M.
The Adventures of Philip (1861–2)
MRS BAYNES   **Isabella Shawe**
CHARLOTTE BAYNES   **Isabella Thackeray**

DR GEORGE FIRMIN	E.J. James
PHILIP FIRMIN	W.M. Thackeray
LORD RINGWOOD	Lord Fitzhardinge

The Book of Snobs (1848)

CAPTAIN SHINDY	Stephen Price

The Confessions of Fitz-Boodle (1852)

KALBSBRATEN	Weimar, Germany
OTTILIA VON SCHLIPPENSCHLOPP	Jenny von Pappenheim
DOROTHEA VON SPECK	Melanie von Spiegel

'The Curate's Walk', *Punch's Prize Novelists* (1853)

REVD FRANK WHITESTOCKE	William Henry Brookfield

Denis Duval (1864)

FAIRPORT	Fareham, Hampshire

'Dennis Haggarty's Wife', *Men's Wives* (1843)

MRS GAM	Isabella Shawe
JEMIMA GAM	Jane Shawe

Doctor Birch and His Young Friends (1849)

MR PRINCE	Revd Edward Churton

The History of Henry Esmond (1852)

TOM BOXER	John Forster
CASTLEWOOD	Clevedon Court, Somerset
LADY CASTLEWOOD	Jane Brookfield
LORD CASTLEWOOD	William Henry Brookfield
COUNTESS OF CHELSEY'S HOUSE	Queens House, Chelsea, London
HENRY ESMOND	W.M. Thackeray
THE *OBSERVATOR*	The *Examiner*

The History of Pendennis (1848–50)

BLANCHE AMORY	Theresa Reviss
	Cecilia Anne Thynne
MR ARCHER	Thomas Hill
THE BACK KITCHEN	The Cider Cellars, London
MR BACON	Richard Bentley
LAURA BELL	Jane Brookfield
BLOUNDELL	Henry Matthew
MR BUNGAY	Henry Colburn
CHATTERIS	Exeter, Devon
CLAVERING ST MARY	Ottery St Mary, Devon
LORD COLCHICUM	2nd Earl of Lonsdale
MR DOLPHIN	Alfred Bunn
FAIROAKS	Larkbeare House, Ottery St Mary, Devon
HARRY FOKER	Andrew Arcedeckne
EMILY FOTHERINGAY	Frances Eleanor Ternan
DR GOODENOUGH	John Elliotson
MR HODGEN	William Gribben Ross

MIROBOLANT	**Alexis Benoit Soyer**
MAJOR PENDENNIS	**Merrick Shawe**
ARTHUR PENDENNIS	**Cuthbert Edward Ellison**
	Charles Lamb Kenney
	W.M. Thackeray
HELEN PENDENNIS	**Anne Carmichael-Smyth**
REVD DR PORTMAN	**Revd Sidney Cornish**
	Revd Francis Huysh
CAPTAIN SHANDON	**William Maginn**
REVD MR SMIRKE	**Revd Sidney Cornish**
EDWARD STRONG	**Henry Glynn**
CAPTAIN GRANBY TIPTOFF	**Granby Hales Calcraft**
GEORGE WARRINGTON	**George Malcolm Crawford**
	George Stovin Venables
MR WENHAM	**John Wilson Croker**

The Kickleburys on the Rhine (1850)

SERJEANT LANKIN	**Frederick Gale**
ROUGETNOIRBOURG	**Homburg, Hesse, Germany**

Lovel the Widower (1860)

DICK BEDFORD	**Samuel James**
THE *MUSEUM*	**The *National Standard***

The Memoirs of Barry Lyndon Esq. (1844)

BARRY LYNDON	**Andrew Robinson Stoney**
HONORIA, COUNTESS OF LYNDON	**Mary Eleanor, Countess of Strathmore**

Mrs Perkins's Ball (1847)

MISS BUNION	**Letitia Elizabeth Landon**

The Newcomes (1854–5)

FRED BAYHAM	**William Proctor Bolland**
THE CAVE OF HARMONY	**The Cider Cellars, London**
	The Coal Hole, London
MARQUIS OF FARINTOSH	**4th Marquis of Bath**
121 FITZROY SQUARE	**37 Fitzroy Square, London**
MR GANDISH	**Henry Sass**
GREYFRIARS	**Charterhouse**
MARTHA HONEYMAN	**Anne Becher**
LITTLE NADAB	**Charles Sloman**
MRS MACKENZIE (THE 'CAMPAIGNER')	**Isabella Shawe**
ETHEL NEWCOME	**Countess of Airlie**
	Sarah ('Sally') Baxter
COLONEL THOMAS NEWCOME	**Charles Montaubon Carmichael**
	Henry Carmichael-Smyth
	Sir Richmond Shakespear

'Notes on the North What-d'ye-Callem Election' (1841)

MR BOUNCER	**James Farrer**
FRANCIS BRITTON	**John Bowes**

BRITTON HALL	**Streatlam Castle, County Durham**
COCKLETON	**Hartlepool, County Durham**
LORD GEORGE CRAMLEY	**Lord Harry Vane**
MR HARTINGTON	**Mr Witham**
STUFFINGTON	**Darlington, County Durham**

'Our Street' (1848)

POCKLINGTON SQUARE	**Kensington Square, London**
WADDILOVE STREET	**Young Street, Kensington, London**

'The Proser IV – On a Good-Looking Young Lady' (1850)

ERMINIA	**Virginia, Countess Somers**
TIMOTHEUS	**Sir Henry Taylor**

'Round About the Christmas Tree' (1899)

BOBBY MISTLETOE	**Robert Follett Synge**

A Shabby Genteel Story (1840)

GEORGE BRANDON	**Henry Matthew**
ANDREA FITCH	**John Brine**

Vanity Fair (1847–8)

HARRIET CRAWLEY	**Harriet Butler**
SIR PITT CRAWLEY	**Sir William Chaytor**
	Lord Rolle
WILLIAM DOBBIN	**John Allen**[2]
GAUNT SQUARE	**Berkeley Square, London**
	Cavendish Square, London
	Manchester Square, London
GEORGE OSBORNE	**Arthur Somerset**
MISS PINKERTON'S ACADEMY	**Dr Turner's School, Chiswick Mall, London**
PUMPERNICKEL	**Weimar, Germany**
AMELIA SEDLEY	**Jane Brookfield**
	Anne Carmichael-Smyth
	Isabella Thackeray
JOHN SEDLEY	**Robert Langslow**
JOSEPH SEDLEY	**George Trant Shakespear**
BECKY SHARP	**Sydney, Lady Morgan**
	Theresa Reviss
MARQUIS OF STEYNE	**Lord Fitzhardinge**
	3rd Marquess of Hertford
MR WAGG	**Theodore Hook**
MR WENHAM	**John Wilson Croker**

The Virginians (1857–9)

HESTER LAMBERT	**Anne Isabella, Lady Ritchie**
LUCY LAMBERT	**Harriet Thackeray**

The Yellowplush Correspondence (1837) and later works

CHARLES JEAMES YELLOWPLUSH	**John Henry Skelton**

THIRKELL, Angela
High Rising (1933)
GEORGE KNOX   **E.V. Lucas**
LAURA MORLAND   **Angela Thirkell**
TONY MORLAND   **Lance Thirkell**

Marling Hall (1942)
MISS BUNTING   **Miss Bennet**

Miss Bunting (1945)
MISS BUNTING   **Miss Bennet**

Northbridge Rectory (1941)
NORTHBRIDGE   **Chipping Camden, Gloucestershire**

Wild Strawberries (1934)
LADY EMILY LESLIE   **Lady Wemyss**

TOMLINSON, H.M.
All Our Yesterdays (1930)
LANGHAM   **C.F. Masterman**

TRILLING, Lionel
The Middle of the Journey (1947)
GIFFORD MAXIM   **Whittaker Chambers**

TROLLOPE, Anthony
The Bertrams (1859)
MISS TODD   **Frances Power Cobbe**

Can You Forgive Her? (1864)
MR FINESPIN   **William Gladstone**
WILLIAM MILDMAY   **John, 1st Earl Russell**
PLANTAGENET PALLISER   **6th Duke of Newcastle**
      Chichester Parkinson-Fortescue
      John, 1st Earl Russell
DUKE OF ST BUNGAY   **Lord Lansdowne**
MR TURNBULL, MP   **John Bright**
THE UNIVERSE   **The Cosmopolitan Club, London**

The Duke's Children (1879–80)
THE BEAR GARDEN   **The Garrick Club, Covent Garden, London**

WILLIAM MILDMAY   **John, 1st Earl Russell**
PLANTAGENET PALLISER   **John, 1st Earl Russell**

'Father Giles of Ballymoy' (1867)
ARCHIBALD GREEN   **Anthony Trollope**

Framley Parsonage (1861)
LORD BROCK   **Lord Palmerston**
LORD DE TERRIER   **Lord Derby**
EMILY DUNSTABLE   **Frances Eleanor Trollope**

SIDONIA	**Benjamin Disraeli**

He Knew He was Right (1869)

MISS STANBURY	**Fanny Bent**

Is He Popenjoy? (1878)

MARCHIONESS OF BROTHERTON	**Fabia, Lady Stanley**

The New Heir (1871)

SIR THOMAS UNDERWOOD	**Anthony Trollope**

'The O'Conors of Castle Conor' (1861)

ARCHIBALD GREEN	**Anthony Trollope**

Orley Farm (1861–2)

MR CHAFFANBRASS	**William Ballantine**
ORLEY FARM	**Julian's Hill, Middlesex**

The Palliser novels: *Can You Forgive Her?* (1864–5), *Phineas Finn* (1867–9), *The Eustace Diamonds* (1871–3), *Phineas Redux* (1873–4), *The Prime Minister* (1875–6), and *The Duke's Children* (1879–80)

WILLIAM MILDMAY	**John, 1st Earl Russell**
PLANTAGENET PALLISER	**John, 1st Earl Russell**

Phineas Finn (1869)

LORD CHILTERN	**Lord Camelford**
	8th Duke of Devonshire
MR DAUBENY	**Benjamin Disraeli**
PHINEAS FINN	**Edward Robert King-Harman**
	Joe Parkinson
	Chichester Parkinson-Fortescue
	Sir John Pope-Hennessy
MR GRESHAM	**William Gladstone**
WILLIAM MILDMAY	**John, 1st Earl Russell**
PLANTAGENET PALLISER	**John, 1st Earl Russell**

Phineas Redux (1874)

PHINEAS FINN	**Edward Robert King-Harman**
	Joe Parkinson
	Chichester Parkinson-Fortescue
	Sir John Pope-Hennessy
WILLIAM MILDMAY	**John, 1st Earl Russell**
PLANTAGENET PALLISER	**John, 1st Earl Russell**

The Small House at Allington (1864)

JOHNNY EAMES	**Anthony Trollope**

The Three Clerks (1857)

SIR GREGORY HARDLINES	**Sir Charles Edward Trevelyan**
CHARLEY TUDOR	**Anthony Trollope**
SIR WARWICK WEST END	**Stafford Northcote, 1st Earl of Iddesleigh**

The Warden (1855)

PESSIMUS ANTICANT	**Thomas Carlyle**

BARCHESTER	**Salisbury, Wiltshire**
	Winchester, Hampshire
BARSET	**Somerset**
HIRAMS HOSPITAL	**St Cross Hospital, Winchester**
THE *JUPITER*	*The Times*
MR POPULAR SENTIMENT	**Charles Dickens**
TOM TOWERS	**George Stovin Venables**

The Way We Live Now (1875)

AUGUSTUS MELMOTTE	**Albert Grant**
	George Hudson

TROLLOPE, Frances
The Blue Belles of England (1842)

BRADLEY	**Sir Edwin Landseer**
ROLFE	**Thomas James Mathias**

Michael Armstrong, the Factory Boy (1840)

PARSON BELL (OF FAIRLY)	**Revd G.S. Bull**
DEEP VALLEY MILL	**Litton Mill, Derby**
ELGOOD SHARPTON	**Ellice Needham**

Three Cousins (1847)

BISHOP SOLWAY	**Charles Richard Sumner**

The Vicar of Wrexhill (1840)

REVD WILLIAM JACOB CARTWRIGHT	**Revd J.W. Cunningham**

TRUMBO, Dalton
Washington Jitters (1936)

DEWEY BRONSON	**Hugh S. Johnson**
DR BURGHLIMIT	**Francis E. Townsend**
REVD DR LAUGHLIN	**Father Charles Coughlin**
ED MEHAFFERTY	**James A. Farley**
WILLIS RANDALL, I	**William Randolph Hearst**
DOWNIE SINCERE	**Upton Sinclair**
FRITZ WEENER	**Felix Frankfurter**

TURNER, Reginald
Davray's Affairs (1906)

HANS BRANDERS	**Max Beerbohm**

Samson Unshorn (1909)

IDA COURTNEY	**Julia Frankau**

TURNER, W.J.
The Aesthetes (1927)

LADY VIRGINIA CARAWAY	**Lady Ottoline Morrell**

TWEED, Thomas Frederic
Gabriel Over the White House (1933)

JUDSON CUMMING HAMMOND	**Warren G. Harding**

UPDIKE

U

UPDIKE, John
The Centaur (1963)
GEORGE CALDWELL   **Wesley Updike**

V

VAN VECHTEN, Carl
Nigger Heaven (1926)
RUSSETT DURNWOOD   **H.L. Mencken**

Parties (1930)
DAVID WESTLAKE   **F. Scott Fitzgerald**
RILDA WESTLAKE   **Zelda Fitzgerald**

Peter Whiffle: His Life and Works (1922)
EDITH DALE   **Mabel Dodge Luhan**
PETER WHIFFLE   **Carl Van Vechten**

The Tattooed Countess (1926)
COUNTESS ELLA NATTATORINI   **Mahala Dutton Benedict Douglas**

VIDAL, Gore
The Judgment of Paris (1952)
JIM   **Denham Fouts**

VOYNICH, Ethel
The Gadfly (1897)
GEMMA (JENNIFER) WARREN   **Charlotte Mary Wilson**

W

WALPOLE, Hugh
The Cathedral (1922)
POLCHESTER   **Truro, Cornwall**

Fortitude (1913)
HENRY GALLEON   **Henry James**
MRS LAUNCE   **Marie Belloc Lowndes**

Hans Frost (1929)
JANE ROSE   **Virginia Woolf**

John Cornelius: His Life and Adventures (1937)
ARCHIE BERTRAND   W. Somerset Maugham
CHARLIE CHRISTIAN   Harold Cheevers

Mr Perrin and Mr Traill (1911)
MOFFATTS   Epsom College, Surrey

WARD, Mrs Humphry
Delia Blanchflower (1915)
MISS DEMPSEY   Josephine Butler
SIR WILFRID LANG   Lewis Harcourt, 1st Viscount
GERTRUDE MARVELL   Christabel Pankhurst
MONK LAWRENCE   Nuneham House, Oxfordshire

Eleanor (1899)
THE AMBASSADOR   1st Marquis of Dufferin and Ava
MR BELLASIS   Henry James
ELEANOR BURGOYNE   Pauline de Beaumont
EDWARD MANISTY   François René de Chateaubriand

Helbeck of Bannisdale (1898)
BANNISDALE   Levens Hall, Cumbria
     Sizergh Castle, Cumbria

The History of David Grieve (1891)
RICHARD ANCRUM   Travers Madge
ELISE DELAUNAY   Marie Bashkirtseff
SANDY GRIEVE   Julian Huxley

Lady Connie (1916)
MR WENLOCK   Mark Pattison

Lady Rose's Daughter (1903)
MR COURTENAY   Evelyn Abbott
LADY HENRY DELAFIELD   Marquise du Deffand
JULIE LE BRETON   Julie de Lespinasse
MR MONTRESOR   Anne-Robert Jacques Turgot
CAPTAIN HENRY WARKWORTH   Jacques, Comte de Guibert

Marcella (1894)
MARCELLA BOYCE   Mrs Humphry Ward
     Beatrice Webb
BROWN'S BUILDINGS, MAINE STREET   Peabody Buildings, London
MAXWELL COURT   Ashridge Park, Hertfordshire
     Tring, Hertfordshire
MELLOR PARK   Hampden House, Buckinghamshire
VENTURIST SOCIETY   Fabian Society
LADY WINTERBOURNE   Anne Frederica, Countess of
     Wemyss

The Marriage of William Ashe (1905)
WILLIAM ASHE   Lord Melbourne
LADY KITTY BLACKWATER   Lady Caroline Lamb

Miss Bretherton (1884)
ISABEL BRETHERTON — Mary Anderson

Robert Elsmere (1888)
LAETITIA DARCY — Harriet Cradock
HENRY GREY — T.H. Green
EDWARD LANGHAM — H.F. Amiel
Mark Pattison
CATHERINE LEYBURN — Laura Lyttelton
ROSE LEYBURN — Margot Asquith
Emilia Francis Pattison
MURESWELL RECTORY — Peper Harow, Surrey
THE PROVOST — Benjamin Jowett
ROGER WENDOVER — Mark Pattison

Sir George Tressady (1896)
LORD FONTENOY — Lord Randolph Churchill
SIR GEORGE TRESSADY — William Stratford Dugdale

WARD, Robert Plumer
De Vere; or The Man of Independence (1827)
LADY CLANELLAN — Lady Grenville
MR FLOWERDALE — Robert Plumer Ward
DR HERBERT — Cyril Jackson
LORD MOWBRAY — 4th Duke of Newcastle
MR RIVERS — Robert Plumer Ward
MR WENTWORTH — Lord Bolingbroke
George Canning
William Pitt, 1st Earl of Chatham
William Pitt, the Younger

WARREN, Robert Penn
All the King's Men (1946)
WILLIE STARK — Huey P. Long

At Heaven's Gate (1943)
BOGAN MURDOCK — Luke Lea
SERGEANT MILL PORSUM — Sergeant Alvin Cullum York

WARREN, Samuel
Ten Thousand a Year (1841)
LORD BULFINCH — John, 1st Earl Russell
MR QUICKSILVER — Lord Brougham
VENOM TUFT — Abraham Hayward
SIR CHARLES WOLSTENHOLME — Lord Lyndhurst

WATSON, Lily
The Vicar of Langthwaite (1893)
PHILIP HAWTHORNE — S.G. Green
DR YORKE — James Acworth

WATTS-DUNTON, Theodore
Aylwin (1899)

CYRIL AYLWIN	**Alfred Eugene Watts**
HENRY AYLWIN	**Theodore Watts-Dunton**
PHILIP AYLWIN	**James Orlando Watts**
T. D'ARCY	**Dante Gabriel Rossetti**
D'ARCY'S HOUSE	**Queens House, Chelsea, London**
DE CASTRO	**Charles Augustus Howell**
HURSTCOTE MANOR	**Kelmscot Manor, Oxfordshire**
RAXTON CHURCH	**Pakefield Church, Suffolk**
SYMONDS	**Frederick Richards Leyland**
WILDERSPIN	**James Smetham**
THE YOUNG SECRETARY	**George Hake**

WAUGH, Alec
The Loom of Youth (1917)

BULLER	**G.M. Carey**
CLAREMONT	**Henry Robinson King**
FERNHURST	**Sherborne School, Dorset**

WAUGH, Evelyn
Black Mischief (1932)

AZANIA	**Abyssinia**
SIR SAMSON COURTENEY	**Sir Sidney Barton**
ANGELA LYNE	**Irene Clarice, Lady Dunn**
BASIL SEAL	**Basil Murray**
	Peter Rodd

Brideshead Revisited (1945)

ANTHONY BLANCHE	**Harold Acton**
	Brian Howard
BRIDESHEAD	**Castle Howard, North Riding, Yorkshire**
	Madresfield Court, Malvern, Worcestershire
SEBASTIAN FLYTE	**Alastair Graham**
	Hugh Lygon
LORD MARCHMAIN	**William, 6th Earl Beauchamp**
	Hubert Duggan
REX MOTTRAM	**Brendan Bracken**
MR RYDER	**Arthur Waugh**
MR SAMGRASS	**Maurice Bowra**

Decline and Fall (1928)

LADY CIRCUMFERENCE	**Jessie Graham**
EDGAR GRIMES	**W.R.B. Young**
DAVID LENNOX	**Cecil Beaton**
LLANABBA CASTLE	**Arnold House, Llanddulas, Denbighshire**
MILES MALPRACTICE	**Robert Gathorne-Hardy**

JACK SPIRE	Sir J.C. Squire

A Handful of Dust (1934)

MRS BEAVER	Syrie Maugham
JAMES TODD	Mr Christie[2]

Helena (1950)

SAINT HELENA	Penelope Betjeman

Love Among the Ruins (1953)

PARSNIP	W.H. Auden

The Loved One (1948)

SIR AMBROSE ABERCROMBIE	Sir Aubrey Smith
WHISPERING GLADES	Forest Lawn, Glendale, California

The Ordeal of Gilbert Pinfold (1957)

GILBERT PINFOLD	Evelyn Waugh
ROGER STILLINGFLEET	Christopher Sykes[2]

Put Out More Flags (1942)

ANGELA LYNE	Irene Clarice, Lady Dunn
PARSNIP	W.H. Auden
BASIL SEAL	Basil Murray
	Peter Rodd
AMBROSE SILK	Brian Howard

Scoop (1938)

LORD COPPER	Lord Beaverbrook
PENSION DRESSLER	Hefts, Ethiopia
SIR JOCELYN HITCHCOCK	Sir Percival Phillips
ISHMAELIA	Abyssinia
BASIL SEAL	Basil Murray
	Peter Rodd
ALGERNON STITCH	Alfred Duff Cooper
JULIA STITCH	Lady Diana Cooper

The *Sword of Honour* trilogy: *Men at Arms* (1952), *Officers and Gentlemen* (1955), and *Unconditional Surrender* (1961)

BELLAMY'S	White's Club, London
TOMMY BLACKHOUSE	Sir Robert Laycock
SIR RALPH BROMPTON	Sir Harold Nicolson
GERVASE CROUCHBACK	Henry Scrope
CORPORAL-MAJOR LUDOVIC	Cyril Connolly
BEN RITCHIE-HOOK	General Adrian Carton de Wiart
	Major-General Albert St Clair-Morford
EVERARD SPRUCE	Cyril Connolly
ALGERNON STITCH	Alfred Duff Cooper
JULIA STITCH	Lady Diana Cooper
SURVIVAL	*Horizon*
TRIMMER	Simon Fraser, Lord Lovat
TURTLES CLUB	Boodles Club, London

Vile Bodies (1930)
ANCHORAGE HOUSE
MRS MELROSE APE
LOTTIE CRUMP
AGATHA RUNCIBLE
SHEPHEARD'S HOTEL

Londonderry House, London
Aimée Semple McPherson
Rosa Lewis
Elizabeth Ponsonby
Cavendish Hotel, London

WEBSTER, Jean
Daddy Long-Legs (1912)
JERUSHA ('JUDY') ABBOTT

Adelaide Crapsey

WELLS, H.G.
Ann Veronica (1909)
GODWIN CAPES
ANN VERONICA STANLEY

PETER STANLEY
WILKINS

H.G. Wells
Amber Blanco White
Catherine ('Jane') Wells
Hubert Bland
H.G. Wells

Apropos of Dolores (1938)
DOLORES WILBECK

Odette Keun

The Autocracy of Mr Parham (1930)
MR PARHAM
SIR BUSSY WOODCOCK

H.G. Wells
Lord Beaverbrook

Boon (1915)
REGINALD BLISS
GEORGE BOON
TOMLINSON KEYHOLE
WILKINS

Arnold Bennett
H.G. Wells
Sir William Robertson Nicoll
H.G. Wells

The Bulpington of Blup (1933)
THEODORE BULPINGTON

Ford Madox Ford

The History of Mr Polly (1910)
ALFRED POLLY

Frank Wells
H.G. Wells
Joseph Wells

In the Days of the Comet (1906)
PARLOAD

Sir Richard Gregory

Joan and Peter (1918)
OSWALD SYDENHAM

Sir Harry Johnston

Kipps (1905)
HARRY CHITTERLOW
ARTHUR KIPPS
MASTERMAN
EDWIN SHALFORD

Sidney Bowkett
H.G. Wells
George Gissing
Edwin Hyde

Love and Mr Lewisham (1900)
GEORGE EDGAR LEWISHAM

Sir Richard Gregory
H.G. Wells

Marriage (1912)
'AUNT' PLESSINGTON   **Beatrice Webb**
HUBERT PLESSINGTON   **Sidney Webb**

Mr Britling Sees It Through (1916)
HUGH BRITLING   **H.G. Wells**
MARY BRITLING   **Catherine ('Jane') Wells**
COUNTESS OF FRENSHAM   **Frances, Lady Warwick**
MRS HARROWDEAN   **Countess Russell**
MATCHINGS EASY   **Little Easton, Essex**
RAEBURN   **C.F. Masterman**

The New Machiavelli (1911)
ALTIORA BAILEY   **Beatrice Webb**
OSCAR BAILEY   **Sidney Webb**
BROMSTEAD   **Bromley, Kent**
WILLIE CRAMPTON   **Sir Charles Philips Trevelyan**
MR EVESHAM   **A.J. Balfour**
FRED NEAL   **J.L. Garvin**
THE PENTAGRAM CLUB   **The Coefficients**
MRS REMINGTON   **Sarah Wells**
ARTHUR REMINGTON   **Joseph Wells**
MARGARET REMINGTON   **Catherine ('Jane') Wells**
RICHARD REMINGTON   **H.G. Wells**
WILLERSLEY   **Graham Wallas**

The Passionate Friends (1913)
STELLA SUMMERSBY SATCHEL   **Dorothy Richardson**

The Sea Lady (1902)
MR BUNTING   **Arthur Frederick Popham**
MRS BUNTING   **Florence Popham**
HARRY CHATTERIS   **Henry J.C. ('Harry') Cust**

The Secret Places of the Heart (1922)
V.V. GRAMMONT   **Margaret Sanger**
SIR RICHMOND HARDY   **H.G. Wells**
MARTIN LEEDS   **Rebecca West**

Tono-Bungay (1909)
BLADESOVER   **Uppark, South Harting, Sussex**
CAPTAIN OF THE *MAUD MARY*   **Joseph Conrad**
SIDNEY EWART   **Walter Low**
     R.A.M. ('Bob') Stevenson
THE HON. BEATRICE NORMANBY   **Violet Hunt**
MR PONDEREVO   **Mr Cowap**
MRS PONDEREVO   **Mrs Cowap**
     Sarah Wells
EDWARD PONDEREVO   **George Gissing**
     Whitaker Wright
GEORGE PONDEREVO   **H.G. Wells**
MARION PONDEREVO   **Isabel Wells**

THE SACRED GROVE	The Academy
WIMBLEHURST	Midhurst, Sussex

The Wheels of Chance (1896)

J.E. HOOPDRIVER	H.G. Wells

The Wonderful Visit (1895)

DR CRUMP	William Collins
LADY HAMMERGLOW	Miss Fetherstonhaugh
SIDDERMORTON	South Harting, Sussex

The World of William Clissold (1926)

CLEMENTINA	Odette Keun
WILLIAM CLISSOLD	H.G. Wells
HELEN	Rebecca West

WERTENBAKER, Charles
The Death of Kings (1954)

LOUIS BRANDON	Henry Luce

WEST, Anthony
Heritage (1984)

GRÄFIN ESSLING-STERLINGHOVEN	Odette Keun
NAOMI SAVAGE	Rebecca West
RICHARD SAVAGE	Anthony West
MAX TOWN	H.G. Wells

WEST, Nathanael
A Cool Million (1934)

NATHAN 'SHAGPOKE' WHIPPLE	Calvin Coolidge

The Day of the Locust (1933)

SHRIKE	H.L. Mencken

WHARTON, Edith
'After Holbein', *Certain People* (1930)

EVELINA JASPAR	Caroline Webster Astor

The Age of Innocence (1920)

JULIUS BEAUFORT	August Belmont
	George Alfred Jones
SILLERTON JACKSON	William Travers
	Egerton Winthrop
CATHERINE MANSON MINGOTT	Mary Mason Jones
AUGUSTA WELLAND	Lucretia Jones

'The Eyes', *Tales of Men and Ghosts* (1910)

ANDREW CULWIN	Walter Berry
	Morton Fullerton

'False Dawn', *Old New York* (1924)

LEWIS RAYCIE	George Frederic Jones
	Charles Eliot Norton

The House of Mirth (1905)
LAWRENCE SELDEN

Walter Berry
Eliot Gregory
Egerton Winthrop

'The Letters', *Tales of Men and Ghosts* (1910)
VINCENT DEERING **Morton Fullerton**

'The Pretext' (1908)
GUY DAWLISH **Sir John Pollock**

A Son at the Front (1923)
BOYLSTON **Ronald Simmons**
JOHN CRAMPTON **Royall ('Peter') Tyler**

'The Verdict', *The Hermit and the Wild Woman* (1908)
JACK GISBURN **Jack Curtis**

WHATELY, Elizabeth Jane
Maude; or The Anglican Sister of Mercy (1869)
MISS MELTON **Priscilla Lydia Sellon**
DOCTOR OLDACRE **J.H. Newman**

WHITLOCK, Brand
Big Matt (1928)
WESLEY BLAKE **Warren G. Harding**

WHYTE-MELVILLE, G.J.
Captain Digby Grand: An Autobiography (1851)
DIGBY GRAND **Sir Henry Maxse**

WILDE, Oscar
'The Model Millionaire' (1891)
BARON HAUSBERG **Baron James Mayer de Rothschild**
ALAN TREVOR **Eugène Delacroix**

The Picture of Dorian Gray (1891)
DORIAN GRAY **John Gray**[2]
LORD HENRY WOOTTON **Lord Ronald Leveson-Gower**

WILKINSON, Louis
The Buffoon (1916)
EUNICE DINWIDDIE **Hilda Doolittle**
EDWARD RAYNES **Louis Wilkinson**
RAOUL ROOT **Ezra Pound**
REGGIE TRYERS **Thomas Henry Lyon**
JACK WELSH **John Cowper Powys**

WILLIAMSON, Henry
The Golden Virgin (1957)
TENBY JONES **Augustus John**

The Innocent Moon (1961)
Tenby Jones   **Augustus John**

The Pathway (1928)
Mary Ogilvie   **Ida Laetitia Williamson**

The Power of the Dead (1963)
Edward Cornelian   **Edward Garnett**
Thomas Morland   **John Galsworthy**

WILSON, Angus
Late Call (1964)
Arthur Calvert   **William Johnstone Wilson**

The Old Men at the Zoo (1961)
Matthew Price   **William King**

WODEHOUSE, P.G.
The Gold Bat (1904)
Wrykyn   **Dulwich College, London**

The Head of Kay's (1905) and others
Mr Higgs   **Seymour Hicks**

Mike (1909) and others
Rupert Psmith   **Rupert D'Oyly Carte**

My Man Jeeves (1919) and others
Bertram ('Bertie') Wooster   **John Wodehouse, 3rd Earl of Kimberley**

Something Fresh (1915) and others
Blandings Castle   **Corsham Court, Wiltshire**

WOLFE, Thomas
Look Homeward, Angel (1929)
Altamont   **Asheville, North Carolina**
Helen Gant Barton   **Mabel Wheaton**
Hugh Barton   **Ralph Wheaton**
Edward Pettigrew ('Buck') Benson   **W.S. Bernard**
Dixieland   **Old Kentucky Home, Asheville, North Carolina**

Eliza Gant   **Julia Wolfe**
Eugene Gant   **Thomas Wolfe**
Luke Gant   **Fred Wolfe**
Stephen Gant   **Frank Wolfe**
W.O. Gant   **William Oliver Wolfe**
Pearl Hines   **Pearl Shope**
Max Isaacs   **Max Israel**
Laura James   **Clara Paul**
John Dorsey Leonard   **J.M. Roberts**
Margaret Leonard   **Margaret Roberts**
Pulpit Hill   **Chapel Hill, North Carolina**

'PAP' RHEINHARDT   'Daddy' Hildebrand
BOB STERLING   Edmund Burdick
JUDGE WEBSTER TAYLOE   Webster Sondley
VERGIL WELDON   Horace Williams

Of Time and the River (1935)
ALTAMONT   Asheville, North Carolina
ANN   Helen Harding
HELEN GANT BARTON   Mabel Wheaton
HUGH BARTON   Ralph Wheaton
BLACKSTONE   Greenville, South Carolina
ELINOR   Marjorie Fairbanks
ELIZA GANT   Julia Wolfe
EUGENE GANT   Thomas Wolfe
LUKE GANT   Fred Wolfe
STEPHEN GANT   Frank Wolfe
W.O. GANT   William Oliver Wolfe
PROFESSOR HATCHER   George Pierce Baker
ABE JONES   Abe Smith
JOHN HUGH WILLIAM MACPHERSON   John Francis Amherst Cecil
    MARRIOTT
MURPHY FAMILY   Casey Family
HUNTER PASTON   Vincent Astor
BASCOM PENTLAND   Henry A. Westall
JOEL PIERCE   Olin Dows
SCHOOL FOR UTILITY CULTURES   New York University
FRANCIS STARWICK   Kenneth Raisbeck
ROBERT WEAVER   Henry Stevens

The Web and the Rock (1939)
JERRY ALSOP   John Skally Terry
ROSALIND BAILEY   Elinor Wylie
GEHEIMRAT BECKER   Erich Lexer
RICHARD BRANDELL   Richard Mansfield
STEPHEN HOOK   Thomas Beer
ALMA JACK   Edla Bernstein
ESTHER JACK   Aline Bernstein
FREDERICK JACK   Theodore Bernstein
LIBYA HILL   Asheville, North Carolina
JOE LINDER   Joseph Frankau
HUNTER GRISWOLD MCCOY   Edward Kidder Graham
SEAMUS MALONE   Ernest Boyd
HUGH MACPHERSON MARRIOTT   John Francis Amherst Cecil
AUNT MAW   Julia Wolfe
PINE ROCK COLLEGE   Chapel Hill, North Carolina
DICK PROSSER   Will Harris
    Robert Parker Rumley
JAMES HEYWARD ('JIM') RANDOLPH   Bill Folger
HYMAN RAWNG   Horace Liveright
MR ROSEN   Edwin Goodman
RANDY SHEPPERTON   Ralph Wheaton

STEIN & ROSEN	Bergdorf-Goodman Company, New York
PAUL VAN VLEECK	Carl Van Vechten
RANDOLPH WARE	Edwin Greenlaw
AMELIA WEBBER	Julia Wolfe
GEORGE WEBBER	Thomas Wolfe
JOHN WEBBER	William Oliver Wolfe
FRANK WERNER	Philip Moeller

You Can't Go Home Again (1940)

AMY CARLETON	Emily Vanderbilt
HUNT CONROY	F. Scott Fitzgerald
FOXHALL EDWARDS	Maxwell Perkins
PLATO GRANT	Horace Williams
FRANZ HEILDIG	Heinrich Ledig-Rowohlt
ALMA JACK	Edla Bernstein
LIBYA HILL	Asheville, North Carolina
PIGGY LOGAN	Alexander Calder
LLOYD MCHAIG	Sinclair Lewis
HENRY MALLOWS	George Bellows
LILY MANDELL	Mina Kirstein Curtiss
HUGH MACPHERSON MARRIOTT	John Francis Amherst Cecil
DAISY PURVIS	Daisy Lavis
RANDY SHEPPERTON	Ralph Wheaton
ELSE VON KOHLER	Thea Voelcker
GEORGE WEBBER	Thomas Wolfe

WOOD, Mrs Henry
East Lynne (1861)

LADY ISABEL VANE	Lady Augusta Fane

WOOLF, Virginia
Jacob's Room (1922)

JACOB FLANDERS	Thoby Stephen

Mrs Dalloway (1925)

CLARISSA DALLOWAY	Katharine ('Kitty') Maxse
SALLY SETON (LADY ROSSITER)	Madge Vaughan
LUCREZIA ('REZIA') WARREN SMITH	Lydia Lopokova
PETER WALSH	Sir Harry Stephen
HUGH WHITBREAD	Philip Morrell

Night and Day (1919)

MRS HILBERY	Anne Isabella, Lady Ritchie
KATHERINE HILBERY	Vanessa Bell
TREVOR HILBERY	Sir Richmond Ritchie
	Sir Leslie Stephen
WILLIAM RODNEY	Walter Headlam

Orlando (1928)

ARCHDUCHESS HARRIET AND ARCHDUKE HARRY OF FINSTER-AR-HORN	Henry G.C. Lascelles, 6th Earl of Harewood

NICHOLAS GREENE	**Edmund Gosse**
THE HOUSE	**Knole, Kent**
ORLANDO	**Victoria Sackville-West**
PRINCESS MAROUSHA ('SASHA') ROMANOVICH	**Violet Trefusis**
MARMADUKE BONTHROP SHELMERDINE	**Sir Harold Nicolson**
MR S.W.	**Sydney Waterlow**

To the Lighthouse (1927)

WILLIAM BANKES	**Walter Headlam**
LILY BRISCOE	**Vanessa Bell**
AUGUSTUS CARMICHAEL	**Joseph Wolstenholme**
THE LIGHTHOUSE	**Godrevy Lighthouse, Cornwall**
MR RAMSAY	**Sir Leslie Stephen**
MRS RAMSAY	**Julia Stephen**
JAMES RAMSAY	**Adrian Stephen**
PRUE RAMSAY	**Stella Duckworth**

The Voyage Out (1915)

HELEN AMBROSE	**Vanessa Bell**
RIDLEY AMBROSE	**Sir Leslie Stephen**
CLARISSA DALLOWAY	**Katharine ('Kitty') Maxse**
RICHARD DALLOWAY	**J.W. Hills**
TERENCE HEWET	**Thoby Stephen**
ST JOHN HIRST	**Lytton Strachey**
WILLIAM PEPPER	**Frederick Waymouth Gibbs**
RACHEL VINRACE	**Virginia Woolf**

The Waves (1931)

BERNARD	**Desmond MacCarthy**
NEVILLE	**Lytton Strachey**
PERCIVAL	**Thoby Stephen**

WOOLSON, Constance Fenimore
Anne (1883)

HORTENSE-PAULINE MOREAU	**Madame Chagaray**

'A Florentine Experiment' (1880)

TRAFFORD MORGAN	**Henry James**

Y

YATES, Edmund
Broken to Harness (1864)

KATE MELLON	**Catherine ('Skittles') Walters**

Land at Last (1866)

WILLIAM BOWKER	**William Proctor Bolland**

YEATS, W.B.
John Sherman (1891)

BALLAH	**Sligo, Ireland**
REVD WILLIAM HOWARD	**Lionel Johnson**
MRS SHERMAN	**Susan Yeats**
JOHN SHERMAN	**Henry Middleton**
	W.B. Yeats

YONGE, C.M.
Abbeychurch (1844)

ELIZABETH WOODBOURNE **Charlotte Yonge**

Countess Kate (1862)

COUNTESS KATE **Charlotte Yonge**

The Daisy Chain (1856)

DR MAY	**Dr James Yonge**
ETHEL MAY	**Charlotte Moberly**

The Heir of Redclyffe (1853)

MR SHENE **William Dyce**

YOUNG, Stark
The Torches Flare (1928)

EUGENE OLIVER **William Faulkner**

2

Real Names

A

ABBOTSBURY, Dorset A village near the coast, eight miles north-west of Weymouth.

ABBOTSEA in Thomas Hardy, Wessex novels and tales (1871–95)

Identified on a map prepared by Thomas Hardy which hangs in the Dorset County Museum, Dorchester. The map, however, bears the following inscription in Hardy's hand: 'It is to be understood that this is an imaginative Wessex only and that the places described under the names here given are not portraits of any real places, but visionary places which may approximate to the real places more or less.'

ABBOTT, Evelyn (1843–1901) Educated at Balliol College, Oxford, in 1866 he had a spinal accident which paralysed his lower limbs for life. In 1870–3 he was a master at Clifton, and in 1874–1901 he was a Fellow of and tutor at Balliol.

MR COURTENAY in Mrs Humphry Ward, *Lady Rose's Daughter* (1903)

'Dear Mrs Ward, . . . I cannot help writing to tell you how profoundly I am touched by your description of Evelyn Abbott in "Lady Rose's Daughter"; he was my cousin; the year before he died I had given up my work in order to live with him entirely. On reading tonight your description of "Mr Courtenay", the happiest days of my life rise so vividly before me. I must write and thank you. Thank you most sincerely, Yours truly, Mary Abbott' (from 103 Eaton Square, 23 March 1903, laid in copy of *Lady Rose's Daughter* from the library of Mrs Humphry Ward (in the possession of the compiler)).

ABERCORN, James Hamilton, 1st Duke of (1811–85) In 1832 he married Louisa Jane (**Abercorn**, below) daughter of the 6th Duke of Bedford. They had seven sons and seven daughters; all the daughters married peers: two dukes, one marquess and four earls.

DUKE OF LOTHAIR in Benjamin Disraeli, *Lothair* (1870)

Identified in 'Key to *Lothair*', *Notes and Queries* 183 (12 September 1942): 173.

ABERCORN, Louisa Jane, Duchess of (1812–1905) Daughter of the 6th Duke of Bedford, she married the Duke of **Abercorn**. In 1894 a photograph was taken of the Duchess with her 101 descendants.

DUCHESS OF LOTHAIR in Benjamin Disraeli, *Lothair* (1870)

Identified in 'Key to *Lothair*', *Notes and Queries* 183 (12 September 1942): 173.

ABERNETHY, John Abercorn (1764–1831) Surgeon. He studied at St Bartholomew's Hospital, London, and from 1815 to 1827 was a surgeon there. He was famous as an anatomist and lecturer, and extended the operation for aneurism that was first developed by John Hunter.

DR VON SPITTERGEN in Benjamin Disraeli, *Vivian Grey* (1826–7)

Identified as Ab—n—thy in a key given in a pamphlet published in 1827 by William Marsh. This key is discussed by Lucien Wolf in his notes to *Vivian Grey*, 1904 (centenary edn), Vol. II, p. 364, with the conclusion that Disraeli was not responsible for the key.

ABINGDON, Berkshire

BABINGTON in Dorothy Richardson, *Pilgrimage* (1915–67)

'The name of her birthplace was ... troublesome. She alternated between Babingdon and Babington, finally settling on the latter' (Gloria G. Fromm, 1977, *Dorothy Richardson: a biography*, London, pp. 68–9).

ABYSSINIA Now called Ethiopia.

AZANIA in Evelyn Waugh, *Black Mischief* (1932)

'Evelyn was at some pains ... to disown any intention of caricaturing Ethiopia in his fictitious Empire of Azania ... [but] Ethiopia is the backbone of this fiction, and there are details ... which were manifestly taken from recent Ethiopian history' (Christopher Sykes, 1975, *Evelyn Waugh*, London: Collins, p. 119).

ISHMAELIA in Evelyn Waugh, *Scoop* (1938)

'The scene is Abyssinia again' (Sykes, op. cit., p. 176).

The ACADEMY A monthly periodical founded in 1869 by Charles Edward Appleton, in 1871 it became a fortnightly publication, with early contributors including Matthew **Arnold** and Mark **Pattison**. In 1896 it was taken over by an American patent-medicine tycoon, Morgan Richards, who bought it as a present for his daughter, Pearl Craigie (the novelist 'John Oliver Hobbes'). 'She ... called in Lewis Hind ... and under his guidance the *Academy* [prospered]' (John Gross, 1969, *The Rise and Fall of the Man of Letters*, London, p. 213). In 1922 the *Academy* was absorbed by the *English Review*.

THE SACRED GROVE in H.G. Wells, *Tono-Bungay* (1909)

'There is a satirical echo of the whole episode in *Tono-Bungay*, where Uncle Ponderero acquires control of "a representative organ of British intellectual culture", *The Sacred Grove*' (Gross, op. cit., p. 214).

ACHEW, James Known as James Starr. He lived with Sybil **Da Costa**, and they had a daughter. On 6 November 1929, he murdered Da Costa in a fit of insane jealousy and then attempted suicide; he was tried and condemned to death, his plea of insanity being rejected by Mr Justice Avory. Although his appeal was also rejected, he was finally reprieved. It emerged at his trial that his real name was Achew. William Plomer lodged in Achew's house in Bayswater, London, in 1929.

PAUL FERNANDEZ in William Plomer, *The Case is Altered* (1932)

'Later I wrote a novel on the circumstances of the crime, *The Case is Altered*' (*The Autobiography of William Plomer*, 1975, London: Jonathan Cape, p. 243).

ACTON, Harold (b. 1904) English writer. Born in Florence, he was educated at Eton and at Christ Church, Oxford, and was a friend and contemporary at Oxford of Evelyn **Waugh**, Brian **Howard** and Henry **Green**. He lived for seven years in Peking and afterwards at his villa, La Pietra, outside Florence. He published volumes of verse and was the author of *Memoirs of an Aesthete* (1948) and *The Bourbons of Naples* (1956)

ANTHONY BLANCHE in Evelyn Waugh, *Brideshead Revisited* (1945)

'On the book's appearance Evelyn's friends unanimously identified Blanche with Harold Acton, and since Evelyn gave his character a cosmopolitan background, an Eton education and made him an undergraduate of Christ Church, all of which was literally true of Harold Acton, and as he furthermore put into Blanche's mouth some genuine sayings of Harold Acton, made Blanche the central figure of some authentic Acton incidents, and portrayed him as the ruling aesthete of Oxford in the 1920s the identification was inevitable' (Christopher Sykes, 1975, *Evelyn Waugh*, London: Collins, p. 254). 'There are characters in my novels – "Ambrose Silk", "Anthony Blanch" [sic] – whom people to his annoyance and to mine, have attempted to identify with him. There are a few incidental similarities. . . . But in neither of the characters mentioned did I attempt a portrait of Harold' (Evelyn Waugh, 1964, *A Little Learning . . . an autobiography*, London: Chapman and Hall, p. 196). *See also* **Howard**, Brian.

ACTON HOUSE, Felton, Northumberland

CADOVER in E.M. Forster, *The Longest Journey* (1907)

'[T]he book did not sell, and an uncle [W.H. Forster] . . . bought a number of remainders . . . and sent them to those of my relations whom they were most likely to upset. It was this same uncle . . . whose house up in Northumberland provided the architecture and the atmosphere for Cadover' (Introd. to *The Longest Journey*, 1960, London: Oxford University Press, p. xiv). A photograph of the house is in Wilfred Stone, 1966, *The Cave and the Mountain: a study of E.M. Forster*, London: Oxford University Press, Pl. 23.

ACWORTH, James (1798–1883) Educated at Glasgow University, he received his LLD in 1847. During 1823–35 he was Minister of the Baptist Church at Leeds, and was subsequently President of Baptist College at Horton, Bradford (1835–59), and Rawdon, near Leeds (1859–63). After 1863 he lived in Scarborough.

DR YORKE in Lily Watson, *The Vicar of Langthwaite* (1893)

'In her novel . . . Lily Watson . . . provided lifelike portraits of Acworth . . . [who] appears as Dr Yorke, massive in mind and body' (A.C. Underwood, 1947, *A History of the English Baptists*, London: Baptist Union Publication Department, p. 236 n. 1).

ADAM, William Patrick (1823–81) Educated at Rugby and at Trinity College, he was called to the Bar. During 1853–8 he was Secretary to Lord Elphinstone in India, then from 1859 to 1880 he was an MP, being Liberal Whip between 1874 and 1880. In 1880 he became Governor of Madras.

GEORGE ARTHUR in Thomas Hughes, *Tom Brown's Schooldays* (1857)

'Arthur is supposedly a composite of Theodore Walrond, W.P. Adam, and August Orlebar' (Edward C. Mack and W.H.G. Armytage, 1952, *Thomas Hughes: the life of the author of* Tom Brown's Schooldays, London: Ernest Benn, p. 94). *See also* **Orlebar**, August; **Walrond**, Theodore.

ADAMS, Franklin Pierce (1881–1960) American journalist, known as 'F.P.A.'. During 1922–31 he wrote a column entitled 'The Conning Tower' in the New York *World*. He later worked on the New York *Herald Tribune* and the New York *Post*. He was a member of the group of writers who used to meet in the 1920s at the Algonquin Hotel, New York.

JOEL CRABTREE in Anita Loos, *But Gentlemen Marry Brunettes* (1927)

'Anyone familiar with the group would have had no trouble identifying Miss Loos' Crabtree as FPA' (John Keats, 1971, *You Might as Well Live: the life and times of Dorothy Parker*, London: Secker & Warburg, p. 121; originally published 1970, New York: Simon & Schuster).

ADAMS, Henry (1838–1918) Novelist. Son of Charles Francis Adams and grandson of the sixth president of the United States. He taught at Harvard University, and in 1872 married Marian Hooper (**Adams**, below). He was the author of, among others, *Mont-St-Michel and Chartres* (1904) and *The Education of Henry Adams* (1907).

ALFRED BONNYCASTLE in Henry James, *Pandora* (1884)

'I don't see why I shouldn't do the "self-made girl" . . . [the action] must take place in New York. Perhaps indeed Washington would do. This would give me a chance to do Washington. . . . I might even *do* Henry Adams and his wife' (*The Notebooks of Henry James*, 1947, ed. F.O. Matthiessen and K.B. Murdock, New York, p. 56). 'James sketched the Adams family with his lightest hand' (ibid.).

THORNTON HANCOCK in F. Scott Fitzgerald, *This Side of Paradise* (1920)

'Thornton Hancock is Henry Adams – I didn't do him thoroughly, of course – but I knew him when I was a boy' (to Maxwell Perkins, 26 July 1919, reproduced in *The Letters of F. Scott Fitzgerald*, 1964, ed. Andrew Turnbull, London: Bodley Head, p. 138).

MADELEINE LEE in Henry Adams, *Democracy* (1880)

See under **Adams**, Marian. *See also* **Lawrence**, Mrs Bigelow.

ADAMS, Marian (1843–85) Known as 'Clover'. She was the daughter of Dr R.W. **Hooper** and Ellen Sturgis, and in 1872 married Henry Adams; she committed suicide during a depressive illness after her father's death.

MRS BONNYCASTLE in Henry James, *Pandora* (1884)

See under **Adams**, Henry.

ESTHER DUDLEY in Henry Adams, *Esther* (1884)

'The central figure is once again a woman, the model obviously Marion Adams' (Ernest Samuels, 1958, *Henry Adams: the middle years*, Cambridge, Mass., p. 238).

MADELEINE LEE in Henry Adams, *Democracy* (1880)

'In the person of the heroine, Adams drew not only the portrait of his wife . . . but also more tellingly the portrait of himself' (Ernest Samuels, op. cit., pp. 69–70). *See also* **Adams**, Henry; **Lawrence**, Mrs Bigelow.

ADAMS, Theodore A medical student at the University of Michigan *c.*1916, he later became an obstetrician.

FATHER PFAFF in Sinclair Lewis, *Arrowsmith* (1925)

Identified in Mark Schorer, 1961, *Sinclair Lewis: an American life*, New York: McGraw-Hill, p. 418.

ADELBODEN, Switzerland Situated in the Bernese Oberland. Dorothy Richardson spent a holiday there in January 1908.

OBERLAND in Dorothy Richardson, *Pilgrimage* (1915–67)

'Oberland is . . . Adelboden' (John Rosenberg, 1973, *Dorothy Richardson: the genius they forgot*, London, p. 21).

THE ADELPHI A literary periodical founded in London by J. Middleton **Murry** in 1923 and controlled by him until 1948. Sir Richard **Rees** was the Editor from 1930 until 1936.

ANTICHRIST in George Orwell, *Keep the Aspidistra Flying* (1936)

The identification is based upon obvious parallels.

D'ADELSWÄRD, Comte Jacques *See* **Fersen**, Count.

AFFPUDDLE, Dorset A village three miles east of Puddletown.

EAST EGDON in Thomas Hardy, *The Return of the Native* (1878)

Identified in F.B. Pinion, 1968, *A Hardy Companion*, London: Macmillan.

AGBRIGG, Yorkshire A suburb of Wakefield, where Thomas Gissing's wife and family moved after his death in 1871.

BANBRIGG in George Gissing, *A Life's Morning* (1888)

'The only book in which he describes the landscape of his childhood with any sort of precision is *A Life's Morning*. . . . "Banbrigg" is Agbrigg' (Gillian Tindall, 1974, *The Born Exile: George Gissing*, London, p. 30).

AGNEW, Sir Andrew (1793–1849) Leader of the abortive parliamentary movement in 1823 to 'protect the Lord's Day'.

CHEVALIER ANDRÉ AGNEAU in Lord Brougham, *Albert Lunel* (1844)

Identified in Brougham's hand in the copy of *Albert Lunel* belonging to Michael Sadleir, formerly in the possession of Frederick Locker, and clearly originally Brougham's own copy.

AINSLIE, Juliet (1865–1925) Third daughter of Mrs Molesworth. In 1898 she married Julian Grant-Duff Ainslie.

JULIAN ('HOODIE') CARYLL in Mrs Molesworth, *Hoodie* (1882)

'[She] presented her daughter Juliet as the heroine of *Hoodie* . . . [in which] her sense of artistic achievement blinded to the effect the story might have on the unfortunate Juliet, whose daughter writes: "My poor mother had tantrums, and *Hoodie* was rather written about her, and she was told this and suffered agonies thinking everyone would know, when it was published"' (Roger Lancelyn Green, 1961, *Mrs Molesworth*, London, pp. 43-4).

AINSWORTH, Alfred Richard (1879–1959) He was a contemporary of E.M. Forster at King's College, Cambridge, and a member of the Apostles, a club at Cambridge University. He was on the Board of Education from 1908 to 1940 and was Deputy-Secretary in 1939. He was married to the sister of G.E. Moore, the philosopher.

STEWART ANSELL in E.M. Forster, *The Longest Journey* (1907)

'Ansell . . . is – in externals at least – a portrait of A.R. Ainsworth. . . . (He was never a close friend of Forster's, and I suspect that, when it comes to Ansell's role as Rickie's conscience, there is more of H.O. Meredith in the portrait)' (P.N. Furbank, 1977, *E.M. Forster: a life*, Vol. I: *The Growth of the Novelist (1879–1914)*, London: Secker & Warburg, p. 77). *See also* **Meredith**, H.O.

AIRLIE, Countess of (1829–1921) Daughter of the 2nd Lord Stanley of Alderley, she married the 5th Earl Airlie. See *The Stanleys of Alderley: their letters between the years 1851–65*, 1939, ed. Nancy Mitford, London: Chapman and Hall.

ETHEL NEWCOME in W.M. Thackeray, *The Newcomes* (1854–5)

'The thought that such favourites of his as Blanche Airlie and Sally Baxter, who both served as models for Ethel Newcome, might . . . sacrifice themselves to Mammon by making a marriage of convenience had long moved him to indignant remonstrance' (Gordon Ray, 1958, *Thackeray: the age of wisdom*, p. 242). *See also* **Baxter**, Sally.

The ALBANY, Piccadilly, London A small eating house in Piccadilly in the 1860s and 1870s, frequented by Henry James on his first visit to London.

THE RED LION in Henry James, *A Passionate Pilgrim* (1875)

'It is incorporated into the opening pages of "A Passionate Pilgrim", where it figures as "The Red Lion" (Leon Edel, 1953, *Henry James: the untried years, 1843–1870*, p. 291).

D'ALBERT-DURADE, François (1804–86) A painter in whose house George Eliot lodged in Geneva during the winter of 1849–50. He was 'not more than 4 feet high with a deformed spine – the result of an accident in his boyhood . . . but a finely formed head' (letter to Mr and Mrs Bray, 24 October 1849). Mainly a portrait painter, in 1850 he painted George Eliot, whose *Adam Bede*, *The Mill on the Floss*, *Silas Marner*, *Romola*, and *Scenes of Clerical Life* he translated into

French. He and his wife became George Eliot's close friends and they corresponded with her until the end of her life.

PHILIP WAKEM in George Eliot, *The Mill on the Floss* (1860)

'In M. D'Albert, a very superior man ... she found a highly desirable daily companion. He was an artist by profession, and it is whispered that he suggested some of the traits in the character of ... Philip Wakem' (Mathilde Blind, 1883, *George Eliot*, p. 53). '[A]nother candidate [as the original] has lately come to light, another painter, whom Marian Evans met in 1845 at her half sister's house in Baginton. To Mrs Bray's letter to her sister Sara Hennell we owe the acount of this affair. "She says she was talking to you about a young artist she was going to meet at Baginton. Well, they did meet. . . and she thought him the most interesting young man she had seen and superior to all the rest of mankind; the third morning he made proposals through her brother-in-law Mr Houghton ... in short, he seemed desperately smitten and begged permission to write to her. She granted this and came to us brimful of happiness ... we liked his letters to her very much – simple, earnest, unstudied. She refused anything like an engagement on so short an acquaintance, but would have much pleasure to see him as a friend etc. So he came to see her last Wednesday evening, and ... did not seem to her half so interesting as before, and the next day she made up her mind that she could never love or respect him enough to marry him. ... So she wrote to him to break if off. ...." It is possible that two widely separated sources have combined here. But I believe we are more likely to find the germ of Maggie's love for Philip in the emotional experience of this affair than in her relations with a Swiss dwarf old enough to be her father, whose wife she always affectionately called Maman' (Gordon Haight, 1958, 'George Eliot's originals', in *From Jane Austen to Joseph Conrad: essays collected in memory of James T. Hillhouse*, 1958, ed. R. Rathburn and M. Steinmann, Jun., Minneapolis, Minn.: University of Minnesota Press, pp. 188–9). The name of the second young painter is not known.

ALBION HOUSE, Marlow, Buckinghamshire It was rented by the **Shelleys** in the summer of 1817.

NIGHTMARE ABBEY in Thomas Love Peacock, *Nightmare Abbey* (1818)

'Peacock's picture of the bustling madcap household of ... *Nightmare Abbey* ... is drawn from his impressions of Albion House during this high summer, and for the sake of fiction he turned its gothic battlements into a mystic tower ... and imported not only Byron but also Coleridge into the household' (Richard Holmes, 1974, *Shelley: the pursuit*, London: Weidenfeld & Nicolson, pp. 374–5).

ALCOTT, Abigail May (1800–77) Daughter of Colonel Joseph **May**, in 1830 she married Bronson **Alcott**; Louisa May Alcott was their daughter.

MRS MARCH ('MARMEE') in Louisa M. Alcott, *Little Women* (1868) and sequels

'"Marmee" ... is copied from Mrs Alcott' (Humphrey Carpenter and Mari Prichard (eds), 1984, *The Oxford Companion to Children's Literature*, Oxford: Oxford University Press, s.v. Alcott).

ALCOTT, Anna Bronson (1831–93) Daughter of Bronson and Abigail May **Alcott**.

MEG MARCH in Louisa M. Alcott, *Little Women* (1868) and sequels

'Amy, Jo, Beth, and Meg are portraits of the four Alcott sisters, May, Louisa May, Elizabeth and Anna' (Humphrey Carpenter and Mari Prichard (eds), 1984, *The Oxford Companion to Children's Literature*, Oxford: Oxford University Press, s.v. Alcott).

ALCOTT, Bronson (1799–1888) American educationalist and philosopher. After a struggle to obtain acceptance for his educational ideas, in 1859 he was appointed Superintendent of the Concord schools, finally establishing the Concord School of Philosophy (1879–88), which exercised a profound influence on education in the United States. He was the author of *Observations on the Principles and Methods of Infant Instruction* (1830), amongst others. In 1830 he married Abigail May (**Alcott**, above); their daughters were Anna Bronson **Alcott**, Louisa May **Alcott**, Elizabeth **Alcott** and May **Alcott**.

MR COLCORD in Nathaniel Hawthorne, *Dr Grimshawe's Secret* (1883)

'[On Beacon Street] . . . [Louisa Alcott] might . . . discuss Hawthorne's use of [Bronson Alcott] as a character [Mr Colcord] in *Dr Grimshawe's Secret*' (M.B. Stern, 1952, *L.M. Alcott*, p. 302). The likeness is unmistakable. *See also* **Bradford**, George Partridge.

MR MARCH in Louisa M. Alcott, *Little Women* (1868) and sequels

'[T]he failure of Bronson Alcott to provide for his family was recast . . . into the March father's having lost all his money "in trying to help an unfortunate friend"' (Humphrey Carpenter and Mari Prichard (eds), 1984, *The Oxford Companion to Children's Literature*, Oxford: Oxford University Press, s.v. Alcott).

ALCOTT, Elizabeth (1835–58) Daughter of Bronson and Abigail May **Alcott**.

BETH MARCH in Louisa M. Alcott, *Little Women* (1868) and sequels

See under **Alcott**, Anna Bronson.

ALCOTT, Louisa May (1832–88) American children's writer. She was born in Germantown, Philadelphia, the daughter of Bronson and Abigail May **Alcott**. During the Civil War, she worked as a nurse in a Union hospital and in 1864 she published her first work, *Hospital Sketches*, which was drawn from her experiences of the war. The *Little Women* series of novels was published between 1868 and 1886. She died on the day of her father's funeral.

JO MARCH in Louisa May Alcott, *Little Women* (1868) and sequels

See under **Alcott**, Anna Bronson.

ALCOTT, May (1840–79) Daughter of Bronson and Abigail May **Alcott**.

AMY MARCH in Louisa M. Alcott, *Little Women* (1868) and sequels

See under **Alcott**, Anna Bronson.

ALDERSHOT, Hampshire

QUARTERSHOT in Thomas Hardy, *Jude the Obscure* (1895)

Identified in F.B. Pinion, 1968, *A Hardy Companion*, London: Macmillan.

ALDINGTON, Richard (1892–1962) Poet, novelist and biographer. In 1912, with Hilda Doolittle (H.D.) and Ezra **Pound**, he became one of the original Imagists. He married H.D. in 1913, and in 1916 enlisted in the Royal Sussex Regiment and served in France and Flanders, but separated from H.D. in 1919, having formed an attachment to Dorothy **Yorke**. In 1928 he left England for France, and between 1935 and 1947 he lived mainly in the USA. He formed a liaison with Brigit **Patmore**, but married Netta Patmore, Brigit's daughter-in-law, in 1938 after his divorce from H.D. In 1947 he returned to France. He was the author of *Death of a Hero* (1929), *Portrait of a Genius, but . . . a life of D.H. Lawrence* (1950), *Pinorman, Personal Recollections of Norman Douglas, Orioli and Prentice* (1954) and *Lawrence of Arabia* (1955), all of which provoked controversy.

RAFE ASHTON in H.D. (Hilda Doolittle), *Bid Me To Live* (1960)

Identified by Helen McNeil in *Bid Me to Live*, 1984, pp. viii–ix, and by Perdita Schaffner, ibid., Afterword, p. 187.

ROBERT CUNNINGHAM in D.H. Lawrence, *Aaron's Rod* (1922)

'Aldington is Robert Cunningham' (H.T. Moore, 1980, *The Priest of Love: a life of D.H. Lawrence*, rev. edn, Harmondsworth: Penguin, p. 362; originally published 1955 as *The Intelligent Heart: the story of D.H. Lawrence*, London: Heinemann).

ARNOLD MASTERS in John Cournos, *Miranda Masters* (1926)

'In . . . *Miranda Masters* John Cournos gives us some sense of how deeply committed H.D. was to Richard Aldington in the early years of their marriage' (Janice S. Robinson, 1982, *H.D.: the life and work of an American poet*, Boston, p. 62).

RICHARD NICHOLSON in May Sinclair, *Mary Olivier* (1919)

'A description of him exists in the character of Richard Nicholson' (Barbara Guest, 1985, *Herself Defined: the poet H.D. and her world*, London: Collins, p. 63; originally published 1984, Garden City, NY: Doubleday).

ALDRICH, Thomas Bailey (1836–1907) American novelist. Born in Portsmouth, New Hampshire, where he spent part of his boyhood, he settled in Boston in 1865. Between 1866 and 1874 he was Editor of *Every Saturday*.

TOM BAILEY in T.B. Aldrich, *The Story of a Bad Boy* (1870)

'. . . his semi-autobiographical novel' (James D. Hart (ed.), 1965, *The Oxford Companion to American Literature*, New York: Oxford University Press, p. 18).

ALEXANDER, F. Matthias (1869–1955) Originally a professional reciter in Tasmania and Melbourne, he devised a system for muscular control after developing some difficulty in voice production. In 1904 he travelled to England to publicize his technique, and there built up a substantial connection with the stage and performing musicians.

JOSEPH MILLER in Aldous Huxley, *Eyeless in Gaza* (1936)

'Here also – shown as Dr Miller, the "elderly little man, short and spare", who had "a mouth like an inquisitor's" – is Matthias Alexander' (Ronald W. Clark, 1968, *The Huxleys*, London: Heinemann, p. 237). *See also* **Heard**, Gerald; **Pennell**, Theodore.

ALEXANDRA FEODOROVNA, Empress of Russia (1872–1918) Daughter of Grand Duke Louis of Hesse-Darmstadt and granddaughter of Queen Victoria, in 1894 she married Tsar Nicholas II. She was murdered, together with her husband and children, by the Bolsheviks at Ekaterinburg.

MADAME ZALENSKA ('THE LADY') in Elinor Glyn, *Three Weeks* (1907)

'The rumour went about that it was . . . a true story. . . . It was . . . reported that the Czar had mentioned *Three Weeks* as being a book about his wife . . . . [A] man [Elinor] met the following year in America . . . said that the Dowager Empress of Russia, despairing of an heir, had sent her daughter-in-law off on a yacht with "Paul" [the name of the hero of the novel] nine months before the birth of the Czarevich. . . . The American insisted on the story, asserting that "Paul" was an Englishman and had in fact died in his arms. . . . It was not until 1910, when [Elinor] went to Russia, that she came to realise that she might in . . . *Three Weeks*, have stumbled on something dangerously close to the truth' (Anthony Glyn, 1968, *Elinor Glyn: a biography*, rev. edn, London: Hutchinson, p. 132; originally published 1955, London: Hutchinson).

ALISON, Sir Archibald (1792–1867) Of Possil House near Glasgow. From 1834 he was Sheriff of Lanarkshire. In 1845 he defeated Macaulay by forty-eight votes to be elected Lord Rector of Marischal College Aberdeen, and in 1852 he became Lord Rector of Glasgow University. He was the author of *History of Europe During the French Revolution (1833–42)*, published in ten volumes.

MR WORDY in Benjamin Disraeli, *Coningsby* (1844)

'He is drawn by Disraeli . . . as Mr Wordy' (Frederic Boase, 1892, *Modern English Biography*, Vol. I, col. 47).

ALLAM, Mary Ellen Renshaw ('Polly') She married James Lawrence, D.H. Lawrence's uncle; after his death in a mining accident she married James Allam.

ELIZABETH BATES in D.H. Lawrence, 'Odour of Chrysanthemums' (1914)

'Mrs Holroyd [in *The Widowing of Mrs Holroyd*, a dramatization of 'Odour of Chrysanthemums'] was an aunt of mine – she lived in a tiny cottage just up the line from the railway crossing at Brinsley, near Eastwood' (to Rolf Gardiner, 3 December 1926, reproduced in *The Letters of D.H. Lawrence*, 1932, ed. Aldous Huxley, London: Heinemann, p. 675).

ALLAN, James Gordon (1820–85) Educated at Edinburgh University, he was called to the Bar in 1844, in the chambers of Edwin **James**. After the disbarred James had fled to New York, Allan was reduced to grave poverty; his fellow barristers subscribed a sum that enabled him to emigrate to New Zealand, where he practised at the Bar and became a well-known figure in Wellington. He was said to be a fine French scholar and to have spent some years in France as a young man.

SYDNEY CARTON in Charles Dickens, *A Tale of Two Cities* (1859)

'It was at 2 Dr Johnson's Buildings in the Temple that Stryver, Q.C., and Memory Carton had their working chambers, and in real life their names were Edwin James and Gordon Allan. . . . Soon after [Edwin James left England] Gordon Allan was found at his "high chamber in a well of houses almost starving". The generosity of his brother barristers gave four hundred pounds to equip him with books and clothing, to help him to start a new career in another land' (Sir Edward Clark, 1914, 'Charles Dickens and the law', *Cornhill Magazine* (NS) 36 (May): 649). Information about Allan in Wellington from Charles Wilson, 1914, 'The originals of Sydney Carton and Stryver, Q.C.', *The Dickensian* (November): 301. Dates of birth and death supplied by Jill Moller of the Alexander Turnbull Library, National Library of New Zealand.

ALLBUTT, Sir Thomas Clifford (1836–1925) Physician. Educated at Gonville & Caius College, Cambridge, and at St George's Hospital, London, he became a consulting physician in Leeds in 1861, and in 1864 was a physician at Leeds General Infirmary. Between 1892 and 1925 he was Regius Professor of Physic at Cambridge. In 1868 he met G.H. **Lewes** and became his and George Eliot's friend.

TERTIUS LYDGATE in George Eliot, *Middlemarch* (1871–2)

'There is only the most superficial resemblance between Dr Allbutt and Dr Lydgate. . . . [H.D.] Rolleston (*The Right Honourable Thomas Clifford Allbutt: a memoir*, 1929, London: Macmillan) summarizes the evidence pp. 59–62. Professor A.T. Kitchel, discussing it in . . . *Quarry for Middlemarch* (Berkeley and Los Angeles, 1950, pp. 2–5) concludes that, while more than one physician contributed to the portrait, the "personality and early career of Dr Allbutt seems to me the most probable 'germ' of young Lydgate"' (*The George Eliot Letters*, 1956, ed. Gordon Haight, Vol. IV, London: Oxford University Press, p. 471 n. 7). '[T]here are many sides to Lydgate, and possibly Nankivell, Allbutt and Clarke all contributed towards George Eliot's conception of him' (Gordon S. Haight, 1958, 'George Eliot's originals', in *From Jane Austen to Joseph Conrad: essays collected in memory of James T. Hillhouse*, 1958, ed. R. Rathburn and M. Steinmann, Jun., Minneapolis, Minn.: University of Minnesota Press, p. 190). *See also* **Clarke**, Edward; **Nankivell**, Charles Benjamin.

ALLEN, Charles (b. *c.*1850) Assistant to A.R. **Wallace** on his voyages in the Malay Archipelago, he remained behind when Wallace returned to England. In 1888 he became the owner of the Perseverance Estate, three miles out of Singapore and extending over more than a thousand acres.

STEIN in Joseph Conrad, *Lord Jim* (1900)

'Conrad . . . was not drawing solely upon Wallace for his character of Stein, for Allen . . . also contributed' (Norman Sherry, 1966, *Conrad's Eastern World*,

Cambridge, p. 145). *See also* **Bernstein**, Dr; **Lingard**, Captain William; **Mesman**, Mr; **Wallace**, Alfred Russel.

ALLEN, John[1] (1771–1843) He was a physician in Edinburgh in 1791 and became Resident Physician and Librarian at Holland House from 1802 until his death in 1843. Between 1811 and 1820 he was Warden of Dulwich College, and was Master from 1829 until 1845. He was associated with Lord Francis **Jeffrey** on the *Edinburgh Review* and was the author of works on political and historical subjects.

HOIAONSKIM in Lady Caroline Lamb, *Glenarvon* (1816)

Identified in a key found among the papers of John Whishaw, a member of the Holland House circle, printed in *The 'Pope' of Holland House: selections from the correspondence of John Whishaw and his friends, 1813–1840*, ed. Lady Seymour, 1906, p. 151.

ALLEN, John[2] (1810–86) Youngest son of Revd David Allen, Rural Dean and Prebendary of Brecon, he was educated at Westminster and at Trinity College, Cambridge, where he became a close friend of Thackeray and of the poet Edward Fitzgerald. In 1839 he was Chaplain and Lecturer in Divinity at King's College, London, and was one of three original inspectors of schools. He was Vicar of Prees, Shropshire, in 1846, and Archdeacon of Salop in 1847. 'If you were here and could be intimate with John Allen my how you would respect him – the man is just a perfect Saint not more nor less . . . and yet this world would not be so good a world as it is were all men like him: it would be but a timid ascetic place in wh. many of the fine faculties of the soul would not dare to exercise themselves – no man however can escape from his influence wh. is perfectly magnetic' (to Mrs Carmichael-Smyth, 18 January 1840, reproduced in *The Letters and Private Papers of W.M. Thackeray*, Vol. I: *1817–1840*, 1945, ed. Gordon N. Ray, London: Oxford University Press, p. 413).

WILLIAM DOBBIN in W.M. Thackeray, *Vanity Fair* (1847–8)

'Anyone who knew the subject of this memoir and has studied *Vanity Fair* will recognize his portrait . . . in the simple-minded, chivalrous Major Dobbin' (R.M. Crier, 1889, *John Allen*, p. 29; this volume contains a portrait of Allen by Samuel Laurence painted in 1844). 'The pictures of Dobbin in his later life have certainly a great resemblance to one of my father's oldest friends and companions at college. This was Archdeacon Allen' (Lady Ritchie, biog. introd. to *The Works of W.M. Thackeray*, Vol. I: *Vanity Fair*, 1898, London: Smith, Elder, pp. xxviii, xxx).

ALLEN, John and Charles (*fl.* 1842)

AUGUSTUS RICHMOND in George Meredith, *The Adventures of Harry Richmond* (1871)

'[F]or immediate models [for the character of Richmond] he probably used two brothers, John and Charles Allen, sons of a naval officer, who about 1842 assumed the name of "Stuart" and announced that they were legitimate grandsons of Bonnie Prince Charlie' (A. Lionel Stevenson, 1954, *The Ordeal of George Meredith*, London: Peter Owen, p. 176). *See also* **Meredith**, Augustus Urmiston; **Meredith**, Melchisedek.

ALSOP, Joseph (1910–89) American journalist and newspaper columnist. Educated at Groton, he then went on to Harvard. For some time he and his brother Stewart **Alsop** jointly wrote a column for the New York Herald Tribune syndicate; they also wrote several books together. In 1961 Joseph married Susan Mary Patten (**Alsop**, below).

LARNED AINTREY in Warren Miller, *The Sleep of Reason* (1956)

'Peopling [the] roman à clef . . . are the journalistic Alsop brothers and others equally well-known' (Joseph Blotner, 1966, *The Modern American Political Novel*, Austin, Tex., p. 303).

ALSOP, Stewart (1914–74) American journalist and newspaper columnist. Educated at Groton and at Yale, he wrote a column for the New York Herald Tribune, and several books, with his brother Joseph **Alsop**.

PROCTER AINTREY in Warren Miller, *The Sleep of Reason* (1956)

See under **Alsop**, Joseph.

ALSOP, Susan Mary Née Jay. Following the death in 1960 of her first husband William Patten, who worked for the US State Department and was posted to Paris, she married Joseph **Alsop** in 1961.

MILDRED JUNGFLEISCH in Nancy Mitford, *Don't Tell Alfred* (1960)

'Lady Diana Cooper, thinly disguised in the book as Lady Leone, couldn't bear to leave Paris . . . so she . . . returned to the Embassy where she holed up in an unused suite of rooms entertaining the most fashionable people in Paris day and night. And who is providing the sustenance for these gatherings? Susan Mary Patten, whose name in the book is Mildred Jungfleisch' (Susan Mary Alsop, 1976, *To Marietta from Paris, 1945–1960*, London: Weidenfeld & Nicolson, p. 152; originally published 1975, New York: Doubleday).

ALTGELD, John Peter (1847–1902) Born in Germany and taken to Ohio as a child, he moved to Chicago in 1875. In 1886 he was elected to the Superior Court of Cook County, and in 1892 he became Governor of Illinois. He pardoned three of the anarchists who had been found guilty of instigating the Haymarket Riot of 1886, and protested when Grover Cleveland sent US troops into Chicago during the Pullman strike of 1894. He was defeated in 1896 because of his radical sympathies.

GOVERNOR SWANSON in Theodore Dreiser, *The Titan* (1914)

'. . . Governor Swanson (whose prototype was Altgeld)' (F.O. Matthiessen, 1951, *Theodore Dreiser*, London: Methuen, p. 148).

ALVANLEY, William Arden, Lord (1789–1849) He succeeded as 2nd Baron in 1804, and in 1835 fought a duel with Morgan John O'Connell, son of Daniel. 'His constant spirits and good humour, together with his marvellous wit and drollery, made him the delight and ornament of society. . . . He was . . . of a kind and affectionate disposition . . . but . . . to the last degree reckless and profligate about money' (entry for 23 January 1850, *The Greville Memoirs, 1814–1860*, 1938, ed. Lytton Strachey and Roger Fulford, 8 vols, London: Macmillan). He was a member of the set of dandies that surrounded Beau **Brummell**.

LORD ALBANY in Lady Blessington, *The Repealers* (1833)

The full key to characters in *The Repealers* (seventeen in all) is printed in Michael Sadleir, 1933, *Blessington–D'Orsay*, London: Constable, Appendix IV, p. 376, and also appears in Sadleir's *XIX Century Fiction*, 1951, 2 vols, London: Constable, and Los Angels: California University Press, pp. 40–1.

ALLFAIR in Bulwer Lytton, *Paul Clifford* (1830)

Identified in a key set out by Rosina Bulwer Lytton, in a letter of 26 May 1830, reproduced in Michael Sadleir, 1968, *Bulwer and His Wife*, pp. 227–8.

LORD GASCOIGNE in Lady Charlotte Bury, *The Exclusives* (1830)

Identified in *Key to the Royal Novel 'The Exclusives'*, 1830, Marsh & Miller; reproduced in Michael Sadleir, 1951, *XIX Century Fiction*, 2 vols, London: Constable, and Los Angeles: California University Press, pp. 73–4.

AMELIA, Princess (1783–1810) Youngest daughter of George III, she was delicate in health and died after an illness lasting two years.

THE BARONESS in Benjamin Disraeli, *Vivian Grey* (1826–7)

Identified as Her late R.H. The Princess A——a in a key given in a pamphlet published in 1827 by William Marsh. This key is discussed by Lucien Wolf in his notes to *Vivian Grey*, 1904 (centenary edn), Vol. II, p. 364, with the conclusion that Disraeli was not responsible for the key.

AMERY, Leopold Stennett (1873–1955) Conservative politician. From 1899 to 1909 he was on the staff of *The Times*. He was much influenced by Lord **Milner** and was a passionate imperialist. He entered Parliament in 1911 and was Secretary of State for the Colonies from 1924 to 1929, Secretary of State for Dominion Affairs from 1925 to 1929, and Secretary of State for India from 1940 to 1945.

LEWIS ASTBURY in John Buchan, *A Lodge in the Wilderness* (1906)

Identified in a key dated January 1907 in a copy of *A Lodge in the Wilderness*, formerly the property of Grace Keily.

AMIEL, Henri Frédéric (1821–81) Swiss philosopher. He was the author of *Journal intime de l'année 1866* (published in part in 1883–4).

EDWARD LANGHAM in Mrs Humphry Ward, *Robert Elsmere* (1888)

'Langham owes his being entirely to the fact that in 1885 . . . I had published a translation of Amiel's "Journal Intime". All those who felt with me the spell of that most pathetic . . . of the spiritual autobiographies of our day will remember the . . . passages in which Amiel dwells on . . . the paralysis . . . of will power . . . which wrecked his own career. . . . It was that impotence . . . which . . . I tried to realise . . . in the character of Langham' (Introd. to *Robert Elsmere*, 1911 (Westmorland edn), Vol. I, p. xlii). *See also* **Pattison**, Mark.

ANDERSEN, Hans Christian (1805–75) Danish writer. He was the author of the *Fairy Tales* (1835–72). In 1857 he paid a five-week visit to Charles **Dickens** at Gadshill, his place near Rochester. Wilkie Collins stayed there at the same time.

HERR VON MÜFFE in Wilkie Collins, 'The Bachelor Bedroom' (1859)

'A sketch of the four remarkable bachelors who had occupied the bachelor room in the house of one Sir John Giles. The first three are stock figures. The fourth, Herr von Müffe, is Collins's depiction of Andersen, or rather, Collins's excuse for narrating the most bizarre of the incidents in which Andersen became involved during his stay with Dickens, the narration substantially paralleling the recorded accounts of the visit' (Anne Lohrli, 1966, 'Andersen, Dickens and "Herr von Müffe"', *The Dickensian* 62: 9).

ANDERSON, Colin (1904–80) Shipping magnate. Educated at Eton and Oxford he was Chairman of the Royal Fine Art Commission in 1968 and also a trustee of the National Gallery and the Tate Gallery in London.

E.V.C. in Henry Green, *Blindness* (1926)

'In *Blindness* the scenery for the Noat Art Society (that is Eton Society of Arts) marionette show was painted by E.V.C. In reality it was designed and created by Colin Anderson' (M.-J. Lancaster, 1968, *Brian Howard: portrait of a failure*, London: Anthony Blond, p. 121).

ANDERSON, Irwin (1845–1919) Born in Pennsylvania, he moved to Ohio with his father, a prosperous farmer, *c.*1856. In 1873 he married Emma Smith, a 'hired girl' in a local family, but she died in 1895 and he subsequently (*c.*1903) remarried. From 1874 onwards he moved from place to place in Ohio, gradually becoming less prosperous, and in 1886 he was working in Clyde as a sign painter. He died in Dayton, Ohio. He was Sherwood Anderson's father.

WINDY MCPHERSON in Sherwood Anderson, *Windy McPherson's Son* (1916)

'We know that Windy McPherson is a caricature, little more than recognizable, of Anderson's father, Irwin' (Wright Morris, 1965, Introd. to *Windy McPherson's Son*, Chicago and London: University of Chicago Press, p. xi; originally published 1916, London and New York: John Lane).

ANDERSON, Mary (1859–1940) Actress. Born in California, she made her début in Louisville, Kentucky, in 1875, and made a hugely successful début in New York in 1877. In 1883 she made her English début at the Lyceum Theatre, London, but in 1889 she collapsed on the stage and retired from theatre. In 1890 she married Antonio de Navarro and settled in Broadway, Worcestershire, where she became a noted hostess.

ISABEL BRETHERTON in Mrs Humphry Ward, *Miss Bretherton* (1884)

'The situation handled in the book was . . . suggested by the great success of one of the most charming actresses . . . of our . . . day. Nobody who saw Miss Anderson Galatea or Perdita will . . . forget the impression of radiant beauty . . . that she made upon London during her few short seasons' (Introd. to *Miss Bretherton*, 1911 (Westmorland edn), Vol. VIII, p. 224).

EMMELINE LUCAS ('LUCIA') in E.F. Benson, *Queen Lucia* (1920) and others

'The heroine of E.F. Benson's "Lucia" stories is said to be a thinly veiled portrait of Mary Anderson during her years of retirement' (Robert L. Schuyler (ed.), 1958, *Dictionary of American Biography*, Vol. XXII (Suppl. 2), London: Oxford University Press, p. 13). *See also* **Colefax**, Lady.

ANDERSON, Sir Robert (1841–1918) Born in Ireland of Presbyterian stock, he was educated at Trinity College, Dublin. In 1868 he was Home Office Adviser on political crime, and in 1888–1901 he was Assistant Commissioner and Head of the Central Investigation Department (CID). Deeply religious, he was the author of some twenty works on Christianity and the Higher Criticism. His memoirs appeared in 1907.

THE ASSISTANT COMMISSIONER in Joseph Conrad, *The Secret Agent* (1907)

'Certain characteristics of the Assistant Commissioner, however, apparently derive from . . . Sir Robert Anderson, whose memoirs were one of Conrad's acknowledged sources for the novel' (Norman Sherry, 1971, *Conrad's Western World*, Cambridge, p. 299). 'I came upon . . . the rather summary recollections of an Assistant Commissioner of Police, an obviously able man with a strong religious strain in his character who was appointed . . . at the time of the dynamite outrages in London, away back in the eighties. . . . I believe [the author's] name was Anderson' (*The Secret Agent*, 1923 (Uniform edn), London: T. Werner Laurie, p. xi author's note). *See also* **Vincent**, Sir Howard.

ANDERSON, Sherwood (1876–1941) American novelist. Born in Camden, Ohio, he left school at 14 and worked in various jobs before becoming Manager of a paint factory. He left his job and family to become a writer in Chicago. William Faulkner met Anderson in New Orleans in 1926 and it was on Anderson's recommendation that Boni & Liveright published his first novel *Soldiers' Pay*.

DAWSON FAIRCHILD in William Faulkner, *Mosquitoes* (1927)

'The character Dawson Fairchild . . . is unquestionably modelled on Anderson' (John MacCormick, 1971, *American Literature, 1919–1932: a comparative history*, London: Routledge & Kegan Paul, p. 20).

SAM MCPHERSON in Sherwood Anderson, *Windy McPherson's Son* (1916)

'We know . . . that Sam, the bright, ambitious youngster, is closely modelled on the author' (Wright Morris, 1965, Introd. to *Windy McPherson's Son*, Chicago and London: University of Chicago Press, p. xi; originally published 1916, London and New York: John Lane).

ANDREWS, Miss A teacher from 1824 to 1825 at the **Clergy Daughters' School** attended by the Brontë sisters.

MISS SCATCHERD in Charlotte Brontë, *Jane Eyre* (1847)

'The next extract is from a former . . . pupil, who entered the school just as Charlotte Brontë had quitted it. She writes to Mrs Carus-Wilson: ". . . Miss Andrews was my favourite; *she was firm, but invariably kind.* . . ." Miss Andrews is "Miss Scatcherd". . . . It will be seen that . . . if, as the writer supposes . . . the character of "Miss Scatcherd" is a caricature of Miss Andrews, it is a mere libel' (Revd H. Shepheard, 1857, *A Vindication of Clergy Daughters' School, and of the Rev. W. Carus Wilson, from the Remarks in 'The Life of Charlotte Brontë'*, Kirkby Lonsdale, p. 25).

ANDREWS, Edward (d. 1853) A boy prisoner in the Birmingham borough prison who hanged himself as a result of the treatment to which he was subjected by order of the governor, William **Austin**. The disclosures at the inquest led in 1855 to the setting up of a commission of inquiry into the management of the prison.

EDWARD JOSEPHS in Charles Reade, *It is Never Too Late to Mend* (1856)

'The boy, Andrews . . . is (probably with a reminiscence of Fielding) named Josephs' ('The license of modern novelists', *Edinburgh Review* 106 (July 1857): 137).

ANDREWS, Vernon (d. 1920) A young American resident on Capri from 1909 onwards, in June 1909 he accompanied Norman **Douglas** to Sicily and Calabria to distribute the money Douglas had raised in Capri towards the relief of the appalling distress that followed the Messina earthquake.

NIGEL DAWSON in Compton Mackenzie, *Vestal Fire* (1927)

'A portrait of Vernon Andrews was painted by me in *Vestal Fire*, where he is called Nigel Dawson' (Compton Mackenzie, 1966, *My Life and Times, Octave Five, 1915–1923*, London, p. 142).

ANGELI, Helen Rossetti (1879–1969) Daughter of W.M. Rossetti, and cousin of Ford Madox **Ford**. Together with her brother Arthur **Rossetti** and her sister Olive, she published the *Torch: a revolutionary journal of anarchist communism* in the 1890s from her father's house at 3 St Edmund's Terrace, London. The paper was printed in the basement and sold in Hyde Park and at the main railway stations. At the time, their father was Senior Assistant Secretary to the Inland Revenue.

YOUNG LADY ANARCHIST in Joseph Conrad, 'The Informer', *A Set of Six* (1908)

'The "young Lady Amateur of anarchism" is almost certainly based on [Helen Rossetti]' (Norman Sherry, 1971, *Conrad's Western World*, Cambridge, p. 213).

ANNAN, Dumfriesshire

HINTERSCHLAG in Thomas Carlyle, *Sartor Resartus* (1833–4)

'Hinterschlag (smitebehind) is Annan' (J.A. Froude, 1882, *Thomas Carlyle: a history of the first forty years of his life, 1795–1835*, Vol. I, London: Longmans, Green & Co., p. 15).

ANNAN ACADEMY The school in Dumfriesshire attended by Thomas Carlyle from 1806 to 1809.

HINTERSCHLAG GYMNASIUM in Thomas Carlyle, *Sartor Resartus* (1833–4)

'"Sartor Resartus" is generally mythic, but parts are historical [i.e. autobiographical] and among them the first launch of Teufelsdröckh into the Hinterschlag Gymnasium' (J.A. Froude, 1882, *Thomas Carlyle: a history of the first forty years of his life, 1795–1835*, Vol. I, London: Longmans, Green & Co., p. 15).

ANNESLEY, James (1713–60?) *De jure* Baron Altham (1st creation) and *de jure* Earl of Anglesey (1737). He was the son and heir of the 4th Lord Altham. '. . . being an obstruction to the grant of some leases and . . . was removed to an obscure school, whence his death was announced. On his father's death [1727], his uncle Richard (who had assumed the title of Lord Altham) . . . sold him, as a slave, to an American planter. . . . He escaped however, to Jamaica and thence . . . in Sep. 1740, to England. . . . He began an action of ejectment against his uncle, then . . . Earl of Anglesey . . . the jury . . . returned a verdict [in his favour . . . and he] recovered the estates accordingly. Singularly . . . he appears never to have assumed the family honours either in England or . . . Ireland' (G.E.C. (ed.), 1887, *The Complete Peerage of England, Scotland, Ireland, Great Britain and the United Kingdom*, Vol. I, London: George Bell & Sons, p. 116 n. b). 'James Annesley was a favourite fairytale hero of the 18th and 19th centuries; he is so clearly a figure of romance that his name need scarcely be changed' (ibid.).

MR A. in Tobias Smollett, *The Adventures of Peregrine Pickle* (1751) (Chapter 98)

'Smollett devotes a chapter of *Peregrine Pickle* to the story' (ibid.).

JAMES ANNESLEY in Charles Reade, *The Wandering Heir* (1872)

Reade did not trouble to change his hero's name; the novel was first published in Toronto and New York and by Tauchitz on the European continent, and did not appear in England until 1882.

HENRY BERTRAM in Sir Walter Scott, *Guy Mannering* (1815)

'It is presumed that the points of resemblance between the leading incidents in the life of this unfortunate young nobleman and the adventures of Harry Bertram . . . are so evident as to require neither comment nor enumeration to make them apparent to the most cursory reader of the Novel' (G.I.F. (Gilbert French of Bolton), 1840, 'The foundation of Scott's *Guy Mannering*: the adventures of James Annesley', *Gentleman's Magazine* 14 (July): 38–42). *See also* **Maxwell**, Sir Robert; **Routledge**, Henry.

JULIAN CLOUDESLEY in William Godwin, *Cloudesley* (1830)

'The following tale is built upon a fact that occurred about the middle of the last century. I have changed the personages and endeavoured to clothe the story with the colours of the imagination' (advertisement in *Cloudesley*, 1830, p. iii).

JAMES DE ALTAMONT in Anon., *Memoirs of an Unfortunate Young Nobleman* (1743–7)

The *Memoirs* were published in two volumes in 1743; in 1747 the third volume appeared, containing a transcript of Annesley's action against his uncle. 'It is but just that the reader should be informed, that a novel has been already written on this theme, and printed in the year 1743, under the title of "Memoirs of an Unfortunate Young Nobleman, Returned from a Thirteen Years' Slavery in America"' (ibid.).

D'ANSOUIS, Château, Vaucluse Situated on the southern slope of the Luberon, belonging to the Sabran family.

CHÂTEAU DE BELLANDARGUES in Nancy Mitford, *The Blessing* (1951)

Identification based upon private information.

ANSTRUTHER, Lady

LADY ASSHER in George Eliot, 'Mr Gilfil's Love Story', *Scenes of Clerical Life* (1857–8)

'Some of the old families of Nuneaton still treasure well-worn copies of the *Scenes of Clerical Life*, in which are written lists of characters and their real names. One of these lists, made by a resident of the town when the book first appeared, was given to the writer by his son. It corresponds almost identically with another list furnished ... by a descendant of one of the most prominent characters' (Charles S. Olcott, 1911, *George Eliot: scenes and people in her novels*, London, pp. 14–16; the identifications are reproduced in an extended footnote).

ANSTRUTHER, Miss She married Charles **Parker**.

BEATRICE ASSHER in George Eliot, 'Mr Gilfil's Love Story', *Scenes of Clerical Life* (1857–8)

See under **Anstruther**, Lady.

APPLEBY, Joseph (d. 1890) He was the butler at Moore Hall, and was an ex-jockey.

JOHN RANDAL ('MR LEOPOLD') in George Moore, *Esther Waters* (1894)

'... Joseph Appleby, a taciturn, clandestine little man whom there is no necessity to describe here, for he is described in *Esther Waters* under the name of John Randal' (George Moore, 1914, *'Hail and Farewell!': a trilogy*, London: Heinemann, p. 24).

ARACHNE CLUB, London A women's club in Bloomsbury; Dorothy Richardson became a member in 1906.

BELMONT CLUB in Dorothy Richardson, *Pilgrimage* (1915–67)

'The original of this club ... being Dorothy's Arachne Club' (John Rosenberg, 1973, *Dorothy Richardson*, London, p. 119).

ARBROATH, Tayside, Scotland Situated on the south-east coast of Forfarshire.

FAIRPORT in Sir Walter Scott, *The Antiquary* (1816)

'It is the "Fairport" of *The Antiquary*' (*The Letters of Sir Walter Scott*, 1937, ed. H.J.C. Grierson, Vol. XII, London: Constable, p. 117 n. 1).

ARBURY HALL, Warwickshire Seat of the **Newdigate** family since 1586. George Eliot, whose father Robert **Evans** was agent there from 1806 onwards, was born and grew up on the estate.

CHEVEREL MANOR in George Eliot, 'Mr Gilfil's Love Story', *Scenes of Clerical Life* (1857–8)

'Cheverel Manor is a faithful copy of Arbury Hall' (Gordon S. Haight, 1968, *George Eliot: a biography*, Oxford, pp. 220–1).

ARBURY MILL, Warwickshire The mill at **Arbury Hall**.

DORLCOTE MILL in George Eliot, *The Mill on the Floss* (1860)

'Dorlcote Mill [George Eliot] drew from vivid memory of Arbury Mill, close by her birth-place' (Gordon S. Haight, 1968, *George Eliot: a biography*, Oxford, p. 302).

ARCEDECKNE, Andrew (1822–71) Only son of Andrew Arcedeckne (1780–1849) of Glevering Hall, Suffolk. He was Sheriff of Suffolk in 1856 and for eighteen years was commodore of the London Yacht Club. In 1870 he married the actress Jane Elsworthy. He was a member of the **Garrick Club**, London.

HARRY FOKER in W.M. Thackeray, *The History of Pendennis* (1848–50)

'. . . Andrew Arcedeckne, Esq. (the original of Mr Foker don't say so though)' (to Mrs Baxter, 25 August 1858, reproduced in *The Letters and Private Papers of W.M. Thackeray*, 1946, ed. Gordon N. Ray, Vol. IV, London: Oxford University Press, p. 109). 'I was personally acquainted with Andrew Arcedeckne, the original of Foker, in whom he was reproduced in the most ludicrously life-like manner' (Edmund Yates, 1884, *Edmund Yates: his recollections and experiences*, Vol. I, London: R. Bentley & Son, p. 219). '(Thackeray) had gone so far as to give an exact woodcut portrait of him, to Mr Arcedeckne's intense annoyance' (ibid., Vol. II, p. 16).

ARDEN, William *See* **Alvanley**, Lord.

ARISTARCHI BEY, Grégoire (d. 1901) Turkish minister at Washington from 1873 to 1883, he was an enormous social success. At the time of his death he was associated with the Turkish legation in Brussels.

BARON JACOBI in Henry Adams, *Democracy* (1880)

'In the figure of Baron Jacobi, Adams drew upon . . . Grégoire Aristarchi Bey' (Ernest Samuels, 1958, *Henry Adams: the middle years*, Cambridge, Mass., p. 94).

ARLEN, Michael (1895–1956) Born in Bulgaria, the son of an Armenian merchant who emigrated to Lancashire, he was educated at Malvern College. Originally Dikran Kouyoumdjian, in 1922 he was naturalized as Michael Arlen, under which name he had already published novels and short stories. In 1924 he published *The Green Hat*, which was an extraordinarily successful best-seller. In 1928 he married Atalanta, the daughter of the Count Mercati, and settled in the South of France, but in 1939, on the outbreak of war, he returned to England

and became an active air-raid warden. He was injured in an air raid, and in circumstances that reflected little credit on the English he was obliged to give up active war work and withdrew to New York, where he died.

MICHAELIS in D.H. Lawrence, *Lady Chatterley's Lover* (1928)

'He used to go down to the country to visit Lawrence . . . (Lawrence, in fact, later wrote him into Lady Chatterley as Michaelis)' (Michael J. Arlen, 1971, *Exiles*, London: André Deutsch, p. 68).

ARMOUR, Philip Danforth (1832–1901) An American industrialist who built up the meat-packing firm of Armour & Co. of Chicago.

TIMOTHY ARNEEL in Theodore Dreiser, *The Titan* (1914)

'The incident . . . in which Mr Arneel calls the Chicago investors to a meeting at his home is based on such a meeting held at Philip D. Armour's house' (Richard Lehan, 1974, *Theodore Dreiser: his world and his novels*, Carbondale, Ill.: Arcturis Books, p. 102).

ARMSTRONG, Thomas (1832–1911) Painter. He was Art Director of the South Kensington Museum in London from 1881 to 1898, and was a friend of George du Maurier from their student days in Paris.

WILLIAM BAGOT ('LITTLE BILLEE') in George Du Maurier, *Trilby* (1894)

'Thomas Armstrong, who . . . was to figure in *Trilby* as Little Billee' (Marghanita Laski, 1973, *George Eliot and Her World*, London: Thames & Hudson, p. 99). 'Lamont and I . . . used to threaten du Maurier that we would give him away by writing "la verité vraie" about the events described in his story. . . . Lammont's grievance arose from the ridiculous figure he made with his broken French . . . and mine from being left out . . . altogether' (Thomas Armstrong, 1912, 'Reminiscences of Du Maurier', in *Thomas Armstrong, a Memoir*, ed. L.M. Lamont, p. 112). *See also* **Walker**, Frederick.

von ARNIM, Elizabeth *See* **Russell**, Countess.

ARNOLD, Matthew (1822–88) English poet and critic, eldest son of Dr Thomas Arnold of Rugby. Educated at Winchester, Rugby and Balliol College, Oxford, he was elected a fellow of Oriel College in 1845, and in 1847 became Private Secretary to Lord Landsdowne. From 1857 to 1867 he was Professor of Poetry at Oxford; he also spent thirty-five years as a lay inspector of schools, often travelling on the European continent to investigate the state of education there.

MR LUKE in W.H. Mallock, *The New Republic* (1877)

Identified in W.H. Mallock, 1920, *Memoirs of Life and Literature*, pp. 65–6.

ARNOLD, Thomas (1823–1900) Younger son of Dr Thomas Arnold of Rugby, brother of Matthew **Arnold**, father of Mrs Humphry **Ward**, Julia **Huxley** and W.T. **Arnold**. In 1847 he entered the Roman Catholic Church, and from 1856 to 1862 he was Professor of English Literature at Catholic University, Dublin. He left the Church of Rome in 1865, but rejoined in 1876. From 1882 until 1900 he was Professor of English Language at University College, Dublin.

AUBREY GARDEN in Rose Macaulay, *A Tale Told by an Idiot* (1923)

'These Arnolds are perhaps the family in . . . *Told by an Idiot*' (B.J. Harris, 1953–4, 'Emilia Francis Strong: portraits of a lady', *The Nineteenth Century* 8: 91). In view of the opening paragraph of the novel ('One evening . . . Mrs Gordon . . . said . . . "Well, my dears, I have to tell you something. Poor papa has lost his faith again"'), there seems little doubt of the connection.

ARNOLD, William Thomas (1852–1904) Author and journalist. Son of Thomas **Arnold**, he married Henrietta Wale. He wrote on politics and occasionally drama for the *Manchester Guardian* from 1879 to 1898, but was compelled to retire because of spinal disease. He was a Gladstonian liberal, and helped to fund Manchester School of Art. He moved to London in 1899.

MAURICE GARDEN in Rose Macaulay, *A Tale Told by an Idiot* (1923)

The only points of resemblance between W.T. Arnold and Maurice Garden are physical appearance (Arnold was very dark and just under six feet tall), political conviction and profession. *See also under* **Arnold**, Thomas.

ARNOLD HOUSE, Llanddulas, Denbighshire The preparatory school at which Evelyn Waugh was an assistant master from 23 January 1925 until 1 July 1926. In *A Little Learning* Waugh describes it as situated in Flintshire: the diaries correctly place it in Denbighshire (now Clwyd).

LLANABBA CASTLE in Evelyn Waugh, *Decline and Fall* (1928)

'This second extract from Waugh's diary begins with him going off to one of the schools that later figured in *Decline and Fall*. Readers will recognise some correspondences: the crazy local Welsh . . . Mrs Roberts's public house [which existed as such]' ('Evelyn Waugh's private diaries', *Observer* (1 April 1973): 16).

ST ANTHONY'S in Richard Macnaughtan, *The Preparatory School Murder* (1934)

'Richard (Dick) Young . . . was the model for Captain Grimes in *Decline and Fall*. . . . He had written a detective story . . . under the name Richard Macna [sic] using Arnold House as a background' (*The Letters of Evelyn Waugh*, 1980, ed. Mark Amory, p. 616 n.; footnote to letter to John MacDougall). Young presents a very different (indeed idyllic) picture of Arnold House from that painted by Waugh.

The ART STUDENTS' LEAGUE, 57th Street, New York Art school founded in the 1890s.

SYNTHESIS OF ART STUDIES in W.D. Howells, *The Coast of Bohemia* (1893)

'The Synthesis of Art Studies, the school where Howells placed the so-called action of his novel, was in reality The Art Student's League of New York, in its early stages' (Albert Parry, 1933, *Garrets and Pretenders*, New York, pp. 101–2).

ASHBOURNE, Derbyshire

OAKBOURNE in George Eliot, *Adam Bede* (1859)

'"Oakbourne" is Ashbourne' (Marghanita Laski, 1973, *George Eliot and Her World*, London: Thames & Hudson, p. 65).

ASHBURTON, John Dunning, Lord (1731–83) 1st Baron. He was a barrister of liberal principles who defended the English politician John Wilkes in 1763. At one time he was thought to be 'Junius', the radical pamphleteer.

FORESTER in Maria Edgeworth, 'Forester', *Moral Tales for Young People* (1801)

'Forester was probably based on Thomas Day, although he was widely taken for Lord Ashburton' (Marilyn Butler, 1972, *Maria Edgeworth*, Oxford, p. 164 n. 2). *See also* **Day**, Thomas.

ASHEVILLE, North Carolina The birthplace and boyhood home of Thomas Wolfe.

ALTAMONT in Thomas Wolfe, *Look Homeward, Angel* (1929) and *Of Time and the River* (1935)

'The story begins . . . with the arrival of Gant . . . in Altamont, in the State of Old Catawba, which is Asheville, North Carolina' (Robert Penn Warren, 1953, 'The hamlet of Thomas Wolfe', in *The Enigma of Thomas Wolfe*, ed. Richard Walse, Cambridge, Mass., p. 121).

LIBYA HILL in Thomas Wolfe, *The Web and the Rock* (1939) and *You Can't Go Home Again* (1940)

'The first 70 pages are explicitly the narrative of the early life of Monk Webber in Libya Hill and implicitly a variation of the lives of Eugene Gant in Altamont and Tom Wolfe in Asheville' (F.C. Watkins, 1957, *Thomas Wolfe's Characters: portraits from life*, Norman, Okla., p. 86).

ASHLEY, Don Member of a prominent family in Warsaw, Indiana. He had an affair with Cecilia ('Sylvia') **Dreiser** *c*.1885, but abandoned her when she became pregnant.

LESTER KANE in Theodore Dreiser, *Jennie Gerhardt* (1911)

'This event, in a rough way, supplied the Lester Kane–Jennie Gerhardt plot in Dreiser's second novel' (Richard Lehan, 1974, *Theodore Dreiser: his world and his novels*, Carbondale, Ill.: Arcturis Books, p. 12).

ASHRIDGE PARK, Hertfordshire

MAXWELL COURT in Mrs Humphry Ward, *Marcella* (1894)

'. . . from the forlorn propriety of Mellor . . . to the magnificence of the neighbouring estate (perhaps Tring, the Rothschild property . . . or Ashridge Park adjoining Aldbury)' (Enid Huws Jones, 1973, *Mrs Humphry Ward*, London: Heinemann, p. 108). *See also* **Tring**.

ASHTON, Thomas (d. 1831) Brother of Mrs. T.B. Potter, and thus a member of the ruling 'cottonocracy' of Manchester. 'A great sensation was caused by the murder of Mr Thomas Ashton of Werneth, who was found, January 3, dead by the roadside, having been shot through the breast. The murderers were not detected for three years, when one of them turned king's evidence, and it was then found to be a trade outrage. Three men had been hired to shoot him, and received £10 for doing the deed. The motive was not private vengeance, for Mr Ashton was an amiable young man, but a desire to intimidate the masters generally' (W.E.A. Axon, 1886, *The Annals of Manchester*, p. 181).

HARRY CARSON in Elizabeth Gaskell, *Mary Barton* (1843)

'[Mrs Gaskell] was accused of dramatizing, in Barton's murder of young Carson, the murder of young Thomas Ashton. The Ashton family . . . [declared] that Ashton's sister, Mrs T.B. Potter fainted when she read the incident in the novel because she recognised the victim as her brother . . . in 1852, Mrs Gaskell wrote to Sir John Potter (son of Mrs T.B. Potter) . . . that similar incidents had occurred in Glasgow about the same time' (A.B. Hopkins, 1952, *Elizabeth Gaskell: her life and work*, pp. 347–8 n. (to p. 77)).

HENRY WOLSTENHOLME in Elizabeth Stone, *William Langshawe, the Cotton Lord* (1842)

'[The novel] is a direct precursor of *Mary Barton*, an earlier work also founded on the actual murder of the same manufacturer, and also set in Manchester' (K.J. Fielding, 1972, review of Ivan Melada, 'The captain of industry in English fiction, 1821–1871', *The Nineteenth Century* 26 (4): 483).

ASHWORTH, Edmund Lancashire cotton spinner, member of the Anti-Corn League, and magistrate.

MR MILLBANK in Benjamin Disraeli, *Coningsby* (1844)

'. . . said to be the original of Mr Millbank in *Coningsby*' (Frederic Boase, 1892, *Modern English Biography*, Vol. I, p. 97).

ASQUITH, Lady Cynthia (1887–1960) Daughter of the 11th Earl of Wemyss, in 1910 she married Herbert **Asquith** and in 1918 she became Private Secretary to Sir James Barrie. Her diaries (1915–18) were published after her death.

CONSTANCE CHATTERLEY in D.H. Lawrence, *Lady Chatterley's Lover* (1928)

'[H]e used the Asquiths' marriage as a principal source for the Chatterleys. . . . In both cases they married when the bride was twenty-three the groom twenty-nine; Connie, like Lady Cynthia, is of Scots ancestry, Clifford, like Herbert Asquith, has an older brother who is killed in 1916, is shattered by a war wound, and dabbles in literature' (Paul Delany, 1979, *D.H. Lawrence's Nightmare: the writer and his circle in the years of the Great War*, Hassocks, West Sussex: Harvester Press, pp. 170–1 n.).

CARLOTTA FELL (AFTERWARDS LADY LATHKILL) in D.H. Lawrence, 'Glad Ghosts' (1928)

See under **Asquith**, Herbert. *See also* **Brett**, Dorothy.

LADY HEPBURN in D.H. Lawrence, 'The Thimble' (1917)

'Lawrence's story arrived by the morning post. . . . I *was* amused to see the "word-picture" of me. He has quite gratuitously put in the large feet. I think some of his character hints are damnably good. He has kept fairly close to the model in the circumstances. The heroine is twenty-seven, the husband a sometime barrister who has become a lieutenant in the Artillery' (Lady Cynthia Asquith, 31 October 1915, in *Diaries, 1915–1918*, 1923, p. 95). 'The Ladybird' (1923), in which the characters are called Major Basil and Lady Daphne Apsley, is a reworking of 'The Thimble' (see Warren Roberts, 1963, *A Bibliography of D.H. Lawrence*, p. 61).

ASQUITH, Herbert (1881–1947) Poet and barrister. Second son of Herbert Henry **Asquith** and his first wife, Helen, he married Cynthia (**Asquith**, above) in 1910 and served with the artillery during the First World War. His brother Raymond was killed in action in 1916.

SIR CLIFFORD CHATTERLEY in D.H. Lawrence, *Lady Chatterley's Lover* (1928)

See under **Asquith**, Lady Cynthia. *See also* **Sitwell**, Osbert.

MR HEPBURN in D.H. Lawrence, 'The Thimble' (1917)

See under **Asquith**, Lady Cynthia.

LUKE, LORD LATHKILL in D.H. Lawrence, 'Glad Ghosts' (1928)

'This . . . was written . . . in the winter of 1925–26. The chief characters are Herbert and Lady Cynthia Asquith' (L.C. Powell, 1937, *The Manuscripts of D.H. Lawrence: a descriptive catalogue*, Los Angeles, p. 25).

ASQUITH, Herbert Henry, 1st Earl of Oxford and Asquith (1852–1928) He was prime minister from 1908 to 1916, but was forced out by Lloyd George. He was married twice: to Helen Melland in 1877, and to Margot Tennant (**Asquith**, below) in 1894.

MR CALAMY in Aldous Huxley, *Crome Yellow* (1921)

'Poor Asquith was depicted as a *ci-devant* Prime Minister, an old man, feebly toddling across the lawn after any pretty girl' (*Ottoline at Garsington: memoirs of Lady Ottoline Morrell*, 1974, ed. R. Gathorne-Hardy, London: Faber, p. 215).

VICTOR STUBBS in Hugh Kingsmill, 'Disintegration of a Politician', *The Dawn's Delay* (1924)

'After only a few pages it becomes clear that Stubbs is in fact a very clever and witty portrayal of Asquith, containing a deft parody of his manner of speechmaking' (Michael Holroyd, 1964, *Hugh Kingsmill*, London: Unicorn Press, p. 79).

ASQUITH, Margot, Countess of Oxford and Asquith (1865–1945) Born Emma Alice Margaret Tennant. She was the sister of Laura **Lyttelton**, and the second wife of H.H. **Asquith**, whom she married in 1894. She was a member of the group known in London Society as the **Souls**, which included A.J. **Balfour**, Lord **Curzon**, and Lady Elcho.

ROSE LEYBURN in Mrs Humphry Ward, *Robert Elsmere* (1888)

'People say that in *Robert Elsmere* Rose is intended for you' (Benjamin Jowett to Margot Tennant, 28 November 1888, quoted in Margot Asquith, 1920, *Autobiography*, Vol. I, pp. 120–1). *See also* **Pattison**, Emilia Francis.

DODO (LADY CHESTERFIELD) VANE in E.F. Benson, *Dodo* (1893)

'*Dodo* . . . is a totally misleading and exceedingly malicious study of Margot's character (it is doubtful if [Benson] ever met her)'(Mark Bonham Carter (ed.), 1962, Introd. to Margot Asquith, *Autobiography*, p. xxii). 'Frances Horner who knew both parties put *Dodo* by [Asquith's] bed as a warning, when (recently engaged) he went to stay at Mells (he threw it out of the window into the garden)' (ibid., p. xxiii).

ASSOCIATION FOR THE PROMOTION OF SOCIAL SCIENCE   'People interested in the various voluntary bodies that had been formed with the aim of bettering social conditions felt that some co-ordination was necessary, and at a preliminary meeting in Brougham's house instituted the Association. . . . This distinguished body . . . met for the first time in Birmingham in October, 1857. . . . Brougham was elected perpetual president. Every year until 1866 he went to the annual congress' (Frances Hawes, 1957, *Henry Brougham*, p. 292).

PANTOPRAGMATIC SOCIETY in Thomas Love Peacock, *Gryll Grange* (1860)

'The Pantopragmatic Society is The National [sic] Association for the Promotion of Social Science' (*The Novels of T.L. Peacock*, 1963, ed. David Garnett, London: Rupert Hart-Davis, p. 811 n. 3).

ASTLEY, Warwickshire

KNEBLEY in George Eliot, 'The Sad Fortunes of the Revd Amos Barton', *Scenes of Clerical Life* (1857–8)

See under **Anstruther**, Lady.

ASTOR, Caroline Webster (1831–1908) Daughter of Abraham Schermerhorn, she married William Backhouse Astor in 1853: she was the acknowledged leading lady of New York Society and was known as 'The' Mrs Astor. For the last years of her life she lived in seclusion.

EVELINA JASPAR in Edith Wharton, 'After Holbein', *Certain People* (1930)

'This regal creature [Mrs Astor], leader and part founder of the social elite known as "The 400", was thus . . . a first cousin once removed of Edith Wharton, who would draw a somewhat harrowing picture of her in . . . "After Holbein"' (R.W.B. Lewis, 1975, *Edith Wharton: a biography*, London: Constable, p. 13)

ASTOR, Vincent (1891–1959) In 1912 he left Harvard after seven months to take over the management of the Astor estates when his father lost his life in the *Titanic*, leaving him a fortune of $87 million.

HUNTER PASTON in Thomas Wolfe, *Of Time and the River* (1935)

'On the Fourth of July . . . I went with Olin [Dows] to a neighboring estate of . . . a young man named Vincent Astor, who is one of the richest young men in the world. . . . The young man likes to play with every kind of steam engine (he has a miniature railroad on the place) and to set off fireworks. He set off several thousand dollars worth for our delight – they were the loveliest things I've ever seen' (to Margaret Roberts, 8? July 1927, reproduced in *The Letters of Thomas Wolfe*, 1956, ed. Elizabeth Nowell, New York, p. 124). Compare *Time and the River*, ch. 65.

ATHELHAMPTON HALL, Dorset The house is mainly Tudor; the village of Athelhampton lies between Puddletown and Tolpuddle.

ATHELHALL in Thomas Hardy, Wessex novels and tales (1871–95)

Identified on a map prepared by Thomas Hardy which hangs in the Dorset County Museum, Dorchester. *See under* **Abbotsbury**.

ATKINS, Edwin Martin (1809–59) Educated at Rugby and Magdalen College, Oxford, he became Sheriff of Berkshire in 1844 and a Fellow of the Society of Antiquaries in 1857.

THE SQUIRE in Thomas Hughes, *The Scouring of the White Horse* (1859)

'The original of the Squire depicted by Tom Hughes in *The Scoring of the White Horse*' (Frederic Boase, 1892, *Modern English Biography*, Vol. I, col. 102).

ATKINSON, Edward (1837?–1911) Known as 'Atky', he was a wealthy bachelor whose income derived from the family scent and soap business. He lived on the Fowey estuary in a beautiful house crammed with bibelots and was a close friend of Kenneth Grahame. In 1899 he became Commodore of the Fowey Yacht Club: he drowned in a sailing accident.

RAT in Kenneth Grahame, *The Wind in the Willows* (1908)

'[H]is general habits and appearance derive in large measure from "Atky", whose riverside bachelor home and passion for "messing about in boats" struck an immediately responsive chord in Grahame' (Peter Green, 1959, *Kenneth Grahame, 1859–1932*, p. 280). *See also* **Furnivall**, F.J.; **Henley**, W.E.

AUDEN, Wystan Hugh (1907–73) Anglo-American poet and essayist. Born in York, he was educated at Christ Church, Oxford. After Oxford he lived in Berlin, returning to England in 1929 to work as a tutor and schoolteacher. He continued to visit Germany regularly, staying with his friend Christopher Isherwood, with whom he later collaborated on three plays. He later worked at the GPO film unit, where he befriended Benjamin Britten. In 1935 he married Erika Mann, daughter of Thomas Mann, to provide her with a British passport to escape from Nazi Germany. He emigrated to the United States with Isherwood in 1939 and was appointed Associate Professor of Michigan University, becoming an American citizen in 1946. He was appointed Professor of Poetry at Oxford University in 1956.

PARSNIP in Evelyn Waugh, *Put Out More Flags* (1942) and *Love Among the Ruins* (1953)

'The poet Parsnip (vaguely identifiable as W.H. Auden)' (Christopher Sykes, 1975, *Evelyn Waugh*, London: Collins, p. 355).

NIGEL STRANGEWAYS in Nicholas Blake, *A Question of Proof* (1935) and others

'In his early days his detective Nigel Strangeways exhibited certain traits of behaviour which, I am proud to believe, were taken from me' (W.H. Auden, 1972, 'Salute to an old friend' (on the death of Cecil Day-Lewis [Nicholas Blake]), *Sunday Times* (4 June): 40).

HUGH WESTON in Christopher Isherwood, *Lions and Shadows* (1938)

'He was as a young man, always extremely funny, buffoon-like, self-parodying. The best portraits of him in this manner are Isherwood's Hugh Weston in *Lions and Shadows* and Cecil Day-Lewis's [Nicholas Blake] picture of him as Nigel Strangeways' (Stephen Spender, 1973, 'W.H. Auden (1907–1973)', *New Statesman* (5 October)).

AUSTEN, Charles John (1779–1852) Admiral. He was the youngest of Jane Austen's brothers.

WILLIAM PRICE in Jane Austen, *Mansfield Park* (1814)

'There can be very little doubt that her "own particular little brother", Charles, is in some respects the original of William Price' (J.H. Hubback, 1928, 'Pen portraits in Jane Austen's novels', *Cornhill Magazine* (NS) 65 (July): 30).

AUSTEN, Eliza (1761–1813) Daughter of T.S. Hancock, a surgeon, and his wife, Philadelphia, née Austen, who was an aunt of Jane Austen. She was the god-daughter of Warren Hastings and married her cousin, Jane Austen's brother Henry Austen, who was guillotined as the Comte de Feuillide in 1794.

MARY CRAWFORD in Jane Austen, *Mansfield Park* (1814)

'I have come to the conclusion . . . that the character of Mary Crawford may be founded . . . on that of Jane's cousin and sister-in-law, Eliza' (J.H. Hubback, 1928, 'Pen portraits in Jane Austen's novels', *Cornhill Magazine* (NS) 65 (July): 26).

AUSTEN, Sir Francis (1744–1865) Brother of Jane Austen. He served in the East Indies and in the North Sea and Baltic from 1811 to 1814. He became an admiral in 1848, and Admiral of the Fleet in 1863.

CAPTAIN HARVILLE in Jane Austen, *Persuasion* (1818)

'Sir Francis . . . says "I rather think parts of Captain Harville's character were drawn from myself; at least the description of his domestic habits, tastes and occupations have a considerable resemblance to mine"' (J.H. Hubback, 1928, 'Pen portraits in Jane Austen's novels', *Cornhill Magazine* (NS) 65 (July): 25). J.H. Hubback was Sir Francis Austen's grandson and spent his boyhood in his house.

AUSTIN, William He entered the Navy in 1823, being put on half-pay in 1846. In 1850 he was appointed Governor of Birmingham borough prison, succeeding Alexander **Maconochie**, but was sentenced to three months' imprisonment in

1855 after he was tried at Warwick assizes, charged with acts of cruelty against a young prisoner, Edward **Andrews**, who committed suicide in 1853.

MR HAWES in Charles Reade, *It is Never Too Late to Mend* (1856)

'The governor of the prison, Lieut. *Aus*-tin, is represented by Mr Hawes' ('The license of modern novelists', *Edinburgh Review* (July 1857): 137).

AVORY, Sir Horace (1851–1935) Barrister, and judge from 1910. He married Maria Louisa Castle (**Avory**, below) in 1877: Dorothy Richardson was governess to their children.

FELIX CORRIE in Dorothy Richardson, *Pilgrimage* (1915–67)

'[T]he Avorys of Dorothy's own experience have become the Corries' (John Rosenberg, 1973, *Dorothy Richardson: the genius they forgot*, London, p. 82).

AVORY, Maria Louisa, Lady Daughter of Henry Castle, in 1877 she married Sir Horace **Avory**.

ROLLO CORRIE in Dorothy Richardson, *Pilgrimage* (1915–67)

See under **Avory**, Sir Horace.

AYKEROYD, Tabitha (1770?–1855?) Servant to the Brontës from 1824 onwards. She was already a Methodist of many years standing. In 1840 she retired to her sister's cottage with a broken leg, but she returned to the Parsonage in 1843.

HANNAH in Charlotte Brontë, *Jane Eyre* (1847)

'Hannah has some of the characteristics of ... Tabby' (*Jane Eyre*, 1976, ed. Margaret Smith, p. 475 n. 1 (to p. 336)). Mrs Gaskell, describing her first visit to Haworth, wrote: 'One Tabby, aged upwards of 90 sitting in an armchair by the kitchen fire . . .' (to John Forster?, *c.*September 1853, reproduced in *Letters of Mrs Gaskell*, 1966, ed. J.A.V. Chapple and Arthur Pollard, Manchester, p. 246).

AYLWIN, Robert Henry (1885–1931) A member of the teaching staff at Davidson Road School, Croydon, when D.H. Lawrence taught there from 1908 to 1911. He died in New Zealand.

MR ALLPORT in D.H. Lawrence, *The Trespasser* (1912)

'R.H. Aylwin ... appeared as Allport' (H.T. Moore, 1960, *The Intelligent Heart: the story of D.H. Lawrence*, Harmondsworth: Penguin, p. 151; originally published 1955, London: Heinemann).

AYRE, Miss The eldest of the three sisters at whose school in Alexandra Villas, Finsbury Park, London, Dorothy Richardson taught from 1892 to 1893.

DEBORAH PERNE in Dorothy Richardson, *Pilgrimage* (1915–67)

'The eldest Miss Perne is as charming as her original, Miss Ayre' (John Rosenberg, 1973, *Dorothy Richardson: the genius they forgot*, London, p. 77).

AYRTON, Hertha (1854–1923) Born Phoebe Sarah Marks, she was the daughter of a Jewish Polish refugee who was a small watchmaker in Petworth, Sussex. In 1873, as a student, she came to know Madame Barbara **Bodichon**, through whom she met George Eliot *c.*1875. She was educated at Girton College, Cambridge (the fees being lent her in large part by Madame Bodichon), and was the first woman member of the Institution of Electrical Engineers. She was a militant suffragist, and married W.E. Ayrton (1847–1908), the English engineer and inventor, becoming his second wife.

MIRAH COHEN (NÉE LAPIDOTH) in George Eliot, *Daniel Deronda* (1876)

'The second part of *Daniel Deronda* is out, and Miss Orme says that Mrs Lewes has drawn a young Jewess that is in it from me; but I have read that part, and I must say I cannot see the likeness. One thing she says of her, she did once say of me – that is, that her utterance sounds foreign from its distinctness' (Hertha Marks to Barbara Bodichon, 1 March 1876, quoted in Evelyn Sharp, 1926, *Hertha Ayrton, 1854–1923*, London: E. Arnold, p. 38). 'Madame Bodichon replied: "You can tell Miss Orme that the little Jewess was written before you ever saw Mrs Lewes, and she did not take one hint from you"' (ibid., pp. 38–9). 'There is little doubt that George Eliot used many of Miss Marks's personal characteristics in . . . her portrait of Mira. One of Hertha's . . . friends remembers . . . the . . . cloak that she used to wear. . . . This cloak is mentioned more than once in the novel' (ibid., p. 40). *See also* **Shilton**, Sally.

B

BABBAGE, Violet Mary A member of the staff at Davidson Road School, Croydon, when D.H. Lawrence taught there from 1908 to 1911. In August 1909 she went to Cornwall with Agnes **Mason** and Helen **Corke**; it was while the three women were away that Herbert **Macartney** committed suicide.

OLIVIA in D.H. Lawrence, *The Trespasser* (1912)

'Violet Mary Babbage turned up as Olivia' (H.T. Moore, 1960, *The Intelligent Heart: the story of D.H. Lawrence*, Harmondsworth: Penguin, p. 151; originally published 1955, London: Heinemann).

BACON, Joseph (b. 1870) He was a farmer and blacksmith on Walloon Lake, where his father had farmed since 1878. He sold a piece of land to Dr Clarence **Hemingway** *c.*1895; Ernest Hemingway used to go to Michigan to hunt every autumn until he was 15, staying at the Bacon's farm. Bacon was still alive in 1960 and was full of reminiscences of the Hemingway family.

JOE GARNER in Ernest Hemingway, 'Ten Indians', *Men Without Women* (1927)

'The "Joe Garner" in "Ten Indians" resembles Joe Bacon in real life, and everything in this story points to the fact that Joe Garner is modeled after Joe Bacon' (C.C. Montgomery, 1966, *Hemingway in Michigan*, New York, p. 97).

BADCOCK, John Henry (1864–1953) Born in Barnet, Hertfordshire. His family had connections in Abingdon with friends of Dorothy Richardson's family, and he was a partner in the dental practice at 140 Harley Street, London, to which she became a secretarial assistant in 1896. Dorothy Richardson and Badcock formed a close friendship that lasted to the end of their lives, and *Oberland* was dedicated to him.

MR HANCOCK in Dorothy Richardson, *Pilgrimage* (1915–67)

'Dorothy sometimes even referred to [Badcock] as Hancock in her letters' (John Rosenberg, 1973, *Dorothy Richardson: the genius they forgot*, London, p. 104).

BAGNOLD, Enid (1889–1981) Writer and playwright. She was the daughter of Colonel A.H. Bagnold, and in 1920 she married Sir Roderick Jones, who became Chairman of Reuters. She had an affair with Frank **Harris** that is described in *Enid Bagnold's Autobiography (from 1889)* (1969, London: Heinemann).

BARBARA in Hugh Kingsmill, *The Will to Love* (1919)

'The character of Barbara is roughly based on that of Enid Bagnold, who had worked with Kingsmill [under Frank Harris] on *Hearth and Home*' (Michael Holroyd, 1964, *Hugh Kingsmill*, London: Unicorn Press, p. 68). 'As [the novel] proceeds Barbara steadily grows less like . . . Enid Bagnold and more like Hugh Kingsmill' (ibid.).

BAINBRIDGE, Henry Charles (1874–1954) He shared lodgings with F.W. Rolfe in Broadhurst Gardens, London, in 1899. He wrote the biography of Peter Carl Fabergé and was the London representative of the firm.

BAINBRIGGE in F.W. Rolfe, *Nicholas Crabbe* (1958)

Identified by Cecil Woolf in his introduction to *Nicholas Crabbe*, 1958, pp. 5–7.

BAINES The gardener at **Arbury Hall**.

BATES (THE GARDENER) in George Eliot, 'Mr Gilfil's Love Story', *Scenes of Clerical Life* (1857–8)

See under **Anstruther**, Lady.

BAKER, Mr

MR FITCHETT in George Eliot, 'The Sad Fortunes of the Revd Amos Barton', *Scenes of Clerical Life* (1857–8)

'It is a curious fact that even one of the paupers, Mr Fitchett, found an "original" in real life in an old verger named Baker' (Charles S. Olcott, 1911, *George Eliot: scenes and people in her novels*, London: Cassell, p. 23; originally published 1910, New York: Thomas Y. Crowell).

BAKER, George Pierce (1866–1935) From 1910 to 1924 he was Professor of Dramatic Literature at Harvard University, having established a course, called English 47, there in practical playwriting in 1906. Among the students were Eugene O'Neill, Sydney Howard, George Abbott and, in 1920, Thomas Wolfe. He was Director of the School of Fine Arts at Yale University from 1925 to 1933.

PROFESSOR HATCHER in Thomas Wolfe, *Of Time and the River* (1935)

'[T]he fictional portrait of Baker as Professor Hatcher ... damns him with a more unctuous urbanity than he in fact possessed' (Andrew Turnbull, 1968, *Thomas Wolfe: a biography*, London: Bodley Head, p. 46).

BAKER, Guy (1880–1919) Regular Army Officer. He was educated at Rugby School between 1894 and 1896, and became a close friend of Wyndham Lewis, many of whose drawings he bought and bequeathed to the Victoria and Albert Museum. He died in the influenza epidemic.

GUY BUTCHER in Wyndham Lewis, *Tarr* (1918)

'In *Tarr*, Baker is affectionately portrayed as Guy Butcher' (Jeffrey Meyers, 1980, *The Enemy: a biography of Wyndham Lewis*, London: Routledge & Kegan Paul, p. 75).

BAKER, Keziah Landlady of 7 Endsleigh Street, where Dorothy Richardson lodged in London from 1896 while working as a dental secretary in Harley Street.

MRS BAILEY in Dorothy Richardson, *Pilgrimage* (1915–67)

Identified in John Rosenberg, 1973, *Dorothy Richardson: the genius they forgot*, London, p. 211, index to characters in *Pilgrimage*.

BAKUNIN, Michael (1814–76) Russian anarchist. He was the author of *God and the State* (1882), and was Turgenev's prototype for Rudin.

MICHAELIS in Joseph Conrad, *The Secret Agent* (1907)

'Finally, Michaelis has one aspect which is derived from . . . Bakunin. . . . The most striking thing about Michaelis is his size. . . . He "had come out of . . . prison round like a tub. . . ." He had entered prison "young and slim" and left it at "eighteen stone" fifteen years later. . . . This appears to be inspired by Bakunin. . . . When [he] was first imprisoned, he had been a "handsome young dandy of thirty five" but on his release twelve years later he had "aged and coarsened, almost beyond recognition . . . he had swelled enormously in bulk, and now weighed twenty stone"' (Norman Sherry, 1971, *Conrad's Western World*, Cambridge, pp. 272–3). *See also* **Condon**, Edward O'Meara; **Davitt**, Michael.

KARL YUNDT in Joseph Conrad, *The Secret Agent* (1907)

'Karl Yundt . . . is most certainly derived from Michael Bakunin, though not necessarily by any direct route' (ibid., p. 259). *See also* **Most**, Johann.

BALCH, Elizabeth (1843–90) Second daughter of Lewis Penn Witherspoon Balch, Rector of Emmanuel Church, Newport, Rhode Island, and great-granddaughter of John Jay, the first Chief Justice of the United States. As a minor novelist and essayist, she was the author of, amongst other works, *Glimpses of Old English Homes* (1890).

MAMIE CUTTER in Henry James, 'Mrs Medwin' (1903)

'May 7th 1898 . . . the Miss Balch and Lady G. incident' (*The Notebooks of Henry James*, 1947, ed. F.O. Matthiessen and K.B. Murdock, New York, p. 265). 'Identifying Miss Balch . . . is easier than one might suppose. The person who best corresponds to the former is Elizabeth Balch . . . we have here the likely candidate for provider of the *donnée* . . . [and] almost certainly the elements out of which Mamie Cutter was formed' (Bernard Richards, 1980, 'The sources of Henry James's "Mrs Medwin"', *Note and Queries* 225 (June): 226–7).

BALDWIN, William Wilberforce (1850–1910) An American physician who set up a practice in Florence in the 1880s and became internationally famous as a diagnostician. Among his patients were Princess Mary of Teck (later Queen Mary), Edith **Wharton**, Henry James and Alice **James**, whom he visited during her last illness and diagnosed cancer.

SIR LUKE STRETT in Henry James, *The Wings of the Dove* (1902)

In July 1890 Henry James went on a walking tour in Tuscany with Baldwin and an Italian friend of his called Taccini. 'The suffocating summer heat made [them] give up the trip after four days. But the name Taccini was carried . . . into *The Wings of the Dove* – he is the doctor who takes charge of Milly Theale when Sir Luke Strett is in London, and this suggests that in some of his characteristics Sir Luke himself derives from Dr Baldwin' (*Henry James Letters*, 1981, Vol. III, ed. Leon Edel, London: Macmillan, pp. 299–300 n. 1). *See also* **Clark**, Sir Andrew.

BALFOUR, Arthur James (1848–1930) Later 1st Earl of Balfour. A Conservative politician and philosopher, in 1902–5 he was Prime Minister. He wrote *A Defence of Philosophic Doubt* (1879) and other works, and was a member of the coterie known as the **Souls**.

LORD APPIN in John Buchan, *A Lodge in the Wilderness* (1906)

Identified in a key dated January 1907 in a copy of *A Lodge in the Wilderness*, formerly the property of Grace Keily. *See also* **Rosebery**, 5th Earl of.

LORD EDWARD BURNLEY in Rose Macaulay, *Mystery at Geneva* (1922)

'Rose Macaulay wrote an affectionately disrespectful novel entitled *Mystery at Geneva*. . . . Balfour appears as Lord Burnley, author of *Scepticism as a Basis for Faith*' (Kenneth Rose, 1975, *The Later Cecils*, p. 160 n.).

EDWARD CHURCHILL in Joseph Conrad and Ford Madox Ford, *The Inheritors* (1901)

'Various people are . . . portrayed in the book . . . Balfour (treated very sympathetically as the honourable Churchill) . . .' (Jocelyn Baines, 1960, *Joseph Conrad: a critical biography*, London: Weidenfeld & Nicolson, p. 239).

MR EVESHAM in H.G. Wells, *The New Machiavelli* (1911)

'I had a great admiration for Balfour. In *The New Machiavelli* . . . I have a sort of caricature-portrait of him as Evesham in which I magnify him unduly' (H.G. Wells, 1934, *Experiment in Autobiography: discoveries and conclusions of a very ordinary brain since 1866*, London: Victor Gollancz, Cresset Press, p. 773).

HENRY, LORD THORLEY in E.F. Benson, *Robin Linnet* (1919)

Identification based upon private information.

BALLANTINE, William (1812–87) Serjeant-at-law. In 1834 he was called to the Bar at Inner Temple, London. He conducted the prosecution at the trial of Franz Müller in 1864; appeared for the Tichborne claimant at the first stage of legal proceedings in 1874; and successfully defended the Gaekwar of Baroda on a charge of attempted murder in 1875.

MR CHAFFANBRASS in Anthony Trollope, *Orley Farm* (1861–2)

'. . . was the original of Mr Chaffanbrass' (Frederic Boase, 1908, *Modern English Biography*, Vol. IV (suppl.), col. 252).

BALTIMORE, Maryland

BRIDGEPOINT in Gertrude Stein, 'The Good Anna', *Three Lives* (1909)

'Baltimore has been renamed Bridgepoint' (James R. Mellow, 1974, *The Charmed Circle: Gertrude Stein and company*, London: Phaidon Press, p. 72).

BALY, Charles Francis Peyton, and family London dentist. He was the partner of J.H. **Badcock** in the Harley Street practice that employed Dorothy Richardson as a dental secretary from 1896 onwards.

LEYTON ORLY AND FAMILY in Dorothy Richardson, *Pilgrimage* (1915–67)

'The Leyton Orlys (the Peyton Balys)' (John Rosenberg, 1973, *Dorothy Richardson: the genius they forgot*, London, p. 104).

BANKIPORE, Patna The town in India, north-east of Allahabad, that formed the British Section of Patna during the period of which Forster was writing.

CHANDRAPORE in E.M. Forster, *A Passage to India* (1924)

'Chandrapore was suggested geographically by Bankipore, but its inhabitants are imaginary' (Forster, 1957, *A Passage to India*, London: Everyman, p. xxix n. (to ch. 1); originally published 1924, London: E. Arnold).

BANNING, Margaret Culkin (b. 1891) Novelist. She lived at Duluth, Minnesota, and became a friend of Sinclair Lewis's during the brief period (1944–6) that he had a house there.

DIANTHA MARL in Sinclair Lewis, *Kingsblood Royal* (1947)

'[H]is animus toward Margaret Banning [appeared] in the characterization of the matron Diantha Marl' (Mark Schorer, 1963, *Sinclair Lewis: an American life*, London: Heinemann, p. 760; originally published 1961, New York: McGraw-Hill).

BARABAR CAVES Group of seven caves in the Barabar Hills of Bihar; Forster visited them in 1913 and wrote a description of them to his mother. Much later he told P.N. Furbank 'that the caves were "not all that remarkable" until they got into his book. He improved them' (P.N. Furbank, 1977, *E.M. Forster: a life*, Vol. I: *The Growth of The Novelist (1879–1914)*, London: Secker & Warburg, p. 247 n. 2).

MARABAR CAVES in E.M. Forster, *A Passage to India* (1924)

'The scenery is that of the Barabar Hills, near Gaya, and several local legends appear, including that of the Kawa Dol. . . . The caves on the Barabar are, however, known to be Buddhist, and their entrances are not unornamented' (*A Passage to India*, 1957, London: Everyman, p. xxix n. (to ch. xii); originally published 1924, London: E. Arnold). The caves are illustrated in Wilfred Stone, 1966, *The Cave and the Mountain*, London: Oxford University Press, Pl. 28, 29).

BARBARO, Palazzo, Venice Renaissance palazzo, on the Grand Canal, where Daniel Curtis of Boston and his English wife, Ariana, lived from 1885 onwards; they were close friends of Henry James, who stayed with them for long periods.

LEPORELLI PALAZZO in Henry James, *The Wings of the Dove* (1902)

'The Barbaro, with its Tiepolo ceilings, its marble floors, its portraits of the Doges, was to reappear as Milly Theale's Palazzo Leporelli' (Millicent Bell, 1966, *Edith Wharton and Henry James*, London, p. 41).

BARBER, Cicely Frances (1886?–92) Daughter of Sir Philip **Barber**.

DIANA CRICH in D.H. Lawrence, *Women in Love* (1920)

'[I]n 1892 . . . Cecily [sic] died in her seventh year. She drowned in Moorgreen Reservoir as the girl in *Women in Love* drowned in Willey Water' (H.T. Moore,

1960, *The Intelligent Heart: the story of D.H. Lawrence*, Harmondsworth: Penguin, p. 52; originally published 1955, London: Heinemann).

BARBER, Thomas (1843–93) Of **Lamb Close House**. He was the father of Thomas Philip **Barber**, and an owner and director of **Barber Walker & Co.**

THOMAS CRICH in D.H. Lawrence, *Women in Love* (1920)

'[Thomas Barber] . . . carried on his own father's charitable activity among the colliers' families. . . . [He] knew great personal grief. . . . His second son . . . was accidentally killed, in 1890 by his brother. . . . Finally, in 1892 . . . the little girl of the family . . . drowned' (H.T. Moore, 1974, *The Priest of Love: a life of D.H. Lawrence*, rev. edn, London: Heinemann, pp. 34–5; originally published 1955 as *The Intelligent Heart: the story of D.H. Lawrence*, London: Heinemann).

BARBER, Sir (Thomas) Philip (1876–1961) 1st Baronet. Of **Lamb Close House**. He was Director of **Barber Walker & Co.**, became the High Sheriff of Nottinghamshire in 1907, and gave distinguished service during the First World War. His daughter was Cicely **Barber**.

GERALD CRICH in D.H. Lawrence, *Women in Love* (1920)

'A man whose appearance and circumstances Lawrence several times used . . . in his fiction was . . . Sir Thomas Philip Barber. . . . Lawrence knew T.P. Barber only distantly, yet he drew on him for the . . . physical aspects of several of his major characters' (H.T. Moore, 1974, *The Priest of Love: a life of D.H. Lawrence*, rev. edn, London: Heinemann, p. 33; originally published 1955 as *The Intelligent Heart: the story of D.H. Lawrence*, London: Heinemann). 'When Murry read *Women in Love* for the first time . . . he failed to recognise himself . . . as Gerald Crich (encased in the envelope of Thomas Philip Barber . . .)' (ibid, p. 259). *See also* **Murry**, J.M.; **Neville**, G.H.

BARBER WALKER & CO. Colliery owners at East Wood, Nottinghamshire. The Barbers and the Walkers began to take control of the mines district in the eighteenth century, and in 1838 the firm guaranteed £10,000 towards the construction of the Erewash Railway, later the London Midland and Scottish line.

CARSON WAITE & CO. in D.H. Lawrence, *Sons and Lovers* (1913)

'In [*Sons and Lovers* Lawrence] calls Barber Walker and Co. Carson Waite and Co.' (Ada Lawrence and G. Stuart Gelder, 1931, *Young Lorenzo: early life of D.H. Lawrence*, Florence, p. 275).

TEMPEST WARRALL & CO. in D.H. Lawrence, *The White Peacock* (1911)

'Tempest Warrall & Co. is meant to be Barber Walker & Co.' (ibid., p. 273).

BARING, John *See* **Revelstoke**, Lord.

BARING, Maurice (1874–1945) Poet, novelist and man of letters. Son of the 1st and brother of the 2nd Lord Revelstoke, he was educated at Eton and at Trinity College, Cambridge. In 1898–1904 he was in the Diplomatic Service; in

1904–12 he was a special correspondent in Manchuria, Russia, and the Balkans; and in 1915–19 he served in the Royal Air Force.

CARYL BRAMSLEY ('C') in Maurice Baring, *C* (1924)

His career parallels that of C. very closely, and, as in the novel, Lady **Desborough**, whom he loved, was deeply attached to his brother. *See also* **Revelstoke**, Lord.

HORNE FISHER in G.K. Chesterton, *The Man Who Knew Too Much* (1922)

'I have always fancied that Maurice Baring gave [Chesterton] the idea for . . . *The Man Who Knew Too Much*. First in the diplomatic service, then . . . an airman in the war, a member of the great banking family, related to most of the aristocracy and intimate with most of the rest, he is like the hero of the book in a sort of detachment, a slight irony about the world he has not cared to conquer' (Maisie Ward, 1944, *G.K. Chesterton*, London: Sheed & Ward, p. 375). Known as 'Mugger', he was a Roman Catholic convert and a great figure in Cambridge in the early years of the twentieth century.

MONSIGNOR BURNS in Shane Leslie, *The Cantab* (1926)

Identified (as 'Mugger' Barnes) in a key in the hand of Dr Ivor Ramsay, a Kingsman of the year 1920, and later Dean, laid in a copy of *The Cantab*.

BARNES, John and Richard The relationship between these two is unknown, but they were attorneys who practised together, with John being first recorded in practice in Barnard Castle in 1822 and Richard (1807–63) joining him in 1829. John had ceased to practise by 1832, and Richard continued on his own until 1847. Richard's London agents were Smithson, Dunn and Milton, the firm that acted for Dickens from 1837; the letter that Dickens carried with him on his Yorkshire journey was from Charles **Smithson**.

JOHN BROWDIE in Charles Dickens, *Nicholas Nickleby* (1838–9)

'Identified by E.T. Jacques, in "The Original of John Browdie" (1915, *The Dickensian* 11: 296–9), as Richard Barnes. . . . This identification, although generally accepted, seems doubtful. . . . John Barnes . . . seems more likely to have been the "old Yorkshire attorney" referred to by [Dickens]' (*Letters of Charles Dickens*, 1965, ed. Madeline House and Graham Storey, Oxford: Oxford University Press, p. 482 n. 5). 'I went down in an assumed name, taking a plausible letter to an old Yorkshire attorney from another attorney in town, telling him how a friend had been left a widow, and wanted to place her boys at a Yorkshire school. . . . The man of business gave an introduction to one or two schools, but at night he came down to the Inn where I was stopping, and after much hesitation and confusion – he was a large-headed flat-nosed red-faced old fellow – said . . . that the matter had been upon his mind all day – that they were sad places for mothers to send their orphan boys too [sic] – that he hoped I would not give up him as my adviser – but that she had better do anything with them – let them hold horses, run errands . . . rather than trust them there' (to Mrs S.C. Hall, 29 December 1838, reproduced in ibid., pp. 482–3). *See also* **Todd**, Thomas.

BARNEY, Natalie Clifford (1877–1972) She was born in Dayton, Ohio, and educated (in part) at Les Ruches, Mademoiselle **Souvestre**'s school in the forest of Fontainebleau (Mademoiselle Souvestre had left her school by the time Barney attended it). She established a salon in Paris at 20 rue Jacob and became a close friend of Rémy de Gourmont, who nicknamed her 'Amazone'. She wrote poems and novels in French and English and in 1915 she met Romaine **Brooks**, who was her lover until 1968.

EVANGELINE MUSSET in Djuna Barnes, *The Ladies Almanack* (1928)

Identified in Meryle Secrest, 1976, *Between Me and Life: a biography of Romaine Brooks*, London: MacDonald & Jane, p. 335; originally published 1974, Garden City, NY: Doubleday.

VALÉRIE SEYMOUR in Radclyffe Hall, *The Well of Loneliness* (1928)

'. . . Natalie Barney (who lives in *The Well of Loneliness* as Valérie Seymour)' (Una, Lady Troubridge, 1961, *The Life and Death of Radclyffe Hall*, London, p. 83).

BARNSTAPLE, Devon

DOWNSTABLE in Thomas Hardy, 'The Honourable Laura' (1891)

Identified in F.B. Pinion, 1968, *A Hardy Companion*, London: Macmillan.

BARRON, Joseph (1849–84)

JAMES WAIT (THE 'NIGGER') in Joseph Conrad, *The Nigger of the 'Narcissus'* (1897)

'The "Agreement and Account of Crew" of the *Narcissus* has survived and holds some clues. Below the name of Conrad Korzeniowski . . . there is that of Joseph Baron, A.B., aged 35 . . . being illiterate, he signed . . . with a cross. . . . Barron died at sea . . . and as he is the only member of the crew to be listed as having died during the voyage it is safe to assume that he was the "nigger"' (Jocelyn Baines, 1967, *Joseph Conrad: a critical biography*, rev. edn, London: Weidenfeld & Nicolson, p. 76; originally published 1960). It is not certain that Barron was a Negro. *See also* **White**, George.

BARROW, Sir John (1764–1848) 1st Baronet. He started life as a timekeeper at a Liverpool iron foundry, and later became a partner there. In 1796 he accompanied Lord Macartney to the Cape of Good Hope, and remained there until 1802. He was appointed Second Secretary to the Admiralty in 1804, and retained that position until 1845. He was a founder of the Royal Geographical Society in 1830 and wrote accounts of his travels.

MR KILLTHEDEAD in Thomas Love Peacock, *Melincourt* (1817)

George Saintsbury identified Killthedead as Barrow, apparently on the basis of his position at the Admiralty, but Peacock in fact had in mind J.W. Croker, who was Secretary of the Admiralty in 1810. *See also* **Croker**, John Wilson.

BARRY, Iris (1895–1969) Film historian and writer. Born in Birmingham as Iris Crump, from 1918 to 1921 she lived with Wyndham Lewis and had two children with him. She became Film Critic for the *Spectator* in 1923, founded the London Film Society in 1925, and was Film Critic for the *Daily Mail* from 1925 to 1930, whereupon she emigrated to the USA. In 1932 she became a librarian at the Museum of Modern Art, and from 1935 to 1950 she was Director of its film library, which she founded. She married Alan Porter in 1923, but they separated in 1930. She then married John Abbott, Vice-President of the Museum of Modern Art, in 1934, but by the late 1930s they were divorced. Finally, in 1947, she met Pierre Kerroux, who was at that time making a living as a smuggler, at the Cannes Film Festival: they lived together in the south of France until her death.

PRISM DIRKES in Wyndham Lewis, *Tarr* (1918)

'In the final sentences, added at the last moment to *Tarr*, Lewis alludes . . . to Iris . . . "the painted, fine and enquiring face of Prism Dirkes"' (Jeffrey Meyers, 1980, *The Enemy: a biography of Wyndham Lewis*, London: Routledge & Kegan Paul, pp. 90–1).

BARTET, Jeanne Julia (1854–1941) Stage name of J.J. Regnault, the French actress.

MADEMOISELLE VOISIN in Henry James, *The Tragic Muse* (1888–9)

'Feb. 2nd, 1889 . . . I must make a little masterpiece . . . of Nick's visit to Mr Carteret. How much I must put into this! The same of the next chapter, Sheringham's visit to the Comédie Française with Miriam – my impression of Bartet, in her *loge*, the other day in Paris' (*The Notebooks of Henry James*, 1947, ed. F.O. Matthiessen and K.B. Murdock, New York, p. 92). 'Mlle Voisin is, no doubt, drawn from Bartet' (ibid., p. 93).

BARTLETT, Paul (1865–1925) American sculptor. He was born in New Haven, Connecticut, and his father was a sculptor and art critic. He studied in Boston and in Paris, where he exhibited a bust of his grandmother in the Salon at the age of 15. Although he executed a number of commissions in the United States, he remained in Paris until his death.

CLAYSON in W. Somerset Maugham, *The Magician* (1908)

'[I]n [*The Magician*] . . . Bartlett became "Clayson"' (R.L. Calder, 1972, *W. Somerset Maugham and the Quest for Freedom*, London: Heinemann, p. 131).

BARTON, Sir Sidney (1876–1946) Educated at St Paul's School, in 1895 he was in the Consular Service in Peking and in 1911 he was Chinese Secretary at Peking. He was a good Chinese scholar, and collaborated with Sir Edmund Backhouse in a revision of Hillier's *Dictionary of Colloquial Chinese* (1918). From 1922 to 1929 he was Consul-General at Shanghai, and from 1929 until 1936 he was Minister at Addis Ababa.

SIR SAMSON COURTENEY in Evelyn Waugh, *Black Mischief* (1932)

'Barton had the reputation of being a blunt, bold man. . . . After thirty-five years in China, he would end his career as minister in Addis Ababa, and would have the misfortune to be there when Evelyn Waugh visited Abyssinia in 1930: he is thus inevitably identified with that great comic figure, "the Envoy Extraordinary"' (Hugh Trevor-Roper, 1976, *A Hidden Life: the enigma of Sir Edmund Backhouse*, London: Macmillan, p. 128). 'It is said that the picture of the ludicrous British Minister in Azania was contrived in a revengeful spirit following a social snub from the British Legation in Addis Ababa. I find no confirmation of this and Evelyn's diary of 1930 suggests friendly relations with the legation' (Christopher Sykes, 1975, *Evelyn Waugh*, London: Collins, p. 120).

BARTTELOT, Major Edmund Musgrave (1859–87) An officer in the British Army, he served under Wolseley in Egypt in 1882 and in 1887 led the rear guard of the expedition mounted by **Stanley**, the explorer, to rescue Emin Pasha, the missing British administrator. In May 1887 he reached Yambuga on the Aruwimi River, near Stanley Falls, and remained there until his murder in July 1888. During this time he appears to have been guilty of appalling atrocities against the indigenous people.

MR KURTZ in Joseph Conrad, *Heart of Darkness* (1902)

'On the Upper Congo [in 1890] Conrad was in the setting so recently connected with Barttelot . . . of this clever, promising, highly connected young Englishman . . . who so unaccountably "went wrong" in the Congo no satisfying explanation was ever given. The enigma of Barttelot was eventually dropped but, eight years after leaving the Congo, Conrad developed from it the enigma of Kurtz' (Jerry Allen, 1967, *The Sea Years of Joseph Conrad*, London: Methuen, p. 275). *See also* **Hodister**, A.E.C.; **Klein**, G.A.; **Stanley**, H.M.

BASEVI, Nathaniel (1792–1869) Conveyancer. He was the first Jewish barrister to practise in the English courts, and was the first cousin of Benjamin Disraeli, who began life reading law in his chambers at Lincoln's Inn, London.

HARGRAVE GREY in Benjamin Disraeli, *Vivian Grey* (1826–7)

'Hargrave Grey [was] his cousin Nathaniel Basevi' (Benjamin Disraeli, 1904, *Vivian Grey*, Intro. by Lucien Wolf, London: Alexander Moring, p. xxxvi; originally published 1826, London: Henry Colburn).

BASHKIRTSEFF, Marie (1860–84) Born of noble family near Poltava, south Russia, she left Russia with her mother in 1867 for a life divided between France and German spas. She was highly educated and studied painting in Paris, exhibiting at the Salon and corresponding with Maupassant. From girlhood, she kept a *Journal*. She died of tuberculosis.

ELISE DELAUNAY in Mrs Humphry Ward, *The History of David Grieve* (1891)

'Those who know the "Journal of Marie Bashkirtseff" will recognise some of her traits in Elise Delaunay' (Introd. to *The History of David Grieve*, 1911 (Westmorland edn), Vol. I, p. xxxv).

BASINGSTOKE, Hampshire

STOKE-BAREHILLS in Thomas Hardy, *Jude the Obscure* (1895)

Identified in Denys Kay-Robinson, 1972, *Hardy's Wessex Reappraised*, Newton Abbot, and in F.B. Pinion, 1968, *A Hardy Companion*, London: Macmillan.

BATCHELOR, Frances Kate (1867–1941) The eldest sister of Dorothy Richardson, in 1895 she married John Arthur **Batchelor**.

SARAH HENDERSON in Dorothy Richardson, *Pilgrimage* (1915–67)

'Throughout the original manuscript as well as its various revisions, she called Kate by her actual first name (Frances), which Kate never used. But the name did not satisfy her, and at the last moment she must have changed it to Sarah, which occurs in the printed text, but nowhere in the manuscript' (Gloria E. Fromm, 1977, *Dorothy Richardson: a biography*, London, p. 68).

BATCHELOR, John Arthur (1856?–1938) When Charles **Richardson** went bankrupt, in 1895, John Batchelor gave his house in Chiswick to his future parents-in-law. That same year, he married Kate Richardson (**Batchelor**, above), the eldest sister of Dorothy Richardson, and from 1904 onwards provided a home to his father-in-law. He was an amateur church organist and was passionately musical.

BENNETT BRODIE in Dorothy Richardson, *Pilgrimage* (1915–67)

'After [Mr Henderson's] financial crash, [Miriam's parents lived] . . . in the Gunnersbury villa lent them by Sarah's husband (just as . . . Arthur Batchelor had given up his home to the Richardsons)' (John Rosenberg, 1973, *Dorothy Richardson*, London, p. 76).

BATH, John Alexander Thynne, 4th Marquis of (1831–96) He was Ambassador Extraordinary at Lisbon in 1858 and at Vienna in 1867.

LORD CARISBROOKE in Benjamin Disraeli, *Lothair* (1870)

Identified in 'Key to *Lothair*', *Notes and Queries* 183 (12 September 1942): 173.

MARQUIS OF FARINTOSH in W.M. Thackeray, *The Newcomes* (1854–5)

'I was . . . walking up . . . the Champs Elysées when I met Mr Thackeray . . . he recognized a young gentleman on the other side of the street. . . . The stranger . . . crossed over to meet him . . . when they parted . . . Thackeray . . . said to me . . . "that is the Marquis of Farintosh." "And *who* is the Marquis of Farintosh?" I pursued. "Why, the Marquis of Bath, of course", he replied' (Maunsell B. Field, 1874, *Memories of Many Men and Some Women: being personal recollections during the last thirty years*, London, pp. 132–3).

BATTERSEA, Cyril Flower, 1st Baron (1843–1907) Son of Philip William Flower, he was educated at Harrow and at Trinity College, Cambridge. Of advanced Liberal opinions, he sat as a Liberal MP in 1880–92; in 1892 he was raised to the peerage on **Gladstone**'s recommendation. In 1877 he married Constance, daughter and co-heiress with her sister of Sir Anthony de Rothschild, Lionel de **Rothschild**'s brother; in her reminiscences Battersea appears to have grown into a man of great charm, distinguished for taste, hospitality and extravagance.

ERIC WILLIAMS in F.W. Farrar, *Eric; or Little by Little* (1858)

'[A]t Harrow . . . [Cyril] had been specially drawn towards his master, Dr Farrar, later Dean of Canterbury, who fully reciprocated the boy's affectionate devotion, often corresponding with him in the holidays, and even introducing him as the hero in . . . *Eric, or Little by Little'* (Lady Battersea, 1922, *Reminiscences*, p. 167).

BAUDELAIRE, Charles (1821–67) French Symbolist poet. After an unhappy childhood, he travelled to India and stopped at Mauritius, where he met Jeanne Duval who became his mistress and inspiration. He returned to Paris in 1843 and was friendly with Delacroix, Manet and Daumier. He sided with the revolutionaries in 1848, although he was Catholic and aristocratic. An essential feature of his work was his preoccupation with Satanism and the macabre. Eventually turning to drink and opium, he became paralysed and died in poverty.

SPANDREL in Aldous Huxley, *Point Counter Point* (1928)

'Spandrell is said to be modelled on Baudelaire, and if we turn to Huxley's essay on Baudelaire, written about the same time as the novel, we find phrases which describe Spandrell' (Laurence Brander, 1969, *Aldous Huxley: a critical study*, p. 39). In a letter to Robert Nichols, 18 January 1927, Huxley wrote that he had been reading François Porché's recently published *Vie de Baudelaire* and comments: 'What a hellish life – inwardly predestined to hellishness by the man's own character' (reproduced in *Letters of Aldous Huxley*, 1969, ed. Grover Smith, p. 282).

BAXTER, Charles (1848–1919) Writer to the *Signet*, of Edinburgh. He and R.L. Stevenson met and became lifelong friends while Stevenson was still a student at Edinburgh University.

MICHAEL FINSBURY in R.L. Stevenson and Lloyd Osbourne, *The Wrong Box* (1889)

'[H]e was . . . the original of Michael Finsbury' (*RLS: Stevenson's letters to Charles Baxter*, 1956, ed. Delancey Ferguson and Marshall Waingrow, p. ix). 'I am extremely glad you liked *The Wrong Box*. I could not but feel a little alarmed when I thought of what liberties the authors had taken' (Fanny Stevenson to Charles Baxter, 3 February 1890, reproduced in ibid., p. 261).

BAXTER, Sarah ('Sally') (1833–61) Daughter of George Baxter, a warehouse owner of New York. Thackeray became a close family friend while on a lecture tour of the United States in 1852. In 1855 'Sally' Baxter married Frank Hampton, who was mortally wounded at Gettysburg in 1863. She died of tuberculosis.

ETHEL NEWCOME in W.M. Thackeray, *The Newcomes* (1854–5)

'In his picture of Ethel Newcome, as she holds a little court about her at one of the great London balls, Thackeray reproduces some impressions made by [my sister]' (Lucy Baxter, 1904, Introd. to *Thackeray's Letters to an American Family*, London, p. 6). *See also* **Airlie**, Countess of.

BAY ROBERTS, Newfoundland Robert Lowell was the representative of the Society for the Propagation of the Gospel at Bay Roberts from 1843 to 1847.

PETERPORT in R.T.S. Lowell, *The Story of the New Priest in Conception Bay* (1858)

'Bay Roberts was to become . . . "Peterport" in his novel' (H. Blodgett, 1943, 'Robert Traill Spence Lowell', *New England Quarterly* 16 (December): 578).

BEACROFT, Thomas (1871–1925) He was the headmaster at the Pupil–Teacher Centre, Ilkeston, Derby, in 1903 when D.H. Lawrence and a group of friends were attending there. He became Organising Inspector of Elementary Education in Ilkeston.

MR HARBY in D.H. Lawrence, *The Rainbow* (1915)

'Lawrence caricatured [Beacroft] . . . as Mr Harby, bully and tyrant' (H.T. Moore, 1960, *The Intelligent Heart: the story of D.H. Lawrence*, Harmondsworth: Penguin, p. 79; originally published 1955, London: Heinemann).

BEADNELL, Maria (1810–86) Daughter of George Beadnell, a clerk in the bank of Smith, Payne and Smith in Lombard Street, London. Dickens seems to have met her in May 1830, and for the next four years he was passionately in love with her. Her parents apparently learned of John Dickens's financial difficulties and Maria was packed off to a finishing school in Paris; when she returned her feelings had cooled. In February 1855, she (now Mrs Winter) wrote to him, recalling their old friendship. Enraptured, Dickens arranged a meeting, but when he called with Mrs Dickens on 25 February, Mrs Winter was no longer the fascinating sylph of 1834.

FLORA FINCHING in Charles Dickens, *Little Dorrit* (1855–7)

'In May 1855 he began to write *Little Dorrit*, in which there was a Flora to set against its predecessor's Dora, both derived from the same original' (John Forster, 1928, *The Life of Charles Dickens*, ed. J.W.T. Ley, p. 50). 'I am so glad you like Flora. It came into my head one day that we have all had our Flora (mine is living, and extremely fat), and that it was a half serious half ridiculous truth which had never been told. It is a wonderful gratification that everybody knows her' (to the Duke of Devonshire, 5 July 1856, reproduced in Charles Dickens, 1938, *Letters*, ed. Walter Dexter, Vol. II, p. 785).

DORA SPENLOW in Charles Dickens, *David Copperfield* (1849–50)

'I fancy . . . you may have seen in one of my books a faithful reflection of the passion I had for you, and may have thought that it was something to have been loved so well, and may have seen in little bits of "Dora" touches of your old self sometimes and a grace here and there that may be revived in your little girls, years hence, for the bewilderment of some other young lover – though he will never be as terribly in earnest as I and David Copperfield were (to Mrs Winter (Maria Beadnell), 15 February 1855, reproduced in *Letters*, op. cit., p. 629). 'I used to laugh and tell him I had no belief in any but the book Dora, until the sudden reappearance of the real one in his life . . . convinced me there had been a more actual foundation for those chapters of his book than I was ready to suppose' (Forster, op. cit., p. 49). In reply to Forster's scepticism, Dickens wrote: 'No one can imagine what pain the recollection gave me in *Copperfield*. And, just as I can never open that book as I open any other book, I cannot see the face (even at four-and-forty), or hear the voice, without going wandering away over the ashes of all that youth and hope in the wildest manner' (ibid.).

BEALE, Emily Daughter of General Edward Fitzgerald Beale, 'a bonanza miner' of California. They lived in enormous splendour in Decatur House on Lafayette Square, Washington. Miss Beale 'was wont to stroll about with a gigantic staghound on a leash'.

VICTORIA DARE in Henry Adams, *Democracy* (1880)

'Emily Beale quickly recognized herself in . . . Victoria Dare' (Ernest Samuels, 1958, *Henry Adams: the middle years*, Cambridge, Mass., p. 94).

BEAMINSTER, Dorset A small town south of Crewkerne, six miles north of Bridport.

EMMINSTER in Thomas Hardy, Wessex novels and tales (1871–95)

Identified on a map prepared by Thomas Hardy which hangs in the Dorset County Museum, Dorchester. *See under* **Abbotsbury**.

BEARD, Captain John Captain of the barque *Palestine* on her last voyage, to Bangkok in 1882.

CAPTAIN ELIJAH BEARD in Joseph Conrad, 'Youth' (1902)

'Conrad . . . kept the name of the master . . . unaltered, though he made Captain *Elijah* Beard into Captain *John* Beard' (Norman Sherry, 1966, *Conrad's Eastern World*, Cambridge, p. 17).

BEARDMORE, Edward Harry (1869–1932) Son of John **Beardmore**. His brother Frank married Bennett's sister, Fanny Gertrude (known as Sissie).

EDWIN CLAYHANGER in Arnold Bennett, the *Clayhanger* trilogy (1910–16)

'[T]he hero is a sort of Edward Harry Beardmore' (Bennett to his brother-in-law and sister, 22 October 1909, reproduced in Reginald Pound, 1952, *Arnold Bennett: a biography*, London: Heinemann, p. 209). *See also* **Bennett**, Arnold.

BEARDMORE, John (1846–1909) Of Burslem, Staffordshire. He was a neighbour and friend of Enoch **Bennett**, and the father of E.H. **Beardmore**.

DARIUS CLAYHANGER in Arnold Bennett, *Clayhanger* (1910)

'My next hero's father is the Pater plus Mr Beardmore' (Arnold Bennett writing to his brother-in-law and sister, 22 October 1909, reproduced in Reginald Pound, 1952, *Arnold Bennett: a biography*, London: Heinemann, p. 209). *See also* **Bennett**, Enoch; **Shaw**, Charles.

BEARDSALL, George (1825–99) Father of Lydia **Lawrence** and grandfather of D.H. Lawrence, he originated from Nottingham and became a dockyard foreman at Sheerness. He was a noted preacher, and according to Lawrence was associated with William **Booth** in founding the Salvation Army.

GEORGE COPPARD in D.H. Lawrence, *Sons and Lovers* (1913)

'This "galled" man [was] D.H. Lawrence's grandfather George Beardsall' (H.T. Moore, 1960, *The Intelligent Heart: the story of D.H. Lawrence*, Harmondsworth: Penguin, pp. 28–9; originally published 1955, London: Heinemann).

BEARDSALL, Herbert Brother of Lydia **Lawrence** and uncle of D.H. Lawrence, he was the black sheep of the family and kept a pub, the Lord Belper, in Sneinton, in Nottingham.

DANIEL SUTTON in D.H. Lawrence, 'The Primrose Path' (1922)

'Lawrence portrayed his Uncle Herbert as Daniel Sutton . . . he told of . . . [his] unhappiness in marriage, of his journey to Australia . . . of his managing a taxi business in Nottingham, and of working for a sporting paper there, all actual experiences of Herbert Beardsall' (H.T. Moore, 1960, *The Intelligent Heart: the story of D.H. Lawrence*, Harmondsworth: Penguin, p. 41; originally published 1955, London: Heinemann).

BEARDSLEY, Mabel (1871–1916) Sister of Aubrey Beardsley, the English illustrator, she began life as an actress and toured the United States with Arthur Bourchier. In 1903 she married George Bealby Wright, an actor. She died of tuberculosis.

FLORA LUSCOMBE in Ada Leverson, *The Limit* (1911)

'Mabel Beardsley was the original of . . . Miss Luscombe' (Violet Wyndham, 1963, *The Sphinx and Her Circle: a biographical sketch of Ada Leverson, 1862–1933*, London: Deutsch, p. 72). 'What a contrast the two are – Mabel a daisy, Aubrey the most monstrous of orchids' (Oscar Wilde to Ada Leverson, on the first night of *The Importance of Being Ernest*, 14 February 1895, 'Reminiscences, by Ada Leverson', reprinted in Wyndham, op. cit., App., p. 114; originally in *Letters to the Sphinx by Oscar Wilde*, London: Duckworth). But she became more orchidaceous – thus: (5 September 1901) 'Miss Beardsley has also arrived . . . she trails about, all day, in evening dress – low neck, no sleeves, and a train as long as the Rue de l'Hotel de Ville, which she carried swathed over her arm. She creates a great sensation' (Max Beerbohm, 1964, *Letters to Reggie Turner*, ed. Rupert Hart-Davis, London: Rupert Hart-Davis, p. 146). 'Yeats's sequence of poems "Upon a Dying Lady" in *The Wild Swans at Coole* (1919) was addressed to her' (ibid., p. 146 n. 3).

BEATON, Cecil (1904–80) Photographer and stage designer. He attended the same day school in Hampstead as Evelyn Waugh, and later the same preparatory school as George **Orwel**

'David Lennox . . . is a caricature of Cecil Beaton, which Evelyn made unmistakable by telling of a photograph of Mrs Best-Chetwynde's head taken by Lennox from the back. (Cecil Beaton had taken a well known photograph of Margot, Lady Oxford, from the same angle). . . . He disguised the portrait only by adding repellent touches' (Christopher Sykes, 1975, *Evelyn Waugh*, London: Collins, p. 86).

BEATTY, Frank A.M. Superintendent of the police in Baluchistan in 1900. After his retirement from the service he was appointed Sports Secretary of the Quetta Club. He was a notable linguist.

KIM in Rudyard Kipling, *Kim* (1901)

'In my early days in Quetta . . . one of the most forceful personalities there was Frank Beaty [sic]. . . . Many believed him to be the original of Kipling's "Kim"' (Henry Holland, 1958, *Frontier Doctor: an autobiography*, London: Hodder & Stoughton, p. 94). 'Holland arrived in Quetta in 1900. . . . This therefore appears to be a contemporary identification' (Simon Digby to the Editor, 1985, *The Kipling Journal* 59 (235): 56). *See also* **Rattigan**, William.

BEATTY, Pakenham Thomas (1855–1930) Born of Irish parents in Brazil, he was educated in Harrow and in Bonn. He became a friend of Shaw's soon after they both arrived in London as young men: he introduced Shaw to Ned **Donnelly**. Beatty was a keen amateur pugilist.

Cashel Byron in George Bernard Shaw, *Cashel Byron's Profession* (1886)

'Shaw . . . sublimated his interest in boxing by writing a novel about it. Conjuring up his hero by mixing in equal parts the personalities of the flamboyant Beatty and Jack Burke . . .' (Benny Green, 1978, *Shaw's Champions: G.B.S. & prizefighting from Cashel Brown to Gene Tunney*, London: Elm Tree Books, p. 7). *See also* **Burke**, Jack.

Chichester Erskine in George Bernard Shaw, *An Unsocial Socialist* (1887)

In 1884 Beatty published a verse tragedy entitled *Marcia*. 'In *An Unsocial Socialist*, [this] poetic drama (which Shaw had read in manuscript) became *The Patriot Martyrs*, and its author was satirised as Chichester Erskine' (G.B. Shaw, 1965, *Collected Letters, 1874–1897*, ed. Dan H. Laurence, p. 137 n.).

BEAUCHAMP, Annie (1864–1918) Née Dyer, she married Sir Harold Beauchamp (1858–1938) in 1884 and was the mother of Katherine Mansfield.

Linda Burnell in Katherine Mansfield, 'Prelude' (1918) and 'At the Bay' (1921)

'Shortly before the Murrys' move to 2 Portland Villas, Hampstead, on August 8 [1918] Katherine's mother died. Katherine loved and admired her deeply. There are three memorable pictures of her in Katherine's stories, as Linda Burnell . . . as Mrs Sheridan . . . and as Mrs Hammond' (*Katherine Mansfield's Letters to John Middleton Murry, 1913–1922*, 1951, ed. J.M. Murry, London: Constable, p. 308).

Mrs Hammond in Katherine Mansfield, 'The Stranger' (1922)

See above.

Mrs Sheridan in Katherine Mansfield, 'The Garden Party' (1922)

See above.

BEAUCHAMP, William, 6th Earl In 1902 he married Lady Lettice Grovenor (1872–1938). After a career of the utmost distinction, he was obliged, owing to a homosexual scandal, to resign all his official appointments and live abroad from 1931. He was able to return to England, and then to the family seat at **Madresfield Court**, in 1936 after the warrant for his arrest was annulled.

Lord Marchmain in Evelyn Waugh, *Brideshead Revisited* (1945)

It is clear that Lord Beauchamp resembled Lord Marchmain only in that he lived abroad, and that his family seat was Madresfield: 'It's all about a family whose father lives abroad, as it might be Boom [Lord Beauchamp] – but it's not Boom – and a younger son; people will say he's like Hughie, but you'll see he's not really Hughie – and there's a house as it might be Mad, but it isn't really Mad' (Lady Dorothy Lygon, 1973, 'Madresfield and Brideshead', *Evelyn Waugh and His World*, ed. David Pryce-Jones, London, p. 53). *See also* **Duggan**, Hubert.

BEAUFORT, Daniel Augustus (1739–1821) Vicar of Collon, County Louth, Ireland, from 1790 to 1821, he was a neighbour and close friend of Richard Lovell **Edgeworth** and the father of the latter's fourth wife, Frances Anne Beaufort. In 1792 he published a map of Ireland.

Dr Cambrai in Maria Edgeworth, *Ormond* (1817)

'An enlightened Anglican clergyman who acts as a benevolent peacemaker among the hot-tempered partisans of the Irish political scene appears in . . . *Ormond* (Dr Cambrai). As even the French name indicates, he is intended for a portrait of Dr Beaufort' (Marilyn Butler, 1972, *Maria Edgeworth*, Oxford, p. 141 n. 1).

de BEAUMONT, Pauline (1768–1803) Daughter of the Comte de Montmorin, Minister for Foreign Affairs to Louis XVI, in 1786 she married C.F. de Beaumont, whom she divorced in 1800. She was the only survivor in her family of the Terror of 1792; in 1800 she was able to return to Paris, where she met and became the mistress of **Chateaubriand**, assisting him in his work on *Génie du Christianisme*. After the publication and success of the book, he largely abandoned her for (among others) Delphine de Custine. She died in his arms in Rome, her death hastened by grief: she was buried in the Church of St Louis of France, where Chateaubriand erected in her memory a monument, which he had considerable difficulty paying for.

Eleanor Burgoyne in Mrs Humphry Ward, *Eleanor* (1899)

'The story of Eleanor Burgoyne owed its being, so far as I can now recollect, to an old familiarity of mine with the love story of Chateaubriand and Madame de Beaumont' (*The Writings of Mrs Humphry Ward*, Vol. X: *Eleanor*, 1911, London: Smith, Elder, p. ix). '[H]ere as always, the first hint given of a situation and a group of characters, both took their own course, and had soon drifted away . . . completely and independently from their first attachment' (ibid., p. x).

BEAVERBROOK, William Maxwell ('Max') Aitken, Lord (1879–1964) 1st Baron. Newspaper proprietor and politician. Born in Canada, he was the son of a Presbyterian minister and moved to England in 1910. In 1916 he became an MP, was created baronet, played a major part in the overthrow of H.H. **Asquith** and, in December, bought the *Daily Express*: by 1954 the paper's circulation exceeded 4 million copies a day. During the Second World War he became Minister of Aircraft Production (November 1940), and Minister of Supply (1941). He was the author of important works of contemporary political history, and in the late 1920s and early 1930s he took up William Gerhardie.

Lord Copper in Evelyn Waugh, *Scoop* (1938)

'Towering over the journalists who throng the story is ... Lord Copper, an imaginary portrait ... of Lord Beaverbrook whom Evelyn had met, served under spasmodically, but never came to know' (Christopher Sykes, 1975, *Evelyn Waugh*, London: Collins, p. 177).

LORD OTTERCOVE in William Gerhardi, *Jazz and Jasper* (1928)

'In the long run the most valuable action that Lord Beaverbrook ever performed for Gerhardie was to provide him with the prototype of Lord Ottercove in *Doom* and successive novels' (William Gerhardie, 1971, *Pending Heaven*, preface by Michael Holroyd, London: Macdonald, p. 7). *Jazz and Jasper* was reissued in 1947 as *My Sinful Earth* and in 1974 as *Doom*.

THE READER in John Prebble, *The Mather Story* (1953)

John Prebble was on the staff of the *Sunday Express* and 'the Reader' is certainly a portrait or caricature of Lord Beaverbrook, drawn from how close a personal knowledge it is impossible to tell.

LORD WESTERLEIGH in Hugh Kingsmill, *The Return of William Shakespeare* (1929)

'This fantasy ... includes amusing portraits of Lord Beaverbrook under the name of Lord Westerleigh, and of Lord Rothermere' (Michael Holroyd, 1964, *Hugh Kingsmill*, London: Unicorn Press, p. 107).

SIR BUSSY WOODCOCK in H.G. Wells, *The Autocracy of Mr Parham* (1930)

'Sir Bussy Woodcock was a neat caricature of Max Beaverbrook that was made explicit by the David Low cartoons that illustrated the book' (N. MacKenzie and J. MacKenzie, 1973, *The Time-Traveller: the life of H.G. Wells*, London: Weidenfeld & Nicolson, p. 357).

BECHER, Anne (*fl.* 1817) W.M. Thackeray's great-aunt.

MARTHA HONEYMAN in W.M. Thackeray, *The Newcomes* (1854–5)

'The old aunt with whom my grandmother had lived as a child, and to whose care my father also had been sent from India, was still living at Fareham in Hampshire, when my sister and I, children of a fourth generation, succeeded to all the old traditions. . . . We called her aunt Becher, but her other name I do believe was Miss Martha Honeyman' (Anne Thackeray Ritchie, 1898, biog. introd. to *The Works of W.M. Thackeray*, Vol. VIII: *The Newcomes*, London: Smith, Elder, p. xiii).

BECKER, Sir Walter (1855–1927) English shipowner resident in Italy. He was knighted in 1918 for his services in promoting the British cause in Italy, and after the First World Was he gave generously to the British Institute in Florence; he was also active in local charities. He married Thérèse de Martelly in 1895, and in 1919 D.H. Lawrence spent two nights as his guest at his home in Val Salice, near Turin.

SIR WILLIAM FRANKS in D.H. Lawrence, *Aaron's Rod* (1922)

'The original of Sir William Franks was Sir Walter Becker' (H.T. Moore, 1960, *The Intelligent Heart: the story of D.H. Lawrence*, Harmondsworth: Penguin, p.

323; originally published 1955, London: Heinemann). 'To my astonishment I found in [Aaron's Rod] . . . a description of [Lawrence's] visit to my house' (to Norman Douglas, presumably from Sir Walter Becker, reproduced in *Looking Backward*, reprinted in E. Nehls, 1958, *D.H. Lawrence: a composite biography*, Vol. II, Madison, p. 12). 'He portrays myself and my wife, and I grieve to say that we did not impress him at all favourably. . . . My wife he thought proper to compare to Queen Victoria, which . . . was unflattering in . . . that he was evidently . . . alluding . . . to her physical shortcomings' (ibid.).

BECKLEY PARK, Oxfordshire Built in 1540 by Lord Williams of Thame, perhaps as a hunting lodge for Rycote. '[T]he best preserved small house of this date in the county' (Nikolaus Pevsner and Jennifer Sherwood, 1974, *Oxfordshire (Buildings of England* series), Harmondsworth: Penguin, Pl. 50).

CROME in Aldous Huxley, *Crome Yellow* (1921)

'The house and garden . . . in *Crome Yellow* is not Garsington but Beckley Park . . . belonging to our friend Percy Fielding, where we had once taken Aldous to tea' (*Ottoline at Garsington: memoirs of Lady Ottoline Morrell*, 1974, ed. R. Gathorne-Hardy, London: Faber, p. 217). *See also* **Garsington Manor**.

BEER, Thomas (1889–1940) American writer. He was the author of *The Mauve Decade* (1926), and his sister Alice was the close friend of Aline **Bernstein**.

STEPHEN HOOK in Thomas Wolfe, *The Web and the Rock* (1939)

'He was the model for Stephen Hook' (*My Other Loneliness: letters of Thomas Wolfe and Aline Bernstein*, 1983, ed. Suzanne Stutman, Chapel Hill, NC, and London: University of North Carolina Press, p. 313 n. 1).

BEERBOHM, Max (1872–1956) Author and cartoonist. He was educated at Charterhouse and at Merton College, Oxford, and in 1893, through William **Rothenstein**, he joined the circle around the illustrator Aubrey Beardsley and met Oscar **Wilde**. In 1910 he married Florence Kahn (d. 1951), an actress distinguished for her acting in the plays of Ibsen, and moved to Rapallo, Italy, where he lived until his death (except for the period 1939–47).

HANS BRANDERS in Reginald Turner, *Davray's Affairs* (1906)

'Probably Reggie had warned Max that he was to appear, thinly disguised, in *Davray's Affairs*. . . . The passage runs as follows: "Hans Branders was by no means averse from playing a part in the comedy of life himself, but he was quite as pleased to watch the comedy going on"' (Max Beerbohm, 1964, *Letters to Reggie Turner*, ed. Rupert Hart-Davis, London: Rupert Hart-Davis, p. 173 n. 2).

AUBERON QUINN in G.K. Chesterton, *The Napoleon of Notting Hill* (1904)

'In [a] letter of 10 April Reggie [Turner] had written [to Beerbohm] "I have seen your name mentioned in connection with [*The Napoleon of Notting Hill*], but as far as I can make out you are only taken as the central figure from a pictorial point of view, it is not an attempt at drawing your personality." . . . The illustrator, W. Graham Robertson, had drawn all his pictures of Auberon Quin . . . in the likeness of Max, but the character itself is much more Chesterton than Beerbohm' (ibid., p. 173 n. 2). *See also* **Chesterton**, Gilbert Keith.

BEERBOHM TREE, Lady *See* **Tree**, Lady Beerbohm.

BEERBOHM TREE, Sir Herbert *See* **Tree**, Sir Herbert Beerbohm.

BELGIOJOSO, Cristina di Trivulsio, Principessa di (1808–71) Born in Milan, she was the daughter of Marchese Triulzi. In 1825 she married Prince Emilio Barbiano di Belgiojoso d'Este, who had been the lover of **Byron**'s Countess Guiccioli, but the marriage lasted only three years. She was a patriot and writer who, from 1828 onwards, was involved in a revolutionary conspiracy. She was obliged to leave Italy in 1830, whereupon she lived in Paris until 1848. In 1848 she raised volunteer corps for Prince Carlo Alberto of Savoy, and in 1849 she organized nursing corps and hospitals for the wounded. She lived and travelled in Asia Minor and the Near East between 1849 and 1855, and then returned to Italy. She became a friend and supporter of Cavour, the Italian statesman.

Princess Casamassima in Henry James, *The Princess Casamassima* (1886)

'Henry James, who knew and admired Cristina, based his *Princess Casamassima* on her' (C.N. Gattey, 1971, *A Bird of Curious Plumage*, p. xiii). 'Nothing is more curious, as we read her story, than the apparent mixture in her of the love of the thing in itself and the love of all the attitudes and aspects, the eccentricities and superfluities of the thing' (Henry James, 1903, *William Wetmore Story and His Friends*, Vol. I, Edinburgh and London: William Blackwood & Sons, p. 162). *See also* **Obolensky**, Princess.

BELL, Florence (1851–1930) She married Sir Hugh Bell, Baronet, and was the mother of the archaeologist Gertrude Bell. She was a close friend of Elizabeth **Robins**.

Mrs Alsager in Henry James, 'Nona Vincent' (1891)

'Mrs Bell . . . is the quiet Mrs Alsager' (Leon Edel, 1969, *Henry James: the treacherous years, 1895–1901*, London: Hart-Davis, p. 28).

BELL, James Richard (d. 1912) Engineer and bridge-builder. He worked for twenty years in the Public Works Department of India, and in 1886 was Engineer-in-Chief on the Ferozepur Bridge Works.

Findlayson in Rudyard Kipling, 'The Bridge Builders' (1898)

'In a copy of an 1899 edition of *The Day's Work* picked up in Madras was found the following autograph inscription: "My dear Storey, sorry I can't find a better edition. . . . The Ganges is the Sutlej and Kashi is Ferozepur – the Bridge is now called the Kaisarin i Hind. . . . The tale is a farrago of bridge building stories told to R.K. at various times. . . . and Findlayson is your old friend J.R.B. 23.4.03". It seems hardly questionable that J.R.B. is James Richard Bell' (Hilton Brown, 1949, letter to *The Kipling Journal* 16 (92): 15). *See also* **Geddes**, Auckland; **Walton**, Frederick.

BELL, Joseph (1837–1911) Physician and surgeon. He was a consultant at the Edinburgh Infirmary, and taught Conan Doyle when the latter was studying medicine; he was renowned among his students for his quick observation and deductive powers.

SHERLOCK HOLMES in Arthur Conan Doyle, the Sherlock Holmes stories (1890–1927)

'In 1893 ... Robert Louis Stevenson, after meeting ... Sherlock Holmes in print for the first time, asked Conan Doyle in a letter from Samoa: "Only one thing troubles me. Can this be my old friend Joe Bell?" Conan Doyle was quick to tell Stevenson, the press, and the world that the prototype for Sherlock Holmes was indeed Dr Bell' (Irving Wallace, 1956, *The Fabulous Originals*, London, p. 29).

BELL, Vanessa (1879–1961) Painter. She was the daughter of Sir Leslie **Stephen**, and the elder sister of Virginia Woolf. In 1907 she married the art critic Clive Bell (1881–1964), but from 1914 onwards she lived with Duncan **Grant**.

HELEN AMBROSE in Virginia Woolf, *The Voyage Out* (1915)

'... Helen Ambrose, accepted by both Virginia and Vanessa as a portrait in some salient respects of Vanessa' (Jane Dunn, 1990, *A Very Close Conspiracy: Vanessa Bell and Virginia Woolf*, London: Jonathan Cape, p. 88). 'Woolf's understanding of her sister and of her creative process ... aided her in the creation of Helen Ambrose, Mrs Ramsay and Lily Briscoe' (Diane Filby Gillespie, 1988, *The Sisters' Art: the writing and painting of Virginia Woolf and Vanessa Bell*, New York, p. 203).

LILY BRISCOE in Virginia Woolf, *To the Lighthouse* (1927)

See above.

KATHERINE HILBERY in Virginia Woolf, *Night and Day* (1919)

'[T]ry thinking of Katherine as Vanessa, not me' (to Janet Case, 19 November 1919, reproduced in *The Letters of Virginia Woolf, 1912–1922*, 1976, ed. Nigel Nicolson, London: Hogarth Press, p. 400).

MARGARET SCHLEGEL in E.M. Forster, *Howards End* (1910)

See under **Woolf**, Virginia.

BELLAIRS, Revd Mr

REVD MR FELLOWES in George Eliot, 'The Sad Fortunes of the Revd Amos Barton', *Scenes of Clerical Life* (1857–8)

See under **Anstruther**, Lady.

BELLOC LOWNDES, Marie (1868–1947) Herself an author of novels and volumes of reminiscences, she was the sister of the writer Hilaire Belloc and was married to F.L. Lowndes.

MRS LAUNCE in Hugh Walpole, *Fortitude* (1913)

'At a dinner party in ... 1910 Hugh met ... Mrs Belloc Lowndes. ... [L]ater [he] drew her portrait ... as Mrs Launce' (Rupert Hart-Davis, 1952, *Hugh Walpole*, p. 75).

BELLOWS, George (1882–1925) American realistic painter. He studied in New York under Robert Henri.

HENRY MALLOWS in Thomas Wolfe, *You Can't Go Home Again* (1940)

'Henry Mallows . . . is based on George Bellows' (*The Notebooks of Thomas Wolfe*, 1970, ed. Richard S. Kennedy and Paschal Reeves, Chapel Hill, NC: University of North Carolina Press, p. 501 n. 8).

BELMONT, August (1816–90) Born in Rhenish Palatinate, in 1837 he emigrated to the USA, where he established the banking house of August Belmont & Co. and was an art connoisseur and sportsman. He was President of the American Jockey Club.

JULIUS BEAUFORT in Edith Wharton, *The Age of Innocence* (1920)

'The only titans in society [during Edith Wharton's childhood in the 1860s] were the Astors and August Belmont, who dazzled Manhattan with his opulence and who was to appear as Julius Beaufort in *The Age of Innocence*' (Louis Auchincloss, 1972, *Edith Wharton: a woman in her time*, London: Joseph, p. 19). 'When [her sister-in-law] Minnie Jones thought to detect . . . August Belmont in the name and figure of . . . Julius Beaufort, Edith was quick to deny it' (R.W.B. Lewis, 1975, *Edith Wharton: a biography*, London: Constable, p. 431). *See also* **Jones**, George Alfred.

BELSCHES, Williamina (1776–1810) Daughter of Sir John Wishart Belsches (afterwards Stuart) of Fettercairn. Scott first met her in Edinburgh in 1790, and by 1792 he was deeply in love and hoped to marry her. However, in 1796 she became engaged to William Forbes, subsequently the 7th Baronet of Pitsligo, whom she married in January of the following year. Her tutor was James **Mill**, the Scottish philosopher, and her father was his patron. When Mill left Scotland for London in 1802, Sir John Stuart gave him a seat in his post-chaise. Mill named his two eldest children John Stuart and Williamina Forbes for Sir John and his daughter, and in his will Sir John left £500 for the purpose of sending John Stuart Mill to Cambridge. Williamina's son, James David Forbes (1809–68), became a Fellow of the Royal Society of Edinburgh at the age of 19, Professor of Natural Philosophy at the University of Edinburgh at the age of 24, and was Principal of St Andrews in 1860.

MATILDA OF ROKEBY in Sir Walter Scott, *Rokeby* (1813)

'This much of Matilda I recollect, for that is not so easily forgotten, that she was attempted from the existing person and character of a lady who is now no more, so that I am particularly flattered with you distinguishing it from the others, which are in general mere shadows' (to Maria Edgeworth, 15 May 1818, reproduced in *The Letters of Sir Walter Scott*, Vol. V: *1817–1819*, 1933, ed. H.J.C. Grierson, London: Constable, p. 145). 'I can have no doubt that the lady he here alludes to was the object of his own unfortunate first love' (J.G. Lockhart, 1900, *Memoirs of Sir Walter Scott*, Vol. II, London: Macmillan, p. 255).

LILIAS REDGAUNTLET in Sir Walter Scott, *Redgauntlet* (1824)

'The Christian name Wilhelmina seems to have come . . . into fashion in the late eighteenth and early nineteenth centuries. The example which everyone will remember is Walter Scott's first love, the original it is said of Lilias (Greenmantle) in "Redgauntlet"' (C.E.H., 1939, *Notes and Queries* 176 (13 May): 332). 'Her dress was, I should suppose, both handsome and fashionable; but it was much concealed by a walking-cloak of green silk, fancifully embroidered

... and ... furnished with a hood' (*Redgauntlet*, Vol. I, letter VIII). 'The green mantle was Williamina's walking cloak of silk ... with a deep hood' (Edgar Johnson, 1970, *Sir Walter Scott: the great unknown*, London: Hamilton, p. 109).

BELVOIR CASTLE, Leicestershire Situated six miles west of Grantham.

BEAUMANOIR in Benjamin Disraeli, *Coningsby* (1844)

'Beaumanoir, le château splendide où vit la famille de Henry Sydney.' 'Il faut y voir Belvoir Castle où vivaient les ducs de Rutland' (L. Cazanian, 1904, *Le Roman social en Angleterre*, Paris, p. 342 and n. 2).

BELZONI, Giovanni Battista (1778–1823) Italian explorer and archaeologist. He explored Egyptian antiquities, opening the temple of Abu-Simbel and the second pyramid of Giza. In 1818 he lived in Craven Hill, London, being a neighbour of Fanny **Kemble**'s parents. Fanny Kemble recounts how his large handsome face and magnificent auburn beard overtopped the six-foot wall that separated the two gardens. (On the other side of the Kembles lived Beau **Brummell**'s sister Mrs Blackshaw; see Fanny Kemble, 1879, *Record of a Girlhood*, Vol. I, p. 60).

FRANCIS BARONI THE ELDER in Benjamin Disraeli, *Tancred* (1847)

'The Baronis, father and son ... are modelled after ... Giovanni Battista Belzoni. Like ... Belzoni the elder Baroni ... is [an] ... itinerant Italian showman ... who with his wife gives *tableaux-vivants* ... all over Europe but especially in the Low Countries. ... Sidonia becomes his patron as Burkhardt ... became Belzoni's. Baroni's son ... has Belzoni's gift for Eastern languages ... and wide experience as traveller and confidential agent in the Near East' (Curtis Dahl, 1958, 'Baroni in Disraeli's *Tancred*', *Notes and Queries* 203: 152).

BENAVIDES (*fl.* 1820) 'A freelance on the southern frontier of Chile during the wars of the Revolution' (to Cunninghame Graham, 30 March 1923, reproduced in G. Jean-Aubrey, 1927, *Joseph Conrad: life and letters*, Vol. II, London: Heinemann, p. 299).

GASPAR RUIZ in Joseph Conrad, 'Gaspar Ruiz', *A Set of Six* (1908)

'I found the seed of it in Capt. Basil Hall, R.N. "Journal of the Years 1820, -21, -22" [Basil Hall, 1824, *Extracts from a Journal, Written on the Coasts of Chili Peru and Mexico, in the Years 1820, 1821, 1822*, Edinburgh]. ... The original of Gaspar Ruiz is a man calle Benavides. ... Hall gives him a page or two. ... I had to invent all his story, find the motives, for his changes of sides, – and the scenery of the tale' (ibid.). Compare this with John Miller, 1829, *Memoirs of General Miller in the Service of Peru*, 2nd edn, London: Longman Rees; originally published 1828, London; see Norman Sherry, 1971, *Conrad's Western World*, Cambridge, pp. 138 ff., p. 412 nn. 6, 9.)

BENÉT, James Walker (d. 1928) Colonel in the US Army. In 1909, the year that Sinclair Lewis first visited **Benicia**, he was Commanding Officer of Benicia base (near San Francisco). He was the father of the writers William Rose Benét and Stephen Vincent Benét.

COLONEL HAVILAND in Sinclair Lewis, *The Trail of the Hawk* (1915)

The identification is based upon obvious parallels.

BENÉT, Theresa Frances Née Thompson. She married William Rose Benét in 1912.

NORA RAFFERTY in William Rose Benét, *The Dust Which is God* (1941)

'Nora Rafferty's prototype was Miss Theresa Thompson, sister of Kathleen Norris' (Mark Schorer, 1963, *Sinclair Lewis: an American life*, London: Heinemann, p. 157; originally published 1961, New York: McGraw-Hill).

BENICIA, California South of Vallejo, it was the site of a small army base and arsenal first set up in 1849. In 1909 it was under the command of Colonel James W. **Benét**.

SAN SPIRITO in Sinclair Lewis, *The Trail of the Hawk* (1915)

The identification would seem obvious as Sinclair Lewis visited it with William Rose Benét in 1909.

BENNET, Miss Governess in the family of Lady Helen Smith of Bere Court, Hampshire, to whom she was known as 'Benny'. By 1941, when Angela Thirkell spent a weekend there, Benny had retired and was living as a member of the household.

MISS BUNTING in Angela Thirkell, *Marling Hall* (1942) and *Miss Bunting* (1945)

'When her . . . hostess, Lady Helen Smith, read the novel she was distressed and furious to find in it a portrait of her beloved governess lightly disguised under a very similar name. She was afraid that Benny would discover it, since she was plainly described down to the smallest detail. . . . Lady Helen bought up and destroyed all the copies she could find in the district. And she didn't invite Angela to spend another weekend at Bere' (M. Strickland, 1977, *Angela Thirkell: portrait of a lady novelist*, London: Duckworth, pp. 136–7).

BENNETT, Andrew Percy (1866–1943) British Acting Consul-General in Zurich from 1899 to 1918, Minister to Panama from 1919 to 1923, and Minister to Costa Rica from 1920 to 1923.

SERGEANT-MAJOR BENNETT in James Joyce, *Ulysses* (1922)

'Originally Joyce intended to make Consul-General Bennett and Henry Carr the two drunken, blasphemous and obscene soldiers who knock Stephen Dedalus down in the 'Circe' episode; but he eventually decided that Bennett should be the sergeant-major, with authority over Private Carr' (Richard Ellmann, 1982, *James Joyce*, rev. edn, Oxford: Oxford University Press, p. 459).

BENNETT, Arnold (1867–1931) English novelist, playwright and journalist. Born in Hanley in the Staffordshire Potteries, the son of an Enoch and Sarah **Bennett**. At 21 he left his job with his father's firm, and went to London, where he worked as a clerk before establishing himself as a writer. He became Assistant Editor of *Woman* magazine in 1893, and Editor in 1896. He lived in

Paris from 1903 to 1912, marrying Marguerite Soulie in 1907. He became a close friend of Lord **Beaverbrook**, and served as Director of Propaganda in the Ministry of Information in 1918. He separated from his wife in 1921, and had a daughter with the companion of his later years, Dorothy Cheston. He died from typhoid.

MR BARBECUE SMITH in Aldous Huxley, *Crome Yellow* (1921)

'[T]he preoccupation of . . . Mr Barbecue Smith with his daily production of words may well be . . . culled from Huxley's observation of Arnold Bennett, with whom he had become friendly in 1919' (George Woodcock, 1972, *Dawn and the Darkest Hour: a study of Aldous Huxley*, London: Faber & Faber, p. 81).

REGINALD BLISS in H.G. Wells, *Boon* (1915)

'The character of Reginald Bliss, someone not unlike Wells's friend Arnold Bennett, was introduced to edit the posthumous remains of George Boon' (Lovat Dickson, 1972, *H.G. Wells*, Harmondsworth: Penguin, p. 241).

EDWIN CLAYHANGER in Arnold Bennett, the *Clayhanger* trilogy (1910–16)

'August 31st [1913] . . . Clayhanger [contained] something of me as a boy' (*The Journals of Arnold Bennett*, 1932, ed. Sir Newman Flower, Vol. II, London: Cassell, p. 67). *See also* **Beardmore**, Edward Harry.

TASKER JONES in May Sinclair, *Tasker Jones: The Real Story* (1916)

'[Bennett] was said to be the model for the unpleasant journalist who is the eponymous hero of her novel' (*Letters of Arnold Bennett*, 1968, ed. James Hepburn, Vol. II, London: Oxford University Press, p. 327 n. 274).

RICHARD LARCH in Arnold Bennett, *The Man from the North* (1898)

'[T]he portrait of Richard, wandering alone to the theatre, eating alone, longing for society, certainly reflects [Bennett's] . . . first months [in London]' (Margaret Drabble, 1974, *Arnold Bennett: a biography*, London: Weidenfeld & Nicolson, p. 49).

LORD RAINGO in Arnold Bennett, *Lord Raingo* (1926)

'Raingo is doubtless more nearly a portrait of Bennett himself than of anyone else' (*Letters of Arnold Bennett*, 1970, ed. James Hepburn, Vol. III, London: Oxford University Press, p. 276 n. 300). *See also* **Rhondda**, 1st Viscount; **Rickards**, Edwin Alfred.

SAMUEL SHODBUTT in Wyndham Lewis, *The Roaring Queen* (1973)

'The identification of S.S. as Arnold Bennett . . . is unmistakeable' (R.T. Chapman, 1973, *Wyndham Lewis: fictions and satires*, London: Vision Press, p. 119).

VERNON SPROTT in William Gerhardi, *Jazz and Jasper* (1928)

'Arnold Bennett . . . in the guise of Vernon Sprott, is described as "a writer of talent but a merchant of genius"' (William Gerhardie, 1974, *Doom* (reissue of *Jazz and Jasper*), preface by Michael Holroyd, London: Macdonald, p. xi).

BENNETT, Enoch (1843–1902) Solicitor. He married Sarah Longson (**Bennett**, below) and was Arnold Bennett's father.

DARIUS CLAYHANGER in Arnold Bennett, *Clayhanger* (1910)

'My next hero's father is the Pater plus Mr Beardmore – a steam printer' (Arnold Bennett writing to his brother-in-law and sister, 22 October 1909, reproduced in Reginald Pound, 1952, *Arnold Bennett: a biography*, London: Heinemann, p. 209). 'The [last] illness of Enoch Bennett is chronicled with relentless truth in *Clayhanger*' (Pound, ibid., p. 121). *See also* **Beardmore**, John; **Shaw**, Charles.

BENNETT, Sarah (1840–1914) Daughter of Robert Longson, she married Enoch **Bennett** in 1866 and was the mother of Arnold Bennett.

MRS CLARA HAMPS in Enoch **Bennett** in 1866 and was the mother of Arnold Bennett.

MRS CLARA HAMPS in Arnold Bennett, the *Clayhanger* trilogy (1910–16)

'Auntie Hamps was not of course modelled on Mrs Bennett ... but the circumstances of [his mother's] death were used by Bennett nevertheless. In his journal for 20 November [1914] he notes the objects in his mother's bedroom, as he sat with her up in Burslem; some of the same objects are described again in the novel' (Margaret Drabble, 1974, *Arnold Bennett: a biography*, London: Weidenfeld & Nicolson, p. 204). Miss Drabble goes on to describe other resemblances. *See also* **Bourne**, Frances.

BENNETT, Septimus (1866–1926) Youngest brother of Arnold Bennett. He won a scholarship and studied sculpture at South Kensington, London.

CYRIL POVEY in Arnold Bennett, *The Old Wives' Tale* (1908)

'[Arnold Bennett's] younger brother Septimus, the sculptor and modeller ... figures as Cyril Povey in *The Old Wives' Tale*' (Reginald Pound, 1952, *Arnold Bennett: a biography*, London: Heinemann, p. 64).

BENNETT, Sir William Sterndale (1816–75) Song writer and composer. In 1856 he was Professor of Music at Cambridge, and in 1868 he was Principal of the Royal Academy of Music. He was an intimate friend of Mendelssohn, the composer.

STARWOOD BURNEY in Elizabeth Sara Sheppard, *Charles Auchester* (1853)

Identified in Michael Sadleir, 1951, *XIX Century Fiction*, Vol. I, London: Constable, and Los Angeles: California University Press, p. 320; and in an anonymous typed key laid in a copy of the first edition of *Charles Auchester* which is now in the possession of the present author.

BENSON, Arthur Christopher (1862–1925) Son of Archbishop Benson and brother of E.F. and R.H. **Benson**, he was educated at Eton and at King's College, Cambridge, becoming a master at Eton (1883–1903) and a Fellow of Magdalen College, Cambridge (1903). He produced a large number of books of essays, which he himself described as 'solemn, sweet and refined'. These deplorable works transformed Magdalen: one of his devoted female readers showed her gratitude by enabling him to endow the college with courts and with scholarships as he chose, and from being one of the poorest, Magdalen became one of the richest Cambridge colleges.

Wentworth Maine in Mary Cholmondeley, *Prisoners* (1906)

'He had been great friends with [Mary Cholmondeley], and was on the select list of those who might call without making an appointment. . . . They had had many . . . talks together, and now she had put, verbatim, into the mouth of Wentworth, many of his contributions to these conversations. . . . My mother, who thought that Arthur had been grossly and intentionally caricatured . . . called it "a piece of savagery on Mary's part". . . . Arthur, however . . . was hurt and angry' (E.F. Benson, 1940, *Final Edition: an informal autobiography*, London: Longman, pp. 78–9).

BENSON, Eugene (1839–1908) American painter. In 1873 he was resident in Rome, where Henry James visited his studio and saw several careful and conscientious but very uninspired little pictures (*Henry James Letters*, Vol. I: *1843–1875*, 1974, ed. Leon Edel, London and Basingstoke: Macmillan, p. 347). He was the stepfather of Constance **Fletcher**.

Sam Singleton in Henry James, *Roderick Hudson* (1875)

'He may have been the "original" for Singleton' (ibid., p. 349 n. 3).

BENSON, Robert Hugh (1871–1914) Son of E.W. Benson (1829–96), Archbishop of Canterbury from 1882, and brother of E.F. Benson, the author.

Revd Bobugo Bonson in F.W. Rolfe, *The Weird of the Wanderer* (1912)

'[H]e set to work on a new novel *The Weird of the Wanderer* in which he pilloried [Benson] as a dishonourable priest, describing his dress, his personal appearance, his stammering mode of talk, in savage caricature, and lest any should fail to mark his intention he called him the Reverend Bobugo Bonson' (E.F. Benson, 1940, *Final Edition: an informal autobiography*, London: Longman, p. 38).

Father Robert Rolle in Shane Leslie, *The Cantab* (1926)

Identified in a key in the hand of Dr Ivor Ramsay, a Kingsman of the year 1920, and later Dean, laid in a copy of *The Cantab*.

S.H. BENSON LTD Well-known London advertising company responsible for advertising campaigns on behalf of among others, Colman's Mustard ('the Mustard Club') and Guinness ('Guinness is Good for You') in the 1920s and 1930s. Dorothy Sayers and R.A.P. **Bevan** were on the staff in the 1920s.

Pym's Publicity Ltd in Dorothy L. Sayers, *Murder Must Advertise* (1933)

'[The] setting of *Murder Must Advertise* was Benson's in every detail' (R.D. Bloomfield, 1975, *The Times* (7 January): 14).

BENT, Fanny Daughter of the Revd George Bent, Rector of Crediton, she was the first cousin of Mrs Frances **Trollope** (see C. Roy Hudleston, 1949, 'Anthony Trollope's mother', *Notes and Queries* 194 (28 May): 240).

Miss STANBURY in Anthony Trollope, *He Knew He was Right* (1869)

'The Exeter scenes and to some extent also "Aunt Stanbury" herself, were memories of visits paid to Miss Fanny Bent, an old friend of Frances Trollope and of her sons, who lived near the Close' (Michael Sadleir, 1945, *Trollope: a commentary*, 2nd rev. edn, London: Constable, p. 393 n. 1; originally published 1927, London: Constable).

BENTLEY, Richard (1794–1871) Publisher. He founded *Bentley's Miscellany*, which Charles **Dickens** edited, in 1837.

MR BACON in W.M. Thackeray, *The History of Pendennis* (1848–50)

'In sketching old-time literary Bohemia, Thackeray included a number of portraits drawn from life, drawn with such fidelity as to be immediately recognizable. The [publisher] Bentley [is] there as Bacon' (Gordon Ray, 1958, *Thackeray: the age of wisdom*, p. 114).

BERAU, Borneo Village in Dutch East Borneo where Captain **Lingard** had a monopoly of the trade in the 1860s.

PATUSAN, PATUSAN RIVER, in Joseph Conrad, *Lord Jim* (1900)

'. . . Berau, the settlement in Eastern Borneo on the Berau river which was to become Conrad's source for Patusan in *Lord Jim*' (Norman Sherry, 1966, *Conrad's Eastern World*, Cambridge, p. 80).

SAMBIR in Joseph Conrad, *Almayer's Folly* (1895)

'The spelling given in [the Shipping Column of a Singapore newspaper of June 1866] is "Brow" and this agrees with Conrad's when by accident he failed to take the name out of the published text of *Almayer's Folly* and replace it with the fictional "Sambir"' (ibid., p. 95).

BERAU RIVER, Borneo

PANTAI RIVER in Joseph Conrad, *Almayer's Folly* (1895)

'The river that . . . Conrad calls the Pantai was based on the . . . Berau . . . which Conrad had visited as mate of the *Vidar* [1887–8]' (*The Collected Letters of Joseph Conrad*, 1983, ed. F.R. Karl and Laurence Davies, Vol. I, Cambridge: Cambridge University Press, p. 186 n. 3). Conrad wrote to W.H. Chesson, a reader at T. Fisher Unwin [October/November 1894?]: 'Yes – in Borneo but as a matter of reality in my memory it is only a faded stream. I regret to see my own stupid finger pointing for ever to the spot on the map. After all, river and people have nothing true about them – in the vulgar sense – but the names. Any criticism that would look for real description of places and events would be disastrous to that particle of the universe, which is nobody and nothing in the world but myself' (ibid.).

BERE REGIS, Dorset Now a village east of Puddletown, King John often stayed there in the thirteenth century. A portion of the manor estate eventually passed into the hands of the Turberville family and the church contains the Turberville Chapel.

KINGSBERE in Thomas Hardy, Wessex novels and tales (1871–95)

Identified in F.B. Pinion, 1968, *A Hardy Companion*, London: Macmillan, p. 381.

BERESFORD, George Charles (1866–1938) A contemporary and close friend of Kipling as a boy at the United Services College, Westward Ho!

WILLIAM M'TURK in Rudyard Kipling, *Stalky & Co.* (1899)

The title page of his own reminiscences, published in London in 1932, reads *'Schooldays with Kipling*: by G.C. Beresford (M'Turk)'.

BERGDORF-GOODMAN COMPANY, New York A department store on Fifth Avenue.

STEIN & ROSEN in Thomas Wolfe, *The Web and the Rock* (1939)

'[T]he New York store which Wolfe took as his model is Bergdorf-Goodman Company' (P. Reeves, 1965, 'Thomas Wolfe: notes on three characters', *Modern Fiction Studies* 11 (3): 277).

BERKELEY, George Grantley Fitzhardinge (1800–81) Sixth son of the 5th Earl of Berkeley, and brother of Lord **Fitzhardinge** and Lady Caroline **Maxse**. In 1816 he was in the Coldstream Guards, and subsequently he was in the 82nd foot. From 1832 to 1853 he was MP for West Gloucestershire. He was a writer, and in 1836, after the publication in *Fraser's Magazine* of a savage review of his novel *Berkeley Castle*, he assaulted Fraser and fought a duel with William **Maginn**, the writer of the review. That same year, he proposed the admission of women to the gallery of the House of Commons; his proposal was taken up in 1841.

EVERARD ROMFREY in George Meredith, *Beauchamp's Career* (1876)

'Beauchamp's uncle, Everard Romfrey . . . was drawn both as to physical and mental characteristics, from Captain Maxse's maternal uncle, Grantley Berkeley. . . . Everard Romfrey thrashes Dr Shrapnel with "a gold-headed horsewhip". Just so . . . did Grantley Berkeley act in . . . his assault on James Fraser for the libellous review . . . in Fraser's Magazine of *Berkeley Castle*. . . . [He] felled the publisher to the ground and beat him savagely with a . . . gold headed hunting-whip. . . . James Fraser eventually died from . . . the injuries he received' (S.M. Ellis, 1920, *George Meredith*, 2nd edn, London: Grant Richards, pp. 239–40).

BERKELEY SQUARE, London

GAUNT SQUARE in W.M. Thackeray, *Vanity Fair* (1847–8)

'. . . material was supplied by Berkeley Square . . . [including] Lansdowne House' (Joan Stevens, 1969, 'A roundabout ride', *Victorian Studies* 13 (September): 69). *See also* **Cavendish Square; Manchester Square.**

BERLIOZ, Hector (1803–69) French composer. A student of medicine until 1923, he entered the Paris Conservatoire in 1926. He married the Irish actress Harriett Smithson.

FLORIMOND ANASTASE in Elizabeth Sara Sheppard, *Charles Auchester* (1853)

Identified in Michael Sadleir, 1951, *XIX Century Fiction*, Vol. I, London: Constable, and Los Angeles: California University Press, p. 320; and in an anonymous typed key laid in a copy of the first edition of *Charles Auchester* which is now in the possession of the present author.

BERNARD, W.S. Professor of Greek at the University of North Carolina at Chapel Hill. He taught Thomas Wolfe.

EDWARD PETTIGREW ('BUCK') BENSON in Thomas Wolfe, *Look Homeward, Angel* (1929)

'Professor Bernard, who sat for the portrait of "Buck" Benson . . . guided Wolfe through literature which . . . colored much of his later writing' (Richard S. Kennedy, 1962, *The Window of Memory: the literary career of Thomas Wolfe*, Chapel Hill, NC, p. 40).

BERNERS, Gerald Hugh Tyrwhitt-Wilson, Lord (1883–1950) Fifth Baronet and 14th Baron. Musician, artist, painter, writer and wit. He was of considerable wealth and succeeded to the title in 1918. In the 1930s he became the neighbour of the Mitfords at Faringdon House, Oxfordshire, a small country house where, in 1935, he built on Faringdon Hill the last folly in England.

ROBERT MAINWROTH in Osbert Sitwell, 'The Love-Bird' (1930)

'[O]ne can see how Osbert's mind was working in a short story based on the character of Gerald Berners. He called it "The Love-Bird", and the hero, Robert Mainwroth, is a rich, eccentric aristocrat' (John Pearson, 1978, *Façades: Edith, Osbert, and Sacheverell Sitwell*, London: Macmillan, p. 251).

LORD MERLIN in Nancy Mitford, *The Pursuit of Love* (1945) and *Love in a Cold Climate* (1949)

'Nancy was to introduce him as "Lord Merlin" into *The Pursuit of Love*' (Harold Acton, 1975, *Nancy Mitford: a memoir*, London: Hamilton, p. 54).

BERNSTEIN, Dr German naturalist, known to A.R. **Wallace** as a collector for the Leyden Museum, in the Malay Archipelago (1854–62).

STEIN in Joseph Conrad, *Lord Jim* (1900)

'Wallace makes one brief reference to Dr Bernstein. . . . In this . . . Conrad found for . . . Stein a name (. . . the last syllable of Bernstein), a nationality and a career' (Norman Sherry, 1966, *Conrad's Eastern World*, Cambridge, p. 143). *See also* **Allen**, Charles; **Lingard**, Captain William; **Mesman**, Mr; **Wallace**, Alfred Russel.

BERNSTEIN, Aline (1882–1955) Distinguished American stage designer. She was the daughter of Joseph **Frankau**, and in 1902 married stockbroker Theodore **Bernstein**. In 1925 she met Thomas Wolfe and they began an affair that came to an end in 1931; she wrote an account of their relationship in *The Journey Down* (1938). The two central characters are not named, but are called 'he' and 'she' throughout.

ESTHER JACK in Thomas Wolfe, *The Web and the Rock* (1939)

'[I]t was during this period [May–December 1930, while breaking off the affair] that he began developing one of his most successful and sympathetic characters, that of Esther Jack, which was based on Aline Bernstein' (*My Other Loneliness: letters of Thomas Wolfe and Aline Bernstein*, 1983, ed. Suzanne Stutman, Chapel Hill, NC, and London: University of North Carolina Press, p. 293).

BERNSTEIN, Edla Afterwards Cusick. She was the daughter of Aline **Bernstein**.

ALMA JACK in Thomas Wolfe, *The Web and the Rock* (1939) and *You Can't Go Home Again* (1940)

'Wolfe's fictionalized character based upon Edla was referred to as Alma throughout *The Web and the Rock* and *You Can't Go Home Again*' (*My Other Loneliness: letters of Thomas Wolfe and Aline Bernstein*, 1983, ed. Suzanne Stutman, Chapel Hill, NC, and London: University of North Carolina Press, p. 42 n. 2).

BERNSTEIN, Theodore (1873–1958) Born in Bad Ems, Germany, he moved to the USA in 1889 and married Aline Frankau (**Bernstein**, above) in 1902. He was a stockbroker in New York, but in 1929 he lost heavily on the stockmarket. He suffered a stroke in 1952.

FREDERICK JACK in Thomas Wolfe, *The Web and the Rock* (1939)

So identified in *The Notebooks of Thomas Wolfe*, 1970, ed. Richard S. Kennedy and Paschal Reeves, Chapel Hill, NC: University of North Carolina Press, p. 1007, s.v. Jack, Fritz.

BERRY, The Misses Agnes (1764–1852) and Mary (1763–1852), daughters of Robert Berry. Mary Berry was a writer and in 1788 made the acquaintance of Horace Walpole (1717–97), who thenceforward conducted an affectionate correspondence with the sisters. From 1791 onwards they lived at Little Strawberry Hill, a house belonging to Walpole that he bequeathed to them upon his death. Walpole entrusted his literary remains to Robert Berry and the two sisters, and the *Works* appeared in 1798, nominally edited by Robert Berry, but in reality by Mary. In 1810 they published the letters of Madame Du Deffand to Walpole at Strawberry Hill.

THE MISSES OTRANTO in Benjamin Disraeli, *Vivian Grey* (1826–7)

Identified as Misses B—— in a key given in *The Star Chamber* (24 May 1826): 114; reprinted in *Vivian Grey*, 1904 (centenary edn), ed. Lucien Wolf, Vol. II, pp. 361–2. The full name appeared in a reprint of the key published in *Notes and Queries* (29 April 1893). Lucien Wolf concludes that Disraeli was not responsible for the key.

BERRY, Walter van Rensselaer (1859–1927) Lawyer. Born in Paris, he grew up in Albany, New York, as a member of an old New York family, and was distantly related to Edith Wharton's mother. In 1910 he settled in Paris, where he became President of the American Chamber of Commerce. He also became a close friend of the novelist Marcel Proust, and was known as a great lady's man: he was immensely tall, distinguished, cultivated and cold. In 1883 he met Edith Wharton for the first time during a summer at Bar Harbor, Maine; their relationship rapidly deepened, and by his own account (written to Edith Wharton in 1923) he contemplated proposing marriage, but dismissed the idea and left Bar Harbor. They scarcely met again until 1897 when they resumed their friendship. They were widely, but implausibly, supposed to have been lovers, although there was no doubt of their deep mutual attachment, which continued through the years when they both lived in France. He bequeathed to her his library and she was buried beside his grave in Versailles.

ANDREW CULWIN in Edith Wharton, 'The Eyes', *Tales of Men and Ghosts* (1910)

'[I]t has always been assumed that Andrew Culwin – unshakeably self-centered, cultivated but cold-spirited, witty but spiteful, and latently homosexual – was based on Walter Berry. Yet Edith, at the time of writing the tale, had seen next to nothing of Berry for two years, while he was . . . in Cairo' (R.W.B. Lewis, 1975, *Edith Wharton: a biography*, London: Constable, p. 288). *See also* **Fullerton**, W. Morton.

LAWRENCE SELDEN in Edith Wharton, *The House of Mirth* (1905)

'One knows all the people without being able to name one of them. Save I think Walter Berry is the hero' (Winthrop Chanler to his wife, Margaret Terry Chanler, quoted in Lewis, ibid., p. 153). *See also* **Gregory**, Eliot; **Winthrop**, Egerton.

BERTZ, Eduard (1853–1931) Born in Potsdam, he was educated at the Universities of Leipzig and Tübingen. He joined the German Socialist party, and in 1877 was arrested and obliged to flee to Paris. He moved to London in 1878 and became acquainted with Gissing as the result of inserting an advertisement in the personal column of a London newspaper, requesting an English gentleman, eager for scholarly companionship, to reply through the paper's offices; Bertz and Gissing became close friends. He emigrated to Rugby, Tennessee, in 1881 to join the community founded there by Thomas **Hughes**, but he returned to England in 1883 when the community went bankrupt, and returned to Germany in 1884. He was a freelance critic and essayist, and published studies of Theodor Storm and Walt **Whitman**.

JULIAN CASTI in George Gissing, *The Unclassed* (1884)

'[Gissing] used this episode in *The Unclassed* . . . in which Julian Casti . . . responds to Osmund Waymark's advertisement' (*Letters of George Gissing to Eduard Bertz, 1887–1903*, 1961, ed. Arthur C. Young, London: Constable, p. xx n. 2).

SCHMIDT in Morley Roberts, *The Private Life of Henry Maitland* (1912)

Identified in an 'Index of Recurring Pseudonyms' in the 1958 edition of *The Private Life of Henry Maitland*, ed. Morchard Bishop, p. 255. *See also* footnote to the novel, p. 101.

BESSBOROUGH, Lady (1761–1821) Daughter of the 1st Earl Spencer, she married the 3rd Earl Bessborough in 1780, becoming the Countess of Bessborough. She was the sister of Georgiana, Duchess of Devonshire (who was married to the 5th Duke of **Devonshire**), and the mother of Lady Caroline Lamb.

Lady Margaret Buchanan and Mrs Seymour in Lady Caroline Lamb, *Glenarvon* (1816)

Identified in a key found among the papers of John Whishaw, a member of the Holland House circle, printed in *The 'Pope' of Holland House: selections from the correspondence of John Whishaw and his friends, 1813–1840*, ed. Lady Seymour, 1906, p. 151. *See also* **Devonshire**, Elizabeth, Duchess of; **Kinnaird**, Maria; **Melbourne**, Lady.

BESSIE MILLIE The Stromness sibyl encountered by Scott during his voyage with the Scottish Lighthouse Commissioners in 1814. Scott describes her in his diary of the voyage, which is printed in J.G. Lockhart, 1900, *Memoirs of Sir Walter Scott*, Vol. II, London: Macmillan, pp. 397–8).

Norna of the Fitful Head in Sir Walter Scott, *The Pirate* (1821)

'Bessie herself was Norna's prototype, answering well to the picture of the hag in the novel' (W.S. Crockett, 1912, *The Scott Originals: an account of notables and worthies, the originals of characters in the Waverley Novels*, Edinburgh and London: T.N. Foulis, p. 303).

BESTE, C.W.L.

Mason in Rudyard Kipling, *Stalky & Co.* (1899)

Identified in the caption to a photograph reproduced in the June 1981 issue of *The Kipling Journal*: 'Masters at the United Services College . . . in Kipling's day' (*The Kipling Journal* 48 (218): 21).

BETJEMAN, Sir John (1906–84) English poet, broadcaster and architectural writer. Born in Highgate, London, he attended Marlborough School and Magdalen College, Oxford, which he left without taking his degree. After teaching cricket at a preparatory school, he began to write for the *Architectural Review* and then became the editor of the *Shell Guides* in 1934. He published his first volume of poetry, *Mount Zion*, in 1931. He married Penelope Chetwode (**Betjeman**, below) in 1933. He was appointed Poet Laureate in 1972.

Paul Fotheringay in Nancy Mitford, *Christmas Pudding* (1932)

'My new book [*Christmas Pudding*] is jolly good. . . . Betjeman is co-hero' (Nancy Mitford to Harold Acton, 4 December 1931, quoted in Harold Acton, 1975, *Nancy Mitford: a memoir*, London: Hamilton, p. 37).

BETJEMAN, Penelope (b. 1910) Daughter of Field Marshal Lord Chetwode, in 1933 she married John **Betjeman**. She was received into the Roman Catholic Church in 1948 and was a passionate horsewoman.

Saint Helena in Evelyn Waugh, *Helena* (1950)

'[Evelyn Waugh] told me and other friends that the character of Helena was modelled on her. I do not disbelieve this, but apart from the taste for horses the resemblance is not easy to detect' (Christopher Sykes, 1975, *Evelyn Waugh*, London: Collins, p. 330).

BEVAN, Charles Oliver Son of a Church of England parson, he was educated at King Edward's School, Birmingham, and was at Trinity Hall, Cambridge, from 1892 to 1895. He took Holy Orders, and from 1905 to 1930 he was Assistant Master at Eton. He and Aldous Huxley lived at The Old Christopher from 1917 to 1918 when Huxley was teaching at Eton.

REVD ROGER PETHERTON in Aldous Huxley, 'Happily Ever After' (1920)

'Bevan was depicted as the Rev. Roger Petherton' (*The Letters of Aldous Huxley*, 1969, ed. Grover Smith, p. 157 n. 140).

BEVAN, Robert Alexander Polhill (1901–74) Son of Robert Bevan, the painter, he was educated at Westminster and at Christ Church, Oxford. In 1923 he joined S.H. **Benson Ltd**, eventually becoming Chairman: he was the inventor of the slogan 'Guiness is good for you'. During the Second World War, he served in the Navy. He was the author of *Robert Bevan, 1865–1925* (1965), and of a *catalogue raisonné* of his father's works.

MR INGLEBY in Dorothy L. Sayers, *Murder Must Advertise* (1933)

'Asked about the characters in the book, Bevan once said to me . . . "Ingleby? – Well, I suppose Ingleby was me"' (R.D. Bloomfield, 1975, *The Times* (7 January): 14).

BIDDER, George Parker (1806–78) Engineer and mathematician. The son of a stonemason, as a boy he was exhibited about England by his father as the 'calculating phenomenon' and he was educated at Edinburgh University. In 1834 he was associate with Robert Stephenson in the London to Birmingham Railway and he was a founder of the Electric Telegraph Company in 1846. He designed the Victoria Docks, London, opened in 1856, and was the engineer of the Royal Danish railway, which was opened in 1855. Bidder was also the originator of the railway swing bridge, the first of which was erected at Reedham, in Norfolk.

GEORGE BITZER in Charles Dickens, *Hard Times* (1854)

'George Bitzer . . . is one of Dickens's most grotesque representations of selfish calculation. . . . Dickens may have been employing a cause célèbre among the phrenologists of the 1830s as a source for his calculating traits, and even his name. . . . The specific source appears have been George Parker Bidder . . . practically undisguised the minor name change' (David E.E. Sloane, 1974, 'Phrenology in *Hard Times*: a source for Bitzer', *Dickens Studies Newsletter* 5 (1): 9).

BIG MOOSE LAKE, New York Scene of the murder of Grace **Brown** by Chester **Gillette** in 1906.

BIG BITTERN in Theodore Dreiser, *An American Tragedy* (1925)

'Dreiser ... altered even the names and places of the case with reluctance ... from Big Moose Lake, where the real murder took place, to his own Big Bittern' (Ellen Moers, 1970, *Two Dreisers*, London: Thames & Hudson, p. 199; originally published 1969, New York: Viking).

BIGELOW, William Sturgis (1850–1926) Only child of Henry Jacob Bigelow, the well-known Boston surgeon, and Susan Sturgis, he was the first cousin of Marian **Adams**. In 1882, after a brief infatuation with Emily **Beale**, he settled in Japan and became a Buddhist. He formed an important collection of Japanese works of art, which he presented to the Boston Museum of Fine Arts.

MR WHARTON in Henry Adams, *Esther* (1884)

'Wharton's troubled career owed some of its features to ... William Sturgis Bigelow' (Ernest Samuels, 1958, *Henry Adams: the middle years*, Cambridge, Mass., p. 246). *See also* **La Farge**, John; **Saint-Gaudens**, Augustus.

BINET, George-Jules-Ernst (1865–1949) French painter. Born in Le Havre, he became the pupil of Cormon and of Raphaël **Collin** in Paris and exhibited in the Paris Salon between 1889 and 1939.

FOINET in W. Somerset Maugham, *Of Human Bondage* (1915)

'... can be identified with ... Binet' (D.W. Buchanan, 1936, *James Wilson Morrice*, Toronto, p. 71).

BINGHAM, Tom Herring (1877–92) He attempted to save Cicely **Barber** as she was drowning.

DR BRINDELL in D.H. Lawrence, *Women in Love* (1920)

'[T]he young Dr Brindell who in the novel dived after [Diana Crich] in an attempt to save her was actually the young son of Dr Bingham of Alfreton; like his prototype, he drowned when [Cicely Barber] seized him around the neck and pulled him under' (H.T. Moore, 1980, *The Priest of Love: a life of D.H. Lawrence*, rev. edn, Harmondsworth: Penguin, p. 54; originally published 1955 as *The Intelligent Heart: the story of D.H. Lawrence*, London: Heinemann).

BINNEY, Revd Thomas (1798–1874) Born in Newcastle on Tyne, from 1813 to 1820 he was apprenticed to a bookseller. He trained for the ministry at Wymondley College, Hertfordshire, and in 1823 ministered at the Old Meeting, Bedford. From 1829 to 1869 he was Pastor of the congregation at King's Weigh House, founding the Colonial Missionary Society in 1836. He was a noted preacher, and twice Chairman of the Congregational Union of England and Wales. In 1853 he published *Is It Possible to Make the Best of Both Worlds: a book for young men*, which sold at the rate of a hundred a day for many months.

THOMAS BRADSHAW in Mark Rutherford, *The Revolution in Tanner's Lane* (1887)

'... a tribute to Thomas Binney' (Valentine Cunningham, 1975, *Everywhere Spoken Against: dissent in the Victorian novel*, Oxford: Clarendon Press, p. 264).

CANON BURNEY in Eliza Tabor, *The Master of Marton* (1864) and *Diary of a Novelist* (1870)

'He is introduced as Canon Burney into the novels . . . by Eliza Tabor' (Frederic Boase, 1892, *Modern English Biography*, Vol. I, p. 281).

BIRD, William (b. 1889) Born in Buffalo, New York, and educated at Trinity College, Hartford, Connecticut, in 1919 he founded the Consolidated Press Association and in 1920 travelled to Paris as its European manager. He had had an interest in printing since childhood, and in Paris he acquired a hand press and started printing English books: the imprint was the Three Mountains Press. In spring 1922 he met Ernest Hemingway at the Genoa Economic Conference, and on his return to Paris, at his suggestion, saw Ezra **Pound**, who agreed to become Editor at the press. Later in the same year Hemingway introduced Bird to Robert **McAlmon** and the two joined forces to found the publishing house of Contact Editions, which remained active in Paris until 1926, when Bird sold his printing press to Nancy **Cunard**. In 1933 he became Chief Foreign Correspondent for the *New York Sun*. He went to live in Tangier in 1945.

JAKE BARNES in Ernest Hemingway, *The Sun Also Rises* (1926)

The second draft of the novel, later discarded on the advice of Scott Fitzgerald, opened with biographies of the principal characters. For Jake Barnes, Hemingway 'is evidently following rather closely the history of Bill Bird' (Carlos Baker, 1969, *Ernest Hemingway: a life story*, New York, p. 589 n. 'Jake Barnes's personal history'). Little of this detail remains in the final version, but Barnes's conversational style echoes Bird's, and his method of getting rid of unwanted visitors was the same (see Baker, ibid., p. 179). *See also* **Hemingway, Ernest**.

BIRKBECK SCHOOLS Founded in 1848 by William Ellis, the friend of the social reformer John Stuart Mill (1806–73), to educate the children of the poor to fulfil their economic function in an industrial society. For a description of their curriculum and method, see Henry Morley, 1852, 'Rational schools', *Household Words* (25 December).

GRADGRIND SCHOOL in Charles Dickens, *Hard Times* (1854)

'Were there such schools in which "the elements of Political Economy" were taught? . . . The answer is that Dickens was right . . . elementary schools of the Gradgrind variety *did* exist at this time' (Robin Gilmour, 1967, 'The Gradgrind School: political economy in the classroom', *Victorian Studies* 11 (2): 212).

BIRLING PLACE, Kent Located near West Malling, it is a Tudor building with later additions and was formerly the seat of the Nevill family (see Nikolaus Pevsner, 1976, *West Kent and the Weald* (*Buildings of England* series), Harmondsworth: Penguin, p. 172).

MANOR FARM, DINGLEY DELL, in Charles Dickens, *The Pickwick Papers* (1836–7)

Identified by S.J. Rust, 1928, 'The real Dingley Dell', *The Dickensian* 24 (June): 225 ff.). *See also* **Cob Tree Manor**.

BIRMINGHAM Native town of Joseph **Chamberlain**.

BIRCHESTER in W.H. Mallock, *The Old Order Changes* (1886)

'"Japhet Snapper" . . . [is] portrayed as taking cruel advantage of the "Birchester" (Birmingham) workers whose interests he pretends to uphold' (R.L. Wolff, 1977, *Gains and Losses: novels of faith and doubt in Victorian England*, London: John Murray, p. 490). *See also* **Arnold**, Matthew.

BIRSTALL, Yorkshire For more information, see Nikolaus Pevsner, 1970, *West Riding (Buildings of England* series), Harmondsworth: Penguin.

BRIARFIELD in Charlotte Brontë, *Shirley* (1849)

'Immediately upon the publication of [*Shirley*], Briarfield was identified by all acquainted with the district, as Birstall' (Herbert Wroot, 1906, *The Persons and Places of the Brontë Novels*, Bradford, p. 77).

BIRT, John Headmaster of King's School, Canterbury, from 1816 to 1832, he was a poor disciplinarian; he resigned, allegedly because his wife had deserted him.

DR STRONG in Charles Dickens, *David Copperfield* (1849–50)

'Dickens . . . grafted Dr Birt's domestic unhappiness on to the genial temperament of Mr Wallace, Dr Birt's successor' (K.R. Cramp, 1952, 'Dr Strong of Canterbury', *The Dickensian* 48 (June): 119). '[A] letter has recently been published, in which Dickens told the School's first historian that he had never even heard of Birt, so any resemblance must be "purely accidental"' (Philip Collins, 1963, *Dickens and Education*, London: Macmillan, p. 118). *See also* **Valpy**, Richard; **Wallace**, George.

BISHOP, John Peale (1892–1944) Contemporary of F. Scott Fitzgerald and Edmund Wilson, the novelist, at Princeton. From 1922 to 1933 he lived in France, and then returned to Massachusetts, USA. He published little work of his own.

THOMAS P. D'INVILLIERS in F. Scott Fitzgerald, *This Side of Paradise* (1920)

'I have had numerous comments from Princeton about putting J—— into the book as Thomas P. D'Invilliers' (to Frances Newman, 6 February 1921, reproduced in *The Letters of F. Scott Fitzgerald*, 1964, ed. Andrew Turnbull, London: Bodley Head, p. 469). A footnote identifies J—— as John Peale Bishop.

von BISMARCK, Otto Eduard Leopold, Prince Bismarck-Schönhausen, Duke of Laue (1815–98) Prusso-German statesman. After studying agriculture and law, he entered the Prussian parliament, where he became known as an ultra-royalist. He was Prussian member of the German diet of Frankfurt in 1851, Minister to St Petersburg in 1859 and to Paris in 1862. During the Franco-Prussian war (1870–1) he was the spokesman of Germany and dictated peace terms to France. He was made a prince and Chancellor of the new German Empire in 1871, and spent the years afterwards making it secure against outside aggressors. In 1879 he formed the Austro-German Treaty of Alliance. In 1890 he resigned the chancellorship because he disapproved of the policy of the Emperor William II, but they became reconciled in 1894.

COUNT FERROL in Benjamin Disraeli, *Endymion* (1880)

Identified in 'Key to *Endymion*', *Notes and Queries* 83 (24 October 1942): 263; identifications attributed to G.E. Buckle.

BLACK HALL, St Giles, Oxford The home of Harriet **Morrell**.

POYNTON in Henry James, *The Spoils of Poynton* (1897)

'Black Hall is the house used by Henry James in his "Spoils of Poynton"' (*Oxford Chronicle* (6 February 1925): 13; article describing the sale of the contents of the house following Mrs Morrell's death).

BLACKIE, Robert (1853–1937) Son of the owner of an engineering business in Liverpool, he moved to Essex *c.*1880 and bought considerable property in the district around Clacton-on-Sea. He married Elizabeth, daughter of Rowland **Rees** and aunt of Ivy Compton-Burnett; Elizabeth was a strong Methodist.

HERBERT BLACKWOOD in I. Compton-Burnett, *Dolores* (1911)

'The originals of both [Dr Cassell and Herbert Blackwood] may be easily identified among Ivy's own acquaintance. ... Ivy's family background provided her ... with the complex series of intermarriages between Blackwoods and Huttons' (Hilary Spurling, 1974, *Ivy When Young: the early life of I. Compton-Burnett, 1884–1919*, London: Gollancz, p. 170).

SIR GODFREY HASLAM in I. Compton-Burnett, *Men and Wives* (1931)

'He was known as "Squire" to his Compton Burnett nephews and nieces ... resembling at any rate in this respect Sir Godfrey Haslam ... who also came of dissenting stock, had inherited an industrial fortune ... [and] purchased a country house.... Like Sir Godfrey, Robert Blackie was fond of delivering long extempore prayers to his family in private' (Spurling, ibid., p. 73).

BLACKMORE, Edward (1799–1879) Solicitor. He was the junior partner in 1823 of Ellis and Blackmore, Gray's Inn, London, where Dickens was office boy from 1827 to 1828. In 1827 Blackmore was lodging with Dickens's great-aunt at 16 Berners Street, London. From 1841 to 1846 he was a partner with Bern and Senior in the Strand before moving in 1846 to a firm in Alresford, Hampshire. In 1928 he married Mary Lear.

MR TULKINGHORN in Charles Dickens, *Bleak House* (1852–3)

'Blackmore himself was thought by some who knew him to ... have exhibited some of the traits of Mr Tulkinghorn' (William J. Carlton, 1952, 'Mr Blackmore engages an office boy', *The Dickensian* 48 (September): 165; this article is based on a manuscript of reminiscences written by Mr Blackmore in 1870 for the publisher J.C. Hotten). Mr Tulkinghorn's chambers were at 58 Lincoln's Inn Fields, London, 'formerly a house of state ... let off in sets of chambers now'; it was the address of John **Forster**.

BLAINE, James Gillespie (1830–93) American statesman. He was a Member of Congress from 1863 to 1876 and became a senator in 1876 despite being charged with corruption as a result of the 'Mulligan letters' scandal. In 1880 he was Secretary of State under President Garfield, and in 1884 he ran as Republican presidential candidate; however, he was defeated by Grover

Cleveland. He was Secretary of State under President Harrison from 1889 to 1892. It was Blaine who as a young journalist in the 1850s first gave currency to the name Republican.

SILAS P. RATCLIFFE in Henry Adams, *Democracy* (1880)

'The portrait of . . . Blaine as Ratcliffe was the most easily recognized [of those in the novel]. . . . The physical description . . . fitted closely, especially the steely glint of the eyes. . . . But the thinly disguised political history made the identification certain' (Ernest Samuels, 1958, *Henry Adams: the middle years*, Cambridge, Mass., pp. 89, 90).

BLAIR, Eileen (1905–45) Née O'Shaughnessy. Educated at St Hugh's College, Oxford, she married Eric Blair (George **Orwell**) in 1936. During the Second World War she worked in the Public Relations Department of the Ministry of Food; Lettice Cooper also worked there at that time.

ANN DRAKE in Lettice Cooper, *Black Bethlehem* (1947)

'The character of Ann . . . is clearly based on Eileen' (Bernard Crick, 1981, *George Orwell: a life*, London: Secker & Warburg, p. 297; originally published 1980, London: Secker & Warburg).

BLAKE HALL, Mirfield, Yorkshire Near Huddersfield, it was the home of Joshua Ingham, the Elder, father of Joshua and Mary **Ingham**. The house was a centre for Methodist preachers at the time of Benjamin Ingham, the founder of the Inghamites.

WELLWOOD HOUSE in Anne Brontë, *Agnes Grey* (1847)

'[Anne Brontë's] experiences at Blake Hall are described in *Agnes Grey*' (Raleigh Trevelyan, 1972, *Princes Under the Volcano*, London: Macmillan, p. 45).

BLANCHE, Mademoiselle A teacher at the Pensionnat Héger. 'Mademoiselle Blanche's character is so false and so contemptible I can't force myself to associate with her' (Charlotte Brontë to Emily Brontë, 2 September 1843, quoted in Herbert Wroot, 1906, *The Persons and Places of the Brontë Novels*, Bradford, p. 194).

ZÉLIE DE ST PIERRE in Charlotte Brontë, *Villette* (1853)

'Mademoiselle St Pierre . . . doubtless found [her] prototype in Mademoiselle Blanche' (Wroot, ibid.).

BLANCO WHITE, Amber (1887–1981) Daughter of William Pember Reeves, who had been High Commissioner for New Zealand in London and was subsequently Director of the London School of Economics, she was educated at Girton College, Cambridge. After an affair with H.G. Wells, during which she had a daughter, she married George Rivers Blanco White.

ANN VERONICA STANLEY in H.G. Wells, *Ann Veronica* (1909)

'[W]e were lent a . . . house in Chipping Campden . . . owned by Mrs Amber Blanco White (who had been the original of Ann Veronica . . .)' (Beatrice, Lady Glenavy, 1964, *Today We Will Only Gossip*, London: Constable, p. 107; a photograph of Mrs Blanco White, taken in 1917, faces p. 160). *See also* **Wells, Catherine Amy.**

BLAND, Hubert (1856–1914) Founder member of the **Fabian Society.** He married Edith Nesbit, the writer of children's books, and *c.*1900 they lived at Dymchurch, not far from the Wellses at **Sandgate.** Himself a man of many amours, he accused Wells of the attempted seduction of one of his daughters.

PETER STANLEY in H.G. Wells, *Ann Veronica* (1909)

'In Mr Stanley, Ann Veronica's father, there are unmistakeable echoes of Hubert Bland' (Lovat Dickson, 1972, *H.G. Wells*, Harmondsworth: Penguin, p. 160).

BLAND-SUTTON, Sir John (1855–1936) Consulting surgeon at the Middlesex Hospital, London. He was a personal friend of Kipling.

SIR JAMES BELTON in Rudyard Kipling, 'The Tender Achilles' (1932)

'Under the pseudonym of Sir James Belton he drew a . . . word-portrait of him in "The Tender Achilles" which all surgeons who knew J.B.S. would instantly recognise' (Victor Bonney, 1947, 'The ephemeral, the passing and the recondite in the works of Rudyard Kipling', *The Kipling Journal* 14 (83): 7).

BLANDFORD FORUM, Dorset

SHOTTSFORD FORUM in Thomas Hardy, Wessex novels and tales (1871–95)

Identified on a map prepared by Thomas Hardy which hangs in the Dorset County Museum, Dorchester. *See under* **Abbotsbury.**

de BLAQUIERE, John, Baron (1732–1812) Son of a French emigrant, he was Secretary of Legation in France 1771–2, Chief Secretary in Ireland 1772–7, an MP in the Irish Parliament 1773–1800, and an MP in the United Kingdom Parliament 1801–3. He was created Baronet in 1784 and was raised to the Irish peerage at the time of the Union in 1800. He was very popular in Ireland and effected many improvements in Dublin. He remained in Ireland until his death.

SIR ULICK O'SHANE in Maria Edgeworth, *Ormond* (1817)

'The early sketches to *Ormond* describe Sir Ulick as resembling two men, Sir John de Blaquiere and "T.P." [Sir Thomas Pakenham]' (Marilyn Butler, 1972, *Maria Edgeworth*, Oxford, p. 249). *See also* **Pakenham,** Admiral Sir Thomas.

BLEAK HALL, St Albans, Hertfordshire As late as 1919 the house was in the countryside, but by 1953 it had been engulfed by the town and was surrounded by other houses. It stands in Catherine Street and Normandy Road, and is an early eighteenth-century house with five bays and two storeys (see Nikolaus Pevsner, 1977, *Hertfordshire* (*Buildings of England* series), Harmondsworth: Penguin, pp. 327–8).

BLEAK HOUSE in Charles Dickens, *Bleak House* (1852–3)

'Bleak Hall answers almost entirely to [the] details of description given by Dickens. It is on a hill, it is approached by a long drive . . . there are three gables in the roof; also the near proximity of an old brickfield. The farm at the back . . .

was owned at one time by a person named "Dickins". The village schoolmaster to-day is named "Dickens". Does it not seem that the novelist had some distant relatives here whom he visited, and during which visit . . . he gained an intimate knowledge of Bleak Hall?' (Revd H. Bodell Smith, 1919, 'Bleak Hall, Kensworth, Herts. Is it the original Dickens's "Bleak House"?', *The Dickensian* 15 (October): 198; the article was reprinted from *The Unitarian Monthly* (June 1919) and was illustrated by a photograph of the house). A later article in *The Dickensian* points out that until 1842 the house was used as a workhouse, and it was not named Bleak Hall until it was purchased for private residence in 1852. The name was subsequently changed to Old Hall; it did not revert to Bleak Hall until it was bought by the owner in 1919. The earliest mention of the house as Bleak Hall is subsequent to the publication of the earlier parts of Bleak House (see T.W. Tyrrell, 1920, 'Bleak House and its suggested prototypes', *The Dickensian* 16 (January): 40–1). *See also* **Great Nast Hyde**.

BLESSINGTON, Charles John Gardiner, Lord (1782–1829) First Earl of Blessington. In 1818 he married Marguerite Farmer (**Blessington**, below).

Lord Rosbrin in Lady Morgan, *Florence Macarthy* (1818)

'Sydney Morgan had caricatured him cruelly as "Lord Rosbrin" in . . . *Florence Macarthy* . . . representing him as stage-struck to the point of lunacy, always dressing up in flamboyant fancy costume, and with a mind like "a tablet, upon which memory – the genius of fools – made some traces" (Michael Sadleir, 1947, *Blessington–D'Orsay: a masquerade*, London: Constable, p. 44; originally published 1933, London: Constable).

Lord Sandyford in John Galt, *Sir Andrew Wylie* (1822)

'The second edition was inscribed to my amiable friend the Earl of Blessington, in consequence of a remark which his Lordship made to me when he was reading it; speaking of Lord Sandyford's character, he observed, that it must be very natural, for, in the same circumstances, he would have acted in a similar manner, and he seemed not to have the least idea that he was himself the model of the character' (John Galt, quoted in 'Illustrations, anecdotes and critical remarks', appended to *Sir Andrew Wylie*, 1841, Edinburgh and London: Blackwood, p. 462).

BLESSINGTON, Marguerite Gardner, Lady (1789–1849) Countess of Blessington. Writer. Born in County Tipperary, Ireland, in 1804 she married Captain Farmer; however, she left him after three months, and in 1817 he was killed in a drunken orgy. In 1818 she married Lord **Blessington**, and in 1822 they embarked on a tour of the European continent, accompanied by Count **D'Orsay** with whom she was thenceforward closely associated. In 1823 she met and fascinated **Byron** in Genoa. Lord Blessington died in Paris in 1829 and in 1831 Lady Blessington returned to England, becoming the centre of a circle of the most distinguished men of intellect of the day and supporting herself by writing. In March 1849 she was obliged by financial losses to leave England.

Lady Doubtful in Benjamin Disraeli, *Vivian Grey* (1826–7)

Identified in a key given in *The Star Chamber* (24 May 1826): p. 114; reprinted in *Vivian Grey*, 1904 (centenary edn), Vol. II, ed. Lucien Wolf, pp. 361–2. Lucien Wolf concludes that Disraeli was not responsible for the key.

CONSTANCE, COUNTESS OF ERPINGHAM in Bulwer Lytton, *Godolphin* (1833)

'[T]he reader might readily conceive that Constance and Godolphin are meant to be Lady Blessington and Count D'Orsay. . . . But although there are some resemblances, the comparison cannot be carried far' (M.W. Rosa, 1936, *The Silver-Fork School: novels of fashion preceding* Vanity Fair, New York, pp. 95–6). Byron told Countess Guiccioli that he was studying Lady Blessington as a model for Lady Adeline Amundeville in *Don Juan*, Cantos 13 and 14. Lord and Lady William Russell, however, felt that they were the originals of Lord Henry and his wife, and the resemblance irritated them and diverted their friends (see Georgiana Blakiston, 1972, *Lord William Russell and His Wife, 1815–1846*, London: John Murray, p. 181 n.).

BLOCK, Katharine S.

MISS CLIFF in I. Compton-Burnett, *Dolores* (1911)

Identified in a key given in the back of a copy of *Dolores*, signed 'H.M. Cam, 1912' in the front (Dr Helen Cam was a student at Holloway in Ivy Compton-Burnett's last two years there). The key was printed in Hilary Spurling, 1974, *Ivy When Young: the early life of I. Compton Burnett, 1884–1919*, London: Gollancz, App. II, p. 280.

BLOOM, Joseph Dublin dentist in the time of James Joyce's youth.

LEOPOLD BLOOM in James Joyce, *Ulysses* (1922)

'Bloom was the name of two or three families who lived in Dublin when Joyce was young. One Bloom . . . had been converted to Catholicism in order to marry a Catholic woman; they had . . . a son, Joseph . . . a dentist . . . renowned for his wit. Joyce deliberately confuses Joseph Bloom the dentist with Leopold in one chapter, and in another he lists as one of Leopold's old addresses 38 Lombard Street, which was actually Joseph Bloom's address' (Richard Ellmann, 1982, *James Joyce*, rev. edn, Oxford: Oxford University Press, p. 375). *See also* **Byrne**, John Francis; **Chance**, Charles; **Hunter**, Alfred H.; **Jackson**, Holbrook; **Joyce**, James; **Joyce**, John Stanislaus; **Mayer**, Teodoro; **Popper**, Leopoldo; **Schmitz**, Ettore.

BLUNDESTON, Suffolk A village three and a half miles north-west of Lowestoft.

BLUNDERSTONE in Charles Dickens, *David Copperfield* (1849–50)

'The original of Blunderstone was Blunderstone [sic]' (John Forster, 1928, *The Life of Charles Dickens*, ed. J.W.T. Ley, p. 542 n. 345). 'In the two letters in which [Dickens] mentions [Blundeston] he does not say or imply that he has ever been there' (Philip Collins, 1965, '*David Copperfield* and East Anglia', *The Dickensian* 61 (January): 48). Dickens himself said that he associated the East Anglian characters of *David Copperfield* with the very bones of Chatham. 'I went down into that part of the country on the Seventh of January last year, when I was meditating the story, and chose Blunderstone [sic] for the sound of its name' (to W.W.F. De Cerjat, 29 December 1849, reproduced in *Letters of Charles Dickens*, 1981, Vol. V, ed. Graham Storey and K.J. Fielding, Oxford: Oxford University Press, p. 682). 'Lowestoft I know, by walking over there from Yarmouth, when I went down on an exploring expedition, previous to Copperfield . . . I saw the name "Blunderstone" [sic] on a direction post between it and Yarmouth, and took it from the said direction-post for the book' (to the Hon. Mrs Richard Watson, 27 August 1853, reproduced in *Letters of Charles Dickens*, 1938, ed. Walter Dexter, Vol. II, p. 484).

BLUNT, Ellen Lloyd Key (1821–84) Born in Washington, DC, she was the daughter of Francis Scott Key, composer of 'The Star Spangled Banner'. In 1846 she married Simon Fraser Blunt of the United States Navy, but she was later widowed. She wrote a novel entitled *Bread*, and in 1861 she went to Paris, where she appeared in scenes from Shakespeare (in English) under the patronage of Théophile Gautier. She remained in Paris throughout the Commune, having abandoned the stage for Society.

MRS BLUNT in Joseph Conrad, *The Arrow of Gold* (1919)

'The four people whose actual names [Conrad] used in "the story dealing with facts" were Captain Blunt, Mrs Blunt, Dominic Cervoni and Monsieur Georges' (Jerry Allen, 1967, *The Sea Years of Joseph Conrad*, London: Methuen, p. 76; see Allen, ibid., ch. VII, *passim*.

BLUNT, Wilfrid Scawen (1840–1922) Born in Petworth, West Sussex, he was the cousin of George Wyndham. As a young man he joined the Diplomatic Service, and in 1863, *en poste* in Paris, he became the lover of 'Skittles' (Catherine **Walters**) to whom his first two volumes of verse were addressed. In 1869 he married **Byron**'s granddaughter, Lady Anne Noel, and retired from the Diplomatic Service. In 1873 they began their travels in Turkey, which led to his involvement in the politics of the Middle East. They subsequently explored Arabia together, and also travelled in Egypt and India; all that they saw reinforced Blunt's hatred of British Imperialism. In 1885 he found a cause nearer home and took up Irish Nationalism, which he passionately supported for the next twenty years, even serving a brief term of imprisonment. He was one of the **Souls**.

HENRY SCROPE in Richard Aldington, *All Men are Enemies* (1933)

'[T]he character . . . had been suggested by Wilfrid Blunt, whom I had met pre-1914 through Yeats and Ezra Pound' (Richard Aldington, 1954, *Pinorman*, p. 186). Traces of Blunt appear in Shaw's *Heartbreak House* in both Hector Hushabye and Captain Shotover.

BODENHEIM, Maxwell (1893–1954) Born in Mississippi, he moved to Chicago and then to Greenwich Village in New York, where he spent the rest of his life. He wrote Imagist verse, novels and plays (in one of which he collaborated with Ben **Hecht**). He became an alcoholic and, with his third wife, was murdered by the lunatic who was lodging with them.

JO BOSHERE in Ben Hecht, *A Jew in Love* (1930)

'Two of [Ben Hecht's] novels, *Count Bruga* and *A Jew in Love*, lampooned ... Maxwell Bodenheim' (Dorothy Parker, 1976, *The Portable Dorothy Parker*, Harmondsworth: Penguin, p. 539 n.).

COUNT BRUGA in Ben Hecht, *Count Bruga* (1926)

See above.

BODICHON, Barbara (1827–91) Illegitimate daughter of Benjamin Leigh-Smith, the radical MP who was a strong advocate of women's rights. In 1857 she married Dr Eugene Bodichon, who practised medicine in Algeria and worked for the abolition of slavery. She proposed the plan of and endowed Girton College, Cambridge, and from 1853 onwards was a close friend of George Eliot.

ROMOLA DE BARDI in George Eliot, *Romola* (1863)

'It was Marian [i.e. George Eliot] who revealed that Romola was based on Barbara Bodichon' (Marghanita Laski, 1973, *George Eliot and Her World*, London: Thames & Hudson, p. 82).

BODKIN, Michael 'Sonny' (d. 1903) A young man who, in 1903, courted Nora **Joyce** in Galway, even though he was dying of tuberculosis. When 'Nora resolved to go to Dublin ... [he] stole out of his sickroom, in spite of the rainy weather, to sing to her under an apple tree and bid her goodbye. He died soon after' (Richard Ellmann, 1982, *James Joyce*, rev. edn, Oxford: Oxford University Press, p. 243).

MICHAEL FUREY in James Joyce, 'The Dead', *Dubliners* (1914)

'[M]odel for Michael Furey' (ibid., p. 821, s.v. Bodkin).

de BOIGNE, Adèle, Comtesse (1781–1866) Born Adèle d'Osmond, she married the Comte de **Boigne**.

COMTESSE DE MONTERESSO in Joseph Conrad, *Suspense* (1925)

'Conrad retained for his heroine not only the christian name, Adèle, borne by the Comtesse de Boigne, but the circumstances of her life, her marriage, her father's life, their connection with Sir John Legard ... their temper and the fantastic career of her husband, Count de Boigne' (G. Jean-Aubry, 1925, 'The inner history of Conrad's *Suspense*', *Bookman's Journal* 13 (49): 7). Conrad's source was the *Memoirs of the Comtesse de Boigne*, almost certainly in the English translation published in 1907 (see Jocelyn Baines, 1967, *Joseph Conrad: a critical biography*, rev. edn, London: Weidenfeld & Nicolson, p. 492 n. 123; originally published 1960).

de BOIGNE, Benoit, Comte (1751–1830) Born in Chambéry, where his father was a furrier, he became a soldier of fortune. In 1780 he arrived in India and amassed a vast wealth in the service of Mahadji Sindhia. After this potentate's death he returned to Europe and married Adèle d'Osmond (de **Boigne**, above), but they separated soon after. He ended his days in solitude in a château outside Chambéry.

COUNT DE MONTERESSO in Joseph Conrad, *Suspense* (1925)

See under de **Boigne**, Comtesse.

BOLINGBROKE, Henry St John, Lord (1678–1751) 1st Viscount. Statesman. In 1714 he was dismissed from office upon the accession of George I; he was impeached and attainted, and fled to France, but returned to England in 1723 and became an opponent of Robert **Walpole**. At the end of his life he retired again to France. He was the author of *The Patriot King* (1738).

MR WENTWORTH in Robert Plumer Ward, *De Vere; or The Man of Independence* (1827)

'Wentworth was designed by Ward as a composite of Pitt, Canning and Bolingbroke: the anecdotes are Pitt's; the love of letters and conversation, Canning's; the remainder, Bolingbroke's' (M.W. Rosa, 1936, *The Silver-Fork School: novels of fashion preceding* Vanity Fair, New York, p. 68). *See also* **Canning**, George; **Pitt**, William; **Pitt**, William, the Younger.

BOLLAND, William Proctor (1816?–63) Son of Sir William Bolland, Baron of the Court of Exchequer, he was educated at Eton and became a barrister of the Inner Temple, London. '[A] big, heavy, handsome man of much peculiar humour' (Edmund Yates, 1884, *Edmund Yates: his recollections and experiences*, Vol. I, London: R. Bentley & Son, p. 238), he was a member of the Fielding Club founded in 1852 by Thackeray and others in Henrietta Street, Covent Garden, London.

FRED BAYHAM in W.M. Thackeray, *The Newcomes* (1854–5)

'He was the original of Fred Bayham' (ibid.).

WILLIAM BOWKER in Edmund Yates, *Land at Last* (1866)

'I ventured to reproduce him as William Bowker in *Land at Last*' (ibid.).

BOMPAS, Mr Serjeant (d. 1844) Serjeant-at-law in 1827, he originally practised at Bristol before moving to London and entering the Court of Common Pleas: his practice consisted largely of assault cases. 'He often repeats himself, but this is not an accidental thing . . . impenetrable indeed must be the heads of the jury, if he do not succeed in hammering into them the points to which he attaches the greatest importance. . . . In person he is tall and stoutly made. His countenance is of a sandy complexion' (James Grant, 1837, *The Bench and the Bar*, London, pp. 185–6). Grant was a gallery reporter, a colleague of Dickens's. He states that at the time of his writing, Bompas was less than 50 years old. When Bompas died leaving a family in straitened circumstances, the Bar Society settled a competence on them.

MR SERJEANT BUZFUZ in Charles Dickens, *The Pickwick Papers* (1836–7)

'Notoriously the [model] for . . . Buzfuz' (John Butt and Kathleen Tillotson, 1957, *Dickens at Work*, London: Methuen, p. 72). *See also* **Phillips**, Charles.

BOND, Mr

RICHARD PRATT in George Eliot, 'Janet's Repentance', *Scenes of Clerical Life* (1857–8)

See under **Anstruther**, Lady.

BOND, Sir Edward

(1844–1920) He achieved a double first at Oxford and was a Fellow of Queen's College. He had sufficient private means to lead a life of unpaid public service and was one the leaders of the Charity Organisation movement, as well a director of the East End Dwellings Company. From 1895 to 1906 he was Conservative MP for Nottingham. George Eliot knew Bond; he was for a time engaged to be married to Octavia Hill, whose sister Gertrude was the wife of G.H. **Lewes**'s son Charles. In the event, he never married.

DANIEL DERONDA in George Eliot, *Daniel Deronda* (1876)

'A fine figure of a man with handsome features, large soulful grey eyes, attractively set in dark pencilled brows and long silken lashes, he alternated cultured comments with thrilling silences; and was the beloved of the philanthropic set. Indeed, it was said that George Eliot had him in mind in the characterisation of the most romantic of her heroes' (Beatrice Webb, 1929, *My Apprenticeship*, p. 227 n.). *See also* **Goldsmid**, Colonel Albert; **Gurney**, Edmund; **Lewes**, G.H.; **Louis**, Alfred Hyman.

BOODLES CLUB, London

TURTLES CLUB in Evelyn Waugh, the *Sword of Honour* trilogy (1952–61)

'. . . Boodles – the bow-windowed St James's club, accorded in *Officers and Gentlemen* the . . . *alias* of "Turtles"' (Oliver Knox, 1968–9, 'A desperate conversation with Evelyn Waugh', *Cornhill Magazine* 177: 181).

BOOKSTAVER, May

She was a protégé of Mabel **Haynes**. In 1900–1 Gertrude Stein met her at Miss Haynes's flat in Baltimore and, it would appear, had an affair with her. Gertrude Stein's letters to Miss Bookstaver have not survived, and in 1932, when the manuscript of *Q.E.D.* was discovered, Alice B. Toklas, in a rage, tore up all Miss Bookstaver's letters to Gertrude Stein. In 1907, Miss Bookstaver arranged the publication of *Three Lives* by the Grafton Press of New York: the book included the story 'Melanctha'.

MELANCTHA HERBERT in Gertrude Stein, 'Melanctha', *Three Lives* (1909)

'Gertrude's interest in her two Negro characters is in . . . their love affair, which re-enacts, in heterosexual terms, the Lesbian affair between Adele and Helen in *Q.E.D.*. . . . Melanctha . . . is a more complex and carefully realised version of Helen' (James R. Mellow, 1974, *The Charmed Circle: Gertrude Stein and company*, London: Phaidon Press, p. 73). 'In April, 1908, Mabel [Weeks] reported to Gertrude that "May doesn't in the least recognize herself in Melanctha, though she says that all those talks between Jeff and Melanctha are practically verbatim"' (ibid., p. 127).

HELEN THOMAS in Gertrude Stein, *Things As They Are* (1950)

'In the book [written in 1903 as *Q.E.D.*] May [Bookstaver] became Helen Thomas. . . . From Miss Toklas [Dr Leon Katz] learnt that in the writing of the book Gertrude had literally transcribed passages from the correspondence to create portions of the book's dialogue' (ibid., p. 59).

BOOTH, Sir Felix (1775–1850) Baronet. He headed the distillers Booth Co. and provided funds for Captain Ross's voyage of discovery in north-east America in 1828.

Mr Juggins in Benjamin Disraeli, *Coningsby* (1844)

'A distiller, £2000 man; but would not agree to any annual subscriptions' (*Notes and Queries* (8th series) 3 (13 May 1893): 363). The identification apparently rests on the word 'distiller'.

BOOTH, General William (1829–1912) Founder of the Salvation Army. In 1865 he started the Christian Mission in Whitechapel, London; the title of Salvation Army was adopted for it in 1878.

The Panjandrum of Philanthropy in Arthur Morrison, *A Child of the Jago* (1896)

'The "Panjandrum of philanthropy, a mummer of the market place" i.e. General William Booth of the Salvation Army' (P.J. Keating, 1969, biog. study prefaced to *A Child of the Jago*, London: MacGibbon & Kee, p. 31).

BOOTT, Francis (1813–1904) American amateur composer, particularly of songs. Born in Boston, he was long a resident in Italy at the Villa Castellani on Bellosguardo, outside Florence. He was the father of Elizabeth **Duveneck;** after her death he returned with her husband and child to Boston.

Gilbert Osmond in Henry James, *The Portrait of a Lady* (1880)

'A not other than lonely and bereft American, addicted to the arts and endowed for them, housed to an effect of long expatriation in a massive old Florentine villa with a treasured and tended little daughter by his side, *that* was the germ which . . . the case of Frank Boott had been appointed to plant deep down in my vision of things. . . . Then at last after years it raised its own head into the air and found its full use for the imagination. An Italianate bereft American with a little moulded daughter in the setting of a massive old Tuscan residence was at the end of years exactly what was required by a situation of my own – conceived in the light of the Novel; and I *had* it there, in the authenticated way . . . at once all the more because my admirable old friend had given it to me and none the less because he had no single note of character or temper, not a grain of the non-essential, in common with my Gilbert Osmund' (Henry James, 1914, *Notes of a Son and Brother*, New York, pp. 481–2).

BORGATTI, Renata Pianist. Daughter of Giuseppe Borgatti, the Italian Wagnerian tenor.

Cléo Gazay in Compton Mackenzie, *Extraordinary Women* (1928)

'I painted her portrait as Cléo Gazay in *Extraordinary Women*' (Compton Mackenzie, 1966, *My Life and Times, Octave 5, 1915–1923*, p. 152).

BORN, Charles (b. 1855) First mate of the *Otago*, Conrad's first command, on her voyage from Bangkok to Sydney in 1888.

MR BURNS in Joseph Conrad, *The Shadow-Line* (1917)

'In *The Shadow Line* [Conrad] gave the first mate, drawn from life, the name Burns, but the man's real name, Born, slipped once [in fact twice] into the manuscript' (J.D. Gordan, 1941, *Joseph Conrad: the making of a novelist*, Cambridge, Mass., p. 37).

BORTHWICK, Peter (1804–52) Educated at Edinburgh University, he was MP for Evesham in 1835–47, and was opposed to the abolition of slavery. In 1850–2 he was Editor of the *Morning Post*.

BOOTS AT CHRISTOPHERS HOTEL in Benjamin Disraeli, *Coningsby* (1844)

Identified in a key in *Notes and Queries* (8th series) 3 (13 May 1893): 363. 'Boots' is precisely what he sounds – the boot boy at Christophers, the inn at Eton. '[T]here were many members of Young England not included in "Coningsby" – Mr Peter Borthwick (etc.)' (Lord Lamington, 1890, *In the Days of the Dandies*, Edinburgh and London: Blackwood, pp. 89–90). *See also under* **Bright**, John.

BOSCASTLE, Cornwall A small town on the coast, two miles from St Juliot.

CASTLE BOTEREL in Thomas Hardy, *A Pair of Blue Eyes* (1873)

Identified in F.B. Pinion, 1968, *A Hardy Companion*, London: Macmillan.

BOSS, Mrs Servant to Reginald Worsley, Samuel Butler's first cousin.

MRS JUPP in Samuel Butler, *The Way of All Flesh* (1903)

'Boss . . . was the original of Mrs Jupp' (H. Festing Jones, 1919, *Samuel Butler, Author of* Erewhon, 2 vols, London: Macmillan, p. 392).

BOURCHIER, James David (1850–1920) A correspondent in the Balkan peninsula for *The Times*, his headquarters were first in Athens and subsequently in Sofia (1892–1918). 'Another master who was mercilessly ragged was Mr Bourchier, who was deaf, and afterwards a famous *Times* correspondent at Sofia – a man who could do what he liked with the Bulgars, but who could not manage a division of Eton boys. The boys took mice into his schoolroom, and ultimately he had to go away' (Maurice Baring, 1922, *The Puppet Show of Memory*, London: Heinemann, p. 104).

STANISLAUS RICHARD DUCROS in Maurice Baring, *Friday's Business* (1932)

'Baring's novel is founded on the story of J.D. Bourchier' (Anthony Powell, 1978, *To Keep the Ball Rolling: the memoirs of Anthony Powell*, Vol. II: *Messengers of Day*, London: Heinemann, p. 185).

BOURDIN, Martial (1867–94) French journeyman tailor who was carrying the bomb whose explosion constituted the **Greenwich Bomb Outrage**; he died of his injuries. His brother-in-law, H.B. Samuels, was the Editor of the Anarchist journal *Commonweal* and wrote an enthusiastic obituary for *Commonweal* (10 March 1894).

AUGUSTIN MYERS in Isabel Meredith, *A Girl Among the Anarchists* (1903)

'[The novel] gave . . . a thinly disguised account of the Greenwich explosion. The account is very close to Nicoll's [in his pamphlet *The Greenwich Mystery*] as regards . . . the supplying of sulphuric acid to Bourdin (called Augustin Myers) by Samuels' (Ian Watt (ed.), 1973, 'The political and social background of *The Secret Agent*', in *The Secret Agent: a casebook*, London: Macmillan, p. 236). For further information about Nicoll's pamphlet, see note under **Samuels**, H.B.

STEVIE in Joseph Conrad, *The Secret Agent* (1907)

Anderson describes how Bourdin, Stevie's counterpart, escaped surveillance at the crucial moment: 'I never spent hours of greater anxiety than during one afternoon in February, 1894, when information reached me that . . . Bourdin had left his shop in Soho with a bomb in his pocket. . . . His . . . objective was the very last place the police would have thought of watching, namely Greenwich Observatory' (Sir Robert Anderson, 1910, *The Lighter Side of My Official Life*, London: Hodder & Stoughton, pp. 175–6).

BOURGET, Paul (1852–1935) French novelist and man of letters. He spent some time in England in 1884.

MONSIEUR FAUBOURG in Maurice Baring, 'A Luncheon Party', *Half a Minute's Silence and Other Stories* (1925)

'Most of the guests were people well known in London . . . all, of course, furnished with pseudonyms and so presented that though they were easy to identify no one can have been hurt' (Ethel Smyth, 1938, *Maurice Baring*, London and Toronto: Heinemann, p. 136).

BOURNE, Frances (d. 1913) Younger sister of Arnold Bennett's mother, she was the daughter of Robert Longson, a weaver of Glossop who in 1860 opened a tailor's shop (**Longson's**) in St John's Square, Burslem; Frances worked there, and Bennett described her as being one of the most powerful, attractive and formidable characters he had ever encountered.

MRS CLARA HAMPS in Arnold Bennett, the *Clayhanger* trilogy (1910–16)

'The younger girl married . . . Ezra Bourne and became Auntie Bourne in Arnold Bennett's life and Mrs Hamps in his novels' (Reginald Pound, 1952, *Arnold Bennett: a biography*, London: Heinemann, p. 49). *See also* **Bennett**, Sarah.

BOURNEMOUTH, Dorset Seaside resort on the Dorset–Hampshire border.

SANDBOURNE in Thomas Hardy, Wessex novels and tales (1871–95)

Identified on a map prepared by Thomas Hardy which hangs in the Dorset County Museum, Dorchester. *See under* **Abbotsbury**.

BOWEN, Stella (1893–1947) Born and brought up in Adelaide, Australia, she moved to England in 1914 and studied painting under Walter **Sickert**. In 1918 Ford Madox **Ford** was introduced to her by Ezra **Pound**, and they became lovers. They had a daughter two years later, and in 1922 they moved to Paris. Their liaison ended in 1928. She returned to England with her daughter in 1932, and from then on supported herself by painting portraits. A Frenchwoman who knew her in Paris in the 1920s described her as 'L'être le moins égoiste que j'ai connu.'

MRS BRADDOCKS in Ernest Hemingway, *The Sun Also Rises* (1926)

'A few [on the Left Bank] in Paris, saw that Braddocks and his wife were based on . . . Ford and Stella Bowen' (Carlos Baker, 1969, *Ernest Hemingway: a life story*, New York, p. 179).

LOIS HEIDLER in Jean Rhys, *Postures* (1928)

'How literal Jean Rhys's representation of Stella is is indicated by the fact that in *Postures* . . . Lois says of Marya, "It's appalling . . . to think of the difference money makes to a woman's life . . ." and in *Drawn from Life* . . . Stella says of Jean, "[knowing her] taught me that the only really unbridgeable gulf in human society is between the financially solvent and the destitute . . ."' (Arthur Mizener, 1971, *The Saddest Story: a biography of Ford Madox Ford*, London: Bodley Head, p. 583 n. 13; originally published 1971, Cleveland: World Publishing). Stella Bowen had certainly read the novel; in 1924 Ford and she had invited Jean Rhys to live with them, an arrangement which had led to her affair with Ford.

BOWEN'S COURT, Kildorsey, County Cork, Ireland 'A stone house which only Bowens had lived in since its completion in 1775. Elizabeth [Bowen] inherited it from her father in 1930. She sold it in 1959, and the new owner pulled it down' (*The Letters of Virginia Woolf, 1932–35*, 1979, ed. Nigel Nicolson, Vol. V, London: Hogarth Press, p. 298, n. 1).

DANIELSTOWN in Elizabeth Bowen, *The Last September* (1929)

'Danielstown . . . is Bowen's Court' (ibid., p. 304 n. 3).

BOWER, Tony An American who was a friend of Cyril and Jean **Connolly** and was with them in Paris in 1937 when he met Isherwood.

RONNY in Christopher Isherwood, *Down There on a Visit* (1962)

'Tony [was] later to appear, affectionately caricatured as . . . "Ronny", in *Down There on a Visit*' (Christopher Isherwood, 1977, *Christopher and His Kind*, London: Eyre Methuen, p. 202).

BOWES, John (1811–85) Of Streatlam Castle. Son of John, 10th Earl of Strathmore, he was MP for South Durham in 1832–47. He won the Derby three times and the Two Thousand Guineas twice; in 1853 he won the Two Thousand Guineas, the Derby and the St Leger.

FRANCIS BRITTON in W.M. Thackeray, 'Notes on the North What-d'ye-Callem Election' (1841)

Identified in *Letters and Private Papers of W.M. Thackeray*, 1945, ed. Gordon N. Ray, Vol. II, London: Oxford University Press, p. 27 n. 49.

BOWKETT, Sidney (1866–1936) Playwright. Born in Presteigne, he was the son of a draper; the family later moved to Bromley in London. From 1873 onwards he was a contemporary and close friend of H.G. Wells at the Bromley Academy, and in the late nineteenth and early twentieth century had some success with light plays. He died in Southwark, London.

HARRY CHITTERLOW in H.G. Wells, *Kipps* (1905)

'[Wells] loitered a good deal around . . . Bromley . . . sometimes with . . . Sidney Bowkett, who later . . . provided Wells with the model for Chitterlow' (N. Mackenzie and J. Mackenzie, 1973, *The Time Traveller: the life of H.G. Wells*, p. 21).

BOWRA, Maurice (1898–1971) Scholar, critic, and wit. Educated in Cheltenham and at New College, Oxford, he was Warden of Wadham College from 1938 to 1970. He was perhaps the most influential figure in the Oxford of his day, and almost every writer who passed through the university from the 1920s until his death owed him some debt. He was of wide scholarship, a brilliant administrator, of steady principle, a radical in politics, a free-thinker in religion, and wielded a coruscating and sometimes profound wit.

MR SAMGRASS in Evelyn Waugh, *Brideshead Revisited* (1945)

'Contrary to his usual custom, Evelyn was annoyed when his friends did not recognise the material whence he contrived the portrait. Samgrass is Maurice Bowra. . . . "I hope", [Bowra] would [say] . . . "you spotted *me*. What a piece of artistry that is – best thing in the whole book"' (Christopher Sykes, 1975, *Evelyn Waugh*, London: Collins, p. 254). Bowra's comment on *Sword of Honour* was 'A Waugh to end Waugh'.

BOWRING, Sir John (1792–1872) British diplomat. Initially a clerk in a London mercantile house in 1811, he became the first Editor of the *Westminster Review* in 1924 (James **Mill** refused the job). In 1833–7 he was sent by the government on a commercial mission to Belgium and the Near East. In 1835–7 he was MP for Clyde boroughs, and in 1838 he was a founding member of the Anti-Corn Law League. In 1841 he was MP for Bolton, Manchester, and in 1847 he was Consul at Canton. In 1854 he became pleni-potentiary to China and Governor of Hong Kong, and in 1855 he established commercial and diplomatic relations with Siam; he returned to England in 1860. He edited and wrote the introductory memoir (described by Leslie **Stephen** as 'the worst biography in the language') to the works of Bentham, of whom he was a close friend. He was a Fellow of the Royal Society.

THE OLD RADICAL in George Borrow, *The Romany Rye* (1857)

'One of the most puzzling problems [in the career of George Borrow] has always been his intense hatred for Sir John Bowring, "The Old Radical", of *The Romany Rye*' (G.F. Bartle, 1963, 'George Borrow's "Old Radical"', *Notes and Queries* 208: 242; this article discusses the relations between Borrow and Sir John Bowring at length).

BOYD, Ernest (1887–1946) Irish-born literary critic. In 1913 he went to the United States with the British Consular Service, and in 1920 returned there as a resident. In 1928 his French wife, Madeleine, became Thomas Wolfe's literary agent, selling *Look Homeward, Angel* to Charles Scribner & Son in 1929.

SEAMUS MALONE in Thomas Wolfe, *The Web and the Rock* (1939)

'Wolfe later satirized Boyd as Seamus Malone' (*The Notebooks of Thomas Wolfe*, 1970, ed. Richard S. Kennedy and Paschal Reeves, Vol. I, Chapel Hill, NC: University of North Carolina Press, p. 287).

BOYLAN, Blazes

HUGH ('BLAZES') BOYLAN in James Joyce, *Ulysses* (1922)

'Boylan's father was a horse dealer. . . . Boylan is a flashy dresser and has just managed a prize fighter. . . . There was [in Dublin] . . . a horse dealer during the 'nineties who bore the name Boylan, and had Blazes or Blazer for a nickname. Joyce took his name, and perhaps borrowed the occupation and appearance of the character from another man named Ted Keogh' (Richard Ellmann, 1982, *James Joyce*, rev. edn, Oxford: Oxford University Press, p. 378). *See also* **Kennedy**, Hugh Boyle; **Keogh**, Ted.

BRABANT, Robert Henry (1781?–1866) Physician. Practising in Edinburgh in 1821, Thomas **Moore** and S.T. **Coleridge** were among his patients. His daughter Elizabeth Rebecca ('Rufa') in 1843 married Charles Hennel, author of *Inquiry Concerning the Origins of Christianity* (1838) and brother of Cara Bray of Rosehill, Coventry, who was George Eliot's close friend. George Eliot met Brabant through the Brays and paid a prolonged visit to his house at Devizes in November 1843; the visit ended, according to John **Chapman**, in Mrs Brabant saying that 'she should never enter the house again, or if she did she, Mrs Brabant, would instantly leave it' (see Gordon S. Haight, 1968, *George Eliot*, Oxford, p. 50).

EDWARD CASAUBON in George Eliot, *Middlemarch* (1871–2)

'Eliza Lynn, who visited Dr Brabant in 1847 under much the same circumstances, was convinced that he was the original of Mr Casaubon. . . . She describes him as "a learned man who used up his energies in thought and desire to do, rather than in actual doing, and whose fastidiousness made his work something like Penelope's web. Ever writing and re-writing, correcting and destroying, he never got farther than the introductory chapter of a book which he intended to be epoch-making, and the final destroyer of superstition and theological dogma [Eliza Lynn Linton, 1899, *My Literary Life*, London: Hodder & Stoughton, p. 43]' (ibid., pp. 50–1). See Richard Ellmann, 1973, 'Dorothea's husbands', in *Golden Codgers*, London: Oxford University Press, pp. 20–1, for arguments against this identification. *See also* **Bryant**, Jacob; **Eliot**, George; **Mackay**, R.W.; **Pattison**, Mark; **Spencer**, H.

BRACEBRIDGE, Charles Holt (1799–1872) Of Atherstone Hall, Warwickshire. In April 1859 he wrote to Blackwood (George Eliot's publisher) in connection with the claim of Joseph Liggins that he was the author of *Adam Bede*; Blackwood's denials left him unmoved.

MR BROOKE in George Eliot, *Middlemarch* (1871–2)

'It is tempting to believe that some of his traits are glanced at in the character of Mr Brooke' (*The George Eliot Letters*, 1954, ed. Gordon S. Haight, Vol. III, London: Oxford University Press, p. 53 n. 3).

BRACKEN, Brendan (1901–58) Born in Ireland, he was shipped off to Australia in 1916 and educated in Sydney. In 1919 he returned to England and financed himself for two terms at Sedbergh School, then made his way into journalism and publishing. By 1925 he was a director of Eyre & Spottiswoode and knew Winston **Churchill**, who remained his lifelong patron and friend. In 1940 he was appointed Churchill's Parliamentary Private Secretary, and in 1941 he became Minister of Information. In 1945 he served as First Lord of the Admiralty and was MP for the safe Tory seat of Bournemouth; he was raised to the peerage in 1952. Bracken's origins were wrapped in a mystery that he did nothing to dispel, actively encouraging, it is said, the rumour that he was Churchill's illegitimate son. There were those who found his charm irresistible, and those, like Waugh, to whom he represented all that was most false and detestable in the world of his day.

REX MOTTRAM in Evelyn Waugh, *Brideshead Revisited* (1945)

'He is closely modelled on Brendan Bracken. Evelyn frequently denied this, but I once cornered him, telling him that he had rather spoilt the portrait by giving Mottram black hair instead of Brendan's red hair. ... He capitulated and admitted that Mottram was indeed Bracken' (Christopher Sykes, 1975, *Evelyn Waugh*, London: Collins, p. 252). Sykes goes on to point out that without Bracken's support Waugh would not have obtained the three months' leave of absence from active service that enabled him to write the novel. His denial may have been prompted by feelings of guilt.

BRADDOCK, Frances (d. 1731 or 1739)

CHLOE MARTINWARD in George Meredith, *A Tale of Chloe* (1879)

'Chloe's real-life original was a Miss Fanny Braddock, sister of the General Braddock best known for his American disaster' (Carl H. Ketcham, 1966, 'Meredith at work: "The Tale of Chloe"', *The Nineteenth Century* 21 (3): 236).

BRADDON, Mary Elizabeth (1837–1915) Writer of 'sensation' novels, of which the most famous was *Lady Audley's Secret* (1862). She married John Maxwell, her publisher, in 1874, and was a first cousin of John Delane, Editor of *The Times*.

JANE HIGHMORE in Henry James, 'The Next Time' (1898)

'The successful sister (Mrs Highmore) . . . is fearfully ugly. She marries perhaps a publisher, or (if that is too like Miss Braddon), a man of business who makes bargains for her' (entry for 4 June 1895, in *The Notebooks of Henry James*, 1947, ed. F.O. Matthiessen and K.B. Murdock, New York, p. 202). 'One of the characters was to be drawn from Miss Braddon as the story was first contemplated but one gathers from the above book that she got crowded out in the end' (private letter from Mr Henry Maxwell to Mr John Sandoe, 24 August 1971; Mr Maxwell is Miss Braddon's grandson). Professor Kathleen Tillotson described the portrait as instantly recognizable. (In appearance as in spouse,

Mrs Highmore is clearly more Braddon than Ward.) *See also* **Ward**, Mrs Humphry.

BRADENHAM, Buckinghamshire The country house of Isaac **D'Israeli**.

Hurstley in Benjamin Disraeli, *Endymion* (1880)

'Endymion Ferrars . . . is the son of a financially ruined Tory politician manqué forced to retire to a remote country house, Hurstley (clearly Bradenham)' (Robert Blake, 1966, *Disraeli*, London: Eyre & Spottiswoode, p. 736).

BRADFORD, George Partridge (1807–90) Classical scholar. He was a member of **Brook Farm**. 'He is so afraid of infringing upon somebody else's will, that he becomes exceedingly troublesome by . . . his very anxiety not to give trouble' (Nathaniel Hawthorne, 1941, *English Notebooks*, ed. Randall Stewart, New York and London: Modern Languages Association of America, p. 16).

Mr Colcord in Nathaniel Hawthorne, *Dr Grimshawe's Secret* (1883)

'Hawthorne appears to have had Bradford in mind in his characterization of Colcord' (ibid., p. 631 n. 102). There is an extended sketch of Bradford on a visit to the Hawthornes in Liverpool in 1854 in the *English Notebooks*, ibid., pp. 75–7. *See also* **Alcott**, Bronson.

BRADFORD, Selina Louise Bridgeman, Countess of (1819–94) Daughter of the 1st Lord Forester and granddaughter of the 3rd Duke of Rutland, she married the 7th Earl of Bradford in 1844. She inherited the Manners good looks and was a noted beauty of her day. Disraeli met her and her elder sister Anne (Lady Chesterfield) in the 1830s and was on friendly terms with both throughout his married life; in the summer of 1873, some months after the death of his wife, the friendship took a new turn and his feelings for Lady Bradford became deeply romantic. He embarked on a correspondence, which ended only a month before his death, writing sometimes daily, or seeing her, in London, two or three times a week. There are indications that at first Lady Bradford found his attentions irksome, but by the end of his life she clearly both accepted and returned his affection.

Lady Montfort in Benjamin Disraeli, *Endymion* (1880)

'I think there are features of Lady Palmerston in her youth in . . . [Lady Mountfort], and some traits of devotion drawn from some-one else' (Lord Beaconsfield to Queen Victoria, reproduced in *The Letters of Queen Victoria*, 1928 (2nd series), ed. G.E. Buckle, Vol. III, London: John Murray, p. 195; the editor's footnote reads: 'Presumably Lady Bradford'). *See also* **Norton**, Caroline; **Palmerston**, Lady.

BRADLAUGH, Charles (1833–91) A free-thinker and politician, he began life as a private soldier in the army, but in 1853 became a clerk in a solicitor's office in London. Shortly afterwards he embarked on propaganda for free thought and political reform, and in 1880 he was elected MP for Northampton but was unable to take his seat, being refused the right to affirm instead of swearing on the Bible. He was re-elected three times before he was finally, when re-elected in 1885, allowed to take his seat in 1886; he represented Northampton until his death. From 1874 to 1885 he was closely associated with the theosophist Annie Besant in her campaign for birth-control.

LUKE RAEBURN in Edna Lyall, *Donovan* (1882) and *We Two* (1884)

'[T]he Queen wishes to know if the character and life of Raeburn are not taken from some real atheist orator and leader. The Queen thought the Dean might know' (Queen Victoria to Randall Davidson, then Dean of Windsor, 18 May 1887, reproduced in G.K.A. Bell, 1935, *Randall Davidson, Archbishop of Canterbury*, London: Oxford University Press, p. 90). The Dean could not tell her. 'I do not intend Raeburn for Bradlaugh; none of the characters are meant for photograph of living people, but I know Mr Bradlaugh personally, and quite admit that the history of Raeburn's persecutions and even the broad outlines of the character were to a great degree suggested to me by the study of his life. The Secularists consider Raeburn to be a life-like portrait of their leader; to my mind he is what Mr Bradlaugh might have been had the circumstances of his life been less hard' (Ed Lyall to Buxton Moorish, 25 February 1886, reproduced in J.M. Escreet, 1904, *The Life of Edna Lyall*, London: Longman, p. 62).

BRADLEY, Francis Herbert (1846–1924) Philosopher. He was a fellow of Merton College, Oxford, and a follower of the German philosopher Hegel. In 1910 he met Elinor Glyn while wintering at St Raphael, in the south of France, and they struck up a friendship that lasted to the end of her life. They exchanged signed copies of their works, and sat side by side, he reading *His Hour* (he had already read *Three Weeks*) and she reading *Appearance and Reality*. Later he read *Halcyone* in manuscript, correcting the spelling as he read.

ARNOLD CARLYON in Elinor Glyn, *Halcyone* (1912)

'Cheiron (Arnold Carlyon), the professor, was a loving portrait of Bradley' (Anthony Glyn, 1968, *Elinor Glyn: a biography*, rev. edn., London: Hutchinson, p. 205; originally published 1955, London: Hutchinson).

BRADLEY, Revd James Chesterton (1818?–1913) Graduating BA from Oxford in 1841, he was Perpetual Curate at Oakden near Haworth in 1845, Curate of All Saints, Paddington, in 1847–55, Curate of Corfe Castle, Dorset, in 1856–62, and Rector of Sutton under Brailes, Warwickshire, in 1863–1903.

DAVID SWEETING in Charlotte Brontë, *Shirley* (1849)

'Mr Bradley takes pleasure in the fact that he was drawn as Mr Sweeting, and in an interview . . . which appeared in the *Dewsbury Reporter*, Dec. 12th and 19th, 1896, [he] stated that he was in the Oakworth days a player of the flute, and the fact that Mr Sweeting was said to perform on that instrument fastened the character of Sweeting on him' (Herbert Wroot, 1906, *The Persons and Places of the Brontë Novels*, Bradford, p. 129).

BRAGGIOTTI, Mario (b. 1908?) Composer, pianist and conductor. An American born in Italy, as a young musician in 1926 he stayed on the Riviera with Gerald and Sara **Murphy** and fell mildly in love with Zelda **Fitzgerald**.

TOMMY BARBAN in F. Scott Fitzgerald, *Tender is the Night* (1934)

'Oddly enough, the character of Tommy, or rather some of the mannerisms of Tommy, were taken from Mario Braggiotti, the brother of Stiano. It would be a delightful coincidence if Stiano played the part [in a dramatized version of the novel]' (to Mrs Mary Leonard Pritchett, 4 March 1938, reproduced in *The Letters of F. Scott Fitzgerald*, 1964, ed. Andrew Turnbull, London: Bodley Head, p. 570). *See also* **Hitchcock**, Thomas; **Jozan**, Edouard.

BRANDOLINI, Contessa Cristiana Née Agnelli, of the great industrial family of Turin, she married Count Brandolino Brandolini in 1947 and was a close friend of Nancy Mitford.

Northey Mackintosh in Nancy Mitford, *Don't Tell Alfred* (1960)

'Northey is Christiana Brandolin [sic] talking like Debo' (Nancy Mitford to Handasyde Buchanan, 7 September 1960, quoted in Harold Acton, 1973, *Nancy Mitford: a memoir*, London: Hamilton, p. 140). *See also* **Devonshire**, Deborah, Duchess of.

BRANDRETH, Alice Mary (1854–1929) Daughter of Mr and Mrs Brandreth of Elvaston Place, South Kensington, London. Her cousin, Dr Gordon of Pixholme, Box Hill, Surrey, was a neighbour of Meredith, and from the age of 13 she knew the novelist, who became a close friend of her parents. In 1878 she married Dr Gordon's son, J.E.H., who was killed in 1893 in a riding accident; in 1898 she married J.G. Butcher, QC, MP for York, later Lord Danesfort. She introduced R.L. **Stevenson** to Meredith. She was also a cousin of Harold **Nicolson**.

Cecilia Halkett in George Meredith, *Beauchamp's Career* (1876)

'A good many of our mutual friends suggested both to Mr Meredith and to me that Cecilia Halkett . . . was taken from myself . . . and one day I asked him if there was any truth in the suggestion, and he said . . . that few authors entirely copy a living character, but that I had been conventionally brought up, and, being the only child of my parents, would doubtless have the same views as Cecilia, and under their influence refuse to marry any one of whom my father and mother did not entirely approve' (Lady Butcher, 1919, *Memories of George Meredith, OM*, London: Constable, p. 41). S.M. Ellis thought that there were slight grounds for supposing Alice Brandreth to be the original of Cecilia Halkett (see *George Meredith*, 1920, London, p. 239 n. 1).

BRAXFIELD, Robert Macqueen, Lord (1722–99) Scottish judge. In 1780 he became Lord of the Justiciary, and in 1788 he became Lord Justice Clerk.

Adam Weir (Lord Hermiston) in R.L. Stevenson, *Weir of Hermiston* (1896)

'Lord Hermiston is believed to be drawn from Robert Macqueen, Lord Braxfield' (Sir Paul Harvey (ed.), 1967, *The Oxford Companion to English Literature*, Oxford: Oxford University Press, p. 878).

The BREACH, Eastwood, Nottinghamshire The block of miners' dwellings to which D.H. Lawrence's parents moved in 1887.

The Bottoms in D.H. Lawrence, *Sons and Lovers* (1913)

'Lawrence remembered that place well; he wrote of it most fully in *Sons and Lovers*, where the Breach is called the Bottoms' (H.T. Moore, 1960, *The Intelligent Heart: the story of D.H. Lawrence*, Harmondsworth: Penguin, p. 34; originally published 1955, London: Heinemann).

BREMNER, Isabel (1883–1917)   A friend and contemporary of Ivy Compton-Burnett at Royal Holloway College from 1902 to 1905.

FELICIA MURRAY in I. Compton-Burnett, *Dolores* (1911)

'One would guess ... that ... Miss Bremner (who had "been told 'I am' in it" by other Hollowegians who had ... recognized the likeness) was the original for Dolores' astute and witty companion, Felicia Murray' (Hilary Spurling, 1974, *Ivy When Young: the early life of I. Compton-Burnett, 1884–1919*, London: Gollancz, p. 173).

BRENAN, Gerald (1894–1987)   English novelist and writer. For some years deeply in love with Dora **Carrington**, in 1931 he married Gamel **Woolsey**. He lived most of his life in Spain.

RANDAL PIXLEY in Llewellyn Powys, *Love and Death* (1939)

The identification is based upon obvious parallels.

BRENNAN, Austin (1846?–1928)   Dry goods merchant from Rochester, New York. Some time before 1896, he married Mary Frances ('Mame') **Dreiser**, and gave a home to her father, John **Dreiser**. He later lived mainly in Greenwich Village and was helped financially in his old age by his brother-in-law, Theodore Dreiser.

WALTER TISDALE in Theodore Dreiser, *Dawn* (1931)

'... Austin Brennan (called Walter Tisdale in *Dawn*)' (R. Lehan, 1974, *Theodore Dreiser: his world and his novels*, Carbondale, Ill.: Arcturis Books, p. 10).

BRENTNALL, Alfred Woolston (1834?–1924)   Cashier for **Barber Walker & Co.** until 1922.

MR BRAITHWAITE in D.H. Lawrence, *Sons and Lovers* (1913)

'Mr Braithwaite was in life Alfred Woolston Brentnall' (H.T. Moore, 1974, *The Priest of Love: life of D.H. Lawrence*, rev. edn, London: Heinemann, p. 27; originally published 1955 as *The Intelligent Heart: the story of D.H. Lawrence*, London: Heinemann).

ALFRED BRICKNELL in D.H. Lawrence, *Aaron's Rod* (1922)

'Alfred Bricknell was Alfred Brentnall' (ibid.).

BRETT, Hon. Dorothy Eugénie (1891–1977)   Painter. Daughter of the 2nd Viscount Esher, she studied at the Slade School of Fine Art, London. In 1915 she became a friend of the Lawrences, and in 1924 she went with them to Taos, New

Mexico. After the Lawrences left she remained in the United States for the rest of her life.

EDITH CLOWES in Gilbert Cannan, *Mendel* (1916)

'Portraits of Edward Marsh, Brett, Carrington, Augustus John and C.R.W. Nevinson are also to be found in the book' (Diana Farr, 1978, *Gilbert Cannan: a Georgian prodigy*, London: Chatto & Windus, p. 40).

CARLOTTA FELL (AFTERWARDS LADY LATHKILL) in D.H. Lawrence, 'Glad Ghosts' (1928)

'Carlotta Fell, who began as Dorothy Brett, came to resemble Lady Cynthia [Asquith]' (H.T. Moore, 1960, *The Intelligent Heart: the story of D.H. Lawrence*, Harmondsworth: Penguin, p. 431; originally published 1955, London: Heinemann). *See also* **Asquith**, Lady Cynthia.

MISS JAMES in D.H. Lawrence, 'The Last Laugh' (1928)

'[Murry] is Marchbanks in "The Last Laugh" as Brett is Miss James, hearing device and all' (ibid., p. 411).

JENNY MULLION in Aldous Huxley, *Crome Yellow* (1921)

'Brett was evoked by Aldous . . . in the character of Jenny' (Sybille Bedford, 1973, *Aldous Huxley: a biography*, Vol. I, London: Chatto & Windus, p. 71).

LAURA RIDLEY in D.H. Lawrence, 'St Mawr' (1925)

'This was the story whose leading character was identified by Catherine Carswell as Brett' (Moore, op. cit., p. 411). Quite clearly a portrait of Miss Brett; the deafness is omitted and the inquisitiveness retained. '[Brett] had never ridden in her life. Her father . . . had kept a racing stable, but he never let his daughter learn to ride. . . . Now her greatest wish was to have a horse and ride across the desert with Lorenzo; and pretty soon she had her desire and he was teaching her to ride. He taught her to have an imaginative relationship with the horse . . . to feel the flow between the horse and herself' (Mabel Dodge Luhan, 1932, *Lorenzo in Taos*, New York, pp. 168–9).

MARY HENRIETTA URQUHART in D.H. Lawrence, 'The Princess' (1925)

'I doubt not that the truth smote . . . Dorothy Brett when she read 'The Princess'. Here was little of portraiture, still less of summing up. But what an inescapable reading of the pulse of a life' (Catherine Carswell, 1932, *The Savage Pilgrimage: a narrative of D.H. Lawrence*, London: Chatto & Windus, p. 106).

BREWSTER, Achsah (1878–1945) Painter. Née Barlow, in 1910 she married Earl **Brewster**.

VALERIE MELVILLE in D.H. Lawrence, 'Things' (1933)

See under **Brewster**, E.H.

BREWSTER, Earl Henry (1878–1957) American painter. Born in Ohio, he studied art in Cleveland and New York. In 1910 he married Achsah Barlow (**Brewster**, above); they lived in Sicily, and in 1921 they met Lawrence on Capri. In 1922 they moved to Ceylon and persuaded Lawrence to stay with them at

Kandy. The friendship continued until Lawrence's death. After 1935 they lived in India; Brewster was a student of Buddhism.

ERASMUS MELVILLE in D.H. Lawrence, 'Things' (1933)

'On Capri [in 1921 Lawrence] met some new friends who were to remain staunch friends to the end of his life: Earl and Achsah Brewster, two Americans. ... They were interested in painting and in Buddhism, these two Jamesian expatriates whom Lawrence years later satirized in his story "Things"' (H.T. Moore, 1960, *The Intelligent Heart: the story of D.H. Lawrence*, Harmondsworth: Penguin, p. 349; originally published 1955, London: Heinemann). 'Have a most amusing story of mine in *American Bookman* – called *Things* – you'll think it's you, but it isn't. I shall bring it along' (D.H. Lawrence to Earl Brewster, 13 September 1928, reproduced in E. Brewster and A. Brewster, 1934, *D.H. Lawrence: reminiscences and correspondence*, London: Martin Secker, p. 179).

BRIDGEMAN, Selina *See* **Bradford**, Countess of.

BRIDLINGTON, Yorkshire Known as Burlington in 1839, when Charlotte Brontë spent a week there in the autumn with Ellen **Nussey**.

BRETTON in Charlotte Brontë, *Villette* (1853)

'Here, in all probability, Charlotte situated in after years "the clean and ancient town of Bretton"' (Winifred Gérin, 1967, *Charlotte Brontë*, Oxford, p. 155).

BRIDPORT, Dorset Situated fifteen miles west of Dorchester.

PORT-BREDY in Thomas Hardy, Wessex novels and tales (1871–95)

Identified on a map prepared by Thomas Hardy which hangs in the Dorset County Museum, Dorchester. *See under* **Abbotsbury**.

BRIGHT, John (1811–89) Orator and statesman. He was a leader of the Anti-Corn Law League, which was formed in 1839, and was a free-trade agitator with Richard **Cobden**. He was a member of the Peace Society.

JAWSTER SHARP in Benjamin Disraeli, *Coningsby* (1844)

'In *Key to the Characters in Coningsby*, published in 1844 by Sherwood, Gilbert & Piper, the names of the originals are indicated by the first and last letters of the surname or title, but in *A New Key to the Characters in Coningsby*, issued by W. Strange (no date), the names of the originals are in nearly all instances printed in full, the names of the characters not being reprinted. The two lists are combined' (*Notes and Queries* (8th series) 3 (13 May 1893): 363; the key is reprinted there).

JOB THORNBERRY in Benjamin Disraeli, *Endymion* (1880)

On 7 February 1881, Queen Victoria wrote to Lord Beaconsfield saying that she had just finished *Endymion* and could 'trace several characters. Were you not thinking of ... Mr Bright in Job Thornberry?' On 10 February, Beaconsfield replied that Thornberry's oratory was an impression of the style of Cobden: 'All the rest is typical: traits perhaps of Mr Bright' (reproduced in *The Letters of*

Queen Victoria, 1928 (2nd series), Vol. III, London: John Murray, p. 195). *See also* **Cobden**, Richard; **Potter**, Thomas Bayley.

MR TURNBULL, MP in Anthony Trollope, *Can You Forgive Her?* (1864) and sequels

'[Trollope admitted] that Turnbull was John Bright' (Michael Sadleir, 1927, *Trollope: a commentary*, London: Constable, p. 416). In fact, in a letter to the *Daily Telegraph* in 1869, Trollope declared: 'In the character of Mr Turnbull ... I depicted Mr Bright neither in his public nor his private character' (reproduced in Anthony Trollope, 1951, *Letters*, ed. Bradford Booth, London: Oxford University Press, p. 241; reprinted 1979, London: Greenwood Press). For a discussion of this whole episode, see J.R. Dinwiddy, 1967–8, 'Who's who in Trollope's political novels', *The Nineteenth Century* 21: 42–5).

BRINE, John Grant An eccentric Scottish painter living in Paris in the 1830s; Thackeray met him in the circle of Evans Eyre Crowe. He left Paris for Madrid, and shortly after moved to London, where he worked as an illustrator on the newly founded *Illustrated London News* and *Punch* from 1842 until his death from tuberculosis. He is said to have taught the English artist Birket Foster figure drawing. He was still alive in 1844.

ANDREA FITCH in W.M. Thackeray, *A Shabby Genteel Story* (1840)

'[Sir Joseph Crowe's account of Brine's character and accoutrements, in his *Reminiscences*] reminds one irresistibly of ... Andrea ... Fitch' (*The Letters and Private Papers of W.M. Thackeray*, Vol. I: *1817–1840*, 1945, ed. Gordon N. Ray, London: Oxford University Press, p. 510).

BRINSLEY COLLIERY Located north of Eastwood; A.J. **Lawrence**, D.H. Lawrence's father, worked there as a 'butty'.

SELBY in D.H. Lawrence, *Sons and Lovers* (1913)

'Selby is Brinsley Colliery' (Ada Lawrence and G. Stuart Gelder, 1931, *Young Lorenzo: early life of D.H. Lawrence*, Florence, p. 275).

BRITISH ASSOCIATION FOR THE ADVANCEMENT OF SCIENCE
Founded in 1831 at York 'to give a stronger impulse and more systematic direction to scientific inquiry'. It met annually, at a different university or town each year. Great importance was attached to the hospitality and social gatherings involved in the annual meetings, and gradually general feeling grew that the association was vulgarizing science rather than popularizing it.

MUDFOG ASSOCIATION FOR THE ADVANCEMENT OF EVERYTHING in Charles Dickens, *The Mudfog Papers* (1837–8)

'Dickens changed the British Association for the Advancement of Science into the Mudfog Association for the Advancement of Everything' (G.A. Chaudhury, 1974, 'The Mudfog Papers', *The Dickensian* 70 (May): 105).

PICKWICK CCLUB in Charles Dickens, *The Pickwick Papers* (1836–7)

'The whole of [ch. 1] is a skit on the British Association' (T.W. Hill, 1947, 'Notes on *The Pickwick Papers*', *The Dickensian* 44 (December): 29).

BRITTON, Jack (1885–1962) American boxer 1904–30. He was the World Welterweight Champion in 1915, 1916 and 1919–22; he lost only 25 of 320 contests.

JACK BRENNAN in Ernest Hemingway, 'Fifty Grand', *Men Without Women* (1927)

'Jack Brennan . . . was modelled on a man Hemingway admired: Jack Britton, who, as Hemingway was to tell Lilian Ross, "kept on his toes and moved around and never let them hit him solid"' (Sheridan Baker, 1967, *Ernest Hemingway*, p. 62).

BROADCASTING HOUSE, London Headquarters of the BBC. George Orwell worked there from 1941 to 1943, in the Indian and South-east Asian Sections.

MINISTRY OF TRUTH in George Orwell, *Nineteen Eighty-four* (1949)

'He made free use of the BBC's physiognomy in constructing *Nineteen Eighty-Four*'s Ministry of Truth, but he never seriously suggested that one was a step to the other' (Eileen Bernard Crick, 1980, *George Orwell: a life*, London: Secker & Warburg, p. 284).

BROADHEAD, William (*c.*1819–79) He was Secretary of the Saw Grinders Union at Sheffield from 1848, and Treasurer of the United Kingdon Alliance of Organised Trades. He kept an inn until 1867, and went to America in 1869 but failed to find employment. He then became a grocer in Sheffield until his death.

GEORGE GROTAIT in Charles Reade, *Put Yourself in His Place* (1870)

'He is the villain under name of Grotait of Charles Reade's novel *Put yourself in his place*' (Frederic Boase, *Modern English Biography*).

BROADLANDS, Romsey, Hampshire Situated 1 mile south of Romsey, it was originally the seat of the St Barbe family, and was later that of Lord Palmerston. It was extensively altered by Capability Brown *c.*1767–8 and by Henry Holland in 1788.

DEANSLEIGH PARK in Thomas Hardy, 'Lady Mottisfont' (1891)

Identified in F.B. Pinion, 1968, *A Hardy Companion*, London: Macmillan.

BRODIE, William (1741–88) A cabinet-maker in Edinburgh and one of the ordinary deacon councillors of the city by day, he was a thief and gambler by night and led a gang of burglars who broke into the Excise Office in Canongate. He was tried be Lord Braxfield and hanged after one of his confederates turned King's evidence. In 1880 Stevenson and W.E. Henley wrote a *Deacon Brodie; or The Double Life*, which was produced (without success) in Aberdeen, London, Montreal and New York.

DR HENRY JEKYLL / EDWARD HYDE in R.L. Stevenson, *The Strange Case of Dr Jekyll and Mr Hyde* (1886)

'It was Deacon Brodie who fathered Dr Jekyll. . . . A cabinet made by Brodie stood in Stevenson's nursery in Edinburgh, so that from early childhood he was familiar with the story' (John Hampden, 1948, Introd. to *Dr Jekyll and Mr Hyde*, pp. 15–16). 'The story had for Robert Louis Stevenson a strong attraction. As early as 1864 he prepared the draft of a play founded upon it . . . "Deacon Brodie, or the Double Life", written in collaboration with . . . W.E. Henley, and published in 1892. It may even be that the conception of "Dr Jekyll and Mr. Hyde" was suggested to Stevenson by his study of the dual nature . . . exemplified in his earlier hero' (*The Trial of Deacon Brodie*, 1906, ed. William Roughead, Edinburgh, p. 10). 'Mr Robert Louis Stevenson arrived in New York on Wednesday last. . . . A *Herald* reporter caught Mr Stevenson at a favourable moment and subjected him to an interview from which we glean much that is interesting. . . . "There is a great difference of opinion as to what suggested . . . 'The Strange Case of Dr Jekyll and Mr Hyde' and 'Deacon Brodie'. Well this has never been properly told. On one occasion I was very hard up for money . . . I thought and thought, and tried hard to find a subject. . . . At night I dreamed the story . . . [but] all I dreamed about Dr Jekyll was that one man was being pressed into a cabinet, when he swallowed a drug and changed into another being . . . 'Deacon Brodie'! I certainly didn't dream that, but in the room in which I slept when a child in Edinburgh there was a cabinet . . . from the hands of the original Deacon Brodie"' ('Notes', 1887, *Critic* 8 (193): 133)

BROMLEY, Kent

BROMSTEAD in H.G. Wells, *The New Machiavelli* (1911)

'The first third of [*The New Machiavelli*] is a magnificent re-creation of Wells's own boyhood in Bromley' (Lovat Dickson, 1972, *H.G. Wells*, Harmondsworth: Penguin, p. 220).

BROMLEY-DAVENPORT ARMS, Ellastone, Staffordshire

DONNITHORNE ARMS, HAYSLOPE, in George Eliot, *Adam Bede* (1859)

'The Donnithorne Arms still exists . . . [and] is known . . . as the Bromley-Davenport Arms. It stands at the entrance to the village of Ellastone' (Charles S. Olcott, 1911, *George Eliot: scenes and people in her novels*, London: Cassell, p. 63; originally published 1910, New York: Thomas Y. Crowell).

BRONSON, Katherine De Kay (d. 1901) American friend of Henry James who lived in Venice. She died in Florence.

MRS PREST in Henry James, *The Aspern Papers* (1888)

'. . . the all-knowing Mrs Prest (a re-creation of the benevolent Mrs Bronson . . .)' (Leon Edel, 1963, *Henry James: the middle years, 1884–1894*, p. 160).

BRONTË, Anne (1820–49) English novelist, who wrote under the name Acton Bell. The sister of Charlotte and Emily Brontë, she was governess to the Ingham family at Blake Hall in 1839, and to the Robinsons at Thorpe Green Hall from 1841 to 1845. She left the latter post when her brother Branwell became emotionally involved with Mrs Robinson.

CAROLINE HELSTONE in Charlotte Brontë, *Shirley* (1849)

'Finally there was a change in Caroline's character. Even the colour of her eyes and hair came to resemble Anne's in the end. An interesting thesis, [Holgate,

1962, *The Structure of Shirley*, Brontë Society Transactions] has appeared to show how, by the time Anne was dead and the third volume begun, Charlotte discarded her heroine's earlier traits – the superficial resemblance . . . to Ellen Nussey . . . to make of Caroline a tribute to her sister Anne, as Shirley was a tribute to Emily' (Winifred Gérin, 1967, *Charlotte Brontë*, Oxford, pp. 289–90). *See also* **Nussey**, Ellen.

MARY RIVERS in Charlotte Brontë, *Jane Eyre* (1847)

'Her sisters [Emily and Anne] now [1845] became the focal point of her life. How she saw them at that time, she set down in *Jane Eyre* in the picture she painted of Diana and Mary Rivers' (Winifred Gérin, 1967, *Charlotte Brontë*, Oxford, p. 303). 'In the flash of "her dark and deep eye" as "Mary" read a passage to her taste, Charlotte gave us a glimpse of her sister' (Winifred Gérin, 1971, *Emily Brontë*, Oxford, p. 146).

BRONTË, Charlotte (1816–55) English novelist, who wrote under the name Currer Bell. Sister of Anne and Emily **Brontë**, and daughter of Patrick Brontë, perpetual curate of Haworth, Yorkshire. She was sent with four of her sisters to the **Clergy Daughter's School** in Cowan Bridge, where two of her sisters died. She was a teacher from 1835 to 1838, and a governess from 1839 to 1841. In 1842 she went with Emily to study languages at the Pensionnat Héger in Brussels, but they returned after a year when their aunt died. Charlotte went back alone to Brussels to teach English, and formed an unhappy and unreciprocated attachment to Constantin **Héger**. After her return to Haworth, she attempted and failed to start a school with her sisters. After the death of her brother and sisters, she married her father's curate Arthur Bell **Nicholls** in 1854, but died during pregnancy the following year.

LUCY SNOWE in Charlotte Brontë, *Villette* (1853)

'In character and person Lucy Snowe resembles her creator closely and . . . many of the incidents of the story are identifiable as . . . Charlotte Brontë's own experiences' (Herbert E. Wroot, 1906, *The Persons and Places of the Brontë Novels*, Bradford, p. 172). 'I am not leniently disposed towards Miss "Frost" [at one time the name Charlotte Brontë proposed for Lucy Snowe]: from the beginning, I never meant to appoint her lines in pleasant places' (Charlotte Brontë to George Smith, 3 November 1852, quoted in Mrs Gaskell, *The Life of Charlotte Brontë*, Vol. II, London: Smith, Elder, ch. 26).

BRONTË, Emily Jane (1818–48) English novelist and poet, who wrote under the name Ellis Bell. She was the sister of Charlotte and Anne **Brontë**. In 1837 she became a governess in Halifax and in 1842 attended the Pensionnat Héger with Charlotte. She was deeply attached to the wild moorland scenery of her home, which was vividly evoked in her work, especially her one novel, *Wuthering Heights*. She died of tuberculosis.

SHIRLEY KEELDAR in Charlotte Brontë, *Shirley* (1849)

'I told her of——'s admiration of "Shirley", which pleased her, for the character of Shirley was meant for her sister Emily, about whom she is never tired of talking, nor I of listening' (Mrs Gaskell, 'parts of a letter I wrote at the time', to an unknown recipient, reproduced in *The Letters of Mrs Gaskell*, 1966, ed. J.A.V. Chapple and Arthur Pollard, Manchester, p. 249).

DIANA RIVERS in Charlotte Brontë, *Jane Eyre* (1847)

See under **Brontë**, Anne.

BRONTË, Maria (1813–25) Eldest of the Brontë sisters.

HELEN BURNS in Charlotte Brontë, *Jane Eyre* (1847)

'There is a tablet put up in the communion railing [in Haworth church] . . . Maria Bronte – May 1825, aged 12 (the original of Helen Burns in "Jane Eyre". She and the next sister died of fever at the Clergy School)' (Mrs Gaskell, to an unknown correspondent (John Forster?) after her first visit to Haworth [September 1853], reproduced in *The Letters of Mrs Gaskell*, 1966, ed. J.A.V. Chapple and Arthur Pollard, Manchester, p. 246). 'You are right in having faith in the reality of Helen Burns's character; she was real enough. I have exaggerated nothing there. I refrained from recording much that I remember respecting her, lest the narrative should sound incredible' (Charlotte Brontë to W.S. Williams, 28 October 1847, reproduced in T.J. Wise and J.A. Symington (eds), 1932, *The Brontës: their lives, friendships & correspondence*, Vol. II, p. 151).

BROOK FARM, Massachusetts A co-operative community established in 1841 by the 'Transcendental Club', at West Roxbury, Massachusetts. George Ripley acted as President, and among those involved were Theodore **Parker**, Bronson **Alcott**, Hawthorne and Elizabeth **Peabody**. In 1844 Brook Farm became a Fourierite Phalanx, but the community broke up in 1847 when a fire partially destroyed the buildings.

BLITHEDALE in Nathaniel Hawthorne, *The Blithedale Romance* (1852)

'In the "Blithedale" of this volume, many readers will probably suspect a faint and not very faithful shadowing of Brook Farm, in Roxbury, which (now a little more than ten years ago) was occupied and cultivated by a company of socialists. The Author does not wish to deny, that he had this Community in his mind, and that (having had the good fortune, for a time, to be personally connected with it) he has occasionally availed himself of his actual reminiscences, in the hope of giving a more lifelike tint to the fancy-sketch in the following pages' (preface to *The Blithedale Romance*, 1852).

BROOK STREET UNITARIAN CHAPEL, Knutsford, Cheshire

BENSON'S CHAPEL in Elizabeth Gaskell, *Ruth* (1853)

'[Mrs Gaskell's] affection for [Brook Street Chapel] was later expressed in the loving description of the Reverend Thurston Benson's chapel in *Ruth*' (A.B. Hopkins, 1952, *Elizabeth Gaskell: her life and work*, p. 21).

BROOKE, Sir James (1803–68) Rajah of Sarawak. Born in Benares, he was educated at Norwich, but *c*.1819 he ran away from school and joined the infantry in Bengal. He served in the Burma war and in 1830 resigned from the service of the East India Company. He first visited Borneo in 1838, returning in 1840 to take part in suppressing a rebellion. In 1841, at the invitation of the governor (Muda Hassim), he was made Rajah of Sarawak and assumed the government of the country. He finally left Borneo in 1863.

JIM in Joseph Conrad, *Lord Jim* (1900)

'[I]n the second half of the novel, Conrad's source changed from A.P. Williams to Jim Lingard. But Conrad could know little about Jim Lingard or his way of life, and was therefore forced to make the source a composite one. Thus he drew upon the inspiration of Brooke for the success of his hero' (Norman Sherry, 1966, *Conrad's Eastern World*, Cambridge, p. 138). *See also* **Lingard**, William James; *Williams*, Augustine Podmore.

TOM LINGARD in Joseph Conrad, *The Rescue* (1920)

'The conception of Lingard in *The Rescue* apparently owed much to the diaries and letters of the Rajah James Brooke of Sarawak' (J.D. Gordan, 1941, *Joseph Conrad: the making of a novelist*, Cambridge, Mass., p. 46). *See also* **Lingard**, Captain William.

BROOKE, Rupert (1887–1915) Poet. He was the son of a master at Rugby who was the first Fellow of King's College, Cambridge, not to have been an Etonian. He was educated at Rugby and at King's College, Cambridge, where he was a contemporary of Shane Leslie. He was also a contemporary and acquaintance of Ronald Firbank.

ADOLPHUS BRIGGS in Shane Leslie, *The Cantab* (1926)

Identified in a key in the hand of Dr Ivor Ramsay, a Kingsman of the year 1920, and later Dean, laid in a copy of *The Cantab*.

WINSOME BROOKES in Ronald Firbank, *Vainglory* (1915)

'. . . the futile poet, the character called Winsome Brookes (patterned on Rupert Brooke)' (M. Benkovitz, 1970, *Ronald Firbank*, Cambridge, p. 269).

BASIL DOYE in Rose Macaulay, *Non-combatants and Others* (1916)

'Basil . . . resembles Rupert in many ways' (C. Babington-Smith, 1972, *Rose Macaulay*, p. 70). Rose Macaulay had known Rupert Brooke from childhood (in Rugby), but she came to know him well after her family moved in 1906 to Shelford, outside Cambridge, when he was an undergraduate. After the outbreak of the First World War she hardly saw him again.

MICHAEL in Rose Macaulay, *The Secret River* (1909)

'In . . . *The Secret River*, which she wrote in 1908, when Rupert was twenty-one, and she twenty-seven, the hero is a young poet just turned twenty. It may well have been as early as this that she came under the spell of his . . . personality' (C. Babington-Smith, op. cit., p. 61).

BROOKFIELD, Jane Octavia (1821–96) Daughter of Sir Charles Elton of **Clevedon Court**, in 1841 she married W.H. **Brookfield**. She knew Thackeray through her husband, but their friendship did not become close until 1848. They corresponded for three years and saw each other constantly but in 1851 Brookfield and Thackeray quarrelled bitterly and Brookfield insisted that the friendship should end; from that time they met and corresponded only infrequently.

LAURA BELL in W.M. Thackeray, *The History of Pendennis* (1848–50)

'Mrs Brookfield ... figured [in *Pendennis*] in the person of his heroine Laura Bell' (Gordon N. Ray, 1952, *The Buried Life*, p. 93).

LADY CASTLEWOOD in W.M. Thackeray, *The History of Henry Esmond* (1852)

'During the next three months [December 1851–March 1852], as Thackeray wrote the last eight chapters of the first book of *Esmond* and the first two chapters of the second, he again lived through the whole course of the Brookfield affair and made it a part of his novel. ... Lady Castlewood he thought of ... as Mrs Brookfield' (ibid., pp. 86–7).

AMELIA SEDLEY in W.M. Thackeray, *Vanity Fair* (1847–8)

'You know you are only a piece of Amelia – my mother is another half; my poor little wife *y est pour beaucoup*' (W.M. Thackeray to Mrs Brookfield, 30 June 1848, reproduced in *The Letters and Private Papers of W.M. Thackeray*, 1945, ed. Gordon N. Ray, Vol. II, London: Oxford University Press, p. 394). *See also* **Carmichael-Smyth**,Anne; **Thackeray**, Isabella.

BROOKFIELD, William Henry (1809–74) Son of a Dissenting solicitor, in 1829 he met Thackeray in Cambridge and became his friend. He took orders and in 1841 he became Curate of St James's, Piccadilly, and St Luke's, in Berwick Street, and married Jane Elton (**Brookfield**, above). His marriage was not a success: his wife was extravagant and he allegedly neglected her. He became a fashionable preacher at Berkeley Chapel, Mayfair, and in 1848 he became an inspector of schools, resigning in 1864 to become Rector of Somerby-with-Hainby in Lincolnshire.

LORD CASTLEWOOD in W.M. Thackeray, *The History of Henry Esmond* (1852)

'Thackeray noted with sardonic amusement that the pages most quoted in early reviews were those in which he had described Brookfield's neglect of his wife. "How mad poor Tomkins must be at the press selecting those passages", he wrote' (Gordon Ray, 1958, *The Age of Wisdom*, p. 189).

REVD FRANK WHITESTOCKE in W.M. Thackeray, 'The Curate's Walk', *Punch's Prize Novelists* (1853)

'[In] "The Curate's Walk" ... Brookfield appears as the Rev. Francis Whitestocke' (*The Letters and Private Papers of W.M. Thackeray*, 1945, ed. Gordon N. Ray, Vol. II, London: Oxford University Press, p. 326 n. 116). 'I send you two bottles for this evening's drinking, by ... little Harrie [his daughter]. ... She does not in the least know for what purpose (except to act as a mere bottle holder) she waits tonight upon the wife of the Rev'd Francis Whitestocke' (Thackeray to Mrs Brookfield, December 1847?, ibid., Vol. II, p. 326).

BROOKS, Georgie Well-known Key West barrister and politician of the 1930s.

ROBERT ('BEE-LIPS') SIMMONS in Ernest Hemingway, *To Have and Have Not* (1937)

'Bee-Lips . . . was drawn to the life from Georgie Brooks' (Carlos Baker, 1969, *Ernest Hemingway: a life story*, New York, p. 295; Baker gives the source of his identification on p. 619 n. 'E.H.'s eccentrics in the Morgan novels').

BROOKS, John Ellingham (d. 1929) Greek scholar and translator. He was a long-term resident of Capri, where for some time he shared the Villa Cercola with E.F. Benson, Norman Douglas, Compton **Mackenzie** and Somerset Maugham. He first met Somerset Maugham as a student in Heidelberg. In 1903 he married Romaine Goddard (**Brooks**, below), but they separated in 1904. He remained on Capri until he died.

ERNEST EAMES in Norman Douglas, *South Wind* (1917)

'Brooks may have served as the original of Mr Ernest Eames' (Edward Nehls, 1958, *D.H. Lawrence: a composite biography*, Vol. II, Madison, p. 454 n. 39).

G. ETHERIDGE HAYWARD in W. Somerset Maugham, *Of Human Bondage* (1915)

'In "Looking Back" Maugham identifies [the young man who was the basis for Hayward] as "Ellingham Brooks"' (R.L. Calder, 1972, *W. Somerset Maugham and the Quest for Freedom*, London: Heinemann, p. 100).

BROOKS, Phillips (1835–93) Born in Boston, he was the second cousin of Henry Adams. He was an Episcopalian parson in Philadelphia in 1859–69 and at Trinity Church, Boston, in 1869–91, and Bishop of Massachusetts in 1891–3. He was a noted preacher and wrote the Christmas carol 'O Little Town of Bethlehem' for his Sunday School in 1868.

STEPHEN HAZARD in Henry Adams, *Esther* (1884)

'For the character of Hazard, Adams drew liberally upon . . . Phillips Brooks' (Ernest Samuels, 1958, *Henry Adams: the middle years*, Cambridge, Mass., p. 241).

BROOKS, Reginald Shirley (d. 1888) Son of C.W. Shirley Brooks, Editor of *Punch*. He was on the staff of the *Sporting Times* (The Pink 'Un) from 1876 to 1888 and used the pseudonym 'Peter Blobbs'.

MORDAUNT RIVERS in Frank Danby, *A Babe in Bohemia* (1889)

'[Brooks] is depicted as . . . Mordaunt Rivers' (Frederic Boase, 1908, *Modern English Biography*, Vol. IV, col. 507).

BROOKS, Romaine (1874–1970) Painter. Daughter of Henry Goddard and Ella Waterman of Philadelphia, who divorced soon after her birth. In 1899 she went to Capri, and in 1902, when her mother died, she inherited a large fortune. She married J.E. **Brooks** in 1903, but they separated in 1904; she continued to pay him a small allowance. She settled in Paris in 1905 and had a passionate friendship with Gabriele D'Annunzio from 1910 to 1915. She met Natalie Clifford **Barney** and began a liaison that lasted until 1968. She died in Nice.

OLIMPIA LEIGH in Compton Mackenzie, *Extraordinary Women* (1928)

'Romaine appears in *Extraordinary Women* to illustrate, by her own behavior, the inanities of others . . . [she] is not a very attractive figure . . . what Romaine thought of this view of her is not known; but, since she does not bother to mention Olimpia Leigh in her memoirs, she was probably not convinced' (Meryle Secrest, 1976, *Between Me and Life: a biography of Romaine Brooks*, London: MacDonald & Jane, pp. 303–4; originally published 1974, Garden City, NY: Doubleday).

BROOKS, Van Wyck (1886–1963) American critic and essayist. He grew up in Plainfield, New Jersey, where Maxwell **Perkins** was his friend from boyhood and was later his contemporary at Harvard.

COOKE in Conrad Aiken, 'The Orange Moth' (1925)

'Aiken pictured Yeats as "Butler", an old portraitist eager to have Brooks, or "Cooke", sit for him because he was taken with the . . . young writer's "honest blue eyes" and "lovely face . . . of an innocence indescribable"' (J. Hooper, 1977, *Van Wyck Brooks*, Amherst, p. 72; the portrait is reproduced on p. 3).

BROUGHAM, Eleanor (1822–39) Daughter of Lord **Brougham**.

EMMELINE DE MOULIN in Lord Brougham, *Albert Lunel* (1844)

'The passages in Vol. III describing the heroine (Brougham's daughter who died in 1839) are heavily scored in the margin [of Michael Sadleir's copy which almost certainly originally belonged to Brougham himself]' (Sadleir, 1951, *XIX Century Fiction*, Vol. I, London: Constable, and Los Angeles: California University Press, p. 57). Brougham built himself a château at Cannes that was named for his daughter, Château Eleanor Louise – hence Château Lunel.

BROUGHAM, Henry Peter Brougham, Lord (1778–1868) 1st Baron Brougham and Vaux. Educated in Edinburgh, he was one of the founders of the *Edinburgh Review*. He was called to the English Bar in 1808 and defended Queen Caroline of Brunswick in 1820. In 1825 he founded the **Society for the Diffusion of Useful Knowledge**, and in 1828 he played a large part the foundation of London University. He established the Judicial Committee of the Privy Council and the Central Criminal Court in 1830–4. After Dugald **Stewart** (who taught him) said he was the ablest man he had ever known, his political career came to a halt in 1834, when the Whig government was voted out.

MONSIEUR BALAYE in Lord Brougham, *Albert Lunel* (1844)

Identified in Brougham's hand in the copy of *Albert Lunel* belonging to Michael Sadleir, formerly in the possession of Frederick Locker, and clearly originally Brougham's own copy.

SIR JOSEPH BOWLEY in Charles Dickens, *The Chimes* (1844)

'[Brougham] was, it seems, probably one of the models for . . . Sir Joseph Bowley' (Robert L. Patten, 1970, 'Portraits of Pott: Lord Brougham and *The Pickwick Papers*', *The Dickensian* 60 (September): p. 217 n. 3).

GEORGE BROUGHTON in W. Massie, *Sydenham; or Memoirs of a Man of the World* (1830)

'In Volume two . . . Brougham (Broughton) . . . [conducts] the destinies of the Whigs' (M.W. Rosa, 1936, *The Silver-Fork School: novels of fashion preceding* Vanity Fair, New York, p. 81 n. 3).

LORD FACING-BOTH-WAYS in Thomas Love Peacock, *Gryll Grange* (1860)

'Lord Brougham [is] intended. Dr Folliott compared Brougham to Mr Facing-both-ways . . . in *Pilgrim's Progress* [in *Crotchet Castle*, chapter II]' (*The Novels of T.L. Peacock*, 1948, ed. David Garnett, London: Rupert Hart-Davis, p. 811 n. 2).

MR FOAMING FUDGE in Benjamin Disraeli, *Vivian Grey* (1826–7)

Identified as Mr B——m in a key given in *The Star Chamber* (24 May 1826): 114; reprinted in *Vivian Grey*, 1904 (centenary edn), ed. Lucien Wolf, Vol. II, London, pp. 361–2. The full name appears on a copy of the key held in the British Museum. Lucien Wolf concludes that Disraeli was not responsible for the key.

THE LEARNED FRIEND in Thomas Love Peacock, *Crotchet Castle* (1831)

'The most notorious [of the public characters figuring in the *Crotchet Castle*] is of course Lord Brougham, or the Learned Friend . . . all the incidents of his career singled out for ridicule are those of the past twelve years. . . . These . . . are . . . his appointment of commissioners to inquire into charity abuses . . . the foundation of the Society for the Diffusion of Useful Knowledge . . . his defection from the Whigs . . . and . . . his elevation to the peerage' (Martin Freeman, 1911, *Thomas Love Peacock*, London: Martin Secker, pp. 305–6).

MR POTT in Charles Dickens, *The Pickwick Papers* (1836–7)

'Mr Pott . . . was unmistakably founded on Lord Brougham. His original description in a draft number of *Pickwick Papers* might have been a description of the statesman himself. This was afterwards toned down a little; but even so the likeness was instantly recognisable to Dickens' contemporaries. . . . And the personality of Mr Pott bore . . . a grotesque resemblance to that of the great Whig chancellor' (Edwin Pugh, 1912, *The Dickens Originals*, London and Edinburgh: T.N. Foulis, p. 97). 'In [Pl. 14 of the original part issue] Pott is made out as clearly as any of the other principal characters, but with a difference . . . with his long, narrow face, piercing eyes, bulbous-tip nose, down-turned mouth, and sunken cheeks, [it] seems a much more specific and particular portrait. In fact it is, for in Mr Pott, Browne has depicted Henry Peter Brougham, Baron Brougham and Vaux' (Patten, op. cit., p. 212). For the one-volume edition of 1837, Brown etched a second plate, and all resemblance to Brougham disappeared. Brougham was much caricatured – his nose appeared on the cover of *Punch* as late as 1964 – not of course as Mr Punch, but on a mask with upturned face which one of the imps in the border is dragging by a string.

MR QUICKSILVER in Samuel Warren, *Ten Thousand a Year* (1841)

'He is the "Mr Quicksilver" . . . in Warren's *Ten Thousand a year*' (Hon. Vicary Gibbs (ed.), 1912, *The Complete Peerage of England, Scotland, Ireland, Great Britain and the United Kingdom*, Vol. II, rev. edn, London: St Catherine Press, p. 342 n.).

BROUGHTON, Rhoda (1840–1920) English novelist.

KATE CHESTER in Rhoda Broughton, *Not Wisely, But Too Well* (1867)

'Friday, January 8th, 1909 . . . Miss Sains told me that she had known Rhoda Broughton, who had sisters who didn't treat her properly, and that the ill-used sister in her early books was herself' (*The Journals of Arnold Bennett*, 1932, ed.

Sir Newman Flower, Vol. I, London: Cassell, p. 305). Miss Sains was a woman Bennett met while staying at a hotel at Vevey in the winter of 1908–9.

ELLINOR LE STRANGE in Rhoda Broughton, *Cometh Up as a Flower* (1867)

See above.

BROUN, Sir Richard (1801–58) 8th Baronet. In 1840–58 he was Honorary Secretary of the Committee of the Baronetage for sustaining rights and privileges of the Order. He projected the London Necropolis and the national mausoleum at Woking which was incorporated in 1852.

SIR VAVASOUR FIREBRACE in Benjamin Disraeli, *Sybil* (1845)

'Even [Disraeli's] most fantastic inventions like Sir Vavasour Firebrace . . . the man who sought to revive the non-existent rights of baronets to sit in Parliament, were copied from life. There really was a man, Sir Richard Broun . . . who pursued this unpromising cause' (Robert Blake, 1969, *Disraeli*, 2nd edn, London: Oxford University Press; originally published 1966, London: Eyre & Spottiswoode, p. 219).

BROWDER, Earl (1891–1973) American Communist. He joined the Communist Party in 1919 and became General Secretary in 1930. He was the Communist nominee for president of the United States in 1936 and 1940, but was expelled from the party as a 'social imperialist' in 1946.

ELMER WEEKS in John Dos Passos, *Adventures of a Young Man* (1939)

'[He] suggests Earl Browder both in position and appearance' (Joseph Blotner, 1966, *The Modern American Political Novel*, Austin, Tex., p. 313 n. 19).

BROWN, Grace ('Billy') (d. 1906) She was a secretary in a skirt factory in Cortland, New York, which belonged to an uncle of Chester **Gillette**. Gillette seduced her and in 1906 she became pregnant. He persuaded her to accompany him on a tour of the lakes of upstate New York: at Big Moose Lake, he took her out in a boat, hit her over the head with a tennis racket and watched her drown.

ROBERTA ('BERT') ALDEN in Theodore Dreiser, *An American Tragedy* (1925)

'Dreiser . . . altered even the names and places of the case with reluctance . . . that of the real victim – Grace ('Billy') Brown to his Roberta ('Bert') Alden' (Ellen Moers, 1970, *Two Dreisers*, London: Thames & Hudson, p. 199; originally published 1969, New York: Viking).

BROWN, Hannah (1808?–78) Née Meredith. Originally the governess of Miss Burdett Coutts (from 1821 onwards), she remained her life-long friend. She lived with Miss Coutts until her marriage in 1844 to Dr William Brown, and then moved next door to 80 Piccadilly, London. Dr Brown died while on holiday in France in 1855.

ROSA DARTLE in Charles Dickens, *David Copperfield* (1849–50)

'It was from one of his lady friends, very familiar to him indeed, he copied her peculiarity of never saying anything outright, but hinting it merely and making more of it that way' (John Forster, 1928, *Life of Dickens*, ed. J.W.T. Ley, p. 556).

'The Forster collection in the Victoria and Albert Museum Library contains two copies of the Charles Dickens edition of the novels, one with pencilled notes by Forster himself . . . *David Copperfield* is one of the most fully annotated and it is here that Forster refers again to Rosa Dartle's origin. Twice the name "Mrs Brown" appears in connexion with her: as a marginal note against her first speech in the novel (ch. 20, p. 177) just after Dickens's allusion to her habit of hinting, and on the blank page at the end of Volume I, where he writes, "Mrs Brown (Dartle)". We may assume that "Mrs Brown" is the "lady friend" referred to in the *Life*; moreover . . . it seems likely that she is to be identified with the Mrs Brown, formerly Hannah Meredith' (Margaret Cardwell, 1960, 'Rosa Dartle and Mrs Brown', *The Dickensian* 56: 29–30). Not long before her marriage, Mrs Brown fell seriously ill and was tended by the nurse who served as the prototype of Mrs Gamp.

BROWN, William Slater (b. 1892?) Educated at Columbia University, he shared an apartment with E.E. Cummings in New York in 1918 and again (after the Armistice) in 1919–20; they travelled together in Europe in 1921. In 1925 he was on the staff of the periodical *Broom*.

B. (OR W.S.B.) in E.E. Cummings, *The Enormous Room* (1922)

'Bill is the "B" or "WSB" in Cummings' *The Enormous Room*. During World War I they were both volunteers in the Norton–Hayes Ambulance Service, and they were both jailed (in "the enormous room") on suspicion of being pro-German, partly because they grew mustaches and were not very neat, partly because they spoke French and preferred the company of the French *poilus* to that of the other Americans' (Susan Jenkins Brown, 1969, *Robber Rocks: letters and memories of Hart Crane, 1923–32*, Middletown, Conn., p. 24).

BROWNE, James (1830–81?) Painter. Known as 'Jim', in 1869 he was living with his two sisters in South Kensington, London, painting huge canvases. He came to know George Moore, at that time living in Alfred Terrace, South Kensington; it was through Browne that Moore first became interested in painting.

MR BARTON in George Moore, *Muslin* (1915)

'More than a glimpse of Jim Browne is given in the ridiculous figure of Mr Barton' (Joseph Hone, 1936, *The Life of George Moore*, London: Victor Gollancz, p. 36).

BROWNING, Oscar (1837–1923) Educated at Eton and at King's College, Cambridge, in 1865–75 he was History Master at Eton; he was dismissed on charges (described by *The Dictionary of National Biography* (London: Oxford University Press) as 'unsubstantiated') of misconduct. He returned to King's as a lecturer in history and later as a University lecturer. He was a tremendous figure in the college, and was the subject of innumerable anecdotes. He was a formidable snob and a dedicated radical.

OLIVER BROWNLOW in Shane Leslie, *The Cantab* (1926)

Identified in a key in the hand of Dr Ivor Ramsay, a Kingsman of the year 1920, and later Dean, laid in a copy of *The Cantab*.

BROWNING, Robert (1812–89) English poet. He was born in Camberwell, South London, the son of a Bank of England clerk. Much travelled in his youth, he began publishing poems in 1833. He married the poet Elizabeth Barrett in 1846 and for the sake of her health they moved to Italy, where their son was born in 1849. After the death of his wife in 1861, he settled in England with his son Robert Barrett, who became a painter and sculptor.

CLARE VAWDREY in Henry James, 'The Private Life' (1891)

'James stated in his preface [to Vol. XVII of the New York edition (1909) of his works] that Robert Browning . . . had furnished the starting point for Vawdrey' (*The Notebooks of Henry James*, 1947, ed. F.O. Matthiessen and K.B. Murdock, New York, p. 110). The 'statement' runs from p. xii to p. xv of the preface; not until the penultimate sentence is 'the fresh sane man . . . who had written the immortal things' identified as Browning.

BROWNRIGG, Captain

GENTLEMAN BROWN in Joseph Conrad, *Lord Jim* (1900)

'[It is] likely that [Conrad] took some aspects of the incident [of Gentleman Brown] from Belcher. . . . Gentleman Brown's arrival at Patusan is similar to Belcher's arrival at Gunung Tabur; and the name Gentleman Brown – and in part his nature – appears to derive from Captain Brownrigg, whom Belcher had come to Berau to rescue' (Norman Sherry, 1966, *Conrad's Eastern World*, Cambridge, p. 155). The narrative referred to is the *Narrative of the Voyage of H.M.S. Samarang During the Years 1843–46* (1848, London) by Captain Sir Edward Belcher.

BRUDENELL, Lord *See* **Cardigan**, 7th Earl of.

BRUMMELL, George Bryan ('Beau') (1778–1840) The greatest of all the dandies. His grandfather, who was in business in Bury Street in St James's, London, also let lodgings: one of his lodgers, Charles Jenkinson (afterwards Lord Liverpool), obtained for his son a clerkship in the Treasury, which enabled him to amass a fortune. He in his turn sent his son, George, to Eton where, in 1791, he was in the IVth Form with William Lamb, afterwards Lord **Melbourne**, and Charles Stewart, afterwards 3rd Marquis of **Londonderry**. He then went on to Oriel College, Oxford. He became a friend of the Prince Regent. In 1816 he retired to France, in debt; he died in a lunatic asylum in Caen.

JULIUS VON ASSLINGEN in Benjamin Disraeli, *Vivian Grey* (1826–7)

Identified as M——s of L—d—y in a key given in a pamphlet published in 1827 by William Marsh. This key is discussed by Lucien Wolf in his notes to *Vivian Grey*, 1904 (centenary edn, Vol. II, London, p. 364), with the conclusion that Disraeli was not responsible for the key.

HENRY BEAUCHAMP in T.H. Lister, *Arlington* (1832)

'The picturesque dandy, Henry Beauchamp, obviously drawn from Brummell, is endowed with physical beauty and a genius for style' (M.W. Rosa, 1936, *The Silver-Fork School: novels of fashion preceding* Vanity Fair, New York, p. 72).

RICHARD BEAUMONT in W. Massie, *Sydenham; or Memoirs of a Man of the World* (1830)

'Volume one is purely social, dealing with such notables as Brummell (Mr Beaumont)' (Rosa, op. cit., p. 81 n. 3).

HON. MR LISTLESS in Thomas Love Peacock, *Nightmare Abbey* (1818)

'This draws of course on the well-known Windermere anecdote of Beau Brummell' (Howard Mills, 1969, *Peacock: his circle and his age*, Cambridge, p. 156 n. 2). The incident referred to occurs in chapter 5, where Mr Listless asks his valet: 'Fatout! When did I think of going to Cheltenham and did not go?' *See also* **Skeffington**, Sir Lumley.

JOHN RUSSELTON in Bulwer Lytton, *Pelham* (1828)

'Russelton, a character based intimately and accurately on Brummell' (Derek Marlow, 1969, *A Single Summer with L.B.*, p. 239 n.).

MR TREBECK in T.H. Lister, *Granby* (1826)

'Captain Jesse in his *Life of Brummell* (... 1844) ... declares that "Trebeck" was intended as a portrait of the Beau. If this were indeed the case, Lister was no portraitist, a conclusion hard to accept in the face of the novelist's successful presentation of Lady Caroline Lamb' (Michael Sadleir, 1933, *Bulwer and His Wife*, London: Constable, p. 111).

BRUNO, Guido (1884–1942) Of Czech or German origin, he was the son of a rabbi and moved to Greenwich Village in 1906. He issued a number of little magazines, including a series called *Bruno's Chapbooks*, of which Djuna Barnes's *Book of Repulsive Women* (1915) was No. 20. At that time he was financed by Charles Edison, son of the inventor.

FELIX VOLKBEIN in Djuna Barnes, *Nightwood* (1936)

'Guido Bruno is of note in the life of Djuna Barnes because she modelled the character of Felix Volkbein ... largely upon him' (Andrew Field, 1983, *The Formidable Miss Barnes*, London: Secker & Warburg, p. 14).

BRUSSELS

VILLETTE in Charlotte Brontë, *Villette* (1853)

'The thinnest possible veil of disguise covers ... the real identity of the city of Villette.... It is hardly possible that the careful reader should ... stand in doubt that the city of Brussels is the real scene of the story' (Herbert Wroot, 1906, *The Persons and Places of the Brontë Novels*, Bradford, p. 160).

BRYANT, Jacob (1715–1804) Classical scholar. Educated at Eton, he was a Fellow of King's College, Cambridge, and in 1756 was Secretary to the Duke of Marlborough. He published treatises on mythology and Homeric questions, in one of which he denied that the city of Troy ever existed, and was the author of *A New System; or An Analysis of Ancient Mythology* (1804).

EDWARD CASAUBON in George Eliot, *Middlemarch* (1871–2)

'Bryant's theory of the Phoenicians . . . of the . . . Cabiri . . . and of Dagon the fish god . . . are all behind Mr Casaubon's researches. It was as if George Eliot had Bryant ready in case she was suspected of deriding a living comparative mythologist' (Richard Ellmann, 1973, 'Dorothea's husbands', in *Golden Codgers*, London: Oxford University Press, p. 22). *See also* **Brabant**, R.H.; **Eliot**, George; **Mackay**, R.W.; **Pattison**, Mark; **Spencer**, Herbert.

BRYN MAWR COLLEGE, Pennsylvania Situated near Philadelphia, it was founded as a college for women by the Society of Friends in 1880.

FERNHURST in Gertrude Stein, *Fernhurst* (1971)

'. . . a fictional account of [an] unhappy love affair, drawn . . . largely from . . . gossip encountered in Mabel Haynes's circle of Bryn Mawr graduates . . . [concerning] a triangular relationship involving the dean of Bryn Mawr . . . Carey Thomas. . . . The dean of [the] story . . . presides over the college of Fernhurst' (James R. Mellow, 1974, *The Charmed Circle: Gertrude Stein and company*, London: Phaidon Press, p. 65).

BUCHAN, John (1875–1940) 1st Baron Tweedsmuir. Novelist and diplomat. He was with the South African High Commission in 1901–3, and was Governor-General of Canada in 1935–40. He wrote novels of adventure, notably *The Thirty-nine Steps* (1915).

HUGH SOMERVILLE in John Buchan, *A Lodge in the Wilderness* (1906)

Identified in a key dated January 1907 in a copy of *A Lodge in the Wilderness*, formerly the property of Grace Keily.

BUCHANAN, Sir George (1854–1924) Diplomat. In 1910–18 he was Ambassador at St Petersburg, and in 1919–21 he was Ambassador at Rome.

SIR HERBERT WITHERSPOON in W. Somerset Maugham, 'His Excellency', *Ashenden; or The British Agent* (1928)

'Sir Herbert Witherspoon . . . is based to some degree on Sir George Buchanan' (R.L. Calder, 1922, *W. Somerset Maugham and the Quest for Freedom*, London: Heinemann, p. 201).

BUCHANAN, James William (1792–1846) He was a lawyer in Nuneaton, Warwickshire, and Clerk of the parish. He played a leading part in the controversy between Evangelicals and conservative members of the established church that raged in Nuneaton from 1828 to 1831. He married Nancy Wallington (**Buchanan**, below) in 1825. The accident that befell Mr Dempster in 'Janet's Repentance' in fact befell Mr Buchanan in 1840, shortly after the death of his wife. He recovered, however, and survived his wife by six years.

ROBERT DEMPSTER in George Eliot, 'Janet's Repentance', *Scenes of Clerical Life* (1857–8)

'The Buchanans appear as the Dempsters in all the "keys" to the originals of "Janet's Repentance" which circulated in Warwickshire after its publication in 1857' (Gordon S. Haight, 1968, *George Eliot*, Oxford, p. 10). 'There are *two* portraits in Clerical Scenes . . . first *Amos Barton* . . . second *Dempster*, whose original has been dead twenty years or more' (George Eliot to Charles Bray, 19 September 1859, reproduced in *The George Eliot Letters*, 1954, ed. Gordon S. Haight, Vol. III, London: Oxford University Press, pp. 156–7).

BUCHANAN, Nancy (1803–40) Daughter of Nancy **Wallington**, in 1825 she married James William **Buchanan**.

JANET DEMPSTER in George Eliot, 'Janet's Repentance', *Scenes of Clerical Life* (1857–8)

See under **Buchanan**, J.W.

BUCK, E.E. ('Gene') (1885–1957) Song-writer and producer. Born in Detroit he later worked with the theatre manager Florenz Ziegfeld and in 1925 was a neighbour of Scott and Zelda **Fitzgerald** in Great Neck. He died at Manhasset, Long Island, New York.

LOU GREGG in Ring Lardner, 'The Love Nest' (1926)

'A source of amusement for Fitzgerald and Lardner was the behavior of Gene Buck, a songwriter of almost impenetrable egocentricity. . . . Lardner wrote Buck into . . . "The Love Nest"' (Matthew J. Bruccoli, 1981, *Some Sort of Epic Grandeur: the life of F. Scott Fitzgerald*, London: Hodder & Stoughton, p. 178).

BUCKINGHAM HOUSE, Old Shoreham, Sussex For more information, see Nikolaus Pevsner, 1970, *Sussex (Buildings of England* series), Harmondsworth: Penguin, pp. 287–8. For 200 years it was the home of the Bridgers, a family of squires; they were close friends of the young George Moore, who frequently stayed at the house.

WOODVIEW in George Moore, *Esther Waters* (1894)

'When Moore first went to stay with [the Bridgers] the old Squire was still alive and lived in the big house called Buckingham, a park of 70 acres, the scene of the opening of *Esther Waters*' (Joseph Hone, 1936, *The Life of George Moore*, London: Victor Gollancz, p. 43).

BUCKNILL, William Surgeon. He practised in Nuneaton, Warwickshire, and attended Robert **Evans**, George Eliot's father, from 1836 onwards.

MR PILGRIM in George Eliot, 'The Sad Fortunes of the Revd Amos Barton', *Scenes of Clerical Life* (1857–8)

See under **Anstruther**, Lady.

BUDE, Cornwall A small watering place fourteen miles north of St Juliot.

STRATLEIGH in Thomas Hardy, *A Pair of Blue Eyes* (1873)

Identified in F.B. Pinion, 1968, *A Hardy Companion*, London: Macmillan.

BUDGEN, Frank (1882–1971) Painter and author. He wrote *James Joyce and the Making of Ulysses* (1934). In 1918 he met Joyce in Zurich and became one of his closest friends.

W.B. MURPHY in James Joyce, *Ulysses* (1922)

'[Joyce] amused himself by borrowing a bit (a very small bit) of Frank Budgen for the wily sailor in the [Eumaeus] episode' (Richard Ellmann, 1982, *James Joyce*, rev. edn, Oxford: Oxford University Press, p. 500).

BULL, Mr

MR PHIPPS in George Eliot, 'Janet's Repentance' and 'The Sad Fortunes of the Revd Amos Barton', *Scenes of Clerical Life* (1857–8)

See under **Anstruther**, Lady.

BULL, Revd George Stringer (1799–1865) Son of John Bull, Rector of Pentlow, Essex, in 1811 he entered the Royal Navy and in 1818 he went to Sierra Leone as a missionary schoolmaster. He was ordained in 1823 and became Curate of Hessle, near Hull, and in 1826 he was Curate of Bierley, near Bradford. He lived in Birmingham from 1840 to 1864, and then lived in Almeley, Herefordshire, until he died. He was a close friend of the reformers Michael Sadler (1780–1835) and Richard Oastler (1789–1861), and was associated with both in the struggle for the abolition of child labour and the fight for the Ten Hours Bill.

PARSON BELL (OF FAIRLY) in Frances Trollope, *Michael Armstrong, the Factory Boy* (1840)

In February 1839, Mrs Trollope set off with her son Tom for the North of England to collect material for a novel about the question of factory reform. 'In Bradford [they] met John Wood, a philanthropic worsted spinner. . . . At Wood's residence they were also introduced to another local champion of the factory children, the Rev. G.S. Bull, the . . . incumbent of Bierley, who appears in *Michael Armstrong* under the thin disguise of "Parson Bell of Fairly" in Yorkshire' (W.H. Chaloner, 1969, 'Mrs Trollope and the early factory system', *Victorian Studies* 4 (7): 161).

The BULL HOTEL, Nuneaton, Warwickshire

THE RED LION in George Eliot, 'Janet's Repentance', *Scenes of Clerical Life* (1857–8)

'The Bull Hotel in Nuneaton . . . played an important part in "Janet's Repentance" as the "Red Lion" of Milby' (Charles S. Olcott, 1911, *George Eliot: scenes and people in her novels*, London: Cassell, p. 36; originally published 1910, New York: Thomas Y. Crowell).

BULLER, Charles, the Elder (1774–1848) Sixth and youngest son of John Buller of Morval, near Looe, Cornwall. He joined the revenue department of the East India Company in Calcutta, returning to England *c*.1812. He became MP for West Looe in 1826. He married Isabella Barbara Kirkpatrick (**Buller**, below).

GRAF ZÄHDARM in Thomas Carlyle, *Sartor Resartus* (1833–4)

'As regards the identification of Graf Zähdarm, it should be observed that in the lady's [Mrs Edward Strachey's] copy of *Sartor* there stand in her handwriting, the words "Charles Buller, senior"' (George Strachey, 1892, 'Carlyle and the "Rose-goddess"', *The Nineteenth Century* 32 (September): 475). *See also under* **Buller**, Isabella Barbara.

BULLER, Charles, the Younger (1806–48) Elder son of Charles and Isabella **Buller**. He was a pupil of Thomas Carlyle in 1822–5, and was his disciple and friend in adult life. He was also a friend of the social reformer John Stewart Mill (1806–73) and was a radical in politics; he became MP for Liskeard. From 1832 to 1848 he was Secretary to Lord Durham and is supposed to have written much of his *Report on the Affairs of British North America* (1839). 'A great tower of a fellow, six feet three in height, a yard in breadth' (Carlyle to his mother, 10 November 1831).

Towgood ('Toughgut') in Thomas Carlyle, *Sartor Resartus* (1833–4)

'"The story of the book," said Mrs Strachey to her son, "is as plain as a pikestaff. . . . Toughgut is young Charles Buller . . ."' (George Strachey, 1892, 'Carlyle and the "Rose-Goddess"', *The Nineteenth Century* 32 (September): 474).

BULLER, Isabella Barbara (d. 1849) Daughter of Major-General William Kirkpatrick, sister of Julia **Strachey** and cousin of Kitty **Kirkpatrick**. She married Charles **Buller**, Senior, and was the mother of Arthur and Charles **Buller**: Theresa **Reviss** was her granddaughter. She became acquainted with Carlyle in 1822 through Edward **Irving**; Carlyle acted as tutor to her two elder sons in 1822–5, and remained her friend to the end of her life.

Gräfin Zähdarm in Thomas Carlyle, *Sartor Resartus* (1833–4)

'"The story of the book," said Mrs Strachey to her son, "is as plain as a pikestaff. . . . The Zähdarms are your uncle and aunt Buller . . ."' (George Strachey, 1892, 'Carlyle and the "Rose-Goddess"', *The Nineteenth Century* 32 (September): 474).

BULWER, Edward George Lytton *See* **Lytton**, 1st Baron.

BULWER, William Henry Lytton Earle (1801–72) Diplomat. Created Baron Dalling and Bulwer in 1871, he was best known as Sir Henry Lytton; he was the brother of Edward Bulwer, 1st Baron **Lytton**. In 1824 he was in Greece, acting for the revolutionary committee, and in 1827–30 he was in the Foreign Service. He was Liberal MP for Wilton in 1830, Coventry in 1831, and Marylebone in 1835. From 1835 to 1865 he was Ambassador at Madrid and Washington, and in 1868 he was Minister at Florence.

Augustus Tremaine Bertie in Benjamin Disraeli, *Endymion* (1880)

Identified in 'Key to *Endymion*', *Notes and Queries* 83 (24 October 1942): 263; identifications attributed to G.E. Buckle.

BUMP, Marjorie (b. 1901?) Daughter of the owner of Bump and McCabe's Hardware Store in Petoskey, Michigan, in 1919 she was a high-school girl with red hair and to one small boy seemed to be the prettiest girl in the world; she had come up to help wait on tables at the chicken-dinner establishment run by Mrs Elizabeth Dilworth at Pinehurst Cottage, Horton Bay. The Dilworths had been friends of the Hemingways since 1903.

MARJORIE in Ernest Hemingway, 'The End of Something', *In Our Time* (1925)

'Marge . . . was real enough to Bill [Smith] – she was Marjorie Bump . . . but the brush-off of the story is a good deal harder to get at' (D. St John, 1972, 'Interview with Hemingway's "Bill Gorton"', in B.D. Sarason, *Hemingway and the Sun Set*, Washington, DC, p. 166).

BUNN, Alfred (1796–1860) Stage manager at Drury Lane Theatre, London, in 1823, he managed Birmingham Theatre in 1826. In 1833–48 he was Manager of Drury Lane and Covent Garden theatres, introducing orchestra stalls (their first appearance) at Drury Lane in 1833. He went bankrupt in 1840, and in 1845 he became an early Catholic convert. He made his début in New York in 1852 and was the author of the libretto of *The Bohemian Girl* and other operas by Balfe.

MR DOLPHIN in W.M. Thackeray, *The History of Pendennis* (1848–50)

'I can also remember Alfred Bunn, and always thought that Thackeray must have sketched the portrait of Mr Dolphin . . . from him' (Edmund Yates, 1884, *Edmund Yates: his recollections and experiences*, Vol. I, London: R. Bentley & Son, pp. 24–5).

BUNSEN, Christian Karl Josias von Bunsen, Baron (1791–1860) He was the Prussian envoy in Great Britain in 1842–54.

THE —— AMBASSADOR in Charles Kingsley, *Alton Locke* (1850)

'"The —— ambassador" to whom Acton is presented at the Dean's reception, is Baron Bunsen' (M.F. Thorp, 1937, *Charles Kingsley, 1819–1875*, Princeton and London, p. 75).

BUNTING, Revd Jabez (1779–1858) Wesleyan methodist. He studied medicine and was admitted to the ministry *c.*1799. He organized the connection and completed its severance from the Anglican church.

REVD JABES BRANDERHAM in Emily Brontë, *Wuthering Heights* (1847)

'The original of this caricature is . . . likely to have been the Revd Jabez Bunting . . . [who was] known to Mr Brontë' (Winifred Gérin, 1971, *Emily Brontë*, Oxford, p. 81).

BURCHIELLO, Domenico (1404–49) Original surname di Giovanni, he was a Florentine barber-poet who was known especially for his burlesque sonnets and obscure humour.

NELLO in George Eliot, *Romola* (1863)

'Nello . . . is an almost literal copy of Domenico Burchiello. . . . The description of his shop . . . was taken from the establishment of Burchiello, a picture of which may be seen in the Medici Gallery. Nello differs from his predecessor only in . . . that he did not claim to be a poet' (Charles S. Olcott, 1911, *George Eliot: scenes and people in her novels*, London: Cassell, p. 132; originally published 1910, New York: Thomas Y. Crowell).

BURDETT, Sir Francis (1770–1844) English politician. Educated at Westminster and Oxford, he was in Paris during the early part of the French Revolution. In 1793 he married Sophia Coutts, and in 1796 he became an MP, advocating Parliamentary reform and opposing the war with France. In 1807–37 he was MP for Westminster, and in 1810 and 1820 he was imprisoned on political charges. After the Reform Bill, he became more conservative in his views, and in 1837–44 he was Tory MP for North Wiltshire.

MOBBING FRANCIS in Bulwer Lytton, *Paul Clifford* (1830)

Identified in a key set out by Rosina Bulwer Lytton, in a letter of 26 May 1830, reproduced in Michael Sadleir, 1968, *Bulwer and His Wife*, London: Constable, pp. 227–8.

BURDICK, Edmund (1899?–1918) Of Asheville, North Carolina. He was Wolfe's room-mate in his sophomore year at Chapel Hill University. He died of congenital heart disease.

BOB STERLING in Thomas Wolfe, *Look Homeward, Angel* (1929)

'The university's *Carolina Magazine* has described the death of . . . Edward [sic] Burwick, whom Wolfe calls Bob Sterling' (Floyd C. Watkins, 1957, *Thomas Wolfe's Characters: portraits from life*, Norman, Okla., p. 17).

BURGES, William (1827–81) Architect. Son of Alfred Burgess, marine engineer and a member of the firm of Walker, Burgess & Cooper which took over the completion of the East Bute Docks at Cardiff for the trustees of the young Lord Bute *c.*1855. William Burgess was trained by Edward Blore and Digby Wyatt and met Lord **Bute** in 1865; in 1868 he was commissioned by him to restore Cardiff Castle, a task that occupied him for the rest of his life. He designed, and from 1875 directed, the restoration of Castell Coch, Lord Bute's property a few miles outside Cardiff, up the valley of the River Taff. 'One of the most Gothic of the Gothicists. ... He was small and facetious ... very short-sighted, with an eyeglass that kept dropping out ... he owned a couple of medieval outfits which he wore on occasions in his rooms in Buckingham Street' (Mark Girouard, 1971, *The Victorian Country House*, Oxford: Clarendon Press, pp. 125–6). Rossetti wrote of him: 'There's a babyish party named Burges, Who from infancy hardly emerges, If you had not been told, He's disgracefully old, You would offer a bull's-eye to Burges (quoted in Girouard, ibid., p. 126). Both houses are illustrated in Girouard.

GEORGIUS OLDHOUSEN in Robert Kerr, *His Excellency The Ambassador Extraordinary* (1879)

'The character of Master Georgius Oldhousen . . . is said to have been inspired by Burges' (ibid., p. 125 n. 3).

BURKE, Jack (d. 1913) Lightweight boxer. He had the reputation of being able to survive the marathon contests that were often fought in the nineteenth-century ring.

CASHEL BYRON in George Bernard Shaw, *Cashel Byron's Profession* (1886)

'Shaw ... sublimated his interest in boxing by writing a novel about it. Conjuring up his hero by mixing in equal parts the personalities of ... Beatty and ... Jack Burke ... Shaw ... on 12 April 1882, settled down to five foolscap pages a day' (Benny Green, 1978, *Shaw's Champions: G.B.S. & prizefighting from Cashel Brown to Gene Tunney*, London: Elm Tree Books, p. 7). *See also* **Beatty**, **Pakenham**.

BURKE, Kenneth (1897–1962) American critic. Born in Pittsburgh, he was educated at Columbia University. He was Music Critic for *Dial* magazine and then for the *Nation*. He studied the theory of literary forms and was the author of *A Grammar of Motives* (1945) and *A Rhetoric of Motives* (1950).

O'BRIAN in Robert McAlmon, *Post Adolescence* (1923)

'O'Brian is Kenneth Burke' (Robert E. Knoll (ed.), 1962, *McAlmon and the Lost Generation: a self-portrait*, Lincoln, Nebr.: University of Nebraska Press, p. 108).

BURKE, Mike Section foreman at the railway yard at Spuyten Duyvil on the Hudson River. Theodore Dreiser worked under him in the summer of 1903.

THE MIGHTY ROURKE in Theodore Dreiser, *Twelve Men* (1919)

'He was to include Mike in *Twelve Men* as "The Mighty Rourke"' (F.O. Matthiessen, 1951, *Theodore Dreiser*, London: Methuen, p. 101).

BURNE-JONES, Edward (1833–98) English painter. Born Jones, he was the son of an impoverished frame-maker in Birmingham. He studied at Exeter College, Oxford, where he met Dante Gabriel **Rossetti** and William Morris, the latter becoming his closest friend. In 1860 he married Georgiana Macdonald, aunt of Rudyard Kipling; Angela Thirkell was his granddaughter. He was a member, from its inception in 1861, of Morris, Marshall & Company (later Morris & Company), for which he designed tapestries and stained glass.

THE LAMA in Rudyard Kipling, *Kim* (1901)

The happiest days of Kipling's unhappy childhood in England were spent with the Burne-Joneses. 'If Kipling expressed his deepest feelings for his uncle anywhere, it was surely in *Kim*. Who else is the old lama, whose life is a quest which others do not understand, who can draw with pen and ink in a way that is almost lost to the world, who shows Kim his art "not for pride's sake, but because thou must learn", and who tells stories that hold him spell-bound? ... In fact, Kipling returned to the manuscript of Kim immediately after Burne-Jones's death' (Penelope Fitzgerald, 1975, *Edward Burne-Jones*, London: Joseph, p. 275).

BURNETT, David (1931–71) Writer. Son of Whit **Burnett** and Martha Foley, he was educated at Columbia University and at the Sorbonne. In 1958–71 he edited *The Best American Short Stories*, and in 1950–2 he edited *New Story Magazine*, in which Jean Genet, Terry Southern and James Baldwin were first published in the USA.

WALT FITZPATRICK in Jack Kerouac, *The Subterraneans* (1958)

Identified in 'Character key to the Duluoz Legend', in Barry Gifford and Lawrence Lee, 1979, *Jack's Book*, pp. 322–32.

BURNETT, Henry (1812–93) Singer and music teacher. As a young boy he sang before the court in Brighton, standing on a table, while the gout-stricken George IV was wheeled into the room wrapped in flannel and bandages. In 1832 he met Fanny Dickens (1810–48), Charles Dickens's sister, when they were both students at the Royal Academy of Music, and married her in 1837. He went on to the operatic stage, and in 1838 he joined Macready's company at Covent Garden. In 1841 he abandoned his stage career, because of religious scruples, and never again entered a theatre or opera house. He settled in Manchester.

NICHOLAS NICKLEBY in Charles Dickens, *Nicholas Nickleby* (1838–9)

'A strong impression prevailed in Manchester circles that Mr Burnett was the ideal of Nicholas Nickleby. In the picture where Mantalini is seen working at the "demnation" mangle the stooping figure of Nicholas is said to be an excellent portrait of Mr Burnett in his prime' (W.E.A.A., 1883, 'The original of Paul Dombey', *The Palatine Notebook*, Vol. III, p. 208; reprinted in 1910 in *The Dickensian* 6 (January): 9). 'That "Phiz" should have taken Mr Burnett as his model for one drawing does not appear to be probable. The face is so sketchy that it might seem to be the portrait of many, or nobody at all' (ibid.).

BURNETT, Henry Augustus ('Harry') (1839–49) Eldest son of Dickens's elder sister Fanny and Henry **Burnett**, he was an invalid from birth.

PAUL DOMBEY in Charles Dickens, *Dombey and Son* (1846–8)

'The "little deformed child", Harry, was a singular child – meditative and quaint in a remarkable degree. He was the original, as Mr Dickens told his sister, of little "Paul Dombey". Harry had been taken to Brighton, as "little Paul" is represented to have been and had there ... given utterance to thoughts quite as remarkable ... as those which are put into the lips of Paul Dombey.... He died in the arms of a dear, dear, nephew of mine since passed away, John Griffin' (James Griffin, 1883, *Memories of the Past*, London: Hamilton, Adams, p. 209). James Griffin was the minister of Rusholme Road Chapel, Manchester, of which Henry and Fanny Burnett were members; by Fanny's wish he officiated at her funeral. According to Professor Tillotson this passage is the earliest evidence of this tradition (see K. Tillotson, 1956, *Novels of the Eighteen-Forties*, Oxford, p. 194 n.).

BURNETT, Swan (1847?–1906) Opthamologist. He married Frances Hodgson in 1873, after meeting her in 1865 when the Hodgson family went to live at New Market, Tennessee, where Swan's father was the local doctor. They were divorced in 1898, and in 1904 he married Margaret Brady.

GRIFFITH DONNE in Frances Hodgson Burnett, *Dolly* (1877)

'Griffith Donne ... is certainly Swan Burnett' (Ann Thwaite, 1974, *Waiting for the Party: the life of Frances Hodgson Burnett, 1849–1924*, London: Secker & Warburg, p. 36).

BURNETT, Vivian (1876–1937) Second son of Swan **Burnett** and Frances Hodgson Burnett. He died in a sailing accident, collapsing after having saved his four companions.

CEDRIC ERROLL, LORD FAUNTLEROY in Frances Hodgson Burnett, *Little Lord Fauntleroy* (1886)

'Frances remembered the origins of *Little Lord Fauntleroy* like this . . . "One day I had an idea. I will write a story about [Vivian]. . . . It is not a portrait; but, certainly, if there had not been Vivian there would not have been Fauntleroy", [a friend] heard Frances tell people' (Ann Thwaite, 1974, *Waiting for the Party: the life of Frances Hodgson Burnett, 1849–1924*, London: Secker & Warburg, p. 90). 'The illustrations . . . were based on a photograph of Vivian taken . . . in 1884' (ibid., p. 92).

BURNETT, Whit (1899–1973) American journalist and writer. He founded the periodical *Story* in Vienna in 1931, and in 1933 he transferred it to New York. He was an editor for various publishers from 1949 to 1973.

BENNETT FITZPATRICK in Jack Kerouac, *The Subterraneans* (1958)

Identified in 'Character key to the Duluoz Legend', in Barry Gifford and Lawrence Lee, 1979, *Jack's Book*, pp. 322–32.

BURNS, Harry H. (1905–79) Professor of English at the University of Washington, Seattle. Ernest Hemingway first met him in Key West in the summer of 1936 and christened him MacWalsey. The two men kept in touch and in 1951 Burns visited Hemingway in Havana.

JOHN MACWALSEY in Ernest Hemingway, *To Have and Have Not* (1937)

'This eccentric educator . . . was based on a rough approximation of Professor Harry Burns and Arnold Gingrich' (Carlos Baker, 1969, *Ernest Hemingway: a life story*, New York, p. 295). 'E.H. later apologized to Burns for having introduced the character of MacWalsey: Harry H. Burns to author, Aug. 3, 1963' (ibid., 619 n. 'E.H's eccentrics in the Morgan novel'). *See also* **Gingrich**, Arnold.

BURROUGHS, Joan Vollmer Née Adams, she married W.S. **Burroughs**.

JANE CARMODY in Jack Kerouac, *On the Road* (1957)

Identified in 'Character key to the Duluoz Legend', in Barry Gifford and Lawrence Lee, 1979, *Jack's Book*, pp. 322–32.

BURROUGHS, Julie Daughter of W.S. **Burroughs**.

DODIE CARMODY in Jack Kerouac, *On the Road* (1957)

Identified in 'Character key to the Duluoz Legend', in Barry Gifford and Lawrence Lee, 1979, *Jack's Book*, pp. 322–32.

BURROUGHS, William, Junior Son of W.S. **Burroughs**.

RAY CARMODY in Jack Kerouac, *On the Road* (1957)

Identified in 'Character key to the Duluoz Legend', in Barry Gifford and Lawrence Lee, 1979, *Jack's Book*, pp. 322–32.

BURROUGHS, William Seward (b. 1914) Novelist. Born in St Louis, Mississippi, he was educated at Harvard. He became a heroin addict in 1944 and was the author of *Junkie* (1953), *The Naked Lunch* (1959), and other works. His grandfather was the inventor of the Burroughs calculating machine. He married Joan Vollmer Adams (**Burroughs**, above), whom he accidentally shot and killed during a drunken party game in Mexico City in 1951.

FRANK CARMODY and OLD BULL LEE in *On the Road* (1957), WILL DENNISON in *The Town and the City* (1950), BULL HUBBARD in *Book of Dreams* (1960) and *Desolation Angels* (1965), and 'WILL' HUBBARD in *Vanity of Duluoz* (1968), all by Jack Kerouac

Identified in 'Character key to the Duluoz Legend', in Barry Gifford and Lawrence Lee, 1979, *Jack's Book*, pp. 322–32.

BURROWS, Alfred (1864–1948) Father of Louisa **Burrows**, he was a draughtsman in a lace factory and in 1899 qualified as a teacher; in 1907 he taught handicrafts for the Leicestershire County Council and he ran a village carving class which made the reredos in St Catherine's Church, Cossall. In 1908 he moved from Cossall to Quorn. He was married to Louisa Burrows.

WILLIAM BRANGWEN in D.H. Lawrence, *The Rainbow* (1915)

'Alfred Burrows was the original of Ursula's father in *The Rainbow*, the dreamy, Ruskinized young man who loves Gothic carvings' (H.T. Moore, 1960, *The Intelligent Heart: the story of D.H. Lawrence*, Harmondsworth: Penguin, p. 79; originally published 1955, London: Heinemann).

BURROWS, Louisa ('Louie') (1888–1962) Born in Ilkeston, Derbyshire, she was the daughter of Alfred **Burrows** and his wife Louisa. They lived at Church Cottage, Cossall, near Ilkeston, and later moved to Quorn, Leicestershire. In 1903 she met D.H. Lawrence when they were attending a pupil–teacher centre at Ilkeston (1903–5); they became engaged in 1910, but the engagement was broken off in February 1912. In 1911–24 she was Headmistress of Quorn Church of England school, later Headmistress of another Leicestershire school. In 1940 she married Frederick Heath, and in 1941 she retired from teaching.

URSULA BRANGWEN in D.H. Lawrence, *The Rainbow* (1915)

'I also felt that the character [of Ella, later called Ursula] was inclined to fall into two halves. . . . It came of trying to graft on to the character of Louie the character, more or less, of Frieda' (to Edward Garnett, 29 January 1914, reproduced in *The D.H. Lawrence Letters*, Vol. II: *1913–1916*, 1982, ed. George T. Zytaruk and James T. Boulton, Cambridge: Cambridge University Press, p. 142). *See also* **Lawrence**, Frieda.

BURTON, Mr

MR BUDD in George Eliot, 'Janet's Repentance', *Scenes of Clerical Life* (1857–8)

See under **Anstruther**, Lady.

BURTON, Mrs Of Boston, later of California.

CORNELIA THORNWELL in Upton Sinclair, *Boston* (1928)

'[A]n elderly lady, socially prominent in Boston ... she enjoyed telling me odd stories about the tight little group of self-determined aristocrats who ruled the ... city. ... Mrs Burton had come to California, seeking a new life, and I delighted her by saying that she would be my heroine – "the runaway grandmother", I would call her' (*The Autobiography of Upton Sinclair*, 1963, London: W.H. Allen, pp. 254–5; originally published 1962, New York: Harcourt, Brace & World). 'Sinclair's principal character is Cornelia Thornwell the "runaway grandmother"' (Joseph Blotner, 1966, *The Modern American Political Novel*, Austin, Tex., p. 287).

BURTON, Mrs F.C. She married F.C. Burton, who in 1887 was a major in the Bengal Lancers stationed at Peshawar. She met Kipling in Simla in 1866.

LUCY HAUKSBEE in Rudyard Kipling, *Plain Tales from the Hills* (1888)

'Nearby [in an exhibition of Kipling memorabilia held at The Elms, Rottingdean, Sussex, 1951] were four ... interesting exhibits. The first was a letter from R.K. to Mrs Burton ... in 1887 at Peshawar. It concerns [the] dedication of *Plain Tales from the Hills* to "the wittiest woman in India", who by this letter was for the first time definitely identified as Mrs Burton' (Owen Tweedy, 1951, 'R.K. and Rottingdean: "The Elms" exhibition', *The Kipling Journal* 18 (100): 11). In 1888 Kipling wrote, to a Mrs Hill: 'Mrs Hauksbee's departure ... was postponed from the 13th to the 27th [April] and now that I have read the passenger list of the steamer of that date I see why'; Mrs Burton duly appears in the list for the 27th, sailing without her husband. It is not possible to identify the reason (see Betty Miller and R.L. Green, 1961, 'Mrs Hauksbee and "The wittiest woman in India"', in R.L. Green (ed.), *The Readers' Guide to Rudyard Kipling's Work*, Sect. I, London: Kipling Society, p. 5).

BURTON, Sir Richard (1821–90) Explorer and translator. Born in Torquay, Devon, he was educated in Europe and England; he was expelled from Oxford. He discovered Lake Tanganyika in Africa with the explorer John Hanning Speke in 1858 and was knighted in 1886. He translated *The Perfumed Garden* and *Kama Sutra* and married Isabella Arundell (1831–96).

RICHARD BLUNDELL in Morley Roberts, *A Son of Empire* (1899)

'Drawn as Richard Blundell in Morley Roberts's novel' (Frederic Boase, *Modern English Biography* (suppl.)).

BURY, Lady Charlotte Susan Maria (1775–1861) Scottish novelist, youngest daughter of the 5th Duke of Argyll and one of the beautiful Gunning sisters. In 1796 she married Colonel John Campbell. In 1809 she became lady-in-waiting to Caroline, Princess of Wales. In 1818 she married Revd Edward John **Bury**, Rector of Lichfield, Hampshire. She was thought to be the author of *Diary Illustrative of the Times of George IV* and she wrote sixteen novels.

LADY MARGARET CARLTON in M. Spencer Stanhope, *Almacks* (1826)

Identified in Michael Sadleir, 1951, *XIX Century Fiction*, London: Constable, p. 331; reprinted from *Literary Gazette* (9 December 1826)).

BURY, Revd Edward John   Rector of Lichfield, Hampshire. He was the husband of Lady Charlotte **Bury**, whom he married in 1809.

ARCHDEACON CARLTON in M. Spencer Stanhope, *Almacks* (1826)

Identified in Michael Sadleir, 1951, *XIX Century Fiction*, London: Constable, p. 331; reprinted from *Literary Gazette* (9 December 1826)).

BUSBY, Mr   A civic official at Kingston-upon-Thames, Surrey.

MARTIN TINMAN in George Meredith, *The House on the Beach* (1877)

'An . . . important element was . . . derived from [Meredith's] friend Hardman's comic anecdotes about a pompous civic official at Kingston, one Busby, whom Meredith transformed into Martin Tinman, the . . . bailiff of Crikswich' (A. Lionel Stevenson, 1954, *The Ordeal of George Meredith*, London: Peter Owen, p. 209).

BUSBY, Thomas   (1755–1838)   Composer, journalist and parliamentary reporter. He was joint Editor of a musical dictionary, and the author of one of the 'Rejected Addresses' written for the reopening of Drury Lane Theatre, London, in 1812. He also published (by subscription) a translation of Lucretius.

THE EDITOR OF THE UNIVERSAL REVIEW (OXFORD) in George Borrow, *Lavengro* (1851)

'To whom . . . does Borrow's description apply? Clearly it must be to someone who possessed fiddles, composed tunes, had some reputation . . . in music and worked for Sir Richard Phillips. The description fits exactly . . . Thomas Busby, Mus. Doc.' (A. Boyle, 1951, 'Portraiture in *Lavengro*', *Notes and Queries* 196 (13 October): 454). The article rejects at length the identification of the Editor with either William Gifford or John Carey. *See also* **Carey**, John ; **Gifford**, William.

BUSBY HALL, Carlton-in-Cleveland, North Yorkshire   Situated near Stokesley, it was the property of the Marwood family since 1587; in 1764 it was destroyed by fire and rebuilt, and it is now divided into flats.

GROBY in Ford Madox Ford, *Parade's End* (1924–8)

'Groby house is apparently modeled on Busby Hall' (Richard Gill, 1972, *Happy Rural Seat*, p. 275 n. 49). The house is illustrated in Gill (ibid.) between pp. 170 and 171.

BUSH, Harriet   (b. 1815)   Eldest daughter of Revd James Bush, Rector of South Luffenham, Rutland, Leicestershire. In 1838, when on a reading party in the Lake District, Froude met her and fell in love with her; with considerable difficulty he overcame the objections of his father to an engagement and a brief period of happiness ensued, but it was shattered when Mr Bush forbade the marriage. Archdeacon Froude had felt in duty bound to communicate to him the information that his son had contracted debts at Oxford amounting to some £400. The marriage was forbidden and Harriet compelled to promise that she would never see Froude again as long as she remained unmarried; she subsequently married Revd A.R. Webster.

EMMA HARDINGE in J.A. Froude, 'The Spirit's Trials', *Shadows of the Clouds* (1847)

Identified in W.H. Dunn, 1961, *James Anthony Froude*, Vol. I, Oxford, p. 53.

BUSHE, Charles Kendal (1767–1843) Irish judge. Educated at Trinity College, Dublin, he opposed the union. In 1805–22 he was Solicitor-General for Ireland, and in 1822–41 he was Chief Justice of King's Bench.

LORD CHIEF JUSTICE in Maria Edgeworth, *Patronage* (1814)

'The real men and women who made appearances [in the novels] . . . included the lawyer Charles Kendal Bushe (Lord Chief Justice) in *Patronage*' (Marilyn Butler, 1972, *Maria Edgeworth*, Oxford, p. 248).

BUTE, John Patrick Crichton-Stuart, Lord (1847–1900) He became the 3rd Marquis when his father died in 1848. He was immensely rich (in 1873 his income was £151,000 a year), with large estates in Scotland and around Cardiff, including Cardiff dock, whose construction his father had begun the year of his death. In 1868, on attaining his majority, he converted to Roman Catholicism, and in the same year he commissioned William **Burges** to undertake the restoration of Cardiff Castle, a monument of the Victorian Gothic imagination. In 1900, when both patron and architect were dead, the work was still uncompleted. In 1875 he was made a Knight of the Order of the Thistle. A man of wide reading and great learning, he was described as 'tall, handsome, strong-willed and capable, but very shy and reserved' (Mark Girouard, 1971, *The Victorian Country House*, Oxford: clarendon Press, p. 125). His portrait shows a deeply sad man in the garb of a medieval friar.

LOTHAIR in Benjamin Disraeli, *Lothair* (1870)

'I sate between the German Ambassador and the Duke of Manchester. . . . Next to him was Lothair, who had travelled up from the wilds of Scotland to show his gratitude for his Thistle. He had other hardships to endure, for it is his lent! and of course he could eat nothing but fish. He managed pretty well, for he instructed his attendant to secure for him a large dish of well-sauced salmon and that sustained him during all the courses. Claud Hamilton sate next to Lothair and talked well, and made him talk' (to Lady Bradford, 25 February 1875, reproduced in *The Letters of Disraeli to Lady Bradford and Lady Chesterfield*, 1929, ed. Marquis of Zetland, Vol. I, London: Ernest Benn, p. 206).

BUTLER, Edward R. A city boss of St Louis from 1898 onwards: 'Edward R. Butler, better known as "Colonel Ed", or "Colonel Butler", or just "Boss" . . . an Irishman by birth, a master horseshoer by trade . . . he certainly was the ruler of St Louis during the Republican administration of Ziegenheim' (Lincoln Steffens, 1904, *The Shame of the Cities*, pp. 105–6). He was still the city Boss when Dreiser interviewed him in 1903 for the *St Louis Globe-Democrat*.

EDWARD BUTLER in Theodore Dreiser, *The Financier* (1912)

'Edward Butler, modelled on a city politician Dreiser interviewed in St Louis' (Richard Lehan, 1974, *Theodore Dreiser: his world and his novels*, Carbondale, Ill.: Arcturis Books, p. 104).

BUTLER, Fanny (1808–73) Daughter of Philip Jordan Worsley, a sugar refiner of Arnos Vale, Bristol, she married Thomas **Butler** in 1831.

MRS OWEN in Samuel Butler, *The Fair Haven* (1873)

'Mrs Owen is Mrs Butler as like as he could get her, occasionally perhaps exaggerated' (H. Festing Jones, 1919, *Samuel Butler, Author of* Erewhon, Vol. I, London: Macmillan, p. 177).

CHRISTINE PONTIFEX in Samuel Butler, *The Way of All Flesh* (1903)

See under **Butler**, Thomas.

BUTLER, Harriet (1770?–1847) Née Cowper. Thackeray's maternal grandmother: shortly after the birth of his mother in 1792 she eloped with Colonel E.W. Butler of the Bengal Artillery and married him in 1800 after the death of her husband. After Thackeray lost his fortune, she came to his assistance and they became much attached to each other.

HARRIET CRAWLEY in W.M. Thackeray, *Vanity Fair* (1847–8)

'It may be surmised that Thackeray did not go far afield for his model when he drew old Miss Crawley. ... Living with him in 1847 was his maternal grandmother, Harriet Butler ... a selfish and imperious old lady to the worldly follies of whose youth had succeeded beads and prayer-books' (biog. memo. in *The Letters and Private Papers of W.M. Thackeray*, Vol. I: *1817–1840*, 1945, ed. Gordon N. Ray, London: Oxford University Press, p. cv).

BUTLER, Josephine Elizabeth (1828–1906) In 1866 she went with her husband to live in Liverpool, where she established homes for working girls and prostitutes. In 1869–85 she was Secretary to the Ladies' National Association for Repeal of the Contagious Diseases Act; it was repealed in 1886. She worked for reform of the law affecting white-slave traffic in countries on the European continent.

MISS DEMPSEY in Mrs Humphry Ward, *Delia Blanchflower* (1915)

'Miss Dempsey is Josephine Butler' (Georgia Dunbar, 1953, 'The faithful recorder: Mrs Humphry Ward and the background of her novels', unpublished Ph.D. dissertation, Columbia University).

BUTLER, Samuel (1835–1902) English author, painter and musician, son of Thomas and Fanny **Butler**, and the grandson of Dr Samuel **Butler**. Born in Langar Rectory, near Bingham, Nottinghamshire, and educated at Shrewsbury and at St John's College, Cambridge, he moved to New Zealand, where he became a sheep farmer, returning to Britain in 1864. He wrote the utopian novel, *Erewhon* (1872), and his autobiography, *The Way of All Flesh*, was published posthumously in 1903.

MR EMERSON in E.M. Forster, *A Room with a View* (1908)

'Mr Emerson . . . is probably partly based on Butler' (P.N. Furbank, 1978, *E.M. Forster: a life*, Vol. II: *Polycrates' Ring (1914–1970)*, London: Secker & Warburg, p. 3 n. 2).

EDWARD OVERTON in Samuel Butler, *The Way of All Flesh* (1903)

'Both Ernest Pontifex and Edward Overton are portraits of Butler, the narrator being Butler as a man of sixty-five, and the hero being also Butler as a child, a boy, a youth, and a man' (H. Festing Jones, 1919, *Samuel Butler: the author of* Erewhon, Vol. I, London: Macmillan, p. 21).

JOHN PICKARD OWEN in Samuel Butler, *The Fair Haven* (1873)

'[H]e drew John Pickard Owen's character, childhood, and youth from his own' (H. Festing Jones, op. cit., Vol. I, p. 177).

ERNEST PONTIFEX in Samuel Butler, *The Way of All Flesh* (1903)

See above under EDWARD OVERTON.

JONATHAN SWIFT in I. Compton-Burnett, *More Women than Men* (1933)

'[I. Compton-Burnett's] fifth novel contains what I take to be a portrait of Butler himself, modelled so closely on material taken from Festing Jones' *Samuel Butler: A Memoir* that it is hard to believe it was not meant as a discreet but deliberate tribute' (Hilary Spurling, 1974, *Ivy When Young: the early life of I. Compton-Burnett, 1884–1919*, London: Gollancz, p. 267). A very slight sketch.

BUTLER, Dr Samuel (1774–1839) He was Headmaster of Shrewsbury School in 1798–1836, and became Bishop of Lichfield and Coventry in 1836. He was the father of Thomas **Butler** and the grandfather of Samuel Butler.

GEORGE PONTIFEX in Samuel Butler, *The Way of All Flesh* (1903)

'George Pontifex . . . was intended for Dr Butler, with his profession altered' (H. Festing Jones, 1919, *Samuel Butler, Author of* Erewhon, Vol. I, London: Macmillan, p. 21). 'Certainly . . . not a portrait of Dr Butler; he is but a reproduction . . . derived from what Canon Butler had told [his son]' (ibid., p. 23). 'Reading his grandfather's papers and correspondence [in 1889] had inspired Butler with an almost Chinese reverence for his ancestor, and showed him that his previous opinion had been wrong. This meant that . . . George Pontifex . . . was a libel. . . . He . . . intended to ease his conscience by altering that part of his book; but other things occupied him, and he never did it' (ibid., Vol. II, p. 73).

BUTLER, Thomas (1806–86) Father of Samuel Butler, he married Fanny Worsley (**Butler**, above) in 1831. From 1834 to 1874 he held the living of Langar-with-Bramston, Nottinghamshire, and in 1876 he retired to Shrewsbury.

THEOBALD PONTIFEX in Samuel Butler, *The Way of All Flesh* (1903)

'Theobald and Christina [are] portraits of his own father and mother as accurate as he could make them, with no softening or exaggeration' (H. Festing Jones, 1919, *Samuel Butler: author of* Erewhon, Vol. I, London: Macmillan, p. 19). 'When [Butler] was five, Fanny Butler, not expecting to recover from her last confinement, wrote a letter addressed "To my two dear boys", which did not come into Butler's hands until after her death . . . just in time for him to put it, word for word, into *The Way of All Flesh*, only changing the names Sam and Tom to Ernest and Joey' (Philip Henderson, 1953, *Samuel Butler*, p. 6).

BUTLER, William (1727–1815) Linen-draper of Kenilworth, Warwickshire. In 1760 he married Lucy Broxsell: they were the parents of Dr Samuel **Butler**.

JOHN PONTIFEX in Samuel Butler, *The Way of All Flesh* (1903)

'John Pontifex . . . is Butler's great-grandfather, by hearsay, with his trade altered' (H. Festing Jones, 1919, *Samuel Butler: the author of* Erewhon, Vol. I, London: Macmillan, p. 21). 'Professor Sale, whose acquaintance Butler made in New Zealand . . . told me that he remembered . . . an old village carpenter . . . somewhere in Warwickshire, near Knowle. This old man . . . had made an organ. He and his friend played on their instrument . . . [and] asked Professor to play to them: they particularly wished to hear, and accordingly he played, "Before Jehovah's awful throne". . . . Professor Sale told this anecdote to Butler, who, no doubt, appropriated it; and . . . elaborated John Pontifex' (ibid., pp. 22–3). 'It is not probable that John Pontifex is much like . . . William Butler. . . . Butler can only have reproduced what he had heard of him' (ibid., p. 22).

BUTLER, Revd William (d. 1843) Vicar of Frampton in 1800, he was a friend of the Prince Regent.

REVD BILLY TOOGOOD in Thomas Hardy, 'Audrey Satchel and the Parson' (1894)

Identified in F.B. Pinion, 1968, *A Hardy Companion*, London: Macmillan.

BYNNER, Witter (1881–1968) American poet. He met the Lawrences in New Mexico in 1922 and travelled with them in Mexico in 1923.

OWEN RHYS in D.H. Lawrence, *The Plumed Serpent* (1926)

'When *The Plumed Serpent* was issued . . . [it] at once became evident . . . that Owen Rhys . . . was I' (W. Bynner, 1953, *Journey with Genius*, London and New York: Peter Nevill, p. 57). '[T]he Owen is not *all* of you, Hal, and also there is something else that isn't you' (Frieda Lawrence to Witter Bynner, 10 November 1929, reproduced in Frieda Lawrence, 1961, *The Memoirs and Correspondence*, ed. E.W. Tedlock, London: Heinemann, p. 239).

BYRNE, John Francis (1879–1960) He attended Belvedere College and University College Dublin with Joyce and became his close friend. In 1910 he emigrated to the USA, where he became Financial Editor of the *Daily News Record* (New York City). In 1927, on a return visit to Europe, he visited Joyce in Paris. He was the author of *Silent Years*, reminiscences in particular of Joyce and of the Troubles.

LEOPOLD BLOOM in James Joyce, *Ulysses* (1922)

'One night Joyce asked me to go for a walk with him. . . . We walked Dublin that night and early morning . . . we arrived [at 7 Eccles Street, where Byrne was living] about three in the morning. . . . I put my hand in the back pocket of my trousers for the . . . key, but the key wasn't there' (J.F. Byrne, 1953, *Silent Years*, New York, p. 157). Byrne goes on to recount how he climbed in, and continues: 'This incident is described in Joyce's *Ulysses*'. *See also* **Bloom**, Joseph; **Chance**, Charles; **Hunter**, Alfred H.; **Jackson**, Holbrook; **Joyce**, James; **Joyce**, John Stanislaus; **Mayer**, Teodoro; **Popper**, Leopoldo; **Schmitz**, Ettore.

CRANLY in James Joyce, *A Portrait of the Artist as a Young Man* (1916)

'It was late in October 1898 that Joyce first dubbed me Cranly' (ibid., p. 43). 'I was, from the outset, charmed by his appearance and touched by his conversation, and I am glad that I experienced these reactions before I knew that J.F. Byrne was Joyce's *Cranly*' (Harvey Breit, 1953, foreword to J.F. Byrne, *Silent Years*, p. ix). The frontispiece to *Silent Years* is a photograph of 7 Eccles Street.

BYRON, Anne Isabella, Lady (1792–1860) Daughter of Sir Ralph Milbanke, the brother of Lady **Melbourne**, and thus the cousin of William Lamb, later the 2nd Lord **Melbourne**. She first met Lord **Byron** in 1812, when she was visiting her aunt at Melbourne House; they were married on 1 January 1814, and their daughter Augusta Ada was born on 10 December 1814, but on 15 January 1815 she left London for her parents' home in Yorkshire. She never saw Byron again, and in 1816 a legal deed of separation was signed immediately before Byron left England. He depicted her as Donna Iñez in *Don Juan* (1819). In 1855 she came to know the young George **MacDonald**, to whom she left a small legacy; his novel *David Elginbrod* (1863) is dedicated to her memory.

LADY BERNARD in George MacDonald, *The Vicar's Daughter* (1872)

'In . . . *The Vicar's Daughter*, he drew her as Lady Bernard' (Ethel Colburn Mayne, 1929, *The Life and Letters of Anne Isabella, Lady Noel Byron*, London: Constable, p. 333).

MISS MONMOUTH in Lady Caroline Lamb, *Glenarvon* (1816)

'This letter [Byron to Lady Caroline Lamb, 1 May 1812] refers to the future Lady Byron, the "Miss Monmouth" of *Glenarvon*' (*The Letters and Journals of Lord Byron*, 1898, ed. Rowland E. Prothero, Vol. II, p. 118 n. 4). Also identified in a key found among the papers of John Whishaw, a member of the Holland House circle; printed in *The 'Pope' of Holland House: selection from the correspondence of John Whishaw and his friends, 1813–1840*, 1906, ed. Lady Seymour, p. 151.

BYRON, George Gordon Byron, Lord (1788–1824) English poet. Son of Captain 'Mad Jack' Byron and the heiress, Catherine Gordon, he became 6th Baron Byron of Rochdale at the age of nine. He was educated at Harrow and Trinity College, Cambridge. In 1809 he set out on his grand tour, spending much of his time in Albania and Greece. He had a scandalous affair with Lady Caroline **Lamb**, then in 1815 he married the heiress Anne Isabella Milbanke (**Byron**, above), who left him the following year, after the birth of their daughter, Ada. He was suspected of having an incestuous relationship with his half sister Augusta Leigh. Resuming his travels, he met **Shelley** in Switzerland, and his liaison with Claire **Clairmont** resulted in a daughter, Allegra, who died in 1822. In 1823 he went to fight for Greek independence from the Turks, and died of marsh fever at Missolonghi without ever having fought.

LORD HAROLD AUGUSTUS in Anon., *Harold the Exile* (1819)

'An anonymous three-volume novel based on the early life of Byron. . . . The obvious purpose of the book is to explain Byron's separation from Lady Byron' (Wilfred S. Dowden, 1951, 'Harold the exile: another item in the list of Byroniana', *Notes and Queries* 196 (13 October): 447). The author would seem to have had no personal acquaintance with Byron.

LORD CADURCIS in Benjamin Disraeli, *Venetia* (1837)

'The genius and personality of Byron are assigned to Cadurcis; but the external circumstances of Byron's life are apportioned almost equally between Cadurcis and Herbert . . . his unhappy marriage . . . and 'Ada'. . . are transferred to Herbert. . . . Both poets are involved in a common end – the end in fact of Shelley' (W.F. Monypenny, 1910, *The Life of Benjamin Disraeli, Earl of Beaconsfield*, Vol. I, London: John Murray, p. 363).

MR CYPRESS in Thomas Love Peacock, *Nightmare Abbey* (1818)

'Mr Cypress is well-known to be a caricature of Byron' (Martin Freeman, 1911, *Thomas Love Peacock*, London: Martin Secker, p. 210).

DE VERE in Lady Morgan, *Florence Macarthy* (1818)

'The hero De Vere is unmistakably Byron' (Blackwell cat. A1041, 1976).

LORD GLENARVON in Lady Caroline Lamb, *Glenarvon* (1816)

'Glenarvon and Vivian are of course Lord Byron. . . . The work is a strange farrago, and only curious from containing some of Lord Byron's genuine letters – the last in which he rejects her love and implores an end to their connexion, directed and sealed by Lady Oxford, is a most astonishing performance to publish' (Lady Holland to Mrs Creevey, 21 May 1816, reproduced in *Creevey Papers*, 1903, ed. Sir Herbert Maxwell, Vol. I, pp. 254, 255). '[I]f the authoress had written the truth, and nothing but the truth – the whole truth – the romance would not only have been more romantic, but more entertaining. As for the likeness, the picture can't be good – I did not sit long enough' (Byron to Thomas Moore, 5 December 1816, reproduced in George Gordon Byron, 1976, *Letters and Journals*, Vol. V: *1816–1817, So Late into the Night*, ed. Leslie A. Marchand, London: John Murray). Also identified in a key found among the papers of John Whishaw, a member of the Holland House circle; printed in *The 'Pope' of Holland House: selection from the correspondence of John Whishaw and his friends, 1813–1840*, 1906, ed. Lady Seymour, p. 151.

LODORE in Mary Wollstonecraft Shelley, *Lodore* (1835)

'Mrs Hare admired *Lodore* amazingly; so do I, or should I, if it were not for that modification of the beastly character of Lord Byron of which you have composed Lodore. I stick to *Frankenstein*, merely because that vile spirit does not haunt its pages as it does in all your other novels . . . now as Raymond, now as Lodore' (Claire Clairmont to Mary Shelley, reproduced in Florence A. Marshall, 1889, *The Life and Letters of Mary Wollstonecraft Shelley*, Vol. II, London: Bentley & Son, p. 265; no date is given).

LORD RAYMOND in Mary Wollstonecraft Shelley, *The Last Man* (1826)

See above.

LORD RUTHVEN in J.W. Polidori, *The Vampyre: A Tale* (1819)

'The next day . . . John Polidori began a short novel on the macabre adventures of two Englishmen in London and Greece. . . . Its heroes must be accurately drawn. . . . Living models for his characters must therefore be sought. . . . The model he sought joined him for tea on the balcony [i.e. Lord Byron, with whom he was travelling as personal physician in June 1816]' (Derek Marlowe, 1973, *A Single Summer with L.B.*, Harmondsworth: Penguin, p. 111).

Count Vivian in Lady Caroline Lamb, *Glenarvon* (1816)

See above under Lord Glenarvon.

BYRON, Robert (1905–41) Traveller, art critic and historian. Educated at Eton and at Oxford, he was the author of *The Byzantine Achievement* (1929) and *The Road to Oxiana* (1937), and other works. He was drowned on the way to Egypt during the Second World War.

Albert Gates in Nancy Mitford, *Highland Fling* (1931)

'Albert Gates . . . was suggested by Robert's cult of Victoriana' (Harold Acton, 1975, *Nancy Mitford: a memoir*, London: Hamilton, p. 22). *See also* **Lees-Milne**, J.

Ben Gore in Henry Green, *Blindness* (1926)

'Robert Byron commemorated the impact of the Eton Society of Arts . . . [in] 1926 in a review of . . . *Blindness* in the Oxford magazine, *Cherwell* . . . (signed "B.G." because the character of those initials in *Blindness* was largely based on himself)' (M.-J. Lancaster, 1968, *Brian Howard: portrait of a failure*, London: Anthony Blond, p. 119).

C

CACOPARDO, Francesco Italian friend and landlord of D.H. Lawrence.

FRANCESCO MARASCA in D.H. Lawrence, *The Lost Girl* (1920)

'... [Lawrence's] friend ... upon whom some of the externals of Ciccio's appearance may be based' (*The Lost Girl*, 1981, ed. John Worthen, Cambridge, p. 378 n. 122: 29).

CAFÉ ROYAL, London A restaurant much frequented during the early 1920s by writers and artists.

CAFÉ POMPADOUR in D.H. Lawrence, *Women in Love* (1920)

'Chapter XXVIII, "Gudrun in the Pompadour", is ... drawn from current happenings. Early in September 1916 Lawrence learned of an incident at the Café Royal between Katherine Mansfield and a group loudly making fun of ... [the] recently published *Amores*. ... The chapter based on the Café Royal incident can only have been added as an afterthought' (E. Delavenay, 1972, *D.H. Lawrence: the man and his work, 1885–1919*, p. 391).

CAIRO, Illinois Dickens twice passed Cairo on his return journey by steamboat down the Ohio in 1842; on neither journey did he land.

EDEN in Charles Dickens, *Martin Chuzzlewit* (1843–4)

'... Cairo, the "Eden" of *Chuzzlewit*, described in *American Notes*, ch. 12' (*Letters of Charles Dickens*, 1974, ed. Madeline House, Graham Storey and Kathleen Tillotson, Vol. III, Oxford: Oxford University Press, p. 195 n. 2).

CALCRAFT, Granby Hales (1800–55) Brother of Sir Henry **Calcraft**, he served in the Army from 1824 to 1833 and was MP for Wareham from 1831 to 1832. Like Thackeray, he was a member of the **Garrick Club** in London. He died in New York.

CAPTAIN GRANBY TIPTOFF in W.M. Thackeray, *The History of Pendennis* (1848–50)

'[H]e had ... in *Pendennis*, made a sketch of a former member [of the Garrick], Captain Granby Calcraft, under the name of Captain Granby Tiptoff' (Edmund Yates, 1884, *Edmund Yates: his recollections and experiences*, Vol. II, London: R. Bentley & Son, p. 16).

CALCRAFT, Sir Henry (1836–96) He joined the Board of Trade as a clerk in 1852 and became permanent Secretary in 1866. He retired in 1893.

HUGO BOHUN in Benjamin Disraeli, *Lothair* (1870)

Identified in 'Key to *Lothair*', *Notes and Queries*, 183 (12 September 1942): 173.

MR PINTO in Benjamin Disraeli, *Lothair* (1870)

'[Henry Calcraft] is drawn as Mr Pinto in Disraeli's *Lothair*, 1871 [sic]' (Frederic Boase, 1892, *Modern English Biography*, Vol. I (suppl.)).

CALCRAFT, William (1800–79) The City of London's executioner from 1829 to 1874, he hanged the **Mannings**, among many others. He had previously been a shoemaker, a watchman and a butler. He was said to be a devoted father and grandfather and a lover of pet animals.

DENNIS in Charles Dickens, *Barnaby Rudge* (1841)

'CD may have drawn on him for Dennis' (*Letters of Charles Dickens*, 1981, Vol. V, ed. Graham Storey and K.J. Fielding, Oxford: Oxford University Press, p. 653 n. 3).

CALDER, Alexander (1898–1976) American sculptor and the deviser of mobiles. On 3 January 1930, Aline Bernstein gave a party at her apartment on Park Avenue in order that he might give a performance of his flying circus.

PIGGY LOGAN in Thomas Wolfe, *You Can't Go Home Again* (1940)

'[Calder later] referred to Wolfe as having made "some nasty remarks on my performance . . . in a long winded book"' (Carole Klein, 1980, *Aline*, p. 248).

CALLANAN, Mrs Née Flynn, she was the sister of Mrs **Lyons** and the mother of Mary Ellen **Callanan**; they were the great-aunts and cousin, respectively, of James Joyce. They kept the Misses Flynn school at 15 Usher's Island, where every year they entertained the Joyces, and John **Joyce** carved the goose and made the speech.

MISS KATE MORKAN in James Joyce, 'The Dead', *Dubliners* (1914)

'In Joyce's story Mrs Callanan and Mrs Lyons . . . become the spinster ladies, the Misses Morkan' (Richard Ellmann, 1982, *James Joyce*, rev. edn, Oxford: Oxford University Press, pp. 245–6).

CALLANAN, Mary Ellen Daughter of Mrs **Callanan**.

MARY JANE in James Joyce, 'The Dead', *Dubliners* (1914)

'Mary Ellen Callanan becomes Mary Jane' (Richard Ellmann, 1982, *James Joyce*, rev. edn, Oxford: Oxford University Press, pp. 245–6).

CALLANDER, Mrs Alice Daughter of Lieutenant-Colonel J.C. Craigie-Halkett of Cramond, Edinburgh. In 1876 she married G.F.W. Callander of Ardkinglas, County Argyll. She became a lady-in-waiting to Queen Victoria. She was a sister-in-law to Lady Archibald Campbell (Janey Sevilla **Campbell**) and a friend of Vernon Lee during the 1880s when the latter visited London as a young woman.

LADY ATALANTA WALKENSHAW in Vernon Lee, 'Lady Tal', *Vanitas* (1892)

'Mrs Callander was the original of Lady Tal' (Peter Gunn, 1964, *Vernon Lee, 1856–1935*, London: Oxford University Press, p. 127).

CALLES, Plutarco Elias (1877–1945) Dictator of Mexico from 1924 to 1934. Originally regarded as a left-wing revolutionary, he moved to the right after seizing power.

SOCRATES TOMÁS MONTES in D.H. Lawrence, *The Plumed Serpent* (1926)

'This character is based on Plutarco Elias Calles' (*The Plumed Serpent*, 1983, ed. Ronald G. Walker, Harmondsworth: Penguin, p. 485 n. 7).

CAME WOOD, Dorset Situated two miles south of Dorchester. The Damers lived at Winterbourne-Came House, and one of them, who later became the 1st Earl of Dorchester, bought Milton Abbey in 1752.

DAMER'S WOOD in Thomas Hardy, *The Trumpet Major* (1880)

Identified in F.B. Pinion, 1968, *A Hardy Companion*, London: Macmillan.

CAMELFORD, Cornwall A small town situated about five miles inland from Trebarwith, on the main road north from Wadebridge to Bude.

CAMELTON in Thomas Hardy, *A Pair of Blue Eyes* (1873)

Identified in F.B. Pinion, 1968, *A Hardy Companion*, Londond: Macmillan.

CAMELFORD, Thomas Pitt, Lord (1774–1804) A great-nephew of Prime Minister Lord Chatham, he was the 2nd Baron Camelford. He entered the Navy in 1789, and after a stormy career, including a court martial, his name was struck off the list of commanders. He subsequently lived in London, where 'he achieved extraordinary notoriety' (*The Dictionary of National Biography*, London: Oxford University Press) by the disorderliness of his life. He was killed in a duel.

LORD CHILTERN in Anthony Trollope, *Phineas Finn* (1869)

'[T]here appears to be little doubt that Lord Chiltern is a lightly disguised representation of Lord Camelford' (Nikolai Tolstoy, 1978, *The Half-Mad Lord*, p. 143). *See also* **Devonshire**, 8th Duke of.

CAMERON, Elizabeth Née Sherman, she was the niece of Senator John Sherman and of General W.T. Sherman, and in 1878 married Senator James Donald Cameron. Marian Adams described her in 1881 as 'very pretty, not more than twenty-four ... staying with the fair Emily [Beale, in Washington]'. The Adams's saw her frequently, and Henry Adams became devoted to her.

CATHERINE BROOKE in Henry Adams, *Esther* (1884)

'Her fresh, dewy-eyed charm recalls ... Elizabeth Cameron, whose extreme youth and beauty had captivated Adams and his wife' (Ernest Samuels, 1958, *Henry Adams: the middle years*, Cambridge, Mass., p. 244).

CAMERON OF LOCHIEL, Sir Donald Walter (1876–1951) Twenty-fifth Chief of the Clan Cameron, in 1906 he married Lady Hermione Grahame, daughter of the 5th Duke of Montrose.

Donald MacDonald of Ben Nevis in Compton Mackenzie, *The Monarch of the Glen* (1941)

'Cameron of Lochiel, thought by some to be depicted as Ben Nevis, was delighted' (J.I.M. Stewart, 1977, 'Out of the North Wind' (review of a reissue of *The Monarch Glen* and other novels), *Times Literary Supplement* (9 September): 1068).

CAMFIELD PLACE, Essendon, Hertfordshire The house is outside the village, situated about four miles east of Hatfield.

Mr McGregor's Garden in Beatrix Potter, *The Tale of Peter Rabbit* (1902) and others

'We go for a walk through the kitchen garden where Peter Rabbit lived. The hole in the wall is still exactly as it was in Beatrix Potter's day when her grandfather owned the house' ('A life in the day of Barbara Cartland', 1978, *Sunday Times*, magazine section (28 May): 86). Barbara Cartland (Mrs McCorquodale) lives at Camfield Place. '"Peter Rabbit's potting shed and the actual geraniums were in Hertfordshire" (Camfield Place)' (Beatrix Potter to her publishers, quoted in Margaret Lane, 1946, *The Tale of Beatrix Potter*, London and New York: Frederick Lane, p. 127). *See also* **Fawe Park**; **Gwaynynog**.

CAMPBELL, Janey Sevilla (d. 1923) Known as Lady Archibald Campbell, she was the daughter of J.H. Callander of Stirling and was a ward of the 8th Duke of Argyll. In 1869 she married the latter's son, Lord Archibald Campbell, and became the mother of the 10th Duke. She was keenly interested in amateur theatricals, giving performances in a garden at Coombe, near Kingston, and was a close friend of the poets **Swinburne** and **Watts-Dunton**.

Alice Oke in Vernon Lee, 'Oke of Okehurst' (1890)

'It is most probable that Vernon Lee had Lady Archie in mind for the character of Mrs Alice Oke' (Peter Gunn, 1964, *Vernon Lee, 1856–1935*, London: Oxford University Press, p. 129).

CAMPBELL, Thomas (1777–1844) Scottish poet and journalist. Son of a Glasgow merchant and educated at Glasgow University, he went to Edinburgh to study law but was drawn to the reading and writing of poetry. After marrying and settling in London he determined on a literary career. In 1820 he delivered a course of lectures at the Surrey Institution and from 1820 to 1930 he edited *New Monthly Magazine*.

Mr MacLaurel in Thomas Love Peacock, *Headlong Hall* (1816)

'MacLaurel . . . may be taken to represent . . . Campbell' (J.B. Priestley, 1927, *Thomas Love Peacock*, London: Macmillan, p. 33). *See also* **Wilson**, John.

4 CAMPBELL RD, Havelock Park, Southsea

Downe Lodge in Rudyard Kipling, 'Baa, Baa, Black Sheep' (1888)

Identified in R.L. Green (ed.), 1961, 'Notes on "Baa, Baa, Black Sheep"', in *The Readers' Guide to Rudyard Kipling's Work*, Sect. I, London: Kipling Society, pp. 374–7.

CANFIELD, Roy Bishop (1874–1932) Specialist in diseases of the ear, nose and throat, he was a surgeon at the Rockefeller Institute, New York.

Roscoe Geake in Sinclair Lewis, *Arrowsmith* (1925)

Identified in Mark Schorer, 1961, *Sinclair Lewis: an American life*, New York: McGraw-Hill, p. 418.

CANFORD MANOR, Dorset Situated near Wimborne. Part of the old manor, known as 'John of Gaunt's kitchen', still exists.

Chene Manor in Thomas Hardy, Wessex novels and tales (1871–95)

Identifed on a map prepared by Thomas Hardy which hangs in the Dorset County Museum, Dorchester. *See under* **Abbotsbury**.

CANNAN, Gilbert (1884–1955) Novelist and playwright. Educated at Cambridge, in 1908 he was called to the Bar. He was a dramatic critic from 1908 to 1910, and he helped found Manchester Repertory Theatre with John **Drinkwater**. He was the author of a translation of Romain Rolland's *Jean Christopher* and of many novels including *Mendel*. At one time he was Private Secretary to the novelist J.M. Barrie, who from 1894 to 1909 was married to the actress Mary Barrie (née Ansell, 1867?–1950). She and Cannan began a liaison, and married in 1910; at first the couple lived on an allowance from Barrie, but they were later divorced. In 1914 they were neighbours, at Chesham, of D.H. and Frieda **Lawrence**, with whom Mary continued to be a friend until they left Europe. Cannan became insane.

Frederick Rodney in Compton Mackenzie, *The Four Winds of Love: The South Wind* (1937)

'In a letter to [E. Nehls] . . . Sir Compton Mackenzie wrote: "... in my novel . . . Frederick Rodney is an impression of Gilbert Cannan. . . . Apart from names and places most of it is factually and conversationally exact"' (E. Nehls, 1957, *D.H. Lawrence: a composite biography*, Vol. I, Madison, p. 570 n. 41). The identification of Mary Cannan as Jane Rodney is obvious from all descriptions, as is that of Summertune, Essex, with Chesham, Buckinghamshire, near which was the millhouse where the Cannans lived. 'After luncheon [in October 1914] Gilbert rewarded me . . . by taking me off into the windmill . . . in which he ground out the long scenes of windy novels which had followed his first' (David Garnett, 1955, *The Golden Echo*, Vol. II: *The Flowers of the Forest*, London: Chatto & Windus, p. 8). In *Fanny's First Play* (1911) Bernard Shaw drew an unflattering portrait of Cannan, as the dramatic critic Gilbert Gunn.

CANNELL, Kitty Born in New York State, she was educated at the University of Toronto and at the Sorbonne. She married Skipwith Cannell, a minor poet, but they were divorced *c.*1926. She then married Roger Vitrac, the French poet and playwright. She trained as a ballet dancer and became an actress, appearing at the Provincetown Playhouse. While in Paris with her first husband during the 1920s, she came to know Ezra **Pound**, Ford Madox **Ford**, Aragon and the Dadaists and Surrealists. In the early 1920s she had an affair with Harold **Loeb**, which ended in some bitterness.

FRANCES CLYNE in Ernest Hemingway, *The Sun Also Rises* (1926)

'The book made Kitty Cannell so angry that she took to her bed for three days ... she was ... enraged by the portrait of Frances Cline [sic]. ... She saw at once that Ernest had listened carefully to her conversational style, which was highly individualized and unmistakeable. He had then projected it upon the character and experience of a Jewish secretary who had worked with Loeb in the editing of *Broom*' (Carlos Baker, 1969, *Ernest Hemingway: a life story*, New York, p. 179).

LILY LUBOW in Harold Loeb, *The Way It Was* (1959)

'[F]ictitious names were given [to some of the] characters in Loeb's memoir. Kitty Cannell became Lily Lubow' (B.D. Sarason, 1972, *Hemingway and the Sun Set*, Washington, DC, p. 17).

CANNING, George (1770–1827) English statesman. Born in London, he was educated at Eton and at Christ Church, Oxford. His mother, widowed in 1771, became an actress and remarried twice, and he was brought up by his uncle, Stratford Canning, father of Lord Stratford de Redcliffe. He was an MP from 1794 onwards and in 1807 he became Foreign Secretary, but in 1809 he fought a duel with Castlereagh and resigned from office. In 1816 he became President of the India Board, resigning in 1821. In 1822 he again became Foreign Secretary, and in 1827 he was Prime Minister and Foreign Secretary. He favoured Greek independence and attempted to reform the Corn Laws, and in 1799–1801 he brought out the 'Anti-Jacobin', 'perhaps the most brilliant success of its kind on record. The intention ... was to make the revolutionary party appear ridiculous' (*The Dictionary of National Biography*, London: Oxford University Press). In 1800 he married Miss Joan Scott, sister of the Duchess of Portland, thereby achieving independence.

VINCENT ANSTRUTHER in W. Massie, *Sydenham; or Memoirs of a Man of the World* (1830)

'In volume two ... Canning (Anstruther) ... [conducts] the destinies of the Whigs' (M.W. Rosa, 1936, *The Silver Fork School: novels of fashion preceding* Vanity Fair, New York, p. 81 n. 3).

MR ANYSIDE ANTIJACK in Thomas Peacock, *Melincourt* (1817)

He appears in chapter 39; in *The Novels of T.L. Peacock*, 1963, ed. David Garnett, London: Rupert Hart-Davis, p. 309), the footnote (3) identifies him as Canning: his name is a reference to the *Anti-Jacobin*.

MR CHARLATAN GAS in Benjamin Disraeli, *Vivian Grey* (1826–7)

Identified as Rt. Hon. G. (C——g) in a key given in *The Star Chamber* (24 May 1826): 114; reprinted in *Vivian Grey*, 1904 (centenary edn), ed. Lucien Wolf, Vol. II, London, pp. 361–2. The full name appears on a copy of the key held in the British Museum. Lucien Wolf concludes that Disraeli was not responsible for the key.

Mr Wentworth in Robert Plumer Ward, *De Vere; or The Man of Independence* (1827)

'Few men have enjoyed better opportunities for observing . . . Mr Canning than the author of De Vere. . . . Let us, therefore, indulge ourselves with contemplating . . . the picture of that great man. . . . In Wentworth Mr Ward has drawn a noble likeness of this distinguished individual' ('Mr Canning from De Vere', *The Literary Gazette* (7 April 1827): 209). On the publication of this article, Ward wrote to Canning, who replied: '[W]ould it be honest . . . not to add that . . . the avowals of your letter of yesterday are as gratifying as the apologies are superfluous?' (E. Phipps, 1850, *Memoirs of . . . Robert Plumer Ward*, Vol. II, p. 160). *See also* **Bolingbroke**, Lord; **Pitt**, William; **Pitt**, William, the Younger.

CANTERBURY Maugham attended the King's School located in Canterbury.

Tercanbury in W. Somerset Maugham, *Of Human Bondage* (1915)

'In Philip's experiences at King's School, in "Tercanbury" (an anagram of Canterbury), Maugham paints a damning picture of English public schools of the time' (R.L. Calder, 1972, *Somerset Maugham and the Quest for Freedom*, London: Heinemann, pp. 95–6).

CAPEL, Monsignor Thomas John (1836–1911) Rector of the University College at Kensington, London, which was set up by Cardinal Edward Henry **Manning** in 1874 in an attempt to found a Catholic University in England; Capel had already founded a Catholic school for boys in Kensington. The enterprise foundered; no books or accounts had been kept and Capel was bankrupt for £28,000. In 1883 he appealed to Rome against his suspension as a priest in the diocese of Westminster, but in 1887 he was in fact suspended *a divinis*. He emigrated to America and died in Sacramento. It was Monsignor Capel who received Lord **Bute** into the Catholic Church.

Monsignor Catesby in Benjamin Disraeli, *Lothair* (1870)

'Do you remember two tall, rather gigantic Misses Jenkinson . . .? One of them has become the devoted companion of the dear, deluded Denbighs and coached by Monsignor Capel (Catesby) was living with them, on the point of entering Holy Church' (to Lady Bradford, 29 December 1876, reproduced in *The Letters of Disraeli to Lady Bradford and Lady Chesterfield*, 1929, ed. Marquis of Zetland, Vol. I, London: Ernest Benn, p. 97).

CAPELLO, Palazzo, Venice Located on the Rio Marin, where Constance **Fletcher** lived.

The Palazzino in Henry James, *The Aspern Papers* (1888)

'The palace James had in mind for this tale is the Capello on the Riva Marin near the railway station, "the old pink-faced, battered-looking and quite homely and plain (as things go in Venice) old Palazzino. It has a garden behind it"' (note from James to Alvin Langdon Coburn, the photographer who supplied the photographs for the New York edn; see Leon Edel, 1963, *Henry James: the middle years, 1884–1894*, p. 331 n. (to *The Aspern Papers*, Bk. 3: Bellosguardo)).

CAPOLOZZI, Signor Magistrate at Alfonsine, near Bologna, in the 1890s, when Giuseppe **Orioli** was a boy, helping his father in his inn. '[A] horrible creature from South Italy, lame and sickly and red-haired, and hated to such an extent by everybody ... socialist and Catholic alike, that he asked to be transferred. ... Later on he ... was appointed Magistrate at Capri' (G. Orioli, 1937, *Adventures of a Bookseller*, Florence, p. 23).

SIGNOR MALIPIZZO in Norman Douglas, *South Wind* (1917)

'I must ... confess that Signor Malipizzo is meant for an unflattering portrait of the then ... magistrate on Capri, a ... ruffian called Capolozzi, who nearly had me in the lock-up once or twice' (preface to *South Wind*, 1925, New York, p. vi).

CAPRI

NEPENTHE in Norman Douglas, *South Wind* (1917)

'The social atmosphere is distilled out of Capri ... as it always should have been and as it never, alas, yet was or will be. I have taken what liberties I pleased with the place' (Introd. to *South Wind*, 1942, New York).

SIRENE in Compton Mackenzie, *Vestal Fire* (1927)

Mackenzie never attempted to conceal the fact that *Vestal Fire* was based on a series of events that took place on Capri in the period 1912–22.

CARCO, Francis (1886–1958) Poet and novelist. Born François Carcopino-Tusoli in New Caledonia, he was living in Paris in 1910. He became a friend of J.M. Murry who, when visiting France in 1914, introduced him to Katherine Mansfield; in early 1915 he had a brief affair with her in France.

DUPONT in J.M. Murry, *Still Life* (1916)

'In ... *Still Life* the character of Dupont, who is Carco's fictional equivalent, tells "Morry" that he must never love a woman more than three or four days' (A. Alpers, 1980, *The Life of Katherine Mansfield*, London: Jonathan Cape, p. 176).

RAOUL DUQUETTE in Katherine Mansfield, 'Je ne parle pas français' (1920)

'The subject, I mean *lui qui parle*, is of course taken from Carco and Gertler, and God knows who' (K. Mansfield to J.M. Murry, writing from Bandol, 4 February 1918, reproduced in Alpers, op. cit., p. 272). Murry, who edited *Katherine Mansfield's Letters to John Middleton Murry, 1913–1922* (1951), replaces both names with a dash on p. 151).

CARDIGAN, James Thomas Brudenell, 7th Earl of (1797–1868) Previously known as Lord Brudenell, he succeeded to the title in 1837. He was a cavalry officer, but owing to his domineering temper he was in constant conflict with his fellow officers. He was a Tory MP from 1818 to 1837, and commanded the Light Cavalry brigade in the Crimea, destroying it in the famous charge against the enemy at Balaclava in 1854. He was appointed Lieutenant-General in 1861. He married Elisabeth, née Tollemache, the ex-wife of Lieutenant-Colonel Christian Johnstone, in 1826, but they separated in 1846 and divorced in 1858. That same year he married Adelina de Horsey (b. 1824), of whom the famous demi-mondaine Catherine **Walters** is alleged to have said, 'Let us drink to the health of the head of my profession, the Countess of Cardigan.'

LORD EVERINGHAM in Benjamin Disraeli, *Coningsby* (1844)

Identified in *La Jeune Angleterre . . . avec deux clefs explicatifs des personnages* (1846, Paris); however, it is difficult to imagine the basis of this identification. *See also* **Clarendon**, 4th Earl of.

LORD ORMONT in George Meredith, *Lord Ormont and His Aminta* (1894)

'[T]he characteristics of Lord Ormont were undoubtedly drawn from the Earl of Cardigan . . . the . . . leader of the Light Brigade . . . at Balaclava' (S.M. Ellis, 1920, *George Meredith*, 2nd edn, London, p. 294).

CAREY, Godfrey Muhun (d. 1927) Assistant Master at Sherborne School from 1897 to 1927.

BULLER in Alec Waugh, *The Loom of Youth* (1917)

'Appears . . . as "The Bull", the games master' (*The Diaries of Evelyn Waugh*, 1976, ed. Michael Davie, London: Wiedenfeld & Nicolson, p. 93 n. 2).

CAREY, John (1756–1829) Classical scholar. He edited a number of classical texts.

THE EDITOR OF THE UNIVERSAL REVIEW (OXFORD) in George Borrow, *Lavengro* (1851)

'I find in *Lowndes Manual*, that an edition of Quintilian was published in 1822. The editor was John Carey . . . I submit . . . that Carey was the editor and that Quintilian was Quintilian. Though Borrow puts a translation instead of an edition, he did not appear to have opened the book' (Sir Leslie Stephen, 1899, letter to *Literature* (8 April), see A. Boyle, 1951, 'Portraiture in Lavengro', *Notes and Queries* 196 (13 October): 454). *See also* **Busby**, Thomas; **Gifford**, William.

CARFAX, Oxford

THE FOURWAYS, CHRISTMINSTER, in Thomas Hardy, *Jude the Obscure* (1895)

Identified in Denys Kay-Robinson, 1972, *Hardy's Wessex Reappraised*, Newton Abbot, and in F.B. Pinion, 1968, *A Hardy Companion*, London: Macmillan.

CARINTHIA, Margaret, Duchess of (1318–69) Called Maultasch, she was the daughter of Henry, Duke of Carinthia; in 1330 she married John Henry, Prince of Bohemia, but discarded him in 1341 and in 1342 married Louis, son of the Emperor. In 1335 she inherited Carinthia and Tyrol, but in 1363 she was forced to abdicate in favour of the Austrian Habsburgs. She was the subject of Leon Feuchtwanger's novel *The Ugly Duchess* (1923).

THE DUCHESS in Lewis Carroll, *Alice's Adventures in Wonderland* (1865)

'A glance at the portrait of *The Ugly Duchess* by the . . . Flemish painter Quintin Matsys . . . leaves little doubt that it served as the model for Tenniel's duchess. Matsys's duchess is popularly supposed to be Margaretha Maultasch. . . . (See "A Portrait of the Ugliest Princess in History" by W.A. Baillie-Grohman,

Burlington Magazine, April 1921)' (Lewis Carroll, 1965, *The Annotated Alice*, introd. and notes by Martin Gardner, Harmondsworth: Penguin, p. 82 n. 1). *See also* **Wilberforce**, Samuel.

CARLINGFORD, Baron *See* **Parkinson-Fortescue**, Chichester Samuel.

CARLISLE HOUSE, Soho, London Located at the west end of Carlisle Street, it was formerly the town house of the Howards, Earls of Carlisle. It was built *c.*1690 and was bought by Angelo, the famous fencing and riding master, *c.*1770. By the mid-nineteenth century it was let out in tenements, and was the place of work of a cabinet maker in 1905. It was totally destroyed during the Second World War.

DR MANETTE'S HOUSE in Charles Dickens, *A Tale of Two Cities* (1859)

'Those who have ... inquired ... have expressed the opinion ... that Carlisle House was the actual house [where Dr Manette lodged] ... one of the noblest late seventeenth-century interiors now remaining in London' ('Doctor Manette's House', *The Dickensian* 1 (August 1905): 209–10; reprinted from the *Daily Graphic* (4 July 1905)). *See also* 1 **Greek Street**.

CARLYLE, James (1758?–1832) Of Ecclefechan, Dumfriesshire. He married Margaret Aitken (**Carlyle**, below); they were the parents of Thomas Carlyle.

ANDREAS FUTTERAL in Thomas Carlyle, *Sartor Resartus* (1833–4)

'Under the thinnest possible veil ... we find portraits of his parents in Father Andreas and Gretchen' (W. Howie Wylie, 1881, *Thomas Carlyle*, p. 23).

CARLYLE, Jane Baillie Welsh (1801–66) She married Thomas Carlyle in 1826, having previously been in love with Edward **Irving**.

BLUMINE in Thomas Carlyle, *Sartor Resartus* (1833–4)

The arguments for accepting Mrs Carlyle as the original of Blumine are detailed by Alexander Carlyle in *The Love Letters of Thomas Carlyle and Jane Welsh Carlyle* (1909, Vol. II, London and New York: John Lane, pp. 373–8 and 400). *See also* **Gordon**, Margaret; **Kirkpatrick**, Catherine Aurora.

CARLYLE, Margaret (d. 1853) Née Aitken, she married James **Carlyle** and was the mother of Thomas Carlyle.

GRETCHEN CARLYLE in Thomas Carlyle, *Sartor Resartus* (1833–4)

See under **Carlyle**, James.

CARLYLE, Thomas (1795–1881) Scottish historian and essayist. After graduating from Edinburgh University in 1813 he studied for the Secessionist Church, but then turned to teaching. He began to write articles in 1818; he studied German literature, writing a biography of Schiller and translating Goethe's *Wilhelm Meister*. He was acquainted with **Coleridge**, Hazlitt and Thomas **Campbell**. In 1826 he married Jane Baillie Welsh (**Carlyle**, above) and moved to Edinburgh, where he contributed to the *Edinburgh Review*. He refused an honour from **Disraeli** and was buried, at his own request, in his birthplace, Ecclefechan, Dumfriesshire, rather than in Westminster Abbey.

PESSIMUS ANTICANT in Anthony Trollope, *The Warden* (1855)

'That Carlyle was generally felt as a dominant force in the forties ... hardly needs illustration. ... He might be Trollope's "Mr Pessimus Anticant", but he remained "Our dear old English Homer – Homer in prose" whose nods must be forgiven' (K. Tillotson, 1954, *Novels of the Eighteen-Forties*, pp. 150, 152).

DONALD GORDON in W.H. Mallock, *The New Republic* (1877)

'Among the principal guests ... [is] ... Carlyle (Donald Gordon)' (G. Faber, 1957, *Jowett*, p. 376). 'It is sometimes suggested that Donald Gordon's original is Carlyle. ... But this will not do. For in the ... text [first published in 1876 in the magazine *Belgravia*] Carlyle had been plainly present as Mr Rokeby. Rokeby is, however, dropped from the book version' (J. Lucas, 1975, Introd. to *The New Republic*, Leicester, pp. 25–6). Lucas goes on to suggest that Carlyle disappeared from the novel because Mallock had paid him a visit, which had not gone well. According to George Saintsbury, Mallock talked freely for a considerable time, Carlyle smoking his pipe in silence. 'When the visitor rose to depart, Thomas conducted him most politely to the door. Then only did he open the lips of wisdom to say "Oh man! but ye're a poor creature"' (G. Saintsbury, 1923, *A Second Scrapbook*, p. 180 n. 1). *See also* **Macdonald**, George.

SANDY MACKAYE in Charles Kingsley, *Alton Locke* (1850)

'Both in speech and in thought Mackaye is clearly modelled on Carlyle, whom Kingsley had known ever since living in Chelsea' (R.B. Martin, 1959, *The Dust of Combat: a life of Charles Kingsley*, London: Faber & Faber, pp. 115–16). Kingsley's father was the Rector of Chelsea, and his Rectory in Church Street was just around the corner from the Carlyles' house in Cheyne Row.

ST BARBE in Benjamin Disraeli, *Endymion* (1880)

On 7 February 1881, Queen Victoria wrote to Lord Beaconsfield saying: 'I have just finished *Endymion* and have been much interested in it. I trace several characters. ... Did you know Carlyle? (*The Letters of Queen Victoria*, 1851, p. 194 n. 2). He replied on 10 February: 'The year after I offered the Grand Cross to Carlyle ... he expressed to Lady Marian [Alford] his wish to make my acquaintance, and accordingly that took place. It was a very successful interview, and I contemplated cultivating his society, so far as I could, for I was then your Majesty's servant, and had little time for many things that should not have been omitted. Carlyle, however ... behaved so unnecessarily discourteously, both about the Indian Empire question, and still more about the Turkish war, writing even letters in the newspapers, that I cared not more to see him' (*The Letters of Queen Victoria*, 1928 (2nd series), Vol. III, ed. G.E. Buckle, London: John Muray, pp. 195–6). It is apparent that the Queen instantly identified St Barbe as Carlyle, and Beaconsfield accepted the identification. *See also* **Hayward**, Abraham; **Thackeray**, W.M.

DIOGENES TEUFELSDRÖCKH in Thomas Carlyle, *Sartor Resartus* (1833–4)

'He [i.e. James Carlyle, his father] took me down to Annan Academy on the Whitsunday morning, 1806; I trotting at his side in the way alluded to in

Teufelsdröckh' (Thomas Carlyle, 1881, *Reminiscences*, ed. J.A. Froude, Vol. I, London: Longman, p. 58). 'Asked him [i.e. Carlyle] concerning his early history, as compared with Teufelsdröckh's . . . the indivisible suit of yellow serge is historical, into which he had daily to insinuate himself' (entry for 6 June 1842, *Memories of Old Friends: being extracts from the journals and letters of Caroline Fox*, 1882, ed. H.N. Pym, Vol. I, London: Smith, Elder, pp. 310–11).

TREGARVA in Charles Kingsley, *Yeast* (1848)

'. . . two Carlylean personalities, Tregarva and Sandy Mackaye' (K. Tillotson, 1954, *Novels of the Eighteen-Forties*, Oxford, p. 153). But whereas, in Sandy Mackaye, Kingsley largely reproduces Carlyle's manner of speech and personal idiosyncrasies, Tregarva, the noble gamekeeper, merely echoes his thought.

CARMICHAEL, Charles Montaubon (1790–1870) Born Carmichael-Smyth, he dropped the Smyth in 1842. He was the younger brother of Henry **Carmichael-Smyth** and in 1841 married Mary Graham. Mary had been brought up by Anne **Carmichael-Smyth**, who was her aunt, Charles's sister-in-law, and Thackeray's mother. The marriage proved to be unhappy, and Thackeray was finally compelled to break off all association with Mary, although he continued to see Charles.

COLONEL THOMAS NEWCOME in W.M. Thackeray, *The Newcomes* (1854–5)

'[I]t was from this old Indian officer (who continued to wear long mustachios many years after the fashion had been abandoned) that [Thackeray] derived the conception of Colonel Newcome's appearance upon which Doyle based his drawings' (*The Letters and Private Papers of W.M. Thackeray*, Vol. I: *1817–1840*, 1945, ed. Gordon N. Ray, London: Oxford University Press, p. cxi). *See also* **Carmichael-Smyth**, Henry; **Shakespear**, Sir Richmond.

CARMICHAEL-SMYTH, Anne (1792–1864) Formerly Thackeray, née Becher, she was the mother of W.M. Thackeray and the daughter of an Indian Civil Servant. When she was young she fell deeply in love with Henry W. **Carmichael-Smyth**, but her relatives, who opposed the marriage, intercepted his letters and told her he was dead. In 1810 she married Richmond Thackeray; one evening he brought home to dine a young officer in the Engineers – Carmichael-Smyth. Mrs Thackeray fainted and the story was revealed to her husband; he died in 1815 and, not long after, she married Carmichael-Smyth. In 1838–61, owing to financial losses, they lived in Paris, and for a number of years cared for Thackeray's two daughters, during the early period of their mother's illness and before he could himself give them a home.

HELEN PENDENNIS in W.M. Thackeray, *The History of Pendennis* (1848–50)

'When you come to London I hope you will come and see me. Mrs Pendennis is living with me. (She is my mother.)' (to Arthur Hugh Clough, 24 November 1848, reproduced in *The Letters and Private Papers of W.M. Thackeray*, 1945, ed. Gordon N. Ray, Vol. II, London: Oxford University Press, p. 457).

AMELIA SEDLEY in W.M. Thackeray, *Vanity Fair* (1847–8)

'You know you are only a piece of Amelia – my mother is another half' (to Mrs Brookfield, 30 June 1848, reproduced in Ray, op. cit., p. 394). *See also* **Brookfield, Jane; Thackeray**, Isabella.

CARMICHAEL-SMYTH, Henry (1780–1861) Brother of Charles **Carmichael**, he married Anne Thackeray (**Carmichael-Smyth**, above) in 1817, some years after first courting her, and following the death of her first husband. He thus became W.M. Thackeray's stepfather.

COLONEL THOMAS NEWCOME in W.M. Thackeray, *The Newcomes* (1854–5)

'When *The Newcomes* was coming out, I said to Thackeray "I see where you got your Colonel." "To be sure you would", he replied, "Only I had to *angelicise* the old boys a little." By this he meant his stepfather . . . and *his* younger brother, General Charles Carmichael' (letter to Alexander F. Baillie, from David Freemantle Carmichael, nephew of the two officers, quoted in A.F. Baillie, 1901, *The Oriental Club and Hanover Square*, London: Longman, Green, p. 72). 'Half of Colonel Newcome is downstairs now – the other half is in London' (to Mrs Gore, writing from Tunbridge Wells, 27 August 1870, reproduced in *The Letters and Private Papers of W.M. Thackeray*, 1946, ed. Gordon N. Ray, Vol. IV, London: Oxford University Press, p. 196). *See also* **Carmichael**, Charles Montauban; **Shakespear**, Sir Richmond.

CARNERA, Primo (b. 1907) Born in the village of Segnals, north-east of Venice, he grew to be nearly six feet tall, weighing 260 pounds. At the age of 16 he joined a circus, but in 1928 was discovered by Paul Journée, the veteran French heavyweight, who persuaded him to train as a boxer. During the next year he engaged in a number of fights in Europe, and in 1929 he went to the United States. By 1933 he was a contender for the heavyweight championship and defeated the holder, Jack Sharbey, by a knockout in the sixth round. In June 1934 he lost his title to Max Baer, but continued fighting until he was decisively beaten by Joe Louis in June 1935. He was not by temperament a fighter: 'an easy-going, good-natured sort . . . [he was] a gullible prey for scheming exploiters' (Nat Fleisher, 1961, *The Heavyweight Championship*, p. 213). After the Second World War he took up wrestling, and with the advent of television he made a fortune to compensate for the millions he had been cheated out of in the boxing ring.

TORO MOLINA in Budd Schulberg, *The Harder They Fall* (1947)

'A boy named Bud Schulberg . . . wrote a novelized life of Primo Carnera full of strange distortion due to the fear of libel and Carnera said to a friend of mine, "I wish so much Mr Schulberg would have come to me because I could have told so much more interesting things"' (to Arthur Mizener, 22 April 1950, reproduced in *Ernest Hemingway Selected Letters, 1917–1961*, 1981, ed. Carlos Baker, London: Granada, p. 690).

CARNEY, Mary

MAGGIE CASSIDY in Jack Kerouac, *Maggie Cassidy* (1959) and *Vanity of Duluoz* (1968)

'[*Maggie Cassidy*] becomes the story of that first love affair between Jack Kerouac (alias Jack Duluoz) and Mary Carney (alias Maggie Cassidy)' (review of *Maggie Cassidy*, *Times Literary Supplement* (13 September 1974): 971).

MARY GILHOOLEY in Jack Kerouac, *The Town and the City* (1950)

Identified in 'Character key to the Duluoz Legend', in Barry Gifford and Lawrence Lee, 1979, *Jack's Book*, pp. 322–32.

CARR, Henry (1894–1962) Born in Sunderland, he grew up in County Durham and in 1911 went to Canada. In 1915 he volunteered for military service and served on the Western Front in the Canadian Black Watch, but he was badly wounded and taken prisoner. He was 'exchanged' and sent to Zurich, where he obtained a small post in the consulate in Zurich. While there he encountered Joyce, and in 1918 the two became involved in a quarrel over an amateur production of *The Importance of Being Ernest* which eventually ended in litigation.

PRIVATE CARR in James Joyce, *Ulysses* (1922)

'Originally Joyce intended to make Consul-General Bennett and Henry Carr the two drunken, blasphemous and obscene soldiers who knock Stephen Dedalus down in the 'Circe' episode; but he eventually decided that Bennett should be the sergeant-major, with authority over Private Carr' (Richard Ellmann, 1982, *James Joyce*, rev. edn, Oxford: Oxford University Press, p. 459). A full account of Carr's life – he returned to England in 1934 and remained until his death – the quarrel and Joyce's revenge was given in the programme notes for the production of Tom Stoppard's *Travesties* at the Aldwych Theatre, London, in 1974–5.

CARRINGTON, Dora (1883–1932) Painter. She studied at the Slade School of Fine Art, London. Passionately in love with Lytton **Strachey**, in 1921 she married Ralph Partridge, and the three subsequently lived, as it were, in a ménage à trois. She nursed Strachey throughout his last illness, and committed suicide shortly after he died.

BETTY BLYTH in Wyndham Lewis, *The Apes of God* (1930)

'Plunkett [Lytton Strachey] took up with Betty Blyth, his Carrington-like girl friend' (Michael Holroyd, 1968, *Lytton Strachey*, Vol. II, London: Heinemann, p. 195).

MARY BRACEGIRDLE in Aldous Huxley, *Crome Yellow* (1921)

'Aldous Huxley ... made some use ... of Carrington's personality in his portrayal of Mary Bracegirdle in *Crome Yellow*. "Pink and childish", Huxley describes her. "Her short hair, clipped like a page's, hung in a bell of elastic gold about her cheeks. She had large china blue eyes, whose expression was one of ingenuous and often puzzled earnestness"' (Holroyd, op. cit., p. 187 n. 1).

ETHEL CANE in D.H. Lawrence, 'None of That' (1928)

'According to D.H. Lawrence, a close friend of Gertler's who took Carrington as the prototype of Ethel Cane in ... "None of That", she was incapable of real love' (Holroyd, op. cit., p. 187). 'Carrington takes you [D.H. Lawrence] aside and begins archly to ask you about flowers. You are looking at her keenly. And I think you used her later in your story "None of that"' (Dorothy Brett, 1933, *Lawrence and Brett*, p. 28).

MINETTE DARRINGTON in D.H. Lawrence, *Women in Love* (1920)

'Minnie Channing . . . shares with Dora Carrington the doubtful honour of having served as model for Minette' (E. Delavenay, 1972, *D.H. Lawrence: the man and his work, 1885–1919*, p. 278). *See also* **Channing** Minnie.

GRETA MORRISON in Gilbert Cannan, *Mendel* (1916)

'[In the summer of 1916] Gilbert Cannan [was] busy writing *Mendel*, his novel built round the Gertler–Carrington love-affair' (Holroyd, op. cit., p. 200).

CARROLL, Lewis *See* **Dodgson**, Charles Lutwidge.

CARSWELL, Catherine (1879–1946) Scottish writer. Née MacFarlane, in 1903 she married H.M. Jackson, but the marriage was annulled in 1908, and in 1915 she married Donald **Carswell**. From 1914 she was a devoted friend of D.H. Lawrence; she was a reviewer for the *Glasgow Herald* until 1915, when she lost her position after writing favourably about Lawrence's *The Rainbow*.

ISABEL PERVIN in D.H. Lawrence, 'The Blind Man' (1922)

'Friends have assured me that the woman in 'The Blind Man' was suggested by me, and it may be so. There was nothing superficially like me in her, and nothing that could not be easily refuted. Yet somewhere the truth smote me' (Catherine Carswell, 1932, *The Savage Pilgrimage: a narrative of D.H. Lawrence*, London: Chatto & Windus, p. 106).

CARSWELL, Donald (1882–1940) Scottish barrister, journalist and writer. He was blinded during the First World War. In 1915 he married Catherine Jackson (**Carswell**, above).

ALEXANDER HEPBURN in D.H. Lawrence, 'The Captain's Doll' (1923)

'For the Scottish officer, Lawrence probably borrowed the surface of Donald Carswell, whom he asked about some details of the uniform' (H.T. Moore, 1960, *The Intelligent Heart: the story of D.H. Lawrence*, Harmondsworth: Penguin, p. 352; originally published 1955, London: Heinemann). *See also* **Lawrence**, D.H.

CARTER, Frederick Painter and etcher. In January 1924 D.H. Lawrence visited him at Pontesbury, Shropshire, and in 1929 he visited Lawrence at Bandol. He was the author of *D.H. Lawrence and the Body Mystical*, and he had a common interest with Lawrence in the symbolism of the Apocalypse.

MR CARTWRIGHT in D.H. Lawrence, 'St Mawr' (1925)

'Lawrence used several of the people at Pontesbury as minor characters, including Carter himself, who appears as Cartwright' (H.T. Moore, 1960, *The Intelligent Heart: the story of D.H. Lawrence*, Harmondsworth: Penguin, p. 409; originally published 1955, London: Heinemann).

CARTON DE WIART, General Adrian (1880–1963) Son of a lawyer in Brussels, he spent most of his childhood in Egypt and was educated at the Oratory School, Edgbaston, and at Balliol College, Oxford, but went down without a degree in order to serve in Paget's Horse in the Boer War. He was subsequently commissioned in the 4th Dragoon Guards and served in India and Somaliland (where he lost an eye). In 1915 he won the Victoria Cross in the Battle of the Somme, and in 1918 he led a military mission to Poland, at that time fighting simultaneously the Bolsheviks, Germans, Ukrainians, Lithuanians, and Czechs. Resigning his commission, between the two World Wars he remained in Poland, living on the Pripet Marshes. In 1939 he returned to England and took part in the Norwegian campaign. In 1941, on his way to Yugoslavia, he was captured by the Italians and was not released until 1943. Between 1943 and 1946, he ended his military career advising Chiang Kai-She in China. 'As a "grand blessé" he was in a class by himself' (*The Times* (6 January 1963)): twice wounded in the Boer War and eight times in the First World War, he was a startling figure, with one arm and a black patch over one eye. To his divisional staff he was known as Old Flamer. Waugh knew him as both were members of **White's Club** in London.

Ben Ritchie-Hook in Evelyn Waugh, the *Sword of Honour* trilogy (1952–61)

'The redoubtable character Brigadier Ritchie-Hook ... was no other than the V.C. general I had come to meet [General Carton de Wiart]' (Lord Lovat, 1978, *March Past*, p. 175). *See also* **St Clair-Morford**, A.

CARUS-WILSON, William (1791–1859) Founder of the **Clergy Daughters' School** at Cowan Bridge in 1823, later at Casterton; the school was attended by the Brontë sisters.

Mr Brocklehurst in Charlotte Brontë, *Jane Eyre* (1847)

'[Charlotte Brontë] saw only one side, and that the unfavourable side of Mr Wilson; but many of those who knew him, assure me of the wonderful fidelity with which his disagreeable qualities ... are represented' (Mrs Gaskell, 1857, *The Life of Charlotte Brontë*, London: Smith, Elder, ch. IV). In *Thornycroft Hall* (1863) Emma Jane Worboise gives an account of the Clergy Daughters' School, which she herself attended, and introduces Carus-Wilson under his own name. She describes him as her 'second father and the kindest man she ever knew'.

CASEY, Joseph Of Kilkenny. Cousin of James Stephens (1825–1901), the chief founder of the Fenians, he was one of four brothers who were all active in the Irish revolutionary movement. He was described by Michael **Davitt** as having 'a leaning towards dynamite and a decided taste for absinthe' (W. O'Brien and Desmond Ryan, 1948, *Devoy's Post-Bag, 1871–1928*, Vol. II, p. 161). In September 1867 he was involved in the Manchester prison rescue; thereafter he was imprisoned in Clerkenwell with Colonel J.O'S. Burke, whence an unsuccessful attempt was made to rescue them. After his release he went to Paris, where he and his brothers fought in the French army in 1870–1. He remained in Paris, working as a compositor on *Galignani's Messenger* and later on the European edition of the New York *Herald Tribune*. He met Joyce in a Paris café in 1903 and the two became friends.

KEVIN EGAN in James Joyce, *Ulysses* (1922)

'In *Ulysses*, where Casey is called Kevin Egan . . . Stephen remembers with pity their lunches together' (Richard Ellmann, 1982, *James Joyce*, rev. edn, Oxford: Oxford University Press, p. 126).

CASEY FAMILY Thomas Wolfe lodged with the family during his last year at Harvard (1922–3).

MURPHY FAMILY in Thomas Wolfe, *Of Time and the River* (1935)

'In his last year, at 21 Trowbridge Street, he lived in the downstairs front room of Mrs D.J. Casey, whose family became the "Murphys"' (R.S. Kennedy, 1962, *The Window of Memory: the literary career of Thomas Wolfe*, Chapel Hill, p. 67). 'Mr Wang', the Chinese lodger, was a Mr Thong (ibid.).

CASSADY, Carolyn Née Robinson, she was educated in Bennington and at Denver University, and in 1947 she married Neal **Cassady**, becoming his second wife; the marriage lasted until his death.

CAMILLE in Jack Kerouac, *On the Road* (1957)

Identified in 'Character key to the Duluoz Legend', Barry Gifford and Lawrence Lee, 1979, *Jack's Book*, pp. 322–32. Cathy and Jamie Cassady, her daughters, appear in the novel as Amy and Joanie Moriarty.

CASSADY, Neal (d. 1968) Railroad brakesman. As a boy, he went through a series of reform schools. To Kerouac, whom he first met in 1947, he became 'the archetypal American man' (R.A. Hipkiss, 1976, *Jack Kerouac: prophet*, Kansas, p. 32).

LEROY in *The Subterraneans* (1958), DEAN MORIARTY in *On the Road* (1957), and CODY POMERAY in *The Dharma Bums* (1958), *Visions of Cody* (1960), *Big Sur* (1962) and *Desolation Angels* (1965), all by Jack Kerouac

Identified in 'Character key to the Duluoz Legend', Barry Gifford and Lawrence Lee, 1979, *Jack's Book*, pp. 322–32.

CASTANO, Pietro (Sometimes 'Peter'.) During the 1920s he was the proprietor of the **Castano's Restaurant**, formerly Previtali's. Powell describes him as small and round, with a little moustache. He had served during the First World War as a cook to one of the battalions of the 60th Rifle Brigade.

FOPPA in Anthony Powell, *A Dance to the Music of Time* (1951–76)

'A genre picture of Castano, his restaurant, the club [upstairs], appears in *A Dance to the Music of Time*, as Foppa's. [He] was far the nicest restaurateur I have ever come across. He was a compulsive gambler, and used to play cards with his friends in the club on the first floor. . . . There was a Russian-billiards table, as in the novel, and it was true, as represented there, that Castano occupied his spare time with trotting-races, in which he himself took part. Unfortunately, these expensive pursuits constrained him at last to give up the Greek Street restaurant. I last heard of him, just before the outbreak of war, running a coffee-stall in Battersea' (Anthony Powell, 1978, *To Keep the Ball Rolling: the memoirs of Anthony Powell,* Vol. II: *Messengers of Day,* London: Heinemann, p. 168).

CASTANO'S RESTAURANT, Soho, London Situated on Greek Street. 'This Italian restaurant entered through a curtain of coloured beads, ran to about a dozen tables on the ground floor, and stood three or four doors down from the archway leading into Manette Street. It is now no more. When I first knew the place it was called Previtali' (A. Powell, 1972, 'Constant Lambert', *The Times* (30 December): 9).

FOPPA'S RESTAURANT in Anthony Powell, *A Dance to the Music of Time* (1951–76)

'In his biography of Lambert, Richard Shead forces an issue by stating categorically that "Foppa's" . . . is Castano's. . . . Without going at length into the diverse methods used by novelists in setting up their puppets, the "short answer" is that "Foppa's", restaurant and proprietor, present, as part of the background of the novel, a genre picture of naturalistic treatment done from life' (Powell, ibid.).

The CASTELLO, Portofino, Italy

SAN SALVATORE in 'Elizabeth', *The Enchanted April* (1922)

'Elizabeth Mary, Countess Russell, published in 1898 [sic] her immensely successful novel, which had the Castello . . . as its setting' (Harold Nicolson to Victoria Sackville-West, 1 February 1934, reproduced in Harold Nicolson, 1966, *Diaries and Letters, 1930–1939,* ed. Nigel Nicolson, London: Collins, p. 16 n. 2). In fact it was *Elizabeth and Her German Garden* that was published in 1898.

CASTLE GATE, Nottingham The street where D.H. Lawrence held his first job, in 1901, with J.H. Haywood Ltd.

SPANIEL ROW in D.H. Lawrence, *Sons and Lovers* (1913)

'Lawrence . . . gave Castle Gate the name of an actual nearby street Spaniel Row' (H.T. Moore, 1960, *The Intelligent Heart: the story of D.H. Lawrence,* Harmondsworth: Penguin, p. 57; originally published 1955, London: Heinemann).

CASTLE HOWARD, North Riding, Yorkshire The seat of the Earls of Carlisle. In 1699 the then Earl of Carlisle commissioned Vanbrugh to prepare designs for a mansion to replace the castle destroyed by fire in 1693. Vanbrugh was at the time a captain in the marines and the author of two successful plays (*The Relapse* and *The Provoked Wife*), but of no architectural training or experience whatever. He was almost immediately joined in the work by Nicholas Hawksmoor, who had been Sir Christopher Wren's clerk since 1679. The two would seem to have been jointly responsible for the building, of which Pevsner says: 'it is on the scale of major princely palaces on the Continent' (*Yorkshire: North Riding,* 1966, (*Buildings of England* series), Harmondsworth: Penguin, p. 109). 'The total impression is eminently festive' (ibid.). The building was gravely damaged in 1940 in an air raid, the dome and great hall being destroyed; they were, however, restored.

BRIDESHEAD in Evelyn Waugh, *Brideshead Revisited* (1945)

'The original of Brideshead can doubtfully be traced to many great houses which Evelyn knew, but I fancy that a strong contribution was made by Castle Howard. The surmounting and majestic lantern . . . may well have suggested the dome of Brideshead, and the fountain facing [the] south front is of the proportions and magnificence of the fountain described in the book. The details of the latter fountain, however, were taken from the great fountain in the Piazza Navona in Rome, as Evelyn told me' (Christopher Sykes, 1975, *Evelyn Waugh*, p. 252). The fountain at Castle Howard was the work, not of Vanbrugh, but of Prince Albert's favourite sculptor, John Thomas. Waugh visited Castle Howard in March 1937, when spending Holy Week at Ampleforth (see *The Diaries of Evelyn Waugh*, 1976, ed. Michael Davie, London: Wiedenfeld & Nicolson, p. 420). *See also* **Madresfield Court**.

CASTLEROSSE, Valentine Edward Charles Browne, Lord (1891–1943) Known as Lord Castlerosse until 1941, when he succeeded as Earl of Kenntare. From 1926 onwards he wrote 'The Londoner's Log' for the *Sunday Express*.

LORD DE JONES in William Gerhardi, *Jazz and Jasper* (1928)

'Lord Castlerosse . . . appears as Lord de Jones' (William Gerhardi, 1974, *Doom* (reissue of *Jazz and Jasper*, preface by Michael Holroyd, London: Macdonald, p. xi).

LORD MACKWORTH in Arnold Bennett, *Lilian* (1922)

'In . . . *Lilian*, Castlerosse appears as Lord Markworth [sic]' (G.M. Thomson, 1973, *Lord Castlerosse: his life and times*, p. 85).

REGINALD, 11TH EARL OF MOUNT WYROC in Michael Arlen, *Young Men in Love* (1927)

'Michael Arlen . . . knew Valentine and put him down in a novel. . . . [His] portrait ran as follows: "Reginald, eleventh Earl of Mount Wyroc, [etc.]"' (Thomson, op. cit., p. 84).

CATHCART, Elizabeth, Lady (d. 1789) Daughter of Thomas Mabyn, she married four times: to James Fleet of Tewin, Hertfordshire; Joseph Sabine of Tring; Lord Cathcart in 1739; and Colonel Hugh **MacGuire** in 1745. This last husband, when she refused to hand over to him her property and jewels, abducted her to his 'love castle in the fastnesses of Ireland' (Burke, *Peerage*), i.e. in County Fermanagh, where he kept her imprisoned until his death in 1764.

LADY RACKRENT in Maria Edgeworth, *Castle Rackrent* (1800)

'The details of the marriage . . . are taken from an authentic incident in another Irish family. . . . [The] episode appears so incredible that Maria is obliged to add a footnote giving her source, the imprisonment of Lady Cathcart by her husband, Col. Hugh MacGuire' (Marilyn Butler, 1972, *Maria Edgeworth*, Oxford, p. 241). See also *Gentleman's Magazine* 59 (August 1780): 766–7; Edward Ford, 1876, *Tewin-Water; or The Story of Lady Cathcart*, Enfield.

The CAVE OF THE GOLDEN CALF, London   A cabaret theatre club off Regent Street, established in 1912 by Frida, second wife of August Strindberg. Wyndham **Lewis** contributed decorations and scenic designs in his pre-war Vorticist style.

THE NIGHTCLUB in Ford Madox Ford, *The Marsden Case* (1923)

'The Nightclub is clearly based on Frida Strindberg's Cave of the Golden Calf' (Jeffrey Meyers, 1980, *The Enemy: a biography of Wyndham Lewis*, London: Routledge & Kegan Paul, p. 30). 'Madame', the owner of The Nightclub, is equally clearly based on Madame Strindberg.

CAVENDISH HOTEL, London   Situated at 81 Jermyn Street. In 1902, Rosa **Lewis** bought it and ran it until her death in 1952. Furnished like a country house and containing some fine pieces (including superb Chinese Chippendale mirrors brought by Lord Ribblesdale), it was run as a mixture of private house and club. One suite was reserved for King Edward VII, and between the death of his first wife and his second marriage Lord Ribblesdale kept a set of rooms there, as did Sir William Eden, the father of Lord Avon. From 1918 the hotel was the London headquarters of Tommy **Hitchcock** and the other members of the American polo team. The most resplendent of its rooms was known as the Elinor Glyn Room; Lord Kitchener dined in it the night before he set sail on his last voyage, in the *Hampshire*. The Cavendish continued throughout the 1920s and 1930s to minister to the Bright Young People and their children, but the cooking and amenities went steadily downhill. During the Second World War it was bombed twice; in 1962 it was pulled down and replaced by a Cavendish Hotel that does not resemble the original at all.

BENTINCK HOTEL in Carroll Carstairs, *A Generation Missing* (1938)

'[Rosa Lewis] now [after the outbreak of the First World War] made a great fuss of all the young Americans who had enlisted under the British colours. Among these was Carroll Carstairs, who joined the Grenadier Guards and was severely wounded. In the novel which he subsequently wrote, he gives a contemporary picture of the hotel, the Bentinck' (Daphne Fielding, 1964, *The Duchess of Jermyn Street*, p. 95).

SACKVILLE HOTEL in Shane Leslie, *The Anglo-Catholic* (1929)

'In *The Anglo-Catholic* [Rosa Lewis] appears as Louisa who, when introducing people staying in her hotel (the Sackville), is described as "rinsing them like a sauce through the duller guests"' (Fielding, op. cit., p. 169).

SHEPHEARD'S HOTEL in Evelyn Waugh, *Vile Bodies* (1930)

'Evelyn Waugh finally cooked the writers' goose as far as Rosa was concerned with his portrait of . . . "Shepheard's Hotel"' (Fielding, op. cit., p. 133).

CAVENDISH SQUARE, London

GAUNT SQUARE in W.M. Thackeray, *Vanity Fair* (1847–8)

'Gaunt Square must be Cavendish Square' (Joan Stevens, 1969–70, 'A roundabout ride', *Victorian Studies* 13: 67). *See also* **Berkeley Square; Manchester Square**.

CAVENDISH-BENTINCK, Prudentia Penelope (d. 1896) Daughter of Charles Powell Leslie of Glaslough, Monahan, in 1850 she married George Cavendish-Bentinck who, as an MP from 1859 until his death, was a friend and supporter of Disraeli. She was known in Society as 'Britannia'; their house in Grafton Street, London, contained a fine collection of French and Italian pictures.

APOLLONIA GILES in Benjamin Disraeli, *Lothair* (1870)

'July 13 [1870] – we did not get home till late and found that the Cavendish-Bentincks had already sat down to dinner . . . but . . . altogether I enjoyed my dinner and a party afterwards. Evidently Apollonia, as Dizzy calls her in *Lothair*, understands society' (*The Journals of Lady Knightley of Fansley*, 1915, ed. Julia Cartwright, London, p. 200).

CECIL, John Francis Amherst (1890–1954) Son of Lord William Cecil, he was in the Diplomatic Service. In 1924 he married Cornelia Vanderbilt of Biltmore Estate, North Carolina, becoming her first husband, but they were divorced in 1934.

JOHN HUGH WILLIAM MACPHERSON MARRIOTT in Thomas Wolfe, *Of Time and the River* (1935)

'He has four names because Wolfe modeled his character on John Francis Amherst Cecil, the first husband of Cornelia Vanderbilt' (*The Notebooks of Thomas Wolfe*, 1970, ed. Richard S. Kennedy and Paschal Reeves, Chapel Hill, NC: University of North Carolina Press, p. 503 n. 9). In *The Web and the Rock* and *You Can't Go Home Again* the name is shortened to Hugh Macpherson.

HUGH MACPHERSON MARRIOTT in Thomas Wolfe, *The Web and the Rock* (1939) and *You Can't Go Home Again* (1940)

See above.

CERNE ABBAS, Dorset A small town situated seven miles north of Dorchester. In the hill just outside the town, cut down to the chalk, is the figure of the Cerne giant, bearing a club 120 feet in length. The town contains the ruins of a Benedictine abbey, and a splendid tithe barn.

ABBOTSCERNEL in Thomas Hardy, Wessex novels and tales (1871–95)

Identifed on a map prepared by Thomas Hardy which hangs in the Dorset County Museum, Dorchester. *See under* **Abbotsbury**.

CERVI, Orazio He was a model for the sculptor Hanro Thornycroft in London. He owned a house at Picinisco in the Abruzzi mountains where, in December 1919, D.H. Lawrence and his wife spent about ten days.

PANCRAZIO CALIFANO in D.H. Lawrence, *The Lost Girl* (1920)

'. . . the Italian farmer Orazio Cervi (Pancrazio in the novel)' (H.T. Moore, 1960, *The Intelligent Heart: the story of D.H. Lawrence*, Harmondsworth: Penguin, p. 325; originally published 1955, London: Heinemann).

CERVONI, Dominic (1834–90) An officer on board the *Saint-Antoine* in which Conrad sailed from July 1876 to February 1877 on a round voyage from Marseilles to Port-au-Prince. '[A] man destined to play a considerable part in Conrad's life; indeed, perhaps, the most important part . . . Conrad has drawn a portrait of him in *The Mirror of the Sea*, 1923 (Uniform edn), p. 162–3). . . . He . . . crops up constantly in Conrad's work under different names. He was Conrad's true initiator into the life of the sea' (G. Jean-Aubry, 1927, *Joseph Conrad: life and letters*, Vol. I, London: Heinemann, pp. 35–6).

DOMINIC in Joseph Conrad, *The Arrow of Gold* (1919)

'I never tried to conceal the origins of the subject matter of this book . . . but some reviewers indulged themselves with a sense of triumph in discovering in it my Dominic of "The Mirror of the Sea" under his own name (a truly wonderful discovery)' (*The Arrow of Gold*, 1924 (Uniform edn), p. viii, author's note).

NOSTROMO in Joseph Conrad, *Nostromo* (1904)

'. . . mainly Nostromo is what he is because I received the inspiration for him in my early days from a Mediterranean sailor. Those who have read certain pages of mine will see at once what I mean when I say that Dominic, the padrone of the *Tremolino*, might under given circumstances have been a Nostromo' (*Nostromo*, 1923 (Uniform edn), p. xii, author's note).

JEAN PEYROL in Joseph Conrad, *The Rover* (1923)

'In *The Rover* Jean Peyrol is undoubtedly an old Dominic' (G. Jean-Aubry, op. cit., p. 37 n. 1).

ATTILIO PIESCHI in Joseph Conrad, *Suspense* (1925)

'[H]ow can we fail to recognise in Attilio Fieschi [sic], a new incarnation of Dominic Cervoni?' (G. Jean-Aubry, 1925, 'The inner history of Conrad's *Suspense*', *Bookman's Journal* 13 (49): 8).

CHAGARAY, Madame Headmistress and proprietor of a school for girls in New York in the mid-nineteenth century.

HORTENSE-PAULINE MOREAU in Constance Fenimore Woolson, *Anne* (1883)

'As a child . . . I heard much of "old New York", for even my Plattsburg grandmother had gone to school there, at "the late celebrated Madame Chagaray's," as Henry James called it in one of his stories. . . . Miss Woolson, who was also a pupil there . . . described the school in *Anne* as Madame Moreau's where "the extreme of everything called accomplishment" was taught . . . this included . . . Italian . . . actually taught by Lorenzo da Ponte, who had written the libretto of *Don Giovanni* and of . . . *Figaro* and *Cosi fan tutte* as well. Julia Ward Howe had been his pupil at Madame Chagaray's, that good-hearted little old Frenchwoman whom everyone called Tante, with a plain black dress and a shrewd face' (Van Wyck Brooks, 1954, *Scenes and Portraits*, p. 61).

CHAMBERLAIN, Joseph (1836–1914) Statesman. Born in Birmingham, he began his career in municipal politics and became MP for Birmingham in 1876.

He was a colleague of John Bright and served in the Cabinet under Gladstone, but left the Liberal Party over the question of home-rule for Ireland. In 1895 he became a member of the Conservative cabinet under Lord Salisbury and was Secretary of State for the Colonies at the time of the Boer War. He retired from public life in 1906.

Jos. Choselwit in Sir Harry Johnston, *The Gay-Dombeys* (1919)

'Jos Choselwit [is a portrait] of Mr Chamberlain' (Sir Harry Johnston to John Gunther, quoted in J. Gunther, 1925, 'Multiple Sir Harry Johnston', *Bookman* 57 (November): 309).

Charles Gurnard in Joseph Conrad and Ford Madox Ford, *The Inheritors* (1901)

Identified in Jocelyn Baines, 1967, *Joseph Conrad: a critical biography*, London: Weidenfeld & Nicolson, p. 239; origianlly published 1960.

Japhet Snapper in W.H. Mallock, *The Old Order Changes* (1886)

'. . . "Japhet Snapper", the Liberal Radical Leader, a vitriolic caricature of Joseph Chamberlain' (R.L. Wolff, 1977, *Gains and Losses: novels of faith and doubt in Victorian England*, London: John Murray, p. 490).

CHAMBERLAIN, Revd Thomas (1810–92) Vicar of St Thomas the Martyr, Oxford, from 1842 until he died. He was Honorary Canon of Christ Church, Oxford, in 1882, and with the help of a band of enthusiastic curates he set himself to reforming his poor and neglected parish. He founded a sisterhood, and was a Tractarian and ritualist.

Mr Chesterfield in Felicia Skene, *St Albans; or The Prisoners of Hope* (1853)

'. . . an idealized portrait of Mr Chamberlain' (M.M. Maison, 1916, *Search Your Soul, Eustace*, p. 51).

CHAMBERS, Alan (1882–1946) Son of Edmund and brother of Jessie **Chambers**, as a boy and young man he was a close friend of D.H. Lawrence. In 1910 he married Lawrence's cousin Aloina Reeve, née Lawrence, and subsequently emigrated to Canada.

Edgar Leivers in D.H. Lawrence, *Sons and Lovers* (1913)

'Edgar [was] apparently modelled after Alan Chambers' (H.T. Moore, 1960, *The Intelligent Heart: the story of D.H. Lawrence*, Harmondsworth: Penguin, p. 100; originally published 1955, London: Heinemann).

George Saxton in D.H. Lawrence, *The White Peacock* (1911)

'The man I have been working with in the hay is the original of my George' (to Blanche Jennings, 30 July 1908, reproduced in *The Letters of D.H. Lawrence*, 1979, ed. James T. Boulton, Vol. I, Cambridge: Cambridge University Press, p. 65). Lawrence had spent the two preceding weeks haymaking with Alan Chambers. *See also* **Neville**, George H.

CHAMBERS, Edmund (1863–1946) He married Sarah Ann Oates, who attended the same chapel as Lydia **Lawrence** and became her close friend. He was the father of Jessie and Alan **Chambers**, and *c*.1898 became the tenant of **Haggs Farm**, Eastwood, Nottinghamshire.

MR LEIVERS in D.H. Lawrence, *Sons and Lovers* (1913)

'Lawrence rarely brings him into the foreground, yet his personality is familiar to readers of *The White Peacock* (Mr Saxton) and of *Sons and Lovers* (Mr Leivers)' (E. Delavenay, 1972, *D.H. Lawrence: the man and his work, 1885–1919*, p. 20).

MR SAXTON in D.H. Lawrence, *The White Peacock* (1911)

See above.

CHAMBERS, Jessie (1887–1944) Daughter of Edmund and sister of Alan **Chambers**, she lived with her parents at **Haggs Farm**. In 1900 she became a close friend of D.H. Lawrence, and in 1915 she married John R. Wood. She was the author ('E.T') of *D.H. Lawrence: a personal record* (1935).

MIRIAM LEIVERS in D.H. Lawrence, *Sons and Lovers* (1913)

'Jessie Chambers . . . was the prototype for Miriam in *Sons and Lovers*' (*The Letters of D.H. Lawrence*, 1979, ed. James T. Boulton, Vol. I, Cambridge: Cambridge University Press, p. 22 n. 2).

MURIEL in D.H. Lawrence, 'A Modern Lover' (1934)

'. . . Jessie (clearly recognisable as Muriel, a name by which he sometimes called her)' (E. Delavenay, 1972, *D.H. Lawrence: the man and his work, 1885–1919*, p. 65).

HERMIONE RODDICE in D.H. Lawrence, *Women in Love* (1920)

'Jessie . . . recognised herself in the Hermione of the novel. [See letters to Delavenay, printed in Appendix IV of the French version of the work.] (Delavenay, op. cit., p. 67). *See also* **Morrell**, Lady Ottoline.

EMILY SAXTON in D.H. Lawrence, *The White Peacock* (1911)

'Sometimes . . . I hear, casually, something of his [Lawrence's] Nottinghamshire home and its people. His talk is like an appendix to *The White Peacock*. . . . The original of Emily, I gather is . . . Jessie Chambers' (Helen Corke, 1975, *In Our Infancy*, Cambridge, p. 179).

CHAMBERS, Whittaker (1901–61) Born in Philadelphia and educated at Long Island and at Columbia University, he joined the Communist Party and became foreign news editor of the New York *Daily Worker*. In 1938 he left the Communist Party and became Senior Editor of *Time Magazine*. In 1939 he alleged that in 1937–8 Alger Hiss, then in the US State Department, had passed confidential state documents to the Soviet Union. Hiss denied the allegation in 1948 to the Congressional Committee on Un-American Activities, and in a grand-jury investigation into espionage the Department of Justice called both Hiss and Chambers as witnesses. Hiss was indicted for perjury and in the subsequent trial Whittaker Chambers was the chief witness for the prosecution: at the first trial the jury disagreed; at the second trial, in 1950, Hiss was found guilty.

WEBSTER CALHOUN in Warren Miller, *The Sleep of Reason* (1956)

'Among the stable of inventive informers [is] Webster Calhoun (who has a farm as well as doubly-familiar initials)' (Joseph Blotner, 1966, *The Modern American Political Novel*, Austin, Tex., p. 303).

GIFFORD MAXIM in Lionel Trilling, *The Middle of the Journey* (1947)

'*The Middle of a Journey* was published ... a year or more before Whittaker Chambers ... accused Alger Hiss of turning over ... State Department documents to the Soviet Union. . . . Recently I wrote Trilling to inquire whether he had any personal acquaintance with the two antagonists, and his reply of May 22, 1972 is . . . of interest . . . as illuminating the way in which authors make use of the material in their own lives. "I did not mean to write a novel . . . only a long, short story. . . . But it seemed to need something else, and in response to that need Gifford Maxim, which is to say Whittaker Chambers, presented himself. . . . I had had some acquaintance with Chambers at college. . . . In the very early thirties he was a figure of some importance in the Communist Party. . . . In 1930 or 1931, he 'went underground'. . . . His connections . . . were with the Russian apparatus, rather than with the American party. . . . Around 1934 or 1935, he . . . 'broke'. In his attempts to 'establish an identity', which the novel makes much of, he turned to his old friends, who believed . . . that he was in mortal danger. The novel's representation of Chambers is pretty liberal"' (Frederick Warburg, 1973, *All Authors are Equal*, pp. 125, 126).

CHAMBERS, William (1800–83) Apprenticed to an Edinburgh bookseller in 1814, in 1819 he opened his own bookstall and later, with his brother Robert, he founded the publishing firm of W.R. Chambers of Edinburgh. They published *Chambers Journal* (1832), a popular three-ha'penny weekly, and *Chambers Encyclopedia* (1859). From 1865 to 1869, he was Lord Provost of Edinburgh. His sister Janet, in 1846, married W.H. Wills, who later became Dickens's personal secretary and one of his most trusted personal friends, and Assistant Editor of *Household Words* and *All the Year Round*.

JOSIAH BOUNDERBY in Charles Dickens, *Hard Times* (1854)

'William, as is well known, unconsciously sat to Dickens for his portrait of Bounderby in "Hard Times". He was always talking of the poverty of his youth, and hinting ... at the genius which had raised him to eminence. He used to give lectures describing the miseries of a poor lad, who had had to "thole" (toil) for his livelihood, and had afterwards, by diligence and merit, made a great figure in the world; and the peroration ... used to be always "I was *that Boy*"' (James Payn, 1884, 'Some literary recollections, VI', *Cornhill Magazine* (NS) 2 (May): 488).

CHANCE, Charles A friend of James Joyce's father, John Stanislaus Joyce, with whom he once went on a retreat.

LEOPOLD BLOOM in James Joyce, *Ulysses* (1922)

'In the variety of his jobs, in the profession of his wife, Chance fitted the description of Bloom' (Richard Ellmann, 1982, *James Joyce*, rev. edn, Oxford: Oxford University Press, p. 375). *See also* **Bloom**, Joseph; **Byrne**, John Francis; **Hunter**, Alfred H.; **Jackson**, Holbrook; **Joyce**, James; **Joyce**, John Stanislaus; **Mayer**, Teodoro; **Popper**, Leopoldo; **Schmitz**, Ettore.

C.P. McCoy in James Joyce, 'Grace', *Dubliners* (1914) and *Ulysses* (1922)

'This man is first mentioned in . . . "Grace" under the name of C.P. McCoy . . . as having been a clerk in the Midland Railway, a canvasser for advertisements for *The Irish Times* and *Freeman's Journal*, a town traveler for a coal firm on commission, a private enquiry agent, a clerk in the office of the sub-sheriff, and secretary to the City Coroner. His wife had been a soprano and still taught children to play the piano. . . . These facts all point to McCoy's actual prototype, Charles Chance' (Ellmann, op. cit.).

CHANCE, Mrs Charles She sang in Dublin under the name of Madame Marie Tallon. She was married to Charles **Chance**.

MARION ('MOLLY') BLOOM in James Joyce, *Ulysses* (1922)

'Charles Chance's wife was one of the models for Molly Bloom' (Richard Ellmann, 1982, *James Joyce*, rev. edn, Oxford: Oxford University Press, p. 133 n.). 'The concert name of Mrs Charles Chance, "Madame Marie Tallon", bears a deliberate resemblance to Madame Marion Tweedy, Mrs Bloom's concert name' (ibid. p. 375). *See also* **Dillon**, Mamie; **Joyce**, Nora; **Popper**, Amalia; **Santos**, Signora.

CHANLER, Mrs Winthrop ('Daisy') Daughter of Luther Terry, an American painter who worked in Rome, she was a close friend of Edith **Wharton**.

MRS LAWRENCE in F. Scott Fitzgerald, *This Side of Paradise* (1920)

'Fay's . . . friends, to whom he introduced . . . Fitzgerald, included Mrs Winthrop Chanler . . . who appears briefly in *This Side of Paradise* as Mrs Lawrence' (H.D. Piper, 1966, *F. Scott Fitzgerald*, p. 47).

CHANNING, Minnie (b. 1894) Daughter of Robert Stuart Channing, a mechanical engineer, in December 1916 she married Philip **Heseltine** (Peter Warlock), but they separated *c.*1923. They had one son.

MINETTE DARRINGTON in D.H. Lawrence, *Women in Love* (1920)

'Minnie Channing . . . shares with Dora Carrington the doubtful honour of having served as model for Minette' (E. Delavenay, 1972, *D.H. Lawrence: the man and his work, 1885–1919*, p. 278). *See also* **Carrington**, Dora.

CHANNON, Sir Henry ('Chips') (1897–1958) Born in Chicago, he went to Europe as a young man and moved in London Society. His diaries were published after his death.

ELLIOTT TEMPLETON in W. Somerset Maugham, *The Razor's Edge* (1944)

'I saw much of Somerset Maugham. . . . He has put me into a book, "The Razor's Edge" and when I dined with him, I asked him why he had done it, and he explained, with some embarrassment, that he had split me into three characters, and then written a book about all three. So I am Elliott Templeton, Larry, himself the hero of the book, and another' (*Chips: the diaries of Sir Henry Channon*, 1967, ed. Robert James, London: Weidenfeld & Nicolson, p. 392). 'It is easy to see that Maugham, caught unexpectedly, extricated himself with the preposterous explanation that Channon provided the raw material for all three characters. Had he not been guilty of using him for Templeton, it would have been much easier to simply deny everything' (R.L. Calder, 1972, *W. Somerset Maugham and the Quest for Freedom*, London: Heinemann, p. 237). *See also* **May**, Henry.

CHAPALA, Mexico The small town where the Lawrences rented a house (Zaragoza 4) from May to 27 July 1923, and where between May and June D.H. Lawrence wrote the first draft of *The Plumed Serpent*.

SAYULA in D.H. Lawrence, *The Plumed Serpent* (1926)

'Sayula is Lawrence's fictional name for Chapala' (D.H. Lawrence, 1983, *The Plumed Serpent*, ed. Ronald G. Walkey, Harmondsworth: Penguin, p. 488 n. 10). 'Here we are, in our own house – a long house with no upstairs. . . . Just outside the gate the big Lake of Chapala. . . . Chapala village is small with a market place. . . . Also three hotels because this is a tiny holiday place for Guadalajara' (D.H. Lawrence to Knut Merrild, 3 May 1923, quoted in E. Nehls, 1958, *D.H. Lawrence: a composite biography*, Vol. II, Madison, pp. 232–3).

CHAPEL HILL, North Carolina Home of the University of North Carolina.

PINE ROCK COLLEGE in Thomas Wolfe, *The Web and the Rock* (1939)

'Only about 50 pages are given to Webber at Pine Rock College, a subject anticipated by Wolfe's life at Chapel Hill and Eugene Gant's at Pulpit Hill' (Floyd C. Watkins, 1957, *Thomas Wolfe's Characters: portraits from life*, Norman, Okla., p. 86).

PULPIT HILL in Thomas Wolfe, *Look Homeward, Angel* (1929)

'Chapel Hill is Pulpit Hill' (Watkins, op. cit., p. 7).

CHAPIN & GORE, Chicago The saloon where L.A. **Hopkins** was employed as Manager in the 1880s.

FITZGERALD & MOY in Theodore Dreiser, *Sister Carrie* (1900)

'Chapin and Gore's became Fitzgerald and Moy's' (R.H. Elias, 1970, *Theodore Dreiser*, p. 107).

CHAPMAN, Edward (1804–80) Publisher. He was the partner of William **Hall** in the firm of Chapman and Hall, publishers of *Pickwick*, and was the more literary of the partners.

THE BACHELOR FRIEND in Charles Dickens, 'The Nice Little Couple', *Sketches of Young Couples* (1840)

'Mr Chirrup has a bachelor friend, who lived with him in his days of single blessedness . . . and . . . whenever you dine with Mr and Mrs Chirrup, you meet the bachelor friend. . . . [T]he bachelor friend . . . was Edward Chapman' (Arthur Waugh, 1930, *A Hundred Years of Publishing: being the story of Chapman & Hall Ltd*, pp. 65, 66).

CHAPMAN, Fanny Sister of Mrs Bigelow **Lawrence**.

SYBIL ROSS in Henry Adams, *Democracy* (1880)

'The formal models of Mrs Madeleine Lee and her sister Sybil were . . . Mrs Bigelow Lawrence . . . and her sister Fanny Chapman' (Ernest Samuels, 1958, *Henry Adams: the middle years*, Cambridge, Mass., p. 93).

CHAPMAN, John (1821–94) Born in Nottingham, he was the son of William Chapman, who kept a druggist and grocer's shop. He trained as a watchmaker and later qualified as a physician and surgeon in Paris and at St George's Hospital, London. In 1851–94, he was the Editor and proprietor of the *Westminster Review*, and for many years he kept the upper part of his offices at 142 Strand, London, as a boarding-house where many literary persons lodged, including George **Eliot**, Hale White ('Mark Rutherford') and **Emerson**. It has been alleged that George Eliot, when she lived in his house in the early 1850s, was his mistress.

MR WOLLASTON in Mark Rutherford, *The Autobiography of Mark Rutherford* (1881)

'It may be assumed . . . that Chapman is the original of Wollaston' (John Grigor, 1902, '"Mark Rutherford" and "George Eliot"', *Notes and Queries* (9th series) 10 (13 September): 204).

CHAPMAN, Lovina (d. 1919) Proprietress of the Hotel Tiaré, Tahiti.

TIARÉ JOHNSON in W. Somerset Maugham, *The Moon and Sixpence* (1919)

'Lovina Chapman . . . (Tiaré Johnson in the novel) . . . was well known to travelers in the South Seas and to readers the world over, for nearly every book about the South Pacific written in the first two decades of the century has an account of her and her hotel' (Richard A. Cordell, 1969, *Somerset Maugham: a writer for all seasons*, Bloomington and London: Indiana University Press, p. 105). In the account of the Hotel Tiaré in *A Writer's Notebook* (1949), Maugham describes her affectionately, giving her name as Madame Lovaina (p. 128).

CHAPMAN, Thomas (1798–1885) Partner in the firm of John Chapman & Co., ship and insurance brokers in Leadenhall St., London. In 1835–81 he was Chairman of Lloyd's Registry of British and foreign shipping. He was also Chairman of Devonshire House sanatorium, which was founded in 1842 by D.T. Southwood Smith in York Terrace. In 1844 he found a job for Augustus Dickens in his office.

MR DOMBEY in Charles Dickens, *Dombey and Son* (1846–8)

'[W]e may as well allude to the Character of Dombey, the hero of Mr Dickens' last completed novel; this is well known as intended to represent a shipowner and merchant "not a hundred miles" from Leadenhall Street, in whose office a relative of the novelist is clerk. . . . When the first number appeared the likeness was readily recognised by this wealthy merchant's relatives, and he was christened Dombey on the spot' (Thomas Powell, 1849, *The Living Authors of England*, New York, pp. 158–9). 'Thomas Powell [for many years confidential clerk in John Chapman & Co., from whom he embezzled a large sum] was responsible for the assertion that Dickens's model for Mr Dombey was Thomas Chapman. ... Although Dickens was at pains to forestall any such identification even before the first number of Dombey was written, and Forster characterized it as absurd, an anonymous writer in Lloyd's List and Shipping Gazette [3 January 1928, p. 6] thought it not impossible' (W.J. Carlton, 1968, 'A note on Captain Cuttle', *The Dickensian* 64 (September): 154). Powell bolted to America in spring 1849 when a warrant was issued for his arrest on charges of defalcation. The identification is described by Kathleen Tillotson as 'absurd' (see *The Letters of Charles Dickens*, 1977, Vol. IV, ed. Kathleen Tillotson, Oxford: Oxford University Press, p. 586 n. 3). 'The man for Dombey, if [Habelot] Browne could see him, the class man to a T, is Sir A—— E——, of D——'s' (Dickens to Forster, 18 July 1846, quoted in John Forster, 1928, *Life of Dickens*, ed. J.W.T. Ley, p. 405). Browne was the illustrator; the likeness can only have been physical, and in any case Sir A—— E—— is unidentifiable (see *Letters*, op. cit., p. 586). '[W]ith ... Mr Thomas Chapman, the chairman of Lloyd's, he held frequent kindly intercourse, and ... few things more absurd or unfounded have been invented, even of Dickens, than that he found any part of the original of Mr Dombey in the nature, the appearance, or the manners of this excellent and much valued friend' (Forster, op. cit., p. 326).

CHARLEMONT, James Caulfield, Lord (1728–99) Irish statesman. Fourth Viscount and 1st Earl of Charlemont. He was an associate of Grattan, and the leader of the Irish Volunteers. He opposed Catholic emancipation and the union.

LORD Y. in Maria Edgeworth, 'Ennui', *Tales of Fashionable Life* (1809)

'The real men and women who made appearances ... included ... Lord Charlemont (Lord Y—— in *Ennui*' (Marilyn Butler, 1972, *Maria Edgeworth*, Oxford, p. 248).

CHARLES, Mrs J.W. Née Merrill, later Frost, she was the sister-in-law of W.B. **Smith**. In 1899, when her sister Katharine Drake Smith died of tuberculosis, the widowed Mrs Frost went to care for the four children. In 1902 she married Dr Charles, although she continued to have charge of the Smith children. In 1912 she and her husband bought a farmhouse at Horton Bay on Lake Charlevoix, Michigan, about three miles from the Hemingways' summer house on the shores of Walloon (Bear) Lake. Here the Smith children spent their holidays and their friendship with the young Ernest **Hemingway** began.

LYDIA RUMFORD (AUNT LYDE) in John Dos Passos, *Chosen Country* (1951)

Identified in Carlos Baker, 1969, *Ernest Hemingway: a life story*, New York, p. 654 n. 'E.H. on Dos Passos's "Chosen Country"'.

CHARLEVILLE, Catherine Maria Bury, Lady Née Dawson, she was the widow of James Tisdall and married the 1st Earl **Charleville**. She was a leader in Society in Dublin and in London, where she held a salon in Charleville House, Cavendish Square.

LADY ABBERVILLE in Lady Blessington, *The Repealers* (1833)

'There seems good reason to suspect that this piece of vicious portraituter Harriet]' (Michael Sadleir, 1933, *Blessington–D'Orsay: a masquerade*, London: Constable, pp. 209–10).

CHARLEVILLE, Charles William Bury, Lord (1764–1835) Irish Representative Peer. The 1st Earl of Charleville, from 1812 to 1833 he was President of the Royal Irish Academy, and in 1814 he became a Fellow of the Royal Society and a Fellow of the Society of Antiquaries. He married Catherine Maria Tisdall (**Charleville**, above).

LORD ABBERVILLE in Lady Blessington, *The Repealers* (1833)

'As for "Lord Abberville", he is even more arguably Charleville in caricature' (Michael Sadleir, 1933, *Blessington–D'Orsay: a masquerade*, London: Constable, p. 210).

CHARMINSTER, Dorset A village about three miles north of Dorchester, on the road to Sherborne.

CHARMLEY in Thomas Hardy, *Under the Greenwood Tree* (1872)

Identified in F.B. Pinion, 1968, *A Hardy Companion*, London: Macmillan.

CHARNOCK, Richard Stephen (1820–99?) Lawyer and littérateur. He edited Bradshaw's *Illustrated Handbook to Spain and Portugal, 1865–1899*.

HIPPIAS FEVEREL in George Meredith, *The Ordeal of Richard Feverel* (1859)

'Hippias Feverel, the dyspeptic wine-bibber and author of scholarly treatises, recalled Richard Charnock' (A. Lionel Stevenson, 1954, *The Ordeal of George Meredith*, London: Peter Owen, p. 64). 'Mr Lionel Robinson tells me that Charnock was a "character", a real antiquarian of doubtful morals and for many years one of the "old boys" of the Arundel Club of Bohemian ways and days. Meredith put him (much disguised) into *Richard Feverel* as the uncle' (Edward Clodd, 1916, *Memories*, p. 142).

CHARTERHOUSE An English public school, formerly in the City of London, but now at Godalming, Surrey.

GREYFRIARS in W.M. Thackeray, *The Newcomes* (1854–5)

'On December 12, 1854 ... Thackeray who was present [at Founder's Day at Charterhouse] for chapel, [the Founder's Day] oration, and dinner, spoke ... in the evening ... avowing ... that the prospect of a speech had hindered his digestion and spoilt his dinner; and before leaving the table he said to some about him, "I shall put all this in my book" (See J.W. Irvine, 1893, 'A Study for Colonel Newcome', *The Nineteenth Century* 34 (October): 588–9). He was as good as his word; see Chapter 75 of *The Newcomes*, "Founder's Day at Greyfriars"' (*The Letters and Private Papers of W.M. Thackeray*, 1945, ed. Gordon Ray, Vol. III, London: Oxford University Press, p. 406 n. 127).

LE CHAT BLANC, Paris Restaurant on rue d'Odessa, Montparnasse.

LE CHIEN NOIR in W. Somerset Maugham, *The Magician* (1908)

'Soon after my arrival [in Paris, 1904], Gerald Kelly took me to . . . Le Chat Blanc . . . and from then on I dined there every night. I have described the place elsewhere, and in some detail in the novel to which these pages are meant to serve as preface' (W. Somerset Maugham, 1956, 'A fragment of autobiography', preface to *The Magician* (collected edn), London, p. vii).

CHATEAUBRIAND, François René, Vicomte de (1768–1848) French writer and statesman. In 1791–2 he travelled in North America, and when he returned to France he fought in the French Royalist Army. Between 1792 and 1800 he lived in London, where he wrote his *Essai sur les Révolutions* (1797). In 1802 he published *Génie du christianisme* and in 1803 he was appointed Secretary to the Rome embassy, serving under Napoleon. In 1804, while in exile, he travelled in the Middle East and North Africa. In 1822 he was Ambassador to Great Britain, in 1823–4 he was Minister of Foreign Affairs, and in 1827 he was Ambassador to Rome.

MILES FANNING in Aldous Huxley, 'After the Fireworks' (1930)

'When [Chateaubriand] was sixty . . . a very young girl at a watering-place came and threw herself at his head. He wrote her a most exquisite letter, which is extant. And there the matter ended, even though she did invade his house one evening. With my usual sadism, I thought it would be amusing to give it the cruel ending. And as one couldn't use Chateaubriand himself – that monstrous pride and loneliness and, underneath the burning imagination, that emotional aridity would have been impracticable to handle – I made the hero one of those people . . . who know how to shirk natural consequences and . . . give Nemesis the slip' (Aldous Huxley to a correspondent, quoted in George Woodcock, 1972, *Dawn and the Darkest Hour: a study of Aldous Huxley*, London: Faber & Faber, p. 166).

EDWARD MANISTY in Mrs Humphry Ward, *Eleanor* (1899)

'The story of Eleanor Burgoyne owed its being, so far as I can now recollect, to an old familiarity . . . with the love story of Chateaubriand and Madame de Beaumont' (*The Writings of Mrs Humphry Ward*, Vol. X: *Eleanor*, 1911, London: Smith, Elder, p. ix). Mrs Humphry Ward goes on to explain (ibid., p. x) that the character of Manisty is not based on that of Chateaubriand although his role and situation are similar; so, incidentally, is his physical appearance.

CHAYTOR, Sir William (1771–1847) Of Croft, Yorkshire and Witton Castle, County Durham, he was created baronet in 1831.

SIR PITT CRAWLEY in W.M. Thackeray, *Vanity Fair* (1847–8)

'In Surtees' autograph-book is a letter from Mr, afterwards Sir, William Chaytor of Witton Castle, across the corner of which is pencilled, "The original of Sir Pitt Crawley in . . . *Vanity Fair*"' (R.S. Surtees and E.D. Cuming, 1924, *Robert Smith Surtees, 1803–1864*, p. 264). 'I heard a story the other day of our most earnest and genial humorist [Thackeray] . . . "I like your novel [*Vanity Fair*] exceedingly", said a lady; "the characters are so natural – all but the baronet, and he surely is overdrawn: it is impossible to find such coarseness in his rank of life!". The artist laughed. "And that character", said he, "is almost the only exact portrait in the whole book"' (Charles Kingsley, 1851, *Yeast*, p. 20). *See also* **Rolle**, Lord.

LORD SCAMPERDALE in R.S. Surtees, *Mr Sponge's Sporting Tour* (1853)

'The family likeness between . . . Sir Pitt Crawley . . . and . . . Lord Scamperdale . . . must have been remarked by all who are familiar with the two novels. . . . May we not fairly conclude that Mr Chaytor served also as a model for Lord Scamperdale?' (Surtees and Cuming, op. cit., p. 264).

CHEEVERS, Harold (b. 1893) A constable in the Metropolitan Police. From 1924 to 1941 he was Hugh Walpole's driver, factotum, companion and friend.

CHARLIE CHRISTIAN in Hugh Walpole, *John Cornelius: His Life and Adventures* (1937)

'For the character called Charlie Christian, Harold was the model' (Rupert Hart-Davis, 1952, *Hugh Walpole*, p. 371).

CHELTENHAM LADIES' COLLEGE Founded in 1853, the Principal was Dorothea Beale from 1858 to 1906, and from 1912 to 1915 Margaret Kennedy was a pupil.

CLEEVE COLLEGE in Margaret Kennedy, *The Constant Nymph* (1924)

'The school to which Tessa . . . [was] sent [was] modelled on Cheltenham, with little attempt at disguise' (Violet Powell, 1983, *The Constant Novelist: a study of Margaret Kennedy, 1896–1967*, p. 62).

CHERRY HINTON, Cambridgeshire A village on the outskirts of Cambridge; it is now a suburb.

CHERRYUMPTON in Shane Leslie, *The Cantab* (1926)

Identified in a key in the hand of Dr Ivor Ramsay, a Kingsman of the year 1920, and later Dean, laid in a copy of *The Cantab*. *See also* **Trumpington**.

CHESHAM, Buckinghamshire

SUMMERTUNE, ESSEX, in Compton Mackenzie, *The Four Winds of Love: The South Wind* (1937)

See under **Cannan**, Gilbert.

CHESTERFIELD, Philip Dormer Stanhope, Lord (1694–1773) Diplomat and statesman. The 4th Earl of Chesterfield, he was chiefly famous for the letters he addressed almost daily to his natural son.

SIR JOHN CHESTER in Charles Dickens, *Barnaby Rudge* (1841)

'As a picture of Lord Chesterfield, of course, upon whom he was modeled, he is pure caricature' (Edgar Johnson, 1953, *Charles Dickens, His Tragedy and Triumph*, Vol. I, p. 333). The identification is an old one and was current from the first appearance of the character.

CHESTERTON, Gilbert Keith (1874–1936) Poet, novelist and critic. He was much influenced by his friendship with Hilaire Belloc, and in 1922 he was received into the Roman Catholic Church.

DR GIDEON FELL in John Dickson Carr, *The Mad Hatter Mystery* (1933) and others

'Dr Fell is G.K. Chesterton' (Erik Routley, 1972, *The Puritan Pleasures of the Detective Story*, p. 139).

AUBERON QUINN in G.K. Chesterton, *The Napoleon of Notting Hill* (1904)

'The illustrator, W. Graham Robertson, had drawn all his pictures of Auberon Quinn ... in the likeness of Max, but the character itself is much more Chesterton than Beerbohm' (Max Beerbohm, 1964, *Letters to Reggie Turner*, ed. Rupert Hart-Davis, London: Rupert Hart-Davis, p. 160 n. 2). *See also* **Beerbohm, Max.**

CHHATARPUR, India Formerly a small state some 250 miles to the south-west of Allahabad, in the Bundekhand Agency.

MAU in E.M. Forster, *A Passage to India* (1924)

'The scenery and architecture of Mau were derived from two small Central Indian states, Chhattarpore and Dewas. Its inhabitants are imaginary, and there is, in particular, no original for the aged Rajah' (*A Passage to India*, 1957, London: Everyman, p. xxix, author's note (to ch. xxxiii); originally published 1924, London: E. Arnold). The decayed summer palace of the Maharajah was in fact called Mau and in *Goldsworthy Lowes Dickinson* (1938, p. 139), Forster describes how 'Dickinson and his host drove out to another palace, Mau, a lovely ruin on a lake'. *See also* **Dewas.**

CHHATARPUR, Vishnwarath Singh Bahadur, Maharajah of (1866–1932) Like Syed Ross Masood, he had been the pupil of Theodore Morison. In 1912 Forster, accompanied by Lowes Dickinson and Robert Trevelyan, visited him for the first time, then in 1921 Forster returned. In 1924, Joe Ackerley spent a period as his Secretary, which provided the basis of *Hindoo Holiday*. 'The passions of his life were philosophy, friendship and beautiful boys' (P.N. Furbank, 1977, *E.M. Forster: a life*, Vol. I: *The Growth of the Novelist (1879–1914)*, London: Secker & Warburg, p. 235).

MAHARAJAH OF CHHOKRAPUR in J.R. Ackerley, *Hindoo Holiday* (1932)

'A[ckerley] had called the State of Chhatarpur "Chhokrapur". But as he wrote in the Preface, dated March 1952, to the second ... edition of *Hindoo Holiday*: "The state of Chhokrapur, if indeed it ever existed, has dissolved away in the new map of India." In the next year when Forster published *The Hill of Devi* ... he took it for granted ... that everybody now knew that A[ckerley]'s "Maharajah of Chhokarpur" was a straight portrait of the Maharajah of Chhatarpur' (*The Letters of J.R. Ackerley*, 1975, ed. Neville Braybrooke, p. 134 n. 2).

NARAYAN GODBOLE in E.M. Forster, *A Passage to India* (1924)

'Godbole is ... modeled on a friend' (E.M. Forster, quoted in an interview, in K. Natwar-Singh (ed.), 1964, *E.M. Forster: a tribute*, New York, p. xii). 'The friend ... could be the Maharajah of Chhatarpur' (Wilfred Stone, 1966, *The Cave and the Mountain: a study of E.M. Forster*, London: Oxford University Press, p. 319 n.). 'Although most critics have assumeD that the friend ... is the Rajah of Dewas, it now seems clear that Forster had in mind the ruler of Chhatarpur' (R.J. Lewis, 1979, *E.M. Forster's Passages to India*, New York, p. 46). 'In March 1913 at a reception in Lahore, Forster met a Brahmin called Mr Godbole – "What a name!" he exclaimed in his diary. After the reception, the two strolled in the public gardens, and Mr Godbole sang to him' (Furbank, op. cit., p. 249).

CHICHESTER HOUSE, Brighton   Located in Chichester Terrace, close to Sussex Square. From at least 1837 to 1843 it was occupied by the Revd Dr George Proctor, who there ran an Academy for Young Gentlemen.

BLIMBER'S in Charles Dickens, *Dombey and Son* (1846–8)

'The general acceptance in Brighton of Chichester House as the novelist's choice [for a suitable house in which to place Dr Blimber's school] seems to be well founded. ... The authority for the identification of Chichester House as Blimber's was a verbal statement . . . made by Harrison Ainsworth to a member of the well-known Brighton family of Barrett-Lennard. Ainsworth and Dickens were intimate friends in their early years of authorship, and in later years [Ainsworth] lived in Brighton, not far from the house he thus identified' (T.B. Powell, 1924, 'Blimber's and Brighton', *The Dickensian* 20 (April): 93). The house still stands. *See also* **Everard, E; King, J.C.; Wick House**, Brighton.

CHILDERS, Mary Alden (1877?–1964)   Daughter of Dr Hamilton Osgood, of Boston, Massachusetts, she had a permanent limp as the result of a spinal injury. In 1904 she married Robert Erskine Childers. Her father's wedding present was a yacht, the *Asgard*, in which she and her husband ran guns from Germany to Ireland for the Easter Rising of 1916. After her husband's execution in 1922 by the Irish National Army, she continued to live in Ireland.

ADRIENNE TONER in Anne Douglas Sedgwick, *Adrienne Toner* (1921)

In her copy of the novel, Lady Young (daughter of Sir Courtney Ibert, under whom Childers had worked as a clerk in the House of Commons) wrote on the title page, below the title: 'Mrs Erskine Childers'. I owe this information to Lady Young's daughter, Mrs Rachel Mathew.

CHILD'S BANK, Strand, London

TELLSON'S BANK in Charles Dickens, *A Tale of Two Cities* (1859)

'It is generally accepted that "Tellson's Bank by Temple Bar" is Child's Bank, whose premises still occupy the same site' (T.W. Hill, 1945, 'Notes on *A Tale of Two Cities*', *The Dickensian* 41: 70, ch. 3 n. 1).

CHILVERS COTON, Warwickshire   A village about one mile south of Nuneaton where George Eliot was baptized and her parents are buried.

SHEPPERTON in George Eliot, 'The Sad Fortunes of the Revd Amos Barton', *Scenes of Clerical Life* (1857–8)

See under **Anstruther**, Lady.

CHIPPING CAMDEN, Gloucestershire

NORTHBRIDGE in Angela Thirkell, *Northbridge Rectory* (1941)

'The novel opens with one of her most accomplished pieces of descriptive writing, of the High Street of Chipping Camden' (M. Strickland, 1977, *Angela Thirkell: portrait of a lady novelist*, London: Duckworth, p. 133). It is the High Street of Northbridge.

CHISHOLM, Caroline (1808–77) Née Jones, she married Archibald Chisholm, an officer in the Madras Native Infantry, in 1830 and established a school at Madras for soldiers' daughters in 1832. In 1841 she opened a school for female immigrants in Sydney, and in 1842 she published a pamphlet entitled *Female Immigration*. She returned to London in 1846 to promote her schemes for emigration, and in 1850 she met Dickens. That same year she joined the Roman church. From 1854 to 1866 she was in Australia, continuing her work, and then returned to England; she died in London.

MRS JELLYBY in Charles Dickens, *Bleak House* (1852–3)

'In her unconcern for her children, Mrs Jellyby was suggested by Mrs Caroline Chisholm, whose Australian emigration schemes Dickens had aided' (Edgar Johnson, 1953, *Charles Dickens*, Vol. II, p. 768). 'I dream of Mrs Chisholm and her housekeeping. The dirty faces of her children are my continual companions' (4 March 1850, reproduced in *Letters from Charles Dickens to Angela Burdett Coutts, 1841–1865*, 1953, ed. E. Johnson, London: Jonathan Cape, p. 166).

CHITOR, Rajasthan, India A ruined city situated some seventy miles from Udaipur.

COLD LAIRS in Rudyard Kipling, *The Jungle Books* (1894–5)

'Chitor . . . the principal model for Cold Lairs' (Angus Wilson, 1977, *The Strange Ride of Rudyard Kipling*, caption to Pl. 30).

CHRIST CHURCH, Oxford College founded by Cardinal Wolsey (*c*.1475–1530). Attached to the Cathedral, it was originally named Cardinal's College.

CARDINAL COLLEGE, CHRISTMINSTER, in Thomas Hardy, *Jude the Obscure* (1895)

Identified in Denys Kay-Robinson, 1972, *Hardy's Wessex Reappraised*, Newton Abbot, and in F.B. Pinion, 1968, *A Hardy Companion*, London: Macmillan. Hardy took the name from Harrison Ainsworth's *Windsor Castle*.

CHRISTIE, Mr[1] Police officer in the Punjab in the mid-nineteenth century. Born in India, in 1867 he was Assistant Superintendent of Police at Armitsar and was praised in the Annual Report of Police Administration as active and able. In 1871, although described as sharp, acute and an excellent linguist, he bungled a major investigation and was transferred. From 1873 he is no longer mentioned in the Report, and is said to have retired to the Kangra Valley. His own account of one of his exploits may be found in the article in *The Readers' Guide to Rudyard Kipling's Work* (1961).

STRICKLAND in Rudyard Kipling, *Plain Tales from the Hills* (1888)

'By those familiar with the Punjab of 1870–80 the original of "Strickland" was identified with at least two police officers. The first [was] a pure-blooded Afghan. . . . Unfortunately, none of his achievements were recorded. . . . The other . . . was Christie' (R.E. H[arbord], 1961, 'Strickland', in R.L. Green (ed.), *The Readers' Guide to Rudyard Kipling's Work*, Sect. I, London: Kipling Society, Preface No. 4, p. 16). *See also* **Goad**, Horace B.

CHRISTIE, Mr[2] A religious fanatic encountered by Waugh in the Brazilian jungle in 1933.

JAMES TODD in Evelyn Waugh, *A Handful of Dust* (1934)

'20 January, 1933. Arrived at Christie's ranch at 4 o'clock. . . . He had been to see the "elect", found them few but hard to count as no bodies' (*The Diaries of Evelyn Waugh*, 1976, ed. Michael Davie, London: Weidenfeld & Nicolson, pp. 366–7). 'The origin of the story . . . was in a brief rest he enjoyed . . . at the ranch of Mr Christie. . . . Christie was a religious enthusiast, manifestly half-mad. . . . EvelyN had stripped [him] of his religious ecstasy and substituteD a mania for the work of Charles Dickens. . . . It has been suggested by Frederick J. Stopp . . . that the story was influenced by thoughts of the mysterious disappearance of Colonel Fawcett' (Christopher Sykes, 1975, *Evelyn Waugh*, London: Collins, p. 137). 'Mr Christie, transformed into "Mr Todd", is the chief protagonist of the penultimate episode of *A Handful of Dust*' (ibid., p. 130).

CHRIST'S COLLEGE, Cambridge C.P. Snow was elected a fellow of the College in 1930.

THE COLLEGE in C.P. Snow, *The Masters* (1951)

'[The] death in 1936 [of the Master of Christ's College] was the prelude to an election which, through its fictional dramatization, has become more widely known than any other of a comparable kind in this century. . . . [W]hen . . . *The Masters* was published, it was clear . . . that the general background bore close similarities to that of the Christ's election in 1936' (F.W. Dillistone, 1975, *Charles Raven*, pp. 191–2).

CHUMLEY, Old Coachman on the *Commodore*, the Chatham to London coach, from the 1820s onwards. He is alleged to have said, 'If the Railway blows up, where are you? Now if a coach overturns, *there* you are!'

TONY WELLER in Charles Dickens, *The Pickwick Papers* (1836–7)

'. . . to some extent the original of Old Weller' (Jack Lindsay, 1950, *Charles Dickens*, p. 43).

CHURCH STREET, Nuneaton, Warwickshire

ORCHARD STREET, MILBY, in George Eliot, 'Janet's Repentance', *Scenes of Clerical Life* (1857–8)

See under **Anstruther**, Lady.

CHURCHILL, Lord Randolph (1849–95) Conservative politician. Youngest son of the 7th Duke of Marlborough, he was an MP from 1874 until 1895 and was the leader of a group of conservatives known as 'The Fourth Party'. He was the father of Winston **Churchill**.

ROLFE BELLARMINE in Justin McCarthy and Mrs Campbell Praed, *The Rebel Rose* (1888)

'Do you remember that we had him a great deal on our minds when we were picturing the parliamentary career of Rolf [sic] Bellarmine in *The Rebel Rose?*' (*Our Book of Memories: letters of Justin McCarthy to Mrs Campbell Praed*, 1912, London: Chatto & Windus, p. 391).

LORD FONTENOY in Mrs Humphrey Ward, *Sir George Tressady* (1896)

'[W]hen writing *Sir George Tressady* in 1895, at the time of Churchill's death, Mrs Humphrey Ward used him as the model for her political Mephistopheles, Lord Fontenoy' (R.F. Foster, 1981, *Lord Randolph Churchill*, p. 6).

PRESIDENT OF THE NATIONAL LABOUR PROTECTION LEAGUE in J. St Loe Strachey, *The Great Bread Riots* (1890)

'In . . . St Loe Strachey's anti-Fair Trade Squib *The Great Bread Riots*, Churchill appears as the unnamed President of the National Labour Protection League' (Foster, op. cit., p. 6).

LORD REGINALD WOODSTOCK in W.F. Rae, *The American Duchess* (1890–1)

'He is Lord Reginald Woodstock in *An American Duchess*' (Foster, op. cit., p. 5).

CHURCHILL, Winston (Leonard) Spencer (1874–1965) English statesman. He was educated at Harrow and Sandhurst, and gazetted to the 4th Hussars in 1895. He became Conservative MP for Oldham in 1900, but joined the Liberals in 1906. From 1908 to 1910 he was President of the Board of Trade, and he became Home Secretary in 1910. From 1919 to 1921 he was Secretary of State for War and Air and from 1924 to 1929 he was Chancellor of the Exchequer. In May 1940 he became head of the Coalition government. He was defeated in the 1945 election but became Prime Minister again in 1951 at the age of 77. He resigned in 1955 but remained a back-bencher almost to the end of his life. He was also a noted writer, his *History of the English-Speaking Peoples* being published in four volumes between 1956 and 1958.

HEREWARD BLENHEIM in Maurice Baring, 'A Luncheon Party', *Half a Minute's Silence and Other Stories* (1925)

'Most of the guests were people well known in London. . . . Mr Winston Churchill and others – all, of course furnished with pseudonyms and so presented that though they were easy to identify no one can have been hurt' (Ethel Smyth, 1938, *Maurice Baring*, London and Toronto: Heinemann, p. 136).

Both from his name and his bearing, Blenheim is easily recognizable as Churchill.

TOM HOGARTH in Arnold Bennett, *Lord Raingo* (1926)

'Thursday, December 2nd [1926] . . . Savoy Hotel for the dinner of the Other Club. . . . Churchill said to me: "Receive the congratulations of Tom Hogarth" (over my row with Birkenhead)' (*The Journals of Arnold Bennett*, 1933, ed. Sir Newman Flower, Vol. III, London: Cassell, p. 175).

SIR HENRY MERRIVALE in Carter Dickson, *The Plague Court Murders* (1934) and others

'Sir Henry Merrivale . . . is Churchill' (Erik Routley, 1972, *The Puritan Pleasures of the Detective Story*, p. 139). 'Merrivale . . . was not inspired by Churchill but developed some of his traits in later books' (Chris Steinbrunner and Otto Penzler, 1976, *Encyclopedia of Mystery and Detection*, p. 287).

CHURTON, Revd Edward (1800–74) Born in Middleton Cheney, Northamptonshire, he was the son of the Archdeacon of St Davids and was educated at Charterhouse and at Christ Church, Oxford. He was a master at Charterhouse during the period *c.*1824–30 and was Headmaster of Hackney Church of England School in 1830–4. In 1835–74 he was Rector of Grayke, Yorkshire, becoming Prebendary of York Cathedral in 1841 and Archdeacon of Cleveland in 1846, and was the author of works on theology and history. Thomas Mozley recalls that when meeting Thackeray one day, he told him that he had just had a talk with Churton; Thackeray exclaimed, 'O tell me where he is that I may fall down and kiss his toe. I do love that man' (Mozley, 1882, *Reminiscences Chiefly of Oriel College and the Oxford Movement*, Vol. I, p. 63). He was also described as the 'single really excellent clergyman and teacher at Charterhouse' (Martin Tupper).

MR PRINCE in W.M. Thackeray, *Doctor Birch and His Young Friends* (1849)

'Thackeray had drawn Churton's portrait in *Dr Birch and his Young Friends*' (*The Letters and Private Papers of W.M. Thackeray*, Vol. I: *1817–1840*, 1945, ed. Gordon N. Ray, London: Oxford University Press, pp. 25–6 n. 28).

The CIDER CELLARS, London A singing tavern at 20 Maiden Lane, Covent Garden, next to the stage-door of the Adelphi Theatre. It was kept by William Rhodes, brother of the keeper of the **Coal Hole**, and by his widow after his death. W.G. **Ross** sang there. It was later converted into a synagogue.

THE BACK KITCHEN in W.M. Thackeray, *The History of Pendennis* (1848–50)

'It . . . was the prototype of the Back Kitchen' (Edmund Yates, 1884, *Edmund Yates: his recollections and experiences*, Vol. I, London: R. Bentley & Son, p. 167). Yates frequented the tavern as a young Post Office clerk between 1847 and 1852.

THE CAVE OF HARMONY in W.M. Thackeray, *The Newcomes* (1854–5)

'A typical evening [for Thackeray in 1832] would begin . . . at one of the taverns of the period . . . the most interesting of them all was the Cider Cellars . . . which had included among its . . . patrons . . . Professor Porson and Dr Raine, Master of Charterhouse. . . . In the first chapter of *The Newcomes* he drew a famous picture of this establishment as it was in the early 1830s' (Gordon N. Ray, 1955, *Thackeray: a biography*, Vol. I: *The Uses of Adversity, 1811–1846*, London: Oxford University Press, p. 155). *See also* The **Coal Hole**.

CLAIRMONT, Claire (1798–1879) Born Clara Mary Jane, she was the daughter of Mary Jane, the second wife of William **Godwin**, and was the half-sister of Mary Wollstonecraft **Shelley**. At the age of 15, and at Shelley's invitation, Claire accompanied Mary and Shelley when they eloped, and a triangular relationship developed, which endured until Shelley's death. She had an affair with **Byron**, when he joined the group in Switzerland, and in 1817 they had a daughter, Allegra. The liaison ended when the Shelleys returned to England and Byron continued to Venice. Allegra died in 1822.

JULIANA BORDEREAU in Henry James, *The Aspern Papers* (1888)

'Florence, January 12th, 1887 . . . Hamilton (V.L.'s brother) told me a curious thing of Capt. Silsbee – the Boston art-critic and Shelley-worshipper. . . . Miss Claremont [sic] . . . was living, until lately, here in Florence, at a great age, 80 or thereabouts, and with her lived her niece, a younger Miss Clairmont – of about 50. Silsbee knew that they had interesting papers – letters of Shelley's and Byron's – he had known it for a long time and cherished the idea of getting hold of them. To this end he laid the plan of going to lodge with the Misses Clairmont – hoping that the old lady . . . would die while he was there, so that he might then put his hands upon the documents. . . . He carried out this scheme. . . . The old woman *did* die – and then he approached the younger one . . . on the subject of his desires. Her answer was – "I will give you all the letters if you marry me!" H. says that Silsbee *court encore*. Certainly there is a little subject there' (*The Notebooks of Henry James*, 1947, ed. F.O. Matthiessen and K.B. Murdock, New York, pp. 71–2). H. was Eugene Lee-Hamilton and V.L. Vernon Lee. *See also* **Wykoff**, Miss.

CELINDA ('STELLA') TOOBAD in Thomas Love Peacock, *Nightmare Abbey* (1818)

'In *Nightmare Abbey* . . . Scythrop's dilemma is that of Shelley between Harriet and Mary, with the character of Claire Clairmont substituted for Mary' (Newman Ivey White, 1947, *Shelley*, Vol. I, p. 705 n. 47). *See also* **Hitchener**, Elizabeth; **Shelley**, Mary Wollstonecraft.

CLAIRMONT, Paula ('Pauline') (1825–91) Daughter of Charles Clairmont and niece of Claire **Clairmont**, she settled with her aunt in Florence in the 1860s and remained with her (with occasional absences) until her death in 1879. Pauline died while walking in the mountains.

TITA ('TINA') BORDEREAU in Henry James, *The Aspern Papers* (1888)

See under **Clairmont**, Claire. Unlike Tita, Paula Clairmont in fact sold some of the letters she inherited, to Captain Silsbee and to H. Buxton Forman.

CLANCY, George A friend and contemporary of James Joyce at University College, Dublin.

DAVIN in James Joyce, *A Portrait of the Artist as a Young Man* (1916)

'The only person who ever addressed me so [i.e. by his forename] (of my companions or friends) was my poor friend George Clancy (Davin in the *Portrait*). This is carefully pointed out in the book. He was afterwards Mayor of Limerick and dragged out of bed by the Black and Tans in the night and shot in the presence of his wife' (to Giorgio and Helen Joyce, 5 February 1935, reproduced in *The Letters of James Joyce*, 1957, Vol. I, ed. Stuart Gilbert, London: Faber & Faber, p. 357).

CLANCY, John 'Long John Clancy', Sub-sheriff of Dublin. From 1894 he was a neighbour of the Joyce family.

LONG JOHN FANNING in James Joyce, *Ulysses* (1922)

'Further down [North Richmond Street] . . . lived Long John Clancy . . . who appears under his own name in *Finnegans Wake* and in a thin disguise in *Ulysses* as Long John Fanning' (Richard Ellmann, 1982, *James Joyce*, rev. edn, Oxford: Oxford University Press, p. 43).

CLANRICARDE, Ulick John de Burgh, 1st Marquess of (1802–74) He married the daughter of George **Canning**. '[In 1847 he was a] tall thin aristocratic man, bald and blank, wearing . . . tight pantaloons, striped silk socks and pumps' (Edmund Yates, 1884, *Edmund Yates: his recollections and experiences*; see Hon. Vicary Gibbs (ed.), 1926, *The Complete Peerage of England, Scotland, Ireland, Great Britain and the United Kingdom*, Vol. III, rev. edn, London: St Catherine Press, p. 237 n. e).

MARQUESS OF CARABAS in Benjamin Disraeli, *Vivian Grey* (1826–7)

Identified as Marquess of C—— in a key given in *The Star Chamber* (24 May 1826): 114; reprinted in *Vivian Grey*, 1904 (centenary edn), Vol. II, London, pp. 361–2. The full name appears on a copy of the key held in the British Museum. Lucien Wolf concludes that Disraeli was not responsible for the key. *See also* **Grenville**, Lord, 2nd Marquis of Chandos; **Murray**, John[1].

CLARENDON, Catherine, Countess of (1810–74) She was married to the 4th Earl of **Clarendon**; it was said of her: 'She is the best, most sensible, inoffensive wife that can be' (Harriet, Countess of Granville, in H.A. Doubleday and Lord Howard de Walden (eds), *The Complete Peerage of England, Scotland, Ireland, Great Britain and the United Kingdom*, Vol. VIII, rev. edn, London: St Catherine Press, p. 271 n. c).

LADY EVERINGHAM in Benjamin Disraeli, *Coningsby* (1844)

Identified in a key in *Notes and Queries* (8th series) 3 (13 May 1893): 363. *See also under* **Bright**, John.

CLARENDON, George William Frederick Villiers, 4th Earl of (1800–70) Diplomat. Born in London and educated at Cambridge, he became Ambassador at Madrid in 1833 and Lord Privy Seal in 1840. In 1853–8, the time of the Crimean War, he was Secretary of State for Foreign Affairs. He was married to Catherine, Countess of **Clarendon**.

LORD EVERINGHAM in Benjamin Disraeli, *Coningsby* (1844)

Identified in a key in *Notes and Queries* (8th series) 3 (13 May 1893): 363. *See also under* **Bright**, John. *See also* **Cardigan**, 7th Earl of.

CLARK, Sir Andrew (1826–93) Physician. He trained in Dundee and Edinburgh and was a physician at the London Hospital in 1866–86. Regarded as the leading physician of his day, he attended **Gladstone** and Edward VII, and was President of the Royal College of Physicians from 1885 until his death. Alice **James** was one of his patients. He was created Baronet in 1883.

SIR LUKE STRETT in Henry James, *The Wings of the Dove* (1902)

'Sir Andrew . . . probably served as one of the models for Sir Luke Strett' (Jean Strouse, 1981, *Alice James*, p. 299). *See also* **Baldwin**, William Wilberforce.

CLARK, Captain Joseph Lucas (b. 1836) Captain of SS *Jeddah*, the pilgrim ship that was crippled near the Gulf of Aden in 1880. Together with other European members of the crew, he deserted her; the subsequent Court of Enquiry at Singapore deprived him of his master's certificate for three years. He was still alive in 1895.

CAPTAIN ARCHBOLD in Joseph Conrad, *'Twixt Land and Sea*, 'The Secret Sharer' (1912)

'It is a surprising fact that . . . in *Lord Jim* Conrad . . . did not use the character of the master of the *Jeddah*. . . . But Conrad did not forget Clark and he makes his appearance as Captain Archbold of the *Sephora*' (Norman Sherry, 1966, *Conrad's Eastern World*, Cambridge, p. 260). 'Clark's grandson . . . has confirmed that Conrad's Captain Archbold is in appearance the same as his grandfather' (ibid. p. 261).

CLARKE, Charles Cowden (1787–1877) Bookseller, lecturer, journalist and writer. In 1828 he married Victoria, daughter of the composer Vincent Novello, and he was a friend of Leigh **Hunt** and the essayist Charles Lamb. While an assistant at the Enfield school of which his father was the founder and headmaster, he taught the poet John Keats, who was a pupil there from 1803 to 1811, and became his friend. It was Cowden Clarke who sent the sonnet 'On first opening Chapman's Homer' to Leigh Hunt, who published it in the *Examiner*.

LAWRENCE BOYTHORN in Charles Dickens, *Bleak House* (1852–3)

'[P]erhaps the best portrait of him came from . . . Charles Dickens. When *Bleak House* was being issued in parts, Clarke's wife and friends found it impossible to believe that Dickens had not drawn Boythorn directly from him. Actually the novelist had seen little of Clarke at the time' (Richard D. Altick, 1948, *The Cowden Clarkes*, p. 79). *See also* **Landor**, Walter Savage.

CLARKE, Christiana (1814–59) Née Evans, and known as Chrissey, she was the sister of George Eliot and in 1837 married Edward **Clarke**, with whom she had nine children. Edward died of tuberculosis and, after his death, her brother

Isaac **Evans** allowed her to continue living in the house, once her own but which he had inherited, but did little to provide for her children.

CELIA BROOKE in George Eliot, *Middlemarch* (1871–2)

'Chrissey's clothes were always tidy ... and she had that "habitual care of whatever she held in her hands" that was to be seen in Celia Brooke' (Gordon S. Haight, 1968, *George Eliot*, London, p. 10).

LUCY DEANE in George Eliot, *The Mill on the Floss* (1860)

'Chrissey was Lucy' (Marghanita Laski, 1973, *George Eliot and Her World*, London: Thames & Hudson, p. 74). *See also* **Garner**, Bessie.

GRITTY MOSS in George Eliot, *The Mill on the Floss* (1860)

'Chrissey appears ... I believe, in the very different guise of Mr Tulliver's sister, Gritty Moss. . . . Isaac Evans could hardly have read the chapter describing Mr Tulliver's visit to his sister Gritty Moss without recalling his own less generous treatment of ... Chrissey Clarke' (Gordon S. Haight, 1958, 'George Eliot's originals', in *From Jane Austen to Joseph Conrad: essays collected in memory of James T. Hillhouse*, ed. R. Rathburn and M. Steinmann, Jun., Minneapolis, Minn.: University of Minnesota Press, p. 190).

CLARKE, Edward (1809–52) Surgeon. Of Meriden, Warwickshire, he married George Eliot's sister Christiana Evans (**Clarke**, above) in 1837. In 1845 he went bankrupt. He died of tuberculosis.

TERTIUS LYDGATE in George Eliot, *Middlemarch* (1871–2)

'A far likelier prototype [than Sir T.C. Allbutt] can be seen in George Eliot's brother-in-law Edward Clarke, who like Lydgate was better born than the other country surgeons, went bankrupt with a debt of £1,000, and died young' (Gordon S. Haight, 1968, *George Eliot*, p. 448). *See also* **Allbutt**, Sir Thomas Clifford; **Nankivell**, Charles Benjamin.

CLARKE, John (b. *c*.1787) Circus proprietor. In 1820 he rode before George IV at the Pavilion in Brighton on a mare called Laura who died, in 1856, at the age of 44 years. Clarke performed at the principal fairs throughout England.

SLEARY in Charles Dickens, *Hard Times* (1854)

'Old Jack Clarke, a notability in his way as a circus proprietor was, I have good cause to believe, the model who sat for "Sleary" in ... *Hard Times*. Many of Clarke's personal characteristics are faithfully pictured in that character; and the physical defect of his gruff asthmatic voice, though not quite turning the *S* into *th*, so nearly produced that effect, that no combination of type could reproduce it better than that which the great novelist adopted' (C.W. Montague, 1881, *Recollections of an Equestrian Manager*, p. 90).

CLATFORD HALL, Wiltshire Situated on the southern side of the old London–Bristol road, two miles west of Marlborough.

SHAKEFOREST TOWERS in Thomas Hardy, 'What the Shepherd Saw' (1913)

Identified in F.B. Pinion, 1968, *A Hardy Companion*, London: Macmillan.

CLAVEL, Gilbert He was a resident on Capri *c.*1907 and died in Positano.

MARTEL in Compton Mackenzie, *Vestal Fire* (1927)

'A deformed young Swiss, with pushful and almost offensive manners. . . . His vulgarity was mitigated . . . by a considerable love of natural history. . . . There is a caricature of him . . . as the ebullient Belgian hunchback called Martel in . . . *Vestal Fire*' (Norman Douglas, 1933, *Looking Back*, Vol. I, p. 35).

CLAY, James (1804–73) Educated in Winchester and at Balliol College, Oxford, in 1821–30 he took leading parts in opera performed by amateurs in Florence when Lord Burghesh was British Minister. In 1830 he travelled in the Holy Land with Disraeli, and in 1847–53 and 1857–73 he was MP for Hull and was a thorough-going Reformer. He was also the finest whist and picquet player of his time.

CECIL CASTLEMAINE in G.A. Lawrence, *Sans Merci; or Kestrels and Falcons* (1866)

'He is described under the name of Castlemaine in G.A. Lawrence's . . . *Sans Merci*' (Frederic Boase, 1892, *Modern English Biography*, Vol. I).

CLAY, Sir William (1791–1869) From 1832 to 1857 he was MP for Tower Hamlets, and from 1839 to 1841 he was Secretary to the Board of Control. A Liberal, he was in favour of extension of the suffrage, the ballot and Triennial Parliaments, and voted for the abolition of Church Rates. He was a cousin of James **Clay**.

SIR JOSEPH WALLINGER in Benjamin Disraeli, *Coningsby* (1844)

Identified in a key in *Notes and Queries* (8th series) 3 (13 May 1893): 363. *See also under* **Bright**, John.

CLEMENTS, Robert E. (b. 1895?) Born in Texas, he became a real estate broker in Long Beach, California. In 1934 he joined Francis **Townsend** to promote through local clubs Old Age Revolving Pensions Ltd, whose programme, The Townsend Plan, was to remove the elderly from the labour market by paying pensions of $200 a month. In 1935 he was in touch with Father **Coughlin**, and in 1936 he left the Townsend movement, taking with him $50,000 as his share in the *Townsend Weekly*.

LEE SARASON in Sinclair Lewis, *It Can't Happen Here* (1935)

Identified in Arthur M. Schlesinger, Jun., 1961, *The Politics of Upheaval (The Age of Roosevelt, III)*, p. 89.

CLERGY DAUGHTERS' SCHOOL, Cowan Bridge, Lancashire Founded in 1824 by Revd William **Carus-Wilson**, it was attended by the Brontë sisters in 1824–5, and was moved to Casterton in 1933.

LOWOOD SCHOOL in Charlotte Brontë, *Jane Eyre* (1847)

'The account of Lowood School . . . was studied from the old Clergy Daughter's School at Cowan Bridge' (Herbert E. Wroot, 1935, *Sources of Charlotte Brontë's Novels: persons and places*, Shipley, Yorks., p. 11). 'Miss Brontë . . . said to me, that she should not have written what she did of Lowood . . . if she had thought the place would have been so immediately identified with Cowan's Bridge, although there was not a word in her account . . . but what was true at the time when she knew it' (Mrs Gaskell, 1857, *The Life of Charlotte Brontë*, London: Smith, Elder, ch. IV). An account of the Clergy Daughters' School will be found in Emma Jane Worboise, 1863, *Thornycroft Hall*. The heroine attended the school for two years, in 1844–6, and she gives a very different account from that in *Jane Eyre* (although porridge still played a large part in the diet). Miss Worboise is, however, describing the school after its removal to Casterton; the school is described by name and no attempt is made to disguise it.

CLERICI, Enrico

GIORGIO VIOLA in Joseph Conrad, *Nostromo* (1904)

'Conrad might have heard from Cunninghame Graham of a similar Italian innkeeper in South America, or he might have read of him in Graham's collection *Thirteen Stories*. . . . In this book, a sketch called "Cruz Alta" contains the following account: "Two days we passed in Ytapna resting our horses, and I renewed my friendship with Enrico Clerici, an Italian, who had served with Garibaldi." . . . The parallels between Giorgio Viola and Enrico Clerici are obvious' (Norman Sherry, 1971, *Conrad's Western World*, Cambridge, pp. 150–1). *See also* **Garibaldi**, Giuseppe; **Giuliolo**, Giovanni.

CLERK, Sir George (1787–1867) Sixth Baronet. Of Penicuik, he was the son of Sir John Clerk and became Tory MP for Midlothian from 1811 to 1832 and was also an MP in 1835–52. He was Secretary to the Treasury in 1834–5 and 1841–5, and was Vice-President of the Board of Trade in 1845–6. He became a Peelite in 1846.

MR EARWIG in Benjamin Disraeli, *Coningsby* (1844)

Identified in a key in *Notes and Queries* (8th series) 3 (13 May 1893): 363. *See also under* **Bright**, John.

CLERK, William (1771–1847) Son of John **Clerk of Eldin**, and brother of Lord Eldin the Judge, he became Clerk of the Jury Court in Edinburgh. He was a college friend of Sir Walter Scott, and remained a close friend until Scott's death.

SIR ARTHUR REDGAUNTLET (DARSIE LATIMER) in Sir Walter Scott, *Redgauntlet* (1824)

'I have no sort of doubt that William Clerk was, in the main, Darsie Latimer' (J.G. Lockhart, 1900, *Memoirs of Sir Walter Scott*, Vol. I, London: Macmillan, p. 136) *See also* **Kerr**, Charles.

CLERK OF ELDIN, John (1728–1812) Writer on naval tactics. He was the younger son of Sir John Clerk and the father of William **Clerk**. Of him, Admiral Rodney said, 'There is one Clerk . . . who has taught us all to fight, and appears to know more of the matter than any of us. If ever I meet the French fleet I mean to try his way.' He worked his naval tactics out sailing a fleet of model boats on the pond at Eldin.

JONATHAN OLDBUCK in Sir Walter Scott, *The Antiquary* (1816)

'Many traits of the elder Clerk were, his son had no doubt, embroidered on the character of George Constable in the composition of Jonathan Oldbuck. The old gentleman's enthusiasm for antiquities was often played on by these young friends but more effectually by his elder son (Lord Eldin), who . . . used to amuse himself with manufacturing mutilated heads, which, after being buried for a convenient time in the ground, were accidentally discovered . . . and received by the laird with great honour as valuable accessions to his museum' (J.G. Lockhart, 1900, *Life of Sir Walter Scott*, London, Vol. I, pp. 126–7). *See also* **Constable** George, the Elder; **Gordon**, Alexander; **Ramsay of Ochtertyre**, John.

CLERMONT-TONNERRE, Elisabeth, Duchesse de (b. 1875) Daughter of duc Agenor de Gramont, in 1896 she married Philibert, Marquis (later duc) de Clermont-Tonnerre. She was a close friend of the novelist Proust and had a long liaison with Nathalie Clifford **Barney**.

CLITORESSA, DUCHESS OF NATESCOURT in Djuna Barnes, *The Ladies Almanack* (1928)

Identified in Meryle Secrest, 1976, *Between Me and Life: a biography of Romaine Brooks*, London: MacDonald & Jane, p. 335; originally published 1974, Garden City, NY: Doubleday.

CLEVEDON COURT, Somerset A house of the early fourteenth century, it was for 250 years the home of the Elton family, and was also the family home of Jane **Brookfield**.

CASTLEWOOD in W.M. Thackeray, *The History of Henry Esmond* (1852)

'Supposedly the "Castlewood" of *Henry Esmond*' (*The Letters of John Addington Symonds*, 1967, ed. H.M. Schueller and R.L. Peters, Vol. I, Detroit, p. 272 n. 6).

CLIFFORD, William Kingdon (1845–79) Mathematician and metaphysician. Educated at King's College, London, and at Trinity College, Cambridge, he was a Fellow of the latter from 1868 to 1871. In 1871 he became Professor of Applied Mathematics at University College London. According to *The Dictionary of National Biography* (London: Oxford University Press), he conceived of consciousness as being built up out of simple elements of 'mind-stuff'. He died of tuberculosis.

MR SAUNDERS in W.H. Mallock, *The New Republic* (1877)

Identified in W.H. Mallock, 1920, *Memoirs of Life and Literature*, London: Chapman and Hall, pp. 65–6.

CLIFFORD'S INN, London The meetings of the Fabian Society were held there in its early days.

ANSELM'S INN in Dorothy Richardson, *Pilgrimage* (1915–67)

'The [meeting] . . . in "Anselm's Inn" is very like the Fabian meetings in Clifford's Inn. . . . Wells's own description of such a meeting in his autobiography is an interesting parallel' (John Rosenberg, 1973, *Dorothy Richardson*, London, p. 117).

CLIVEDEN, Buckinghamshire Designed by Sir Charles Barry for the Duke of Sutherland in 1850, it was sold to the Duke of Westminster, and later, in 1893, was bought by Viscount Astor. It was situated on the Thames, 'in the Cinquecento style, and reminiscent of the villas of Genoese noblemen' (Nikolaus Pevsner, 1960, *Buckinghamshire (Buildings of England* series), Harmondsworth: Penguin, Pl. 61 (a)).

TOAD HALL in Kenneth Grahame, *The Wind in the Willows* (1908)

'Toad Hall . . . contains elements from . . . Cliveden' (Peter Green, 1959, *Kenneth Grahame, 1859–1932*, p. 240). *See also* **Harleyford Manor; Mapledurham House**.

CLODD, Edward (1840–1930) Banker and author. He was Chairman of the Rationalist Press Association and a friend of many distinguished scientific and literary men whom he entertained at his home at Aldeburgh, Suffolk.

EDMUND RODEN in Morley Roberts, *The Private Life of Henry Maitland* (1912)

Identified in an 'Index of Recurring Pseudonyms' in the 1958 edition of *The Private Life of Henry Maitland*, ed. Morchard Bishop, p. 255.

CLOVELLY, Devon

ABERALVA in Charles Kingsley, *Two Years Ago* (1857)

'Most of the action is laid in Devon at Clovelly (here called Aberalva)' (R.B. Martin, 1959, *The Dust of Combat: a life of Charles Kingsley*, London: Faber & Faber, p. 203).

CLUN, Shropshire

ONITON in E.M. Forster, *Howards End* (1910)

'[Oniton] is *Clun* . . . I walked there, over Clun Forest, from Newton [i.e. Newtown] (Montgomery), and walked on next day [11 April 1907] to Ludlow' (E.M. Forster to William Plomer, 20 November 1960, reproduced in introd. to *Howards End*, 1973 (Abinger edn), p. viii).

CLUSERET, Gustave Paul (1823–1900) French soldier and politician. He served in Garibaldi's expedition against the Kingdom of the Two Sicilies in 1860, and in the Union Army in 1862 during the American Civil War. In April 1871 he was a member of the Commune of Paris, and he became Minister of War; from 1871 to 1884 he was exiled from France. In 1888 he was a member of the Chamber of Deputies.

CAPTAIN BRUGES in Benjamin Disraeli, *Lothair* (1870)

'A good many persons here may have heard of General Cluseret. He is a very remarkable man. . . . He was, I believe, the original of the "General" whom Lord Beaconsfield describes with so much appreciation in *Lothair*' (J.A. Froude, addressing the 5th annual meeting of the Liberty and Property Defence League,

25 November 1887, quoted in W.H. Dunn, 1963, *J.A. Froude: a biography*, Vol. II, Oxford, p. 555).

The COAL HOLE, London A singing tavern in a court off the Strand, perhaps Fountain Court. It was later the Occidental Tavern. In the 1840s and early 1850s, it was kept by one John Rhodes, whose brother was the Landlord of the **Cider Cellars**. The Coal Hole never had the reputation of its rivals and was the first to succumb to the change in public taste.

THE CAVE OF HARMONY in W.M. Thackeray, *The Newcomes* (1854–5)

'From my recollection of Rhodes and his room, I imagine that he was Hoskins, the landlord of the Cave of Harmony . . . only, in my time at least, the singing at the Coal Hole was confined to professionals, and no visitor would have been allowed to volunteer a song, as did the Colonel' (Edmund Yates, 1884, *Edmund Yates: his recollections and experiences*, Vol. I, London: R. Bentley & Son, p. 166). *See also* The **Cider Cellars**.

COB TREE MANOR, Sandling, Kent The house, much modernized, still existed in 1978.

MANOR FARM, DINGLEY DELL, in Charles Dickens, *The Pickwick Papers* (1836–7)

'[G]enerally it is agreed that "Cob Tree", a house at Sandling in the parish of Boxley, midway between Aylesford and Maidstone, was the original [of Manor Farm]' (C.T. Roade, 1921, 'Roundabout Maidstone and Muggleton', *The Dickensian* 17 (April): 70). *See also* **Birling Place**.

COBBE, Frances Power (1822–1904) Philanthropist, publicist and religious writer. Born in Ireland, into 'a family which counted five archbishops and a bishop amongst its connections' (*The Dictionary of National Biography*, London: Oxford University Press), she was an anti-vivisectionist and an advocate of degrees and votes for women, and in 1878 she promoted the Matrimonial Causes Act. She was of ample proportions and great good humour, and was an indefatigable traveller.

MISS TODD in Anthony Trollope, *The Bertrams* (1859)

'Miss Todd is said to have been modelled on Frances Power Cobbe' (Michael Sadleir, 1927, *Trollope: a commentary*, London: Constable, p. 384 n.).

COBDEN, Richard (1804–65) English economist and politician. From 1838 to 1847 he was the foremost leader of the Anti-Corn Law League, which was founded in 1838. He was MP for Stockport, Manchester, from 1841 to 1847, and for the West Riding of Yorkshire from 1847 to 1857. He was elected for Rochdale in 1859.

JOB THORNBERRY in Benjamin Disraeli, *Endymion* (1880)

'In pages 261–2, second volume [Vol. II, ch. XXVI], I have endeavoured to convey my impression of the style of Mr Cobden as an orator. All the rest is typical' (Lord Beaconsfield to Queen Victoria, 10 February 1881, reproduced in *The Letters of Queen Victoria*, 1928 (2nd series), ed. G.E. Buckle, Vol. III, London: John Murray, p. 195). *See also* **Bright**, John; **Potter**, Thomas Bayley.

COBRIDGE, Burslem, Staffordshire The suburb of Burslem where Arnold Bennett's father Enoch built a house in 1879.

BLEAKRIDGE in Arnold Bennett, the *Clayhanger* trilogy (1910–16)

'Cobridge is Bleakridge in *Clayhanger*' (Reginald Pound, 1952, *Arnold Bennett: a biography*, London: Heinemann, p. 53).

COCHRANE, Admiral Thomas (1775–1860) Scottish naval commander. Styled Lord Cochrane until 1931, he joined his first ship, the *Hind*, in 1793. As commander of the *Speedy* in 1800–1, he captured more than fifty vessels; he also made successful cruises off the Azores in 1805, and in the Bay of Biscay in 1806. He became MP for Honiton in 1806 and for Westminster in 1808, but stood unsuccessfully in 1807. He exposed abuses in the Admiralty and in 1814 was falsely accused of complicity in a stock exchange fraud, and was consequently expelled from the Navy, Parliament and the Order of Bath. He took charge of the Chilean navy in 1818 and proceeded to secure the independence of Chile, Peru and Brazil, and took command of the Greek navy in 1827–8. He was eventually, in 1832, reinstated in the British Navy, and in 1851 was made an admiral. Frederick Marryat served under him on the *Impérieuse* in 1806 and 1809. Cochrane was buried in Westminster Abbey, London.

CAPTAIN SAVAGE in Frederick Marryat, *Peter Simple* (1834)

'Frederick Marryat . . . fashioned his Captain Savage after the dramatic figure of . . . Thomas Cochrane, the tenth Earl of Dundonald' (Irving Wallace, 1956, *The Fabulous Originals*, p. 251).

The COEFFICIENTS A London dining club founded in 1902 at the suggestion of Beatrice **Webb**. Its members included L.S. **Amery**, Lord Grey of Fallodon, J.B.S. **Haldane**, Henry Newbolt, Lord **Milner**, Bertrand **Russell**, Sidney **Webb** and H.G. Wells.

THE PENTAGRAM CLUB in H.G. Wells, *The New Machiavelli* (1911)

'There is . . . in the . . . book a remote sketch of the Coefficients as the "Pentagram Club"' (H.G. Wells, 1969, *An Experiment in Autobiography*, pp. 773–4).

COHN (or KOHN) A watch-maker whom G.H. **Lewes** met as a young man, when a member of the Philosophers Club in Red Lion Square. He was described by Lewes in an article in the *Fortnightly Review* (April 1866), and thence the character of Mordecai was generally, and wrongly, supposed to be derived from him.

MORDECAI COHEN in George Eliot, *Daniel Deronda* (1876)

'[T]he character was immediately connected with Kohn or Cohn. . . . Lewes repeatedly declared that no resemblance existed between . . . Mordecai and Cohn, . . . "a highly impressive man, but without any specifically Jewish enthusiasm"' (Gordon S. Haight, 1968, *George Eliot*, Oxford, p. 489). *See also* **Deutsch**, Emanuel; **Louis**, Alfred Hyman.

COHN, Roy Marcus (b. 1927) Born in New York City and educated at Columbia University, he enjoyed a brilliant career as a student and young lawyer. In 1948 he was admitted to the New York State Bar, and in 1953–4 he was Chief Counsel for the Permanent Sub-committee on Investigations (under the Government Operations Committee) with G. David **Schine** as 'chief consultant'. Their most notorious undertaking for the Committee was a tour of US Embassies in Europe in 1953, checking the libraries maintained in them by the US Information Agency, for subversive material. He subsequently had a successful career as a more conventional lawyer.

R. JOHN BURKE in Warren Miller, *The Sleep of Reason* (1956)

'People in [the] *roman à clef* . . . [include] . . . Cohn and Schine figures' (Joseph Blotner, 1966, *The Modern American Political Novel*, Austin, Tex., p. 303). Burke is easily recognizable as Cohn, both from his name (from the notorious criminal), and from his activities in the novel and his perhaps excessively demonstrated affection for Hare.

COKE, Lady Anne (1803–44) Née Lady Anne Keppel, she married Thomas William **Coke** in 1822, becoming his second wife; after his death, she married Edward **Ellice** in 1843.

LADY GLENMORE in M. Spencer Stanhope, *Almacks* (1826)

'The character of Lady Glenmore has almost been identified, by Disraeli among others, with Lady Ann [sic] Coke, Lord Glenmore being accepted as portraying Coke of Norfolk' (E.M. Oddie, 1935, *Portrait of Ianthe*, p. 339). *See also* **Digby**, Jane.

COKE, Thomas William, 1st Earl of Leicester (1752–1842) Known as Coke of Norfolk, or Coke of Holkham, he was a fervent Whig and was MP for Norfolk in 1776–84, 1790–1807 and 1807–32. He was created 1st Earl of Leicester in 1837 and in 1775 he married his cousin Jane Lenox Dutton, but she died in 1800; Jane **Digby** was their granddaughter. In 1822 he married Lady Anne Keppel (**Coke**, above) who was then 18 years of age. He was the most eminent agriculturalist of his time.

LORD GLENMORE in M. Spencer Stanhope, *Almacks* (1826)

See under **Coke**, Lady Anne.

COLBURN, Henry (d. 1855) Publisher. He published the first edition of *Evelyn's Diary* (1818), and followed it, in 1825, with the first edition of Pepys's diary.

MR BUNGAY in W.M. Thackeray, *The History of Pendennis* (1848–50)

'The publishers Bentley and Colburn are [in *Pendennis*] as Bacon and Bungay' (Gordon Ray, 1958, *Thackeray: the age of wisdom*, p. 114).

COLE, Sir Henry (1808–82) Designer, writer and civil servant. Educated at Christ's Hospital, in 1836 he was Assistant Keeper at the Public Record Office. He was a moving spirit behind the Great Exhibition of 1851, and in 1852 was appointed General Superintendent of Marlborough House, the headquarters of the Department of Practical Art, set up to promote the study of industrial design for pottery, textiles and other manufactured products. In 1853–73 he was

Secretary of the Department; he gathered together a distinguished body of designers, including Owen Jones, author of *The Grammar of Ornament* and decorator of the Khedive's palace in Egypt, and Ralph Wornum, the Keeper of the National Gallery and saviour of the Turner collection. The aim of the department, and of the group as a whole, was to purge Victorian design of its grosser vulgarities. He was the inventor of the adhesive postage stamp.

THE THIRD GENTLEMAN in Charles Dickens, *Hard Times* (1854)

'Dickens was satirizing the doctrines of the newly-formed Department of Practical Art, and ... the figure of the "third gentleman" originated as a caricature of its superintendent Henry Cole' (K.J. Fielding, 1953, 'Charles Dickens and the Department of Practical Art', *Modern Language Review* 48 (3): 272). 'Perhaps the only persons to understand exactly what Dickens meant were the new officials themselves. Cole ... seems to have written him a friendly letter of protest' (ibid., p. 274). Professor Collins points out that this was not the only occasion when Dickens used a novel for a private joke (see Philip Collins, 1963, *Dickens and Education*, London: Macmillan, p. 157).

COLE, Rufus (1872–1966) Bacteriologist and pathologist. In 1909 he became Director of the hospital at the Rockefeller Center, New York; he retired in 1937.

RIPPLETON HOLABIRD in Sinclair Lewis, *Arrowsmith* (1925)

Identified in Mark Schorer, 1961, *Sinclair Lewis: an American life*, New York: McGraw-Hill, p. 418. *See also* **Rous**, Peyton.

COLEFAX, Sybil, Lady (1874–1950) Daughter of an officer in the Bengal Civil Service, and niece of W.R. **Greg**, she became a hostess who specialized in the capture of the famous. Osbert **Sitwell** used to call her house (Argyle House, on a corner of King's Road in Chelsea, London, opposite his own) 'the Lion's Corner House'. She married Sir Arthur Colefax, a highly regarded and successful Chancery barrister; in 1929 she lost all her money in the stock-market crash in the United States, and her husband simultaneously lost his hearing and his practice at the Bar. She thereupon turned to and became an enormously fashionable (and hard-working) interior decorator.

LOTTIE in Mary Borden, 'To Meet Jesus Christ', *Four O'Clock* (1926)

'On the last occasion when I met [W. Somerset Maugham] at Sybil's [Lady Colefax's] ... he was in great form. The atmosphere was somewhat tense because Mary Borden had just published ... "To Meet Jesus Christ", in which the principal character bore a suspicious resemblance to Sybil' (Beverley Nichols, 1966, *A Case of Human Bondage*, p. 54).

EMMELINE LUCAS ('LUCIA') in E.F. Benson, *Queen Lucia* (1920) and others

'He [Benson] claimed that the characters were drawn from figures in his past, that he himself was variously Miss Mapp or Lucia (though the latter seems to be based partly on the relentless hostess Lady Colefax)' (E.F. Benson, 1988, *Final Edition: an informal autobiography*, intro. by Hugo Vickers, London: Hogarth Press; originally published 1940, London: Longman). *See also* **Anderson**, Mary.

AMY STRICKLAND in W. Somerset Maugham, *The Moon and Sixpence* (1919)

'Mrs Strickland bears a considerable resemblance to the prominent social hostess of the time, Lady (Sybil) Colefax' (R.L. Calder, 1972, *Somerset Maugham and the Quest for Freedom*, London: Heinemann, p. 138). Lady Colefax was also portrayed by Osbert Sitwell in his verses 'At the House of Mrs Kinfoot'.

COLERIDGE, Samuel Taylor (1772–1834) English poet. Son of a vicar, and initially destined for the church, he was educated at Christ's Hospital and at Jesus College, Cambridge, where he studied classics until an unhappy love affair prompted him to enlist in the 15th Light Dragoons, from which he was bought out under an 'insanity clause' by his brother. He befriended Robert **Southey** in 1794, and they became brothers-in-law when Coleridge married Sarah Fricker in 1795 and Southey married her sister Elizabeth. In 1797 he met William and Dorothy *Wordsworth* and in 1800 he moved with them to the Lake District. Having taken opium during periods of sickness and depression, he became addicted to the drug. By 1811 he was estranged from his wife and had broken with Wordsworth. From 1816 until his death he lived in Highgate in the household of a surgeon, Dr James Gillman.

FERDINANDO FLOSKY in Thomas Love Peacock, *Nightmare Abbey* (1818)

'This gentleman [Mr Flosky], of course, is Coleridge' (Martin Freeman, 1911, *Thomas Love Peacock*, London: Martin Secker, p. 207).

MOLEY MYSTIC in Thomas Love Peacock, *Melincourt* (1817)

'On their travels . . . Forester and Fax meet "a recluse genius" in the Coleridgean Mr Moley Mystic. . . . The speeches he is given are . . . a kind of anthology culled from the *Statesman's Manual* [1816], and thus a literal presentation of Coleridge's own propositions. . . . There has been a misconception that Peacock attempts to *characterise* Coleridge in Mr Mystic. It is true that the sage "talked for three hours without intermission" – a much publicised feature of Coleridge's real-life conversation. But otherwise Mystic is not endowed with the kind of characteristics that should suggest a portrait' (Marilyn Butler, 1979, *Peacock Displayed*, pp. 89–90). David Garnett's footnote on the first appearance of Mr Mystic reads 'Coleridge' (see *The Novels of T.L. Peacock*, 1948, ed. David Garnett, London: Rupert Hart-Davis, p. 147 n. 2).

EDMUND OLIVER in Charles Lloyd, *Edmund Oliver* (1798)

'The incidents of Coleridge's life about this period . . . are to be found (with what modifications I know not) in the novel of *Edmund Oliver*, written by the late Charles Lloyd' (T. de Quincey, 1970, *Recollections of the Lakes and Lake Poets*, Harmondsworth: Penguin, p. 60).

MR PANSCOPE in Thomas Love Peacock, *Headlong Hall* (1816)

'[A character] based on an insufficient knowledge of Coleridge' (*Headlong Hall*, 1948, ed. David Garnett, p. 21 n. 4).

FRANK SALTRAM in Henry James, 'The Coxon Fund' (1894)

'Feb. 3rd 1894 . . . in reading Dykes Campbell's book on Coleridge . . . I was infinitely struck with the suggestiveness of S.T.C's figure . . . for pictorial treatment. . . . There was a point, as I read, at which I seemed to see a little story' (*The Notebooks of Henry James*, 1947, ed. F.O. Matthiessen and K.B. Murdock,

New York, p. 152; the genesis of 'The Coxon Fund' is discussed in detail on pp. 152–64). 'The wondrous figment of that genius [i.e. Coleridge] had long haunted me ... yet it is none the less true that ... Frank Saltram ... pretends to be of his great suggester no more than a dim reflexion and above all a free rearrangement. More interesting ... than the man ... is the S.T. Coleridge *type*' (Henry James, 1935, *The Art of the Novel: critical prefaces*, p. 229).

MR SKIONAR in Thomas Love Peacock, *Crotchet Castle* (1831)

'Mr Skionar, or Coleridge ... now acts his last part in the Peacockian comedies' (Freeman, op. cit., pp. 307–8).

COLES, Jack A friend of Ernest Hemingway and of John Dos Passos, in 1936 he brought his new wife (**Coles**, below) to Key West.

JAMES LAUGHTON in Ernest Hemingway, *To Have and Have Not* (1937)

'The Laughtons were thinly disguised portraits of Jack Coles and his wife' (Carlos Baker, 1969, *Ernest Hemingway: a life story*, New York, p. 295). Baker describes this identification as 'a surmise, based on EH to Dos Passos, April 12, 1936' (ibid., p. 619 n. 'EH's eccentrics in the Morgan novel').

COLES, Mrs Jack Married to Jack **Coles** in 1936, she was described by Hemingway to Dos Passos as a crop-haired woman with a bad complexion and the build of a lady wrestler.

MRS JAMES LAUGHTON in Ernest Hemingway, *To Have and Have Not* (1937)

See under **Coles**, Jack.

COLLIER, Lady Born Elizabeth Fryer, in 1781 she married Admiral Sir George Collier (1738–95), becoming his second wife; they had six children.

LADY AUGUSTA SELWYN in Lady Caroline Lamb, *Glenarvon* (1816)

'Lady Augusta [is] Lady Jersey and Lady Collier' (Lady Holland to Mrs Creevey, 21 May 1816, quoted in *Creevey Papers*, 1903, ed. Sir Herbert Maxwell, Vol. I, p. 254). Also identified in a key found among the papers of John Whishaw (a member of the Holland House circle), printed in *The 'Pope' of Holland House: selections from the correspondence of John Whishaw and his friends, 1813–1840*, ed. Lady Seymour, 1906, p. 151. *See also* **Jersey**, Countess of.

COLLIER, Constance (1880–1955) Née Hardie, she married Julian L'Estrange. From 1901 to 1907, she was a member of Sir Herbert Beerbohm Tree's company at His Majesty's Theatre, and in 1908–12 she performed on the New York stage. She was briefly engaged in 1903–4 to Max Beerbohm, with whom she spent the summer of 1903 in Dieppe.

ZULEIKA DOBSON in Max Beerbohm, *Zuleika Dobson* (1911)

'Constance Collier ... is supposed to have been the model for Zuleika Dobson. I asked Max about this, and he told me she was not. The actual model was a girl he had known who died of consumption. But Max ... implored me, "Please, don't say anything about this. Let her think that she was". I promised. To her dying day, Constance Collier thought that she was the model for Zuleika' (S.N. Behrman, 1960, *Conversation with Max*, p. 90).

COLLIN, Raphaël (1850–1916) He was a pupil in the atelier of Bouguereau, and subsequently in that of Cabanel, where his fellows included Jules Bastien-Lepage and Benjamin Constant. He exhibited in the Paris Salon from 1873 or 1875.

MICHEL ROLLIN in W. Somerset Maugham, *Of Human Bondage* (1915)

'. . . can be identified with Raphel Colin [sic]' (D.W. Buchanan, 1936, *James Wilson Morrice*, Toronto, p. 71).

COLLINGS, Beatrice Sister of Lady Preston, whose husband Sir Harry Preston was the owner of the Royal York Hotel at Brighton when Arnold Bennett stayed there in 1910 while writing *Clayhanger*.

THE HOUSEKEEPER in Arnold Bennett, the *Clayhanger* trilogy (1910–16)

'[T]he housekeeper [at the Royal Sussex Hotel] is Miss Beatrice Collings, my wife's sister' (Sir Harry Preston, 1936, *Leaves from My Unwritten Diary*, London: Hutchinson, p. 46).

COLLINS, William A doctor at South Harting, Sussex, when Wells was a boy at **Uppark**. In 1887, he attended Wells when he developed tuberculosis.

DR CRUMP in H.G. Wells, *The Wonderful Visit* (1895)

'The book is a satire on the squirearchy . . . Lady Hammerslow . . . Sir John Gotch . . . the village doctor interested only in the angel's deformed shoulder blades . . . all remind one that the setting is South Harting . . . while . . . Dr Collins [and the rest] are being ironically depicted' (Lovat Dickson, 1972, *H.G. Wells*, Harmondsworth: Penguin, p. 86). In fact Dr Collins was 'an able and sympathetic man who later became professionally eminent' (N. Mackenzie and J. Mackenzie, 1973, *The Time Traveller: the life of H.G. Wells*, London, p. 72).

COLLITON HOUSE, Dorchester, Dorset

HIGH-PLACE HALL in Thomas Hardy, *The Mayor of Casterbridge* (1886)

Identified in F.B. Pinion, 1968, *A Hardy Companion*, London: Macmillan.

The COLONIAL OFFICE

THE CIRCUMLOCUTION OFFICE in Charles Dickens, *Little Dorrit* (1855–7)

See under **Stephen**, Sir James.

COLVIN, Lady Born Frances Jane Featherstonhaugh, she married Mr Sitwell, a clergyman, and in 1901 she married Sir Sidney **Colvin**.

MRS BARTON TRAFFORD in W. Somerset Maugham, *Cakes and Ale* (1930)

'The lion-hunting Mrs Barton Trafford and her husband are undoubtedly thinly disguised representations of Mr and Mrs Sidney Colvin' (R.L. Calder, 1972, *W. Somerset Maugham and the Quest for Freedom*, London: Heinemann, p. 183).

COLVIN, Sir Sidney (1845–1927) A Fellow of Trinity College, Cambridge, in 1868, he was Slade Professor of Fine Art, Cambridge, in 1873–85, Director of the Fitzwilliam Museum in 1876–83, and Keeper of the Department of Prints and Drawings at the British Museum, London, in 1883–1912. In 1901 he married Frances Jane Sitwell (**Colvin**, above). Both Sir Colvin and his wife were close friends of R.L. Stevenson, whose letters Sir Sidney edited.

BARTON TRAFFORD in W. Somerset Maugham, *Cakes and Ale* (1930)

See under **Colvin**, Lady.

COMPTON-BURNETT, Guy (1885–1905) Elder son of Dr James *Compton-Burnett* and his second wife, Katharine *Compton-Burnett*. Ivy Compton-Burnett was his sister.

FABIAN CLARE in I. Compton-Burnett, *The Present and the Past* (1953)

'Guy and Noel Compton-Burnett are described in the persons of Fabian and Guy Clare . . . (Ivy's sisters confirm that this is an exact likeness of their own brothers)' (Hilary Spurling, 1974, *Ivy When Young: the early life of I. Compton-Burnett, 1884–1919*, London: Gollancz, p. 59 n.). 'Ivy's two younger sisters maintain emphatically that her books contain no hint of a portrait of Guy: "The quality was the same, but never the character"' (ibid., p. 116).

COMPTON-BURNETT, Dame Ivy (1892–1969) English novelist. Born in Pinner, Middlesex, she graduated in classics from Royal Holloway College, London University. Her brother Noel was killed in the First World War. Following the war she suffered a mental and physical breakdown, and two of her sisters committed suicide in 1917. She lived with the writer Margaret Jourdain from 1919 until the latter's death in 1951.

DUDLEY GAVESTON in I. Compton-Burnett, *A Family and a Fortune* (1939)

'Dudley's illness . . . closely follows the course of Ivy's own [in the influenza epidemic of 1918]. His strength, like hers, had been undermined by what his family call "the troubles", he too had gone away by himself and been discovered alone, barely conscious, close to delirium and fighting for breath' (H. Spurling, 1974, *Ivy When Young: the early life of I. Compton-Burnett, 1884–1919*, London: Gollancz, p. 257).

DOLORES HUTTON in I. Compton-Burnett, *Dolores* (1911)

'[T]he heroine herself . . . evidently in some sense embodies her creator' (Spurling, op. cit., p. 173).

COMPTON-BURNETT, James (1840–1901) Homeopath. He was the son of a farm labourer of Red Lynch near Salisbury, who later moved and set up as a coal and corn dealer in Southampton. He contrived to read medicine in Vienna and Glasgow, and in 1872 he became a homeopath and one of the most distinguished practitioners in London. He was Ivy Compton-Burnett's father.

CHRISTIAN STACE in I. Compton-Burnett, *Brothers and Sisters* (1929)

'Christian Stace is the first of Ivy's doctors . . . and the one who most closely resembles her father' (Hilary Spurling, 1974, *Ivy When Young: the early life of I. Compton-Burnett, 1884–1919*, London: Gollancz, p. 94).

COMPTON-BURNETT, Katharine (1855–1911) Daughter of Rowland **Rees**, in 1883 she married James **Compton-Burnett**, becoming his second wife. They had seven children, of whom Ivy Compton-Burnett was the eldest.

ELIZA HERIOT in I. Compton-Burnett, *The Last and the First* (1970)

'Sophia [Stace] is the first and closest but far from the only descendant of Mrs Compton-Burnett in her daughter's books. To the very end . . . Ivy . . . distributed among her characters touches taken from her mother. . . . But the two who most nearly resemble the original pattern come quite close together near the end of their creator's life, Eliza Mowbray . . . and Eliza Heriot' (Hilary Spurling, 1974, *Ivy When Young: the early life of I. Compton-Burnett, 1884–1919*, London: Gollancz, p. 127). By no means can either be said to be a portrait of Mrs Compton-Burnett, except in so far as each embodies an aspect' (ibid.).

SOPHIA HUTTON in I. Compton-Burnett, *Dolores* (1911)

'Ivy's mother was by this time [1911] too weak to resent, perhaps even to identify, the portrait of herself as Mrs Hutton' (Spurling, op. cit., p. 184).

ELIZA MOWBRAY in I. Compton-Burnett, *A Father and His Fate* (1957)

See above under ELIZA HERIOT.

SOPHIA STACE in I. Compton-Burnett, *Brothers and Sisters* (1929)

'She . . . had "the high, arched nose and high, arched brow, the full blue eye and short but finished build" which . . . Ivy passed on to Sophia Stace' (Spurling, op. cit., p. 30). 'Ivy's sisters confirm that this is an exact likeness of their mother' (ibid., p. 288 n. 18). '. . . in both looks and character the nearest Ivy ever came to a direct portrait of her mother' (ibid., pp. 109–10).

COMPTON-BURNETT, Noel (1887–1916) Second son of Dr James *Compton-Burnett* and brother of Ivy Compton-Burnett, he was a Fellow of Kings College, Cambridge. In 1915 he married Tertia Beresford (**Compton-Burnett**, below), but he was killed at Bazentin-le-Petit on the Somme on 14 July 1916.

GUY CLARE in I. Compton-Burnett, *The Present and the Past* (1953)

See under **Compton-Burnett**, Guy.

ROBIN STACE in I. Compton-Burnett, *Brothers and Sisters* (1929)

'Noel, in so far as one may judge from his letters and from his sister's borrowings from him for Robin Stace . . . had a smoother temperament than hers' (Hilary Spurling, 1974, *Ivy When Young: the early life of I. Compton-Burnett, 1884–1919*, London: Gollancz, p. 241).

COMPTON-BURNETT, Tertia (1890–1956) Third daughter of J.J. Beresford, Rector of Easton Grey, Wiltshire, and sister of J.B. Beresford, who was Noel

Compton-Burnett's closest friend at Cambridge. In 1915 she married Noel Compton-Burnett, and after his death she married Horace Mann.

RUTH GIFFARD in I. Compton-Burnett, *More Women Than Men* (1933)

'A painting of her by Margot Asquith's sister Lucy Graham Smith, is so like the description of Ruth Giffard ... that one can only suppose Tertia sat for both portraits' (Hilary Spurling, 1974, *Ivy When Young: the early life of I. Compton Burnett, 1884–1919*, London: Gollancz, p. 212).

CONDON, Edward O'Meara Alias Shore, Irish American Fenian. One of the four Manchester Martyrs, who in 1867 were condemned to death for the murder of a policeman while attempting to rescue two well-known Fenians (Colonel Kelly and Captain Deasy) from the police van in which they were being taken to gaol in Manchester. As a result of the intercession of the American Ambassador in London, Condon was reprieved because he had been unarmed.

MICHAELIS in Joseph Conrad, *The Secret Agent* (1907)

'[The] attack on a police van [ch. vi in the novel] is given as an anarchist incident, but Conrad is actually making use of a Fenian incident – the then famous ... event of the Manchester Martyrs. ... Just as in the novel "three ring-leaders got hanged". ... And a fourth, Condon (alias Shore) ... was given a last minute reprieve, his sentence being commuted to ... life imprisonment' (Norman Sherry, 1971, *Conrad's Western World*, Cambridge, pp. 261, 263). *See also* **Bakunin**, Michael; **Davitt**, Michael.

CONE, Claribel (1864–1929) Sister of Etta **Cone** and daughter of Herman Cone, a German Jewish immigrant to the USA who founded a wholesale grocery business, which was sold by his sons when he retired; they invested the proceeds in textile mills from which the two sisters derived their incomes. In 1892, Claribel trained as a doctor, but she never practised. She and Etta met Leo and Gertrude **Stein** in Baltimore and became lifelong friends; under their influence the sisters began to collect modern art, and they later bought a number of pictures from the Stein collections. Etta bequeathed their pictures to the Baltimore Museum of Art upon their death.

MARTHA in Gertrude Stein, 'Two Women' (1925)

'"Two Women", her portrait of Claribel and Etta Cone, is typical of her early method. ... The names that Gertrude ... chose for Claribel and Etta are significant ... for Claribel ... she finally chose ... Martha and for Etta she chose Ada' (James R. Mellow, 1974, *The Charmed Circle: Gertrude Stein and company*, London: Phaidon Press, p. 132).

CONE, Etta (1870–1949) Sister of Claribel **Cone**.

ADA in Gertrude Stein, 'Two Women' (1925)

See under **Cone**, Claribel.

CONKLIN, Asa An unsuccessful Chicago real-estate agent who, in 1890, hired Theodore Dreiser to work for him. '[H]e cared nothing for business, everything for religion' (E. Moers, 1970, *Two Dreisers*, London: Thames & Hudson, p. 292; originally published 1969, New York: Viking).

ASA GRIFFITHS in Theodore Dreiser, *An American Tragedy* (1925)

'In [*Dawn*], his autobiography, Dreiser wrote unequivocally that the "living prototype" of Asa Griffiths was a "defeated and worn out religious fuzzy-wuzzy" named Asa Conklin' (Moers, op. cit.). *See also* **Dreiser**, John Paul.

CONNOLLY, Albrecht Brother of Vincent *Connolly*, from 1893 to 1844 he was a contemporary of James Joyce at Belvedere College, Dublin.

VINCENT HERON in James Joyce, *A Portrait of the Artist as a Young Man* (1916)

'Albrecht Connolly was the fop of Belvedere College. . . . But in *A Portrait* Joyce combines Albrecht's attire and his [brother's] face to compose . . . Heron' (Richard Ellmann, 1982, *James Joyce*, rev. edn, Oxford: Oxford University Press, p. 750 n. 77). *See also* **Connolly**, Vincent.

CONNOLLY, Cyril (1903–74) Critic and writer. He was educated at the same preparatory school (St Cyprians, Eastbourne) as George **Orwell** and Cecil **Beaton**, and at Eton and Oxford, where his contemporaries included Anthony Powell, Harold **Acton**, and Brian **Howard**. He founded and became Editor of the periodical *Horizon* (1939–50) until its end, and then became a reviewer (1950–74) on the *Sunday Times*. He was married three times, first in 1930 to Jean Bakewell (**Connolly**, below).

CORPORAL-MAJOR LUDOVIC in Evelyn Waugh, the *Sword of Honour* trilogy (1952–61)

'When Evelyn told Nancy Mitford that Ludovic was based on Cyril Connolly, he was deliberately misleading her. . . . Ludovic's pensées . . . are cruelly close to the aphorisms . . . in . . . *The Unquiet Grave*. Otherwise Ludovic . . . bears no relation to Cyril' (Christopher Sykes, 1975, *Evelyn Waugh*, London: Collins, pp. 421–2).

ED SPAIN in Nancy Mitford, *The Blessing* (1951)

'Ed Spain, "the Captain", a leading London intellectual, is based on Cyril Connolly' (Harold Acton, 1975, *Nancy Mitford: a memoir*, London: Hamilton, p. 86).

EVERARD SPRUCE in Evelyn Waugh, the *Sword of Honour* trilogy (1952–61)

'Spruce is manifestly based on Cyril Connolly, and his monthly magazine *Survival* on Cyril's . . . magazine *Horizon*. Cyril was much hurt when the book came out and asked Ann Fleming to tell him candidly whether Everard Spruce was a caricature of himself. Ann candidly replied that there could be no question about it, just as there could be no question that Ludovic's pensées were based on his own aphorisms' (Sykes, op. cit., p. 426).

CONNOLLY, Jean (1911–50) Novelist under the name Barbara Skelton. Née Bakewell, she was an American and was at one time very beautiful. On 1930 she married Cyril **Connolly**; upon their divorce she returned to New York and in 1946 married Laurence Vail, who had previously been married to the millionairess Peggy Guggenheim and to the novelist Kay Boyle.

RUTHIE in Christopher Isherwood, *Down There on a Visit* (1962)

'Jean . . . [was] later to appear, affectionately caricatured as "Ruthie" . . . in *Down There on a Visit*' (Christopher Isherwood, 1977, *Christopher and His Kind*, London: Eyre & Methuen, p. 202).

CONNOLLY, Vincent Brother of Albrecht **Connolly**, from 1893 to 1844 he was a contemporary of James Joyce at Belvedere College, Dublin.

VINCENT HERON in James Joyce, *A Portrait of the Artist as a Young Man* (1916)

See under **Connolly**, Albrecht.

CONRAD, Jessie (1873–1936) Née George, she married Joseph Conrad in 1896.

WINNIE VERLOC in Joseph Conrad, *The Secret Agent* (1907)

'[T]here is a certain similarity between the character of Jessie Conrad as it is revealed in her books on her husband and that of Winnie Verloc' (Norman Sherry, 1971, *Conrad's Western World*, Cambridge, p. 366). 'In terms of physical appearances, there are also some similarities between Winnie and Jessie Conrad' (ibid., p. 368).

CONRAD, Joseph (1857–1924) Polish-born British novelist. Born Josef Teodor Konrad Nalecz Korzeniowski in Berdichev, in the Polish Ukraine. His father was a revolutionary, exiled to Vologda in 1862. In 1878, Joseph joined an English merchant ship, and in 1884 he gained his certificate as a master, and was naturalized. For the following ten years he sailed between Singapore and Borneo, apart from an interval in the Belgian Congo. In 1896, he married Jessie George (**Conrad**, above), and they settled in Ashford, Kent, where Conrad spent the rest of his life in seclusion.

WALTER ARGALLO in Max Beerbohm, 'Walter Argallo and Felix Ledgett', *A Variety of Things* (1928)

'[The story] describes how a noble and sombre man of genius [Argallo], suggested by Conrad, after years of neglect, achieves the fame which is his due' (David Cecil, 1964, *Max: a biography*, p. 418).

ARMAND in John Galsworthy, 'The Doldrums', *Forsytes, Pendyces and Others* (1935)

'[T]the hero is the first mate, by the name of Armand, obviously modelled on Korzeniowski' (Z. Najder, 1983, *Joseph Conrad: a chronicle*, Cambridge: Cambridge University Press, p. 157).

SIMON BRANSDON in Ford Madox Ford, *The Simple Life Limited* (1911)

'The only comprehensive . . . (though unreliable) account of how Conrad came to know and marry Jessie . . . George is to be found in . . . *The Simple Life Limited*. Conrad is represented . . . as Simeon Brandetski . . . who settles in England . . .

he changes his name to Simon Bransdon and becomes a writer' (Najder, op. cit., p. 191).

CAPTAIN OF THE *MAUD MARY* in H.G. Wells, *Tono-Bungay* (1909)

'[T]he resemblances of the captain of the *Maud Mary* to Conrad are too close and numerous to be anything other than deliberate. . . . It is hardly possible that Conrad should have remained aware of this caricature, which is not merely ludicrous but malicious' (Bernard Bergonzi, 1973, *The Turn of a Century*, p. 98).

CONSTABLE, George, the Elder (1719–1803) An old friend of Sir Walter Scott's father, he was 'educated to the law, but retired upon his independent property, and generally residing near Dundee'. Scott, as a child, first met him in 1777 when staying with Miss Janet Scott, his aunt, in Prestonpans.

JONATHAN OLDBUCK in Sir Walter Scott, *The Antiquary* (1816)

'He had many of those peculiarities of temper which long afterwards I tried to develop in the character of Jonathan Oldbuck. It is very odd, that though I am unconscious of anything in which I strictly copied the *manners* of my old friend, the resemblance was nevertheless detected by George Chalmers, Esq., solicitor, London, an old friend, both of my father and Mr Constable, and who affirmed to my late friend Lord Kinedder, that I must needs be the author of *The Antiquary* since he recognised the portrait of George Constable' (Walter Scott, note (dated 1826) to autobiog. fragment of 1808, in J.D. Lockhart, 1900, *Memoirs of Sir Walter Scott*, vol. I, London: Macmillan, p. 18–19 n. 1). 'It is one of the very few of my works of fiction which contains a portrait from life . . . a fact detected at the time by . . . Mr Chalmers. . . . When he read the *Antiquary* [he] told my friend William Erskine that he was now perfectly satisfied that Walter Scott . . . was the author of these mysterious works of fiction for that the character of Jonathan Oldbuck . . . was drawn from the late George Constable of Wallace Craigie of Dundee. . . . I was extremely surprized at this detection. For I thought I had taken the utmost care to destroy every trace of personal resemblance' (to Basil Hall, 27 October 1831, reproduced in *The Letters of Sir Walter Scott*, 1937, ed. H.J.C. Grierson, Vol. XII, London: Constable, pp. 36–37). *See also* **Clerk of Eldin**, John; **Gordon**, Alexander; **Ramsay of Ochtertyre**, John.

CONSTABLE, George, the Younger Colonel in the Bengal Artillery. He was the nephew of George **Constable**, the Elder.

HECTOR M'INTYRE in Sir Walter Scott, *The Antiquary* (1816)

'George, son of David Constable, brother of the Antiquary . . . was the prototype of . . . Captain Hector M'Intyre' (W.S. Crockett, 1912, *The Scott Originals: an account of notables and worthies, the originals of characters in the Waverley novels*, Edinburgh and London: T.N. Foulis, p. 127).

CONSTABLE, Matilda Sister of George **Constable**, the Elder.

GRISELDA OLDBUCK in Sir Walter Scott, *The Antiquary* (1816)

'The original of the Antiquary's "most discreet sister Griselda" . . . is held to be Constable's sister, Matilda' (W.S. Crockett, 1912, *The Scott Originals: an account of notables and worthies, the originals of characters in the Waverley novels,* Edinburgh and London: T.N. Foulis, p. 127).

CONWAY, Mrs Hearn James Joyce's childhood governess from 1887 to 1891. She inherited a fortune, but she married a member of staff of the Bank of Ireland, and he deserted her, taking her money with him.

Mrs Dante Riordan in James Joyce, *A Portrait of the Artist as a Young Man* (1916) and *Ulysses* (1922)

'Even Molly Bloom acknowledges this quality [a fairly good education] in "Mrs Riordan" (that is, Mrs Conway) in *Ulysses* . . . but supposes none the less that her husband "was glad to get shut of her"' (Richard Ellmann, 1982, *James Joyce,* rev. edn, Oxford: Oxford University Press, p. 748 n. 12).

COOK, Francis She was a sculpture cleaner and lived at 2 **Woburn Buildings**, London, over whose shop Dorothy Richardson and Miss **Moffatt** lodged in 1906.

Mr Perrance in Dorothy Richardson, *Pilgrimage* (1915–67)

See John Rosenberg, 1973, *Dorothy Richardson*, London, p. 212, index s.v. Perrance.

COOKE V. FYNNEY **(1844) C.59** A case held in the Chancery Court, concerning a farm at the Lane End, Leek, Staffordshire. There were eighteen defendants.

Gridley Case in Charles Dickens, *Bleak House* (1852–3)

'"The case of Gridley," said Dickens in the preface to *Bleak House*, "is in no essential altered from one of actual occurrence." Although this assertion was made in 1853, and Dickensians have known for the last forty years that the litigation referred to was brought to Dickens's notice by a pamphlet, . . . "The Court of Chancery: its Inherent Defects", issued in 1849 by William Challinor, solicitor, the case of "actual occurrence" has never been identified. Now, however, I have ascertained that it was Cooke v. Fynney, 1844' (E.T. Jacques, 1917, 'Dickens and the Court of Chancery', *The Dickensian* 13 (January): 16).

COOLIDGE, Calvin (1872–1933) Thirtieth President of the United States. The son of a Vermont farmer and storekeeper, he became a lawyer and then Governor of Massachusetts from 1919 to 1920, where he decisively used the state militia to break the Boston police strike in 1919. He was Vice-President from 1921 to 1923, succeeding Warren Harding as President on the latter's death. He was re-elected in 1924, and began a term as President that lasted until 1929 and which was noted for economic prosperity.

Nathan 'Shagpoke' Whipple in Nathanael West, *A Cool Million* (1934)

'[In the early part of the novel] he is a broad comic caricature of Calvin Coolidge' (Joseph Blotner, 1966, *The Modern American Political Novel*, Austin, Tex., p. 245).

COOMBE WARREN, Surrey '[A] solid Victorian house looking across the North Downs toward the Epsom grandstand' (Richard Gill, 1972, *Happy Rural Seat*, p. 116), it was built by John Galsworthy's father.

ROBIN HILL in John Galsworthy, *The Man of Property* (1906)

'Coombe Warren – or at least the setting and the grounds – was in fact Galsworthy's model for Robin Hill' (ibid.).

COOPER, Alfred Duff, 1st Viscount Norwich (1890–54) Politician, diplomat and author. In 1919 he married Lady Diana Manners (**Cooper**, below), and in 1924 he became MP for Oldham. In 1937 he became First Lord of the Admiralty, but resigned in 1938 because he was unable to accept the Munich agreement. In 1944 he was the British representative with the French Committee of Nation Liberation in North Africa, and in November 1944 he became Ambassador in Paris.

ALGERNON STITCH in Evelyn Waugh, *Scoop* (1938) and the *Sword of Honour* trilogy (1952–61)

'[T]he very lightly drawn background figure of Algernon Stitch bears a decided resemblance to . . . Alfred Duff Cooper' (Christopher Sykes, 1975, *Evelyn Waugh*, London: Collins, p. 170).

COOPER, Lady Diana, Viscountess Norwich (1892–1986) Née Manners, she was the daughter of the Duchess of Rutland and Harry **Cust**. She was a famous beauty and in 1911 she played the Madonna in Reinhardt's production of *The Miracle*. In 1919 she married Alfred Duff **Cooper**; she accompanied him to Algiers in 1944, and was with him in Paris in 1944–7. After Duff Cooper's death, she reverted to the style of Lady Diana Cooper.

LADY ARTEMIS HOOPER in D.H. Lawrence, *Aaron's Rod* (1922)

'Lady Diana Manners . . . is barely disguised as Lady Artemis Hooper' (E. Delavenay, 1972, *D.H. Lawrence: the man and his work, 1885–1919*, p. 448).

LADY LEONE in Nancy Mitford, *Don't Tell Alfred* (1960)

'. . . Lady Diana Cooper, thinly disguised in the book as Lady Leone' (Susan Mary Alsop, 1976, *To Marietta from Paris, 1945–1960*, London: Weidenfeld & Nicolson, p. 152; originally published 1975, New York: Doubleday). Of course I couldn't really let myself go about Lady Leone who has been so kind to me' (Nancy Mitford to Handasyde Buchanan, 7 September 1960, quoted in Harold Acton, 1975, *Nancy Mitford: a memoir*, London: Hamilton, p. 140).

RUBY, LADY MACLEAN in Enid Bagnold, *The Loved and Envied* (1951)

'Though Duff [Cooper] would never allow that the character . . . in *The Loved and Envied* had any likeness to Diana, I don't admit that husbands know best. I think when I wrote: "No one liked to be excluded. No one could afford to leave alone such a dispenser of life: everyone fed at the spring" I didn't do badly' (*Enid Bagnold's Autobiography (from 1889)*, 1969, London: Heinemann, p. 215).

LADY QUEENIE PAULLE in Arnold Bennett, *The Pretty Lady* (1918)

'[O]n 2 July [1918] he dined at the Savoy with Beaverbrook . . . and Diana Manners . . . and the conversation turned, embarrassingly, to whether or not Diana Manners was the original of Queenie in *The Pretty Lady*. The two had not met before, and Bennett knew of her and her reputation only through gossip. . . . It was the Countess of Chell situation all over again [see **Sutherland**,

Duchess of]; clearly . . . Bennett could repudiate the charge, as he didn't know her personally, but equally clearly he had caught something of her character through hearsay. Lady Diana herself could see the resemblance, and reports the uncanny experience of living through incidents similar to those in the novel, which Bennett could not have known from anyone' (Margaret Drabble, 1974, *Arnold Bennett: a biography*, London: Weidenfeld & Nicolson, pp. 235–6).

JULIA STITCH in Evelyn Waugh, *Scoop* (1938) and the *Sword of Honour* trilogy (1952–61)

'1936 . . . Monday, 12 October—Friday, 16 October. On Thursday 15th made a very good start with the first page of a novel describing Diana's early morning' (*The Diaries of Evelyn Waugh*, 1976, ed. Michael Davie, London: Weidenfeld & Nicolson, p. 409). 'The reader who knows the book will recognize the opening scene in which Mrs Stitch . . . is shown beginning and organizing her day. None of his friends doubted, or could doubt, that Mrs Stitch was a caricaturist's impression of Diana Cooper. . . . Not only did Diana recognize her image . . . but she rejoiced in it' (Christopher Sykes, 1975, *Evelyn Waugh*, London: Collins, p. 170). 'To Diana Cooper's great delight, Mrs Stitch was revived [in *Officers and Gentlemen*] from *Scoop*, but given here "treatment in depth" and a key role' (ibid., p. 375).

COOPER, Thomas[1] (1805–92) Born in Leicester, from 1820 to 1840 he worked as a shoemaker, schoolmaster and journalist. In 1841 he joined the Chartists and conducted their newspaper, the *Midland Counties Illuminator*. He was imprisoned for sedition and conspiracy between 1843 and 1845, and in 1845 he composed *The Purgatory of Suicides: a prison rhyme*, dedicated to Thomas Carlyle. In 1848 he formed a friendship with Charles Kingsley and corresponded with him until Kingsley's death; he was converted, largely by Kingsley, to Christianity. He was baptized in 1859 and lectured on the proofs of the Christian religion.

ALTON LOCKE in Charles Kingsley, *Alton Locke* (1850)

'Alton Locke's character is said to be based upon that of Thomas Cooper. . . . Branded as a Chartist and Atheist, Thomas Cooper . . . fought nobly with his religious and political doubts. . . . This was the man Kingsley took as the hero of his book – though in personal appearance they did not resemble each other, for Thomas Cooper was a tall, handsome man, while Alton is puny' (Laura Hain Friswell, 1905, *In the Sixties and Seventies*, p. 115). 'Locke himself is probably an amalgam of the two [i.e. Thomas and Walter] Coopers' (R.B. Martin, 1959, *The Dust of Combat: a life of Charles Kingsley*, London: Faber & Faber, p. 113). *See also* **Cooper**, Walter.

COOPER, Thomas[2] (d. 1918) He was the owner of the house in Lynn Croft Road, Eastwood, Nottinghamshire, to which D.H. Lawrence's parents moved in 1902. He lived next door at No. 97, and his daughters, Frances and Gertrude, were members of 'the Pagans', a group of Lawrence's friends.

AARON SISSON in D.H. Lawrence, *Aaron's Rod* (1922)

'Lynn Croft . . . was to serve . . . as a model for Aaron's residence in *Aaron's Rod*. Indeed . . . Thomas Cooper was to serve as the model for at least the outward aspects of Aaron. . . . Like [him], Tom Cooper was . . . a flautist and piccolo player; and like Aaron he was a check-weighman' (H.T. Moore, 1960, *The Intelligent Heart: the story of D.H. Lawrence*, Harmondsworth: Penguin, p. 69; originally published 1955, London: Heinemann).

COOPER, Walter Scottish Chartist. He lectured on Strauss and worked as a tailor, in 1850 becoming the manager of the Tailors' Association shop set up in Castle Street, London, by the Christian Socialists. Charles Kingsley saw him frequently during this period and obtained from him background information for *Alton Locke*. Originally an agnostic, he was later converted to orthodox Christianity and became Vicar's Warden at All Saints, Margaret Street, London. In 1860 he was convicted of misappropriation of the funds of the Working Tailors and sentenced to prison.

ALTON LOCKE in Charles Kingsley, *Alton Locke* (1850)

See under **Cooper**, Thomas[1].

COPE, Sir John (1768–1851) 11th Baronet, of Bramshill Park, Hampshire. A solicitor until 1806, he succeeded his brother in the Baronetcy in 1812. He was Master of Foxhounds until the year of his death, and was Patron of the Living of Eversley, where from 1844 Charles Kingsley was Rector. He had been a crony of the Prince Regent.

SQUIRE LAVINGTON in Charles Kingsley, *Yeast* (1848)

'[H]e furnished a good many of the features for the portrait of Squire Lavington' (Margaret Farrand Thorp, 1937, *Charles Kingsley, 1819–1875*, p. 29).

CORFE CASTLE, Dorset Situated half-way between Wareham and Swanage.

CORVSGATE CASTLE in Thomas Hardy, Wessex novels and tales (1871–95)

Identified on a map prepared by Thomas Hardy which hangs in the Dorset County Museum, Dorchester. *See under* **Abbotsbury**.

CORFE MULLEN, Dorset A village about two miles west of Wimborne Minster on the Dorchester road.

ELM-CRANLYNCH in Thomas Hardy, 'The First Countess of Wessex' (1891)

Identified in F.B. Pinion, 1968, *A Hardy Companion*, London: Macmillan.

CORKE, Helen (1882–1972) Writer. When she was a schoolteacher, she met and became a close friend of D.H. Lawrence in 1908–12, through her colleague Agnes **Mason**. She fell in love with H.B. **Macartney** and after his death showed Lawrence the memoir she had written of the five days she had spent with Macartney at Freshwater, Isle of Wight, immediately before his suicide. She never saw Lawrence again after he left England in 1912 with Frieda Weekley (**Lawrence**). In later life, she published textbooks, a novel, four studies of Lawrence and Jessie **Chambers** (who became her friend), and an autobiography.

ELLIS BROOKE in Helen Corke, *Neutral Ground* (1933)

'Lawrence returned from his summer holidays . . . to find Helen Corke in a state of shock from a personal diaster. . . . Ellis Brooke . . . similarly suffers from shock' (H.T. Moore, 1960, *The Intelligent Heart: the story of D.H. Lawrence*, Harmondsworth: Penguin, p. 118; originally published 1955, London: Heinemann). 'Ellis Brooke, the heroine of . . . *Neutral Ground*, has become involved with a married man, her violin teacher – a situation repeated in . . . *The Trespasser*. In both these novels the man persuades the girl to go away with him for a holiday, during which they make themselves miserable. After their return . . . the man kills himself. . . . Lawrence took [*The Trespasser*] from parts of *Neutral Ground* long before Helen Corke completed and published her novel' (ibid., pp. 118–9). 'The only part of the *Neutral Ground* papers written before *The Trespasser* appears on pp. 227 to 236 of *Neutral Ground*. This brief five days' diary was L's [Lawrence's] inspiration for his work, and his expansion of it occupies 193 pages of the original . . . edition' (Helen Corke to H. T. Moore, 20 May 1951, quoted in Moore, op. cit., p. 150).

HELENA VERDEN in D.H. Lawrence, *The Trespasser* (1912)

'[Lawrence] returns to the subject of my Freshwater Diary later – comes with the request that he may take and expand its theme' (Helen Corke, 1975, *In Our Infancy*, Cambridge, p. 178). The 'Freshwater Diary' is printed in *In Our Infancy*, the autobiography that gives a complete account of the genesis of *The Trespasser*.

CORKE, Mary Boyle, Lady (1748?–1840) Née Monckton, she was the daughter of the 1st Viscount Galway and in 1786 married the 8th Earl of Corke, becoming his second wife. As a young woman, she knew Dr Johnson (who said to her, 'Dearest, you are a dunce'). She was noted 'for her eccentricities and as a leader of fashion' (G.E.C. (ed.), 1889, *The Complete Peerage of England, Scotland, Ireland, Great Britain and the United Kingdom*, Vol. III, London: George Bell & Sons).

LADY BELLAIR in Benjamin Disraeli, *Henrietta Temple* (1837)

'We shall find her appearing in *Henrietta Temple* as Lady Bellair' (W.F. Monypenny, 1910, *The Life of Benjamin Disraeli, Earl of Beaconsfield*, Vol. I, London: John Murray, p. 234 n. 1).

CORNISH, Revd Sidney (1800?–74) He was Headmaster of King's School in Ottery St Mary, Devon, from 1824 to 1863, and Vicar of Ottery St Mary from 1841 to 1874.

REVD DR PORTMAN in W.M. Thackeray, *The History of Pendennis* (1848–50)

'It has usually been assumed, that Dr Cornish was the original of Dr Portman' (Gordon N. Ray, 1955, *Thackeray: a biography*, Vol. I: *The Uses of Adversity, 1811–1846*, London: Oxford University Press, p. 454 n. 14). Ray discusses and discards this identification.

REVD MR SMIRKE in W.M. Thackeray, *The History of Pendennis* (1848–50)

'Of Thackeray's impressions of Cornish, unless we ungraciously assume that something of him may be found in the Revd Mr Smirke of *Pendennis*, there remains only an offhand query of later life: "How's that jovial fellow Cornish?"' (Ray, op. cit., p. 106).

CORNWALL MANSIONS

CUMBERLAND MANSIONS (FORMERLY RESIDENCES) in Morley Roberts, *The Private Life of Henry Maitland* (1912)

Identified in an 'Index of Recurring Pseudonyms' in the 1958 edition of *The Private Life of Henry Maitland*, ed. Morchard Bishop, p. 255.

CORRIGAN, Joseph The New York magistrate who found G. Bronson Howard guilty of carrying a deadly weapon after Howard threatened a musical comedy star with a knife.

CORNIGAN in George Bronson Howard, *God's Man* (1915)

'When [Howard] wrote . . . *God's Man* . . . he christened his villain Cornigan and on one page spelled it "Corrigan" to make sure that nobody would misunderstand. The magistrate . . . sued the publisher for two hundred thousand dollars' (Alva Johnston, 1953, *The Incredible Mizners*, London, pp. 150–1).

CORRY, James Of Shantonagh, County Monaghan. He married Mary Ruxton, the sister of John Ruxton (of Black Castle, County Meath) who married R.L. **Edgeworth**'s sister, Margaret. The relationship between the Edgeworths and the Ruxtons was very close; Maria Edgeworth had visited Shantonagh, and the household is described in a letter of 3 July 1808 (reproduced in *Maria Edgeworth: chosen letters*, 1966, ed. F.V. Barry, London: Faber & Faber, pp. 153–5).

CORNELIUS O'SHANE in Maria Edgeworth, *Ormond* (1817)

'Corny was based on James Corry. . . . Maria anxiously enquired of her aunt how far she might go in reproducing his peculiarities' (Marilyn Butler, 1972, *Maria Edgeworth*, Oxford, pp. 250; the letter is reproduced on p. 251).

CORSHAM COURT, Wiltshire Situated near Bath, it was built in 1582 by Thomas Smythe and had various owners until 1745, when it was bought by Paul Methuen of Bradford-on-Avon. In 1749 its front was remodelled, and in 1760 it was added to by Capability Brown. Further additions were made in 1800 by John *Nash*, and in 1845 part of his additions were pulled down and replaced by Bellamy. Gardens were laid out by Brown in 1761 and by **Repton** in 1799. It is now a college of art.

BLANDINGS CASTLE in P.G. Wodehouse, *Something Fresh* (1915) and others

'In shape and size and messuages Wodehouse's Blandings Castle owes a good deal to his boyhood memory of Corsham. . . . The young Pelham, spending school holidays with a clergyman uncle nearby, was taken to Corsham to skate on the lake, and the image of the great house remained on the retina of his inward eye' (Richard Usborne, 1976, *Wodehouse at Work to the End*, p. 114).

CORSO, Gregory (b. 1930) American poet. He was the author of *Gasoline* and others, and was a member of the 'Beat' movement.

YURI GLIGORIC in *The Subterraneans* (1958), and RAPHAEL URSO in *Book of Dreams* (1960) and *Desolation Angels* (1965), all by Jack Kerouac

Identified in 'Character key to the Duluoz Legend', in Barry Gifford and Lawrence Lee, 1979, *Jack's Book*, pp. 322–32.

CORTLAND, New York Town in Upstate New York in which an uncle of Chester **Gillette** owned a skirt factory where both Gillette and Grace **Brown** were employed.

Lycurgus in Theodore Dreiser, *An American Tragedy* (1925)

'After intermittent schooling and a variety of jobs and travels, Gillette found his way to . . . Cortland . . . (Lycurgus in the novel)' (Ellen Moers, 1970, *Two Dreisers*, London: Thames & Hudson, p. 199; originally published 1969, New York: Viking).

COSGRAVE, Vincent (1878–1927) A contemporary and friend of James Joyce at University College Dublin, he was '[c]ommitted to idleness and rancorous unsuccess' (Richard Ellmann, 1966, *James Joyce*, London: Oxford Paperbacks, p. 65). While still at the College, he observed that 'Joyce is the most remarkable man any of us have met' (ibid.). In 1904 he attempted, without success, the conquest of Nora Barnacle. He drowned in the Thames River in London and was believed to have committed suicide.

Vincent Lynch in James Joyce, *A Portrait of the Artist as a Young Man* (1916) and *Ulysses* (1922)

'If you see Cosgrave tell him that he is in my novel under the name of Lynch' (to Stanislaus Joyce, 4 April 1905, reproduced in *The Letters of James Joyce*, 1966, Vol. II, ed. Richard Ellmann, London: Faber & Faber, p. 87).

The COSMOPOLITAN CLUB, London Founded in 1851 by Robert Morier, then a clerk in the Privy Council Office, 'as a Sunday evening gathering of his friends, of which membership was later to become a much coveted honour'. At first the Club met in his rooms in New Bond Street, then it subsequently migrated to G.F. Watts's studio.

The Universe in Anthony Trollope, *Can You Forgive Her?* (1864) and sequels

'"Feb. 20 [1852] . . . To Morier's. There Prince Nicholas of Nassau, Arthur Russell, Reeve, F. Egerton, Layard . . ." The reference to the gathering at Morier's rooms is Fortescue's first mention of the Cosmopolitan Club . . . As "The Universe" it plays a prominent part in . . . *Phineas Redux* of which Fortescue is largely the hero' ('. . . *and Mr Fortescue': a selection from the diaries from 1851 to 1862 of Chichester Fortescue, Lord Carlingford*, 1958, ed. O.W. Hewett, London: John Murray, pp. 30–1).

COSSALL, Nottinghamshire

Cossethay in D.H. Lawrence, *The Rainbow* (1915)

'Cossethay is the village of Cossal [sic], home of Louie's father [Alfred **Burrows**]' (E. Delavenay, 1972, *D.H. Lawrence: the man and his work*, p. 369).

COSTA, Sir Michael (1810–84) Composer. Born and trained at Naples, he was Conductor from 1830 to 1846 at King's Theatre, London; Director of Music at

Covent Garden in 1846; and Conductor of Philharmonic Concerts in 1847–54. In 1871 he was Director of the Italian opera in London.

St Michel in Elizabeth Sara Sheppard, *Charles Auchester* (1853)

Identified in Michael Sadleir, 1951, *XIX Century Fiction*, Vol. I, London: Constable, and Los Angeles: California University Press, p. 320.

COTTESBROOKE HALL, Northamptonshire Situated nine miles slightly north-west of Northampton, just off the road to Husbands Bosworth, it was built for Sir John Langham between 1702 and 1713 (see Nikolaus Pevsner, 1973, *Northamptonshire (Buildings of England* series), Harmondsworth: Penguin, pp. 163–4, Pl. 97).

Mansfield Park in Jane Austen, *Mansfield Park* (1814)

'Mansfield Park was identified . . . by Sir Frank Mackinnon a few years ago, as being a house called Cottesbrooke Hall. . . . In the *Times Literary Supplement* of Dec. 10, 1931, Dr R.W. Chapman published this information. As the estate came into the market in 1935, I . . . induced a neighbour of mine to motor me there to see it. . . . In what we call "reality" . . . the name of the owners of Mansfield Park was Langham. . . . The Hall was built by the fourth Baronet, Sir John Langham. . . . That beautiful and stately house in the great park we visited . . . saw the stairs on which Edmund found the little Fanny weeping, the breakfast room in which she wrote her letter to her brother William, and her room upstairs with its empty grate. Then downstairs we went into the library with the billiard room adjoining, which was the scene of the rehearsal of *Lovers' Vows*. . . . Was Jane Austen ever at Cottesbrooke Hall? There is good reason to believe . . . that she was acquainted with the Sir James Langham of the time, and that her brother, Henry Austen, was familiar with his family. It may be that he supplied her with the necessary plans and information. . . . But anyone who has made this most delightful of all Jane Austen pilgrimages, will find it difficult to believe she had not been there herself, so accurately does she describe all the details' (Logan Pearsall Smith, 1936, *Jane Austen, Reperusals and Recollections*, pp. 368–9 n.). *See also* **Godmersham Park**.

COTTON, George Edward Lynch (1813–66) Educated at Westminster and at Trinity College, Cambridge, from 1852 to 1858 he was Headmaster of Marlborough college and completely reorganized it. Between 1858 and 1866 he was Bishop of Calcutta and established schools in Bengal for the education of the middle classes. He drowned in the Gorai river and his body was never recovered.

The Young Master in Thomas Hughes, *Tom Brown's Schooldays* (1857)

'In the book which beyond any other will keep fresh in the minds of future generations the picture of the school-life at Rugby, it will be remembered that the crisis of the story is brought about by . . . a young master. . . . That "young master" was Cotton' (Sophia Cotton, 1871, *Memoir of George Edward Lynch Cotton, D.D.*, pp. 12–13).

COUGHLIN, Father Charles (b. 1891) Born in Hamilton, Ontario, in 1916 he was ordained as a Roman Catholic priest, becoming a parish priest in Royal

Oak, Michigan, from 1926 to 1966. In 1930 he became a national figure as a broadcaster, and in 1934 launched his own network, the National Union for Social Justice; by 1936 he claimed nine million supporters. He became increasingly anti-Semitic and increasingly hostile to Roosevelt, and by 1941 he was almost pro-Fascist; in 1942 he was forbidden by the Catholic hierarchy to broadcast.

REVD DR LAUGHLIN in Dalton Trumbo, *Washington Jitters* (1936)

'The Rev. Dr Laughlin, founder of the National Association for Just Living . . . [is an obvious caricature] of . . . the Rev. Charles E. Coughlin' (Joseph Blotner, 1966, *The Modern American Political Novel*, Austin, Tex., p. 132).

BISHOP PAUL PRANG in Sinclair Lewis, *It Can't Happen Here* (1935)

Identified in Arthur M. Schlesinger, 1961, *The Politics of Upheaval (The Age of Roosevelt, III)*, p. 89.

COUGHLIN, John He was a Chicago alderman during the 1890s.

MICHAEL TIERNAN in Theodore Dreiser, *The Titan* (1914)

'Among Dreiser's papers are lengthy notes on . . . John Coughlin and Michael . . . Kenna (the Chicago aldermen who are the models for Michael Tiernan and Patrick Kerrigan)' (Richard Lehan, 1974, *Theodore Dreiser: his world and his novels*, Carbondale, Ill.: Arcturis Books, p. 98).

COULON, Auguste Of French origin, he was a jeweller living in Balham, London, in 1894. He was the secret agent particularly connected with Inspector William **Melville**, the officer in charge of the investigations into the **Greenwich Bomb Outrage**. Mrs Helen Angeli remembered him as a 'disgusting looking man . . . [who] was mixed up in a murder and bolted to France' (Norman Sherry, 1971, *Conrad's Western World*, Cambridge, p. 322).

ADOLF VERLOC in Joseph Conrad, *The Secret Agent* (1907)

'The relationship between Melville and Coulon . . . closely parallels that between Heat and Verloc' (ibid., p. 320). *See also* **Krieger**, Adolf P.; **Samuels**, Henry B.

COURNOS, John (1881–1966) American novelist. Born in Russia, he lived in England from 1912 to 1930.

JOHN GOMBAROV in John Cournos, *Miranda Masters* (1926)

'Then Gombarov (Cournos) continues . . .' (Barbara Guest, 1985, *Herself Defined: the poet H.D. and her world*, London: Collins, p. 84; originally published 1984, Garden City, NY: Doubleday).

IVAN LEFSKY in H.D. (Hilda Doolittle), *Bid Me To Live* (1960)

'[Cournos's] hostility towards H.D. is revealed in a letter written in great bitterness over the minor role he is given in H.D.'s *Bid Me to Live*' (J.S. Robinson, 1982, *H.D.: the life and work of an American poet*, Boston, p. 176).

COURTENAY, Louisa (1812–1904) Only daughter of Philip Courtenay (1785–1841), QC and MP for Bridgewater (1837–41), she was described by a cousin as a 'great lady of the old school with a widespread acquaintance amongst the famous people of her day' (*Selected Letters of Sydney Smith*, 1956, ed. Nowell C. Smith, No. 862, p. 292 n. 1).

MISS ISABELLA CURRENT ('AUNT BEL') in George Meredith, *Evan Harrington* (1860)

'She was a friend of Peacock; probably the model for his "Miss Ilex" . . . and certainly for his son-in-law Meredith's "Aunt Bel"' (*Letters*, op. cit.).

MISS ILEX in Thomas Love Peacock, *Gryll Grange* (1860)

See above.

COUTTS, Harriot (1777–1837) Daughter of Matthew Mellon, a lieutenant in the Madras Native Infantry, and Sarah, an Irish cottier's daughter who subsequently became a milliner in Corke and re-married Mr Entwhistle, a strolling player. Harriot joined the troupe as a child and in 1795 made her first appearance on the London stage as Lydia Languish in *The Rivals* at Drury Lane: she was highly successful. In 1805 she was supposed to have become the mistress of Thomas Coutts, and after his first wife died on 4 January 1815, Harriot married him; he died in 1822, leaving his wife as his 'universal legatee'. In 1827 she married William Aubrey de Vere, 9th Duke of St Albans, he being 26 years old and she 50. She was renowned for her liberal charity (details of her will are to be found in the *Annual Register*, 1837, p. 201).

MRS MILLION in Benjamin Disraeli, *Vivian Grey* (1826–7)

Identified as Mrs C. in a key given in *The Star Chamber* (24 May 1826): 114; reprinted in *Vivian Grey*, 1904 (centenary edn), Vol. II, London: Alexander Moring, pp. 361–2. The full name appears on a copy of the key held in the British Museum. Lucien Wolf concludes that Disraeli was not responsible for the key. *See also* **Powles**, John Diston.

COVARRUBIAS, Miguel (1902–57) Mexican artist. He became an acquaintance of D.H. Lawrence during his visit to Mexico City accompanied by Witter Bynner in 1923.

SEÑOR GARCÍA in D.H. Lawrence, *The Plumed Serpent* (1926)

'The young Mexican who was accompanying the party figures in the book as a composite of Covarrubias and a youthful professor. . . . Covarrubias, then a disciple of Rivera, was always stoutly defending his master' (Witter Bynner, 1953, *Journey with Genius*, London and New York: Peter Nevill, p. 30). The youthful professor is not further identified.

COVENTRY, Warwickshire In the early nineteenth century its chief industries were tape-weaving and watch-making.

TREBY MAGNA in George Eliot, *Felix Holt, the Radical* (1866)

'The links between Treby Magna and Coventry are close' (Valentine Cunningham, 1975, *Everywhere Spoken Against: dissent in the Victorian novel*, Oxford: Clarendon Press, p. 183).

MIDDLEMARCH in George Eliot, *Middlemarch* (1871–2)

'Middlemarch is, no doubt, Coventry' (Anna T. Kitchel (ed.), 1950, *Quarry for 'Middlemarch'*, Berkeley and Los Angeles, p. iv; suppl. to *The Nineteenth Century* 4).

COWAP, Mr A chemist in whose shop in Midhurst, Sussex, H.G. Wells worked for a month in 1881.

MR PONDEREVO in H.G. Wells, *Tono-Bungay* (1909)

'I have . . . drawn largely on this shop, and my experiences in it, in describing aunt and uncle Ponderevo. . . . Cowap, like Uncle Ponderevo, really did produce a heartening Cough Linctus' (H.G. Wells, 1934, *Experiment in Autobiography: discoveries and conclusions of a very ordinary brain since 1866*, London: Victor Gollancz, Cresset Press, p. 138).

COWAP, Mrs Wife of the chemist for whom H.G. Wells worked in 1881.

MRS PONDEREVO in H.G. Wells, *Tono-Bungay* (1909)

See under **Cowap**, Mr.

COWARD, Sir Noël Pierce (1899–1973) English actor, dramatist and composer of light music. He began his professional stage career at the age of 14 in *Peter Pan* and subsequently appeared in many plays, often his own, as well as in films. He was the author of several plays, all marked by his gift for witty society dialogue, and also composed music for many revues.

NIGEL FARRADAY in Charles Brackett, *Entirely Surrounded* (1934)

'The scene is our island and all the characters will be painfully recognizable. . . . Thaddeus Hulbert . . . makes his first appearance playing backgammon with an English actor at a party' (to Noël Coward, August 1934, reproduced in *Letters of Alexander Woolcott*, 1946, pp. 109–10). This 'English actor' is easily identifiable as Coward.

NIGEL FLEET in Beverley Nichols, *Death to Slow Music* (1956)

'"Nigel" was wholly based on Noel Coward. . . . He was delighted with the book, presumably because I gave him the star part. I made him the murderer!' (Beverley Nichols to M.C. Rintoul, 17 November 1978).

COWELL, George Weaver. Resident in Preston from the late 1830s, he was a Methodist and teetotaller. In 1848 he played an important part in the Chartist movement in North Lancashire, and with Mortimer **Grimshaw** was one the leaders of the **Preston Strike**. He opened a small shop in Preston, but was involved in the politics of labour until he disappeared from public view in 1861.

NICHOLAS HIGGINS in Elizabeth Gaskell, *North and South* (1855)

'Compared with Dickens [in *Hard Times*], the characters are far more real. Higgins is closer to Cowell than Slackbridge is to Grimshaw' (H.I. Dutton and J.E. King, 1981, *'Ten Per Cent and No Surrender': the Preston Strike, 1853–1854*, p. 200).

COWLISHAW, William Harrison ('Harry') (1870–1957) He married Lucy Garnett, sister of Edward **Garnett**, and in 1896 designed the Garnetts' house, The Cearne, at Limpsfield. He also designed the house of Ford Madox Ford's sister, Katharine Lamb, in County Galway in 1927. Ford Madox Ford shared his flat when visiting London in 1894.

MR MAJOR in Ford Madox Ford, *The Simple Life Limited* (1911)

Identified in Arthur Mizener, 1971, *The Saddest Story: a biography of Ford Madox Ford*, Cleveland: World Publishing, p. 558 n. 12.

COY, Edward Harris (1888–1935) Educated at Yale, he was a superb athlete and footballer. In 1913 he eloped with and married Sophie Meldrim, daughter of General Meldrim, President of the American Bar Association. He entered business, and following his divorce in 1924 he married, in 1925, Jeanne Eagels, the actress who played Sadie Thompson in the New York production of 'Rain'; in 1928 they were divorced and he married Lottie Bruhn. Jeanne Eagels died in 1929 as the result of heroin addiction. He moved to California, and after the Wall Street Crash he was for a short time a Fuller Brush salesman; he went bankrupt in 1933. He died of a heart attack.

TED FAY in F. Scott Fitzgerald, 'The Freshest Boy' (1935)

'As late as 1928, he appeared, barely concealed behind the name Ted Fay . . . in . . . "The Freshest Boy"' (Paul Wagner, 1970, 'I just can't see daylight', in *Fitzgerald/Hemingway Annual*, Washington, DC, p. 62).

COYOACÁN, Mexico A village to the south of Mexico City in the 1920s.

TLACOLULA in D.H. Lawrence, *The Plumed Serpent* (1926)

'Fictional name for Coyoacán' (*The Plumed Serpent*, 1983, ed. Ronald G. Walker, Harmondsworth: Penguin, p. 485 n. 4).

CRADDOCK, Mr

BENJAMIN LANDOR in 'Janet's Repentance', and MR PHIPPS in 'The Sad Fortunes of the Revd Amos Barton', both in George Eliot, *Scenes of Clerical Life* (1857–8)

See under **Anstruther**, Lady.

CRADDOCK, Mrs

MRS WOODCOCK in George Eliot, 'The Sad Fortunes of the Revd Amos Barton', *Scenes of Clerical Life* (1857–8)

See under **Anstruther**, Lady.

CRADOCK, Harriet (1809–84) Daughter of Thomas Lister of Armitage Park, Staffordshire, she was the half-sister of T.H. Lister. In 1837–44 she was Maid of

Honour to Queen Victoria, being the only maid of honour in the Queen's reign who was neither the daughter nor the granddaughter of a peer. In 1844 she married her cousin the Revd E.H. Grove, who in 1849 changed his name to Cradock and was Principal of Brasenose College, Oxford, in 1852–86. She was the author of a number of novels, and died at Cowley Park, near Oxford.

LAETITIA DARCY in Mrs Humphry Ward, *Robert Elsmere* (1888)

'She was a poignant conversationalist and observer of books, men and company. Mr Jowett delighted in her society and inscribed some lines in her album about the bee which, though small in size, is great in energies. Afterwards she figures in *Robert Elsmere'* (Walter Sichel, 1923, *The Sands of Time*, p. 131).

CRAIG, Edward Gordon (1872–1966) Actor and stage designer. Son of Ellen Terry and E.W. Godwin, the architect, in 1889–98 he acted with Irving's company at the Lyceum Theatre, London. In 1903 he abandoned acting and became a designer and producer, working in Berlin, in Florence with Duse, and in Russia with the Moscow Art Theatre. In 1908 he settled in Florence. He had an immense influence on theatrical production in Europe and America.

CHARLES MANN in Gilbert Cannan, *Mummery* (1916)

'[T]he scene designer in [this novel] is clearly based on Gordon Craig, whom Gilbert had met before the war. . . . I doubt that anyone has given us a better picture of Gordon Craig' (Diana Farr, 1978, *Gilbert Cannan: a Georgian prodigy*, London: Chatto & Windus, p. 164).

CRAIG, Captain James (1854–1929) In 1886 he became Master of the *Vidar* based in Singapore and sailing under the Dutch flag. Conrad signed on as a mate in August 1887 and made five or six voyages with the ship.

CAPTAIN FORD in Joseph Conrad, *Almayer's Folly* (1895)

'Another figure who apparently stood for a thumbnail sketch ... was the Captain of the *Vidar*, who appeared as Captain Ford. . . . From an inadvertent reference in one of Conrad's letters he can be identified as Captain Craig' (J.D. Gordan, 1941, *Joseph Conrad: the making of a novelist*, Cambridge, Mass., pp. 46–7).

CRAIGHALL, Perthshire Seat of the Ratray family. Scott visited it in 1792 with William **Clerk**, a connection of the Ratrays.

TULLY-VEOLAN in Sir Walter Scott, *Waverley* (1814)

'From the position of this striking place, as Mr Clerk at once perceived, and as the author afterwards confessed to him, that of Tully-Veolan was very faithfully copied' (J.G. Lockhart, 1900, *Memoirs of Sir Walter Scott*, Vol. I, London: Macmillan, p. 183). *See also* **Ravelston House**.

CRANBORNE, Dorset A small market town south of the Blandford–Salisbury road east of the Pentridge Hills.

CHASEBOROUGH in Thomas Hardy, Wessex novels and tales (1871–95)

Identified on a map prepared by Thomas Hardy which hangs in the Dorset County Museum, Dorchester. *See under* **Abbotsbury**.

CRANE, Stephen (1871–1900) American author. He lived in England in 1897–8 and 1899, becoming friendly with Joseph **Conrad**, H.G. **Wells** and others.

MR HANGBIRD in Ford Madox Ford, *The Simple Life Limited* (1911)

Identified in Arthur Mizener, 1971, *The Saddest Story: a biography of Ford Madox Ford*, Cleveland: World Publishing, p. 558 n. 12.

WILLIAM HAWKER in Stephen Crane, *The Third Violet* (1897)

'When they came to write autobiographical fiction ... Crane and Dreiser portrayed themselves as artists, not writers, in the nineties' (Ellen Moers, 1970, *Two Dreisers*, London: Thames & Hudson, p. 42; originally published 1969, New York: Viking). Crane's autobiographical novel is identified as *The Third Violet* (1897) (see ibid., p. 326 n. 21).

CRAPSEY, Adelaide (1874–1914) American poet. Daughter of Algernon Sidney Crapsey, an Episcopal clergyman of Rochester, New York, who in 1906 was deposed from the ministry for heresy (he was a Christian Socialist, but his heresy apparently consisted in denying the Virgin birth). She was educated at Vassar, where she formed a close friendship with Jean Webster which lasted to the end of her life. She taught at Smith College, Northampton. She was deeply interested in problems of metre and invented the 'cinquain'. Her only book of verse (*Verse*) was edited by Jean Webster and published posthumously. She died of tuberculosis.

JERUSHA ('JUDY') ABBOTT in Jean Webster, *Daddy Long-Legs* (1912)

'She had as a room-mate [at Vassar] Jean Webster. ... Much later, Jean Webster said that she had had Adelaide in mind while she was writing *Daddy Long-Legs*, and this is probably true of many of the "Patty" sketches as well' (M.E. Osborn, 1933, *Adelaide Crapsey*, Boston, Mass., p. 28).

CRAWFORD, Fleury A prostitute in Dublin in the early years of the twentieth century.

FLORRY TALBOT in James Joyce, *Ulysses* (1922)

'[Mrs Bella Cohen's] girls were probably modelled on contemporary prostitutes. Florry Talbot, for instance, was probably Fleury Crawford' (Richard Ellmann, 1982, *James Joyce*, rev. edn, Oxford: Oxford University Press, p. 368).

CRAWFORD, George Malcolm (1816–85) Born at Chelsfield Court Lodge, he inherited enormous debts upon the death of his father. A barrister from 1837 to 1850, in 1853 he succeeded Scurlle Morton as the Paris correspondent of the *Daily News*, retaining this appointment until his death. He was an intimate of the statesman Thiers and the politician Gambetta, and died as a result of a wasp sting.

GEORGE WARRINGTON in W.M. Thackeray, *The History of Pendennis* (1848–50)

'There is something of you in Warrington, but he is not fit to hold a candle to you' (Thackeray to G.M. Crawford, December 1850, in a letter sent with a presentation copy of *Pendennis*, reproduced in *The Letters and Private Papers of W.M. Thackeray*, 1945, ed. Gordon N. Ray, Vol. II, London: Oxford University Press, pp. 721–2). *See also* **Venables**, G.S.

CRAWFURD, Oswald (1834–1909) Diplomat and literary figure of the 1890s. In 1894 he was Chairman of the Board of Directors of Chapman and Hall, publishers of several of his books. In 1890 he met Violet Hunt, with whom he had a love affair, and in 1892, at his home, Ada Leverson first met Oscar Wilde. His wife died in 1899 and in 1902 he married Lita Bronne, daughter of Hermann von Flesch Branninjen.

ROBERT ASSHETON in Violet Hunt, *Sooner or Later* (1904)

'The equivalent of Willy [Colette's first husband] in Violet's life was a married man of . . . "good social position". He also had literary tastes . . . when he was free to marry again he did not marry Violet, who loved him tenaciously, but someone else. . . . [He was] the "Robert Assheton" of *Sooner or Later* [and] died in Switzerland, at Clarens, though not before he had contributed an article to *The English Review*' (Douglas Goldring, 1943, *South Lodge*, pp. 80–1). Crawfurd in fact died at Montreux.

CREAGHE, Dr Originally from Dublin, in the 1890s he started a doctor's practice in a slum district in Sheffield, where he led a 'No Rent Campaign' among his neighbours, 'who took it up eagerly'; he carried a personal banner inscribed 'No God nor Master' to meetings. He edited and published the *Sheffield Anarchist* until, failing to make a living in Sheffield, he moved to London and then emigrated to Argentina. He settled in Buenos Aires, where he set up another paper, *La Protesta*. As an old man he took part in the revolt of the peons in Mexico in 1907.

THE PROFESSOR in Joseph Conrad, *The Secret Agent* (1907)

'Conrad's Professor could well be based on some aspects of Creaghe's history and character' (Norman Sherry, 1971, *Conrad's Western World*, Cambridge, p. 431 n. 12). *See also* **Dillon**, Luke; **Mezzeroff**, 'Professor'; **Most**, Johann; **Rossetti**, Arthur.

CRICHTON, Charles

LORD PETER WIMSEY in Dorothy L. Sayers, *Murder Must Advertise* (1933)

See under **Whelpton**, Eric.

CROCKETT, Samuel Rutherford (1859–1914) Scottish popular novelist. Educated at Edinburgh University and New College, Edinburgh, he became a Free Church minister. After some popular success he resigned the ministry to become a full-time writer in 1895. He was a writer of the so-called 'kailyard school', along with Ian Maclaren and J.M. Barrie, whose books tended to promote a sentimental image of small-town life in Scotland.

CALLAN in Joseph Conrad and Ford Madox Ford, *The Inheritors* (1901)

Identified in Jocelyn Baines, 1967, *Joseph Conrad: a critical biography*, rev. edn, London: Weidenfeld & Nicolson, p. 239; originally published 1960.

CROCKFORD, William (1775–1844) Starting life as a fishmonger, in 1827 he set up Crockford's Club, nextdoor to **White's Club** in St James's Street, London, and in a few years amassed a fortune of £1,200,000.

GENERAL ARTHUR FENTIMAN in Dorothy L. Sayers, *The Unpleasantness at the Bellona Club* (1928)

'The circumstances of Mr Crockford's death inspired Dorothy Sayers to write . . . *The Unpleasantness at the Bellona Club*. The old man was left sitting in his favourite chair for all to see as if he were alive when he had died a day earlier. Large sums had been wagered on his horse in the Derby and it would have been a disaster for backers if the colt had been compulsorily scratched owing to his owner's death' (Edward Mayer, 1977, 'Crockford's: the rise and fall of a card club', *The Times* (29 August): 6). 'Disraeli in "Sybil" [1845] has painted to the life the scene in the rooms, on the eve of the Derby, when Rat-trap was favourite and Caravan was fancied' (A.I. Shand, 1897, 'Lord Alvanley', *Cornhill Magazine* (NS) 3 (August): 165). Disraeli gives the rooms no name. (Caravan, owned by Lord Suffield, came second in the Derby in 1837; Lord Berners's brown colt Phosphorus landed the race in the last two or three strides.)

BOND SHARPE in Benjamin Disraeli, *Henrietta Temple* (1837)

'[T]here is Mr Bond Sharpe, apparently drawn from Crockford' (W.F. Monypenny, 1910, *The Life of Benjamin Disraeli, Earl of Beaconsfield*, Vol. I, London: John Murray, p. 343).

CROFTS, William Carr (1846–1912) Born in Hampstead, London, he was the son of a barrister and educated at Bedford School and at Merton and Brasenose Colleges, Oxford, where he was Captain of the College Eight rowing team and twice won the Diamond Sculls. He gained a third in Greats, his course at Oxford. He taught in a preparatory school before joining United Services College at Westward Ho!, in 1875, where he was Senior Classics Master and taught Latin and English Literature to Kipling, **Dunsterville** and **Beresford**; Kipling later sent him copies of all publications and newspaper cuttings from India. He resigned in 1892 over differences with Cornell **Price** about the management of the school, and thenceforward moved from post to post as a private tutor and as a partner in Lunn's travel agency. He settled in lodgings in Sark, where he was drowned while swimming in November, it being his practice to bathe throughout the year.

MR KING in Rudyard Kipling, *Stalky & Co.* (1899)

'"King" is . . . chiefly built upon William Crofts . . . it was Crofts who guided Kipling's taste in English Literature' (Charles Carrington, 1955, *Rudyard Kipling: his life and work*, pp. 32–3). Also identified in the caption to a photograph reproduced in the June 1981 issue of *The Kipling Journal*: 'Masters at the United Services College . . . in Kipling's day' (*The Kipling Journal* 48 (218): 21). *See also* **Haslam**, F.W.

CROKER, John Wilson (1780–1857) Reviewer for the *Quarterly Review*, he was also author of the notoriously hostile review of Keats's *Endymion* in 1818. From 1809 he was Secretary to the Admiralty, and he coined the term 'Conservative'. He was the friend and factotum of the 3rd Marquis of Hertford, who bequeathed to him £20,000 and the contents of his cellar.

CONWAY TOWNSEND CRAWLEY in Lady Morgan, *Florence Macarthy* (1818)

'Lady Morgan depicted him in . . . *Florence Macarthy* as Councillor Crawley' (Frederic Boase, *Modern English Biography*).

MR KILLTHEDEAD in Thomas Love Peacock, *Melincourt* (1817)

'Based upon John Wilson Croker' (*The Novels of T.L. Peacock*, 1948, ed. David Garnett, London: Rupert Hart-Davis, p. 260 n. 2). *See also* **Barrow**, Sir John.

MONSIEUR LA CROASSE in Lord Brougham, *Albert Lunel* (1844)
Identified in Brougham's hand in the copy of *Albert Lunel* belonging to Michael Sadleir, formerly in the possession of Frederick Locker, and clearly originally Brougham's own copy.

NICHOLAS RIGBY in Benjamin Disraeli, *Coningsby* (1844)

Identified in a key in *Notes and Queries* (8th series) 3 (13 May 1893): 363. In 1849 Disraeli found himself sitting next to Croker at a public dinner. He wrote: '. . . Mr Croker and myself were not socially acquainted. I had never seen him since I was a boy. Nor was he the person, who ought to assume, that a character in one of my books, which he deemed odious, was intended for himself. He behaved like a man of the world . . . I treated him with great consideration, & spoke enough, but not too much, & took care never to break into cordiality, which I should have done under ordinary circumstances with so eminent [a] man, met under such conditions' (*Disraeli's Reminiscences*, 1975, ed. Helen M. Swartz and Marvin Swartz, London: Hamilton, p. 39).

VIVIDA VIS in Benjamin Disraeli, *Vivian Grey* (1826–7)

Identified as J.W. C——, Esq. in a key given in *The Star Chamber* (24 May 1826): 114; reprinted in *Vivian Grey*, 1904 (centenary edn), ed. Lucien Wolf, Vol. II, London: Alexander Moring, pp. 361–2. The full name appeared in a reprint of the key published in *Notes and Queries* 3 (29 April 1893). Lucien Wolf concludes that Disraeli was not responsible for the key.

MR WENHAM in W.M. Thackeray, *Vanity Fair* (1847–8) and *The History of Pendennis* (1848–50)

'Croker [reappears] as the sycophant Wenham' (Malcolm Elwin, 1932, *Thackeray: a personality*, p. 124).

CROSBIE, Andrew (1735–85) Scottish advocate. He was recognized as one of the most eloquent pleaders of the time, but he took to drink and dissipation and died in solitary poverty.

PAUL PLEYDELL in Sir Walter Scott, *Guy Mannering* (1815)

'We feel no little pleasure in presenting the original of a character so important as . . . Pleydell. He is understood to be the representative of Mr Andrew Crosbie'

(Robert Chambers, 1884, *Illustrations of the Characters of Waverley*, p. 32). This identification has been widely accepted; however, 'as Crosbie had been dead thirty years before the novel was published, Scott cannot have known him personally' (*The Letters of Sir Walter Scott*, Vol. V: *1817–1819*, 1933, ed. H.J.C. Grierson, Vol. V, London: Constable, p. 251 n. 1). *See also* **Rolland**, Adam.

CROSBY, Enoch (1750–1835) A New England shoemaker who served George Washington as a spy in the American War of Independence, working for the statesman John Jay's Committee of Safety.

HARVEY BIRCH in James Fenimore Cooper, *The Spy* (1821)

'A gentleman of good standing . . . who has long enjoyed the friendship . . . of Mr Cooper, informed the writer . . . on the authority of Mr Cooper himself, that the *outline* of the character of Harvey Birch, was actually sketched from that of Enoch Crosby . . . [and] we think no one can peruse the following pages without being convinced that Enoch Crosby was the original model from which that character was formed. It is highly probable, however, that Mr Cooper never saw Crosby. . . . But . . . we understand it was at Mr Jay's residence that . . . *The Spy* was first conceived. . . . This venerable patriot . . . could furnish Mr Cooper with every requisite material for the character of Harvey Birch' (H.L. Barnum, 1828, *The Spy Unmasked; or Memoirs of Enoch Crosby, alias Harvey Birch . . . being an authentic account of the secret services which he rendered his country during the Revolutionary War* (taken from his own lips, in shorthand), New York, pp. ix–xi).

CROSBY, Harry (1898–1929) Born in Boston, he was the nephew of the financier J.P. Morgan and the cousin of Walter van Rensselaer **Berry**. From 1917 to 1918 he served in France in the American Field Service Ambulance Corps and was awarded the Croix de Guerre. In 1922 he married Polly, the divorced wife of Richard Peabody (she was known as Caresse Crosby), and from then on lived in Paris. He founded Black Sun Press and published D.H. **Lawrence** and Hart Crane. He was contributor to *Transition*, and in 1929 became Assistant Editor. He was rich, a poet and a womanizer, and on 10 December 1929, in New York, he shot and killed his mistress and himself instead of going to tea with J.P. Morgan.

ANTONY LISTER in Kay Boyle, *My Next Bride* (1934)

'*My Next Bride*, Kay Boyle's novel about Harry, was . . . dedicated to Caresse. . . . In it a young lady much like Miss Boyle is subjected to the generosities and eccentricities of a would-be painter, Antony Lister, who has too much money for his own good and kills himself in New York' (Geoffrey Woolff, 1977, *Black Sun: the brief transit and violent eclipse of Harry Crosby*, p. 299 n.)

CROSS, John Walter (1840–1924) Banker. He first met George Eliot when she was in Rome with G.H. **Lewes** in 1869, three months before she began work on *Middlemarch*. By 1872 he was in charge of their investments and business affairs and he became a close friend of the family, being referred to as 'Nephew'. He was at Lewes's bedside the day before his death in 1878, and in May 1880 he married George Eliot; he was the author of *Life of George Eliot*.

WILL LADISLAW in George Eliot, *Middlemarch* (1871–2)

'In Ladislaw, a fantasy of middle age, indulged because innocuous, the character is deprived of her usual controls. She allows herself to idealize him ... the new image of Ladislaw took her unawares, as a result of the luxuriantly fantasied encounter in Rome with her young admirer and future husband' (Richard Ellmann, 1973, 'Dorothea's husbands', in *Golden Codgers*, London: Oxford University Press, p. 16).

CROWLEY, Aleister (1875–1947) Originally Edward Alexander, he was a writer on and dabbler in the occult. He was expelled from the occultist Order of the Golden Dawn, of which W.B. **Yeats** was also a member, and founded his own order, the Silver Star. He was later expelled from Italy because of rumours about his unorthodox practices. He married Rose Kelly (**Crowley**, below) in 1903 and was a close friend of Gerald Hamilton, with whom he at one time shared a flat in Berlin.

J. CRONSHAW in W. Somerset Maugham, *Of Human Bondage* (1915)

'That weird charlatan ... Aleister Crowley, later to be immortalized as Cronshaw' (Richard A. Cordell, 1969, *Somerset Maugham: a writer for all seasons*, Bloomington and London: Indiana University Press, p. 32). *See also* **Morrice**, James Wilson.

OLIVER HADDO in W. Somerset Maugham, *The Magician* (1908)

'Though Aleister Crowley served ... as the model for Oliver Haddo, it is by no means a portrait of him.... Crowley, however, recognized himself... and wrote a full-page review of the novel in *Vanity Fair*, which he signed "Oliver Haddo"' (W. Somerset Maugham, 1956, 'A fragment of autobiography', preface to *The Magician* (collected edn), p. x). 'Oliver Haddo is very closely modelled on Crowley; almost the only physical difference is that he is much taller. Otherwise he is Crowley to the life, though viewed sensationally' (Maurice Richardson, 1978, 'The mystic Mountebank' (review of a reprint of *The Magician*), *Times Literary Supplement* (26 May): 577). The article contains an account of the three occasions on which Richardson met Crowley, once in the company of Gerald Hamilton.

DR TRELAWNEY in Anthony Powell, *A Dance to the Music of Time* (1951–76)

'Is not that prophet of the higher life, Dr Trelawney ... is he not Aleister Crowley?' (Julian Symons, 1966, *Critical Occasions*, London, pp. 76–7).

CROWLEY, Rose (d. 1932) Sister of Sir Gerald **Kelly**, in 1903 she married Aleister **Crowley** within two weeks of meeting him; they divorced in 1909 and she married Dr Goymley.

MARGARET DAUNCEY in W. Somerset Maugham, *The Magician* (1908)

'*The Magician*, said Sir Gerald [Kelly], was basically the story of [the marriage between Rose Kelly and Aleister Crowley] ... and of the strange domination of Crowley over his future wife' (R.L. Calder, 1972, *W. Somerset Maugham and the Quest for Freedom*, London: Heinemann, p. 75).

CROWN INN, Marnhull, Dorset

THE PURE DROP INN, MARLOTT, in Thomas Hardy, Wessex novels and tales (1871–95)

'This was Hardy's fictional name for the Crown Inn' (D.F. Barber, 1968, *Concerning Thomas Hardy*, p. 127 n. 1). The inn appears to have been commonly known by Hardy's fictional name. Thus, Hardy's chauffeur H.L. Voes wrote: 'The "Pure Drop" at Marnhull was an inn for which he had great fondness. Even if we did not enter for a meal I always had to stop and look at it' (ibid.).

CUCKFIELD PLACE, Sussex Situated west of Haywards Heath, now Cuckfield Park, it was originally Elizabethan (see Nikolaus Pevsner, 1970, *Sussex* (*Buildings of England* series), Harmondsworth: Penguin, pp. 478–9).

ROOKWOOD HALL in W. Harrison Ainsworth, *Rookwood: A Romance* (1834)

'[Cuckfield Place] is the real Rookwood Hall. . . . The general features of the venerable structure . . . are carefully delineated with, I think, entire accuracy' (W.H. Ainsworth, quoted in S.M. Ellis, 1911, *William Harrison Ainsworth and His Friends*, Vol. I, p. 232).

CUDLIPP, Annie Ericsson Assistant Editor on the *Delineator* in 1909 when Dreiser was Managing Editor. She was the mother of Thelma **Cudlipp** and was violently opposed to Dreiser's affair with her daughter, which she succeeded in breaking up by reporting it to the directors of Butterick. She committed suicide.

EMILY DALE in Theodore Dreiser, *The 'Genius'* (1915)

'As Mrs Dale kidnaps Suzanne . . . Mrs Cudlipp kidnapped Thelma'(Richard Lehan, 1974, *Theodore Dreiser: his world and his novels*, Carbondale, Ill.: Arcturis Books, p. 126).

CUDLIPP, Thelma (b. 1893?) Dreiser fell violently in love with her in 1909, but in 1910 she was moved to England by her mother, Annie Ericsson **Cudlipp**, and in 1918 she married Edwin Grosvenor, a distinguished lawyer. Her husband died in 1930, and in 1933 she married Charles Seymour Whitman, who had been Governor of New York in 1915–18; he died in 1947.

SUZANNE DALE in Theodore Dreiser, *The 'Genius'* (1915)

'In *The "Genius"* Dreiser faithfully rendered his love affair with Thelma Cudlipp, even to the extent of using the same letters he wrote Thelma' (Richard Lehan, 1974, *Theodore Dreiser: his world and his novels*, Carbondale, Ill.: Arcturis Books, p. 126).

CULLEN, Florence ('Flossie') (1879–1924) Daughter of George **Cullen**.

ALVINA HOUGHTON in D.H. Lawrence, *The Lost Girl* (1920)

'The Alvina Houghton of the novel . . . was also taken from life: at least the outward circumstances of her existence were. Like Alvina Florence (Flossie) Cullen became a nurse' (H.T. Moore, 1960, *The Intelligent Heart: the story of D.H. Lawrence*, Harmondsworth: Penguin, pp. 49–50; originally published 1955,

London: Heinemann). 'Although Lawrence drew so much on fact, Alvina is his own creation' (Ada Lawrence and G. Stuart Gelder, 1931, *Young Lorenzo: early Life of D.H. Lawrence*, Florence, p. 274).

CULLEN, George (1845–1915) Draper, mine owner and cinema proprietor. He was the owner of London House, Nottingham Road, Eastwood, when D.H. Lawrence lived there as a boy and a young man.

JAMES HOUGHTON in D.H. Lawrence, *The Lost Girl* (1920)

'James Haughton [sic] was George Cullen, a remarkable man whose ideas of clothing were quite foreign to those of the miners and their wives' (Ada Lawrence and G. Stuart Gelder, 1931, *Young Lorenzo: early Life of D.H. Lawrence*, Florence, p. 273).

CULLEN, Father James A. He was in charge of the retreat at Belvedere that began on 30 November 1896.

PREACHER AT THE RETREAT in James Joyce, *A Portrait of the Artist as a Young Man* (1916)

'In identifying Father Cullen as the preacher of the sermons in the retreat Thomas Bodkin says: "Father Cullen's phrasing was characteristic. . . . He had a habit of addressing his congregation as 'my dear little brothers in Jesus Christ', which always struck me as a repellent mode of address"' (Richard Ellmann, 1982, *James Joyce*, rev. edn, Oxford: Oxford University Press, pp. 48–9 n.).

CULLEN, Lucy (1836–1904) Born in Loughborough, Leicestershire, she married George **Cullen** *c.*1867. She died after a long illness.

CLARISS HOUGHTON in D.H. Lawrence, *The Lost Girl* (1920)

'Clariss Houghton is DHL's recreation of Mrs Lucy Cullen' (*The Lost Girl*, 1981, ed. John Worthen, p. 362 n. 2:35).

CUMMINGS, Edith Of Chicago. Both her father, Mark, and her brother, Dexter, were distinguished golf players, and in 1923 she won the Women's Golf Championship of the United States. There is a portrait of her in H.B. Martin, 1936, *Fifty Years of American Golf*, New York, facing p. 351. She was a schoolfriend of Ginevra **King**.

JORDAN BAKER in F. Scott Fitzgerald, *The Great Gatsby* (1925)

'Jordan of course was a great idea (perhaps you know its Edith Cummings)' (to Max Perkins, 20 December 1924, reproduced in *Dear Scott/Dear Max: the Fitzgerald–Perkins correspondence*, 1971, ed. John Kuehl and Jackson R. Bryer, New York, p. 90).

CUMNOR, Oxfordshire A village to the west of Oxford.

LUMSDON in Thomas Hardy, *Jude the Obscure* (1895)

Identified in Denys Kay-Robinson, 1972, *Hardy's Wessex Reappraised*, Newton Abbot, and in F.B. Pinion, 1968, *A Hardy Companion*, London: Macmillan.

CUNARD, Maud ('Emerald'), Lady Born in San Francisco, she married Sir Bache Cunard and was the mother of Nancy **Cunard**. She became a close friend of George Moore, the novelist, and of the conductor Sir Thomas Beecham. She was a known hostess and a patron of the arts, particularly music.

MRS MAISIE WELLESLEY-CROOK in Wyndham Lewis, *The Roaring Queen* (1973)

'It seems to me likely that many hostesses went to her making. Part of her, though, is probably derived ... from ... Lady Cunard' (Walter Allen, 1973, Introd. to *The Roaring Queen*, p. 20).

CUNARD, Nancy (1896–1965) Poet. Daughter of Sir Bache Cunard and Maud ('Emerald') **Cunard**, although many people thought that her real father was George Moore, the novelist. One of the Bright Young Things, she was a passionate anti-fascist and spent much of her time in France, at one time being the mistress of Louis Aragon, the French communist poet and novelist.

BABY BUCKTROUT in Wyndham Lewis, *The Roaring Queen* (1973)

'According to Mrs Wyndham Lewis, in a letter to the present publisher, "Nancy Cunard was the main figure in the book." By this I assume she means Baby Bucktrout ... but whether one would have spotted Baby as Nancy Cunard without Mrs Lewis' word for it I do not know' (Walter Allen, 1973, Introd. to *The Roaring Queen*, pp. 17–18).

IRIS MARCH in Michael Arlen, *The Green Hat* (1924)

'In [*The Green Hat*] Miss Cunard appeared as Iris March' (Hugh Ford (ed.), 1968, *Nancy Cunard*, p. 60). *See also* **Twysden**, Lady.

LUCY TANTAMOUNT in Aldous Huxley, *Point Counter Point* (1928)

'... there again are the shades of Nancy Cunard whom this time he did not attempt to do at all, Lucy Tantamount is any stylized siren of the 1920s; what he did was the tale ... of a young man's unrequited physical passion for a woman he dislikes' (Sybille Bedford, 1973, *Aldous Huxley*, Vol. I, London: Chatto & Windus, p. 202). '[Maria] minded *Point Counter Point* – his killing the child – it was all too lifelike and horrible – and the love affair with Lucy was A's affair with N.C. I think Maria hardly forgives it' (D.H. Lawrence to E.H. Brewster, winter 1928, quoted in Bedford, op. cit., p. 207).

CONSTANCE TOWNSEND in Richard Aldington, 'Now Lies She There', *Soft Answers* (1932)

In her introduction to the Virago edition of H.D.'s *Bid Me To Live* (1984), Helen McNeil says (p. x) that Lady Cunard was crudely satirized in *Soft Answers*. Much cruder, crueller and more obvious is the portrait of her daughter in the same story.

MYRA VIVEASH in Aldous Huxley, *Antic Hay* (1923)

In 1922 or thereabouts Huxley had fallen in love with Nancy Cunard, whom he had known since 1917; the affair seems to have lasted about 6 months, until brought abruptly to an end by Maria who carried him off to Italy at 12 hours' notice. 'They [Aldous and Maria Huxley] went straight to Italy. There ... Aldous wrote *Antic Hay*. He wrote it all down, Maria said, he wrote it all out;

it was over' (Bedford, op. cit., p. 138). 'But *is* . . . Myra Viveash really in the least like Nancy? . . . Mrs Viveash has been given Nancy's voice and Nancy's walk . . . there is also a version of the famous *regard* . . . yet Mrs Viveash is . . . Nancy Cunard . . . turned into a type' (ibid., pp. 143–4).

CUNNINGHAM, Revd J.W. (1780–1861) Known as 'Velvet Cunningham' in reference to his book of verse, *The Velvet Cushion* (1810, 10th edn 1816), he was educated at St John's College, Cambridge. He was Curate of Clapham until 1811, and was then Vicar of Harrow until he died. He was a prominent Evangelical, and Fitzjames Stephen, the jurist, was his son-in-law.

Revd William Jacob Cartwright in Frances Trollope, *The Vicar of Wrexhill* (1840)

'More than one view was expressed about the character of Fitzjames's father-in-law. Fanny Trollope savagely caricatured him in *The Vicar of Wrexhill*' (Noel Annan, 1951, *Leslie Stephen*, p. 51 n.).

CUNNINGHAM, Marjorie (d. 1941) Head of the German department at Royal Holloway College in 1900–6, she was subsequently Warden of Trinity Hall, Dublin.

Miss Dorrington in I. Compton-Burnett, *Dolores* (1911)

Identified in a key given in the back of a copy of *Dolores*, signed 'H.M. Cam, 1912' in the front (Dr Helen Cam was a student at Holloway in Ivy Compton-Burnett's last two years there). The key was printed in Hilary Spurling, 1974, *Ivy When Young: the early life of I. Compton Burnett, 1884–1919*, London: Gollancz, App. II, p. 280.

CUNNINGHAME GRAHAM, Robert Bontine (1852–1936) Scottish politician and author. Son of a Scottish laird, he was the leader of the dock strike in 1887. He was an anarchist and travelled extensively, particularly in Latin America. He became a lifelong friend of Joseph Conrad after writing him an enthusiastic letter in 1897 upon the publication of 'An outpost of progress'.

Charles Gould in Joseph Conrad, *Nostromo* (1904)

'There are certain parallels between Charles Gould and R.B. Cunninghame Graham which tempt one to suggest that Conrad had his friend in mind as a model for this character' (Norman Sherry, 1971, *Conrad's Western World*, Cambridge, p. 149).

CURLEY, James Michael (1874–1958) Politician. Born in Boston, Massachusetts he was the child of Irish immigrants. After entering politics in 1898, he was elected Mayor of Boston three times and to Congress twice, and became Governor of Massachusetts in 1934. He was constantly accused of corruption and was charged and convicted twice. A progressive administrator, as mayor during the 1920s his social legislation anticipated the New Deal.

Francis Skeffington in Edwin O'Connor, *The Last Hurrah* (1956)

'Almost every commentator on this novel has remarked that Skeffington and his city appear to be based upon . . . Curley . . . and Boston' (Joseph Blotner, 1966, *The Modern American Political Novel*, Austin, Tex., p. 82 n. 48).

CURRAN, Constantine P. (b. 1883) He was a contemporary at University College, Dublin, and lifelong friend of James Joyce. In later life he was Registrar of the Supreme Court.

GABRIEL CONROY in James Joyce, 'The Dead', *Dubliners* (1914)

'For Gabriel's personality there is among Joyce's friends another model. This was Constantine Curran, nicknamed "Cautious Con"' (Richard Ellmann, 1982, *James Joyce*, Oxford: Oxford University Press, p. 247). *See also* **Joyce**, John Stanislaus.

DONOVAN in James Joyce, *A Portrait of the Artist as a Young Man* (1916)

'Constantine P. Curran was goodhearted and controlled; Joyce granted his cleverness as well. *A Portrait* represents him as interested in food (he was inclined to be fat)' (Ellmann, op. cit., p. 63). Mr Ellmann does not in so many words identify Donovan with Curran, but the identification seems clear from this quotation.

CURRIE, John (1884–1914) Portrait painter. He murdered his mistress and then committed suicide.

JAMES LOGAN in Gilbert Cannan, *Mendel* (1916)

See under **Lawrence**, D.H.

CURRIE, Mary, Lady (1843–1905) Writer of verse under the pseudonym of 'Violet Fane'. She was the daughter of Sir Charles Lamb of Beauport Park in Sussex by a disastrous marriage with Charlotte Gray, daughter of a Chichester draper; Lamb was the half-brother of Lord Eglinton and was a deeply chivalrous young man, who took part in the **Eglinton Tournament** and had rescued his bride from the clutches of her employer, an Indian rajah, who was determined to seduce her. In 1864 Mary married Henry Singleton, but by 1877 she had become the mistress of Philip Currie, whom she married in 1893, after Singleton's death. In 1880 she had a brief, violent affair with Wilfrid Scawen **Blunt** which inspired some of his *Love Sonnets of Proteus* (1881). Maurice **Baring**, who had been Third Secretary at the Embassy in Rome under Philip Currie, said of her 'she had a quiet, plaintive, half-deprecating way of saying the slyest, and sometimes the most enormous things' (*The Puppet Show of Memory*, 1922, London: Heinemann, p. 246).

MRS SINCLAIR in W.H. Mallock, *The New Republic* (1877)

'Mrs Sinclair was the beautiful "Violet Fane". . . . She was perfect in features, slight as a sylph in figure, and her large dark eyes alternately gleamed with laughter and were vague as though she was listening for a voice from some vague beyond' (W.H. Mallock, 1920, *Memoirs of Life and Literature*, London: Chapman and Hall, pp. 65, 96).

CURTIS, Jack Painter. Son of Daniel Curtis, the owner of the Palazzo **Barbaro**, he was an American and painted Venetian and oriental genre subjects, and during 1881–96 he exhibited in Paris, Florence, Venice and London. He married Lise Rotch, née Colt, and settled at Beaulieu. He was a close friend of Sargent.

JACK GISBURN in Edith Wharton, 'The Verdict', *The Hermit and the Wild Woman* (1908)

'"The Verdict" has to do with a popular American painter who . . . accepts the fact that he is no more than second-rate, marries a rich widow, and settles down to . . . life on the French Riviera. This was almost a point-by-point replica of . . . Ralph Curtis. . . . [His wife], who could hardly have been pleased by the portrait of her as a woman of beaming stupidity, took enduring offense' (R.W.B. Lewis, 1975, *Edith Wharton: a biography*, London: Constable, p. 193).

CURTIS, O'Leary (d. late 1920s) A Dublin newspaper man who was known to James and Stanislaus Joyce in 1904. 'Gogarty calls O'Leary Curtis "the Japanese Jesus"' (*The Complete Dublin Diary of Stanislaus Joyce*, 1971, ed. George H. Healey, Ithaca and London: Cornell University Press, p. 13).

O'MADDEN BURKE in James Joyce, 'A Mother', *Dubliners* (1914) and *Ulysses* (1922)

'Curtis . . . is the O'Madden Burke of "The Mother" in *Dubliners* and of the "Aeolus" episode in *Ulysses*' (ibid. p. 13 n. 4).

CURTISS, Mina Kirstein Associate Professor of English at Smith College, Massachusetts. She was the daughter of a successful Boston businessman and was the sister of Lincoln Kirstein, the founder (and Editor) of the literary periodical *Hound and Horn* and founder of the School of American Ballet in 1933. She was a friend of Aline **Bernstein** and met Thomas Wolfe on board the *Olympic* in 1926, when he first met Mrs Bernstein.

LILY MANDELL in Thomas Wolfe, *You Can't Go Home Again* (1940)

'She is the model for the character Lily Mandell' (*The Notebooks of Thomas Wolfe*, 1970, ed. Richard S. Kennedy and Paschal Reeves, Chapel Hill, NC: University of North Carolina Press, p. 386 n. 23).

CURZON, George Nathaniel, Lord, Marquis Curzon of Kedleston (1859–1025) Educated at Eton and at Balliol College, Oxford, he was one of the **Souls**. Between 1887 and 1894 he travelled widely in the East, and was Viceroy of India from 1899 to 1905; he resigned as the result of a disagreement with Lord Kitchener on the powers of the Commander-in-Chief *vis-à-vis* the civil government. In 1915 he joined the Coalition government, and in 1919–24 he was Foreign Secretary; in 1923 he was bitterly disappointed at not succeeding Bonar Law as Prime Minister. Elinor Glyn met Curzon (then a widower) in 1908 and fell violently in love with him, but the affair came to an end in 1916 when without warning Curzon announced his engagement to Mrs Alfred Duggan. He and Elinor Glyn never met again.

JOHN DERRINGHAM in Elinor Glyn, *Halcyone* (1912)

'[W]e are given many indications of the personage who inspired John Derringham. Like Curzon, he ... had been Captain of the Oppidans at Eton. ... Like Curzon, he was an ambitious politician' (Anthony Glyn, 1968, *Elinor Glyn: a biography*, rev. edn, London: Hutchinson, p. 205; originally published 1955, London: Hutchinson).

CUSACK, Michael (1847–1907) Founder of the Gaelic Athletic Association in 1884.

THE CITIZEN in James Joyce, *Ulysses* (1922)

'George [Clancy] brought Joyce to meet Cusack a few times, and Joyce liked him little enough to make him model the narrow-minded and rhetorical Cyclops [i.e. The Citizen] in *Ulysses*' (Richard Ellmann, 1982, *James Joyce*, rev. edn, Oxford: Oxford University Press, p. 61). 'Cusack used to refer to himself as "Citizen Cusack" (*The Letters of James Joyce*, 1966, Vol. II, ed. Richard Ellmann, London: Faber & Faber, p. 210 n. 6).

CUST, Henry J.C. ('Harry') (1861–1917) Politician and journalist. Educated at Eton and at Trinity College, Cambridge, he was an MP during the periods 1890–5 and 1900–6. Between 1892 and 1896 he edited the *Pall Mall Gazette*. He was one of the **Souls** and was the father of Lady Diana **Cooper**.

HARRY CHATTERIS in H.G. Wells, *The Sea Lady* (1902)

'Chatteris is a promising young politician, a sort of mixture of Harry Cust and any hero in any novel by Mrs Humphry Ward' (H.G. Wells, 1934, *Experiment in Autobiography: discoveries and conclusions of a very ordinary brain since 1866*, London: Victor Gollancz, Cresset Press, p. 468). Wells had written for the *Pall Mall Gazette*; it was Cust who introduced him into the literary world, and Chatteris closely resembles the Cust of the autobiography.

CUTTY SARK A tea clipper built in 1869 for Captain Jock Willis. It continued to sail until 1922 and now lies beside Greenwich Pier in London.

SEPHORA in Joseph Conrad, 'The Secret Sharer', *'Twixt Land and Sea* (1912)

'The story is based on an incident which happened on board the *Cutty Sark* in 1880' (Jocelyn Baines, 1960, *Joseph Conrad: a critical biography*, London: Weidenfeld & Nicolson, p. 355).

D

DA COSTA, Sybil (d. 1929) She passed as the wife of James **Achew** and kept a lodging house in Bayswater, London, where William Plomer was one of her tenants. She was murdered by her husband on 26 November 1929.

BERYL FERNANDEZ in William Plomer, *The Case is Altered* (1932)

'Later I wrote a novel on the circumstances of the crime. *The Case is Altered* had some success' (*The Autobiography of William Plomer*, 1975, London: Jonathan Cape, p. 243).

DAL MONTE, Toti (1893–1975) Italian soprano. She made her debut at La Scala, Milan, in 1916, sang Gilda under Toscanini in 1921, and sang with the Chicago Opera from 1924 to 1928. She joined Dame Nellie Melba for her farewell tour in Australia, and in 1949 she retired.

BABA LETOILE in Beverley Nichols, *Evensong* (1932)

Identification based on information from the author.

DALRYMPLE, Janet (d. 1669) Daughter of James Dalrymple, 1st Viscount Stair and Lady **Stair**, she was alleged to have betrothed herself to Archibald, 3rd Lord **Rutherford**, but on 12 August 1669, under pressure from her mother, she married his nephew, David Dunbar, heir of Sir David Dunbar of Baldoon, instead. She died just one month later, on 12 September; her husband married again, and Rutherford died unmarried in 1685.

LUCY ASHTON in Sir Walter Scott, *The Bride of Lammermoor* (1819)

'. . . [Lord Stair's] eldest daughter, Janet Dalrymple, the original of Scott's Bride, who, according to popular tradition, stabbed her bridegroom on their wedding night and died a few days afterwards, a . . . maniac' (W.S. Crockett, 1912, *The Scott Originals: an account of notables and worthies, the originals of characters in the Waverley Novels*, Edinburgh and London: T.N. Foulis, p. 254). Stair's daughter did not in fact murder her husband, but 'it is more than likely . . . that something untoward did happen in connection with the marriage, for Scott's and Macaulay's is not the sole tradition, and traditions more or less similar could hardly have originated without cause' (ibid., p. 255).

DALY, Father James, SJ

FATHER DOLAN in James Joyce, *A Portrait of the Artist as a Young Man* (1916)

'Father Dolan was in real life Father James Daly, the efficient prefect of studies at Clongowes for thirty years, and a martinet. Joyce was to speak of him later . . . as "lowbred"' (Richard Ellmann, 1982, *James Joyce*, rev. edn, Oxford: Oxford University Press, p. 28). Soon after Joyce arrived at Clongowes he was unjustly beaten by Father Daly, for having allegedly broken his spectacles in order to avoid working. The incident profoundly affected him and figures in *A Portrait*.

DANIEL, Charles (*fl.* 1941) Publisher. He ran a small publishing company in London during the first thirty years of the twentieth century, and published *Crank*, a periodical to which Dorothy Richardson contributed her earliest reviews. In 1920 he published D.H. **Lawrence**'s play *Touch and Go*. He married Florence Woolland (d. *c.*1921).

GEORGE TAYLOR in Dorothy Richardson, *Pilgrimage* (1915–67)

'[Miriam] and Wilson argue about [the] unconventional publisher Taylor (Charles Daniel)' (John Rosenberg, 1973, *Dorothy Richardson*, London, p. 118)

DARLING, Donald (b. 1907) He lived in Spain and ran a tourist business in Barcelona from 1930. In 1939 he worked in a camp for Spanish refugees in Perpignan with Peter **Rodd** and Nancy Mitford, and after the German invasion of France he reached England and then worked in Spain and Gibraltar for the Special Services, organizing lines of escape for RAF personnel until 1944. In June 1944 he was in Paris, working for the War Office and the Foreign Office, and from 1946 to 1960 he was Information and Political Officer in Brazil for the Central Office of Information. He retired and returned to London in 1960 and became a freelance writer.

ROBERT PARKER in Nancy Mitford, *The Pursuit of Love* (1945)

'Peter has two helpers, one called Donald Darling is a young man who owned a travel agency in Barcelona and is now of course ruined. He only thinks of the refugees although his own future is in as much of a mess as theirs' (Nancy Mitford to her mother, 16 May 1939, reproduced in Harold Acton, 1975, *Nancy Mitford: a memoir*, London: Hamilton, p. 44). 'Mr Donald Darling . . . appears as Robert Parker in *The Pursuit of Love*' (ibid., p. 45).

DARLINGTON, County Durham

STUFFINGTON in W.M. Thackeray, 'Notes on the North What-d'ye-Callem Election' 1841

Identified in *Letters and Private Papers of W.M. Thackeray*, 1945, ed. Gordon N. Ray, Vol. II, London: Oxford University Press, p. 27 n. 49.

DARLINGTON, Father Joseph, SJ (1850–1939) Dean of Studies at University College, Dublin. When Joyce announced that he proposed to follow the career of letters, Father Darlington asked whether there was not 'some danger of perishing of inanition in the meantime' (Richard Ellmann, 1982, *James Joyce*, rev. edn, Oxford: Oxford University Press, p. 140).

DEAN OF STUDIES in James Joyce, *A Portrait of the Artist as a Young Man* (1916)

'His mildly disapproving eye followed Joyce for four years, and Joyce's mildly disapproving eye has followed Darlington, the dean of studies in *Stephen Hero* and *A Portrait*, into eternity' (Ellmann, op. cit., p. 58). Joyce reworked the exchange described above in ch. 5 of *A Portrait* (see ibid., p. 140 n.). 'The long scene with the dean of studies in *A Portrait* [lighting the fire] . . . happened not to Joyce but to [J.F. Byrne, as he points out in *Silent Years* pp. 33 ff.]' (ibid., p. 289 n.).

DARROW, Clarence Seward (1857–1938) American lawyer. Born in Kinsman, Ohio, in 1878 he was admitted to the Ohio Bar and to the Chicago Bar. In 1894 he defended Eugene **Debs** in the Railroad Union case, and during 1902–3 he was Chief Counsel for the unions in the anthracite strike trials at Scranton, Pennsylvania. In 1924 he defended the murderers Nathan Leopold and Richard Loeb, and in 1925 he was defending Counsel in the Dayton, Tennessee, evolution trial. In 1932 he defended the Scottsboro Negroes.

ELISHA CROFT in John Dos Passos, *Chosen Country* (1951)

'. . . a lawyer named Elisha Croft who is evidently modelled on Clarence Darrow' (Iain Colley, 1978, *Dos Passos and the Fiction of Despair*, London: Macmillan, p. 136).

DARTINGTON, Devon Located near Totnes.

DARLING in James Anthony Froude, 'The Spirit's Trials', *Shadows of the Clouds* (1847)

'For an understanding of the story we need [to] remember . . . that Darling is Dartington the home of the Froudes' (W.H. Dunn, 1961, *James Anthony Froude*, Oxford, p. 53).

DAS, Sarat Chandra (1849–1917) In 1874 he was Headmaster of the Bhutia boarding school at Darjeeling in India. He studied Tibetan with a lama who taught there, and in 1879 the two men started out to visit Lhasa but were forced to return; they reached Lhasa in 1881 and wrote reports of the journey, and in 1960 the reports were still an authority on the subject. *The Readers' Guide to Rudyard Kipling's Work* (R.L. Green (ed.), 1961, Sect. I, London: Kipling Society, p. 211) describes him as a Pundit, or member of the Indian Survey Department. In 1884–5 he visited Sikkim and Peking. He was the author of a Tibetan Grammar and of a Tibetan English Dictionary (1902).

HURREE CHANDER MOOKERJEE in Rudyard Kipling, *Kim* (1901)

'. . . partly drawn from Sarat Chandra Das' (ibid.).

DAUGHERTY, Harry M. (1860–1941) Born in Ohio, he was engaged in local Republican politics. In 1890–4 he was a Member of the Ohio legislature and had already acquired an unsavoury reputation; he was one of President **Harding**'s so-called Ohio Gang and was believed to have been indispensable in securing his election to the presidency. From 1921 to April 1924 he was the US Attorney-General; he was twice charged with bribery and defrauding the government, but escaped indictment because he had destroyed the documents concerned.

BARNEY BROCKWAY in Upton Sinclair, *Oil!* (1927)

See below.

DAN LURCOCK in Samuel Hopkins Adams, *Revelry* (1926)

'Dan Lurcock is the real if not the titular Attorney General in [*Revelry*] whereas in [*Oil*] Barney Brockway is both' (Joseph Blotner, 1966, *The Modern American Political Novel*, Austin, Tex., p. 116).

DAVENPORT, Thomas Donald (1792–1851) Stage name of Thomas Donald. After beginning life as a lawyer, he became the Manager of Richmond Theatre, Surrey, and was thereafter Manager of a circuit of theatres including those at Norwich and Portsmouth. In 1849 he took his family to America; he launched his daughter, the actress Jean Davenport (**Lander**), in New York and retired from the stage. He died in Cincinnati.

Vincent Crummles in Charles Dickens, *Nicholas Nickleby* (1838–9)

'Caricatured by Dickens . . . as Vincent Crummles' (Frederic Boase, *Modern English Biography*, Vol. V, col. 26). 'Dickens drew his portraits . . . from the company of a then well-known theatrical manager named Davenport. . . . Edmund Yates maintained that Dickens had at one time been a member of Davenport's company in Portsmouth' (Otis Skinner, 1915, 'The original of the Infant Phenomenon' (interview), *The Dickensian* 11 (May): 134; reprinted from *Boston Sunday Herald* (21 March 1915)).

DAVIDSON, James Scottish Border farmer, of Hyndlee, near Jedburgh.

Dandie Dinmont in Sir Walter Scott, *Guy Mannering* (1815)

'[I]t is certain that the James Davidson, who carried the name of Dandie to his grave with him . . . was first pointed out to Scott by Mr Shortreed . . . several years after the novel had established the man's celebrity all over the Border; some accidental report about his terriers, and their odd names, have alone been turned to account in the original composition of the tale' (J.G. Lockhart, 1900, *Memoirs of Sir Walter Scott*, Vol. I, London: Macmillan, p. 168). 'I have been at the spring circuit . . . and there I was introduced to a man whom I never saw in my life before, namely the proprietor of all the Pepper and Mustard family – in other words, the genuine Dandie Dinmont. . . . In truth, I knew nothing of the man, except his odd humour of having only two names for twenty dogs. But there are lines of general resemblance among all these hill men, which there is no missing; and Jamie Davidson of Hyndlea certainly looks Dandie Dinmont remarkably well. He is much flattered with the compliment, and goes uniformly by the name among his comrades, but has never read the book' (to David Terry, 18 April 1816, reproduced in *The Letters of Sir Walter Scott*, 1933, ed. H.J.C. Grierson, Vol. IV, London: Constable, pp. 216–17). '[Scott] made something of [Davidson] for short though their interview was, it was during it that he pencilled off . . . the store-farmer . . . in the beginning of the first *Tales of My Landlord* . . . which appeared shortly after [i.e. *The Black Dwarf*, 1816]. Young Mr Pringle of Whitebank was present at the interview, and he told me that great part of what Jamie Davidson then said . . . is there not in substance merely, but that we have the actual words and phrases he made use of' (Robert Shortreed, quoted in W.E. Wilson, 1932, 'The making of the "Minstrelsy". Scott and Shortreed in Liddesdale', *Cornhill Magazine* (NS) 73 (September: 273). *See also* **Elliott**, Willie; **Laidlaw**, James; **Park**, Archibald; **Thorburn**, James.

DAVIS, Marion (1898–1961) A star in the days of the silent film, she began as a cinema dancer and appeared in one or two silent films. In 1937 she abandoned her career when taken under the protection of William Randolph **Hearst**.

Virginia Maunciple in Aldous Huxley, *After Many a Summer* (1939)

'Hearst's young woman friend, Marion Davis, was, at least to contemporary Californians, as recognizable as she is in Orson Welles's film [*Citizen Kane*]' (Sybille Bedford, 1973, *Aldous Huxley*, Vol. I, London: Chatto & Windus, p. 379). Sybille Bedford is quoting Lawrence Clark Powell, librarian of the University of California and Huxley's friend. *See also* **Goddard**, Paulette.

DAVITT, Michael (1846–1906) Founder of the Irish Land League in 1879, having earlier been a member of the Fenian Brotherhood, which he joined in 1866; he served two periods of penal servitude, in 1870–7 and 1881–2. He was an MP in 1882, 1892 and 1895–9.

MICHAELIS in Joseph Conrad, *The Secret Agent* (1907)

'[I]t seems clear that in terms of his purity of spirit, his gentleness and his optimism, all the result of his term of imprisonment, Michaelis is based upon Davitt' (Norman Sherry, 1971, *Conrad's Western World*, p. 269). *See also* **Bakunin**, Michael; **Condon**, Edward O'Meara.

DONAL MOORE in Edna Lyall, *Doreen* (1904)

'The character of Donal Moore . . . is founded on that of Michael Davitt, though one or two personal details I have purposely altered' (Edna Lyall to C.E. Maurice, 1895, quoted in J.M. Escreet, 1904, *The Life of Edna Lyall*, London: Longman, p. 148). Michael Davitt was a personal friend of Edna Lyall's, and advised her on the background of *Doreen*.

DAVY, Jane, Lady (1780–1855) Daughter of Charles Kerr, the younger son of William Kerr of Kelso, she was a blood-relative of Sir Walter Scott. In 1799 she married Shuckburgh Apreece, heir to a baronetcy, but he died in 1807 and in 1810 she accompanied Scott on a tour of the Western Isles: he described her as 'a fashionable little woman, who travels rather *to say she has seen* than *to see*' (to J.S.B. Morritt, 9 August 1811, reproduced in *The Letters of Sir Walter Scott*, 1932, ed. H.J.C. Grierson, Vol. II, London: Constable, p. 368). In 1812 she married Sir Humphrey Davy, and after he died in 1829 she became a prominent figure in Society in Paris and London, being much disliked by Maria Edgeworth, who described Davy as 'the martyr of matrimony'.

LADY ANGELICA HEADINGHAM in Maria Edgeworth, *Patronage* (1814)

'Lady Angelica may . . . have had connections with . . . the wealthy widow Mrs Apreece' (Marilyn Butler, 1972, *Maria Edgeworth*, Oxford, p. 254). *See also* **White**, Lydia.

DAX, Alice (1878–1959) Born in Liverpool, in 1905 she married Henry Dax and moved to Nottinghamshire. An emancipated woman, she was an enthusiast for socialism and women's rights and knew Mrs Pankhurst, Keir Hardie and Annie Besant. In 1912 she and her husband moved to Mansfield, Nottinghamshire, and in 1951 she emigrated to Australia.

CLARA DAWES in D.H. Lawrence, *Sons and Lovers* (1913)

'The letter from Alice Dax, found among . . . [Frieda Lawrence's] papers, not only emphasises her importance in Lawrence's life, just before he met Frieda, but clarifies the nature of Paul's struggle for fulfilment with "Clara", for whom she was the real life counterpart, in *Sons and Lovers'* (Frieda Lawrence, 1961, *The Memoirs and Correspondence*, ed. E.W. Tedlock, London: Heinemann, p. 432 n.). Alice Dax's letter of 23 January 1935 (ibid., pp. 245–8) makes clear that Mrs Dax was Lawrence's mistress.

DAY, Thomas (1748–89) Author and barrister. Educated at Charterhouse and at Corpus Christi, Oxford, he became friends with R.L. **Edgeworth** while studying law in London. He was a follower of Rousseau, and at his farm at Anningsley, Surrey, he attempted to practise his schemes for moral and social reform among the poor. He educated two orphan girls, intending to marry one of them; in the event he married neither, but instead married Esther Milnes, an heiress, in 1778.

FORESTER in Maria Edgeworth, 'Forester', *Moral Tales for Young People* (1801)

'Forester was probably based on Thomas Day, although he was widely taken for Lord Ashburton' (Marilyn Butler, 1927, *Maria Edgeworth*, Oxford, p. 164 n. 2). *See also* **Ashburton**, Lord.

CLARENCE HERVEY in Maria Edgeworth, *Belinda* (1801)

'Maria Edgeworth has taken two series of events from her father's youth – Sir Francis Delaval's life and death, and Thomas Day's attempt to train a wife – and fitted them to the format of Fanny Burney's first two novels' (Butler, op. cit., p. 309).

DEBS, Eugene Victor (1855–1926) American politician. Born in Terre Haute, Indiana, he was a locomotive fireman in 1870–4 and in 1880 became National Secretary and Treasurer to the Brotherhood of Locomotive Firemen. In 1894 he was a leader in the Pullman strike in Chicago and was sentenced to six months' imprisonment for contempt of court. In 1897 he organized the Socialist Democratic Party of America, and stood as the Socialist candidate for president five times. In 1918 he was sentenced to ten years' imprisonment for violation of the Espionage Act, but was released in 1921 by order of President **Harding**.

ERNEST EVERHARD in Jack London, *The Iron Heel* (1908)

'. . . a composite . . . of Eugene Debs, Ernest Untermann and Jack London' (Joseph Blotner, 1966, *The Modern American Political Novel*, Austin, Tex., p. 151 n. 22). *See also* **London**, Jack; **Untermann**, Ernest.

DEFFAND, Marie de Vichy-Chamrond, Marquise du (1697–1780) Educated in a Paris convent, she married the Marquis du Deffand; after they separated she became a French salon hostess and was a friend and corespondent of Voltaire, Montesquieu and Horace Walpole. After she lost her sight in 1753, Julie de **Lespinasse** lived with her, but they parted when they quarrelled ten years later.

LADY HENRY DELAFIELD in Mrs Humphry Ward, *Lady Rose's Daughter* (1903)

See under de **Lespinasse**, Julie.

DE KLEINE, William (1877–1951) He was Director of the American Red Cross from 1928 to 1942 and was a pioneer in the field of public health.

ALNUS PICHERBOUGH in Sinclair Lewis, *Arrowsmith* (1925)

Identified in Mark Schorer, 1961, *Sinclair Lewis: an American life*, New York: McGraw-Hill, p. 418.

DE KRUIF, Rhea Elizabeth Daughter of George Frederick Barbarin, a pharmacist of Freetown, Michigan, she was educated in Ann Arbor, Michigan, and in 1922 married Paul De Kruif.

LEORA TOZER in Sinclair Lewis, *Arrowsmith* (1925)

'Of one character Novy would have approved fully. That was Leora. In her he would have detected, as many have done, a replica of Rhea' (Paul De Kruif, 1962, *The Sweeping Wind: a memoir*, London: Rupert Hart- Davis, p. 109). *See also* **Summers**, Edith.

DELACROIX, Ferdinand Victor Eugène (1798–1863) French painter. He was born in Charenton, the son of Charles Delacroix, who had been foreign minister under the Directory. He studied under Guérin and was a fellow pupil of Géricault. His work was inspired by dramatic historical events and, latterly, his travels in the Orient. Often viewed as a rebel in the art world because of his departure from a traditional classical style, he was an expert colourist. He was a friend of George Sand, whom he painted, and he kept a daily journal from the age of 23 until the year of his death.

ALAN TREVOR in Oscar Wilde, 'The Model Millionaire' (1891)

See under de **Rothschild**, Baron James Mayer.

DELAVAL, Sir Francis (1727–71) MP for Hindon in 1751 and for Andover in 1754, in 1761 he married Isabella, the widow of Lord Nassau Paulet and daughter of the Earl of Thanet. Horace Walpole described him as one of the three most fashionable men in London, while Lord Chesterfield described him as 'that most consummate puppy and impudent jackanapes'. Richard Lovell **Edgeworth** met him in 1766 and saw much of him during the following two years.

LADY DELACOUR in Maria Edgeworth, *Belinda* (1801)

'Many years later Maria was to draw on many features of Delaval's life and death ... the fashionable notoriety, the outward appearance of gaiety, the private confession to a young friend, the pain in the chest the gay world knew nothing of ... for ... Lady Delacour in *Belinda*' (Marilyn Butler, 1972, *Maria Edgeworth*, Oxford, p. 29).

DELCOMMUNE, Alexandre (1855–1922) Born in Namur, Belgium, he was the elder brother of Camille **Delcommune**. In 1873 he went to Africa, and in 1883–4 he was Manager of the factory, and later the station of Boma, capital of the Congo Free State. He was the leader of expeditions of exploration that culminated in 1890–2 in the **Katanga Expedition**.

MANAGER'S UNCLE in Joseph Conrad, *Heart of Darkness* (1902)

'[T]he manager's uncle ... is based on Alexandre Delcommune' (Norman Sherry, 1971, *Conrad's Western World*, Cambridge, pp. 85–6).

DELCOMMUNE, Camille (1859–92) Younger brother of Alexandre **Delcommune**, in 1883 he went to Africa. He was Acting Company Manager at Kinshasa (Congo) when Conrad arrived in 1890, and conceived a violent, and reciprocated, antipathy towards Conrad.

MANAGER in Joseph Conrad, *Heart of Darkness* (1902)

'As soon as [he] arrived at Kinchassa he was received by the person whom Conrad calls "the manager".... This manager ... was Camille Delcommune. ... The physical portrait which Conrad traces of him corresponds perfectly with the photographs ... in the Belgian magazines of the time. ... Conrad ... despised this man heartily' (G. Jean-Aubry, 1927, *Joseph Conrad: life and letters*, Vol. I, London: Heinemann, pp. 132–3).

DE LISLE, Ambrose Lisle March Phillipps (1809–78) Of Garendon Park, Leicestershire. He was a Roman Catholic convert and was a supporter of Young England outside the House of Commons.

EUSTACE LYLE in Benjamin Disraeli, *Coningsby* (1844)

Identified in a key in *Notes and Queries* (8th series) 3 (13 May 1893): 363. *See also under* **Bright**, John.

DELIUS, Frederick (1862–1934) English composer. He entered Leipzig Conservatory in 1886, but was more influenced by his fellow pupil Grieg than by his teachers. After 1890 he lived mostly in France composing a variety of musical works, including operas, concertos, choral and orchestral pieces. In 1924 he became paralysed and totally blind but produced a group of final works with the assistance of Eric Fenby, who was his amanuensis from 1928 onwards.

SOPHUS JONSEN in C.F. Keary, *The Journalist* (1898)

'Keary's book is very good. He has taken an awful lot of sayings out of my mouth for Johnson [sic]' (to Jelka Rosen, 28 November 1898, reproduced in *Delius: a life in letters*, Vol. I: *1862–1908*, 1984, ed. Lionel Carley, London: Scolar and The Delius Trust, p. 137 n. 3).

DEMPSEY, George Stanislaus He was a lay teacher of English composition at the Jesuit Belvedere College, Dublin, where James Joyce was his pupil, from 1893 to 1898; the two corresponded in later years.

MR TATE in James Joyce, *A Portrait of the Artist as a Young Man* (1916)

'The lay teacher of English composition was George Stanislaus Dempsey.... Joyce treats him well enough under the name of "Mr Tate"' (Richard Ellmann, 1982, *James Joyce*, rev. edn, Oxford: Oxford University Press, p. 36).

DENNIS, Gypsy A London stenographer who became engaged to W. Ernest Lawrence *c*.1901; in 1901 he took her to Eastwood, Nottinghamshire, on a visit to his family.

Louisa Lily Denys Western in D.H. Lawrence, *Sons and Lovers* (1913)

'Gypsy (the Louisa Lily Denys Western of *Sons and Lovers*) . . .' (H.T. Moore, 1960, *The Intelligent Heart: the story of D.H. Lawrence*, Harmondsworth: Penguin, p. 56; originally published 1955, London: Heinemann). 'I heard [Lawrence] tell mother, in a voice that was clearly an unconscious imitation of his mother's, how Ernest and his fiancée had spent a fortnight's holiday with them, and that it had proved something of a strain' (E.T. [Jessie Chambers], 1935, *D.H. Lawrence: a personal record*, p. 26).

DENT, Yorkshire A village near Sedbergh, where the Compton-Burnett family spent the summer of 1908 in the vicarage.

Millfield in I. Compton-Burnett, *Dolores* (1911)

'Dolores' home in a country village [owed] something perhaps to the summer of 1908 spent by the Compton Burnetts at Dent' (Hilary Spurling, 1974, *Ivy When Young: the early life of I. Compton-Burnett, 1884–1919*, London: Gollancz, p. 167). *See also* **Great Clacton**.

DENT, Edward Joseph (1876–1957) Musicologist. Educated at Eton and at King's College, Cambridge, from 1928 to 1948 he was Professor of Music at Cambridge. He translated a number of operas including *The Marriage of Figaro*, *Don Giovanni*, *The Magic Flute*, *The Trojans* and *Fidelio*. He was active in the International Society for Contemporary Music, and was Governor of Sadler's Wells Theatre and Director of Covent Garden Opera Trust. He was deeply interested in the presentation of opera in English.

Philip Herriton in E.M. Forster, *Where Angels Fear to Tread* (1905)

'Philip Herriton I modelled on Professor Dent. He knew this, and took an interest in his own progress' (E.M. Forster, interviewed in 1952, quoted in P.N. Furbank and F.J.H. Haskell, 1972, *Writers at Work: the Paris Review interviews*, selected by Kay Dick, Harmondsworth: Penguin, p. 13). *See also* **Forster**, E.M.

DENYS DE MONTFORT, Pierre (1768–post 1820) French conchologist. He was the author (with others) of *Histoire naturelle . . . des mollusques* (1801–5).

Asterias in Thomas Love Peacock, *Nightmare Abbey* (1818)

'Asterias appears to be a caricature of Denys-Montfort' (Norma L. Rudinsky, 1975, 'Source of Asterias's paean to science in Peacock's *Nightmare Abbey*', *Notes and Queries* 220: 68). *See also* **Sinclair**, Sir John.

DERBY, Edward George Geoffrey Smith Stanley, Lord (799–1869) 14th Earl of Derby. Statesman. Educated at Eton and at Christ Church College, Oxford, he was a Whig MP in 1822–44, Irish Secretary 1830–3 and Colonial Secretary 1833–4. In 1835 he joined the Conservative opposition, and in 1841–4 was again Colonial Secretary. He was Prime Minister in 1852, 1858–9 and 1866–68 and, with Disraeli, he carried the Reform Bill of 1867.

Lord De Terrier in Anthony Trollope, *Framley Parsonage* (1861)

'Among the more powerful of the giants [in Parliament] is . . . Lord De Terrier (Lord Derby)' (C.L. Cline, 1944, '*Coningsby* and three Victorian novelists', *Notes and Queries* 186 (15 January): 42).

DERBYSHIRE

STONYSHIRE in George Eliot, *Adam Bede* (1859)

'[Derbyshire] is Stonyshire in the novel' (Charles S. Olcott, 1911, *George Eliot: scenes and people in her novels*, London: Cassell, p. 65; originally published 1910, New York: Thomas Y. Crowell).

DE ROS, Henry (1793–1839) Son of Lady Henry Fitzgerald née Boyle, he lived at Boyle Farm, where he gave riotous and notorious parties. In 1837 he brought a libel action against John Cumming (a well-known clubman of the day), who declared that Lord de Ros cheated habitually and successfully at cards. De Ros lost his case and retired to the European continent, returning to England to die a few months later in St John's Wood, London. He was an intimate friend of Charles **Greville**, whose diary (*The Greville Memoirs, 1814–1860,* 1938, ed. Lytton Strachey and Roger Fulford, Vol. III, London: Macmillan, pp. 317–31) contains an agonized account of the scandal and the trial.

HARRY FINISH in Bulwer Lytton, *Paul Clifford* (1830)

Identified in a key set out by Rosina Bulwer Lytton, in a letter of 26 May 1830, reproduced in Michael Sadleir, 1968, *Bulwer and His Wife*, pp. 227–8.

DESBOROUGH, Ethel Anne Priscilla Grenfell, Lady (1867–1952) Known as 'Ettie', she was the daughter of the Hon. Julian Fane and in 1887 married W.H. Grenfell, who was created Baron Desborough in 1905. Of her three sons, two, Julian (the poet) and Billy, were killed during the First World War, while Ivo was killed in a motor accident in 1926. '[In] the years before 1914 . . . she held a position in the world of wit and fashion that nobody has occupied since. . . . [In] the closing years of the last century . . . many of those who gave colour to that epoch were her most frequent visitors' (David Cecil, 1952, *The Times* (30 May): 8).

LADY AMYSFORT in John Buchan, *A Lodge in the Wilderness* (1906)

Identified in a key dated January 1907 in a copy of *A Lodge in the Wilderness*, formerly the property of Grace Keily.

LEILA BUCKNELL in Maurice Baring, *C* (1924)

'There is a novel by . . . Maurice Baring . . . in which the hero and heroine are like Ettie [Desborough] and John Baring. . . . The novel is called, curiously or significantly *C* ("C" being one of the code names in Ettie's and John Baring's letters)' (Nicholas Mosley, 1976, *Julian Grenfell: his life and times, 1888–1915*, London: Weidenfeld & Nicolson, p. 45). *See also* **Lytton**, Countess of.

DUCHESS OF HERTFORDSHIRE in Max Beerbohm, 'Maltby and Braxton', *Seven Men* (1919)

'[T]he Duchess of Hertfordshire [is] Lady Desborough' (David Cecil, 1964, *Max: a biography*, p. 341).

DESHON, Florence (1894–1922) A stage and screen actress from 1917 to 1921, she was the mistress of Max Eastman and at one time was involved in a relationship *à trois* with Eastman and Charlie Chaplin. She died in an accident that was widely supposed to be suicide.

ERNESTINE DE JONGH in Theodore Dreiser, 'Ernestine', *A Gallery of Women* (1929)

'Ernestine de Jongh is modelled upon Florence Deshon' (Richard Lehan, 1969, *Theodore Dreiser: his world and his novels*, London and Amsterdam: Feffer & Simons, p. 264 n. 11).

DEUTSCH, Emanuel (1829–73) Born in Silesia, he was educated by his uncle (a rabbi) and at the University of Berlin, then moved to England where in 1855–70 he was employed as an assistant librarian in the British Museum. In 1866 he met George Eliot and gave her lessons in Hebrew. He was the author of an essay on the Talmud, published in the *Quarterly Review* in 1867, and in 1869 he conceived an enthusiasm for the Jewish National Home during visits to the Near East. He died of cancer in Alexandria.

MORDECAI COHEN in George Eliot, *Daniel Deronda* (1876)

'[His death] occurred just as George Eliot was planning her new novel; and memories of poor Deutsch are woven through her conception of the dying Mordecai' (Gordon S. Haight, 1968, *George Eliot*, Oxford, p. 471). *See also* **Cohn (or Kohn)**; **Louis**, Alfred Hyman.

DE VALERA, Éamon (1882–1975) Prime Minister of the Irish Free State 1937–48, 1951–4 and 1957–9, and President of the Republic of Ireland 1959–73. Born in Brooklyn, New York, he grew up in County Limerick, Ireland, and was educated at Blackrock College, Dublin. He was imprisoned after taking a leading part in the Easter Rising in 1916 and became MP for East Clare after his release from prison the following year. He formed a Republican opposition party in 1926 and in 1927 that party entered the Lower House of Parliament, the Dáil. As Prime Minister of the Irish Free State he had a new constitution ratified in 1937, thereby gaining the country's independence from Britain.

SHAUN in James Joyce, *Finnegans Wake* (1939)

'[Joyce] was excited to learn that Éamon De Valera had eye trouble and was born in 1882 . . . and [he appears] in *Finnegans Wake* . . . as one of the models for Shaun' (Richard Ellmann, 1982, *James Joyce*, rev. edn, Oxford: Oxford University Press, p. 622). *See also* **Ford**, John; **Joyce**, Stanislaus.

DE VEER, Carel (*fl.* 1887) A Dutchman who lived with Olmeijer in Berau, Germany. He had a broken wrist and a weakness for alcohol.

PETER WILLEMS in Joseph Conrad, *An Outcast of the Islands* (1896)

'*An Outcast* grew from the impression of a man whom Conrad met at Olmeijer's house in Berouw. Though the man's name may have been De Veer, the novelist called the character Willems' (J.D. Gordan, 1941, *Joseph Conrad: the making of a novelist*, Cambridge, Mass., pp. 103–4). 'The man who suggested Willems to me was not particularly interesting in himself. My interest was aroused by his dependent position, his strange, dubious status of a mistrusted, disliked, worn-out European living on the reluctant toleration of that settlement hidden in the heart of the forest-land' (*An Outcast of the Islands*, 1923 (Uniform edn), p. ix n.). *See also* **Wallace**, Alfred Russel.

DEVIN, Thomas (*c*.1868–1937) An official in the city cleansing department of the Dublin Corporation, he was a friend of John Stanislaus Joyce and Alfred Bergan. His sons were James Joyce's friends.

JACK POWER in James Joyce, 'Grace', *Dubliners* (1914) and *Ulysses* (1922)

'[He] would have been a fine pianist if he had studied as he had a very agreeable touch on the keys. . . . He comes into *Ulysses* under the name of Mr Power and also into *Dubliners*' (to Alfred Bergan, 25 May 1937, on hearing of Devin's death, reproduced in *The Letters of James Joyce*, 1966, Vol. III, ed. Richard Ellmann, London: Faber & Faber, p. 399).

DEVONSHIRE, Deborah Cavendish, Duchess of (b. 1920) Née Mitford, she was the youngest daughter of Lord **Redesdale** and the sister of Nancy Mitford. In 1941 she married Lord Andrew Cavendish, who succeeded his father as 11th Duke of Devonshire in 1950.

NORTHEY MACKINTOSH in Nancy Mitford, *Don't Tell Alfred* (1960)

'Northey is Christiana Brandolin talking like Debo' (Nancy Mitford to Handasyde Buchanan, 7 September 1960, quoted in Harold Acton, 1975, *Nancy Mitford: a memoir*, London: Hamilton, pp. 140–1). *See also* **Brandolini**, Contessa Christiana.

LINDA RADLETT in Nancy Mitford, *The Pursuit of Love* (1945) and *Love in a Cold Climate* (1949)

'I used to call my sister Debo Linda-May can't tell you why, so I used it, as Linda is more *like* her than anybody' (Nancy Mitford to Laura Propper of the Oxford University Press, 12 December 1972, unpublished MS).

DEVONSHIRE, Elizabeth Cavendish, Duchess of (1759–1824) Daughter of Frederick, 4th Earl of Brist and Bishop of Derry, she married John Thomas Foster in 1776. She was the mistress of the 5th Duke of **Devonshire** for many years and married him in 1809, becoming his second wife; after his death in 1811 she lived abroad. The historian Ed Gibbon, who proposed marriage to her in 1787, said she was 'a mortal for whom the wisest man, historic or medical, would throw away two or three worlds if he had them in possession'.

LADY MARGARET BUCHANAN in Lady Caroline Lamb, *Glenarvon* (1816)

Identified in a key found among the papers of John Whishaw, a member of the Holland House circle, printed in *The 'Pope' of Holland House: selections from the correspondence of John Whishaw and his friends, 1813–1840*, ed. Lady Seymour, 1906, p. 151. *See also* **Bessborough**, Lady; **Kinnaid**, Maria.

DEVONSHIRE, Spencer Compton Cavendish, 8th Duke of (1833–1908) Known as the Marquess of Hartington until he became the 8th Duke of Devonshire in 1891, he was educated at Trinity College, Cambridge, and became a Liberal MP in 1857. He was Secretary of State for War in 1866 and

Secretary of State for India in 1880–2, and was a Liberal Unionist. In 1892, after a long liaison, he married Louise, widow of the 7th Duke of Manchester.

LORD CHILTERN in Anthony Trollope, *Phineas Finn* (1869)

'[T]he red-haired, red-faced, shaggy and untamable Lord Chiltern ... represents Trollop's snapshot at the Lord Hartington of his own day, who died eighth Duke of Devonshire' (T.H.S. Escott, 1913, *Anthony Trollope*, London: John Lane, p. 259). *See also* **Camelford**, Lord.

DEVONSHIRE, William Cavendish, 5th Duke of (1748–1811) A Whig grandee, he was celebrated for his phlegm. In 1774 he married Georgiana, eldest daughter of the 1st Earl Spencer; she died in 1806 and in 1809 he married Lady Elizabeth Foster (**Devonshire**, below). His daughters became Lady **Granville** and Lady **Morpeth**.

DUKE OF CLAVERTON in W. Massie, *Sydenham; or Memoirs of a Man of the world* (1830)

Identification based on obvious parallels – clearly an intentional portrait.

DEVONSHIRE, William George Spencer Cavendish, 6th Duke of (1790–1858) Son of the 5th Duke of **Devonshire**, he was described as 'good-looking but unfortunately very deaf' (G.E.C. (ed.), 1890, *The Complete Peerage of England, Scotland, Ireland, Great Britain and the United Kingdom*, London: George Bell & Sons). He employed the architect Sir Joseph Paxton (1801–65) as manager of his estates, and was described as 'the model of the old English noble of his time' (9th Duke of Argyll, 1907, *Passages from the Past*, p. 76). He died unmarried.

DUKE OF ALTAMONTE in Lady Caroline Lamb, *Glenarvon* (1816)

Identified in a key found among the papers of John Whishaw, a member of the Holland House circle, printed in *The 'Pope' of Holland House: selections from the correspondence of John Whishaw and his friends, 1813–1840*, ed. Lady Seymour, 1906, p. 151.

BACHELOR BILL in Bulwer Lytton, *Paul Clifford* (1830)

Identified in a key set out by Rosina Bulwer Lytton in a letter of 26 May 1830, reproduced in Michael Sadleir, 1968, *Bulwer and His Wife*, pp. 227–8. 'The Duke of Devonshire was so pleased with the caricature of himself in Paul Clifford that he left his name on the author as "Bachelor Bill"' (Owen Meredith, 1883, *The Life, Letters and Literary Remains of Edward Bulwer, Lord Lytton*, Vol. II, p. 249).

DEVONSHIRE HOUSE, London Residence of the Dukes of Devonshire in Piccadilly; it is no longer standing.

CASTLE DELAVAL in Lady Caroline Lamb, *Glenarvon* (1816)

Identified in a key found among the papers of John Whishaw, a member of the Holland House circle, printed in *The 'Pope' of Holland House: selections from the correspondence of John Whishaw and his friends, 1813–1840*, ed. Lady Seymour, 1906, p. 151.

CLAVERTON HOUSE in W. Massie, *Sydenham; or Memoirs of a Man of the World* (1830)

'In Volume two . . . the scene shifts to Devonshire House (Claverton House in the novel)' (M.W. Rosa, 1936, *The Silver-Fork School: novels of fashion preceding 'Vanity Fair'*, New York, p. 81 n. 3).

DEWAS, Central India Located some thirty miles to the north-east of Indore. In 1913, Forster visited the Maharajah, who became one of his closest Indian friends; he returned in 1921 to spend six months as the Maharajah's Secretary.

MAU in E.M. Forster, *A Passage to India* (1924)

'The scenery and architecture of Mau were derived from two small Central Indian states, Chhattapore and Dewas. Its inhabitants are imaginary. . . . The Krishna festival closely follows the great celebration of Gokal Ashtami, which I attended for nine days in the palace of Dewas State Senior, and which was the strangest and strongest Indian experience ever granted me' (*A Passage to India*, 1957, London: Everyman, pp. xxix–xxx n.; originally published 1925, London: E. Arnold). *See also* **Chhatarpur.**

DEWEY, Thomas Edward (1902–71) Lawyer and politician. He was Governor of New York State from 1942 to 1954, and was the Republican nominee for US president in 1944 and 1948.

GOVERNOR OF NEW YORK in James Reichley, *Hail to the Chief* (1960)

Identified in Joseph Blotner, 1966, *The Modern American Political Novel*, Austin, Tex., p. 129.

DIBRELL, John A young American from Texas who was living in Chapala, Mexico, when the Lawrences were there in 1923.

DON RAMÓN CARRASCO in D.H. Lawrence, *The Plumed Serpent* (1926)

'Dibrell's belief in the Indians, their liking for him and his handsome easy leadership among them, had, I am certain, much to do with Lawrence's concept of Don Ramon' (Witter Bynner, 1953, *Journey with Genius*, London and New York: Peter Nevill, p. 121). *See also* **Vasconcelos,** José.

DICK, Margaret Catherine (1827?–79) Of Madeira Hall, Ventnor, Isle of Wight.

MISS HAVISHAM in Charles Dickens, *Great Expectations* (1860–1)

'A local legend has circulated for many years that a Miss Margaret Dick of "Madeira Hall" . . . was the original of Miss Havisham. . . . The story was told to . . . the present owner . . . soon after he purchased the property in 1948, by two old ladies who had heard it from Miss Dick's doctor. Miss Dick, like Miss Havisham, had been jilted on her wedding day; had left the wedding feast untouched; and had turned night into day, never leaving the house during daylight until her death' (R.J. Hutchings, 1965, 'Dickens at Bonchurch', *The Dickensian* 61: 97). Dickens rented a house in Bonchurch, Isle of Wight, in the summer of 1849 when he was busy on *David Copperfield*; there he was the neighbour, and became the friend, of Miss Dick's father Captain Samuel Dick, of the Royal Navy. It is indeed possible that Captain Dick supplied a name for Mr Dick in *Copperfield*. Miss Dick took herself off to Madeira Hall in the autumn of 1860. It is not possible to prove that Dickens revisited Bonchurch, but there are indications that he may have done so at about that time, and picked up the story when working on *Great Expectations*. *See also* **Joachim**, Martha; **White Woman of Berners Street**.

DICK, Quentin (1777–1858) Educated at Trinity College, Dublin, he was called to the Irish Bar. He was MP for West Looe, Cornwall, 1803–6; Cashel 1807–9; Orford, Suffolk, 1826–30; Maldon, Essex, 1830–47; and Aylesbury 1848–52. Upon his death he left a fortune of between two and three million pounds which he accrued in the East Indies.

Mr Ormsby in Benjamin Disraeli, *Coningsby* (1844) and *Tancred* (1847)

Identified in a key in *Notes and Queries* (8th series) 3 (13 May 1893): 363. *See also under* **Bright**, John. *See also* **Irving**, John.

DICKENS, Charles (1812–70) English author. Born in Portsmouth, the son of John **Dickens**. When his father was imprisoned for debt in the Marshalsea, Charles, at the age of 12, was sent to work in a blacking factory. In 1827 he worked as an office boy in a firm of attorneys, studied shorthand, and became a reporter of debates in the House of Commons. In 1833 he became parliamentary journalist for the *Morning Chronicle*, and also wrote sketches for a variety of journals, including *The Monthly Magazine*, edited by his friend George Hogarth. In March 1986, the first number of *The Pickwick Papers* appeared, and in the same month he married Hogarth's eldest daughter, Catherine, with whom he had seven sons and three daughters. In 1857 he met Ellen **Ternan**; his admiration for the young actress contributed to the deterioration of his marriage, and he separated from his wife in 1858. He travelled widely throughout the 1860s, giving public readings of his own works. He died suddenly, leaving his last novel, *The Mystery of Edwin Drood*, unfinished.

David Copperfield in Charles Dickens, *David Copperfield* (1849–50)

'Many guesses have been made since [Dickens's] death, connecting David's autobiography with his own. . . . There is not only truth in all this, but it will . . . be seen that the identity went deeper than any had supposed, and covered experiences not less startling in the reality than they appear to be in the fiction' (John Forster, 1928, *The Life of Charles Dickens*, ed. J.W.T. Ley, p. 5). 'I have my mother's authority for saying . . . that the story [i.e. the autobiographical fragment given to Forster and printed in his life] was . . . read to her . . . by my father, who . . . intimated his intention of publishing it . . . as a portion of his autobiography. From this purpose she endeavoured to dissuade him . . . and he eventually decided that he would be satisfied with working it into *David Copperfield*' (Charles Dickens, the Younger, 1892, Introd. to *David Copperfield*, p. xx).

Mr Gushy in Benjamin Disraeli, *Endymion* (1880)

Identified in 'Key to *Endymion*', *Notes and Queries* 83 (24 October 1942): 263; identifications attributed to G.E. Buckle.

MR POPULAR SENTIMENT in Anthony Trollope, *The Warden* (1855)

'Perhaps, however, Mr Sentiment's greatest attraction is in his second rate characters . . . they walk and talk like men and women . . . yes, live, and will live till the names of their calling shall be forgotten in their own, and Buckett and Mrs Gamp will be the only worlds left to us to signify a detective police officer or a monthly nurse' (*The Warden*, 1855, London: Longman, Brown, Green, ch. XV, p. 244–5).

DANIEL QUILP in Charles Dickens, *The Old Curiosity Shop* (1840–1)

'Quilp was, in a sense . . . Dickens himself as seen by the eyes of Mrs Hogarth' (Thomas Wright, 1935, *Life of Charles Dickens*, London: Herbert Jenkins, p. 131). *See also* **Grimaldi**, Giuseppe; *Prior*, 'Donkey'.

ROBERT SMITHERS in Charles Dickens, 'Making a Night of It', *Sketches by Boz* (1836)

'Those two clerks, Thomas Potter and Robert Smithers . . . are very interesting for several reasons. The most important is that they are completely alive. The second is that Robert Smithers is a miniature self-portrait of Charles Dickens' (Ernest Boll, 1940, 'The Sketches by Boz', *The Dickensian* 36: 70). 'It has . . . been suggested that the figure on the extreme right of Cruikshank's plate for this sketch represents Dickens' (Malcolm Morley, 1964, 'Revelry by night', *The Dickensian* 40: 98 n.). Mr Morley rejects both identifications.

DICKENS, Elizabeth[1] (1745?–1824) Née Ball, she was the grandmother of Charles Dickens. She was in the service of the family of Lord Crewe throughout her life, becoming the housekeeper at Crewe Hall; she married William Dickens, the butler at Crewe Hall, in 1781.

MRS ROUNCEWELL in Charles Dickens, *Bleak House* (1852–3)

'[She figures as Mrs Rouncewell, the housekeeper at Chesney Wold in *Bleak House*' (A.T. Butler and Arthur Campling, 1949, 'The Dickens ancestry: some new discoveries', *The Dickensian* 45 (March): 70).

DICKENS, Elizabeth[2] (1789–1863) Née Barrow, she married John **Dickens** in 1809. Charles Dickens was her son.

MRS MICAWBER in Charles Dickens, *Nicholas Nickleby* (1838–9)

The link between Mrs Dickens and Mrs Micawber is the brass plate in ch. XI: in 1822 Dickens's parents rented 4 Gower Street North, and a large brass plate on the door announced 'Mrs Dickens's Establishment', for his mother intended to open a girl's school there. 'Nobody ever came to the school, nor do I recollect that anybody ever proposed to come, or that the least preparation was made to receive anybody' (autobiog. fragment, in John Forster, 1928, *Life of Charles Dickens*, ed. J.W.T. Ley, p. 13). The house has been demolished.

MRS NICKLEBY in Charles Dickens, *Nicholas Nickleby* (1838–9)

'Mrs Nickleby herself, sitting bodily before me in a solid chair, once asked whether I really believed there ever was such a woman' (to Richard Lane, 2 January 1844, reproduced in *Letters of Charles Dickens*, 1977, Vol. I, ed. Kathleen Tillotson, Oxford: Oxford University Press, p. 5). The footnote (11) identifies

'Mrs Nickleby herself' as Elizabeth Dickens and continues: 'The identification is traditional, and is clearly implied by Forster'. Forster quotes Dickens, writing to Leigh Hunt: 'The character [i.e. Skimpole] is not you. . . . Under similar disguises my own father and mother are in my books' and adds 'The distinction is that the foibles of Mr Micawber and of Mrs Nickleby . . . make neither of them . . . less loveable' (Forster, op. cit., p. 551).

DICKENS, John (1785?–1851) Father of Charles Dickens. From 1805 to 1825 he was an assistant clerk in the Navy pay office, but he was perpetually in financial straits and in 1824 he was imprisoned for debt. He left the pay office and became a journalist, and in 1828 was a parliamentary reporter. In 1839, Dickens established him in the country, and in 1845, when Dickens assumed control of the proposed *Daily News* (founded by Paxton and his friends, including George **Hudson**), John Dickens was appointed to take charge of the reporting staff and discharged his duties with the greatest efficiency until his last illness. He was described in the early days of the paper as 'a gentleman of most enviable stamina', and, later, as 'short, portly, obese, fond of a glass of grog, full of fun, never given to much locomotion, but sitting as chairman, and looking carefully to the regular marking and orderly despatch to the printers of the numerous manuscripts thrown off at lightning speed by the men from the gallery' (Sir Joseph Crowe, 1895, *Reminiscences of Thirty-five Years of My Life*, London: John Murray, p. 69).

WILLIAM DORRIT in Charles Dickens, *Little Dorrit* (1855–7)

'John Dickens is the source for Mr Micawber; he also becomes, later, the source for William Dorrit' (W. Oddie, 1967, 'Mr Micawber and the redefinition of experience', *The Dickensian* 63: 109).

WILKINS MICAWBER in Charles Dickens, *David Copperfield* (1849–50)

'[T]he feeling of the creator of Micawber, as he . . . remembered the foibles of his original, found its counterpart in that of his readers for the creation itself. . . . Nobody likes Micawber less for his follies; and Dickens liked his father more, the more he recalled his whimsical qualities' (John Forster, 1928, *Life of Dickens*, ed. J.W.T. Ley, p. 552). 'We know more about John Dickens from *David Copperfield* . . . than from any other source. It is worth noting that Micawber's face in the illustration to this Chapter [XVII] (his first appearance in a picture), bears a distinct resemblance to the face of John Dickens' (T.W. Hill, 1943, 'Notes to *David Copperfield*', *The Dickensian* 39: 86 n.4 (to ch. XVII)).

DICKINSON, The Misses May, Hettie and Janet Lowes Dickinson, daughters of Lowes Cato Dickinson and his wife Ellen, née Williams. They were the sisters of Goldsworthy Lowes **Dickinson**.

HELEN AND MARGARET SCHLEGEL in E.M. Forster, *Howards End* (1910)

'The three Miss Dickinsons condensed into two Miss Schlegels' (E.M. Forster, interviewed by P.N. Furbank and F.J.H. Haskell, 1953, 'The art of fiction', *The Paris Review* 1: 37). 'Your three sisters – seen as it were with a sideways glance and then refocused – did help towards my two. That's almost as much as I can recollect . . . of the odd process, but May was, perhaps, more definitely Margaret than anyone else was anything else in those two worlds, though Janet entered in too' (E.M. Forster to G.L. Dickinson, 17 March 1931, quoted in Oliver Stallybrass, 1973, Introd. to *Howard's End*, p. ix). *See also* **Woolf**, Virginia.

DICKINSON, Emily Elizabeth (1830–86) American poet. Born in Amherst, Massachusetts, the daughter of a successful lawyer and congressman, she was educated at Amherst Academy and Mount Holyoke Female Seminary. From the age of 23 she withdrew from social contact, and by the age of 30 she had become an almost total recluse, never leaving her father's house and garden, dressing completely in white, and carrying on her friendships through written correspondence. Only seven of the nearly 2,000 poems that she produced were published during her lifetime.

MERCY PHILBRICK in Helen Hunt Jackson, *Mercy Philbrick's Choice* (1876)

'[The] novel . . . is said to be a fictional study of her friend Emily Dickinson' (James D. Hart (ed.), 1965, *The Oxford Companion to American Literature*, New York: Oxford University Press, s.v. Jackson). The novel was in fact written before she met Emily Dickinson.

ALISON STANHOPE in Susan Glaspell, *Alison's House* (1930)

'Alison Stanhope is considered to represent Emily Dickinson' (Hart, op. cit., s.v. *Alison's House*).

DICKINSON, Goldsworthy Lowes (1862–1932) Educated at Charterhouse and at King's College, Cambridge, he was the son of Lowes Cato Dickinson, the portrait painter, who had been a friend of the Pre-Raphaelites and was, with F.D. Maurice, a founder of the Christian Socialist movement. He was the brother of May, Hettie and Janet ('The Misses') **Dickinson**. As a close friend of E.M. **Forster** and of Roger Fry, the artist, he was connected with the Bloomsbury group. In 1887 he was a Fellow of King's College.

MR LOCKSON in Shane Leslie, *The Cantab* (1926)

Identified in a key in the hand of Dr Ivor Ramsay, a Kingsman of the year 1920, and later Dean, laid in a copy of *The Cantab*.

DICKS, Laura (1871–1959) Known as Blor, she was born in and died in Egham, and was nanny to the Mitford family.

NANNY in Nancy Mitford, *The Blessing* (1951)

'Useless to pretend that the Nanny in *The Blessing* is not based on Blor. She has all her mannerisms and many of her prejudices, but she is a caricature' (Nancy Mitford, 1962, 'Blor', in *The Water Beetle*, London: Hamish Hamilton, p. 14).

DIGBY, Jane (1807–81) Daughter of Admiral Sir Henry Digby and the granddaughter of Thomas **Coke** of Norfolk, in 1824 she married the 1st Earl of **Ellenborough**, but he divorced her in 1830 on the grounds of adultery with Prince Felix Schwarzenberg. In 1832, in Munich, she married Baron Venningen, who committed suicide when she left him, and in 1841 she married Count Spyro Theotoky and settled in Greece. In 1853 she left Athens for Syria, where she finally settled with the Sheikh Abdul Medjnel el Mezrab: she married him and remained with him until her death.

LADY GLENMORE in M. Spencer Stanhope, *Almacks* (1826)

'The character appears to be a blend of both Lady Ann [Coke] and Lady Ellenborough' (E.M. Oddie, 1935, *Portrait of Ianthe*, p. 339). *See also* **Coke**, Lady Anne.

LADY GLENMORE in Lady Charlotte Bury, *The Exclusives* (1830)

Identified in *Key to the Royal Novel 'The Exclusives'*, 1830, Marsh & Miller; reproduced in Michael Sadleir, 1951, *XIX Century Fiction*, 2 vols, London: Constable, and Los Angeles: California University Press, pp. 73–4.

LADY WALMER in Lady Blessington, *The Two Friends* (1835)

'[I]n these volumes, we have many allusions ... to the story of Lady Ellenborough, whom the authoress has caused to sit to her for her sketch of "Lady Walmer"' ('A quintette of novels', *Fraser's Magazine* 11 (April 1835): 476).

DILHORNE, Lord *See* **Manningham-Buller**, Reginald.

DILKE, Sir Charles Wentworth (1843–1911) 2nd Baronet, he was the Son of Sir Charles Dilke, who won the friendship of the Prince Consort while acting as a member of the executive committee of the Great Exhibition. His grandfather (also Charles Wentworth) was the close friend of Keats, Charles Lamb, and Thomas Hood, and was the owner and Editor of the *Athenaeum*. He began attending Trinity Hall, Cambridge, in 1862 and was President of the Union. After travelling around the world he entered politics and was MP for Chelsea from 1868 to 1886. A radical and a republican, he was much influenced by the social reformer J.S. Mill and allied himself with Chamberlain. His political career was destroyed by the Crawford–Dilke divorce case, and in 1886 he resigned his parliamentary seat. The divorce case was one of the great scandals and mysteries of the period, and for the rest of his life Dilke struggled to collect evidence to clear his name. His first wife died in 1874 after the birth of a son following only two years of marriage, and in 1885 he married Emilia **Pattison**. He claimed, with justice, to have known everyone of distinction in the second half of the nineteenth century, and not only in England. Disraeli spoke of him as 'the coming man on the other side'.

ENDYMION FERRARS in Benjamin Disraeli, *Endymion* (1880)

'Lord Beaconsfield told me that he had been very anxious to meet me, since he had taken the liberty of writing about me without my leave in his novel *Endymion*, and that he thought we were never destined to meet' (Charles Dilke, 1917, memoir, in Stephen Gwynn and G. M. Tuckwell, *Life of the Rt. Hon. Sir Charles Dilke*, Vol. I, p. 410). The meeting took place on 30 January 1881. 'Lady Chesterfield guessed at the original of "Endymion". Beaconsfield rallied her on her perspicacity – "I never was more surprised than when you told me who was the original of Endymion. I thought he was the last person who could have been fixed on"' (*Letters of Disraeli to Lady Bradford and Lady Chesterfield*, 1929, ed. Marquis of Zetland, Vol. II, London: Ernest Benn, p. 301). The date of the letter is not given, but it was written apparently between 28 November and 7

December 1880. Writing to Lord Beaconsfield on 7 February 1881, the Queen asked, 'How is it that your hero should be a Whig?', to which Beaconsfield replied: 'Endymion was not intended for a hero. . . . I did not wish him to be an interesting character: he has no imagination and very controlled passion: but he has great patience, perseverance, judgment, and tact. . . . He is in fact rather a plodder, and I thought quite good enough to be a Whig' (10 February 1881, reproduced in *Letters of Queen Victoria*, 1928 (2nd series), ed. G.E. Buckle, Vol. III, London: John Murray, p. 195). A very adequate description of Dilke.

DILLING, Elizabeth

Mrs Gimmitch in Sinclair Lewis, *It Can't Happen Here* (1935)

Identified in Arthur M. Schlesinger, Jun., 1961, *The Politics of Upheaval (The Age of Roosevelt III)*, p. 89.

DILLON, Luke (b. 1848) An Irish-American terrorist, he was involved in the dynamite outrages in London during the 1890s, but was never captured by the police. It was his habit to carry dynamite on his person.

The Professor in Joseph Conrad, *The Secret Agent* (1907)

'The person Conrad seems to have used as a source here was Luke Dillon' (Norman Sherry, 1971, *Conrad's Western World*, Cambridge, p. 283). Professor Sherry was unable to discover how Conrad came to know of Dillon, but suggests that either Roger Casement or Cunninghame Graham might have spoken of him (see Sherry, op. cit., p. 285). *See also* **Creaghe**, Dr; **Mezzeroff**, 'Professor'; **Most**, Johann; **Rossetti**, Arthur.

DILLON, Mamie Daughter of Matt Dillon, an old friend of the Joyce family who is also mentioned in *Ulysses*.

Marion ('Molly') Bloom in James Joyce, *Ulysses* (1922)

'For the Spanish quality in [Molly Bloom] Joyce drew upon one of the many daughters of Matt Dillon. . . . This daughter had been in Spain, smoked cigarettes, and was considered a Spanish type' (Richard Ellmann, 1982, *James Joyce*, rev. edn, Oxford: Oxford University Press, p. 376). 'I want . . . any information you have about the Dillons (Matt Dillon and his bevy of daughters, Tiny, Floey, Atty, Sara, Nannie and Mamie, especially the last, the cigarette smoker and Spanish type.)' (to Josephine Murray, wife of William Murray, and his aunt by marriage, [12 October 1921], reproduced in *The Letters of James Joyce*, 1957, Vol. I, ed. Stuart Gilbert, London: Faber & Faber, p. 174). *See also* **Chance**, Mrs Charles; **Joyce**, Nora; **Popper**, Amalia; **Santos**, Signora.

DISRAELI, Benjamin, 1st Earl of Beaconsfield (1804–81) British statesman and novelist. Born in London, eldest son of Isaac **D'Israeli**, who, although Jewish, had his son baptized in 1817. In 1826 he published his first novel *Vivian Grey*, and after travelling in Europe, he stood for Parliament in 1931, losing four elections before becoming MP for Maidstone in 1837. He became Prime Minister in February 1868, but resigned in December of that year. He returned to power in 1874 and in 1875 he made Britain half-owner of the Suez Canal. In 1876 he conferred on Queen Victoria her new title of Empress of India and in the same year he was made Earl of Beaconsfield and went to the Upper House. He is buried at Hughendon in Buckinghamshire, his family home. After his wife's death in 1873, he formed a deeply romantic attachment to Selina, Countess of **Bradford**, writing to her sometimes daily.

MR DAUBENY in Anthony Trollope, *Phineas Finn* (1869)

'[Trollope] admitted that the Tory leader Daubeny was Disraeli (then in opposition to Gladstone)' (Michael Sadleir, 1945, *Trollope: a commentary*, 2nd rev. edn, London: Constable, p. 418; originally published 1927, London: Constable).

CONTARINI FLEMING in Benjamin Disraeli, *Contarini Fleming* (1832)

'One of Benjamin Disraeli's autobiographical heroes – Contarini Fleming . . .' (B.R. Jerman, 1960, *The Young Disraeli*, London: Oxford University Press, p. 38).

VIVIAN GREY in Benjamin Disraeli, *Vivian Grey* (1826–7)

'In *Vivian Grey* I have portrayed my active and real ambition' (Disraeli in his diary, 1833–4, reproduced in Robert Blake, 1966, *Disraeli*, London: Eyre & Spottiswoode, p. 38). 'No doubt he had in mind the Vivian Grey of the first three books – not the rather absurd figure of melodrama who figures at the end of the fourth' (ibid.).

ROBERT ORANGE in John Oliver Hobbes, *The School for Saints* (1897) and *Robert Orange* (1900)

'Robert is an idealized and Catholicized Disraeli' (Margaret Maison, 1961, *Search Your Soul, Eustace: a survey of the religious novel in the Victorian age*, p. 165).

SIDONIA in Benjamin Disraeli, *Coningsby* (1844)

'"Sidonia" stands for several types in addition to Disraeli's own' (Walter Sichel, 1904, *Disraeli: a study in personality and ideas*, London: Methuen, p. 122 n. 1). *See also* de **Rothschild**, Adolph; de **Rothschild**, Baron James Mayer; de **Rothschild**, Lionel; **Urquhart**, David.

SIDONIA in Anthony Trollope, *Framley Parsonage* (1861)

'Later in the book, chapter 18, when real politics give way to imaginary politics . . . [Lord Brock's] successful rivals are Lord de Terrier and Sidonia, who are clearly Derby and Disraeli' (R.W. Chapman, 1948, 'Personal names in Trollope's political novels', in *Essays Mainly on the Nineteenth Century Presented to Sir Humphrey Milford*, p. 76).

D'ISRAELI, Isaac (1766–1848) He was the father of Benjamin Disraeli and was the anonymous author of *Curiosities of Literature* (1791) and other works.

HORACE GREY in Benjamin Disraeli, *Vivian Grey* (1826–7)

'Horace Grey was his father' (Lucien Wolf, 1904, Introd. to *Vivian Grey*, 1904 (centenary edn), London: Alexander Moring, p. xxxvi; originally published 1826, London: Henry Colburn).

MR SHERBORNE in Benjamin Disraeli, *Vivian Grey* (1826–7)

Identified as Mr D'Is—i, sen., in a key given in a pamphlet published in 1827 by William Marsh. This key is discussed by Lucien Wolf in his notes to *Vivian*

Grey (1904 (centenary edn), Vol. II, London: Alexander Moring, p. 364), who concludes that Disraeli was not responsible for the key.

DISS, Norfolk

DEERBROOK in Harriet Martineau, *Deerbrook* (1839)

'I have over and over again heard ... that Diss was Deerbrook' (to Harriet Martineau, 7 December 1859, reproduced in *The Letters of Mrs Gaskell*, 1966, ed. J.A.V. Chapple and Arthur Pollard, Manchester, p. 909). Mrs Gaskell implies in her next sentence that she does not necessarily accept the identification. 'One acquires one's materials,' she writes, 'unconsciously as it were.'

DODGSON, Charles Lutwidge (Lewis Carroll) (1832–98) English author and mathematician, who wrote under the name of Lewis Carroll. Born near Warrington the third of eleven children, he was educated at Rugby and at Christ Church, Oxford, where he was a mathematics lecturer from 1855 to 1881. He took orders in 1861. His most famous book, *Alice in Wonderland*, was published in 1865, and appears to have been inspired by a boating trip which Dodgson took with the young **Liddell** children, daughters of the Dean of Christ Church Henry Liddell, in the summer of 1862. A sequel, *Through the Looking-Glass and What Alice Found There*, followed in 1871, and the two books, with their fantastical settings, upside-down logic and refreshing lack of moralizing, proved to be vastly successful with Victorian children and subsequent generations.

THE WHITE KNIGHT in Lewis Carroll, *Through the Looking-Glass* (1872)

'Many Carrollian scholars have surmised, and with good reason, that Carroll intended the White Knight to be a caricature of himself' (*The Annotated Alice*, 1970, with introd. and notes by Martin Gardner, Harmondsworth: Penguin, p. 296).

DONNELLY, Ned (b. 1844) George Bernard Shaw's 'professor' of boxing, he was himself a pupil of Nat Langham. Shaw met him through Pakenham **Beatty** and attended his gymnasium in London.

NED SKENE in George Bernard Shaw, *Cashel Byron's Profession* (1886)

'Around the time he and Shaw first met, Donnelly published a small manual on the art of boxing (Self Defence)' (Benny Green, 1975, *Shaw's Champions: G.B.S. & prizefighting from Cashel Brown to Gene Tunney*, London: Elm Tree Books, pp. 5–6). In 1882, Shaw settled down to write *Cashel Byron's Profession*, 'drawing heavily on Donnelly for his portrait of Ned Skene' (ibid., p. 7).

DOOLITTLE, Hilda (H.D.) (1886–1961) Poet and novelist. Born in Bethlehem, Pennsylvania, she was the daughter of a professor of astronomy. In 1901 she met Ezra **Pound**, who became a close friend, and in 1904–6 she attended Bryn Mawr College. She left America for Europe in 1911 and settled in London, marrying Richard **Aldington** in 1913; they became friends with D.H. and Frieda **Lawrence**, and in 1918 she met the novelist Bryher (Winifred Ellerman), with whom she formed a close friendship. She and Richard Aldington separated in

1919 and were finally divorced in 1937. An early Imagist, she had her first poems published in 1913.

JULIA ASHTON in H.D. (Hilda Doolittle), *Bid Me to Live* (1960)

'Julia is of course H.D.' (Perdita Schaffner, 1984, 'A profound animal', in *Bid Me to Live*, p. 186). Perdita Schaffner is H.D.'s daughter.

JULIA CUNNINGHAM in D.H. Lawrence, *Aaron's Rod* (1922)

'Julia . . . is H.D.: the "tall stag of a thing"' (Barbara Guest, 1985, *Herself Defined: the poet H.D. and her world*, London: Collins, p. 89; originally published 1984, Garden City, NY: Doubleday).

EUNICE DINWIDDIE in Louis Wilkinson, *The Buffoon* (1916)

'In *The Buffoon*, H.D. is called Eunice Dinwiddie' (Guest, op. cit., p. 44).

MIRANDA MASTERS in John Cournos, *Miranda Masters* (1926)

'*Miranda Masters* . . . portrays [John Cournos's] relationship to H.D. during the war years' (Janice Robinson, *H.D.*, Boston, p. 42).

DORCHESTER, Dorset County town.

CASTERBRIDGE in Thomas Hardy, Wessex novels and tales (1871–95)

'It might be urged that my Casterbridge . . . is not Dorchester – not even the Dorchester as it existed sixty years ago, but a dream-place that never was outside an irresponsible book. Nevertheless, when somebody said to me that "Casterbridge" is a sort of essence of the town as it used to be, "a place more Dorchester than Dorchester itself", I could not absolutely contradict him' (Thomas Hardy on receiving the freedom of Dorchester, 16 November 1910, quoted in F.E. Hardy, 1972, *The Life of Thomas Hardy, 1840–1928*, p. 351).

DORION, Charles T. A young lawyer who was admitted to a practice in Minnesota in 1902. In 1905 he was in the town of Sauk Center, where he met and became friendly with the young Sinclair Lewis. He had no success there and stayed for only one year.

GUY POLLOCK in Sinclair Lewis, *Main Street* (1920)

'Charles T. Dorion . . . was the genesis and prototype of Guy Pollock' (Mark Schorer, 1963, *Sinclair Lewis*, London: Heinemann, p. 102; originally published 1961, New York: McGraw-Hill).

DORMAN-SMITH, E.E. (1895–1969) Afterwards Dorman O'Gowan, called Chink. Of a landed family in County Cavan, he was educated at Uppingham and Sandhurst. He joined the Northumberland Fusiliers and during the First World War he gained a very distinguished record. He was a brigadier in 1938 and became Chief of Staff to General Auchinleck in North Africa, and was subsequently Director of Military Training at General Headquarters in India. In 1918 he met Ernest Hemingway in Milan, where he was Officer-in-Charge of the British troops stationed in the city; they became warm friends and saw a good deal of each other between 1922 and 1926. When Dorman-Smith was stationed in Cologne in the Army of Occupation, Hemingway visited him there and gathered material for two of the sketches in *In Our Time*. Dorman-Smith went to Paris on leave or joined the Hemingways on trips to the mountains that Hemingway described many years later in 'A False Spring' (*A Moveable Feast*); he was godfather to their son John ('Bumby'). In 1924 Hemingway, on his first visit to the fiesta at Pamplona, went fishing with Bill **Smith** in the Burguele: they met Dorman-Smith, who was setting out to walk through Andorra with John **Dos Passos** and Robert **McAlmon**. In later life they met infrequently, although their friendship lasted until Hemingway's death.

WILSON-HARRIS in Ernest Hemingway, *The Sun Also Rises* (1926)

'This admirable figure who is modeled on Edward Dorman-Smith' (G.T. Gordon, 1972, 'Hemingway's Wilson-Harris', in *Fitzgerald–Hemingway Annual, 1972*, Washington, DC, p. 237).

D'ORSAY, Alfred Guillaume Gabriel, Count (1801–52) Portrait painter. In 1821 he visited England for the coronation of George IV, and in 1831 he joined Lady **Blessington** in establishing a fashionable coterie in London; he left London for Paris in 1849, driven out by debt.

SIR GERALD DENBIGH in T.H. Lister, *Arlington* (1832)

'*Arlington* . . . is notable chiefly for its . . . presentation of two types of dandies . . . the intellectual and the picturesque. Of the two, the intellectual, Sir Gerald Denbigh, who is probably drawn in part from D'Orsay, is the more interesting' (M.W. Rosa, 1936, *The Silver-Fork School: novels of fashion preceding 'Vanity Fair'*, New York, p. 71).

PERCY GODOLPHIN in Bulwer Lytton, *Godolphin* (1833)

'[T]he reader might readily conceive that Constance and Godolphin are meant to be Lady Blessington and Count D'Orsay. . . . But although there are some resemblances, the comparison cannot be carried far' (Rosa, op. cit., pp. 95–6).

COUNT ALCIBIADES DE MIRABEL in Benjamin Disraeli, *Henrietta Temple* (1837)

'[T]he [portrait] . . . of Count Alcibiades de Mirabel, a delightful picture of d'Orsay to whom the book is dedicated, [has] an attractive sparkle' (Robert Blake, 1966, *Disraeli*, London: Eyre & Spottiswoode, p. 144).

PAULET in W. Massie, *Sydenham; or Memoirs of a Man of the World* (1830)

'Volume one is purely social, dealing with such notables as . . . D'Orsay (Mr Paulet)' (Rosa, op. cit., p. 81 n. 3).

DICK SWIVELLER in Charles Dickens, *The Old Curiosity Shop* (1840–1)

For a number of years D'Orsay was unable to leave Gore house except on Sundays, for fear of being taken up for debt. Surely Dickens borrowed from his friend both this and the faint shadow of the dandy which hangs about Swiveller. I owe this suggestion to Professor Kathleen Tillotson.

DOS PASSOS, John R. (1844–1917) Born in Philadelphia, he was of Portuguese descent. He fought in the Civil War and in 1865 was admitted to the Philadelphia Bar, being transferred to New York City in 1867. After a successful start at the criminal Bar, he took up commercial practice and became a successful corporation lawyer. In 1910, after a long liaison and following the death of his first wife, a Roman Catholic, he married Mrs Lucy Madison: John Dos Passos was their son.

JAMES KNOX POLK PIGNATELLI in John Dos Passos, *Chosen Country* (1951)

'My relations with my father whom I came to admire greatly before he died . . . were much too complicated to go into here. For a *fictional* approximation see Chosen Country: the Pignatelli family' (John Dos Passos to Melvin Landsberg, 12 August 1964, quoted in Landsberg, 1972, *Dos Passos' Path to USA*, Boulder, p. 6).

DOS PASSOS, John Roderigo (1896–1970) American novelist. Son of John R. Dos Passos, he was brought up in Chicago and educated at Harvard University. He served in the Norton–Hayes Ambulance Corps during the First World War and met Hemingway in Italy in 1918. During the 1920s he lived in Paris, and in 1929 he married Katie Smith (**Dos Passos**, below); he remarried after her death. He was a writer with a strong social conscience.

RICHARD GORDON in Ernest Hemingway, *To Have and Have Not* (1937)

'Gingrich warned [in 1936] that the book clearly libeled Dos Passos through the figure of Richard Gordon' (Carlos Baker, 1969, *Ernest Hemingway: a life story*, New York, p. 298). *See also* **Fisher**, Edward.

BILL GORTON in Ernest Hemingway, *The Sun Also Rises* (1926)

'EH also borrowed elements from . . . Dos Passos. Dos had discovered Mme Lecomte and her restaurant on the Isle-St-Louis during his days with the Norton–Hayes Ambulance' (Baker, op. cit., p. 594 n. 'Identification of characters in "The Sun Also Rises"'). *See also* **Smith**, Bill; **Stewart**, Donald Ogden.

JAY PIGNATELLI in John Dos Passos, *Chosen Country* (1951)

The novel is almost entirely autobiographical, apart from those elements in it that Dos Passos took from his wife's memories of her childhood in Michigan. In it he describes his strange life as a child wandering about Europe with his mother, paints a vivid portrait of his father and gives an account of his experiences in France during the war (see '. . . Jay Pignatelli, Dos Passos' semi-autobiographical figure . . . in *Chosen Country*', in Melvin Landsberg, 1972, *Dos Passos' Path to USA*, Boulder, p. 8).

DOS PASSOS, Katharine ('Katie') Foster (1891–1947) Sister of Bill **Smith** and Y.K. **Smith**, like her brothers she was a close friend of Ernest **Hemingway** from childhood; she introduced him to his first wife, Hadley, and was a close friend of his second, Pauline (they were both from St Louis). 'Her most arresting feature was her eyes, which were green as a cat's, and almost made you think she could see in the dark' (Carlos Baker, 1969, *Ernest Hemingway: a life story*, New York, p. 25). She first met Dos Passos at Hemingway's house at Key West in 1928, and they married in 1929. She was killed in a terrible motor accident in which Dos Passos lost an eye.

LULIE HARRINGTON in John Dos Passos, *Chosen Country* (1951)

Identified in Baker, op. cit., p. 654 n. 'E.H. on Dos Passos's "Chosen Country"'.

DOUGLAS, Lord Alfred (1870–1945) Poet. Known as 'Bosie', he was the son of the 8th Marquess of Queensberry. He was a close friend of Oscar Wilde; it was a postcard delivered by his father at Wilde's club that compelled Wilde to initiate the action for libel which finally led, in 1895, to his own conviction and imprisonment on a charge of homosexual conduct. Wilde's devotion to Lord Douglas continued until his death.

LORD REGINALD HASTINGS in Robert Hichens, *The Green Carnation* (1894)

'*The Green Carnation* . . . was a novel in which the two principal characters are recognisable portraits of Oscar and Bosie' (Violet Wyndham, 1963, *The Sphinx and Her Circle: a biographical sketch of Ida Leverson, 1862–1933*, London: Deutsch, p. 43).

DOUGLAS, Frances, Lady (1750–1817) Née Scott, she was the daughter of Lord Dalkeith; after her father's death, her mother married Charles Townsend, the Whig politician, who was devoted to his step-daughter. In 1784 she married Mr Douglas, the successful claimant in the famous Douglas case: in 1790 he became the 1st Baron Douglas of Douglas. In 1799 she became one of Sir Walter Scott's closest friends.

JEANIE DEANS in Sir Walter Scott, *The Heart of Midlothian* (1818)

'It was suggested by Lady Louisa Stuart [Lady Douglas's cousin, and one of Scott's closest friends] that Lady Douglas's character helped to mould Scott's creation of Jeanie Deans' (*The Letters of Sir Walter Scott*, 1933, ed. H.J.C. Grierson, Vol. IV, London: Constable, p. 450 n.). Lady Louisa Stuart wrote to Scott, in 1818: 'Is it possible that you had at all in your eye what my wishes pointed to, when I wrote to you last winter? If not, you will think the question strange; yet, with all the differences of situation . . . refinement, &c, . . . there was a strong likeness of character: the same steady attachment to rectitude, the same simplicity and singleness of heart, the same inward humility . . . the same strong, plain, straightforward understanding always hitting exactly right. . . . Let me dream that you designed this resemblance, whether you did or not' (quoted in F. MacCunn, 1909, *Sir Walter Scott's Friends*, p. 204). *See also* **Walker**, Helen.

DOUGLAS, Mahala Dutton Benedict She married Walter Douglas, founder of the Quaker Oats Company; when he died in the *Titanic* disaster, she inherited his fortune. She lived at Cedar Rapids, Iowa, where she befriended the young Carl Van Vechten. A woman of advanced views, she was not considered proper company for the young. In 1943 Gertrude **Stein** and Alice B. Toklas lunched with her 'at her vast estate near Minneapolis': the luncheon is described in *The Alice B. Toklas Cook Book*, and the recipe for one of the dishes they had, Lobster Archiduc, is given there.

COUNTESS ELLA NATTATORINI in Carl Van Vechten, *The Tattooed Countess* (1926)

'[T]hey were entertained at the baronial estate of Mrs Walter Douglas . . . the original model, so Gertrude and Alice believed, of . . . *The Tattooed Countess*' (James P. Mellon, 1974, *The Charmed Circle: Gertrude Stein and company*, p. 396).

DOUGLAS, Norman (1868–1952) Writer. Born in Thüringen, he was educated in Uppingham and Karlsruhe and spent a short time in the Foreign Service (mainly in Russia). In 1896 he resigned and set up house in the Villa Maya at Posilipo. After marrying in 1898 and divorcing in 1904, he settled on Capri. Between 1910 and 1916 he lived in London, where he was Assistant Editor of the *English Review*. After the First World War he returned to Italy, living mainly in Florence until 1937. He spent the Second World War in England, and in 1946 he went back to Capri, remaining there for the rest of his life. His life was much complicated by his pederasty, which enforced frequent bolts from the law, from province to province in Italy, and sometimes from country to country.

JAMES ARGYLE in D.H. Lawrence, *Aaron's Rod* (1922)

'Do you think Douglas will identify himself with Argyle and be offended? I should think not' (to Martin Secker, 23 November 1921, reproduced in *The Letters of D.H. Lawrence*, 1987, Vol. IV, ed. W. Roberts, J.T. Boulton and E. Mansfield, Cambridge: Cambridge University Press, p. 129). 'If you really must modify Argyle – I think he is so funny . . . you can do so at your discretion' (to Thomas Seltzer, 26 November 1921, ibid., p. 131).

DONALD MCDOUGALL in Osbert Sitwell, *Donald McDougall* (1958)

'There were also portraits of his more famous friends . . . most memorable of all, Norman Douglas (given the alias of Donald McDougall), the "complete realisation, spiritually, of that ideal of ancient China, the Old Scamp"' (John Pearson, 1978, *Façades: Edith, Osbert, and Sacheverell Sitwell*, London: Macmillan, p. 458).

DUNCAN MAXWELL in Compton Mackenzie, *Vestal Fire* (1927)

'Norman Douglas appears in these pages as Duncan Maxwell' (inscription in the author's hand in a copy of *Vestal Fire* offered for sale in Blackwell's catalogue, Oxford, A1067).

MR SCOGAN in Aldous Huxley, *Crome Yellow* (1921)

'There is something of Norman Douglas in old Scogan. . . . I knew Douglas quite well in the twenties in Florence' (Aldous Huxley, interviewed by George Wickes and Roy Frazer, 1960, 'The art of fiction, XXIV', *Paris Review* 23 (spring): 76). *See also* **Russell**, Bertrand.

DOUGLAS, Sholto

ROBERT KEMP in F.W. Rolfe, *Nicholas Crabbe* (1958)

Identified by Cecil Woolf in his introduction to *Nicholas Crabbe*, 1958, pp. 5–7.

DOUHAULT, Adelaide-Marie-Rogres-Lusignan de Champignelles, Marquise de (*c*.1741–1817).

LAURA FAIRLIE in Wilkie Collins, *The Woman in White* (1860)

The plot of the novel was taken from the celebrated case of the widowed Marquise de Douhault, who in 1787 was drugged by her brother and nephew and incarcerated under a false name in the Salpétrière, the asylum in Paris. Her death was presumed and her estate passed on to them. Wilkie Collins found the case recounted in Maurice Méjan, 1808, *Recueil des Cause Célèbres*, Vol. III, pp. 5 f., and in Méjan, 1809, ibid., Vol. VI, pp. 5–92, which were in his library (see Clyde C. Hyder, 1939, *Publications of the Modern Language Association* 54: 297 ff.).

DOVEDALE, Staffordshire   A dale in the Peak District, north-west of Ashbourne, it is a sheltered limestone gorge.

Eagledale in George Eliot, *Adam Bede* (1859)

'"Eagledale" is Dovedale' (Marghanita Laski, 1973, *George Eliot and Her World*, London: Thames & Hudson, p. 65).

DOWS, Olin   (b. 1904?) He first met Wolfe at Harvard in 1923 before leaving to go to Yale School of Fine Arts. Between 1924 and 1928, Wolfe often visited him at Rhinebeck, his family's estate on the Hudson River.

Joel Pierce in Thomas Wolfe, *Of Time and the River* (1935)

'Joel Pierce in *Of Time and the River*' (Andrew Turnbull, 1968, *Thomas Wolfe: a biography*, London: Bodley Head, p. 117).

D'OYLY CARTE, Rupert   (1876–1948) Son of Richard D'Oyly Carte, the producer of Gilbert and Sullivan's operas, he was educated at Winchester and became Chairman of the Savoy, Berkeley, and New Claridges hotel companies. He was the proprietor of the D'Oyly Carte Opera Company.

Rupert Psmith in P.G. Wodehouse, *Mike* (1909) and others

'The character of Psmith . . . is the only thing in my literary career which was handed to me on a plate with watercress round it. . . . Psmith came to me ready-made. A cousin of mine, who had been at Winchester, happened to tell me one night of Rupert D'Oyly Carte . . . a schoolmate of his. . . . [He] was long, slender, always beautifully dressed and very dignified. His speech was what is known as orotund, and he wore a monocle. He habitually addressed his fellow Wykehamists as "Comrade", and if one of the masters chanced to inquire as to his health, would reply, "Sir, I grow thinnah and thinnah." . . . I was writing a serial for . . . *The Captain* at the time, and to remove the character I had planned and put Psmith in his place was . . . the work of a moment' (P.G. Wodehouse, 1974, preface to *The World of Psmith*, London: Barrie & Jenkins, p. v).

DRAYSON, Alfred Wilks   (1826?–1901) Mathematician and astronomer. He spent two years at Greenwich Observatory in London, and was on the staff of the Royal Military Academy at Woolwich from 1858 until 1873. He was resident at Southsea in 1882–9 and came to know Arthur Conan Doyle, with whom he investigated psychic phenomena.

Professor James Moriarty in Arthur Conan Doyle, the Sherlock Holmes stories (1890–1927)

'The professor is described [in 'The Final Problem'] as a remarkable mathematician and author of a brilliantly abstruse work on asteroids; these elements of the character are drawn from Conan Doyle's mathematician-astronomer friend . . . Major-General Drayson, a specialist in asteroids' (Charles Higham, 1876, *The Adventures of Conan Doyle*, p. 113). *See also* **Moriarty**, George; **Payn**, James; **Worth**, Adrian.

DREISER, Cecilia ('Sylvia') Youngest sister of Theodore Dreiser, in around 1885 she had an illegitimate child as the result of an affair with Don **Ashley** of Warsaw, Indiana. She married Hide Ishima, a photographer of Newark, New Jersey, and was still alive in 1944.

AMY in Theodore Dreiser, *Dawn* (1931)

'Dreiser . . . referred to her as "Amy" in *Dawn*' (Richard Lehan, 1969, *Theodore Dreiser: his world and his novels*, London and Amsterdam: Feffer & Simons, p. 12).

JENNIE GERHARDT in Theodore Dreiser, *Jennie Gerhardt* (1911)

'Jennie's story is the composite story of Dreiser's sisters Mame and Sylvia. . . . To . . . incidents [from Mame's life] Dreiser added the story of Sylvia which roughly parallels the Jennie–Lester Kane plot' (Lehan, op. cit., p. 83). *See also* **Dreiser**, Mary Frances.

DREISER, Emma Wilhelmina (d. 1937) Second sister of Theodore Dreiser. She had two children, but her marriage to L.A. **Hopkins** was unhappy.

JANET in Theodore Dreiser, *Dawn* (1931)

'Dreiser wrote about her early years in *Dawn*, where he called her Janet' (Richard Lehan, 1969, *Theodore Dreiser: his world and his novels*, London and Amsterdam: Feffer & Simons, p. 10).

CAROLINE MEEBER in Theodore Dreiser, *Sister Carrie* (1900)

'From the sexual adventures of his sister Em, first with a Chicago architect and then with the . . . saloon-manager named Hopkins, Dreiser would draw the outlines of Carrie's story. . . . But Em completely lacked the artistic flair that characterised . . . most of the Dreiser children . . . [she] grew fat and matronly and weepy . . . and . . . exhibited none of [Carrie's] talent or . . . drive. . . . Em is not Sister Carrie' (Ellen Moers, 1970, *Two Dreisers*, London: Thames & Hudson, p. 79; originally published 1969, New York: Viking).

DREISER, John Paul (1821–1900) Father of Theodore Dreiser. Born in Mayen, near Coblenz, he emigrated to America in 1844 and settled in Sullivan, Indiana, where he owned a woollen mill. He lost everything when the mill was destroyed by fire, and thereafter descended into poverty. He was a bigoted Catholic, prey to severe depression. He married Sarah Schönäb (**Dreiser**, below) in 1848, and at the end of his life he lived with his daughter Mame (Mary Frances **Dreiser**) and her husband Austin **Brennan**.

SOLON BARNES in Theodore Dreiser, *The Bulwark* (1946)

'The Solon Barnes who might once have been a harsh portrayal of his father, or even a gently ironic one, now became his father lovingly transformed into the embodiment of Dreiser's own feeling of affection' (Robert H. Elias, 1970, *Theodore Dreiser*, pp. 298–9).

MR GERHARDT in Theodore Dreiser, *Jennie Gerhardt* (1911)

'[Jennie's] father is to the last inflection the picture of [Dreiser's] father, except as he is a bigoted Lutheran instead of Catholic' (Dorothy Dudley, 1933, *Dreiser and the Land of the Free*, p. 240).

ASA GRIFFITHS in Theodore Dreiser, *An American Tragedy* (1925)

'Asa is modeled on . . . (Asa Conklin) . . . he is also modeled on his own father, as a discarded version of *An American Tragedy* proves' (Richard Lehan, 1969, *Theodore Dreiser: his world and his novels*, London and Amsterdam: Feffer & Simons, p. 4). *See also* **Conklin**, Asa.

DREISER, Marcus Romanus ('Rome') (d. 1940) Second brother of Theodore Dreiser, he was a railroad man, tipsy and coarse mouthed. When Dreiser was five or six years old, Rome took him out on the Wabash River in a rowing boat and rocked the boat to frighten him. 'The child thought he was going to fall in the water and drown, and he began to scream; Rome grinned . . . and went on rocking. Dreiser told this story often. . . . He said that "for some four or five years afterwards I could not view any considerable body of water without having brought back to me most clearly that particular sensation of something that could and might destroy me"' (Ellen Moers, 1970 *Two Dreisers*, London: Thames & Hudson, p. 217; originally published 1969, New York: Viking; see Dreiser, 1931, *Dawn*, New York, p. 28). From the mid-1920s until his death, Rome was supported entirely by Theodore.

STEWART BARNES in Theodore Dreiser, *The Bulwark* (1946)

'Surely from Rome also derived some of the wildness of Stewart Barnes' (Moers, op. cit., p. 218).

SEBASTIAN ('BASS') GERHARDT in Theodore Dreiser, *Jennie Gerhardt* (1911)

'Sebastian . . . Gerhardt . . . is a sentimentalized version of Rome' (Moers, op. cit., p. 218). *See also* **Dresser**, Paul.

DREISER, Mary Frances ('Mame') (1861–1944) Eldest of Theodore's sisters. While a young woman in Terre Haute, she became the mistress of a prominent local politician who had procured the release from prison of her brother Paul **Dresser**. She went to Chicago and married Austin **Brennan**, then moved to New York. In the latter part of her life she was largely dependent on her brother.

ELEANOR in Theodore Dreiser, *Dawn* (1931)

'[I]n *Dawn* . . . he refers to Mame as Eleanor' (Richard Lehan, 1969, *Theodore Dreiser: his world and his novels*, London and Amsterdam: Feffer & Simons, p. 9).

JENNIE GERHARDT in Theodore Dreiser, *Jennie Gerhardt* (1911)

See under **Dreiser**, Cecilia.

ESTA GRIFFITHS in Theodore Dreiser, *An American Tragedy* (1925)

'Esta . . . (modelled on Mame)' (Lehan, op. cit., p. 155).

DREISER, Sara Osborne White ('Jug') (1869?–1942) School teacher. She met Theodore Dreiser in 1893 on the Chicago train, and married him in 1898, becoming his first wife; they separated in 1910.

ANGEL BLUE in Theodore Dreiser, *The 'Genius'* (1915)

'When he put his own wife into ... *The "Genius"* he had named her ... Angel Blue' (Ellen Moers, 1970, *Two Dreisers*, p. 212).

RUTH in Arthur Henry, *An Island Cabin* (1902)

'Jug ... [is] referred to herein as ... Ruth' (Robert H. Elias, 1970, *Theodore Dreiser*, p. 322 n. 1).

DREISER, Sarah Schönäb (1833–90) The daughter of a Pennsylvania Dutch couple of the Mennonite faith, she married John Paul **Dreiser** in 1848; they had thirteen children, including Theodore Dreiser.

MRS GERHARDT in Theodore Dreiser, *Jennie Gerhardt* (1911)

'Mrs Gerhardt is modeled on Dreiser's mother' (Richard Lehan, 1969, *Theodore Dreiser: his world and his novels*, London and Amsterdam: Feffer & Simons, p. 83).

ELVIRA GRIFFITHS in Theodore Dreiser, *An American Tragedy* (1925)

'Mrs Dreiser was to appear in many ... of Dreiser's works. Particularly in *An American Tragedy* (as Mrs Asa Griffiths)' (Lehan, op. cit., p. 3).

DREISER, Theodore Herman Albert (1871–1945) American novelist. Born in Terre Haute, Indiana, the son of John Paul and Sarah Schönäb **Dreiser**, and one of thirteen children, he left home for Chicago at the age of 15. After a number of odd jobs he became a journalist with the *Chicago Globe*. In 1894 he moved to New York, where he worked as an editor for Butterick, a company specializing in women's magazines. Dreiser's reputation was harmed by his jealousy of Sinclair **Lewis**'s receipt of the 1930 Nobel Prize for Literature and his alleged plagiarism of a book on Russia by Lewis's wife, Dorothy Thompson.

WILLARD KANE in Theodore Dreiser, *The Bulwark* (1946)

'Dreiser obviously modelled Kane on himself' (Richard Lehan, 1969, *Theodore Dreiser: his world and his novels*, London and Amsterdam: Feffer & Simons, p. 223).

TOM in Arthur Henry, *An Island Cabin* (1902)

'Dreiser ... [is] referred to herein as Tom' (Robert H. Elias, 1970, *Theodore Dreiser*, p. 322 n. 1).

EUGENE WITLA in Theodore Dreiser, *The 'Genius'* (1915)

'When they came to write autobiographical fiction ... Crane and Dreiser portrayed themselves as artists, not writers, in the nineties' (Ellen Moers, 1970, *Two Dreisers*, London: Thames & Hudson, p. 42; originally published 1969, New York: Viking). Dreiser's autobiographical novel is identified as *The 'Genius'* (see Moers, op. cit., p. 326 n. 21). *See also* **Shinn**, Everett; **Sonntag**, William Louis.

DREISER, Theresa (1864–97) Third of Theodore Dreiser's sisters, she was killed in an accident.

RUTH in Theodore Dreiser, *Dawn* (1931)

'Theresa, whom Dreiser refers to as "Ruth" in *Dawn* . . .' (Richard Lehan, 1969, *Theodore Dreiser: his world and his novels*, London and Amsterdam: Feffer & Simons, p. 10).

DRESSER, Paul (1857–1911) Song-writer. He composed 'On the Banks of the Wabash', the words of which were written by his brother Theodore Dreiser.

SEBASTIAN ('BASS') GERHARDT in Theodore Dreiser, *Jennie Gerhardt* (1911)

'[Jennie's] brother, Bass, [is] modelled upon Paul Dresser' (Richard Lehan, 1969, *Theodore Dreiser: his world and his novels*, London and Amsterdam: Feffer & Simons, p. 83). *See also* **Dreiser**, Rome.

DRINKWATER, John (1822–1937) Playwright and poet. He was the author of *Abraham Lincoln* (1918) and the co-founder, with Sir Barry Jackson, of the Birmingham Repertory Theatre and, with Gilbert **Cannan**, of the Manchester Repertory Theatre.

JASPER GIBBONS in W. Somerset Maugham, *Cakes and Ale* (1930)

'Fred Bason, the author of *Fred Bason's Diaries* (1950, 1952) . . . declared [to Allen B. Brown] that John Drinkwater . . . considered Gibbons a cruel caricature of himself' (Allen B. Brown, 1960, 'Substance and shadow: the originals of the characters in *Cakes and Ale*', *Papers of the Michigan Academy of Science, Arts and Letters* 45: 444 n. 20). *See also* **Phillips**, Stephen.

DRUCE FARM, Puddletown, Dorset

WEATHERBURY UPPER FARM in Thomas Hardy, *Far from the Madding Crowd* (1874)

'The original of Boldwood's farm is Druce Farm; the house was built in 1867' (F.B. Pinion, 1968, *A Hardy Companion*, London: Macmillan, p. 504). *See also* **Waterston House**.

DRUMMOND, Rose Emma Miniaturist. Daughter of Samuel Drummond, she was an Associate of the Royal Academy, where she exhibited from 1815 to 1835.

MISS LA CREEVY in Charles Dickens, *Nicholas Nickleby* (1838–9)

'The original of Miss La Creevy, the good-natured little miniature painter, was probably Miss Rose Emma Drummond, to whom, in 1835, Dickens sat for his portrait on ivory . . . executed as an engagement gift to his future wife, and . . . now (1897) in the possession of Mrs Perugini' (F.G. Kitton, 1897, *The Novels of Charles Dickens: a bibliography and sketch*, London, p. 51). *See also* **Mannin**, Mary Anne.

DUCKWORTH, Robinson (1834–1911) Son of Robinson Duckworth of Liverpool, he was educated at University College, Oxford, and became a Fellow of Trinity College, Oxford, in 1860. He became Chaplain-in-Ordinary to the Queen, and Canon of Westminster, and held a number of appointments (tutorial or clerical) connected with the royal family. His brother Sir Dyce Duckworth was a distinguished physician. He was an early friend of C.L. Dodgson (Lewis

Carroll) and was the other adult present on the rowing party on 4 July 1862 when Dodgson first told the story of *Alice*.

THE DUCK in Lewis Carroll, *Alice's Adventures in Wonderland* (1865)

'Mr Duckworth . . . who gave his name to the "Duck" in the "Pool of Tears"' (Caryl Hargreaves, 1932, 'Alice's recollections of Carrollean days', *Cornhill Magazine* (NS) 73 (July): 3). Caryl Hargreaves was the son of Alice Hargreaves, née Liddell. '[A] note is pasted into a presentation copy of the 1866 *Alice* bearing the inscription: "R. Duckworth, with the sincere regards of the Author in memory of our voyage"' (*Letters of Lewis Carroll*, 1979, ed. Morton N. Cohen, Vol. I, p. 63 n. 1).

DUCKWORTH, Stella (1869–97) Daughter of Julia **Stephen** by her first marriage, she was Virginia Woolf's half-sister.

PRUE RAMSAY in Virginia Woolf, *To the Lighthouse* (1927)

'After Julia Stephen's death . . . Stella Duckworth took over the management of the household. When Vanessa [Stephen] was considered old enough for this responsibility Stella married. "Prue Ramsay, leaning on her father's arm, was given in marriage", is how Virginia refers to this in *To the Lighthouse*' (Aileen Pippett, 1955, *The Moth and the Star: a biography of Virginia Woolf*, Boston and Toronto, p. 24).

DUDLEY, Lord *See* **Ward**, John William.

DUFF-GORDON, Sir Alexander (1811–72) Third Baronet. Educated at Eton, in 1840 he married Lucie Austin (**Duff-Gordon**, below); Janet **Ross** was their daughter. He became a senior clerk in the Treasury, and in 1856 became Commissioner of the Inland Revenue. He and his wife entertained a distinguished literary circle that extended from Dickens to George Meredith (a country neighbour at Box Hill) and included Thackeray, Caroline **Norton** and Ouida.

EARL OF ARCHIESTOWN ('LORD ARCHIE') in Ouida, *Friendship* (1878)

Lord Archie is not identified as Sir Alexander Duff-Gordon in Eileen Bigland, 1951, *Ouida: the passionate Victorian*. He is, however, unmistakably intended as a sketch. He had attended Etoile's parties in Paris as Sir Alexander had attended Ouida's in London and, like Duff-Gordon, he gave her an introduction to his daughter in Italy. The portrait is drawn with great affection. Duff-Gordon died shortly after Ouida went to live in Florence.

SIR FRANK JOCELYN in George Meredith, *Evan Harrington* (1860)

'Sir Frank and Lady Jocelyn were my father and mother' (Janet Ross, 1912, *The Fourth Generation*, London: Constable, pp. 50–1).

DUFF-GORDON, Lucie, Lady (1821–69) Daughter of the distinguished jurist John Austin and Sarah, née Taylor, of Norwich, who was a cousin of the writer Harriet Martineau. She married Sir Alexander **Duff-Gordon** in 1840 and their daughter was Janet **Ross**. She was obliged to spend her later life in Egypt after developing tuberculosis in 1862.

LADY DUNSTANE in George Meredith, *Diana of the Crossways* (1884)

'Meredith was well aware of Caroline (Norton) and Lady Duff Gordon's great friendship. So much so that Lady Dunstane, the faithful and beloved friend of Diana in the book, was based on her (as was also Lady Jocelyn in *Evan Harrington*' (Alice Acland, 1948, *Caroline Norton*, London: Constable, p. 171).

LADY JOCELYN in George Meredith, *Evan Harrington* (1860)

See above, and also under **Duff-Gordon**, Sir Alexander.

DUFFERIN AND AVA, Frederick Temple Hamilton-Temple Blackwood, 1st Marquis of (1826–1902) English statesman. Born in Florence and educated at Eton and at Christ Church, Oxford, he was a direct descendant of Richard Brinsley **Sheridan** and wrote *Letters from High Latitudes* (1856). He was the Governor-General of Canada in 1872–8, and Ambassador at St Petersburg in 1879 and at Constantinople in 1881. In 1882–3 he reconstructed the administration in Egypt, and he was Governor-General of India in 1884–8, and Ambassador at Rome in 1888–91 and at Paris in 1891–6. He suffered a loss of money and reputation as Chairman of London and Globe Finance Corporation in 1901.

THE AMBASSADOR in Mrs Humphry Ward, *Eleanor* (1899)

'In the sketch of the "Ambassador" in "Eleanor" there are some points caught from the living Lord Dufferin, so closely indeed that before the book came out, I sent him the proofs, and asked his leave – which he gave at once, in one of the graceful little notes of which he was always master' (Mrs Humphry Ward, 1918, *A Writer's Recollections*, New York and London: Harper & Bros, p. 277).

DUGDALE, William Stratford (1828–82) Of Merevale Hall, Warwickshire, in 1871 he married Alice, youngest daughter of Sir Charles Trevelyan. He died from injuries received while attempting to rescue a party of miners trapped in a disaster in a coal mine he owned.

SIR GEORGE TRESSADY in Mrs Humphry Ward, *Sir George Tressady* (1896)

'The death of Sir George Tressady ... was no fictional contrivance: it was the death of [Stratford] Dugdale ... a friend of the Ward family' (Enid Huws Jones, 1973, *Mrs Humphry Ward*, London: Heinemann, p. 115).

DUGGAN, Hubert (1904–43) He was the stepson of Lord **Curzon**, and his father was the owner of immense properties in Argentina. He was educated at Eton, where he was the contemporary and close friend of Anthony Powell. The Duggans were a Catholic family, but at the time of his death Hubert Duggan had not practised his religion for many years. He was one of Waugh's closest friends.

LORD MARCHMAIN in Evelyn Waugh, *Brideshead Revisited* (1945)

In Evelyn Waugh's diary for 12 and 13 October 1943, he describes Duggan's death and his own successful efforts to bring him to a priest to administer absolution and the sacrament of Extreme Unction (see *The Diaries of Evelyn Waugh*, 1976, ed. Michael Davie, London: Weidenfeld & Nicolson, pp. 552–3). 'The whole of this incident, altered in detail to suit the story . . . was eight months later to be described in what was probably the most famous scene of *Brideshead Revisited*' (Christopher Sykes, 1975, *Evelyn Waugh*, London: Collins, pp. 234–5). *See also* **Beauchamp**, William.

CHARLES STRINGHAM in Anthony Powell, *A Dance to the Music of Time* (1951–76)

'Hubert Duggan's demeanour at school – though not in later life – contributes something to . . . Stringham in my novel' (Anthony Powell, 1976, *To Keep the Ball Rolling: the memoirs of anthony powell*, Vol. I: *The Infants of Spring*, London: Heinemann, p. 98). 'During the summer term [of 1926], my last at Oxford, I had to visit London. It was arranged that Hubert Duggan and I should dine together. . . . In Duggan's quarters, that evening, took place the scene which suggested the sequence in *A Question of Upbringing*, where Stringham puts off the Narrator for dinner. . . . The occasion represents the last moment in the novel when Duggan might be said to have any direct bearing on Stringham's doings as described' (ibid., p. 196).

DULWICH COLLEGE, London A public school in the south-east suburbs; it was founded in 1619 by the actor-manager Edward Alleyn.

WRYKYN in P.G. Wodehouse, *The Gold Bat* (1904)

'Wrykyn . . . is Dulwich, a Dulwich not situated in a London suburb but in the country' (P.G. Wodehouse, 1953, *Performing Flea*, introd. W. Townend, London: Herbert Jenkins, p. 11).

DUNCAN, Alexander (1708–95) Minister of Smailholm, Roxburghshire, from 1743 onwards, he was the author of various religious works and of a history of the revolution of 1688. Scott first met him when staying at Sandyknowe as a child and continued to pay him yearly visits when he was a young man.

JOSIAH CARGILL in Sir Walter Scott, *St Ronan's Well* (1823)

'According to Lockhart [Josiah Cargill] was drawn from Dr Alexander Duncan' (W.S. Crockett, 1912, *The Scott Originals: an account of notables and worthies, the originals of characters in the Waverley Novels*, Edinburgh and London: T.N. Foulis, p. 329). *See also* **Lawson**, George.

DUNCAN, Robert (b. 1919) American poet. Born in Oakland, California, he was educated at the University of California. As a poet he was much influenced by Ezra **Pound**.

GEOFFREY DONALD in Jack Kerouac, *Desolation Angels* (1965)

Identified in 'Character key to the Duluoz Legend', Barry Gifford and Lawrence Lee, 1979, *Jack's Book*, pp. 322–32.

DUNCOMBE, Thomas Slingsby (1796–1861) English politician. He began his political life in 1821 as a Whig, but from 1834 onwards became steadily more radical and by the 1840s was a supporter of the Chartists (although opposed to the use of physical force). He was MP for Finsbury from 1834 to 1861.

CHARLES, LORD ARLINGTON in Lady Blessington, *The Two Friends* (1835)

'First and foremost John Duncombe suggested himself to [the author's] imagination . . . but what should she call him? Oh! he lives in Arlington Street – Lord Arlington!' ('A quintette of novels', *Fraser's Magazine* 11 (April 1835): 474).

DUNN, Irene Clarice, Lady (1900–77) Née Richards. One of the theatre impresario C.B. Cochran's Young Ladies, she had a great success in *Manhattan*. In 1917, at the age of 16, she married Lord Drumlaning (later the 11th Marquess of Queensberry), nephew of Lord Alfred **Douglas**. They were divorced in 1925, and in 1926 she married the Canadian millionaire Sir James Dunn, he being more than twice her age; the ceremony, in what the gossip writers described as a runaway match, took place in Paris with Lord **Beaverbrook** (then Max Aitken) as the only witness. In 1942, after another divorce, she married Captain Murrough O'Brien of the Irish Guards; in 1951, this too ended in divorce, and in 1955 she embarked on her last marriage, to T.F.J. Hanbury, the racehorse trainer.

ANGELA LYNE in Evelyn Waugh, *Black Mischief* (1932) and *Put Out More Flags* (1942)

Identification based on private information.

DUNSTER, Somerset A small town west of the Quantock Hills.

MARKTON in Thomas Hardy, *A Laodicean* (1881)

'Hardy's map of Wessex and a historical quotation relating to Stancy Castle indicate that this is Dunster' (F.B. Pinion, 1968, *A Hardy Companion*, London: Macmillan, p. 401). '"A Laodicean" was first published in 1881. . . . Looking over the novel at the present much later date, I hazard the conjecture that its sites, mileages and architectural details can hardly seem satisfactory to the investigating topographist, so appreciable a proportion of these features being but the baseless fabrics of a vision' (Hardy, 1912, PS to introd. to *A Laodicean*).

DUNSTER CASTLE, Somerset

STANCY CASTLE in Thomas Hardy, *A Laodicean* (1881)

'Rather imaginary, though Hardy's map of Wessex and his quotation from Collinson's *History of Somerset* (I, xiii) identify [Stancy Castle] as Dunster Castle' (F.B. Pinion, 1968, *A Hardy Companion*, London: Macmillan, p. 479).

DUNSTERVILLE, Lionel Charles (1865–1946) Major-General. He was a contemporary of Kipling at the United Services College, Westward Ho! (1875–83), and was his lifelong friend.

ARTHUR CORKRAN ('STALKY') in Rudyard Kipling, *Stalky & Co.* (1899)

'The titles of two of his . . . books, *Stalky's Reminiscences* (1928, London) and *Stalky Settles Down* (1932, London) are evidence of the continuing adult identification with the schoolboy role Kipling made famous in *Stalky and Co.*' (R. Collins and R. Collins, 1965, '"Exiles" in India: an early Kipling variant', *Notes and Queries* 210: 306 n. 1). Also identified in the caption to a photograph reproduced in the June 1981 issue of *The Kipling Journal*: 'Masters at the United Services College . . . in Kipling's day' (*The Kipling Journal* 48 (218): 21).

DUTERME, Robert Marine engineer. In 1902 he was the manager of a foundry near Tunis.

PAUL DUFRÉNOIS in Norman Douglas, *Fountains in the Sand* (1912)

'I have no clear recollection of him, but he helped, I think, to form the character of "Paul Dufrénois"' (Norman Douglas, 1934, *Looking Back: an autobiographical excursion*, Vol. II, London: Chatto & Windus, p. 378).

DUTTON, Charles

DONKIN in Joseph Conrad, *The Nigger of the 'Narcissus'* (1897)

'Another member of the crew [of the *Narcissus* in 1884] was an A.B. named Charles Dutton who also [like the "nigger"] signed his name with a cross . . . although Conrad himself could not have come in contact with him it may be that talk among the crew provided him with material for Donkin' (Jocelyn Baines, 1967, *Joseph Conrad: a critical biography*, rev. edn, London: Weidenfeld & Nicolson, p. 76; originally published 1960).

DUVENECK, Elizabeth (1846–88) Daughter of Francis **Boott** who, after the early death of his wife, brought her up in a sort of reclusive solitude at Bellosguardo, outside Florence. She married Frank Duveneck, who according to the artist John Singer Sargent was the greatest painter of his generation. 'Lizzie is as sweet and good as ever. . . . [She] still has the attribute of making you fancy from her deadly languid passivity at times, that she is acutely miserable. But she is evidently very happy' (Henry James to William James, 8 January 1873, reproduced in *Henry James Letters*, Vol. I: *1843–1875*, 1974, ed. Leon Edel, London: Macmillan, p. 325).

PANSY OSMOND in Henry James, *The Portrait of a Lady* (1880)

'More than a year after Lizzie's death Alice James wrote in her journal: "Henry says he misses Lizzie Duveneck more and more." This was true. She had been a certain kind of American girl – the quiet gentle Europeanized *jeune fille*, not the daisy but the pansy, and he had much feeling for her. She was to remain enshrined . . . in the delicate beauty of Pansy Osmond' (Leon Edel, 1963, *Henry James: the middle years, 1884–1894*, p. 187). The frontispiece to Edel, *Henry James: the early years, 1870–1881* is a photograph encaptioned 'Francis Boott and Lizzie (*ca.*1850) in Italy. "Osmund and Pansy" from a photograph.'

DYCE, William (1806–64) Painter. He first exhibited at the Royal Academy in 1827 and originated the Pre-Raphaelite school of painting in 1828 with 'Madonna and Child'. He was commissioned to paint frescoes in the House of Lords and in the Queen's Robing Room, but he did not complete the commission. He was Professor of Fine Arts at King's College, London, from 1844 onwards, and was a leader in the High Church movement.

MR SHENE in C.M. Yonge, *The Heir of Redclyffe* (1853)

'"Mr Shene" was probably based on William Dyce, who was a friend of C.M. Yonge's friend Keble and was painting *Sir Galahad adoring the San Greal* for the Queen's Robing Room in 1851, exactly when *The Heir of Redclyffe* was being written' (Mark Girouard, 1981, *The Return to Camelot*, New Haven and London, p. 300 n. 6). The reference is to a passage in ch. XXX of the novel, where Mr Shene, the painter, is struck by an expression on the hero's face which is exactly what he wants for Sir Galahad 'when he kneels to adore the San Greal'.

DYETT, Edwin (1896?–1917) A temporary sub-lieutenant in the Royal Navy Reserve, he was court-martialled for cowardice shown at the Battle of the Ancre on 13 November 1916 (the battle in which Lieutenant-Colonel Bernard Freyberg won the Victoria Cross), and was shot on 5 January 1917. The case was the subject of an article in *John Bull*, and the matter was raised in Parliament by Philip Morrell in 1919.

HARRY PENROSE in A.P. Herbert, *The Secret Battle* (1919)

'Penrose . . . was based on Edwin Dyett. . . . There was every reason for A.P. Herbert to know the facts. He was serving in the Royal Naval Division at the time. . . . The details of the case . . . were deliberately disguised . . . but in two . . . respects they tallied with the allegations made in John Bull and in Parliament. The vital testimony that led to him being found guilty was attributed to a witness who had a personal grudge against him – and the summary of evidence was handed to the prisoner's friend only the day before the trial' (William Moore, 1974, *The Thin Yellow Line*, London: Cooper, p. 202).

E

EARDLEY-WILMOT, Sir John Eardley (1783–1847) Conservative politician. MP for Warwickshire North from 1832 until 1842, when he became Governor of Van Diemen's Land, he declared that he would vote for triennial parliaments and the ballot if Parliament did not secure electors free exercise of their franchise, and that he would resign his seat if required to do so by his constituents.

SIR BAPTIST PLACID in Benjamin Disraeli, *Coningsby* (1844)

Identified in a key in *Notes and Queries* (8th series) 3 (13 May 1893): 363. *See also under* **Bright**, John.

EAST CHALDON (or CHALDON HERRING), Dorset The village known by both names; it lies about two miles inland and slightly to the west of Lulworth Cove.

CHALDON in Thomas Hardy, 'The Distracted Preacher' (1888)

Identified in F.B. Pinion, 1968, *A Hardy Companion*, London: Macmillan.

EAST OAKLAND, California A town across the bay from San Francisco. From 1850 to 1892 it was the home of Gertrude Stein.

GOSSOLS in Gertrude Stein, *The Making of Americans* (1925)

'The name she chose to replace Oakland . . . was Gossols' (James R. Mellow, 1974, *The Charmed Circle: Gertrude Stein and Company*, London: Phaidon Press, p. 116).

EASTGATE HOUSE, Rochester, Kent It was built in the High Street in 1590 for Sir Peter Bucke, paymaster in the Navy.

NUN'S HOUSE, CLOISTERHAM, in Charles Dickens, *Edwin Drood* (1870)

'Eastgate House appears in . . . *Edwin Drood.* "In the midst of Cloisterham stands the Nun's House"' (John Oliver, 1978, *Dickens' Rochester*, p. 57).

WESTGATE HOUSE in Charles Dickens, *The Pickwick Papers* (1836–7)

'Eastgate House is the model for Westgate House . . . transposing the house from Rochester to Bury St Edmunds is consistent with [Dickens's] style' (Oliver, op. cit., p. 57).

EASTON, Portland, Dorset A village on the east side of the Isle of Portland.

EAST QUARRIERS in Thomas Hardy, *The Well-Beloved* (1897)

Identified in F.B. Pinion, 1968, *A Hardy Companion*, London: Macmillan.

EASTWICK, Edward Backhouse (1814–83) Orientalist and diplomatist. In 1859 he served in the India Office, and from 1860 to 1863 he was Secretary of

Legation at the Persian court. In 1863 and 1867 he was the commissioner for arranging a Venezuelan loan, and between 1868 and 1874 he was MP for Penryn and Falmouth. He translated numerous Hindustani classics from Persian, and was the author of *Venezuela; or Sketches of Life in a South American Republic* (1868).

SIR JOHN in Joseph Conrad, *Nostromo* (1904)

'Sir John in *Nostromo* as the representative of "material interests" from abroad is based upon Eastwick and his similar function' (Norman Sherry, 1971, *Conrad's Western World*, Cambridge, p. 172).

EASTWOOD, Nottinghamshire The village in which D.H. Lawrence was born and lived as a child.

BELDOVER in D.H. Lawrence, *The Rainbow* (1915)

'[I]n *The Rainbow* and *Women in Love* ... Eastwood is called Beldover' (H.T. Moore, 1960, *The Intelligent Heart: the story of D.H. Lawrence*, Harmondsworth: Penguin, pp. 89–90; originally published 1955, London: Heinemann). *See also* **Quorn**.

BESTWOOD in D.H. Lawrence, *Sons and Lovers* (1913)

'The "Bestwood" of "Sons and Lovers" is Eastwood although there is a village and colliery named Bestwood not very far away' (Ada Lawrence and G. Stuart Gelder, 1931, *Young Lorenzo: early life of D.H. Lawrence*, Florence, p. 275).

EBERWICH in D.H. Lawrence, *The White Peacock* (1911)

'Eberwich is Eastwood and so accurate are his descriptions that those who know the district are able to follow him almost step by step' (Lawrence and Gelder, op. cit., p. 272).

TEVERSHALL in D.H. Lawrence, *Lady Chatterley's Lover* (1928)

Wragby Hall, as described by Lawrence, '"stood on an eminence in a rather fine old park of trees", and from there the smoke and steam of the nearest colliery could be seen – as well as "the raw straggle of Tevershall village", or Eastwood' (Moore, op. cit., p. 25).

WOODHOUSE in D.H. Lawrence, *The Lost Girl* (1920)

'Woodhouse, DHL's recreation of his home town Eastwood' (*The Lost Girl*, 1981, ed. John Worthen, Cambridge, p. 361 n. 1:3).

EASTWOOD BRITISH SCHOOL, Nottinghamshire The primary school where, from 1902 to 1904, D.H. Lawrence worked as a pupil-teacher.

ST PHILIP'S in D.H. Lawrence, *The Rainbow* (1915)

'In *The Rainbow* [Lawrence] has described under the name of St Philip's the drab mock-Gothic stone building' (E. Delavenay, 1972, *D.H. Lawrence: the man and his work ... 1885–1919*, p. 17).

EBDELL, Revd Bernard Gilpin (d. 1829) Between 1786 and 1829 he was Vicar of Chilvers Coton and Astley, Warwickshire, where George Eliot grew up; he baptized her. In 1801 he married Sally **Shilton**.

Revd Maynard Gilfil in George Eliot, 'Mr Gilfil's Love Story' and 'The Sad Fortunes of the Revd Amos Barton', , *Scenes of Clerical Life* (1857–8)

'Maynard Gilfil . . . she [George Eliot] had known in the Reverend Bernard Gilpin Ebdell . . . the plot is entirely imaginary' (Gordon S. Haight, 1968, *George Eliot*, Oxford, p. 221). *See also under* **Anstruther**, Lady.

ECCLEFECHAN, Dumfriesshire The birthplace of Thomas Carlyle.

Entepfuhl in Thomas Carlyle, *Sartor Resartus* (1833–4)

'Asked him concerning his early history, as compared with Teufelsdrockh's. . . . The description of Entepfuhl is identical with that of his (Carlyle's) native village' (entry for 6 June 1842, *Memories of Old Friends: being extracts from the journals and letters of Caroline Fox*, 1882, ed. H.N. Pym, Vol. I, London: Smith, Elder, pp. 310–11).

EDER, David (1865–1936) Pioneer psychoanalyst in England. In 1914 he and his wife Edith (née Low) became friends of the Lawrences; Edith Eder's niece, Ivy Low, married Maxim **Litvinov**, the Soviet politician and diplomat. Eder was a leading Zionist and was closely associated with Chaim Weizmann, the Israeli statesman.

Benjamin Cooley in D.H. Lawrence, *Kangaroo* (1923)

'Frieda [Lawrence] has said that Dr Eder . . . helped compose the character' (H.T. Moore, 1960, *The Intelligent Heart: the story of D.H. Lawrence*, Harmondsworth: Penguin, p. 364; originally published 1955, London: Heinemann). *See also* **Koteliansky**, S.S.; **Monash**, Sir John.

EDGEWORTH, Francis (1809–46) He was Maria Edgeworth's half-brother, and took over the management of the Edgeworth's town estate from her in 1839. He was the twenty-first child of R.L. **Edgeworth**, and the fifth by the latter's marriage to Frances Beaufort.

Granville Beauclerc in Maria Edgeworth, *Helen* (1834)

'Beauclerc's character owes much to . . . Francis Edgeworth, who was talented but impulsive and wayward' (Marilyn Butler, 1972, *Maria Edgeworth*, Oxford, p. 470).

EDGEWORTH, Honora (1774–90) Elder of the two children of R.L. **Edgeworth** by his second wife, Honora Sneyd, she was perhaps the most obviously talented of all the Edgeworth children. She married Francis Beaufort, and like her mother and aunt she died of tuberculosis.

Caroline Percy in Maria Edgeworth, *Patronage* (1814)

'Caroline . . . [derived] from [Maria's] stepsister Honora' (Marilyn Butler, 1972, *Maria Edgeworth*, Oxford, p. 248). *See also under* **Edgeworth**, Maria.

EDGEWORTH, Maria (1767–1849) Irish novelist. Born in Oxfordshire, she was the third child and eldest daughter of R.L. **Edgeworth** by his marriage to Anna Maria Elers. She was educated in England but returned to Ireland in 1872. She acted as governess to her many younger brothers and sisters and collaborated with her father on several books about education. Her first novel, *Castle Rackrent*, was published in 1800, to immediate success which resulted, among other things, in a proposal of marriage from the Swedish Count Edelcrantz, which she turned down for the sake of her father. After his death in 1817, she did little more writing, but administered the family property and became involved in philanthropic work.

ROSAMOND PERCY in Maria Edgeworth, *Patronage* (1814)

'The impetuous Rosamond [derived] from Maria herself' (Marilyn Butler, 1972, *Maria Edgeworth*, Oxford, p. 248). 'The evidence for identifying Maria with Rosamond and Honora with Caroline is a pencilled note in a family copy of *Patronage*, and the family tradition handed down by Mrs H.J. Butler, daughter of Maria's youngest stepbrother' (ibid., n. 1).

EDGEWORTH, Richard (1764–96) Eldest child of R.L. **Edgeworth** by Anna Maria Elers, he was educated at Lyons and Charterhouse. In 1779 he went to sea, and in 1783 he deserted his ship; his father refused to allow him to return home and he settled in South Carolina. He married Elizabeth Knight, the daughter of a Methodist hatter. He was Maria Edgeworth's brother.

GODFREY PERCY in Maria Edgeworth, *Patronage* (1814)

'Godfrey . . . who suffers from an excess of party spirit, ultimately derived from Maria's eldest brother, Richard' (Marilyn Butler, 1972, *Maria Edgeworth*, Oxford, p. 248).

EDGEWORTH, Richard Lovell (1744–1817) Inventor and educationist of Edgeworthstown, County Longford, Ireland. Son of Richard Edgeworth and Jane Lovell, he was married four times: in 1764 he married Anna Maria Elers, daughter of Paul **Elers**; in 1773 he married Honora Sneyd; in 1780 he married Elizabeth Sneyd; and in 1798 he married Frances Anne Beaufort. In total he had twenty-two children, including Maria Edgeworth, his third child. He was a close friend of the members of the Lunar Society and of Thomas **Day**, with whom he studied at Corpus Christi, Oxford. He invented a caterpillar-wheeled tractor, a form of telegraph and many other mechanical devices. From 1782 he lived on his estate at Edgeworthstown and devoted himself to its management and to the education of his children, being assisted in both undertakings by Maria. He also took an active part in politics, advocating parliamentary reform.

LADY DAVENANT in Maria Edgeworth, *Helen* (1834)

'Lady Davenant in *Helen*. . . in part resembles him' (Marilyn Butler, 1972, *Maria Edgeworth*, Oxford, p. 247 n. 5, p. 477).

COUNCILLOR MOLYNEUX in Maria Edgeworth, 'Rosanna', *Popular Tales* (1804)

'He is Mr Percival . . . Councillor Molyneux . . . and Mr Percy' (Butler, op. cit., p. 247).

MR PERCIVAL in Maria Edgeworth, *Belinda* (1801)

See above.

MR PERCY in Maria Edgeworth, *Patronage* (1814)

See above under Councillor Molyneux.

EDGEWORTH HOUSE, Finsbury Park, London The address of the school in North London that was run by the Misses **Ayre**. Dorothy Richardson taught there in 1892–3.

Wordsworth House in Dorothy Richardson, *Pilgrimage* (1915–67)

'Edgeworth House is translated to Wordsworth' (Gloria G. Gomm, 1977, *Dorothy Richardson: a biography*, London, p. 101).

EDGHILL, Ernest Arthur (d. 1912) Educated at Eton and at King's College, Cambridge, like poor Edge he had a dazzling career at Cambridge, winning two firsts – one in theology – and seven prizes, but no fellowship. His father was Honorary Chaplain to the King, and he himself took holy orders and became a curate in Hornsey, London. He 'devoted his life', says the King's Register, 'to the welfare of poor boys', and died as a result of an accident in a boys' camp.

Edge in Shane Leslie, *The Cantab* (1926)

Identified in a key in the hand of Dr Ivor Ramsay, a Kingsman of the year 1920, and later Dean, laid in a copy of *The Cantab*.

The *EDINBURGH REVIEW* A Whig periodical that was published from 1802 until 1929.

The *Praise-All Review* in Benjamin Disraeli, *Vivian Grey* (1826–7)

Identified in a key given in a pamphlet published in 1827 by William Marsh. This key is discussed by Lucien Wolf in his notes to *Vivian Grey* (1904 (centenary edn), Vol. II, London: Alexander Moring, p. 364), with the conclusion that Disraeli was not responsible for the key. But compare: 'You know the system of the Edinburgh Gentlemen is universal attack, they praise none' (to the Revd John Becher, 26 February 1808, reproduced in George Gordon Byron, 1973, *Letters and Journals*, Vol. I: *In My Hot Youth*, ed. Leslie Marchand, London: John Murray, p. 157). In a subsequent letter to Hobhouse, Byron described himself as cut to atoms by a review by Brougham published in the *Edinburgh*.

EGGARDON HILL, Dorset Located five miles north-east of Bridport and crowned with a prehistoric camp.

Haggardon in Thomas Hardy, *The Trumpet Major* (1880)

Identified in F.B. Pinion, 1968, *A Hardy Companion*, London: Macmillan.

EGGERS, Frank Hague Nephew of Frank **Hague**, who installed him as his successor, as Mayor of New Jersey, in control of the Democratic party machine; in 1949 he was defeated and ousted.

Ed Coyle in Francis T. Field, *McDonough* (1951)

'[Boss Coyle's] son Ed . . . [suggests] . . . Frank Hague Eggers' (Joseph Blotner, 1966, *The Modern American Political Novel*, Austin, Tex., p. 80 n. 45).

EGLINTON, Hugh Montgomerie, 12th Earl of (1739–1819) Lord Lieutenant of Ayrshire, he was the largest landowner of the district of Irvine. He rebuilt the castle of Eglinton, which was some two miles north of Irvine, and constructed Ardrossan Harbour and the Paisley Canal.

THE EARL in John Galt, *The Provost* (1822)

'The Earl of Eglinton, Galt's model' (*The Provost*, 1973, ed. Ian A. Gordon, London: Oxford University Press, p. 155 n. 7).

EGLINTON TOURNAMENT 'In 1839 [the 13th Earl of Eglinton] held a magnificent tournament, carried out in the ancient style, at Eglintoun Castle, Lady Seymour (born Sheridan), afterwards Duchess of Somerset, being the Queen of Beauty. The cost, which was expected not to exceed £2,000, amounted to some £40,000' (Hon. Vicary Gibbs and H.A. Doubleday (eds), *The Complete Peerage of England, Scotland, Ireland, Great Britain and the United Kingdom*, Vol. V, rev. edn, London: St Catherine Press, p. 26 n. b).

THE MONTFORT TOURNAMENT in Benjamin Disraeli, *Endymion* (1880)

The description of the Montfort tournament is in fact a description of the Eglinton tournament, even to the detail of the cost.

EISENHOWER, Dwight D. (1890–1969) Born in Texas, he was Commander-in-Chief of allied forces in Western Europe during the Second World War. He became Republican President of the USA in 1953, and remained in that position until 1961.

LUCAS P. STARBUCK in James Reichley, *Hail to the Chief* (1960)

Identified in Joseph Blotner, 1966, *The Modern American Political Novel*, Austin, Tex., p. 129.

EL FUERTE A village on Lake Chapala, Mexico.

ORILLA in D.H. Lawrence, *The Plumed Serpent* (1926)

'. . . fictional name for El Fuerte' (*The Plumed Serpent*, 1983, ed. Ronald G. Walker, Harmondsworth: Penguin, p. 492 n. 1).

ELAND, John Arnold Bennett's first friend in London, he was a shorthand clerk in Le Brasseur & Oakley and was probably three or four years older than Bennett.

MR AKED in Arnold Bennett, *The Man from the North* (1898)

'[W]hen I first came to London . . . I'd no social relations whatever . . . except one clerk in the office, a fellow named Eland who had a passion for bibliography'(22 September 1925, reproduced in *Arnold Bennett's Letters to His Nephew*, 1935, ed. R. Bennett, London: Heinemann, p. 149). Mr Aked is also a bibliophile.

ELDON, John Scott, 1st Earl of (1751–1838) He became Attorney-General in 1793, and Lord Chief Justice of Common Pleas in 1799. From 1801 until 1806, and from 1807 until 1838, he was Lord Chancellor, holding the longest tenure of the office by any one person. In 1806 he was Adviser to Caroline, Princess of Wales, and also became Adviser to the Prince of Wales, later George IV. He was an active opponent of the Reform Bill, and was a Tory of Tories: Lord Campbell wrote that 'he defended every abuse and absurdity which disgraced our jurisprudence' (G.E.C. (ed.), 1890, *The Complete Peerage of England, Scotland, Ireland, Great Britain and the United Kingdom*, Vol. III, London: George Bell & Sons).

OLD BAGS in Bulwer Lytton, *Paul Clifford* (1830)

Identified in a key set out by Rosina Bulwer Lytton, in a letter of 26 May 1830, reproduced in Michael Sadleir, 1968, *Bulwer and His Wife*, pp. 227–8.

LORD PAST CENTURY in Benjamin Disraeli, *Vivian Grey* (1826–7)

Identified as Earl of E——n in a key given in *The Star Chamber* (24 May 1826): 114; reprinted in *Vivian Grey*, 1904 (centenary edn), ed. Lucien Wolf, Vol. II, London: Alexander Moring, pp. 361–2. The full name appears on a copy of the key held in the British Museum. Lucien Wolf concludes that Disraeli was not responsible for the key.

ELERS, Paul Son of John Philip Elers, the potter who introduced salt glazing into Staffordshire. He was the father of Anna Maria, the first wife of Richard Lovell **Edgeworth**, and thus Maria Edgeworth's grandfather.

SIR CONNOLLY ('CONDY') RACKRENT in Maria Edgeworth, *Castle Rackrent* (1800)

See Bevis Hillier, 1970, 'Antiques', *Harpers Bazaar* (April): 64.

ELIOT, George (1819–1880) Mary Ann (Marian) Evans, afterwards Cross. English novelist, born in Warwickshire, the daughter of a land agent, Robert **Evans**. In 1836 her mother died and she took charge of the household, and in 1841 the family moved to Coventry. She travelled extensively on the European continent and prepared the first English translation of Feuerbach's *Essence of Christianity*. She became Managing Editor of the *Westminster Review*, moving to London where she met Herbert **Spencer** and George Henry **Lewes**. She formed a relationship with Lewes that lasted until his death in 1878, although they never married as his wife refused to divorce him. In May 1880 she married John Walter **Cross**, a banker twenty years her junior. She died a few months later.

DOROTHEA CASAUBON (NÉE BROOKE) in George Eliot, *Middlemarch* (1871–2)

'Dorothea is perhaps her own idealized self' (Anna T. Kitchel (ed.), 1950, preface to *Quarry for Middlemarch*, Berkeley and Los Angeles, p. iv; suppl. to *The Nineteenth Century* 4). *See also* **Pattison**, Dorothea Wyndlow; **Pattison**, Emilia Francis.

EDWARD CASAUBON in George Eliot, *Middlemarch* (1871–2)

'F.W.H. Myers, in the *Century Magazine* of November, 1891 (23:60), related that when asked where she had found Casaubon, "with a humourous solemnity, which was quite in earnest, nevertheless, she pointed to her own heart". . . . What must be sought is not a Casaubon, but casaubonism, and this George Eliot found, as Flaubert found *le bovarysme*, in herself. Casaubonism is the entombing of the senses in the mind's cellarage. As a young woman George Eliot was liable to this iniquity, and all her life she was capable of what Myers called "almost morbid accesses of self-reproach"' (Richard Ellmann, 1973, 'Dorothea's husbands: some biographical speculations', *Times Literary Supplement* (16 February): 165). *See also* **Brabant,** R.H.; **Bryant,** Jacob; **Mackay,** R.W.; **Pattison,** Mark; **Spencer,** Herbert.

THERESA in Mark Rutherford, *The Autobiography of Mark Rutherford* (1881)

'The *Bookman* for August [1902] . . . contains two articles of exceptional interest: (1) "George Eliot as I Knew Her", by Mr Hale White [i.e. Mark Rutherford]; and (2) "Sir Leslie Stephen's George Eliot", by Mr James Douglas. . . . Mr Hale White tells us that between 1852 and 1855 he and Miss Evans lived at [John] Chapman's . . . bearing out my contention that Theresa . . . is a portrait of George Eliot' (John Grigor, 1902, '"Mark Rutherford" and "George Eliot"', *Notes and Queries* (9th series) 10 (13 September): 204–5). Grigor cites a number of parallel passages from the *Bookman* article and from the *Autobiography,* which certainly lend colour to the identification. E.S. Merton, 1950, 'The autobiographical novels of Mark Rutherford', *The Nineteenth Century* 5 (3) makes the same identification and quotes a letter from Hale White to the *Athenaeum* (8 December 1894): 790: 'She occupied two dark but very quiet rooms at the end of a long passage . . . but she had her meals with the family. . . . She never reserved herself but always said what was best in her at the moment . . . consequently she found out what was best in everybody. I have not heard better talk than hers, even when there was nobody to listen but myself and the Chapman family.'

MAGGIE TULLIVER in George Eliot, *The Mill on the Floss* (1860)

'There is good reason for reading autobiography in the childhood of Tom and Maggie Tulliver, who were born in the same years as [George Eliot and her brother Isaac]' (Gordon S. Haight, 1968, *George Eliot,* Oxford, p. 5).

ELIOT, Thomas Stearns (1888–1965) American-born British poet, critic and dramatist. Born in St Louis, Missouri, he studied philosophy at Harvard, leaving without taking a degree. He left America in 1914, and studied briefly in Germany, at the Sorbonne, and at Merton College, Oxford. He settled in London, teaching at Highgate School, reviewing books for the *Times Literary Supplement,* and working at Lloyds Bank before becoming a director of the publishing firm Faber & Faber. In 1915 he married Vivien Haigh-Wood, but in 1932 they separated; she was confined in a mental hospital until her death in 1947. Encouraged by Ezra **Pound,** he published his first collection of poems, *Prufrock and Other Observations,* in 1917, and his well-known and influential work *The Wasteland* was published by Leonard and Virginia **Woolf** at the Hogarth Press in 1922. He converted to Catholicism in 1927. In 1948 he was awarded the Nobel Prize for Literature and the Order of Merit. He married Valerie Fletcher in 1957.

JEREMY PRATT CIBBER in Richard Aldington, *Stepping Heavenward* (1931)

'*Stepping Heavenward* . . . is a biting lampoon of Eliot, now transformed into Jeremy Pratt Sybba (later Cibber) . . . the portrayal of Vivian Eliot as Miss Adele Paleologue, whom Cibber marries, must have stung him' (C. Doyle, 1989, *Richard Aldington: a biography,* Basingstoke and London: Macmillan, pp. 146, 147).

ELIZABETH *See* **Russell**, Countess.

ELKINS, William Lukens (1832–1903) Born in West Virginia and educated in Philadelphia. After the discovery of oil in Pennsylvania, between 1861 and 1880 he surveyed the oil region and organized many oil companies. Along with P.A.B. **Widener**, he was involved in the public transport system of Philadelphia. Upon his death he left a fortune of $25,000,000.

ANSON MERRILL in Theodore Dreiser, *The Titan* (1914)

'Elkins (the . . . Merrill of the novel)' (Richard Lehan, 1974, *Theodore Dreiser: his world and his novels*, Carbondale, Ill.: Arcturis Books, p. 98).

ELLASTONE, Staffordshire Situated on the Derbyshire border of Staffordshire, east of Stoke on Trent. It was the home of the first wife of Robert **Evans** (George Eliot's father) and the seat of the Bromley Davenport family.

HAYSLOPE in George Eliot, *Adam Bede* (1859)

'Treddleston is *not* Ellastone. Hayslope is, with a difference. But no one who is not an artist knows how experience is wrought up in writing any form of poetry' (to Charles Bray, 19 September 1859, *The George Eliot Letters*, 1954, ed. Gordon S. Haight, Vol. III, London: Oxford University Press, p. 156).

ELLENBOROUGH, Edward Law, 1st Baron (1750–1818) Educated at Charterhouse and Cambridge, he was a barrister at Lincoln's Inn in 1780, and in 1788 he became leading counsel for Warren Hastings, the English administrator in India who was acquitted after a seven-year trial of charges brought against him by the Whig opposition. In 1801 he was MP for Newtown, Isle of Wight, and in 1802 he became Lord Chief-Justice, resigning in 1818.

LORD OLDBOROUGH in Maria Edgeworth, *Patronage* (1814)

'I have redde "Patronage" it is full of praises of Lord Ellenborough!!! from which I infer near & dear relations at the bar' (Lord Byron to John Murray, 11 January 1814, reproduced in George Gordon Byron, 1975, *Letters and Journals*, Vol. IV: *Wedlock's the Devil*, ed. Leslie Marchand, London: John Murray, p. 25). 'In . . . *Patronage*, the Lord Chief Justice, Lord Oldborough, is idealised as a benevolent judge' (ibid., n. 1). *See also* **Stuart**, William; **Walpole**, Sir Robert.

ELLENBOROUGH, Edward Law, 1st Earl of (1790–1871) Son of the 1st Baron **Ellenborough**, he became an MP in 1813 and in 1828 was the Lord Privy Seal. In 1841 he became Governor-General of India but was recalled in 1844. He was created Earl and in 1846 was First Lord of the Admiralty under Sir Robert **Peel**. In 1813 he married the sister of Lord Castlereagh, and in 1824 he married Jane **Digby**, whom he divorced in 1830.

LORD GLENMORE in Lady Charlotte Bury, *The Exclusives* (1830)

Identified in *Key to the Royal Novel 'The Exclusives'*, 1830, Marsh & Miller; reproduced in Michael Sadleir, 1951, *XIX Century Fiction*, 2 vols, London: Constable, and Los Angeles: California University Press, pp. 73–4.

LONG NED in Bulwer Lytton, *Paul Clifford* (1830)

Identified in a key set out by Rosina Bulwer Lytton, in a letter of 26 May 1830, reproduced in Michael Sadleir, 1968, *Bulwer and His Wife*, pp. 227–8.

ELLICE, Edward (1781–1863) Known as 'Bear' Ellice, from his connection with Hudson's Bay Company and the fur trade. He was elected MP for Coventry four times, and between 1832 and 1834 was Secretary at War. He was one of the founders of the Reform Club in 1836. A considerable figure in society, he was a friend of Sir Francis **Burdett** and of Cam Hobhouse, 1st Baron Broughton, the British statesman, and was a connection, by marriage, of **Byron**. In 1843 he married his second wife, Lady Leicester (Lady Anne **Coke**).

MR ERRICE in Lady Blessington, *The Repealers* (1833) and *The Belle of a Season* (1840)

'He appears in . . . *The Belle of the [sic] Season*, as Mr Errice' (*The Letters and Journals of Lord Byron*, 1904, ed. R.E. Prothero, Vol. VI, p. 90).

ELLIOTSON, John (1791–1868) Physician. In 1831 he became Professor of Medicine at London University, and between 1834 and 1838 he was Senior Physician at University College Hospital, whose foundation he was greatly involved in. He was also the founder and first president of the Phrenological Society, but after he began to practise mesmerism in 1837 he was compelled to resign his chair. In 1849 he founded the London Mesmeric Infirmary in Weymouth St. He was a friend of **Dickens** and of Thackeray, and was personal physician to the latter, who dedicated *Pendennis* to him. 'A dark, sombre taciturn, powerful-looking man, with coal-black hair, and a beard as black, fringing round his face', wrote Hawthorne, meeting him in London in 1856 (Nathaniel Hawthorne, 1941, *English Notebooks*, ed. Randall Stewart, New York and London: Modern Languages Association of America, p. 317).

DR GOODENOUGH in W.M. Thackeray, *The History of Pendennis* (1848–50)

'Elliotson figures as Dr Goodenough' (*The Letters and Private Papers of W.M. Thackeray*, 1946, ed. Gordon N. Ray, Vol. IV, London: Oxford University Press, p. 275 n. 44). 'Mr and the Misses Pendennis request the honour of Doctor Goodenough's company to dinner tomorrow' (Thackeray to Dr Elliotson, 23 September 1862, ibid.).

ELLIOTT, Willie (*fl.* 1792) A farmer, of Millburnholm in Liddesdale, Roxburghshire. Scott was taken to his farm in the autumn of 1792 by Robert **Shortreed**, who was his wife's cousin, during their journey through Liddesdale in search of ballads.

DANDIE DINMONT in Sir Walter Scott, *Guy Mannering* (1815)

'According to Mr Shortreed, this good man . . . was the great original of Dandie Dinmont. As he seems to have been the first of these upland sheep-farmers that Scott ever visited, there can be little doubt that he sat for some parts that inimitable portraiture' (J.G. Lockhart, 1900, *Memoirs of Sir Walter Scott*, Vol. I, London: Macmillan, p. 168). '[F]rom what passed between Sir Walter and me some time ago, there cannot be a doubt that he had Willie o'Millburn in his eye when he drew the Character' (J.E. Shortreed, 1932, 'Conversations with my father on the subject of his tours with Sir Walter Scott in Liddesdale', reprinted in W.E. Wilson, 'The making of the "Minstrelsy"', *Cornhill Magazine* (NS) 73 (September): 272). *See also* **Davidson**, James; **Laidlaw**, James; **Park**, Archibald; **Thorburn**, James.

ELLIS, Ann She kept an eating house near Doctors' Commons in the City of London.

MRS BARDELL in Charles Dickens, *The Pickwick Papers* (1836–7)

'Mrs Bardell is reputed to have been drawn . . . from Mrs Ann Ellis' (F.G. Kitton, 1897, *The Novels of Charles Dickens: a bibliography and sketch*, London, pp. 19–20).

ELLIS, Catherine Matilda, Lady (1794–1847) Née Meredith, she was George Meredith's aunt and married Sir Samuel Burdon **Ellis**.

MRS STRIKE in George Meredith, *Evan Harrington* (1860)

'The Ellises, of course, were the originals of Major and Mrs Strike' (S.M. Ellis, 1920, *George Meredith*, 2nd edn, London: Grant Richards, p. 27).

ELLIS, Charles Rose, 1st Baron Seaford (1771–1845) An MP from 1793 until 1826, he was head of the West Indian interest and a friend of **Canning**. He was created Baron Seaford in 1826.

ANTILLES in Benjamin Disraeli, *Vivian Grey* (1826–7)

Identified in a key given in a pamphlet published in 1827 by William Marsh. This key is discussed by Lucien Wolf in his notes to *Vivian Grey*, 1904 (centenary edn), Vol. II, London: Alexander Moring, p. 364), with the conclusion that Disraeli was not responsible for the key. 'A slight error is the ascription of the original of Antilles to a Mr C— E—, whereas the initials should be C.R.E., standing for Charles Rose Ellis, the highest authority in Parliament on the West-Indian Islands, often called the Antilles' (B.N. Langdon-Davies, 1904, Introd. to *Vivian Grey*, London: Alexander Moring, p. xxxi; originally published 1826, London: Henry Colburn).

ELLIS, Edward (b. 1789?) Senior partner in the firm of Ellis & Blackmore, solicitors, of 1 Holborn Court (later South Square), Gray's Inn, London, where Dickens was an office boy in 1827.

MR PERKER in Charles Dickens, *The Pickwick Papers* (1836–7)

'Edward Ellis . . . had some of the peculiarities attributed to Mr Perker, being in particular an inveterate snuff-taker' (William J. Carlton, 1952, 'Mr Blackmore engages an office boy', *The Dickensian* 48 (September): 163; based on the manuscript of Edward Blackmore, 'Reminiscences of Charles Dickens', written in 1870).

ELLIS, George Hasted George Meredith's first cousin, son of Sir Samuel Burdon **Ellis**.

CROSSJAY PATTERNE in George Meredith, *The Egoist* (1879)

'[Augustus Meredith's] sister's son, the original of Crossjay Patterne in *The Egoist*' (S.M. Ellis, 1920, *George Meredith*, 2nd edn, London: Grant Richards, p. 137).

ELLIS, Captain Henry (1835–1908) He was Master-Attendant at Singapore and, as such, was in complete control of the port from 1873 to 1888. It was he who, in 1888, gave Conrad his first command.

CAPTAIN ELLIOT in Joseph Conrad, *Lord Jim* (1900) and 'The End of the Tether' (1902)

See below.

CAPTAIN ELLIS in Joseph Conrad, *The Shadow-Line* (1917)

'It may seem odd that Conrad, having disguised Ellis's identity by means of the fictional name of Elliott in two stories, should give the man's real name in *The Shadow-Line*. A possible reason is that Captain Ellis was alive when the first two stories were published' (Norman Sherry, 1966, *Conrad's Eastern World*, Cambridge, p. 165).

ELLIS, Sir Samuel Burdon (1782–1865) He married Catherine Matilda Meredith (**Ellis**, above).

MAJOR STRIKE in George Meredith, *Evan Harrington* (1860)

See under **Ellis**, Lady.

ELLISON, Cuthbert Edward A contemporary of Charles **Kingsley** at Cambridge, he was a member of the Young England party, and later shared chambers in Inner Temple, London, with Thackeray. In 1848, he was one of the founders of *Politics for the People*, a short-lived journal published by the Christian Socialists.

ARTHUR PENDENNIS in W.M. Thackeray, *The History of Pendennis* (1848–50)

'[T]here is one more of our [the Christian Socialists of 1848] promoters whom I cannot pretermit, as his position amongst us was quite unique, – Cuthbert E. Ellison. . . . Ellison was our "swell". Very good looking, always faultlessly dressed, most courteous in manner . . . it seemed quite a condescension for such a superior-looking being to take his seat in our midst. . . . Your interest in him will, I know, be excited when I say that he was the original of Arthur Pendennis' (J.M. Ludlow, 1894, 'The Christian Socialists of 1848 and the following years II', *Economic Review* 4: 34–5). *See also* **Kenney**, C.L.; **Thackeray**, W.M.

ELWES, John (or John Meggott) (1714–89) He was a celebrated miser who was MP for Berkshire from 1774 to 1787. He was heir to his uncle, Sir Harvey Elwes, and changed his name to Elwes from Meggott.

JOHN SCARVE in W. Harrison Ainsworth, *The Miser's Daughter* (1842)

'The most significant reappearance of John Elwes in literature [is to be found in] certain episodes of William Harrison Ainsworth's *The Miser's Daughter*. . . . Parallels in phrase and action may best be organised according to the sequence of episodes in *The Miser's Daughter*' (Coleman O. Parsons, 1946, 'Harrison Ainsworth's use of John Elwes in "The Miser's Daughter"', *Notes and Queries* 191 (24 August): 68, 69). Elwes's first appearance in literature is Edward Topham's *The Life of the Late John Elwes, Esquire*, first published in the *World*, it appeared in twelve editions between 1790 and 1805. See Parsons, op. cit., which follows in detail Ainsworth's debt to this source.

ELWOOD, John Rudolph (d. 1931?) He was a contemporary and friend of James Joyce at University College, Dublin, where he studied medicine.

TEMPLE in James Joyce, *A Portrait of the Artist as a Young Man* (1916)

'Dr Ellwood [sic] is the original of Temple in the Portrait' (to Harriet Shaw Weaver, 28 March 1928, *The Letters of James Joyce*, 1966, Vol. II, ed. Richard Ellmann, London: Faber & Faber, p. 174).

The EMBASSY CLUB, Soho, London A night-club that was fashionable in the 1920s.

THE LOYALTY CLUB in Michael Arlen, *The Green Hat* (1924)

'"The Loyalty" – recognizable as the Embassy Club, at which the smartest people, including young princes, then danced to the blues – was depicted almost table by table' (M. Bellasis, 1971, in T. Williams and Helen M. Palmer (eds), *The Dictionary of National Biography, 1951–1960*, London: Oxford University Press, s.v. Arlen).

EMBLEY HOUSE, Romsey, Hampshire

FERNELL HALL in Thomas Hardy, 'Lady Mottisfont' (1891)

Identified in F.B. Pinion, 1968, *A Hardy Companion*, London: Macmillan.

EMERSON, Ralph Waldo (1803–82) American essayist, poet and transcendental philosopher. Born in Boston, he graduated from Harvard in 1821. In 1829 he became pastor of a Unitarian church in Boston and married his first wife, Ellen Louisa Tucker (d. 1832). His radical views on the Last Supper forced him to resign his pulpit. His visit to **Carlyle** in 1833 prompted the correspondence that was to last for thirty-eight years. In 1835 he married his second wife, Lydia Jackson (1802–92).

MARK WINSOME in Herman Melville, *The Confidence Man* (1857)

'[I]t is, I think, demonstrably true that Melville used Emerson as the pattern of the mystic [Winsome] in . . . *The Confidence-man*. . . . [The mystic is described in detail]. . . . The details are exact, and the general impression explicit. . . . The physical description . . . is very close to what an observer would have seen in a survey of Emerson in the middle of the century' (Egbert S. Oliver, 1946, 'Melville's picture of Emerson and Thoreau in "The Confidence-Man"', *College English* 8 (2): 62).

EPSOM COLLEGE, Surrey The public school at which Hugh Walpole was a member of staff in 1908.

MOFFATTS in Hugh Walpole, *Mr Perrin and Mr Traill* (1911)

'Mr Perrin's school may have been situated on a carefully described Cornish sea-coast, but to anyone who knew anything of Epsom and the staff there in recent years its identity was unmistakeable' (Rupert Hart-Davis, 1952, *Hugh Walpole*, p. 83).

D'ERLANGER, Catherine, Baroness Née de Rochegnde, she married Baron Emile d'Erlanger. Shortly before the First World War, he bought Falconwood at Woolwich, where the Baroness became the neighbour and friend of Enid Bagnold, but the friendship ended abruptly when she recognized her portrait in *Serena Blandish*.

COUNTESS FLOR DI FOLIO in Enid Bagnold, *Serena Blandish* (1924)

When Enid Bagnold came to describe the Baroness's arrival at Falconwood, she exclaimed: 'Does no one quote from their own books? I shall' (*Enid Bagnold's Autobiography (from 1889)*, 1969, London: Heinemann, p. 108). She then quotes the passage in ch. 2 of *Serena Blandish* describing the Countess Flor di Folio.

ERSKINE, James Alexander Wedderburn St Clair ('Hamish') (1909–74) The second son of the 5th Earl of Rosslyn, he was a close friend of Nancy Mitford, to whom he was engaged for a time. He was awarded the Military Cross in the Second World War, during which he was taken prisoner and subsequently escaped. His aunts were Millicent, Duchess of **Sutherland**; Sybil, Countess of **Westmorland**; Frances, Lady **Warwick**; and Lady Angela **Forbes**.

SIR RODERICK ('BOBBY') BOBBIN in Nancy Mitford, *Christmas Pudding* (1932)

'My new book is jolly good, all about Hamish at Eton. "All father's sisters married well, thank God," is his opening remark' (Nancy Mitford to Harold Acton, 4 December 1931, quoted in Harold Acton, 1975, *Nancy Mitford: a memoir*, London: Hamilton, p. 37). In *Christmas Pudding* (ch. VII), he in fact says, 'Father's sisters all married well, as it happens, which leaves me quite nicely connected'.

ESTERHÁZY, Prince Paul Anton (1786–1866) He was the Austrian Ambassador in London between 1815 and 1818 and again between 1830 and 1838. He returned to Hungary and joined the nationalist movement in 1842, and became Minister for Foreign Affairs in 1848. He was subsequently Minister in Rome, until 1851, and was a minister with no portfolio between 1861 and 1866. He married the niece of George III's wife in 1816.

PRINCE HUNGARY in Benjamin Disraeli, *Vivian Grey* (1826–7)

Identified as Prince E—— in a key given in *The Star Chamber* (24 May 1826): 114; reprinted in *Vivian Grey*, 1904 (centenary edn), ed. Lucien Wolf, Vol. II, London: Alexander Moring, pp. 361–2. The full name appears on a copy of the key held in the British Museum. Lucien Wolf concludes that Disraeli was not responsible for the key.

THE RUSSIAN ARCHDUKE in Benjamin Disraeli, *Vivian Grey* (1826–7)

Identified as Es—h—y in a key given in a pamphlet published in 1827 by William Marsh. This key is discussed by Lucien Wolf in his notes to *Vivian Grey* (1904 (centenary edn), Vol. II, London: Alexander Moring, p. 364), who concludes that Disraeli was not responsible for the key.

ETON COLLEGE, Berkshire

NOAT in Henry Green, *Blindness* (1926)

'[Brian Howard] belonged to a set of boys who gained much from Eton because of the little they gave. There was Harold Acton . . . his brother William, Robert Byron . . . the two Messels, Anthony Powell . . . and Henry Green, who described them in his novel, *Blindness*' (Cyril Connolly, 1938, *Enemies of Promise*, p. 318).

ETON SOCIETY OF ARTS, Eton College, Berkshire It was founded by Brian **Howard** and the art critic Alan Clutton-Brock.

NOAT ART SOCIETY in Henry Green, *Blindness* (1926)

'Robert Byron commemorated the impact of the Eton Society of Arts as long ago as 1926 in a discursive review of . . . *Blindness*, in the Oxford magazine *Cherwell*, under the title of "Henry Yorke and the Eton Society of Arts". . . . He quotes an account of the "Noad [sic] Art Society" continuing with: "The E.S.A. was founded jointly by Brian Howard . . . and Alan Clutton Brock. . . . The whole brunt of [the] initial difficulties fell on Henry Yorke"' (M.-J. Lancaster, 1968, *Brian Howard: portrait of a failure*, London: Anthony Blond, p. 119). According to Henry Yorke (Henry Green) himself, 'Harold Acton and Brian, who were great rivals, started the Eton Society of Arts, which met once a week for two years and I was the Secretary . . .' (ibid., p. 120).

EUSTON, Margaret She was married to Matthew Baillie, 'the last of gipsies [who] could steal a horse from under the owner if he liked, but always left the saddle and bridle; a thorough gentleman in his way, and six feet four in stature'.

MEG MERRILIES in Sir Walter Scott, *Guy Mannering* (1815)

'By the way my uncle has told me since I came here that the wife of that Matthew Baillie, Margaret Euston by name, was the original of Sir W. Scott's "Meg Merrilies"' (*Letters and Memorials of Jane Welsh Carlyle*, 1883, ed. J.A. Froude, Vol. II, London: Longman, p. 54). *See also* **Gordon**, Jean.

EVANS, Anne (d. 1856) Superintendent of the **Clergy Daughters' School**, Cowan Bridge, when the Brontë sisters were there as pupils in 1824 and 1825. She married the Revd Mr Harben, and they emigrated to the United States *c.*1843.

MISS TEMPLE in Charlotte Brontë, *Jane Eyre* (1847)

'The description of the sweet dignity and benevolence of Miss Temple was a just tribute to the merits of one whom all who knew her appear to hold in honour' (Mrs Gaskell, 1857, *The Life of Charlotte Brontë*, London: Smith, Elder, ch. IV). 'This lady was Miss A. Evans' (Herbert Wroot, 1935, *Sources for Charlotte Brontë's Novels: persons and places*, Shipley, Yorks., p. 69). *See also* **Thompson**, Jane.

EVANS, Christiana (1788?–1836) Née Pearson, she was from a family of substantial farmers in Warwickshire, and was the sister of Anne **Garner**, Elizabeth **Johnson** and Mary **Everard**. In 1813 she married Robert **Evans**, becoming his second wife; George Eliot was their daughter.

Mrs Hackit in George Eliot, 'The Sad Fortunes of the Revd Amos Barton', *Scenes of Clerical Life* (1857–8)

'Mrs Hackit was identified [in Warwickshire] as Mrs Robert Evans, though Mrs Evans could not have attended the deathbed of "Milly" who died after her, in November 1836' (Marghanita Laski, 1973, *George Eliot and Her World*, London: Thames & Hudson, p. 55). *See also under* **Anstruther**, Lady.

EVANS, Elizabeth (1776–1849) Née Tomlinson. A lace-maker of Nottingham, in 1797 she underwent a spectacular conversion, falling to the ground like one dead. She became a Methodist preacher, being so valuable a hand in the factory where she worked that she was able to combine the two occupations as she wished. In 1804 she married Samuel **Evans**, and they settled at Wirksworth, Derbyshire. As a result of the Wesleyan ban on women preachers, they associated with the Primitive Methodists, eventually joining the Derby Faith Folk. She was George Eliot's aunt by marriage.

Dinah Morris in George Eliot, *Adam Bede* (1859)

'The germ of "Adam Bede" was an anecdote told me by my Methodist Aunt Samuel . . . an anecdote from her own experience. We were sitting together one afternoon during her visit to me at Griffe, probably in 1839 or 40, when it occurred to her to tell me how she had visited a condemned criminal, a very ignorant girl who had murdered her child and refused to confess – how she stayed with her praying, through the night and how the poor creature at last broke into tears and confessed her crime. My Aunt afterwards went with her in the cart to the place of execution, and she described to me the great respect with which this ministry of hers was regarded by the official people about the gaol. The story, told by my aunt with great feeling, affected me deeply, and I never lost the impression of that afternoon and our talk together' (entry for 30 November 1858 in autograph journal, 1854–61, reproduced in *The George Eliot Letters*, 1954, ed. Gordon S. Haight, Vol. II, London: Oxford University Press, p. 502). 'You see how she suggested Dinah, but it is not possible you should see as I do how entirely her individuality differed from Dinah's' (to Sara Hemmel, 7 October 1859, *Letters*, op. cit., Vol. III, pp. 174–6). The 'unhappy girl' was Mary **Voce** and the account of the episode, which was published in the Nottingham *Journal* (20 March 1802) is to be found reprinted in the edition of *Adam Bede* edited by G.S. Haight (1948, New York). 'The equation between Dinah Morris and Mrs Evans became a firm folk belief, written into the Primitive Methodist record, and testified to by a tablet in the Methodist Chapel at Wirksworth ("Erected . . . to the memory of Elizabeth Evans . . . known to the world as 'Dinah Bede'")' (Valentine Cunningham, 1976, *Everywhere Spoken Against: dissent in the Victorian novel*, Oxford: Clarendon Press, p. 153).

EVANS, George[1] (1740–1830) Village carpenter, of Roston Common, Norbury, Derby. He married Mary Leech and they had eight children, including George, Robert and Samuel **Evans**. He died at the age of 90 in the house of his son William, at **Ellastone**, Staffordshire. He was George Eliot's paternal grandfather.

Thias Bede in George Eliot, *Adam Bede* (1859)

'Though Robert Evans's father died . . . in 1830 at the age of ninety, he has been widely named as the original of "Thias Bede"' (Marghanita Laski, 1973, *George Eliot and Her World*, London: Thames & Hudson, p. 65). 'Beyond the fact that [George and Mary Evans] were the parents of Robert Evans, there is little, if anything, to suggest that this couple were . . . the originals of Thias and Lisbeth Bede' (Charles S. Olcott, 1911, *George Eliot: scenes and people in her novels*, London: Cassell, p. 67; originally published 1910, New York: Thomas Y. Crowell).

EVANS, George[2] Eldest son of George **Evans**[1], he took to drink and died young at Rocester, Derbyshire.

THIAS BEDE in George Eliot, *Adam Bede* (1859)

'George Evans . . . has been widely named as the original of "Thias Bede" – but it is tempting to substitute his eldest son George' (Marghanita Laski, 1973, *George Eliot and Her World*, London: Thames & Hudson, p. 65). 'The incident . . . was taken from real life; an uncle of George Eliot met the death of Thias Bede, having been drowned in a few inches of water while intoxicated' (Charles S. Olcott, 1911, *George Eliot: scenes and people in her novels*, London: Cassell, p. 67; originally published 1910, New York: Thomas Y. Crowell).

EVANS, Herbert Arthur (1846–1923) Educated at Marlborough and at Balliol College, Oxford, he was Assistant Master at the United Services College, Westward Ho!, from 1879 to 1894. He was on the staff of Rylands Library, Manchester, between 1895 and 1897, and was subsequently a private tutor. He was the author of *Highways and Byways in Oxford and the Cotswolds* (1905), and he founded the natural history society at Westward Ho! and promoted the school's theatricals.

MR HARTOPP in Rudyard Kipling, *Stalky & Co.* (1899)

'A more sympathetic teacher [than 'Prout'] was Mr H.A. Evans ("Hartopp")' (Charles Carrington, 1955, *Rudyard Kipling: his life and work*, p. 32). Also identified in the caption to a photograph reproduced in the June 1981 issue of *The Kipling Journal*: 'Masters at the United Services College . . . in Kipling's day' (*The Kipling Journal* 48 (218): 21).

EVANS, Isaac (1816–90) Second son of Robert and Christiana **Evans**. He was George Eliot's brother.

TOM TULLIVER in George Eliot, *The Mill on the Floss* (1860)

'Isaac was Tom' (Marghanita Laski, 1973, *George Eliot and Her World*, London: Thames & Hudson, p. 74).

EVANS, Robert (1773–1849) Born in Ellastone, Staffordshire, he was land agent to the **Newdigate** family of Arbury, Warwickshire, for many years. In 1813 he married Christiana Pearson (**Evans**, above), who became his second wife; George Eliot was their daughter.

ADAM BEDE in George Eliot, *Adam Bede* (1859)

'The character of Adam, and one or two incidents connected with him, were suggested by my Father's early life' (entry for 30 November 1858 in autograph journal, reproduced in 'History of Adam Bede', *The George Eliot Letters*, 1954, Gordon S. Haight, Vol. II, London: Oxford University Press, p. 503).

CALEB GARTH in George Eliot, *Middlemarch* (1871–2)

'Caleb is her [George Eliot's] father' (Anna T. Kitchel (ed.), 1950, *Quarry for Middlemarch*, Berkeley and Los Angeles, p. iv; suppl. to *The Nineteenth Century* 4).

MR HACKIT in George Eliot, 'The Sad Fortunes of the Revd Amos Barton', *Scenes of Clerical Life* (1857–8)

See under **Anstruther**, Lady.

EDWARD TULLIVER in George Eliot, *The Mill on the Floss* (1860)

'The strong affection of Mr Tulliver is but a reflection of [George Eliot's] father's love. . . . [This] love is the sole element of reality here reproduced' (Charles S. Olcott, 1911, *George Eliot: scenes and places in her novels*, London: Cassell, pp. 88, 89; originally published 1910, New York: Thomas Y. Crowell). *See also* **Pagden**, John.

EVANS, Samuel (1777–1858) Son of George **Evans**[1], he was also the brother of Robert **Evans** and married Elizabeth Tomlinson (**Evans**, above) in 1804. He was a carpenter and converted to Methodism in 1795. He was George Eliot's uncle.

SETH BEDE in George Eliot, *Adam Bede* (1859)

'Robert's brother Samuel was accepted as the original of Seth; and his wife Elizabeth . . . as Dinah . . . the memorial tablet to them set up in the Wesleyan Chapel in Wirksworth in 1873 unequivocally makes the identifications' (Marghanita Laski, 1973, *George Eliot and Her World*, London: Thames & Hudson, p. 65).

EVERARD, Revd E. A Doctor of Divinity, in 1822 he was Curate at St Nicholas, the parish church of Brighton. He began to take pupils *c.*1827, and by 1830 he had a school at Wick House which, from the aristocratic birth of the pupils, was known as 'The Young House of Lords'. The school continued until 1837, when Dr Everard disappears from the local directories, although it is possible that his son was running another school in the town at the end of the decade.

DR BLIMBER in Charles Dickens, *Dombey and Son* (1846–8)

'The probability is that Dickens took the outlines from his knowledge of Everard's celebrated Academy, filled in the details by the aid of his fertile imagination, and . . . placed it at some suitable house on the Brighton front' (T.B. Powell, 1924, 'Blimber's and Brighton', *The Dickensian* 20 (April): 93). *See also* **King**, J.C.

EVERARD, Mary (1771–1844) Daughter of Isaac Pearson of Old Castle Farm, Astley, Warwickshire, she married John Everard of Attleborough. She was the sister of Christiana **Evans** and thus the maternal aunt of George Eliot.

JANE GLEGG (NÉE DODSON) in George Eliot, *The Mill on the Floss* (1860)

'There is a portrait of Mrs Everard in a lace cap and her best "front" of glossy curls over a handsome face that one sees instantly to be Mrs Glegg's' (Gordon S. Haight, 1958, 'George Eliot's originals', in R.C. Rathburn and M. Steinmann, Jun. (eds), *From Jane Austen to Joseph Conrad*, Minneapolis, p. 189). The portrait is reproduced in Charles S. Olcott, 1911, *George Eliot: scenes and people in her novels*, London: Cassell; originally published 1910, New York: Thomas Y. Crowell.

EVERHARD, Mr

THOMAS JEROME in George Eliot, 'Janet's Repentance', *Scenes of Clerical Life* (1857–8)

See under **Anstruther**, Lady.

EVERSHOT, Dorset A village twelve miles north-west of Dorchester.

EVERSHEAD in Thomas Hardy, Wessex novels and tales (1871–95)

Identified on a map prepared by Thomas Hardy which hangs in the Dorset County Museum, Dorchester. *See under* **Abbotsbury**.

The *EXAMINER* A London literary periodical founded by Leigh **Hunt** and his brother John. It was published from 1808 until 1880, and was edited between 1847 and 1855 by John **Forster**.

THE *OBSERVATOR* in W.M. Thackeray, *The History of Henry Esmond* (1852)

'[In chapter 5 of the second book, Thackeray] included a veiled but unmistakeable allusion to Forster . . . and to his campaign against the *English Humourists* in the *Examiner*, which appears as *The Observator*' (Gordon Ray, 1958, *Thackeray: the age of wisdom*, p. 197). The passage was omitted from the revised edition of *The History of Esmond* (1858).

EXETER, Devon

CHATTERIS in W.M. Thackeray, *The History of Pendennis* (1848–50)

'Chatteris (which is Exeter)' (H.C. Minchin, 1928, 'Thackeray in the Temple', *Cornhill Magazine* (NS) 65 (September): 290).

EXONBURY in Thomas Hardy, Wessex novels and tales (1871–95)

Identifed on a map prepared by Thomas Hardy which hangs in the Dorset County Museum, Dorchester. *See under* **Abbotsbury**.

F

FABER, Frederick William (1814–63) A friend of **Wordsworth**, George **Smythe** and Lord John **Manners**, he met the latter in 1838 when acting as a tutor in a household in Ambleside. He was ordained in 1837 and joined the Church of Rome in 1845. On hearing of this, Augustus Stafford wrote to John Manners: 'I was talking to the wife of one of our divines about his going over. "Oh", she said, "I am not in the least surprised at his turning Papist. Have you seen the catalogue [of the sale of his goods at the Rectory of Elton]? The man must be mad. 26lb of black pepper! Was ever such a quantity heard of in a small establishment – and Cayenne in proportion! I shouldn't be surprised if the fool had turned Turk! 26lb of black pepper!"' (Charles Whibley, 1925, *Lord John Manners*, Vol. I, London, p. 73).

AUBREY ST LYS in Benjamin Disraeli, *Sybil* (1845)

'[Disraeli] has drawn a picture of "Young England" Anglicanism in "St Lys" of *Sybil*, the prototype of whom was Faber' (Walter Sichel, 1904, *Disraeli: a study in personality and ideas*, London: Methuen, p. 126). The identification was accepted in W.F. Monypenny, 1912, *Life of Benjamin Disraeli*, Vol. II, London, p. 170.

FABIAN SOCIETY A socialist society founded in London in 1883–4, aimed at 'reconstructing society on the highest moral principles after long taking of counsel'. The Society rejected Marxism. Among its early members were G.B. Shaw, Beatrice and Sidney Webb, and H.G. Wells.

THE LYCURGANS in Dorothy Richardson, *Pilgrimage* (1915–67)

'Miriam attends Lycurgan (Fabian) meetings' (John Rosenberg, 1973, *Dorothy Richardson*, London, p. 117).

VENTURIST SOCIETY in Mrs Humphry Ward, *Marcella* (1894)

'Venturist (Fabian)' (Enid Huws Jones, 1973, *Mrs Humphry Ward*, London: Heinemann, p. 103).

FAGIN, Bob An orphan who worked in Warren's Blacking Warehouse and showed great kindness to Dickens when working with him.

MICK WALKER in Charles Dickens, *David Copperfield* (1849–50)

'Mick Walker's portrait was drawn from Bob Fagin' (*David Copperfield*, 1903 (autograph edn), ed. F.G. Kitton, p. 390 n. (to p. 207)).

FAHNESTOCK, Ernest (d. 1918) Inventor. He was the younger son of Edith, sister of Frances Hodgson Burnett, and her first husband, Pleasant Fahnestock of Knoxville.

JOSEPH HUTCHINSON in Frances Hodgson Burnett, *T. Tembaron* (1913)

'Ernest had been . . . the inspiration of a number of characters in Frances' books – including Joseph Hutchinson' (Ann Thwaite, 1973, *Waiting for the Party: the life of Frances Hodgson Burnett, 1849–1924*, p. 240).

FAIRBANKS, Marjorie   One of the two women from Boston who, with Kenneth **Raisbeck**, went on a tour of France with Thomas Wolfe in 1925. Mrs Fairbanks had left behind a husband and child, and on her return to the United States she became divorced. She subsequently remarried, becoming Mrs Crocker. Wolfe was still in touch with her in 1936.

ELINOR in Thomas Wolfe, *Of Time and the River* (1935)

'Marjorie Fairbanks, Helen Harding and Kenneth Raisbeck accompanied Wolfe . . . in 1925. Wolfe made use of this experience . . . in the adventures of Eugene Gant with Elinor, Ann, and Starwick' (*The Notebooks of Thomas Wolfe*, 1970, ed. Richard S. Kennedy and Paschal Reeves, Chapel Hill, NC: University of North Carolina Press, p. 443 n. 26).

FAIRLIE, Gerard   (1900?–83) Soldier, journalist and novelist. He was an officer in the Scots Guards for six years, and worked with the French Resistance during the Second World War. He was a sports correspondent for *The Times*, and published his first novel in 1927.

HUGH ('BULL-DOG') DRUMMOND in Sapper (H.C. McNeile), *Bull-dog Drummond* (1920) and others

'It was in a radio broadcast a few years before his early death in 1937 that Sapper informed his audience that he had based Bulldog [sic] Drummond on Fairlie though as Fairlie himself was wont to point out, the character had much of Sapper himself in it and must have been at least partially realized in the author's mind by the time he met Fairlie . . . in 1919' (obituary notice, 1983, *The Times* (19 April): 14).

FAITHFULL, Starr   (d. 1931) She was the stepdaughter of a retired chemical engineer and lived with her family in an apartment on St Mark's Place in New York. She was to be seen around the speakeasies of the town, and on 9 June 1931 New York newspapers reported that her body had been washed up on Long Beach, Long Island. She was sexually assaulted when she was a child.

GLORIA WANDROUS in John O'Hara, *BUtterfield 8* (1935)

'O'Hara used Starr Faithfull as the model for Gloria Wandrous' (Finis Farr, 1974, *O'Hara: a biography*, p. 178).

FALKNER, Fanny   (1789?–1808) She was Peacock's first love: they met near Chertsey, Berkshire, and became engaged, but her parents disapproved. She was hastily married to someone else and died the following year. Peacock's grand-daughter stated that to the end of his life he wore a locket containing her hair.

ANTHELIA MELINCOURT in Thomas Love Peacock, *Melincourt* (1817)

'Anthelia has been variously stated to have been an idealisation of Peacock's first love and of Jane Gryffydh' (*The Novels of T.L. Peacock*, 1948, ed. David Garnett, London: Rupert Hart-Davis, p. 106 n. 1). *See also* **Gryffydh**, Jane.

FALKNER, William Cuthbert (1825–89) Mississippi army officer, lawyer, railroad builder and author. He wrote *The White Rose of Memphis*, which was 'a best seller in its day' (John Faulkner, 1963, *My Brother Bill*), a play that had a short run on Broadway, a travel book and a book of verse. He was William Faulkner's grandfather.

COLONEL JOHN SARTORIS in William Faulkner, *The Unvanquished* (1938)

'Prototype of Colonel Sartoris' (James D. Hart (ed.), 1965, *The Oxford Companion to American Literature*, New York: Oxford University Press, s.v. Falkner).

FANE, Lady Augusta (1786–1871) She was the second daughter of John, 10th Earl of Westmorland, and the sister of Sarah Sophia, Countess of Jersey. In 1804 she married John, Lord Boringdon, who was created Viscount Boringdon and Earl of Morley in 1815. In May 1808 she eloped with the Rt. Hon. Sir Arthur Paget, Ambassador to the Ottoman Porte, and they were married in February 1809: he was recalled in May of the same year and retired on a pension of £2,000.

LADY ISABEL VANE in Mrs Henry Wood, *East Lynne* (1861)

'*East Lynne* is simply the true story of Lady Augusta Fane, one of the most beautiful women of her day, who ran away from her husband Lord Morley. She left her little baby, but came back ten years later as a nurse, when the child, Lord Boringdon, was dying, and took care of him to the end, her broken-hearted husband recognising her, but never letting her know he had done so. These facts my father had from Thackeray who told them to Mrs Henry Wood, who founded *East Lynne* on the story' (J.O. Field, 1926, *More Uncensored Recollections*, p. 281). This reference is given in Hon. Vicary Gibbs (ed.), 1926, *The Complete Peerage of England, Scotland, Ireland, Great Britain and the United Kingdom*, Vol. III, London: St Catherine Press, s.v. Morley. The child died near Paris, in November 1817.

FANE, John *See* **Westmorland**, 11th Earl of.

FAREHAM, Hampshire Thackeray's maternal great-grandmother and grandmother, Mrs Becher, lived in this small town; he was in their care when he was a small boy at school in England and his parents were in India.

FAIRPORT in W.M. Thackeray, *Denis Duval* (1864)

'Fareham . . . the Fairport of *Denis Duval*' (*The Letters and Private Papers of W.M. Thackeray*, Vol. I: *1817–1840*, 1945, ed. Gordon N. Ray, London: Oxford University Press, p. 4 n. 7).

FARLEY, James Aloysius (b. 1888) American politician. He was Chairman of the Democratic National Committee from 1932 to 1940, and was the US Postmaster-General from 1933 to 1940.

ED MEHAFFERTY in Dalton Trumbo, *Washington Jitters* (1936)

'Trumbo made wholesale borrowings from life . . . Ed Mehafferty [suggests] Jim Farley' (Joseph Blotner, 1966, *The Modern American Political Novel*, Austin, Tex., p. 132).

FARR HOUSE, Dorset Situated one and a half miles west of Wimborne.

YEWSHOLT LODGE in Thomas Hardy, 'Barbara of the House of Grebe' (1891)

Identified in F.B. Pinion, 1968, *A Hardy Companion*, London: Macmillan.

FARRELL, James Thomas (1904–1979) American novelist, short-story writer, critic and essayist. He was born in Chicago and paid for himself to be educated at the University there. He lived in Paris during the 1930s. His style owed much to that of Sherwood **Anderson** and also drew from the naturalist tradition of Zola. He published more than fifty novels in all.

DANNY O'NEILL in James T. Farrell, *A World I Never Made* (1936) and others

'The identity of Danny O'Neill has always been transparently clear. Step by step [his] early years parallel those of Farrell himself' (Nelson Manfred Blake, 1969, *Novelists' America: fiction as history, 1910–1940*, Syracuse, NY, p. 197).

FARRER, James (1812–79) Son of J.W. Farrer, Master in Chancery. In 1847–57 and 1859–65 he was MP for South Durham.

MR BOUNCER in W.M. Thackeray, 'Notes on the North What-d'ye-Callem Election' (1841)

Identified in *Letters and Private Papers of W.M. Thackeray*, 1945, ed. Gordon N. Ray, Vol. II, London: Oxford University Press, p. 27 n. 49.

FAULKNER, William (1897–1962) American novelist, born near Oxford, Mississippi. He was rejected by the US Army when America entered the First World War, but became a pilot in the Canadian Flying Corps. After the war he attended the University of Mississippi. He published his first novel, *Soldier's Pay*, with the help of Sherwood Anderson in 1926. He married in 1929, and in the same year took a job as a coal-heaver on night-work at the local power station during which time he wrote *As I Lay Dying*. His later novels established his reputation as a major figure in modern American fiction and he was awarded the Nobel Prize for Literature in 1949.

DAVID in Sherwood Anderson, 'A Meeting South', *Death in the Woods* (1933)

'Sherwood Anderson's use of William Faulkner as David, the war-scarred southern poet in "A Meeting South" ... has long been recognized' (Hubert McAlexander, Jun., 1972, 'William Faulkner: the young poet in Stark Young's *The Torches Flare*', *American Literature* 3 (4): 647).

EUGENE OLIVER in Stark Young, *The Torches Flare* (1928)

'The character Eugene Oliver ... strongly suggests the young Faulkner. The setting of the novel is clearly Oxford, Mississippi ... but the most striking local touch is the minor character Oliver, the young student-poet. ... The physical resemblance is pronounced. Oliver's genealogy, however, provides an even stronger clue' (Hubert McAlexander, Jun., 1972, 'William Faulkner: the young poet in Stark Young's *The Torches Flare*, *American Literature* 3 (4): 647).

FAWE PARK, Cumbria Near Keswick. A country house, overlooking Derwentwater, where the Potter family spent the summer of 1903.

MR McGREGOR'S GARDEN in Beatrix Potter, *The Tale of Peter Rabbit* (1902) and others

'The garden in *Benjamin Bunny* was at Fawe Park, Keswick' (Beatrix Potter to her publishers; see Margaret Lane, 1946, *The Tale of Beatrix Potter*, London and New York: Frederick Lane, p. 128). *See also* **Camfield Place; Gwaynynog**.

FAWLEY, Berkshire

MARYGREEN in Thomas Hardy, *Jude the Obscure* (1895)

Identified in Denys Kay-Robinson, 1972, *Hardy's Wessex Reappraised*, Newton Abbot, and in F.B. Pinion, 1968, *A Hardy Companion*, London: Macmillan. '[In 1923 Hardy and his wife, returning from Oxford] paused . . . at Fawley, that pleasant Berkshire village described in [*Jude the Obscure*] under the name of Marygreen. Here some of Hardy's ancestors were buried, and he searched fruitlessly for their graves in the little churchyard. His father's mother . . . had spent the first thirteen years of her life here as an orphan child . . . and her memories of Fawley were so poignant that she never cared to return to the place after she had left it as a young girl. The surname of Jude was taken from this place' (F.E. Hardy, 1972, *The Life of Thomas Hardy, 1840–1928*, p. 420).

FAY, Monsignor Sigourney

MONSIGNOR DARCY in F. Scott Fitzgerald, *This Side of Paradise* (1920)

'[Monsignor Darcy] was, of course, my best friend, the Monsignor Sigourney Fay to whom the book was dedicated. He was known to many Catholics as the most brilliant priest in America. The letters in the book are almost transcriptions of his own letters to me' (to Frances Newman, 26 February 1921, reproduced in *The Letters of F. Scott Fitzgerald*, 1964, ed. Andrew Turnbull, London: Bodley Head, p. 469).

FECKLESS FANNIE A crazed creature who wandered the Scottish country-side in the late eighteenth century.

MADGE WILDFIRE in Sir Walter Scott, *The Heart of Midlothian* (1818)

'Madge was modelled (with differences) from Feckless Fannie. . . . Joseph Train collected all the available information about her' (W.S. Crockett, 1912, *The Scott Originals: an account of notables and worthies, the originals of characters in the Waverley Novels*, Edinburgh and London: T.N. Foulis, p. 244).

FELLEY MILL, Nottinghamshire Located three miles north of Underwood The back of **Haggs Farm** overlooks it.

STRELLEY MILL in D.H. Lawrence, *The White Peacock* (1911)

'Turn to the left [on the Alfreton Road], towards Underwood, and go till you come to the lodge gate by the reservoir – go through the gate, and up the drive to the next gate, and continue on the footpath just below the drive on the left – on through the wood to Felley Mill (The White Peacock Farm)' (*The Letters of D.H. Lawrence*, 1932, ed. Aldous Huxley, London: Heinemann, p. 374). *See also* **Haggs Farm**.

FENTON, Frederick He was best man to Jack **Hale** at his marriage to Jessie Richardson in 1895. At that time he was intending to join the Community of the Resurrection, and was deeply attracted to Dorothy Richardson. He was subsequently married, and reappeared in her life at intervals for many years.

MR GROVE in Dorothy Richardson, *Pilgrimage* (1915–67)

'Mr Grove, the strange intense young man who is based on the character of Fred Fenton' (John Rosenberg, 1973, *Dorothy Richardson*, London, p. 106).

FERLINGHETTI, Lawrence (b. 1920) American poet and publisher. In 1955 he founded City Lights Books, San Francisco; he was the author of *A Coney Island of the Mind* (1958) and others.

LORENZO MONSANTO in *Big Sur* (1962), LARRY O'HARA in *The Subterraneans* (1958), and DANNY RICHMAN in *Book of Dreams* (1960) and *Visions of Gerard* (1963), all by Jack Kerouac

Identified in 'Character key to the Duluoz Legend', in Barry Gifford and Lawrence Lee, 1979, *Jack's Book*, pp. 322–32.

FEROZE, Dr Dhunjabhi Mullan (1874–1959) Family doctor of Ada **Lawrence** in Ripley, he attended D.H. Lawrence, who grew to like him warmly.

DR SHERARDY in D.H. Lawrence, *Aaron's Rod* (1922)

'We had a second turn-to yesterday – and at half past eleven went roaring off . . . to Dr Feroze's – he is a Parsee – and drank two more bottles of muscatel, and danced in his big empty room till we were staggered' (to Katherine Mansfield, 27 December 1918, reproduced in *The D.H. Lawrence Letters*, 1984, Vol. III, ed. J.T. Boulton and A. Robertson, Cambridge: Cambridge University Press, p. 571; written from Ripley, near Derby). 'It was probably [Dr Feroze] . . . who provided the conception of the character Sherardy' (E. Nehls, 1957, *D.H. Lawrence: a composite biography*, Vol. I, Madison, p. 580 n. 215).

FERSEN, Baron Jacques d'Adelswärd-Fersen, Comte (1879–1923) Son of a rich steel magnate, he was a member of the family of Count Hans Fersen, who aided Marie Antoinette and Louis XVI in their attempt to flee from France in 1791. He was imprisoned in Paris for offences against schoolboys; after his release 'he settled on Capri where he built a villa and entertained lavishly' (Mark Holloway, 1976, *Norman Douglas*, p. 504 n. 66), but rumours of the Parisian scandal reached the island and he was banished. In 1913, when the decree of banishment was revoked, Kate and Saidée **Wolcott-Perry** gave a dinner party in his honour. In 1914 they toured the Far East with him; he returned addicted to opium, and later took to cocaine.

COUNT MARSAC LÄGERSTROM in Compton Mackenzie, *Vestal Fire* (1927)

'There is a full length portrait of him as "Count Marsac" in . . . *Vestal Fire*' (Norman Douglas, 1934, *Looking Back*, p. 358).

FETHERSTONHAUGH, Miss Of **Uppark**, South Harting, Sussex; H.G. Wells's mother was her housekeeper there in the 1880s.

LADY HAMMERGLOW in H.G. Wells, *The Wonderful Visit* (1895)

'The book is a satire on the squirearchy . . . Lady Hammerslow patronizing the angel, Sir John Gotch . . . the village doctor . . . all remind one that the setting is South Harting, while Miss Fetherstonhaugh, Sir Edward [sic] King, Dr Collins . . . are being ironically depicted' (Lovat Dickson, 1972, *H.G. Wells*, Harmondsworth: Penguin, p. 86).

FIELD, Charles Frederick (1805?–74) Starting life as a Bow Street runner, he rose to be Chief Inspector of the Metropolitan detective police. He retired in 1851 and became a private investigator. Dickens formed a friendship with him in 1851, and he was the novelist's guide around the slums of East London. On one occasion he took a group of young Guards officers on a similar tour (*see* **Lascar Sal**); one of them described him then as 'a little wizened man who carried no more formidable weapon than a small umbrella with a little white ivory crook as a handle' (F. Wellesley, 1947, *Recollections of a Soldier Diplomat*, p. 74).

INSPECTOR BUCKET in Charles Dickens, *Bleak House* (1852–3)

'Mr Charles Dickens has made much use of Mr Field's experiences in Inspector Bucket of the *Bleak House*' ('A detective in his vocation', *The Times* (17 September 1853): 11; reprinted from the *Bath Chronicle*). '[I]t seems clear that [Dickens] saw Bucket as Field, and endowed him with Field's peculiar yet limited sagacity, his energy, his good nature, his mannerisms, and above all with his intimate knowledge of the haunts of vice' (John Butt and Kathleen Tillotson, 1957, *Dickens at Work*, London: Methuen, p. 198).

TOM FORSTER in Hain Friswell, *One of Two* (1871)

'A well-known person, in his way a celebrity, and a link of the past, as an old Bow-Street runner, described in Mr Friswell's *One of Two*, has just passed away' (*Publishers' Circular* (16 October 1874): 738). Field seems quite recognizable as Tom Forster, the Bow-Street runner known as 'Old Daylight'. Field also appeared as Inspector Wield in a number of articles in *Household Words* in 1850 and 1851. '[I]n Numbers 63 and 64 . . . he appears again, the last time under his proper name of Field' (Butt and Tillotson, op. cit., p. 197).

FIGSBURY RINGS, Wiltshire An Iron Age fort, situated about five miles north-east of Salisbury.

CADBURY RINGS in E.M. Forster, *The Longest Journey* (1907)

'[The "Cadbury Rings"] are really the Figsbury Rings . . . which Forster visited on September 12, 1904, and many times thereafter' (Wilfred Stone, 1966, *The Cave and the Mountain: a study of E.M. Forster*, London: Oxford University Press, p. 206).

FINA, Santa (*fl.* 1253) A saint depicted in two frescoes by Ghirlandaio in the Collegiate Church, San Gimignano. For six years she lay in one position on a plank; when, after her death, her body was removed, white violets were found growing where she had lain.

SANTA DEODATA in E.M. Forster, *Where Angels Fear to Tread* (1905)

'Santa Deodata is in reality Santa Fina' (Wilfred Stone, 1966, *The Cave and the Mountain: a study of E.M. Forster*, London: Oxford University Press, p. 173 n.).

FINCH, John Seymour Wynne (1845–1906) The younger son of Charles Wynne Finch of Voelas, County Denbigh, he was a major in the Royal Horse Guards. He was very handsome, elegant in his dress and something of a wit. He met Elinor Glyn *c.*1900, and she allegedly fell passionately in love with him.

SIR ANTHONY THORNHIRST in Elinor Glyn, *The Reflections of Ambrosine* (1902)

'Seymour Wynne Finch, when he read the book, had no difficulty in recognizing himself. . . . At a houseparty at Wynyard that year Lady Londonderry had him announced . . . as Sir Antony Thornhirst' (Anthony Glyn, 1955, *Elinor Glyn: a biography*, London: Hutchinson, p. 100).

FINSBURY PARK, North London

BANBURY PARK in Dorothy Richardson, *Pilgrimage* (1915–67)

Identified in John Rosenberg, 1973, *Dorothy Richardson*, p. 207, s.v. Finsbury Park.

FIRBANK, (Arthur Annesley) Ronald (1886–1926) English novelist. He was born in London and educated at Uppingham and Cambridge, where he converted to Catholicism. After leaving Cambridge without a degree he travelled widely in Europe and North Africa, publishing his first work, a collection of short stories, in 1905.

ALGY BANNISTER in R.H. Benson, *The Conventionalists* (1908)

'Despite changes of incidental detail Algy is clearly recognisable as Firbank. During his lifetime veiled hints were dropped by a couple of writers, but it was not until 1938 that Firbank's contemporary Shane Leslie explicitly identified Algy with Firbank. Benson prized his conversion of this clever undergraduate, and, wrote Leslie, "not content with sketching his penitent, he leaped into his own pages under his own name and triumphantly converted his own hero over again"' (David Dougill, 1973, 'Firbank: a long look', *Books and Bookmen* 18 (8): 36).

LAMBERT ORME in Harold Nicolson, *Some People* (1927)

'In Madrid [in 1905, Firbank] saw a great deal of Nicolson . . . [this] association was adequate to provide . . . material . . . for . . . Lambert Orme. Nicolson said that his account in *Some People* of his meeting with Lambert Orme was "more or less accurate" . . . and . . . definitely gave some idea of what Firbank seemed at that age to a rather conventional person' (Miriam Benkovitz, 1968, *Ronald Firbank*, New York, p. 65).

FISHER, Edward American writer. He was the author of a number of novels and was ghost-writer for some of the principals of the New Deal.

RICHARD GORDON in Ernest Hemingway, *To Have and Have Not* (1937)

'One-half of Hemingway's fictional character, Richard Gordon' (List of Contributors, 1975, *Connecticut Review* 8 (2): 5; Fisher contributes an article entitled 'What Papa Said', which deals with the great Labor Day Hurricane of 1935 in which a number of veterans were drowned in a workcamp at Matecumbe Key, Florida). *See also* **Dos Passos**, John.

FISHER, Revd John (b. 1834?) Vicar of Higham on the Hill, Warwickshire.

REVD MARTIN CLEVES in George Eliot, 'The Sad Fortunes of the Revd Amos Barton', *Scenes of Clerical Life* (1857–8)

See under **Anstruther**, Lady.

FITZGERALD, Frances Scott ('Scottie') (b. 1921) F. Scott and Zelda Fitzgerald's daughter.

CECILIA BRADY in F. Scott Fitzgerald, *The Last Tycoon* (1941)

'[Scott] said . . . "I sort of combined you [Budd Schulberg] with my daughter Scottie for Cecilia"' (Budd Schulberg, 1974, *The Four Seasons of Success*, p. 134). *See also* **Schulberg**, Budd.

HONORIA WALES in F. Scott Fitzgerald, 'Babylon Revisited' (1935)

'You earned some money for me this week because I sold "Babylon Revisited", in which you are a character, to the pictures' (to his daughter, 25 January 1940, *The Letters of F. Scott Fitzgerald*, 1964, ed. Andrew Turnbull, London: Bodley Head, p. 64).

FITZGERALD, Francis Scott Key (1896–1941) American novelist. He was born in St Paul, Minnesota and educated at Newman School, New Jersey, and Princeton. In 1917 he left Princeton before graduating to take up a commission in the US Army. While stationed in Montgomery, Alabama, he met Zelda Sayre (**Fitzgerald**, below). After the war, he moved to New York City, working briefly for an advertising agency. He achieved instant success with the publication of his first novel, *This Side of Paradise*, in 1920, and shortly afterwards he married Zelda. They adopted a frenzied and extravagant lifestyle, and saw themselves as representatives of the 'Jazz Age'. They moved to France in 1924, meeting Ernest Hemingway and Gertrude **Stein**, and spent the next five years travelling back and forth between Europe and America. Zelda suffered from continuing mental illness from 1930 until her death, and Scott described his own mental and physical exhaustion in a number of confessional essays, including 'The Crack-up', which was published in *Esquire* magazine in 1936. He worked sporadically as a Hollywood screenwriter, but only completed one screenplay, and on one occasion was fired because of his drinking. While Zelda was in hospital in North Carolina, he became involved with the columnist Sheilah **Graham**. He died of a heart attack in her apartment.

JOEL COLES in F. Scott Fitzgerald, 'Crazy Sunday' (1935)

Part of this story is based on an incident in Hollywood in 1931: at a party at Irving Thalberg's, Fitzgerald was drunk and performed at great length an unfunny humorous song of his own called 'Dog'. It was not a success. A more accurate version than 'Crazy Sunday' is to be found in Dwight Taylor, 1959, *Joy Ride*, New York, pp. 240–50. *See also* **Taylor**, Dwight.

HUNT CONROY in Thomas Wolfe, *You Can't Go Home Again* (1940)

'Given Wolfe's method of transposing people into his novels, it was inevitable that he would make use of Fitzgerald, who became Hunt Conroy' (M.J. Bruccoli, 1981, *Some Sort of Epic Grandeur: the life of F. Scott Fitzgerald*, London: Hodder & Stoughton, p. 311).

RICHARD DIVER in F. Scott Fitzgerald, *Tender is the Night* (1934)

'For his external qualities use anything of Gerald [Murphy], Ernest [Hemingway], Ben Finny, Archie McLiesh [sic], Charley McArthur [sic] or myself. He looks, though, like me' (general plan of *Tender is the Night*, see Bruccoli, op. cit., p. 337). *See also* **Murphy**, Gerald.

JAY GATSBY in F. Scott Fitzgerald, *The Great Gatsby* (1925)

'You are right abut Gatsby being blurred and patchy. I never at any one time saw him clear myself – for he started as one man I knew and then changed into myself – the amalgam was never complete in my mind' (to John Peale Bishop, 9 August 1925, reproduced in *The Letters of F. Scott Fitzgerald*, 1964, ed. Andrew Turnbull, London: Bodley Head, p. 358).

MANLEY HALLIDAY in Budd Schulberg, *The Disenchanted* (1950)

'Although Mr Schulberg insists that Manley Halliday was not intended to be a literal portrait of Fitzgerald, the two continue to be identified with one another' (H.D. Piper, 1966, *F. Scott Fitzgerald*, pp. 250–1).

JULIAN in Ernest Hemingway, 'The Snows of Kilimanjaro', *The Fifth Column and the First Forty-nine Stories* (1938)

'Harry's friend Julian (who was called Scott Fitzgerald in the first printed version . . . [*Esquire*, 6 August 1936] had been wrecked by the leisure class. . . . He thought the rich "a splendid glamorous race and when he found out they weren't it wrecked him just as much as any other thing wrecked him"' (C. Baker, 1972, *Hemingway: the writer as artist*, Princeton, pp. 208–9).

IVOR KELLY in Mary Deasy, *The Boy Who Made Good* (1955)

'The narrative makes it clear that the characteristics of Ivor and Stella Kelly are indebted to Scott and Zelda Fitzgerald' (Joseph Blotner, 1966, *The Modern American Political Novel*, Austin, Tex., p. 50). Fitzgerald is transmogrified into an idealistic politician.

DAVID KNIGHT in Zelda Fitzgerald, *Save Me the Waltz* (1932)

'It was . . . a bitter attack on Fitzgerald, who was thinly disguised in her manuscript as Amory Blaine' (Piper, op. cit., p. 191). The name was later changed to David Knight.

BASIL DUKE LEE in F. Scott Fitzgerald, 'A Night at the Fair' (1957)

'. . . in addition to Fitzgerald himself, who is of course the model for Basil' (F. Scott Fitzgerald, 1957, *Afternoon of an Author*, introd. and notes by Arthur Mizener, Princeton, p. 15). 'The identification between Basil and Fitzgerald is close; the chief episodes were drawn from author's experience' (Bruccoli, op. cit., p. 266).

ABE NORTH in F. Scott Fitzgerald, *Tender is the Night* (1934)

'Abe, composite portrait of Fitzgerald and . . . Ring Lardner' (K. Cross, 1949, *Scott Fitzgerald*, p. 87). *See also* **Lardner**, Ring.

ANTHONY PATCH in F. Scott Fitzgerald, *The Beautiful and Damned* (1922)

'[The] suggestion that the book is biographical was also encouraged by Hill's . . . easily recognizable portraits of the Fitzgeralds on the dust-wrapper. . . . [But] Gloria and Anthony were not the Fitzgeralds; they were what the spoiled priest in Fitzgerald thought the Fitzgeralds might become' (Arthur Mizener, 1951, *The Far Side of Paradise: a biography of F. Scott Fitzgerald*, p. 124).

DAVID WESTLAKE in Carl Van Vechten, *Parties* (1930)

'David and Rilda (who are contemporary portraits of the Fitzgeralds) in . . . *Parties*' (Mizener, op. cit., p. 122).

FITZGERALD, Maurice (1835–78)

ADRIAN HARLEY in George Meredith, *The Ordeal of Richard Feverel* (1859)

'Adrian . . . like many of Meredith's most narrowly and symbolically controlled creations – had [a model] in real life: [he] was based on Maurice Fitzgerald, nephew of Edward Fitzgerald' (Gillian Beer, 1970, *Meredith: a change of masks*, p. 203 n. 11).

FITZGERALD, Zelda (1900–48) Née Sayre, she married F. Scott Fitzgerald in 1920. She had her first nervous breakdown in 1930, and was hospitalized periodically from then until her death.

ALABAMA BEGGS in Zelda Fitzgerald, *Save Me the Waltz* (1932)

'In her story Zelda Fitzgerald appears as Alabama Beggs, a glamour girl from the Deep South' (H.T. Moore, 1968, Introd. to *Save Me the Waltz*, p. ix; see this introd., *passim*, for a discussion of the relationship between the characters in the novel, those in F. Scott Fitzgerald's *Tender is the Night*, and their prototypes).

SALLY CARROL in F. Scott Fitzgerald, 'The Ice Palace' (1921)

'Like Sally Carrol . . . who is a portrait of her, she want[ed] to live where things happen on a big scale' (Arthur Mizener, 1951, *The Far Side of Paradise*, p. 77). 'I had been an amateur before [*This Side of Paradise* was accepted for publication]; in October, when I strolled with a girl [Zelda] among the stones of a Southern graveyard, I was a professional and my enchantment with certain things she felt and said was already paced by an anxiety to set them down in a story – it was called *The Ice Palace* and it was published later' (F. Scott Fitzgerald, 1945, *The Crack-Up*, New York, p. 86).

ROSALIND CONNAGE in F. Scott Fitzgerald, *This Side of Paradise* (1920)

'I'm deadly curious to see if Hill's picture [for the dust-jacket] looks like the real Rosalind' (to Maxwell Perkins, 10 January 1920, reproduced in *The Letters of F. Scott Fitzgerald*, 1964, ed. Andrew Turnbull, London: Bodley Head). 'I married the Rosalind of the novel' (to Shane Leslie, 6 August 1920, reproduced in *Letters* op. cit., p. 142).

Nɪᴄᴏʟᴇ Dɪᴠᴇʀ in F. Scott Fitzgerald, *Tender is the Night* (1934)

'Beneath the Murphy's façade (for the Divers'. . . *style* was that of the Murphys) Fitzgerald had explored his relations with Zelda' (Andrew Turnbull, 1962, *Scott Fitzgerald*, p. 218). *See also* **Murphy**, Sara.

Sᴛᴇʟʟᴀ Kᴇʟʟʏ in Mary Deasy, *The Boy Who Made Good* (1955)

See under **Fitzgerald**, F. Scott.

Gʟᴏʀɪᴀ Pᴀᴛᴄʜ in F. Scott Fitzgerald, *The Beautiful and Damned* (1922)

'"Gloria", [Fitzgerald] wrote his daughter years later, "was much more trivial and vulgar than your mother. . . . I naturally used many circumstantial events of our early married life. However the emphases were entirely different. We had a much better time than Anthony and Gloria did"' (Arthur Mizener, 1951, *The Far Side of Paradise: a biography of F. Scott Fitzgerald*, p. 125).

Mɪɴɴᴀ Sᴛᴀʜʀ in F. Scott Fitzgerald, *The Last Tycoon* (1941)

'Stahr's dead wife, Minna, was Zelda' (M.J. Bruccoli, 1981, *Some Sort of Epic Grandeur: the life of F. Scott Fitzgerald*, London: Hodder & Stoughton, p. 467). 'The elements of Stahr's emotional situation were drawn from Fitzgerald's life' (ibid.).

Rɪʟᴅᴀ Wᴇsᴛʟᴀᴋᴇ in Carl Van Vechten, *Parties* (1930)

See under **Fitzgerald**, F. Scott.

FITZHARDINGE, William Fitzhardinge Berkeley, Lord (1786–1867) Of Berkeley Castle, Gloucestershire. Son of Frederick Augustus, 5th Earl of Berkeley, and Mary Cole, whom the Earl married in 1796, he was the brother of G.F. **Berkeley** and Lady Caroline **Maxse**. On his father's death, he 'succeeded, under settlement, to the vast estates of the family', but was not held to have proved his legitimacy (which depended on a marriage alleged to have taken place between his parents in 1785). Thenceforward he styled himself Colonel Berkeley. On the coronation of William IV he was created Baron Segrave, and in 1841 he became 1st Earl Fitzhardinge. As Colonel Berkeley, he was notorious in the annals of sport, fashion and scandal. The actress Maria Foote (who married the 4th Earl of **Harrington** in 1831) was for some time his mistress. On his death the *Morning Leader* (17 October 1857) published an article referring to his dissipations and the marvellous eloquence of his objurgations, and concluded 'he will be remembered as a sort of tenth-rate Rochester, who but for his noble birth might have been a Boots' (Hon. Vicary Gibbs and H.A. Doubleday (eds), *The Complete Peerage of England, Scotland, Ireland, Great Britain and the United Kingdom*, Vol. V, rev. edn, London: St Catherine Press, p. 410 n.).

Lᴏʀᴅ Rɪɴɢᴡᴏᴏᴅ in W.M. Thackeray, *The Adventures of Philip* (1861–2)

See below.

Mᴀʀǫᴜɪs ᴏꜰ Sᴛᴇʏɴᴇ in W.M. Thackeray, *Vanity Fair* (1847–8)

'Lord Steyne was merely taken from a wicked nobleman. If Thackeray had anyone in his eye it was Lord Fitzhardinge drawn in '*Philip* as Lord Ringwood' (note in an elderly hand, regrettably in ink, on p. 223 of the London Library copy of W.F. Monypenny, 1912, *Life of Benjamin Disraeli*, Vol. II, London). *See also* **Hertford**, 3rd Marquess of.

37 FITZROY SQUARE, London This house forms part of the great centre piece on the south side of the square, which, together with the east side, was an Adam design of 1793–8. It was much damaged in the Second World War, but has been restored, with the three houses, 36–38, being thrown into one; the exterior has been preserved, with the huge window of what was, from 1966 until his death, the studio of the painter Ford Madox Brown.

121 FITZROY SQUARE in W.M. Thackeray, *The Newcomes* (1854–5)

'There was I all alone in my grandfather's studio in the great house once inhabited by Thackeray's Colonel Newcome' (Ford Madox Ford, 1938, *Mightier Than the Sword*, p. 192). Ford is describing how, in 1881 as a child eight years old, he entertained the Russian novelist Turgenev at 37 Fitzroy Square, his grandfather's house.

FLEETWOOD, Lancashire A seaside place where Mrs Molesworth's parents had a small house, to which they used to send their children for part of the year.

SANDYSHORE in Mrs Molesworth, *'Carrots': Just a Little Boy* (1878)

'The Stewarts managed to send their children to the seaside. . . . [The place] is described in *Carrots*. . . . The place described is Fleetwood' (R. Lancelyn Green, 1961, *Mrs Molesworth*, pp. 19, 20).

FLEISCHMANN, Marthe (1885–1950) A young Swiss woman whom James Joyce encountered in Zurich, in December 1918. She was the mistress of an engineer, Rudolf Hitpold, but Joyce conducted a clandestine correspondence with her, signing his letters with a Greek 'e'. Like Gerty MacDowell, she had a slight limp.

MARTHA CLIFFORD in James Joyce, *Ulysses* (1922)

'In *Ulysses* Marthe Fleischmann is one of the prototypes of the limping Gerty MacDowell . . . and in part the prototype of Bloom's penpal Martha Clifford, to whom, as Joyce emphasizes, Bloom is always careful to write with Greek *e*'s' (Richard Ellmann, 1966, *James Joyce*, London: Oxford Paperbacks, p. 463).

GERTIE MACDOWELL in James Joyce, *Ulysses* (1922)

See above.

FLEMING, George *See* **Fletcher**, Constance.

FLETCHER, Constance (1858–1938) Novelist and playwright under the name of George Fleming. Of American parentage, she was long a resident in Venice in the Palazzo Capello, where she 'lived with her old and infirm mother and her mother's second husband, Eugene **Benson**, a painter whom James had known in Rome' (Leon Edel, 1972, *Henry James: the master, 1901–1916*, p. 342). It was said that she was once engaged to Byron's grandson, Lord Lovelace (see Lind Simon, 1978, *Alice B. Toklas*, p. 82). It was for her that Alfred Sassoon, the father of the poet, abandoned his wife. In 1911 she was a hugely fat, golden-haired, deaf woman with big blue eyes (Simon, ibid.).

Mrs Harvey in Henry James, 'Broken Wings' (1903)

'How many characters, do you know, were suggested by real people? [Was] Constance Fletcher [adumbrated] in "Broken Wings"?' (Logan Pearsall Smith to Ethel Sands, 19 March 1943, quoted in John Russell, 1950, Introd. to *A Portrait of Logan Pearsall Smith*, pp. 156–7). In 1900, when 'Broken Wings' was first published in a periodical, Constance Fletcher was still moving in fashionable circles. Pearsall Smith would seem to have identified Mrs Harvey from Miss Fletcher's circumstances at the time of her death.

FLETCHER, John Gould (1886–1950) American poet. Born in Arkansas, he was educated at Harvard University. He was influenced by the Symbolists. In 1908, he settled in London. He was a Fabian, and met Ezra **Pound** in 1913 and joined the Imagists. He was the protégé of Amy Lowell. He returned to Arkansas, where he became a leader of the Agrarians. In 1939 he was awarded the Pulitzer Prize for *Selected Poems* (1938).

Roy Christopher in John Cournos, *Miranda Masters* (1926)

'. . . Roy Christopher (John Gould Fletcher)' (Barbara Guest, 1985, *Herself Defined: the poet H.D. and her world*, London: Collins, p. 84; originally published 1984, Garden City, NY: Doubleday).

FLEUR-DE-LIS INN, Cranbourne, Dorset

Flower-de-Luce in Thomas Hardy, *Tess of the d'Urbervilles* (1891)

Identified in F.B. Pinion, 1968, *A Hardy Companion*, London: Macmillan.

FLEXNER, Simon (1863–1946) Pathologist. Between 1903 and 1935 he was Director of the laboratories of the Rockefeller Institute, New York; between 1920 and 1925 he was Director of the Institute.

A. DeWitt Tubbs in Sinclair Lewis, *Arrowsmith* (1925)

Identified in Mark Schorer, 1961, *Sinclair Lewis: an American life*, New York: McGraw-Hill, p. 418.

FLOWER, Cyril *See* **Battersea**, 1st Baron.

FLYNN, Lefty A former Yale football star and a movie actor, he was married to Nora **Flynn**.

Cedric Killian in F. Scott Fitzgerald, 'The Intimate Strangers' (1935)

See under **Flynn**, Nora.

FLYNN, Nora Born in Langhorne, she married Lefty **Flynn**; the couple were friends of F. Scott Fitzgerald and were living at Tryon, North Carolina, when Fitzgerald went there to be treated for tuberculosis in 1935. Of her two sisters, one, Nancy (1879–1964), became Lady Astor, the British politician, and the other was Mrs Charles Dana Gibson, the original 'Gibson Girl'.

SARA KILLIAN in F. Scott Fitzgerald, 'The Intimate Strangers' (1935)

'"The Intimate Strangers" was a thinly disguised account of the Flynn's marital histories. They recognised themselves in the story, but were not upset' (M.J. Bruccoli, 1981, *Some Sort of Epic Grandeur: the life of F. Scott Fitzgerald*, London: Hodder & Stoughton, p. 396).

FOLGER, Augustine William ('Bill') He was a member of the University of North Carolina football team that defeated the University of Virginia in 1916. In 1923 Wolfe briefly shared a flat with him in New York while waiting to hear the verdict of the Theatre Guild on his play *Welcome to Our City*.

JAMES HEYWARD ('JIM') RANDOLPH in Thomas Wolfe, *The Web and the Rock* (1939)

'. . . Jim Randolph, fictional counterpart of football hero Augustine William Folger' (Richard Walser, 1965, 'An early Wolfe essay – and the downfall of a hero', *Modern Fiction Studies* 11 (3): 271).

FORBES, Alexander (1678–1762) 4th (and last) Baron Forbes of Pitsligo, he succeeded to the title in 1690. In 1705 he protested against the Union; he subsequently no longer attended Parliament. He was 'out' in 1715, and in 1718 was in exile in Leyden. In 1745, although old and asthmatic, he raised a company of 150 mounted gentlemen for Prince Charles. After the failure of the rebellion, he was attainted, his title and estates were forfeited to the Crown, and he was forced into hiding for many years. In his youth he was the friend of Fénélon, and 'he was religious, amiable, loyal and courageous' (GEC, Vol. I, p. 551 n. c). In 1734 he published *Essays, Moral and Philosophical*.

BARON BRADWARDINE in Sir Walter Scott, *Waverley* (1814)

'The person who held the situation in the rebel army which in the novel has been assigned to the Baron, namely, the command of their few cavalry, was Alexander, fourth Lord Forbes of Pitsligo. . . . It is not unworthy of remark, that the supporters of Lord Pitsligo's arms were two bears proper; which circumstance, connected with the great favour in which these animals were held by Bradwardine, brings the relation between the real and the fictitious personages very close' (Robert Chambers, 1884, *Illustrations of the Author of Waverley*, pp. 5, 6). *See also* **Oliphant**, Laurence[1]; **Stuart of Invernahyle,** Alexander.

FORBES, Lady Angela (1876–1950) Daughter of the 4th Earl of Rosslyn, she was also the sister of Millicent, the Duchess of **Sutherland**, and Sybil, Countess of **Westmorland**; the half-sister of Frances, Lady **Warwick**; and an aunt of Hamish **Erskine**. In 1896 she married James Forbes, but they separated, amicably, in 1904; she became the mistress of Lord Ribblesdale and of Lord Wemyss. For an account of her life, see *The Diaries of Lady Cynthia Asquith*, 1969, London, pp. 501-2, and also her own reminiscences.

ELIZABETH in Elinor Glyn, *The Visits of Elizabeth* (1900)

'I am not sure whether I should have been inordinately proud, or a little bit ashamed, of my photograph being used as the prototype of Elizabeth. . . . On the other hand it was head-turning to have had such an attractive heroine built upon what Mrs Glyn imagined to be my characteristics' (Angela Forbes, 1922, *Memories and Base Details*, p. 79).

MRS SHAMEFOOT in Ronald Firbank, *Vainglory* (1915)

Mrs Shamefoot's shop derives remotely from 'My Shop', a flower shop that Lady Angela at one time ran. 'Firbank had patronized Lady Angela's shop, and he thought [her] "amusing and clever". In 1921 he considered collaborating on a book with her' (Mirian J. Benhovitz, 1970, *Ronald Firbank*, p. 120).

FORBES-MOSSE, Irene (d. 1948) The granddaughter of Bettina von Arnim, she was married first to Graf Oriola, and then to Colonel Forbes-Mosse. She was a cousin of Professor Lujo Brentano, the economist. From 1906 until *c.*1918 she rented part of Vernon Lee's property in Florence, 'Palmerino'.

IRAIS in 'Elizabeth', *Elizabeth and Her German Garden* (1898)

'Mrs Forbes-Mosse was the original of Ira [sic] in *Elizabeth and Her German Garden*' (Peter Gunn, 1964, *Vernon Lee, 1856–1935*, London: Oxford University Press, p. 186).

FORD, Elsie *See* **Hueffer**, Elsie.

FORD, Ford Madox (1873–1939) Novelist, poet and editor. He was the son of Frances Hueffer, the music critic of *The Times*, and the grandson of the painter Ford Madox Brown. He founded the *English Review*, which he edited from December 1908 until early 1910, publishing in it the first short stories of D.H. **Lawrence**, as well as contributions by Henry James, **Hardy** and H.G. Wells. He was a great womanizer; although twice married, he lived for many years outside matrimony with Violet **Hunt**, and later with Stella **Bowen**. Of his other affairs the most literarily productive was that with Jean Rhys in 1924. In the 1920s he lived largely in Paris, where he edited the *Transatlantic Review*, and during his last years he lived much in the United States.

EDWARD ASHBURNHAM in Ford Madox Ford, *The Good Soldier* (1915)

'Ford and Edward both have a dread of scenes in public places. Edward shares one of Ford's most touching traits . . . an inability to defend himself. . . . Edward and Dowell have more in common than Fordian traits. They are psychological doubles' (Thomas C. Moser, 1980, *The Life in the Fiction of Ford Madox Ford*, Princeton, p. 28).

HENRY BRADDOCKS in Ernest Hemingway, *The Sun Also Rises* (1926)

'After the fiesta in Pamplona . . . Bill [Smith] went to Paris for a short time. . . . While in Paris, he received a letter from Hem dated July 27, 1925. . . . He didn't mention *The Sun Also Rises* by name . . . but it was obvious that he was working on that novel . . . he said . . . that the story was fairly funny and that he had Ford Madox Ford in it as Braddocks' (D. St John, 1972, 'Interview with Hemingway's "Bill Gorton"', in B.D. Sarason, *Hemingway and the Sun Set*, Washington, DC, p. 186).

THEODORE BULPINGTON in H.G. Wells, *The Bulpington of Blup* (1933)

'Theodore Bulpington, though his life parallels Ford's only in a general way, gets his character from Wells' conception of Ford' (Arthur Mizener, 1971, *The Saddest Story: a biography of Ford Madox Ford*, Cleveland: World Publishing, p. 293).

MERTON DENSHER in Henry James, *The Wings of the Dove* (1902)

'[I]t was established sufficiently between us that in the longish, leanish, fairish Englishman who was Morton [sic] Densher in *The Wings of the Dove*, [James] had made an at least external portrait of myself at a time when he had known me only vaguely and hadn't imagined that in the ordinary course of things the acquaintance would deepen' (Ford Madox Ford, 1938, *Mightier than the Sword* (US title *Portraits from Life*), p. 24). *See also* **Fullerton**, W. Morton; **Seaman**, Sir Owen.

JOHN DOWELL in Ford Madox Ford, *The Good Soldier* (1915)

'Dowell would seem to fit Ford's prescription of the author's self' (Moser, op. cit., p. 160). *See also above under* Edward Ashburnham.

THE FRIEND IN PARIS in Joseph Conrad, 'The Informer', *A Set of Six* (1908)

'[I]t would seem likely that [Ford] had not a little influence upon the conception of Conrad's stories dealing with anarchism. . . . His function would be "introductory" . . . but it was a sufficiently important function for Conrad to make some acknowledgement of it in an Author's Note, and, I believe, to introduce a fictional figure actually based on Ford into one of the stories. . . . It is at the beginning of "The Informer" that Ford appears, I think, in his particular role. . . . "My friend in Paris is a collector, too. . . . He collects acquaintances"' (Norman Sherry, 1971, *Conrad's Western World*, Cambridge, p. 209).

HORATIO GUBB in Ford Madox Ford, *The Simple Life Limited* (1911)

'. . . unquestionably a self-portrait' (Moser, op. cit., p. 95). *See also* **Pinker**, J.B.; **Wells**, H.G.

H.J. HEIDLER in Jean Rhys, *Postures* (1928)

'*Postures* . . . the novel [Jean Rhys] wrote about her affair with Ford' (Mizener, op. cit., p. 345).

HÜBNER in Edward de Nève, *Barred* (1932)

'Another view of the Ford–Rhys relationship [from that in Jean Rhys's novel *Postures* or *Quartet*] is provided in a . . . novel . . . by de Nève. In its way de Nève's book is more directly personal than *Quartet*, and, as a reflection of actual events, seemingly more candid' (Thomas F. Staley, 1979, *Jean Rhys: a critical study*, p. 12.

COUNT SERGIUS MIHAILOVICH MACDONALD in Ford Madox Ford, *The New Humpty-Dumpty* (1912)

Identified in Mizener, op. cit., pp. 223–7.

MR SHOBBE in Richard Aldington, *Death of a Hero* (1929)

'*Death of a Hero* . . . contains a malicious portrait of Ford in his pre-war days. . . . Possibly the sympathetic portrayals by Douglas Goldring [*The Last Pre-Raphaelite*, 1948] and [Frank] MacShane [*The Life and Work of Ford Madox Ford*, 1965] need to be complemented by Aldington's representation of Ford as Mr Shobbe' (Bernard Bergonzi, 1973, *The Turn of a Century*, pp. 143, 144).

FORD, James

SHEM in James Joyce, *Finnegans Wake* (1939)

See under **Ford**, John.

FORD, John

SHAUN in James Joyce, *Finnegans Wake* (1939)

'In all his books Joyce makes his characters out of both real and mythical types, but in *Finnegans Wake* he does this much more explicitly than elsewhere. So . . . Shem and Shaun were based in part upon two feeble minded hangers-on, James and John Ford, who lived in Dublin on the North Strand. They were known as 'Shem and Shaun' and were famous for their incomprehensible speech and shuffling gait. Their only occupations were bringing the hurley sticks on to the field for the hurley teams and carrying two of Hely's sandwich signs' (Richard Ellmann, 1966, *James Joyce*, London: Oxford Paperbacks, p. 562). *See also* **De Valera**, Éamon; **Joyce**, Stanislaus.

FORDINGTON, Dorset A village, practically a suburb, on the south-eastern side of Dorchester on the Frome. From 1829 until 1880, Henry **Moule** was the Vicar. Hardy knew it well, and all the sons of the family, particularly Horace **Moule**, were his close friends.

DURNOVER in Thomas Hardy, Wessex novels and tales (1871–95)

Identifed on a map prepared by Thomas Hardy which hangs in the Dorset County Museum, Dorchester. *See also under* **Abbotsbury**.

FOREMAN, Mrs Somerset Maugham's landlady at 11 Vincent Square, Westminster, London; she lived in the house until her death during the Second World War.

MRS HUDSON in W. Somerset Maugham, *Cakes and Ale* (1930)

'While I was at St Thomas's Hospital I lived in furnished rooms at 11 Vincent Square, Westminster. My landlady was a character. I have drawn a slight portrait of her in . . . *Cakes and Ale*' (W. Somerset Maugham, 1949, *A Writer's Notebook*, p. 9; on the next page he gives her name).

FOREST LAWN, Glendale, California A large cemetery, ostentatiously landscaped and adorned with reproductions of famous works of art. It was established in 1917 by a banker, Hubert L. Eaton.

WHISPERING GLADES in Evelyn Waugh, *The Loved One* (1948)

'And then we have of course the passing evocation of the Beverly Pantheon – Forest Lawn, the Western necropolis immortalized a few years later by another

English novelist Aldous did not read (though he's been heard to say that he enjoyed *Vile Bodies*' (Sybille Bedford, 1973, *Aldous Huxley: a biography*, Vol. I, London: Chatto & Windus, p. 379).

FORMOSA PLACE, Cookham, Berkshire Seat of Sir George Young, 2nd Baronet, of whom Kingsley was a friend and frequent visitor.

THE PRIORY in Charles Kingsley, *Yeast* (1848)

A tradition in the Young family; identification based on private information.

FORRESTAL, James (1892–1949) Educated at Princeton, he was Under-Secretary of the Navy in 1940–4, Secretary 1944–7, and Secretary of Defense 1947–9. He was a strong advocate of the Cold War. He committed suicide.

ROGER THURLOE in John Dos Passos, *The Great Days* (1958)

'Interviewer: I suppose a . . . more direct characterization [than that of Ivy **Lee**] occurs . . . with Roger Thurloe modelled as he is on Forrestal? Dos Passos: That's closer to being an effort to produce a characterization of a living person . . . than most of the others. I had met Forrestal a couple of times, but even so the characterization is pretty far off' (Dos Passos, interviewed by David Sanders, 1969, 'The Art of Fiction, XLIV', *Paris Review* 12 (46): 158).

FORSTER, Edward Morgan (1879–1970) English novelist and critic. He was born in London and educated at Tonbridge School and King's College, Cambridge. In 1901 he was elected to the Apostles, through which he met members of what later became the Bloomsbury Group. After graduating he travelled with his mother to Italy and Greece. On his return, he founded the *Independent Review* with Lowes **Dickinson** in 1903. In 1905, he spent several months in Nassenheide, Germany, as tutor to the children of Elizabeth von Arnim (later Countess **Russell**). In 1912, he visited India, where he developed a loathing for British imperialism. He joined the International Red Cross after the outbreak of the First World War, and served in Alexandria, where he met the poet C.P. Cavafy. He returned to India in 1921 as secretary and companion to the Maharajah of the native state of Dewas Senior. His two visits to India resulted in the publication of his novel *A Passage to India* in 1925, for which he was awarded the Tait Black Memorial Prize. He became first President of the National Council of Civil Liberties in 1934. He was elected a Fellow of King's College in 1946, and refused a knighthood in 1949. His novel *Maurice*, a detailed exploration of a homosexual relationship, was published posthumously in 1971.

BENJAMIN DEXTER in Graham Greene, 'The Third Man' (1958)

'. . . the great English writer Dexter, whose literary character bore certain echoes of the gentle genius of Mr E.M. Forster' (Graham Greene, 1958, Introd. to 'The Third Man' in *The Third Man and the Fallen Idol*, p. 5).

FREDERICK ('RICKIE') ELLIOT in E.M. Forster, *The Longest Journey* (1907)

'Interviewer: Do any of your characters represent yourself at all? Forster: Rickie more than any. Also Philip. And Cecil . . . has got something of Philip in him' (Forster, interviewed in 1952, quoted in P.N. Furbank and F.J.H. Haskell, 1972,

Writers at Work: the Paris Review interviews, selected by Kay Dick, Harmondsworth: Penguin, p. 14).

PHILIP HERRITON in E.M. Forster, *Where Angels Fear to Tread* (1905)

See above. See also **Dent**, Edward Joseph.

CECIL VYSE in E.M. Forster, *A Room with a View* (1908)

See above under FREDERICK ELLIOT.

FORSTER, Emily Née Nash. Married to E.M. Forster, she was an heiress and was much older than her husband 'and plain and foolish into the bargain' (P.N. Furbank, 1977, *E.M. Forster*, Vol. I: *The Growth of the Novelist (1879–1914)*, London: Secker & Warburg, p. 64). He gave her a terrible time.

CHARLOTTE BARTLETT in E.M. Forster, *A Room with a View* (1908)

'Miss Bartlett was my Aunt Emily – they all read the book but they none of them saw it' (Forster, interviewed in 1952, quoted in P.N. Furbank and F.J.H. Haskell, 1972, *Writers at Work: the Paris Review interviews*, selected by Kay Dick, Harmondsworth: Penguin, p. 13).

FORSTER, John (1812–76) Historian and man of letters. Son of a Newcastle butcher, he was educated at the local grammar school and at University College London. He developed a passionate interest in the theatre, and became the dramatic critic of the *Examiner*; he was its Editor from 1847 to 1855. He became a biographer of and the closest friend of Dickens. By 1836, the time of his first meeting with Dickens, probably at the house of Harrison Ainsworth, he had a remarkable circle of friends including Leigh **Hunt**, Lord Bulwer **Lytton** and Macready. From 1837 he read, either in manuscript or proof, every line that Dickens wrote, and was asked for and gave advice, which was not always accepted, in every difficulty or crisis. Between 1834 and 1856 he lived at 58 Lincoln's Fields, London. He was briefly engaged to Letitia Landon in 1835, but the engagement was broken off, and in 1856 he married the widow of Henry **Colburn**, the publisher. His most notorious superficial characteristic was an astonishing rudeness.

TOM BOXER in W.M. Thackeray, *The History of Henry Esmond* (1852)

'His most carefully meditated work, in which he had included a veiled but unmistakeable allusion to Forster, who figures as Mr Congreve's man Tom Boxer, and to his campaign against the *English Humourists* in the *Examiner*, which appears as the *Observator*' (Gordon Ray, 1958, *Thackeray: the age of wisdom*, p. 197). The passage (Vol. II, ch. 15) was omitted from the 1858, revised edition of *The History of Henry Esmond* (London: Smith, Elder).

FUZBOZ in Lady Lytton, *Cheveley; or The Man of Honour* (1839)

'Lady Bulwer Lytton describes him as Fuzboz in her *Cheveley*' (Jack Lindsay, 1950, *Charles Dickens*, p. 151).

MR PODSNAP in Charles Dickens, *Our Mutual Friend* (1864–5)

'All Forster's acquaintances recognized his mannerisms embedded in Podsnap – the indignant flush, the sweeping gesture of dismissal – but nobody who knew him doubted his entire inability to see himself there. It is not impossible, however, that they were wrong' (Edgar Johnson, 1953, *Charles Dickens*, Vol. II, p. 1053). On 28 July 1864, 'just around the time that the chapter on Podsnap appeared ... "Forster fluttered about in the Athenaeum," Dickens wrote to Georgina, "as I conversed in the hall ... and pretended to not to see me – but I saw in every hair of his whisker (left hand one) that he saw Nothing Else"' (ibid.). 'Podsnap is Dickens's reaction to the reproving pressure of Forster's respectability and is based, though not completely yet *fundamentally* and in many points of detail, on the characteristics of Dickens's closest friend' (James A. Davies, 1974, 'Forster and Dickens: the making of Podsnap', *The Dickensian* 70 (374): 152). The article goes on to list points of resemblance.

FORSTER, William Houley (1855–1910) He was the youngest of the ten children of Charles Forster, Rector of Stinsted, Essex, and was E.M. Forster's uncle. He married Emily **Nash**, and in the 1880s settled at Acton House, Northumberland, into which he soon introduced a rival woman.

MRS EMILY FAILING in E.M. Forster, *The Longest Journey* (1907)

'Uncle Willie turned into Mrs Failing. He was a bluff and simple character (*correcting himself*) – bluff without being simple' (Forster, interviewed in 1952, quoted in P.J. Furbank and F.J.H. Haskell, 1972, *Writers at Work: the Paris Review interviews*, selected by Kay Dick, Harmondsworth: Penguin, p. 13). *See also* **Russell**, Countess.

FORTESCUE, Chichester *See* **Parkinson-Fortescue**, Chichester Samuel.

FORTUNE'S WELL, Portland, Dorset The small town on the Isle of Portland, where the road from the mainland reaches the island.

STREET OF WELLS in Thomas Hardy, Wessex novels and tales (1871–95)

Identifed on a map prepared by Thomas Hardy which hangs in the Dorset County Museum, Dorchester. *See under* **Abbotsbury**.

FOSTER, John A friend of Edward Chapman (1804–80) of Chapman and Hall, Dickens's publishers. He and Chapman, in 1836, conceived the notion of a 'monthly something' to be written around a series of comical plates to be drawn by Robert Seymour. From this idea came *The Pickwick Papers*.

SAMUEL PICKWICK in Charles Dickens, *The Pickwick Papers* (1836–7)

'I may as well claim what little belongs to me in the matter, and that is the figure of Pickwick. Seymour's first sketch was of a long, thin man. The present immortal one he made from my description of a friend of mine at Richmond, a fat old beau who would wear, in spite of the ladies' protests, drab tights and black gaiters. His name was John Foster' (Edward Chapman to Charles Dickens, 7 July 1849, quoted in John Forster, 1928, *Life of Charles Dickens*, pp. 75–6). The name 'Pickwick' was supplied by Dickens himself, from Moses Pickwick, a stage-coach proprietor of Bath (Forster, op. cit., p. 74 n.). *See also* **Rawes**, Robert Booth.

FOURIE, Ben '[A] taciturn young man ... who served ... as mechanic-cum-assistant hunter' (Carlos Baker, 1969, on Ernest Hemingway's Kenya safari in 1933–4, *Ernest Hemingway: a life story*, p. 303).

DAN in Ernest Hemingway, *The Green Hills of Africa* (1935)

'To give his story the air of fiction he had changed most of the names ... Ben Fourie was Dan' (ibid., p. 316).

FOUTS, Denham (1912?–49) In his time he was described as 'the most expensive male prostitute in the world'. By his own account he was born on the wrong side of the tracks in Jacksonville, Florida; he moved to Europe and in 1933 became the lover of Peter Watson (later the backer and Art Editor of the periodical *Horizon*). They lived together in Paris in the rue du Bac, but Fouts was in England in 1939 and in 1940 he returned to the United States, taking the greater part of Watson's valuable art collection with him. By the end of the Second World War he had sold the entire collection to maintain his heroin habit, although he spent a short period of the war as a cook in a camp for conscientious objectors (together with Christopher Isherwood). He returned to join Watson in Paris in 1946, but in 1947 he was obliged to leave Paris when Watson gave up his apartment. He moved to Rome, where he died after collapsing with a heart attack in the hotel that he was staying at.

JIM in Gore Vidal, *The Judgment of Paris* (1952)

'There is a brilliant vignette of Denham in ... *The Judgement [sic] of Paris*. He appears very much in character wearing a blazer on the terrace of the Flore and afterwards dissolving into one of those long sad swoons which he had come to need' (Michael Wishart, 1977, *High Diver*, p. 60).

SOPHIE MACDONALD in W. Somerset Maugham, *The Razor's Edge* (1944)

'Denham loved Toulon. We sometimes bought opium there. He claimed to be the model for Sophie, the hopelessly self-destructive opiumaniac drunken girl in ... *The Razor's Edge*, who also went to Toulon for drugs. Certainly Maugham had been fascinated by Denham, and there was a great resemblance, of which Denham was strangely proud' (Wishart, op. cit., p. 54).

PAUL in Christopher Isherwood, *Down There on a Visit* (1962)

'Isherwood gives a very accurate picture of Denham ... thinly disguised as "Paul" in ... *Down There on a Visit*' (Wishart, op. cit., p. 49).

FOWLER, Ludlow Sebring (1896–1961) Born in Warwick, New York, he was Fitzgerald's contemporary at Princeton and best man at his wedding. He became a distinguished member of the New York Bar. He married Elsie Blatchford in 1926.

ANSON HUNTER in F. Scott Fitzgerald, 'The Rich Boy' (1926)

'I have written a ... story about you called *The Rich Boy* – it is so disguised that no one except you and me and maybe two of the girls concerned would recognize ... but it is in a large measure the story of your life. ... It is frank, unsparing but sympathetic and think you will like it' (to Ludlow Fowler, March 1925, reproduced in *The Correspondence of F. Scott Fitzgerald*, 1980, ed. Matthew

J. Bruccoli and M.M. Duggan, New York, p. 35). Fitzgerald showed the story to Fowler before publication and agreed to some alterations, which in the event were not made until it was collected in book form. 'Everyone seems to have recognized you in *The Rich Boy*' (to Ludlow Fowler, summer 1926, ibid., p. 200).

FOX, Daniel Miller He was Mayor of Philadelphia from 1869 to 1872: 'the year 1871 was one of numerous disturbances ... due largely to the inferior and undisciplined character of the police force during the three years that followed Mr Fox's election as Mayor' (J.T. Scharf and T. Westcott, 1884, *History of Philadelphia, 1609–1884*, Vol. I, Philadelphia, p. 837).

JACOB BORCHARDT in Theodore Dreiser, *The Financier* (1912)

'. . . Mayor Fox (Jacob Borchardt in the novel)' (Richard Lehan, 1974, *Theodore Dreiser: his world and his novels*, Carbondale, Ill.: Arcturis Books, p. 98).

FOX, Elizabeth *See* **Ilchester**, Countess of.

FOX, Stephen *See* **Ilchester**, 1st Earl of.

FOX RIVER, Michigan Located near Seney in the north of the state.

TWO-HEARTED RIVER in Ernest Hemingway, 'Big Two-Hearted River', *In Our Time* (1925)

'This Quarter ... is publishing a long fishing story of mine ... called Big Two Hearted River. ... The river in it is really the Fox above Seney' (to Dr C.E. Hemingway, 20 March 1925, reproduced in *Ernest Hemingway Selected Letters 1917–1961*, 1981, ed. Carlos Baker, London: Granada, p. 153).

FOX-STRANGWAYS, Charles Redlynch (1761–1836) He was the brother of the 2nd Earl of Ilchester, and for many years was Rector of Maiden Newton, Dorset, and of Rewe, Devon.

HON. AND REVD MR OLDHAM in Thomas Hardy, 'The Grave by the Handpost' (1913)

'Reference to Hutchins [*History ... of the Country of Dorset*] shows that Mr Oldham was Charles Redlynch Fox Strangways' (F.B. Pinion, 1968, *A Hardy Companion*, London: Macmillan, p. 427).

FOXWARREN PARK, Surrey Located near Cobham, it was designed in 1855 by Charles Buxton (of the Norfolk Quaker tribe of Buxtons, Gurneys, and Barclays) for himself, with the help of Frederic Barnes of Ipswich. It was a house of formidable hideousness (see Nikolaus Pevsner, 1962, *Surrey* (*Buildings of England* series), Harmondsworth: Penguin, Pl. 47(b)).

WATERBATH in Henry James, *The Spoils of Poynton* (1897)

'There would be the particular type and taste of the wife the son would have chosen ... out of a Philistine, a tasteless, a hideous house; the kind of house the very walls and furniture of which constitute a kind of anguish for such a woman as I suppose the mother to be. That kind of anguish occurred to me, precisely, as a subject, during the two days I spent at Fox Warren [sic] ... a month or so ago' (entry for 24 December 1893, in *The Notebooks of Henry James*, 1947, ed. F.O. Matthiessen and K.B. Murdock, New York, p. 137). The entry relates the anecdote from which grew the whole plot of the novel.

FRAMPTON, Dorset A village about four miles south of Marden Newton, on the Dorchester road.

SCRIMPTON in Thomas Hardy, 'Audrey Satchel and the Parson' (1894)

Identified in F.B. Pinion, 1968, *A Hardy Companion*, London: Macmillan.

FRANCHETTI, Mimi

ROSALBA in Compton Mackenzie, *Extraordinary Women* (1928)

'Rosalba was modeled on Mimi Franchetti, daughter of a Baron who had composed several operas, whose mother had been a beauty of such rarity and renown that when she appeared in her box at the opera the rest of the audience would turn in their chairs to stare at her. Rosalba was just as beautiful' (Meryle Secrest, 1976, *Between Me and You: a biography of Romaine Brooks*, London: MacDonald & Jane, p. 287; originally published 1974, Garden City, NY: Doubleday).

FRANCIS, David Rowland (1850–1927) He was Governor of Missouri from 1887 to 1893, US Secretary of the Interior from 1896 to 1897, and US Ambassador to Russia from 1916 to 1918.

WILBUR SCHÄFER in W. Somerset Maugham, 'Behind the Scenes', *Ashenden; or The British Agent* (1928)

'"Mr Wilbur Schafer" [is based to some degree] on Francis' (R.L. Calder, 1972, *W. Somerset Maugham and the Quest for Freedom*, London: Heinemann, p. 201).

FRANKAU, Joseph (d. 1898) A Shakespearean actor on the New York stage in the late nineteenth century, his greatest success was in Steel MacKaye's *Hazel Kirke* (1880, New York). His daughter was Aline **Bernstein**.

JOE LINDER in Thomas Wolfe, *The Web and the Rock* (1939)

'In all of Wolfe's manuscripts Joseph Frankau is given the name Joe Lindau. Wolfe's second editor, Edward Aswell, altered the name to Linder' (R.S. Kennedy, 1962, *The Window of Memory: the literary career of Thomas Wolfe*, Chapel Hill, NC, p. 228 n. 69).

FRANKAU, Julia (1864–1916) She was the author of a number of novels under the name Frank Danby, and was the mother of Gilbert Frankau, the novelist. She described herself in *Who's Who* as 'educated at home by Mme Paul Lafargue, elder daughter of Karl Marx'.

IDA COURTNEY in Reginald Turner, *Samson Unshorn* (1909)

'Stanley Weintraub [in *Reggie: a portrait of Reginald Turner*, 1965] believes that . . . Ida Courtney . . . is "an Ada Leverson type", but the details fit Mrs Julia Frankau . . . much more closely than they do the Sphinx' (Charles Burkhart, 1973, *Ada Leverson*, New York, p. 27).

FRANKFURTER, Felix (1882–1965) Born in Vienna, he was a professor at Harvard Law School from 1914 to 1939 and was an associate justice of the US Supreme Court between 1939 and 1962. He was known as a supporter of civil liberties and was the founder of the American Civil Liberties Union.

FRITZ WEENER in Dalton Trumbo, *Washington Jitters* (1936)

'Trumbo made wholesale borrowings from life . . . Fritz Weener [suggests] Felix Frankfurter' (Joseph Blotner, 1966, *The Modern American Political Novel*, Austin, Tex., p. 132).

FRANKLIN, Francis (1773?–1852) Converted by James Jinton, Pastor of the New Road Baptist Church, Oxford, he was baptized at Abingdon in 1793 and became a student at Bristol Baptist Academy in 1797. He was Minister of the Cow Lane Baptist Chapel in Coventry from 1798 to 1852, and his daughters, Mary and Rebecca, were the Misses Franklin whose school in Warwick Row, Coventry, George Eliot attended as a pupil from 1832 to 1836; on Sundays, all the pupils went to Cow Lane Chapel to hear Mr Franklin preach.

RUFUS LYON in George Eliot, *Felix Holt, the Radical* (1866)

'George Eliot . . . drew a lifelike picture of Franklin, who is the original of Rufus Lyon' (A.C. Underwood, 1947, *A History of the English Baptists*, London: Baptist Union Publication Department, p. 174 n.). Allegedly Lyon's appearance was drawn from Franklin, with his large head, small body and prominent, short-sighted eyes, and apparently 'in Franklin's study . . . the books were arranged like Rufus Lyon's in rows on the floor, and . . . he walked up and down these passages composing sermons' (Valentine Cunningham, 1976, *Everywhere Spoken Against: dissent in the Victorian novel*, Oxford: Clarendon Press, p. 185). *See also* **Sibree**, John.

FRAZER, Sir James (*c.*1854–1941) Social anthropologist and author. Educated at Glasgow University and at Trinity College, Cambridge, he was a Fellow from 1879 to 1941. He wrote *The Golden Bough* (1890), and was Professor of Social Anthropology at Liverpool from 1907 to 1922.

MR BRAZIER in Shane Leslie, *The Cantab* (1926)

Identified in a key in the hand of Dr Ivor Ramsay, a Kingsman of the year 1920, and later Dean, laid in a copy of *The Cantab*.

FRAZIER, Richard He was an itinerant fiddler, travelling in Lancashire in the first decade of the nineteenth century.

SAMUEL WELLER in Charles Dickens, *The Pickwick Papers* (1836–7)

'Few serving men have been more popular than Sam Weller: though for our part we liked him fully as much in his original . . . character of Fiddling Dick, in the . . . pages of the "Itinerant". With such a large amount of literary capital in his possession, Mr Dickens might have well spared a trifle by way of acknowledgment to poor Ryley' (R.W. Procter, 1880, *Memorials of Bygone Manchester*, p. 122). The reference is to S.W. Ryley's description of Richard Frazier, whom he encountered and employed while travelling in the North as an itinerant actor. The impudence and the Wellerisms were both to be seen in

Frazier (see ch. 27–31, S.W. Ryley, 1817, *The Itinerant*, Vol. VI, pp. 230–346). *See also* **Vale**, Samuel.

FREER He was a warden in the Birmingham borough prison in 1853.

FRY in Charles Reade, *It is Never Too Late to Mend* (1856)

'Freer, one of the warders, is called Fry' ('The license of modern novelists', *Edinburgh Review* (July 1857): 137).

FREIESLEBEN, Captain (1861–90) In command of the steamer *Florida* (of the fleet of the Société Belge pour le Commerce du Haut Congo) trading on the Congo in 1890, he was shot at Tchumbiri by the son of the chief of the local tribe. Conrad was appointed to the command of the *Florida* in his place.

CAPTAIN FRESLEVEN in Joseph Conrad, *Heart of Darkness* (1902)

'Freiesleben, the captain whom Conrad replaced, appears under the spelling Fresleven' (Ian Watt, 1980, *Conrad in the Nineteenth Century*, p. 137).

FRÉTIGNY A young sculptor whom Conrad knew in Marseilles in 1875.

PRAX in Joseph Conrad, *The Arrow of Gold* (1919)

'He also knew ... Frétigny who appears in ... *The Arrow of Gold*, under the name Prax' (G. Jean-Aubry, 1947, *The Sea-Dreamer: a definitive biography of Joseph Conrad*, p. 63).

FRICK, Henry Clay (1849–1919) American industrialist. He was Chairman of Carnegie Steel Corporation from 1889 to 1900, and Managing Head of the company during the Homestead strike; in 1901 he played an important part in the formation of the United States Steel Corporation.

HENRY MARVIN in I.K. Friedman, *By Bread Alone* (1901)

'Henry Marvin ... is no less able and no more unscrupulous than his prototype, Carnegie's manager at the Homestead Mill' (Walter B. Rideout, 1956, *The Radical Novel in the United States, 1900–1954*, Cambridge, Mass., p. 17).

FROME RIVER Rising at Evershot, it flows through Maiden Newton, past Dorchester and Wareham to Poole Harbour.

THE BLACKWATER in Thomas Hardy, Wessex novels and tales (1871–95)

Identified on a map prepared by Thomas Hardy which hangs in the Dorset County Museum, Dorchester. *See also under* **Abbotsbury**. Hardy sometimes calls it the Var, from its British name' (F.B. Pinion, 1968, *A Hardy Companion*, London: Macmillan, p. 336).

FROST, Catherine (1860?–1948) She was Senior Lecturer in Mathematics at Royal Holloway College from 1887 to 1907; the jubilee booklet *Royal Holloway College 1887–1937* describes her as 'demurely concealing a bagful of mirth and mimicry' (p. 28).

MISS GREENLOW in I. Compton-Burnett, *Dolores* (1911)

'Miss Frost . . . who [reappears] in *Dolores* as . . . the humorous Miss Greenlow' (Hilary Spurling, 1974, *Ivy When Young: the early life of I. Compton-Burnett, 1884–1919*, London: Gollancz, p. 173).

FROUDE, Charlotte (1813?–1860) Daughter of Pascoe Grenfell and the sister of Frances **Kingsley**, in 1949 she married J.A. **Froude**, becoming his first wife.

ARGEMONE LAVINGTON in Charles Kingsley, *Yeast* (1848)

'One [of the four daughters of Pascoe Grenfell] . . . married Lord Wolverton, one . . . Lord Sidney Godolphin Osborne . . . and a fourth sister, easily recognizable as . . . Argemone, became Mrs Froude' (obituary notice of J.A. Froude, probably by Max Muller, 1894, *The Times* (22 October): 7). *See also* **Kingsley**, Frances; **Mansfield**, Caulia.

FROUDE, Eliza Margaret ('Isy') *See* von **Hügel**, Baroness.

FROUDE, James Anthony (1818–94) Son of Robert Hurrell **Froude**, he was the brother of the tractarian Richard Hurrell Froude and uncle of W.H. Mallock. He was educated at Westminster and Oriel College, Oxford, and in 1849 married his first wife, Charlotte Grenfell (**Froude**, above). He was a Fellow of Exeter College, Oxford, but after the publication of *The Nemesis of Faith* (1849), which was publicly burned by William Sewell (at that time Sub-Rector of Exeter), he resigned his fellowship. He was a disciple of **Carlyle**, being his chief literary executor, author of his biography and editor of his *Reminiscences*. From 1892 to 1894 he was Regius Professor of Modern History at Oxford.

EDWARD FOWLER in James Anthony Froude, 'The Spirit's Trials', *Shadows of the Clouds* (1847)

'Of the accuracy of Froude's narrative [of his school-days at Westminster] written in the 1890's [and forming part of an unpublished autobiographical fragment], there can be no question. It is . . . corroborated by an account of his life at Westminster, as recalled by him when he was in residence at Oxford, which he published in 1847. In this painful story, purportedly fiction, it should be kept in mind that Edward Fowler is the name Froude used for himself' (W.H. Dunn, 1961, *James Anthony Froude: a biography*, Oxford, Vol. I, p. 35).

MARKHAM SUTHERLAND in James Anthony Froude, *The Nemesis of Faith* (1849)

'Markham Sutherland . . . is just as much Froude as Edward Fowler' (R.L. Wolff, 1977, *Gains and Losses: novels of faith and doubt in Victorian England*, London: John Murray, p. 392). Arthur Audley in Clough's poem *The Bothie of Toper-na-Fuosich* (1848) was recognized by contemporaries as a portrait of Froude.

FROUDE, Revd John (1777–1852) He was Vicar of Knowstone with Molland, North Devon, from 1804 to 1852. He kept a pack of harriers, hunting three days a week and shooting three days.

PARSON CHOWNE in R.D. Blackmore, *The Maid of Sker* (1872)

'This unspeakable oaf is buried at Knowstone. He left his two parishes, like himself, in a heathen and lawless condition. He is Parson Chowne' (W.G. Hoskins, 1978, *Devon*, p. 144).

FROUDE, Robert Hurrell (1770–1859) From 1799 until his death he was Rector of Denbury and of Dartington, Devon, and in 1820 he was Archdeacon of Totnes. He was the father of J.A. Froude.

CANON FOWLER in James Anthony Froude, 'The Spirit's Trials', *Shadows of the Clouds* (1847)

'Canon Fowler [is] the archdeacon' (R.L. Wolff, 1977, *Gains and Losses: novels of faith and doubt in Victorian England*, London: John Murray, p. 392).

FRYSTON HALL, Ferrybridge, Yorkshire It was the family seat of Richard Monckton **Milnes**, but is no longer standing.

DICKIEFIELD in Laurence Oliphant, *Piccadilly* (1870)

'When *Piccadilly* first appeared in *Blackwood's Magazine* . . . it was recognised that Dickiefield . . . was a picture of Fryston Hall' (James Pope-Hennessy, 1951, *Monckton Milnes: the flight of youth, 1851–1885*, p. 142).

FULLER, Margaret (1810–50) Journalist, critic and social reformer. Born in Massachusetts, as a young woman she was a member of the transcendentalist circle around Emerson, and for a time was one of the editors of their journal *Dial*. She moved to Europe in 1846 and settled in Rome, becoming involved in the revolution of 1848. She married the Marchese Angelo Ossoli, but in 1849, after the suppression of the Roman Republic, she fled the city, sailing for America with her husband and infant son in 1850; all three were drowned when the ship foundered off Fire Island. She wrote *Woman in the Nineteenth Century* (1845).

ZENOBIA in Nathaniel Hawthorne, *The Blithedale Romance* (1852)

'One needs only to read Hawthorne's life and letters, as published by his son, to realize that Zenobia was certainly Hawthorne's version of Margaret Fuller' (Katharine Anthony, 1922, *Margaret Fuller*, p. 90).

FULLERTON, Bailie (1735?–1825?) He was Town Councillor for fifty years and was three times Provost of the Royal Burgh of **Irvine**. He was still alive, although a nonagenarian, in 1825, when he signed the Town Council minutes confirming that he had conferred the freedom of the Burgh on John Galt.

JAMES PAWKIE in John Galt, *The Provost* (1822)

'Galt had left Irvine as a boy of ten [in 1789]. But . . . he remembered . . . Bailie Fullerton. . . . By 1821 he must be long dead. He would form a convenient starting-point for a . . . portrait of "Mr Pawkie", a small-town politician' (Ian A. Gordon (ed.), 1973, introd. to *The Provost*, London: Oxford University Press, p. xii).

FULLERTON, William Morton (1865–1952) Son of a New England Congregational minister, he was educated at Phillips Academy and at Harvard. In 1890, he went to England and joined the staff of *The Times*, and from 1891 to 1911 was based in *The Times*'s Paris office; Paris remained his base for the rest of his life, although he later left *The Times* for *Figaro*. A small, dark, appealing man, he had a penchant for majestic women: in 1890, while in London, he became the lover of Margaret Brooke, the Ranee of Sarawak; in 1903 he married a singer at the Paris Opera Comique, but divorced her in 1904; and for many years he was involved in a liaison with yet another woman, who was not above a little blackmail. There was also an abortive engagement to a cousin, and in addition he had various homosexual liaisons. He had formed a warm friendship with Henry James when he arrived in London in 1890 with an introduction from Charles Eliot **Norton**; in 1907 James introduced him to Edith Wharton and they had become lovers by 1908, remaining friends to the end of her life. He was in Paris throughout both world wars and lived his last years largely on the proceeds of the sale of letters from his distinguished friends; not those from Mrs Wharton, however – these are not to be found.

ANDREW CULWIN in Edith Wharton, 'The Eyes', *Tales of Men and Ghosts* (1910)

'The traces of Fullerton are there to recognize in the portrait of Culwin: what might be called a sort of sexual indecisiveness, the sense of unrealized literary gifts, the cunning use of language in conversation; even more, the engagement to a first cousin, followed by flight to Europe and absolute silence. One of the phrases used about Culwin . . . is taken almost verbatim from Fullerton's report to his Harvard class secretary of 1910' (R.W.B. Lewis, 1975, *Edith Wharton: a biography*, London: Constable, p. 288). *See also* **Berry**, Walter van Rensselaer.

VINCENT DEERING in Edith Wharton, 'The Letters', *Tales of Men and Ghosts* (1910)

'"The Letters" . . . is a mélange of incidents culled from Edith Wharton's and Fullerton's lives, separately and together. . . . Deering, indeed is almost to a detail an ironic though tempered portrait of Morton Fullerton' (Lewis, op. cit., pp. 286, 287).

MERTON DENSHER in Henry James, *The Wings of the Dove* (1902)

'The centre of emotion in this novel is fixed in Merton Densher, a figure not unlike James's Parisian friend W. Morton Fullerton . . . [who] . . . lived a life similar to James's hero. He was curious about this character, for he wrote to James inquiring whether Densher was modelled on a man named T.A. Cook. "Ah, que non" James responded. . . . The personality of Morton Fullerton and the use of the name Merton, permits us to speculate that the Parisianized journalist had grounds for his enquiries' (Leon Edel, 1972, *Henry James: the master, 1901–1916*, p. 124). *See also* **Ford**, Ford Madox; **Seaman**, Sir Owen.

FURLEY, Mary Having left a workhouse because of the ill-treatment she suffered there, she was unable to earn enough money to feed herself and her baby, so she attempted to drown herself; however, she was rescued but the baby slipped from her arms and drowned. She was found guilty of wilful murder and was condemned to death at the Old Bailey, London, on 16 April 1844; the Home Secretary subsequently commuted the sentence to seven years' transportation.

MARGARET ('MEG') VECK in Charles Dickens, *The Chimes* (1844)

'There can be little doubt that [this case] was . . . in Dickens's mind when he came to write of Meg's desperate flight to the river. . . . Certainly many of the book's readers were reminded of Mary Furley . . . a reviewer in the Chartist organ, *The Northern Star*, wrote . . . "At length, she [Meg] turns . . . and hastens to the river's brink: a true picture of Mary Furley, and too many hapless ones who, like her, have been driven to destruction"' (Michael Slater, 1970, 'Dickens's tract for the Times', in Michael Slater (ed.), *Dickens 1970: centenary essays*, p. 104).

FURNIVALL, Frederick James (1825–1910) Scholar and editor. He was an enthusiastic oarsman from youth, a barrister of Gray's Inn in 1849, a member of the Christian Socialists, a friend of John Ruskin, and an outspoken agnostic. In 1854 he helped to found the Working Man's College, London, and taught there. He was one of the originators of the *New Oxford Dictionary*, a founder of the Early English Text Society, and edited the works of Chaucer and the Percy Ballads. In 1867 he lost his fortune in the failure of Overend and Gurney's bank. Kenneth Grahame met him in 1875 and joined his New Shakespeare Society, being Honorary Secretary from 1880 to 1891.

PAN in Kenneth Grahame, *The Wind in the Willows* (1908)

'Furnivall also provided one aspect of the appearance and *mise en scène* of Pan. . . . Professor Livingston Lowes describes "an island in the Thames, where, of a Sunday afternoon, [Furnivall] used to recline against a tree, like a glorious old British river-God with white and curling beard' (Peter Green, 1959, *Kenneth Grahame, 1859–1932*, p. 280).

RAT in Kenneth Grahame, *The Wind in the Willows* (1908)

'His sculling expeditions and loaded luncheon hampers recall an older, more eccentric, friend – Dr Furnivall' (Green, op. cit., p. 280). *See also* **Atkinson, Edward; Henley**, W.E.

G

GAINSBOROUGH, Lincolnshire

ST OGG'S in George Eliot, *The Mill on the Floss* (1860)

'It was not until September [1859] in Lincolnshire, that [the Leweses] found that . . . Gainsborough [could supply] St Oggs' (Marghanita Laski, 1973, *George Eliot and Her World*, London: Thames & Hudson, p. 72).

GALE, Frederick (1823–1904) Solicitor and parliamentary agent. He was a friend of Thackeray, and was with him in Germany in September 1850.

SERJEANT LANKIN in W.M. Thackeray, *The Kickleburys on the Rhine* (1850)

'I dined with the Elliots yesterday, only Mr Helps and Mr Gale (Sergt Lankin of the Kicklebury book)' (Mrs Brookfield to her husband, 8 January 1851, reproduced in *The Letters and Private Papers of W.M. Thackeray*, 1945, ed. Gordon N. Ray, Vol. II, London: Oxford University Press, p. 735 n. 18).

GALLAHER, Fred

IGNATIUS GALLAHER in James Joyce, 'A Little Cloud', *Dubliners* (1914) and *Ulysses* (1922)

'The Gallaher family was one Joyce knew well. . . . The [member of the family] who appears most prominently in [his] writings is Mrs Gallaher's brother-in-law Fred. Joyce calls him Ignatius Gallaher, and in . . . 'A Little Cloud' and in *Ulysses* gives an accurate account of him' (Richard Ellmann, 1966, *James Joyce*, London: Oxford Paperbacks, pp. 46, 47 n.). *See also* **Gogarty**, Oliver St John.

GALSWORTHY, Ada Nemesis Pearson Cooper (b. 1864) She was probably the illegitimate daughter of Dr Emanuel Cooper of Norwich, and in 1891 she married Arthur Galsworthy, John Galsworthy's cousin. The latter fell in love with her and they lived together from 1905, marrying that same year, after she was divorced.

IRENE FORSYTE in John Galsworthy, *The Man of Property* (1906)

'The story of Irene is of course the story of Ada. . . . Ada herself completely accepted the identification' (Catherine Dupré, 1976, *John Galsworthy*, p. 114).

GALSWORTHY, John (1867–1933) English novelist and playwright. He was born in Coombe in Surrey and was educated at Harrow and New College, Oxford. He was called to the Bar in 1890 but decided to travel instead. In the course of his travels, he met Joseph **Conrad** and they became friends. He published his first work, a collection of short stories (*From the Four Winds*) in 1897. He wrote a number of novels, including the celebrated *Forsyte Saga* and produced more than thirty plays. He won the Nobel Prize for Literature in 1932.

THOMAS MORLAND in Henry Williamson, *The Power of the Dead* (1963)

'Galsworthy is pictured as the patronising Thomas Morland' (George Jefferson, 1982, *Edward Garnett*, p. 243).

GAMBLE, Susan Guttridge In 1859 she married Charles **Yerkes**. They had six children and were divorced in 1881.

LILLIAN SEMPLE in Theodore Dreiser, *The Financier* (1912)

'Dreiser . . . was faithful to his sources in portraying Yerkes' first wife, Mrs Gamble – whom he called Mrs Semple' (Richard Lehan, 1974, *Theodore Dreiser: his world and his novels*, Carbondale, Ill.: Arcturis Books, p. 104).

GANS, Bird Daughter of Solomon and Pauline Stein, she was Gertrude Stein's cousin. She married Howard Gans, who remained on friendly terms with Gertrude and Leo Stein until their deaths.

JULIA DEHNING in Gertrude Stein, *The Making of Americans* (1925)

'A character based on . . . Bird Stein, later Bird Gans' (James R. Mellow, 1974, *The Charmed Circle: Gertrude Stein and company*, London: Phaidon Press, p. 116).

GAPON, Georgi Appolonovich (1870?–1906) Called 'Father' Gapon, he was educated for the priesthood and began mission work among the factory population of St Petersburg. He became a Russian revolutionary and organized trades unions. On Bloody Sunday 1905 he led a crowd to the Tsar's palace to present a petition, but the crowd was fired at by the troops; he escaped to London.

FATHER ZOSIM in Joseph Conrad, *Under Western Eyes* (1911)

'It is easy enough to identify Father Zosim with Father Gapon' (Jocelyn Baines, 1967, *Joseph Conrad: a critical biography*, rev. ed, London: Weidenfeld & Nicolson, p. 371; originally published 1960).

GARCÍA, Manuel (1775–1832) Spanish tenor and singing master. Born in Seville, he later became famous as a singing teacher in Paris and London, with his methods forming the basis of modern teaching; he created roles in several Rossini operas. He was the father of Maria **Malibran** and Pauline **Viardot**.

JOSEPH CERINTHEA in Elizabeth Sara Sheppard, *Charles Auchester* (1853)

Identified in an anonymous typed key laid in a copy of the first edition of *Charles Auchester* which is now in the possession of the present author.

GARENDON PARK, Leicestershire A seventeenth-century hall that was bought in 1683 by Sir Ambrose Phillipps, whose two nephews designed and built a Palladian south front. In 1796 the hall passed to the March family, who took the name of Phillipps, and in 1862 it was inherited by Ambrose March Phillipps **de Lisle**.

ST GENEVIÈVE (SEAT OF EUSTACE LYLE) in Benjamin Disraeli, *Coningsby* (1844)

'St Geneviève as described by Disraeli was "a pile of modern building in the finest style of Christian architecture" complete with a great hall equipped with "rich roof . . . gallery and screen". Disraeli's description was almost certainly inspired by the designs which . . . Augustus Welby Pugin had prepared in 1841 for rebuilding Garendon. . . . The designs were never carried out' (Mark Girouard, 1981, *The Return to Camelot*, p. 84). 'The designs are now in the Drawing Collection of the Royal Institute of British Architects' (ibid., p. 297 n. 60).

GARIBALDI, Giuseppe (1807–82) Italian revolutionary hero and leader of the Risorgimento. In 1834, he took part in Mazzini's 'Young Italy' movement and was condemned to death for participating in an abortive attempt to seize Genoa. He escaped to South America where he married Anita Riveira de Silva with whom he had three children, and took part in the Rio Grande rebellion. He returned to Italy during the 1848 revolution and defended Rome against the French. In 1860 he conquered Sicily and Naples for the new unified Kingdom of Italy.

Giorgio Viola in Joseph Conrad, *Nostromo* (1904)

'Viola . . . derives in part from the lives and careers of two followers of Garibaldi, but significantly, he is in his appearance and character Garibaldi *himself*' (Norman Sherry, 1971, *Conrad's Western World*, Cambridge, p. 158). *See also* **Clerici**, Enrico; **Giuliolo**, Giovanni.

GARNER, Anne Daughter of Isaac Pearson, of Old Castle Farm, Astley, Warwickshire, she was the sister of Christiana **Evans** and married George Garner of Sole End, Astley.

Susan Deane (née Dodson) in George Eliot, *The Mill on the Floss* (1860)

'The Garners, originals of the Deanes, were . . . cheerful folk living comfortably at Sole End' (Gordon S. Haight, 1958, 'The George Eliot originals', in *From Jane Austen to Joseph Conrad: essays collected in memory of James T. Hillhouse*, ed. R. Rathburn and M. Steinmann, Jun., Minneapolis, Minn.: University of Minnesota Press, p. 189).

GARNER, Bessie Daughter of George and Anne **Garner**.

Lucy Deane in George Eliot, *The Mill on the Floss* (1860)

'[The Garners'] daughter Bessie seems a more likely prototype of Lucy Deane than George Eliot's sister Chrissey, who is traditionally assigned the part' (Gordon S. Haight, 1958, 'The George Eliot originals', in *From Jane Austen to Joseph Conrad: essays collected in memory of James T. Hillhouse*, ed. R. Rathburn and M. Steinmann, Jun., Minneapolis, Minn., University of Minnesota Press, p. 190). *See also* **Clarke**, Christiana.

GARNETT, Constance (1862–1946) Née Black, she married Edward **Garnett** in 1889. She translated Dostoevsky, Chekhov and Turgenev.

Mrs Butler in David Garnett, *Beany-Eye* (1935)

'Mrs Butler is in fact Constance Garnett' (review, *Times Literary Supplement* (10 October 1935): 626).

Miss Stobhall in Ford Madox Ford, *The Simple Life Limited* (1911)

Identified in Arthur Mizener, 1971, *The Saddest Story: a biography of Ford Madox Ford*, Cleveland: World Publishing, p. 559 n.12. *See also* **Garnett**, Olive.

GARNETT, Edward (1868–1937) Critic, essayist and dramatist. Son of Richard Garnett, he became Keeper of Printed Books in the British Museum. He was also a publisher's reader for Fisher Unwin, Heinemann, Duckworth and Jonathan Cape, and in this capacity his discoveries included Galsworthy, D.H. **Lawrence**, W.H. Hudson and Conrad. He married Constance Black (**Garnett**, above) in 1889 and was David Garnett's father.

Philip Bosinney in John Galsworthy, *The Man of Property* (1906)

'It was from Edward that Galsworthy drew Bosinney . . . which gives a certain piquancy to the violent discussion, published in their correspondence, in which Edward assailed Jack for not understanding Bosinney's character and Bosinney's creator defended himself as best he might' (David Garnett, 1953, *The Golden Echo*, London: Chatto & Windus, p. 70).

Christopher Brandon in Olivia Shakespear, *The Journey of High Honour* (1895)

'Christopher, as soon as I had discovered his approximate age, put on the form of a certain ungainly, long-suffering and freckled publisher's reader' (to Olivia Shakespear, 28 November 1894, reproduced in *The Letters of W.B. Yeats*, 1954, ed. Allan Wade, p. 241). 'Possibly his friend Edward Garnett' (ibid., n. 1).

James Butler in David Garnett, *Beany-Eye* (1935)

'. . . Mr Butler is the triumph of the book: Mr Garnett has never surpassed this memory . . . of his father, whom he exhibits . . . as a man of a lovable yet wilful temperament, patient at one moment, irascible at the next, almost irrationally fearless and when frightened absolutely courageous' (review, *Times Literary Supplement* (10 October 1935): 626).

Edward Cornelian in Henry Williamson, *The Power of the Dead* (1963)

'Edward is Edward Cornelian – an overbearing literary critic' (George Jefferson, 1982, *Edward Garnett*, p. 243).

Lea in Joseph Conrad and Ford Madox Ford, *The Inheritors* (1901)

'I value the book for the portrait of Edward, as Lea the publisher's reader, which shows the regard in which he was held by the collaborators' (Garnett, op. cit., p. 64).

Mr Parmont in Ford Madox Ford, *The Simple Life Limited* (1911)

'. . . Mr Parmont (who stands for Garnett)' (Z. Najder, 1983, *Joseph Conrad: a chronicle*, Cambridge: Cambridge University Press, p. 191).

GARNETT, Olive (b. 1871) She was the sister of Edward **Garnett** and was a neighbour and friend of Ford Madox Ford from childhood.

Miss Stobhall in Ford Madox Ford, *The Simple Life Limited* (1911)

'When Olive Garnett termed *The Simple Life Limited* "scandalous", she may have meant something besides Ford's treatment of . . . herself as the tactless, strident, puritanical . . . Miss Stobhall' (Thomas C. Moser, 1980, *The Life in the Fiction of Ford Madox Ford*, Princeton, p. 307). *See also* **Garnett**, Constance.

GARRARD, Violet Florence ('Flo') As a child she had been an inmate of the house in Southsea where the Kipling children lodged while their parents were in India. In 1880 or thereabouts they encountered each other in London and renewed their friendship. By 1890 she was sharing a studio with a Miss Mabel Price in Paris, where Kipling visited them.

MAISIE in Rudyard Kipling, *The Light that Failed* (1890)

'She has been identified rightly or wrongly, with Violet Florence Garrard . . . by Professor [Charles] Carrington' (R.E. Harbord (ed.), 1970, *The Readers' Guide to Rudyard Kipling's Work*, Sect. V, London: Kipling Society, p. 2157). The identification is commonly accepted.

The GARRICK CLUB, Covent Garden, London Founded in 1831 as a club in which 'actors and men of education might meet on equal terms'. Count **d'Orsay** and Samuel **Rogers** were among its original members; later members included **Thackeray** and Trollope.

THE BEAR GARDEN in Anthony Trollope, *The Duke's Children* (1879–80)

'How well he renders the political and social atmosphere, how aptly he characterizes the Garrick Club, of which he was so fond, as the "Bear Garden"' (Walter Sichel, 1923, *The Sands of Time*, London, p. 219).

GARSINGTON MANOR, Oxfordshire Situated about five miles south-east of Oxford, from 1915 to 1927 it was the home of Philip and Lady Ottoline **Morrell** from which they entertained a distinguished literary and artistic circle including Lytton **Strachey**, Bertrand **Russell**, D.H. Lawrence and Virginia **Woolf**; here both Aldous and Julian **Huxley** met their future wives.

BIRCH END in Gilbert Cannan, *Pugs and Peacocks* (1921)

A Garsington house party on the outskirts of Cambridge; the exterior of the house in no way resembles the original, but the interior had much in common.

BREADALBY in D.H. Lawrence, *Women in Love* (1920)

'In the "Breadalby" chapter Birkin proclaims the inequality of man, echoing the author's conversations with Russell and Ottoline, in a pure caricature of the old Garsington weekends' (E. Delavenay, 1972, *D.H. Lawrence: the man and his work*, p. 420).

CROME in Aldous Huxley, *Crome Yellow* (1921)

'The war comes . . . [Peter Greenow] sets off to carry out his landwork on the farm of a country estate. It is the first appearance of Garsington Manor in Huxley's fiction, and already it bears the name of Crome' (George Woodcock, 1972, *Dawn and the Darkest Hour: a study of Aldous Huxley*, London: Faber & Faber, p. 69). *See also* **Beckley Park**.

DODDERINGHAM OLD HALL in Osbert Sitwell, 'Triple Fugue' (1924)

This is unmistakably Garsington, house party, hostess and all, transported, like Birch End (*see above*), to the outskirts of Cambridge.

GARVIN, James Louis (1868–1947) Editor of the London *Observer* between 1908 and 1942.

FRED NEAL in H.G. Wells, *The New Machiavelli* (1911)

'There could be only one original for Neal . . . J.L. Garvin, who was then very much to the fore, and whose articles were being widely discussed' Lovat (Dickson, 1972, *H.G. Wells*, Harmondsworth: Penguin, p. 219).

GASELEE, Sir Stephen (1762–1839) He was a member of Gray's Inn, London; as a young barrister he was said to have laid a friend 100 to 1 in guineas that he would never reach the bench. He became a judge in 1824 and duly paid the 100 guineas to the executor of his long-deceased friend (see *Gentleman's Magazine* (September 1839)). He retired in 1837.

MR JUSTICE STARELEIGH in Charles Dickens, *The Pickwick Papers* (1836–7)

'He . . . is said to have been the original of the . . . judge represented by Dickens . . . under the name of Justice Stareleigh' (G.S. Boase, 1890, in Leslie Stephen (ed.), *The Dictionary of National Biography*, London: Oxford University Press). 'The physical likeness between him and Stareleigh was as marked as the resemblance of the name' (W.S. Holdworth, 1928, *Charles Dickens as a Legal Historian*, New Haven, Conn., p. 76). 'It is noteworthy that he resigned in the Hilary Term, 1837 – shortly after the appearance of the trial scene in *Pickwick*' (ibid.).

GASKELL, Julia (1846–1908) The youngest of the four daughters of Mrs Gaskell, the author.

PAULINA MARY HOME in Charlotte Brontë, *Villette* (1853)

'In seeking an original for [Paulina] . . . biographers and commentators . . . have wholly overlooked the recent and powerful impression that Julia Gaskell had made upon [Charlotte Brontë] at the very time she was writing the opening chapters of *Villette*. It seems . . . likely that she was the original of Paulina. . . . The porcelain fragility of portrait and original is too strikingly similar . . . not to evoke the comparison' (Winifred Gérin, 1969, *Charlotte Brontë*, Oxford, pp. 492, 493). *See also* **Whipp**, Fanny.

GATES, Elmer (1859?–1923) American inventor and experimental psychologist. Born in Dayton, Ohio, and educated privately, he set up a private laboratory near Washington where, *inter alia*, he allegedly trained dogs to distinguish seven shades of red and eight of green. In 1900, Dreiser interviewed him and wrote an article on his work; however, no publisher could be found.

BOB AMES in Theodore Dreiser, *Sister Carrie* (1900)

'He may have recorded his admiration for the Washington "investigator" in his portrait of Bob Ames' (Ellen Moers, 1970, *Two Dreisers*, London: Thames & Hudson, p. 161; originally published 1969, New York: Viking).

GATHORNE-HARDY, Robert (1902–73) He was the son of the Earl of Cranbrook. For many years he worked in association with Logan Pearsall Smith, the writer, and in 1949 he published his recollections of him. He was a distinguished bibliophile and edited the memoirs of Lady Ottoline **Morrell**.

MILES MALPRACTICE in Evelyn Waugh, *Decline and Fall* (1928)

'In the first edition the name of Miles Malpractice was very close to the name of a living person [Martin Gaythorn-Brodie]. For fear of libel it was changed in the second edition' (Christopher Sykes, 1975, *Evelyn Waugh*, London: Collins, p. 86).

GAUGUIN, (Eugène Henri) Paul (1848–1903) French Post-Impressionist painter. He was born in Paris and lived there as a successful stockbroker and art collector until 1883, when he exhibited his own work with the help of Camille Pissarro. Driven by the desire to give up everything for painting, he left his wife and children and went to Pont Aven in Brittany, where he became the leader of a group of painters. He lived in Tahiti from 1891 to 1901 and in the Marquesas Islands. Both places greatly influenced his style of painting.

CHARLES STRICKLAND in W. Somerset Maugham, *The Moon and Sixpence* (1919)

'This novel was suggested by the life of Paul Gauguin' (Introd. to *The Moon and Sixpence*, 1935 (collected edn), p. v). 'Many years ago I wrote a novel called The Moon and Sixpence. In that I took a famous painter, Paul Gauguin, and, using the novelist's privilege, devised a number of incidents to illustrate the character I had created on the suggestions afforded me by the scanty facts I knew about the French artist' (W. Somerset Maugham, 1949, *The Razor's Edge*, p. 1). *See also* **John**, Augustus.

GEDDES, Auckland (1831–1908) Civil engineer. From 1857 to 1869 he was engaged on railway work in India, in close association with Robert Brown. Brown died in 1869, whereupon Geddes returned to England. He was married in 1871, and from 1871 to 1882 he was the head of an engineering firm in India. In 1882 he made his final return to England. He was the father of the first Lord Geddes.

FINDLAYSON in Rudyard Kipling, 'The Bridge Builders' (1898)

'The friendship [with Brown] must have been of no ordinary kind, because many years later . . . Kipling told how he had met Auckland Geddes and, having heard many tales of the Geddes–Brown association, used them as prototypes for the two engineers in . . . 'The Bridge Builders' (Auckland Geddes, 1952, *The Forging of a Family*, pp. 89–90). I have been unable to trace any confirmation of this identification; possibly Kipling himself made it in conversation with Geddes, whom he may well have known. *See also* **Bell**, J.R.; **Walton**, Frederick.

GELL, Sir William (1778–1836) Archaeologist. In 1801 he visited Troy, and in 1814 he became Chamberlain to Queen Caroline, giving evidence on her behalf in 1820; thenceforward he lived in Italy.

THE PHILOSOPHER OF THE VILLA PLINIANA in Benjamin Disraeli, *Vivian Grey* (1826–7)

Identified as Sir W. G—ll in a key given in a pamphlet published in 1827 by William Marsh. This key is discussed by Lucien Wolf in his notes to *Vivian Grey* (1904 (centenary edn), Vol. II, London: Alexander Moring, p. 364), with the conclusion that Disraeli was not responsible for the key.

GELLHORN, Martha Journalist and novelist. Educated at Bryn Mawr, she met Hemingway in Key West, Florida, in 1936 and went to Spain with him in 1937. Between 1938 and 1940, she covered the war in Finland for *Celliers* magazine, and in November 1940 she married Hemingway, becoming his third wife. They were divorced in 1945 and she later married T.S. Matthews. Like all Hemingway's wives, she came from St Louis.

DOROTHY BRIDGES in Ernest Hemingway, 'The Fifth Column', *The Fifth Column and the First Forty-nine Stories* (1938)

'The lady correspondent of the play, Dorothy Bridges, bore an unmistakeable resemblance to Martha Gellhorn. She was a tall, handsome blonde with long smooth legs, a curiously cultivated accent, and a college degree. Like Martha, she disliked dirt, displayed a passion for making rooms homelike, and even owned a silver-fox cape' (Carlos Baker, 1969, *Ernest Hemingway: a life story*, New York, p. 321).

GEMMELLS, Andrew (1688?–1793) He was a licensed beggar. He served for a time in the army and fought at Fontenoy. He died and was buried at Roxburgh, supposedly aged 105.

EDIE OCHILTREE in Sir Walter Scott, *The Antiquary* (1816)

'Having . . . given an account of the genus and species to which Edie Ochiltree appertains, the author may add that the individual he had in his eye was Andrew Gemmells, an old mendicant . . . who was many years since well known . . . in the vales of Gala, Tweed, Ettrick, Yarrow, and the adjoining country. The author has in his youth repeatedly seen and conversed with Andrew, but cannot in fact remember whether he held the rank of Blue-Gown' (Sir Walter Scott, advertisement to *The Antiquary*, 1900 (Border edn), pp. xiv, xv, note added in 1828). In fact, according to Robert Chambers, Gemmells was a Blue-Gown, i.e. a King's Bedesman, one of an order of mendicants to whom the King of Scotland distributed alms, in return for prayers for the royal welfare; each member received a new blue cloak each year on the King's birthday, together with a badge, and was licensed to beg throughout Scotland.

GEORGE IV (1760–1830) At the age of 18 he had an affair with an actress called Mrs Robinson, and at 20 he married a Roman Catholic called Mrs Fitzherbert, although the marriage was later annulled. He married Princess Caroline of Brunswick in 1795; parliament made it a condition that he do so before it paid off his debts of £650,000. He tried to divorce Caroline, but public opinion rallied behind her and she died, still married, in 1821. He became Prince Regent in 1811 owing to the insanity of his father, George III. He succeeded to the throne in 1820 and was a great dandy and connoisseur.

GENTLEMAN GEORGE in Bulwer Lytton, *Paul Clifford* (1830)

Identified in a key set out by Rosina Bulwer Lytton in a letter of 26 May 1830, reproduced in Michael Sadleir, 1968, *Bulwer and His Wife*, pp. 227–8.

MARQUIS OF SNOWDON in W. Massie, *Sydenham; or Memoirs of a Man of the World* (1830)

'Volume one is purely social, dealing with such notables as . . . the Prince, (Lord Snowdon)' (M.W. Rosa, 1936, *The Silver Fork School: novels of fashion preceding 'Vanity Fair'*, New York, p. 81 n. 3).

GERTLER, Mark (1891–1939) Painter. Born in Spitalfields, he studied at the Slade School of Fine Art, London, and fell violently in love with Dora **Carrington**. He committed suicide.

GOMBAULD in Aldous Huxley, *Crome Yellow* (1921)

'Gertler was almost certainly D.H. Lawrence's model for the sculptor Loerke in *Women in Love*, and the original for the painter Gombauld in Aldous Huxley's *Crome Yellow*' (Michael Holroyd, 1968, *Lytton Strachey*, Vol. II, London: Heinemann, p. 189 n.).

MENDEL KÜHLER in Gilbert Cannan, *Mendel* (1916)

Documents illustrating the reception of *Mendel* by some of the characters are to be found in *Mark Gertler: selected letters*, 1965, ed. Noel Carrington, pp. 253–6. *See also under* **Carrington**, Dora.

LOERKE in D.H. Lawrence, *Women in Love* (1920)

See above under GOMBAULD.

GHEZZI, Father Charles, SJ He was a lecturer in Italian at University College, Dublin, in 1898, and taught James Joyce.

ALMIDANO ARTIFONI in James Joyce, *Ulysses* (1922)

'Ghezzi was sympathetic to [Joyce], and the two men retained an affection for each other. Ghezzi appears in Joyce's books with a benign character and the euphonious name of Almidano Artifoni' (Richard Ellmann, 1966, *James Joyce*, London: Oxford Paperbacks, p. 61).

GIANNI, Giovanni Captain of a steamboat.

GIOVANNI GIANNI in Samuel Butler, *Erewhon* (1872)

'[Butler] was abroad from 17th August to 21st September; his route . . . took him through Antwerp . . . Paris, Mâcon, Turin . . . Florence, Leghorn, thence by steamer to Genoa. . . . The captain of the steamer was Giovanni Gianni, and Butler used him for the captain of the ship in which Mr Higgs and Arowhena were picked up in Chapter XXV [XXVIII of the revised edition of 1901] of *Erewhon*' (H. Festing Jones, 1919, *Samuel Butler: author of* Erewhon, 2 vols, London: Macmillan, p. 117).

GIBBS, Frederick Waymouth (1821–98) He was educated at King's College School, London, and at Trinity College, Cambridge, where he was an 'Apostle', and from 1845 to 1853 he was a Fellow of Trinity. In 1848 he was called to the

Bar, and he became a member of Lincoln's Inn, London. He acted as tutor to the Prince of Wales and Prince Alfred between 1851 and 1860, having been recommended to Prince Albert by Sir James **Stephen**; Gibbs had been brought up with Leslie and Fitzjames Stephen.

WILLIAM PEPPER in Virginia Woolf, *The Voyage Out* (1915)

'Mr Gibbs was an old friend of the Stephen family and at more or less regular intervals used to come and dine with them at Hyde Park Gate. He had been tutor . . . to the Prince of Wales . . . and in spite or because of this was a bit of a bore – I think Mr Pepper . . . has some of his characteristics. On the nights when [he] came to dinner, towards ten o'clock, Stephen would start groaning and saying at intervals quite audibly: "O why doesn't he go; O why doesn't he go' (Leonard Woolf, 1964, *Beginning Again*, pp. 92–3 n.). Extracts from his diaries for 1851–6, and photographs, prefaced by the account of his character which Sir James Stephen furnished to the Prince Consort, are to be found in *Cornhill Magazine* 165: 105 ff.

GIFFORD, Anna Younger sister of C.B. **Mansfield** and of Caulia **Mansfield**.

HONORIA LAVINGTON in Charles Kingsley, *Yeast* (1848)

'Kingsley told me once that in *Yeast* . . . Anna Gifford [had been his type] for Honoria, but the latter by no means does justice to her model' (J.M. Ludlow, quoted in R.B. Martin, 1959, *The Dust of Combat: a life of Charles Kingsley*, London: Faber & Faber, p. 99). *See also* **Kingsley**, Frances.

GIFFORD, William (1756–1826) He was self-taught, beginning as a ploughboy, then working as a boy on a Brixham trawler, and later being apprenticed to a shoe-maker (hence Peacock's name for him). In 1779 friends sent him to Exeter College, Oxford, and in 1797 and 1798 he was Editor of *Anti-Jacobin*. He became the first editor of the **Quarterly Review**, a position he held from 1809 to 1824, translated Juvenal and Persius, and edited works of Massinger, Ben Johnson, and Ford. Scott describes him as 'a little man, dumpled up together, and so ill-made as to seem almost deformed, but with a singular expression of talent in his countenance' (entry for 18 January 1827 in *Journal*).

THE EDITOR OF THE *UNIVERSAL REVIEW* (OXFORD) in George Burrow, *Lavengro* (1851)

'My information is positive that the prototype of [The Editor] was William Gifford, translator of Juvenal, 1802, 3rd edition, 1817' (W.E. Knapp, 1900, *Lavengro*, p. 564 n. (to p. 208), reproduced in A. Boyle, 1951, 'Portraiture in Lavengro', *Notes and Queries* 196 (13 October): 453, 454; this article quotes Sir Leslie Stephen in a letter to *Literature* (8 April 1899) pointing out the extreme implausibility of this identification). *See also* **Busby**, Thomas; **Carey**, John.

MR VAMP in Thomas Love Peacock, *Melincourt* (1817)

'Gifford . . . started life as a shoemaker's apprentice' (*The Novels of T.L. Peacock*, 1948, ed. David Garnett, London: Rupert Hart-Davis, p. 171 n. 2).

GILLETTE, Chester (1881?–1908) He was found guilty in 1906 of the murder of Grace **Brown**, an employee in his uncle's skirt factory in upstate New York; he was condemned to death and executed.

CLYDE GRIFFITHS in Theodore Dreiser, *An American Tragedy* (1925)

'[Dreiser] freely and fully admitted his debt to the prototype.... Clyde Griffiths was born of ... Chester Gillette. There was more to Dreiser's hero, of course. There was Dreiser himself. For, while ... Gillette's background was middle-class ... Griffiths was ... savagely poor as Dreiser himself had once been. Further, the details of the first half of the book differed from fact, though in the later chapters Dreiser drew heavily from Gillette's correspondence with Grace Brown' (Irving Wallace, 1956, *The Fabulous Originals*, p. 3).

GILLINGHAM, Dorset A town located four miles north-west of Shaftesbury.

LEDDENTON in Thomas Hardy, *Jude the Obscure* (1895)

Identified in Denys Kay-Robinson, 1972, *Hardy's Wessex Reappraised*, Newton Abbot, and in F.B. Pinion, 1968, *A Hardy Companion*, London: Macmillan.

GINGRICH, Arnold (1903–72) Born in Pennsylvania, he met Ernest Hemingway in 1933. He was the founder of *Esquire* and was its Editor from 1933 to 1945; Hemingway was a regular contributor between 1933 and 1939. Gingrich married Jane **Mason** in 1955, after his first wife died.

JOHN MACWALSEY in Ernest Hemingway, *To Have and Have Not* (1937)

'This eccentric educator was based on a rough approximation of Professor Harry Burns and Arnold Gingrich' (Carlos Baker, 1969, *Ernest Hemingway: a life story*, New York, p. 295). Baker explains that the identification of Burns and Gingrich as prototypes for MacWalsey is based on the fact that elements of the description fit both men as they looked in the summer of 1936 (see ibid., p. 619 n. 'E.H's eccentrics in the Morgan novel'). *See also* **Burns**, Harry.

GINSBERG, Allen (b. 1926) American poet. Born in Newark, New Jersey, his father was a poet and his mother was a left-wing Russian emigrée. He was the author of *Kaddish* (1961), *Howl* (1956) and others, and was associated with the 'Beat' movement in San Francisco.

IRWIN GARDEN in *Big Sur* (1962), ALVAH GOLDBROOK in *The Dharma Bums* (1958), LEON LEVINSKY in *The Town and the City* (1950), CARLO MARX in *On the Road* (1957), and ADAM MOORAD in *The Subterraneans* (1958), all by Jack Kerouac

Identified in 'Character key to the Duluoz Legend', in Barry Gifford and Lawrence Lee, 1979, *Jack's Book*, pp. 322–32.

GISSING, George Robert (1857–1903) English novelist. He was born in Wakefield, Yorkshire, and was educated at Owens College (now the University of Manchester). He was expelled from the college in 1876 and sent to prison for a month for stealing money to give to a young woman, Marianne ('Nell') Harrison, apparently to keep her off the streets. He went to America in disgrace, but returned to England in 1877, where he met up again with Nell (Marianne **Gissing**, below). They married in 1879, but separated after a few years. Gissing was single-minded and hard-working, and had few friends apart from H.G. Wells, who came from a similar background. In 1890 he married Edith Underwood, and they had two sons, but again the marriage failed and they separated in 1897. In 1898 he went to Paris and met Gabrielle **Fleury**; together they moved to the South of France, where he spent the rest of his life.

WILL CURGENVEN in Morley Roberts, *The Degradation of Geoffrey Alwith* (1895)

'Will Curgenven, of course, was Maitland' (Morley Roberts, 1958, *The Private Life of Henry Maitland*, ed. Morchard Bishop, pp. 67, 68). That is to say, Curgenven is a portrait of Gissing. In *The Private Life of Henry Maitland* the writer (J.C.H. – i.e. Morley Roberts) describes his novel, *The Fate of Hilary Dale*. It is identified in a footnote, by the editor, as *The Degradation of Geoffrey Alwith*.

HENRY MAITLAND in Morley Roberts, *The Private Life of Henry Maitland* (1912)

'. . . a veiled portrait of Gissing in which the veils were so transparent that they hid nothing' (Morchard Bishop, 1958, introduction to *The Private Life of Henry Maitland*, p. 1).

MASTERMAN in H.G. Wells, *Kipps* (1905)

'In the middle of the book, he introduced the character of Masterman . . . whose manner of life and tragic death were closely modelled on George Gissing' (N. Mackenzie and J. Mackenzie, 1973, *The Time Traveller: the life of H.G. Wells*, p. 193).

GOODWIN PEAK in George Gissing, *Born in Exile* (1892)

'Peak is myself – one phase of myself' (20 May 1892, reproduced in *The Letters of George Gissing to Eduard Bertz, 1887–1903*, 1961, ed. Arthur C. Young, London: Constable, p. 153).

EDWARD PONDEREVO in H.G. Wells, *Tono-Bungay* (1909)

'Wells, in Tono-Bungay, actually describes, fairly accurately, the last stage of Gissing's illness' (Henry Hick, 1973, *Recollections of George Gissing*, ed. Pierre Coustillas, p. 12). *See also* **Wright**, Whitaker.

MAURICE QUAIN in Morley Roberts, *Maurice Quain* (1897)

'[A]t least once, in a now forgotten book, *Maurice Quain*, Roberts himself drew a portrait of Gissing' (Gillian Tindall, 1974, *The Born Exile: George Gissing*, p. 195).

OSMUND WAYMARK in George Gissing, *The Unclassed* (1884)

'Joseph Anderson . . . wrote a long review of the American edition of *The Unclassed* (1896, New York), in which he said ". . . *The Unclassed* reveals many . . . of the sad and smarting experiences that have been Gissing's own, and there constantly comes through the . . . thought that Waymark . . . and the interesting sad-eyed man . . . in the frontispiece are one and the same" (*Boston Evening Transcript*, 2 July 1896, p. 6)' (*Letters* op. cit., p. 219 n. 559).

GISSING, Margaret (1857–1903) The elder of the two sisters of George Gissing. Like her mother, she was a Unitarian. In 1896 Gissing took his elder son Walter (then four years old) to Wakefield, to be cared for and brought up by Margaret and Ellen Gissing. The sisters opened a small school for young children, which Walter attended, c.1898.

MIRIAM BASKE in George Gissing, *The Emancipated* (1890)

'Madge Gissing thought, probably rightly, that the character was modelled on her' (Gillian Tindall, 1974, *The Born Exile: George Gissing*, p. 208).

GISSING, Marianne Helen ('Nell') (1858?–88) Née Harrison. Thought to be a prostitute, she married George Gissing in 1879. It was a disastrous marriage; she became a hopeless drunk, and by 1883 they had separated. She died in circumstances of the greatest squalor.

MARIAN HILTON in Morley Roberts, *The Private Life of Henry Maitland* (1912)

The identification is made by Morton Bishop in the 1958 edition of *The Private Life of Henry Maitland*, p. 29.

CARRIE MITCHELL in George Gissing, *Workers in the Dawn* (1880)

'Carrie Mitchell, of whom Nell was the prototype' (M.C. Donnelly, 1954, *George Gissing: grave comedian*, Cambridge, Mass., p. 57).

GISSING, Walter Leonard (1891–1916) The elder son of George Gissing, who removed him from his mother, Edith, to the care of his aunts, Ellen and Margaret Gissing; he was brought up by them in Wakefield, Yorkshire. He was killed in the Battle of the Somme.

HUGHIE ROLFE in George Gissing, *In the Year of the Jubilee* (1894) and *The Whirlpool* (1897)

'His portraits of Walter in *In the Year of Jubilee* and *The Whirlpool* are particularly touching' (Gillian Tindall, 1974, *The Born Exile: George Gissing*, p. 251).

GIULIOLO, Giovanni ('Leggero') 'A native of Maddelena, he had served in the Piedmontese navy for seven years and deserted in Monterides in 1839, and later joined the Italian legion there' (John Parris, 1962, *The Lion of Caprera*, p. 109; see Norman Sherry, 1971, *Conrad's Western World*, Cambridge, p. 154).

GIORGIO VIOLA in Joseph Conrad, *Nostromo* (1904)

'... Leggero would appear to be the source for Viola who had also been "wounded in the defence of the Roman Republic"' (ibid., p. 154). *See also* **Clerici, Enrico; Garibaldi**, Giuseppe.

GLADSTONE, William Ewart (1809–98) English statesman. He was born in Liverpool and educated at Eton and Christ Church, Oxford. He was Tory MP for Newark, 1832–45; served in Peel's administration as a Junior Lord of the Treasury, 1834–5; and had responsibility for the Royal Mint, 1841–5. In 1847 he re-entered parliament as MP for the University of Oxford. He was still a Tory at this time, but the Corn Law agitation sparked off a political change-of-heart, and he became a formidable orator railing against social injustice. In 1852, he was made Chancellor of the Exchequer, and after a number of parliamentary upheavals caused by the problems of constitutional reform and the Irish insurrection, he became Liberal Prime Minister in 1868. He lost power in 1874, and concentrated on his literary studies for a couple of years, but he returned to politics as MP for Midlothian, and regained the premiership in 1880 after a landslide Liberal victory. He lost power to Lord Salisbury for a few months in 1886, and was later defeated over the question of Home Rule for Ireland. Although he was returned to office in 1992, his declining health forced him to resign in 1894.

MR FINESPIN in Anthony Trollope, *Can You Forgive Her?* (1864)

'The identification of Finespin with Gladstone has been suggested before; and I have no doubt that the fictional Chancellor of the Exchequer was a deliberate caricature of the real one – the name, of course, reflecting Gladstone's reputation for sophistry' (J.R. Dinwiddy, 1967, 'Who's who in Trollope's political novels', *The Nineteenth Century* 22 (June): 37).

MR GRESHAM in Anthony Trollope, *Phineas Finn* (1869)

'... though in former novels [i.e. previous to *The Prime Minister*] certain well-known political characters such as ... Gladstone, have been taken as models for such fictitious personages as ... Gresham, it has only been as to their political tenets. There is nothing of personal characteristic here' (to Mary Holmes, 15 June 1876, reproduced in *The Letters of Anthony Trollope*, 1951, ed. Bradford Booth, London: Oxford University Press, p. 355).

OSWALD MILLBANK in Benjamin Disraeli, *Coningsby* (1844)

'Oswald Millbank is in part painted from the young Gladstone' (Walter Sichel, 1904, *Disraeli: a study in personality and ideas*, London: Methuen, p. 122 n. 1). 'The resemblance, if any, was purely accidental' (W.F. Moneypenny, 1912, *The Life of Benjamin Disraeli, Earl of Beaconsfield*, Vol. II, p. 202 n. 2). *See also* **Walter**, John.

Atelier GLEYRE, Paris The studio of the painter Charles **Gleyre**, where he taught from 1843 onwards: Gleyre's pupils included Renoir, Monet and Sisley, together with an English contingent including Du Maurier and Edward **Poynter**.

CHEZ CARREL in George Du Maurier, *Trilby* (1894)

'In ... *Trilby* ... George du Maurier described [Gleyre's] atelier, which he called "Chez Carrel"' (Gordon Fleming, 1978, *The Young Whistler, 1834–66*, p. 126).

GLEYRE, Charles (1806–74) Swiss painter. He studied in Italy and travelled in Greece and Egypt. He taught at Delaroche's school in Paris. Monet, Renoir and Sisley were among his pupils.

KAMI in Rudyard Kipling, *The Light that Failed* (1890)

'During the year 1890 [Kipling] was seeing much of his relatives, the Poynters. ... Their father Edward ... had many tales to tell of his younger days in Paris of the eighteen-sixties, when he was the model pupil at Gleyre's ... studio. While Poynter practised line ... Monet, at the other end of the room ... applied himself to pure colours. Gleyre (whom Kipling calls "Kami") ... merely said "Continuez, mes enfants"' (C.E. Carrington, 1970, 'The Light that Failed: a problem', in R.E. Harbord (ed.), *The Readers' Guide to Rudyard Kipling's Work*, Sect. V, London: Kipling Society, p. 2240). *See also* Atelier **Gleyre**.

GLOVER, James ('Jimmy') (1861–1931) Conductor, composer and music critic. Born in Dublin, he was the grandson of J.W. Glover, the editor of Moore's *Irish Melodies*. He received a musical education in France, and was a conductor at Drury Lane, London, from 1897 to 1920.

MONTGOMERY in George Moore, *A Mummer's Wife* (1885)

'Jimmy Glover, a fat man, formerly chief musical conductor at Drury Lane . . . introduced himself to me at the Savoy last night, saying that he had given to George Moore . . . the details and the chief facts . . . for the opening chapter (Potteries) . . . of *A Mummer's Wife*. . . . Glover said he was the original of Montgomery in the novel' (Arnold Bennett in his Journal, 10 March 1930, reproduced in Reginald Pound, 1952, *Arnold Bennett: a biography*, London: Heinemann, p. 67).

GLYN, Elinor (1864–1943) Writer. Neé Sutherland, she married Clayton Glyn in 1892, and they had two daughters. By 1908 Clayton had lost his fortune and Elinor had to support the family by writing: her greatest success was *Three Weeks* (1907). In 1908 she met Lord **Curzon**, for whom she developed a passion, with the attachment lasting until 11 December 1916, when she read of his engagement to Mrs Alfred Duggan in *The Times*. (For more information about her involvement with Lord Curzon, *see* **Montacute House**). Her husband died in 1915, and she spent a great part of the First World War in France. In 1920 she went to Hollywood, where she supervised the filming of her novels and wrote the novel *It*, which, with Clara Bow as the star, became her most famous film.

HALCYONE LA SARTHE in Elinor Glyn, *Halcyone* (1912)

'Halcyone herself is, of course, yet another self-portrait of the authoress . . . idealised almost to the point of incredibility' (Anthony Glyn, 1955, *Elinor Glyn: a biography*, London: Hutchinson, p. 204).

GLYNN, Henry (d. 1859) He first met Thackeray on 9 August 1844 at breakfast with Eliott Warburton: 'a very pleasant Mr Glyn with stories about the war in Spain' (Diary, reproduced in *The Letters and Private Papers of W.M. Thackeray*, 1945, ed. Gordon N. Ray, Vol. II, London: Oxford University Press, p. 148). He went to New York *c*.1854, and died there; Thackeray offered to pay half the funeral expenses.

EDWARD STRONG in W.M. Thackeray, *The History of Pendennis* (1848–50)

'A friend of mine is coming to NY, to whom I shall give a letter. He is a queer fellow, the original of the Chevalier Strong in *Pendennis*' (Thackeray to Elizabeth Strong, 18 July 1854, ibid., Vol. III, p. 380). 'Mine I think was the last house he was in in London, and his almost the last face I saw as I left New York [in 1856] . . . a character something like his I put into one of my stories. Of course he recognized it; and laughed and told me he thought the captain of my story was a very fine fellow' (Thackeray to John H. Bewley of New York, 31 October 1859, ibid., n. 72).

GOAD, Horace B. (d. 1896) He was the son of Major S.B. Goad, one of the largest property owners in Simla, owning thirty-three properties in 1870. He entered the police, being known as the smartest officer in the North West

Province, and was in the service of Simla Municipality from 1877 to 1897. He had an extraordinary knowledge of the native language and customs, and a genius for disguising himself. He committed suicide.

STRICKLAND in Rudyard Kipling, *Plain Tales from the Hills* (1888)

'Horace . . . became "Strickland" in *Plain Tales from the Hills*' (A. Mason, 1963, 'Kipling's association with India', in R.E. Harbord (ed.), *The Readers' Guide to Rudyard Kipling's Work*, Sect. II, London: Kipling Society, p. 660). *See also* **Christie**, Mr.

GODDARD, Paulette (b. 1915) Hollywood film actress. She was married four times: first, to Edgar James; to Charlie Chaplin in 1936; to Burgess Meredith in 1944; and to Erich Maria Remarque (d. 1971) in 1958. In 1936 she starred in Charlie Chaplin's film *Modern Times*.

VIRGINIA MAUNCIPLE in Aldous Huxley, *After Many a Summer* (1939)

'Aldous [while in California] had developed a little sneaker for Paulette which is rather given away by the heroine of *After Many a Summer Dies the Swan*. Her physical description fits Paulette to a T; she even wears the white sharkskin tennis garments affected by Mrs Chaplin' (Anita Loos, 1979, *Kiss Hollywood Goodbye*, Harmondsworth: Penguin, p. 154). An implausible identification. *See also* **Davis**, Marion.

GODINTON, Kent Near Ashford. (See John Newman, 1969, *West Kent and the Weald*, Harmondsworth: Penguin, pp. 283 ff.).

OKEHURST in Vernon Lee, 'Oke of Okehurst' (1890)

'In . . . 1885 [Vernon Lee] . . . had stayed with the Alfred Austins at Swinford Old Manor, near Ashford. . . . The Austins lived in the dower house on the Goddington [sic] estate; and it was Goddington . . . which furnished Vernon Lee with the background for . . . *Oke of Okehurst*' (Peter Gunn, 1964, *Vernon Lee, 1856–1935*, London: Oxford University Press, p. 124).

GODMERSHAM PARK, Kent Situated in the Stour Valley, it was built in 1732 for Thomas Brodnax, afterwards (on inheriting a fortune) Knight. It became the home of Jane Austen's brother, Edward Austen Knight. For a photograph of the hall, see Nikolaus Pevsner, *North-East and East Kent* (*Buildings of England* series), Harmondsworth: Penguin, Pl. 85. It was bought in 1936 and restored by Mr and Mrs Robert Tritton, and sold in 1983 when Mrs Tritton died.

MANSFIELD PARK in Jane Austen, *Mansfield Park* (1814)

'The house was probably the model for Mansfield Park' (Geraldine Norman, 1983, *The Times* (13 April): 12). *See also* **Cottesbrooke Hall**.

GODREVY LIGHTHOUSE, Cornwall Situated in St Ives Bay.

THE LIGHTHOUSE in Virginia Woolf, *To the Lighthouse* (1927)

'We had a superb drive over the moor to Zennor . . . to St Ives; where I saw my Lighthouse' (to V. Sackville-West, 8? May 1930, reproduced in *The Letters of*

Virginia Woolf, 1978, ed. Nigel Nicolson, Vol. IV, London: Hogarth Press, p. 165). 'Godrevy Lighthouse . . . the model for the one in *To the Lighthouse*' (ibid., n. 4).

GODWIN, William (1756–1836) Political philosopher and novelist. He was the author of *Political Justice* (1793), *Caleb Williams* (1794), and others. In 1797 he married Mary **Wollstonecraft**, and their daughter was Mary **Shelley**; in 1801 he married Mrs Mary Jane Clairmont, who was the mother of Claire **Clairmont**.

ALPHONSE FRANKENSTEIN in Mary Wollstonecraft Shelley, *Frankenstein; or The Modern Prometheus* (1818)

'In the biographical . . . ancestry of this ideal father William Godwin undoubtedly had a share' (Christopher Small, 1972, *Ariel Like a Harpy: Shelley, Mary and Frankenstein*, p. 105). *See also* **Lind**, James.

FREDERIC GLENMURRAY in Mrs Amelia Opie, *Adeline Mowbray; or The Mother and Daughter* (1804)

'. . . a travesty of the story of Godwin and Mary, but there is no doubt that it used their experience and held them up to ridicule' (Claire Tomalin, 1977, *The Life and Death of Mary Wollstonecraft*, Harmondsworth: Penguin, p. 92).

GOGARTY, Oliver St John (1878–1957) Surgeon, man of letters, and wit. He practised in Dublin, and then lived in New York from 1939 to 1957. From 1902 to 1904 he was an inseparable friend of James Joyce.

IGNATIUS GALLAHER in James Joyce, 'A Little Cloud', *Dubliners* (1914)

'Joyce also associated Gallaher with Gogarty, and wrote to Stanislaus on the occasion of Gogarty's marriage, "Long health to Ignatius Gallaher!"' (Richard Ellmann, 1966, *James Joyce*, London: Oxford Paperbacks, p. 228 n.). *See also* **Gallaher**, Fred.

BUCK MULLIGAN in James Joyce, *Ulysses* (1922)

'[In 1904] Synge drove with Quinn to AE's house in Rathgar, where Quinn met Joyce's future Buck Mulligan, Oliver St John Gogarty, "a good looking well dressed young fellow"' (B.L. Reid, 1969, *The Man from New York: John Quinn and his friends*, New York, p. 30).

THE GOLDEN BOUGH 1890 ff. Sir James Frazer's great work on social anthropology.

THE SILVER APPLE in Shane Leslie, *The Cantab* (1926)

Identified in a key in the hand of Dr Ivor Ramsay, a Kingsman of the year 1920, and later Dean, laid in a copy of *The Cantab*.

GOLDMAN, Emma (1869–1940) Born in Russia, she moved to the USA in 1886, and from 1889 to 1906 was a close friend of Johann **Most** and became identified with the anarchist party. She was sentenced to a year's imprisonment in 1893, and was sentenced to a further two years in 1917. In 1919 she went to Russia, but she was deeply disillusioned by the USSR and returned to the USA. She met Theodore Dreiser in Paris in 1926.

ERNITA BARTRAM in Theodore Dreiser, 'Ernita', *A Gallery of Women* (1929)

'After he dined with Emma in 1926 . . . he used her story – or at least the spirit of it – in the portrait of Ernita' (Richard Lehan, 1974, *Theodore Dreiser: his world and his novels*, Carbondale, Ill.: Arcturis Books, p. 172).

SOPHIA GOLDSTEIN in I.K. Friedman, *By Bread Alone* (1901)

'[In the Homestead strike] the Anarchist virago . . . who had formerly escaped from St Petersburg to New York and had . . . come to Chicago at the time of the Haymarket riot . . . villainously persuades a young Pole to attempt the assassination of Marvin' (W.B. Rideout, 1956, *The Radical Novel in the United States, 1900–1954*, Cambridge, Mass., p. 16). This is clearly a portrait of Emma Goldman, including her part in Alexander Berkman's attempted assassination of H.C. Frick; at the time Berkman (who was indeed a Pole) was 22 years of age.

GOLDSMID, Colonel Albert (1846–1904) Born in Poona, he was the son of H.E. Goldsmid, a distinguished Bombay civilian. He was married in 1879, and at one time associated with Theodore Herzl in the movement for achieving a Jewish National home. His entry in *Who's Who* includes the sentence: 'present at the battle of Paardeberg (horse killed)'.

DANIEL DERONDA in George Eliot, *Daniel Deronda* (1876)

'Herzl's diary for 1895 recounts a conversation in which Colonel Albert Goldsmid told him, "I am Deronda." Goldsmid was born a Christian in India, the son of baptized Jews; but, when a lieutenant in the Bengal Fusiliers, he decided "to return to my ancestral stock" and went over to Judaism. ". . . My wife was also a Christian of Jewish origin [she was a daughter of F. Hendriks]. I eloped with her, contracted first a free marriage in Scotland; then she had to turn Jewess, and we were married in synagogue." . . . His daughter, the Dowager Baroness Swaythling, wrote in 1949 that her father's connection with Deronda "was just a romance and has no real foundation in fact"' (Gordon S. Haight, 1968, *George Eliot*, Oxford, pp. 488–9). It is clear from the date of Colonel Goldsmid's marriage that his story cannot have any connection with the origins of Daniel Deronda. *See also* **Bond**, Edward; **Gurney**, Edmund; **Lewes**, G.H.; **Louis**, Alfred Hyman.

GOLDSMITH, Oliver (1728–74) Irish poet, novelist, dramatist and man of letters. He was born in Pallasmore, County Longford, Ireland. He unsuccessfully studied for the Church. In 1752 he went to study medicine at Edinburgh, but left without a degree. He spent some time travelling in Europe, returning to England in 1756. He did various odd jobs until he published his first work in 1759. He wrote for various periodicals including Smollett's *British Magazine*. *The Vicar of Wakefield*, the novel that established his reputation, was published in 1766.

CHARLES MELL in Charles Dickens, *David Copperfield* (1849–50)

'Oliver Goldsmith, when a young man in London, was employed temporarily in the school of Mr Milnes in Peckham. . . . Goldsmith's chief hobby was flute-playing and he became popular with the boys by telling them stories . . . and performing on the flute. He was, however, wilfully deficient in dignity, and on one particular occasion he had cause to regret this failing. After playing a tune he waxed enthusiastic over the art of music, describing it as . . . a valuable accomplishment for a gentleman; whereupon one of the boys . . . enquired whether he regarded himself as a gentleman. . . . Forster's "Life of Goldsmith", dedicated to . . . Dickens was published in 1848, and it is a reasonable assumption that it was read by the novelist. In the spring of 1849 Dickens began to write *David Copperfield*, and Mr Mell, the flute-playing assistant of Mr Creakle . . . appears early in the tale. We can almost perceive the mental process by which Dickens draws the character of Mr Mell from the Goldsmith incident' (E. Basil Lupton, 1920, 'Oliver Goldsmith as the prototype of Mr Mell', *The Dickensian* 16 (July): 133). *See also* **Taylor,** Mr.

GOMME, James For many years he was a manservant to Anthony Powell's parents.

ALBERT in Anthony Powell, *A Dance to the Music of Time* (1951–76)

'James was our cook . . . and some of his remarks as Albert are authentic' (Anthony Powell, 1976, *To Keep the Ball Rolling: the memoirs of Anthony Powell*, Vol. I: *The Infants of Spring*, London: Heinemann, p. 54).

GOOD, Sarah One of those found guilty at the Salem witchcraft trials and executed in 1692.

MATHEW MAULE in Nathaniel Hawthorne, *The House of the Seven Gables* (1851)

See under **Noyes,** Nicholas.

GOODMAN, Edwin (1876–1953) He was the founder (1901) and proprietor (1903) of the New York department store, Bergdorf-Goodman.

MR ROSEN in Thomas Wolfe, *The Web and the Rock* (1939)

'There can be little doubt that Edwin Goodman served as the principal prototype for "Mr Rosen"' (P. Reeves, 1965, 'Thomas Wolfe: notes on three characters', *Modern Fiction Studies* 11 (3): 278).

GORDON, Alexander (1692?–1754?) Antiquary. Educated at the University of Aberdeen, he later studied music in Italy and became known as 'Singing Sandie'. He was the author of the 'Hinerarium Septentionale' (1726) and was acquainted with Sir John Clerk of Penicuik. In 1736 he was Secretary to the Society of Antiquaries, and in 1741 he went to South Carolina as Secretary to the Governor; he died there.

JONATHAN OLDBUCK in Sir Walter Scott, *The Antiquary* (1816)

'Another person who added a few points to Oldbuck was "Sandy Gordon", author of . . . the very folio which Monkbarns carried in the dilatory coach to Queens ferry' (Andrew Lang, 1900, Introd. to *The Antiquary* (Border edn), p. xxix; the points of resemblance are fully set out on pp. xxix–xxx). *See also* **Clerk of Eldin,** John; **Constable,** George, the Elder; **Ramsay of Ochtertyre,** John.

GORDON, Jean (*c*.1670–*c*.1745) She was a gypsy of Kirk-Yetholm in the Cheviots. She married in her teens and had many sons, all of whom were said to have been hanged. Scott once encountered her granddaughter, Madge Gordon, who was said to resemble her exactly, and never forgot her: 'My memory is haunted by a solemn resemblance of a woman of more than female height, dressed in a long red cloak.' Jean Gordon died as the result of a ducking.

MEG MERRILIES in Sir Walter Scott, *Guy Mannering* (1815)

'I am like poor Jean Gordon, the prototype of Meg Merrilees who was ducked to death at Carlisle for being a Jacobite, and till she was smothered outright, cried out every time she got her head above water, *Charlie yet'* (to J.W. Croker, 19 March 1826, *The Letters of Sir Walter Scott*, 1935, ed. H.J.C. Grierson, Vol. IX, London: Constable, p. 474). 'The individual gypsy upon whom the character of Meg Merrilies was founded was well known about the middle of the last century by the name of Jean Gordon' (Introd. to *Guy Mannering*, 1901 (Border edn), p. xxxix). (Scott used both possible spellings of Merrilies.) *See also* **Euston**, Margaret.

GORDON, Margaret (1798–1878) Born in Charlottetown, Prince Edward Island, the daughter of an army surgeon who died in 1803, she was adopted by her aunt, Mrs Usher, and was brought up in Kirkaldy, Fife; in 1806, her mother married another army surgeon stationed in Halifax. She met Thomas Carlyle through Edward **Irving** when both men were teaching at Kirkaldy Grammar School. Shortly after they met, he left the area, but Carlyle had fallen in love with her and they corresponded. In 1820, she went to London, and in 1824 she married Alexander Bannerman, a banker who became governor of Prince Edward Island in 1851 and of the Bahamas in 1854.

BLUMINE in Thomas Carlyle, *Sartor Resartus* (1833–4)

'From ... *Sartor* may be quoted many passages which apply in detail to Margaret Gordon' (R.C. Archibald, 1910, *Carlyle's First Love*, p. 89). R.C. Archibald (op. cit.) sets out most forcibly the arguments for accepting Margaret Gordon as the original of Blumine. These arguments had previously been considered and demolished by Alexander Carlyle in *The Love Letters of Thomas Carlyle and Jane Welsh Carlyle*, 1909, ed. Alexander Carlyle, Vol. II, London and New York: John Lane, pp. 387–400). *See also* **Carlyle**, Jane Welsh; **Kirkpatrick**, Catherine Aurora.

GORDON-LENNOX, Cosmo (1869–1921) Actor, known as Charles Stuart. He was the grandson of the 5th Duke of Richmond, and he wrote plays and adapted from the French. In 1898 he married the actress Marie Tempest.

HARRY DEFREYNE in Ada Leverson, *The Limit* (1911)

'It was from him that the character of Henry Defreyne ... was derived' (Violet Wyndham, 1963, *The Sphinx and Her Circle: a biographical sketch of Ada Leverson, 1862–1933*, London: Deutsch, p. 74).

GORE, Cecilia *See* **Thynne**, Cecilia Anne.

GORTCHAKOFF, Prince Alexander Mikhailovich (1798–1883) Russian diplomat. Minister of Foreign Affairs, at one time he was the lover of Frances Anne, Marchioness of **Londonderry**. He first met Disraeli in Berlin in 1878, telling him that he had only come to the Conference to make his acquaintance, because Lady Londonderry had always mentioned him in her letters; he said that she had thought he would be prime minister, and, if so, hoped the two would be friends.

PRINCE XTMNPQRTOSKLW in Benjamin Disraeli, *Vivian Grey* (1826–7)

Identified as Prince G—t—f in a key given in *The Star Chamber* (24 May 1826): 114; reprinted in *Vivian Grey*, 1904 (centenary edn), ed. Lucien Wolf, Vol. II, London: Alexander Moring, pp. 361–2. The full name appeared in a reprint of the key published in *Notes and Queries* 3 (29 April 1893). Lucien Wolf concludes that Disraeli was not responsible for the key.

GOSFORD CASTLE, County Armagh, Ireland 'Said to be the first mock-Norman castle built in the British Isles' (A. Powell, 1980, *Faces in My Time*, p. 105). Powell was stationed there in 1940 while serving in the Welch Regiment.

CASTLE MALLOCK in Anthony Powell, *The Valley of Bones* (1964)

'The place figures as Castle Mallock in *The Valley of Bones*' (ibid.).

GOSSE, Edmund (1849–1928) Man of letters. He was the son of the zoologist Philip Gosse and from 1865 to 1875 worked in the catalogue section of the British Museum. In 1875 he was a translator for the Board of Trade, and from 1904 to 1914 he was Librarian to the House of Lords. He contributed a weekly article to the *Sunday Times* from 1918 to 1928, and was also the author of *Father and Son* and others. He introduced Ibsen, the Norwegian dramatist, to the British public.

PROFESSOR JAMES CRISCROSS in Osbert Sitwell, 'Triple Fugue' (1924)

'Society, as Osbert Sitwell would reiterate . . . in "Triple Fugue" (with Gosse appearing as Professor Criscross), was becoming "exceptionally artistic"' (Ann Thwaite, 1984, *Edmund Gosse*, p. 407).

RICHARD GILES in Maurice Baring, 'A Luncheon Party', *Half a Minute's Silence and Other Stories* (1925)

'Most of the guests [at "The Luncheon Party"] were people well known in London . . . Mr Gosse . . . and others – all, of course, furnished with pseudonyms and so presented that though they were easy to identify no one can have been hurt' (Ethel Smyth, 1938, *Maurice Baring*, London and Toronto: Heinemann, p. 136). Gosse is easily recognizable as Giles.

NICHOLAS GREENE in Virginia Woolf, *Orlando* (1928)

'Nicholas Greene you will recognise as Gosse' (Vita Sackville-West to Harold Nicolson, 11 October 1928, reproduced in Victoria Glendinning, 1983, *Vita: the life of V. Sackville West*, p. 202).

ALLGOOD NEWTON in W. Somerset Maugham, *Cakes and Ale* (1930)

'Allgood Newton is Maugham's caricature of the critic and man of letters Sir Edmund Gosse' (R.L. Calder, 1972, *W. Somerset Maugham and the Quest for Freedom*, London: Heinemann, p. 183).

GOULD, Gerald (1885–1936) Literary critic. For many years he was a reader for the publishing firm of Victor Gollancz and Chief Novel Reviewer for the *Observer*.

GEOFFREY BELL in Wyndham Lewis, *The Roaring Queen* (1973)

'There is . . . the reference . . . to "Geoffrey Bell . . . reader for *Hector Gollywog and Ogpu*, who in his capacity of novel critic of the *Sunday Messenger* writes the most glowing accounts of the books that reach him . . . from the firm to which he belongs, as reader. . . ." This could only refer to . . . Gerald Gould' (Walter Allen, Introd. to *The Roaring Queen*, 1973, p. 7).

GOW, John Son of William Gow who settled in Stromness in 1716, he went to sea and took to piracy, seizing command of the ship in which he was serving as Second Mate in 1724. He was captured and executed in London in 1725. *A Life of Gow* (1724) is attributed to Defoe.

CAPTAIN CLEMENT CLEVELAND in Sir Walter Scott, *The Pirate* (1821)

'It was from Bessie Hillie, the Stromness sibyl, that Scott heard the story of John Gow the pirate, on whose . . . career he founded his Captain Cleveland' (W.S. Crockett, 1912, *The Scott Originals: an account of notables and worthies, the originals of characters in the Waverley novels*, Edinburgh and London: T.N. Foulis, p. 303).

GRAD, Avice Veronica (1885–*c*.1957) Née Leslie Jones. In 1906 she was living at the **Arachne Club** and studying at the Royal Academy of Dramatic Art (RADA). She met Dorothy Richardson, and in 1907 was arrested after taking part in the Easter Sunday march of the suffragettes; she was imprisoned in Holloway, London. In 1908 she married Benjamin **Grad**, but was later divorced. She ran a hostel for prostitutes in Lambeth, London, and during the Second World War and after she ran a hostel in Streatham for homeless families. She remained a close friend of Dorothy Richardson until the novelist's death.

AMABEL SHATOV in Dorothy Richardson, *Pilgrimage* (1915–67)

'Amabel . . . is very reminiscent of Veronica Grad. Miriam even calls [her] by the same pet name "Babinka" that Dorothy used for Veronica' (John Rosenberg, 1873, *Dorothy Richardson*, London, p. 138).

GRAD, Benjamin (before 1886–after 1948) Son of a Jewish lawyer in Russia, he met Dorothy Richardson in 1896 when they lived at the same house in Endsleigh Street, London. She declined his proposals and, in 1907, he married Veronica Leslie Jones (**Grad**, above), but they separated *c*.1918 and were divorced. By 1916 he was an active Zionist. In 1942 he was interned in France, but he returned to Britain in 1946.

MICHAEL SHATOV in Dorothy Richardson, *Pilgrimage* (1915–67)

'A character based on Benjamin Grad, as letters confirm' (John Rosenberg, 1973, *Dorothy Richardson*, p. 111).

GRAHAM, Alastair (b. 1904) Son of Jessie **Graham**, he was educated at Wellington College and at Brasenose College, Oxford, and in 1924 attended the Bartlett School of Architecture at London University. He was appointed honorary attaché at Athens in 1928, but in 1929 he was transferred to Cairo and from 1933 onwards he lived as a recluse on the Welsh coast. He was Evelyn Waugh's closest friend between 1924 and 1929; it was through him and his uncle (Willie Low) that Waugh was introduced to the **Cavendish Hotel**. In September 1924 he became a Roman Catholic, and during the Second World War he was attached to the US Navy.

SEBASTIAN FLYTE in Evelyn Waugh, *Brideshead Revisited* (1945)

'A stronger contribution [than that of Hugh Lygon] was made by memories of [Waugh's] Oxford friendship with Alastair Graham. This assertion . . . relies on Waugh's own testimony and is supported by the curious fact that in the manuscript the name Alastair sometimes occurs in the place of Sebastian' (Christopher Sykes, 1975, *Evelyn Waugh*, London: Collins, p. 252). In Waugh's autobiography, *A Little Learning . . . an autobiography* (1964, London: Chapman and Hall), Graham appears under the name of Hamish Lennox. *See also* **Lygon**, Hugh.

GRAHAM, Arthur Smith

CAPTAIN THEOPHANES CLAYFOOT in F.W. Rolfe, *Nicholas Crabbe* (1958)

Identified by Cecil Woolf in his introduction to *Nicholas Crabbe*, 1958, pp. 5–7.

GRAHAM, Edward Kidder (1876–1918) He was Professor of English at the University of North Carolina from 1908 to 1914, Acting President from 1913 to 1914, and President from 1914 to 1918. Thomas Wolfe was a freshman at the University of North Carolina during this latter period.

HUNTER GRISWOLD MCCOY in Thomas Wolfe, *The Web and the Rock* (1939)

'Twenty years later Wolfe would paint an uncomplimentary picture of Graham as Hunter-Griswold McCoy' (Andrew Turnbull, 1968, *Thomas Wolfe: a biography*, London: Bodley Head, p. 327 n. 4).

GRAHAM, Jessie (1862?–1934) Youngest daughter of Andrew Low of Savannah, Georgia, she was also the granddaughter of W.H. Stiles, the American *Charge d'affaires* in Vienna in 1848. Her brother Willie inherited £750,000 and settled in England, becoming the intimate friend of Edward VII, whom he entertained at his country house in Warwickshire. He was a great favourite with Mrs Rosa **Lewis**, and for many years maintained rooms at the **Cavendish Hotel**.

LADY CIRCUMFERENCE in Evelyn Waugh, *Decline and Fall* (1928)

'[Alastair Graham's] mother was high-tempered, possessive, jolly and erratic. (She later was the model for "Lady Circumference" in my first novel)' (Evelyn Waugh, 1964, *A Little Learning . . . an autobiography*, London: Chapman and Hall, p. 192). 'The picture Waugh drew of Lady Circumference, in a felt hat, at the school sports in *Decline and Fall* is "quite a good likeness", according to Alastair Graham' (*The Diaries of Evelyn Waugh*, 1976, ed. Michael Davie, London: Weidenfeld & Nicolson, p. 799, index s.v. Graham, Jessie).

GRAHAM, Sheilah (1904–88) Journalist and author (Lily Sheil). Brought up in a London orphanage, she emigrated to New York in 1933 and in 1935 moved

to California. She met Scott Fitzgerald in 1937 and cared for him to the end of his life.

KATHLEEN in F. Scott Fitzgerald, *The Last Tycoon* (1941)

'Kathleen is . . . Sheilah, barely disguised; he left the manuscript to her, but she gave it to Scottie' (David Shipman, 1988, 'Sheilah Graham' (obituary), *The Independent* (21 November): 13).

GRAHAME, Alistair (1900–20) Known as 'Mouse', he was the only child of Kenneth Grahame and suffered from congenital cataract. He was educated at Rugby (where he stayed for only one term), Eton, and Christ Church, Oxford. He was run over and killed by a train, in circumstances suggesting suicide.

MR TOAD in Kenneth Grahame, *The Wind in the Willows* (1908)

'Every evening Mr Grahame told Mouse an unending story dealing with the adventures of the little animals whom they met in their river journeys . . . Mouse's own tendency to exult in his exploits was gently satirized in Mr Toad' (Miss Constance Smedley, quoted in Peter Green, 1959, *Kenneth Grahame, 1859–1932*, p. 269).

GRAHAME, Kenneth (1859–1932) Scottish children's writer. He was born in Edinburgh and educated at St Edward's School in Oxford. In 1876 he entered the Bank of England as a clerk. He became its secretary in 1898 and retired in 1903 on health grounds. His first published work, *Pagan Papers* (1893), demonstrated his deft sympathy with the child mind which was to culminate in his celebrated work, *The Wind in the Willows*. He married in 1899, and had a son, Alastair (**Grahame**, above).

KENNETH O'LYMPOS in F.W. Rolfe, *Nicholas Crabbe* (1958)

Identified by Cecil Woolf in his introduction to *Nicholas Crabbe*, 1958, pp. 5–7.

GRAHAME, Sophie She was resident on Capri and died of pneumonia, which she contracted while attending the funeral of Colonel Bryan **Palmes**.

EFFIE MACADAM in Compton Mackenzie, *Vestal Fire* (1927)

'The "Effie" of [*Vestal Fire*]' (Norman Douglas, 1933, *Looking Back*, p. 99).

GRAMONT, Ida, Duchesse de (b. 1802) She was the sister of Count d'Orsay, 'and like him in petticoats' (Disraeli to his sister, 14 October 1842).

DUCHESSE DE G——T in Benjamin Disraeli, *Coningsby* (1844)

Identified in a key in *Notes and Queries* (8th series) 3 (13 May 1893): 363. *See also under* **Bright**, John.

GRANT, Albert (1830–99) Known as Baron Grant. Born in Gottheimer, he was MP for Kidderminster from 1865 to 1868 and from 1874 to 1880. In 1868, Victor Emmanuel conferred on him the title of Baron Grant. He bought Leicester Square in London, converted it into a public garden and, in 1874, handed it over to the metropolitan Board of Works. He is said to have been the pioneer of company promotions: 'by collecting lists of clergymen, widows and the like he discovered a large body of investors who were anxious for money, incautious and inexperienced' (G.M. Young, 1977, *Portrait of an Age*, annot. edn by George Kitson Clarke, p. 367 n. 3, signed GKC). He thus raised £24,000,000, of which £20,000,000 was lost. He died in comparative poverty, enmeshed in a series of bankruptcy actions.

AUGUSTUS MELMOTTE in Anthony Trollope, *The Way We Live Now* (1875)

'In 1873 Trollope started to write *The Way We Live Now*, instigated, as he said in his *Autobiography*, "by what I conceived to be the commercial profligacy of the age." The career of his character Melmotte was in many ways not unlike that of Baron Grant' (ibid.). *See also* **Hudson**, George.

GRANT, Daniel and William (1780?–1855) and (1769?–1842) Along with two other brothers, John and Charles, they set up a calico printing business near Bury, *c*.1800. They moved to Manchester and in 1806 bought the printworks belonging to Sir Robert Peel, at Ramsbottom. The firm, William Grant and Brothers, was well known for its care for its employees. Dickens met Daniel and William in Manchester at a dinner given by Harrison Ainsworth in November 1838; in the preface to the first edition of *Nicholas Nickleby*, he unwarily announced that the Brothers Cheeryble still lived, still dispensing their unbounded charity, with the result that he received a flood of begging letters to be forwarded to them.

CHEERYBLE BROTHERS in Charles Dickens, *Nicholas Nickleby* (1838–9)

'One of the noble hearts who sat for the Cheeryble Brothers is dead. . . . I am told that it appears from a memorandum found among [his] papers, that in his life time he gave away in charity £600,000 . . . !' (to C.C. Felton, 29 April 1842, reproduced in *Letters of Charles Dickens*, 1974, Vol. III, ed. Madeline House, Graham Storey and Kathleen Tillotson, Oxford: Oxford University Press, p. 216). W.H. Elliott . . . argues that [Dickens] united in Brother Charles the appearance of . . . William with the buoyant speech of . . . Daniel and made Brother Ned speak in the tranquil and self-controlled manner of William' (ibid., n. 2).

GRANT, Duncan (1885–1978) Painter. He was the first cousin of Lytton **Strachey** and was a member of the Bloomsbury group; he lived with Vanessa **Bell** from 1914 onwards.

DUNCAN FORBES in D.H. Lawrence, *Lady Chatterley's Lover* (1928)

'It seems certain that a memory of [Lawrence's] visit to Duncan [Grant's] studio [in 1915] inspired the passage at the end of Chapter XVIII of *Lady Chatterley's Lover*. Mellors . . . is taken to the studio of Duncan Forbes, "a dark-skinned taciturn Hamlet of a fellow with straight black hair and a weird Celtic conceit of himself"' (David Garnett, 1955, *The Golden Echo*, Vol. II: *Flowers of the Forest*, London: Chatto & Windus, p. 37).

MAURICE RHODES in Francis King, *A Domestic Animal* (1970)

The identification is based upon private information.

GRANT, Revd Joseph Brett (1821?–79) Headmaster of the Grammar School at Haworth, Yorkshire, for a short time he acted as Curate to Mr Brontë, succeeding the Revd J.W. **Smith**. In 1845 he was appointed Incumbent and afterwards Vicar of Oxenhope (near Keighley), where he remained until his death.

JOSEPH DONNE in Charlotte Brontë, *Shirley* (1849)

'He was the prototype of "Joseph Donne"' (T.J. Wise and J.A Symington (eds), 1932, *The Brontës: their lives, friendships and correspondence*, Vol. II, p. 17). 'The very curates, poor fellows! show no resentment: each . . . finds solace for his own wounds in crowing over his brethren. Mr Donne was, at first, a little disturbed; for a week or two he was in disquietude, but he is now soothed down; only yesterday I had the pleasure of making him a comfortable cup of tea, and seeing him sip it with revived complacency. It is a curious fact that, since he read "Shirley", he has come to the house oftener than ever, and been remarkably meek, and assiduous to please. . . . I quite expected to have one good scene at least with him; but as yet nothing of the sort has occurred' (Charlotte Brontë to W.S. Williams, 19 March 1850, ibid., Vol. III, p. 90).

GRANTLEY, Katherine Buckner Norton, Lady (1848?–97) She was the daughter of Commodore W.H. McVickar, of New York. On 5 November 1879 she married Richard Brinsley Norton, 5th Baron Grantley; the decree of her divorce from Major Charles Grantley Campbell Norton had only been made absolute the previous day. The divorce case had been something of a sensation and was reported in *The Times* (27 February 1879).

MRS MEDWIN in Henry James, 'Mrs Medwin' (1903)

'On 7 May 1898 James [in his *Notebooks*] records a *donnée* for a story: "The Miss Balch and Lady G. incident." . . . We can be fairly confident in identifying Lady G. (the original, in a situational sense, of Mrs Medwin), since she is specified as 'Lady G. . .ly [on p. 295 of the *Notebooks*, 1947, New York]. Looking through *Burke's Peerage* the most likely candidate is Lady Grantley' (Bernard Richards, 1980, 'The sources of Henry James's "Mrs Medwin", *Notes and Queries* (NS) 27 (3): 228).

GRANVILLE, Harriet Leveson-Gower, Lady (1785–1862) Daughter of the 5th Duke of **Devonshire** and his wife Georgiana, and the sister of Lady **Morpeth**. In 1809 she married Granville Leveson-Gower, afterwards the 1st Earl Granville, who had for many years been the lover of her aunt, Lady **Bessborough**.

SOPHIA SEYMOUR in Lady Caroline Lamb, *Glenarvon* (1816)

Identified in a key found among the papers of John Whishaw, a member of the Holland House circle, printed in *The 'Pope' of Holland House: selections from the correspondence of John Whishaw and his friends, 1813–1840*, 1906, ed. Lady Seymour, p. 151. 'Sophia [is] Lady Granville, who had 6 years ago a passion for working fine embroidery, and she marks most atrociously her marriage with Lord Granville' (Lady Holland to Mrs Creevey, 21 May 1816, quoted in *The Creevey Papers*, 1970, ed. John Gore, p. 162). In fact Sophia Seymour does not marry in the novel; it is Frances Seymour who does, and her bridegroom, Lord Trelawney, is clearly based on Lord Morpeth. Sophia Seymour is obviously an ill-natured portrait of Lady Granville as a girl.

GRANVILLE SQUARE, London Located in Clerkenwell.

RICEYMAN SQUARE in Arnold Bennett, *Riceyman Steps* (1923)

'Transporting [T. James's bookshop] bodily to [London], he inserted it into . . . Granville Square, where so far as the residents could remember there had never been a bookshop' (Louis Tillier, 1969, *Studies in the Sources of Arnold Bennett's Novels*, Paris, p. 144).

GRATZ, Rebecca (1781–1869) Daughter of Michael Gratz, a Jewish merchant in Philadelphia, she became a close friend of Mathilda Hoffmann of New York, the girl whom Washington Irving loved and who died at the age of 18. In 1817, when Irving visited Scott at Abbotsford, he told Scott the story of Rebecca Gratz: she only loved one of her suitors and he was a Gentile, so she never married, but devoted her life to work among the poor of Philadelphia. Her portrait, by Mabone, shows her as a great beauty.

REBECCA in Sir Walter Scott, *Ivanhoe* (1819)

'One of the first copies [of Ivanhoe] was dispatched to Irving along with a letter in which the question was put "How do you like your Rebecca? Does the Rebecca I have pictured, compare well with the pattern given?"' (W.S. Crockett, 1912, *The Scott Originals: an account of notables and worthies, the originals of characters in the Waverley Novels*, Edinburgh and London: T.N. Foulis, p. 294).

GRAVES, Caroline Elizabeth (*c.*1834–95) Née Courtenay, she was married to George Graves. Wilkie Collins, walking home late one night *c.*1859 through North London with some friends, heard the piercing scream of a 'young and beautiful woman dressed in flowing white robes that shone in the moonlight', who rushed out of a villa and 'seemed to float rather than run' towards them and 'paused . . . in an attitude of supplication and terror'. Collins pursued her, and discovered that she had been kept a prisoner, under hypnotic influence, by a wicked man (see R.L. Woolf, 1971, *Strange Stories*, Boston, p. 20). She became Collins's mistress, but in 1868 she married Joseph Clow. Collins then had four children with Martha Rudd, known as Mrs Dawson; however, Caroline returned to him in the 1870s, and they resumed their ménage until his death. She was later buried with him in his grave.

ANNE CATHERICK in Wilkie Collins, *The Woman in White* (1860)

'The dramatic first appearance of Caroline Graves . . . inspired *The Woman in White*' (ibid., p. 20).

GRAVES, Robert von Ranke (1895–1985) English poet, novelist and critic. He was born in Wimbledon and educated at Charterhouse. Like Siegfried Sassoon, he served with the Royal Welch Fusiliers on the Somme. In 1925, shattered by his experiences during he war, he met Laura Riding with whom he lived and collaborated until 1939. Apart from a year as Professor of English at Cairo University in 1926, he earnt his living by writing. He married his second wife, Beryl Hodge, and settled permanently in Majorca in 1946. He was elected Professor of Poetry at Oxford in 1961.

DAVID CROMLECH in Siegfried Sassoon, *Memoirs of an Infantry Officer* (1930)

'After an encounter at Mametz Wood . . . the battalion is withdrawn to rest . . . behind the line. There is time for George [Sherston] to renew acquaintance with "David Cromlech" (Robert Graves)' (Paul Fussell, 1979, *The Great War and Modern Memory*, p. 97).

GRAY, Cecil (1895–1951) Composer and music critic. In 1917 he was in Cornwall, where he was the neighbour of and became the friend of the Lawrences, whom he met through Philip **Heseltine**. He was a close friend of Heseltine and was eventually his biographer. He had a brief affair with H.D. in 1918, and she bore a daughter, whose father she never acknowledged.

WILFRED RENNELL in John Cournos, *Miranda Masters* (1926)

'In his novel *Miranda Masters* John Cournos . . . presents a Cecil Gray character as an artist who wants Miranda . . . to model for him. . . . "Barely a week had elapsed before Miranda and Wilfred were on their way to his studio cottage among the Welsh hills"' (Janice S. Robinson, 1982, *H.D.: the life and work of an American poet*, Boston, p. 175).

CYRIL SCOTT in D.H. Lawrence, *Aaron's Rod* (1922)

'Cecil Gray is Cyril Scott' (H.T. Moore, 1974, *The Priest of Love: a life of D.H. Lawrence*, rev. edn, London: Heinemann, p. 362; originally published 1955, as *The Intelligent Heart: the story of D.H. Lawrence*, London: Heinemann).

VANE in H.D. (Hilda Doolittle), *Bid Me to Live* (1960)

Identified by Helen McNeil in the introduction to *Bid Me to Live*, 1984, pp. viii–ix and in the same edition by Perdita Schaffner, Afterword, p. 187.

GRAY, John[1] (*c*.1770–1837) Known as 'Daft Jock Gray'. A native of Ettrick, he later moved with his father to Selkirk: 'a half-witted wandering crazy sort of a creature' (*Waverley Anecdotes*, 1841 (new edn), p. 63).

DAVIE GELLATLEY in Sir Walter Scott, *Waverley* (1814)

'Jock Gray is familiarly known through an extent of fifty miles in the shires of Peebles, Selkirk and Roxburgh; and there are collateral evidences from the inhabitants of these parts, of his being supposed to be the original. Jock has been frequently seen residing with his parents, by persons living at the present day, long before the publication of "Waverley". His character and habits were well known, and were at once recognised on the appearance of the novel . . . as almost the precise counterpart of Davie's' (ibid., pp. 63–4). Jock was simply an idiot or innocent, but clearly a particularly amiable one. Although he was not usually got up in the high style of Davie Gellatly, he habitually wore knee-breeches, bright red garters, enormous buttons and the tallest possible hats. Of the two suggested prototypes he certainly seems the more likely; Scott knew him both at Ashestiel and in the early days at Abbotsford. *See also* **Hinves**, David.

GRAY, John[2] (1866–1934) He was for a time employed in the General Post Office and the Foreign Office. He met Oscar Wilde and wrote *Silverpoints*, which was published in 1893 under the supervision of Charles Ricketts. In 1890 he became a Roman Catholic, and subsequently took religious orders and wrote mainly religious verse. He lived in Edinburgh with André Raffalovich.

DORIAN GRAY in Oscar Wilde, *The Picture of Dorian Gray* (1891)

'Once at least [in Edinburgh towards the end of 1914, Firbank] visited Father John Gray . . . who had been the friend of Aubrey Beardsley and reputedly the origin of Dorian Gray' (Miriam J. Benkovitz, 1969, *Ronald Firbank*, New York, p. 131).

GREAT CLACTON, Essex A village on the Essex coast where Robert **Blackie** and many other connections of the Compton-Burnett family lived and owned property.

MILLFIELD in I. Compton-Burnett, *Dolores* (1911)

'Dolores' home in a country village owed something perhaps to . . . Dent . . . and rather more to the topography of Great Clacton. . . . Actual details of life . . . were unmistakeably supplied by the doings of Ivy's own evangelical relations' (Hilary Spurling, 1974, *Ivy When Young: the early life of I. Compton-Burnett, 1884–1919*, London: Gollancz, pp. 167, 168). *See also* **Dent.**

GREAT NAST HYDE, Hertfordshire A house in the village of Nast Hyde, one and three quarter miles south-west of Hatfield. It was an early seventeenth-century brick mansion of two storeys with gables; it also has nineteenth-century additions, but still retains the original hall, the staircase and the parlour (see Nikolaus Pevsner, 1977, *Hertfordshire* (Buildings of England series), Harmondsworth: Penguin, p. 258).

BLEAK HOUSE in Charles Dickens, *Bleak House* (1852–3)

'The house which readily fits in with the description [in the novel] is Great Nast Hyde. . . . The interior . . . exactly fits the description given in the same chapter . . . it only remains for me to add that Great Nast Hyde is known to old inhabitants as "Bleak House". It . . . is the only house in Hertfordshire which answers to Dickens's description of Esther's house' (W.C. Day, 1930, 'The original of "Bleak House"', *The Dickensian* 26 (spring): 121–2). The same article adds that an old gardener remembers that the turret of the house still contained a revolving light in his lifetime; in 1930 it still contained the bell that rang as Esther Summerson approached the house. *See also* **Bleak Hall.**

GREATHAM, Sussex The village where Wilfrid **Meynell** built houses for members of his family; the Lawrences lived there from 21 January to the end of July 1915 in a cottage lent to them by Viola Meynell.

CROCKHAM in D.H. Lawrence, 'England, My England' (1915)

'Lawrence used . . . environment from real life . . . – [including] the Greatham scene – as a basis for his story' (Francis Meynell, 1971, *My Lives*, p. 87). The story first appeared in the *English Review* (1915); the version in the volume of short stories (1922) is a revision made at Taormina in 1921 in which the resemblances to Greatham and the Meynells are much emphasized.

1 GREEK STREET, Soho, London The shell of the house was built in 1746, and fittings were added in the 1750s when Richard Beckford (uncle of the author of *Vathek*) bought it. Since 1862, it has been occupied by a charitable society, St Barnabas-in-Soho. 'The interior is easily the finest in Soho' (Nikolaus Pevsner, 1973, *London*, Vol. II: *South*, rev. Bridget Cherry (*Buildings of England* series), Harmondsworth: Penguin).

DR MANETTE'S HOUSE in Charles Dickens, *A Tale of Two Cities* (1859)

'The house fits [the] description [of Dr Manette's house] exactly' (A.E. Reffold, 1963, 'Dr Manette in Soho: some new notes and suggestions', *The Dickensian* 59 (September): 173). The article sets out at some length the correspondences between 1 Greek Street and Dr Manette's house, as described in the novel. *See also* **Carlisle House.**

GREEN, Henry (Henry Vincent Yorke) (1905–73) English novelist. Educated at Eton and at Oxford, he left the latter at the end of his second year to go into the family business in Birmingham. He started there as a labourer and eventually became the Managing Director and Chairman of the British Chemical Plant Manufacturers' Association. He wrote nine novels, with his last, *Doting*, being published in 1952.

JOHN HAYE in Henry Green, *Blindness* (1926)

The first section of *Blindness* is described as the 'Diary of John Haye, Secretary to the Noat Art Society'. Henry Green was the Secretary of the Eton Society of Arts (see M.-J. Lancaster, 1968, *Brian Howard: portrait of a failure*, London: Anthony Blond, p. 120).

GREEN, Samuel Gosnell (1822–1905) Baptist minister and bibliophile. In 1844 he joined the Baptist ministry, and was President of the Baptist college at Rawdon, near Leeds, from 1863 to 1876. In 1876 he was Editor, in 1881 Editorial Secretary, and in 1899 Historian of the Religious Tract Society. He became President of the Baptist Union in 1895, and in 1899 he assisted Mrs Rylands in forming the John Rylands Library in Manchester.

PHILIP HAWTHORNE in Lily Watson, *The Vicar of Langthwaite* (1893)

'In her novel . . . Lily Watson, S.G. Green's daughter, provided lifelike portraits of . . . Green [who] . . . appears . . . as Philip Hawthorne, gentle and scholarly' (A.C. Underwood, 1947, *A History of the English Baptists*, London: Baptist Union Publication Department, p. 236 n. 1).

GREEN, Thomas Hill (1836–82) He was Whyte Professor of Moral Philosophy at Oxford from 1878 to 1882. He married Charlotte, sister of J.A. **Symonds**, in 1871.

HENRY GREY in Mrs Humphry Ward, *Robert Elsmere* (1888)

'"The parting with the Christian mythology is the rending asunder of bones and marrow" – words which I have put into Grey's mouth – were words of Mr Green's to me' (Mrs Humphry Ward to W.E. Gladstone, 17 April 1888, quoted in Janet Penrose Trevelyan, 1923, *Life of Mrs Humphrey Ward*, London, p. 63).

GREENE, Sir William Graham Cousin of Kathleen Isherwood, Christopher Isherwood's mother.

THE COMMISSIONER in Graham Greene, *It's a Battlefield* (1934)

'My uncle Graham Greene, who had been Secretary to the Admiralty under Mr Churchill during the First World War, and was one of the founders of Naval Intelligence, lent a little of his stiff inhibited bachelor integrity to the character of the Assistant Commissioner. He had no experience of the Far East – that was to be mine nearly 20 years later, a curious foreshadowing' (Introd. to *It's a Battlefield*, 1970 (collected edn), London: Heinemann and Bodley Head. In the first edition of 1934 he is 'The Commissioner'.

GREENLAW, Edwin (1874–1931) From 1913 to 1918 he was Professor of English at the University of North Carolina; from 1918 to 1925 he was Kenan Professor of English; from 1920 to 1925 he was Dean of the Graduate School; and from 1925 to 1931 he was Professor of English at Johns Hopkins University. He taught Thomas Wolfe.

RANDOLPH WARE in Thomas Wolfe, *The Web and the Rock* (1939)

'. . . a character based on Edwin Greenlaw' (Richard S. Kennedy, 1962, *The Window of Memory: the literary career of Thomas Wolfe*, Chapel Hill, NC, p. 55 n. 12).

GREENOUGH, Horatio (1805–52) American sculptor. In 1825 and 1826 he studied in Italy, and between 1828 and 1851 he had a studio in Florence.

ANGELO in Theodore S. Fay, *Norman Leslie: A Tale of the Present Times* (1835)

'[He] seems to be drawn in part from . . . Horatio Greenough, to whom Fay carried a letter of introduction [on his visit to Florence in 1834]' (Nathalia Wright, 1965, *American Novelists in Italy*, Philadelphia, p. 67).

GREENVILLE, South Carolina

BLACKSTONE in Thomas Wolfe, *Of Time and the River* (1935)

'. . . the . . . name Wolfe gives to Greenville' (Floyd C. Watkins, 1957, *Thomas Wolfe's Characters*, Norman, Okla., p. 55).

GREENWAY, Devon A Georgian house in an idyllic setting four and a half miles from Dartmouth, up the river Dart, on the left bank opposite Dittisham. The home of Agatha Christie and her husband, Sir Max Mallowan, from 1938 until her death; the grounds were planted with flowering shrubs.

NASSE HOUSE in Agatha Christie, *Dead Man's Folly* (1956)

'A description of Greenway has been given by Agatha . . . in her novel *Dead Man's Folly*, where familiar landmarks in the garden can be identified' (Max Mallowan, 1977, *Mallowan's Memoirs*, p. 203).

GREENWAY, Mr

MR LANDOR in 'The Sad Fortunes of the Revd Amos Barton' and MR PITTMAN in 'Janet's Repentance', both in George Eliot, *Scenes of Clerical Life* (1857–8)

See under **Anstruther**, Lady.

GREENWICH BOMB OUTRAGE 1894. Perpetrated by Martial **Bourdin**.

THE BOMB OUTRAGE in Joseph Conrad, *The Secret Agent* (1907)

'The source for the basic incident of *The Secret Agent* was . . . an actual episode from anarchist history. The bomb outrage in the novel . . . was based upon the Greenwich Bomb Outrage which took place in 1894. . . . That this was his source has never been denied except by Conrad himself, and he was not consistent about his denial' (Norman Sherry, 1971, *Conrad's Western World*, Cambridge, p. 228).

GREENWOOD, Harold He was tried and acquitted in 1920 at Carmarthen, Wales, on a charge of murdering his wife.

HENRY HUTTON in Aldous Huxley, 'The Gioconda Smile' (1922)

'Meanwhile I have a choice specimen of detective-story realisms in *The English Review* for August – variations on the theme of the Greenwood case' (Aldous Huxley to Julian Huxley, 26 August 1921, reproduced in *Letters of Aldous Huxley*, 1969, ed. Grover Smith, p. 202).

GREENWOOD, Joseph Goudge (1821–94) He was the first Professor of Classics and History at Owens College, Manchester, in 1850, and was Principal from 1857 to 1889.

PROFESSOR LITTLE in Morley Roberts, *The Private Life of Henry Maitland* (1912)

Identified in an 'Index of Recurring Pseudonyms' in the 1958 edition of *The Private Life of Henry Maitland*, ed. Morchard Bishop, p. 255.

GREG, William Rathbone (1809–81) Educated at Edinburgh University, he was later a mill owner for eighteen years. He was the Commissioner of Customs in 1856, and of Her Majesty's Stationery Office from 1864 to 1877. He was the author of *Rocks Ahead* (1874), and was the brother-in-law of Walter Bagehot and the uncle of Lady **Colefax**.

EDWARD FAIRFAX ROCHESTER in Charlotte Brontë, *Jane Eyre* (1847)

'Greg was supposed to have been the inspiration for Rochester in *Jane Eyre*' (Anne Fremantle, 1971, *Three-Cornered Heart*, p. 30). This was told to Anne Fremantle by her mother, daughter of Sir Monstuart Grant Duff, in whose family it was a commonly accepted tradition. Greg certainly looked like Rochester; George Eliot described him in 1852 as 'a short man with a hooked nose and an imperfect enunciation through defective teeth, but his brain is large, the anterior lobe very fine and a moral region to correspond. Black, wiry, curly hair and every indication of a first-rate temperament. But when you see him across the room, you are unpleasantly impressed, and can't believe he wrote his own books' (to Mr and Mrs Charles Bray, 26 April 1852, reproduced in *The George Eliot Letters*, 1954, ed. Gordon S. Haight, Vol. II, London: Oxford University Press, p. 21). 'He is very pleasing, but somehow or other he frightens me dreadfully' (6 November 1852, ibid., p. 66).

GREGORY, Eliot (1854–1915) He was a man-about-town and essayist, and published a collection of essays on the manners of society. He was a friend of Edith Wharton in New York and Paris.

LAWRENCE SELDEN in Edith Wharton, *The House of Mirth* (1905)

'Fond as she was of her Walter Benys . . . her Eliot Gregorys . . . and Selden has a little of each – she knew they had insufficient blood in their veins' (R.W.B. Lewis, 1975, *Edith Wharton: a biography*, London: Constable, p. 155). *See also* **Berry**, Walter van Rensselaer, **Winthrop**, Egerton.

GREGORY, Sir Richard (1864–1952) Author and scientific journalist. From 1893 to 1919 he was Assistant Editor of *Nature*, and was then Editor until 1938. He was the son of John Gregory, who was a poet, cobbler, Wesleyan and social reformer, and was a contemporary of H.G. Wells at the Normal School of Science, South Kensington; Wells became his lifelong friend. He had a particular interest in astronomy in his early life.

GEORGE EDGAR LEWISHAM in H.G. Wells, *Love and Mr Lewisham* (1900)

'Some of [the] detail is borrowed from the experiences of Richard Gregory, who had done in fact what Lewisham does in this fiction – married a girl on his guinea-a-week student's allowance. But mainly it is Wells's own story' (Dickson, 1972, *H.G. Wells*, Harmondsworth: Penguin, p. 128). *See also* **Wells**, H.G.

PARLOAD in H.G. Wells, *In the Days of the Comet* (1906)

'Parload is an amateur astronomer plainly based both in physical appearance and in other detail on . . . Richard Gregory' (Lovat Dickson, op. cit., p. 181).

GREIN, Clara She was a resident on Capri *c*.1907.

MADAME STEYNLIN in Norman Douglas, *South Wind* (1917)

'A hospitable and romantic lady who . . . might not be gratified to learn that she had contributed her share towards the formation of . . . "Madame Steynlin"' (Norman Douglas, 1933, *Looking Back*, p. 146).

GRENVILLE, George Nugent *See* **Nugent of Carlanston**, Lord.

GRENVILLE, Mary Temple-Nugent-Brydges-Chandos, Lady (1795–1862) Née Campbell, she married Lord **Grenville**.

DUCHESS OF AGINCOURT in Benjamin Disraeli, *Coningsby* (1844)

See under **Grenville**, Lord, 2nd Duke of Buckingham and Chandos.

LADY CLANELLAN in Robert Plumer Ward, *De Vere; or The Man of Independence* (1827)

'We might . . . at least inquire, whether the amiable Lady Clanellan does not find something like a prototype in the equally amiable Duchess of Buckingham' (*Literary Gazette* (31 March 1827): 193).

GRENVILLE, Richard Plantagenet Temple-Nugent-Brydges-Chandos, Lord, 2nd Duke of Buckingham and Chandos (1797–1861) He was the son of the 1st Duke of Buckingham (Lord **Grenville**, below). MP for Buckinghamshire from 1818 to 1839, he was considered a leader of the landed interest in the House of Commons. He married Mary Campbell (**Grenville**, above), and was known as the Marquess of Chandos from 1822 to 1839, and then succeeded to the dukedom; within eight years he was a ruined man and all his possessions (including Stowe) were sold. He died at the Great Western Hotel, Paddington, London, leaving an estate of less than £200.

DUKE OF AGINCOURT in Benjamin Disraeli, *Coningsby* (1844)

'He is the "Duke of Agincourt" and his wife "the Duchess" in Disraeli's *Coningsby*' (Hon. Vicary Gibbs (ed.), 1912, *The Complete Peerage of England, Scotland, Ireland, Great Britain and the United Kingdom*, Vol. II, rev. edn, London: St Catherine Press, p. 410 n. (a)).

GRENVILLE, Richard Temple-Nugent-Brydges-Chandos, Lord, 2nd Marquess of Chandos and 1st Duke of Buckingham (1776–1839) He was MP for Buckinghamshire from 1797 to 1813, when he succeeded to the marquessate, and in 1822 was created duke, being the only one ever created by George IV. From 1813 until his death he was Lord Lieutenant of Buckinghamshire.

MARQUESS OF CARABAS in Benjamin Disraeli, *Vivian Grey* (1826–7)

Identified in a key given in a pamphlet published in 1827 by William Marsh, and discussed by Lucien Wolf in his notes to *Vivian Grey* (1904 (centenary edn), Vol. II, London: Alexander Moring, pp. 364). 'The Key probably meant the Marquess of Chandos [Lord **Grenville**, above] . . . a friend of Disraeli's and the leader of the landed Conservatives from 1818 to 1839. [But] Disraeli meant, if anyone, the father of this Marquess, in 1826 Duke of Buckingham and Chandos' (Benjamin Disraeli, 1904, *Vivian Grey*, ed. B.N. Langdon-Davies, London: Alexander Moring, p. 862 n. 1; originally published 1826, London: Henry Colburn). *See also* **Clanricarde**, 1st Marquess of; **Murray**, John[1].

GREPPI, Count Giuseppe (1819–1921) Italian diplomat. He began his diplomatic career in Vienna under Metternich, and in 1840 was appointed Diplomatic Adviser to Napoleon's widow, Marie-Louise. He was Italian Ambassador to Paris during the regime of Napoleon III, and was later Italian Minister at Constantinople and Ambassador at St Petersburg. He died while attending a race meeting in Milan. Ernest Hemingway met him at Stresa in 1918.

COUNT GREFFI in Ernest Hemingway, *A Farewell to Arms* (1929)

'[He] appears unchanged in the novel as Count Greffi. Throughout the manuscript, his name is spelled Creppi; the spelling was not changed until the *Scribner's Magazine* galleys [of the serialization] were being proofed' (M.S. Reynolds, 1976, *Hemingway's First War: the making of* A Farewell to Arms, Princeton, NJ: Princeton University Press, p. 166).

GREVILLE, Charles (1794–1865) He was Clerk to the Council from 1821 to 1859, and was Manager of the Duke of York's racing stable. His diaries were first published in 1875.

DORSET WILMERS in George Meredith, *Diana of the Crossways* (1884)

'The book opens with an analysis . . . of the journalistic comments of Henry Wilmer's [sic] cousin Dorset Wilmers (i.e. Henry Greville's brother Charles, author of the Greville memoirs)' (Alice Acland, 1948, *Caroline Norton*, London: Constable, pp. 171, 172).

GREVILLE, Henry (1801–72) Brother of Charles **Greville**, he was in the diplomatic service. His own *Leaves from a Diary* were published 1883–4.

HENRY WILMERS in George Meredith, *Diana of the Crossways* (1884)

'The book opens with an analysis of *Leaves from the Diary of Henry Wilmers* (i.e. *Leaves from the Diary of Henry Greville)*' (Alice Acland, 1948, *Caroline Norton*, London: Constable, pp. 171–2).

GREY, Constance Gwladys, Lady *See* **Ripon**, Marchioness of.

GRIERSON, Sir Robert (1655?–1733) Laird of Lag, Galloway, he was notorious for his severity towards Covenanters; he presided at the trial and execution of the 'Wigtown martyrs', and was fined and imprisoned after the Revolution. He died at Dumfries.

SIR ROBERT REDGAUNTLET in Sir Walter Scott, *Redgauntlet* (1824)

'Grierson is the Sir Robert Redgauntlet of Wandering Willie's tale in ... *Redgauntlet*' (*The Dictionary of National Biography*, Vol. XXIII, London: Oxford University Press, p. 222, s.v. Grierson).

GRIGSBY, Emilie Busbey (b. 1880) She was the daughter of a confederate officer and Sue Grigsby of Kentucky. Charles T. **Yerkes** installed her in a five-storey mansion in New York.

BERENICE FLEMING in Theodore Dreiser, *The Titan* (1914)

'Emilie Grigsby figures in *The Titan* as Berenice Fleming' (Leon Edel, 1972, *Henry James: the master, 1901–1916*, p. 183). She asserted that she was James's inspiration for the character of Milly Theale in *The Wings of the Dove*, in spite of all his denials.

GRIMALDI, Giuseppe (d. 1788) Father of Joseph Grimaldi, the famous actor, pantomimist and clown, he moved to England from Genoa as dentist to Queen Charlotte in 1860. Soon after his arrival, he resigned his position and began giving lessons in dancing; he became Ballet-Master of Drury Lane Theatre and Sadler's Wells, London, and *primo buffo*.

DANIEL QUILP in Charles Dickens, *The Old Curiosity Shop* (1840–1)

'There is another possible source for some elements of Quilp's behaviour in the *Memoirs of Joseph Grimaldi*, edited by Dickens and published in February 1838. The character of Grimaldi's father appears to have strong affinities with that of Quilp' (G.M. Watkins, 1971, 'A possible source for Quilp', *Notes and Queries* 216: 411). *See also* **Dickens**, Charles; **Prior**, 'Donkey'.

GRIMSBURY FARM, Berkshire Located on Long Lane, Hermitage, near Newbury. In 1918 and 1919 it was the farm of Cecily **Lambert** and Violet **Monk**.

BAILEY FARM in D.H. Lawrence, 'The Fox' (1923)

'[The] setting of "The Fox"' (E. Nehl, 1957, *D.H. Lawrence: a composite biography*, Vol. I, Madison, caption to photograph of Grimsbury Farm facing p. 454).

GRIMSHAW, Mortimer (1825?–69) He was from Great Harwood, Lancashire, where his father had been involved in radical politics earlier in the century. In 1852 he was involved in a campaign in Royton (near Oldham) for the enforcement of the factory acts, and along with George **Cowell** he was a leader of the **Preston Strike**. He died of 'phthisis' (progressive wasting disease), and although he was described on his death certificate as a cotton power loom weaver, in the early part of the 1850s he was actually engaged almost entirely in the politics of labour. He was a considerable orator, known as 'the Thunderer of Lancashire'.

SLACKBRIDGE in Charles Dickens, *Hard Times* (1854)

'Slackbridge ... is almost certainly based on Mortimer Grimshaw ... characterized ... as a brash insensitive mob orator. ... This picture is ... drawn from the incidents Dickens witnessed at the delegates' meeting [he attended during his visit to Preston] on Sunday [29 January 1854]. ... [The] image, however ... is very misleading' (H.I. Dutton and J.E. King, 1981, *'Ten Per Cent and No Surrender': the Preston Strike, 1853–1854*, p. 198).

GROSVENOR, Sibell Mary, Lady (1855–1929) Afterwards Lady Sibell Wyndham. Née Lumley, she was the youngest daughter of the 9th Earl of Scarborough. In 1874 she married Victor, Earl Grosvenor, heir to the first Duke of Westminster; he died on 22 January 1884, and in 1887 she married George Wyndham, later Chief Secretary for Ireland.

MARGARET, LADY VANDELEUR, in Henry James, 'The Path of Duty' (1884)

For James's account of the origin of the plot of this story, *see under* **Sutherland**, Duchess of.

GROSVENOR, Susan Daughter of the Hon. Norman Grosvenor, she married John Buchan in 1907.

LADY FLORA BRUME in John Buchan, *A Lodge in the Wilderness* (1906)

'[Buchan] put [Susan Grosvenor] into *A Lodge in the Wilderness* as Lady Flora Brume' (Janet Adam Smith, 1965, *John Buchan*, p. 160). Also identified in a key dated January 1907 in a copy of *A Lodge in the Wilderness*, formerly the property of Grace Keily.

GROVE, Harriet

EMILY GIROUETTE in Thomas Love Peacock, *Nightmare Abbey* (1818)

'Miss Emily Girouette, whose marriage to another man had occasioned her lover much grief ... is Harriet Grove, of whom Shelly wrote in 1811: "She is gone. ... She is lost to me forever. She is married – married to a clod of earth"' (Martin Freeman, 1911, *Thomas Love Peacock*, London: Martin Secker, pp. 201, 202).

GRYFFYDH, Jane (1789–1851) Daughter of John **Gryffydh**, she met Thomas Love Peacock in 1808; they were married in 1819.

ANTHELIA MELINCOURT in Thomas Love Peacock, *Melincourt* (1817)

'Anthelia has been variously stated to have been an idealisation of Peacock's first love and of the Welsh girl, Jane Gryffydh, whom he afterwards married' (*The Novels of Thomas Love Peacock*, 1948, ed. David Garnett, London: Rupert Hart-Davis, p. 106 n. 1). *See also* **Falkner**, Fanny.

GRYFFYDH, John (d. 1812) Father of Jane **Gryffydh** and father-in-law of Thomas Love Peacock, he was the Rector of Festiniog and Maentwrog, Merionethshire, from 1787 onwards. Peacock always referred to him as Dr Gryffydh, but although he graduated in 1776 from Jesus College, Oxford, he never in fact took his doctorate.

MR CRANIUM in Thomas Love Peacock, *Headlong Hall* (1816)

'It is probably not . . . far-fetched to see in the enthusiastic Mr Cranium a caricature of Dr Gryffydh holding forth on some favourite subject' (Martin Freeman, 1911, *Thomas Love Peacock*, London: Martin Secker, p. 96). But the real connection between Dr Gryffydh and Mr Cranium is that both had the misfortune to suffer a severe fall, Mr Cranium (ch. VIII) from a tower, and Dr Gryffydh down the Black Cataract or Rhaiad Du, about a mile from Maentwrog, which he was climbing by moonlight with Peacock; both were saved by a hazel bush (see letter to E.T. Hookham, 22 March 1810, reproduced in Thomas Love Peacock, 1934, *Works* (Halliford edn), Vol. VIII, p. 182).

GUIBERT, Jacques, Comte de (1743–1790) French soldier and writer. He served in the Seven Years War, and became Field Marshal in 1786. Julie de **Lespinasse** was his mistress.

CAPTAIN HENRY WARKWORTH in Mrs Humphry Ward, *Lady Rose's Daughter* (1903)

'Julie uses her social influence for Warkworth, as Julie de Lespinasse used hers for the Comte Guibert . . . her lover is sordidly false to her, as was the Comte Guibert to the earlier Julie' (Introd. to *Lady Rose's Daughter*, 1911 (Westmorland edn), p. ix).

GULLY, James Manby (1808–83) Born in Kingston, Jamaica, and completing his education at Edinburgh University in 1829, he was a physician in London from 1830 to 1842 and practised hydrotherapy at Malvern, Worcestershire, between 1842 and 1871. He became very friendly with Mrs C.D.T. Bravo, and in 1876 he was a witness in the Bravo poison case; that same year his name was removed from the medical register.

DR GULLSON in Charles Reade, *It is Never Too Late to Mend* (1856)

'Appears as Dr Gullson in . . . *It is Never Too Late to Mend* (Frederic Boase, 1892, *Modern English Biography*, Vol. I, col. 1257).

GURNEY, Edmund (1847–88) Educated privately and at Trinity College, Cambridge, he was a Fellow in 1872 and subsequently studied music (1872–5), medicine (1877–81) and law (1881–3). He founded the Society for Psychical Research in 1882 and was the author of *The Power of Sound* (1880). He married Kate Sibley (**Gurney**, below) in 1877: 'They have a pretty house in Brompton. . . . Mrs Gurney who is, as you know, a gardener's daughter whom he has educated . . . is a . . . beautiful young woman . . . with fine manners. Edmund Gurney is supposed to be marvellously handsome but to me is more like a fine butler with a dash of guardsman, with a very undecided manner' (Vernon Lee to her mother, Mrs Paget, 1882, quoted in Peter Gunn, 1964, *Vernon Lee, 1856–1935*, London: Oxford University Press, p. 84). He died as a result of a narcotic overdose in a Brighton hotel. George Eliot met Gurney at Trinity College in 1873.

DANIEL DERONDA in George Eliot, *Daniel Deronda* (1876)

'I have always fancied – though without any evidence – that some touches in Deronda were drawn from . . . Edmund Gurney, a man of remarkable charm of character and as good-looking as Deronda' (Leslie Stephen, 1902, *George Eliot*, p. 191). *See also* **Bond**, Edward; **Goldsmid**, Colonel Albert; **Lewes**, G.H.; **Louis**, Alfred Hyman.

GURNEY, Kate Née Sibley, she married Edmund **Gurney**.

ANNE BROWN in Vernon Lee, *Miss Brown* (1884)

'*Miss Brown* was regarded from the first as a *roman à clef*. William Morris and Edmund Gurney had both educated girls to be their wives' (Peter Gunn, 1964, *Vernon Lee, 1856–1935*, London: Oxford University Press, p. 102). *See also* **Morris**, Jane.

GUTHRIE, Pat 'A tall dissipated Scot with narrow shoulders and a wide-ranging thirst' (Carlos Baker, 1969, *Ernest Hemingway: a life story*, New York, p. 145). He was reputedly the lover of Duff **Twysden** in 1925 in Paris, and his liaison with Lady Twysden seems to have come to an end *c*.1926. He was permanently in financial difficulties and was an alcoholic; he finally committed suicide.

MICHAEL CAMPBELL in Ernest Hemingway, *The Sun Also Rises* (1926)

'Pat Guthrie, the model for Mike Campbell' (B.D. Sarason, 1972, *Hemingway and the Sun Set*, Washington, DC, pp. 47–8).

GUTIÉRREZ, Carlos (b. 1878) A Cuban fisherman whom Ernest Hemingway met in 1932 on his first visit to Havana. Several times in the previous fifteen years, he had taken more marlin than any other local fisherman, using a handline with the bait lashed at different levels. He became Hemingway's chief consultant and instructor in the habits of game fish, and they fished together until 1936; by then Gutiérrez had become three-quarters blind and quite deaf. In 1935 he told Hemingway the story on which the novel is based, and Hemingway used it in the first article he wrote for the magazine *Esquire* ('On the blue water', *Esquire* (April 1936)), but it remained in his mind as unfinished business until he wrote *The Old Man and the Sea* in 1950.

SANTIAGO in Ernest Hemingway, *The Old Man and the Sea* (1952)

'[Hemingway] was momentarily agitated when Carlos Baker wrote to remind him of an old letter to Max Perkins in which he had mentioned Carlos Gutiérrez as one distant prototype of Santiago' (Carlos Baker, 1969, *Ernest Hemingway: a life story*, New York, p. 502). Gutiérrez, like Santiago, would allow the hooked fish to exhaust itself towing the boat. *See also* **Saunders**, Eddie.

GWAYNYNOG, Denbighshire Home of Beatrix Potter's uncle Fred Burton. It formerly belonged to the Myddleton family who, in 1774, had entertained the Thrales and Dr Johnson; to commemorate the visit, Mr John Myddleton erected an urn in the garden.

MR MCGREGOR'S GARDEN in Beatrix Potter, *The Tale of the Flopsy Bunnies* (1909)

'It was this . . . garden . . . that came back to her . . . as the perfect setting for the tale of the 'Flopsy Bunnies' (Margaret Lane, 1978, *The Magic Years of Beatrix Potter*, p. 85). 'Peter was so composite . . . in locality that I have found it troublesome to explain its various sources. . . . I called the garden at Gwaynynog "Mr McGregor's garden" when I used it for the backgrounds in *Flopsy Bunnies*; so as Uncle Fred Burton used to say, "Leave it at that!"' (Beatrix Potter to her publishers, quoted in Margaret Lane, 1946, *The Tale of Beatrix Potter*, London and New York: Frederick Lane, pp. 127–8). *See also* **Camfield Place; Fawe Park**.

GWINN, Mary An 1890's member of the faculty at **Bryn Mawr College**. She was a protégée of Carey **Thomas**, with whom she had been childhood friends and had studied in Germany; each of them had an affair with Alfred **Hodder**, who eventually married Mary.

JANET BRUCE in Gertrude Stein, *Fernhurst* (1971)

'[Gertrude Stein's] Miss Gwinn is named Janet Bruce' (James R. Mellow, 1974, *The Charmed Circle: Gertrude Stein and company*, London: Phaidon Press, p. 66).

CORA DOUNOR in Gertrude Stein, *The Making of Americans* (1925)

'Five years later, she embedded the *Fernhurst* story . . . into the . . . narrative of . . . *The Making of Americans*. At that point she changed the [name] . . . of Janet Bruce to . . . Cora Dounor' (ibid., p. 67).

GWYTHER, Emma (1802?–36) She was married to Revd John **Gwyther**.

AMELIA ('MILLY') BARTON in George Eliot, 'The Sad Fortunes of the Revd Amos Barton', *Scenes of Clerical Life* (1857–8)

'[Mr Gwyther's] wife Emma, whose sad story was locally well known, is buried in Chilvers Coton Churchyard. Her fictional name is that of a sister of Sir Roger Newdigate's second wife' (Marghanita Laski, 1973, *George Eliot and Her World*, London: Thames & Hudson, p. 55).

GWYTHER, Revd John (d. 1873) He completed a BA at St John's College, Cambridge, in 1828, and was Curate of the parish of Chilvers Coton, home of George Eliot's father, between 1831 and 1841. He was much influenced by Charles Simeon, the evangelical clergyman, and on his arrival at Chilvers Coton, after a period in Birmingham, he proceeded with great zeal to initiate

Evangelical reforms. He moved from Warwickshire to Sheffield, and then to Fewston, Yorkshire, where he died.

REVD AMOS BARTON in George Eliot, 'The Sad Fortunes of the Revd Amos Barton', *Scenes of Clerical Life* (1857–8)

'[Amos Barton] was drawn from keen observation of the Rev. John Gwyther . . . who had officiated at her mother's funeral and her sister's wedding . . . the episode in Chapter 1, where Amos interrupted the wedding psalm actually occurred on 12 February 1832, when Robert Evans noted [it] in his Journal' (Gordon S. Haight, 1968, *George Eliot*, Oxford, pp. 211, 212). 'I heard a curious thing about Amos Barton, namely that it is the actual life of a clergyman named Gwythir [sic] who at the time the incidents occurred lived at a place called, I think, Coton, in one of the Midland counties and who is now vicar of a small parish in Yorkshire. Indeed his daughter wrote to a lady, a friend of mine, telling her to be sure to read the story as it was their family history' (Joseph Langford to John Blackwood, the publisher, 16 February 1857, quoted in Haight, op. cit., p. 220). 'We are as assured that I am intended by Amos Barton as I am of the Truth of any Fact soever' (John Gwyther to the Editor of *Blackwoods*, 13 June 1859, reproduced in *The George Eliot Letters*, 1954, ed. Gordon S. Haight, Vol. III, London: Oxford University Press, p. 84). 'There are *two* portraits in *Clerical Scenes*: they are first, *Amos Barton* . . . (I thought "Amos" was dead)' (George Eliot to Charles Bray, 19 September 1859, ibid., pp. 156–7).

H

H——, Rachel A village girl of Hardy's youth.

ARABELLA DONN in Thomas Hardy, *Jude the Obscure* (1895)

'March 1 [1888]. Youthful recollections of four village beauties . . . 3. Rachel H——, and her rich colour, and vanity, and frailty, and clever artificial dimple-making. [She is probably in some respects the original of Arabella in Jude the Obscure]''' (entry in Hardy's journal, quoted in F.E. Hardy, 1972, *The Life of Thomas Hardy, 1840–1928*, p. 206; the square brackets are reproduced from the original text).

HACKETT, Mr

MR SPRATT in George Eliot, 'The Sad Fortunes of the Revd Amos Barton', *Scenes of Clerical Life* (1857–8)

See under **Anstruther**, Lady.

HADDON HALL, Derbyshire

MARTINDALE CASTLE in Sir Walter Scott, *Peveril of the Peak* (1823)

'[In 1815 Scott] . . . visited Haddon Hall . . . upon the great hall of this mansion . . . and the adjoining bedroom . . . Scott later modeled Lady Peveril's rooms in *Peveril of the Peak*' (Edgar Johnson, 1970, *Sir Walter Scott: the great unknown*, London: Hamilton, p. 506).

HAFOD HOUSE, Cardiganshire Seat of Thomas **Johnes**, who had it rebuilt in 1786 by architect Thomas Baldwin. Additions were done by Nash, but in 1807 it was destroyed by fire. It was rebuilt again by Baldwin, and in 1832 it was bought and much altered by the Duke of Newcastle before being sold to Sir Henry de Hoghton. It was later partially demolished to make way for projected additions by Salvin. It was damaged again by fire in 1932 and was destroyed in 1950.

HEADLONG HALL in Thomas Love Peacock, *Headlong Hall* (1816)

'It appears probable that the description of Headlong Hall and of its owner was inspired by Hafod House and grounds, which belonged to Colonel Johnes. . . . Hafod House was burnt down in 1807 and Peacock saw the ruins [in 1811]' (*The Novels of T.L. Peacock*, 1948, ed. David Garnett, London: Rupert Hart-Davis, p. 22 n. 1). Geoffrey Grigson has suggested that the spectacle of Hafod House (seen on his walking tour in Wales in 1794) was an element in Coleridge's vision of Kubla Khan (see 'Kubla Khan in Wales', 1946–7, *Cornhill* 162: 278). *See also* **High Elms**.

HAGGS FARM, Nottinghamshire Situated at Underwood, it was the home of the **Chambers** family. 'The farm lies about a mile and a half from Eastwood on the edge of a little wood standing on either side of Willey Water Brook' (E. Delavenay, 1972, *D.H. Lawrence: the man and his work, 1885–1919*, p. 20).

STRELLEY MILL in D.H. Lawrence, *The White Peacock* (1911)

'Strelley Mill . . . is the Haggs, transplanted' (ibid., p. 89). *See also* **Felley Mill**.

WILLEY FARM in D.H. Lawrence, *Sons and Lovers* (1913)

'Lawrence did not even know the Chambers family until he was fifteen and used to walk . . . to their farm . . . the Willey Farm of *Sons and Lovers*' (H.T. Moore, 1960, *The Intelligent Heart: the story of D.H. Lawrence*, Harmondsworth: Penguin, p. 35; originally published 1955, London: Heinemann).

HAGUE, Frank Mayor of Jersey City from 1919 to 1947, he controlled the Democratic machine. His power eventually covered most of Hudson County and extended into the rest of Jersey City and even beyond. He ran his machine, often by telephone from Florida, until the defeat, in 1949, of Frank Hague **Eggers**, the nephew he had installed upon his own retirement in 1947.

BOSS COYLE in Francis T. Field, *McDonough* (1951)

'Boss Coyle . . . [suggests] Boss Frank Hague' (Joseph Blotner, 1966, *The Modern American Political Novel*, Austin, Tex., p. 80 n. 45).

HAJJI BABA He was a young Persian who was taken to England in 1811 by Sir Haxford Jones, the British Plenipotentiary, to study medicine; he remained in England until 1819, and Morier had contact with him during his stay.

HAJJI BABA in James Morier, *The Adventures of Haji Baba of Ispahan* (1824)

'We can surely assert that Morier probably borrowed the name of the Persian youth. Morier knew the real Hajji Baba when the latter was just about the same age as the fictitious one, and they both were apprenticed to physicians' (Arthur J. Weitzman, 1970, 'Who was Haji Baba?', *Notes and Queries* 215: 179).

HAKE, George (d. before 1914) Younger brother of T. St E. Hake.

THE YOUNG SECRETARY in Theodore Watts-Dunton, *Aylwin* (1899)

Identified in T. St E. Hake, 1902, 'Aylwin', *Notes and Queries* (9th series) 9 (7 June): 450–2, and 10 (2 August): 89–91; reprinted in *Aylwin* (World's Classics), 1914, Oxford, App. II.

HAKE, Revd George (1784–1848) Vicar of Chilvers Coton, Warwickshire. Between 1829 and 1844 he also held livings at Rocester and Ellastone, Staffordshire. He left Cambridge without a degree. He forced John **Gwyther** to leave Coton because he wished to give the curacy to his brother Henry. 'The Rev. George Hake was originally a soldier who entered the church rather late in life. He was an *evangelical* preacher; very ugly, stuttering, and rather obese; very poor, and unscrupulous about getting into debt, which he did to a considerable extent; supposed to conceal some meanness under a rather excessive air of benevolence; and generally *dis*respected by his Staffordshire parishioners' (to Mrs Charles Bray, 3? October? 1859, reproduced in *The George*

Eliot Letters, 1954, ed. Gordon S. Haight, Vol. III, London: Oxford University Press, p. 171).

REVD MR CARPE in George Eliot, 'The Sad Fortunes of the Revd Amos Barton', *Scenes of Clerical Life* (1857–8)

'Carpe's prototype [was] the Reverend George Hake' (Gordon S. Haight, 1968, *George Eliot*, Oxford, p. 217). *See also under* **Anstruther**, Lady.

HALDANE, John Burdon Sanderson (1892–1964) Eminent biologist and geneticist. He was the son of J.S. **Haldane**.

JAMES SHEARWATER in Aldous Huxley, *Antic Hay* (1923)

'[At Garsington] also shone Aldous Huxley, an old friend from Eton days who . . . was to pillory J.B.S. as the Shearwater of *Antic Hay*' (Ronald Clark, 1968, *J.B.S: the life and work of J.B.S. Haldane*, p. 57).

HALDANE, John Scott (1860–1936) Physiologist. He was the father of J.B.S. **Haldane** and Naomi Mitchison, mother of Geoffrey **Mitchison**.

LORD EDWARD TANTAMOUNT in Aldous Huxley, *Point Counter Point* (1928)

'My father [J.S. Haldane] is in a sense the original of Lord Edward in *Point Counter Point*' (Naomi Mitchison, quoted in *Aldous Huxley, 1894–1963: a memorial volume*, 1965, ed. Julian Huxley, p. 53).

HALE, Jessie Abbott (1874–1962) Youngest daughter of Charles Richardson, she was Dorothy Richardson's sister. In 1895 she married Robert Thomas **Hale** ('Jack'). After an unsettled life in England, where amongst other things they ran a boarding house at Hastings, in 1903 they emigrated to Texas, where they settled.

HARRIETT HENDERSON in Dorothy Richardson, *Pilgrimage* (1915–67)

'[Harriett's] engagement to Gerald . . . refers us back to Jessie Richardson and Jack Hale . . . whose subsequent vicissitudes . . . were, by Jessie Hale's own account, accurately reflected in *Pilgrimage*' (John Rosenberg, 1973, *Dorothy Richardson*, London, p. 76).

HALE, Robert Thomas ('Jack') In 1895 he married Jessie Richardson (**Hale**, above), youngest sister of Dorothy Richardson.

GERALD DUCAYNE in Dorothy Richardson, *Pilgrimage* (1915–67)

See under **Hale**, Jessie Abbott

HALES, Harold Keates (1868–1942) A school friend of Arnold Bennett. He was MP for Hanley from 1931 to 1935.

EDWARD HENRY ('DENRY') MACHIN in Arnold Bennett, *The Card* (1911)

'Harold Hales is coming to see me today, for tea. What a scene! He is convinced that he is the original of the Card. (He is.) And he is intensely proud of this' (19 January 1920, reproduced in *Arnold Bennett's Letters to His Nephew*, 1935, ed. R. Bennett, London: Heinemann, pp. 13–14). 'The Card himself is clearly a fictitious character. . . . It's doubtful whether Bennett was thinking much of [Hales] when he invented Denry' (Margaret Drabble, 1974, *Arnold Bennett: a biography*, London: Weidenfeld & Nicolson, p. 159).

RICHARD POVEY in Arnold Bennett, *The Old Wives' Tale* (1908)

'Hales . . . no doubt furnished many of the ideas for Dick Povey, for instance, the cyclist and the balloonist in *The Old Wives' Tale*' (ibid.).

HALL, Alice (b. 1880?) A friend of D.H. Lawrence when they were both attending a teacher training course at Ilkeston, she lived at Eastwood, Nottinghamshire, and was one of the group known as 'the Pagans'. She married White Holditch, a Quaker.

ALICE GALL in D.H. Lawrence, *The White Peacock* (1911)

'In Eastwood offence was taken, particularly by the family of Alice Hall (portrayed in the novel under the too closely similar name of Alice Gall)' (E. Delavenay, 1972, *D.H. Lawrence: the man and his work . . . 1885–1919*, p. 75). 'Her husband, White Holditch, threatened a lawsuit' (H.T. Moore, 1960, *The Intelligent Heart: the story of D.H. Lawrence*, Harmondsworth: Penguin, p. 146; originally published 1955, London: Heinemann).

BEATRICE WYLD in D.H. Lawrence, *Sons and Lovers* (1913)

'The next time Lawrence put Alice into a novel he gave her the quite different name of Beatrice Wyld' (Moore, op. cit., p. 146).

HALL, Marguerite Radclyffe (1886–1943) English novelist and poet. Born in Bournemouth, she was educated at King's College, London, and in Germany. She won the Tait Black Memorial Prize and the Femina Vie Heureuse for *Adam's Breed*, which was published in 1926. Her open treatment of lesbianism in *The Well of Loneliness* provoked a trial for obscenity. The book was banned and an appeal refused, despite the support of many eminent writers, including E.M. **Forster**, Virginia **Woolf** and Arnold **Bennett**.

LADY BUCK-AND-BALK in Djuna Barnes, *The Ladies Almanack* (1928)

Identified in Meryle Secrest, 1976, *Between Me and Life: a biography of Romaine Brooks*, London: MacDonald & Jane; originally published 1974, Garden City, NY: Doubleday, p. 335.

RORY FREEMANTLE in Compton Mackenzie, *Extraordinary Women* (1928)

'Rory Freemantle, supposedly modeled on Radclyffe Hall' (Secrest, op. cit., p. 290). 'Every one of the characters in *Extraordinary Women* is an exact portrait with a single exception; Rory Freemantle is a composite creation of my own' (Compton Mackenzie, 1966, *My Life and Times, Octave Four*, p. 138).

STEPHEN GORDON in Radclyffe Hall, *The Well of Loneliness* (1928)

'. . . many of Stephen Gordon's feelings and reactions, though practically none of her circumstances or experiences, were her own' (Una, Lady Troubridge, 1961, *The Life and Death of Radclyffe Hall*, p. 103).

HALL, Samuel Carter (1800–89) He was Editor of the Art Union Monthly from 1839 to 1880 and was married to Anna Maria Hall, the novelist.

SETH PECKSNIFF in Charles Dickens, *Martin Chuzzlewit* (1843–4)

'"'No', said Mr Pecksniff, keeping his hand in his waistcoat as though he were ready on the shortest notice to produce his heart." This sentence amusingly describes a trick Mr Hall had of putting his right hand inside the velvet jacket which he usually wore, buttoned by one button at the waist' (Charles C. Osborne, 1906, 'Mr Pecksniff and his prototype', *Independent Review* (September): 330). C.C. Osborne was for many years the private secretary of Miss Burdett-Coutts and knew S.C. Hall – 'When Mr Hall . . . went to lecture in the United States he was . . . heralded by the American press as the prototype of Pecksniff; *Punch* also referred to him as Pecksniff, and to the Art Union as "Pecksniffery", whereupon Mr Hall threatened a libel action' (F.G. Kitton, 1897, *The Novels of Charles Dickens: a bibliography and sketch*, London, pp. 92–3).

HALL, William (1801–47) Publisher. He was a partner of Edward **Chapman** in the firm of Chapman and Hall, who printed Dickens's first published work in the *Monthly Magazine* (December 1833).

MR CHIRRUP in Charles Dickens, 'The Nice Little Couple', *Sketches of Young Couples* (1840)

'"The Nice Little Couple", in the *Sketches of Young Couples*, are none other than the junior partner in Chapman and Hall and his wife' (Arthur Waugh, 1930, *A Hundred Years of Publishing: being the story of Chapman & Hall Ltd*, p. 6).

HAMILTON, Elizabeth (1758–1816) Author. She was the sister of Charles Hamilton, the orientalist, and lived mainly in Edinburgh, where she was something of a leader of intellectual society. Her novel, *Memoirs of Modern Philosophers* (1800), was a satire on Godwin and his followers. Although unmarried, she was known as Mrs Hamilton.

MRS DELANEY in Mary Martha Sherwood, *Caroline Mordaunt; or The Governess* (1853)

'Mary Butt met [Mrs Hamilton in Bath] . . . [and] gives an amusing account of [a] rout [that they both attended] in her novel, *Caroline Mordaunt*. . . . Caroline . . . has just entered the household of Mrs Delaney (Mrs Hamilton)' (Mona Wilson, 1938, *Jane Austen and Some Contemporaries*, p. 175).

HAMILTON, Gerald (1890–1970) Son of Frank Souter, a Shanghai merchant, he was born in Shanghai and educated at Rugby, and changed his name by deed poll. After an early life of great luxury, he ran through his money and was subsequently in perpetual financial straits.

ARTHUR NORRIS in Christopher Isherwood, *Mr Norris Changes Trains* (1935)

'[Auden] advised me to try to meet Gerald Hamilton. "Christopher Isherwood used him as . . . Arthur Norris . . ." he told me. "But there's a great deal more material hidden in *that* man"' (Robin Maugham, 1972, *Escape from the Shadows*, p. 203; see also Gerald Hamilton, 1969, *The Way It Was With Me*, ch. 4.) 'Christopher first met Gerald Hamilton in the winter of 1930–31. . . . It seems to me that [he] "recognized" . . . Hamilton as Arthur Norris, his character-to-be, almost as soon as he set eyes on him' (Christopher Isherwood, 1977, *Christopher and His Kind, 1929–1939*, London: Eyre Methuen, pp. 60, 62).

HAMMERSLEY, Violet (1877–1964) Daughter of William Peere Williams Freeman, second Secretary at the Paris Embassy from 1873 to 1878. Her father died in 1884, but the family remained in Paris for some years. She was a childhood friend of W. Somerset **Maugham**, whose mother was her godmother. She married Arthur Hammersley, a banker, and was painted by Wilson Steer and Duncan **Grant**. Her half-sister was the Comtesse Costa de Beauregard of Fontaines les Nonnes, Seine et Marne. At the end of her life she lived at Totland Bay, Isle of Wight, in a house decorated by Duncan Grant and Boris Anrep. She was a close friend of Nancy Mitford, who described her, Madame Costa and Fontaines in 'Portrait of a French Country House', *The Water Beetle* (1962, London: Hamish Hamilton). There is a description of her and her house on the Isle of Wight in Robin Maugham, 1966, *Somerset and All the Maughams*, p. 103; she herself left a description of Fontaines at the end of the nineteenth century in 'A Childhood in Paris', *Orpheus*, 1949, Vol. II.

LADY BEECH in Nancy Mitford, *Pigeon Pie* (1940)

Mrs Hammersley always addressed Miss Mitford as 'Child' and, like Lady Beech, she certainly could discourse 'of Oscar, Aubrey, Jimmy, Algernon, Henry, Max, Willie, Osbert and the rest' (private information).

MURIEL CHITTY in Osbert Sitwell, 'That Flesh is Heir to . . .' (1930)

'Sitwell caricatured her as a germ-carrier in his story "That Flesh is Heir to . . ."' (Harold Acton, 1975, *Nancy Mitford: a memoir*, London: Hamilton, pp. 67–8).

MRS O'DONOVAN in Nancy Mitford, *The Blessing* (1951)

'Mrs O'Donovan . . . is based on Mrs Hammersley' (Acton, op. cit., p. 86).

HAMMETT, Dashiel (1894–1961) American writer of detective fiction. The best known of his novels was *The Thin Man* (1934). Well known for his left-wing sympathies, he was among those who appeared before Senator **McCarthy**'s Committee of Investigation (in 1953).

DARTNELL HARNETT in Warren Miller, *The Sleep of Reason* (1956)

He is identifiable from the initials and by his behaviour, which closely parallels that of Hammett before McCarthy. 'On only one occasion, however, had any witness fallen asleep on the stand. This was the writer of detective stories, Dartnell Harnett, who dozed off during a Mugonnigle question that lasted fifteen minutes. He woke up in time to say "no"' (*The Sleep of Reason*, 1956, p. 103).

HAMPDEN HOUSE, Buckinghamshire Situated in Great Hampden, and the home of John Hampden in the seventeenth century, it was rented by the Humphry Wards in the summer of 1889. The doorway dates from the thirteenth century, but the greater part of the house is eighteenth-century Gothic (see

Nikolaus Pevsner, 1960, *Buckinghamshire* (*Buildings of England* series), Harmondsworth: Penguin).

MELLOR PARK in Mrs Humphry Ward, *Marcella* (1894)

'I have said something already in the introduction to an earlier novel of the beautiful . . . house whence John Hampden rode to . . . Chalgrove Field. . . . The long . . . avenue . . . on which Marcella looks out, in the opening scene of the book was ours' (Introd. to *Marcella*, 1911 (Westmorland edn), Vol. I, pp. xi–xvi; there is an illustration facing p. 4).

HANLEY, Staffordshire

COKETOWN in Charles Dickens, *Hard Times* (1854)

'Coketown, which you can see today for yourself in all its grime in the Potteries (the real name of it is Hanley in Staffordshire on the London and North Western Railway) . . . is not . . . a patch of slum. . . . Coketown is the whole place' (Bernard Shaw, 1912, Introd. to *Hard Times* (Waverley edn), p. vii). *See also under* **Preston Strike**.

HANNAY, Arthur (1854–1927) London solicitor. He was an early motoring enthusiast and married Alice Hannay, a painter; they used to spend the summers at Dieppe in the Villa Séjour on the hill by the castle overlooking Dieppe. Their friends included **Whistler** and **Sickert**.

JAMES PETHEL in Max Beerbohm, 'James Pethel', *Seven Men* (1919)

'Yes: you were quite right, by the way: it *was* Hannay whose driving suggested the idea to me' (Max Beerbohm, 1964, *Letters to Reggie Turner*, ed. Rupert Hart-Davis, London: Rupert Hart-Davis, p. 240).

HANNAY, James (1827–73) Novelist, journalist and man of letters. Beginning as a midshipman in the Royal Navy from 1840 to 1845, in 1846 he became a reporter with the *Morning Chronicle*. He edited the poetical works of Edgar Allan Poe, and was Consul at Barcelona from 1868 to 1873.

EGLINTON CONYERS in Cecil Hay, *The Club and the Drawing Room* (1870)

'He is described under the name of Eglinton Conyers in The Club and the Drawing Room by Cecil Hay' (Frederic Boase, 1892, *Modern English Biography*, Vol. I, col. 1320).

HAPGOOD, Hutchins (1869–1944) Journalist. Born in Chicago, he later worked there and in New York and was the author of realistic novels and an autobiography. In 1917–18 he and Mary **Pyne** became close friends, though not lovers.

J.J. in Theodore Dreiser, 'Esther Norn', *A Gallery of Women* (1929)

'I don't know' he wrote, 'who it was that told my old friend Theodore Dreiser that I was carrying on an affair with Mary. . . . But as I found out years afterwards, he sat down and wrote a story about Mary and me – Mary was wronged and seduced, I was . . . a regular Svengali figure, romantically evil . . . he made a picture of a number of realistic details . . . which made it clear . . .

that I was intended' (Hutchins Hapgood, 1972, *A Victorian in the Modern World*, p. 430).

HARCOURT, Lewis, 1st Viscount (1863–1922) Politician. Son of Sir William Harcourt, from 1910 to 1915 he was Secretary of State for the Colonies. He was opposed to the suffragette movement.

SIR WILFRID LANG in Mrs Humphry Ward, *Delia Blanchflower* (1915)

'The burning of Monk Lawrence . . . is based on the actual burning of Nuneham House, owned by the anti-suffragette cabinet minister, Lewis Harcourt' (Georgia Dunbar, 1953, 'The faithful recorder: Mrs Humphry Ward and the background of her novels', unpublished Ph.D. dissertation, Columbia University, p. 250).

HARCOURT, Sir William (1827–1904) Statesman. Of Plantagenet descent, he was educated at Cambridge, where he was an Apostle. He was called to the Bar in 1854, and in 1859 he married Thérèse, daughter of T.H. Lister. He became Liberal MP in 1868, and was Solicitor-General in 1873–4, Home Secretary in 1880–5, and Chancellor of the Exchequer in 1882–94. Lady Waldegrave said she thought him the handsomest man she knew, except for Julian Fane, and that he was 'like a hawk ready to pounce on his prey'.

SIR ETHELRED in Joseph Conrad, *The Secret Agent* (1907)

'The most vivid description of him is to be found in *The Secret Agent*, where he appears as Sir Ethelred. . . . Conrad has also suggested the inflections of his deep smooth voice and his laconic interruptions of anyone conveying information . . . and his habit of relapsing into a sort of absentminded loftiness. The only detail in [the] description to which my memory demurs is the word "pale", for towards the end of his life his complexion was a very deep pink' (Desmond MacCarthy, 1931, 'Sir William Harcourt', *Portraits*, p. 128). 'I came upon . . . the . . . recollections of an Assistant Commissioner of the Police. . . . I won't even try to explain why I should have been arrested by a . . . passage of about seven lines, in which the author . . . reproduced a short dialogue . . . with the Home Secretary. I think it was Sir William Harcourt then. . . . The phrase . . . that struck me most was Sir W. Harcourt's . . . "All that's very well. But your idea of secrecy over there seems to consist of keeping the Home Secretary in the dark"' (*The Secret Agent*, 1907, p. xi author's note. The reference is to R. Anderson, *Sidelights on the Home Rule Movement*, 1907, p. 89. Compare *The Secret Agent*, ch. VI.

HARDING, Helen (b. 1895?) An American woman from Boston who Wolfe met in 1925 when she and her friend Marjorie **Fairbanks** were in Paris with Kenneth **Raisbeck**.

ANN in Thomas Wolfe, *Of Time and the River* (1935)

'During Wolfe's 1925 trip to Europe, he had fallen in love with a woman named Helen Harding. . . . The experience is recounted fictionally in *Of Time and the River* pp. 680–794 [ch. 76–89]' (*My Other Loneliness: letters of Thomas Wolfe and Aline Bernstein*, 1983, ed. Suzanne Stutman, Chapel Hill, NC, and London: University of North Carolina Press, p. 63 n. 1).

HARDING, Warren Gamaliel (1865–1923) Born in Ohio, he was the twenty-fourth president of the United States, from 1921 to 1923.

WESLEY BLAKE in Brand Whitlock, *Big Matt* (1928)

'His aspect is familiar, for Blake is the first of several figures modeled on Warren G. Harding' (Joseph Blotner, 1966, *The Modern American Political Novel*, Austin, Tex., p. 71). 'Like Harding, Blake is a mid-westerner. His state is not identified, but it has an Indian name' (ibid., n. 31).

JUDSON CUMMING HAMMOND in Thomas Frederic Tweed, *Gabriel Over the White House* (1933)

'Another figure drawn in the image of Warren Gamaliel Harding' (Blotner, op. cit., p. 146).

WILLIS MARKHAM in Samuel Hopkins Adams, *Revelry* (1926)

'The President in the year 1951 [Harry S. Truman] resembles *Revelry's* Willis Markham as Markham had resembled Warren Harding' (ibid., p. 157).

HARDINGE, Charles, 1st Baron Hardinge of Penshurst (1858–1944) He was Ambassador at St Petersburg 1904–6; Permanent Under-secretary of State for Foreign Affairs 1906–10 and 1916–20; and Viceroy of India 1910–16.

ROBERT LESLIE in W.H. Mallock, *The New Republic* (1877)

'Traditionally has been identified with Charles Hardinge ... first Baron Hardinge of Penshurst' (*The New Republic*, 1950, ed. J. Max Patrick, Gainsville, p. xvii). *See also* **Hardinge**, William; **Stephen**, Leslie.

HARDINGE, William Money (1854–1916) Son of a London doctor, he was educated at Westminster and at Balliol College, Oxford. In 1876 he won the Newdigate Prize for a poem on Helen of Troy, but was too ill to declaim it at the Sheldonian. 'There was at Balliol a gentle youth of my time, W.M. Hardinge, the son of an eminent physician. Of delicate health, he passed for a *malade imaginaire*. . . . A disciple of Mallock, he used to recline on his sofa and recite to his friends pages of what he called mysteriously "Mallock's book". This was *The New Republic*' (Shane Leslie, 1930, *Memoir of J.E.C. Bodley*, p. 35).

ROBERT LESLIE in W.H. Mallock, *The New Republic* (1877)

'Leslie is surely based on W.M. Hardinge, Mallock's Oxford friend?' (J. Lucas, 1975, Introd. to *The New Republic*, Leicester, p. 17). *See also* **Hardinge**, Charles; **Stephen**, Leslie.

HARDMAN, Sir William (1828–1890) Educated at Bury Grammar School and at Trinity College, Cambridge, he was called to the Bar in 1852. He lived at Norbiton Hall, Kingston on Thames, and was for many years Chairman of the Surrey Sessions. He was a close friend of Meredith's, and was for some time Editor of the *Morning Post*. For many years he kept a journal, which was published in three volumes (1923–30).

BLACKBURN TUCKMAN in George Meredith, *Beauchamp's Career* (1876)

'There is no doubt that in Blackburn Tuckman we have an authentic and amusing picture of William Hardman' (S.M. Ellis, 1920, *George Meredith*, 2nd edn, London: Grant Richards, p. 240).

HARDY Valet to Harry (later Sir Harry) Preston, host at the Royal York Hotel, Brighton, when Arnold Bennett stayed there in January 1910 while writing *Clayhanger*.

THE PAGEBOY AT THE ROYAL SUSSEX HOTEL in Arnold Bennett, the *Clayhanger* trilogy (1910)

'The pageboy [in *Clayhanger*] is Hardy, my valet' (Sir Harry Preston, 1936, *Leaves from My Unwritten Diary*, London: Hutchinson; quoted in Reginald Pound, 1952, *Arnold Bennett: a biography*, London: Heinemann, p. 214).

HARDY, Emma (d. 1912) Née Gifford. Daughter of a retired solicitor, she met Thomas Hardy at the house of her brother-in-law, the Revd Caddell **Holder**, Rector of St Juliot, Cornwall, when Hardy was engaged in the restoration of the parish church; they were married in 1874. She was of some social pretensions and later became an acute eccentric; for many years the marriage was unhappy. When Hardy first met her, she had literary ambitions and had written a novel.

ELFRIDE SWANCOURT in Thomas Hardy, *A Pair of Blue Eyes* (1873)

'The character and appearance of Elfride have points in common with those of Mrs Hardy in quite young womanhood, a few years before Hardy met her (though her eyes would have been described as deep grey, not as blue); moreover, like Elfride, the moment she was on a horse, she was part of the animal' (F.E. Hardy, 1972, *The Life of Thomas Hardy, 1840–1928*, p. 74).

HARDY, Florence Née Dugdale. Daughter of an Enfield schoolmaster, in 1914 she married Thomas **Hardy**, becoming his second wife, after acting as his secretary for some years.

AMY DRIFFIELD in W. Somerset Maugham, *Cakes and Ale* (1930)

'*Cakes and Ale* has made a huge sensation and is selling like hot cakes. Hugh Walpole bursts into tears when it is mentioned. ... Mrs Thomas Hardy, however, seems quite untouched. I sat by her at luncheon the other day & she talked so exactly out of *Cakes and Ale* that I could hardly believe that she was the genuine thing, not someone who was acting & indeed over-acting the part' (Logan Pearsall Smith to Cyril Connolly, 14 December 1920, reproduced in *A Portrait of Logan Pearsall Smith: from his letters and diaries*, 1950, introd. John Russell, p. 130).

HARDY, Jemima (1813–1904) Daughter of George and Betty (née Swetman) Hand. When her father, who would appear to have been a shepherd, died, he left his wife 'with several children, the youngest only a few months old' (F.E. Hardy, 1972, *Life of Thomas Hardy, 1840–1928*, p. 7). In 1839 she married Thomas Hardy the second, and thenceforth lived at **Higher Bockhampton**; their son was Thomas Hardy the novelist.

ETHELBERTA CHICKEREL in Thomas Hardy, *The Hand of Ethelberta* (1876)

'Ethelberta's London enterprise for her family was suggested by "a rather adventurous scheme" on the part of [Hardy's] mother. . . . Thomas Hardy's maternal grandmother was left a widow with seven children; his mother, before she was married, formed the idea of being a club-house cook and applied to the Earl of Ilchester to assist her. He sent her to his brother in London, where she became a skilful cook, taking her brothers and sisters with her' (F.B. Pinion, 1968, *A Hardy Companion*, London: Macmillan, p. 29).

HARDY, Thomas (1840–1928) English novelist, playwright and poet. He was born in Upper Bockhampton, near Dorchester, and trained as an architect. In 1868, after a problematic relationship with his cousin, Tryphena **Sparks**, he was sent to Cornwall where he met and married Emma Gifford (**Hardy**, above). Most of his celebrated novels were published before 1895, when he turned more to writing poetry and drama. After Emma's death in 1912, he met Florence Dugdale (**Hardy**, above), who became his secretary and general assistant, and then, in 1914, his wife. She published a biography of him after his death.

EDWARD DRIFFIELD in W. Somerset Maugham, *Cakes and Ale* (1930)

'The book is causing some excitement. . . . It is . . . based obviously on Hardy's history' (Lytton Strachey to Dorothy Bussy, November 1930, quoted in Michael Holroyd, 1968, *Lytton Strachey*, Vol. II, London: Heinemann, p. 680). 'Actually Maugham drew the character of Driffield largely from an obscure writer and impecunious journalist who settled in Whitstable with his family in the 1880s and whose name he does not remember' (Richard A. Cordell, 1969, *Somerset Maugham: a writer for all seasons*, 2nd edn, Bloomington and London: Indiana University Press, p. 120).

HENRY KNIGHT in Thomas Hardy, *A Pair of Blue Eyes* (1873)

'Henry Knight . . . was really much more like Thomas Hardy as described in his future wife's diary' (F.E. Hardy, 1972, *The Life of Thomas Hardy, 1840–1928*, p. 74). 'The reading of the lessons at Endelstow Church . . . is certainly autobiographical' (F.B. Pinion, 1968, *A Hardy Companion*, London: Macmillan, p. 384). *See also* **Moule**, Horace M.

EDWARD SPRINGROVE in Thomas Hardy, *Desperate Remedies* (1871)

'Though Hardy insisted that a fellow-architect at Crickmay's office . . . was his prototype, he is in some respects like Hardy. . . . The boating scene [ch. III] . . . is based on Hardy's experiences at Weymouth' (Pinion, op. cit., p. 478).

HARDY, Thomas, the First (1778–1837) Builder and master mason of **Higher Bockhampton** in Stinsford, Dorset, he married Mary Head of Fawley, Berkshire. He was an enthusiastic musician (clarinetist and player of the bass-viol) and reformed the quire, or church musicians, and 'played in the gallery of Stinsford Church at two services every Sunday from 1801–1802 till his death' (F.E. Hardy, 1972, *Life of Thomas Hardy, 1840–1928*, p. 12). He was the grandfather of Thomas Hardy the novelist.

MR YEOBRIGHT in Thomas Hardy, *The Return of the Native* (1878)

'There is no doubt that the description by Fairway in *The Return of the Native* of the bowing of Thomasin's father when lending his services to the choir of

Kingsbere, is a humorous exaggeration of the traditions concerning Thomas Hardy the First's musical triumphs as a locum-tenens' (ibid.).

HARE, Humphrey John Christian (b. 1909) Born in New Zealand. He was the author of a book about the poet **Swinburne**.

RANDOLPH PINE in Nancy Mitford, *The Pursuit of Love* (1945)

Identification based on private information.

HARFORD, John Scandrett (1785–1866) Of Blaise Castle, Gloucestershire. From 1815 to 1817, he made a collection of pictures at Blaise; in 1822 he gave the site of the castle at Lampeter for St Davids College. He became a Fellow of the Royal Society in 1823, and was an MP in 1841 and 1842.

COELEBS in Hannah More, *Coelebs in Search of a Wife* (1809)

'The hero of Hannah More's *Coelebs in search of a wife*' (Frederic Boase, 1892, *Modern English Biography*, Vol. I, col. 1335, 1336).

HARLAND, Henry (1861–1905) An American born in St Petersburg, he had some vogue in America as an author of sensational novels, one entitled *The Yoke of the Thoraks*, under the name of Sidney Lusha. He moved to England and became the Editor of *The Yellow Book* and later the Literary Adviser to John Lane.

SYDNEY THORAH in F.W. Rolfe, *Nicholas Crabbe* (1958)

'Henry Harland . . . appears . . . as Sidney Thorah, – the infamous editor of *The Blue Volume*' (Cecil Woolf, 1958, Introd. to *Nicolas Crabbe*, p. 4).

HARLEYFORD MANOR, Buckinghamshire Situated on the banks of the Thames, one and a half miles south-west of Marlow, it was built in 1755 and its grounds were landscaped by Capability Brown (see Nikolaus Pevsner, 1960, *Buckinghamshire* (*Buildings of England* series), Harmondsworth: Penguin, Pl. 1(b)).

TOAD HALL in Kenneth Grahame, *The Wind in the Willows* (1908)

'Toad Hall . . . contains elements from Harleyford Manor' (Peter Green, 1959, *Kenneth Grahame, 1859–1932*, p. 240). *See also* **Cliveden; Mapledurham House.**

HARPER (or HARPUR), Henry Richard (1798–1870) Of Chilvers Coton, Warwickshire.

MR FARQUHAR in George Eliot, 'The Sad Fortunes of the Revd Amos Barton', *Scenes of Clerical Life* (1857–8)

'He is said to be the original of Mr Farquhar . . . though Farquhar has a wife and two daughters, while Mr Harper died unmarried' (*The George Eliot Letters*, 1954, ed. Gordon S. Haight, Vol. I, London: Oxford University Press, p. 45 n. 6). *See also under* **Anstruther**, Lady.

HARRINGTON, Charles Stanhope, 4th Earl of (1780–1851) Styled Lord Petersham until 1829, he designed the Petersham overcoat and Petersham snuff-mixture.

LORD FITZBOOBY in Benjamin Disraeli, *Coningsby* (1844)

Identified in a key in *Notes and Queries* (8th series) 3 (13 May 1893): 363. *See also under* **Bright**, John. *See also* **Ryder**, Dudley.

HARRIS, Mr

MR BRAND in George Eliot, 'The Sad Fortunes of the Revd Amos Barton', *Scenes of Clerical Life* (1857–8)

See under **Anstruther**, Lady.

HARRIS, Mr and Mrs
Bacon curers of Calne, Wiltshire. Alice **Richardson** was a governess and companion to their family.

MR AND MRS GREEN in Dorothy Richardson, *Pilgrimage* (1915–67)

'[Eve's] employers the Greens . . . correspond to Alice Richardson's employers the Harrises' (John Rosenberg, 1973, *Dorothy Richardson*, London, 1973, p. 109).

HARRIS, Frank
(1856?–1931) Author and adventurer. He ran away to New York at the age of 15 and worked variously as a labourer, bootblack and bellboy, before studying law at the University of Kansas. After returning to England, he became the Editor of the *Evening News* in 1833, of the *Fortnightly Review* from 1886 to 1894, and of the *Saturday Review* from 1894 to 1898. He had a reputation as a liar, boaster and philanderer. He wrote a biography of Oscar Wilde (1916) and an autobiography, *My Life and Loves* (1923–7). Both were fantastical but were with occasional insight; the latter was banned for its pornographic content.

GEORGE EVERARD in Ford Madox Ford, *The Simple Life Limited* (1911)

'Everard has a physical resemblance to Frank Harris' (Arthur Mizener, 1971, *The Saddest Story: a biography of Ford Madox Ford*, Cleveland: World Publishing, p. 558 n. 12).

JOHN JOHNS in Frederic Carrel, *The Adventures of John Johns* (1897)

'The sketch of Frank Harris in *John Johns* is superb. Who wrote the book? It is a wonderful indictment' (Oscar Wilde to Robert Ross, 20 July 1897, reproduced in *The Letters of Oscar Wilde*, 1962, ed. Rupert Hart-Davis, London: Rupert Hart-Davis, p. 624). 'The central character is clearly based upon Harris' (ibid., n. 3).

RALPH PARKER in Hugh Kingsmill, *The Will to Love* (1919)

'Ralph Parker, the leading male figure in the novel . . . is based on the character of Frank Harris' (Michael Holroyd, 1964, *Hugh Kingsmill*, London: Unicorn Press, p. 68).

HARRIS, Thomas Lake
(1823–1906) Spiritualist. Born in Fenny Stratford, Buckinghamshire, he emigrated to Utica, New York, with his parents in 1828. In 1848 he organized the 'independent Christian Congregation' on Swedenborgian principles in New York, and in 1861 he set up a community near Wassaic. In 1859–61 and 1865–6, he visited England, and in 1867 he was

joined in America by Laurence **Oliphant**[2]. With Oliphant's money he was able to move his community to Brocton, on the shores of Lake Erie, but in 1881 he was compelled to restore Oliphant's property. In 1875 he moved to Santa Rosa. He advocated the theory of celestial marriages, and in 1876 he proclaimed his attainment of immortality; his celestial marriages had very strange earthly manifestations.

FATHER JOSEPH in Mary S. Emerson, *Among the Chosen* (1884)

The portrait is immediately recognizable.

DAVID MASOLLAM in Laurence Oliphant, *Masollam* (1886)

'A striking and not unkindly picture of Harris, drawn by Oliphant under the designation of David Masollam, portrays his "leonine aspect"' (*The Dictionary of National Biography*, 1912, Vol. II (Suppl. 2), London: Oxford University Press, p. 217).

HARRIS, Will (d. 1906) Of Asheville, North Carolina. When discovered in bed with the wife of another black man, he killed the husband, shot the policeman who was summoned, and charged through the town shooting at every moving object, killing three men; two days later he was captured, and his dead body was hung from the undertaker's window.

DICK PROSSER in Thomas Wolfe, *The Web and the Rock* (1939)

'Wolfe moulded the situation ... by having the story focus on Dick Prosser. ... [He] invented the series of incidents that opens the story and developed a character very different from the original, Will Harris.... [Finally he] made use of the true story of Will Harris as he had heard it' (R.S. Kennedy, 1962, *The Window of Memory: the literary career of Thomas Wolfe*, Chapel Hill, NC, pp. 316–8). A detailed description of Wolfe's sources for both character and incident will be found in F.C. Watkins, 1957, *Thomas Wolfe's Characters*, Norman, Okla., pp. 102–9. Watkins points out that one of the models was 'the most famous and loved Negro who ever lived in Asheville ... the ... janitor of the Bingham Academy' (ibid., p. 108). His name is not given. *See also* **Rumley**, Robert Parker.

HARRISBURG, Pennsylvania

FORT PENN in John O'Hara, *A Rage to Live* (1949)

'He ... set the story in and around Harrisburg, which he called Fort Penn' (Finis Farr, 1974, *O'Hara: a biography*, p. 211).

HARRISON, Carter Henry (1860–1953) Son of Carter Henry Harrison, who was five times Mayor of Chicago and was assassinated in 1893. He was Publisher and Editor of the *Chicago Times* from 1891 to 1894, and was Democratic Mayor of Chicago in 1897, 1899, 1901, 1903 and 1911–15. He was the leader of the fight against Charles **Yerkes**'s ever-extending control of the city's transport system.

WALDEN LUCAS in Theodore Dreiser, *The Titan* (1914)

'[Dreiser's] readers knew that ... "Lucas" [was a] thinly disguised [portrait] of ... Mayor Carter Henry Harrison II' (Walter T.K. Nugent, 1966, 'Carter H. Harrison and Dreiser's "Walden Lucas"', *Newberry Library Bulletin* 6 (7): 222).

HARRISON, Frederic (1831–1923) Positivist. He was called to the Bar in 1858, and from 1880 to 1905 was President of the English Positivist Committee. He wrote on historical and literary subjects, and from 1877 to 1889 was Professor of Jurisprudence, Constitutional, and International Law for the Council of Legal Education. In 1880 he engaged George **Gissing** as tutor to his sons.

HAROLD EDGEWORTH in Morley Roberts, *The Private Life of Henry Maitland* (1912)

Identified in an 'Index of Recurring Pseudonyms' in the 1958 edition of *The Private Life of Henry Maitland*, ed. Morchard Bishop, p. 255.

HARROWBY, 2nd Earl of *See* **Ryder**, Dudley.

HART, Michael (d. before 1900) Known as 'Monsart', i.e. Monsieur Hart, from his habit of speaking French. He was a friend of John **Joyce**, James Joyce's father, and knew a great deal about racing: 'his great day was that . . . when he "tipped the double" in verse; that is, he predicted the winners of both [the Lincoln and the Grand National]' (Richard Ellmann, 1966, *James Joyce*, London: Oxford Paperbacks, p. 376).

T. LENEHAN in James Joyce, 'Two Gallants', *Dubliners* (1914) and *Ulysses* (1922)

'Lenehan was based mostly on Michael Hart' (ibid., p. 228).

HARTFOOT LANE, Dorset A small village among the chalk hills overlooking the Vale of Blackmoor.

STAGFOOT LANE in Thomas Hardy, Wessex novels and tales (1871–95)

Identified on a map prepared by Thomas Hardy which hangs in the Dorset County Museum, Dorchester. *See under* **Abbotsbury.**

HARTINGTON, Lord *See* **Devonshire**, 8th Duke of.

HARTLEPOOL, County Durham

COCKLETON in W.M. Thackeray, 'Notes on the North What-d'ye-Callem Election' (1841)

Identified in *Letters and Private Papers of W.M. Thackeray*, 1945, ed. Gordon N. Ray, Vol. II, London: Oxford University Press, p. 27 n. 49.

HARTLEY, Grizel (1900–87) Daughter of Sir George Seton Buchanan, Senior Medical Officer at the Ministry of Health, she was educated at St Paul's Girls School and at Girton College, Cambridge. In 1923 she married Hubert Horton-Smith Hartley, who was a master, and later a house master, at Eton.

JENNIFER BAIRD in Rosamund Lehmann, *Dusty Answer* (1927)

'Fictional but recognisable depictions of Grizel appear in *Dusty Answer* (as . . . Jennifer Baird); in John Le Carré's *A Murder of Quality* (as a public school housemaster's wife, Shane Hecht); in *Of Flowers and a Village* (as Delia Lovell . . .)' (P.S.H. Lawrence (ed.), 1991, *Grizel: Grizel Hartley remembered*, Salisbury, p. 131).

SHANE HECHT in John Le Carré, *A Murder of Quality* (1962)

See above.

DELIA LOVELL in Wilfrid Blunt, *Of Flowers and a Village* (1963)

See above.

HARTLEY, Marsden (1877–1943) American expressionist painter and occasional poet. He was born in Lewiston, Maine and trained at the Cleveland School of Art. He travelled extensively in Europe and was heavily influenced by the abstract work of Kandinsky, among others. He became a leading figure in the development of modern American art.

BRANDER OGDEN in Robert McAlmon, *Post Adolescence* (1923)

'Marsden Hartley . . . appears as Brander Ogden – this portrait is particularly illuminating' (Robert E. Knoll, 1959, *Robert McAlmon, Expatriate Publisher and Writer*, Lincoln, Nebr.: University of Nebraska Press, p. 51).

HARTSHEAD, Yorkshire

NUNNELLY in Charlotte Brontë, *Shirley* (1849)

'Nunnelly . . . is Hartshead, in the little Norman church of which Mr Brontë officiated as vicar from 1811 to 1815' (Herbert Wroot, 1935, *Sources of Charlotte Brontë's Novels: persons and places*, Shipley, Yorks., p. 254).

HARVEY, Daisy Elizabeth (1883–1963?) Daughter of George Harvey, metal merchant of Lewisham, she was educated at Lewisham Grammar School, Brunswick, and Howard College, Bedford. At the latter, she met Ivy Compton-Burnett, and in 1902 they arrived at Royal Holloway College on the same day. In 1906 she took her B.Sc. A woman of the same name became a schoolmistress in London and subsequently at Great Crosby, near Liverpool, where she later started a school of her own and died on 4 July 1963 (see Hilary Spurling, 1974, *Ivy When Young: the early life of I. Compton-Burnett, 1884–1919*, London: Gollancz, p. 297 n. 10).

PERDITA KINGSFORD in I. Compton-Burnett, *Dolores* (1911)

'All her contemporaries agree that Ivy had only one close companion at college, a girl named Daisy Harvey, short, plumpish and rather pretty . . . whom she had known at Howard College . . . and it is at least possible that she provided the model for Perdita Kingsford. . . . Miss Bremner at any rate thought that, of all their contemporaries at Holloway, "Miss Harvey was the nearest to Perdita"' (ibid., p. 151).

HASLAM, Francis William Chapman (1848–1924) Born in Cotta, Ceylon, where his father was a translator of the Bible into Sinhalese. He was educated at Rugby and at St John's College, Cambridge, and taught at Westward Ho! until 1879, when he became Professor of Classics at Canterbury College, New Zealand.

MR KING in Rudyard Kipling, *Stalky & Co.* (1899)

'["King"] owes some features to ... F.W. Haslam, who grounded Kipling in Latin during his first two years at school and then departed. ... Haslam introduced Kipling to Horace' (Charles Carrington, 1955, *Rudyard Kipling: his life and work*, p. 33). Also identified in the caption to a photograph reproduced in the June 1981 issue of *The Kipling Journal*: 'Masters at the United Services College ... in Kipling's day' (*The Kipling Journal* 48 (218): 21). *See also* **Crofts**, W.C.

HATHERSAGE, Derbyshire

MORTON in Charlotte Brontë, *Jane Eyre* (1847)

'The village [of Morton] ... has been identified with ... Hathersage in the vale of Derwent, Derbyshire. ... In the novel the place is but slightly disguised. ... The Rev. Henry Nussey ... became vicar of Hathersage in 1844. In [1845] ... he married, and during his honeymoon Miss Ellen Nussey [his sister] went to Hathersage ... and invited her friend Charlotte Brontë to stay with her' (Herbert Wroot, 1935, *The Sources of Charlotte Brontë's Novels: persons and places*, Shipley, Yorks., p. 21).

HATHORNE, John (1640?–1717) An ancestor of Nathaniel Hawthorne, he served as a judge in the Salem witchcraft trials of 1691–2: 'the curse pronounced on him by one of his victims was remembered by his descendants and was blamed for any evil fortune which befell the house' (*The Dictionary of National Biography*, London: Oxford University Press, s.v. Hawthorne, Nathaniel).

COLONEL PYNCHEON in Nathaniel Hawthorne, *The House of the Seven Gables* (1851)

'This circumstance doubtless furnished a hint for that piece of tradition in the book which represents a Pyncheon of a former generation as having persecuted one Maule, who declared that God would give his enemy "blood to drink"' (G.P. Lathrop, 1883, Introd. to *The House of the Seven Gables*, Cambridge, Mass., p. 8). *See also* **Noyes**, Nicholas.

von HATZFELDT, Countess Sophie

BARONESS LUCIE VON CREFELDT in George Meredith, *The Tragic Comedians* (1880)

'[Lassalle's] personal reputation was sullied by his long-standing alliance with the Countess Sophie von Hatzfeldt. ... [She] became Lucie, Baroness von Crefeldt' (A. Lionel Stevenson, 1954, *The Ordeal of George Meredith*, London: Peter Owen, p. 239).

HAUSSÉ, Mademoiselle Governess on the staff of the Pensionnat Héger in Brussels in 1843; she was a colleague of Charlotte Brontë.

HORTENSE MOORE in Charlotte Brontë, *Shirley* (1849)

'The portrait of [Mademoiselle Haussé] as Hortense Moore in *Shirley* was so lifelike that the Wheelwright girls, reading the book years later, exclaimed at the resemblance. It was indeed this clue ... that made them guess the identity of Currer Bell' (Winifred Gérin, 1969, *Charlotte Brontë*, Oxford, p. 235).

HAWKEN, Mr A Cornish landlord at Portcothan in 1915; he boasted of evicting an old woman from one of his cottages.

JAZ TREWHELLA in D.H. Lawrence, *Kangaroo* (1923)

'Hawken ... was probably the inspiration for ... Jaz Trewhella, the sly little Cornishman transplanted to Australia in [*Kangaroo*]' (H.T. Moore, 1960, *The Intelligent Heart: the story of D.H. Lawrence*, Harmondsworth: Penguin, p. 267; originally published 1955, London: Heinemann).

HAWKER, Revd Robert Stephen (1804–75) Poet and clergyman. In 1827 he was the winner of the Newdigate Prize. From 1834 to 1875 he was Vicar of Morwenstow, but was received into the Roman Catholic Church on his death-bed. He wrote *The Quest of the San Graal*.

CANON TREMAINE in Mortimer Collins, *Sweet and Twenty* (1875)

'Delineated in Mortimer Collins' novel ... as Canon Tremaine' (Frederic Boase, 1892, *Modern English Biography*, Vol. I, col. 1385).

HAWKINS, Lewis Weldon (d. 1910) Painter. Born in Stuttgart and brought up in Brussels, he was naturalized as a French citizen. He was a cousin of James **Browne** and in 1873 he met George Moore at Julian's studio in Paris; he became his close friend. He exhibited in the Paris Salons.

HENRY MARSHALL in George Moore, *Confessions of a Young Man* (1888) and others

'The Lewis Ponsonby Marshall of the *Confessions* and of *Hail and Farewell*' (Joseph Hone, 1936, *The Life of George Moore*, London: Victor Gollancz, p. 47). The character's name was later changed to Henry.

LEWIS SEYMOUR in George Moore, *A Modern Lover* (1883)

'No reader ... will doubt that ... Lewis sat for the portrait of the ingenuous but resourceful egoist who is helped all his life by women' (Hone, op. cit., p. 95).

HAWTHORNE, Julian (1846–1934) Son of Nathaniel **Hawthorne**, he was educated in the United States and Europe and spent part of his early life in England. He was a popular novelist.

GEORGE FLACK in Henry James, *The Reverberator* (1888)

'November 17th, 1887 ... [The journalist] means no harm in pumping [the girl], and she means none in telling him everything about her prospective circle. ... The result is a most fearful letter from the young man to his ... newspaper ... a letter as monstrous as Julian H's ... betrayal last winter of J.R.L.' (*The Notebooks of Henry James*, 1947, ed. F.O. Matthiessen and K.B. Murdock, New York, p. 83). 'In October 1886 Julian Hawthorne printed in a New York newspaper his version of a conversation with [James Russell] Lowell about English affairs. Lowell wrote to a friend: "He *knew* that I didn't know he was interviewing me ... though he has remembered some of the subjects (none of my choosing) which we talked about, he has wholly misrepresented the tone and sometimes falsified the substance of what I said"' (ibid., pp. 83, 84 n. 1). Lowell had been, until 1885, the US Ambassador in London.

HAWTHORNE, Nathaniel (1804–64) American novelist and short-story writer. He was born in Salem, Massachusetts, the son of a sea captain who died of yellow fever in 1808. He was brought up by his widowed mother in straitened circumstances. He published his first novel, *Fanshawe*, in 1828 after a period of almost hermetic seclusion. He contributed to a number of journals and in 1837 published his first collection of short stories. His work was not very well received and he was forced in 1839 to accept a position as measurer at the Boston Customs House, a post he held until 1841. In that year he married Sophia Peabody (sister of Elizabeth Palmer **Peabody**), and the following year they settled in Concord; from 1846 to 1849 he was Surveyor of the port of Salem. He wrote prolifically for the following three years, publishing *The Scarlet Letter*, his most famous novel, in 1850. In 1853 he was appointed US Consul for Liverpool and lived in England for four years. He then lived in Italy for two years before returning to the United States in 1960.

MILES COVERDALE in Nathaniel Hawthorne, *The Blithedale Romance* (1852)

'Coverdale is a self-portrait of Hawthorne, but a highly distorted and mocking self-portrait' (Irving Howe, 1961, *Politics and the Novel*, p. 166).

HAWTHORNE, Una Daughter of Nathaniel Hawthorne.

PEARL in Nathaniel Hawthorne, *The Scarlett Letter* (1850)

'[T]here is something that frightens me about the child – I know not whether elfin or angelic but at all events supernatural. . . . I cannot believe her to be my own human child, but a spirit, strangely mingled with good and evil, haunting the house' (Nathaniel Hawthorne, 1932, *American Notebooks*, ed. Randall Stuart, New York, January–June 1849). This identification is generally accepted.

HAYDON, Benjamin Robert (1786–1846) Historical painter. Born in Plymouth, in 1815 he campaigned for the purchase of the Elgin Marbles. He was later imprisoned for debt, and after some years he committed suicide, despite some success with the sale of his larger paintings. His pupils included Landseer and Eastlake, and he was the author of an autobiography and 'Lectures on painting and design'.

THE PAINTER OF THE HEROIC in George Borrow, *Lavengro* (1851)

'It is impossible not to recognise Haydon; the picture given of him – which we first read as a comic exaggeration – is minutely correct, and not one jot more ludicrous than the living original' (Wentwell Elwin, 1853, 'Article on Tom Taylor: *Life of Benjamin Robert Haydon*', *Quarterly Review*: 574). See Angus Fraser, 1971 ('George Borrow and the painter of the heroic', *Notes and Queries* 216: 370) for a discussion of the discrepancies and inaccuracies in Borrow's account of his meeting with Haydon.

HAYES, Mrs (1815?–1905) Née Littlefair, of Manchester. As a young woman, she entered the service of Mrs Henry **Burnett** (Dickens's sister Fanny), and took charge of little Harry **Burnett**.

POLLY TOODLE in Charles Dickens, *Dombey and Son* (1846–8)

'Mrs Hayes, during her connexion with the Burnett family, frequently came under the notice of Charles Dickens, who took great interest in her, and frequently told her that he had used her for a character in more than one of his books' (Arthur Humphreys, 1907, 'The prototype of Polly Toodle', *The Dickensian* 3 (March): 73; the article also shows a photograph encaptioned 'The late Mrs Hayes. The original of Polly Toodle').

HAYES, Rutherford Birchard (1822–93) Nineteenth president of the United States, 1877–81. He was elected after a close and disputed election, his Democratic opponent being Samuel Tilden; the election was decided by an electoral commission, with one vote in Hayes's favour.

OLD GRANITE in Henry Adams, *Democracy* (1880)

'Hayes's feebleness and good intentions lie close to the surface of the sketch as befitted the "third-rate nonentity" of Adams's original estimate. In more questionable taste were the patronizing allusions to Mrs Hayes's provincial morality . . . she barred wine, billiards and cards from the White House and insisted on high necked gowns and long sleeves' (Ernest Samuels, 1958, *Henry Adams: the middle years*, Cambridge, Mass., p. 93). Samuels points out that Old Granite also contains elements taken from Lincoln and Grant.

HAYNES, Edmund Sidney Pollock (1877–1949) Educated at Eton and Balliol, he became an eminent lawyer. He was a cousin by marriage of Aldous Huxley, who wrote of him: 'His death marks the passing . . . of an epoch of history, and, one might almost say, a character in fiction' (Ronald W. Clark, 1968, *The Huxleys*, London: Heinemann, p. 344).

TIMOTHY BARTER in A.P. Herbert, *Holy Deadlock* (1934)

'. . . a dedicated divorce law reformer, and the original of the lawyer in A.P. Herbert's *Holy Deadlock*' (ibid., p. 244).

HAYNES, Mabel She was the leader of a group of graduates of Smith and **Bryn Mawr College** who met in 1900 and 1901 at her apartment in Baltimore for discussion; Gertrude Stein, then in her last years at Johns Hopkins University, joined them. She married a captain, called Hessig, in the Austrian army *c*.1907.

SOPHIE NEATHE in Gertrude Stein, *Things As They Are* (1950)

'Mabel Haynes was transposed into the character of Mabel Neathe' (James R. Mellow, 1974, *The Charmed Circle: Gertrude Stein and company*, London: Phaidon Press, p. 59). In the 1950 edition, 'Mabel Neathe's name was altered to Sophie Neathe to avoid possible identification of the subject' (ibid., p. 484 n. 58).

HAYWARD, Abraham (1801–84) Essayist. In 1845 he was QC at Inner Temple. He contributed to the *Quarterly Review*, the *Edinburgh Review*, *Fraser's Magazine*, and occasionally to *The Times*. He translated Goethe's *Faust* (1831), and was well known as a raconteur: Thomas Carlyle called him 'the cleverest of our second-rate men'.

ST BARBE in Benjamin Disraeli, *Endymion* (1880)

'St Barbe is far more Hayward than Thackeray' (Walter Sichel, 1904, *Disraeli: a study in personality and ideas*, London: Methuen, p. 17 n.). *See also* **Carlyle**, Thomas; **Thackeray**, W.M.

VENOM TUFT in Samuel Warren, *Ten Thousand a Year* (1841)

'Drawn as Venom Tuft in *Ten Thousand a Year*' (Frederic Boase, 1892, *Modern English Biography*, Vol. I, col. 1402).

HAYWOOD, John Harrington (1829?–1912) Owner of J.H. Haywood Ltd, surgical goods manufacturers at 9 Castle Gate, Nottingham, where D.H. Lawrence was employed as a clerk from July to December 1901 after he left Nottingham High School.

THOMAS JORDAN in D.H. Lawrence, *Sons and Lovers* (1913)

'From the boy's first caustic interview with the owner, the experience at Haywood's appears at great length in *Sons and Lovers*' (H.T. Moore, 1960, *The Intelligent Heart: the story of D.H. Lawrence*, Harmondsworth: Penguin, p. 57; originally published 1955, London: Heinemann). '[Lawrence] got the job [at Haywood's], and was paid about thirteen shillings a week. He has described the place in *Sons and Lovers*' (Ada Lawrence and G. Stuart Gelder, 1935, *Young Lorenzo: the early life of D.H. Lawrence*, Florence, p. 71).

HAYWOOD, William Dudley (1869–1928) US labour agitator. In 1896 he joined the Western Federation of Miners, and in 1900 he was dominant in its leadership. He founded the International Workers of the World in 1905, and eventually became national Secretary-Treasure. In 1917 he was arrested on a charge of sedition, and in 1918 was sentenced to twenty years' imprisonment and a fine of $10,000; he was released on bail, pending an appeal, and escaped to the Soviet Union, where he lived for the rest of his life. He lost an eye et the age of 9.

JIM MARSH in Ernest Poole, *The Harbor* (1915)

'[Poole] met Bill Hayward [in 1913] when he came to New York [to organize a strike in the Paterson, New Jersey, silk mills and] accompanied [him] when he went to Paterson and addressed twenty thousand strikers in an open-air meeting. This scene . . . became a part of the climax in *The Harbor*, and Haywood . . . became a model for . . . Jim Marsh' (T.F. Keefer, 1966, *Ernest Poole*, New York, p. 45).

HAZELBURY BRYAN, Dorset A village in the Vale of Blackmoor, under Bulbarrow to the north.

NUTTLEBURY in Thomas Hardy, *Tess of the d'Urbervilles* (1891)

Identified in F.B. Pinion, 1968, *A Hardy Companion*, London: Macmillan.

H.D. *See* **Doolittle**, Hilda.

HEADLAM, Walter (1866–1908) In 1890 he was a Fellow of King's College, Cambridge. He translated Meleager and Aeschylus, and was 'rarely surpassed in Greek versions of English poetry' (*The Dictionary of National Biography*,

London: Oxford University Press). In 1907 he was engaged in a flirtation with Virginia Woolf.

WILLIAM BANKES in Virginia Woolf, *To the Lighthouse* (1927)

'What do I after all feel for Walter Headlam, except that one of these days I shall put him into a novel?' (to Vanessa Bell, 23 March 1919, *The Letters of Virginia Woolf*, 1976, ed. Nigel Nicolson, Vol. II, London: Hogarth Press, p. 338). 'Headlam may have served as a model for Mr Bankes' (Quentin Bell, 1973, *Virginia Woolf*, Vol. I, p. 118 n.).

DR MELEAGER in Shane Leslie, *The Cantab* (1926)

Identified in a key in the hand of Dr Ivor Ramsay, a Kingsman of the year 1920, and later Dean, laid in a copy of *The Cantab*.

WILLIAM RODNEY in Virginia Woolf, *Night and Day* (1919)

'If there was a dash of anybody in Rodney, I think it must have been Walter Headlam' (to J.T. Sheppard, 5 January 1920, reproduced in *Letters*, op. cit., p. 414).

HEALD, Revd William Margetson He was Vicar of Birstall, Yorkshire, for many years in the period when Charlotte Brontë was living in Haworth.

CYRIL HALL in Charlotte Brontë, *Shirley* (1849)

'The sketch of Mr Hall appears to have been based on the person and character of the Rev. William Margetson Heald' (Herbert Wroot, 1935, *Sources of Charlotte Brontë's Novels: persons and places*, Shipley, Yorks., p. 118). '[T]he story goes that either I or my father, I do not exactly know which, are part of "Currer Bell's" stock-in-trade, under the title of Mr Hall, in that Mr Hall is represented as black, bilious, and of dismal aspect, stooping a trifle, and indulging a little now and then in the indigenous dialect ... this seems to sit very well on your humble servant – other traits do better for my good father than myself. However, though I had no idea that I should be made a means to amuse the public, Currer Bell is perfectly welcome to what she can make of so unpromising a subject' (W.M. Heald to Ellen Nussey, 8 January 1850, reproduced in T.J. Wise and J.A. Symington, 1932, *The Brontës: their lives, friendships and correspondence*, Vol. IV, p. 64).

HEARD, Gerald (1889–1971)

JOSEPH MILLER in Aldous Huxley, *Eyeless in Gaza* (1936)

'Under the influence of Gerald Heard, who appears in *Eyeless in Gaza* as Joseph Miller ... Huxley becomes ... concerned with the practical ramifications of mysticism' (Jerome Meckier, 1969, *Aldous Huxley*, p. 154). *See also* **Alexander**, F. Matthias; **Pennell**, Theodore.

AUGUSTUS PARR in Christopher Isherwood, *Down There on a Visit* (1962)

'There's a very crude parody of the way he talks in *Down There on a Visit*, in the character of Augustus Parr' (Isherwood to W.I. Scobie, quoted in George Plumpton (ed.), 1977, *Writers at Work: the Paris Review interviews* (4th series), Harmondsworth: Penguin, p. 229).

WILLIAM PROPTER in Aldous Huxley, *After Many a Summer* (1939)

'In 1937 he [left] England for America where he became a close friend of . . . Aldous Huxley, who portrayed him as the mystic William Propter . . . and, possibly, Bruno Rontini' (Michael Holroyd, 1968, *Lytton Strachey*, Vol. II, London: Heinemann, p. 575 n.).

BRUNO RONTINI in Aldous Huxley, *Time Must Have a Stop* (1944)

See above.

HEARNE, Dr Edwin (1820?–80)

DR SHRAPNEL in George Meredith, *Beauchamp's Career* (1876)

'[Dr Shrapnel's] immediate prototype was an actual Southampton resident, Dr Edwin Hearne, who had been one of Maxse's chief supporters in the election [of 1868]. Hearne's penchant for controversy is indicated by the titles of two of his pamphlets: *Cholera Non-contagious, and the Absurdity of Quarantine Restrictions* and *Thoughts on Medical Education, and the Importance of Relieving Mental Labour from Legal Restrictions*' (A. Lionel Stevenson, 1954, *The Ordeal of George Meredith*, London: Peter Owen, p. 200).

HEARST, William Randolph (1863–1951) Newspaper proprietor. Born in San Francisco, in 1887 he took charge of his father's San Francisco *Examiner*. He built up a chain of newspapers throughout the United States, and later became the owner of film and radio companies. Through his newspapers he conducted violent political campaigns of extreme nationalism, opposing the League of Nations and demanding the suppression of racial minorities. He lived on his estate at San Simeon in California, and for some years his companion was Marion **Davis**.

WILLIS RANDALL I in Dalton Trumbo, *Washington Jitters* (1936)

'Trumbo made wholesale borrowings from life. . . . Willis Randall I [seems to bear some relationship] to William Randolph Hearst' (Joseph Blotner, 1966, *The Modern American Political Novel*, Austin, Tex., p. 132).

JOSEPH PAUL STOYTE in Aldous Huxley, *After Many a Summer* (1939)

'Aldous came as near to making use of living models as he ever did. His Mr Stoyte . . . maintains a private laboratory, researching ways of prolonging human life' (Sybille Bedford, 1973, *Aldous Huxley: a biography*, Vol. I, London: Chatto & Windus, p. 379). Stoyte's castle is 'an almost undisguised version of W. Randolph Hearst's aberration, where the Huxleys spent a fascinated weekend. (Domestic details, such as cotton sheets in a house with an old master in the lift, were imparted in Maria's letters)' (ibid.).

HEATH, Mabel She shared a flat with Ellie ('Johnnie') **Schleussner** in Bloomsbury, London, in 1896.

MAG in Dorothy Richardson, *Pilgrimage* (1915–67)

'Jan and Mag (Johnny Schleussner and Mabel Heath)' (Gloria G. Fromm, 1977, *Dorothy Richardson*, London, p. 129).

HECHT, Ben (1893–1964) American novelist, journalist and playwright. He was a member of the Bohemian literary set in Chicago immediately after the First World War. He later moved to New York, where he became a friend of Maxwell **Bodenheim**, with whom he wrote a play and conducted a well-publicized literary feud; his most successful play was *The Front Page* (1928), written with Charles MacArthur.

BEN HELGIN in Maxwell Bodenheim, *Ninth Avenue* (1926)

'Two of his novels ... lampooned ... Maxwell Bodenheim ... who had lampooned Hecht in his *Ninth Avenue*' (Dorothy Parker, 1971, *A Month of Saturdays*, p. 137 n.).

HEDGECOCK, Bill He was the brother of Bert, who had been handyman to the Garnetts at The Cearne, their house near Limpsfield. The incident upon which the tale is based took place in 1901.

JOE STARLING in David Garnett, *Beany-Eye* (1935)

'An interesting character ... suddenly turned into a raving maniac.... The poor fellow is now in an Asylum' (Edward Garnett to R.B. Cunninghame Graham, 9 February 1901, reproduced in George Jefferson, 1982, *Edward Garnett*, p. 33). 'The "poor fellow" was Bill Hedgecock' (Jefferson, ibid.).

HEFTS, Ethiopia A hotel in Addis Ababa which was the headquarters of most of the Press during the early stages of the Abyssinian war. In 1930, when Waugh first visited Addis for the Coronation of Haile Selassie, it was known as the Deutsches Haus. When he returned in 1938 it had become the Pensione Germanica Bar-dancing, but Heft was still the proprietor.

PENSION DRESSLER in Evelyn Waugh, *Scoop* (1938)

'It figures as the Pension Dressler in *Scoop*' (*The Diaries of Evelyn Waugh*, 1976, ed. Michael Davie, London: Weidenfeld & Nicolson, p. 400 n.).

HÉGER, Madame Claire Zoë (1804–90) She was married to Constantin **Héger** and was the Director of the Pensionnat Héger.

MADAME MODESTE MARIA BECK in Charlotte Brontë, *Villette* (1853)

'It has been frequently asserted that the characteristics of Madame Beck ... were studied from Madame Héger.... On the other hand it has been as emphatically denied that the character in any way resembled Madame Héger.... In spite of this denial information ... from former scholars in Madame Héger's school – Protestant scholars, it is only fair to say – is to the effect that the resemblance between Madame Beck and the real Madame Héger was very great' (Herbert Wroot, 1935, *Sources of Charlotte Brontë's Novels: persons and places*, Shipley, Yorks., pp. 177, 178).

HÉGER, Constantin (1809–96) Principal of the Pensionnat Héger in Brussels, where Charlotte Brontë was a pupil in 1842 and where she was a teacher of English in 1843–4. He was by all accounts a brilliantly gifted teacher. An account of his methods will be found in Mrs Gaskell, 1857, *The Life of Charlotte Brontë*, London: Smith, Elder, ch. XI).

PAUL EMANUEL in Charlotte Brontë, *Villette* (1853)

'In person, manners and characteristics Paul Emanuel was drawn, it is admitted, from M. Héger' (Herbert Wroot, 1935, *Sources of Charlotte Brontë's Novels: persons and places*, Shipley, Yorks, p. 171). '. . . a man of power as to mind, but very choleric and irritable as to temperament; a little black ugly being, with a face that varies in expression. Sometimes he borrows the lineaments of an insane tom-cat, sometimes those of a delirious hyena; occasionally, but very seldom, he discards these perilous attractions and assumes an air not above 100 degrees removed from mild and gentlemanlike' (Charlotte Brontë to Ellen Nussey, from Brussels, May 1842, quoted in T.J. Wise and J.A. Symington, 1932, *The Brontës: their lives, friendships and correspondence*, Vol. I, p. 259).

HEINEMANN, William (1863–1920) Publisher. Son of a naturalized German-Jewish father, in 1890 he set up his own publishing house in London. He became one of the most distinguished of English publishers, his authors including **Conrad, Wells, Galsworthy**, W. Somerset **Maugham** and Flora Annie Steel, whose best-selling novel *On the Face of the Waters* he accepted after it had been rejected by Macmillan.

MR HIRSCH in Flora Annie Steel, *A Sovereign Remedy* (1906)

'She includes a portrait partly based on . . . William Heinemann . . . the traits are too obvious to be ignored. Mr Hirsch is a business man of German-Jewish origin, "with nothing to show his ancestry or his age except a slight foreign lisp, and a still more slight tendency to size below the last button of his waistcoat". . . . If Flora wished to make a pretence that she was writing in general terms of a clever business man, she should have refrained from making *sole au vin blanc* the favourite dish of Mr Hirsch, as it was of William Heinemann' (Violet Powell, 1981, *Flora Annie Steel*, p. 128).

HELICON HOME COLONY, New Jersey A communal experiment founded in 1906 at Englewood by Upton **Sinclair**. It was abandoned in 1907 when the main building was destroyed by fire.

HALCYON HALL in Harry Kemp, *More Miles* (1926)

The identification is based upon obvious parallels.

HELLMANN, Lillian (1905–84)

NORA CHARLES in Dashiel Hammett, *The Thin Man* (1932)

'So it was a happy day when I was given half the manuscript [of *The Thin Man*] to read and was told that I was Nora' (Lillian Hellmann, 1969, *An Unfinished Woman*, p. 279).

HELLYER, John and Harriet Eustace

MR AND MRS ANDREW COGGLESBY in George Meredith, *Evan Harrington* (1860)

'In 1810 [Louisa Meredith's] sister Harriet Eustace was married to John Hellyer of Newington, Surrey, a brewer. Little authentic information is available concerning the Hellyers beyond the fact that they were the originals of the Andrew Cogglesbys in *Evan Harrington*' (S.M. Ellis, 1920, *George Meredith*, 2nd edn, London: Grant Richards, p. 17).

HEMINGWAY, Clarence Edward (1871–1928) Father of Ernest Hemingway. He was a medical practitioner, and lived, practised and died at Oak Park, Illinois. A teetotaller, devout Christian, and a puritan, in 1896 he married Grace Hall, also of Oak Park, who had trained as an opera singer: they had six children. Like his son, he died by his own hand, blowing out his brains after detecting in himself signs of gangrene consequent upon diabetes.

HENRY ADAMS (THE DOCTOR) in Ernest Hemingway, *In Our Time* (1925)

'[In the first story "Indian Camp"] the doctor, his brother, and his son were clearly modeled on Dr Hemingway, his brother George, and Ernest' (Carlos Baker, 1969, *Ernest Hemingway: a life story*, New York, p. 125). Dr Adams is modelled on Dr Hemingway throughout the book.

NICK'S FATHER in Ernest Hemingway, 'Fathers and Sons', *Winner Take Nothing* (1933)

This is the most extensive portrait of his father that Hemingway ever wrote.

DR WARNER in John Dos Passos, *Chosen Country* (1951)

'Dr Hemingway appeared as Dr Warner' (Baker, op. cit., p. 654 n. 'EH on Dos Passos's "Chosen Country"').

HEMINGWAY, Ernest (1899–1961) American novelist and short-story writer. He was born in Chicago, the son of C.E. **Hemingway**, and educated at Oak Park and River Forest Township High School. In 1917 he worked briefly as a cub reporter on the *Kansas City Star* before joining the Red Cross in 1918. He served as an ambulance driver on the Italian Front and was seriously wounded and twice decorated for his services. He returned to America in 1919, and in 1921 married Hadley Richardson (**Hemingway**, below), the first of his four wives, all of whom hailed from St Louis. He travelled widely in Europe, spending some time in Paris, where he met several of the literati, including Gertrude **Stein**, James **Joyce**, Ezra **Pound** and F. Scott **Fitzgerald**. He published his first collection of short stories in Paris in 1923. In 1927 he married his second wife, Pauline Pfeiffer (**Hemingway**, below), with whom he had two sons, and in 1928, following critical acclaim for his early work, they moved to Key West in Florida. He had a passion for bullfighting, big-game hunting and deep-sea fishing. He visited Spain during the Civil War and described his experiences in *For Whom the Bell Tolls* (1940). In 1940 he divorced Pauline and married Martha **Gellhorn**, whom he divorced in 1945, and in 1946 he married Mary Welsh (**Hemingway**, below). He won the Pulitzer Prize in 1953 and the Nobel Prize for Literature in 1954. Afterwards he wrote very little and his health began to fail. He committed suicide by shooting himself in the mouth.

NICK ADAMS in Ernest Hemingway, *In Our Time* (1925)

'The doctor, his brother, and his son were clearly modeled on Dr Hemingway, his brother George, and Ernest. But the melodramatic circumstances were Ernest's own invention' (Carlos Baker, 1969, *Ernest Hemingway: a life story*, New York, p. 125). The prototype of Nick Adams in all the short stories in which he appears is Hemingway himself, but as Carlos Baker points out, it would be a rash person who would build a biography of Hemingway on the Nick Adams stories.

AHEARN in Irwin Shaw, *The Young Lions* (1948)

'[Hemingway] thought [the novel] a disgraceful and ignoble book. . . . He believed that Shaw had portrayed . . . himself [Hemingway] as . . . Ahearn' (Baker, op. cit., p. 470). The two men had met in London in 1944.

JAKE BARNES in Ernest Hemingway, *The Sun Also Rises* (1926)

'Harold Loeb's version [in *The Way It Was*] of the events on which Hemingway drew for the story . . . does not specifically identify any actual person with the fictional characters. Yet it is clear from his narrative that he associates . . . Hemingway with Jake Barnes' (Carlos Baker, 1972, *Hemingway: the writer as artist*, Princeton, p. 78 n. 9). *See also* **Bird**, William.

CAIRN in Jean Rhys, *Postures* (1928)

'Cairn ([who is] Hemingway)' (Arthur Mizener, 1971, *The Saddest Story: a biography of Ford Madox Ford*, Cleveland: World Publishing, p. 347).

RICHARD CANTWELL in Ernest Hemingway, *Across the River and into the Trees* (1950)

'All the time he had ever spent in Italy, he wrote Buck Lanham, was now paying off. He said that his hero Cantwell was a composite portrait of . . . Sweeny . . . Lanham . . . and most of all himself as he might have been if he had turned to soldiering instead of writing' (Baker, op. cit., p. 475). *See also* **Lanham**, C.T.; **Sweeny**, Charles.

RANDO GRANHAM in Leicester Hemingway, *The Sound of the Trumpet* (1953)

'When Hemingway's younger brother . . . wrote his first novel it was inevitable that one of the characters would be modeled after Ernest. . . . Hemingway appears as war correspondent "Rando Granham"' (W.F. Nolan, 1975, 'The Man Behind the Masks: Hemingway as a fictional character', in *Fitzgerald–Hemingway Annual, 1974*, Englewood, NJ: Prentice-Hall, p. 208).

MAX HARDER in J.W. Beach, *Glass Mountain* (1930)

'The Hemingway character is named "Max Harder"' (Nolan, op. cit., p. 207).

FREDERIC HENRY in Ernest Hemingway, *A Farewell to Arms* (1929)

'It would be foolish to argue that there was no use of biographical experience [in the novel]. Indeed, Hemingway scholars have already established the main correlations between Hemingway's life and the novel. . . . Both Hemingway and Frederic were blown up by trench mortar shells. . . . Both men recuperated in a Milan hospital, where each established a relationship with a nurse. Once in Switzerland, Frederic sticks to terrain that Hemingway knew from experience' (M.S. Reynolds, 1976, *Hemingway's First War: the making of* A

Farewell to Arms, Princeton, NJ: Princeton University Press, p. 169). And both were driving an ambulance. *See also* **McKey**, Edward.

GEORGE ELBERT WARNER in John Dos Passos, *Chosen Country* (1951)

'A big part of it is about Michigan and I am one of the more loathsome characters in it [George Elbert Warner]' (to Charles A. Fenton, 29 July 1952, reproduced in *Ernest Hemingway Selected Letters, 1917–1961*, 1981, ed. Carlos Baker, London: Granada, p. 690; the annotation is Baker's). 'I doubt more than 20 people ever recognized the allusions to Hemingway. (He was George in the book.) But it absolutely infuriated Hemingway' (W.B. Smith to D. St John, 1972, 'Interview with Hemingway's "Bill Gorton"', quoted in B.D. Sarason, *Hemingway and the Sun Set*, Washington, DC, p. 157).

HEMINGWAY, George R. Younger brother of C.E. **Hemingway**, Ernest Hemingway's father.

UNCLE GEORGE in Ernest Hemingway, 'Indian Camp', *In Our Time* (1925)

See under **Hemingway**, C.E.

HEMINGWAY, Hadley (1892–1979) Née Richardson, she grew up in St Louis, Missouri. Her father committed suicide in 1903 and she lived with her mother, caring for her until her death in 1920. She went to school with Kate Smith (later **Dos Passos**), and after her mother's death she accepted an invitation to visit the Smiths in Chicago. She met Hemingway there for the first time, and in 1921 she married him, becoming his first wife; they were divorced in 1927, and in 1933 she married Paul Mowrer.

CATHERINE BARKLEY in Ernest Hemingway, *A Farewell to Arms* (1929)

'The portrait of Catherine Barkley appears to have been influenced by Hemingway's recollection of his first wife' (Carlos Baker, 1972, *Ernest Hemingway: the writer as artist*, Princeton, pp. 98–9 n. 4). 'Hadley Richardson ... contributes heavily to the idyllic winter at Montreux' (M.S. Reynolds, 1976, *Hemingway's First War: the making of* A Farewell to Arms, Princeton, NJ: Princeton University Press, p. 170). *See also* **Jessup**, Elsie; **Hemingway**, Pauline; **Von Kurowsky**, Agnes.

NORMA HARDER in J.W. Beach, *Glass Mountain* (1930)

'The novel is loosely based on Hemingway's first marriage to Hadley (here dubbed "Norma")' (W.F. Nolan, 1975, 'The man behind the masks: Hemingway as a fictional character', in *Fitzgerald–Hemingway Annual, 1974*, Englewood, NJ: New Jersey, p. 207).

HEMINGWAY, Leicester (1915–82) Younger brother of Ernest **Hemingway**, he was the author of a biography entitled *My Brother, Ernest Hemingway*. During the Second World War he served in Europe in the same documentary film unit as Irwin Shaw.

DAN GRANHAM in Leicester Hemingway, *The Sound of the Trumpet* (1953)

'When ... Leicester wrote his first novel ... Hemingway [appeared] as ... "Rando Granham" older brother to "Dan Granham" (Leicester Hemingway)'

(William F. Nolan, 1975, 'The man behind the masks: Hemingway as a fictional character', in *Fitzgerald–Hemingway Annual, 1974*, Englewood, NJ: Prentice-Hall, p. 208).

LEROY KEANE in Irwin Shaw, *The Young Lions* (1948)

'[Hemingway] believed that Shaw had portrayed . . . Leicester Hemingway as . . . Keane' (Carlos Baker, 1970, *Ernest Hemingway: a life story*, New York, p. 470).

HEMINGWAY, Mary (1908–86) Journalist. Née Welsh. She was born in St Louis, the daughter of a lumberjack. In 1932 she joined the *Chicago Daily News* as a reporter, and in 1937 she moved to England during the Spanish Civil War and joined the *Daily Express*. In 1940 she joined the London Bureau of *Time Magazine, Life* magazine and *Future*. She remained in London almost continuously throughout the Second World War until 1944. She was introduced to Ernest **Hemingway** by Irwin Shaw in 1944 and married him in 1946.

LOUISE M'KIMBER in Irwin Shaw, *The Young Lions* (1948)

'[Hemingway] believed that Shaw had portrayed Mary Welsh as . . . Louise' (Carlos Baker, 1970, *Ernest Hemingway: a life story*, New York, p. 470).

HEMINGWAY, Pauline (1895–1951) Née Pfeiffer, she was the daughter of a land-owner of Piggott, Arkansas, and married Ernest Hemingway in 1927, becoming his second wife. They had two sons and were divorced in 1940. She worked for a time on *Vogue*.

CATHERINE BARKLEY in Ernest Hemingway, *A Farewell to Arms* (1929)

'On June 28 [1928] . . . Pauline suffered through eighteen hours of labor that ended with a Caesarean section. . . . Pauline's operation provided the naturalistic basis for [the] conclusion [of the novel]' (M.S. Reynolds, 1976, *Hemingway's First War: the making of* A Farewell to Arms, Princeton, NJ: Princeton University Press, p. 25). *See also* **Jessup**, Elsie; **Hemingway**, Hadley; **Von Kurowsky**, Agnes.

P.O.M. in Ernest Hemingway, *The Green Hills of Africa* (1935)

'To give his story the air of fiction he had changed most of the names . . . Pauline was P.O.M.' (Carlos Baker, 1970, *Ernest Hemingway: a life story*, New York, p. 260).

HENLEY, Oxfordshire A town on the Thames. Ida Blair, George Orwell's mother, lived there with her family from 1904 to 1912.

LOWER BINFIELD in George Orwell, *Coming up for Air* (1939)

'The nostalgia of George Bowling for a happy Edwardian childhood in the opening pages of Part II of *Coming Up for Air* can be seen as very much George Orwell's own. "Lower Binfield" is recognisably Henley' (Eileen Bernard Crick, 1980, *George Orwell: a life*, London: Secker & Warburg, p. 12).

HENLEY, William Ernest (1849–1903) Poet, critic, and dramatist. He was crippled from boyhood and spent 1873–5 in Edinburgh Infirmary. During this time he met and became a close friend of Robert Louis Stevenson. He settled in

London as Editor of *London,* and from 1882 to 1886 he was Editor of *Magazine Art.* In 1889 he was Editor of the *Scots Observer* (later the *National Observer*), where he published Kenneth Grahame's early work.

MR BADGER in Kenneth Grahame, *The Wind in the Willows* (1908)

'Badger . . . contains elements of Henley . . . his weakness for . . . polysyllables off-set by . . . slang, and the gruffness which masked a vast benevolent paternalism' (Peter Green, 1959, *Kenneth Grahame, 1859–1932,* p. 281). *See also* **Portland**, 5th Duke of.

LONG JOHN SILVER in R.L. Stevenson, *Treasure Island* (1883)

'In the 1880s, his life was still dominated by the over-intense friendship with Stevenson which had begun when he was a patient at the Edinburgh Royal Infirmary, and which was to end in estrangement and bad blood, its only lasting memorial the character which he had inspired, Long John Silver' (John Gross, 1969, *The Rise and Fall of the Man of Letters,* p. 150).

RAT in Kenneth Grahame, *The Wind in the Willows* (1908)

'There is a touch of Henley in his blunt dogmatism' (Green, op. cit., p. 280). Henley is portrayed as 'Burly' in R.L. Stevenson's 'Men of Letters', *Memories and Portraits* (1887). *See also* **Atkinson**, Edward; **Furnivall**, F.J.

HENNIKER, Hon. Florence Ellen Hungerford (1855–1923) Writer. Daughter of Richard Monckton **Milnes**, 1st Baron Houghton, in 1882 she married Major-General Arthur Henry Henniker (1855–1912): born Henniker-Major, the youngest son of the 4th Lord Henniker, he had a distinguished military career in the Coldstream Guards, displaying great gallantry in the Boer War. In 1891 she published the first of six novels, and she was also the author of volumes of short stories and a play. She became a friend of Thomas Hardy and his wife, *c.*1893, and a number of his poems arose from the relationship. In 1904 she introduced Hardy to Florence Emily Dugdale (**Hardy**), who became his second wife in 1914.

SUE BRIDEHEAD in Thomas Hardy, *Jude the Obscure* (1895)

'Mrs Hardy [F.E. Hardy] is my authority for the statement that Sue Bridehead was in part drawn from Mrs Henniker' (R.L. Purdy, 1954, *Thomas Hardy: a bibliographical study,* Oxford, p. 345). *See also* **Sparks**, Tryphena.

ELLA MARCHMILL in Thomas Hardy, 'An Imaginative Woman' (1896)

'About this time [1893] Hardy "found and touched up" "An Imaginative Woman" . . . the Solentsea where the heroine stays is Southsea [where Mrs Henniker stayed]; like Mrs Henniker she is interested in Shelley's poetry, and she was the poet's "ideal She" as Mrs Henniker was Hardy's . . . her husband, like Mrs Henniker's, was most unpoetical and connected with weapons of war' (*One Rare Fair Woman: Thomas Hardy's letters to Florence Henniker, 1893–1922,* 1972, ed. Evelyn Hardy and F.B. Pinion, p. 38). The expression 'found and touched up' is Hardy's own (entry for December 1893, in Hardy's Journal; see F.E. Hardy, 1972, *Life of Thomas Hardy,* p. 260). The story was first published in the *Pall Mall Gazette* (April 1894). It is perhaps significant that the heroine's name is Ella, but it is not clear when the story was originally written.

HENRY, Arthur (1867–1938) Novelist and journalist. He was married first to Maude Wood, and then to Anna **Mallon**. He was the city Editor of the *Toledo Blade* when Dreiser met him in Ohio in 1894; they became close friends and he drove Dreiser into writing *Sister Carrie*. In 1901 the Dreisers spent a summer holiday with Henry and Anna Mallon in Henry's cabin on Dumpling Island, off Noank, Connecticut.

WINFIELD VLASTO in Theodore Dreiser, 'Rona Murtha', *A Gallery of Women* (1929)

'Dreiser . . . portrayed . . . Henry . . . as Winnie Vlasto in *A Gallery of Women*' (Richard Lehan, 1974, *Theodore Dreiser: his world and his novels*, Carbondale, Ill.: Arcturis Books, p. 28).

HENRY, Dolly (1894?–1914) She was the mistress of the painter John **Currie**; in a fit of jealousy he killed her and then himself.

NELLY OLIVER in Gilbert Cannan, *Mendel* (1916)

'An important theme is the love-affair between the artist Logan (John Currie) and his mistress (Dolly Henry)' (Diana Farr, 1978, *Gilbert Cannan: a georgian prodigy*, London: Chatto & Windus, p. 140). *See also* **Lawrence**, Frieda.

HENRY, Father William, SJ Rector of Belvedere College, Dublin, at the time that Joyce attended the school.

FATHER BUTLER in James Joyce, 'An Encounter', *Dubliners* (1914)

'In the school play [probably in 1898] [Joyce] . . . parodied all the rector's mannerisms. . . . He was to do so again at the beginning of . . . "An Encounter"' (Richard Ellmann, 1966, *James Joyce*, London: Oxford Paperbacks, p. 57 n.).

HENSEL, Fanny (1805–47) She was the sister of Felix **Mendelssohn** and composed a number of songs herself. She married Wilhelm Hensel, a painter, and was a friend of Pauline **Viardot**.

MARIA CERINTHEA in Elizabeth Sara Sheppard, *Charles Auchester* (1853)

Identified in an anonymous typed key laid in a copy of the first edition of *Charles Auchester* which is now in the possession of the present author. *See also* **Malibran**, Maria.

HENSON, Josiah (1789–1883) Born in Maryland, he was a black slave who, in 1830, escaped to Canada, where he devoted himself to the struggle for cultural and industrial advancement of the American Negro. He met Harriet Becher Stowe in Boston in 1850.

UNCLE TOM in Harriet Becher Stowe, *Uncle Tom's Cabin* (1851–2)

'Reputed to be the original of Uncle Tom' (*Webster's Biographical Dictionary*, 1969, Springfield, Mass.).

HERBERT, Hon. Aubrey Nigel Henry Molyneux (1880–1923) Son of the 4th Earl of Carnarvon. He was an MP between 1911 and 1923, and he was a considerable orientalist. His daughter Laura married Evelyn **Waugh**.

SANDY ARBUTHNOT in John Buchan, *Greenmantle* (1916) and *The Courts of the Morning* (1929)

'The original of Sandy Arbuthnot was certainly Aubrey Herbert and not . . . T.E. Lawrence' (J. Adam-Smith, 1965, *John Buchan*, p. 207 n.). 'With the real Aubrey Herbert in view – an aristocrat who looked like a tramp, a master of languages, a champion of minority views, a hopelessly short-sighted man who had got himself into the B.E.F. [British Expeditionary Force] in 1914 by putting on khaki and joining a battalion of the Irish Guards as it swung out of Wellington Barracks . . . Buchan had little need to invent' (ibid., p. 256). *See also* **Lawrence, T.E.**

HERBERT, Elizabeth, Lady (1821?–1911) She married Sidney **Herbert**, 1st Baron Herbert of Lea, and was the mother of the 14th Earl of Pembroke. She very much disliked 'of Lea' as an addition to her title and never used it. In 1866 she converted to Roman Catholicism.

LADY CHISELHURST in W.H. Mallock, *The Old Order Changes* (1886)

'Lady Herbert seemed to be generally regarded . . . as the type of the English Catholic female aristocracy. . . . As such she is presented in more than one well-known contemporary novel, figuring as Lady St Jerome in *Lothair*, [and] as Lady Chiselhurst in . . . *The Old Order Changes*' (David Hunter-Blair, 1919, *A Medley of Memories*, p. 107).

LADY ST JEROME in Benjamin Disraeli, *Lothair* (1870)

See above.

HERBERT, Sidney, 1st Baron Herbert of Lea (1810–61) Statesman. He was War Secretary during the Crimean War; it was he who invited Florence Nightingale, the English nurse and hospital reformer, to go to Scutari. He killed himself through overworking.

PERCY DACIER in George Meredith, *Diana of the Crossways* (1884)

'At this point Percy Dacier enters Diana's life. He bears a striking resemblance to Sidney Herbert' (Alice Acland, 1948, *Caroline Norton*, London: Constable, p. 175).

SIDNEY WILTON in Benjamin Disraeli, *Endymion* (1880)

Identified in 'Key to *Endymion*', *Notes and Queries* 83 (24 October 1942): 263; identifications attributed to G.E. Buckle.

HEREFORD, Henrietta Charlotte Devereux, Viscountess (d. 1817) Daughter and coheiress of Anthony Keck (formerly Tracy) of Great Tew, Oxon, in 1774 she took the name of Tracy (by Act of Parliament), under the will of her uncle. The same year she married Edward, 12th Viscount Hereford, who died in 1783, leaving no children. Her sister Susan married Lord Elcho, who died in 1808; from then the two widows lived together at Stanway, Gloucestershire, in a house belonging to Lord Elcho's family.

LADY LUDLOW in Elizabeth Gaskell, *My Lady Ludlow* (1858)

'Lady Hereford is supposed to be the original of Lady Ludlow in the story by Mrs Gaskell, who describes her as being a quaint mixture of haughtiness and strong prejudice combined with ... graciousness and good-breeding (Lady Wemyss, 1932, *A Family Record*, p. 29). I can find no trace of any connection between Mrs Gaskell and Lady Hereford, the Wemyss family or Stanway.

HERKIMER COUNTY, New York Located to the south-east of Utica, this area is that described in Edmund Wilson's *Upstate* (ch. 4).

CATARAQUI COUNTY in Theodore Dreiser, *An American Tragedy* (1925)

'Gillette was ... in December 1906, convicted [of murder[by the People of Herkimer County (Cataraqui in the novel)' (Ellen Moers, 1970, *Two Dreisers*, London: Thames & Hudson, p. 200; originally published 1969, New York: Viking).

HERRIARD HOUSE, Hampshire Situated in Herriard, a hamlet about four miles south of Basingstoke.

ICENWAY HOUSE in Thomas Hardy, 'The Lady Icenway' (1891)

'In Hardy's map of Wessex, Icenway House appears to be Herriard House.... George Purefoy Jervoise (1770–1847) of Herriard House married Anna Maria Selina, daughter of Wadham Locke of Rowdeford House, Bromham, near Devizes, Wiltshire, and died without issue. How far the story is founded on fact ... [remains a problem] for research' (F.B. Pinion, 1968, *A Hardy Companion*, London: Macmillan, p. 373).

HERSEY, Marie Of St Paul, Minnesota. She was a friend of F. Scott Fitzgerald from 1915 onwards.

IMOGENE BISSET in F. Scott Fitzgerald, 'The Scandal Detectives' (1935)

'In real life Imogene Bisset was Marie Hersey' (Andrew Turnbull, 1962, *Scott Fitzgerald*, p. 34).

HERTFORD, Francis Charles Seymour-Conway, 3rd Marquess of (1777–1842) A great roué, he married Maria Fagnani in 1798. 'There has been, as far as I know, no such example of undisguised debauchery in the world' (entry for 19 March 1842, *The Greville Memoirs, 1814–1860*, 1938, ed. Lytton Strachey and Roger Fulford, 8 vols, London: Macmillan).

MARQUESS OF GRANDGOUT in Benjamin Disraeli, *Vivian Grey* (1826–7)

Identified as Marq. of H——d in a key given in *The Star Chamber* (24 May 1826): 114; reprinted in *Vivian Grey* (1904 (centenary edn), ed. Lucien Wolf, Vol. II, London, pp. 361–2. The full name appears on a copy of the key held in the British Museum. Lucien Wolf concludes that Disraeli was not responsible for the key.

MARQUIS OF STEYNE in W.M. Thackeray, *Vanity Fair* (1847–8)

'The character of the "Marquis of Steyne" ... is supposed to represent him' (H.A. Doubleday, Duncan Warrand and Lord Howard de Walden (eds), *The Complete Peerage of England, Scotland, Ireland, Great Britain and the United Kingdom*, Vol. VI, rev. edn, London: St Catherine Press, p. 513 n. b). 'His portrait of Lord Steyne owes something to the newspaper accounts of the litigation that followed the death of the third Marquis of Hertford' (Gordon N. Ray, 1955, *Thackeray: a biography*, Vol. I: *The Uses of Adversity, 1811–1846*, London: Oxford University Press, p. 497 n. 18). *See also* **Fitzhardinge**, Lord.

LORD MONMOUTH in Benjamin Disraeli, *Coningsby* (1844)

Identified in a key in *Notes and Queries* (8th series) 3 (13 May 1893): 363. *See also under* **Bright**, John.

HESELTINE, Philip (1894–1930) Composer under the name of Peter Warlock. He was D.H. Lawrence's neighbour in Cornwall in 1916 and 1917. He was an alcoholic and committed suicide.

COLEMAN in Aldous Huxley, *Antic Hay* (1923)

'One of the chief characters in [*Antic Hay*] . . . the young man named Coleman . . . is none other than Philip [Heseltine]. . . . I can even recall quite clearly the occasion on which the central idea for the book presented itself to Huxley. One evening in the summer of 1922 . . . Philip and I came across Huxley in company with Eugene Goossens [and] we all went to Verrey's café . . . for a drink . . . there, in answer to a question asking why he had grown a beard, Philip made a brilliant . . . speech of which the essence is reproduced in the book' (Cecil Gray, 1934, *Peter Warlock*, p. 226). 'It is . . . significant that, deeply though Philip had resented Lawrence's caricature of himself, he was positively delighted with that of Huxley; the reason being that . . . Lawrence's was a caricature of his intrinsic innerself – Philip Heseltine – [while] that of Huxley was a caricature of the fictitious . . . personality which he had built up for himself and as which he wished to be taken by the world – Peter Warlock' (ibid., p. 227). 'Coleman . . . is given Heseltine's beard, taste for composing limericks, intellectual anarchism. If exact portraiture of an existent individual is what the reader requires from a character in a novel . . . Coleman conveys quite a good idea of what Heseltine was like to meet' (Anthony Powell, 1978, *To Keep the Ball Rolling: the memoirs of Anthony Powell*, Vol. II: *Messengers of Day*, London: Heinemann, pp. 147–8).

JULIUS HALLIDAY in D.H. Lawrence, *Women in Love* (1920)

'Ask Don [Donald Carswell] if he thinks any part [of *Women in Love*] libellous – e.g. Halliday is Heseltine, The Pussum is a model called the Puma [i.e. "Minnie" Lucie Channing], and they are taken from life . . .' (to Catharine Carswell, 21 November 1916, reproduced in *The Letters of D.H. Lawrence*, 1984, Vol. III, ed. J.T. Boulton and A. Robertson, Cambridge: Cambridge University Press, p. 36). 'Of course *all* the Halliday–Pussum scenes in *Women in Love* are *purely* fictitious. No shadow of a resemblance to them ever happened, as far as I know' (10 November 1921, reproduced in *Letters from D.H. Lawrence to Martin Secker*, 1970, p. 44). *See also above.*

HETTON LAWN, Gloucestershire Situated at Charlton Kings, now a suburb of Cheltenham, it was the home of Mrs Liddell, mother of H.G. Liddell, Dean of Christ Church, from 1855 to 1891.

LOOKING-GLASS HOUSE in Lewis Carroll, *Through the Looking-Glass* (1872)

'With these facts [i.e. the entries in Dodgson's diary for April 1862 describing a visit to Hetton Lawn] before us, it surely seems more likely that Looking-Glass House was Hetton Lawn' (R. Lancelyn Green, 1969, 'Alice's rail journey', *Notes and Queries* 214: 218).

HICK, Henry Doctor. Son of the chemist from whom George **Gissing**'s father bought his shop in Wakefield, he became a personal friend and doctor of George Gissing. In the 1890s he practised at New Romney and was H.G. **Wells**'s doctor when the latter lived at Sandgate. He married a sister of C.F.A. Voysey, the architect.

DR LAKE in Morley Roberts, *The Private Life of Henry Maitland* (1912)

Identified in an 'Index of Recurring Pseudonyms' in the 1958 edition of *The Private Life of Henry Maitland*, ed. Morchard Bishop, p. 255.

HICKS, Seymour (1871–1949) Light comedian, actor-manager and play-wright. He was involved in building the Globe, Queen's and Aldwych theatres in London, and wrote and produced sixty-four plays. He married Ellaline Terriss.

MR HIGGS in P.G. Wodehouse, *The Head of Kay's* (1905) and others

'One nice character-actor [appears in the Wodehouse school-books]; his name is Higgs, and his model was Wodehouse's friend, Seymour Hicks' (Richard Usborne, 1976, *Wodehouse at Work*, p. 74).

HIGH ELMS, Bracknell, Berkshire

HEADLONG HALL in Thomas Love Peacock, *Headlong Hall* (1816)

'What Bracknell had in common with *Headlong Hall* was a household of abstract philosophers discussing the destiny of man' (Howard Mills, 1969, *Peacock: his circle and his age*, Cambridge, pp. 86–7). *See also* **Hafod House**.

HIGH STREET, Oxford

CHIEF STREET, CHRISTMINSTER, in Thomas Hardy, *Jude the Obscure* (1895)

Identified in Denys Kay-Robinson, 1972, *Hardy's Wessex Reappraised*, Newton Abbot, and in F.B. Pinion, 1968, *A Hardy Companion*, London: Macmillan.

HIGH SUNDERLAND HALL, Yorkshire Located east of Halifax and north of Law Hill. From 1274 it was the home of the Sunderland family, but in 1655 it was forfeited to pay the fine levied for their support of the King in the Civil War. In 1837, when it belonged to the Priestley family, Emily Brontë taught there. The building was remarkable for the heavily carved gateway. It was derelict in 1929.

WUTHERING HEIGHTS in Emily Brontë, *Wuthering Heights* (1847)

'Wuthering Heights is hauntingly reminiscent of High Sunderland Hall. . . . But Emily's knowledge of the place would appear to be confined to the immense façade. . . . The interior "house-rooms" . . . she described . . . belong rather to the Elizabethan farmhouses around Haworth, like Ponden House and Upper

Withins' (Winifred Gérin, 1971, *Emily Brontë*, Oxford, pp. 82–83). *See also* **Top Withins**.

HIGHAM ON THE HILL, Leicestershire A village about three miles north-east of Nuneaton.

TRIPPLEGATE in George Eliot, 'The Sad Fortunes of the Revd Amos Barton', *Scenes of Clerical Life* (1857–8)

See under **Anstruther**, Lady.

HIGHER BOCKHAMPTON, Dorset A hamlet about two miles from Dorchester where Thomas Hardy's family lived for more than a hundred years; he himself was born there.

FAIRLAND in Thomas Hardy, 'An Indiscretion in the Life of an Heiress' (1878)

'Probably Higher Bockhampton' (F.B. Pinion, 1968, *A Hardy Companion*, London: Macmillan, p. 325).

UPPER MELLSTOCK in Thomas Hardy, Wessex novels and tales (1871–95)

'"Mellstock" consists of three hamlets . . . the third "Upper Mellstock", a mile to the north-east of the church. [It corresponds] to . . . Higher Bockhampton' (Pinion, op. cit., p. 410).

HILDEBRAND, 'Daddy' A contemporary of Thomas Wolfe's at J.M. **Roberts**'s school in Asheville, North Carolina.

'PAP' RHEINHARDT in Thomas Wolfe, *Look Homeward, Angel* (1929)

'"Daddy" Hildebrand was called "Pap" Rheinhardt' (R.S. Kennedy, 1962, *The Window of Memory: the literary career of Thomas Wolfe*, Chapel Hill, NC, p. 182).

HILL, The Misses

MARY AND REBECCA LINNET in George Eliot, 'Janet's Repentance', *Scenes of Clerical Life* (1857–8)

See under **Anstruther**, Lady.

HILL, Mrs Jane Seymour Née Cordery. A chiropodist and manicurist of 6 York Gate, Regent's Park, London. In 1849 she was a near neighbour of Dickens. 'A dwarf, she was greatly distressed by what she and others was convinced was a portrait of her as Miss Mowcher, introduced into . . . ch. 22 [of *Copperfield*]' (*Letters of Charles Dickens*, 1981, Vol. V, ed. Graham Storey and K.J. Fielding, Oxford: Oxford University Press, p. 674 n. 5). She wrote Dickens a most distressed letter, and he replied assuring her that the whole design of the character would be altered rather than she should pass another sleepless night (ibid., p. 275) – and altered it duly was.

MISS MOWCHER in Charles Dickens, *David Copperfield* (1849–50)

'I am bound to admit that in the character to which I take it for granted you refer, I have yielded to several little recollections of your general manner, but I assure you that the original of a great portion of that character is well known to me ... and is ... a very different person' (to Mrs Hill, 18 December 1849, ibid., p. 675).

HILL, Thomas (1760–1840) Retired dry-salter and book collector. He entertained literary and theatrical celebrities.

MR ARCHER in W.M. Thackeray, *The History of Pendennis* (1848–50)

'In sketching old time literary Bohemia, Thackeray included a number of portraits from life, drawn with such fidelity as to be immediately recognizable ... Tom Hill is drawn as Archer' (Gordon Ray, 1959, *Thackeray: the age of wisdom*, p. 114).

MR HULL in Theodore Hook, *Gilbert Gurney* (1836)

'He was the original of the amiable know-all Hull in ... *Gilbert Gurney*' (*Letters of Charles Dickens*, 1965, ed. Madeline House and Graham Storey, Vol. I, Oxford: Oxford University Press, p. 329 n. 2).

HILLS, John Walter (1867–1938) Solicitor. In 1897 he married Stella **Duckworth**, who died three months later of peritonitis. He was Conservative MP for Durham City in 1906.

RICHARD DALLOWAY in Virginia Woolf, *The Voyage Out* (1915)

'Her [V. Woolf's] friendships are echoed in certain characters ... Jack Hills in Mr Dalloway' (*The Letters of Virginia Woolf*, 1975, ed. Nigel Nicolson, Vol. I, London: Hogarth Press, p. xxi).

HILLSIDE, Surrey Mr Gidley Robinson's preparatory school near Godalming, to which Aldous Huxley went in 1903.

BULSTRODE in Aldous Huxley, *Eyeless in Gaza* (1936)

'In the early chapters of *Eyeless in Gaza*, Bulstrode is a thinly disguised Hillside. ... The moonlight pastime of sailing little wooden boats in the dammed gutters which ran level with the windows of the cubicle dormitories exactly describes one of our most enjoyed pastimes' (Gervas Huxley, quoted in Julian Huxley (ed.), 1965, *Aldous Huxley, 1894–1963: a memorial volume*, p. 57).

HILLYARD, Samuel (1792–1839) Minister at the Bunyan Meeting, Bedford, he was the fourth pastor in succession from Bunyan himself. He had been trained by Cowper's friend, William Bull of Olney, and was 'passionately attached to the great principles of civil and religious freedom' (John Brown, 1885, *John Bunyan*, p. 423). He advocated and laboured for the abolition of the slave trade and the extension of the franchise.

JAMES HARDEN in Mark Rutherford, *The Revolution in Tanner's Lane* (1887)

'Based on Samuel Hillyard' (Valentine Cunningham, 1976, *Everywhere Spoken Against: dissent in the Victorian novel*, Oxford: Clarendon Press, p. 264).

HINKS, Mr

MR TOMLINSON in George Eliot, 'Janet's Repentance', *Scenes of Clerical Life* (1857–8)

See under **Anstruther**, Lady.

HINVES, David (d. 1838) Valet to W.S. **Rose**. '[H]e lived more than forty years in the service of Mr W.S. Rose. . . . A bookbinder by trade, and a preacher among the Methodists. A sermon heard casually under a tree in the New Forest, had such touches of good feeling and broad humour, that the young gentleman promoted him to be his valet on the spot. He was treated latterly more like a friend than a servant, by his master, and by all his master's intimate friends. Scott presented him with a copy of all his works and Coleridge gave him a corrected (or rather an altered) copy of Christabelle [sic] . . . "as a *small* token of regard"' (J.G. Lockhart, 1900, *Memoirs of Sir Walter Scott*, Vol. II, London: Macmillan, p. 481 n. 1).

DAVIE GELLATLEY in Sir Walter Scott, *Waverley* (1814)

'David Gelatly [sic], whom I take to be a transcript of William Rose's motley follower' (J.B.S. Morritt to Scott, quoted in Lockhart, ibid.; the 'motley follower' is identified in the footnote). It is to be supposed at least that Hinves affected a garish kind of dress, and like David Gellatly, Hinves had 'a habit of answering questions and referring to events by snatches of rhyme' (MacCunn, *The Friends of Sir Walter Scott*, p. 235). *See also* **Gray**, John.

HINZINGER, T.G. He was a general practitioner at Zeeland, Michigan.

T.J.H. SILVA in Sinclair Lewis, *Arrowsmith* (1925)

Identified in Mark Schorer, 1961, *Sinclair Lewis: an American life*, New York: McGraw-Hill, p. 418.

HITCHCOCK, Thomas (1900–44) Son of Thomas Hitchcock of Long Island, he began flying with the Royal Flying Corps before he was 18. During the First World War he was forced down behind German lines and made a spectacular escape from a prison camp. He later joined American flying forces, and after the war he became one of the foremost polo players in America. During the Second World War, he served in the US Army Air Corps; he was killed while test-flying an aeroplane.

TOMMY BARBAN in F. Scott Fitzgerald, *Tender is the Night* (1934)

'He was Tommy Hitchcock in a way, whose whole life is a challenge – who is only interested in realities' (to Mrs Edwina Jarrett, 7 February 1938, reproduced in *The Letters of F. Scott Fitzgerald*, 1964, ed. Andrew Turnbull, London: Bodley Head, p. 566). *See also* **Braggiotti**, Mario; **Jozan**, Edouard.

HITCHENER, Elizabeth

CELINDA ('STELLA') TOOBAD in Thomas Love Peacock, *Nightmare Abbey* (1818)

'[There have been] suggestions that [Stella] was primarily based on Elizabeth Hitchener, who paid a prolonged visit to Shelley and Harriet in 1812' (*Nightmare Abbey*, 1969, ed. Raymond Wright, Harmondsworth: Penguin, p. 19). *See also* **Clairmont**, Claire; **Shelley**, Mary Wollstonecraft.

HOCKING, William Henry (1882?–1955) A young farmer who was a neighbour of the Lawrences in 1816 and 1917 at Higher Tregerthen, Cornwall. Lawrence and he became friends, and Lawrence used to help on his farm.

JOHN THOMAS BURYAN in D.H. Lawrence, *Kangaroo* (1923)

'In *Kangaroo*, Lawrence gave the young farmer the name of John Thomas Buryan' (H.T. Moore, 1960, *The Intelligent Heart: the story of D.H. Lawrence*, Harmondsworth: Penguin, p. 293; originally published 1955, London: Heinemann).

HODDER, Alfred (*fl.*1896) A Harvard graduate with a reputation for brilliance. In the 1890s he taught at **Bryn Mawr College** and became involved in a triangular imbroglio with Carey **Thomas** and Mary **Gwinn**. He eventually divorced his wife and married Miss Gwinn, but died shortly afterwards.

PHILIP REDFERN in Gertrude Stein, *Fernhurst* (1971)

'[T]he Hodder role is given to Philip Redfern' (James R. Mellow, 1974, *The Charmed Circle: Gertrude Stein and company*, London: Phaidon Press, p. 66).

HODISTER, Arthur Eugene Constant (d. 1892) He was engaged by the Comité d'Etudes du Haut-Congo in 1883, and in 1886 was a member of the Sanford exploring expedition. In 1889 he was appointed 'chef de district des Bangalas', they being a race of cannibals who were popular with Europeans as particularly cheap labour. He became an energetic and successful collector of ivory, and in addition he conducted exploring expeditions of a hazardous kind up the Mongala river, in the course of which he discovered a lake. He was opposed to slavery, and was on terms of the deepest friendship and confidence with the natives. At the end of 1890 he returned to Europe, where he was appointed director of the Syndicat Commercial du Katanga, which was planning an expedition intended to plant trading stations in the heart of the Arab country, the object being to divert the Arabs from the slave trade to more general commerce. In 1892 the expedition set out, but its overtures were totally rejected and Hodister was put to death, together with all the European members of his force (see Norman Sherry, 1971, *Conrad's Western World*, Cambridge, pp. 95–111).

MR KURTZ in Joseph Conrad, *Heart of Darkness* (1902)

'If a man even approximating to Kurtz ... existed in the Congo during 1890, Conrad must surely have heard of him. And there was such a man. . . . [He] was Arthur Eugene Constant Hodister, and his character, charisma and success ... suggest that he was at least in part the inspiration for Kurtz' (ibid., p. 95). *See also* **Barttelot**, E.M.; **Klein**, G.A.; **Stanley**, H.M.

HOGARTH, Georgina[1] (1793–1863) Daughter of George Thomson, 'the friend of Burns' and collector of folk music ('national airs'). In 1814 she married George Hogarth, the music critic; their daughters included Georgina and Mary **Hogarth** and Catherine ('Kate') Dickens.

MRS JINIWIN in Charles Dickens, *The Old Curiosity Shop* (1840–1)

'Mrs Hogarth, whose portrait Dickens drew as Mrs Jeniwin [sic] . . . Quilp was in a sense . . . Dickens himself as seen by the eyes of Mrs Hogarth; and the word conflicts between that . . . dwarf and Mrs Jeniwin certainly took place in real life' (Thomas Wright, 1935, *Life of Charles Dickens*, London: Herbert Jenkins, p. 131).

HOGARTH, Georgina[2] (1827–1917) Fourth daughter of George Hogarth, she was the youngest sister of Catherine ('Kate') Dickens. In 1845 she joined Dickens's household at 1 Devonshire Terrace and remained with the family until his death, taking over more and more of the running of the house.

ESTHER SUMMERSON in Charles Dickens, *Bleak House* (1852–3)

'[Esther Summerson was] suggested probably, like Agnes Wickfield, by what Dickens saw of Georgina Hogarth's sacrificial dedication to the welfare of others and her immersion in household duties' (Edgar Johnson, 1952, *Charles Dickens*, Vol. II, p. 766). This kind of identification is difficult to verify or substantiate, but *c*.1913 Leslie Staples visited Miss Hogarth and many years later he wrote an account of what he remembered of their conversation: 'One question did arouse a little asperity. Would she agree that the character of Agnes Wickfield was in part founded upon her? "No, no, no," she replied, "not Agnes. Possibly there is something of me in Esther Summerson, but certainly not Agnes"' (L.C. Staples, 1977, 'Some early memories of the Dickens fellowship', *The Dickensian* 73: 134). However, from as early as 1849 Dickens constantly referred to Georgina as his 'little house-keeper'. This phrase (to which Professor Tillotson drew my attention) is at least a link with both Agnes Wickfield and Esther Summerson, and one which it is difficult to brush to one side. Miss Hogarth, in view of the gossip which had attended Dickens's separation from his wife, would naturally wish to minimize the part she had played in running his household in the earlier years.

AGNES WICKFIELD in Charles Dickens, *David Copperfield* (1849–50)

See above.

HOGARTH, Mary Scott (1819–37) Younger sister of Catherine ('Kate') Dickens. After Kate's marriage, Mary spent long periods with her, first at Furnival's Inn, and subsequently at Doughty Street. On 7 May 1837 she died suddenly, after a family visit to the theatre. Dickens was deeply attached to her and she died in his arms. He was at the time working on *Pickwick* and *Oliver Twist*, and for a month after her death he was unable to continue writing either of them.

ROSE MAYLIE in Charles Dickens, *Oliver Twist* (1837–8)

'The character of Rose Maylie became an idealized portrait of Mary' (Humphrey House, 1949, Introd. to *Oliver Twist*, p. vii). '[Dickens] deleted some phrases in his first description of Rose, including a rhetorical question about a "loved original" which confirms the impression that he had Mary Hogarth in mind' (K. Tillotson, 1966, Introd. to *Oliver Twist*, Oxford, p. xxvii). The deleted passage had appeared at the end of the third paragraph in chapter 29 and read: 'Oh! Where are the hearts which following some halting description of youth and beauty, do not recall a loved original that Time has sadly changed or death resolved to dust' (ibid., p. 187 n. 4).

NELL TRENT ('LITTLE NELL') in Charles Dickens, *The Old Curiosity Shop* (1840–1)

'I have refused several invitations for this week and next, determining to go nowhere till I have done [with the death of little Nell]. I am afraid of disturbing the state I have been trying to get into, and having to fetch it all back again' (Dickens to Forster, 8? January 1841, reproduced in *Letters of Charles Dickens*, 1969, ed. Madeline House and Graham Storey, Vol. II, Oxford: Oxford University Press, p. 182). 'A sentence which shows the sort of effort it was to write ch. 71. Probably, when the time came to write of the death he had had in mind since July (18)40 . . . Dickens found he had deliberately to bring thoughts of Mary Hogarth's death into his mind to produce the "state" he needed to be in' (ibid., n. 1).

HOGG, Thomas Jefferson (1792–1862) He was a contemporary of **Shelley** at University College, Oxford; in 1881, both Hogg and Shelley were sent down for publishing the pamphlet *The Necessity of Atheism*. Hogg joined Shelley and his wife Harriet in Edinburgh and he was called to the Bar. After Shelley and Edward Ellerher Williams drowned, Hogg lived with the latter's widow until his death; they had one daughter. In 1858 he published his biography of Shelley (covering up until 1814), much to the dismay of Shelley's family.

PRINCE ALEXY HAIMATOFF in T.J. Hogg, *Memoirs of Prince Alexy Haimatoff* (1813)

'The book could neither have attracted nor deserved attention while it remained anonymous but at the present day the identification of the imaginary Haimatoff with the real Hogg is a source of no inconsiderable amusement' (Richard Garnett, 1891, in Leslie Stephen (ed.), *The Dictionary of National Biography*, London: Oxford University Press, s.v., Hogg, T.J.). *See also* **Shelley**, P.B.

HUMPHREY HIPPY in Thomas Love Peacock, *Melincourt* (1817)

'Peacock . . . possibly had Hogg in mind as the original of his Humphrey Hippy. . . . There are certain Hogg-like touches, such as Hippy's interest in class and enjoyment of wine, his gout, and . . . his capping of a poetical reference to the music of the winds and the waters and the voice of Miss Melincourt with the reminder of a "pretty concert waiting at the inn" – "the tinkling of cups and spoons, and the divine song of the tea-urn". Readers of Hogg's Shelley will easily find parallels' (Sylvia Norman, 1934, *After Shelley*, p. xi).

MR JENKISON in Thomas Love Peacock, *Headlong Hall* (1816)

'Mr Jenkison's views [are based] partly on Hogg's cautious conservatism' (David Garnett, 1948, Introd. to *Headlong Hall*, p. 8).

HÖHLER, Agnes Venetia (1870–1933) Née Goring, she was the niece of Mrs Molesworth and published four children's stories, rather in her aunt's style.

SYBIL in Mrs Molesworth, *'Carrots': Just a Little Boy* (1878)

'Sybil was Mrs Molesworth's niece, Agnes Venetia Goring' (R. Lancelyn Green, 1961, *Mrs Molesworth*, London, p. 40).

HOKE, Revd Mr

REVD ARCHIBALD DUKE in George Eliot, 'The Sad Fortunes of the Revd Amos Barton', *Scenes of Clerical Life* (1857–8)

See under **Anstruther**, Lady.

HOLDEN, George
Usually called 'Gentleman Holden'. He lived in Whitstable when W. Somerset Maugham lived there as a boy : 'You might say he was one of the industrial aristocrats of the town. . . . A big shipowner, he was, with luggers . . . and schooners that took Kentish coal to Bermuda' (Mr Smith of Whitstable talking to Robin Maugham about the Whistable of Somerset Maugham's boyhood, quoted in R. Maugham, 1966, *Somerset and All the Maughams*, p. 154).

'LORD' GEORGE KEMP in W. Somerset Maugham, *Cakes and Ale* (1930)

'This is almost certainly the original of Lord George Kemp' (R.L. Calder, 1972, *W. Somerset Maugham and the Quest for Freedom*, London: Heinemann, p. 183).

HOLDER, Revd Caddell
(1803–82) Thomas Hardy's brother-in-law.

ALWYN HILL in Thomas Hardy, 'The Duchess of Hamptonshire' (1891)

'As a young man Holder was a curate in Bristol during the terrible cholera visitation. He related that one day . . . he met a . . . young widow, who invited him to call on her . . . he went at tea-time a day or two later. . . . The servant said . . . "Why, sir, you buried her this morning". He found that amongst the . . . funerals . . . he had conducted that day . . . hers had been one' (F.E. Hardy, 1972, *The Life of Thomas Hardy, 1840–1891*, p. 155). 'In the Duchess of Hamptonshire the final irony lies in Alwyn Hill's unawareness of what woman he has performed the burial service for' (David Bonnell Green, 1956, 'A source for Hardy's "The Duchess of Hamptonshire"', *Notes and Queries* 201: 86).

HOLLAND, Elizabeth Vassall Fox, Lady
(1771–1845) Daughter of Richard Vassall and heiress to the West Indian fortune of her grandfather, in 1786 she married Sir Godfrey Webster; their son became Sir Godfrey **Webster**, and their daughter's daughter became Lady **Walpole**. In 1797 she was divorced from Webster, and two days later she married Lord Holland (the correspondent). Thereafter she entertained a brilliant circle of Whig Society at Holland House.

MADAME CAROLINA in Benjamin Disraeli, *Vivian Grey* (1826–7)

Identified as Lady H—ll—d in a key given in a pamphlet published in 1827 by William Marsh. This key is discussed by Lucien Wolf in his notes to *Vivian Grey* (1904 (centenary edn), Vol. II, London, p. 364), with the conclusion that Disraeli was not responsible for the key.

PRINCESS OF MADAGASCAR in Lady Caroline Lamb, *Glenarvon* (1816)

Identified in a key found among the papers of John Whishaw, a member of the Holland House circle, printed in *The 'Pope' of Holland House: selections from the correspondence of John Whishaw and his friends, 1813–1840*, ed. Lady Seymour, 1906, p. 151. '[T]he jokes against me for my love of *aisances* and comforts she has heard laughed at by myself and coterie at my own fireside for years' (Lady

Holland to Mrs Creevy, 21 May 1816, quoted in *The Creevey Papers*, 1979, ed. John Gore, p. 163).

HOLLAND, Samuel He was the maternal grandfather of Mrs Gaskell.

EBENEZER HOLMAN in Elizabeth Gaskell, *Cousin Phillis* (1864)

'Samuel Holland combined the life of land-agent farmer ... with that of preacher. ... That he was actually portrayed in the character of "Farmer Holman" his grandson, later Sir Henry Holland, confirmed' (Winifred Gérin, 1976, *Elizabeth Gaskell*, pp. 11–12).

HOLLOWAY, Pryse Agar (1810–74/5) He was married to Sarah **Holloway**; the Kipling children lodged with the couple in Southsea from 1872 to 1877. He served in the Navy from 1824 to 1829 and was present at the Battle of Navarino in 1827; subsequently, he was probably in the Merchant Navy.

UNCLE HARRY in Rudyard Kipling, 'Baa, Baa, Black Sheep' (1888)

Identified in R.L. Green (ed.), 1961, 'Notes on "Baa, Baa, Black Sheep", in *The Readers' Guide to Rudyard Kipling's Work*, Sect. I, London: Kipling Society, pp. 374–77.

HOLLOWAY, Sarah (d. 1896 or after) She was married to Pryse Agar **Holloway**.

AUNTY ROSA in Rudyard Kipling, 'Baa, Baa, Black Sheep' (1888)

Identified in R.L. Green (ed.), 1961, 'Notes on "Baa, Baa, Black Sheep", in *The Readers' Guide to Rudyard Kipling's Work*, Sect. I, London: Kipling Society, pp. 374–77.

HOLMAN, James Australian labour leader.

WILLIE STRUTHERS in D.H. Lawrence, *Kangaroo* (1923)

'Lawrence probably found in [the *Sydney Bulletin*] the outward model for Willie Struthers, the socialist leader, in the frequent references to the labour leader James Holman' (H.T. Moore, 1960, *The Intelligent Heart: the story of D.H. Lawrence*, Harmondsworth: Penguin, p. 364; originally published 1955, London: Heinemann). *See also* **Hopkin**, William E.

HOLMBURY ST MARY, Surrey Located near Dorking. Forster's Aunt Laura (Forster) lived nearby at West Hackhurst, in the house that he subsequently inherited.

SUMMER STREET in E.M. Forster, *A Room with a View* (1908)

'Summer Street is Holmbury St Mary' (E.M. Forster writing in a copy of *A Room with a View* belonging to the American artist Paul Cadums; see Oliver Stallybrass (ed.), 1977, introd. to *A Room with a View* (Abinger edn), p. xi).

HOLMES, John Clellon (b. 1926) Novelist. He was one of the 'Beat Generation' of writers and was author of *Go*, a novel; *Nothing More to Declare*

(1967), essays and other works. In 1978 he was still living at Old Saybrook, Connecticut, alternating it with the University of Arkansas.

BALLIOL MACJONES in *The Subterraneans* (1958), TOM SAYBROOK in *On the Road* (1957), JAMES WATSON in *Book of Dreams* (1960), and TOM WILSON in *Vanity of Duluoz* (1968), all by Jack Kerouac

Identified in 'Character key to the Duluoz Legend', in Barry Gifford and Lawrence Lee, 1979, *Jack's Book*, pp. 322–32.

HOMBURG, Hesse, Germany

ROUGETNOIRBOURG in W.M. Thackeray, *The Kickleburys on the Rhine* (1850)

'[Homburg is] the Rougetnoirbourg of *The Kickleburys on the Rhine*' (*The Letters and Private Papers of W.M. Thackeray*, 1945, ed. Gordon N. Ray, Vol. II, London: Oxford University Press, p. 691 n. 127).

HOMESTEAD STEEL MILL, Pennsylvania It was the scene of a desperate strike amongst the operatives, who were brutally repressed, in 1902.

MARVIN STEEL MILL in I.K. Friedman, *By Bread Alone* (1901)

'For the main events of the strike Friedman turned to the terrible struggle that had taken place at Homestead . . . only nine years before' (Walter B. Rideout, 1956, *The Radical Novel in the United States, 1900–1954*, Cambridge, Mass., p. 15).

HOOD, Mary Frederica Elizabeth, Lady (1783–1862) Née Mackenzie. The eldest of the six daughters of Francis H., Lord Seaforth, and with her four brothers all dying unmarried, her father's estates passed to her under a deed of entail on his death in 1815. She married twice: first in 1804 to Vice-Admiral Sir Samuel Hood, 1st Baronet (d. 1814); and second in 1817 to the Rt. Hon. James Alexander Stewart, of Glasserton, who took the additional name of Mackenzie.

ELLEN DOUGLAS in Sir Walter Scott, *The Lady of the Lake* (1810)

'"She has the spirit of a chieftainess in every drop of her blood" was Scott's tribute to her; and it lends colour to a theory of [J.B.S] Morrit's [of Rokeby] suggested when he wrote about this time [to Scott]: "By the by, we all think that Ellen Douglas . . . is akin to Lady Hood; and that you certainly drew some of the features from nature" (W. Partington, 1932, *Sir Walter's Post-Bag*, London, p. 57).

HOOK, Theodore (1788–1841) He was Accountant-General for Mauritius from 1813 to 1817, but was dismissed in 1823–5 for deficiencies in the accounts and was imprisoned for his debt to the Crown. He was Editor of *John Bull* between 1820 and 1836, and of the *New Monthly* between 1836 and 1841, and was a famous practical joker.

LUCIAN GAY in Benjamin Disraeli, *Coningsby* (1844)

Identified in a key in *Notes and Queries* (8th series) 3 (13 May 1893): 363. *See also under* **Bright**, John.

MR STANISLAUS HOAX in Benjamin Disraeli, *Vivian Grey* (1826–7)

Identified as T—— H—k in a key given in *The Star Chamber* (24 May 1826): 114; reprinted in *Vivian Grey*, 1904 (centenary edn), ed. Lucien Wolf, Vol. II, London, pp. 361–2. The full name appears on a copy of the key held in the British Museum. Lucien Wolf concludes that Disraeli was not responsible for the key. These identifications are generally accepted.

REGINALD SPARKLE in Lord William Lennox, *The Tuft-Hunter* (1843)

'The best of these attempts [at portraiture] is a slight sketch . . . by Lord William Lennox. . . . Reginald Sparkle . . . appears but once . . . at a dinner-party. . . . It is natural . . . and life-like' (R.H. Dalton Barham, 1853, *Life of Theodore Hook*, p. 252).

LORD VINCENT in Bulwer Lytton, *Pelham* (1828)

'There [is a portrait] . . . of course of Theodore Hook, who appears in nearly every social novel of the time' (Michael Sadleir, 1933, *Bulwer and His Wife*, London: Constable, p. 190). 'My father gave me to understand that Vincent and Guloseton had also their originals in real life; but he did not mention their names' (Owen Meredith, 1883, *Life, Letters and Literary Remains of Edward Bulwer, Lord Lytton*, Vol. II, p. 193). Vincent is clearly based on Hook.

MR WAGG in W.M. Thackeray, *Vanity Fair* (1847–8)

'In *Vanity Fair* he figures as Mr Wagg' (Richard Garnett, 1891, in Leslie Stephen (ed.), *The Dictionary of National Biography*, London: Oxford University Press, s.v. Hook).

HOOPER, Robert William (1810–85) A descendant of a Puritan family that settled in Marblehead, Massachusetts, in 1663, he studied medicine in Europe, but soon gave up practising. His wife, Ellen Sturgis, died in 1848 and he devoted himself to bringing up his two children, becoming particularly close to the younger one, Marian (**Adams**), who married Henry **Adams**; she wrote her father a long weekly letter whenever they were separated.

WILLIAM DUDLEY in Henry Adams, *Esther* (1884)

'Esther . . . lives with her long-widowed father, William Dudley. . . . The parallel with Marian's situation is close. . . . Her father . . . was a professional man, an oculist, and he like Mr Dudley had inherited enough money to be indifferent to his practice' (Ernest Samuels, 1958, *Henry Adams: the middle years*, Cambridge, Mass., p. 239). 'What the faith of her father was is portrayed in the character of Mr Dudley. . . . [He] "had no taste for church-going". In this respect Mr Dudley reflected her father's practice' (ibid., p. 278). Ernest Samuels (ibid., pp. 248, 249) points out the close parallel between Esther Dudley's obsessive attachment to her father, and her feeling of isolation at his death, and Marian Adams's relationship with Doctor Hooper.

HOPE, George Fountain Weare (d. 1930) He was Conrad's oldest English friend and was his neighbour in the village of Stanford-le-Hope in Essex until 1898, when the Conrads moved to Pent Farm near Hythe, Kent.

THE COMPANY DIRECTOR in Joseph Conrad, *Heart of Darkness* (1902)

'There *was* a cruising yawl called the Nellie in which Conrad sailed on the Thames immediately before and immediately after his Congo trip ... [it] belonged to his old friend G.F.W. Hope ... [who in] an unpublished account of his yachting days ... himself points out ... "[Conrad] mentions [the *Nellie*] in *Heart of Darkness* and myself as The Director"' (Norman Sherry, 1971, *Conrad's Western World*, Cambridge, p. 122).

HOPE-JONES, William Born in Peru, he was educated at Eton and at King's College, Cambridge (1903–6). In 1907 he was a mathematics master at Eton.

H.M. HOPINGTON in Shane Leslie, *The Cantab* (1926)

Identified in a key in the hand of Dr Ivor Ramsay, a Kingsman of the year 1920, and later Dean, laid in a copy of *The Cantab*.

HOPKIN, William Edward (1862–1951) Son of a postmaster, he became a colliery clerk, then a cobbler, and then the proprietor of a bookshop. A socialist from youth, he lived in Eastwood and served on the Urban District Council for forty-five years. He was passionately interested in local history and became a lifelong friend of D.H. Lawrence *c*.1905.

WILLIE HOUGHTON in D.H. Lawrence, *Touch and Go* (1919)

'Lawrence ... made Hopkin the Willie Houghton of ... *Touch and Go*' (H.T. Moore, 1960, *The Intelligent Heart: the story of D.H. Lawrence*, Harmondsworth: Penguin, p. 90; originally published 1955, London: Heinemann). He threatened to take me off in a book – he did thoroughly in ... *Touch and Go*' (W.E. Hopkin, 1957, 'Memoir', in E. Nehls (ed.), *D.H. Lawrence: a composite biography*, Vol. I, Madison, p. 73).

WILLIE STRUTHERS in D.H. Lawrence, *Kangaroo* (1923)

'But though the face of Willie Struthers may have been the face of Holman, the voice was often that of William Hopkin' (Moore, op. cit., p. 364). *See also* **Holman**, James.

HOPKINS, L.A. He was the Manager of **Chapin & Gore**'s, a saloon in Chicago, in the early 1880s. He was married and had a young daughter, but he became the lover of Emma **Dreiser**, Theodore Dreiser's sister. In 1886 he stole $3500 from the saloon safe and eloped with Emma to New York, where he started a new life, based on connections with Tammany Hall, under an assumed name. In 1894 Theodore Dreiser returned to New York from Pittsburgh and lodged in Hopkins's flat; he discovered that Hopkins had lost his job after the defeat of Tammany in the municipal elections and was unemployed, becoming unemployable, and persuaded Emma to leave Hopkins (see G. Steinbrecher, Jun., 'Theodore Dreiser's fictional method in *Sister Carrie* and *Jennie Gerhardt*', unpublished thesis, p. 323.)

GEORGE HURSTWOOD in Theodore Dreiser, *Sister Carrie* (1900)

'What Dreiser saw [in 1893 and 1894] was a "dark and shrewd and hawklike person who seemed always to be following me with his eyes". This description would be transferred to ... Hurstwood, along with the outlines of Hopkins' career' (Ellen Moers, 1970, *Two Dreisers*, London: Thames & Hudson, p. 28; originally published 1969, New York: Viking).

HORIZON A literary periodical founded in 1939 by Peter Watson, Stephen **Spender** and Cyril **Connolly**. It was edited by Connolly until it ceased to be published in 1950.

SURVIVAL in Evelyn Waugh, the *Sword of Honour* trilogy (1952–61)

'[Spruce's] monthly magazine *Survival* [is manifestly based] on . . . *Horizon*' (Christopher Sykes, 1975, *Evelyn Waugh*, London: Collins, p. 426).

HORNE, Revd Mr He was Rector of Garsington, Oxon, in 1921.

REVD MR BODIHAM in Aldous Huxley, *Crome Yellow* (1921)

'There were pages and pages taken from a book of sermons by our rector. . . . I always hoped that Mr Horne, our rector, would not read the book' (*Ottoline at Garsington: memoirs of Lady Ottoline Morrell*, 1974, ed. R. Gathorne-Hardy, London: Faber, pp. 215, 217).

HORNER, Thomas (1688–1741) Of Mells Park, Somerset. Son of George Horner, he married Susanna, daughter and heiress of Thomas Strangways of **Melbury House**, Dorset.

THOMAS DORNELL in Thomas Hardy, 'The First Countess of Wessex' (1891)

Identified in F.B. Pinion, 1968, *A Hardy Companion*, London: Macmillan.

HORSLEY, Charles (1821–76) Son of William Horsley, composer and organist of the Charterhouse. In 1829 the Horsleys were friends of the Sheppard family.

CHARLES AUCHESTER in Elizabeth Sara Sheppard, *Charles Auchester* (1853)

'[Charles Horsley] stood as the prototype for Charles Auchester . . . as also did his sister Sophy for the character of Miss Lawrence . . . but these highly imaginary presentments must not in any way be taken for accurate portraits' (*Mendelssohn and His Friends in Kensington: letters from Fanny and Sophy Horsley*, 1934, ed. Rosamund Brunel Gotch, p. 5). *See also* **Joachim**, Joseph.

HORTON INN, Dorset Located on the road from Wimborne to Cranborne.

LORNTON INN in Thomas Hardy, 'Barbara of the House of Grebe' (1891)

Identified in F.B. Pinion, 1968, *A Hardy Companion*, London: Macmillan.

HOWARD, Brian (1905–58) Born of American parents, he was educated at Eton and at Christ Church, Oxford. He was a contemporary of Harold **Acton** and Evelyn Waugh, and while at Eton he edited *The Eton Candle*, assisted by Anthony Powell. In 1931 his *First Poems* were published by Nancy **Cunard** at the Hours Press in Paris. Of Jewish origin, he was an early anti-Fascist. During the Second World War he served in the ranks of the Royal Air Force; he was a notorious homosexual addicted to drink, drugs and extravagance, but he was a man of extraordinary charm, capable of inspiring considerable devotion in his despairing friends. He committed suicide at Nice.

ANTHONY BLANCHE in Evelyn Waugh, *Brideshead Revisited* (1945)

'It is true that the characters in my novels often wrongly identified with Harold Acton were to a great extent drawn from [Brian Howard]' (Evelyn Waugh, 1964, *A Little Learning . . . an autobiography*, London: Chapman and Hall, p. 204). *See also* **Acton**, Harold.

DONALD BUTTERBOY in Wyndham Lewis, *The Roaring Queen* (1973)

'If we can identify Baby Bucktrout with Miss Cunard then we may have some tenuous clue to the identity of the Roaring Queen himself, Donald Butterboy. . . . The modern reader will probably think first of . . . Brian Howard. . . . The possible clue to Butterboy's identity is that Baby Bucktrout is reluctantly engaged to him. . . . Nancy Cunard was never engaged to Brian Howard, but that they were close friends is certain. Indeed, at one time, according to Daphne Fielding [in *Emerald and Nancy*], she declared that she loved him "in every possible way"' (Walter Allen, 1973, Introd. to *The Roaring Queen*, London, pp. 18, 19).

AMBROSE SILK in Evelyn Waugh, *Put Out More Flags* (1942)

'I should, however, like to point out . . . that the two characters in . . . Waugh's novels – "Ambrose Silk" and "Anthony Blanche" – who were largely modelled on Brian are not so close to the original as some people suppose. Ambrose Silk is the closer of the two. Anthony Blanche, besides containing features from one or even two other models, is largely a vulgarization' (Maurice Richardson, 1968, Introd. to M.-J. Lancester (ed.), *Brian Howard: portrait of a failure*, London: Anthony Blond, p. xii). 'I . . . wrote to ask for [Waugh's] permission to quote "Ambrose Silk" . . . and "Anthony Blanche". . . . He replied that it would be misleading to quote from the novels as although the characters . . . were suggested by Brian they were wholly fictitious in that nothing they did or said was actually true of Brian' (Lancaster, op. cit., p. 196). '[Ambrose Silk] is clearly modelled on Brian Howard. He is represented as half-Jewish, as a flashy amateur of modernism in all forms, including fashionable Left-Wing political opinions, and as a homosexual with a special preference for young Germans; all of which was true of Brian Howard in real life. Evelyn drew Brian's features and weaknesses with a care that might be called loving, were it not for the known fact that Evelyn despised and disliked this model intensely' (Christopher Sykes, 1975, *Evelyn Waugh*, London: Collins, p. 207). Howard identified Hans as his German friend Toni, to whom he wrote in 1941, 'Evelyn Waugh has made an absolutely vicious attack on me in his new novel *Put Out More Flags. You* come into it too!' (quoted in Lancaster, op. cit., p. 428).

HOWARD, Edward George Fitzalan, Lord, 1st Baron Howard of Glossop (1818–83) He was Liberal MP for Horsham (1848–53) and for Arundel (1853–68), and was Deputy Earl Marshal of England from 1861 to 1868.

LORD ST JEROME in Benjamin Disraeli, *Lothair* (1870)

Identified in 'Key to *Lothair*', *Notes and Queries* 183 (12 September 1942): 173.

LORD VERE in Benjamin Disraeli, *Coningsby* (1844)

Identified in a key in *Notes and Queries* (8th series) 3 (13 May 1893): 363. *See also under* **Bright**, John. *See also* **Lyttelton**, Lord.

HOWELL, Charles Augustus (1840–90) Born in Portugal the son of an English wine merchant (who also gave drawing lessons) and a Portuguese woman of distinguished family, from 1856 to 1858 he was in England, allegedly training as a civil engineer. He met the **Rossetti** family and from 1858 to 1864 he lived again in Portugal. In 1864 he settled in England, where for some years, *c.*1870, he acted as Secretary to **Ruskin**. He was subsequently a rather dubious dealer or agent acting in particular for D.G. Rossetti, and in 1876 his friendship with Rossetti's family ended, apparently as a result of his liaison with Rosa Corder (the subject of Whistler's 'Arrangement in Black and Brown' now in the Frick Collection, New York). With Rosa Corder, he was alleged to have produced fake Rossetti drawings.

De Castro in Theodore Watts-Dunton, *Aylwin* (1899)

'In *Aylwin* ... he introduces Howell under the name of De Castro' (Helen Rossetti Angeli, 1954, *The Pre-Raphaelite Twilight*, p. 141). 'The most convincing portrait is that by Rossetti, depicting him ... standing beside the lady who is "washing her hands of him", painted from his wife, in the picture "Washing Hands"' (ibid., p. 206). 'Of course to make use of so strange a character as this was a great temptation to me when I wrote 'Aylwyn' [sic]. But in what has been called my "thumbnail portrait of him" I treated the peccadilloes attributed to him in a playful and jocose way' (letter from Watts-Dunton, 1900, quoted in Angeli, op. cit., p. 227).

HOWELLS, William Dean (1837–1920) American man of letters and novelist. He was Editor of *Atlantic Monthly* from 1871 to 1878, and was on the editorial staff of *Harper's Magazine* from 1886 to 1889 and *Cosmopolitan Magazine* in 1891 and 1892. He was a close friend of Henry James.

Lewis Lambert Strether in Henry James, *The Ambassadors* (1903)

The genesis of *The Ambassadors* has been described in great detail by James himself, from the planting of the seed in 1895, to the final revision in the New York Edition of 1908. 'Torquay, October 31st, 1895. I was struck last evening with something that Jonathan Sturges ... mentioned to me: it was only 10 words, but I seemed, as usual, to catch a glimpse of a *sujet de nouvelle* in it. We were talking of W.D.H[owells] and of his having seen him ... 18 months ago in Paris. ... He had scarcely been in Paris, ever, in former days, and he had come there to see his domiciled and initiated son, who was at the Beaux Arts. Virtually in the evening, as it were, of life, it was all new to him: all, all, all. Sturges said he seemed sad ... and I asked him what gave him ... that impression. "Oh – somewhere – I forget, when I was with him – he laid his hand on my shoulder and said *à propos* of some remark of mine: 'Oh, you are young, you are young – be glad of it: be glad of it and *live*. Live all you can: it's a mistake not to. It doesn't so much matter what you do – but live. This place makes it all come over me. I see it now. I haven't done so – and now I'm old. It's too late. It has gone past me – I've lost it. You have time. You are young. Live!'" I amplify and improve a little – but that was the tone. It touches me – I can see him – I can hear him' [James goes on to sketch a novel based on this theme] (*The*

Notebooks of Henry James, 1947, ed. F.O. Matthiessen and K.B. Murdock, New York, pp. 225 ff.). We notice that in the novel the setting for the scene, Gloriam's garden, gradually defines itself as Whistler's garden in the rue de Bac.

HUDSON, George (1800–71) Son of a Yorkshire farmer, he inherited a fortune of £30,000, which he increased by way of a successful drapery business in York. In 1837 and 1846 he was Mayor of York; he became Manager of the York and North Midland Railway Company in 1839, of the Newcastle and Darlington Railway in 1842, and subsequently of the Midland Railway. He was an MP from 1845 to 1859, and when railway shares began to fall in 1847 and he found himself in difficulties, he resorted to paying dividends out of capital, and in 1849 he was obliged to resign from the boards of several companies; he was protected from the law by his position as an MP. In 1854 he retired to the European continent, where he lived rather more modestly until his death.

MR HUMSON in Emma Robinson, *The Gold-Worshippers* (1851)

'If the novels of Bell [see below] and Robinson still have any claims on our attention it is ... because their authors were first in the field, and got on so quickly, in a documentary way, to what was happening on the surface of their society. We can see this in the direct relationship between the Hudson of real life and their fictional characters ... this one to one relationship is even more obvious with Emma Robinson's Hudson figure whom she calls Humson' (Grahame Smith and Angela Smith, 1971, 'Dickens as a popular artist', *The Dickensian* 67 (September): 137).

AUGUSTUS MELMOTTE in Anthony Trollope, *The Way We Live Now* (1875)

'The greatest of the novels in which Hudson was reincarnated is Trollope's *The Way We Live Now*' (R.B. Martin, 1962, *Enter Rumour*, p. 234). *See also* **Grant**, Albert.

MR MERDLE in Charles Dickens, *Little Dorrit* (1855–7)

'Though Merdle resembles Sadleir physically ... he is not, as Sadleir was, of a retiring nature socially, and his lavish dinner parties remind one rather, and would certainly have reminded Dickens's contemporaries, of Hudson the Railway King's notorious entertaining at his house in Knightsbridge' (Smith, op. cit., p. 132). *See also* **Sadleir**, John.

RICHARD RAWLINGS in Robert Bell, *The Ladder of Gold: An English Story* (1850)

'Bell wrote his novel on the fall of Hudson, and it was published ... only a year after Hudson had resigned his chairmanships. ... The inspiration must have been patent to any reader. The reviewer in the January 1851 issue of *Fraser's* wrote that "the chief personage in the story is a railway Croesus, Mr Richard Rawlings. His ascent ... and subsequent fall ... are obviously suggested by the fortunes ... of George Hudson"' (Martin, op. cit., pp. 231–2).

VIGO in Benjamin Disraeli, *Endymion* (1880)

'Mr Vigo, the name under which Hudson walks in ... *Endymion* is "by birth a Yorkshireman, and gifted with all the attributes of that celebrated race"' (Martin, op. cit., p. 232). *See also* **Poole**, Henry George.

HUEFFER, Elsie (1876–1949) Daughter of Dr William Martindale, analytical chemist and compiler of the *Extra Pharmacopoeia*. She first met Ford Madox Ford when she was at boarding school in Folkestone, Kent; they eloped, marrying in 1894, but Ford left her for Violet **Hunt** in 1910.

LEONORA ASHBURNHAM in Ford Madox Ford, *The Good Soldier* (1915)

'[Ford] worked hard to remove from *The Good Soldier* the evidence that it was based on personal experience. . . . [But] less obvious [than the fact that Florence is based on Violet Hunt] but equally pervasive is the influence on Leonora of Ford's view of Elsie Martindale, to whom by this time he was ascribing the same feeling for status, the same dislike of impulsive generosity, the same willingness to disregard traditions and obligations that Leonora shows' (Arthur Mizener, 1971, *The Saddest Story: a biography of Ford Madox Ford*, Cleveland: World Publishing, p. 253).

COUNTESS MACDONALD in Ford Madox Ford, *The New Humpty-Dumpty* (1912)

Identified as Elsie Ford in Arthur Mizener, 1971, *The Saddest Story: a biography of Ford Madox Ford*, Cleveland: World Publishing, pp. 223–7.

von HÜGEL, Anatole, Baron (1854–1928) Second son of Baron Carl von Hügel, Austrian minister at Florence and Brussels, he was born in Florence and educated at Stonyhurst and at Trinity College, Cambridge. He was Curator of the University Museum of Archaeology from 1883 to 1921, and founded the Cambridge University Catholic Association, remaining its first president from 1895 to 1922; he was also President of St Edmund's House, Cambridge, from 1917 to 1920. In 1880 he married Eliza Margaret Froude (von **Hügel**, below).

BARON VON BUGLE in Shane Leslie, *The Cantab* (1926)

'[H]ere [at Baron Anatole's house, Croft Cottage] Catholic Cambridge found a centre' (Maisie Ward, 1937, *The Wilfrid Wards and the Transition*, Vol. II, p. 124). The identity is unmistakable, although Baron Anatole does not figure in the key of Dr Ivor Ramsay.

von HÜGEL, Eliza Margaret ('Isy'), Baroness (1839–1931) Daughter of William Froude, the marine engineer, she was the niece of J.A. **Froude** and a cousin of W.H. Mallock, and married Baron von **Hügel**.

MISS CONSUELO BURTON in W.H. Mallock, *The Old Order Changes* (1886)

'[She] . . . serves as model for one of Mallock's later heroines, Miss Consuelo Burton' (J. Lucas, 1975, Introd. to *The New Republic*, Leicester, p. [19]).

MISS MERTON in W.H. Mallock, *The New Republic* (1877)

'There is absolutely no room for doubt about Miss Merton's original. She is based on Isy Froude . . . later Baroness A. von Hügel. . . . (Some years ago both Miss Helen Mallock and Mr William Froude told me in conversation that Mallock never married partly because he hadn't enough money to support a wife in the manner to which he thought she ought to become accustomed, and partly because Isy was the only woman he ever really loved and she wouldn't have him.)' (Lucas, op. cit., p. [19]).

HUGHES, Revd Hugh (1755?–1830) For fifty-two years he was Curate of Nuneaton, and for thirty-two years he was Headmaster of the Free Grammar School.

REVD MR CREWE in George Eliot, 'Janet's Repentance', *Scenes of Clerical Life* (1857–8)

See under **Anstruther**, Lady.

HUGHES, Richard (1906–84) Australian born journalist. In 1948 he joined the *Sunday Times* as Foreign Manager under Jan Fleming, and from 1956 until his death he lived in Hong Kong.

WILLIAM CAW in John Le Carré, *The Honourable Schoolboy* (1977)

'Hong Kong's press corps has honoured ... Richard Hughes with a bronze effigy of himself. ... The head will be a permanent fixture at the Hong Kong foreign correspondents' club, where the opening scene of ... *The Honourable Schoolboy* is set. Hughes ... is the model for a central character (Craw) in the book' (Anthony Holden, 1978, 'Atticus', *Sunday Times* (23 July): 32).

HUGHES, Thomas (1822–96) English reformer and novelist. Educated at Rugby and at Oriel College, Oxford, he was a Christian Socialist and follower of F.D. Maurice and was active in founding the Working Men's College in Great Ormond Street, London; he was its principal from 1872 to 1883. He was an active organizer of support in England for the Union in the American Civil War and was a close friend of J.R. **Lowell**; he had many other American connections, being strongly in favour of Anglo-American friendship. In 1865 he was Liberal MP for Lambeth, his election campaign being largely organized by George Holyoake, the radical; his election did not cost him a penny because the expenses were met by subscription among his working-class supporters. He supported the Reform League for enfranchisement of the artisan, and was a member of the Trades Union Commission of 1867. With Frederic Harrison, he drew up a minority report and appendix, setting out the arguments in favour of trade unions, which became the foundation of subsequent legislation on the subject. He was also a strong supporter of co-operation and profit-sharing. Between 1868 and 1874 he was MP for Frome, Wiltshire. He later became less radical and joined **Chamberlain**'s Liberal Unionists. Nassau Senior was his brother-in-law.

THOMAS BROWN in Thomas Hughes, *Tom Brown's Schooldays* (1857)

'Hughes never actually convinced anyone that he had drawn other than himself as his hero' (Edward C. Mack and W.H.G. Armytage, 1952, *Thomas Hughes: the life of the author of Tom Brown's Schooldays*, London: Ernest Benn, pp. 93–4).

HULLAH, John Pyke (1812–84) Composer and teacher. From 1858 to 1884 he was the organist at the Charterhouse, London, and in 1840 he organized singing classes on the tonic sol-fa method at Battersea. He was connected with the Academy of Music and achieved a great deal for the musical education of the masses.

LENHART DAVY in Elizabeth Sara Sheppard, *Charles Auchester* (1853)

Identified in an anonymous typed key laid in a copy of the first edition of *Charles Auchester* which is now in the possession of the present author.

HUMBERT, Frédéric (b. 1859) Son of Gustave Humbert, Senator of the French Republic, in 1903 he was convicted, with his wife, of a vast swindle including the flotation of a fraudulent insurance company.

DE BARRAL in Joseph Conrad, *Chance* (1914)

'Perhaps it is not generally known that the Humbert Case served Joseph Conrad as background . . . for the De Barral Case in *Chance*. This is not mere assumption or even deduction on my part. I know because he told me so . . . while *Chance* was actually in the writing' (Warrington Dawson, '13 years – 13 windows', unpublished work in the Dawson Collection in the Duke University Library; see Dale B.J. Randall, 1968, *Joseph Conrad and Warrington Dawson: the record of a friendship*, Durham, NC, p. 42).

HUMES, Mrs Mother of Elizabeth **Humes**.

RACHEL WITT in D.H. Lawrence, 'St Mawr' (1925)

'[Elizabeth Humes's] mother . . . became Mrs Witt, the mother in the story' (H.T. Moore, 1960, *The Intelligent Heart: the story of D.H. Lawrence*, Harmondsworth: Penguin, p. 363; originally published 1955, London: Heinemann).

HUMES, Elizabeth Known as 'Bettina', she was the fiancée of Jan Juta, the South African-born painter who illustrated D.H. Lawrence's *Sea and Sardinia*. She was from the southern states of America, and Lawrence met her in Capri in 1920. In 1923 she was working in Vienna in the office of the American Commercial Commission.

LOUISE CARRINGTON in D.H. Lawrence, 'St Mawr' (1925)

'The portrait of her as the American girl, Lou Carrington, in *St Mawr* is not a malignant one' (H.T. Moore, 1960, *The Intelligent Heart: the story of D.H. Lawrence*, Harmondsworth: Penguin, p. 363; originally published 1955, London: Heinemann).

HUMPHREYS, Ernest A member of the teaching staff at Davidson Road School, Croydon, when D.H. Lawrence taught there from 1908 to 1911.

MR HOLIDAY in D.H. Lawrence, *The Trespasser* (1912)

'Ernest Humphreys, appeared as . . . Haliday [sic]' (H.T. Moore, 1960, *The Intelligent Heart: the story of D.H. Lawrence*, Harmondsworth: Penguin, p. 151; originally published 1955, London: Heinemann).

HUNSWORTH MILL, Yorkshire

HOLLOWS MILL in Charlotte Brontë, *Shirley* (1849)

Charlotte Brontë situates Hollows Mill in a spot between Oakwell Hall and Birstall. 'The mill she actually describes was three miles away on the other side of Birstall, at Hunsworth. Mr Taylor (Hiram Yorke) . . . worked the mill which had been erected by his father, John Taylor, about the year 1785' (Herbert Wroot,

1935, *Sources of Charlotte Brontë's Novels: persons and places*, Shipley, Yorks., p. 85).

HUNT He was a prisoner in Birmingham borough prison in 1853; in 1855 the governor, William **Austin**, was charged with inflicting brutal punishment on him, but he was acquitted.

CARTER in Charles Reade, *It is Never Too Late to Mend* (1856)

'Mr Reade . . . makes a great deal of Mr Austin's conduct towards a man named Hunt (called in the novel Carter)' ('The license of modern novelists', *Edinburgh Review* 106 (July 1857): 141).

HUNT, Frazier (b. 1885) Known as 'Spike', he was Foreign Correspondent for *Cosmopolitan* and other **Hearst** periodicals. In 1921 he met Sinclair Lewis in London; they became close friends.

ROSS IRELAND in Sinclair Lewis, *Dodsworth* (1929)

'Ross Ireland seems to be modeled on Frazier Hunt' (Mark Schorer, 1963, *Sinclair Lewis: an American life*, London: Heinemann, p. 485 n.; originally published 1961, New York: McGraw-Hill).

SOLON RICHARDSON in Grace Hegger Lewis, *Half a Loaf* (1931)

'Hunt appears in *Half a Loaf* as Solon . . . Richardson, foreign correspondent for *The Circle*' (Shorer, op. cit., p. 311 n.).

HUNT, Henry 'Orator' (1773–1835) Radical politician. He farmed in Wiltshire. In 1800 he was fined and imprisoned for challenging a colonel of the yeomanry, and, in 1810, for assaulting a gamekeeper. In 1819 he was imprisoned for two years for his part in the Manchester meeting (Peterloo). From 1830 to 1833 he was MP for Preston. He became a blacking manufacturer, and he always wore a white beaver hat: the white hat became a symbol of radicalism.

GALLIPOT JONES in George Borrow, *Lavengro* (1851)

A variant of ch. xxxiv (later discarded), printed by Clement Shorter in the Norwich edition (1923–4), reads: '[Borrow] . . . [gives] us . . . an admirable portrait – in this case "Orator" Hunt with his white topper' (see A. Boyle, 1951, 'Portraiture in Lavengro', *Notes and Queries* 196 (8 December): 537). 'In another suppressed chapter of Lavengro restored by Knapp in his edition of 1899 Orator Hunt is . . . referred to as "Eolus Jones"' (ibid., p. 538).

HUNT, (William) Holman (1827–1910) English painter. Born in London, he was admitted to the Royal Academy in 1845. Emma **Watkins** sat for him in 1852. Along with Dante Gabriel **Rossetti** and **Millais**, he founded the 'Pre-Raphaelite Brotherhood'. In 1905 he published *Pre-Raphaelitism and the Pre-Raphaelite Brotherhood*, a work that provides a valuable insight into the movement's aims and methods.

MILDMAY STRONG in Robert Barnabas Brough, 'Calmuck', *Heads and Tails* (1859)

'A particularly interesting sale of documents was held on 15 December 1970, when a large collection of Holman Hunt papers was sold. . . . There were . . .

three from Dickens (19–30 April 1858) in which he answers Hunt's complaints about "Calmuck", a story published in *Household Words*. The story was a thinly disguised satirical account of Hunt's relations with his model Emma Watkins, six years earlier, and a recent biographer of Hunt considers that Dickens must have been well aware of this. He did not admit it to Hunt however' ('Dickens at Sotheby's', 1971, *The Dickensian* 67 (363): 90).

HUNT, Leigh (1784–1859) Essayist, journalist and poet. He was a friend of **Shelley**, **Byron** and Keats, and was a neighbour in Chelsea of the **Carlyles**. He was in perpetual financial straits.

JULIAN FIELD in Halcott Glover, *Both Sides of the Blanket* (1945)

A *roman à clef* written by an American connection of Hunt's dealing with the relationship between Thornton Hunt, George Lewes and his wife (who became Thornton Hunt's mistress), and George Eliot. In the novel the Hunts appear as the Fields (see Marghanita Laski, 1973, *George Eliot and Her World*, London: Thames & Hudson, p. 44).

HAROLD SKIMPOLE in Charles Dickens, *Bleak House* (1852–3)

'Skimpole. I must not forget Skimpole. . . . I suppose he is the most exact portrait that ever was painted in words! I have very seldom, if ever, done such a thing. But the likeness is astonishing. I don't think he could possibly be more like himself. It is so awfully true, that I make a bargain with myself "never to do so, any more". There is not an atom of exaggeration or suppression. It is an absolute reproduction of a real man. Of course I have been careful to keep the outward figure away from the fact; but in all else it is the life itself' (Charles Dickens to the Hon. Mrs Richard Watson, 25 September 1853, reproduced in Deshler Welch, 1966, 'Dickens in Switzerland: some unpublished letters and recollections', *Harpers Monthly Magazine* (European edn) 51 (April): 717, 719). The portrait was recognized by Barry Procter and John Forster, who both protested by letter to Dickens. He replied, 'I have again gone over every part of it very carefully, and I think I have made it much less like. I have also changed Leonard to Harold. I have no right to give Hunt pain' (to Forster, 18 March 1852, reproduced in John Forster, 1928, *Life of Charles Dickens*, ed. J.W.T. Ley, p. 550).

HUNT, Margaret (1831–1912) Novelist. She was married to Alfred Hunt, the painter in watercolours, and Violet **Hunt** was their daughter.

MRS WANNOP in Ford Madox Ford, *Parade's End* (1924–8)

'In her girlhood Mrs Hunt was the model for Tennyson's "Margaret". . . . This faint shadowy figure . . . is difficult to reconcile with the figure the elderly Mrs Hunt cut as Valentine Wannop's mother in . . . [Parade's End], that "frightfully inaccurate" old lady who had "written the only novel that's been fit to read since the eighteenth century"' (Arthur Mizener, 1971, *The Saddest Story: a biography of Ford Madox Ford*, Cleveland: World Publishing, p. 141).

HUNT, Violet (1862?–1942) Novelist. Daughter of the painter Alfred William Hunt, she grew up in the **Rossetti** circle and studied painting until she was 28 years old. After 1911 she was known for some years as Mrs Hueffer, although she was never legally married to Ford Madox Ford; they were estranged for many years before his death.

EMILY, LADY ALDINGTON, in Ford Madox Ford, *The New Humpty-Dumpty* (1912)

Identified in Arthur Mizener, 1971, *The Saddest Story: a biography of Ford Madox Ford*, Cleveland: World Publishing, pp. 223–7.

FLORENCE DOWELL in Ford Madox Ford, *The Good Soldier* (1915)

'[Ford] worked hard to remove from *The Good Soldier* the evidence that it was based on personal experience. . . . But there is really no concealing the fact that Florence is based on Violet' (Arthur Mizener, 1972, *The Saddest Story: a biography of Ford Madox Ford*, Cleveland: World Publishing, p. 253).

ROSE NEWALL in Violet Hunt, *Sooner or Later* (1904)

The book describes her love affair with Oswald **Crawfurd**. The identification is based upon obvious parallels.

THE HON. BEATRICE NORMANBY in H.G. Wells, *Tono-Bungay* (1909)

'[Wells] told her that Beatrice of *Tono-Bungay* was modelled on her' (Arthur Mizener, 1971, *The Saddest Story: a biography of Ford Madox Ford*, Cleveland: World Publishing, p. 152).

CLAIRE TEMPLE in Norah Hoult, *There Were No Windows* (1946)

Information supplied by the author. The novel describes Violet Hunt as living during the war at South Lodge on Campden Hill, old, confused and alone.

ROSE WATERFORD in W. Somerset Maugham, *The Moon and Sixpence* (1919)

'Violet Hunt is supposed to be the original of Rose Waterford' (R.L. Calder, 1972, *W. Somerset Maugham and the Quest for Freedom*, London: Heinemann, p. 138).

HUNTER, Alfred H.

LEOPOLD BLOOM in James Joyce, *Ulysses* (1922)

'[A] plan [for a story] which [James Joyce] mentioned to Stanislaus on September 30 [1906] was to be called "Ulysses" and to portray . . . a dark-complexioned Dublin Jew named Hunter who was rumoured to be a cuckold. . . . On December 3 [Joyce] asked [Stanislaus] to write what he remembered of Hunter. (Joyce had only met him twice.)' (Richard Ellmann, 1966, *James Joyce*, London: Oxford Paperbacks, pp. 238–9). 'Several Dubliners helped Joyce to complete his hero. The first was the man named Hunter, about whom he had asked Stanislaus and, later, his aunt Josephine Murray to send him all the details they could remember' (ibid., p. 385). *See also* **Bloom**, Joseph; **Byrne**, John Francis; **Chance**, Charles; **Jackson**, Holbrook; **Joyce**, James; **Joyce**, John Stanislaus; **Mayer**, Teodoro; **Popper**, Leopoldo; **Schmitz**, Ettore.

HURLBERT, William Henry (1827–95) American journalist. Born Hurlbut. He was a friend of James Russell **Lowell** and in the 1850s he published articles in English newspapers in favour of the abolition of slavery. He was also a friend of Charles Kingsley. He was not an entirely estimable character and was alleged to have stolen Lord Goderick's plaid in Lausanne while travelling abroad with

Thomas **Hughes**. In 1857 he joined the *New York Times*; and later became Editor of the *New York World*.

STANLAKE in Charles Kingsley, *Two Years Ago* (1857)

'Kingsley's friend Hurlbert sat for the portrait of . . . Stanlake' (R.B. Martin, 1959, *The Dust of Combat: a life of Charles Kingsley*, London: Faber & Faber, p. 203).

HURN COURT, Bournemouth, Dorset Formerly Heron Court, it is located in Hurn, which is north-east of, and now almost a suburb of, Bournemouth.

ROOKINGTON PARK in Thomas Hardy, *The Hand of Ethelberta* (1876)

Identified in F.B. Pinion, 1968, *A Hardy Companion*, London: Macmillan.

HUSKISSON, William (1770–1830) Statesman. Educated privately in Paris, in 1795 he was Under-Secretary at War, and he was an MP in 1796–1802 and 1804–30. He was Secretary to the Treasury under Pitt in 1804 and 1805, and under Portland from 1807 to 1809, whereupon he resigned with Canning. He was deeply interested in finance and was in favour of free trade, and was President of the Board of Trade from 1823 to 1827. From 1827 to 1829 he was Colonial Secretary. He also supported Catholic emancipation. He was run over and killed by a train at the opening of the Manchester and Liverpool Railway.

MR LIBERAL PRINCIPLES in Benjamin Disraeli, *Vivian Grey* (1826–7)

Identified as Mr H——n in a key given in *The Star Chamber* (24 May 1826): 114; reprinted in *Vivian Grey*, 1904 (centenary edn), ed. Lucien Wolf, Vol. II, London, pp. 361–2. The full name appears on a copy of the key held in the British Museum. Lucien Wolf concludes that Disraeli was not responsible for the key.

THE SALLOW GENTLEMAN in Bulwer Lytton, *Paul Clifford* (1830)

Identified in a key set out by Rosina Bulwer Lytton, in a letter of 26 May 1830, reproduced in Michael Sadleir, 1968, *Bulwer and His Wife*, pp. 227–8.

HUSSEY, R.G. (1883–1953) Pathologist. He was a member of the Rockefeller Institute from 1919 to 1922 and was active in the Red Cross from 1938 to 1944.

MARTIN ARROWSMITH in Sinclair Lewis, *Arrowsmith* (1925)

Identified in Mark Schorer, 1961, *Sinclair Lewis: an American life*, New York: McGraw-Hill, p. 418.

HUTCHINS, Mrs

MRS PATTEN in George Eliot, 'The Sad Fortunes of the Revd Amos Barton', *Scenes of Clerical Life* (1857–8)

See under **Anstruther**, Lady.

HUTCHINS, Sophia (1819–94) Daughter of William Horsley, composer and organist of the Charterhouse, and sister of Charles **Horsley**. In 1829 **Mendelssohn**, on his first visit to England, became intimate with the family, constantly visiting them at 1 High Row, Kensington (now 128 Kensington

Church Street), London. He corresponded with William Horsley, once describing Sophia as 'the fiercely reserved silent girl'.

MISS LAWRENCE in Elizabeth Sara Sheppard, *Charles Auchester* (1853)

'[Charles Horsley's] sister Sophy [sat] for the character of Miss Lawrence' (*Mendelssohn and His Friends in Kensington: letters from Fanny and Sophy Horsley*, 1934, ed. Rosamund Brunel Gotch, p. 5).

HUTTON, Mary Josephine   Sister of Thomas Grindal **Hutton**. Mrs Molesworth may have known their parents in Manchester when their uncle, Professor W.S. **Jevons**, held the Chair of Political Economy at Owens College.

NARCISSA in Mrs Molesworth, *A Christmas Child* (1880)

'*The Cuckoo Clock* is dedicated to the memory of Thomas Grindal Hutton, and to his sister Mary Josephine, the "Narcissa" of *A Christmas Child*' (R. Lancelyn Green, 1961, *Mrs Molesworth*, p. 43).

HUTTON, Thomas Grindal   (1862–75)   Brother of Mary Josephine **Hutton**.

TED in Mrs Molesworth, *A Christmas Child* (1880)

'[*A Christmas Child*] is an actual biography of a real boy whom she knew, and was written and re-written with infinite care ... to achieve accuracy. The original of "Ted" was Thomas Grindal Hutton' (R. Lancelyn Green, 1961, *Mrs Molesworth*, p. 43).

HUXLEY, Julia   (d. 1908)   Daughter of Thomas **Arnold**; she was the sister of Mrs Humphry **Ward** and was the mother of Aldous and Julian **Huxley**.

MAISIE BEAVIS in Aldous Huxley, *Eyeless in Gaza* (1936)

'In novel after novel Huxley returned to Julia's death ... [it] ... pervasively shadows *Eyeless in Gaza* ... the action ... begins in Anthony Beavis's memoirs of his mother and her funeral' (George Woodcock, 1972, *Dawn and the Darkest Hour: a study of Aldous Huxley*, London: Faber & Faber, p. 38). 'For Anthony the death of his mother was the same ... traumatic experience as the death of Julia Huxley for Aldous, but there the resemblance ends, for Maisie Beavis obviously had little in common with Julia Huxley' (ibid., p. 198).

MRS GUMBRIL in Aldous Huxley, *Antic Hay* (1923)

'Julia's sons came to see her for the last time. ... The youngest ... thinly disguised the experience in fiction: "He hadn't known that she was going to die, but when he entered her room, when he saw her lying so weakly in bed, he had suddenly begun to cry, uncontrollably"' (Ronald W. Clark, 1968, *The Huxleys*, London: Heinemann, p. 141).

HUXLEY, Julian   (1887–1975)   He was Aldous **Huxley**'s brother and a distinguished biologist. Julia **Huxley** was his mother. In 1919 he married Juliette Baillot (**Huxley**, below).

SANDY GRIEVE in Mrs Humphry Ward, *The History of David Grieve* (1891)

'To the same beloved sister [Julia Huxley] she was indebted for the . . . tales of her small boy Julian, which enliven the later pages of *David Grieve*; for Sandy Grieve was taken direct from the little grandson of the Professor' (Janet Penrose Trevelyan, 1923, *Life of Mrs Humphry Ward*, pp. 98, 99). 'We are very proud of Julian's apotheosis. . . . The strength of his conviction that people who interfere with his freedom are certainly foolish, probably wicked, is quite Gladstonian' (T.H. Huxley to Mrs Humphry Ward, 1 February 1892, ibid., pp. 100, 107).

HUXLEY, Juliette (b. 1896) Née Baillot, she was born in Switzerland and in 1919 married Julian **Huxley**.

FRÄULEIN MÄRZ in D.H. Lawrence, *Women in Love* (1920)

'Juliette Baillot . . . later to figure as the Fräulein of *Women in Love*' (E. Delavenay, 1972, *D.H. Lawrence: the man and his work*, p. 278).

HUXLEY, Leonard (1860–1933) Father of Aldous and Julian **Huxley**. He taught at Charterhouse and was Assistant Editor and then Editor of the *Cornhill Magazine*.

JOHN BEAVIS in Aldous Huxley, *Eyeless in Gaza* (1936)

'John Beavis . . . seemed so much like . . . Leonard Huxley, that Aldous's stepmother felt impelled to write to him in protest. Huxley's reply [dated 30 November 1936] was a . . . demonstration of the way a fictional character comes into being. "Following a principle which I have always used [he writes] that the only way of rendering . . . the subjective feeling of a person and the objective judgement of other people upon that person is to mingle tragedy with . . . extravagance – I introduced the element of philology. . . . After this it was necessary to fix the personage in time. . . . And here, I am afraid quite unjustifiably, I made use of mannerisms and phrases some of which were recognizably father's"' (George Woodcock, 1972, *Dawn and the Darkest Hour: a study of Aldous Huxley*, London: Faber & Faber, p. 197). The text of the letter is to be found in *The Letters of Aldous Huxley*, 1969, ed. Grover Smith, p. 409. *See also* **Weekley**, Ernest.

HUXLEY, Maria (1898–1955) Née Nys. Born in Belgium, she became the first wife of Aldous Huxley after they met at **Garsington Manor** in 1916. She died of cancer after a prolonged illness.

ELINOR QUARLES in Aldous Huxley, *Point Counter Point* (1928)

'Elinor Quarles, if no portrait [of Maria], is a tender evocation' (Sybille Bedford, 1973, *Aldous Huxley: a biography*, Vol. I, London: Chatto & Windus, p. 204).

HELEN RIVERS in Aldous Huxley, *The Genius and the Goddess* (1955)

'[The novel] was written some months before Maria Huxley died, but she was already approaching her end, with clear knowledge and exemplary calm, and, while Helen is not a portrait of Maria, there is no doubt that Huxley's involvement in Maria's fate had helped to form the view of death that Helen embodied' (George Woodcock, 1972, *Dawn and the Darkest Hour: a study of Aldous Huxley*, London: Faber & Faber, p. 279).

ANNE WIMBUSH in Aldous Huxley, *Crome Yellow* (1921)

'If people . . . said that Anne made them think of Carrington (or Maria Nys) . . . surely then people must also see that all these were conceived in a spirit of light-hearted comedy' (Bedford, op. cit., Vol. I, p. 123).

HUXLEY, Matthew (b. 1921) Son of Aldous and Maria **Huxley**.

PHILIP QUARLES THE YOUNGER in Aldous Huxley, *Point Counter Point* (1928)

'Aldous . . . did . . . Matthew in [Philip and Eleanor Quarles's] child' (Sybille Bedford, 1973, *Aldous Huxley: a biography*, Vol. I, London: Chatto & Windus, p. 202). 'The child in the book has Matthew's ways as a small boy. Like Matthew, he muddles up his longer words. . . . *Like* Matthew; not *Matthew*. . . . The child in the novel dies of meningitis (a death probably suggested by that of the Mitchison's eldest boy the year before)' (ibid., p. 207). *See also* **Mitchison, Geoffrey.**

HUXLEY, Noel Trevenen (1889–1914) Elder brother of Aldous Huxley. He committed suicide.

BRIAN FOXE in Aldous Huxley, *Eyeless in Gaza* (1936)

'Trevenen, who lives on at least partially in the character of the sensitive and over-scrupulous Brian Foxe in *Eyeless in Gaza*, was among his siblings the closest in age and disposition to Aldous' (George Woodcock, 1972, *Dawn and the Darkest Hour: a study of Aldous Huxley*, London: Faber & Faber, p. 46). 'We have Aldous's re-creation of his brother as Brian Foxe . . . (perhaps his only fully intended portrait of an actual person.)' (Sibylle Bedford, 1973, *Aldous Huxley: a biography*, Vol. I, London: Chatto & Windus, p. 40).

HUXLEY, Thomas Henry (1825–95) Zoologist. Father of Leonard **Huxley**, grandfather of Aldous and Julian **Huxley**, and great-grandfather of Matthew **Huxley**.

MR STORKS in W.H. Mallock, *The New Republic* (1877)

'Mr Storks . . . the prosaic . . . [materialist, was] meant for [Professor] Huxley' (W.H. Mallock, 1920, *Memoirs of Life and Literature*, London: Chapman and Hall, p. 65). See J. Max Patrick, 1956, 'The portrait of Huxley in Mallock's "New Republic"', *The Nineteenth Century* 2 (1): 61). Also identified in W.H. Mallock, 1920, *Memoirs of Life and Literature*, London: Chapman and Hall, pp. 65–6.

HUYSH, Revd Francis (1768–1839) Rector of Clysthidon, Devon. In 1831 he was Prebendary of Clutton in Exeter.

REVD DR PORTMAN in W.M. Thackeray, *The History of Pendennis* (1848–50)

'This gentleman, upon whom Thackeray modelled Dr Portman . . . was descended from an ancient Somerset family. . . . The Huyshes lived at Talaton, a few miles south of Larklease, and there was much intercourse between the two families' (Gordon N. Ray, 1955, *Thackeray: a biography*, Vol. I: *The Uses of Adversity, 1811–1846*, London: Oxford University Press, p. 105). *See also* **Cornish, Revd Sidney.**

HYDE, Edwin He was the owner of the Southsea Drapery Emporium of King's Road, Southsea, where H.G. Wells was apprenticed from 1881 to 1883.

Edwin Shalford in H.G. Wells, *Kipps* (1905)

'A contemporary, named Maurice Camkin, wrote to [Wells] late in life recalling their time at Hyde's together. One can see where Wells caught his glimpse of the employer in *Kipps* in Camkin's description of Hyde "walking crab-wise to the counter and all the time washing his hands in invisible soap"' (N. Mackenzie and J. Mackenzie, 1973, *The Time Traveller: the life of H.G. Wells*, p. 41).

HYNDMAN, Henry Mayers (1842–1921) Socialist leader. From 1871 to 1880 he was on the staff of the *Pall Mall Gazette*. In 1881 he played a leading part in the formation of the (Social) Democratic Federation. He opposed the Boer War and in 1916 he left the British Socialist Party to form the National Socialist Party.

Josiah Foreman in W.H. Mallock, *The Old Order Changes* (1886)

'Mr Foreman . . . was a clear caricature of H.M. Hyndman' (P.M. Yarker, 1959, 'W.H. Mallock's other novels', *The Nineteenth Century* 14 (December): 196).

I

ICENING WAY, Dorchester, Dorset The Via Iceniana or Ikenild, a Roman and, later, Saxon Road taking its name from the Iceni of Norfolk, where it started. It runs across England through the Eastern counties to Wantage, where it becomes the Ridgeway, to Dorchester, continuing south to the coast at Melford Regis or Weymouth. For a great part of the way it is known as the Icknield Way.

THE VIA in Thomas Hardy, *The Mayor of Casterbridge* (1886)

'It is the Via which Henchard watched ... from the heights of Mai-Dun [sic]' (F.B. Pinion, 1968, *A Hardy Companion*, London: Macmillan, p. 373).

IDDESLEIGH, Stafford Henry Northcote, 1st Earl of (1818–87) Conservative politician. Born in London, he was educated at Eton and at Balliol College, Oxford, and was called to the Bar in 1847. He was an MP from 1855 to 1884, and was Chancellor of the Exchequer from 1874 to 1880. He succeeded to the title of 8th Baronet in 1851 and was created Earl in 1884.

SIR WARWICK WEST END in Anthony Trollope, *The Three Clerks* (1857)

'Sir Stafford Northcote ... appears in *The Three Clerks* under the feebly facetious name of Sir Warwick West End' (Anthony Trollope, 1883, *An Autobiography*, Vol. I, p. 149).

ILCHESTER, Elizabeth, Countess of (1723–92) Only daughter of Thomas Strangways-Horner, of Mells Park, and Susanna, née **Strangways** of Melbury Sampford. She was the heiress of **Melbury House**, and her second husband became the 1st Earl of **Ilchester**. Her daughter Susan Fox-Strangways eloped with William O'Brien, the actor.

BETTY DORNELL in Thomas Hardy, 'The First Countess of Wessex' (1891)

'"The first Countess of Wessex" was Elizabeth Horner, wife of the first Earl of Ilchester' (R.L. Purdy, 1954, *Thomas Hardy: a bibliographical study*, pp. 66, 67).

ILCHESTER, Stephen Fox, 1st Earl of The eighth but first surviving son of Sir Stephen Fox, Paymaster General to the Forces. He was the intimate friend of Lord Hervey and in 1735 he married Elizabeth (**Ilchester**, above). In 1756 he was created Earl, and in 1758, upon the death of his wife's mother, Susanna **Strangways**-Horner, Strangways was added to the family name.

STEPHEN REYNARD, AFTERWARDS EARL OF WESSEX, in Thomas Hardy, 'The First Countess of Wessex' (1891)

Identified in F.B. Pinion, 1968, *A Hardy Companion*, London: Macmillan.

ILSINGTON FARM, Dorset Located on the south side of the road from Wareham to Tincleton, where it runs through the Frome Valley.

ELSENFORD in Thomas Hardy, 'The Waiting Supper' (1913)

Identified in F.B. Pinion, 1968, *A Hardy Companion*, London: Macmillan.

HMS IMPÉRIEUSE The captured Spanish frigate, commanded by Admiral Thomas **Cochrane**, in which Frederick Marryat served as a First Volunteer in 1806–9.

HMS Dιοмède in Frederick Marryat, *Peter Simple* (1834)

'Lord Cochrane and the Impérieuse . . . were made to appear in [*Peter Simple*] as Captain Savage and the Diomède' (Irving Wallace, 1956, *The Fabulous Originals*, London, p. 254).

INGATESTONE HALL, Essex Originally a manor of the nunnery of Barking, in 1539 it came into the hands of Sir William Petre. It was probably built between 1540 and 1565 (see Nikolaus Pevsner, 1974, *Essex* (*Buildings of England* series), Harmondsworth: Penguin), and although it was altered in the eighteenth century, a large part of the sixteenth-century house remains. It was in the possession of the Petre family for more than 350 years.

Audley Court in M.E. Braddon, *Lady Audley's Secret* (1862)

'I went over . . . to see Lord Petre's other place, Ingatestone, a fascinating Elizabethan manor-house, with a priests' hiding place. . . . It was let in suites to various tenants, one of whom, Miss Braddon, laid there the scene of her most famous novel, *Lady Audley's Secret*. I was much interested in seeing the tower-clock with the one crazy hand, as well as the lime-walk, and the old well down which the golden-haired heroine dropped the unfortunate George Talboys' (David Hunter Blair, 1919, *A Medley of Memories*, p. 100). Like Audley Court, Ingatestone is remarkable for its stepped gables and splendid chimney stacks.

INGHAM, Joshua Eldest son of Joshua Ingham (b. 1802) of **Blake Hall**, Mirfield, Yorkshire. The family consisted of five sons and five daughters and was descended from Ingham Benjamin Ingham, founder of the Wesleyan sect, the Inghamites.

Tom Bloomfield in Anne Brontë, *Agnes Grey* (1847)

'Joshua Ingham is of literary interest, since it was he who in April 1837 engaged Anne Brontë as governess to his two elder children. . . . Her experiences at Blake Hall are described in *Agnes Grey*. . . . Her two awful charges are immortalized as Master Tom Bloomfield and Miss Mary Anne Bloomfield' (Raleigh Trevelyan, 1972, *Princes Under the Volcano*, London: Macmillan, p. 45). 'Their real names were Joshua . . . and Mary' (ibid., p. 481 n. 14).

INGHAM, Mary Sister of Joshua **Ingham**.

Mary Ann Bloomfield in Anne Brontë, *Agnes Grey* (1847)

See under **Ingham**, Joshua.

IPSWICH, Suffolk County town of Suffolk.

Eatanswill in Charles Dickens, *The Pickwick Papers* (1836–7)

'I have . . . been assured by Mr Alfred Morrison . . . that Eatanswill was Ipswich, that his father was one of the candidates, and that Dickens was there in person' (Percy Fitzgerald, 1895, *Bozland: Dickens' places and people*, p. 15). *See also* **Sudbury**.

IRONSIDE, William Edmund, 1st Baron (1880–1959) Field Marshal. Known as 'Tiny', he was in fact six foot four inches. He could speak fourteen languages, including Cape Dutch; he served in the Boer War and escorted General Smuts to Vereenigung, South Africa. Disguised as a Boer transport driver, he acted as an intelligence agent in South West Africa. He also served in the First World War, taking part in the battles of Vimy Ridge and Passchendaele, and in 1918 he commanded the allied forces in Russia. He later went on a military mission to Hungary, and in 1921 was in command of Ismid and North Persian forces. In 1939 he was appointed Chief of the Imperial General Staff, and in May 1940 he was Commander-in-Chief of the home forces to prepare for invasion. He retired in July 1940.

RICHARD HANNAY in John Buchan, *The Thirty-nine Steps* (1915) and others

'The model for Richard Hannay . . . was Ironside . . . whom Buchan had first met in South Africa' (Janet Adam-Smith, 1965, *John Buchan*, p. 293).

IRVINE, Ayrshire A self-governing Royal Burgh; it was the birthplace of John Galt.

GUDETOWN in John Galt, *The Provost* (1822)

'Gudetown: Galt's name for his birthplace' (*The Provost*, 1973, ed. Ian A. Gordon, London: Oxford University Press, p. 153, n. 1 (to p. 1)).

IRVING, Edward (1792–1834) Founder of the Apostolic Church. Son of a tanner at Annan, in 1810–12 he was a schoolmaster at Haddington, near Edinburgh, where he taught Jane Baillie Welsh (**Carlyle**), and later at Kirkcaldy, where he became a friend of Thomas Carlyle, whom he introduced to Jane Welsh; it was through him that Carlyle became a friend of the **Bullers** and the **Stracheys**. In 1822 he moved to London and became famous as a preacher, but in 1832 he was compelled to retire from his ministry in Regent's Square on account of his approval of the speaking of 'Tongues' (which his followers supposed were divinely inspired). Carlyle described him as 'the noblest, largest and brotherliest man' he had ever met. He married Isabella Martin.

PHILISTINE in Thomas Carlyle, *Sartor Resartus* (1833–4)

'"The story of the book," said Mrs Strachey to her son, "is as plain as a pikestaff. . . . Philistine is Irving . . ."' (George Strachey, 1892, 'Carlyle and the "Rose-Goddess"', *The Nineteenth Century* 32 (September): 474).

TOWGOOD in Thomas Carlyle, *Sartor Resartus* (1833–4)

Identified by Alexander Carlyle in *The Love Letters of Thomas Carlyle and Jane Welsh Carlyle*, 1909, ed. Alexander Carlyle, London and New York: John Lane, pp. 364–78, App. B, n. 1. The identification is based on the assumption that the episode depicted is Carlyle's first visit to Haddington and encounter with Jane Welsh in May 1921.

ARTHUR VINCENT in Margaret Oliphant, *Salem Chapel* (1873)

'The Colbys [*The Equivocal Virtue: Mrs Oliphant and the Victorian literary marketplace*, 1966, Conn.] have pointed out general similarities between Vincent and Irving' (Valentine Cunningham, 1975, *Everywhere Spoken Against: dissent in the Victorian novel*, Oxford: Clarendon Press, p. 246).

IRVING, John (d. 1853) He was MP for County Antrim from 1837 to 1845 and was the first president of the Alliance Assurance company; he was a well-known Croesus of the day.

MR ORMSBY in Benjamin Disraeli, *Coningsby* (1844) and *Tancred* (1847)

'I send you "Coningsby", Disraeli's novel, well worth reading, and admirably written. . . . You will recognise . . . Irving in Ormsby' (Lord Palmerston to his brother, the Hon. William Temple, 30 May–5 June 1844, reproduced in Lord Dalling and Bulwer, 1874, *Life of Lord Palmerston*, Vol. III, London, pp. 138–9). *See also* **Dick**, Quentin.

IRWIN, Francis (b. 1861?) Born in Clogher, he was the son of Andrew Irwin of the Royal Ulster Constabulary and entered Trinity College, Dublin, in January 1882. He was a Protestant and was Headmaster of Clifton School, Veco Road, Dalkey, where Joyce taught for a short time in 1904.

GARRETT DEASY in James Joyce, *Ulysses* (1922)

'Irwin is presented under the name of Deasey' (Richard Ellmann, 1966, *James Joyce*, Oxford: London Paperbacks, p. 158). *See also* **Price**, Henry Blackwood.

ISHERWOOD, Christopher William Bradshaw (1904–86) Anglo-American novelist. He was born in High Lane, Cheshire, and educated at Repton School and Corpus Christi College, Cambridge. He taught English in Germany from 1930 to 1933, an experience that formed the basis of his two most celebrated novels *Mr Norris Changes Trains* (1935) and *Goodbye to Berlin* (1939). He was a close friend of W.H. **Auden** and collaborated with him on three plays. In 1939, he emigrated to the United States, settling in California, where he developed an interest in metaphysics and Eastern philosophy, and co-operated on a translation of the *Bhagavad-Gita*. He also worked as a scriptwriter in Hollywood, and taught in various Californian universities. He became an American citizen in 1946.

LAURENCE DARRELL in W. Somerset Maugham, *The Razor's Edge* (1944)

'At one time it was conjectured that in Larry Darrell Maugham was portraying Isherwood. The earlier counterparts of the young man in "The Road Uphill" [an unproduced and unpublished play written c.1924] and as Edward Barnard [in "The Fall of Edward Barnard", a short story written in 1921] make this unlikely. Nevertheless it is possible that Isherwood, whom the author knew at the time of the writing of *The Razor's Edge*, provided some aspects of Larry's character, particularly his faith in his guru' (R.L. Calder, 1972, *W. Somerset Maugham and the Quest for Freedom*, London: Heinemann, p. 241).

ISRAEL, Max The Israels were neighbours of the Wolfes in Woodfin Street, Asheville, and Max Israel was Thomas Wolfe's closest friend as a child.

Max Isaacs in Thomas Wolfe, *Look Homeward, Angel* (1929)

'Wolfe ... changed the name Israel to Isaacs' (*The Notebooks of Thomas Wolfe*, 1970, ed. Richard S. Kennedy and Paschal Reeves, Chapel Hill, NC: University of North Carolina Press, p. 335 n. 37).

ISRAEL, Wilfrid (1899–1943) He was born in London of an Anglo-German family who owned the great Berlin department store 'N. Israel', which he inherited. After Hitler's rise to power, Wilfred Israel devoted himself to organizing the escape of Jews from Germany. He travelled to England in 1938. He was shot down when returning from Portugal, where he had been attempting to arrange the rescue of Jewish refugees through Vichy France.

Bernhard Landauer in Christopher Isherwood, *Goodbye to Berlin* (1939)

'The original of Bernhard Landauer was Wilfrid Israel' (Christopher Isherwood, 1977, *Christopher and His Kind*, London: Eyre Methuen, p. 55).

ISRAELI, Benjamin (1730–1816) Father of Isaac D'Israeli and grandfather of Benjamin Disraeli. He was a native of Cento, near Ferrara, and engaged in the straw-bonnet trade. In 1748 he emigrated to England and became a well-to-do stockbroker. Basevi, the architect, was a connection of his wife's.

Baron Fleming in Benjamin Disraeli, *Contarini Fleming* (1832)

'In *Contarini [Fleming]* ... Baron Fleming is [Disraeli's] grandfather reincarnated as a noble' (Walter Sichel, 1904, *Disraeli: a study in personality and ideas*, London: Methuen, p. 16).

Putney Giles in Benjamin Disraeli, *Lothair* (1870)

'There is a touch also of his grandfather in ... "Mr Putney Giles" ... who "never made difficulties, but always overcame them"' (Sichel, op. cit., p. 16 n.).

IVANCICH, Adriana (b. 1929?) Afterwards von Rex. Descendent of a family that moved to Venice at the end of the eighteenth century from an island off the coast of Dalmatia. Her father was murdered by an unknown person in June 1945, the family's country house was destroyed during the Second World War and her brother was wounded while serving in the Italian army at Alamein; after the Italian surrender to the Allies, he fought in the American Office of Strategic Services as a partisan. Hemingway met her near Cortina in December 1948 and conceived for her a romantic affection.

Renata in Ernest Hemingway, *Across the River and into the Trees* (1950)

'As Renata's prototype, he chose the black-haired, nineteen year old Adriana Ivancich ... [she] was not a countess like Renata, nor was she (except in a remote and schoolgirlish fashion) in love with Ernest' (Carlos Baker, 1969, *Ernest Hemingway: a life story*, New York, p. 476).

J

JACKSON, Cyril (1746–1818) Clergyman and scholar. He was Sub-Preceptor to the elder sons of George III in 1771–6, a preacher at Lincoln's Inn 1776–83, and Dean of Christ Church, Oxford, 1783–1801; as Dean of Christ Church, he had a large share in the 'Public Examination Statute'. He declined the offer of several bishoprics, and in 1804 he helped to bring about the retirement of Henry Addington, the Tory Prime Minister, from the premiership.

DR HERBERT in Robert Plumer Ward, *De Vere; or The Man of Independence* (1827)

'It is impossible not to see that the novelist has designed to draw, under [the name of Dr Herbert], a full-length portrait of the late Cyril Jackson; and upon the whole, we believe that those who knew the Dean best will be little displeased with the shadow' (review of *De Vere*, 1827, *Quarterly Review* 36: 276).

JACKSON, George Vernon (1787–1876) In 1801 he was a midshipman in the Navy, in 1841 he was a captain, and in 1875 he was a retired admiral.

TERENCE O'BRIEN in Frederick Marryat, *Peter Simple* (1834)

'He is said to have been the original of O'Brien in Marryat's novel *Peter Simple*' (Frederic Boase, 1892, *Modern English Biography*, Vol. II, col. 31).

JACKSON, Henry (1839–1921) Educated at Trinity College, Cambridge, he was a Fellow in 1864, Vice-Master in 1914, Regius Professor of Greek in 1906, and received the Order of Merit in 1908.

HENRY JOHNSON in Shane Leslie, *The Cantab* (1926)

Identified in a key in the hand of Dr Ivor Ramsay, a Kingsman of the year 1920, and later Dean, laid in a copy of *The Cantab*.

JACKSON, (George) Holbrook (1874–1948) English journalist, man of letters and bibliophile. He helped to establish the political and literary journal *New Age* with A.R. Orage. He was active in the Fabian Society and published a number of books, including a biography of George Bernard **Shaw** (1907).

LEOPOLD BLOOM in James Joyce, *Ulysses* (1922)

'From the author of *Ulysses* himself, I learned what Mr Bloom looked like. Joyce asked me one day if I would write to Mr Holbrook Jackson . . . and ask him to send me a photograph of himself. . . . Joyce didn't say that he and Jackson had ever met, but I imagine they had. . . . The photograph arrived. I showed it to Joyce. He scrutinized it at some length and seemed disappointed; then, handing it to me, he said: "If you want to know what Leopold Bloom looked like here is someone who resembles him. But," he went on, "the photo is not a good likeness. He doesn't look as much like Bloom in it." Anyhow, I kept the photograph carefully; it was the only one of Mr Bloom I ever had' (Sylvia Beach, 1960, *Shakespeare and Company*, p. 97; the photograph is reproduced as Pl. 16).

See also **Bloom**, Joseph; **Byrne**, John Francis; **Chance**, Charles; **Hunter**, Alfred H.; **Joyce**, John Stanislaus; **Mayer**, Teodoro; **Popper**, Leopoldo; **Schmitz**, Ettore.

JACKSON, Richard Charles (1851–1923) He claimed to be the grandson of Charles Lamb's friend Captain Francis Jackson. He was attached to St Austin's Priory, which was founded in 1878 in the New Kent Road, London, by Revd George Nugée. He was a literary dilettante who wrote, *inter alia*, some indifferent hymns. In 1877 he became friends with Pater, who spent much time at Jackson's house, Grove Park, in Camberwell, London. Jackson was found dead in his house with a half-eaten orange in his hand, amid an extraordinary collection of things, mostly rubbish, with some eight thousand books scattered about.

MARIUS in Walter Pater, *Marius the Epicurean* (1885)

'"I will write a book about you." He did. That book was *Marius the Epicurean* – and Mr Jackson was Marius' (Thomas Wright, 1907, *The Life of Walter Pater*, Vol. II, p. 21). 'It may be that Mr Richard C. Jackson . . . was the original of . . . "Marius the Epicurean", but the claim seems to have been quite unknown until Wright published his biography of Pater in 1907. Those who knew Jackson personally, especially in later years, were aware that he was inaccurate in matters of fact . . . and that his literary vanity was prodigious. *De mortuis, &c*, is an excellent maxim, but in the present case a point of literary history is involved' (*The Times* (30 July 1923)).

JACOB, Alexander M. (1849?–1921) Variously described as an astrologer, magician, conjuror and Russian spy, he was a dealer in precious stones in Simla, where he is said to have arrived in 1871. He was ruined by an action that he brought and won against the Nizam of Hyderabad, who had refused to pay for a diamond brooch Jacob had sold to him – the British Resident having vetoed the purchase as excessively expensive; he was reduced to doing a modest business with Anglo-Indians. He was widely supposed to be in the employ of the Secret Department of the Government of India.

MR EMMANUEL in Newnham Davis, *Jadoo* (1898)

'Colonel Newnham Davis recognised Mr Jacob as a local celebrity, for in . . . *Jadoo* . . . is found the following allusion to this strange character: ". . . where the path joins the broad road there was . . . a pale-faced, fat, black-eyed little man on a Burmese pony . . . 'Who is the little man?' asked Dita. 'Oh! Emanuel. A man who knows more of the mystic secrets of India than any other man'"' (E.J. Buck, 1925, *Simla Past and Present*, Bombay, p. 177).

MR ISAACS in Marion Crawford, *Mr Isaacs* (1882)

'It has long been an open secret . . . that Marion Crawford's "Mr Isaacs" was no other than Mr Jacob. . . . Marion Crawford met Mr Jacob at Simla about 1880 and on May 5th, 1882 . . . Crawford told [his uncle Sam Ward] his recollections of an interesting man he had met at Simla. . . . Ward said "That is a good . . . story and you must write it out immediately." That night he began *Mr Isaacs'* (Buck, op. cit., p. 176).

LURGAN SAHIB in Rudyard Kipling, *Kim* (1901)

'Kipling, too . . . immortalised Mr Jacob as "Lurgan Sahib"' (Buck, op. cit., p. 176).

JAMES, Alice (1848–92) Sister of Henry James, she was a life-long invalid who died of cancer in England. Her constant companion was Katharine **Loring,** whom she met in 1873.

MILLY THEALE in Henry James, *The Wings of the Dove* (1902)

'It seems, by the way, that Henry James had seen quite a good deal of psychiatrists in connection with his sister Alice. I suppose that Alice and her ailments are also behind the Milly Theale situation' (Edmund Wilson to James Thurber, 1959, reproduced in *Letters on Literature and Politics, 1912–1972*, 1977, ed. Elena Wilson, p. 239). *See also* **Temple**, Mary.

JAMES, Edwin John (1812–82) Barrister-at-law. In 1861, after a very successful career, he was disbarred for malpractice, with his liabilities allegedly exceeding £100,000: he made off to New York. In 1858, Edmund Yates had consulted him when he was considering taking legal action against the **Garrick Club**, London, which had decided to expel him for publishing an article attacking Thackeray, a fellow member. Yates described him as a 'fat, florid man, with a large hard face' (Edmund Yates, 1884, *Edmund Yates: his recollections and experiences*, Vol. II, London: R. Bentley & Son, p. 31).

DR GEORGE FIRMIN in W.M. Thackeray, *The Adventures of Philip* (1861–2)

'Thackeray appears to have had James's débâcle in mind when he described the later phases of Dr Firmin's career' (*The Letters and Private Papers of W.M. Thackeray*, 1946, ed. Gordon Ray, Vol. IV, London: Oxford University Press, p. 117 n. 71).

C.J. STRYVER in Charles Dickens, *A Tale of Two Cities* (1859)

'. . . the counsel retained to conduct my case was Edwin James, Q.C. . . . I had many consultations with him. . . . One day I took Dickens – who had never seen Edwin James – to one of these consultations. . . . Dickens was quietly observant. About four months after appeared the early numbers of *A Tale of Two Cities*, in which a prominent part was played by Mr Stryver. After reading the description, I said to Dickens, "Stryver is a good likeness." He smiled. "Not bad, I think" he said, "especially after only one sitting"' (Yates, op. cit., pp. 31–2). *See also* **Wetherell**, Sir Charles.

JAMES, Henry (1843–1916) American novelist. Born in New York, the son of a prominent theologian and philosopher, he spent much of his youth travelling in America and Europe. He briefly studied law at Harvard. In 1865, he began to publish reviews and short stories. In 1875 he settled for a year in Paris, where he met Flaubert and Turgenev. The following year he moved to England, where he met H.G. **Wells**, who became a close friend. James became a British citizen on the outbreak of the First World War.

MR BELLASIS in Mrs Humphry Ward, *Eleanor* (1899)

'I've read carefully every word, and many two or three times, as Mr Bellasis would say – and is Mr Bellasis, by the way, naturally – as it were – H.J. ?????!!!'

(to Mrs Humphry Ward, July 1899, reproduced in *Letters of Henry James*, 1920, ed. Percy Lubbock, Vol. I, pp. 328–9). The answer would appear to be 'No'.

GEOFFREY BELLINGHAM in E.F. Benson, *Robin Linnet* (1919)

Identification based upon private information.

JOHN CHANNON in Percy Lubbock, *The Region Cloud* (1925)

'Percy Lubbock, whose involvement with James as ultimate editor of his letters would be posthumous rather than actual, would write a novel called *The Region Cloud* about a great artist and his disciples, picturing the artist as a powerful vampire, who needed young admirers to feed his incredible egotism. Whether he was thinking of himself and James we do not know: but in the very style of the novel, with its Jamesian imitations . . . Lubbock created a portrait caricature of James of considerable power and a certain amount of truth' (Leon Edel, 1972, *Henry James: the master, 1901–1916*, p. 195). This is not a much-read novel, nor indeed is it highly readable; but the description in the first chapter of John Channon, seen across the room, sitting alone at a table in a French inn, gives a startling impression that one is actually *seeing* James. Indeed, the whole of Austin's first encounter with Channon gives a most vivid and actual picture of James. But after that first glimpse, Channon as a character bears no resemblance to James at all, any more than Bintworth, his magnificent residence, resembles Lamb House.

HENRY GALLEON in Hugh Walpole, *Fortitude* (1913)

'Hugh would later record in *Fortitude* . . . the lessons of the Master; still later we can find the emotion of their meeting . . . in a tale called "Mr Oddy". . . . He named his fictitious novelist, both in novel and tale Henry Galleon; James, in his obesity, his large Johnsonian body set on his short legs, must have seemed like some great old ship. . . . In *Fortitude*, Galleon talks . . . in simplified Walpolian sentences, but we catch the reverberation of the great style; the feeling rings true' (Edel, op. cit., pp. 408–9).

RALPH IMBERT in Henry James, 'The Next Time' (1898)

'It is the old story of my letters to the [*New York Times*] where I had to write to Whitelaw [Reid] that they "were the worst I could do for the money"' (entry for 4 June 1895, in *The Notebooks of Henry James*, 1947, ed. F.O. Matthiessen and K.B. Murdock, New York, pp. 200–1).

JERVASE MARION in Vernon Lee, 'Lady Tal', *Vanitas* (1892)

'Receive from me . . . a word of warning about Vernon Lee . . . she has lately, as I am told (in a volume of tales called *Vanitas* which I haven't yet read), directed a kind of satire at me!!' (Henry James to William James, 20 January 1893, quoted in Peter Gunn, 1964, *Vernon Lee, 1856–1935*, London: Oxford University Press, pp. 138, 139). 'The portrait of my brother . . . is clever enough and I cannot call it exactly malicious. But . . . you will not be surprised to learn that seeing the book has quite quenched my desire to pay you another visit' (William James to Vernon Lee, 11 March 1893, quoted in ibid.).

TRAFFORD MORGAN in Constance Fenimore Woolson, 'A Florentine Experiment' (1880)

'In "A Florentine Experiment" . . . a young American heiress, believing the Henry James character (. . . named Trafford Morgan) to be in love with another woman, trifles with his affections' (Leon Edel, 1962, *Henry James: the conquest of London, 1870–1883*, pp. 418–19). Nothing of Henry James is evident in Trafford Morgan except perhaps his 'rather peculiar eyes' and the fact that the heroine of the story is in love with him as, according to Edel, Miss Woolson was with James.

RALPH ORTH in Gertrude Atherton, 'The Bell in the Fog' (1905)

'*The Bell in the Fog* . . . in the name-story of which the hero is drawn from James' (Simon Nowell-Smith, 1947, *The Legend of the Master*, p. 135 n. 1). Gertrude Atherton dedicated the book to James.

JAMES, Montague Rhodes (1862–1936) Educated at Eton and at King's College, Cambridge, he was Provost of King's from 1905 to 1918 and Provost of Eton from 1918 to 1935. He reconstructed the windows of King's College Chapel and between 1892 and 1935 he catalogued the Western manuscripts at Cambridge, Eton, Westminster Abbey and a number of other libraries. He published studies in Apocryphal literature and wrote ghost stories.

THE PROVOST in Shane Leslie, *The Cantab* (1926)

Identified in a key in the hand of Dr Ivor Ramsay, a Kingsman of the year 1920, and later Dean, laid in a copy of *The Cantab*.

JAMES, Samuel He was Thackeray's manservant from 1850 to 1852, becoming in that short time more of a friend than an employee. In 1852 he emigrated to Australia rather than accompany Thackeray to the United States, but he was still in touch with the family in 1890.

DICK BEDFORD in W.M. Thackeray, *Lovel the Widower* (1860)

'In 1855 [Thackeray] put James into his comedy *The Wolves and the Lamb* as James Howell'. 'When Thackeray turned *The Wolves and the Lamb* into *Lovel the Widower* he made Bedford, as he called the butler of that story, even more like James than Howell had been. In the end Bedford emigrates to Melbourne' (Gordon Ray, 1958, *Thackeray: the age of wisdom*, pp. 10, 435, n. 19).

JAMES, William (1842–1910) American philosopher and psychologist. He was the brother of Henry James. He graduated from Harvard and taught there from 1882. In 1889, he became Professor of Psychology and published *Principles of Psychology* the following year. He wrote several treatises in philosophy and described his views as those of a 'radical empiricist'.

BENJAMIN BABCOCK in Henry James, *The American* (1876)

'Here, at last, William recognized himself. "Your second instalment of *The American* is prime", he wrote. "The morbid little clergyman is worthy of Ivan Sergeyevich [Turgenev]. I was not a little amused to find some of my own attributes in him – I think you found my 'moral reaction' excessive when I was abroad"' (Leon Edel, 1962, *Henry James: the conquest of London, 1870–1883*, p. 259; no date or reference given).

T. JAMES & CO. A bookshop established in 1849 at 34 Bernard Street, Southampton.

T.T. RICEYMAN BOOKSHOP in Arnold Bennett, *Riceyman Steps* (1923)

'On one of our Southampton expeditions, I pointed out an old book shop to Bennett. We plunged into it, and made friends with the bookseller, an eccentric, kindly, elderly man by the name of James – "T. James and Co., 34 Bernard Street, established 1849", as the little labels announced, which he pasted into the corners of the books as soon as he had sold them. . . . We spent many an afternoon in the shop . . . talking to Mr James. At the same time I told Bennett about a servant girl my sister had had and her love affair with a soldier. Out of these two characters and the bookseller, combined with many other factors, Bennett during the following winter wove his *Riceyman Steps*' (Edward Knoblock, 1939, *Round the Room: an autobiography*, p. 314). 'On June 29, 1924, [Bennett] wrote in the yachting diary: "Southampton Water. I went ashore and bought two books at James' (original shop of *Riceyman Steps*)"' (Reginald Pound, 1952, *Arnold Bennett: a biography*, London: Heinemann, p. 301).

JARMAN, Frances Eleanor *See* **Ternan**, Frances Eleanor.

JARRELL, Randall (1914–65) American poet, novelist and critic. He was a consultant in poetry to the Library of Congress between 1956 and 1958, and during this time Kerouac and **Corso** stayed with him. He was killed in a motor accident.

VARNUM RANDOM in Jack Kerouac, *Desolation Angels* (1965)

Identified in 'Character key to the Duluoz Legend', in Barry Gifford and Lawrence Lee, 1979, *Jack's Book*, pp. 322–32.

JARVIS, Elizabeth (b. 1803)

ISOPEL BERNERS in George Borrow, *Lavengro* (1851)

'On July 25th 1803 [at Long Melford] Elizabeth Jarvis "Illeg. Daur. of Elizabeth Jarvis" was baptized. . . . There can be little doubt that this is the record of Isopel Berners' (Andrew Boyle, 1952, 'Portraiture in *Lavengro*', *Notes and Queries* 197 (13 September): 408–9; the article sets out the findings of Mr Ivor N. Evans in the Birth and Death Register at Long Melford as described in the current number of the *Journal of The Gipsy Lore Society*).

JAY, Revd Austin Osborne He was Vicar of Holy Trinity in Shoreditch, London, in 1886, and was the author of *Life in Darkest London and The Social Problem: its possible solution* (1893).

THE REVD HENRY STURT (FATHER STURT) in Arthur Morrison, *A Child of the Jago* (1896)

'Jay's parish was situated on the boundary of Bethnal Green and Shoreditch. . . . The Old Nichol . . . lay at the heart of the parish . . . and it was here that Jay decided to settle . . . in 1886. . . . In the space of ten years [he] raised . . . £25,000 with which he built, in the centre of Old Nichol Street, a church, social club, gymnasium and lodging-house. His greatest achievement, however, was in persuading the newly formed LCC [London County Council] to give high priority on its slum clearance schedules to the Old Nichol, or the Boundary Street Improvement scheme as it was officially called. . . . These details of Jay's life are familiar to readers of *A Child of the Jago* as Morrison faithfully reproduced them in his portrait of Father Sturt' (P.J. Keating, 1969, 'Arthur Morrison', biog. preface to *A Child of the Jago*, London: MacGibbon & Kee, p. 24). The incident in ch. 10, in which Father Sturt shoots the pot of beer into Kiddo Cook's face, comes directly from *Life in Darkest London*, ch. 4).

SS JEDDAH

SS *PATNA* in Joseph Conrad, *Lord Jim* (1900)

'One of the most famous scandals of the East of the 1880s was the case of the pilgrim ship *Jeddah*. . . . Sir Frank Swettenham, in a letter to *The Times Literary Supplement*, 6 September 1923, was the first to suggest that Conrad had based his story of the desertion of the pilgrim ship *Patna* upon the desertion of the pilgrim ship *Jeddah* by her European Master and officers' (Norman Sherry, 1966, *Conrad's Eastern World*, Cambridge, p. 41). The incident took place in August 1880. The *Jeddah* did not of course sink and was towed into Aden by the SS *Antenor*, arriving a day later than her officers who sailed in on the *Scindia*, which had picked them up, reporting that the Jeddah was lost with all her passengers.

JEFFREY, Francis, Lord (1773–1850) Scottish judge and critic. Called to the Scottish Bar in 1794, he a successful lawyer and became Lord Advocate in 1834; he was strongly Whig in his views. He was a co-founder of the **Edinburgh Review** in 1802 and was its Editor until 1829. He was a friend of Sir Walter **Scott**, Thomas Moore, Charles **Dickens** and Thomas Macaulay. He married, as his second wife, the grandniece of John Wilkes, the English politician.

GEOFFREY GALL in Thomas Love Peacock, **Headlong Hall** (1816)

'Et même un personnage apparaît comme le compère et le confrère en iniquité de ceux-là . . . c'est Geoffrey Gall, toujours occupé de la *Revue*, et dont le nom seul suggèrerait pour original Jeffrey de l'*Edinburgh Review* . . . et nous le verrons professer en face de Mr Milestone la même théorie esthétique de l'étonnement qu'avait avancée Jeffrey dans l'*Edinburgh* (Jean-Jacques Mayoux, 1933, *Un épicurien anglais: Thomas Love Peacock*, Paris, p. 148). Richard Garnett's identification of Gall as Gifford is mistaken.

JENKINS, Mrs A.L. An Australian from Perth, Western Australia, she met the Lawrences while sailing from Naples to Ceylon aboard the *Osterley* in February and March 1922; she entertained them in Australia in May of the same year.

VICTORIA CALLCOTT in D.H. Lawrence, **Kangaroo** (1923)

'[Mrs A.L. Jenkins] is possibly the original of Victoria Callcott' (H.T. Moore, 1960, *The Intelligent Heart: the story of D.H. Lawrence*, Harmondsworth: Penguin, p. 363; originally published 1955, London: Heinemann).

JENNINGS, Hargrave (c.1817–90) For many years he was Secretary to James Henry Mapleson, Manager of the Royal Italian Opera. He was the author of a number of novels and works dealing with the occult.

EZRA JENNINGS in Wilkie Collins, *The Moonstone* (1868)

'Said to be the original of Ezra Jennings' (Frederic Boase, 1892, *Modern English Biography*, Vol. II, col. 83).

JENNINGS V. JENNINGS Sometimes written 'Jennens'. Litigation in this case began on the intestate death in 1798 of William Jennens of Birmingham, known as 'William the Rich': he left nearly £1,500,000 in money and shares, and the bulk of his property passed to Lady Andover and Earl Howe, who claimed to be next-of-kin through marriage. Members of the same family held the greater part thereafter, despite efforts to dispute the claim that were said to cost £250,000. In 1915 one of the claimants, David Jennings, died in Wolverhampton Workhouse.

JARNDYCE V. JARNDYCE in Charles Dickens, *Bleak House* (1852-3)

'. . . it was the case on which Dickens based his Jarndyce v. Jarndyce in *Bleak House*' (*The Dickensian* 11 (February 1915): 31). From the phrasing of this note it would appear that litigation continued further.

JERICHO, Oxford A working-class district in the town, west of Woodstock Road.

BEERSHEBA in Thomas Hardy, *Jude the Obscure* (1895)

Identified in Denys Kay-Robinson, 1972, *Hardy's Wessex Reappraised*, Newton Abbot, and in F.B. Pinion, 1968, *A Hardy Companion*, London: Macmillan.

JEROME, Thomas Spencer American Vice-Consul in Capri in the early years of the twentieth century. He was 'a Roman historian of enormous erudition' (Meryle Secrest, 1974, *Between Me and Life: a life of Romaine Brooks*, Garden City, NY: Doubleday, p. 128).

SCUDAMORE in Compton Mackenzie, *Vestal Fire* (1927)

'Those who are anxious to learn about him will find a portrait of him as "Scudamore" in . . . *Vestal Fire*' (Norman Douglas, 1933, *Looking Backward*, p. 418).

JERSEY, Sarah Sophia Child-Villiers, Countess of (1785–1867) Née Fane, she was the eldest daughter of the 10th Earl of Westmorland, and inherited, through her mother, the vast fortune of her grandfather, Robert Child the banker. She was a reigning beauty of her day and married the 5th Earl of Jersey; she was alleged to have preceded Lady Hertford and Lady Conyngham as the mistress of **George IV**. Lady Augusta **Fane** was her younger sister.

COUNTESS OF GUERNSEY in Lady Blessington, *The Repealers* (1833)

Identified in Michael Sadleir, 1933, *Blessington–D'Orsay*, London: Constable, App. IV, p. 376, and in Michael Sadleir, 1951, *XIX Century Fiction*, London: Constable, pp. 40–1.

LADY HAUTON in M. Spencer Stanhope, *Almacks* (1826)

Identified in Michael Sadleir, 1951, *XIX Century Fiction*, London: Constable, p. 331; reprinted from *Literary Gazette* (9 December 1826).

LADY ST JULIANS in Benjamin Disraeli, *Coningsby* (1844) and *Sybil* (1845)

Identified in a key in *Notes and Queries* (8th series) 3 (13 May 1893): 363. 'She appears in . . . *Coningsby* and *Sybil* as "Lady St Julians", by this time a mother of marriageable daughters and a matchmaker of ruthless competence' (Michael Sadleir, 1933, *Blessington–D'Orsay*, London: Constable, pp. 133–4).

LADY AUGUSTA SELWYN in Lady Caroline Lamb, *Glenarvon* (1816)

'Lady Augusta [is] Lady Jersey and Lady Collier' (Lady Holland to Mrs Creevey, 21 May 1816, quoted in *The Creevey Papers*, 1903, ed. Sir H. Maxwell, Vol. I, p. 254). *See also* **Collier**, Lady.

LADY TILNEY in Lady Charlotte Bury, *The Exclusives* (1830)

Identified in *Key to the Royal Novel 'The Exclusives'*, 1830, Marsh & Miller; reproduced in Michael Sadleir, 1951, *XIX Century Fiction*, 2 vols, London: Constable, and Los Angeles: California University Press, pp. 73–4.

ZENOBIA in Benjamin Disraeli, *Endymion* (1880)

'Lady Jersey was the original of "Zenobia" in . . . *Endymion* (S.M. Ellis, 1911, *William Harrison Ainsworth and His Friends*, p. 159 n. 3).

JERSEY CITY, New Jersey

PACKER CITY in Francis T. Shield, *McDonough* (1951)

'Boss Coyle and his son of Packer City, suggest . . . Frank Hague and his nephew . . . of Jersey City' (Joseph Blotner, 1966, *The Modern American Political Novel*, Austin, Tex., p. 80 n. 45).

JESSOP, Augustus (1823–1914) Educated abroad and at Cambridge, he was Headmaster of the Grammar School in Helston, Cornwall, for four years, and was Headmaster of King Edward VI School, Norwich, from 1859 to 1879. After his retirement, he became Rector of Scarning, Norfolk, remaining as such until 1911. He published a great deal, including a biography of Donne and a volume of sermons. In 1861 he wrote to Meredith, apropos a poem that had appeared in a periodical. The two men became friends, and the following year Meredith sent his son Arthur to Jessop's school as a boarder. Jessop had done much to modernize the school but had retained a good deal more religious observance than Meredith could approve. Their religious differences prevented the development of a close intimacy between the two men, but they corresponded until the end of Meredith's life.

REVD MR BARMBY in George Meredith, *One of Our Conquerors* (1891)

'G.M. borrowed Jessop's voice for the Rev. Mr Barmby' (*Letters of George Meredith*, 1970, ed. C.L. Cline, Vol. I, Oxford, p. 213 n. 10). 'In Thun you will see Jessop. . . . But, if you hear him you can't mistake him. Think of a cock-chafer informing the world that his wife has run away from him: – so deep, so desolate, the voice of Jessop . . . the incarnation of three minor canons, primed . . . on port:

– a cathedral voice' (to William Hardman, 10 July 1863, reproduced in *Letters*, op. cit., p. 213). The Hardmans were about to start on a journey to Switzerland.

JESSUP, Elsie American Red Cross nurse; she was in Italy in 1918.

Catherine Barkley in Ernest Hemingway, *A Farewell to Arms* (1929)

'For a while I was sent to Florence to help with the care of a Red Cross worker who had typhoid in an Italian hospital, and there was an American Red Cross nurse on duty in Florence, who was also on this case. Her name was Elsie Jessup, and I believe she was the pattern for some of Hemingway's characterization of Catherine Barkley, as she always carried a cane when in uniform, and had been engaged to an English officer who was killed. . . . When I returned to Milan she went there with me' (Mrs William Stanfield [formerly Miss Von Kurowsky] to C.E. Buckingham, 6 May 1962, reproduced in M.S. Reynolds, 1976, *Hemingway's First War: the making of* A Farewell to Arms, Princeton, NJ: Princeton University Press, p. 175 n. 43). *See also* **Hemingway**, Hadley; **Hemingway**, Pauline; **Von Kurowsky**, Agnes.

JEVONS, William Stanley (1835–82) Economist. Son of Mrs Mary Anne Roscoe, a minor poet whose father, William Roscoe, was the author of *The Butterfly's Ball*. His university studies, which began with chemistry and mathematics and ended with political economy and logic, were interrupted by four years in Australia as Assayer to the Sydney Mint. From 1866 to 1879 he was Professor of Logic, Political Economy and Philosophy at Owens College, Manchester, and from 1876 to 1881 he was Professor of Political Economy at University College London.

The Uncle in Mrs Molesworth, *A Christmas Child* (1880)

'The Uncle in the story who is an expert at "statistics" was William Stanley Jevons' (R. Lancelyn Green, 1961, *Mrs Molesworth*, p. 43).

JOACHIM, Joseph (1831–1907) Hungarian violinist and composer. He was Concert Conductor and Violinist to the King at Hanover from 1854 to 1866, and was Director of Music at the Hochschule in Berlin. In 1868 he was the founder and Director of the Joachim Quartet, which performed Bach, Beethoven and Mozart.

Charles Auchester in Elizabeth Sara Sheppard, *Charles Auchester* (1853)

Identified in Michael Sadleir, 1951, *XIX Century Fiction*, Vol. I, London: Constable, and Los Angeles: California University Press, p. 320. *See also* **Horsley**, Charles.

JOACHIM, Martha (1798?–1850) 'An inquest was held on the 29th [January 1850], on Martha Joachim, a *Wealthy and Eccentric Lady*, late of 27, York-buildings, Marylebone. . . . It was shown in evidence that . . . [in] 1808, her father, an officer in the Life Guards, was murdered and robbed in Regent's Park. A reward of 300L. was offered for the murderer, who was apprehended with the property upon him, and executed. In 1825, a suitor . . . whom her mother rejected, shot himself while sitting on the sofa with her, and she was covered with his brains. From that instant she lost her reason. Since her mother's death, eighteen years ago, she had led the life of a recluse, dressed in white, and never going out' (*Household Narrative of Current Events* (suppl. to *Household Words*, January 1850)).

MISS HAVISHAM in Charles Dickens, *Great Expectations* (1860–1)

'Reading about this eccentric white woman, Dickens must have recalled his own boyhood White woman. . . . Miss Havisham, like Martha Joachim . . . is wealthy, is associated with crime and murder, undergoes an instantaneous breakdown caused by her suitor, becomes a recluse . . . and lives in a house with a walled garden' (Harry Stone, 1969, 'The Genesis of a Novel: *Great Expectations*', in E.W.F. Tomlin (ed.), *Charles Dickens, 1812–1870*, pp. 117, 118). *See also* **Dick**, Margaret Catherine; **White Woman of Berners Street**.

JOHN, Augustus Edwin (1878–1961) Welsh painter. He was born in Tenby, Wales, and studied at the Slade School of Fine Art, London, with his sister Gwen, and in Paris. He was an official war artist during the First World War and also painted many portraits of literary figures such as Thomas **Hardy**.

JOHN BIDLAKE in Aldous Huxley, *Point Counter Point* (1928)

'The sensualist painter John Bidlake . . . is probably modelled on . . . Augustus John' (Jerome Meckier, 1969, *Aldous Huxley*, p. 121).

CALTHROP in Gilbert Cannan, *Mendel* (1916)

'Portraits of Edward Marsh, Brett, Carrington, Augustus John and C.R.W. Nevinson are also to be found in the book' (Diana Farr, 1978, *Gilbert Cannan: a Georgian prodigy*, London: Chatto & Windus, p. 164).

GULLEY JIMSON in Joyce Carey, *The Horse's Mouth* (1944)

'Gulley Jimson . . . may also contain some aspects of John' (Michael Holroyd, 1975, *Augustus John*, Vol. II, pp. 225–6 n. 503). *See also* **Spencer**, Stanley; **Thomas**, Dylan.

TENBY JONES in Henry Williamson, *The Golden Virgin* (1957) and *The Innocent Moon* (1961)

'John is said to be the prototype of characters in several novels . . . Tenby Jones . . . in . . .*The Golden Virgin* and *The Innocent Moon*' (Holroyd, op. cit., pp. 225–6 n. 503).

JOHN LAFCADIO in Margery Allingham, *Death of a Ghost* (1934)

'John is said to be the prototype of . . . the artist in . . . Death of a Ghost' (Holroyd, op. cit., pp. 225–6 n. 503).

OWEN in Aleister Crowley, *The Diary of a Drug Fiend* (1922)

'John is said to be the prototype of . . . the sculptor Owen in . . . *The Diary of a Drug Fiend* (Crowley noted this in his own copy of the novel)' (Holroyd, op. cit., pp. 225–6 n. 503).

ALBERT SANGER in Margaret Kennedy, *The Constant Nymph* (1924)

'John is said to be the prototype of . . . Albert Sanger' (Holroyd, op. cit., pp. 225–6 n. 503).

CHARLES STRICKLAND in W. Somerset Maugham, *The Moon and Sixpence* (1919)

'Of ... *The Moon and Sixpence* John Quinn wrote (9 September 1919): "The description of the artist ... up to the time he leaves France, is obviously based upon a superficial study of Augustus John"' (Holroyd, op. cit., p. 226). *See also* **Gauguin**, Paul.

STRUTHERS in D.H. Lawrence, *Aaron's Rod* (1922)

'Augustus John is the artist Struthers who showed poor manners by talking through an opera performance – Cynthia Asquith recalled that performance, and stopping with Lawrence, on the way, at John's studio ...' (H.T. Moore, 1960, *The Intelligent Heart: the story of D.H. Lawrence*, Harmondsworth: Penguin, p. 300; originally published 1955, London: Heinemann).

JOHN OF CRONSTADT, Father (1821–1908) Born Ioann Sergiev in the district of Archangel, he became an Orthodox Russian priest and ministered to the sick and poor of Cronstadt, allegedly performing miracles.

BAZHAKULOFF in Norman Douglas, *South Wind* (1917)

'Father John of Cronstadt and Rasputin have subscribed their share of elements to the formation of the Russian "Messiah"' (Norman Douglas, 1942, Introd. to *South Wind*, London, p. unnumbered). *See also* **Rasputin**, Grigori Efimovitch.

JOHNES, Thomas (1748–1816) Of **Hafod House**, Cardiganshire. He was the son of Thomas and Elizabeth Johnes of Hafod House and Croft Castle, Herefordshire, and could trace his lineage back without a break to the first prince of the ancient Britons (*fl.* 500 BC). Educated at Eton and at Edinburgh University, he was a contemporary and friend of Sir Uvedale **Price**. In 1783, after his marriage, he went to live at Hafod, which he rebuilt, employing Thomas Baldwin and John **Nash**; the work was completed in 1788, and he was largely influenced by Richard Payne Knight (his cousin) and Sir Uvedale Price in redesigning the landscape. He translated the *Chronicles of Froissart* (1803–5) and the *Memoirs of de Joinville* (1807), and he set up a private press in a neighbouring cottage, from which he issued his works. He was an MP from 1774 to 1816, and became a Fellow of the Royal Society in 1809. For an account of his life, and the building (and rebuilding after a fire in 1807) of Hafod, see Elizabeth Inglis-Jones, 1950, *Peacocks in Paradise*.

HARRY HEADLONG in Thomas Love Peacock, *Headlong Hall* (1816)

'It appears probable that the description of Headlong Hall and of its owner was inspired by Hafod House and grounds, which belonged to Colonel Johnes' (*The Novels of T.L. Peacock*, 1948, ed. David Garnett, London: Rupert Hart-Davis, p. 22 n. 1). *See also* **Madocks**, W.A.

JOHNSON, Elizabeth (d. 1833) Daughter of Isaac Pearson, of Old Castle Farm in Astley, Warwickshire, she married Richard Johnson of Marston Jabbett. She was the sister of Christiana **Evans**, and thus the maternal aunt of George Eliot.

SOPHY PULLETT (NÉE DODSON) in George Eliot, *The Mill on the Floss* (1860)

'Of Aunt Pullet there are fewer traces in George Eliot's biography. . . . The few references [to Mr and Mrs Johnson] concern prolonged illnesses, which perhaps explain the medicine bottles Mr Pullet preserved so carefully' (Gordon S. Haight, 1958, 'George Eliot's originals', in R. Rathburn and M. Steinmann, Jun. (eds) *From Jane Austen to Joseph Conrad: essays collected in memory of James T. Hillhouse*, 1958, Minneapolis, Minn.: University of Minnesota Press, p. 189).

JOHNSON, Hugh S. (1882–1942) American lawyer and army officer. In 1917 he originated the plans for selective draft and supervised its administration. He was Administrator for the National Recovery Administration in 1933 and 1934 and for the Works Progress Administration in New York City in 1935. From 1935 onwards he was a lecturer and journalist.

DEWEY BRONSON in Dalton Trumbo, *Washington Jitters* (1936)

'Trumbo made wholesale borrowings from life. . . . General Dewey Bronson seems to bear some relationship to General Hugh S. Johnson' (Joseph Blotner, 1966, *The Modern American Political Novel*, Austin, Tex., p. 132).

JOHNSON, Lionel Pigot (1867–1902) English poet and critic. He was born in Broadstairs in Kent and educated at Winchester and New College, Oxford. He converted to Catholicism while living in London. He was a friend of Yeats and of Oscar **Wilde** and was greatly influenced by the 'Celtic Twilight'. A heavy drinker, he died as a result of a drunken fall (mentioned in Ezra Pound's 'Hugh Selwyn Mauberley' (1920)).

REVD WILLIAM HOWARD in W.B. Yeats, *John Sherman* (1891)

'Howard . . . closely resembles Lionel Johnson, whom Yeats probably met at the "Fitzroy Settlement" as early as 1888. The small neat figure, neat handwriting, Howard's library: Bourget jostling agreeably with Newman and Chrysostom, are all suggestive' (Ian Fletcher, 1971, 'Review: "William Butler Yeats: John Sherman and Dhoya"', *Notes and Queries* 216: 276).

JOHNSON, Willard (1897–1968) American journalist. He met the Lawrence's in New Mexico in 1922 and travelled with them and Witter **Bynner** in Mexico in 1923. He was the founder and Editor, from 1922 to 1939, of *The Laughing Horse*.

BUD VILLIERS in D.H. Lawrence, *The Plumed Serpent* (1926)

'[W]hen *The Plumed Serpent* was issued . . . [it] at once became evident that . . . Bud Villiers was Johnson' (Witter Bynner, 1953, *Journey with Genius*, London and New York: Peter Nevill, p. 57).

JOHNSTON, Sir Harry (1858–1927) Explorer and administrator. In 1883 he penetrated the Congo basin, where he met and won the friendship of H.M. **Stanley,** and in 1885 he joined the Consular Service and served in Africa. He was British Commissioner for South Central Africa from 1891 to 1896, and was Special Commissioner in Uganda in 1899. He had remarkable linguistic, scientific and artistic gifts, frequently exhibiting at the Royal Academy.

OSWALD SYDENHAM in H.G. Wells, *Joan and Peter* (1918)

'Oswald Sydenham, an African explorer partly derived from . . . Sir Harry Johnston' (Lionel Stevenson, 1967, *History of the English Novel*, Vol. XI, New York, p. 52).

JONES, Bulkeley Owen (b. 1824) Educated at Rugby and at Brasenose College, Oxford, he became Warden of Ruthin in 1851 and was Chancellor of St Asaph in 1897.

'SLOGGER' WILLIAMS in Thomas Hughes, *Tom Brown's Schooldays* (1857)

'The "Slogger" had his original in Buckley [sic] O. Jones' (Edward C. Mack and W.H.G. Armytage, 1952, *Thomas Hughes: the life of the author of Tom Brown's Schooldays*, London: Ernest Benn, p. 94).

JONES, Ethelwyn Sylvia (1883–1948) Daughter of Henry Arthur Jones, the playwright, she was a professional actress from the age of 14 and in 1902 married Vivian Leveaux, a theatrical manager. In 1913 she married Angus McDonell, the second son of the 6th Earl of Antrim.

ROSE DRIFFIELD in W. Somerset Maugham, *Cakes and Ale* (1930)

'The character of Rose is modelled as closely. . . . The original . . . was Ethelwyn Sylvia Jones' (R.L. Calder, 1972, *W. Somerset Maugham and the Quest for Freedom*, London: Heinemann, p. 192).

JONES, George Alfred He was a cousin of Edith Wharton's father, G.F. **Jones**, and became the centre of a family scandal: he was married to a 'bilious brunette' called Harriet (née Coster) and embezzled a great deal of money in order to support his more agreeable mistress in proper style. Having been compelled to repay the entire sum, he retired to the country with his unhappy wife, with whom he set up a small business making dolls.

JULIUS BEAUFORT in Edith Wharton, *The Age of Innocence* (1920)

'No doubt Beaufort also incarnated a portion of her reprehensible cousin George Arthur Jones, who had, like Beaufort, embezzled money to support his mistress' (R.W.B. Lewis, 1975, *Edith Wharton: a biography*, London: Constable, p. 431). *See also* **Belmont**, August.

JONES, George Frederic (1821–82) He married Lucretia Rhinelander (**Jones**, below) and was the father of Edith Wharton.

LEWIS RAYCIE in Edith Wharton, 'False Dawn', *Old New York* (1924)

'George Frederic in love proved himself both persistent and resourceful. He took to stealing down at dawn to a cove where he kept a large rowboat. He improvised a mast – all this can be found in *False Dawn* . . . [and] attached the quilt from his bed as a sail' (R.W.B. Lewis, 1975, *Edith Wharton: a biography*, London: Constable, p. 12). Lewis Raycie did not resemble George Jones physically, but there seem to be points of resemblance in his character. *See also* **Norton**, Charles Eliot.

JONES, James Rhys ('Kilsby') (1813–89) Born near Llandoveny, Carmarthenshire, he was an independent minister in Kilsby, Northamptonshire, from

1840 to 1850, and from 1857 to 1889 he preached in Wales, there being the most popular preacher of the day.

REVD SLINGSBY EDWARDS in M.E. Braddon, *Hostages to Fortune* (1875)

'In ... *Hostages to Fortune* ... he is described under name of Rev. Slingsby Edwards' (Frederic Boase, 1892, *Modern English Biography*, Vol. II, col. 130).

JONES, Revd John Edmund (1797–1831) As Perpetual Curate of the Chapel of Ease at Stockingford, Nuneaton, in 1828, he was an evangelical preacher whose sermons and addresses roused vociferous opposition from conservative churchmen. Maria Lewis, Principal Governess at the school in Nuneaton attended by George Eliot, was one of his ardent disciples.

REVD EDGAR TRYAN in George Eliot, 'Janet's Repentance', *Scenes of Clerical Life* (1857–8)

'Mr Tryan, [the] hero, is an idealized portrait of Mr Jones, the Evangelical curate at Nuneaton' (Gordon S. Haight, 1968, *George Eliot*, Oxford, p. 227). *See also under* **Anstruther**, Lady.

JONES, John William (1869–1950) He was Superintendent School Attendance Officer in Croydon from 1907 to 1936, and was married to Marie (**Jones**). Lawrence lodged with the couple at Colworth Road, Addiscombe, from October 1908 to January 1912.

MR THOMAS in D.H. Lawrence, 'The old Adam' (1934)

'"The old Adam" is a sketch of the Jones family whom Lawrence lodged with durint his Croydon schoolmastership' (H.T. Moore, 1951, *Life and Works of D.H. Lawrence*, p. 122).

JONES, Lucretia (1825?–1901) Daughter of Frederick and Mary Rhinelander; her father died when she was 12 years old. In 1844 she married George Frederic **Jones**; Edith Wharton was their daughter.

AUGUSTA WELLAND in Edith Wharton, *The Age of Innocence* (1920)

'In middle age she was obviously the model for Mrs Welland' (R.W.B. Lewis, 1975, *Edith Wharton: a biography*, London: Constable, p. 24).

JONES, Marie (1869–1950) Wife of John William **Jones**.

MRS THOMAS in D.H. Lawrence, 'The Old Adam' (1934)

See under **Jones**, John William.

JONES, Mary Mason She was married to Isaac Jones and was Edith Wharton's aunt. She built the first great house on Upper Fifth Avenue.

CATHERINE MANSON MINGOTT in Edith Wharton, *The Age of Innocence* (1920)

'Aunt Mary Mason, after living for some years in downtown Waverley Place, startled society by moving almost beyond visibility to . . . Fifth Avenue between Fifty-seventh and Fifty-eighth streets. . . . Here, with advancing years and increasing obesity she lived in a suite off the entry hall. . . . Edith Wharton would have her preside over a good part of *The Age of Innocence* in the guise of ... Mrs Manson Mingott' (R.W.B. Lewis, 1975, *Edith Wharton: a biography*, London: Constable, p. 13).

JONES, William (1786?–1836) Headmaster of Wellington House Academy, the school in Mornington Crescent, London, that Dickens attended between 1824 and 1826.

MR CREAKLE in Charles Dickens, *David Copperfield* (1849–50)

'William Jones, a Welshman and the original of Creakle, seems actually to have possessed the picturesque qualities of a story-book wicked schoolmaster. . . . We have more than Dickens's word for this' (Philip Collins, 1963, *Dickens and Education*, London: Macmillan, p. 11). *See also* **Rotch**, Benjamin.

JOSANNE, Edouard *See* **Jozan**.

JOWETT, Benjamin (1817–93) He was Regius Professor of Greek at Oxford from 1855 to 1893, but he was deprived of the emoluments of the office for ten years after incurring the suspicion of heresy because of his religious views. In 1860 he contributed to *Essays and Reviews* (ed. Bishop Gore); his association with this Liberal exposition of Christian doctrine increased the suspicion of heresy entertained against him. He was deeply opposed to the High Church party in Oxford, represented by **Liddon** and **Pusey**. From 1870 to 1893 he was Master of Balliol College, Oxford, and from 1882 to 1886 he was Vice-Chancellor of Oxford University. He translated Plato, Aristotle and Thucydides.

DR JENKINSON in W.H. Mallock, *The New Republic* (1877)

'Dr Jenkinson was Jowett' (Mallock, 1920, *Memoirs of Life and Literature*, London: Chapman and Hall, p. 66). '[I]n Dr Jenkinson's sermon Mallock scarcely does more than paraphrase – and occasionally even repeat – the words of Jowett's own sermons' (John Lucas, 1975, Introd. to *The New Republic*, Leicester, p. 23).

THE PROVOST in Mrs Humphry Ward, *Robert Elsmere* (1888)

'People say that in *Robert Elsmere* . . . the Provost [is intended] for me' (Jowett to Margot Tennant, 28 November 1888, quoted in *The Autobiography of Margot Asquith*, 1920, pp. 120–1).

JOYCE, James Augustine Aloysius (1882–1941) Irish writer. Born in Dublin, one of sixteen or seventeen children, he was educated at Clongowes Wood College, Kildare, and Belvedere College, Dublin. He taught English in Dalkey until 1914, when he went to Switzerland with his lifelong companion Nora Barnacle (**Joyce**, below). They lived in Zurich throughout the First World War, apart from a spell in Trieste, where he taught at the Berlitz School. They moved to Paris in 1920 with their two children, and *Ulysses* was published there in 1922. Joyce suffered from a lifelong eye complaint, complicated by glaucoma in 1917. He married Nora in 1931, and after his daughter Lucia was diagnosed a schizophrenic in 1932 his general health began to deteriorate. After the outbreak of the Second World War the family returned to Switzerland, where Joyce died after an operation on a duodenal ulcer.

LEOPOLD BLOOM in James Joyce, *Ulysses* (1922)

'A great deal of [Joyce's] own experience became Bloom's. . . . Not all [the] details were unique, but their accumulation is important' (Richard Ellmann, 1982, *James Joyce*, rev. edn, Oxford: Oxford University Press, pp. 373–4). *See also* **Bloom**, Joseph; **Chance**, Charles; **Hunter**, Alfred H.; **Jackson**, Holbrook; **Joyce**, John Stanislaus; **Mayer**, Teodoro; **Popper**, Leopoldo; **Schmitz**, Ettore.

PULLMAN ('PULLEY') in Wyndham Lewis, *The Childermass* (1928)

'I had not yet realised that Pullman had originally been drawn by Lewis as a caricature of James Joyce' (D.G. Bridson, 1969–70, 'The making of *The Human Age*', *Agenda* 7 (3)-8 (1): 164). Bridson is describing the making of the radio production of *The Childermass*, first broadcast 18 June 1951. The work formed part I of the novel and radio drama known as *The Human Age*.

JAMES JULIUS RATNER in Wyndham Lewis, *The Apes of God* (1930)

'The most violently ridiculed figure . . . is James-Julius Ratner, a self-promoting author who is a palpable caricature of James Joyce' (Lionel Stevenson, 1967, *History of the English Novel*, Vol. XI, New York, p. 177).

SHEM in James Joyce, *Finnegans Wake* (1939)

'Of course, Joyce had for models [for Shem and Shaun] also himself [James] and his brother John Stanislaus Joyce Jr.' (Ellmann, op. cit., p. 550).

JOYCE, John Stanislaus (1849–1931) Father of James Joyce. 'This reckless, talented man . . . became identified in his son James's mind with something like the life force itself. . . . He appeared in [Joyce's books] more centrally . . . than anyone except their author' (Richard Ellmann, 1966, *James Joyce*, London: Oxford Paperbacks, p. 20).

LEOPOLD BLOOM in James Joyce, *Ulysses* (1922)

'In *Ulysses* he . . . enters into Bloom and the narrator of the *Cyclops* episode' (Ellmann, op. cit., p. 21). *See also* **Bloom**, Joseph; **Byrne**, John Francis; **Chance**, Charles; **Hunter**, Alfred H.; **Jackson**, Holbrook; **Joyce**, James; **Mayer**, Teodoro; **Popper**, Leopold; **Schmitz**, Ettore.

GABRIEL CONROY in James Joyce, 'The Dead', *Dubliners* (1914)

'In the later stories [in *Dubliners*], besides contributing to Farington ['Counterparts'], he is also in Henchy [and] Hynes ['Ivy Day in the Committee Room'], Kernan, ['Grace'], and Gabriel Conroy' (Ellmann, op. cit., p. 20). *See also* **Curran**, Constantine.

SIMON DEDALUS in James Joyce, *A Portrait of the Artist as a Young Man* (1916)

'In *A Portrait of the Artist* he is Simon Dedalus' (Ellmann, op. cit., p. 20).

HUMPHREY CHIMPDEN EARWICKER in James Joyce, *Finnegans Wake* (1939)

'In *Finnegans Wake*, John Joyce is the chief model for Earwicker' (Ellmann, op. cit., p. 21).

JOYCE, Nora (1884–1951) Née Barnacle. She married James Joyce in 1931; their first walk together was on the evening of 16 June 1904, the date of the action of *Ulysses*.

MARION ('MOLLY') BLOOM in James Joyce, *Ulysses* (1922)

'[Joyce] had a model at home for Molly's mind. Nora Joyce had a similar gift for concentrated, pungent expression, and Joyce delighted in it as much as Bloom did' (Richard Ellmann, 1959, *James Joyce*, p. 387). *See also* **Chance**, Mrs Charles; **Dillon**, Mamie; **Popper**, Amalia; **Santos**, Signora.

ANNA LIVIA PLURABELLE in James Joyce, *Finnegans Wake* (1939)

'Molly Bloom, once . . . Nora Joyce, became the river Liffey' (Ellmann, op. cit., p. 562). 'The character of Anna Livia was like that of Molly Bloom, but put more emphasis on ultimate attachment. . . . The words which Joyce had earlier applied to woman, "untrustworthy" and "indifferent" were scarcely adequate to convey the total female temperament as he had observed it in Nora during thirty four years' (Ellmann, op. cit., p. 725).

JOYCE, Stanislaus (1884–1955) Second son of John **Joyce**, and younger brother of James Joyce.

MAURICE DAEDALUS in James Joyce, *Stephen Hero* (1944)

'At first [Joyce] allowed Stephen to have one loyal adherent, his brother Maurice, modelled on Stanislaus' (Richard Ellmann, 1966, *James Joyce*, London: Oxford Paperbacks, p. 154). 'I suggested many of the names for the characters on an onomatopoeic principle. . . . I parodied some of the names . . . myself, Morose Maurice . . .' (entry for 29 March 1904, in *The Dublin Diary of Stanislaus Joyce*, 1962, ed. George H. Healey, p. 25 n. 3, MS n. added to the MS of the diary).

JAMES DUFFY in James Joyce, 'A Painful Case', *Dubliners* (1914)

'Like Stanislaus Joyce, Mr Duffy kept a diary, "a little sheaf of papers held together with a brass pin". Stanislaus's diary, also held together with a brass pin, is now in the Cornell University Library' (G.H. Healey (ed.), 1962, preface to *The Dublin Diary of Stanislaus Joyce*, p. 7). 'In Drumcondia [in 1894] . . . Stanislaus had a fight with one of the local boys, "Pisser" Duffy, and was amused when his . . . brother gave the name of Duffy to the hero of "A Painful Case" who in most respects was modelled on Stanislaus' (Ellmann, op. cit., p. 39).

SHAUN in James Joyce, *Finnegans Wake* (1939)

'Of course, Joyce had for models also himself and his brother, John Stanislaus Joyce Jr.' (Ellmann, op. cit., p. 562). *See also* **De Valera**, Éamon; **Ford**, John.

JOZAN, Edouard (b. 1899) As a young naval aviator, in July 1924 he met the Fitzgeralds in St Raphael and formed a romantic attachment for Zelda; allegedly Zelda asked for a divorce, but Jozan later maintained that only a flirtation had been involved. In October 1924, he was transferred to Indo-China, and in 1943–5 he was deported to Germany. He was Vice-Admiral in the French

Navy in 1952, Commandant of naval forces in the Far East in 1954, and in 1959 he retired with the rank of Admiral.

TOMMY BARBAN in F. Scott Fitzgerald, *Tender is the Night* (1934)

'Tommy Barban is an amalgam of five people – Edouard Jozan, Mario Braggiotti, Tommy Hitchcock, Percy Pyne and Denny Holden' (Matthew J. Bruccoli, 1981, *Some Sort of Epic Grandeur: the life of F. Scott Fitzgerald*, London: Hodder & Stoughton, pp. 341–2). *See also* **Braggiotti**, Mario; **Hitchcock**, Thomas.

JACQUES CHEVRE-FEUILLE in Zelda Fitzgerald, *Save Me the Waltz* (1932)

'Both Fitzgeralds wrote fictionalized versions of the events' (Bruccoli, op. cit., p. 199). Chevre-Feuille is the name Zelda gave her lover in her version. Fitzgerald appears to have spelt Jozan as 'Josanne' both in his *Ledger* and in correspondence with Zelda's psychiatrist (see Andrew Turnbull, 1962, *Scott Fitzgerald*, p. 302 n. 28.) Arthur Mizener (1951, *The Far Side of Paradise*, pp. 162–3) identifies Chevre-Feuille with René Silvy, but Silvy was the son of a local lawyer, and was not an airman.

JUKES, John (1799?–1866) As Pastor of the Old Meeting (later the Bunyan meeting) at Bedford from 1840 onwards, he was the fifth in succession to Bunyan and was successor to Samuel **Hillyard**. 'His great defect was the utter absence of imagination and humour' ('Act Book of the Church at Bunyan Meeting', 1866, p. 92; see Valentine Cunningham, 1976, *Everywhere Spoken Against: dissent in the Victorian novel*, Oxford: Clarendon Press, p. 272 n. 1).

JOHN BROAD in Mark Rutherford, *The Revolution in Tanner's Lane* (1887)

'. . . based on John Jukes' (ibid., p. 265). '[L]ike Jukes, Broad is a big man . . . has a son who goes into the Congregational ministry, and trains young men as missionaries' (ibid., p. 272). Like Broad, Jukes suffered a paralytic stroke, from which he never fully recovered, some years before his death.

JULIAN'S HILL, Middlesex A farmhouse, located near Harrow, to which the Trollope family moved in 1827 from the neighbouring Julians; the move was necessary because of Thomas Trollope's growing financial embarrassment, and in 1830 they moved to a humbler house at Harrow Weald.

ORLEY FARM in Anthony Trollope, *Orley Farm* (1861–2)

'Confessedly the model for "Orley Farm"' (Michael Sadleir, 1945, *Trollope: a commentary*, 2nd rev. edn, London: Constable, p. 65; originally published 1927, London: Constable).

K

KAHN, Otto Herman (1867–1934) Banker and patron of the arts. Born in Germany, he began working with the Deutsche Bank in Berlin in 1888 and later transferred to London and was naturalized as a British citizen. In 1893 he was transferred to New York, and in 1917 took American citizenship. He financed the Metropolitan Opera Company and in 1908 he brought Toscanini to New York; he is described in the *Dictionary of American Biography* (London: Oxford University Press) as 'undoubtedly the greatest patron of the arts that America had yet known'. In 1927–8 he financed the **New Playwrights** in New York.

ADOLPH HERMAN BAUM in John Dos Passos, *Most Likely to Succeed* (1954)

'A . . . fictional characterization of him as Adolph Baum is to be found in . . . *Most Likely to Succeed*' (G.A. Knox and H.M. Stahl, 1964, *Dos Passos and 'The Revolting Playwrights*, Lund, p. 61).

KANE, Matthew (d. 1904) Chief Clerk of the Crown Solicitor's Office, Dublin. He drowned when he was less than 40. His close friend, John Stanislaus **Joyce**, was present at his funeral, along with James Joyce and many others upon whom characters in *Ulysses* were based.

MARTIN CUNNINGHAM in James Joyce, 'Grace', *Dubliners* (1914) and *Ulysses* (1922)

'Matthew Kane was the original of Martin Cunningham. . . . He had a long beard and was fond of oraculating, usually on the basis of misinformation' (Richard Ellmann, 1959, *James Joyce*, p. 138 n.).

KATANGA EXPEDITION Led by Alexandre **Delcommune** in 1890–2, its objective was to explore the river Lomani, a tributary of the Congo.

ELDORADO EXPLORING EXPEDITION in Joseph Conrad, *Heart of Darkness* (1902)

'[In "Heart of Darkness"], Conrad alludes to the arrival at Kinchasa of an expedition, which he describes in the most ironical terms and which he gives the still more ironical name of the Eldorado Exploring Expedition. . . . This expedition is not an invention. . . . It was the Katanga expedition and was under the command of Alexandre Delcommune' (G.Jean-Aubry, 1927, *Joseph Conrad: life and letters*, Vol. I, London: Heinemann, p. 138).

KATHA, Upper Burma A small town north of Mandalay to which George Orwell was posted in 1926 as Headquarters Superintendent in the Indian Imperial Police; it was his last posting.

KYAUKTADA in George Orwell, *Burmese Days* (1934)

'The place . . . made an unforgettable impression upon him; some years later he would reproduce it vividly as Kyauktada, the setting for *Burmese Days*' (Peter Stansky and William Abrahams, 1972, *The Unknown Orwell*, p. 169).

KAUWĀDOL, Bihar, India Situated in the Barābar Hills.

KAWA DOL in E.M. Forster, *A Passage to India* (1924)

'The Kawa Dol exists as the Kauwādol, about two miles south of the [Barābar] range of hills, and in the site of an ancient Silabhadra monastery' (Wilfred Stones, 1966, *The Cave and the Mountain*, London: Oxford University Press, p. 300 n.; see also Pl. 30 for an illustration).

KAY-SHUTTLEWORTH, Ughtred James (1844–1939) Son of Sir James Kay-Shuttleworth, he became the 1st Baron Shuttleworth when he was raised to the Peerage in 1902. He was MP for Hastings from 1869 to 1880 and for Clitheroe from 1885 to 1902, and Under-Secretary of State for India in 1886 and Parliamentary Secretary to the Admiralty from 1892 to 1895.

SIR WILLOUGHBY PATTERNE in George Meredith, *The Egoist* (1879)

The identification was generally accepted at the time, and is based here upon private information.

KEEPER The Brontës' house-dog, acquired in 1838. In fact he was controlled only by Emily Brontë and at her funeral he walked with Mr Brontë at the head of the small procession, entering the family pewbox and remaining with him throughout the service.

TARTAR in Charlotte Brontë, *Shirley* (1849)

'Ellen Nussey described Emily as habitually kneeling on the hearth, reading a book, with her arm around Keeper; both recollections are confirmed by Charlotte's picture of Shirley' (Winifred Gérin, 1971, *Emily Brontë*, Oxford, p. 156).

KEITH, Anne Murray (1736–1818) Daughter of Robert Keith, Ambassador at Vienna and St Petersburg, and sister of Sir Robert Keith, a distinguished soldier and diplomat who was also Ambassador at Vienna (1772–9). In the latter part of her life she shared a flat in St Georges Square with her cousin Lady Balcarres, widow of the 5th Earl and mother of Lady Anne Barnard. She was a mine of information about the past and Scott, whose parents were her neighbours, was devoted to her until her death.

MARTHA BETHUNE BALIOL in Sir Walter Scott, 'The Highland Widow', *Chronicles of the Canongate* (1827) (1st series)

'[T]he lady termed ... Mrs Bethune Baliol was designed to shadow out ... the interesting character of a dear friend of mine, Mrs Murray Keith' (preface to *Chronicles of the Canongate*, 1831 (Border edn), ed. Andrew Lang, Vol. XXIV, p. 330).

MRS SYDNEY HUME in Anon., *Probation and Other Tales* (1832)

'There is a novel called "Probation", now long forgotten written by [Mrs Murray Keith's] little ward after she was grown to be a woman. The dignified old lady with the white hair, of cordial approach and benevolent aspect ... is Anne Keith as she appeared to the affectionate veneration of a younger generation' (Florence McCunn, 1909, *Sir Walter Scott's Friends*, pp. 28–9).

KELLY, Sir Fitzroy (1796–1880) Barrister. He was at Lincoln's Inn, London, in 1824, being standing Counsel to the Bank of England and the East India Company, and appeared in a number of *causes célèbres*, including the Graham case. He was Tory MP for Ipswich from 1837 to 1841, Cambridge from 1843 to 1847, and East Suffolk from 1852 to 1866. In 1845–6 and 1852 he was Solicitor-General, in 1858–9 he was Attorney-General, and from 1866 to 1880 he was Lord Chief Baron; he was knighted in 1845.

BAR in Charles Dickens, *Little Dorrit* (1855–7)

'I shall beg, when you have read the present number, to enquire whether you consider "Bar" an instance, in reference to KF, of a suggested likeness in not many touches?' (Dickens to Forster, quoted in John Forster, *Life of Charles Dickens*, 1929, ed. J.W.T. Ley, p. 625). Forster continues: 'The likeness no one could mistake ... "the insinuating Jury-droop, and persuasive double eye glass"'. It was Forster's practice to alter initials in cases of this sort. '"Bar" was taken from Fitzroy Kelly ... and was acknowledged to be a singularly good likeness' (Charles Dickens, the Younger, 1899, Introd. to *Little Dorrit*, p. xxxvi).

HORATIO FIZKIN in Charles Dickens, *The Pickwick Papers* (1836–7)

'The opposing candidate was Mr Kelly, afterwards Sir Fitzroy Kelly, who in [the] story, bears the name of Fizkin' (Percy Fitzgerald, 1895, *Bozland: Dickens's places and people*, p. 15).

KELLY, Sir Gerald Festus (1879–1972) Portrait painter. Educated at Eton and at Cambridge, he studied painting in Paris in 1901 where he met Degas, Renoir, Monet and Cézanne. He was President of the Royal Academy from 1949 to 1954. He was a close friend of W. Somerset Maugham.

GRIFFITHS in W. Somerset Maugham, *Of Human Bondage* (1915)

'Gerald Kelly served partly as the model for Griffiths' (Richard A. Cordell, 1969, *Somerset Maugham: a writer for all seasons*, Bloomington and London: Indiana University Press, p. 94).

LIONEL HILLIER in W. Somerset Maugham, *Cakes and Ale* (1930)

'Kelly also admired "She" [the actress Ethelwyn Sylvia Jones], and painted her portrait, which Maugham described in the book as the work of "Lionel Hillier"' (Derek Hudson, 1975, *For Love of Painting: the life of Sir Gerald Kelly, K.C.V.O., P.R.A.*, p. 30).

FREDERICK LAWSON in W. Somerset Maugham, *Of Human Bondage* (1915)

'In [*Of Human Bondage*] Kelly [appears as] "Lawson"' (R.L. Calder, 1972, *W. Somerset Maugham and the Quest for Freedom*, London: Heinemann, p. 131).

O'MALLEY in W. Somerset Maugham, 'His Excellency', *Ashenden; or The British Agent* (1928)

'In ... "His Excellency", Maugham provided the most unequivocal of his many fictional portrayals of Kelly, whom he presented as "the young Irish painter called O'Malley"' (Hudson, op. cit., p. 39). *Ashenden* is dedicated to Kelly.

KELLY, John Of Tralee. A member of the Land League, he was imprisoned several times. He was a friend of John Stanislaus Joyce and in 1887 was a visitor at his house at 1 Martello Terrace, Bray.

JOHN CASEY in James Joyce, *A Portrait of the Artist as a Young Man* (1916)

'Another visitor [at Bray] . . . was John Kelly of Tralee, who appears in *A Portrait of the Artist* under the name of John Casey' (Richard Ellmann, 1966, *James Joyce*, London: Oxford Paperbacks, pp. 23, 24).

KELMSCOT MANOR, Oxfordshire The home of the poet William Morris (1834–96) from 1876 until his death.

HURSTCOTE MANOR in Theodore Watts-Dunton, *Aylwin* (1899)

Identified in T. St E. Hake, 1902, 'Aylwin', *Notes and Queries* (9th series) 9 (7 June): 450–2, and 10 (2 August): 89–91; reprinted in *Aylwin*, 1914 (World's Classics), Oxford, App. II.

KEMBLE, Frances Anne ('Fanny') (1809–93) Daughter of the actor Charles Kemble and niece of the actress Sarah Siddons, she first appeared on stage as Juliet at Covent Garden, London, in 1829. In 1834, when on tour in the United States with her father, she married Pierce Butler, the owner of a Georgian plantation. She resumed her maiden name after their divorce in 1849 and retired to Lenox, Massachusetts, near Pitsfield, where Herman Melville had his home from 1850 to 1863. She remained in Lenox until 1868 and in 1877 she returned to England. During the latter part of her life she supported herself through her writings.

GONERIL in Herman Melville, *The Confidence Man* (1857)

'The character Goneril takes on an added significance in being Melville's caricature of a widely known contemporary . . . the Shakespearean actress . . . Fanny Kemble' (Egbert S. Oliver, 1945, 'Melville's Goneril and Fanny Kemble', *New England Quarterly* 18 (December): 490). Melville uses the history of Fanny Kemble's life with Pierce Butler and their divorce as a background to the Goneril episode in chapters 13 and 14 of the novel.

KEMBLE, Henry (1812–57) Brother of Fanny **Kemble**. In 1832 he gazetted *Ensign*, but was transferred almost immediately to the 67th (South Hampshire) Regiment and was out of England for almost nine years; he spent a good deal of his time away in Ireland. It appears that he became engaged to Miss Thackeray *c.*1841, but in 1853 he was confined in Mr Stillwell's private lunatic asylum, Moorcroft House at Hillingdon, Middlesex, where he died, supposedly of 'general paralysis of the insane'.

MORRIS TOWNSEND in Henry James, *Washington Square* (1881)

'February 21st [1879]. Mrs Kemble told me last evening the history of her brother H[enry]'s engagement to Miss T[hackeray]. H.K. was a young ensign . . . very handsome ("beautiful") said Mrs K., but very luxurious and selfish, and without a penny to his name. Miss T. was a dull, plain, common-place girl, only daughter of the Master of King's Coll., Cambridge, who had a handsome private fortune (£4000 a year). She was very much in love with H.K., and was of that slow, sober, dutiful nature that an impression once made upon her, was made for ever. Her father disapproved strongly (and justly) of the engagement and informed her that if she married young K. he would not leave her a penny of his money. It was only in her money that H. was interested. . . . Miss T. . . . asked Mrs K. what she would advise her to do – Henry K. having taken the ground that if she would hold on and marry him the old Doctor would after a while relent and they would get the money. (It was in this belief that he was holding on to her.) Mrs K. advised the young girl by *no means* to marry her brother. . . . Miss T. reflected a while; and then, as she was much in love with [him], she determined to disobey her father and take the consequences. Meanwhile H.K., however, had come to the conclusion that the father's forgiveness was not to be counted upon. . . . *Then* all his effort was to disentangle himself. He went off, shook himself free of the engagement, let the girl go. She was deeply wounded – they separated. Some few years elapsed – her father died and she came into his fortune. She never received the addresses of another man – she always cared in secret for Henry K. – but she was determined to remain unmarried. K. lived about the world in different military stations, and at last, at the end of 10 years (or more), came back to England – still a handsome, selfish, impecunious soldier. One of his other sisters, Mrs S[artoris] then attempted to bring on the engagement again – knowing that Miss T. still cared for him. . . . K. again . . . paid his addresses to Miss T. She refused him – it was too late. And yet, said Mrs K., she cared for him – and she would have married no other man. But H.K.'s selfishness had over-reached itself and this was the retribution of time' (*The Notebooks of Henry James*, 1947, ed. F.O. Matthiessen and Kenneth B. Murdock, New York, pp. 12–13). The editors add a note: 'The characters sketched here bear considerable resemblance to Catherine Sloper and Morris Townsend. . . . The outlined situation is also fairly similar to the central one in [*Washington Square*], but James took the theme and fitted it to an entirely different background and milieu out of his own experience' (see Bruce Dickins, 1961, 'The story of Washington Square', *Times Literary Supplement* (13 October)).

KEMBLE, John Philip (1757–1823) Son of Roger Kemble, brother of the actress Sarah Siddons, and uncle of Fanny **Kemble**, he was educated for the Roman Catholic priesthood but became an actor. He appeared at Drury Lane Theatre in London from 1783 to 1802, playing more than 120 parts. In 1802 he became Manager of Covent Garden Theatre; it was destroyed by fire in 1808 and he reopened it in 1812. In 1817 he retired to Switzerland, where he died.

DORRIFORTH (AFTERWARDS LORD ELMWOOD) in Elizabeth Inchbald, *A Simple Story* (1791)

'[Mrs Inchbald] was an enthusiastic admirer of my uncle John, and . . . Dorriforth is supposed to have been intended by her as a portrait of him' (Fanny Kemble, 1879, *Records of a Girlhood*, Vol. II, pp. 49–50).

KEMP, Alexander (b. *c*.1770) The 'poet' responsible for the rhymes advertising the products of the **Warren's Blacking Warehouse** *c*.1824.

MR SLUM in Charles Dickens, *The Old Curiosity Shop* (1840–1)

'It is a reasonable theory that ... in Alexander Kemp we possibly have the original of "Mr Slum"' (W. Partington, 1938, 'The Blacking Laureate: the identity of Mr Slum, a pioneer in publicity', *The Dickensian* 34: 201). At the time that Dickens was employed in Warren's Blacking Warehouse it was owned by George and managed by James Lamert, his cousins, who had bought the business from one Jonathan Warren, cousin of the more famous Jonathan in the same line of business. 'The rivalry of Robert Warren by Jonathan's representatives, the cousins George and James, was carried to wonderful extremes in the way of advertisement; and they were all very proud, [Dickens] told me, of the cat scratching the boot, which was *their* house's device. The poets in the house's regular employ he remembered too, and made his first study from one of them for the poet in Mrs Jarley's wax-work' (John Forster, 1928, *Life of Charles Dickens*, ed. J.W.T. Ley, pp. 35–6).

KEMP, Harry (1883–1960) 'The tramp poet'. Born in Ohio, he later lived in Greenwich Village and married Mary **Pyne**.

DOANE in Theodore Dreiser, 'Esther Norn', *A Gallery of Women* (1929)

Identification based upon obvious parallels.

KENNA, Michael He was a Chicago alderman during the 1890s.

PATRICK KERRIGAN in Theodore Dreiser, *The Titan* (1914)

'John Coughlin and Michael ... Kenna (the Chicago aldermen who are the models for Michael Tiernan and Patrick Kerrigan)' (Richard Lehan, 1974, *Theodore Dreiser: his world and his novels*, Carbondale, Ill.: Arcturis Books, p. 98).

KENNEDY, Miss Daughter of Benjamin Hall **Kennedy**.

MISS SKINNER in Samuel Butler, *The Way of All Flesh* (1903)

'During luncheon [with Professor Kennedy, while accompanying Butler on a visit to Cambridge in 1880] I [Festing Jones] sat next one of the daughters of the professor, and there occurred between us the conversation about music and "the simple chord of Beethoven" which Butler reproduced in *The Way of All Flesh* (chapter lxxxvi) as having taken place between Miss Skinner and Ernest' (H. Festing Jones, 1919, *Samuel Butler: author of* Erewhon, 2 vols, London: Macmillan, pp. 347–8).

KENNEDY, Benjamin Hall (1804–89) Headmaster of Shrewsbury from 1836 to 1866 and Regius Professor of Greek at Cambridge from 1867 to 1889, he is described in *The Concise Dictionary of National Biography* as 'the greatest classical master of the century', and wrote *Latin Primer* (1843).

DR SAMUEL SKINNER in Samuel Butler, *The Way of All Flesh* (1903)

'A reminiscence of his ... old schoolmaster, Dr Kennedy ... as faithful as he could make it' (H. Festing Jones, 1919, *Samuel Butler: author of* Erewhon, 2 vols, London: Macmillan, p. 32). 'Butler sent *Unconscious Memory* to ... Dr Kennedy ... in acknowledging [the book Kennedy] wrote Butler a letter, 2nd December 1880, applying to his critics the three Greek words which Dr Skinner applied to Ernest's critics. "Ernest remembered [scleroi], and knew that the other words were of like nature, so it was all right" (chapter LXXXVI)' (ibid., pp. 347–8).

KENNEDY, Hugh Boyle (1879–1936) A contemporary of James Joyce at University College, Dublin, he became First Chief Justice in the Irish Free State and President of the Supreme Court of Justice in the Free State in 1924.

HUGH ('BLAZES') BOYLAN in James Joyce, *Ulysses* (1922)

'Boylan's first name is not Blazes, as he is always called, but Hugh; and the provenance of this name is diverting. It is likely that Joyce had in mind his classmate . . . the prim and proper Hugh Boyle Kennedy' (Richard Ellmann, 1966, *James Joyce*, London: Oxford Paperbacks, p. 389). *See also* **Boylan**, Blazes; **Keogh**, Ted.

KENNEDY, Lucy (1859–1925) Daughter of George Marwood of Little Busby Hall, Cleveland, she was the sister of Arthur **Marwood** and the aunt of Margaret Kennedy. In 1882 she married Charles Napier Kennedy.

FLORENCE CHURCHILL in Margaret Kennedy, *The Constant Nymph* (1924)

'That the pretentious Florence should be clearly modelled on his own mother may not have distressed [George Kennedy] unduly' (Violet Powell, 1983, *The Constant Novelist: a study of Margaret Kennedy, 1896–1967*, p. 56).

KENNEY, Charles Lamb (1821–81) Son of the dramatist James Kenney and godson of Charles Lamb, in 1837 he became a clerk in the General Post Office and in 1840 worked for *The Times*. He was Secretary to Sir Joseph Paxton during the organization of transport services to the Crimea, and in 1858 was Secretary to Ferdinand de Lesseps. He later worked on the *Standard* and also wrote a number of plays, adapted foreign operas and wrote songs. He was one of the wittiest men of his time.

ARTHUR PENDENNIS in W.M. Thackeray, *The History of Pendennis* (1848–50)

'Nor must I forget to mention a visitor who used to come to Kensington in the very early days of Pendennis. He was a rather short good-looking young man, with a fair, placid face . . . and one day after dinner . . . my father pulled out his sketch-book and began to make a drawing of his guest. This was a young literary man just beginning his career; his name was Charles Lamb Kenney, and we were told that he was to be the hero of the new book, or rather, that the hero of the new book was to look like Mr Kenney' (Lady Ritchie, 1898, biog. introd. to *The Works of W.M. Thackeray*, Vol. II: *Pendennis*, London: Smith, Elder, p. xxxiii). *See also* **Ellison**, Cuthbert; **Thackeray**, W.M.

KENSINGTON SQUARE, London

POCKLINGTON SQUARE in W.M. Thackeray, 'Our Street' (1848)

'[Thackeray] knew intimately the Kensington world of the 1840s . . . and he preserved it for posterity in . . . *Our Street*, where Kensington Square . . . [is] faithfully presented under the [name] of Pocklington Square' (Gordon Ray, 1958, *Thackeray: the age of wisdom*, p. 4).

KENT, Constance Emily (b. 1844) Her half-brother Frances Saville Kent was murdered when he was 4 years old: she confessed to his murder in 1865 and was condemned to death but was reprieved and remained in prison until 1885. Following her release she disappeared.

HELENA LANDLESS in Charles Dickens, *Edwin Drood* (1870)

'Neither [Mr J. Lindsay] nor any other writer that I have seen appears to have noticed what must have been obvious to contemporaries, that Helena was modelled mainly, if not entirely, on Constance Kent' (E.O. Winstedt, 1950, 'Helena Landless', *Notes and Queries* 195 (22 July): 325). *See also* **Ternan**, Ellen Lawless.

KENTON STREET, Bloomsbury, London The street in which Ellie **Schleussner** shared a flat with another woman in 1896.

KENNETT STREET in Dorothy Richardson, *Pilgrimage* (1915–67)

'Kennett Street (probably Kenton Street, in fact)' (John Rosenberg, 1973, *Dorothy Richardson*, London, p. 103).

KEOGH, Ted

HUGH ('BLAZES') BOYLAN in James Joyce, *Ulysses* (1922)

'Joyce . . . perhaps borrowed the occupation and appearance of [this] character from [a] man named Ted Keogh. Keogh ran a junk shop . . . in almost exactly the same location as the hawker's car where Bloom buys *The Sweets of Sin* for Molly. . . . Keogh in 1909 was, like his father, a horse dealer; he dressed expensively and habitually wore a straw hat; and when Joyce visited Dublin Keogh was managing a well known prizefighter' (Richard Ellmann, 1966, *James Joyce*, London: Oxford Paperbacks, p. 389). *See also* **Boylan**, Blazes; **Kennedy**, Hugh Boyle.

KEPPEL, Alice (d. 1947) Daughter of Sir William Edmonstone, in 1891 she married the Hon. George Keppel and from 1898 to 1910 she was the mistress of Edward VII. Violet **Trefusis** was her daughter.

ROMOLA CHEYNE in Victoria Sackville-West, *The Edwardians* (1930)

'. . . (for "Romola Cheyne" read "Alice Keppel")' (Philippe Julian, 1976, *The Life of Violet Trefusis*, p. 12).

KEROUAC, Jack (1922–69) Novelist. Born in Lowell, Massachusetts, the son of French-speaking Quebecois parents, he did not learn to speak English until he was 6 years old. He won a football scholarship to Columbia University, but left to spend the early years of the Second World War working as a mechanic in Hartford and later as a sports journalist on the *Lowell Star*. In 1942 he worked briefly in Washington on the construction of the Pentagon. He then joined the merchant marines, and in 1943 enlisted in the US Navy but was discharged after a month. He described his group of friends, which included Allen **Ginsberg** and Gary **Snyder**, as the 'Beat Generation'. His novels were largely autobiographical.

Jack Duluoz in *Maggie Cassidy* (1959), Jack in *Book of Dreams* (1960), Peter Martin in *The Town and the City* (1950), Leo Percepied in *The Subterraneans* (1958), and Ray Smith in *The Dharma Bums* (1958), all by Jack Kerouac

Identified in 'Character key to the Duluoz Legend', in Barry Gifford and Lawrence Lee, 1979, *Jack's Book*, pp. 322–32.

Sal Paradise in Jack Kerouac, *On the Road* (1957)

'Sal Paradise (a self-portrait by Kerouac)' (James D. Hart (ed.), 1983, *The Oxford Companion to American Literature*, New York and Oxford: Oxford University Press, p. 558, s.v. *On the Road*). Also identified in Gifford and Lee, op. cit., pp. 322–32.

KERR, Charles (1767–1821) Of Abbotrule, Roxburghshire. A schoolfellow and distant relative of Scott, he was his close friend at Edinburgh University, and in 1789 was a writer to the *Signet*. He married the daughter of a merchant in the Isle of Man, whither he had repaired to evade his creditors; his father disinherited him and packed him off to Jamaica, but when his father died in 1792 he inherited Abbotrule. He joined the Army as a recruiting officer in 1795 and was compelled to sell Abbotrule and adopt the Army as his permanent profession. On 6 June 1830, Scott wrote in his journal: 'I remember [Colin] Mackenzie] was one of a small party at College, that formed ourselves into a club called the Poetical society. The other members were Charles Kerr of Abbotrule (a singular being), Colin M'Laurin (insane), Colin [Mackenzie] and I, who have luckily kept our wits.' In 1792 Kerr introduced to Scott his cousin Robert **Shortreed**, who became his companion in the 'Liddesdale raids', which provided the material for *The Minstrelsy of the Scottish Border*.

Sir Arthur Redgauntlet (Darsie Latimer) in Sir Walter Scott, *Redgauntlet* (1824)

'I could easily trace many ... coincidences between [Kerr's] letters [to Scott, dating from 1786] and [*Redgauntlet*] ... though ... I have no ... doubt that William Clerk was, in the main, Darsie Latimer' (J.G. Lockhart, 1900, *Memoirs of Sir Walter Scott*, Vol. I, London: Macmillan, p. 136). '[T]he character of Charles Kerr as revealed in his curious letters must have equally [with William Clerk] inspired the account of that early friendship ... in *Redgauntlet*. It is readily granted that Kerr is flattered by the portrait of Darsie Latimer; but, nevertheless, there are other points which make the resemblance more than accidental' (Wilfred Partington, 1932, *Sir Walter's Post-Bag*, p. 312). *See also* **Clerk**, William.

KEUN, Odette (1888–1978) Born in Constantinople, she was the daughter of a Dutch diplomat and had a Greek mother. She became a nun in a Dominican convent, then after three years returned to Constantinople, and later became a journalist and novelist in Paris. She travelled in Russia after the Revolution, and wrote *Sous Lenine*. In 1924 she met H.G. Wells, with whom she set up house near Grasse in the south of France until they parted in 1932.

Clementina in H.G. Wells, *The World of William Clissold* (1926)

'Though H.G. dedicated the book to Odette, she was hurt by the implication that she was a woman of easy virtue like Clementina' (N. Mackenzie and J. Mackenzie, 1973, *The Time Traveller: the life of H.G. Wells*, p. 344).

GRÄFIN ESSLING-STERLINGHOVEN in Anthony West, *Heritage* (1984)

'. . . based on Wells's . . . mistress, Odette Keun' (Hilary Spurling, 1984, 'Family vendetta', review of *Heritage*, *Observer* (3 June): 22).

DOLORES WILBECK in H.G. Wells, *Apropos of Dolores* (1938)

'Odette Keun . . . wrote for *Time and Tide*, when the autobiography appeared [1934], a series of articles analyzing him and his novels in a merciless way. . . . He did not seem to mind . . . but took his revenge in a biting, witty little novel . . . *Apropos of Dolores*' (Lovat Dickson, 1969, *H.G. Wells*, p. 13).

KIDD, Dorothy Second daughter of J.J. Beresford, Rector of Easton Grey, in 1916–17 she shared a flat in Bayswater, London, with Ivy Compton-Burnett. In 1917 she married Alan Kidd.

TULLIA CALDERON in I. Compton-Burnett, *Elders and Betters* (1944)

'Dorothy had never forgiven her mother for, as she said, "taking the easy way out of Easton Grey". This was a kind of truculence which Ivy . . . perhaps passed on to Tullia Calderon. . . . One cannot help suspecting in Tullia's boastfulness echoes of much that must have amused her creator in Dorothy' (Hilary Spurling, 1974, *Ivy When Young: the early life of I. Compton-Burnett, 1884–1919*, London: Gollancz, p. 249).

KIMBERLEY, John Wodehouse, 3rd Earl of (1883–1941) He was killed in an air-raid.

BERTRAM ('BERTIE') WOOSTER in P.G. Wodehouse, *My Man Jeeves* (1919) and others

'Lord Kimberley was Winston Churchill's private secretary [in 1941]. . . . P.G. Wodehouse was his cousin and the character of Bertie Wooster was very probably based on him' (Daphne Fielding, 1964, *The Duchess of Jermyn Street*, p. 185).

KING, Clarence (1842–1901) Geologist. In 1862 he rode across the United States to work in the mines of the Comstock Lode and California. He was the first head of the United States Geological Survey and was the author of *Mountaineering in the Sierra Nevada*. He was a close friend of Henry Adams.

GEORGE STRONG in Henry Adams, *Esther* (1884)

'Esther is the centre of a group of five characters. One of them is her cousin George Strong . . . as incurably facetious and high-spirited as . . . Clarence King, who obviously supplies [his] main features' (Ernest Samuels, 1958, **Henry Adams: the middle years**, Cambridge, Mass., p. 239).

KING, Ginevra (b. 1899) Born in Lake Forest, Illinois, and from a wealthy family. In 1914 she met Fitzgerald while on a visit to St Paul, and in 1918 she married William Hamilton Mitchell. She was divorced in 1937, and that same year visited Santa Barbara and saw Fitzgerald in Hollywood.

ISABELLE BARGÉ in F. Scott Fitzgerald, *This Side of Paradise* (1920)

'I used to write endless letters throughout sophomore and junior years [at Princeton] to Ginevra King of Chicago and Westover, who later figured in *This Side of Paradise*' (to Frances Scott Fitzgerald, 8 October 1937, reproduced in *The Letters of F. Scott Fitzgerald*, 1964, ed. Andrew Turnbull, London: Bodley Head, p. 19).

JOSEPHINE PERRY in F. Scott Fitzgerald, 'First Blood' (1930) and others

'The Josephine stories, based on Ginevra King . . .' (M.J. Bruccoli, 1981, *Some Sort of Epic Grandeur: the life of F. Scott Fitzgerald*, London: Hodder & Stoughton, p. 125).

KING, Henry Robinson (d. 1935) He was the father of Mary, Cecil Day-Lewis's first wife. Assistant Master at Sherbourne, he taught J.C. **Powys**, who speaks of him with great affection in his *Autobiography* (1934).

CLAREMONT in Alec Waugh, *The Loom of Youth* (1917)

'"Crusoe", as he was known at the school, or "Claremont" as he became when transmuted into the . . . "dear old fellow" of *The Loom of Youth*, was one of the school's rare civilizing influences' (Sean Day-Lewis, 1980, *C. Day-Lewis: an English literary life*, p. 17).

KING, Joseph Charles (1795?–1854) Father of Louisa **King**, he kept a small school at 9 Northwick Terrace, St John's Wood, London. Among his pupils were the children of the artists Landseer and Cattermole, and of the actor Macready (his intimate friend), together with Dickens's sons Charles (1844–9, with interruptions) and Walter. He used methods of teaching that were far in advance of his time and had 'no academic mustiness'. 'He was a connoisseur and collector of engravings . . . and had a fine library' (K. Tillotson, 1978, 'Louisa King and Cornelia Blimber', *The Dickensian* (May): 91).

DR BLIMBER in Charles Dickens, *Dombey and Son* (1846–8)

'I was myself . . . at a school in St John's Wood where the master was assisted by his daughter . . . a thorough classical scholar – an arrangement which . . . just suggested the Blimber notion, although in matters of detail there was not the slightest likeness between the two families' (Charles Dickens, the Younger, 1892, Introd. to *Dombey and Son* (biog. edn), p. xix). '[2 September 1847, from Broadstairs] Charley and Wally have been taken to school this morning in high spirits, and at London Bridge will be folded in the arms of Blimber' (to John Forster, quoted in John Forster, 1928, *Life of Dickens*, ed. J.W.T. Ley, p. 464). But as Philip Collins points out (see Philip Collins, 1963, *Dickens and Education*, London: Macmillan, p. 29), the name may simply have been a family joke. However, 'it has been asserted that Dr Blimber's character and manner were suggested by the Dickens boys' imitations of the "suave and mellifluous personage" of their teacher' (ibid.). '[I]t is almost true to say that Dickens reversed the characteristics of Mr King's school for Dr Blimber's' (Tillotson, op. cit., p. 91). *See also* **Everard**, E.

KING, Louisa (1827?–94) One of Joseph **King's** three daughters, in 1849 she was teaching Greek to boys in her father's school. She had two stories published in *Household Words* (1854 and 1855), and in 1857 she married James Martin Menzies.

CORNELIA BLIMBER in Charles Dickens, *Dombey and Son* (1846–8)

'I had myself some knowledge of Miss Blimber' (John Forster, 1928, *Life of Dickens*, Vol. V, vii, p. 485). John Forster speaks of personal acquaintance. '[T]here is one undisputed connection between the Blimber establishment and the . . . school in St John's Wood which Charley and Wally were attending. The proprietor . . . was . . . assisted by his daughter . . . [but] the evidence we have suggests . . . that Miss Louisa King bore little resemblance . . . to . . . Miss Cornelia Blimber' (Philip Collins, 1963, *Dickens and Education*, London: Macmillan, p. 30).

KING, William Augustus Henry (1894–1958) Ceramics expert. From 1926 to 1954 he was a member of staff at the British Museum in London, and in 1952–4 he was Deputy Keeper of the Department of British and Medieval Antiquities. He was a friend of and Literary Executive to Norman **Douglas**, and 'went through most of Douglas' books with him, page by page and line by line . . . in other words a meticulous editor' (Mark Holloway, 1976, *Norman Douglas*, p. 457). He married Dorothy Elizabeth ('Viva') Booth.

MATTHEW PRICE in Angus Wilson, *The Old Men at the Zoo* (1961)

' . . . the character of Matthew & his attachment to his parrots coming from the devotion of the British Museum keeper to the ceramic collection' (author's inscription in copy of the book, see Bertram Rota, 1982, catalogue no. 226, p. 63).

KING, Revd William Hutchinson (1792–1866) He was Curate of Nuneaton, Warwickshire, from 1831 to 1839 and Perpetual Curate of St Luke's, Manchester, from 1839 to 1851.

REVD MR ELY in George Eliot, 'The Sad Fortunes of the Revd Amos Barton', *Scenes of Clerical Life* (1857–8)

See under **Anstruther**, Lady.

KING-HARMAN, Edward Robert (1838–88) Educated at Eton, he was later a member of the 60th Rifles and from 1878 to 1888 was a colonel with Roscommon militia. He unsuccessfully contested parliamentary elections in 1870, 1880 and 1885, but was MP for County Sligo from 1877 to 1880, County Dublin from 1883 to 1885, and the Isle of Thanet from 1885 to 1888. He was Parliamentary Under-Secretary for Ireland.

PHINEAS FINN in Anthony Trollope, *Phineas Finn* (1869) and *Phineas Redux* (1874)

'In another Irishman Trollope found the original of Phineas Finn. . . . This was Mr King-Harman. Trollope first met him in the old Arts Club . . . [with] Mr Marcus Stone' (T.H. Escott, 1906, 'Anthony Trollope: an appreciation and reminiscence', *Fortnightly Review*: 1100, 1101). The dates make it obvious that Trollope can only have drawn on King-Harman's character and not on the details of his career. *See also* **Parkinson**, Joe; **Parkinson-Fortescue**, Chichester; **Pope-Hennessy**, Sir John.

The KING OF PRUSSIA, Dorchester, Dorset The public house that stood in the High Street; the old building has been demolished.

THE THREE MARINERS in Thomas Hardy, *The Mayor of Casterbridge* (1886)

'[The "Three Mariners"] inn was the "King of Prussia"' (F.B. Pinion, 1968, *A Hardy Companion*, London: Macmillan, p. 269).

KINGLAKE, Alexander William (1809–91) English historian. Born in Devon, he was educated at Eton and at Trinity College, Cambridge, and was called to the Bar in 1837. Following his travels in the East and the Crimea, respectively, he wrote *Eothen* (1844) and *Invasion of the Crimea* (1863–87).

WESTLAKE in George Meredith, *Diana of the Crossways* (1884)

'Caroline's various admirers . . . are also sketched in. There is . . . Westlake, the distinguished writer who is also an Oriental traveller (Kinglake)' (Alice Acland, 1948, *Caroline Norton*, London: Constable, p. 179).

The KING'S HEAD, Chigwell, Essex

THE MAYPOLE INN in Charles Dickens, *Barnaby Rudge* (1841)

'What is now known as the King's Head, Chigell, was in 1841 a private house – a large gabled building (adjoining the old inn) which [Dickens] probably had in mind when describing the Maypole in *Barnaby*' (*Letters of Charles Dickens*, 1969, ed. Madeline House and Graham Storey, Vol. II, Oxford: Oxford University Press, p. 243 n. 3).

KING'S SCHOOL, Canterbury

DR STRONG'S SCHOOL in Charles Dickens, *David Copperfield* (1849–50)

'The link between the novel and the school is at least acknowledged in Canterbury itself, for in the brochure *The King's School, Canterbury*, it is thus expressed – "Probably the King's scholar of widest renown is one David Copperfield, for Dr Strong's school . . . could have been no other than the King's School"' (K.R. Cramp, 1952, 'Dr Strong of Canterbury', *The Dickensian* 48: 119). *See also* **Reading School**.

Mr KING'S SCHOOL, St John's Wood, London

BLIMBER'S in Charles Dickens, *Dombey and Son* (1846–8)

See under **King**, J.C. *See also* **Chichester House; Wick House**.

KINGSLEY, Charles (1819–75) Novelist and Anglican clergyman. Born at Holne vicarage, Dartmoor, and educated at Magdalene College, Cambridge, in 1844 he became Curate, and later Rector, of Eversley, Hampshire. He was tutor to Edward VII as the Prince of Wales, and in 1860 became Regius Professor of Modern History at Cambridge. In 1869 he resigned his professorship and was appointed Canon of Chester. He travelled to the West Indies in 1869–70, and was appointed Canon of Westminster and Chaplain to Queen Victoria in 1873. His published works include *Alton Locke* (1850) and *Westward Ho!* (1855). He married Frances Grenfell (**Kingsley**, below).

LANCELOT SMITH in Charles Kingsley, *Yeast* (1848)

'Lancelot .. is recognizable as Kingsley's idea of himself at the time he met [his future wife], and even has Kingsley's own stammer in moments of stress' (R.B. Martin, 1989, *The Dust of Combat: a life of Charles Kingsley*, London: Faber & Faber, p. 84).

BISHOP SYNESIUS in Charles Kingsley, *Hypatia* (1853)

'To the biographer of Kingsley there is a character in *Hypatia* who is of special interest. Bishop Synesius . . . bears a striking resemblance to Kingsley himself' (Susan Chitty, 1974, *The Beast and the Monk: a life of Charles Kingsley*, p. 154).

KINGSLEY, Frances (b. 1814) Née Grenfell, she was the sister of Charlotte **Froude** and married Charles Kingsley.

ARGEMONE LAVINGTON and HONORIA LAVINGTON in Charles Kingsley, *Yeast* (1848)

'Argemone clearly has much in common with Fanny, who indicated in her own copy of [*Yeast*] that Argemone's meeting with her lover was parallel to her own. . . . John Martineau and Max Müller, both close friends of the Kingsleys, were sure that Argemone was Charlotte and Honoria Fanny' (R.B. Martin, 1959, *The Dust of Combat: a life of Charles Kingsley*, London: Faber & Faber, pp. 94, 95). 'One [of the four daughters of Pascoe Grenfell] married . . . Charles Kingsley. This last was the Honoria of "Yeast"' (obituary notice of J.A. Froude, probably by Max Müller, 1894, *The Times* (22 October): 7). 'I have been much amused lately . . . in reading a *Times* obituary notice of J.A. Froude . . . to see a quite different identification of the two characters laid down ex cathedra, the identification of Mrs Kingsley with Honoria being simply ludicrous' (J.M. Ludlow, quoted in Martin, op. cit., p. 95). *See also* **Froude**, Charlotte; **Gifford**, Anna; **Mansfield**, Caulia.

KINGSLEY, George Henry (1827–92) Brother of Charles Kingsley. He read medicine at Edinburgh University in 1846, and in 1848 he was active during the cholera epidemic in England. He fought on the Paris barricades and travelled extensively.

TOM THURNALL in Charles Kingsley, *Two Years Ago* (1857)

'[H]is activity in combating the outbreak of cholera in England [in 1848] was commemorated by his brother Charles in the portrait of Tom Thurnall' (*The Dictionary of National Biography*, 1892, London: Oxford University Press).

KINGSLEY, Henry (1830–76) Novelist and journalist. Youngest brother of Charles Kingsley, he was educated at King's College School in London and at Worcester College, Oxford. He was a gold prospector in Australia from 1953 until 1958 and wrote *Recollections of Geoffrey Hamlyn* (1859) and *Ravenshoe* (1861), amongst others. In 1869–70 he edited the *Edinburgh Daily Review*.

LORD OAKSHOTT in Henry Kingsley, *Oakshott Castle* (1873)

'Oakshott is exactly what I should be if I had got the money. In my late miserable poverty I amused myself by thinking what I should be if I was rich. The result was Oakshott, a greater fool even than myself. Surely that is legitimate fiction' (Henry Kingsley to G.L. Craik, 1873, quoted in S.M. Ellis, 1931, *Henry Kingsley: 1830–1876*, p. 189).

KINGSLEY, Sarah Maria (1942–1922) Née Haselwood, she married Henry Kingsley.

MISS LEE in Henry Kingsley, *Silcote of Silcotes* (1867)

'The chief interest of the story is that the governess, Miss Lee, is said to be a portrait of his wife, who at the time when he married her was governess in the house of the Rev Gerald Blunt, rector of Chelsea' (Angela Thirkell, 1951, 'The works of Henry Kingsley', *The Nineteenth Century* 5 (4): 280).

KINGSMILL, Hugh, (Hugh Kingsmill Lunn) (1889–1949) Novelist and biographer. Son of Sir Henry Lunn, the founder of the travel agency, he was educated at Harrow, Oxford and Dublin. His works included a biography of Frank **Harris**.

RODERICK CORY in Hugh Kingsmill, *The Will to Love* (1919)

'Hugh Kingsmill himself appears early on in the book in the minor character of Roderick Cory' (Michael Holroyd, 1964, *Hugh Kingsmill*, London: Unicorn Press, p. 68).

MAX FISHER in William Gerhardi, *Pending Heaven* (1930)

'Novel . . . written round the character of Hugh Kingsmill under the name of Max Fisher' (*The Best of Hugh Kingsmill*, 1971, ed. Michael Holroyd, p. 399).

CYRIL MEARS in Hugh Kingsmill, *The Will to Love* (1919)

'[He] makes a brief reappearance as Cyril Mears' (Holroyd, op. cit., p. 399).

BENJAMIN POLMONT in Hugh Kingsmill, 'The End of the World', *The Dawn's Delay* (1924)

'Polmont, Kingsmill's most successful and complete portrayal of himself in fiction' (Holroyd, op. cit., p. 75). Kingsmill had difficulty in depicting any character other than himself and he appears in all his novels.

KINGSTON, Dorset Village situated south of Corfe Castle.

KINGSCREECH in Thomas Hardy, *Old Mrs Chundle* (1929)

Identified in F.B. Pinion, 1968, *A Hardy Companion*, London: Macmillan.

KINGSTON MAURWARD HOUSE, Stinsford, Dorset During Hardy's childhood, it was the home of Mrs Julia Augusta Martin, who claimed to have taught him his letters; his first school was one that she established in Lower Bockhampton.

KNAPWATER HOUSE in Thomas Hardy, *Desperate Remedies* (1871)

Identified in F.B. Pinion, 1968, *A Hardy Companion*, London: Macmillan.

TOLLAMORE HOUSE in Thomas Hardy, 'An Indiscretion in the Life of an Heiress' (1878)

Identified in F.B. Pinion, 1968, *A Hardy Companion*, London: Macmillan.

KINNAIRD, Mrs Maria Singer. Properly Maria Keppel, for several years she lived with **Byron**'s friend and banker Douglas Kinnaird, as his common-law wife; she appears in Byron's letters as Mrs K. and used the name Kinnaird. In 1818 the association seems to have broken up and Kinnaird made a settlement on her. Byron wrote to Kinnaird, 'all I know is that she made your house very pleasant to your friends' (23 April 1818, reproduced in George Gordon Byron, 1976, *Letters and Journals*, Vol. VI: *1818–19, The Flesh is Frail*, 1976, ed. Leslie Marchand, London: John Murray, p. 33).

LADY MARGARET BUCHANAN and MRS SEYMOUR in Lady Caroline Lamb, *Glenarvon* (1816)

Identified in a key found among the papers of John Whishaw, a member of the Holland House circle, printed in *The 'Pope' of Holland House: selections from the correspondence of John Whishaw and his friends, 1813–1840*, 1906, ed. Lady Seymour, p. 151. *See also* **Bessborough**, Lady; **Devonshire**, Elizabeth, Duchess of; **Melbourne**, Lady.

KINSHASA, Zaire Formerly Léopoldville, Belgian Congo.

THE CENTRAL STATION in Joseph Conrad, *Heart of Darkness* (1902)

'On 2 August [1890] Conrad arrived at Kinshasa, which was the main base for navigation on the upper Congo, and corresponds to Marlow's Central Station. He found that the steamer which he was supposed to command . . . had been damaged; unlike Marlow . . . [he] did not spend three months repairing his command, but . . . left . . . the next day . . . on . . . the *Roi des Belges*' (Ian Watt, 1980, *Conrad in the Nineteenth Century*, pp. 135–6).

KIOWA RANCH, San Cristobal, New Mexico A ranch situated about seventeen miles above Taos that probably belonged to John Evans, son of Mabel Dodge **Luhan**; she bought it back from him in 1924 and gave it to Frieda **Lawrence**, receiving in exchange the manuscript of *Sons and Lovers*. The Lawrence's moved with Dorothy **Brett** to the ranch on 5 May.

LAS CHIVAS in D.H. Lawrence, 'St Mawr' (1925)

'The little one-story white cottage seemed to have flown over from New England. Surrounding them was, actually, a white picket fence to keep the animals out, and there was one tall pine tree in the yard! You have read all about it in St Mawr, haven't you . . .?' (Mable Dodge Luhan, 1932, *Lorenzo in Taos*, New York, p. 191).

KIPLING, Alice Macdonald ('Trix') (1868–1948) Sister of Rudyard Kipling, she married Lieutenant-Colonel J.M. Fleming.

JUDY in Rudyard Kipling, 'Baa, Baa, Black Sheep' (1888)

Identified in R.L. Green (ed.), 1961, 'Notes on "Baa, Baa, Black Sheep", in *The Readers' Guide to Rudyard Kipling's Work*, Sect. I, London: Kipling Society, pp. 374–7.

KIPLING, Elsie (1896–1976) Daughter of Rudyard Kipling, she married George Bambridge in 1924. In 1932 they settled at Wimpole Hall in Cambridge but she was widowed in 1943.

UNA in Rudyard Kipling, *Puck of Pook's Hill* (1906) and *Rewards and Fairies* (1910)

'Every year from 1900 to 1905 they spent the winter in South Africa. . . . On one visit the children brought up a lion cub as a pet after which their father nicknamed them "Una" and "Dan", after "Una" . . . in the *Faerie Queen* and Daniel of the Lion's Den. As "Dan" and "Una" they became known to thousands of readers. Elsie is vividly portrayed in . . . *Gloriana* and *Marklake Witches*' (Charles Carrington, 1976, 'Obituary: Elsie Bambridge', *The Kipling Journal* 42 (200): 20).

KIPLING, John (1897–1915) Son of Rudyard Kipling, he was killed in the Battle of Loos.

DAN in Rudyard Kipling, *Puck of Pook's Hill* (1906) and *Rewards and Fairies* (1910)

See under **Kipling**, Elsie.

KIPLING, Rudyard (1865–1936) English writer. Born in Bombay and educated at the United Services College, Westward Ho!, Devon, he returned to India as a journalist in 1880. After some early success with his writing, he settled in London in 1889. In 1892 he married Caroline Balestier, and they lived for a time in her native Vermont. In 1899 they finally settled in England. He won the Nobel Prize for literature in 1907.

BEETLE in Rudyard Kipling, *Stalky & Co.* (1899)

'The curve in the shoulder region and an apparently small head close to the shoulders earned [Kipling] the nickname of "The Beetle"; but this appellation was current only amongst a few, although used throughout in *Stalky and Co.*' (G.C. Beresford, 1936, *Schooldays with Kipling*, p. 21). Also identified in the caption to a photograph reproduced in the June 1981 issue of *The Kipling Journal*: 'Masters at the United Services College . . . in Kipling's day' (*The Kipling Journal* 48 (218): 21).

PUNCH in Rudyard Kipling, 'Baa, Baa, Black Sheep' (1888)

Identified in R.L. Green (ed.), 1961, 'Notes on "Baa, Baa, Black Sheep", in *The Readers' Guide to Rudyard Kipling's Work*, Sect. I, London: Kipling Society, pp. 374–77.

KIRKBY LONSDALE, Westmorland Located two miles from Cowan Bridge (see Nikolaus Pevsner, 1967, *Cumberland and Westmorland* (*Buildings of England* series), Harmondsworth: Penguin, pp. 260 ff.).

LOWTON in Charlotte Brontë, *Jane Eyre* (1847)

'... based on Kirkby Lonsdale' (**Jane Eyre**, 1976, ed. Margaret Smith, p. 468 n. (to p. 87)).

KIRKPATRICK, Catherine Aurora ('Kitty') (1802–89) Daughter of William Achilles Kirkpatrick by his marriage to a princess of the family of the Nizam of Hyderabad, she was the cousin of Julia **Strachey** and of Isabella **Buller**. In 1824, in the company of Edward **Strachey** and Carlyle, she went to France, and in 1829 she married Captain James Winslow Phillipps of the 7th Hussars.

BLUMINE in Thomas Carlyle, *Sartor Resartus* (1833–4)

'In 1847 ... Mrs Elizabeth Mercer [Mrs Phillipps]. A conversation ... took place, which Mrs Mercer later reported as follows: She was arranging books in the library one morning when she turned to me and said: "Lizzie, have you ever read *Sartor Resartus* by Carlyle?" "No, I had not." "Well, get it, and read the 'Romance'. I am the heroine and every word of it is true"' (Mrs Mercer, 1894, 'Carlyle and the "Blumine" of Sartor Resartus', *Westminster Review* 144 (August): 164–5; see C.R. Sanders, 1953, *The Strachey Family, 1588–1932*, Durham, NC, p. 126). 'That Blumine personified Miss Kirkpatrick has always passed in the family for a certainty, requiring no more discussion than the belief that Nelson stands on the column in Trafalgar Square' (George Strachey, 1892, 'Carlyle and the "Rose-goddess"', *The Nineteenth Century* 32 (September): 475). C.R. Sanders (op. cit., pp. 122 ff.) sets out the arguments for accepting Kitty Kirkpatrick as the original of Blumine. *See also* **Carlyle**, Jane Welsh; **Gordon**, Margaret.

KIRKUP, Seymour Stocker (1778–1880) Painter. He was acquainted with William Blake and Benjamin Robert **Haydon**. and was present at the funerals of both Keats and **Shelley**. He was the leader of a literary circle in Florence.

DR ORMSKIRK in Nathaniel Hawthorne, *Dr Grimshawes Secret* (1883)

'Dr Ormskirk and his daughter Elsie are modelled after ... Seymour Kirkup and the child Imogen in his house, whom Hawthorne had met in Florence [in 1858]' (Nathalia Wright, 1965, *American Novelists in Italy*, Philadelphia, p. 154).

KLEIN, Georges Antoine (1863–90) Commercial agent for the Société anonyme Belge du Haut Congo, where he arrived in May 1890 at Stanley Falls. In September of the same year he died of dysentery on board Conrad's ship *Roi des Belges* and was buried at Tchumbiri.

MR KURTZ in Joseph Conrad, *Heart of Darkness* (1902)

'It is impossible to assert without definite proof that the resemblance between Kurtz and Klein is *complete* but there can be little doubt ... that these two beings ... had much more in common than a mere similarity of names' (G. Jean-Aubrey, 1927, *Joseph Conrad: life and letters*, Vol. I, London: Heinemann, p. 136). '[I]n the manuscript ... Conrad starts by writing Klein and then changes to Kurtz' (Jocelyn Baines, 1969, *Joseph Conrad: a critical biography*, p. 117). *See also* **Barttelot**, E.M.; **Hodister**, A.E.C.; **Stanley**, H.M.

KNOLE, Kent The family seat of the Sackvilles and Sackville-Wests since 1566.

CHEVRON in Victoria Sackville-West, *The Edwardians* (1930)

'Sebastian . . . discusses the future of Chevron – Knole . . . with his sister Viola. . . . The first two chapters [of *The Edwardians*] . . . describing . . . the organisation and running of a great country house, give a detailed and probably highly accurate description of life at Knole as [Vita Sackville-West] knew it in the first decade of this century' (Michael Stevens, 1973, *V. Sackville-West: a critical biography*, p. 56).

THE HOUSE in Virginia Woolf, *Orlando* (1928)

'You made me cry with your passages about Knole, you wretch' (V. Sackville-West to Virginia Woolf, on first reading *Orlando*, 11 October 1928, reproduced in *The Letters of Virginia Woolf*, 1977, ed. Nigel Nicolson, Vol. III, London: Hogarth Press, p. 575).

KNOTT, Newman 'A needy and seedy individual who presented himself at the office [of Ellis and Blackmore, solicitors] every week to draw an allowance of seven shillings made by a friend. Formerly a prosperous tenant farmer near Chichester, his expensive tastes had ruined him, and the shifts to which he resorted in an endeavour to anticipate his weekly allowance were a source of great amusement to Dickens' (W.J. Carlton, 1952, 'Mr Blackmore engages an office boy', *The Dickensian* 48 (September): 165; based on Edward Blackmore, 1870, 'Reminiscences of Charles Dickens', unpublished MS).

NEWMAN NOGGS in Charles Dickens, *Nicholas Nickleby* (1838–9)

'Blackmore was convinced that [Noggs] was Newman Nott' (Carlton, ibid.).

KNOXVILLE, Tennessee

DELISLEVILLE in Frances Hodgson Burnett, *In Connection with the De Willoughby Claim* (1899)

'Knoxville in 1895 [when Mrs Hodgson and her children arrived there from England] was a sad place. Years later Frances described it as Delisleville in her novel, *In Connection with the De Willoughby Claim*' (Ann Thwaite, 1974, *Waiting for the Party: the life of Frances Hodgson Burnett, 1849–1924*, London: Secker & Warburg, p. 26).

KNUTSFORD, Cheshire

CRANFORD in Elizabeth Gaskell, *Cranford* (1853)

'Knutsford did duty not only as the original of *Cranford*. It reappears under the name of Dunscomb in "Mr Harrison's Confessions" [*Lizzie Leigh and Other Tales*, 1855], as Barford in "The Squire's Story" [ibid.], as Hamley in *A Dark Night's Work* [1863]; as Eltham in *Cousin Phillis* [1865] and as Hollingford in *Wives and Daughters* [1866]' (A.B. Hopkins, 1952, *Elizabeth Gaskell: her life and works*, p. 13).

MALLINGFORD in Mrs Molesworth, *Lover and Husband* (1870)

'Mrs Molesworth does not seem to have taken kindly to the rarefied social atmosphere of . . . "Cranford"; and indeed she pilloried it . . . as "Mallingford" in her first novel' (Roger Lancelyn Green, 1961, *Mrs Molesworth*, p. 33).

KOLTSOV, Mihail (1898–1942) *Pravda's* leading foreign correspondent. He went to Spain in September 1936 and returned to Russia in the late summer of 1937, together with all the other Russian advisers and generals; most disappeared, not only from Spain, but from history. Koltsov survived, only to be arrested in 1938 and die in prison in 1942; Khrushchev, however, rehabilitated his ghost, and his diaries were published in Russia in 1951.

Karkov in Ernest Hemingway, *For Whom the Bell Tolls* (1940)

'I remember a Russian I knew named Michel Koltzov who I put in a book . . . under the name of Kharkov' (to Bernard Berenson, 14 October 1952, reproduced in *Ernest Hemingway Selected Letters, 1917–1961*, 1981, ed. Carlos Baker, London: Granada, p. 788).

KORITSCHONER, Hans An Austrian trader in East Africa, the description of Hemingway's encounter with him while on safari is almost literally true: in 1925 Koritschoner had read the poems and the short story 'The Undefeated' which had been published in the German periodical *Der Querschnitt*. He later became a government ethnologist.

Kandisky in Ernest Hemingway, *The Green Hills of Africa* (1935)

'The Austrian trader there called Kandisky was actually named Hans Koritschoner' (Carlos Baker, 1973, *Hemingway: the writer as artist*, Princeton, p. 29 n. 7). In 1938 he wrote to Hemingway, remembering the meeting (see Carlos Baker, 1969, *Ernest Hemingway: a life story*, New York, p. 610 n. 'Meeting Hans Koritschoner').

KOTELIANSKY, Samuel Solomnovich (1882–1955) A Russian Jew, he was born in a ghetto village in the Ukraine and moved to London from the University of Kiev shortly before the First World War. He earned his living by translating. He was a close friend of D.H. Lawrence, Mark **Gertler** and Leonard Woolf.

Benjamin Cooley in D.H. Lawrence, *Kangaroo* (1923)

'His representation as the Australian leader Benjamin Cooley . . . [lays] stress on his tall and strong figure and [shows] him as "a remarkable and formidable man"' (E. Delavenay, 1972, *D.H. Lawrence: the man and his work*, p. 282). '[I]n a letter Lawrence denied [that Koteliansky was the original of Cooley], as he usually did' (H.T. Moore, 1955, *The Intelligent Heart: the story of D.H. Lawrence*, London: Heinemann, p. 292). *See also* **Eder**, David; **Monash**, Sir John.

Maxim Libidnikov in D.H. Lawrence, *Women in Love* (1920)

'Maxim Libidnikov . . . may have been partly a portrait of Koteliansky' (Moore, op. cit., p. 239). *See also* **Litvinov**, Maxim.

KREYMBORG, Alfred (1883–1966) New York poet and playwright. He was the 'founder of *Others* (the others who were not published in Harriet Monroe's

Poetry); co-founder with Harold Loeb of the periodical *Broom'* (Robert E. Knoll (ed.), 1962, *McAlmon and the Lost Generation: a self-portrait*, Lincoln, Nebr.: University of Nebraska Press, p. 375).

REGINALD CRACKYE in Robert McAlmon, *Post Adolescence* (1923)

Identified in ibid., p. 108.

KRIEGER, Adolf P. (b. 1851) Born in the United States, in 1880 he shared lodgings with Conrad, and it seems probable that Conrad lodged with him and his wife Mary between voyages during the period 1881–6. They remained friends until at least 1904 and Conrad dedicated *Tales of Unrest* (1898) to him, but the friendship was latterly soured by a dispute over a loan from Krieger to Conrad which, after three years, still remained undischarged.

ADOLF VERLOC in Joseph Conrad, *The Secret Agent* (1907)

'[A]s I believe, Adolf Verloc is in part based upon . . . Krieger' (Norman Sherry, 1971, *Conrad's Western World*, Cambridge, p. 327). 'Finally, I think Conrad had Krieger's physical appearance in mind when he described Verloc' (ibid., p. 239). 'I believe the Kriegers' marital situation was the basis of the Verloc's' (ibid., p. 363). *See also* **Coulon**, Auguste; **Samuels**, Henry B.

KROG, Fritz Educated at the University of Missouri, in 1909 he became the nominal Editor of the *Bohemian*, a bankrupt periodical bought by Dreiser, who was at that time Editor of the Butterick Group's *Delineator*. In 1913 he fell in love with Ann **Watkins** and attempted to force her at gunpoint to go off with him. As his conduct grew wilder, he found himself before the courts; Dreiser intervened on his behalf and he was put on probation.

ERNEST SCHEIB in Theodore Dreiser, 'Emmanuela', *A Gallery of Women* (1929)

'Emanuela's escape from Scheib is based upon an experience Ann Watkins had with Fritz Krog' (Richard Lehan, 1974, *Theodore Dreiser: his world and his novels*, Carbondale, Ill.: Arcturis Books, p. 264 n. 12).

KROPOTKIN, Princess Alexandra Daughter of Peter **Kropotkin**.

ANASTASIA ALEXANDROVNA LEONIDOV in W. Somerset Maugham, 'Love and Russian Literature', *Ashenden; or The British Agent* (1928)

'"Anastasia Alexandrovna" [is based to some degree] on Alexandra Kropotkin' (R.L. Calder, 1972, *W. Somerset Maugham and the Quest for Freedom*, London: Heinemann, p. 201).

KROPOTKIN, Prince Peter Alexeivich (1842–1921) Russian anarchist and social philosopher. Born in Moscow, he spent five years in Siberia on military service, and then returned to Moscow to study mathematics, while acting as Secretary to the Geographical Society. In 1872 he became involved with the International Workingman's Association. Arrested and imprisoned in Russia in 1874, he escaped to England in 1876. In Lyon in 1883 he was condemned to five years' imprisonment for anarchism, but was released in 1886 and lived in

England until the outbreak of revolution prompted him to return to Russia in 1917.

PETER IVANOVICH in Joseph Conrad, *Under Western Eyes* (1911)

'[S]ome facets of Peter Ivanovich, such as his sentimental feminism, may be a guying of Kropotkin' (Jocelyn Baines, 1967, *Joseph Conrad: a critical biography*, rev. edn, London: Weidenfeld & Nicolson, p. 372; originally published 1960). 'Prince Kropotkin ... gave me a description of Anarchy that was more like Heaven upon earth than anything else, with laws of order, peace and beauty enforced by a vast army of Christian hearted atheists' (Anne Thackeray Ritchie to her husband, describing a luncheon party at the Misses Gaskells', Manchester, 14 November 1891, reproduced in *Letters of Anne Thackeray Ritchie*, 1924, ed. Hester Ritchie, London: John Murray, p. 217). *See also* **Tolstoy**, Count.

L

LABOUCHÈRE, Henry du Pré (1831–1912) Radical journalist and politician. He was in the Diplomatic Service from 1854 to 1864, and was MP for Windsor (1865–6; unseated on appeal), Middlesex (1867–8) and Northampton (1880–96; with Charles Bradlaugh as his colleague 1880–91). He married the actress Henrietta Hodson in 1868 and in 1870 he acquired control of Queen's Theatre for her benefit. He founded the weekly journal *Truth* in 1876.

HENLEIGH MALLINGER GRANDCOURT in George Eliot, ***Daniel Deronda*** (1876)

'With these names [of influential newspaper proprietors of the nineties] one must bracket the original of George Eliot's "Grandcourt" in *Daniel Deronda*, Mr Henry Labouchère' (T.H.S. Escott, 1898, *Personal Forces of the Period*, pp. 189, 190).

TOMMY TRESSEL in Justin McCarthy and Mrs Campbell Praed, ***The Rebel Rose*** (1888)

'Tommy Tressel . . . was modelled mainly upon the late Mr Henry Labouchère' (*Our Book of Memories: letter of Justin McCarthy to Mrs Campbell Praed*, 1912, London: Chatto & Windus, p. 51).

LAÇENAIRE, Pierre-François (1800–36) French psychopathic killer. Born at Francheville, near Lyons, he was the son of a silk merchant. After failing to settle in any employ in his native town, he went to Paris, where he engaged in journalism, robbery and murder; his life was ended on the guillotine. He is described in the *Nouvelle biographie générale* of 1858 as small, frail and sallow, with a high forehead, an averted gaze and a mocking smirk.

MONSIEUR RIGAUD in Charles Dickens, ***Little Dorrit*** (1855–7)

'The greatest influences on the French, Swiss and Italian scenes of the novel . . . were Dickens's own personal experiences in those countries, from 1844 onwards. . . . Rigaud . . . may owe something to . . . Wainewright . . . but infinitely more to . . . Laçenaire . . . a debt that includes Rigaud's deliberate theatricality' (H.P. Schucksmith, 1979, Introd. to *Little Dorrit*, Oxford, p. xv). *See also* **Napoleon III**; **Wainewright**, Thomas Griffiths.

LACOCK ABBEY, Wiltshire Founded as an abbey for Augustinian Canonesses in 1229, it was dissolved in 1539 and, later in the sixteenth century, came into the possession of the Talbot family. It was here, in the nineteenth century, that W.H. Fox Talbot made his photographic inventions. A certain proportion, more than of any other English nunnery, according to Pevsner, of the original abbey remains. In the eighteenth century a fine dining-room was added and the hall was Gothicized, the roof being decorated with the coats of arms of the then owner, Ivry Talbot (see Nikolaus Pevsner, 1975, *Wiltshire* (*Buildings of England* series), Harmondsworth: Penguin, Pl. 31, 55; and, extensively, H. Avray Tipping, *English Homes*, Period II, Vol. I: *Early Tudor, 1485–1558*, pp. 361–85).

TOPPING ABBEY in George Eliot, *Daniel Deronda* (1876)

'Lacock in particular gave [George Eliot] the details of Sir Hugo Mallinger's Topping Abbey' (Gordon S. Haight, 1968, *George Eliot*, Oxford, p. 475). *See also* **Maxstoke Priory**.

LA FARGE, John (1835–1910) Artist and author. Born in New York, he studied painting with Couture in Paris in 1856 and met the Pre-Raphaelites. In 1876 he executed murals for Trinity Church, Boston, and in 1886 he travelled in the Far East with Henry Adams. He also designed and manufactured stained glass.

MR WHARTON in Henry Adams, *Esther* (1884)

'Wharton lives for art. The most complex figure of the [central] group [of characters], he reflects the challenge of John La Farge's personality' (Ernest Samuels, 1958, *Henry Adams: the middle years*, Cambridge, Mass., p. 240). *See also* **Bigelow**, William Sturgis; **Saint-Gaudens**, Augustus.

LAFAYETTE COUNTY, Mississippi

YOKNAPATAWPHA COUNTY in William Faulkner, the Yoknapatawpha novels (1929–36)

'Nearly all Faulkner's novels ... take place in a small imaginary area of Mississippi called Yoknapatawpha County, a place which bears a striking resemblance to Lafayette County ... where William Faulkner has lived most of his life' (Arthur Mizener, 1959, 'The promises of life', *The Listener* 61 (12 February): 284).

LA FOLLETTE, Robert Marion (1855–1925) United States politician. He was a member of the United States House of Representatives from 1885 to 1889 and was elected Governor of Wisconsin in 1901, remaining in that post until 1907. In 1905 he was elected Senator, and at that point resigned from his position as governor. He was a senator for twenty years and was a leader of progressives and radicals. He sponsored the resolution authorizing congressional investigation into the Teapot Dome oil lease.

SENATOR WELLING in S.H. Hopkins, *Revelry* (1926)

'In *Revelry* ... Adams fictionalizes or withholds most of the names, dates and places. In *Oil!* Upton Sinclair supplies them so that [*Oil!*] can be read as a kind of key to [*Revelry*]' (Joseph Blotner, 1966, *The Modern American Political Novel*, Austin, Tex., p. 113). 'Adams makes Senator Welling the ... man who brings about a Congressional investigation; Sinclair gives the credit to Senator La Follette' (ibid., p. 116).

LA GUARDIA, Fiorello Henry (1882–1947) Born in New York, he was a Republican member of the House of Representatives from 1917 to 1921 and from 1923 to 1933. He was Mayor of New York from 1933 to 1945, being elected three times.

GEORGE DE ANGELIS in Stephen Endicott, *Mayor Harding of New York* (1931)

'. . . clearly based on Fiorello La Guardia' (Joseph Blotner, 1966, *The Modern American Political Novel*, Austin, Tex., p. 125).

LAIDLAW, Catherine (d. 1817) She was married to James **Laidlaw**.

AILIE DINMONT in Sir Walter Scott, *Guy Mannering* (1815)

See under **Laidlaw**, James.

LAIDLAW, James Farmer of Blackhouse, Yarrow, Selkirkshire. He was the husband of Catherine **Laidlaw** and the father of William, who was a steward at Abbotsford from 1817 until 1832. James Hogg, the poet, was shepherd at Blackhouse for some ten years. Scott first met the family in 1801, when ballad-hunting in Liddesdale with James **Skene**.

DANDIE DINMONT in Sir Walter Scott, *Guy Mannering* (1815)

'I have the best reason to believe that the . . . character of Dandie . . . [and] of his wife and some, at least, of the . . . peculiarities of the ménage at Charlieshope were filled up from Scott's observation . . . of . . . the early home of his dear friend, William Laidlaw' (J.G. Lockhart, 1900, *Memoirs of Sir Walter Scott*, Vol. I, London: Macmillan, pp. 168–9). It is to be supposed that the 'best reason' was something let fall by Scott himself. 'The author may here remark that the character of Dandie Dinmont was drawn from no individual' (*Guy Mannering*, 1901 (Border edn), ch. xxiii, author's note). *See also* **Davidson**, James; **Elliott**, Willie; **Park**, Archibald; **Thorburn**, James.

LAING, Allan Stewart (1788–1862) Son of James Laing of the Isle of Dominica. From 1820 to 1837 he was a magistrate at Hatton Garden police court, London; he was removed by the Home Secretary because of his bad temper.

MR FANG in Charles Dickens, *Oliver Twist* (1837–8)

'In my next number of Oliver Twist, I must have a magistrate, and casting about for a magistrate whose harshness and insolence would render him a fit subject to be "shewn up" I have . . . stumbled upon Mr Laing. . . . I know the man's character perfectly well, but as it would be necessary to describe his appearance also, I ought to have seen him, which . . . I have never done. In this dilemma it occurred to me that perhaps I might under your auspices be smuggled into the Hatton Garden office for a few moments some morning' (Charles Dickens to Thomas Haines (a reporter at the Mansion House police office), 3 June 1837, reproduced in *Letters of Charles Dickens*, 1965, ed. Madeline House and Graham Storey, Vol. I, Oxford: Oxford University Press, p. 267).

NUPKINS in Charles Dickens, *The Pickwick Papers* (1836–7)

'Nupkins is Laing the London magistrate' (Jack Lindsay, 1900, *Charles Dickens*, p. 434).

LAMANTIA, Philip (b. 1927) San Francisco poet.

DAVID D'ANGELI in *Desolation Angels* (1965), and FRANCIS DA PAVIA in *The Dharma Bums* (1958), both by Jack Kerouac

Identified in 'Character key to the Duluoz Legend', in Barry Gifford and Lawrence Lee, 1979, *Jack's Book*, pp. 322–32.

LAMAR, Lucius Quintus Cincinnatus (1825–93) American politician and lawyer. He was a nephew of Mirabeau Buonaparte Lamar, who was the second president of the Republic of Texas (1838–41). In 1855 he settled in Mississippi. He was twice Member of the House of Representatives (1857–60 and 1873–7), he served in the Confederate Army during the Civil War, and was Confederate Commissioner in Europe in 1862 and 1863. He was a United States senator (1877–85); Secretary of the Interior (1885–8); and Associate Justice to the Supreme Court (1888–93). Henry Adams became his intimate friend in Washington, describing him as having become 'one of the calmest, most reasonable and most amiable Union men in the United States, and quite unusual in social charm' (*Education of Henry Adams*; see *Letters of Mrs Henry Adams*, 1937, ed. Ward Thoron, p. 246 n.).

BASIL RANSOM in Henry James, *The Bostonians* (1884)

'John Hay told James that Lucius Q.C. Lamar ... whom James had met in Washington, seemed to recognize something of himself in the character. James confessed that he was "in it a little, for I met him once or twice ... and he is one of the very few Mississippians with whom I have had the pleasure of conversing"' (Leon Edel, 1963, *Henry James: the middle years, 1884–1894*, p. 77).

LAMB, Lady Caroline (1785–1828) Author. Née Ponsonby, she was the only daughter of the 3rd Earl of Bessborough and Lady **Bessborough**, and in 1805 married William Lamb, afterwards 2nd Viscount **Melbourne**. In 1813 she became passionately infatuated with Lord **Byron**, with whom she had a nine-month affair, and when she met Byron's funeral procession in 1824 she sustained a shock from which she never fully recovered. She separated from her husband in 1825. She was the author of three novels.

LADY KITTY BLACKWATER in Mrs Humphry Ward, *The Marriage of William Ashe* (1905)

'Perhaps the best-known novel in which she occurs is Mrs Humphry Ward's *The Marriage of William Ash* [sic]; the story of William Lamb, Lady Caroline, Lady Melbourne, and Byron and Lady Byron transmuted into the later nineteenth century' (Elizabeth Jenkins, 1932, *Lady Caroline Lamb*, p. 276).

LADY CALANTHA DELAVAL in Lady Caroline Lamb, *Glenarvon* (1816)

'Smarting at Lord Byron's neglect, she wrote and published in May [1816] a novel called *Glenarvon* in which she was the heroine called Calanthe [sic]' (Mabell, Countess of Airlie, 1921, *In Whig Society, 1775–1818*, pp. 183–5). Also identified in a key found among the papers of John Whishaw, a member of the Holland House circle, printed in *The 'Pope' of Holland House: selections from the correspondence of John Whishaw and his friends, 1813–1840*, 1906, ed. Lady Seymour, p. 151.

LADY HARRIET DUNCAN in T.H. Lister, *Granby* (1826)

'The fascination of her character ... has inspired several writers with the desire to reproduce it. .... *Granby* ... is ... perhaps the best ... the sketch has the interest of a portrait drawn from life, and the conversation of Lady Harriet Duncan has a perceptible echo of that of Lady Caroline Lamb' (Jenkins, op. cit., p. 276).

MRS FELIX (AMALIA) LORRAINE in Benjamin Disraeli, *Vivian Grey* (1826–7)

'Mrs Lorraine … [is] alleged without much basis to be a portrait of Lady Caroline Lamb' (Robert Blake, 1969, *Disraeli*, 2nd edn, London: Oxford University Press, p. 39). Also identified in a key given in a pamphlet published in 1827 by William Marsh. 'Together with this [key] was given a reprint of the key to the first part, in which the character of Mrs Felix Lorraine … was identified with Lady Caroline Lamb' (Lucien Wolf in his notes to *Vivian Grey*, 1904 (centenary edn), Vol. II, pp. 364). Lucien Wolf concluded that Disraeli was not responsible for the key.

LADY MERCER in J.W. Polidori, *The Vampyre: A Tale* (1819)

'Lady Mercer, who … did all but put on the dress of a mountebank, to attract his notice' (*The Vampyre*, quoted in Derek Marlowe, 1973, *A Single Summer with L.B.*, Harmondsworth: Penguin, p. 111); the footnote reads 'An allusion to … Caroline Lamb.'

LADY MONTEAGLE in Benjamin Disraeli, *Venetia* (1837)

'Lady Caroline Lamb, who appears in the book as Lady Monteagle' (W.F. Monypenny, 1910, *The Life of Benjamin Disraeli, Earl of Beaconsfield*, Vol. I, London: John Murray, p. 363).

LAMB, Henry (1883–1960) Painter. One of a distinguished academic family, he qualified in medicine at Guy's Hospital, London, in 1916 and served in the First World War as a medical officer. He abandoned medicine for painting and studied under Augustus **John**; in 1940 he was an Associate of the Royal Academy, and in 1949 he became a Royal Academician. He was also a gifted pianist. In 1906 he married Nina Euphemia Lamb: they separated soon afterwards and divorced in 1926. In 1928 he married Lady Pansy Pakenham.

LEWIS DODD in Margaret Kennedy, *The Constant Nymph* (1924)

'On his first appearance he wears an unusual number of waistcoats and a yellow muffler, indisputably trademarks of Henry Lamb. Physical traits, pallor, a lined face, a thin mouth, immensely expressive hands, could also be drawn from the same pattern. There the resemblance ceases' (Violet Powell, 1983, *The Constant Novelist: a study of Margaret Kennedy, 1896–1967*, pp. 57–8).

LAMB CLOSE HOUSE, Eastwood, Nottinghamshire Home of the **Barber** family, of **Barber Walker & Co.**, coal-owners.

HIGHCLOSE in D.H. Lawrence, *The White Peacock* (1911)

'[Lamb Close House] appeared in Lawrence's first novel, *The White Peacock*, as Highclose' (H.T. Moore, 1960, *The Intelligent Heart: the story of D.H. Lawrence*, Harmondsworth: Penguin, p. 51; originally published 1955, London: Heinemann).

LILLEY CLOSE in D.H. Lawrence, *Touch and Go* (1919)

'[I]n . . . *Touch and Go* . . . some of the scenes took place at Lilley Close, home of the mine-owning Barlows' (H.T. Moore, 1960, *The Intelligent Heart: the story of D.H. Lawrence*, Harmondsworth: Penguin, pp. 51–2; originally published 1955, London: Heinemann).

SHORTLANDS in D.H. Lawrence, *Women in Love* (1920)

'In *Women in Love*, Lamb Close was Shortlands' (H.T. Moore, 1960, *The Intelligent Heart: the story of D.H. Lawrence*, Harmondsworth: Penguin, p. 51; originally published 1955, London: Heinemann).

WRAGBY HALL in D.H. Lawrence, *Lady Chatterley's Lover* (1928)

'[T]he portrait of Wragby Hall in *Lady Chatterley's Lover* . . . looks strangely like Lamb Close' (H.T. Moore, 1960, *The Intelligent Heart: the story of D.H. Lawrence*, Harmondsworth: Penguin, p. 52; originally published 1955, London: Heinemann). *See also* **Renishaw House**.

LAMB HOUSE, Rye, East Sussex The home of Henry **James** from 1897 until his death in 1916, after which it became the home of E.F. Benson, until 1940. A picture of Lamb House, captioned 'Mr Longdon's', was used as the frontispiece of the New York edition of James's *The Awkward Age* (1909)' (Leon Edel, 1969, *Henry James: the treacherous years, 1895–1901*, London: Rupert Hart-Davis, p. 237).

MALLARDS in E.F. Benson, *Queen Lucia* (1920) and others

'Mallards, where Lucia lived, was a faithful delineation of Lamb House, where I lived' (E.F. Benson, 1940, *Final Edition: an informal autobiography*, London: Longman, p. 271).

LAMBERT, Mr Brother of Cecily **Lambert**.

HENRY GRENFEL in D.H. Lawrence, 'The Fox' (1923)

'At this time [1918] . . . a brother of mine was home on sick leave from the East Africa War Zone and spent some of the time at the farm. . . . (He was the soldier referred to in D.H.L.'s story.) But far from having any amorous feelings towards the lady (my cousin), he actively disliked her, and moreover was years younger with no particular interest in girls at home, having an attachment in South Africa. I believe between them they did mutilate a tree, but . . . I don't really remember much about it' (memoir written by Cecily Lambert in 1955, quoted in E. Nehls, 1957, *D.H. Lawrence: a composite biography*, Madison, Vol. I, p. 466).

LAMBERT, Cecily Afterwards Minchin. She farmed Grimsbury Farms, Long Lane, Hermitage, Berkshire, with her cousin Violet **Monk** during the First World War. The two cousins became friends with the Lawrences when the latter were living in Dollie **Radford**'s cottage at Hermitage in 1918–19.

JILL BANFORD in D.H. Lawrence, 'The Fox' (1923)

'For his human figures . . . Lawrence took two girls he knew . . . near Hermitage. . . . [T]hese girls – whose real names were Violet Monk and Cecily Lambert – became Nellie March and Jill Banford' (H.T. Moore, 1960, *The Intelligent Heart:*

the story of D.H. Lawrence, Harmondsworth: Penguin, pp. 303–4; originally published 1955, London: Heinemann). *See also* **Radford**, Margaret.

LAMBERT, Constant (1905–51) English composer. He studied at the Royal College of Music under Vaughan Williams, and while still a student he was commissioned by Diaghilev, the Russian impresario, to write the ballet *Romeo and Juliet*, which was first performed at Monte Carlo in 1926; he was the first English composer to be commissioned by Diaghilev. His later works included *Music for Orchestra* (1927) and *The Rio Grande* (1929), and the ballets *Horoscope* (1938) and *Tiresias* (1951). He was Conductor of the Camargo Society (1930), from which developed the Vic-Wells (later Sadler's Wells) Ballet of which he was Musical Director until 1947. He was the author of *Music Ho!* (1934).

HUGH MORELAND in Anthony Powell, *A Dance to the Music of Time* (1951–76)

'Dark, rather than fair, he has the Bronzino-type features of Lambert's "Bluecoat" portrait by his father. . . . If I have been skilful enough, lucky enough, to pass on an echo of Lambert's incomparable wit, then "Moreland" is like him; in other respects the things that happen to "Moreland" approximate to the things that happened to Lambert only insomuch as all composers' lives have something in common' (Anthony Powell, 1972, 'Constant Lambert', *The Times* (30 December).

LAMERT, Dr Matthew (1774–1848) Born in Germany he had a distinguished and adventurous career as an Army surgeon and in 1830 became Deputy Inspector-General of Military Hospitals. In 1821 he married Mrs Mary Allen (née Barrow), the widowed elder sister of Dickens's mother. They moved to Cork, Ireland, but Mary died in 1822, and in 1824 he married Susanna Travers.

DR SLAMMER in Charles Dickens, *The Pickwick Papers* (1836–7)

'Mary, the eldest daughter of Charles Banow . . . took for her second husband, an army-surgeon, whose son James . . . had a turn for private theatricals; and as his father's quarters were at the ordnance-hospital . . . he had plenty of room in which to get up his entertainments. The staff-doctor himself played his part, and his portrait will be found in *Pickwick*' (John Forster, 1928, *Life of Charles Dickens*, ed. J.W.T. Ley, pp. 6–7). 'Dr Slammer, of course' (ibid., p. 19 n. 16).

LAMINGTON, Alexander Dundas Ross Cochrane-Wishart-Baillie, Lord (1816–99) He was one of the founders, along with George **Smythe**, of the Young England party in the 1840s, and from 1841 to 1880 was MP for various constituencies. He was created 1st Baron Lamington in 1880, and was the author of *In the Days of the Dandies* (1890) and a number of novels.

SIR CHARLES BUCKHURST in Benjamin Disraeli, *Coningsby* (1844)

Identified in a key in *Notes and Queries* (8th series) 3 (13 May 1893): 363. *See also under* **Bright**, John.

LAMONT, Thomas Reynolds (1826–98) Scottish genre painter and watercolourist. He studied in Paris at the same time as Du Maurier, with whom he shared a studio, and exhibited four works at the Royal Academy. After 1880 he lived in London and on his estates near Greenock in Scotland. He appears to have given up painting in the 1880s.

SANDY MCALLISTER ('THE LAIRD') in George Du Maurier, *Trilby* (1894)

'There seemed to be an idea abroad that all the characters in [Trilby] . . . were drawn from life, and this belief was confirmed by the excellent portrait of my friend Lamont as the Laird' (Thomas Armstrong, 1912, 'Reminiscences of Du Maurier', in *Thomas Armstrong, A Memoir*, ed. L.M. Lamont, p. 111). *See also* **Millais**, John Everett.

LANDER, Jean Margaret (1829–1903) Actress. Born at Wolverhampton, she was the daughter of T.D. **Davenport** and first appeared on the stage in 1837 as Jean Davenport at the Richmond Theatre, Surrey, in the title role of *Richard III*! She toured in England and Ireland, on the European continent and in America, and in 1849 she paid a second visit to America with such success that she decided to make that country her home. In 1860 she married General Frederick West Lander, a member of a distinguished Massachusetts family, but he died in 1862 as the result of wounds received in the Civil War. She resumed her career on the stage as Mrs Lander, and her last appearance was on 1 January 1877, as Hester Prynne in her own dramatization of *The Scarlet Letter*. She was described as a 'small, beautifully formed lady, with a sweet expressive face, and a voice as clear as a bell' (*New York Herald* (7 February 1865)).

NINETTA CRUMMLES (THE 'INFANT PHENOMENON') in Charles Dickens, *Nicholas Nickleby* (1838–9)

'More than once, I tried to draw her out about *Nicholas Nickleby* and the widely-circulated story that she had been the model of the Infant Phenomenon. The subject was uncongenial to her, for she passed it by' ('The original of the Infant Phenomenon', 1915, interview with Otis Skinner, *The Dickensian* 11 (May): 134).

LANDON, Letitia Elizabeth (1802–38) Poet under the initials L.E.L. She was the author of a number of novels and was visited in her lodgings by William **Maginn**, who helped her compose her verses, get them published, and puffed them as they appeared. There ensued a scandal, as the result of which her engagement to John **Forster** was broken off. In 1838 she married George Maclean, Governor of Cape Coast Castle, where she arrived in August, only to die in October from a dose of prussic acid.

MISS BUNION in W.M. Thackeray, *Mrs Perkins's Ball* (1847)

'She figures we cannot but believe, in Thackeray's inimitable portrait of Miss Bunion' (Logan Pearsall Smith, 1936, *Reperusals and Re-collections*, p. 186).

LANDOR, Walter Savage (1775–1864) Poet and writer. He lived in Florence from 1821 to 1835 and in Bath from 1838 to 1858, whereupon he returned to Florence and remained there until his death. He was among Dickens's close friends from 1839 onwards and stood godfather to his second son, Walter Landor.

LAWRENCE BOYTHORN in Charles Dickens, *Bleak House* (1852–3)

'Mr Boythorn is (between ourselves) a most exact portrait of Walter Savage Landor' (to the Hon. Mrs Richard Watson, 6 May 1852, reproduced in *Letters of Charles Dickens*, 1988, ed. Graham Storey, Kathleen Tillotson and Nina Burgis, Vol. VI, Oxford: Oxford University Press, p. 666). 'If you were the man I took you for . . . you would come to Paris and amaze the weak walls of the house I haven't yet with that steady snore of yours, which I once heard piercing the door of your bedroom on Devonshire Terrace, reverberating all the bell-wire in the hall, so getting outside into the street, playing Eolian harps among the area railings, and going down the New Road like the blast of a trumpet' (to W.S. Landor, 22 November 1846, reproduced in *Letters of Charles Dickens*, 1977, ed. Kathleen Tillotson, Vol. IV, Oxford: Oxford University Press, p. 661); the footnote (2) reads: 'The sound is recalled in *Bleak House*, ch. 9, where Esther is "awakened by Mr Boythorn's lusty snoring".'). *See also* **Clarke**, Charles Cowden.

LANDSEER, Sir Edwin (1802–73) English painter and sculptor. He first exhibited at the Royal Academy at the age of 13. He sculpted the bronze lions at the foot of Nelson's Column in Trafalgar Square in London. His subjects were mostly animals and he was wildly successful until his health broke down in the 1860s.

BRADLEY in Frances Trollope, *The Blue Belles of England* (1842)

'Mrs Trollope's book *is* clever, do you not admit? And Bradley is Edwin Landseer!' (11 January 1842, reproduced in *Elizabeth Barrett to Miss Mitford*, 1954, ed. Betty Miller, London: John Murray, p. 99).

LANE, John (1854–1925) Publisher.

SLIM SCHELM in F.W. Rolfe, *Nicholas Crabbe* (1958)

'Before the end of February he presented himself to his publisher Slim Schelm [John Lane] (a tubby pot-bellied bantam, scrupulously attired and looking as though he had been suckled on bad beer)' (Donald Weeks, 1971, *Corvo*, p. 173). Also identified by Cecil Woolf in his introduction to *Nicholas Crabbe*, 1958, pp. 5–7.

LANGAN, John He was a steward at Richard Lovell **Edgeworth**'s town house from 1782 onwards.

THADY M'QUIRK in Maria Edgeworth, *Castle Rackrent* (1800)

'The real-life origin of Thady McQuirk – Edgeworth's steward John Langan – is well known, since Maria for once made no secret of it. "The only character drawn from the life . . . is Thady himself. . . . He was an old steward (not very old, though, at that time, I added to his age)"' (Marilyn Butler, 1972, *Maria Edgeworth*, Oxford, p. 240).

LANGAR, Nottinghamshire Home of Samuel Butler when he was a boy, his father holding the living of Langar-with-Bramston.

BATTERSBY and CRAMPSFORD in Samuel Butler, *The Way of All Flesh* (1903)

'The general atmosphere of Battersby [is] . . . as faithfully as he could do it, reproduced from Langar. Paleham and Crampsford are also both drawn from Langar' (H. Festing Jones, 1919, *Samuel Butler: author of* Erewhon, 2 vols, London: Macmillan, pp. 24–5).

LANGLEY MILL, Nottinghamshire Situated west of Eastwood.

LUMLEY in D.H. Lawrence, *The Lost Girl* (1920)

'DHL's recreation of Langley Mill, an industrial . . . settlement with (*c*.1910) two iron foundries and a railway wheel and wagon works' (*The Lost Girl*, 1981, ed. John Wathen, Cambridge, p. 373 n. 87:15). '*The Lost Girl* begins in Eastwood – the cinematograph show being in Langley Mill' (to H.A. Piehler, 17 April 1925, reproduced in *The Letters of D.H. Lawrence*, 1932, ed. Aldous Huxley, London: Heinemann, p. 633).

LANGSLOW, Robert (d. 1853) He was called to the Bar in 1823, and from 1832 to 1838 he was Attorney-General of Malta. In 1840 he became Judge of the District Court of Colombo, Ceylon, but he was suspended from office in 1843 and removed in 1844. He was married to a cousin of Thackeray's: 'In the rich, they [his wife and himself] everywhere saw oppression and insolence – in the poor, worth and excellence fettered by misery and degradation; and . . . he has ever waged a crusade against his superiors in office. . . . The government of Ceylon have at last . . . determined on suspending him from his office as judge. . . . The natives of Colombo seem to be unanimous in his favour. . . . But . . . it is most melancholy to see a man . . . sacrificing his all, £1,200 a year, for mistaken principles' (William Ritchie to Miss Augusta Trimmer (later his wife), 23 January 1844, reproduced in *The Ritchies in India . . . Correspondence of William Ritchie*, 1920, ed. Gerald Ritchie, pp. 127–8). The remainder of Langslow's life was spent in England, where he endeavoured fruitlessly to obtain redress for his grievances' (*Letters and Private Papers of W.M. Thackeray*, 1945, ed. Gordon N. Ray, Vol. II, London: Oxford University Press, p. 195 n. 14).

JOHN SEDLEY in W.M. Thackeray, *Vanity Fair* (1847–8)

'It seems likely that certain traits of old Sedley after his ruin are drawn from Langslow' (ibid.).

LANHAM, Charles Trueman ('Buck') (1902–78) Officer in the United States Army. Ernest Hemingway first met him in Normandy, where Lanham was commanding the 22nd Regiment, 4th Infantry. As War Correspondent for *Collier's Magazine*, Hemingway was with the regiment in France, Belgium and Germany, where in the Hürtgen forest it sustained 2,678 casualties in eighteen days. In March 1945, Lanham was promoted to Brigadier-General, and in September he returned to Washington as Chief of Information and Education in the War Department. He remained a firm and close friend until Hemingway's death.

RICHARD CANTWELL in Ernest Hemingway, *Across the River and Into the Trees* (1950)

'[Hemingway wrote to Lanham] that his hero Cantwell was a composite portrait of . . . Charlie Sweeney . . . Lanham, the hard-driving West Pointer, and himself' (Carlos Baker, 1969, *Ernest Hemingway: a life story*, New York, p. 475). *See also* **Hemingway**, Ernest; *Sweeny*, Charles.

LANHYDROCK HOUSE, Cornwall A seventeenth-century house situated two miles south of Bodmin that was partly destroyed by fire but restored in the nineteenth century. It is remarkable for its formal gardens.

ENDELSTOW HOUSE in Thomas Hardy, *A Pair of Blue Eyes* (1873)

'Much of [the description of Endelstow House] is drawn from Lanhydrock House' (F.B. Pinion, 1968, *A Hardy Companion*, London: Macmillan, p. 319).

LANSDOWNE, Henry Petty-Fitzmaurice, Lord (1780–1863) Whig statesman. He was Chancellor of the Exchequer under Grenville in 1806 and was leader of the opposition from 1807 onwards. He entered cabinet in 1827, but resigned in 1828. He was President of the Council under Lord Grey in 1830, and thenceforward intermittently until 1841; he obtained the same office under Lord John Russell in 1846, remaining in that post until 1852. He was in cabinet without office, and was a supporter of the abolition of slavery. He succeeded to the title of 3rd Marquis of Landsdowne in 1809.

DUKE OF ST BUNGAY in Anthony Trollope, *Can You Forgive Her?* (1864) and sequels

'I should say that St Bungay is meant to be "a great Whig duke" rather than a specific portrait, but that ... in the two passages which describe St Bungay's political position [in *Can You Forgive Her* and *Phineas Finn*], Trollope did to some extent use Lansdowne as a model' (J.R. Dinwiddy, 1967–8, 'Who's who in Trollope's political novels', *The Nineteenth Century* 22: 42).

LARDNER, Ring (1885–1933) Sports journalist, short-story writer and humorist.

ABE NORTH in F. Scott Fitzgerald, *Tender is the Night* (1934)

'Abe, composite portrait of Fitzgerald and ... Ring Lardner' (K. Cross, 1949, *Scott Fitzgerald*, p. 87). *See also* **Fitzgerald**, F. Scott.

LARKBEARE HOUSE, Ottery St Mary, Devon The home of Thackeray's mother and stepfather, Major and Mrs **Carmichael-Smyth**, from 1827 to 1835.

FAIROAKS in W.M. Thackeray, *The History of Pendennis* (1848–50)

'In *Pendennis* ... Larkbeare becomes Fairoaks' (*The Letters and Private Papers of W.M. Thackeray*, 1945, ed. Gordon N. Ray, Vol. I, London: Oxford University Press, p. 13 n. 2).

LASCAR SAL Known also as Opium Sal, in the 1860s she kept an opium den in the neighbourhood of Whitechapel that Dickens visited. In 1869, Frederick Wellesley (1844–1931), at the time a young officer in the Coldstream Guards, left an account of a visit c.1864, when he and a group of brother officers were escorted to the den by Charley **Field**: '[The den] belonged to a woman known as "Sally the Opium Smoker". Her hair was perfectly white and she appeared to be very aged. She was lying on her bed close to the wall and by her side was a long narrow shelf on which several white mice were running about. The other beds ... in the middle of the room, were occupied by Lascar sailors ... when we reached the street Field asked us how old we imagined Sally to be, and we all guessed various ages, eighty being the lowest. We were then told that [she] was but twenty six years old' (Frederick Wellesley, 1947, *Recollections of a Soldier-Diplomat*, pp. 75–6).

PRINCESS PUFFER in Charles Dickens, *Edwin Drood* (1870)

'The scene of Jasper's opium smoking [was] a court just beyond the churchyard of St George's-in-the-East, Stepney. The Rev. Harry Jones, rector from 1873 to 1882, mentions that the old crone was known as Lascar Sal, and was living at the time he wrote (1875)' (F.G. Kitton, 1897, *The Novels of Charles Dickens: a bibliography and sketch*, London, p. 231). 'I ought to tell you, perhaps, that the opium smoking I have described, I saw (exactly as I have described it, penny ink-bottle and all) down in Shadwell this last autumn. A couple of the Inspectors of Lodging Houses knew the woman and took me to her as I was making a round with them to see for myself the working of Lord Shaftesbury's Bill' (to Sir John Bowring, 5 May 1870, *Letters of Charles Dickens*, 1938, ed. Walter Dexter, Vol. III, p. 775). All three of the references above are cited in Philip Collins, 1964, 'Inspector Bucket visits the Princess Puffer', *The Dickensian* 60: 89 n. 2.

LASCELLES, Henry G.C., 6th Earl of Harewood Known as Viscount Lascelles until he succeeded his father as Earl of Harewood in 1929, he inherited a vast fortune from his godfather the last Earl of Clanricarde, who was a notorious miser. From 1911 to 1913 he was violently in love with Victoria **Sackville-West**, and in 1922 he married Princess Mary, only daughter of George V.

ARCHDUCHESS HARRIET AND ARCHDUKE HARRY OF FINSTER-AR-HORN in Virginia Woolf, *Orlando* (1928)

'Lord Lascelles appears in *Orlando* as the Archduchess Harriet' (*The Letters of Virginia Woolf*, 1977, ed. Nigel Nicolson, Vol. III, London: Hogarth Press, p. 433 n. 2).

LASSALLE, Ferdinand (1825–64) German socialist and revolutionary activist. He died from wounds received in a duel with a Count von **Racowitz**, who had married Lassalle's earlier love, Helene von Dönniges (**Racowitza**).

SIGISMUND ALVAN in George Meredith, *The Tragic Comedians* (1880)

'My dreadful study of Lassalle and his lass' (to Louisa Lawrence, 11 April 1880, reproduced in *Letters of George Meredith*, 1970, ed. C.L. Cline, Vol. II, Oxford, p. 656). 'In *The Tragic Comedians* [Meredith] shows the genuine and growing richness of love between a man and a woman (in history Ferdinand Lassalle and Helene von Dönniges). ... Meredith's sources were Helene von Racowitza's *Meine Beziehungen zu Ferdinand Lassalle* and J.M. Ludlow's article "Ferdinand Lassalle, the German Social Democrat" in the *Fortnightly Review*' (Gillian Beer, 1970, *Meredith: a change of masks*, p. 137).

LAUNCESTON, Cornwall Situated just over the border from Devon, about four miles north-east of Bodmin Moor.

Sᴛ Lᴀᴜɴᴄᴇ's in Thomas Hardy, *A Pair of Blue Eyes* (1873)

Identified in F.B. Pinion, 1968, *A Hardy Companion*, London: Macmillan.

LAURIE, Sir Peter (1779–1861) A saddler who made a fortune supplying saddles to the Indian Army. In 1832 he was Lord Mayor of London, and from 1839 to 1861 he was Chairman of the Union Bank. He was also a Middlesex magistrate.

Aʟᴅᴇʀᴍᴀɴ Cᴜᴛᴇ in Charles Dickens, *The Chimes* (1844)

'In creating Alderman Cute [Dickens] set out to attack a particular contemporary figure ... Sir Peter Laurie ... [who] had rendered himself particularly obnoxious to humanitarian opinion by his campaign, begun in 1841, to "put down" suicide' (Michael Slater, 1970, 'Dickens's tract for *The Times*', in M. Slater (ed.) *Dickens 1970: centenary essays*, p. 116). 'When I came to consider these things [Sir Peter Laurie's declaration that Jacob's Island, as described in *Oliver Twist*, did not exist], I was inclined to make this preface the vehicle of my humble tribute to Sir Peter Laurie. But I am restrained by a very painful condition. ... For Sir Peter Laurie, having been himself described in a book (as I understand he was, one Christmastime, for his conduct on the seat of justice), it is but too clear that there CAN be no such man!' (Dickens, 1850, preface to *Oliver Twist* ('First cheap' edn), p. viii).

LAVIS, Daisy She was Thomas Wolfe's charwoman at 75 Ebury Street in London from October 1930 until February 1931. She shared with the Russian doctor on the floor below.

Dᴀɪsʏ Pᴜʀᴠɪs in Thomas Wolfe, *You Can't Go Home Again* (1940)

'... the charwoman ... Mrs Lavis, was to become ... Daisy Purvis' (*The Notebooks of Thomas Wolfe*, 1970, ed. Richard S. Kennedy and Paschal Reeves, Chapel Hill, NC: University of North Carolina Press, p. 527).

LAWRENCE, Ada (1887–1948) Afterwards Clarke. Younger sister of D.H. Lawrence. She was co-author, with Stuart Gelder, of *Young Lorenzo: early life of D.H. Lawrence* (1932).

Lᴇᴛᴛɪᴇ Bᴇᴀʀᴅsᴀʟʟ in D.H. Lawrence, *The White Peacock* (1911)

'Lettie, at least in the early chapters, is a close portrait of [Lawrence's] sister Ada' (E. Delavenay, 1972, *D.H. Lawrence: the man and his work . . . 1885–1919*, p. 89).

LAWRENCE, Mrs Bigelow A neighbour of Marion and Henry Adams in Massachusetts.

Mᴀᴅᴇʟᴇɪɴᴇ Lᴇᴇ in Henry Adams, *Democracy* (1880)

'The journal models of Mrs Madeleine Lee and her sister Sybil were the elegant Mrs Bigelow Lawrence ... and her sister Fanny Chapman. Blaine's platonic devotion to Mrs Bigelow once inspired Marian Adams to comment, "If Blaine were a widower, she would not long be a widow"' (Ernest Samuels, 1958, *Henry*

Adams: the middle years, Cambridge, Mass., p. 93). *See also* **Adams**, Henry; **Admas**, Marian.

LAWRENCE, David Herbert (1885–1930) English writer. Born in Eastwood, Nottinghamshire, the son of a miner. He won a scholarship to Nottingham High School, but left to work for a manufacturer of surgical goods. He became a schoolmaster for a time, but after the success of his first novel, *The White Peacock* (1911), he decided to make his living by writing. In 1912 he eloped to Germany with Frieda Weekley (**Lawrence**, below) and they married in 1914 after her divorce. In 1915 he was prosecuted for obscenity on the publication of *The Rainbow* and he left England in 1919, settling first in Mexico and then in Italy, where he eventually died of tuberculosis.

CYRIL BEARDSALL in D.H. Lawrence, *The White Peacock* (1911)

'I have just sent up to Mr Hueffer my novel . . . which is much altered. I have added a third part, have married Lettie and Leslie and George and Meg, and Emily to a stranger and myself [i.e. Cyril Beardsall] to nobody' (to Blanche Jennings, 1 November 1909, reproduced in *The Letters of D.H. Lawrence*, 1979, ed. J.T. Boulton, Vol. I, Cambridge: Cambridge University Press, p. 141; footnote 4 identifies 'myself' as Cyril Beardsall).

RUPERT BIRKIN in D.H. Lawrence, *Women in Love* (1920)

'Birkin . . . may in part be reasonably identified with certain parts of Lawrence' (H.T. Moore, 1951, *The Life and Works of D.H. Lawrence*, p. 156).

CECIL BYRNE in D.H. Lawrence, *The Trespasser* (1912)

'. . . his self-portrait as Cecil Byrne in *The Trespasser*' (Moore, op. cit., p. 79).

FREDERICK ('FREDERICO') in H.D. (Hilda Doolittle), *Bid Me to Live* (1960)

Identified by Helen McNeil in the introduction to *Bid Me to Live*, 1984, pp. viii–ix, and by Perdita Schaffner, in the afterword, p. 187.

DERRICK HAMILTON in Helen Corke, *Neutral Ground* (1933)

'He [D.H. Lawrence] is also the Derrick Hamilton of Helen Corke's novel, *Neutral Ground* . . . when published the book contained an author's note which said . . . "The autobiographical section of this story . . . is a revision of papers, written at intervals during 1910, 1911, 1912, upon some of which Lawrence based his novel *The Trespasser*"' (Moore, op. cit., p. 82).

ALEXANDER HEPBURN in D.H. Lawrence, 'The Captain's Doll' (1923)

'For the Scottish Officer, Lawrence probably borrowed the surface of Donald Carswell . . . but at the end the character becomes Lawrence himself' (H.T. Moore, 1980, *The Priest of Love: a life of D.H. Lawrence*, rev. edn, Harmondsworth: Penguin, p. 431; originally published 1955 as *The Intelligent Heart: the story of D.H. Lawrence*, London: Heinemann). *See also* **Carswell**, Donald.

KINGHAM in Aldous Huxley, *Two or Three Graces* (1926)

'In "Two or Three Graces" Kingham (supposed to be a caricature of Lawrence) tells the writer: "Your great defect is spiritual impotence . . ."' (Sisirkumar Ghose, 1962, *Aldous Huxley*, p. 61). 'Kingham . . . was concocted before I knew

[Lawrence] – at least I'd only seen him once' (Aldous Huxley to Floyd Starkey, quoted in Sybille Bedford, 1973, *Aldous Huxley: a biography*, Vol. I, London: Chatto & Windus, p. 202).

RAWDON LILLY in D.H. Lawrence, *Aaron's Rod* (1922)

'Lawrence and Frieda disport themselves in this exalted company as Lilly and Tanny' (E. Delavenay, 1972, *D.H. Lawrence: the man and his work, 1885–1919*, p. 448).

JAMES LOGAN in Gilbert Cannan, *Mendel* (1916)

'. . . some of L's speeches I recognized' (to S.S. Koteliansky, prior to 12 December 1916, reproduced in Frieda Lawrence, 1961, *The Memoirs and Correspondence*, 1961, ed. E.W. Tedlock, London: Heinemann, p. 218). 'L' is Lawrence. Logan is based on John Currie, in so far as concerns his appearance and the events of his life – or rather, death. The ideas he expresses and the language in which he expresses them are pure Lawrence. But a great deal of this indifferent novel is sub-Lawrentian. *See also* **Currie**, John.

DAVID MARSH in James L. Grant, *Male and Female* (1933)

'. . . based on Lawrence's life, as the author explains in his prefatory note' (G.F. Sims, 1973?, catalogue 85, item no. 334 (antiquarian books)). '[T]he reader who expects from this book a complete life of Lawrence, must . . . be doomed to disappointment. The book makes no pretension to be a literal interpretation of . . . places, incidents and people as they entered into the life of Lawrence' (preface to *Male and Female*, 1933, p. ix).

CYRIL MERSHAM in D.H. Lawrence, 'A Modern Lover' (1934)

'The . . . short story "A Modern Lover" . . . provides an interesting self-portrait of Lawrence at this time [Christmas 1909]. The hero, Cyril Mersham (who has so many points in common with the Cyril/Lawrence of *The White Peacock*) . . . returns to the farmhouse home of his friend Muriel' (Delavenay, op. cit., p. 64).

MARK MORIER in D.H. Lawrence, 'Glad Ghosts' (1928)

'Morier, who is Lawrence, complains that all the guests at dinner mutter inaudibly, whereas the plain fact is that he was going deaf' (Richard Aldington, 1950, Introd. to *The Woman Who Rode Away*, Harmondsworth: Penguin, p. 9).

MARK RAMPION in Aldous Huxley, *Point Counter Point* (1928)

'Rampion is just some of Lawrence's notions on legs. The actual character of the man was incomparably queerer and more complex than that' (Aldous Huxley to Floyd Starkey, quoted in Bedford, op. cit., p. 202).

DAVID RAYNER in Compton Mackenzie, *The Four Winds of Love: The South Wind* (1937)

'In a letter to [E. Nehls] (12 March 1953), Sir Compton Mackenzie wrote: "You will find an impression of Lawrence in . . . *The Four Winds of Love, The South Wind*. . . . I called Lawrence Daniel Rayner' (E. Nehls, 1957, *D.H. Lawrence: a composite biography*, Madison, Vol. I, p. 570 n. 41).

EDWARD SEVERN in D.H. Lawrence, 'The Old Adam' (1934)

'Lawrence himself is Edward Severn' (Moore, *Life and Works*, op. cit., p. 122). '[The] setting is clearly that of Lawrence's Croydon years as the lodger in the home of Mr and Mrs Jones' (Delavenay, op. cit., p. 111).

RICHARD LOVAT SOMERS in D.H. Lawrence, *Kangaroo* (1923)

'[M]any pages and scenes of *Kangaroo* ... show the strange battle of wills between [Lawrence] and his wife when, after nearly ten years of marriage, he laboured ... unavailingly to prove to her that the basis of marriage is not perfect love, but perfect submission of the wife to the husband' (Richard Aldington, 1950, Introd. to *Kangaroo*, Harmondsworth: Penguin, p. 9).

LAWRENCE, Frieda (1879–1956) Second daughter of Baron Friedrich von **Richthofen**. In 1899 she married Ernest **Weekley**, a head of the Department of Modern Languages at Nottingham University and D.H. Lawrence's former French instructor, with whom she had two daughters and a son. She met Lawrence in April 1912, and a month later they eloped. They were married in 1914 after her divorce from Weekley. After Lawrence's death in 1930, Weekley invited Frieda to became his wife again. In 1950 she married Angelo Ravagli, whom she and Lawrence had met when they rented the Villa Bernarda from him in 1925.

URSULA BRANGWEN in D.H. Lawrence, *The Rainbow* (1915)

'I also felt that the character was inclined to fall into two halves. ... It came of trying to graft on to the character of Louie [Burrows] the character, more or less, of Frieda' (to Edward Garnett, 29 January 1914, reproduced in *The Letters of D.H. Lawrence*, Vol. II: *1913–1916*, 1981, ed. George T. Zytaruk and James T. Boulton, Cambridge: Cambridge University Press, p. 142). *See also* **Burrows**, Louisa.

KATHERINE FARQUHAR in D.H. Lawrence, 'The Border Line' (1928)

'The woman [Alan Anstruther] had married ... was undisguisedly Frieda, and her journey to Strasbourg ... was the Lawrences' journey east [in February 1924]' (H.T. Moore, 1960, *The Intelligent Heart: the story of D.H. Lawrence*, Harmondsworth: Penguin, p. 404; originally published 1955, London: Heinemann).

ELSE FREDERICK in H.D. (Hilda Doolittle), *Bid Me to Live* (1960)

Identified by Helen McNeil in the introduction to *Bid Me to Live*, 1984, pp. viii–ix, and by Perdita Schaffner in the afterword, p. 187.

PAULA JABLONOWSKY in D.H. Lawrence, 'Love Among the Haystacks' (1930)

'The indifference with which she beats her employer the vicar is perhaps the most typical of all the features which make of her a barely disguised version of Frieda von Richthofen' (E. Delavenay, 1972, *D.H. Lawrence: the man and his work* ... *1885–1919*, p. 189).

LYDIA LENSKY (AFTERWARDS BRANGWEN) in D.H. Lawrence, *The Rainbow* (1915)

'Her personality is, of course, a skilful transposition of that of Frieda, from whose behaviour and past life Lawrence has borrowed widely' (Delavenay, op. cit., p. 360).

TANNY LILLY in D.H. Lawrence, *Aaron's Rod* (1922)

See under **Lawrence**, D.H.

KATY MAARTENS in Aldous Huxley, *The Genius and the Goddess* (1955)

'[My conception of the goddess] is very clear to me, because I used to know very well a specimen of the breed. This was Frieda Lawrence . . . Frieda (and Katy is a non-German and less Rabelaisian specimen of Frieda) was a woman of enormous strength and vitality. . . . Everything that Katy–Frieda does, she does with her whole heart. I feel that, in essence, this person I knew and then re-imagined in another context is solidly there' (to Nancy Kelly, 21 November 1957, reproduced in *Letters of Aldous Huxley*, 1969, ed. Grover Smith, pp. 830–2).

PAULA MOEST in D.H. Lawrence, 'New Eve and Old Adam' (1934)

'Nowhere has Lawrence painted so realistic a portrait of his wife as in these pages' (Delavenay, op. cit., p. 190).

NELLY OLIVER in Gilbert Cannan, *Mendel* (1916)

'I heard a day or two ago from Mrs Carswell that there was a portrait of me in "Mendel". I suppose I am the murdered woman. We live and learn, I never recognized myself!' (to S.S. Koteliansky, prior to 12 December 1916, reproduced in Frieda Lawrence, 1961, *The Memoirs and Correspondence*, ed. E.W. Tedlock, London: Heinemann, p. 218). *See also* **Henry**, Dolly.

MARY RAMPION in Aldous Huxley, *Point Counter Point* (1928)

'Rampion and Mary . . . took most of their features from Lawrence and Frieda' (George Woodcock, 1972, *Dawn and the Darkest Hour: a study of Aldous Huxley*, London: Faber & Faber, p. 157).

COUNTESS JOHANNA ('HANNELE') ZU RASSENTLOW in D.H. Lawrence, 'The Captain's Doll' (1923)

'Frieda . . . [was a ready-made original] for the Countess Hannele' (Moore, op. cit., p. 352).

HILDEGARDE RAYNER in Compton Mackenzie, *The Four Winds of Love: The South Wind* (1937)

In Mackenzie's autobiography, *My Life and Times: Octave 4* (1965), he describes a visit to the Lawrences in Chesham in almost exactly the words he had used in the novel to describe the visit paid to the Rayners.

HARRIET SOMERS in D.H. Lawrence, *Kangaroo* (1923)

'[The] Somers–Harriet contest is . . . marvellously true to the characters of Lawrence and his wife' (Richard Aldington, 1950, Introd. to *Kangaroo*, Harmondsworth: Penguin, p. 9).

LAWRENCE, John Arthur (1846–1924)   He married Lydia Beardsall (**Lawrence**, below) in 1875; D.H. Lawrence was their son. He worked at **Brinsley Colliery** from the age of 7 until his death.

FRANK BEARDSALL in D.H. Lawrence, *The White Peacock* (1911)

'This estranged father is clearly John Arthur Lawrence, slightly raised in social status' (E. Delavenay, 1972, *D.H. Lawrence: the man and his work . . . 1885–1919*, p. 90).

WALTER MOREL in D.H. Lawrence, *Sons and Lovers* (1913)

'Morel was John Arthur Lawrence' (Ada Lawrence and G. Stuart Gelder, 1931, *Young Lorenzo: early life of D.H. Lawrence*, Florence, p. 11).

LAWRENCE, Lydia (1851–1910) Daughter of George **Beardsall**. She became a schoolteacher and in 1875 she married John Arthur **Lawrence**. D.H. Lawrence was their son.

GERTRUDE MOREL in D.H. Lawrence, *Sons and Lovers* (1913)

'Gertrude Coppard was Lydia Beardsall' (Ada Lawrence and G. Stuart Gelder, 1931, *Young Lorenzo: early life of D.H. Lawrence*, Florence, p. 11).

LAWRENCE, Thomas Edward (1888–1935) Educated at Jesus College, Oxford, he became a member of the British archaeological team that worked on excavations at Carkemish, Syria, from 1911 to 1914. He worked for the Arab Bureau from 1914 to 1916, and was Adviser to the Emir Faisal for the following two years. He raised Arab levies and in 1918 he broke up Turkish armies and led Arab troops up to Damascus. In 1921 and 1922 he was Adviser on Arab Affairs to the Colonial Office. He obtained the appointment of Faisal as king of Iraq and of Abdullah as ruler of Transjordan. From 1922 to 1935 he served in the ranks of the Royal Air Force under the assumed name of T.E. Shaw. He was a Research Fellow of All Souls, Oxford, and was the author of *The Seven Pillars of Wisdom* (1935). He was killed in a motorcycling accident in Dorset.

SANDY ARBUTHNOT in John Buchan, *The Courts of the Morning* (1929)

'Sandy . . . who so distinctly was *not* T.E. Lawrence in the earlier books, has now come to be very like him. A "tallish" man in *Greenmantle*, he has shrunk . . . down to T.E. Lawrence's five foot four inches, and he is saddled with Lawrence's "finical conscience"' (J. Adam Smith, 1965, *John Buchan*, p. 262). *See also* **Herbert**, Aubrey.

LAWRENCE, William Ernest (1878–1901) Second son of John Arthur and Lydia **Lawrence**, and elder brother of D.H. Lawrence. At the age of 21 he went to London.

WILLIAM MOREL in D.H. Lawrence, *Sons and Lovers* (1913)

'The real role of elder brother . . . is given by Lawrence . . . to the [second] son, William Ernest, whom the novelist calls William Morel . . . the first part of *Sons and Lovers* contains a detailed description of his youth' (E. Delavenay, 1972, *D.H. Lawrence: the man and his work . . . 1885–1919*, p. 7). 'Ernest – William of "Son [sic] and Lovers"' (Ada Lawrence and G. Stuart Gelder, 1931, *Young Lorenzo: early life of D.H. Lawrence*, Florence, p. 29).

LAWSON, Cecil (1851–82) Landscape painter. His mother, Elizabeth Lawson, attempted to entertain Shaw in her house in Chelsea, London, in 1880.

CYRIL SCOTT in George Bernard Shaw, *Immaturity* (1930)

'. . . the prototype, for Cyril Scott' (G.B. Shaw, 1965, *Collected Letters, 1874–1897*, ed. Dan H. Laurence, p. 28 n.). 'Lawson was a genius: I met him a few times about 11 or 12 years ago; and he suggested to me one of the characters in my first novel. . . . That is, the character is a rude character of him; I do not mean that he suggested it verbally' (to James Stanley Little, 26 August 1889, reproduced in ibid., p. 220).

LAWSON, George (1749–1820) He was Professor of Theology in the associate secession (Burgher) Church of Scotland from 1787 to 1820 and was said to have known the Scriptures by heart. He was the author of *Exposition of the Book of Proverbs* (1821).

JOSIAH CARGILL in Sir Walter Scott, *St Ronan's Well* (1823)

'. . . is said to have been the original of Josiah Cargill' (*Collected Letters of Thomas and Jane Welsh Carlyle*, 1970, Vol. I, Durham, NC, p. 357 n. 50). *See also* **Duncan,** Alexander.

LAWSON, John Howard (1894–1977) American playwright and screenwriter. Born Simon Levy. He was serving as an ambulance driver during the First World War when he met Dos Passos, who became a close friend. In the 1920s he wrote plays and became a committed Marxist, and in 1927 was one of the **New Playwrights**. In 1928 he went to Hollywood and in 1933 he became the first president of the Screen Writers' Guild. In 1934 he joined the Communist Party, and in 1948 he was one of the Hollywood Ten subpoenaed to appear before the House Committee of Un-American Activities; in 1950 he was sentenced to one year's imprisonment for refusing to co-operate. He was blacklisted and went to Mexico.

J.E.D. MORRIS in John Dos Passos, *Most Likely to Succeed* (1954)

'Dos Passos's highly jaundiced afterthoughts about his New Playwright friends and Lawson in particular are contained in . . . *Most Likely to Succeed*' (D. Aaron, *Writers on the Left*, New York, p. 441 n. 10). Morris is an easily recognizable portrait of Lawson. The character is described by G.A. Knox and H.M. Stahl in *Dos Passos and "The Revolting Playwrights"* (1964, Lund, p. 88) as a 'composite and representative figure'.

LAYARD, Brownlow Villiers (d. 1853) Born in Dublin, he was MP for Carlow from 1841–7. He committed suicide.

GINGERLY BROWN in Benjamin Disraeli, *Coningsby* (1844)

Identified in a key in *Notes and Queries* (8th series) 3 (13 May 1893): 363. *See also under* **Bright**, John.

LAYARD, John (1891–1972) Anthropologist. Educated at King's College, Cambridge, he was a pupil of the anthropologist and psychologist W.H.R. Rivers, with whom he visited Malekula, New Hebrides, in 1914–15; he published his conclusions twenty-five years later in *The Stones of Malekula*. He was a follower of Homer Love, and in later life he was a follower of Jung and became an analytical psychologist. **Auden** and Isherwood met him in Berlin and acquired from him the theories of Georg Groddsale, who held that diseases arise from elements in the human personality rather than from purely physical causes. Layard was psychologically unstable and in 1939 attempted suicide by shooting himself in the mouth; the attempt was a failure and he recovered completely. He was a distant cousin of Sir A.H. Layard, the archaeologist.

BARNARD in Christopher Isherwood, *Lions and Shadows* (1938)

'While in Berlin, Wystan [Auden] had met the anthropologist John Layard – "Barnard" in *Lions & Shadows*' (Christopher Isherwood, 1976, *Christopher and His Kind*, New York, p. 9).

EDWARD BLAKE in Christopher Isherwood, *The Memorial* (1932)

'Christopher Isherwood was so fascinated by the story [of the attempted suicide] that he put a version of it into his novel *The Memorial*, basing his account on what Layard told him about the experience' (Humphrey Carpenter, 1981, *W.H. Auden: a biography*, p. 101).

LAYCOCK, Sir Robert (1907–68) Chief of combined operations in 1943–8. He was the son of Brigadier-General Sir Joseph Laycock, who at one time was the lover of Daisy, Countess of Warwick. In 1935 he married Angela Dudley Ward.

TOMMY BLACKHOUSE in Evelyn Waugh, the *Sword of Honour* trilogy (1952–61)

'Sir Robert Laycock (the Tommy Blackhouse of the novels), one of the few soldiers . . . whom Evelyn unconditionally admired' (Eric Newby, 1973, 'Lush places', *Evelyn Waugh and His World*, ed. David Pryce-Jones, p. 94). 'The real life and career of Bob Laycock were dissimilar to those of . . . the invented Tommy Blackhouse, but if Evelyn had never met Bob I think the picture of Tommy Blackhouse would have been different' (Christopher Sykes, 1975, *Evelyn Waugh*, London: Collins, p. 375).

LEA, Luke (1879–1945) Newspaper publisher and United States Democrat Senator. In 1907 he founded *Nashville Tennessean*. In the 1920s he controlled an empire of banks, insurance companies and property; the structure collapsed in 1930, and in 1931 he was convicted, with his oldest son, of conspiracy to defraud the Central Bank and Trust Company of Asheville, North Carolina. In 1934 he was sentenced to a term of imprisonment; he was paroled in 1936 and in 1937 he was granted a full pardon.

BOGAN MURDOCK in Robert Penn Warren, *At Heaven's Gate* (1943)

'Twenty-seven men in all were indicted, including Colonel Luke Lea . . . who . . . served as a model for the villain of . . . *At Heaven's Gate*' (F.C. Watkins, 1957, *Thomas Wolfe's Characters: portraits from life*, Norman, Okla., p. 123–4).

LEACH, Sir John (1760–1834) He was MP for Seaford from 1806 to 1816 and became Vice-Chancellor of England in 1818, Master of the Rolls in 1827, and a member of the judicial committee of the Privy Council in 1833.

MONSIEUR VELOUR in Lord Brougham, *Albert Lunel* (1844)

'[In Michael Sadleir's copy of *Albert Lunel*] in Brougham's hand, are identifications of certain characters. Thus ... Vol. III ... p. 155 [identifies] M. Velour with Sir John Leach' (Michael Sadleir, 1951, *XIX Century Fiction*, Vol. I, London: Constable, and Los Angeles: California University Press, p. 57).

LEBEL, Joachim-Joseph (b. 1807) Director of the boarding house of the Athénée Royale, the boys' school in Brussels adjoining the Pensionnat Héger, where Charlotte Brontë was a pupil and later a governess from 1842 to 1844. He had emigrated from France as a refugee from the July Revolution.

MONSIEUR PELET in Charlotte Brontë, *The Professor* (1857)

'M. Pelet was not only drawn from life, he was depicted with startling veracity so far as externals are concerned; and I am assured by those who knew him that no character in the Brussels chapters of the two books [*Villette* and *The Professor*] has been presented with greater truth as to appearance and style. M. Pelet was no other than M. Lebel' (Marion H. Spielmann, 1916, 'Charlotte Brontë in Brussels', *Times Literary Supplement* (13 April): 178).

LEBENDER, Lena From 1897 to 1902 she was housekeeper to Gertrude and Leo Stein at 215 East Biddle Street, Baltimore, when both, and later Gertrude alone, were studying medicine at Johns Hopkins University.

ANNA in Gertrude Stein, 'The Good Anna', *Three Lives* (1909)

'Anna ... is patterned directly after Lena Lebender ... with her two dogs, Jack and Rags ... now named Peter and Rags' (James R. Mellow, 1974, *The Charmed Circle: Gertrude Stein and company*, London: Phaidon Press, p. 72).

LE BLANC, Thomas John (1894–1948) Professor of Preventative Medicine. In 1919 and 1920 he was a member of the Rockefeller Institute, and in 1920 and 1921 he was a field scientist for the Rockefeller Foundation. He worked with the United States Government on promoting public health awareness.

TERRY WICKETT in Sinclair Lewis, *Arrowsmith* (1925)

Identified in Mark Schorer, 1961, *Sinclair Lewis: an American life*, New York: McGraw-Hill, p. 418. *See also* **Lewis**, Sinclair; *Northrop*, J.H.

LE BRASSEUR & OAKLEY Solicitors in New Court, Lincoln's Inn, London, where Arnold Bennett was a clerk from 1889 to 1893; the firm flourished in Great Russell Street well into the present century.

CURPET & SMYTHE in Arnold Bennett, *The Man from the North* (1898)

'The life of the solicitor's office is to be found in the novel, too, down to the exact salary of twenty-five shillings; Le Brasseur and Oakley are transformed into Curpet and Smythe' (Margaret Drabble, 1975, *Arnold Bennett: a biography*, London: Weidenfeld & Nicolson, p. 49).

LEDIG-ROWOHLT, Heinrich (1908) German publisher. Born in Leipzig, he was the illegitimate son of Ernst Rowohlt of Rowohlt Verlag, and in 1931 he joined his father's publishing house in Berlin. An editor in the firm, he became

Thomas Wolfe's closest friend in Germany, and was subsequently Managing Director of Rowohlts.

FRANZ HEILDIG in Thomas Wolfe, *You Can't Go Home Again* (1940)

'The character, Franz Heildig . . . is based on Ledig' (*Beyond Love and Loyalty: the letters of Thomas Wolfe and Elizabeth Nowell*, 1983, ed. R.S. Kennedy, p. 44 n.).

LEDRU-ROLLIN, Alexandre Auguste (1807–74) French lawyer and populist politician. In 1848 he was Minister of the Interior in the provisional government, and in 1849, after leading an armed insurrection, he escaped to London, where he lived in exile until 1870.

FELIX DROLLIN in Benjamin Disraeli, *Lothair* (1870)

Identified in 'Key to *Lothair*', *Notes and Queries* 183 (12 September 1942): 173.

LEE, Ivy Ledbetter (1877–1934) American publicist. One of the earliest public relations officers, in 1903 he was Publicity Manager for Seth Low in the campaign for the mayoralty of New York, and in 1912 he took on the Pennsylvania Railroad Company; other clients were J.D. Rockefeller, Bethlehem Steel Company, the Chrysler company and the ITR Company of New York. He visited Russia twice, and strongly advocated US recognition of the Soviet government.

J. WARD MOOREHOUSE in John Dos Passos, *U.S.A.* (1938)

'*Interviewer* . . . in . . . *42nd Parallel* . . . J. Ward Moorehouse . . . might be taken . . . as based on Ivy Lee . . .? *Dos Passos* Well, Ivy Lee did have something to do with Moorehouse because I met Ivy Lee in Moscow . . . when I was writing the book . . . I had several rather interesting conversations with him. . . . I had done the first few chapters . . . before I went, and then J. Ward Moorehouse was just emerging. I think those conversations . . . probably had something to do with his completed portrait' (Dos Passos, interviewed by David Sanders, 1969, 'The art of fiction XLIV', *The Paris Review* 12 (46): 157–8).

LEEK, Staffordshire

AXE and MANEFOLD in Arnold Bennett, *Anna of the Five Towns* (1902)

'"Manefold" and "Axe" are the same town (of which I changed the name), and that town is Leek' (to John Squire, 18 April 1915, reproduced in *Letters of Arnold Bennett*, 1968, ed. James Hepburn, Vol. II, London: Oxford University Press, p. 364).

LEES-MILNE, James (b. 1908) Writer. Educated at Eton and at Magdalen College, Oxford, from 1936 to 1966 he was on the staff of the National Trust. He was a lifelong friend and correspondent of Nancy Mitford.

ALBERT GATES in Nancy Mitford, *Highland Fling* (1931)

Identification based upon private information. *See also* **Byron**, Robert.

LEGARD, Jane, Lady (d. 1833) Née Aston, of Aston, Cheshire, in 1782 she married Sir John **Legard**.

LADY LATHAM in Joseph Conrad, *Suspense* (1925)

'Conrad even retained the exact [maiden] name "Aston" of Lady Legard, who in the novel becomes Lady Latham [née Aston]' ((G. Jean-Aubry, 1925, 'The inner history of Conrad's *Suspense'*, *Bookman's Journal* 13 (49): 7 n.).

LEGARD, Sir John (*c.*1758–1807) 6th Baronet of Garston, Yorkshire. In 1782 he married Jane Aston (**Legard**, above); they had no children.

SIR CHARLES LATHAM in Joseph Conrad, *Suspense* (1925)

'. . . Sir John Legard (who . . . becomes Sir Charles Latham)' (G. Jean-Aubry, 1925, 'The inner history of Conrad's *Suspense'*, *Bookman's Journal* 13 (49): 7).

LEIGH, Geraldine (1845–1915) Daughter of Henry Francis Leigh (b. 1820, youngest child of Augusta Leigh, and **Byron**'s nephew), she was born four months after her parents' marriage. In 1882 she inherited Byron's estate jointly with a cousin.

GWENDOLEN HARLETH in George Eliot, *Daniel Deronda* (1876)

'The saddest thing to be witnessed [in the gambling rooms of the Kursaal at Homburg] is the play of Miss Leigh, Byron's grand niece, who is only 26 years old, and is completely in the grip of this mean, money-raking demon. It made me cry to see her fresh young face among the hags and brutally stupid men around her' (to John Blackwood, 4 October 1872, *The George Eliot Letters*, 1955, ed. Gordon S. Haight, Vol. V, London: Oxford University Press, p. 314). 'In his journal for 26 Sept. Lewes speaks of her as "having lost 500£ looking feverish and excited. Painful sight!"' (ibid., n. 6). 'In his review of Cross [*Life of George Eliot*] in the *Nineteenth Century* (17 March 1885), Lord Acton says: 'a young woman over whom George Eliot wept in the gambling rooms at Homburg, and who remembers the meeting, served as the model for Gwendolen' (ibid.).

LEIGH, John Porter Coal and corn merchant of Hackney, London. He lived in Lea Bridge Road, Lower Clapton, London, and his daughter Mary Anne was the friend of Maria **Beadnell**.

OCTAVIUS BUDDEN (FORMERLY BAGSHAW) in Charles Dickens, 'Mr Minns and His Cousin', *Sketches by Boz* (1836)

'Leigh . . . was the original of Octavius Bagshaw in "A Dinner in Poplar Walk" (Octavius Budden when the tale was renamed "Mr Minns and his Cousin" for *Sketches)'* (*Letters of Charles Dickens, 1820–1839*, 1965, ed. Madeline House and Graham Storey, Oxford: Oxford University Press, p. 2 n. 5).

LEIGH, Mrs J.P. She was married to John Porter **Leigh**.

MRS JOSEPH PORTER in Charles Dickens, 'Mrs Joseph Porter', *Sketches by Boz* (1836)

'Marianne Leigh, the girl who made mischief between Dickens and Maria Beadnell . . . lived at Clapton, her mother is supposed to be presented in the malicious Mrs Joseph Porter' (John Butt and Kathleen Tillotson, 1957, *Dickens at Work*, London: Methuen, p. 48 n. 1). 'Mrs Leigh . . . is referred to in the earlier part of the *Bill of Fare* as "A Curry, smart, hot and biting," while [Dickens] in her epitaph writes: "'Bout scandal or spreading reports without need Of course I'd say nothing – how could I indeed?" which points at once to the sketch "Mrs Joseph Porter"' (J.H. Stonehouse, 1931, *Green Leaves*, p. 13).

LEIGHTON, Frederic, Lord (1830–96)   Painter. Born in Scarborough, Yorkshire, he was the son of a doctor and studied in Europe. He was President of the Royal Academy from 1878 to 1896. He became the 1st Baron Leighton of Stretton. He died unmarried.

MONSIEUR KIOWSKI in Adelaide Kemble, *A Week in a French Country-House* (1867)

'Miss Barrington told me that . . . the painter . . . is Leighton' (entry for 14 December 1874, in *The Journals of Lady Knightley of Fawsley*, 1915, ed. Julia Cartwright, p. 216). Leighton illustrated the book; like Kiowski he spoke perfect French, and indeed German and Italian.

LORD MELLIFONT in Henry James, 'The Private Life' (1891)

'These reflections [on Robert Browning and Lord Leighton] became . . . "The Private Life". . . . Lord Mellifont is a man whose personality pervades English life' (Leon Edel, 1963, *Henry James: the middle years, 1884–1894*, pp. 214, 215).

GASTON PHOEBUS in Benjamin Disraeli, *Lothair* (1870)

Identified in 'Key to *Lothair*', *Notes and Queries* 183 (12 September 1942): 173.

LENNOX, Lord William Pitt (1799–1881)   Miscellaneous writer and novelist. Son of the 4th Duke of Richmond, he was the brother of the 5th Duke and married the opera singer Mary Ann Paton (afterwards Wood) in 1824; they were divorced in 1831. He was MP for King's Lynn from 1831 to 1835.

LORD PRIMA DONNA in Benjamin Disraeli, *Vivian Grey* (1826–7)

Identified as Lord Wm. L—— in a key given in *The Star Chamber* (24 May 1826): 114; reprinted in *Vivian Grey*, 1904 (centenary edn), ed. Lucien Wolf, Vol. II, pp. 361–2. The full name appears on a copy of the key held in the British Museum. Lucien Wolf concludes that Disraeli was not responsible for the key.

LEONARD, Benny (1896–1947)   World lightweight champion. In the fight for the welterweight championship at the New York Hippodrome on 26 June 1922, he met Jack **Britton** and fouled him in the thirteenth round of a fifteen-round contest; Britton thereby won the fight on a foul.

WALCOTT in Ernest Hemingway, 'Fifty Grand', *Men Without Women* (1927)

'The . . . story . . . was based on the welterweight championship bout . . . on June 26, 1922' (Carlos Baker, 1969, *Ernest Hemingway: a life-story*, New York, p. 157). *See also* **Walker**, E.M.

LEOPOLD I, King of the Belgians (1790–1865)   Fourth son of Francis Frederick, Duke of Saxe-Coburg Saalfeld, he was elected the first king of independent Belgium in 1831. He was an uncle of Queen Victoria.

THE KING OF LABASSECOEUR in Charlotte Brontë, *Villette* (1853)

'There can be little doubt that the character of the King of Labassecoeur ... represents the attempts of Charlotte Brontë to arrive at an understanding of the character and temperament of Leopold I, King of the Belgians, by facial study, on some unrecorded occasion when [she] found herself in the royal presence' (Herbert Wroot, 1935, *Sources of Charlotte Brontë's Novels: persons and places*, Shipley, Yorks., p. 186).

LEOPOLD II, King of the Belgians (1865–1909) Son of **Leopold I**. In 1884 he was granted sovereignty over the Congo by the Berlin Congress, but he was generally censured for the oppression of natives of the region.

DUC DE MERSCH in Joseph Conrad and Ford Madox Ford, *The Inheritors* (1901)

Identified in Jocelyn Baines, 1967, *Joseph Conrad*, p. 239.

de LESPINASSE, Julie (1732–76) The natural daughter of the Countess D'Albon, for ten years she was companion to Madame du **Deffand**, through whom she became a friend of the philosopher d'Alembert. She was the mistress of the Marquis de Mora and of the Comte de **Guibert**; her letters to the latter were published as the *Lettres de Mlle de Lespinasse*.

JULIE LE BRETON in Mrs Humphry Ward, *Lady Rose's Daughter* (1903)

'Some years before the story of *Lady Rose's Daughter* was planned and written, I was struck in reading Sainte-Beuve's study of Julie de Lespinasse by the dramatic possibilities of the situation involved in the well-known quarrel between Mlle de Lespinasse and Madame du Deffand' (Introd. to *Lady Rose's Daughter*, 1911 (Westmorland edn), p. vii). 'With regard to Julie's subsequent story, no doubt the passion felt by her prototype for M. de Guibert contributed something' (ibid., p. ix).

LETCOMBE BASSETT, Oxfordshire A village on the northern side of the hills between Fawley, Berkshire and Wantage.

CRESSCOMBE in Thomas Hardy, *Jude the Obscure* (1895)

Identified in Denys Kay-Robinson, 1972, *Hardy's Wessex Reappraised*, Newton Abbot, and in F.B. Pinion, 1968, *A Hardy Companion*, London: Macmillan.

LETCOMBE REGIS, Oxfordshire A village located between Letcombe Bassett and Wantage.

FENSWORTH in Thomas Hardy, *Jude the Obscure* (1895)

Identified in Denys Kay-Robinson, 1972, *Hardy's Wessex Reappraised*, Newton Abbot, and in F.B. Pinion, 1968, *A Hardy Companion*, London: Macmillan.

LEVENS HALL, Cumbria Situated south of Kendal, it was the largest Elizabethan house in Cumberland or Westmorland (see Nikolaus Pevsner, 1967, *Westmorland (Buildings of England* series), Harmondsworth: Penguin, pp. 268

ff.). Mrs Humphry Ward spent March to May there in 1897, working on *Helbeck of Bannisdale*.

BANNISDALE in Mrs Humphry Ward, *Helbeck of Bannisdale* (1898)

'Bannisdale ... is compounded of Levens, and of Sizergh' (introd. to *The Writings of Mrs Humphry Ward*, Vol. IX: *Helbeck of Bannisdale*, 1911 (Westmorland edn), London: Smith, Elder, p. xvi). *See also* **Sizergh Castle**.

LEVERSON, Ada (1862–1933) Novelist. She was the friend and protector of Oscar **Wilde**.

THE SIB in Wyndham Lewis, *The Apes of God* (1930)

'Lewis is also very severe with ... Ada Leverson (the Sib), who is the reigning pet of Lord Osmund and supplies him with saucy gossip about the figures of the 1890s' (Jeffrey Meyers, 1980, *The Enemy: a biography of Wyndham Lewis*, London: Routledge & Kegan Paul, p. 176).

EDITH OTTLEY in Ada Leverson, *Love's Shadow* (1908) and others

'Edith Ottley ... may be seen ... to personify – insofar as any character does or can ... the woman Ada Leverson felt herself to be' (Colin MacInnes, quoted in Violet Wyndham, 1963, *The Sphinx and Her Circle: a biographical sketch of Ada Leverson, 1862–1933*, London: Deutsch, p. 35).

LEVERSON, Mrs George The daughter of a 'dignitary of the Church of England, she became the second wife of George Leverson, Ada Leverson's father-in-law.

LADY KELLYNCH in Ada Leverson, *Bird of Paradise* (1914)

'A composite portrait drawn by Ada of her mother-in-law and her step-mother-in-law' (Violet Wyndham, 1963, *The Sphinx and Her Circle: a biographical sketch of Ada Leverson, 1862–1933*, London: Deutch, pp. 17, 18). *See also* **Leverson**, Henrietta.

LEVERSON, Henrietta (d. 1890) Née Johansson. She was the first wife of George Leverson, and was the mother-in-law of Ada Leverson.

MARY CROFTON ('AUNT WILLIAM') in Ada Leverson, *The Twelfth Hour* (1907)

'Aunt William ... was taken from Henrietta' (Violet Wyndham, 1963, *The Sphinx and Her Circle: a biographical sketch of Ada Leverson, 1862–1933*, London: Deutch, p. 17).

LADY KELLYNCH in Ada Leverson, *Bird of Paradise* (1914)

See under **Leverson**, Mrs George.

LEVESON-GOWER, Lord Ronald (1845–1916) Fourth son of the 2nd Duke of Sutherland.

LORD HENRY WOOTTON in Oscar Wilde, *The Picture of Dorian Gray* (1891)

'When ... *The Picture of Dorian Gray* was published, the Venice crowd [of 1890] instantly recognised Lord Ronnie, as the original of ... Lord Henry Wootton'

(Jehanne Wake, 1988, *Princess Louise, Queen Victoria's Unconventional Daughter*, p. 302).

LEWES, George Henry (1817–78) Writer. Born in London, he went to Germany in 1838 for two years to study the language and literature. Upon his return to London he wrote contributions for the *Morning Chronicler* and the *Penny Encyclopaedia*. From 1851 to 1854, in association with Thornton Hunt, he was Editor of the *Leader*, and in 1865 he founded the *Fortnightly Review*. He wrote *The Life and Works of Goethe* (1855), and also published various works on physiology and psychology. In 1841 he married Agnes Jervis, with whom he had four sons, but from 1854 he lived with George Eliot, as her *de facto* husband.

DANIEL DERONDA in George Eliot, *Daniel Deronda* (1876)

'An examination of Lewes' autobiographical introduction to an 1866 article on Spinoza [*Fortnightly Review* 4: 385–406] ... raises the strong possibility that Lewes may have been the prototype for Deronda. ... Lewes, writing about his own youth, remembers ... "a small club of students [that held] weekly meetings in ... a tavern in Red Lion Square, Holborn." ... [He] recalls ... that his group was composed of men of diverse types. ... Eliot creates a situation closely corresponding to Lewes' account when she introduces Deronda to the group in the smoke-filled parlour of the Hand and Banner for the first time. ... Clearly Lewes' autobiographical account and George Eliot's fictional account correspond with an exactitude that cannot be overlooked' (Hannah Goldberg, 1957, 'George Henry Lewes and *Daniel Deronda*', *Notes and Queries* 202: 357–8). *See also* **Bond**, Edward; **Goldsmid**, Colonel Albert; **Gurney**, Edmund; **Louis**, Alfred Hyman.

LEWIS, Grace Hegger She married Sinclair Lewis in 1914, they were divorced in 1928, and in 1933 she married Telesforo Casanova de Ojea.

FRAN DODSWORTH in Sinclair Lewis, *Dodsworth* (1929)

'The model for this portrait is obvious enough' (Mark Schorer, 1963, *Sinclair Lewis: an American life*, London: Heinemann, p. 517; originally published 1961, New York: McGraw-Hill). 'Gossip still has it that during rehearsals [of the dramatized version], Lewis repeatedly misspoke [the] name [of the actress playing Fran] and would call out to her, "Come on, Gracie, you can be much bitchier than that!"' (ibid., p. 596).

MADELINE FOX in Sinclair Lewis, *Arrowsmith* (1925)

'Both Madeline Fox and Joyce Lanyon ... bear certain biographical resemblances to Mrs Lewis' (Schorer, op. cit., p. 420).

SUSAN HALE in Grace Hegger Lewis, *Half a Loaf* (1931)

The identification is based upon obvious parallels.

JOYCE LANYON in Sinclair Lewis, *Arrowsmith* (1925)

See above under MADELINE FOX.

RUTH WINSLOW in Sinclair Lewis, *The Trail of the Hawk* (1915)

'The details of the life they lived [at Port Washington, Long Island, in 1914] are to be found . . . in the last chapters of *The Tail of the Hawk*' (Schorer, op. cit., p. 215). 'The courtship of Ruth Winslow has the character of his own' (ibid., p. 223).

LEWIS, Percy Wyndham (1882–1957) Artist and writer. He was a leader of the Vorticist movement, and in 1920 he met James Joyce in Paris (a meeting engineered by Ezra **Pound**); their relations became cool after Lewis attacked Joyce in his book *Time and the Western Man* (1927).

HENRY DEBINGHAM in Edith Sitwell, *I Live Under a Black Sun* (1937)

'Wyndham Lewis is the villain, Henry Debingham, looking like "a rather sinister, piratic, formidable Dago"' (John Pearson, 1978, *Façades: Edith, Osbert and Sacheverell Sitwell*, London: Macmillan, p. 324).

PROFESSOR JONES in James Joyce, *Finnegans Wake* (1939)

'Lewis is the model for Professor Jones and for the Ondt that is outwitted by the Joycean Gracehoper' (Jeffrey Meyers, 1980, *The Enemy: a biography of Wyndham Lewis*, London: Routledge & Kegan Paul, p. 141).

THE ONDT in James Joyce, *Finnegans Wake* (1939)

See above.

LEWIS, Rosa (1867–1952) She was the proprietor of the **Cavendish Hotel** from 1902 to 1952. She furnished and ran the hotel like a country house: one signed the visitors' book on leaving, not on arrival. 'You treat my house like an hotel', she cried to one of her guests. A superlative cook, she started life in the kitchens of the Comte de Paris at Sheen House, and until the outbreak of the First World War would go to the houses of her patrons and cook their grand dinners and their ball suppers. Both as a cook and as a woman, she was a great favourite with Edward VII, and as a young woman she was said to have the most beautiful neck and shoulders in London. In middle and later life she had the largest collection of dud cheques, and it was her practice to add the bills of her more impecunious clients on to the accounts of those who could afford to pay both.

LOTTIE CRUMP in Evelyn Waugh, *Vile Bodies* (1930)

'Only two identifications can be made [in *Vile Bodies*] . . . the [second] is of . . . Lottie Crump . . . with Mrs Lewis. Lottie's manner of speech and manner of running her hotel were identical with those of Rosa Lewis. [She] was infuriated by the book . . . [and], as I can testify personally, after the appearance of [the novel] she forbade Evelyn the house' (Christopher Sykes, 1975, *Evelyn Waugh*, London: Collins, p. 100).

MRS OLIVER in Carroll Carstairs, *A Generation Missing* (1938)

'In [his] novel . . . he gives a contemporary picture of the hotel . . . and its owner, "Mrs Oliver"' (Daphne Fielding, 1964, *The Duchess of Jermyn Street*, p. 95).

LOUISA ROSE in Shane Leslie, *The Anglo-Catholic* (1929)

'In *The Anglo-Catholic* she appears as Louisa' (Fielding, op. cit., p. 169). And a very good, affectionate and exact portrait it is.

LEWIS, Sinclair (1885–1951) American novelist. Born in Sauk Center, Minnesota, he was educated at Overlin College and at Yale. In 1914 he married Grace Hegger (**Lewis**, above), but they divorced in 1928. He later married Dorothy Thompson. He refused the Pulitzer Prize for *Arrowsmith*, but accepted the Nobel Prize for Literature in 1930 and was the first American writer to receive it.

FRANK ARCHER in Bernard de Voto, *We Accept With Pleasure* (1934)

'De Voto . . . could not resist creating a character, Frank Archer . . . in the image of Sinclair Lewis' (Mark Schorer, 1963, *Sinclair Lewis: an American life*, London: Heinemann, p. 287; originally published 1961, New York: McGraw-Hill).

CARL ERICSON in Sinclair Lewis, *The Trail of the Hawk* (1915)

'Carl Ericson, for whom Lewis himself in some ways was the prototype' (Schorer, op. cit., p. 158).

JULIUS 'RED' FLATMAN in Harry Kemp, *More Miles* (1926)

'Harry Kemp attempted to memorialize him as . . . Julius "Red" Flatman, in his now forgotten autobiographical novel *More Miles*' (Schorer, op. cit., p. 77).

TIMOTHY HALE in Grace Hegger Lewis, *Half a Loaf* (1931)

'[Sinclair Lewis] as represented by the protagonist, Timothy Hale' (Schorer, op. cit., p. 209).

LARRY HARRIS in William Rose Benét, *The Dust Which is God* (1941)

'Benét left two recollections of their friendship at Carmel, one . . . in his poeticized autobiography . . . where Harry Lewis appears as Larry Harris' (Schorer, op. cit., p. 148 n.).

CAROL KENNICOTT in Sinclair Lewis, *Main Street* (1920)

'Later, Charles Breasted was to ask him the question direct . . . "What about Carol Kennicott – isn't she a portrait of you?" He seemed startled and said that only a very few people had guessed her identity. "Yes," he added, "Carol is 'Red' Lewis – always groping for something she isn't capable of attaining, always dissatisfied"' (Schorer, op. cit., p. 286 n.).

LLOYD McHAIG in Thomas Wolfe, *You Can't Go Home Again* (1940)

'There are modifications in minor facts to disguise the prototype of McHaig but they are transparent, and the general account . . . is substantially literal. The physical portrait of Lewis is perfect and no less is the representation of his behaviour' (Schorer, op. cit., p. 558).

CASS TIMBERLANE in Sinclair Lewis, *Cass Timberlane* (1945)

'It is his own thinly veiled love story' (Schorer, op. cit., p. 738).

TERRY WICKETT in Sinclair Lewis, *Arrowsmith* (1925)

Lewis and Hemingway had both been staying at the Gritti Palace in Venice in March 1949, when Hemingway was writing *Across the River and Into the Trees* (1950). '[When] the novel was published, it was widely assumed that Lewis had found a ... place in the dramatis personae as a certain anonymous "son of a bitch" ... observed by Colonel Cantwell in Harry's Bar' (Schorer, op. cit., p. 780). *See also* **Le Blanc**, T.J.; **Northrop**, J.H.

LEWIS, Revd W. Reuben He was Minister of the Congregational Church at St Neots, Huntingdonshire, until his resignation in 1851.

REVD THEOPHILUS CARDEW in Mark Rutherford, *Catharine Furze* (1893)

'Clyde Binfield has suggested to me that the plot of *Catharine Furze*, where Rev. Mr Cardew, an evangelical Anglican, neglects his wife to pay court to Catharine, could have been generated by a scandal at St Neots Congregational Church. The minister, W. Reuben Lewis, resigned (28 Feb. 1831) and admitted ... "certain indiscretions". A committee of inquiry, presided over by Jukes of Bedford, found a Mrs Joyce guilty of receiving "improper" letters from the Rev. Lewis. He subsequently went to Australia. In the novel, Mr Cardew goes to a "far distant" parish' (Valentine Cunningham, 1976, *Everywhere Spoken Against: dissent in the Victorian novel*, Oxford: Clarendon Press, p. 275 n. 2).

LEXER, Erich (1867–1937) Distinguished German surgeon. In 1928 he was appointed to the Chair of Surgery in Munich and he was Director of the München-Schwäbing Hospital. He treated Wolfe for the head injury he received during the Oktoberfest of 1928.

GEHEIMRAT BECKER in Thomas Wolfe, *The Web and the Rock* (1939)

'On ... September 30 [1928 in Munich] ... Wolfe had his celebrated fight with a group of German revelers. The following day he entered a hospital ... [and] was treated by Geheimrat Lexer. Wolfe immediately determined to make literary capital of his misfortune. ... After his release he continued to work on the hospital scenes, portions of which ... finally appeared ... as Chapter 48 of *The Web and the Rock*' (*The Notebooks of Thomas Wolfe*, 1970, ed. Richard S. Kennedy and Paschal Reeves, Chapel Hill, NC: University of North Carolina Press, p. 197; see also p. 201 (entry for October 10)).

LEYLAND, Frederick Richards (1831–92) Founder of the Leyland line of steamers, of Liverpool. He was the last man in Liverpool, and probably England, who wore frills habitually. He lived in London at 49 Princes Gate, where the Peacock Room was painted by **Whistler**; the decorations included a caricature of Leyland as a grasping bird with its claws on a pile of money.

SYMONDS in Theodore Watts-Dunton, *Aylwin* (1899)

Identified in T. St E. Hake, 1902, 'Aylwin', *Notes and Queries* (9th series) 9 (7 June): 450–2, and 10 (2 August): 89–91; reprinted in *Aylwin* (World's Classics), 1914, Oxford, App. II.

LIDDELL, Alice Pleasance (1852–1934) Second daughter of Henry Liddell, Dean of Christ Church, Oxford, in 1880 she married Reginald Hargreaves. Her sisters were Louisa, Edith, Rhoda and Violet **Liddell**.

ALICE in Lewis Carroll, *Alice's Adventures in Wonderland* (1865) and *Through the Looking-Glass* (1872)

'Rainald [Knightley] and I and Alice Liddell – a most fascinating girl, the original of *Alice in Wonderland* – dined with Prince Leopold in his own rooms' (entry for Whit-Sunday 1875, in *The Journal of Lady Knightley of Fawsley*, 1915, ed. Julia Cartwright, p. 278). 'One point, which was not settled for a long time and until after many trials and consultations, was whether Alice ... should have her hair cut straight across her forehead as Alice Liddell had always worn it, or not. Finally it was decided that Alice in Wonderland should have no facial resemblance to her prototype' (Caryl Hargreaves, 1932, 'Alice's recollections of Carrollian days', *Cornhill Magazine* (NS) 73 (July): 9). 'Her own story in her own words' (op. cit.: 1).

LACIE in Lewis Carroll, *Alice's Adventures in Wonderland* (1865)

'The three children figure in the Dormouse's story as "Elsie" (L.C. for Louisa Charlotte), "Lacie" (anagram of "Alice") and "Tillie" (short for Matilda, Edith's nickname)' (R.L. Green, 1948, 'Lewis Carroll and the making of Alice', *Notes and Queries* 193 (10 July): 301).

LIDDELL, Edith (1854–76) Third daughter of Henry Liddell, Dean of Christ Church, Oxford, she became engaged to Anthony Harcourt of Nuneham, but died before she was married. Her sisters were Louisa, Alice, Rhoda and Violet **Liddell**.

TILLIE in Lewis Carroll, *Alice's Adventures in Wonderland* (1865)

See under **Liddell**, Alice Pleasance.

LIDDELL, Louisa Charlotte (1849–1930) Eldest daughter of Henry Liddell, Dean of Christ Church, Oxford, in 1874 she married William Baillie Skene of Pitlour. Her sisters were Alice, Edith, Rhoda and Violet **Liddell**.

ELSIE in Lewis Carroll, *Alice's Adventures in Wonderland* (1865)

See under **Liddell**, Alice Pleasance.

THE LORY in Lewis Carroll, *Alice's Adventures in Wonderland* (1865)

'Louisa Charlotte ... becomes the Lory in "The Pool of Tears"' (Caryl Hargreaves, 1939, 'Alice's recollections of Carrollian days', *Cornhill Magazine* (NS) 73 (July): 3).

LIDDELL, Rhoda (1858–1949) Fourth daughter of Henry Liddell, Dean of Christ Church, Oxford. Her sisters were Louisa, Alice, Edith and Violet **Liddell**.

THE ROSE in Lewis Carroll, *Through the Looking-Glass* (1872)

'The Rose – Alice's small sister Rhoda' (R.L. Green, 1969, 'Alice's rail-journey', *Notes and Queries* 214: 218).

LIDDELL, Violet (1864–1927) Fifth daughter of Henry Liddell, Dean of Christ Church, Oxford. Her sisters were Louisa, Alice, Edith and Rhoda **Liddell**.

THE VIOLET in Lewis Carroll, *Through the Looking-Glass* (1872)

'In addition to the three Liddell girls, of whom Carroll was so fond, there were two younger . . . sisters, Rhoda and Violet. They appear . . . as the Rose and Violet' (*The Annotated Alice*, 1970, with introd. and notes by Martin Gardner, Harmondsworth: Penguin, p. 203).

LIDDON, Henry Parry (1829–90) Educated at King's College School, London, and at Christ Church, Oxford, from 1870 to 1882 he was Ireland Professor of Exegesis at Oxford. He became Canon and Chancellor, respectively, of St Paul's Cathedral, London, in 1870 and 1886, and for twenty years his sermons there were a central fact of London life. He was an associate of Keble and **Pusey**.

DR SEYDON in W.H. Mallock, *The New Republic* (1877)

'Mallock has Liddon in mind when Lady Ambrose remarks that Seydon preaches beautiful sermons' (John Lucas, 1975, Introd. to *The New Republic*, Leicester, pp. 23–4). *See also* **Pusey**, E.B.

LIEVEN, Christopher Andreivich, Prince (d. 1839) Minster Plenipotentiary in Berlin in 1810, in 1812 he became Russian Ambassador in London, being recalled in 1834 and appointed Governor to the young Prince Alexander (later Tsar Alexander II). He accompanied the Prince on his travels and died in Rome. He married Dorothea Khristorovna (**Lieven**, below).

THE RUSSIAN AMBASSADOR in Benjamin Disraeli, *Coningsby* (1844)

Identified in a key in *Notes and Queries* (8th series) 3 (13 May 1893): 363. *See also under* **Bright**, John.

LIEVEN, Dorothea Khristorovna (1784–1857) Sister of General Alexander Khristorovich, who later became Minister of Police under Tsar Nicholas I, in 1810 she married Count (later Prince) **Lieven**. In 1828 she was appointed dame d'honneur to the Tsarina and created 'Princess'. 'She was celebrated in the diplomatic world by her talents and knowledge of public affairs, and during her residence in London no society was more sought after' (*Journal of Mary Frampton*, 1886, p. 150). When she was in England from 1812 to 1834, she was the mistress of Prince **Metternich**. After the death of her husband in 1839, she settled in Paris; she was the mistress of the French statesman Guizot from 1837 until her death.

COMTESSE LEINSENGEN in Lady Charlotte Bury, *The Exclusives* (1830)

Identified in *Key to the Royal Novel 'The Exclusives'*, 1830, Marsh & Miller; reproduced in Michael Sadleir, 1951, *XIX Century Fiction*, 2 vols, London: Constable, and Los Angeles: California University Press, pp. 73–4.

THE RUSSIAN AMBASSADRESS in Benjamin Disraeli, *Coningsby* (1844)

Identified in a key in *Notes and Queries* (8th series) 3 (13 May 1893): 363. *See also under* **Bright**, John.

LIFE MAGAZINE A US periodical, largely photographic, that was founded in 1936 by Henry Robinson **Luce**.

VITAL in William Brinkley, *The Fun House* (1961)

'Whenever any of [Luce's employees] wrote a book, [Mrs Luce] would give him a ... copy. ... The collection grew to number several novels that caustically depicted a Luce-like publishing empire' (John Kobler, 1968, *Henry Luce*, p. 258; a footnote lists *The Fun House* among these novels).

LIND, James (1736–1812) Born in Gorgie, near Edinburgh, in 1778 he married Anne Elizabeth Mealey, companion to the Duchess of Portland at Bulstrode; they had five children. Educated at Edinburgh University, in 1770 he became a Fellow of Edinburgh College of Physicians, and in 1775 he became a Fellow of the Royal Society. In 1772 he was chosen as one of the scientists to accompany James Cook in the *Resolution*; he spent heavily on equipping himself with scientific instruments for the voyage, but the arrangements fell through and his expenses were never recovered. In 1782 he settled in Windsor, where he was acquainted with the Royal Family. He came into contact with many of the boys at Eton, including **Shelley**, who said of him: 'I owe to that man far, ah! far more than I owe to my father; he loved me and I shall never forget our long talks' (Thompson Cooper, 1893, in Leslie Stephen (ed.), *The Dictionary of National Biography*, London: Oxford University Press, s.v. Lind, J.).

ALPHONSE FRANKENSTEIN in Mary Wollstonecraft Shelley, *Frankenstein; or The Modern Prometheus* (1818)

'In the biographical ... ancestry of this ideal father William Godwin undoubtedly had a share; but more probably was owed ... to Dr Lind' (Christopher Small, 1972, *Ariel Like a Harpy: Shelley, Mary and Frankenstein*, p. 105). *See also* **Godwin**, William.

MONSIEUR GOTHA in T.J. Hogg, *Memoirs of Prince Alexy Haimatoff* (1813)

'The venerable pedagogue Gotha seems to have been suggested by Shelley's account of Dr Lind' (Richard Garnett, 1891, in Leslie Stephen (ed.), *The Dictionary of National Biography*, London: Oxford University Press, s.v. Hogg, T.J.).

WALDMAN in Mary Wollstonecraft Shelley, *Frankenstein; or the Modern Prometheus* (1818)

'He also enters into the person of Waldmann [sic]' (Small, op. cit., p. 104). 'He lives on in Shelley's verse as the old hermit in "Laon and Cyntha"' (*The Dictionary of National Biography*, London: Oxford University Press).

LIND, Jenny (1820–77) Swedish soprano. She studied under **García** and in 1849 retired from opera, then devoting herself to concert singing and oratorio. She became naturalized as a British subject in 1859 and settled in England.

CLARA BENETTE in Elizabeth Sara Sheppard, *Charles Auchester* (1853)

Identified in Michael Sadleir, 1951, *XIX Century Fiction*, Vol. I, London: Constable, and Los Angeles: California University Press, p. 320; and in an anonymous typed key laid in a copy of the first edition of *Charles Auchester* which is now in the possession of the present author.

LINGARD, Captain William Known as the Rajah Laut (King of the Sea), a name that he gave to his last ship, he was a captain and trader sailing from

Singapore from the 1860s onwards; he had a monopoly of the trade in Berau. The first recorded mention of him dates from 1861, but nothing is known of him after 1887.

Tom Lingard in Joseph Conrad, *Almayer's Folly* (1895)

'How far the stories are founded upon fact . . . cannot here be determined; but it is certain that Captain Thomas Lingard, the "Rajah Laut" . . . was well known for many years in the Eastern Isles as . . . a man of strong and upright character. At the same time, the man as he is here set before us is not an accurate portrait of the man as he was' (A.K., 1896, review of *Almayer's Folly* and of *An Outcast of the Islands, Indian Magazine and Review* 27 (306): 301). Norman Sherry gives the real Lingard's name as 'William' (see Norman Sherry, 1966, *Conrad's Eastern World*, Cambridge, p. 102). *See also* **Brooke**, Sir James.

Stein in Joseph Conrad, *Lord Jim* (1900)

'. . . the man known to Conrad as having established trading posts at Berau and Bulungan was Captain Lingard. Lingard was, like Stein, a merchant adventurer. . . . Conrad. . . was not drawing solely upon Wallace for his character of Stein . . . for . . . Lingard . . . contributed' (Sherry, op. cit., pp. 144–5). *See also* **Allen**, Charles; **Bernstein**, Dr; **Mesman**, Mr; **Wallace**, Alfred Russel.

LINGARD, William James ('Jim') (1862–1921) Nephew of Captain William **Lingard**, he joined his uncle in the East *c*.1876. By 1887 he represented Lingards at the trading station of Berau and was a person of some influence in the trading area of Berau and Bulungan in North Borneo.

Jim in Joseph Conrad, *Lord Jim* (1900)

'According to Mr Cools [a resident in Berau since 1904] Jim Lingard was called Tuan Jim and, according to Captain Craig, Lord Jim by the officers of the Vidar "thanks to the swaggering manner he assumed"' (J.D. Gordon, 1941, *Joseph Conrad: the making of a novelist*, Cambridge, Mass., p. 58). 'It was not a swaggering manner of a physique that Conrad found in Jim Lingard, but the devotion of a native woman and a native servant, possibly his name, his position and influence in the jungle and the general inexplicableness of his being in Berau at all' (Norman Sherry, 1966, *Conrad's Eastern World*, Cambridge, pp. 135–6). 'The analogies between the Jim of *Lord Jim* and Jim Lingard are based on . . . inevitable similarities [elements to be found in the lives of most European settlers at that time]' (Z. Najder, 1983, *Joseph Conrad: a chronicle*, Cambridge: Cambridge University Press, p. 100). *See also* **Brooke**, Sir James; **Williams**, Augustine Podmore.

LISZT, Franz (1811–86) Hungarian composer and pianist. He first played in public at the age of nine and was sent to study in Vienna. He settled in Paris in 1823, though he made a number of trips to England between 1824 and 1827. Between 1835 and 1839 he lived with the Comtesse d'Agoult with whom he had three children, including a daughter Cosima, who married Wagner. In 1847 he met Princess Carolyne zu Sayn-Wittgenstein and they lived together for some years. In 1848 he went to Weimar to direct opera and concerts and to teach, but resigned in 1861. In 1865 he received minor orders in the Church of Rome and was known as Abbé.

JULIUS KLESMER in George Eliot, *Daniel Deronda* (1876)

'Franz Liszt has been generally accepted as the model since 1885, when Lord Acton asserted positively that he "became Klesmer". ["George Eliot's Life", *The Nineteent Century* (17 March 1885): 483]. When George Eliot knew Liszt . . . in his forty-third year it was his sweetness, tenderness and benignity that impressed her. None of these qualities can be seen in . . . Klesmer, nor do his . . . features resemble . . . Liszt's' (Gordon S. Haight, 1968, *George Eliot*, p. 489). *See also* **Rubinstein**, Anton.

LITTLE EASTON, Essex The home of H.G. Wells and his wife from 1912 to 1930.

MATCHINGS EASY in H.G. Wells, *Mr Britling Sees It Through* (1916)

'The background to the story is Little Easton' (N. Mackenzie and J. Mackenzie, 1973, *The Time-Traveller: the Life of H.G. Wells*, p. 310).

LITTON MILL, Derby Located near Tideswell, about four miles north-west of Bakewell.

DEEP VALLEY MILL in Frances Trollope, *Michael Armstrong, the Factory Boy* (1840)

'[O]wned by Ellice Needham . . . the setting of Litton Mill "at the bottom of a sequestered glen, and surrounded by rugged rocks, remote from any human habitation", answers completely to that of Deep Valley Mill' (W.H. Chaloner, 1960, 'Mrs Trollope and the early factory system', *Victorian Studies* 4 (2): 164). The description of Litton Mill comes from John Brown's *Memoir of Robert Blincoe* (1828), which describes the sufferings of a boy apprentice at Litton Mill. 'The real name of this valley (which most assuredly is no creation of romance) is not given, lest an action for libel should be the consequence' (Mrs Trollope, 1840, *Michael Armstrong*, Vol. II, p. 149 n.).

LITVINOV, Maxim Maximovich (1876–1951) Russian diplomat. In 1918 he was the Russian diplomatic representative in London, and from 1930 to 1939 he was the USSR Commissar to Foreign Affairs; he was dismissed in 1939 but reappointed in 1941, and remained in the position until 1946. In 1916 he married Ivy Low, daughter of Walter **Low**.

MAXIM LIBIDNIKOV in D.H. Lawrence, *Women in Love* (1920)

'When *Women in Love* came out . . . Litvinov may have been surprised to find in it a minor character named Maxim Libidnikov' (H.T. Moore, 1960, *The Intelligent Heart: the story of D.H. Lawrence*, Harmondsworth: Penguin, p. 302; originally published 1955, London: Heinemann). *See also* **Koteliansky**, S.S.

LIVERIGHT, Horace (1886–1933) American publisher. He was the founder (1918) and President of Boni & Liveright, and the Publisher of *The Modern Library*. He published the works of Ernest **Hemingway**, Theodore **Dreiser** and others, and in 1928 rejected Thomas Wolfe's *Look Homeward, Angel*.

HYMAN RAWNG in Thomas Wolfe, *The Web and the Rock* (1939)

'The publisher to whom Wolfe had first submitted *Look Homeward, Angel*. Wolfe was angry about the rejection. . . . Later he satirized Liveright as Mr Rawng' (*The Notebooks of Thomas Wolfe*, 1970, ed. Richard S. Kennedy and Paschal Reeves, Chapel Hill, NC: University of North Carolina, p. 386 n. 24). The editor who read the manuscript and wrote the letter of rejection was R.S. Smith; perhaps he was the original Mr Rawng.

LLOYD, James

RODERICK ROBTHETILL in Thomas Love Peacock, *Crotchet Castle* (1831)

'Roderick Robthetill [was] modelled on . . . [Rowland Stephenson's] clerk James Lloyd who absconded from London in December 1828 and sailed for Savannah' (*Crotchet Castle*, 1969, ed. Raymond Wright, Harmondsworth: Penguin, p. 279 n. 4 (to ch. XI)).

LLOYD GEORGE, David (1863–1945) Welsh statesman. He became a solicitor and began his political career in 1890 as an advanced Liberal for Carnarvon Boroughs. He was President of the Board of Trade from 1905 to 1908, and Chancellor of the Exchequer from 1908 to 1915. He was appointed Minister of Munitions in 1915 and in 1916 became War Secretary, superseding **Asquith** as coalition Prime Minister and remaining in office until 1922. In 1921 he negotiated with Sinn Fein and conceded the first Irish Free State, which ultimately led to his own downfall and that of the Liberal party the following year. He remained an MP until his death, in which year he was also made 1st Earl of Dwyfor.

ANDY CLYTH in Arnold Bennett, *Lord Raingo* (1926)

'Andy Clyth plays in the political career of . . . Raingo the part Lloyd George is supposed to have played in the career of D.A. Thomas [i.e. Lord Rhondda]. . . . As to Clyth's great speech in the House of Commons about the Manpower Bill, the quotations . . . from it in the novel are actually taken from the speech Lloyd George delivered . . . on April 9th, 1919' (Louis Tillier, 1969, *Studies in the Sources of Arnold Bennett's Novels*, pp. 164–5).

LOCKHART, John Gibson (1794–1854) Educated at Glasgow University and at Balliol College, Oxford, he was called to the Bar and in 1817 became a contributor to *Blackwood's Magazine*. He was Editor of the *Quarterly Review* from 1825 to 1853, and in 1825 and 1826 he was involved with John **Murray** and Disraeli in the daily newspaper, the *Representative*, which failed after just six months. In 1820 he married Sophia, elder daughter of Sir Walter **Scott**, and in 1837–8 he published *Life of Scott*. He was the author of four novels.

FREDERICK CLEVELAND in Benjamin Disraeli, *Vivian Grey* (1826–7)

'Cleveland . . . is clearly Lockhart' (Robert Blake, 1966, *Disraeli*, London: Eyre & Spottiswoode, p. 39).

LOCKHART, John Hugh (1821–1831) Elder son of J.G. **Lockhart** and his wife Sophia, Sir Walter Scott's daughter. He was delicate from infancy.

HUGH LITTLEJOHN in Sir Walter Scott, *Tales of a Grandfather* (1827–9)

'[T]he Hugh Little John of Scott's *Tales of a Grandfather*' (*The Dictionary of National Biography*, London: Oxford University Press, s.v. Lockhart, J.G.). 'All here ... not forgetting little John Hugh or as he is popularly stile[d] Hugh Littlejohn send loving remembrances' (to Joanna Baillie, 18 July 1823, reproduced in *The Letters of Sir Walter Scott*, 1935, ed. H.J.C. Grierson, Vol. VIII, London: Constable, p. 58).

LOCKIE LONGLEGS (*fl.* 1817) A Scot of eccentric appearance, he was presented to Washington Irving by Sir Walter **Scott** during Irving's visit to Abbotsford in 1817.

ICHABOD CRANE in Washington Irving, 'The Legend of Sleepy Hollow', *The Sketch Books of Geoffrey Crayon, Gent* (1820)

'The recent publication of a new letter from Irving to Walter Scott ["Washington Irving to Walter Scott: two unpublished letters", *Studies in Scottish Literature* 3 (October 1965): 116] ... suggests that [the] description [of the physical appearance of Crane] ... was inspired by an experience which [Irving] had during his 1817 visit at Abbotsford. In this letter, written (3 Nov. 1819) while Irving was working on *The Sketch Book*, [Irving] referred ... to his introduction from Scott to "that worthy wight Lockie Longlegs, whose appearance I shall never forget striding along the profile of the knoll in his red nightcap, with his flimsy garments fluttering about him"' (Benn Harris McClary, 1968, 'Ichabod Crane's Scottish origin', *Notes and Queries* 213: 29).

LOEB, Harold (b. 1891) A member of the American banking family; his mother was a Guggenheim. As a young man, he founded and edited the avant-garde magazine *Broom*. During the 1920s he was in Paris and became a friend of Ernest Hemingway; he was one of those who pressed Boni & Liveright to publish *In Our Time* (1925). In 1925 he was one of the party at the fiesta Pamplona, and wrote his own account in *The Way It Was* (1959).

ROBERT COHN in Ernest Hemingway, *The Sun Also Rises* (1926)

'Harold Loeb's version ... does not specifically identify any actual person with the fictional characters. Yet it is clear from his narrative that he associates ... himself (remotely) with Robert Cohn' (Carlos Baker, 1969, *Ernest Hemingway: a life story*, New York, p. 93 n. 28). Also identified in a hand-written key 'given me by Hemingway', on the fly-leaf of a copy of *The Sun Also Rises* owned by Mrs Louis Henry Cohn.

LOEB, Jacques (1859–1924) Biologist. Born in Mayen, Germany, he moved to the United States in 1891, where he became a professor at Chicago, California, and the Rockefeller Institute for Medical Research, successively. He was the originator of the theory of tropism, accounting for certain behavioural phenomena.

MAX GOTTLIEB in Sinclair Lewis, *Arrowsmith* (1925)

'Loeb seems to have changed the image of the laboratory scientist ... through the character of Max Gottlieb ... drawn after Loeb' (Ellen Moers, 1970, *Two Dreisers*, London: Thames & Hudson, p. 241; originally published 1969, New York: Viking). *See also* **Novy**, Frederick.

LOFTUS, Marie Cecilia ('Cissy') (1876–1943) Music hall singer and actress. The daughter of the actress Marie Loftus, she made her début at the Oxford Music Hall in 1893 and played Peter Pan in the 1905 revival. In 1894 she married Justin Huntly McCarthy, the novelist, historian and dramatist, but their marriage was dissolved in 1899; she married A.W. Waterman in 1926. Max Beerbohm, writing to Reggie **Turner** in 1893, professed a passion for her, and Shaw said she had beauty, genius and a personality that touched the audience.

JENNY MERE in Max Beerbohm, *The Happy Hypocrite* (1897)

'Jenny Mere . . . and we recall that Mistress Mere was one of Max's names for her – is the Cissey he used to watch from the stalls of the theatre' (David Cecil, 1964, *Max: a biography*, p. 150).

LOMASNEY, 'Czar' Martin (1859–1932) Mayor of Boston. He dominated Democrat politics in Boston between 1892 and 1915.

HUGHIE DONNELLY in Joseph Dineen, *Ward Eight* (1936)

'A strong resemblance exists between Hughie Donnelly and . . . Lomasney' (J. Blotner, 1966, *The Modern American Political Novel*, p. 76 n. 39).

LOMBARD, Warren P. (1855–1939) Professor of Physiology at the University of Michigan from 1892 to 1923.

JOHN A. ROBERTSHAW in Sinclair Lewis, *Arrowsmith* (1925)

Identified in Mark Schorer, 1961, *Sinclair Lewis: an American life*, New York: McGraw-Hill, p. 418.

LONDON, Jack (John Griffith) (1876–1916) American novelist. Born in San Francisco, he was the son of an itinerant astrologer and a spiritualist. He made a living by many legal and illegal means, including robbing the oyster beds, working in a canning factory and a jute mill, signing on a sealing ship at the age of 17, which took him to the Arctic and Japan, and joining the Klondike gold rush of 1897. His experiences provided material for his works, which brought him wealth and success in his lifetime, although he is thought to have committed suicide.

MARTIN EDEN in Jack London, *Martin Eden* (1909)

'His autobiographical hero, Martin Eden' (Kunitz and Haycraft, 1942, *Twentieth Century Authors*, New York, p. 845, s.v. London).

ERNEST EVERHARD in Jack London, *The Iron Heel* (1908)

'According to Ernest Untermann, who spent several years with London on his ranch after 1910, Everhard was a composite of three people: Jack London, Eugene V. Debs, and Untermann himself' (Philip S. Foner (ed.), 1958, *Jack London: American rebel*, Berlin, p. 114). *See also* **Debs**, E.V.; **Untermann**, Ernest.

LONDON HOUSE, Eastwood, Nottinghamshire A drapery owned by George **Cullen** when D.H. Lawrence lived in Eastwood as a boy and a young man.

MANCHESTER HOUSE in D.H. Lawrence, *The Lost Girl* (1920)

'[George Cullen's] shop, London House, named by Lawrence, Manchester House, was stocked with beautiful creations bought by him in London' (Ada Lawrence and G. Stuart Gelder, 1931, *Young Lorenzo*, Florence, p. 273).

LONDONDERRY, Charles Vane-Tempest-Stewart, Lord (1851–1915) He succeeded to the title of 6th Marquess of Londonderry in 1884. He was Viceroy of India from 1886 to 1889, and from 1902 to 1905 he was the first President of the Board of Education. In 1875 he married Theresa Susey Helen (**Londonderry**, below).

LORD TEMPLECOMBE in Victoria Sackville-West, *The Edwardians* (1930)

See under **Londonderry**, Lady.

LONDONDERRY, Charles William Stewart, 3rd Marquis of (1778–1854) Afterwards Vane, he was the half-brother of Lord Castlereagh. From 1794 to 1810 he had a distinguished military career, and in 1814 he was Ambassador at Vienna during the Congress.

COLONEL VON TRUMPETSON in Benjamin Disraeli, *Vivian Grey* (1826–7)

Identified as M——s of L—d—y in a key given in a pamphlet published in 1827 by William Marsh. This key is discussed by Lucien Wolf in his notes to *Vivian Grey* (1904 (centenary edn), Vol. II, p. 364), with the conclusion that Disraeli was not responsible for the key.

LONDONDERRY, Frances Anne Emily Stewart, 3rd Marchioness of (1800–65) In 1819 she married the 3rd Marquis of **Londonderry**. She was a noted hostess of her day, and at one time was the mistress of Prince **Gortchakoff**.

MARCHIONESS OF ALMACKS in Benjamin Disraeli, *Vivian Grey* (1826–7)

Identified as Marchioness of L——y in a key given in *The Star Chamber* (24 May 1826): 114, reprinted in *Vivian Grey* (1904 (centenary edn), ed. Lucien Wolf, Vol. II, pp. 361–2. The full name appears on a copy of the key held in the British Museum. Lucien Wolf concludes that Disraeli was not responsible for the key.

LONDONDERRY, Theresa Susan Helen Vane-Tempest-Stewart, Lady (1856–1919) Eldest daughter of the 19th Earl of Shrewsbury, she was known to her intimate friends as Nellie. One of the reigning beauties of her day, she married Lord **Londonderry** in 1875 and became a great Society hostess and a member of the Prince of Wales's set. The catastrophe of the Londonderrys' married life was well known in Society. The generally current version of events (set out in *Edwardians in Love*) is that Lady de Grey (*see* **Ripon**) came into possession of a packet of letters addressed by Harry **Cust** (with whom she herself was passionately in love) to Lady Londonderry and sent them in an anonymous package to Lord Londonderry. He re-wrapped the package enclosing a note reading 'Henceforth we do not speak', and the parcel was placed on his wife's dressing table. From that day, it was alleged, the Londonderrys spoke to each other only in public, and even when he lay dying he would not see his wife. She died in the influenza epidemic that followed the First World War.

LADY GARRIBARDINE in Elinor Glyn, *The Career of Katherine Bush* (1917)

'[Katherine Bush] took a job as personal secretary to Lady Garribardine (a portrait of Theresa, Lady Londonderry)' (Anthony Glyn, 1955, *Elinor Glyn: a biography*, London: Hutchinson, p. 235).

LADY RODFITTEN in Max Beerbohm, 'Maltby and Braxton', *Seven Men* (1919)

'Lady Rodfitten [is probably] Theresa, Marchioness of Londonderry' (David Cecil, 1964, *Max: a biography*, p. 341).

LADY TEMPLECOMBE in Victoria Sackville-West, *The Edwardians* (1930)

'Vita Sackville-West depicted the Londonderrys in . . . *The Edwardians*, calling them the Roehamptons and the Templecombes' (Anita Leslie, 1972, *Edwardians in Love*, p. 136). Miss Leslie was mistaken – they were not the Roehamptons; *see* **Westmorland**, Countess of.

LONDONDERRY HOUSE, London A Park Lane town house owned by the Marquess of Londonderry. Originally built *c*.1765 but remodelled in 1825–8 by Benjamin and Philip Wyatt, externally it is 'a very quiet, not very distinguished square building of two and a half storeys', but internally '1825 at its grandest' (Nikolaus Pevsner, 1973, *London*, Vol. I: *Cities of Westminster and London*, rev. edn, ed. R. Cloth (*Buildings of England* series), Harmondsworth: Penguin, p. 618 n.). The great ballroom, on the first floor, with skylights, was originally the sculpture gallery. It was demolished in the 1960s and replaced by the Londonderry Hotel (see ibid.; ballroom ill. Pl. 141).

ANCHORAGE HOUSE in Evelyn Waugh, *Vile Bodies* (1930)

'Lady Londonderry [in the 1920s and 1930s] lived in state and splendour . . . every eve of session [of the Houses of Parliament] she held a reception at Londonderry House and, wearing the Waterloo jewels, received her guests at the top of the double staircase' (Janet Adam Smith, 1935, *John Buchan*, p. 312). 'There is an account of such an occasion at "Anchorage House" in . . . *Vile Bodies*' (ibid., n.).

LONG, Huey Pierce (1893–1935) Governor of Louisiana from 1928 to 1931, he became a United States senator in 1931 but was assassinated in 1935.

HOMER T. 'CHUCK' CRAWFORD in John Dos Passos, *Number One* (1943)

'[O]bvious elements in this *roman à clef* include Crawford's start as a county road commissioner and subsequent rise to membership on the State Utilities Commission. He manages to get his state delegation accredited over the claim of a rival faction at the national convention, as Long had done in 1932' (J. Blotner, 1966, *The Modern American Political Novel*, p. 216 n. 52).

WILLIE STARK in Robert Penn Warren, *All the King's Men* (1946)

'My politician hero . . . Willie Stark, was quickly equated with the late senator Huey P. Long. . . . For better or for worse, Willie Stark was not Huey Long. . . . Certainly, it was the career of Long and the atmosphere of Louisiana that suggested the play that was to become the novel. But suggestion does not mean identity. . . . I did not, and do not, know what Long was like' (R. Penn Warren, 1953, 'A note to *All the King's Men*', *Swanee Review* 61: 479–80; reprinted as introd. to Modern Library edn).

BERZELIUS ('BUZZ') WINDRIP in Sinclair Lewis, *It Can't Happen Here* (1935)

Identified in Arthur M. Schlesinger, Jun., 1961, *The Politics of Upheaval (The Age of Roosevelt, III)*, p. 89. *See also* **Winrod**, G.B.

LONGSON'S, St John's Square, Burslem, Staffordshire A draper's shop in **Burslem** that belonged to Robert Longson, Arnold Bennett's maternal grandfather. Bennett's mother and his aunt, later Frances **Bourne**, served behind the counter.

BAINES'S in Arnold Bennett, *The Old Wives' Tale* (1908)

'The shop . . . is immortalised in *The Old Wives' Tale*' (Reginald Pound, 1959, *Arnold Bennett: a biography*, London: Heinemann, p. 49). 'The shop was, and still is, in the centre of Burslem. . . . It stands at the bottom end of St John's Square and now houses a bookmaker, but the building itself is largely unchanged' (Margaret Drabble, 1975, *Arnold Bennett: a biography*, London: Weidenfeld & Nicolson, p. 28).

LONGTON, Staffordshire

LONGSHAW in Arnold Bennett, *Anna of the Five Towns* (1902)

'Longton became Longshaw' (Margaret Drabble, 1975, *Arnold Bennett: a biography*, London: Weidenfeld & Nicolson, p. 4).

LONSDALE, William Lowther, 1st Earl of (1757–1844)

LORD LOWERSDALE in Benjamin Disraeli, *Vivian Grey* (1826–7)

Identified as Lord L—— in a key given in *The Star Chamber* (24 May 1826): 114, reprinted in *Vivian Grey* (1904 (centenary edn), ed. Lucien Wolf, Vol. II, pp. 361–2. The full name appears on a copy of the key held in the British Museum. Lucien Wolf concludes that Disraeli was not responsible for the key.

LONSDALE, William Lowther, 2nd Earl of (1787–1872) Known as Lord Lowther until he succeeded his father in 1844, he was a Fellow of the Royal Society. From 1808 to 1841 he was an MP and held a number of political offices, including that of Postmaster-General in 1841. He was allegedly refused the office of prime minister, twice, on the grounds that it would interfere with his private life. In 1831, Carlyle described him to Jane Carlyle as 'Red-bearded, red-skinned, with clear grey eyes and light hair . . . somewhat the manners of a respectable Cumberland yeoman . . . very limited, honest and Toryish . . . remarkable . . . as the first lord I ever sat with' (*Collected Letters*, 1976, ed. C.R. Sanders, Vol. V, Durham, NC: Duke University Press, p. 385). A passionate collector of fine porcelain, and of actresses, to the end of his life he was a man of the most exquisite urbanity.

LORD COLCHICUM in W.M. Thackeray, *The History of Pendennis* (1848–50)

'Lord Lonsdale [reappears] as Lord Colchicum' (Malcolm Elwin, 1932, *Thackeray*, p. 124). The Lonsdale livery was bright yellow.

LORD ESKDALE in Benjamin Disraeli, *Coningsby* (1844)

Identified in a key in *Notes and Queries* (8th series) 3 (13 May 1893): 363. *See also under* **Bright**, John.

LORD ESKDALE in Benjamin Disraeli, *Tancred* (1847)

'Lord Lonsdale ("Lord Eskdale" in *Tancred*)' (Robert Blake, 1969, *Disraeli*, 2nd edn, London: Oxford University Press, p. 379).

LOONEY The beadle in Salisbury Square, London, during the 1850s.

MOONEY in Charles Dickens, *Bleak House* (1852–3)

'Mooney, the beadle . . . had a prototype in a real beadle of the name of Looney. I am indebted to Mr Thomas Catling . . . ex-editor of "Lloyd's News", for some information concerning him. He says:– "I remember Looney, the beadle, in Salisbury Square. He used to sprinkle it with water conveyed by a hose, and the delight of the boys of the time was to get hold of the hose and turn the water on Looney. . . . The poor beadle's life was not a happy one, for he was continually being harassed by the printers' devils from Fleet Street and the surrounding neighbourhood. Undoubtedly Dickens knew this Looney"' (W. Matchett, 1919, 'Another Dickens original', *The Dickensian* 15 (October): 198).

LOPOKOVA, Lydia (1891–1981) Ballet dancer. Born in St Petersburg into a family of dancers, she became a member of the Diaghilev Russian Ballet Company. In 1918 she met John Maynard Keynes, whom she married in 1925, and with whom she helped found the Vic-Wells ballet (now Sadlers-Wells).

LUCREZIA ('REZIA') WARREN SMITH in Virginia Woolf, *Mrs Dalloway* (1925)

'Here we are back from . . . Studland. . . . I wanted to observe Lydia as a type for Rezia; and did observe one or two facts' (entry for 11 September 1923, *The Diary of Virginia Woolf*, Vol. II: *1920–1924*, 1978, ed. Anne Olivier Bell, London: Hogarth Press, p. 265). The Woolfs had been the guests of Maynard Keynes, together with Lopokova, Raymond Mortimer and George Rylands.

LOPUKHIN, Aleksey Aleksandrovich (1864–1927) Of liberal inclinations, he was Director of the Department of Police in Russia from 1902 to 1905. In 1906 he uncovered the printing of pogrom proclamations in the police department, and in 1908 he informed the revolutionary journalist Burtsev (1862–1942) of the services to the Secret Police of the *agent provocateur* Azev; in 1909 he was sentenced to hard labour for this offence, with his sentence subsequently being commuted to exile. He was pardoned and reinstated in 1911, and from 1913 he was Vice-Director of the Petersburg Commercial Bank. He published his memoirs in 1923.

COUNCILLOR MIKULIN in Joseph Conrad, *Under Western Eyes* (1911)

'Councillor Mikulin is based at least in part on Lopukhin and is given the same fate' (Jocelyn Baines, 1967, *Joseph Conrad: a critical biography*, rev. edn, London: Weidenfeld & Nicolson, p. 371; originally published 1960).

LORING, Frank Boston publisher. In 1880 he pirated an American edition of Henry James's tale *A Bundle of Letters*.

M<small>R</small> W<small>ENTWORTH</small> in Henry James, *The Europeans* (1878)

'[Y]es, Mr Wentworth *was* a reminiscence of Mr Frank Loring, whose frosty personality I had always in my mind in dealing with this figure' (to Elizabeth Boott, 30 October 1878, *Henry James Letters*, 1978, ed. Leon Edel, Vol. II, London: Macmillan, p. 189).

LORING, Katharine Peabody (1849–1943) Of Boston and Pride's Crossing, Massachusetts. She met Alice **James**, Henry James's sister, in 1873, and by 1879 had become her devoted companion, accompanying her on a visit to England in 1881. They returned to England in 1884, and Katherine remained there until Alice's death in 1892. She was a woman of great strength of will and intellect.

O<small>LIVE</small> C<small>HANCELLOR</small> in Henry James, *The Bostonians* (1884)

'If Henry spoke of Alice's "independence" [in 1883, after the death of their father], he nevertheless noted the extent to which she leaned upon her powerful friend Katharine Loring. . . . He was to observe this relationship closely. One might say that the figure of Olive Chancellor . . . had appeared upon the novelist's very doorstep' (Leon Edel, 1962, *Henry James: the conquest of London, 1870–1883*, London: Rupert Hart-Davis, pp. 498–9). 'The kind of intense, exclusive relationship Alice and Katharine had developed became so common between upper-class single women in late nineteenth-century America that people called it "a Boston marriage"' (Jean Stone, 1981, *Alice James*, p. 200).

LOUIS, Alfred Hyman (1829?–1915) Born in Birmingham into a Jewish family, he was the son of Hyman Tobias Louis, a merchant. He was educated at King Edward's School, where he was a contemporary of E.W. Benson (later Archbishop of Canterbury), and attended Trinity College, Cambridge, in 1847, but went down without a degree in 1850. In 1851 he was admitted as a member of Lincoln's Inn, where he met F.D. Maurice, then Chaplain to the Inn, and was baptized by him (evidence exists in Maurice's family papers). He went to the United States in 1869 and returned there again in 1876. While in New York, he was mistaken for the writer G.H. **Lewes**, and it seems that he took no steps to correct the misapprehension. In 1880 he was back in London, and in 1897 he was again in New York, but by this time was an eccentric pauper. He met E.A. Robinson, the American poet, and in 1903 he returned to England. He converted to catholicism through Alice and Wilfrid **Meynell**, but returned to Judaism in his latter years. He met George Eliot when he visited John **Chapman** in 1851. He died in poverty.

M<small>ORDECAI</small> C<small>OHEN</small> in George Eliot, *Daniel Deronda* (1876)

'He . . . claimed [in a conversation with E.A. Robinson in New York in 1897] to be the original of Mordecai' (H. Hagedorn, 1938, *Edwin Arlington Robinson: a biography*, New York, p. 162). *See also* **Cohn (or Kohn)**; **Deutsch**, Emanuel.

D<small>ANIEL</small> D<small>ERONDA</small> in George Eliot, *Daniel Deronda* (1876)

'Louis . . . claimed friendship with George Eliot and said that he was her model for Daniel Deronda' (R.B. Martin, 1959, *The Dust of Combat: a life of Charles*

Kingsley, London: Faber & Faber, p. 143). *See also* **Bond**, Edward; **Goldsmid**, Colonel Albert; **Gurney**, Edmund; **Lewes**, G.H.

RAPHAEL ABEN EZRA in Charles Kingsley, *Hypatia* (1853)

'The model for Raphael was ... Alfred Hyman Louis. ... Kingsley told [Thomas] Hughes; Raphael was suggested to me by Louis, and I am so fond of him that he who touches him, touches me' (Martin, op. cit., p. 143). Louis was the original of Captain Craig, in Edwin Arlington Robinson's poem of that name (see H. Hagedorn, 1938, *Edwin Arlington Robinson*).

Hotel du LOUVRE, Singapore Known as the 'Tingel Tangel', it was a local edition of a Continental dance hotel in Singapore in the 1890s where Austrian girls wearing white muslin dresses with coloured sashes played in a string band.

SCHOMBERG'S HOTEL in Joseph Conrad, *Victory* (1915) and *Lord Jim* (1900)

Norman Sherry came across a description of this dance hall in *One Hundred Years of Singapore*, 1921, ed. W. Makepeace, G.E. Brooke and R.S.J. Braddell, Vol. II, p. 183; he writes: 'I felt certain that the "Tingel Tangel" ... was Schomberg's Hotel' (Norman Sherry, 1966, *Conrad's Eastern World*, Cambridge, p. 244).

LOVAT, Simon Fraser, Lord (b. 1911) 17th Baron, *de facto* (owing to Attainder) 15th Baron. He was educated at Ampleforth and at Magdalen College, Oxford. He served in the Commandos during the Second World War, taking part in the Lofoten raid and, in 1942, the attack on Dieppe. In 1944 he was severely wounded (as Brigadier) in the invasion of Normandy while leading the First Commando Brigade; he was awarded the Military Cross and Companion of the Distinguished Service Order (DSO). It was he who drove Waugh out of the Commandos in 1943.

TRIMMER in Evelyn Waugh, the *Sword of Honour* trilogy (1952–61)

'For many years now I have been embarrassed to be approached by various members of Lord Lovat's family ... and asked whether the character of Trimmer, the shady hairdresser of Evelyn Waugh's trilogy, was based on their kinsman. Plainly they detected some resemblance, but I could scarcely help them, as I had never met Lord Lovat. It seemed unlikely, I said, as I was not aware that Lord Lovat had ever been a hairdresser, and my father was always most meticulous in his research. Then I learn [from Sir Iain Moncrieffe's introduction to Lovat's *March Past*] that Lord Lovat's branch ... calls itself Fraser by virtue of having changed its name from Frissell ... a curious name for a Highland chief, of course, but suitable in one or two other callings ... as I stare at his ... face on the back cover I am haunted by the idea that Evelyn Waugh might have been right and that it *is* the face of a Hairdresser acting the part of an aristocrat' (Auberon Waugh, 1978, 'Hairdressers' revolution', *Books and Bookmen* (December): 11, 13). This article, a review of a batch of books including Andrew Barrow's *Gossip 1920–1970* and Lord Lovat's *March Past*, deals with the social revolution of the preceding fifty years. The passages dealing with Lord Lovat are clearly dictated by a touching filial piety. There is obviously some connection between Trimmer and Lord Lovat, but Trimmer seems to be a figure Waugh constructed to stick pins into. He may be an instrument of revenge; he is not a likeness.

LOW, Elena Daughter of Francis Low of Boston, Massachusetts, in 1874 she married Gerald Raoul de Courcy Perry, son of Sir William Perry and for many years Consul in Venice, who was knighted in 1900 after a distinguished career in the Consular Service. From 1883 to 1893 she lived in Odessa, and from 1893 to 1903 she was resident in Antwerp. Henry James met her in Rome in 1873.

CHRISTINA LIGHT in Henry James, *Roderick Hudson* (1875)

'In Elena Lowe [sic] . . . Henry had found an image for the heroine of his first important novel. When he came to create her he gave her a name which seems to echo the original: Christina Light' (Leon Edel, 1962, *Henry James: the conquest of London, 1870–1833*, London: Rupert Hart-Davis, p. 114).

LOW, Walter (1864?–95) Son of Maximilian Low, he became Editor of the *Educational Times* (owned by the College of Preceptors). His daughters, Ivy and Barbara, married Maxim **Litvinov** and David **Eder**, respectively. He was a close friend of H.G. Wells between 1890 and 1895.

SIDNEY EWART in H.G. Wells, *Tono-Bungay* (1909)

'Chiefly with Walter Low, whose portrait appears as Ewart in *Tono-Bungay* . . . he shared the confidences of his unhappy married life' (Lovat Dickson, 1969, *H.G. Wells: his turbulent life and times*, p. 45).

LOWE, Joe (d. 1935) A war veteran, he was a member of the Civilian Conservation Corps working in Florida in September 1935, building a road and bridges near Key West. He frequented **Sloppy Joe's** bar.

EDDY MARSHALL in Ernest Hemingway, *To Have and Have Not* (1937)

'Joe Lowe the original of the Rummy in that story of mine "One Trip Across" was drowned at the Ferry Slip' (to Maxwell Perkins, 7 September 1935, reproduced in *Ernest Hemingway Selected Letters, 1917–1961*, 1981, ed. Carlos Baker, London: Granada, p. 423). The letter gives an account of the hurricane that struck Key West in September 1935, claiming between seven hundred and one thousand victims, Joe Lowe being one. 'One Trip Across' became the first chapter of *To Have and Have Not*.

LOWELL, Amy (1874–1925) American poet. Born in Brookline, Massachusetts, into an extremely wealthy family, she travelled extensively in Europe during her youth. She published several volumes of verse from 1912 onwards, and was a leading figure in the Imagist movement.

MARY DOWELL in H.D. (Hilda Doolittle), *Bid Me to Live* (1960)

Identified by Helen McNeil in the introduction to *Bid Me to Live*, 1984, pp. viii–ix, and by Perdita Schaffner in the afterword, p. 187.

LOWELL, James Russell (1819–91) American poet, essayist and diplomat. From 1857 to 1861 he was Editor of *Atlantic Monthly*, and in 1864, with Charles

Eliot **Norton**, he was Editor of *North American Review*. He was the United States Minister to Spain from 1877 to 1880, and to Great Britain from 1880 to 1885.

THE AMERICAN AMBASSADOR in Henry James, *The Sense of the Past* (1917)

'Before . . . [the hero's] possible disappearance into history, he has a long talk with the American Ambassador to London whom James set down in the image of the most significant of the American envoys he had known at the court of St James's – James Russell Lowell' (Leon Edel, 1969, *Henry James: the treacherous years, 1895–1901*, London: Rupert Hart-Davis, p. 315).

NATHAN GORE in Henry Adams, *Democracy* (1880)

'A disabused historian retired from politics . . . he has frequently been taken as a portrait of James Russell Lowell' (Irving Howe, 1961, *Politics and the Novel*, p. 177). An unconvincing identification: Lowell was not what is generally thought of as a politician, he was scarcely a historian, and he did not retire until he was 66. *See also* **Motley**, John Lothrop.

LOWELL, Robert (1917–77) American poet. Born in Boston, Massachusetts, he was educated at Harvard, Kenyon College and Louisiana State University. He was a conscientious objector during the Second World War and served six months' imprisonment. He was awarded the Pulitzer Prize for Poetry in 1947. He married Jean Stafford in 1940, Elizabeth Hardwick in 1949, and Caroline Blackwood in 1972; all three women were writers.

JIM PREWITT in Peter Taylor, '1939' (1960)

'In the story two Kenyon students – the first person narrator and his friend Jim Prewitt (Lowell) – set off to see their girlfriends in New York' (Ian Hamilton, 1983, *Robert Lowell*, p. 61).

LOWER BOCKHAMPTON, Dorset Located east of Dorchester.

LOWER MELLSTOCK in Thomas Hardy, Wessex novels and tales (1871–95)

'"Mellstock" . . . consists of three hamlets . . . the second, with the school and post-office, more than half a mile to the east [of the first] . . . [it corresponds] to . . . Lower Bockhampton' (F.B. Pinion, 1968, *A Hardy Companion*, London: Macmillan, p. 410). Also identified on a map prepared by Thomas Hardy which hangs in the Dorset County Museum, Dorchester. *See under* **Abbotsbury**.

LOWNDES, James 'A charming South Carolinian, who, after serving in the Confederate Army with the rank of colonel . . . settled in Washington and there practised law' (*Letters of Mrs Henry Adams*, 1937, ed. Ward Thoron, p. 240 n. 2). He became an intimate friend of Henry and Marian **Adams**.

JOHN CARRINGTON in Henry Adams, *Esther* (1884)

'He was supposed to be portrayed as "Carrington" in *Democracy*' (ibid.).

LOWTHER, William, 2nd Earl of Lonsdale *See* **Lonsdale**, 2nd Earl of.

LUCAS, Edward Verrall (1868–1938) Journalist, essayist and critic. He wrote a biography of Charles Lamb and edited his letters. In 1914 he was Chairman of Methuen, and it was probably on his recommendation that they published D.H. **Lawrence**'s *The Rainbow*. He was the brother of Perceval **Lucas**.

GEORGE KNOX in Angela Thirkell, *High Rising* (1933)

'[One passage in the novel] suggests that George Knox, or the man he was modelled on – probably E.V. Lucas – was more important to Angela than purely literary friendship would indicate' (M. Strickland, 1977, *Angela Thirkell: portrait of a lady novelist*, London: Duckworth, p. 81).

LUCAS, James (1813–74) Known as the 'Hertfordshire Hermit'. He inherited from his parents Elmwood at Redcoats Green, midway between Hitchin and Stevenage; after his mother's death in 1849 he became increasingly eccentric and barricaded his house, which fell into ruin, occupying only the small back scullery. He wore only a blanket fastened by a wooden skewer and subsisted on bread and cheese washed down with water, gin and wine. In 1851 he was examined by the lunacy commissioners, one of whom, John **Forster**, found that 'so far from being insane the Hermit was a man of most acute intellect' (see A.E. Brookes Cross, 1930, 'Truth about Mr Mopes', *The Dickensian* 26 (spring): 126). Dickens visited him while staying with Lord Lytton at Knebworth in 1861.

TOM MOPES in Charles Dickens, 'Tom Tiddler's Ground' (1861)

'Mr Mopes is but a transparent disguise for one Mr James Lucas, or as he was known locally, Squire Lucas, the Hertfordshire Hermit' (ibid., p. 123).

LUCAS, Madeline (1881?–1975) Daughter of Wilfrid **Meynell** and his wife Alice, she married Percy **Lucas** and was the mother of Sylvia **Lucas**.

WINIFRED in D.H. Lawrence, 'England, My England' (1915)

See under LUCAS, Perceval.

LUCAS, Perceval Drewett (1879–1916) Genealogist. Brother of E.V. **Lucas** and husband of Madeline **Lucas**; his daughter was Sylvia **Lucas**. His ruling passion in life was Morris dancing. He died of wounds in France.

EGBERT in D.H. Lawrence, 'England, My England' (1915)

'In ... "England, My England" Lawrence used personalities and environment from real life ... [among them] my sister Madeline [and] her husband Percy Lucas. ... Egbert (Percy) is made an unhappy ... man ... driven to the war by the unhappiness of his marriage' (Francis Meynell, 1971, *My Lives*, p. 87).

LUCAS, Sylvia (b. 1909) Daughter of Perceval and Madeline **Lucas**, she was educated at St Paul's Girls School and at Somerville College, Oxford.

JOYCE in D.H. Lawrence, 'England, My England' (1915)

'In his story ... Lawrence used ... [my sister's] daughter Sylvia ... as a basis ... in all-too-real life Sylvia, six years old, had fallen on a sickle and irreparably crippled herself. Lawrence ... attributes [this] falsely and cruelly to the carelessness of her father. In fact ... Percy was abroad at the time of the accident' (Francis Meynell, 1971, *My Lives*, p. 87).

LUCE, Henry Robinson (1898–1967) Publisher. Born in China, he was the son of missionaries. In 1922, with Briton Hadden, a friend from Yale, he founded *Time magazine* (first issue March 1923). In 1930 he founded *Fortune*, and in 1936 he founded *Life*. He was a proponent of the Cold War, and was a strong supporter of Chiang Kai-Shek when he was in the Far East.

LOUIS BRANDON in Charles Wertenbaker, *The Death of Kings* (1954)

'[In 1939] I suggested that we get Luce for an evening. . . . Luce accepted my invitation to dinner, but then, characteristically, turned it inside out: we were to dine with him, at his apartment. . . . I think there were five of us . . . John Osborne, Charley Wertenbaker, Bob Fitzgerald, Frank Norris and myself. (Wertenbaker gave a description of the evening in *The Death of Kings*, but he rearranged what happened and of course changed all our names)' (T.S. Matthews, 1961, *Name and Address*, p. 242).

EDWARD MASTERSON in John Nixon Brooks, *The Big Wheel* (1949)

Instantly identifiable. 'Whenever any of [Luce's employees] wrote a book, [Mrs Luce] would give [him] a . . . copy. . . . The collection grew to number several novels that caustically depicted a Luce-like publishing empire' (John Kobler, 1968, *Henry Luce*, p. 258; the footnote lists the following titles: Ralph Ingersoll, *The Great Ones*; Charles Wertenbaker, *The Fun House*; John Brooks, *The Big Wheel*).

LUCKCOCK, Mr A magistrate in Birmingham in 1853.

MR WOODCOCK in Charles Reade, *It is Never Too Late to Mend* (1856)

'Mr Luckcock . . . is described as Mr Woodcock' ('The license of modern novelists', *Edinburgh Review* (July 1857): 137).

LUHAN, Mabel Dodge (1879–1962) Born in Buffalo, New York, she was the daughter of Charles and Sarah Ganson and in 1900 married Carl Evans, also of Buffalo, who in 1902 was killed in a hunting accident. In 1903 she married Edwin Dodge, an architect of Boston. They settled in Florence and she became friends with Gertrude **Stein**. In 1912 she was divorced from Edwin Dodge and returned to New York City, where she established a salon at 23 Fifth Avenue. She had a love affair with John Reed, the journalist, and then in 1916 she married the painter Maurice Sterne. They went to Taos to join a colony of artists, and after they were divorced she married Tony Luhan, a Pueblo Indian, in 1923. In 1922 she persuaded D.H. Lawrence to visit Taos; she corresponded with him until his death.

EDITH DALE in Carl Van Vechten, *Peter Whiffle: His Life and Works* (1922)

'[His novels] described a world of . . . attractive and emancipated women like . . . Edith Dale . . . patterned after Mabel Dodge' (James R. Mellow, 1974, *The Charmed Circle: Gertrude Stein and company*, London: Phaidon Press, p. 195).

MARY KITTRIDGE in Max Eastman, *Venture* (1927)

'[S]he appears as Mary Kittridge in . . . *Venture*. Eastman suggests clearly the astonishing variety of activities into which one after another, she dived headlong' (W.G. Rogers, 1968, *Ladies Bountiful*, p. 109).

Mrs Lederman in D.H. Lawrence, 'The Woman Who Rode Away' (1928)

'On the journey [from Los Angeles to Guadalajara in 1923] Lawrence and Gótzsche stopped for a couple of days to visit a Swiss who owned a silver mine near Navajoa; planting Mrs Luhan in this setting, Lawrence wrote about them in 'The Woman Who Rode Away' (H.T. Moore, 1960, *The Intelligent Heart: the story of D.H. Lawrence*, Harmondsworth: Penguin, p. 399; originally published 1955, London: Heinemann). '. . . a story . . . freely based on Mabel Luhan, who called it "that story where Lorenzo thought he finished me up"' (Keith Sagar, 1971, Introd. to D.H. Lawrence, *The Princess and Other Stories*, Harmondsworth: Penguin, p. 7).

LULWORTH COVE, Dorset Situated nine miles east of Weymouth.

Lulwind Cove in Thomas Hardy, Wessex novels and tales (1871–95)

Identified on a map prepared by Thomas Hardy which hangs in the Dorset County Museum, Dorchester. *See under* **Abbotsbury**.

LYGON, Hugh (1904–36) Second son of the 6th Earl **Beauchamp**. In 1923, when he was at Pembroke College, Oxford, he became one of Waugh's close friends. After Oxford, he could make a success of nothing, owing to persistent ill-health, which he refused either to recognize or to have diagnosed or treated. He engaged in a variety of occupations, all involving considerable physical exertion, and in the summer of 1934 he took Waugh with him on an expedition to Spitzbergen, a reconnaissance for the Oxford University Arctic Expedition of 1935–6; the expedition failed to achieve its objectives. He died suddenly while on a motor-tour in Germany in the summer of 1936. He was a man with an extraordinarily sweet disposition.

Sebastian Flyte in Evelyn Waugh, *Brideshead Revisited* (1945)

'His circumstances and something of his appearance was taken in part from Hugh Lygon, as can be stated on Evelyn's own testimony' (Christopher Sykes, 1975, *Evelyn Waugh*, London: Collins, p. 252). *See also* **Graham**, Alastair.

LYKENS, Pennsylvania Situated thirty miles west of Pottsville, it was the home of John O'Hara's maternal grandparents, the Delaneys.

Lyons in John O'Hara, *A Family Party* (1956) and other stories

'Here he worked with memories of Lykens (Lyons in this and other stories)' (Finis Farr, 1974, *O'Hara: a biography*, p. 226).

LYNDHURST, John Singleton Copley, Lord (1772–1863) Born in Boston, Massachusetts, he was the son of the American portrait-painter J.S. Copley. In 1775 his parents, being loyalists, moved to England; he was educated at Trinity College, Cambridge, and in 1804 was called to the Bar. He was Solicitor-General from 1819 to 1824, and in 1820 he conducted the prosecution of Queen Caroline before the House of Lords. He was Attorney-General from 1824 to 1826, and an MP from 1818 to 1827, being created 1st Baron Lyndhurst in 1827. He was Lord Chancellor 1827–30, 1834–5 and 1841–6, but declined a fourth tenure of the office in 1851. He made his last speech in the House of Lords in 1861. A spectacularly handsome man with exquisite manners, he is said to have been the prototype of W.S. Gilbert's 'highly susceptible Chancellor' in *Iolanthe* (see Robert Blake, 1966, *Disraeli*, London: Eyre & Spottiswoode, p. 115).

MONSIEUR DE CHAPELEY in Lord Brougham, *Albert Lunel* (1844)

'[In Michael Sadleir's copy of *Albert Lunel*] in Brougham's hand are identifications of certain characters. Thus . . . vol. III pp. 32 and 156 identify "M. de Chapeley" with Copley Lyndhurst' (Michael Sadleir, 1951, *XIX Century Fiction*, London: Constable, and Los Angeles: California University Press, p. 57).

THE LORD CHANCELLOR in Charles Dickens, *Bleak House* (1852–3)

'The figure of Lord Lyndhurst shines out even through the moral and material fog of Jarndyce v. Jarndyce, as he talks in his private room to Richard Carstone' (J.B. Atlay, 1906, *The Victorian Chancellors*, Vol. I, p. 143).

SIR CHARLES WOLSTENHOLME in Samuel Warren, *Ten Thousand a Year* (1841)

'Of his identity with Sir Charles Wolstenholme . . . there is no room for doubt' (ibid., p. 8).

LYON, Thomas Henry (1869–d. before 1929) Born near Newton Abbot, Devon, he attended Corpus Christi College, Cambridge, from 1890 to 1893. He was a friend and contemporary of John Cowper **Powys**, who became his brother-in-law. Later he lived at Appleton Hall, Cheshire.

REGGIE TRYERS in Louis Wilkinson, *The Buffoon* (1916)

'. . . introduced into the plot as Reggie Tryers' (R.P. Graves, 1983, *The Brothers Powys*, p. 117).

LYONS, Mrs Sister of Mrs **Callanan**.

MISS JULIA MORKAN in James Joyce, 'The Dead', *Dubliners* (1914) and *Ulysses* (1922)

'In Joyce's story Mrs Callanan and Mrs Lyons . . . become the spinster ladies, the Misses Morkan' (Richard Ellmann, 1982, *James Joyce*, rev. edn, Oxford: Oxford University Press, pp. 245–6).

LYONS, Freddy Son of James Joyce's great-aunt, Mrs **Lyons**. He kept a Christmas card shop on Grafton Street in Dublin.

FREDDY MALINS in James Joyce, 'The Dead', *Dubliners* (1914)

'Joyce introduces [Freddy Lyons] as Freddy Malins' (Richard Ellmann, 1966, *James Joyce*, London: Oxford Paperbacks, p. 255).

LYTCHETT MINSTER, Dorset A village five miles east of Wareham, on the road to Poole and Bournemouth.

FLYCHETT in Thomas Hardy, *The Hand of Ethelberta* (1876)

Identified in F.B. Pinion, 1968, *A Hardy Companion*, London: Macmillan.

LYTTELTON, George William, Lord (1817–76) 4th Baron Lyttelton of Frankley.

HARRY CONINGSBY in Benjamin Disraeli, *Coningsby* (1844) and *Tancred* (1847)

Identified (as Lord Littleton) in a key in *Notes and Queries* (8th series) 3 (13 May 1893): 363. *See also under* **Bright**, John. *See also* **Smythe**, George.

LORD VERE in Benjamin Disraeli, *Coningsby* (1844)

'. . . Lord Lyttelton, who appears in the novel as "the calm and sagacious Vere"' (W.F. Monypenny, 1912, *Life of Benjamin Disraeli*, Vol. II, p. 202 n. 1). Also identified in a key in *Notes and Queries* (8th series) 3 (13 May 1893): 363. *See also* **Howard**, Lord Edward.

LYTTELTON, Laura (1862–86) Née Tennant, she was the sister of Margaret **Asquith**, and married Alfred Lyttelton, becoming his first wife. She was the central figure, even after her death during childbirth, of the group known as the **Souls**.

CATHERINE LEYBURN in Mrs Humphry Ward, *Robert Elsmere* (1888)

'People say that . . . Catherine [is intended] for your sister Laura' (Benjamin Jowett to Margot Asquith, 28 November 1888, quoted in *Autobiography of Margot Asquith*, 1920, pp. 120, 121). *Robert Elsmere* is dedicated to the memory of Laura Lyttelton.

LYTTON, Edward George Lytton Bulwer, 1st Baron (1803–1873) Novelist and politician. He was an MP in 1831–41 and 1852–66, and was Secretary for the Colonies in 1858–9. He was a great dandy and the intimate friend of Disraeli from early days. In 1827 he married Rosina Wheeler (**Lytton**, below), but the marriage was a disaster and they separated in 1836; their son became the 1st Earl of **Lytton**. H.F. Chorley described him as 'a thoroughly *sat in* character'.

LORD DE CLIFFORD in Lady Lytton, *Cheveley; or The Man of Honour* (1839)

'What contemporary reader could fail to recognize . . . Bulwer-Lytton in Lord de Clifford?' (M.W. Rosa, 1936, *The Silver Fork: novels of fashion preceding 'Vanity Fair'*, New York, p. 172).

DESBROW in Lady Blessington, *The Two Friends* (1835)

'The author is said to have put Bulwer in . . . as "Desbrow"' (Willard Connelly, 1952, *Count D'Orsay*, p. 228). 'This personage . . . must be Liston [sic] Bulwer. She passes him off under the *alias* Desbrow' ('A quintette of novels', *Fraser's Magazine* 11 (April 1835): 474).

LORD SURBITON in W.H. Mallock, *A Romance of the Nineteenth Century* (1881)

'Into *A Romance of the Nineteenth Century* [Mallock] put a lovingly drawn portrait of the first Lord Lytton – Edward Bulwer-Lytton, the novelist, playwright, and poet, who had died in 1873 – a dandy of the early century, and a finished . . . man of the world. "Lord Surbiton" Mallock called him' (R.L. Wolff, 1977, *Gains and Losses: novels of faith and doubt in Victorian England*, p. 488). *See also* **Milnes**, Richard Monckton.

BERTIE TREMAINE in Benjamin Disraeli, *Endymion* (1880)

Identified in 'Key to *Endymion*', *Notes and Queries* 83 (24 October 1942): 263; identifications attributed to G.E. Buckle. 'Just at the commencement of the spring of 1830 . . . I made the acquaintance of Lytton Bulwer and dined with him at his house in Hertford Street. . . . The other three were Henry Bulwer, Charles Villiers and Alexander Cockburn' (Disraeli writing in the 1860s, reproduced in W.F. Monypenny, 1910, *The Life of Benjamin Disraeli, Earl of Beaconsfield*, Vol. I, London: John Murray, p. 124). 'There is an obvious reminiscence of this party in the dinner given by Mr Bertie Tremaine and his brother, Mr Tremaine Bertie, in chapter 37 of *Endymion*' (ibid., p. 125 n. 1).

LYTTON, Edward Robert Bulwer, 1st Earl of (1831–91) Poet, diplomat and statesman. Son of the 1st Baron **Lytton**, he was educated at Harrow and in Bonn, and later entered the Diplomatic Service. From 1872 to 1874, while Secretary to the Embassy at Paris, he became the close friend of Wilfrid Scawen **Blunt**. In 1876 Disraeli appointed him Viceroy of India, and it was he who proclaimed Queen Victoria Empress of India in 1877. His viceroyalty is chiefly remembered for the disastrous Afghan War of 1879. He left India in 1880 and from 1887 to 1891 he was Ambassador in Paris. He wrote verse under the pseudonym of Owen Meredith.

LORD AIDEN in W.H. Mallock, *The Old Order Changes* (1886)

'"Lord Aiden" – poet, diplomat and sophisticated man of the world – is an affectionate portrait of Robert . . . first Earl of Lytton' (R.L. Wolff, 1977, *Gains and Losses: novels of faith and doubt in Victorian England*, London: John Murray, pp. 490–1).

LYTTON, Pamela Bulwer, Countess of (d. 1971) Née Chichele-Plowden, in 1902 she married the 2nd Earl of Lytton, and in 1910 Julian Grenfell, son of Lady **Desborough**, fell passionately in love with her.

LEILA BUCKNELL in Maurice Baring, *C* (1924)

'The character of Leila . . . which seems so like Ettie [Desborough], was believed by Pamela Lytton's contemporaries to have been taken from her' (Nicholas Mosley, 1976, *Julian Grenfell*, London: Weidenfeld & Nicolson, p. 175). *See also* **Desborough**, Lady.

LYTTON, Richard Warburton (1745–1810) Educated at Harrow School where he became the friend of Dr Parr, who declared him to be 'the best Latin scholar of the day, inferior only to Porson in Greek and to Sir William Jones in Hebrew and oriental languages' (*The Dictionary of National Biography*, London: Oxford University Press). He produced nothing other than one play in Hebrew. His grandson became the 1st Baron **Lytton**.

CLUTTERBUCK in Bulwer Lytton, *Pelham* (1828)

'Although the character of the henpecked Clutterbuck is by no means in all aspects the counterpart of my great grandfather, this . . . portrait of the clerical scholar . . . was undoubtedly suggested by the wasted life of Richard Warburton Lytton' (*The Life Letters and Literary Remains of Edward Bulwer, Lord Lytton*, 1883, Vol. II, pp. 192–3).

LYTTON, Rosina Bulwer, Lady (1804–82) Author. Née Wheeler, in 1827 she married the 1st Baron **Lytton**, but they were separated in 1836; their son was the 1st Earl of **Lytton**. She wrote a number of novels.

LADY DE CLIFFORD in Lady Lytton, *Cheveley; or The Man of Honour* (1839)

'His [de Clifford's] long-suffering wife (Rosina's dream picture of herself)' (Jack Lindsay, 1950, *Charles Dickens*, p. 408).

M

MacALISTER & CO. A firm of ship chandlers in Singapore during the 1880s.

EGSTRÖM & BLAKE in Joseph Conrad, *Lord Jim* (1900)

'It is almost certain that Conrad knew the firm and its premises and made them the originals for the firm and premises of Egström and Blake' (Norman Sherry, 1966, *Conrad's Eastern World*, p. 22).

McALMON, Robert (1896–1956) An expatriate author from the United States, he was in France during the 1920s. He married the novelist Bryher (Winifred Ellerman) in 1921, but they were divorced in 1927. In 1922, with William Carlos Williams, he founded the Contact Publishing Company, which published the periodical *Contact* and **Hemingway**'s first book, *Three Stories & Ten Poems*. He joined William **Bird** in the Three Mountains Press.

DENKA in Kay Boyle, 'I Can't Get Drunk' (1933)

'In a story written about 1928, Kay Boyle has sketched the Robert McAlmon of the late twenties' (*McAlmon and the Lost Generation: a self-portrait*, 1962, ed. Robert E. Knoll, Lincoln, p. 259). In 'Denka' she gives a vivid description of him.

PETER in Robert McAlmon, *Post Adolescence* (1923)

Identified in *McAlmon and the Lost Generation: a self-portrait*, ed. Robert E. Knoll, 1962, Lincoln, Nebr.: University of Nebraska Press, p. 108.

MacARTHUR, Douglas (1880–1964) United States General. Born in Little Rock, Arkansas, during the First World War he commanded the 42nd (Rainbow) Division in France. He retired in 1937, but was recalled to active service as Commander of US forces in the Far East in 1941. In 1942 he was Applied Supreme Commander in the south-west Pacific, and in 1950 and 1951 he was Supreme Commander of United Nations forces in Korea.

DEWEY HAIK in Sinclair Lewis, *It Can't Happen Here* (1935)

Identified in Arthur M. Schlesinger, Jun., 1961, *The Politics of Upheaval (The Age of Roosevelt, III)*, p. 89.

MACARTNEY, Herbert Baldwin (1870?–1909) Violinist. He played in the orchestra at the Gaiety Theatre and at the Opera House in Covent Garden, London. He gave violin lessons to Helen **Corke** and they fell in love. After a difficult relationship lasting five years, they spent five days together in the Isle of Wight in August 1909; Macartney returned home and hanged himself the next morning.

SIEGMUND MACNAIR in D.H. Lawrence, *The Trespasser* (1912)

A full account of the affair, the text of the memoir Helen Corke wrote of their days in Freshwater, and a description of how Lawrence used both the memoir and his conversations with Helen Corke as the basis for *The Trespasser* is to be found in the first volume of her autobiography, *In Our Infancy* (1975, Cambridge). The account of the discovery of Siegmund's body and of his mode of death in the novel exactly reproduces the details revealed at the inquest on the death Macartney's death, reported in the *Surrey Comet* on 14 August 1909.

MACARTNEY, Laura Sister of H.B. **Macartney**. Helen **Corke** introduced her to Lawrence, who went to one or two musical evenings at her home in Purley, Surrey, in 1911.

LAURA BRAITHWAITE in D.H. Lawrence, 'The Witch à la Mode' (1934)

'One occasion [among these musical evenings] . . . is recorded in . . . "The Witch à la Mode"' (*Lawrence in Love: letters to Louie Burrows*, 1968, ed. James T. Boulton, Nottingham, p. 94 n. 1). 'A collection of D.H. Lawrence's short stories published after his death includes . . . "The Witch à la Mode", which recalls that evening. . . . The story . . . is a skilful blend of fact and fiction, with an entirely imaginary denouement' (Helen Corke, 1975, *In Our Infancy*, p. 210).

MACAULAY, Dame (Emilie) Rose (1881–1958) English novelist. Born in Rugby, Warwickshire, she was educated at Oxford High School and Somerville College, Oxford. She won the Tait Black Memorial Prize for *The Towers of Trebizond*, which was published in 1956, following her return to the Anglican faith. She was made a Dame of the British Empire in the year of her death.

ALIX in Rose Macaulay, *Non-combatants and Others* (1916)

'So far as we know Rose hardly saw Rupert again once war began. . . . But we may guess, from . . . *Non-Combatants and Others* . . . that she did encounter him at least a couple more times. . . . She showed "Alix" as secretly in love with Basil Doye [i.e. Rupert Brooke]' (C. Babington-Smith, 1972, *Rose Macaulay*, p. 70).

NAN in Rose Macaulay, *Dangerous Ages* (1921)

'Something of Rose herself can be seen in one of the daughters . . . ("Nan")' (Babington-Smith, op. cit., p. 98).

MACAULAY, Grace (1855–1925) Daughter of Revd W. Conybeare, in 1878 she married George Macaulay, who was then Assistant Master at Rugby. She was the mother of Rose **Macaulay**.

HILARY in Rose Macaulay, *Dangerous Ages* (1921)

'When Grace Macaulay read the book in manuscript she recognised the portrait of herself and was deeply hurt' (C. Babington-Smith, 1972, *Rose Macaulay*, p. 98).

MACAULAY, William Herrick (1853–1936) Dean of King's College, Cambridge. He was a mathematician and the uncle of Rose **Macaulay**.

WILLIAM MASSON in I. Compton-Burnett, *Pastors and Masters* (1925)

'Masson's looks (his character seems to have been pure invention on his author's part) were borrowed from . . . W.H. Macaulay' (Hilary Spurling, 1974, *Ivy When Young: the early life of I. Compton-Burnett, 1884–1919*, London: Gollancz, p. 195).

MacCARTHY, Desmond (1877–1952) English writer and critic. Educated at Eton and at Trinity College, Cambridge, where he read history (taking an *aegrotat*) and was an Apostle. He also became the intimate of the children of Sir Leslie **Stephen** and others who were later to form the Bloomsbury group. Between 1913 and 1928 he acted first as Dramatic Critic and later as Literary Editor on the *New Statesman*, with an interval during the First World War in which he served with the Red Cross, and from 1928 to 1952 he was Senior Literary Critic on the *Sunday Times*. In 1906 he married Mary Warre-Cornish (**MacCarthy**, below).

BERNARD in Virginia Woolf, *The Waves* (1931)

'Bernard has something of Desmond in him. . . . But Bernard is not Desmond; none of Virginia's characters are drawn completely or photographically from life. The final heroic charge against death, "unvanquished and unyielding", was not in Desmond' (Leonard Woolf, 1964, *Beginning Again*, p. 143).

M. FITZGERALD in Mary MacCarthy, *A Pier and a Band* (1918)

'Even when Molly seemed at her most critical of him, Desmond could sympathetically enter into her thoughts and feelings. So also did she understand him. She shows this in her fictional portrait of him under the name of Fitzgerald in . . . *A Pier and a Band*' (*Desmond MacCarthy: the man and his writings*, 1984, introd. David Cecil, p. 25).

CHARLES OSSORY in A.G. Macdonell, *England, Their England* (1933)

'One of [the reviewers on the weekly paper where he was literary editor] was eventually moved to retaliate [for his procrastination] by drawing a satirical picture of him in his celebrated . . . comic novel *England, their England*' (Michael Holroyd, 1967, *Lytton Strachey*, Vol. I, London: Heinemann, p. 124).

McCARTHY, Joseph Raymond (1908–57) American politician. Junior Senator for Wisconsin from 1948 to 1954, he first achieved notoriety as a Red Baiter in a speech delivered at Wheeling, West Virginia, on 9 February 1950. In 1953, after the inauguration of General Eisenhower as President, he set up and became Chairman of the Permanent Subcommittee on Investigations and led the campaign against American Liberals and the left wing in which many innocent people were hunted down and accused of Communism. He was finally 'condemned' by the Senate on a charge of contempt in December 1954.

JOHN ISELIN in Richard Condon, *The Manchurian Candidate* (1959)

See J. Blotner, 1966, *The Modern American Political Novel*, for a discussion of the use of Senator McCarthy by American novelists of the 1950s.

SENATOR MUGONNIGLE in Warren Miller, *The Sleep of Reason* (1956)

See above.

SENATOR O'BRIEN in William L. Shirer, *Stranger Come Home* (1954)

See above.

KANE O'CONNOR in Ernest Frankel, *Tongue of Fire* (1960)

See above.

MacCARTHY, Mary (1882–1953) Daughter of Francis and Blanche **Warre-Cornish**, in 1906 she married Desmond **MacCarthy**.

Perdita Villiers in Mary MacCarthy, *A Pier and a Band* (1918)

'[I]n her novel ... she herself also figures as the heroine, Perdita' (*Desmond MacCarthy: the man and his writings*, 1984, introd. David Cecil, p. 25).

McCARTHY, Mary Therese (1912–89) American novelist and critic. Born in Seattle, Washington, she was orphaned in 1918 and she and her three brothers were brought up by grandparents and other relatives. She graduated from Vassar College, New York in 1933. Her first marriage was to the actor Harold Johnsrud, who died in a fire. In 1938 she married the author and critic Edmund Wilson, who encouraged her to write fiction. Her third marriage, in 1948, was to Bowden Bowater, whom she divorced in 1961 to marry an information officer, James West.

Gertrude Johnson in Randall Jarrell, *Pictures from an Institution* (1954)

'What [Mary McCarthy] was like on the campus of Sarah Lawrence ... can only be surmised from the one piece of possible evidence ... *Pictures from an Institution* ... her detractors are united in their view that Gertrude ... is the spit and image of Mary McCarthy.... [She] says of the fictional portrait: "It didn't resemble me in any way that counted".... She adds that when the book appeared she wrote to Jarrell ... and said that she had heard "that Gertrude was supposed to be me", and that I didn't think so. He wrote back and said, "No, it's me – you know, like Flaubert".... Gertrude does seem to gather under one skin many views of Mary McCarthy that have been expressed by "enemies" (a word she herself uses often for them). ... If Mary McCarthy could not recognize the portrait ... and Randall Jarrell disclaimed it, the reader detects some satiric assaults upon and distortions of her character as a novelist. Her propensity for the fact in fiction, her affection for catalogues ... her customary resort to people she knows well for her characters: all these ring true' (Doris Grumbach, 1967, *The Company She Kept*, pp. 123–6).

McCLELLAN, May Marcy Daughter of General George Brinton McClellan (1826–85), a general in the Civil who stood as Democratic candidate for United States president in 1864 and was defeated by Lincoln. In November 1886 she contributed an article to *The World* (New York) about the friends who had entertained her in Venice. Henry James met her in 1887 when she was in Florence with her mother.

Francina Dosson in Henry James, *The Reverberator* (1888)

'November 17th, 1887. Last winter, in Florence, I was struck with the queer incident of Miss McC.'s writing to the ... *World* that inconceivable letter about the Venetian society whose hospitality she had just been enjoying – and the strange *typicality* of the whole thing. She ... was amazed ... when an outcry and indignation were the result.... It was a striking incident and it seemed to me exactly the theme for a short story' (*The Notebooks of Henry James*, 1947, ed. F.O. Matthiessen and K.B. Murdock, New York, p. 82).

McCLURE, Samuel Sidney (1857–1949) Pioneer of newspaper syndication. Born in Ireland, he was taken to the United States by his mother when he was a child. He founded his syndicate in 1884, and Howells and Stevenson were among the authors he published. In 1903 he founded *McClure's*, which was famous as the original muck-racking journal.

FULKERSON in W.D. Howells, *A Hazard of New Fortunes* (1890)

'Howells . . . portrayed McClure as . . . Fulkerson' (*Dictionary of American Biography, 1946–50*, 1974, New York, p. 517).

JIM PINKERTON in R.L. Stevenson and Lloyd Osbourne, *The Wrecker* (1892)

'He . . . was the original of Pinkerton' (*The Letters of Oscar Wilde*, 1962, ed. Rupert Hart-Davis, London: Rupert Hart-Davis, p. 209 n. 5).

McCORD, Peter B. (d. *c*.1935) He worked in the art department of the St Louis *Globe-Democrat* when Dreiser was a reporter on the paper in 1892. He later worked on the *Philadelphia North American*, and then on the *Newark News* (1902).

PETER in Theodore Dreiser, *Twelve Men* (1919)

See R.H. Elias, 1970, *Theodore Dreiser, Apostle of Nature* (emended edn), p. 313 n. 4).

McCULLOCH, John Ramsay (1789–1864) Professor of Political Economy at London University from 1828 to 1837, he then became Comptroller of Her Majesty's Stationery Office until 1864. He was the author of a number of works on statistics and political economy, and was the propounder of the theory of the 'wage fund'.

LIBERAL SNAKE in Benjamin Disraeli, *Vivian Grey* (1826–7)

Identified as Mr Mc——h in a key given in *The Star Chamber* (24 May 1826): 114, reprinted in *Vivian Grey* (1904, (centenary edn), ed. Lucien Wolf, Vol. II, pp. 361–2. The full name appeared in a reprint of the key published in *Notes and Queries* (29 April 1893). Lucien Wolf concludes that Disraeli was not responsible for the key.

MR MACQUEDY in Thomas Love Peacock, *Crotchet Castle* (1831)

'Mr McQuedy was immediately recognised by contemporaries as McCulloch' (A. Martin Freeman, 1911, *Thomas Love Peacock*, London: Martin Secker, p. 306). *See also* **Mill**, James; **Mushet**, Robert.

MacDONALD, George (1824–1905) Poet, novelist and writer of books for children. Born and educated in Aberdeen, he lived in Manchester from 1853 to 1860 and in London from 1860 to 1905. He was a friend of F.D. Maurice, **Browning, Ruskin** and **Carlyle**, and was deeply religious. His stories for children (*At the Back of the North Wind, The Princess and Curdie*) were exquisitely illustrated by the Pre-Raphaelite artist Arthur Hughes. He dedicated his *David Elginbrod* (1863) to Lady **Byron**.

DONALD GORDON in W.H. Mallock, *The New Republic* (1877)

'One problem remains. If Donald Gordon is not based on Carlyle, who is the original? George Macdonald, I suggest. He and Ruskin had met and become friends in 1863, and it is very possible that Mallock had met him during his own Oxford years, since Macdonald frequently stayed with Ruskin at Oxford' (J. Lucas, 1975, Introd. to *The New Republic*, Leicester, p. 29). This is a much more likely original than Carlyle for the gentle character of Gordon. *See also* **Carlyle**, Thomas.

MACDONALD, James William Bosville (1810–82) Second son of the 3rd Baron Macdonald of Slate and Louisa La Coast (d. 1835), who was the natural daughter of the Duke of Gloucester and Lady Almeria Carpenter. For upwards of thirty years he was Private Secretary to the Duke of Cambridge.

MR MELTON in Benjamin Disraeli, *Coningsby* (1844)

Identified in a key in *Notes and Queries* (8th series) 3 (13 May 1893): 363. *See also under* **Bright**, John.

MACDONALD, Ramsay (1866–1937) He became the first Labour prime minister of Great Britain in 1924, and filled the same position in 1929–31 and 1931–5.

HAMER SHAWCROSS in Howard Spring, *Fame is the Spur* (1940)

The identification is based upon obvious parallels.

MacDONELL OF GLENGARRY, Alexander (1771–1828) He was tried and acquitted for killing Lieutenant Macleod, of the Black Watch, in a duel in 1798. In 1802 he married Rebecca Forbes, the sister of the William Forbes of Pitsligo who had married Williamina **Belsches**. In 1816 he gave an enormous deer hound, **Maida**, to Sir Walter Scott; Maida was Scott's inseparable companion until it died, whereupon Glengarry gave Scott a replacement deer hound, **Nimrod**. Scott said of Glengarry, 'he seems to have lived a century too late' (entry for 14 February 1826, in *Journal*). He always wore the dress of and followed the style of living of his ancestors.

FERGUS MACIVOR in Sir Walter Scott, *Waverley* (1814)

'It is supposed that from Glengarry Scott drew most of the features of Fergus McIvor in *Waverley*' (*The Letters of Sir Walter Scott*, 1933, ed. H.J.C. Grierson, Vol. IV, London: Constable, p. 198 n. 1).

MacGUIRE, Colonel Hugh (d. 1764) In 1745 he married Elizabeth, Lady **Cathcart**; when she refused to hand her property and jewels over to him, he carried her off and immured her in his castle in County Fermanagh until his death.

SIR KIT RACKRENT in Maria Edgeworth, *Castle Rackrent* (1800)

'It was ... by making strict distinction between the *characters* of the people involved (which were drawn from Edgeworth history), and their *actions* (which came from Col. MacGuire and Lady Cathcart) that Maria was able to deny that Sir Kit and his bride were drawn from life' (Marilyn Butler, 1972, *Maria Edgeworth*, Oxford, p. 242).

McHARDY Groom to Sir Roderick and Lady Jones (Enid Bagnold) for ten years.

MR TAYLOR in Enid Bagnold, *National Velvet* (1935)

'McHardy was "Mr Taylor" in . . . *National Velvet*' (*Enid Bagnold's Autobiography (from 1889)*, 1969, London: Heinemann, p. 149).

MACIRONE, Emilia Afterwards Lady Hornby.

EMILIA SANDRA BELLONI in George Meredith, *Sandra Belloni (Emilia in England)* (1864)

'The character and more particularly the physical aspects of Emilia were drawn to a certain extent from Miss Emilia Macirone (Lady Hornby) . . . like [Emilia], Miss Macirone . . . was the daughter of an Italian by an English wife. . . . She was an accomplished musician and sang exquisitely. She was unconventional for her period, and during her voyage to the Crimea, in 1855, used to sing almost every evening to . . . the soldiers and sailors on board. In England . . . she would go out at night in harvest time and sing to the . . . labourers. . . . These incidents were utilised by Meredith in the scene where his Emilia goes to sing . . . [to] the members of the rural Junction Club of Ipley and Hillford' (S.M. Ellis, 1920, *George Meredith*, 2nd edn, London: Grant Richards, pp. 179, 180). 'I gave you once . . . an outline of the real story it is taken from. Of course one does not follow out real stories; and this has simply suggested Emilia to me' (to Janet Ross, 17 May 1861, reproduced in *Letters of George Meredith*, 1970, ed. C.L. Cline, Oxford, p. 80). Early in the letter, Meredith gives the title of the novel as *Emilia Belloni*. Meredith and his first wife had lodged for a time, shortly after their marriage, at the house of Miss Macirone's mother in Weybridge.

MACKAY, Robert William (1803–82) Philosopher and scholar. His work *The Progress of the Intellect as Exemplified in the Religious Development of the Greeks and Hebrews* (1850) was published by John **Chapman** and reviewed by George Eliot in her first article for the *Westminster Review*.

EDWARD CASAUBON in George Eliot, *Middlemarch* (1871–2)

'Mr Mackay was somewhat of an invalid and a nervous man, much absorbed in his studies. I have heard it said that he was the original of George Eliot's *Mr Casaubon*' (Francis Power Cobbe, 1894, *Life of Francis Power Cobbe*, Vol. II, pp. 110, 111). 'After [his marriage at the age of 48] he appeared "rather worse than otherwise", she reported (*The George Eliot Letters*, 1954, ed. Gordon S. Haight, Vol. II, London: Oxford University Press, p. 29). Following his return from a wedding trip to Weymouth, she asked him how he and his wife had liked it. "Not at all, not at all", he replied, "but it was not the fault of the place" (ibid., II, p. 29)' (Richard Ellmann, 1973, 'Dorothea's husbands, some biographical speculations', *Times Literary Supplement* (16 February)). *See also* **Brabant**, R.H.; **Bryant**, Jacob; **Eliot**, George; **Pattison**, Mark; **Spencer**, Herbert.

MACKENZIE, Sir Compton (1883–1972) Novelist. Educated at St Paul's School and at Magdalen College, Oxford, he published his first novel, *The Passionate Elopement* in 1911, followed by *Carnival* (1912) and *Sinister Street* (1913–14, 2 vols). During the First World War he served with the Gallipoli expedition. In 1916 he was a military control officer in Athens, and in 1917 he was Director of the Aegean Intelligence Service. Among other works, after the First World War he published the novels *Vestal Fire* (1927) and *The Four Winds of Love* (1937–45), and the ten-*Octave* autobiography *My Life and Times* (1963–71). He married Faith Stone (**Mackenzie**, below) in 1905. He first met D.H. Lawrence and his wife in 1914 at Chesham and met them again on Capri in 1919–20.

MR CATHCART in D.H. Lawrence, 'The Man Who Loved Islands' (1928)

'[In February 1926 Lawrence went to Capri.] . . . He . . . called at the villa of Faith Mackenzie, who told him her husband was away on the channel island he had rented – about which Lawrence soon wrote "The Man Who Loved Islands"' (H.T. Moore, 1960, *The Intelligent Heart: the story of D.H. Lawrence*, Harmondsworth: Penguin, p. 433; originally published 1955, London: Heinemann). In August 1920 Compton Mackenzie leased Herm and Jethou from the Crown. 'As the result of a protest from Sir Compton Mackenzie ["The Man Who Loved Islands"] was excluded from the English edition of *The Woman Who Rode Away*' (E. Nehls, 1958, *D.H. Lawrence: a composite biography*, Madison, Vol. II, p. 455 n. 44). 'Compton Mackenzie . . . told the author of the present volume (in London in 1950) that Lawrence's fiction often gives a distorted view of his acquaintances because he had a trick of describing a person's setting or background vividly, and then putting into the setting an ectoplasm entirely of his own creation' (Moore, op. cit., p. 240).

CAMERON GEE in D.H. Lawrence, 'Two Blue Birds' (1928)

'[On] 13 May [1926] . . . Lawrence sent . . . "Two Blue Birds" to his agents in London, prophetically speaking of it as "probably . . . another tribulation to you"; indeed, this little satire . . . did not please the Compton Mackenzies any more than "The Man Who Loved Islands" pleased them' (Moore, op. cit., p. 435).

MACKENZIE, Faith Compton Née Stone, she married Compton **Mackenzie** in 1905.

MRS GEE in D.H. Lawrence, 'The Man Who Loved Islands' (1928)

'When [in 1926] Lawrence asked me to dine alone with him at a little restaurant . . . I went gladly because I enjoyed his company. And when we discussed Monty [Compton Mackenzie] I let him talk more frankly than I would have allowed anyone else to do, "because", I wrote in my diary, "I know he loves him". And, of course, I talked myself. . . . To me that night he seemed an angel, and I gave him some of the secrets of my heart . . . some months later a short story appeared . . . which he could not have written if I had not dined with him that night in Capri. A malicious caricature of Monty, and a monstrous perversion of facts, yet the source of it clearly recognisable' (Faith Compton Mackenzie, 1940, *More Than I Show*, p. 34). 'Presumably a reference to "The Man Who Loved Islands" . . . or possibly to "Two Blue Birds"' (E. Nehls, 1959, *D.H. Lawrence: a composite biography*, Madison, p. 660 n. 57).

McKEY, Edward (d. 1918) Artist. He lived in Paris and Italy; he was in Paris when the First World War began and immediately volunteered to drive ambulances for the Italian army. He was killed near Piave in March 1918, being the first of the few members of the American Red Cross killed on the Italian front.

FREDERIC HENRY in Ernest Hemingway, *A Farewell to Arms* (1929)

'In [Charles Bakewell's *The Story of the American Red Cross in Italy* (1920)] Hemingway also could have read of the death of Lieutenant Edward McKey. . . . Certainly some of [McKey's] circumstances were used in the background and circumstances of Frederic Henry' (M.S. Reynolds, 1976, *Hemingway's First War: the making of* A Farewell to Arms, Princeton, NJ: Princeton University Press, pp. 147, 149). *See also* **Hemingway**, Ernest.

MACLAREN-ROSS, Julian (1912–64)

XAVIER FRANCIS TRAPNEL in Anthony Powell, *A Dance to the Music of Time* (1951–76)

'In due course I took some liberties with the theatrically projected personality of Maclaren Ross . . . in constructing the character of X. Trapnel' (Anthony Powell, 1982, *The Strangers All Are Gone*, p. 6).

McLEOD, Arthur William (1885–1956) Schoolteacher. He was D.H.
Lawrence's closest friend on the staff at Davidson Road School in Croydon, London, from 1908 to 1911. He was Headmaster of a series of secondary schools between 1920 and 1946.

MR MACWHIRTER in D.H. Lawrence, *The Trespasser* (1912)

'In the portrait of [Mr MacWhirter] . . . Lawrence gives us a glimpse of . . . A.W. McLeod' (H.T. Moore, 1960, *The Intelligent Heart: the story of D.H. Lawrence*, Harmondsworth: Penguin, p. 151; originally published 1955, London: Heinemann).

HOWARD PHILLIPS in Helen Corke, *Neutral Ground* (1933)

'McLeod appears as Howard Phillips' (*The Letters of D.H. Lawrence*, 1979, Vol. I, ed. James T. Boulton, Cambridge, p. 136 n. 3).

McMANES, James (1822–99) Born in Ireland, he moved to Philadelphia in
1830 and was naturalized as a United States citizen in 1844. From 1866 to 1881 he was the political boss of Philadelphia.

HENRY A. MOLLENHAUER in Theodore Dreiser, *The Financier* (1912)

'James McManes (the Henry A. Mollenhauer in the novel)' (Richard Lehan, 1974, *Theodore Dreiser: his world and his novels*, Carbondale, Ill.: Arcturis Books, p. 98).

MacNEILL, Hugh He was on the staff of the Dublin *Evening Telegraph* at the
time of Joyce's visit in 1909.

PROFESSOR MACHUGH in James Joyce, *Ulysses* (1922)

'MacHugh . . . was . . . Hugh MacNeill, a scholar of the classical modern languages, clever and lazy . . . he had for a time a position as teacher . . . at Maynooth. . . . The title of professor was accorded him out of . . . ironic politeness, for ... he never attained that eminence' (Richard Ellmann, 1966, *James Joyce*, London: Oxford Paperbacks, p. 298).

MACONOCHIE, Alexander (1787–1860) He entered the Royal Navy in 1803 and retired as a captain in 1855. From 1840 to 1845 he was Governor of Norfolk Island, and in 1849 he was Secretary to the Governor of Van Diemen's land. He was the author of a number of pamphlets on penology and was the inventor of the 'mark' system of prison discipline, 'framed to mix persuasion with punishment' (Frederic Boase, 1892, *Modern English Biography*, Vol. II, p. 674). In 1849 he became Governor of Birmingham borough prison, being succeeded in 1850 by William **Austin**.

Mr O'Connor in Charles Reade, *It is Never Too Late to Mend* (1856)

'Captain Maconochie . . . is O'Connor' ('The license of modern novelists', 1857, *Edinburgh Review* (July): 137).

McPHERSON, Aimée Semple (1890–1944) Née Kennedy. Daughter of a Canadian farmer, her family were Salvation Army followers but she 'converted' at the age of 17 and took to the road as an evangelist after the failure of her second marriage. She arrived in Los Angeles in 1918, and by 1923, said her admirers, she had made religion the best-paying business in America. In 1928, the 'Four-Square Gospel and Lighthouse Creed', the sect of which she was the founder, prophet and, so to speak, business manager, had 130 churches in California and 302 in the rest of America. The parent church, the Angelus Temple in Los Angeles, had 14,000 members, not including 2,000 children. In September 1928 she set out for England, to see what she could do for that country.

Mrs Melrose Ape in Evelyn Waugh, *Vile Bodies* (1930)

'"Mrs Ape" is clearly contrived from Aimée Semple MacPherson' (Christopher Sykes, 1975, *Evelyn Waugh*, London: Collins, p. 100).

McTAGGART, John McTaggart Ellis (1866–1925) Philosopher and scholar. Grandson of Thomas Flower Ellis, who was Macaulay's contemporary at Trinity College, Cambridge, and his closest friend throughout his life. In 1896 he was a Fellow of Trinity and was a lecturer in moral sciences from 1897 to 1923. Although he was an exponent of Hegel's philosophy, and an atheist, he nevertheless believed (unlike Boggart) in immortality. In appearance, he closely resembled the March Hare, and as the philosophers G.E. Moore and Bertrand **Russell** were equally like the Dormouse and the Mad Hatter, the trio (who were friends and contemporaries at Cambridge) was collectively known as the Mad Tea Party.

Professor Boggart in Shane Leslie, *The Cantab* (1926)

Identified in a key in the hand of Dr Ivor Ramsay, a Kingsman of the year 1920, and later Dean, laid in a copy of *The Cantab*.

MADGE, Travers (1823–66) Son of Thomas Madge, Unitarian minister of Bury, Norwich and Essex Street, London, he was educated at University College London. He was a town missionary in Norwich in 1845–7 and then became an itinerant preacher. In 1848–50 and 1859–61, he was a teacher at Lower Mosley Street schools in Manchester.

RICHARD ANCRUM in Mrs Humphry Ward, *The History of David Grieve* (1891)

'In the Manchester chapters, and for the character of Ancrum, I owed something to the life of Travers Madge, that martyr and missionary of the Cotton Famine' (Mrs Humphry Ward, 1911, Introd. to *The History of David Grieve* (Westmorland edn), Vol. I, p. xxxiv).

MADOCKS, William Alexander (1773–1828) He was MP for Boston, Lincolnshire, from 1802 to 1820, and for Chippenham from 1820 to 1828. 'Improver, "Chaotic", Architectural and Regional Planner, Reformer, Romantic' (Elizabeth Beazley, 1967, *Madocks and the Wonder of Wales*, title p.): he drained and reclaimed Traeth Mawr in the Bay of Cardigan, Caernarvonshire (1800 and 1824) by the construction of embankments, and in 1805–11 he built and largely designed the town of Tremadoc on the reclaimed land.

HARRY HEADLONG in Thomas Love Peacock, *Headlong Hall* (1816)

'Thomas Love Peacock . . . spent the winter of 1811 in North Wales and knew both Madocks and his schemes. When reading Madocks' letters it is impossible not to be reminded of that impulsive squire of Peacock's creation: "In all the thoughts, words and actions of Squire Headlong, there was a remarkable alacrity of progression, which almost annihilated the interval between conception and execution. He was utterly regardless of obstacles, and seemed to have expunged their very name from his vocabulary . . . he saw no interval between the first step and the last, but pounced upon his object with the impetus of a mountain cataract" *Headlong Hall*, ch. VIII' (Elizabeth Beazley, 1967, *Madocks and the Wonder of Wales*, p. 81). The three philosophers in the novel walk to Tremadoc, see the embankment in process of construction and admire 'the magnificence of the flowing tide', and return to Headlong Hall after having partaken of cold saddle of mutton and sherry at the inn [ch. VII]. *See also* **Johnes, T.**

MADRESFIELD COURT, Malvern, Worcestershire Seat of the **Lygon** family. The original house was Elizabethan, but as it now stands it is largely the work of P.C. Hardwick, who began work on it in 1863. The chapel 'is an exceptionally complete piece of Arts and Crafts decoration of 1902. The furnishing was done by Birmingham craftsmen for Countess Beauchamp, as a wedding present to the 7th Earl. Work went on until 1923' (Nikolaus Pevsner, 1968, *Worcestershire* (*Buildings of England* series), Harmondsworth: Penguin, p. 218).

BRIDESHEAD in Evelyn Waugh, *Brideshead Revisited* (1945)

'There is no resemblance between the landscape and architecture of Brideshead . . . and Madresfield, except for one detail – the art-nouveau decoration of the chapel. Madresfield is a moated house of red brick, of mainly Victorian architecture superimposed on an earlier base, while Brideshead is an epitome in stone of the Palladian style he loved so much' (Lady Dorothy Lygon, 1973, 'Madresfield and Brideshead', *Evelyn Waugh and His World*, ed. David Pryce-Jones, p. 54). *See also* **Castle Howard.**

MAGINN, William (1793–1842) Born in Cork and educated at Trinity College, Dublin, he moved to London in 1823 and secured employment on several Tory periodicals. In 1830 he was instrumental in founding *Fraser's Magazine*, where much of his best work subsequently appeared. In April 1832 he met Thackeray and for a time had a strong influence on his work. He began to drink to excess and died of tuberculosis in a debtor's prison.

Captain Shandon in W.M. Thackeray, *The History of Pendennis* (1848–50)

'Maginn was certainly the original of Captain Shandon. . . . The likeness may not be exact – Thackeray's portraits are never mere photographs – but it is none the less unmistakable' (*The Letters and Private Papers of W.M. Thackeray*, Vol. I: *1817–1840*, 1945, ed. Gordon N. Ray, London: Oxford University Press, p. 192 n. 29).

MAGNUS, Maurice (1876–1920) Journalist and theatrical agent. He was Manager for the dancer Isadora Duncan. He served in the French Foreign Legion; D.H. Lawrence wrote an introduction for his posthumous *Memoirs of the Foreign Legion* in which he stated that Magnus's mother was the illegitimate daughter of the German emperor, which remains in doubt. He committed suicide in Malta.

Mr May in D.H. Lawrence, *The Lost Girl* (1920)

'As a kind of preliminary sketch for the biographical introduction he was to write later for Magnus's Legion *Memoirs*, Lawrence put him into *The Lost Girl* as Mr May' (H.T. Moore, 1960, *The Intelligent Heart: the story of D.H. Lawrence*, Harmondsworth: Penguin, p. 339; originally published 1955, London: Heinemann).

MAHANTONGO STREET, Pottsville, Pennsylvania John O'Hara's father moved his family to 606 Mahantongo Street in December 1910, and John O'Hara grew up there.

Lantenengo Street, Gibbsville, in John O'Hara, *Appointment in Samarra* (1934)

'Mahantongo Street is called Lantenengo Street' (John O'Hara to his brother Tom, 12 February 1934, quoted in Finis Farr, 1974, *O'Hara: a biography*, p. 156).

MAHONEY, Daniel A. (*c.*1895–after 1952) Born in San Francisco of a large Irish Catholic family, he settled in Paris after the First World War. He was homosexual and an abortionist and in 1941 he was forcibly repatriated, although he later returned to Paris, where he died.

Matthew O'Connor in Djuna Barnes, *Ryder* (1928) and *Nightwood* (1936)

'[I]n the end she made out of him her single greatest literary character . . . Dr Matthew-Mighty-grain-of-salt-Dante-O'Connor' (Andrew Field, 1983, *The Formidable Miss Barnes*, p. 137). '[McAlmon] . . . had earlier depicted Mahoney in his 1923 short story "Miss Knight". . . . The story is about a transvestite, but John Glassco [in *Memoirs of Montparnasse*, 1973] . . . confirms that the character is based upon Mahoney' (ibid., p. 135).

MAIDA An enormous deerhound that was presented to Scott by **MacDonell of Glengarry** in 1816: it died in 1824.

ROSWAL in Sir Walter Scott, *The Talisman* (1825)

'It has been stated that Maida provided a model for two hounds in the Waverley novels, viz. "Roswal" in *The Talisman* and "Bevis" in *Woodstock*. See E. Thornton Cook, 1931, *Sir Walter's Dogs*, p. 22' (*The Letters of Sir Walter Scott*, 1935, ed. H.J.C. Grierson, Vol. VIII, London: Constable, p. 409 n.) The identification of Bevis would appear to be mistaken: see **Nimrod**.

MAIDEN CASTLE, Dorset 'Vast prehistoric earthwork or fortress, surrounded with three ramparts, each about sixty feet high, to defend a whole community during a siege.' Located about two miles south-west of Dorchester.

MAI DUN in Thomas Hardy, *The Mayor of Casterbridge* (1886)

Identified in F.B. Pinion, 1968, *A Hardy Companion*, London: Macmillan.

MAIDEN NEWTON, Dorset A village located eight miles north-west of Dorchester.

CHALK NEWTON in Thomas Hardy, Wessex novels and tales (1871–95)

Identified on a map prepared by Thomas Hardy which hangs in the Dorset County Museum, Dorchester. *See under* **Abbotsbury**.

MAIDSTONE, Kent

MUGGLETON in Charles Dickens, *The Pickwick Papers* (1836–7)

'It will go down to posterity as the original of "Muggleton", the scene of the famous cricket match in *Pickwick*' (C.T. Roade, 1921, 'Round about Maidstone and Muggleton', *The Dickensian* 17: 68). *See also* **West Malling**.

MAILER, Norman (b. 1923) American novelist, journalist and polemicist. Born in Long Branch, New Jersey, he was educated at Harvard and served in the Pacific during the Second World War; he wrote *The Naked and the Dead* (1948) following his time there. His work *Armies of the Night* (1968) won the Pulitzer Prize.

HARVEY MARKER in Jack Kerouac, *Desolation Angels* (1965)

Identified in 'Character key to the Duluoz Legend', in Barry Gifford and Lawrence Lee, 1979, *Jack's Book*, pp. 322–32.

MAINLAND, David (1818–1906) Master of a merchantman. He was introduced to Dickens in July 1842 when he went with Thomas **Chapman**, Maclise, Leech and others to see the restored Crosby Hall in Bishopsgate. His career is recounted in W.J. Carlton, 1968, 'A note on Captain Cuttle', *The Dickensian* (September): 152 ff.

CAPTAIN CUTTLE in Charles Dickens, *Dombey and Son* (1846–8)

'Captain Cuttle was one David Mainland' (R.S. Mackenzie, 1870, *Life of Charles Dickens*, p. 202).

MAITLAND, Sir Thomas (1759?–1824) Lieutenant-General. In 1813 he was Governor of Malta, and from 1815 to 1824 he was Commander-in-Chief in the Mediterranean and Lord High Commissioner of the Ionian Island. Nicknamed 'King Tom', he was an eccentric and high-handed man. He died of apoplexy at Malta.

THE GOVERNOR in Frederick Marryat, *Midshipman Easy* (1836)

'It is said he was the Governor in . . . *Midshipman Easy*' (*The Letters of Sir Walter Scott*, 1935, ed. H.J.C. Grierson, Vol. VIII, London: Constable, p. 185 n. 2).

MALHAM TARN HOUSE, Yorkshire Located near Skipton. Kingsley stayed there in the 1850s as the guest of Walter Morrison, the philanthropist.

HARTHOVER PLACE in Charles Kingsley, *The Water Babies* (1863)

'Malham Tarn House . . . was the original of Harthover Place . . . likewise the cliff down which he ran before he plunged into the river to become a water-baby was the nearby Malham Cove. . . . Martin has it that the little black marks made by lichen on the cliff face first gave Kingsley the idea of *The Water-Babies*. A friend asked him what caused the marks and he replied that they might have been made by the sooty feet of a little chimney sweep as he climbed down from the top' (Susan Chitty, 1974, *The Beast and the Monk: a life of Charles Kingsley*, p. 193).

MALIBRAN, Maria (1808–36) Opera singer. She was the daughter of Manuel **García** and the sister of Pauline **Viardot**.

MARIA CERINTHEA in Elizabeth Sara Sheppard, *Charles Auchester* (1853)

Identified in an anonymous typed key laid in a copy of the first edition of *Charles Auchester* which is now in the possession of the present author. *See also* **Hensel, Fanny**.

MALLON, Anna T. She was Arthur **Henry**'s mistress before she married him, becoming his second wife; they were later divorced. In 1901, after the failure of *Sister Carrie*, Dreiser and his wife spent a month with Henry and Anna in Henry's island cabin off the coast of Connecticut.

RONA MURTHA in Theodore Dreiser, 'Rona Murtha', *A Gallery of Women* (1929)

'Dreiser's semi-fictional portrait of Anna Mallon: "Rona Murtha"' (R.H. Elias, 1970, *Theodore Dreiser*, p. 322 n. 1).

NANCY in Arthur Henry, *An Island Cabin* (1902)

'Anna [is] referred to herein as . . . Nancy' (ibid.).

MALLOWAN, Max (1904–78) Distinguished archaeologist. Educated at Lancing, where he was the contemporary of Evelyn **Waugh**, and at New College, Oxford. From 1928 to 1930 he worked under Leonard **Woolley** at Ur. He married Agatha Christie in 1930.

DAVID EMMOTT in Agatha Christie, *Murder in Mesopotamia* (1936)

'In this book I figure as Emmott, a minor but decent character' (Max Mallowan, 1977, *Mallowan's Memoirs*, p. 208).

MALTHUS, Thomas Robert (1766–1834) Clergyman, economist and essayist. He was famous for his theories on population growth.

MR FAX in Thomas Love Peacock, *Melincourt* (1817)

'[T]he situation is further complicated . . . by the introduction of Malthus, in the person of Mr Fax . . . [whose] conversation throughout is based largely on Malthus' second chapter and the early chapters of the Third Book' (Martin Freeman, 1911, *Thomas Love Peacock*, London: Martin Secker, p. 173). However, cf. William F. Kennedy, 1966, 'Peacock's economists: some mistaken identities', *The Nineteenth Century* 21 (2): 185–8, where Kennedy argues that this identification is mistaken because Malthus was politically a Conservative where Mr Fax is a Benthamite Philosophic Radical; he offers no alternative identification.

MANCHESTER

MILTON in Elizabeth Gaskell, *North and South* (1855)

'[T]he strike in *North and South* seems to take place in Manchester' (H.I. Dutton and J.E. King, 1981, *'Ten Per Cent and No Surrender': the Preston Strike, 1853–4*, p. 199). 'The structure of the strike is . . . clearly based on the events in Preston' (ibid., p. 200).

MOORHAMPTON in Morley Roberts, *The Private Life of Henry Maitland* (1912)

Identified in an 'Index of Recurring Pseudonyms' in the 1958 edition of *The Private Life of Henry Maitland*, ed. Morchard Bishop, p. 255.

MANCHESTER SQUARE, London

GAUNT SQUARE in W.M. Thackeray, *Vanity Fair* (1847–8)

'A third square also contributes . . . this is Manchester Square' (Joan Stevens, 1969–70, 'A roundabout ride', *Victorian Studies* 13: 167). *See also* **Berkeley Square; Cavendish Square**.

MANGEOT, André Violinist and teacher of the violin. Of Belgian origin, he was the leader of a quartet in the 1920s and 1930s. He was married to Olive **Mangeot**.

MONSIEUR CHEURET in Christopher Isherwood, *Lions and Shadows* (1938)

Identification based upon private information.

MANGEOT, Olive She was married to André **Mangeot**. In the 1930s she became an active member of various left-wing groups.

MADAME CHEURET in Christopher Isherwood, *Lions and Shadows* (1938)

'Olive Mangeot ("Madame Cheuret" in *Lions and Shadows*)' (Christopher Isherwood, 1977, *Christopher and His Kind*, London: Eyre Methuen, p. 81).

MARGARET LANWIN in Christopher Isherwood, *The Memorial* (1932)

'[Isherwood] had put her doubly into *The Memorial* – in the characters of Margaret Lanwin (Olive as she then was) and of Margaret Scriven (Olive as she might be in later life)' (Isherwood, op. cit., p. 81).

MARY SCRIVEN in Christopher Isherwood, *The Memorial* (1932)

See above.

MANNERS, Lord John, 7th Duke of Rutland (1818–1906) Politician. Known as Lord John Manners until he succeeded his brother, the 6th Duke of **Rutland**, in 1888. An MP from 1841 to 1847 and from 1850 to 1888, he associated with Disraeli, George **Smythe** and others in the Young England Party. He advocated public holidays and the Ten Hour Act, and was in Cabinet under various Tory governments. He was depicted as an old man in Lady Diana **Cooper**'s reminiscences, *The Rainbow Comes and Goes*.

LORD HENRY SYDNEY in Benjamin Disraeli, *Tancred* (1847) and *Coningsby* (1844)

'Some of the charm of the original character is caught in the portrait' (A. Monypenny, 1912, *The Life of Benjamin Disraeli*, Vol. II, p. 163).

GEORGE WALDERSHARE in Benjamin Disraeli, *Endymion* (1880)

Identified in 'Key to *Endymion*', *Notes and Queries* 83 (24 October 1942): 263; identifications attributed to G.E. Buckle. *See also* **Smythe**, George.

MANNIN, Mary Anne (1800–64) Miniature painter in London. Née Millington, she married John Mannin, Professor of Singing, in 1832. She had premises in the Strand in London from 1829 to 1835 and exhibited at the Royal Academy. She painted a miniature of Dickens in 1827.

MISS LA CREEVY in Charles Dickens, *Nicholas Nickleby* (1838–9)

'The evidence of the portrait . . . indicates clearly whom Dickens had in mind when he depicted the character of Miss La Creevy [i.e. Mrs Mannin]' (W.G. Stryvers, 1946, 'Positively the first appearance', *The Dickensian* 44 (March): 93; the miniature is reproduced on p. 89). Miss La Creevy's premises, too, were in the Strand. *See also* **Drummond**, Rose Emma.

MANNING, Henry Edward (1802–92) Cardinal. An Anglican cleric from 1832, in 1851 he joined the Church of Rome. In 1865 he became the Roman Catholic Archbishop of Westminster, and in 1875 he became Cardinal.

CARDINAL GRANDISON in Benjamin Disraeli, *Lothair* (1870)

'The character of Cardinal Grandison in *Lothair* was Disraeli's revenge [for Manning's withdrawal of support from the proposal in 1868 to grant a charter and financial support to a Roman Catholic University in Dublin]' (Robert Blake, 1969, *Disraeli*, 2nd edn, London: Oxford University Press, p. 497).

NIGEL PENRUDDOCK in Benjamin Disraeli, *Endymion* (1880)

'Nigel Penruddock (representing Manning) says in Disraeli's *Endymion*, "No human power has the right to destroy a bishopric"' (J.E. Baker, 1932, *The Novel and the Oxford Movement*, Princeton, p. 2).

MANNING, Maria (1821–49) Née De Roux, she was born in Lausanne and became a lady's maid at Stafford House to Lady Blantyre, the daughter of the Duchess of Sutherland. In 1847, she married Frederick George Manning. In October 1849 the couple were tried at the Old Bailey for the murder of Maria's former lover, Patrick O'Connor; they were found guilty and hanged on 13 November in the presence of a crowd of some 50,000. Dickens, who was present, wrote a passionate letter to *The Times* (14 November 1849): 4): 'I was a witness of the execution . . . this morning. I went there with the intention of observing the crowd . . . I believe that a sight so inconceivably awful as the wickedness and levity of the immense crowd collected at that execution . . . could be imagined by no man.'

HORTENSE in Charles Dickens, *Bleak House* (1852–3)

'Hortense . . . is intended as a portrait of Maria Manning, at whose trial Dickens was present and whose broken English, impatient gestures and volubility he has reproduced with wonderful exactness' (B.B. Valentine, 1923, 'The original of Hortense and the trial of Marcia [sic] Manning for murder', *The Dickensian* 19 (January): 21). At the time of the trial the writer was a schoolboy in London. For her execution Maria Manning wore a black satin gown: it was some time, it is said, before fashionable ladies again wore black satin.

MRS REDGOLD in Emma Robinson, *The Gold-Worshippers* (1851)

Mrs Redgold appears first in chapter IV, paying a visit to Mrs Sparkleton, whose lady's maid she had been. 'She was only at present', writes Miss Robinson, 'a French femme de chambre, who had married an English railway-guard, and, after spending her youth amidst the refinement, splendour and luxury of great households, found herself condemned to poverty and a little hovel of a residence in the Borough for the rest of her life, apparently.' In the last volume we catch a glimpse of her execution, Mrs Redgold in the notorious black gown, in the midst of the hideous throng described by Dickens (chapter III). The novel deals primarily with George **Hudson** and the railway panic of 1845, and the general corruption caused by speculation in railway shares. Hudson figures as Humson, and at the other end of the scale Mrs Redgold, married to a railway guard, is hanged with her husband for murdering a customs man for his railway scrip.

MANNINGHAM-BULLER, Reginald, 1st Baron Dilhorne (1905–80) Solicitor-General from 1951 to 1954, Attorney-General from 1954 until 1962, and Lord Chancellor from 1962 to 1964, he was created Baron in 1962 and Viscount in 1964.

KENNETH WIDMERPOOL in Anthony Powell, *A Dance to the Music of Time* (1951–76)

'Dilhorne is said to be the original of Widmerpool in the Anthony Powell novels' (Alan Watkins, 1978, 'Notebook', *Observer* (18 June): 38).

MANSFIELD, Caulia Elder sister of C.B. **Mansfield** and Anna **Gifford**.

ARGEMONE LAVINGTON in Charles Kingsley, *Yeast* (1848)

'Kingsley told me once that in *Yeast* Caulia Mansfield had been his type for Argemone' (J.M. Ludlow, quoted in R.B. Martin, 1959, *The Dust of Combat: a life of Charles Kingsley*, London: Faber & Faber, p. 95). **See also Froude**, Charlotte; **Kingsley**, Frances.

MANSFIELD, Charles Blackford (1819–55) Chemist. A close friend and contemporary of Charles Kingsley at Cambridge, he was a rigid vegetarian and strict teetaller and joined the Christian Socialists. He discovered a method of extracting benzol from coal-tar, and published *Aerial Navigation* (1850) and, posthumously, *Paraguay, Brazil and the Plate*. He was burnt to death as the result of an accident while conducting an experiment.

FRANK LEIGH in Charles Kingsley, *Westward Ho!* (1855)

'Kingsley himself firmly declared . . . that . . . Frank . . . was Charles Mansfield' (Susan Chitty, 1974, *The Beast and the Monk: a life of Charles Kingsley*, p. 172).

MANSFIELD, Katherine (1888–1923) Short-story writer. Born Katherine Mansfield Beauchamp in Wellington, New Zealand, she was educated at Queen's College, London, and was a cousin of 'Elizabeth', Countess **Russell**. She was very briefly married to George Bowden, and later, in 1918, to John Middleton **Murry**, with whom she had lived since 1912. She contracted tuberculosis and died at Fontainebleau.

GUDRUN BRANGWEN in D.H. Lawrence, *Women in Love* (1920)

'Murry and Katherine Mansfield were assigned the most important roles . . . and in his autobiography [Murry] says . . . "It is probably true that Lawrence . . . found the germ of Gudrun in Katherine" . . . and "a few of the incidents of Katherine's life were taken without any sea-change from Katherine's"' (H.T. Moore, 1951, *Life and Works of D.H. Lawrence*, pp. 158–9; quoting John Middleton Murry).

OPHELIA in D.H. Lawrence, 'Smile' (1928)

'"Smile" [is] obviously based on the death of Katherine Mansfield (with . . . Katherine as . . . Ophelia)' (H.T. Moore, 1960, *The Intelligent Heart: the story of D.H. Lawrence*, Harmondsworth: Penguin, p. 431; originally published 1955, London: Heinemann).

SUSAN PALEY in Aldous Huxley, *Point Counter Point* (1928)

'Susan Paley, who is Katherine, is already dead, and much of the satire against Burlap accuses him of exploiting the memory of his wife' (Jerome Meckier, 1969, *Aldous Huxley*, p. 87).

REINE WILSON in Conrad Aiken, 'Your Obituary, Well Written' (1928)

'Katherine Mansfield . . . is, incidentally, the woman novelist, Reine Wilson, in . . . "Your Obituary, Well Written"' (Walter Allen, 1966, preface to *The Collected Short Stories of Conrad Aitken*, p. vii). In 1916 Francis Carco published in Paris a novel called *Les Innocents*, 'in which Katherine is depicted as "Winnie"' (A. Alpers, 1980, *The Life of Katherine Mansfield*, London: Jonathan Cape, p. 178).

MANSFIELD, Richard (1854–1907) American actor. Born in Berlin, he began his career in England and then in 1882 went to New York. Among his chief roles were Stevenson's Dr Jekyll and Mr Hyde and Rostand's Cyrano de Bergerac; he also played Shylock, Brutus, Richard III and Henry V. In 1906–7, in his last season, he put on the first production in English of *Peer Gynt*, playing the title role.

RICHARD BRANDELL in Thomas Wolfe, *The Web and the Rock* (1939)

'A story . . . by Thomas Wolfe is based on a visit Aline [Bernstein], at fourteen, paid with her father to . . . Richard Mansfield after one of his last performances as Richard III. Aline recalled the visit . . . for Wolfe, who later transcribed it almost literally . . . as a chapter in . . . *The Web and the Rock*' (Carole Klein, 1980, *Aline*, pp. 16–17).

MAPLEDURHAM HOUSE, Oxfordshire Situated on the Thames, now almost on the outskirts of Reading, 'but the village is remote and untouched by modern development' (Nikolaus Pevsner, 1974, *Oxfordshire* (*Buildings of England* series), Harmondsworth: Penguin). One of the largest Elizabethan houses in the county, it was begun *c*.1585, and was much altered internally during the eighteenth and early nineteenth centuries.

TOAD HALL in Kenneth Grahame, *The Wind in the Willows* (1908)

'Toad Hall . . . contains elements from . . . Mapledurham House' (Peter Green, 1959, *Kenneth Grahame, 1859–1932*, p. 24). *See also* **Cliveden; Harleyford Manor**.

MARCER, Joseph F. City Treasurer in Philadelphia, he was involved with C.T. **Yerkes** in the misappropriation of city funds.

GEORGE W. STENER in Theodore Dreiser, *The Financier* (1912)

'Marcer (the George W. Stener of the novel)' (Richard Lehan, 1974, *Theodore Dreiser: his world and his novels*, Carbondale, Ill.: Arcturis Books, p. 98).

MARIO, Jessie Meriton (1832–1906) Born Jessie White, in Gosport, Hampshire, she was the daughter of a shipbuilder. In 1854, during a tour of Italy, she met **Garibaldi** and Mazzini, and in 1857 she edited Orsini's *Memoirs and Adventures*. She was a correspondent in Genoa of the *Daily News*, and was imprisoned for a political offence, but was acquitted and released. In December 1857 she married Captain Alberto Mario, Aide-de-camp to Garibaldi; they followed Garibaldi in the expedition to Sicily, and set up a hospital for 2,000 in Palermo. At Milazzo she ran a hospital for the wounded, and she superintended the ambulances in the army of the Vosges attached to Garibaldi in the Franco-Prussian War. As a young woman she had applied, unsuccessfully, to study medicine at the University of London. She was a correspondent for several American and English newspapers, and in her old age she was reduced to teaching English in Florence. She was a close friend of Madame **Bodichon**.

THEODORA CAMPION in Benjamin Disraeli, *Lothair* (1870)

Identified in 'Key to *Lothair*', *Notes and Queries*, 183 (12 September 1942): 173.

MARION, Cape Cod, Massachusetts

MARMION in Henry James, *The Bostonians* (1884)

'Some weeks before his departure [for England, Henry James] spent a ... week-end at Marion, Cape Cod, visiting Richard Watson Gilder, of the Century, and his wife, who was a sister of Mrs Bronson's. His impressions are incorporated in *The Bostonians*, where Marion is renamed Marmion' (Leon Edel, 1962, *Henry James: the conquest of London, 1870–1883*, London: Rupert Hart-Davis, pp. 506, 507).

MARLBOROUGH DOWNS, Wiltshire Located between Marlborough to the south and Swindon to the north.

MARLBURY DOWNS in Thomas Hardy, 'What the Shepherd Saw' (1913)

Identified in F.B. Pinion, 1968, *A Hardy Companion*, London: Macmillan.

MARNHULL, Dorset A village located slightly north-east of Stalbridge, in the Vale of Blackmore. In the village is the **Crown Inn**, which was used by Hardy.

MARLOTT in Thomas Hardy, Wessex novels and tales (1871–95)

Identified on a map prepared by Thomas Hardy which hangs in the Dorset County Museum, Dorchester. *See under* **Abbotsbury**.

MARS, Miss *See under* **Squire**, Miss.

MARSH, Sir Edward (1872–1953) Educated at Westminster and at Trinity College, Cambridge, where he became a member of the Apostles. In 1896 he joined the Colonial Office, and in 1905 he became Winston **Churchill's** Private Secretary when the latter became Parliamentary Under-Secretary for the Colonies; their association lasted until 1928, with Marsh following Churchill from department to department. At the end of his career he served under J.H. Thomas, the Labour Party minister, retiring in 1935 after a brief stint under the National Government. A descendant of the Prime Minister Spenser Perceval, in 1903 he inherited a small share of the compensation granted to the Perceval family after his assassination. He used this in the patronage of the arts (he built up one of the largest collections of contemporary paintings in England), and the support of contemporary poets and writers. The literary executor of Rupert **Brooke**, he edited his collected works, and from 1912 to 1922 he edited a series of anthologies called *Georgian Poetry*. The last years of his life were devoted to literary work (largely translation) and the enjoyment of theatre.

MATTHEW DEAN in Osbert Sitwell, 'Triple Fugue' (1924)

'[T]he little story "Triple Fugue" was based on another of Osbert's old vendettas – this time with ... Edward Marsh. ... The malicious portrait of Marsh as Matthew Dean was a telling one' (John Pearson, 1978, *Façades: Edith, Osbert, and Sacheverell Sitwell*, London: Macmillan, p. 194). The portrait was exceedingly exact; Marsh's sitting-room, with its walls covered with pictures, was described, as was his appearance, the most remarkable feature of which was the tilting eyebrows and his voice, 'extraordinarily high, lisping, innocent' –

one of the consequences of the attack of mumps which Marsh suffered as a boy. According to Pearson (ibid.), Marsh never forgave Sitwell.

TYLNEY TYSOE in Gilbert Cannan, *Mendel* (1916)

'Portraits of Edward Marsh, Brett, Carrington, Augustus John and C.R.W. Nevinson are also to be found in the book' (Diana Farr, 1978, *Gilbert Cannan: a Georgian prodigy*, London: Chatto & Windus, p. 40). In fact, if Tysoe was intended as a portrait of Marsh, it was not an exact one: he was not married, nor was he a rich man, and he lived in a flat, not in a luxurious house. The only point in which Tysoe resembles him is in being a patron of the arts.

MARSHALL, Dr

DR MARTEL in Joseph Conrad, *Suspense* (1925)

'[T]wo half-pages (*Mémoires de la Comtesse de Boigne*, Vol. II, chap. III and chap. VIII) furnished him with the sketch of Dr Marshall who . . . becomes Dr Martel' (G. Jean-Aubry, 1925, 'The inner history of Conrad's *Suspense'*, *Bookman's Journal* 13 (49): 98).

MARTIN, Joseph United States congressman.

THE CHAIRMAN OF THE NATIONAL CONVENTION in James Reichley, *Hail to the Chief* (1960)

Identified in Joseph Blotner, 1966, *The Modern American Political Novel*, p. 129.

MARTINEAU, Kitty (b. 1882?) Née Savile-Clark, she married Cyril Martineau for love and died soon after. Thought by some to be the most beautiful woman in London, she was a member of Ada Leverson's circle.

FELICITY, LADY CHETWODE in Ada Leverson, *The Twelfth Hour* (1907)

See below.

BERTHA KELLYNCH in Ada Leverson, *Bird of Paradise* (1914)

'The "onlie begetter" of the heroines in Ada's six novels, all of whom were, like Kitty, beautiful, fairly intelligent, sweet-natured, devoid of malice and ambition and only concerned with love' (Violet Wyndham, 1963, *The Sphinx and Her Circle: a biographical sketch of Ada Leverson, 1862–1933*, London: Deutch, p. 35). Mrs Martineau would seem from the description in Mrs Wyndham's book, and the photograph there reproduced, to have been tall, slender and dark. Both Felicity Chetwode and Bertha Kellynch were small, rounded and blonde. But surely they are the heroines? Apart from looks, they fit the bill.

MARTYN, Edward (1859–1923) Irish critic and playwright. He was associated with W.B. Yeats, Lady Gregory and George Moore in founding the Irish Literary Theatre, and in 1914 he founded the Irish Theatre in Dublin. He was President of Sinn Fein from 1904 to 1908.

JOHN NORTON in George Moore, *A Mere Accident* (1887)

'A portrait of Edward Martyn . . . anglicised, rendered wholly aesthetic and much reduced in physical bulk' (Joseph Hone, 1936, *The Life of George Moore*, London: Victor Gollancz, p. 130).

MARTYN, Henry (1781–1812) Missionary. Born in Truro, Cornwall, he was educated at St John's College, Cambridge, becoming a Fellow in 1802. He was Curate to Charles Simeon at Holy Trinity Church, Cambridge; while he was in Cambridge, Patrick Brontë was his friend. He had an attachment to Lydia Grenfell, whose sister Fanny married Charles **Kingsley**, but abandoned thoughts of marriage to go to Bengal as a missionary in 1805. He translated the New Testament and the Prayer Book into Hindustani, the New Testament and the Psalms into Persian, and the Gospels into Judaeo-Persic. He died of fever while on a visit to Persia.

FRANCIS GWYNNE in Holme Lee, *Her Title of Honour* (1871)

'Curiously enough, Henry Martyn has been made the hero of a novel called *The Title of Honour*, published in 1871 by Holm [sic] Lee' (C.K. Shorter, 1905, *Charlotte Brontë and Her Sisters*, p. 170).

ST JOHN EYRE RIVERS in Charlotte Brontë, *Jane Eyre* (1847)

'St John Rivers obviously owes something to Henry Nussey . . . but his more heroic exploits in the East would appear to be derived from the missionary endeavours of Henry Martyn' (Tom Winnifrith, 1973, *The Brontës and their Background*, p. 229 n. 20). *See also* **Nussey**, Henry.

MARWOOD, Arthur (1868–1916) Fourth son of George Marwood of Little Busby Hall, Cleveland, and Frances, née Peel, who was first cousin to Robert **Peel**, the statesman. He was also a first cousin of Lewis **Carroll** and an uncle of Margaret Kennedy, the novelist. '[A] dandy in London and a farmer in Kent' (Violet Hunt, 1926, *The Flurried Years*, p. 28), he was one of Joseph **Conrad**'s closest friends. In 1902 he married Caroline Cranswick (**Marwood**, below).

THE DUKE OF KINTYRE in Ford Madox Ford, *The New Humpty-Dumpty* (1912)

Identified in Arthur Mizener, 1971, *The Saddest Story: a biography of Ford Madox Ford*, Cleveland: World Publishing, pp. 223–7.

CHRISTOPHER TIETJENS in Ford Madox Ford, *Parade's End* (1924–8)

'Tietjens of Groby . . . was admittedly a projection of Marwood' (Douglas Goldring, 1943, *South Lodge*, p. 16).

GERALD LUSCOMBE in Ford Madox Ford, *The Simple Life Limited* (1911)

'Gerald Luscombe . . . exhibits many Marwoodian features' (Thomas C. Moser, 1980, *The Life in the Fiction of Ford Madox Ford*, Princeton, p. 93).

MARWOOD, Caroline (1868?–1952) Née Cranswick, she married Arthur Marwood in 1902; in 1918, two years after his death, she married Walter Pilcher (d. 1941).

EVANGELINE LUSCOMBE in Ford Madox Ford, *The Simple Life Limited* (1911)

'[Gerald Luscombe's] wife is Evangeline (Marwood's Caroline)' (Thomas C. Moser, 1980, *The Life in the Fiction of Ford Madox Ford*, Princeton, p. 93).

MASON, Agnes (1871–c.1950) She was a member of the staff at Davidson Road School in Croydon, London, from 1907 to 1923. Lawrence also taught there, from 1908 to 1912, and although Agnes was rather older than Lawrence, she became much attached to him and watched over his health. She was a close friend of Helen Corke.

LOUISA in D.H. Lawrence, *The Trespasser* (1912)

'Lawrence used his . . . Croydon friends as prototypes for several of his characters . . . Miss Agnes Mason became Louisa' (E. Nehls, 1957, *D.H. Lawrence: a composite biography*, Madison, Vol. I, p. 551 n. 23).

CECILY MORTON in Helen Corke, *Neutral Ground* (1933)

'"Cecily Morton" in . . . *Neutral Ground*' (*The D.H. Lawrence Letters*, 1979, Vol. I, ed. James T. Boulton, Cambridge: Cambridge University Press, p. 194 n. 8).

MASON, Alexander Herbert (1856–95) Lieutenant-Colonel, Royal Engineers. Commissioned in 1874, he arrived in India in 1879, and except for a brief period of service in Egypt and of leave in England, he served there continually. He served in the Second Afghan War and in 1882–4 he was in Lahore as aide-de-camp to the Governor of the Punjab; it is probable that he and Kipling got to know each other at this time. In 1892 he was posted permanently to the Intelligence branch of the Army. He died of typhoid.

COLONEL CREIGHTON in Rudyard Kipling, *Kim* (1901)

'The only name that has been put forward as a possible original for Colonel Creighton is that of Lieut.-Col, Alexander Herbert Mason' (Alexander Mason, 1961, 'Colonel Creighton', *The Readers' Guide to Rudyard Kipling's Work*, Section I, App. II, p. 268).

MASON, George Grant An official of Pan American Airways, he lived in Havana. He and his wife Jane **Mason** were friends of Donald Ogden **Stewart**, through whom they met the Hemingways in 1931 when the three couples crossed the Atlantic on the same liner.

TOMMY BRADLEY in Ernest Hemingway, *To Have and Have Not* (1937)

'Gingrich warned that the book clearly libeled . . . Grant and Jane Mason, who in his view might be mistaken for Tommy and Helene Bradley' (Carlos Baker, 1969, *Ernest Hemingway: a life story*, New York, p. 298).

MASON, Jane She was married to Grant **Mason**. While in Havana, she frequently accompanied Hemingway on his fishing trips. The Masons were later divorced and in 1955 she married Arnold **Gingrich**.

MARGOT MACOMBER in Ernest Hemingway, 'The Short Happy Life of Francis Macomber', *The Fifth Column and the First Forty-nine Stories* (1938)

'[In 1937] Ernest [reminded] Arnold [Gingrich] that Jane Mason had been "flattered" when people said she was the model for Margaret Macomber' (Carlos Baker, 1969, *Ernest Hemingway: a life story*, New York, p. 299).

MASOOD, Syed Ross (1889–1937) Grandson of Sir Syed Ahmed Khan, the founder of the Anglo-Oriental College at Aligarh, he was educated at Aligarh and at New College, Oxford. In 1914 he joined the Imperial Educational Service, and from 1916 to 1928 he was Director of Public Education in Hyderabad State. He became Vice-Chancellor of Aligarh in 1928, and in 1933 he was knighted. As a child, he had joined the household of Sir Theodore Morrison, the distinguished Anglo-Indian official who was Principal of Aligarh (1899–1908) at that time. The Morrisons were friends of Forster's mother, and in 1906, when they were spending a leave at Weybridge, Forster undertook to coach Masood in Latin, preparatory to his going up to Oxford. The two became close friends, with the friendship lasting until Masood's death.

DR AZIZ in E.M. Forster, *A Passage to India* (1924)

'Aziz is modeled on Masood, my greatest Indian friend' (E.M. Forster speaking to K. Natwar-Singh in 1962, quoted in K. Natwar-Singh (ed.), 1964, *E.M. Forster: a tribute*, New York, p. xii).

MASSEY, Gerald (1828–1907) Poet. Put to work at the age of 8, he educated himself, with his first volume of verse being published at Tring, Hertfordshire, in 1848. He joined the Chartists and became a Christian socialist, and in 1875 his complete poetical works were published. Becoming a journalist and popular lecturer, he gave lecture tours in America. He lived for a time in Edinburgh, and from 1862 to 1877 at Little Gaddesden.

FELIX HOLT in George Eliot, *Felix Holt, the Radical* (1866)

'No one indeed can go through the two volumes of Mr Massey's poems without being struck with what struck George Eliot when, as she made no secret, she drew the portrait of their author in Felix Holt – the innate nobility of the character impressed on them' (J. Churton Collins, 1905, *Studies in Poetry and Criticism*, pp. 148–9). 'The low opinion of Gerald Massey that G.E. reveals in these letters [9 March 1854 to Sara Hennell and 15 March 1854 to Charles Bray] should dispel the absurd story that he was the original of Felix Holt' (*The George Eliot Letters*, 1954, ed. Gordon S. Haight, Vol. II, London: Oxford University Press, p. 146 n. 9).

MASTERMAN, Charles Frederick Gurney (1874–1927) Politician, writer and journalist. He was a Liberal MP from 1906 to 1914 and in 1923–4. In 1914–15, he was Chancellor of the Duchy of Lancaster, with a seat in Cabinet, and from 1914 to 1918 he was Director of Wellington House (i.e. propaganda).

LANGHAM in H.M. Tomlinson, *All Our Yesterdays* (1930)

'According to Lucy Masterman her husband was the model for Langham . . . and for Raeburn' (Samuel Hynes, 1968, *The Edwardian Turn of the Mind*, p. 58 n. 2).

RAEBURN in H.G. Wells, *Mr Britling Sees It Through* (1916)

See above.

STEPHEN FENWICK WATERHOUSE in Ford Madox Ford, *Parade's End* (1924–8)

'Waterhouse is basically Ford's conception of Masterman' (Arthur Mizener, 1971, *The Saddest Story: a biography of Ford Madox Ford*, Cleveland: World Publishing, p. 365).

MASTERMAN, George Frederick (1833?–93) Physician. He took the name of Cadogan-Masterman in 1891. In 1856 he served in the Crimea on the medical staff of the 82nd Regiment, and in 1863 he was at General Military Hospital in Asunción, Paraguay. He was caught up in the war between Paraguay and Brazil and was imprisoned in 1867, only being released to leave the country. He returned to England and became a Member of the Royal College of Surgeons in 1871 and a Licentiate of the Royal College of Physicians (Ireland) in 1876. He entered the local government medical service and was Medical Officer of Health for Stourport, Worcestershire, from 1881 to 1893. He was the author of *Seven Eventful Years in Paraguay* (1869).

DR MONYGHAM in Joseph Conrad, *Nostromo* (1904)

'From Masterman, Conrad took most of the names of his characters, including . . . Monygham. Masterman was a doctor and Conrad based his account of Dr Monygham's torture and confession on that of Masterman himself' (Jocelyn Baines, 1969, *Joseph Conrad: a critical biography*, p. 295).

MATADI, Congo The terminal point of navigation on the Lower Congo, where Conrad arrived in July 1890.

THE COMPANY STATION in Joseph Conrad, *Heart of Darkness* (1902)

'[T]o emphasise the inefficiency of Belgian colonisation and increase the isolation of Marlow and Kurtz, the story gives no idea of how far colonisation had proceeded. Thus, at what Marlow calls the Company Station, Matadi, there were in fact some 170 Europeans . . . and much commercial activity' (Ian Watt, 1980, *Conrad in the Nineteenth Century*, p. 140).

MATHIAS, Thomas James (1754–1835) Satirist and Italian scholar. In 1812 he was a librarian at Buckingham Palace, and in 1814 he edited and published Gray's works, an enterprise on which he lost heavily. He went to Italy in 1817; he was described as 'the best Italian scholar since Milton' (*Concise Dictionary of National Biography*, Oxford).

ROLFE in Frances Trollope, *The Blue Belles of England* (1842)

'Thank you my dearest friend, for the *Key* [to *The Blue Belles of Scotland*] . . . I had guessed a good many of the names – . . . I mistook Rolfe for Roscoe instead of Mathias!' (11 January 1842, reproduced in *Elizabeth Barrett to Miss Mitford*, 1954, ed. Betty Miller, London: John Murray, p. 98).

MATTHEW, Henry (1807–61) Son of Revd John Matthew of Kilve, Somerset, he was educated at Cambridge, where Thackeray was intimate with him during his second year. He matriculated at Balliol College, Oxford, in 1825, and in 1830 he enrolled at Sidney Sussex, Cambridge, but took a degree at neither university. From 1843 to 1861 he was Rector of Little Eversholt, Bedfordshire.

BLOUNDELL in W.M. Thackeray, *The History of Pendennis* (1848–50)

'An identification for which there is strong evidence' (Gordon N. Ray, 1955, *Thackeray: a biography*, Vol. I: *The Uses of Adversity, 1811–1846*, London: Oxford University Press, p. 459 n. 44).

GEORGE BRANDON in W.M. Thackeray, *A Shabby Genteel Story* (1840)

'It may be surmised that he supplied some traits of George Brandon' (*The Letters and Private Papers of W.M. Thackeray*, Vol. I: *1817–1840*, 1945, ed. Gordon N. Ray, London: Oxford University Press, p. 151 n. 9). 'I have never known what adversity is or I should be able perhaps to understand his incomprehensible recklessness and quiet with things hanging over him, wh. if discovered might leave him a beggar, an outcast' (Thackeray, Diary, entry for 12 April 1830, ibid., p. 190).

MATTHIESSEN, Francis Otto (1902–50) Professor at Harvard from 1929 to 1950, he edited *The Notebooks of Henry James* along with Kenneth Murdock. He was the author of *American Renaissance* (1941) and other works, and was a liberal politically. He committed suicide.

EDWARD CAVAN in May Sarton, *Faithful are the Wounds* (1955)

'It seems agreed that Cavan bears a strong resemblance to Professor F.O. Matthiessen' (J. Blotner, 1966, *The Modern American Political Novel*, p. 323 n. 33).

MAUDE, Christine (b. 1886) Dancer and actress. She married John Mavrogodarto.

JENNY PEARL in Compton Mackenzie, *Carnival* (1912)

'Christine Maude was the original of Jenny Pearl' (Compton Mackenzie, 1966, *My Life and Times: Octave 5, 1915–1923*, p. 192).

MAUGHAM, Barbara Sophia (1828?–92?) Née von Seidlin, she was the daughter of a German banker and married Revd H.M. **Maugham**.

LOUISE CAREY in W. Somerset Maugham, *Of Human Bondage* (1915)

'She was prim and respectable, kindly but straitlaced. Both [she and her husband] appear with stark clarity as the Reverend William Carey and his wife Louise in . . . *Of Human Bondage* (Robin Maugham, 1966, *Somerset and All the Maughams*, p. 117).

MAUGHAM, Edith Mary (1840–82) Daughter of Major Snell, in 1863 she married Robert Ormond Maugham. She was the mother of W. Somerset Maugham.

MRS CAREY in W. Somerset Maugham, *Of Human Bondage* (1915)

'It is a moving story, but the last episodes were strangely distorted . . . in the opening pages of *Of Human Bondage*' (Robin Maugham, 1966, *Somerset and All the Maughams*, p. 108). 'Once when she was lying in bed . . . and knew she could not live much longer, the thought came to her that her sons when they grew up would not know what she was like when she died, so she called her maid, had herself dressed in an evening gown of white satin and went to the photographers' (W. Somerset Maugham, 1938, *The Summing Up*, p. 18).

MAUGHAM, Frederic Herbert, 1st Viscount (1866–1958) Lord Chancellor of England. Second son of Robert Ormond Maugham and Edith Mary **Maugham**, he was the elder brother of W. Somerset Maugham.

WALTER FANE in W. Somerset Maugham, *The Painted Veil* (1925)

'I don't suppose you have ever read a novel of mine called *The Painted Veil*. I used my brother as my model for the doctor in that story' (W. Somerset Maugham to R.F.V. Heuston, 7 September 1959, quoted in Robin Maugham, 1966, *Somerset and All the Maughams*, p. 186).

MAUGHAM, Revd Henry Macdonald (1828–97) Vicar of Whitstable. He was the uncle with whom W. Somerset Maugham was sent to live when his father died in 1884. He married Barbara Sophia von Seidlin (**Maugham**, above).

REVD WILLIAM CAREY in W. Somerset Maugham, *Of Human Bondage* (1915)

'Maugham's portraits of his uncle, bitter in *Of Human Bondage* and softened in *Cakes and Ale*, are not generous' (R.L. Calder, 1972, *W. Somerset Maugham and the Quest for Freedom*, London: Heinemann, p. 5).

MAUGHAM, Syrie (1879–1955) Daughter of the well-known philanthropist, Dr Thomas Barnardo, in 1901 she married Henry (later Sir Henry) Wellcome, who was twenty-six years her senior. They were divorced in 1915, and in 1916 she married W. Somerset **Maugham**, but the marriage was not a success and Maugham lived in France while his wife lived in London; they were divorced in 1927. She practised as a fashionable interior decorator from 1927 until 1939 and spent the Second World War in America; after her return to England, she carried out only a handful of commissions, all for American clients.

MRS BEAVER in Evelyn Waugh, *A Handful of Dust* (1934)

'Mrs Beaver bears a suspicious resemblance to Syrie' (R.B. Fisher, 1978, *Syrie Maugham*, p. 32).

CYNTHIA STODDARD in Elinor Mordaunt, *Gin and Bitters* (1931)

'"Mrs Cynthia Stoddard" (presumably meant to be Syrie Wellcome)' (R.L. Calder, 1972, *W. Somerset Maugham and the Quest for Freedom*, London: Heinemann, p. 272).

MAUGHAM, William Somerset (1874–1965) British novelist and playwright. Born in Paris of Irish origin, he was educated at the King's School, Canterbury and Heidelberg. He qualified as a surgeon at St Thomas's Hospital, London, and spent a year as a medical practitioner in the London slums. In 1914 he served with a Red Cross unit in France, becoming a secret agent in Geneva and Petrograd, an experience he used in *Ashenden* (1928). He spent two years in a Scottish sanatorium with tuberculosis, then travelled in the Far East before settling in the south of France. He was a British agent again during the Second World War, fleeing from France in 1940 and settling in the United States until 1946.

WILLIAM ASHENDEN in W. Somerset Maugham, *Ashenden; or The British Agent* (1928)

'William Ashenden, who is Somerset Maugham himself' (Jerome Meckier, 1969, *Aldous Huxley*, p. 9).

ARCHIE BERTRAND in Hugh Walpole, *John Cornelius: His Life and Adventures* (1937)

'"Archie Bertrand", although incorporating a number of Maugham's characteristics, is only part of the literary background of the novel' (R.L. Calder, 1972, *W. Somerset Maugham and the Quest for Freedom*, London: Heinemann, pp. 293, 294).

PHILIP CAREY in W. Somerset Maugham, *Of Human Bondage* (1915)

'Except that the hero . . . Philip Carey, suffered from a club foot instead of a stammer, the events from the very first scene, portraying his mother's death, were directly modeled on Maugham's own experience' (Lionel Stevenson, 1967, *History of the English Novel*, Vol. XI, New York, p. 66).

LAURENCE HURLE in Elinor Mordaunt, *Gin and Bitters* (1931)

'There is little of Maugham's real character in Hurle' (Calder, op. cit., p. 293). The English edition, entitled *Full Circle*, was withdrawn when Maugham issued a writ of alleged libel against the author.

GILBERT HEREFORD VAUGHAN in Ada Leverson, *The Limit* (1911)

'Ada Leverson met the young Maugham in the early years of this century . . . she saw the opportunity of sketching him in . . . *The Limit*, as Gilbert Hereford Vaughan. . . . The portrait is accurate' (Calder, op. cit., pp. 290, 291).

MAXIM'S CHINESE RESTAURANT, Soho, London Situated on Gerrard Street, off Shaftesbury Avenue.

CASANOVA'S CHINESE RESTAURANT in Anthony Powell, *A Dance to the Music of Time* (1951–76)

'. . . Maxim's Chinese Restaurant, to some small extent model for Casanova's Chinese Restaurant' (A. Powell, 1978, *To Keep the Ball Rolling: the memoirs of Anthony Powell*, Vol. II: *Messengers of Day*, London: Heinemann, p. 169).

MAXSE, Lady Caroline (1803–86) Daughter of the 5th Earl of Berkeley, in 1829 she married James Maxse of Effingham Hill, Surrey. She was the sister of G.G.F. **Berkeley** and Lord **Fitzhardinge**, and the mother of Sir Henry **Maxse** and F.A. **Maxse**.

LADY CHARLOTTE EGLETT in George Meredith, *Lord Ormont and His Aminta* (1894)

'The character of Lady Charlotte Eglett . . . is said to have been suggested by Lady Caroline Maxse' (S.M. Ellis, 1920, *George Meredith*, 2nd edn, London: Grant Richards, p. 295).

MAXSE, Rear-Admiral Frederick Augustus (1833–1900)   Admiral and political writer. He was the son of Lady Caroline **Maxse** and the brother of Sir Henry **Maxse**.

NEVIL BEAUCHAMP in George Meredith, *Beauchamp's Career* (1876)

'Nevil Beauchamp . . . was a full-length portrait of Maxse' (A. Lionel Stevenson, 1954, *The Ordeal of George Meredith*, London: Peter Owen, p. 193). 'In **Beauchamp's Career** [Meredith] drew my father, and the election described there was the election at Southampton in 1869 [sic] when my father contested the seat – and was defeated. Meredith was there canvassing and he was the shrewdest of observers. There is a list of some of the characters in *Beauchamp's Career* and the people he drew them from' (Viscountess Milner, 1951, *From My Picture Gallery*, p. 72).

MAXSE, Sir Henry (1832–83)   A lieutenant-colonel, he distinguished himself in the Crimea. He left the Army in 1863 and became Lieutenant-Governor of Heligoland, being appointed Governor in 1864. In 1881 he became Governor of Newfoundland. He was the son of Lady Caroline **Maxse** and the brother of F.A. **Maxse**. While attached to the Embassy in Vienna, to the dismay of his family he met and married a German actress, Fräulein von Rudloff.

DIGBY GRAND in G.J. Whyte-Melville, *Captain Digby Grand: An Autobiography* (1851)

'The original of Digby Grand' (to Janet Ross, 19 November 1861, reproduced in *Letters of George Meredith*, 1970, ed. C.L. Cline, Vol. I, Oxford, p. 112).

MAXSE, Katharine ('Kitty') (1867–1922)   Daughter of Vernon Lushington, in 1890 she married L.J. Maxse, son of F.A. **Maxse** and the owner and Editor (1893–1932) of the *National Review*.

CLARISSA DALLOWAY in Virginia Woolf, *The Voyage Out* (1915) and *Mrs Dalloway* (1925)

'Lettice is almost Kitty verbatim; what would happen if she guessed?' (to Vanessa Bell, 10 August 1908, reproduced in *The Letters of Virginia Woolf*, 1975, ed. Nigel Nicolson, Vol. I, London: Hogarth Press, p. 349). '[Lettice was] an earlier name for Clarissa Dalloway, who first appeared in *The Voyage Out*' (ibid., n. 2). 'I remember the night at Rodmell when I decided to give [*Mrs Dalloway*] up, because I found Clarissa in some way tinselly. Then I invented her memories. But I think some distaste for her persisted. Yet, again, that was true to my feeling for Kitty' (entry for 18 June 1925, in Virginia Woolf, 1953, *A Writer's Diary*, ed. Leonard Woolf, London: Hogarth Press, p. 79).

MAXSTOKE PRIORY, Warwickshire   Located near Fillongley.

TOPPING ABBEY in George Eliot, *Daniel Deronda* (1876)

'At Maxstoke Priory near Fillongley, where Marian's [i.e. George Eliot's] Aunt Garner and Uncle Isaac lived, there is, according to the local guide, "a remarkable panelled room with a painted ceiling showing the crests of many families", just as in Sir Hugo's drawing-room' (Marghanita Laski, 1973, *George Eliot and Her World*, London: Thames & Hudson, p. 106). *See also* **Laycock Abbey**.

MAXWELL, Sir Robert (d. 1786) 'A Maxwell of Glenormiston . . . sent his only son and heir to a Jesuit College in Flanders, left his estate in his brother's management and died. The wicked uncle alleged that the heir was also dead. The child, ignorant of his birth, grew up, ran away from the Jesuits at the age of sixteen, enlisted in the French army, fought at Fontenoy, got his colours, and, later, landed in the Moray Firth as a French officer in 1745. He went through the campaign, was in hiding in Lochaber after Drumossie, and in making for a Galloway port, was seized and imprisoned in Dumfries. Here an old woman of his father's household recognized him by "a mark which she remembered on his body". His cause was taken up by friends; but the usurping uncle died, and Sir Robert Maxwell recovered his estates without a lawsuit' (Andrew Lang (ed.), 1901, Introd. to *Guy Mannering* (Border edn), pp. xiv, xv). Lang is abridging an anecdote from the *New Monthly Magazine*, recounted by Robert Chambers, 1884, *Illustrations of the Author of Waverley*, pp. 29–32. According to Chambers, Maxwell settled down as an exemplary landowner and landlord. Towards the end of his life, however, he lost his fortune in speculation and was obliged to sell his estate. He died in Galloway.

HENRY BERTRAM in Sir Walter Scott, *Guy Mannering* (1815)

Robert Chambers describes this story as 'the groundwork of the novel'. In 1859 Mrs Gaskell wrote to Charles Norton, describing a family holiday in 'Auchencairn, a little village on a land-locked bay of the Solway, where we had rooms for a month in an old house . . . close to all the scenery of Guy Mannering, and within a mile of the Maxwells of Orchardston, an ancestor of whom was the lost heir' (reproduced in *Letters of Mrs Gaskell*, 1966, ed. J.A.V. Chapple and Arthur Pollard, Manchester, p. 581). So this tradition was widely known and accepted. Andrew Lang, however, says: 'There is nothing to prove that Scott was acquainted with this adventure' (ibid., p. xv). *See also* **Annesley**, James; **Routledge**, Henry.

MAY, Henry

ELLIOTT TEMPLETON in W. Somerset Maugham, *The Razor's Edge* (1944)

'Chips Channon was not the original of Templeton . . . but Henry May, an old Corniche figure whom I met with Maugham' (Cyril Connolly, 1974, review of Anthony Curtis, *The Patterns of Maugham*, *Sunday Times* (20 January): 31). *See also* **Channon**, Sir Henry.

MAY, Colonel Joseph (1760–1841) Born and raised in Boston, he was a descendant of John May, who emigrated from England in 1640. In 1797 he was elected Colonel of the Boston cadets. He was a partner in a firm of Boston merchants, but trade failed in 1798 and in 1799 he became the first and only Secretary of the Boston Marine Insurance Company. The company was wound up in 1838, and he retired to devote almost half his time to charitable enterprises. He was the father of Abigail May, who married Bronson **Alcott**.

MR LAURENCE in Louisa M. Alcott, *Little Women* (1868) and sequels

'This is the author's own statement:–... "Mr Lawrence [sic] is my grandfather, Colonel Joseph May"' (E.D. Cheney, 1889, *Louisa May Alcott: her life, letters and journals*, p. 193).

MAYA, Villa, Posilipo, Italy Situated in the Bay of Naples and known as the Villa Maia, it was bought by Norman Douglas in 1896 from an Irish marine engineer who was then Director of the Patterson or Guppy works at Naples. In 1885 J.M. Faulkner had joined the Armstrong-Whitworth Company, which had links with the firm of Guppy, and must have visited the Villa. It was still occupied in 1976.

VILLA DE ANGELIS in J. Meade Faulkner, *The Lost Stradivarius* (1895)

'Several of the rooms in my villa, and all the capacious cellars, are of Roman construction. It can therefore boast of a long ancestry and has been much written about; it figures in *The Lost Stradivarius* of which I remember nothing save the mention of a creaking arm-chair' (Norman Douglas, 1934, *Looking Back*, p. 372).

MAYER, Teodoro Publisher (1905–15) of the evening newspaper, *Le Piccolo della Sera*, the principal paper of Trieste, when James Joyce lived there; the newspaper had been founded in 1881 by his father, a Hungarian Jewish peddler. He was a leader of the irredentist movement in Trieste, and later became an Italian senator.

LEOPOLD BLOOM in James Joyce, *Ulysses* (1922)

'Another rival for this honor [that of being the prototype of Bloom] was Teodoro Mayer. ... But there is no evidence that he and Joyce were closely acquainted' (Richard Ellmann, 1982, *James Joyce*, rev. edn, Oxford: Oxford Paperbacks, p. 374 n.). *See also* **Bloom**, Joseph; **Byrne**, John Francis; **Chance**, Charles; **Hunter**, Alfred H.; **Jackson**, Holbrook; **Joyce**, James; **Joyce**, John Stanislaus; **Popper**, Leopoldo; **Schmitz**, Ettore.

MAYTHAM HALL, Rolverden, Kent Located about ten miles from Rye. Frances Hodgson Burnett rented the Hall from 1898 until she left England in 1907.

MISSELTHWAITE MANOR in Frances Hodgson Burnett, *The Secret Garden* (1911)

'Maytham ... provided the lamb, the rose garden and the robin. The Brontës ... and Frances's visit to Lord Crewe's house [Fryston Hall] in 1895 had provided the Yorkshire setting' (Ann Thwaite, 1973, *Waiting for the Party: the life of Frances Hodgson Burnett, 1849–1924*, p. 221).

MEAD, Patrick J. Editor of the Dublin *Evening Telegraph* at the time of Joyce's visit in 1909.

MYLES CRAWFORD in James Joyce, *Ulysses* (1922)

'The personality of Crawford is ... that ... of Mead in 1904 sub-editor, but now editor. ... The description of Mead is mostly literal' (Richard Ellmann, 1966, *James Joyce*, London: Oxford Paperbacks, p. 298).

MEE, Lois   A fellow student with D.H. Lawrence at University College, Nottinghamshire.

Lois in D.H. Lawrence, 'Goose Fair' (1914)

'Do you recognise the people? – a glorified Lois Mee (is she glorified) ...?' (to Louie Burrows, 3? November 1909, reproduced in *The D.H. Lawrence Letters*, 1979, Vol. I, ed. James T. Boulton, Cambridge: Cambridge University Press, p. 142). 'Lois Mee ... presumably is the "Lois" in the story' (ibid., n. 6).

MELBA, Dame Nellie   (1861–1931)   Operatic singer. Born Helen Porter Mitchell in Melbourne, Australia. She performed at Covent Garden, London, in 1888 and was created Dame Commander of the Order of the British Empire in 1927.

Madame Irela in Beverley Nichols, *Evensong* (1932)

Identification based upon private information.

MELBOURNE, Elizabeth Lamb, Lady   (1753?–1818) Daughter of Sir Ralph Milbanke, 5th Baronet, she married the 1st Viscount Melbourne. She was alleged to have been at one time the mistress of the Prince of Wales, and later of the Earl of Egremont, the latter generally being supposed to be the father of her son William Lamb, Lord **Melbourne**. She was an aunt of Lady **Byron** and at 60 years of age she became the friend and confidante of Lord **Byron**, who was then aged 24.

Mrs Seymour in Lady Caroline Lamb, *Glenarvon* (1816)

'Lady Melbourne is also made to appear in the book and is depicted as bigoted and vulgar. She is probably represented under the name of Mrs Seymour' (Mabell, Countess of Airlie, 1921, *In Whig Society, 1775–1818*, p. 184). *See also* **Bessborough**, Lady; **Kinnaird**, Maria.

MELBOURNE, William Lamb, Lord   (1779–1848)   Statesman. 2nd Viscount Melbourne, he was the son of the 1st Viscount and Lady **Melbourne**, and was educated at Eton, Trinity College, Cambridge, and in Glasgow. He became a Whig MP in 1805 and was Prime Minister in 1834 and in 1835–41. In 1805 he married Lady Caroline Ponsonby (**Lamb**).

William Ashe in Mrs Humphry Ward, *The Marriage of William Ashe* (1905)

'... the story of William Lamb ... transmuted into the later nineteenth century' (Elizabeth Jenkins, 1932, *Lady Caroline Lamb*, p. 276).

Lord Avondale in Lady Caroline Lamb, *Glenarvon* (1816)

'[Calantha's] husband, Lord Avondale, otherwise William [Lamb] in spite of the fact that he too is unusually noble-hearted, neglects her, and corrupts her morals by his cynical views' (Lord David Cecil, 1939, *The Young Melbourne and the Story of His Marriage with Caroline Lamb*, p. 190). Also identified in a key found among the papers of John Whishaw, a member of the Holland House circle, printed in the *The 'Pope' of Holland House: selections from the correspondence of John Whishaw and his friends, 1813–1840*, 1906, ed. Lady Seymour, p. 151.

LORD DANNISBURGH in George Meredith, *Diana of the Crossways* (1884)

'"Lord Dannisburgh" is described in authentic (though superficial) terms of Melbourne within the first few pages' (Alice Acland, 1948, *Caroline Norton*, London: Constable, p. 172).

MELBOURNE HOUSE, London Located in Whitehall, it was the house of Lord and Lady **Melbourne** and later became the Scottish Office.

MENTEITH HOUSE in Lady Caroline Lamb, *Glenarvon* (1816)

Identified in a key found among the papers of John Whishaw, a member of the Holland House circle, printed in *The 'Pope' of Holland House: selections from the correspondence of John Whishaw and his friends, 1813–1840*, ed. Lady Seymour, 1906, p. 151.

MELBURY HOUSE, Dorset Located at Melbury Sampford, halfway between Melbury Osmund to the north, and Evershot to the south. The house, part of which dates from the fifteenth century, stands in a large wooded park; it belonged to Lord Ilchester.

KING'S HINTOCK COURT in Thomas Hardy, Wessex novels and tales (1871–95)

Identified on a map prepared by Thomas Hardy which hangs in the Dorset County Museum, Dorchester. *See under* **Abbotsbury**.

MELBURY OSMOND, Dorset A small hamlet about ten miles south of Yeovil, just inside the north-west border of Dorset. Hardy's maternal ancestors, the Swetmans, lived there in a house called Townsend.

KING'S HINTOCK in Thomas Hardy, Wessex novels and tales (1871–95)

Identified on a map prepared by Thomas Hardy which hangs in the Dorset County Museum, Dorchester. *See under* **Abbotsbury**.

MELLS, Somerset Located four miles west of Frome. The Elizabethan manor house, much restored *c.*1900, belonged to the Horner family until after the First World War.

FALLS-PARK in Thomas Hardy, 'The First Countess of Wessex' (1891)

Identified in F.B. Pinion, 1968, *A Hardy Companion*, London: Macmillan. Mells Park, another house in the village that was formerly Horner property, was largely rebuilt by Lutyens for Reginald McKenna in 1923.

MELROSE, Angus 'An adventurer calling himself Dr Angus Melrose – perhaps an assumed name – who had a few months before alighted in Belleville [Illinois] as a lecturer on phrenology ... and incidentally offering his professional services for the healing of all known diseases. ... [He] was over six feet in height, and robust in proportion, with florid face and long nose. Of friendly, social disposition, he was a fluent talker, speaking correct English with a broad Scotch accent. . . . He stated that he had recently graduated in medicine at the Edinburgh University, and having but limited means, to gratify his desire to see America he had recourse to the lecture platform, phrenology and the practice of medicine to defray expenses of touring the country' (J.F. Snyder in *Journal of the Illinois Historical Society*, quoted in W.G. Wilkins, 1911, *Dickens in America*, p. 220).

DR CROCUS in Charles Dickens, *American Notes* (1842)

'He remained in Belleville several months, but though immortalized as "Dr Crocus" . . . very few persons now living retain the slightest recollection of him' (Wilkins, op. cit., pp. 220–1). Dr Snyder, who was a boy at the time, was describing Dickens's trip to Belleville from St Louis in April 1842. According to Russell Hinkley, writing to John Forster from Belleville in April 1874, his real name was Croselong (see W.J. Carlton, 1962, 'Postscripts to Forster', *The Dickensian* 58 (January): 90).

MELVILL, Harry (1866–1936) Son of Sir W.H. Melvill and Elizabeth Theresa, née Lister, daughter of the 2nd Baron Ribblesdale, he was also the step-grandson of Lord John **Russell** and was educated at Harrow and at University College, Oxford. For a brief time he was Secretary to Sir Edgar Vincent (later Lord D'Abernon) when the latter was a governor of the Imperial Ottoman Bank (1889–97). He moved in the circle of painters, writers and members of Society centring on Dieppe in the period before the First World War. A legendary raconteur of Edwardian London, he was described as 'the great conversation geyser', and according to Jacques Emile Blanche, who painted his portrait in 1904 (see J.E. Blanche, 1937, *Portraits of a Lifetime*, p. 108), he was known as 'Mr Chatterbox'.

MR CHERRY-MARVEL in Michael Arlen, *The Green Hat* (1924)

'Caricatured as Mr Cherry-Marvel in *The Green Hat*' (*The Letters of Oscar Wilde*, 1962, ed. Rupert Hart-Davis, London: Rupert Hart-Davis, p. 220 n. 1).

HUGH DEARBORN in Osbert Sitwell, 'The Machine Breaks Down' (1924)

In 1919 Osbert Sitwell, staying in Monte Carlo, met Melvill for the first time. In the spring of 1921, with Aldous Huxley, he made an expedition from Florence to Lucca and there he again encountered Melvill (see John Pearson, 1978, *Façades: Edith, Osbert and Sacheverell Sitwell*, London: Macmillan, p. 164). The story gives an exact description of Melvill, and the incident in the hotel at Lucca took place just as described.

WALTER TILLOTSON in Aldous Huxley, 'The Tillotson Banquet' (1924)

'The whole idea of this rediscovered idol of the nineties was plainly taken from the incident at Lucca with old Harry Melvill. . . . He was cut to the quick when he discovered he was the inspiration of the two stories' (Pearson, op. cit., pp. 171, 172).

MELVILLE, William (1852–1918) Chief Inspector of the Criminal Investigation Department at the time of the **Greenwich Bomb Outrage** of 1894. He described himself in *Who's Who* as having taken an active part in the suppression of anarchism.

CHIEF INSPECTOR HEAT in Joseph Conrad, *The Secret Agent* (1907)

'In some important aspects [Chief Inspector Melville] approximates to Conrad's Inspector Heat' (Norman Sherry, 1971, *Conrad's Western World*, Cambridge, p. 302).

MENCKEN, Henry Louis (1880–1956) American journalist, editor and satirist. He edited *Smart Set* from 1908 to 1923, and between 1924 and 1933 he founded and edited *American Mercury*. He criticized many public figures, was contemptuous of religion, and was the author of a number of varied works, including *American Language* (1918) and *Menckeniana: a schimpflexicon* (1927).

HARRY F. BRANDT in Charles Angoff, *Between Day and Night* (1959) and others

'H.L. Mencken is the apparent source for a number of fictional characterisations. I know of the following – [there follow the names given here]' (J.W. Scheideman, 1973, *Notes and Queries* 219: 142–3).

RUSSETT DURNWOOD in Carl Van Vechten, *Nigger Heaven* (1926)

See above.

SHRIKE in Nathanael West, *The Day of the Locust* (1933)

See above.

MENDELSSOHN, Felix (1809–47) German composer. Born in Hamburg, he was the son of a banker who changed the family name to Mendelssohn-Bartholdy. He first appeared as a pianist at the age of 10, and had written an opera, *Camacho's Wedding*, by the time he was 16. He settled in Berlin in 1841 and founded an Academy of Arts. He was a frequent visitor to England, and produced his *Elijah* in Birmingham in 1846. The following year, however, the shock of his sister Fanny's death caused him to go into a decline, and he died shortly afterwards.

SERAPHAEL in Elizabeth Sara Sheppard, *Charles Auchester* (1853)

Identified in Michael Sadleir, 1951, *XIX Century Fiction*, Vol. I, London: Constable, and Los Angeles: California University Press, p. 320; and in an anonymous typed key laid in a copy of the first edition of *Charles Auchester* which is now in the possession of the present author.

MENDL, Sir Charles (1871–1958) He was a press attaché to the British Embassy in Paris from 1926 to 1940. Gerald **Murphy** and his wife met him in the Antibes in the summer of 1926 and took a fancy to him. His first wife Elsie de Wolfe, of New York, was a notable hostess in Paris during the 1930s. He spent his last years in California.

LUIS CAMPION in F. Scott Fitzgerald, *Tender is the Night* (1934)

'Mendl later turned up in *Tender is the Night* as the homosexual Campion, an unflattering and highly inaccurate portrait' (Calvin Tomkins, 1971, *Living Well is the Best Revenge*, New York, p. 104).

MEREDITH, Augustus Urmiston (1797–1876) George Meredith's father. He inherited the naval outfitters business owned by his own father, Melchisedek **Meredith**, in Portsmouth. He emigrated to Cape Town in 1849 and set up there as a tailor.

EVAN HARRINGTON in George Meredith, *Evan Harrington* (1860)

'As befitted the original of Evan Harrington, Augustus Meredith was more addicted to the society of those in higher circles than that of his neighbours, the tradespeople of the High Street' (S.M. Ellis, 1920, *George Meredith*, 2nd edn, London: Grant Richards, p. 43). 'After the death of George Meredith in 1909, some correspondence was published in *The Cape Times* on the subject of local reminiscences of the novelist's father. . . . Mr B.T. Lawton, of Rondebosch, who had been a customer and friend of Augustus Meredith, wrote that he well remembered how, in 1860, when *Evan Harrington* was appearing serially in *Once a Week* he . . . found the tailor in very low spirits. . . . He asked Mr Lawton if he had seen the new story. "I am very sore about it," said Augustus; "I am pained beyond expression, as I consider it aimed at myself and I am sorry to say that the writer is my own son"' (ibid., pp. 138, 139). *See also* **Meredith**, George.

AUGUSTUS RICHMOND in George Meredith, *The Adventures of Harry Richmond* (1871)

'The fundamental personal element in the book, however, was in the relationship of Harry Richmond with his father, which was essentially that of George Meredith with Augustus' (A. Lionel Stevenson, 1954, *The Ordeal of George Meredith*, London: Peter Owen, p. 184). *See also* **Allen**, John and Charles; **Meredith**, Melchisedek.

MEREDITH, George (1828–1909) Novelist. Born in Portsmouth, he was educated privately in Germany. His first published work was *Chambers's Journal* (1849) and he was a contributor to the *Fortnightly Review*. In 1849 he married Thomas Love *Peacock*'s daughter, Mary Ellen Nicolls (**Meredith**, below), a widow; the marriage was not a successful one.

EVAN HARRINGTON in George Meredith, *Evan Harrington* (1860)

'When Evan . . . set off to seek his fortune, the focus suddenly changed to Meredith's own immediate surroundings. Evan was now a projection of George Meredith himself' (A. Lionel Stevenson, 1954, *The Ordeal of George Meredith*, London: Peter Owen, p. 81). *See also* **Meredith**, Augustus Urmiston.

ARTHUR RHODES in George Meredith, *Diana of the Crossways* (1884)

'[Meredith] put in also a sketch of his own youthful self in the person of Arthur Rhodes, a London law clerk with literary ambitions who fell under Diana's spell' (Stevenson, op. cit., p. 255).

GEOFFREY VIVIAN in G. Lowes Dickinson, *A Modern Symposium* (1905)

'G. Lowes Dickinson portrayed him in the character of Geoffrey Vivian in *A Modern Symposium*' (Stevenson, op. cit., p. 346).

MEREDITH, Hugh Owen (1878–1964) A Fellow of King's College, Cambridge, from 1903 to 1908, he was a contemporary and friend of E.M.

Forster there and was known to his friends as 'Hom'. He was Professor of Political Economy at Queen's University, Belfast, from 1911 to 1946, and was married four times.

STEWART ANSELL in E.M. Forster, *The Longest Journey* (1907)

'[Forster]'s just written his second novel. . . . After the hero (who's Forster himself), the principal figure is Hom' (Lytton Strachey to Duncan Grant, 30 April 1907, quoted in Michael Holroyd, 1971, *Lytton Strachey: a biography*, Harmondsworth: Penguin, p. 353). *See also* **Ainsworth**, A.R.

MEREDITH, Louise Mitchell (b. 1793) Daughter of Melchisedek **Meredith**, she was George Meredith's aunt. In 1811 she married William Harding Read, and in 1834 her daughter married Antonio da Costa Cabral, who subsequently became Marques de Thomar and the Portuguese Ambassador at Rome; the latter couple's son, who styled himself Read Cabral, published a volume of verse in Portuguese.

COUNTESS DE SALDAR in George Meredith, *Evan Harrington* (1860)

'The most remarkable of these girls [George Meredith's aunts, daughters of Melchisedek Meredith], Louisa Mitchell Meredith, was the original of . . . the Countess de Saldar, in *Evan Harrington*' (S.M. Ellis, 1920, *George Meredith*, 2nd edn, London: Grant Richards, p. 24).

MEREDITH, Mary Ellen (1821–61) Daughter of Thomas Love **Peacock**, in January 1844 she married Edward Nicolls, Royal Navy Lieutenant; he was lost at sea in March of the same year. In 1849 she married George Meredith, with whom she had one son, Arthur. In 1851, she left Meredith for the painter Henry Wallis, Meredith having been the model for his painting *The Death of Chatterton*; she and Wallis had a son, Harold (known as Felix).

MARGARET LOVELL in George Meredith, *Rhoda Fleming* (1865)

'As a portrait of a charming, shallow, worldly woman, hardened by early emotional disaster, she is fully convincing; and she is also startlingly like Edward Peacock's sister, Mrs Mary Ellen Nicolls' (A. Lionel Stevenson, 1954, *The Ordeal of George Meredith*, London: Peter Owen, p. 147).

BELLA MOUNT in George Meredith, *The Ordeal of Richard Feverel* (1859)

'George . . . left some heroines . . . who reputedly owe a lot to Mary. There is one special type of ironic, fascinating and sophisticated *femme du monde* who keeps recurring . . . named . . . Mrs Mount in the first book George wrote after their separation' (Diane Johnson, 1973, *The True History of the First Mrs Meredith and Other Lesser Lives*, p. 69).

MEREDITH, Melchisedek (1763–1814) A tailor of Portsmouth, he was the father of Augustus Urmiston **Meredith** and the grandfather of George Meredith. Habitually well dressed, he was known in Portsmouth as 'the Count'.

MELCHISEDEK HARRINGTON in George Meredith, *Evan Harrington* (1860)

'In . . . *Evan Harrington* George Meredith does penance for his own snobbery in concealing the fact that he came of a family of naval outfitting tailors in

Portsmouth. Paying fictional tribute to the character of his grandfather portrayed as "the great Mel" the foxhunting tailor of Lymport . . .' (E. Johnson, 1953, *Charles Dickens*, Vol. II, p. 988).

AUGUSTUS RICHMOND in George Meredith, *The Adventures of Harry Richmond* (1871)

'Richmond Roy had the aristocratic bearing and expansive schemes of Augustus Meredith, with some touches of old Melchizedek added' (A. Lionel Stevenson, 1954, *The Ordeal of George Meredith*, London: Peter Owen, p. 184). *See also* **Allen**, John and Charles; **Meredith**, Augustus Urmiston.

MEREWORTH CASTLE, Kent Situated about ten miles south-west of Maidstone. A ravishing Palladian villa, copied from the Villa Rotonda, it was built by Colen Campbell for John Fane (afterwards the 7th Earl of Westmorland) in the 1720s.

FAIRLADIES in Sir Walter Scott, *Redgauntlet* (1824)

'Charles is said to have held his last council in England at Mereworth. . . . Miss Warrender informs the Editor [Andrew Lang] that Lady Falmouth, to whom . . . the castle belonged, pointed out Prince Charles's room, which he occupied at some time between 1750 and 1762. . . . The father and mother of Lady Falmouth well remembered an old maidservant . . . who had seen and known the Prince there, and recollected him perfectly. In Mereworth Castle, then, we may see the original of Fairladies' (Andrew Lang, 1901, Introd. to *Redgauntlet*, pp. xvii–xviii).

MERRILL, James Ingram (b. 1926) American poet, novelist and playwright. He was the author of *The (Diblos) Notebook* (1965), a book of verse *The Fire Screen* (1969) and others.

MERRILL RANDALL in Jack Kerouac, *Desolation Angels* (1965)

Identified in 'Character key to the Duluoz Legend', in Barry Gifford and Lawrence Lee, 1979, *Jack's Book*, pp. 322–32.

MERRIMAN, Robert (1908?–38) Son of a lumberjack, he worked his way through the University of Nevada and became, briefly, a lecturer in economics at the University of California. In 1936 he visited the Soviet Union on a travelling scholarship, to investigate agricultural problems. He joined the International Brigade of the Spanish Republican Army and in 1937 he commanded the Lincoln Brigade at the battles of Brunete and Jarama; he was killed in March 1938 in the retreat from Belchite.

ROBERT JORDAN in Ernest Hemingway, *For Whom the Bell Tolls* (1940)

'Robert Jordan, the professor from Montana, owed at least something to the courageous figure of Major Robert Merriman . . . the one time professor of Economics from California' (Carlos Baker, 1969, *Ernest Hemingway: a life story*, New York, p. 348).

MESMAN, Mr A Malayan friend of A.R. **Wallace**.

STEIN in Joseph Conrad, *Lord Jim* (1900)

'In *Lord Jim* Conrad modeled the country life of Stein on that of Wallace's friend, Mr Mesman' (Florence Clemens, 1939, 'Conrad's favourite bedside book', *South Atlantic Quarterly* 38: 309). *See also* **Allen**, Charles; **Bernstein**, Dr; **Lingard**, William; **Wallace**, Alfred Russel.

METCALF, John (1717–1810) Commonly known as 'Blind Jack of Knaresborough', he lost his sight at the age of 6 as a result of contracting smallpox. He became well known as a fiddler and a jockey, and was a recruiting sergeant, fighting at Falkirk and Culloden in 1746. He became a road maker and bridge builder, and was prosperous in later life. A biography, with portrait, from his own narrative, was in Scott's library.

WILLIE STEENSON (WANDERING WILLIE) in Sir Walter Scott, *Redgauntlet* (1824)

'Jack seems a character made to Scott's hand, and may, perhaps, have lent some traits to the portrait of Wandering Willie' (*Redgauntlet*, 1901, ed. Andrew Lang, p. 649). *See also* **Williams ap Prichard**.

METTERNICH, Prince Clemens Lothat Wenzel (1773–1859) Austrian statesman. Born in Coblenz, the son of an Austrian diplomat, he was educated in Strasburg and Mainz. He was Austrian minister at Dresden by the age of 28, then at Berlin and, in 1805, at Paris. In 1807 he concluded the Treaty of Fontainebleau, and in 1809 was appointed Foreign Minister. During the French Revolution, the implications of which reached Vienna, he fled to England and in 1851 he retired to his castle on the Rhine.

BECKENDORFF in Benjamin Disraeli, *Vivian Grey* (1826–7)

Identified in a key given in a pamphlet published in 1827 by William Marsh. This key is discussed by Lucien Wolf in his notes to *Vivian Grey* (centenary edn, 1904, Vol. II, p. 364), with the conclusion that Disraeli was not responsible for the key.

MEXBOROUGH, John Charles George Savile, 4th Earl of (1810–99) Known as Lord Pollington until 1860, when he succeeded to the earldom, he was a Tory MP in 1831–2 and 1835–47. In 1842 he married Lady Rachel Walpole (**Mexborough**, below); following her death, in 1861 he married Agnes, daughter of John Raphael. At the time of his death he was the last survivor of the unreformed Parliament. He was one of the best classical scholars of his time.

LORD GAVERSTOCK in Benjamin Disraeli, *Coningsby* (1844)

'He and his first wife are the "Lord and Lady Gaverstock" in ... *Coningsby*' (H.A. Doubleday and Lord Howard de Walden (eds), *The Complete Peerage of England, Scotland, Ireland, Great Britain and the United Kingdom*, Vol. VIII, rev. edn, London: George Bell & Sons, p. 686).

MEXBOROUGH, Rachel Katherine, Countess of (d. 1854) Née Walpole, she was the daughter of the 3rd Earl of Orford, and in 1842 she married the 4th Earl of **Mexborough**.

LADY GAVERSTOCK in Benjamin Disraeli, *Coningsby* (1844)

See under **Mexborough**, 4th Earl of.

MEYNELL, Wilfrid (1852–1948) Journalist. He married the poet and essayist Alice Thompson (1847–1922) in 1877. They were Roman Catholics and were patrons and supporters of Francis Thompson. They built a village at Greatham, Sussex, for their family and were there in May 1915 when the Lawrences were there. Their daughter was Madeline **Lucas**.

MR MARSHALL in D.H. Lawrence, 'England, My England' (1915)

'In . . . "England, My England" Lawrence used personalities and environment from real life – [including] my father – as a basis for his story' (Francis Meynell, 1971, *My Lives*, p. 87).

MEZZEROFF, 'Professor' (*fl.* 1885)

THE PROFESSOR in Joseph Conrad, *The Secret Agent* (1907)

'On the last page of the January 13, 1885 issue [of *Alarm*, an anarchist weekly published in Chicago], the bomb-carrying Professor springs into life. Here, by all appearances, is the original of Conrad's character. "DYNAMITE: Professor Mezzeroff Talks About It and Other Explosives . . . He Carries a Bomb in His Pocket; How the Professor Carries Explosives Around with Him in Street Cars. Collated from the N.Y. 'Voice!'"' (Paul Avrich, 1977, 'Conrad's anarchist professor; an undiscovered source', *Labor History* 18 (3): 400–1). There follows an account by the Professor (who seems to have been associated with an institution in Boston) of his early life, his beliefs and his bomb-carrying practices. *See also* **Creaghe**, Dr; **Dillon**, Luke; **Most**, Johann; **Rossetti**, Arthur.

M'GUCKIN, Barton Operatic tenor. On hearing John Joyce sing in 1875, he said he was the best tenor in Ireland.

BARTELL D'ARCY in James Joyce, 'The Dead', *Dubliners* (1914)

'Bartell d'Arcy, the hoarse singer . . . was based on Barton M'Guckin, the leading tenor in the Carl Rosa company' (Richard Ellmann, 1966, *James Joyce*, London: Oxford Paperbacks, p. 255).

MIDDLESEX COUNTY, New Jersey

LENAPE COUNTY in Francis T. Field, *McDonough* (1951)

'Middlesex County can . . . be read for Field's Lenape County. The earliest recorded inhabitants of New Jersey were a branch of the Algonquin family called the Delaware, or Lenni-Lenape Indians' (J. Blotner, 1966, *The Modern American Political Novel*, p. 80 n. 45).

MIDDLETON, Henry Son of William Middleton (great-uncle of W.B. Yeats), who had bought Elsinore Lodge, at Rosses Point, West Sligo, Ireland, in 1867; the Yeats children spent the summers at Elsinore Lodge with their cousins. He became a noted eccentric and lived alone behind a locked gate at Elsinore with peacocks and a herd of Jersey cows. He was the Henry Middleton of Yeats's poem ('My name is Henry Middleton . . .').

JOHN SHERMAN in W.B. Yeats, *John Sherman* (1891)

'Yeatses, Pollexfens and Middletons . . . are now all gone from Sligo. One of the last of these names to be found in the county was that of Henry Middleton . . . the original of John Sherman' (Joseph Hone, 1962, *W.B. Yeats, 1865–1939*, p. 21). *See also* **Yeats**, William Butler.

MIDHURST, Sussex

WIMBLEHURST in H.G. Wells, *Tono-Bungay* (1909)

'In *Tono-Bungay* . . . young George Ponderevo is taken over from Bladesover . . . to . . . Wimblehurst, which is Midhurst' (Lovat Dickson, 1972, *H.G. Wells*, Harmondsworth: Penguin, pp. 37, 38).

MILBORNE PORT, Somerset A village situated about three miles north-east of Sherborne.

MILL POOL in Thomas Hardy, 'Squire Petrick's Lady' (1891)

Identified in F.B. Pinion, 1968, *A Hardy Companion*, London: Macmillan.

MILES, Mr

MR TOPE in Charles Dickens, *Edwin Drood* (1870)

'The venerable verger at Rochester Cathedral, Mr Miles, believes, with some justification, that he is the original of Mr Tope' (F.G. Kitton, 1897, *The Novels of Charles Dickens: a bibliography and sketch*, London, p. 232).

MILL, James (1773–1836) Economist and philosopher. Born and educated in Scotland, he moved to London in 1802, working as a journalist and editor. He helped to found University College London in 1825 and became an official at India House, where he was a colleague of Peacock. He was the father of the English philosopher and social reformer John Stuart Mill (1806–73).

MR MACQUEDY in Thomas Love Peacock, *Crotchet Castle* (1831)

'A claim can be made that Mill was the model [for MacQuedy] because two statements by MacQuedy can be traced to his book on economics [*Elements of Political Economy*]' (W.F. Kennedy, 1966, 'Peacock's economists: some mistaken identities', *The Nineteenth Century* 21 (2): 189). *See also* **McCulloch**, John Ramsay; **Mushet**, Robert.

MILL STREET, Fordington

MIXEN LANE, DURNOVER, in Thomas Hardy, *The Mayor of Casterbridge* (1886)

Identified in F.B. Pinion, 1968, *A Hardy Companion*, London: Macmillan.

MILLAIS, Sir John Everett (1829–96) Painter. Born in Southampton, he attended the Royal Academy in 1840 (being the youngest-ever student), becoming President in 1896. He studied with Henry Sass, and was one of the founders of the Pre-Raphaelite movement.

SANDY MCALLISTER ('THE LAIRD') in George Du Maurier, *Trilby* (1894)

'The character of "the Laird" was mainly drawn from himself [Millais]' (J.G. Millais, 1899, *The Life and Letters of Sir John Everett Millais*, Vol. II, p. 281). This identification was probably inspired by family pride. *See also* **Lamont**, T.R.

MILLARD, Christopher (1872–1927) Educated at Bradfield and Keble College, Oxford, he was successively a schoolmaster, Assistant Editor of *Burlington Magazine*, Secretary to Robert Ross, and a clerk in the War Office during the First World War. He wrote an account of the trials of Oscar **Wilde** and compiled a bibliography of his writings, under the pseudonym of Stuart Mason, and a bibliography of Lovat Fraser. He became a dealer in rare books after the war; Anthony Powell's mother bought books from him and Powell himself used to frequent his shop when he was a schoolboy on holiday from Eton. He introduced A.J. Symons, author of *The Quest for Corvo*, to Frederick **Rolfe**.

EDGAR DEACON in Anthony Powell, *A Dance to the Music of Time* (1951–76)

'Does not Mr Deacon . . . bear some resemblance in style and appearance to . . . Christopher Millard?' (Julian Symons, 1966, *Critical Occasions*, p. 16).

MILLAY, Edna St Vincent (1892–1951) Poet. Born in Maine and educated at Vassar College, New York, she lived in Greenwich Village during the early 1920s and won the Pulitzer Prize for her 1923 book of verse, *The Harp Weaver and Other Poems*. At one time the novelist Edmund Wilson was in love with her.

VERE ST VITUS in Robert McAlmon, *Post Adolescence* (1923)

Identified in Robert E. Knoll (ed.), 1962, *McAlmon and the Lost Generation: a self-portrait*, Lincoln, Nebr.: University of Nebraska Press, p. 108.

MILLER, Maria Afterwards Robertson. She was a pupil at the Pensionnat Héger in Brussels at the time that Charlotte Brontë was a pupil and later a teacher of English there.

GINEVRA FANSHAWE in Charlotte Brontë, *Villette* (1853)

'The portrait of Ginevra Fanshawe was studied from that of an English girl – Miss Maria Miller – at the Pensionnat Héger. In later years [she] became Mrs Robertson, the wife of an author' (Herbert Wroot, 1935, *Sources of Charlotte Brontë's Novels: persons and places*, Shipley, Yorks., p. 183). Mr Robertson was not a successful author; in 1852 they were settled in Boulogne and his wife was touting for subscriptions to enable his latest work to be published.

MILNER, Alfred, 1st Viscount (1854–1925) Politician. Educated at New College, Oxford, he became High Commissioner for South Africa (1897–1905) and was instrumental in instituting land reforms after the Boer War, although he failed to win the confidence of the Boers. He became a member of the War

Cabinet in 1916 and Secretary of State for War in 1918, and was Secretary of State for the Colonies from 1918 until 1921. He was created Viscount in 1902.

LORD LAUNCESTON in John Buchan, *A Lodge in the Wilderness* (1906)

Identified in a key dated January 1907 in a copy of *A Lodge in the Wilderness*, formerly the property of Grace Keily.

MILNES, Richard Monckton, 1st Baron Houghton (1809–85) Politician. Educated at Trinity College, Cambridge, where he was a member of the Apostles and the intimate of **Tennyson**, Hallam, and **Thackeray**. In 1837 he became a Conservative MP, but he became a Liberal upon **Peel**'s conversion to free trade and advocated mechanics' institutes. From 1882 to 1885 he was President of the London Library; he was celebrated for his wide acquaintance in the world of literature and society, and was also the owner of an extensive and notorious collection of erotica. He was the father of Florence **Henniker**.

AUGUSTUS TREMAINE BERTIE in Benjamin Disraeli, *Endymion* (1880)

'This same "Mr Vavasour" of *Tancred* and "Mr Tremaine Bertie" of *Endymion* had written "We have set agoing a new dining club which promises well." . . . It is no disrespect to . . . the late Lord Houghton to say that the vague eclecticism of his youth scarcely fosters . . . a keen insight . . . well does Disraeli make "Waldershare" . . . exclaim of him . . . "What I do like in him . . . is this revival of the Pythagorean system, and heading a party of science"' (Walter Sichel, 1904, *Disraeli: a study in personality and ideas*, London: Methuen, p. 125). In fact Waldershare is speaking of Bertie Tremaine, i.e. Lord **Lytton**. The identification is based on a misapprehension.

LORD DICKIEFIELD in Laurence Oliphant, *Piccadilly* (1870)

'When *Piccadilly* first appeared in *Blackwood's Magazine* for 1865, it was recognised . . . that the "warm-hearted and eccentric" host, Lord Dickiefield, was a representation of Lord Houghton' (James Pope Henessy, 1951, *Monckton Milnes: the flight of youth, 1851–1885*, p. 142). 'An annotated copy [of *Piccadilly*] from the Fryston library confirms the identification of Houghton ("Dickie Milnes") with Dickiefield' (ibid., n. 1).

LORD SURBITON in W.H. Mallock, *A Romance of the Nineteenth Century* (1881)

'Lord Surbiton is without doubt based on Lord Houghton. Vernon [the hero] describes Surbiton as "the first poet I ever knew; and when I was seventeen, he seemed to me little short of a god," and we know this to have been true of Mallock's relationship with Houghton. Further, Surbiton is described as "the poet, diplomat and dandy," and we are also told that he suffers from indigestion through eating too much. But Mallock models Surbiton on Houghton more . . . significantly, than [these] details can suggest. For Houghton was also, as is well known, the possessor of a large library of erotica. And without doubt it is on this knowledge that Mallock is drawing in his portrait of Surbiton' (John Lucas, 1966, 'Tilting at the moderns: W.H. Mallock's criticisms of the positivist spirit', *Renaissance and Modern Studies* 10: 135–6). *See also* **Lytton**, 1st Baron.

MR VAVASOUR in Benjamin Disraeli, *Tancred* (1847)

'When I published *Coningsby*, he complained to me, that I had not introduced his character among the Young England group. . . . Accordingly when I wrote "Tancred" in which the Young England group reappeared, I sketched the character of Vavasour, & I made it as attractive as I could consistent with that verisimilitude which [was] necessary. I don't know whether he was over-satisfied' (*Disraeli's Reminiscences*, 1975, ed. H.M. Swartz and Marvin Swartz, London: Hamilton, p. 58).

MILTON ABBAS, Dorset

MIDDLETON ABBEY in Thomas Hardy, *The Woodlanders* (1887)

Identified in F.B. Pinion, 1968, *A Hardy Companion*, London: Macmillan.

MINNEAPOLIS, Minnesota

ZENITH in Sinclair Lewis, *Babbit* (1922)

'Zenith . . . is actually Minneapolis, but it is presented as though it were a smaller town' (James T. Farrell, 1975, 'The 1920s', *Fitzgerald–Hemingway Annual, 1974*, Englewood: Prentice-Hall, p. 121).

MIRTIL, Adrien

ADOLPHE BLANC in Radclyffe Hall, *The Well of Loneliness* (1928)

'Adrien Mirtil (who also figured in [*The Well of Loneliness*], slightly idealized, as the gentle and learned Jew) . . .' (Una, Lady Troubridge, 1961, *The Life and Death of Radclyffe Hall*, pp. 83, 84).

MITCHISON, Geoffrey (d. 1927) The first child of Richard and Naomi Mitchison; the latter was the sister of J.B.S. **Haldane** and Huxley had known the family since he was a boy.

PHILIP QUARLES THE YOUNGER in Aldous Huxley, *Point Counter Point* (1928)

'Naomi Mitchison's first child, Geoffrey, who died in 1927, appears as Little Phil' (*Letters of Aldous Huxley*, 1969, ed. Grover Smith, p. 144 n. 130). *See also* **Huxley**, Matthew.

MITFORD, Jessica (b. 1917) Author. Fifth of the six daughters of Lord **Redesdale**, in 1937 she married Esmond Romilly, who was killed in action in 1941; she settled in the United States in 1939, and in 1943 she married Robert Edward Treuhaft. She was the author of *Hons and Rebels* (1960) and *The American Way of Death* (1963). She was the sister of Nancy and Unity **Mitford**.

JASSY RADLETT in Nancy Mitford, *The Pursuit of Love* (1945) and *Love in a Cold Climate* (1949)

This identification is based on a comparison between *Hons and Rebels* and *The Pursuit of Love*, from which it clearly follows.

MITFORD, Nancy Freeman (1904–73) Novelist and writer of historical works. She was the eldest daughter of the 2nd Lord **Redesdale** and sister of Deborah, Duchess of **Devonshire**, Jessica and Unity **Mitford** and Diana Mosley, who married Sir Oswald **Mosley**. In 1933 she married Peter **Rodd**, but they were divorced in 1952.

GRACE, MARQUISE DE VALHUBERT in Nancy Mitford, *Don't Tell Alfred* (1960)

'Grace is more or less me' (Nancy Mitford to Handasyde Buchanan, 7 September 1960, quoted in Harold Acton, 1975, *Nancy Mitford: a memoir*, London: Hamilton, p. 141). There is no evidence that Grace in *The Blessing* was Miss Mitford.

MITFORD, Unity Valkyrie (1914–48) Fourth daughter of Lord **Redesdale** and sister of Nancy and Jessica **Mitford**, she became a passionate adherent of Hitler and the National Socialist movement, and after the outbreak of the Second World War she attempted suicide in Germany by shooting herself. She returned to England, where she remained for the rest of her life.

EUGENIA MALMAINS in Nancy Mitford, *Wigs on the Green* (1935)

'Nancy had made fun of her in . . . *Wigs on the Green* . . . but she always spoke of her with special tenderness' (Harold Acton, 1965, *Nancy Mitford: a memoir*, London: Hamilton, p. 78).

The MITRE HOTEL, Oxford

THE CROZIER HOTEL, CHRISTMINSTER, in Thomas Hardy, *Jude the Obscure* (1895)

Identified in Denys Kay-Robinson, 1972, *Hardy's Wessex Reappraised*, Newton Abbot, and in F.B. Pinion, 1968, *A Hardy Companion*, London: Macmillan.

The MITRE INN, Chatham, Kent The children of John Tribe, the landlord, were friends of the Dickens children c.1820; one of the children, John Tribe, Jun., grew up to be the Mayor of Rochester.

THE CROZIER in Charles Dickens, *Edwin Drood* (1870)

'The Mitre appears . . . in *Edwin Drood*, ch. 18, disguised as "The Crozier"' (*Letters of Charles Dickens*, Vol. I: *1820–1839*, 1965, ed. Madeline House and Graham Storey, Oxford: Oxford University Press, p. 1 n. 1).

MITZICUS, Demetrius Known as 'The Duke of Mitzicus'. He appears to be the painter alluded to by James Charters in *This Must Be the Place* (p. 120) as Mitzi, 'who acted as guide and interpreter for all newly arrived English and Americans'. He was Greek, and although he was almost certainly not a Duke and it is not clear that Mitzicus was his real name, he was possibly the son of a Minister at the Greek Court. He was described as 'small and of slight build and swarthy'. Permanently in financial straits, he arrived in Paris from Florence during the 1920s.

'DUKE' ZIZI in Ernest Hemingway, *The Sun Also Rises* (1926)

'When asked point blank by Bill Hoffmann of Key West whether . . . Duke Zizi was based on a real person Hoffmann had known, Hemingway cooled at once. . . . In real life "Zizi" had a reputation that would have embarrassed Hemingway were he linked in friendship with him. He was of course a Greek. . . . Homosexuality was part of his upbringing. He had studied art in Munich where Hoffmann was a fellow-student. . . . [He] appears to be the very person mentioned in *This Must Be the Place*' (B.D. Sarason, 1972, *Hemingway and the Sun Set*, Washington, DC, pp. 59–60).

MIZNER, Wilson (1876–1933) Playwright, wit and man about New York. Born in Benicia, California, he was the son of Lansing Bond Mizner, the Californian senator and United States diplomat. He married Mary **Yerkes** in 1906.

MILTON LAZARD in George Bronson Howard, 'The Parasite' (1912)

'[Bronson Howard] took the typical revenge of the wronged literary man, writing Mizner up, under the name of Milton Lazard, in . . . "The Parasite"' (Ava Johnson, 1953, *The Incredible Mizners*, p. 101).

MOBERLY, Charlotte (1846–1937) Seventh daughter of George Moberly, Headmaster of Winchester and Bishop of Salisbury, in 1886 she became the first Principal of St Hugh's College, Oxford. She was co-author of *An Adventure* (1911), a report of encountering ghosts at Versailles.

ETHEL MAY in C.M. Yonge, *The Daisy Chain* (1856)

'She is said to be the model for Ethel in *The Daisy Chain*, by her godmother, Charlotte M. Yonge' (*The Letters of Lewis Carroll*, 1979, ed. Morton N. Cohen, Vol. II, p. 1022 n. 1).

MOELLER, Philip (1880–1958) He was a manager of the New York Theater Guild during the late 1920s. He was a friend of Aline **Bernstein** from childhood; they were born in neighbouring houses in New York.

FRANK WERNER in Thomas Wolfe, *The Web and the Rock* (1939)

'How I have thought with nausea of the party at Moeller's the other night' (entry for March 1927, in Thomas Wolfe, 1970, *The Notebooks of Thomas Wolfe*, 1970, ed. Richard S. Kennedy and Paschal Reeves, Chapel Hill, NC: University of North Carolina Press, p. 111). This was the origin of the party described in ch. 30 of *The Web and the Rock,* and clearly Frank Werner, the host, is drawn from Philip Moeller.

MOFFAT, David Halliday (1839–1911) Banker, railroad builder and mine owner. In 1905 he was supposed to be the richest man in Colorado.

DANIEL MELNOTTE in Walter Hurt, *The Scarlet Shadow* (1907)

'"Daniel Melnotte" is clearly intended as a portrait of . . . Moffat' (Walter Rideout, 1956, *The Radical Novel in the United States, 1900–1954*, Cambridge, Mass., p. 303 n. 14).

MOFFATT, Miss A London County Council evening-class teacher with whom Dorothy Richardson shared a flat in **Woburn Buildings**, London, in 1906.

SELINA HOLLAND in Dorothy Richardson, *Pilgrimage* (1915–67)

'The details of life with Miss Holland. . . very closely match those of Miss Moffatt in Woburn Buildings' (John Rosenberg, 1973, *Dorothy Richardson*, London, p. 121).

MOLÉ, Louis Mathieu, Comte (1781–1855) He was Prime Minister of France under Louis Philippe from 1836 to 1839.

COUNT M—É in Benjamin Disraeli, *Coningsby* (1844)

Identified in a key in *Notes and Queries* (8th series) 3 (13 May 1893): 363. *See also under* **Bright**, John.

MOLESWORTH, Lionel Charles (1873–1916) Seventh child and second surviving son of Richard **Molesworth** and his wife Mary Louise. He left Oxford without taking a degree and became a land agent in Cirencester, Gloucestershire.

FABIAN DESART ('CARROTS') in Mrs Molesworth, *'Carrots': Just a Little Boy* (1878)

'Carrots . . . [combines her] youngest son Lionel, aged four, and Bevil, aged about six' (R. Lancelyn Green, 1961, *Mrs Molesworth*, p. 40). *See also* **Molesworth**, Richard Bevil.

MOLESWORTH, Richard (1836–1900) Eldest son of Captain Oliver Molesworth, Royal Artillery, he was the nephew of the 7th Viscount Molesworth. In 1854 he was an ensign in the 19th Regiment of Foot; he was severely wounded in the head during the Crimean War. In 1861 he married Louisa Mary Stewart, but they separated in 1879. He retired from the Army in 1864.

CAPTAIN FRANK DESART in Mrs Molesworth, *'Carrots': Just a Little Boy* (1878)

'*Carrots* . . . presented her own family fairly faithfully. . . . Captain Desart being modelled to some extent on the irascible Major Molesworth (as his daughter Cicely testifies)' (R. Lancelyn Green, 1961, *Mrs Molesworth*, p. 40).

MOLESWORTH, Richard Bevil (1870–98) Sixth child and eldest surviving son of Richard **Molesworth** and his wife Mary Louise. He went to South America in 1889; he died unmarried, on his ranch in Patagonia.

FABIAN DESART ('CARROTS') in Mrs Molesworth, *'Carrots': Just a Little Boy* (1878)

See under **Molesworth**, Lionel Charles.

MOLSON, Dr A physician at Hove who attended the Compton-Burnetts during the first decade of the twentieth century.

DR CASSELL in I. Compton-Burnett, *Dolores* (1911)

'Dr Molson, who recognized himself in Dr Cassell, was filled with such natural resentment that it became for some time a question as to whether he could bring himself to continue in attendance on the family' (Hilary Spurling, 1974, *Ivy When Young: the early life of I. Compton Burnett, 1884–1919*, London: Gollancz, p. 184).

MONASH, Sir John (1865–1931) Born in Melbourne, he practised as a civil engineer. He commanded the 4th Infantry Brigade at Gallipoli in 1915 and the

3rd Australian division at Messines, Passchendaele, Ypres and Amiens in 1916–18, and in 1918 he launched the allied offensive. He became a general in 1930 and retired the same year.

BENJAMIN COOLEY in D.H. Lawrence, *Kangaroo* (1923)

'Reading [in the *Sydney Bulletin*] about … Sir John Monash … Lawrence probably found the outward guise of Ben Cooley: pictures of Monash … show him with the long face Lawrence described; and pictures of him would have appeared in the *Bulletin* at that time' (H.T. Moore, 1960, *The Intelligent Heart: the story of D.H. Lawrence*, Harmondsworth: Penguin, p. 364; originally published 1955, London Heinemann). *See also* **Eder**, David; **Koteliansky**, S.S.

MONBODDO, James Burnett, Lord (1714–99) Scottish judge and anthropologist. Son of a minor Scottish laird, he was educated in Aberdeen, Gröningen and Edinburgh and in 1767 became Lord of Succession. He was a great social light in Edinburgh, and was an excellent and kindly landlord at Monboddo, never raising his rents or dismissing a tenant. He was the author of *The Origin and Progress of Language* (1773–92), in which he maintained 'that language is a human invention … that the orang-utans were not specially distinct from men' (William Knight, 1900, *Lord Monboddo*, p. 22).

SYLVAN FORESTER in Thomas Love Peacock, *Melincourt* (1817)

'The portrayal of Forester does indeed refer back to Monboddo, and not only in his belief in the essential humanity of the great apes. Monboddo's example must also have been the model for Forester's method of running his estate, which is populous and hence un-Malthusian. More generally, Forester's admiration for the manners, literature and philosophy of the ancients is Monboddo-like. Peacock may have got his information about Monboddo's simplicity of life from Boswell or from Lord Woodhouselee, who sketched him affectionately in his *Memoirs of Lord Kames*' (Marilyn Butler, 1977, letter, *Times Literary Supplement* (27 May): 653). *See also* **Shelley**, Percy Bysshe.

MONCINI, Charles and Alice '[The Moncinis were] a French family who made and sold good wine in a neat frame house on Val Vista Street in Sheridan [Wyoming]. … Charles was a trucker at the mines. Alice cooked and served meals. Ernest and Pauline sat on the … porch drinking cold home-brewed beer. … They all spoke French together' (Carlos Baker, 1969, *Ernest Hemingway: a life story*, New York, p. 196).

FONTAN and MADAME FONTAN in Ernest Hemingway, 'Wine of Wyoming', *Winner Take Nothing* (1933)

'Ernest listened intently … whenever it suited him, he would put the Moncinis into a story' (ibid.).

MONK, Violet Afterwards Stevens. During the First World War she farmed Grimsbury Farm, Long Lane, Hermitage, Berkshire, with her cousin Cecily Lambert (later Minchin). She was a friend of the Lawrences when they were living in Dollie **Radford**'s cottage at Hermitage in 1918–19.

NELLIE MARCH in D.H. Lawrence, 'The Fox' (1923)

'For his human figures... Lawrence took two girls he knew... near Hermitage.
... [T]hese girls – whose real names were Violet Monk and Cecily Lambert –
became Nellie March and Jill Banford' (H.T. Moore, 1960, *The Intelligent Heart:
the story of D.H. Lawrence*, Harmondsworth: Penguin, pp. 303–4; originally
published 1955, London: Heinemann).

MONOD, Adolphe Frédéric Théodore (1802–56) Member of a well-known
family of French theologians. He studied at Paris and Geneva and subsequently
became a member of the Protestant faculty at Montauban. In 1847 he was Pastor
of the Reformed Church of Paris; he became widely known as a preacher.

STEPHEN TOURNEUR in Lady Ritchie, *The Story of Elizabeth* (1863)

'Lady Ritchie draws on her recollections of this little French Protestant
world in ... *The Story of Elizabeth*' (*The Letters and Private Papers of W.M.
Thackeray*, 1945, ed. Gordon N. Ray, Vol. III, London: Oxford University
Press, p. 138 n. 207).

MONRO, Robert (d. 1680?) A general, he served for seven years on the
European continent, and in the Civil War he sided with the Scots against Charles
I. He was sent to Ireland as a major-general when the Irish rebellion broke out.
In 1642 he sacked Newry, and in 1646 he was finally defeated by O'Neill at
Benburb; he then came to an understanding with the Royalist party. He was
captured by Monck in 1648 and imprisoned in England until 1654;
thenceforward he lived in Ireland.

DUGALD DALGETTY in Sir Walter Scott, *A Legend of Montrose* (1819)

'Annotations on the margin of Munro's [sic] closely-printed black-letter folio
of *Expeditions and Observations*, preserved in the Advocates' Library [in
Edinburgh] have a suspicious resemblance to Scott's handwriting. This was
probably the copy he used in gathering materials for *A Legend of Montrose*, and
evolving the immortal personality of Dalgetty' (W.S. Crockett, 1912, *The Scott
Originals: an account of notables and worthies, the originals of characters in the
Waverley Novels*, Edinburgh and London: T.N. Foulis, p. 275). *See also* **Skene**,
Martin; **Turner**, Sir James.

MONTACUTE HOUSE, Somerset A magnificent Elizabethan mansion
situated four miles west of Yeovil. Lord **Curzon** took a long lease of the place
in 1915, and its redecoration was supervised for him by Elinor **Glyn**, who spent
much of the winter of 1915–16 on top of ladders in the cold stone house.

MONTISLOPE HOUSE in Thomas Hardy, 'Master John Horseleigh, Knight' (1913)

Identified in F.B. Pinion, 1968, *A Hardy Companion*, London: Macmillan.

MONTAGU, Judith Venetia (b. 1923) Afterwards Grendel. Daughter of Rt.
Hon. Edwin Montagu and Venetia (née Stanley).

LIZ LANGHAM in Martha Gellhorn, *His Own Man* (1961)

Identification based upon private information.

MONTAGUE PLACE, London Located near Limehouse Canal, London E14, it runs between Bazeley Street and Newby Place, parallel with and just south of East India Dock Road.

Brig Place in Charles Dickens, *Dombey and Son* (1846–8)

'I am now convinced that Montague Place can be read Brig Place' (Gwen Major, 1936, 'Captain Cuttle's lodgings', *The Dickensian* 32: 60).

MONTAUTO, Villa, Florence Located in Bellosguardo. It was here that Hawthorne and his family spent the months of August and September 1858. One of the frescoes in the villa contains a figure resembling Donatello of *The Marble Faun*.

Villa Monte Beni in Nathaniel Hawthorne, *The Marble Faun* (1860)

'The Montauto (Monte Beni) villa' (Nathalia Wright, 1965, *American Novelists in Italy*, Philadelphia, p. 165).

Hotel MONTE CARLO, Mexico City An Italian-owned hotel on Calle Uruguay, Mexico City, where Frieda and D.H. Lawrence stayed in 1923 and 1924; it was still there in 1983.

Hotel San Remo in D.H. Lawrence, *The Plumed Serpent* (1926)

'[T]ried a big American hotel and didn't like it: this is a nice little place' (D.H. Lawrence to Bessie Freeman, 24 March 1923, quoted in H.T. Moore, 1960, *The Intelligent Heart: the story of D.H. Lawrence*, Harmondsworth: Penguin, p. 387; originally published 1955, London: Heinemann). 'This hotel is a little Italian place' (the same to the same, 11 April 1923, ibid., p. 388). 'The San Remo of *The Plumed Serpent*' (H.T. Moore and Warren Roberts, n.d., *D.H. Lawrence and His World*, p. 86).

MONTEGUFONI, Castello di, Italy A castle located midway between Siena and Florence, which was bought by Sir George **Sitwell** in 1925 and to which he withdrew permanently; after his death it was inherited by Osbert **Sitwell**.

Palazzo Malaspina in Aldous Huxley, *Those Barren Leaves* (1925)

'24 August 1921 . . . I have a plan to do a gigantic Peacock in an Italian scene. An incredibly large castle – like the Sitwells' at Monte Gufone [sic] . . . the most amazing place I have ever seen in my life – divided up, as Monte Gufone was divided till recently, into scores of separate habitations, which will be occupied, for the purposes of my story, by the most improbable people of every species and nationality' (to Julian Huxley, reproduced in *Letters of Aldous Huxley*, 1969, ed. Grover Smith, p. 202). For the purposes of the novel the Castello was shifted a hundred miles to the north.

MONTPELIER, Maine The estate of the Knox family.

House of the Seven Gables in Nathaniel Hawthorne, *The House of the Seven Gables* (1851)

'A number of parallels will be observed between . . . the Knox estate . . . and the Pyncheon property in the novel' (T.M. Griffiths, 1943, '"Montpelier" and "Seven Gables"', *New England Quarterly* 16: 439).

MOODY, Robert (1909–70) Child psychiatrist. Educated at Bromsgrove School and St Thomas's Hospital, in 1957 he became President of the International Association for Analytical Psychology.

LEE in Christopher Isherwood, *Lions and Shadows* (1938)

'Hector Wintle and Robert Moody (Lee, in *Lions and Shadows*) drew strength [during the Munich crisis of 1938] from their professional status' (Christopher Isherwood, 1967, *Christopher and His Kind*, London: Eyre Methuen, p. 239).

MOONEY, Tom (1882–1942) American Labor leader. Along with W.K. Billings, he was convicted of responsibility for the bomb explosion at San Francisco Preparedness Parade on 22 July 1916; he was condemned to death, but in 1918 his sentence was commuted to life imprisonment. He maintained his innocence and in 1939 he was pardoned and released.

STEVE MANTON in William Rose Benét, *The Dust Which is God* (1941)

'William Rose Benét tells of an evening with Larry Harris [i.e. Sinclair Lewis] when they heard a speech by a labor organizer whom Benét calls Steve Manton (this would seem to have been Tom Mooney)' (Mark Schorer, 1961, *Sinclair Lewis: an American life*, New York: McGraw-Hill, p. 157).

MOORE, John (1729–1802) Physician, man of letters and novelist. He practised in Glasgow and was a friend and doctor to Tobias Smollett. He published books of travel, a history of the French revolution and three novels, and edited Smollett's works, with a memoir.

DR X. in Maria Edgeworth, *Belinda* (1801)

'Dr X is identified in the draft to *Belinda* published as an Appendix to the *Memoir* [of R.L. Edgeworth]' (Marilyn Butler, 1972, *Maria Edgeworth*, Oxford, p. 248 n. 3).

MOORE, Marianne Craig (1887–1972) American poet. Born in Kirkwood, Missouri, and educated at Bryn Mawr College and Carlisle Commercial College, she then taught commercial studies at Carlisle as well as being a private tutor. She contributed to the *Egoist* from 1915 and was Editor of the *Dial* from 1926 until 1929, when the magazine folded. She knew Ezra **Pound** and T.S. **Eliot**, but associated more with the Greenwich Village group, including William Carlos **Williams**.

MARTA WULLUS in Robert McAlmon, *Post Adolescence* (1923)

Identified in Robert E. Knoll (ed.), 1962, *McAlmon and the Lost Generation: a self-portrait*, Lincoln, Nebr.: University of Nebraska Press, p. 108.

MOORE, Thomas (1779–1852) Irish poet. Born in Dublin, the son of a Catholic grocer, he was educated at Trinity College, Dublin, and the Middle Temple. In 1803 he was appointed Registrar of the Admiralty Court, Bermuda, but left a deputy in charge while he toured the USA and Canada. In 1811 he married Bessy Dyke, an actress, and settled in Wiltshire soon after. His Bermuda deputy embezzled some £6,000 and Moore had to flee to Italy to avoid arrest, and thence to Paris. In 1822 he returned to Wiltshire and spent the remainder of his life there. In his lifetime his own poetry was as popular as that of his friend **Byron**.

MR MINUS in Theodore Hook, *The Man of Sorrow* (1809)

'He is sketched under the name of Mr Minus by Theodore Hook in his first novel . . . The Man of Sorrow. By Alfred Allendale' (Frederic Boase, 1892, *Modern English Biography*, Vol. II, col. 955).

MR TRILLO in Thomas Love Peacock, *Crotchet Castle* (1831)

'A character based on Tom Moore' (*Crotchet Castle*, 1969, ed. Raymond Wright, Harmondsworth: Penguin, p. 275 n. 4 (to ch. V)).

MOORGREEN, Nottinghamshire

MINTON in D.H. Lawrence, *Sons and Lovers* (1913)

'Minton is Moorgreen' (Ada Lawrence and G. Stuart Gelder, 1931, *Young Lorenzo: early life of D.H. Lawrence*, Florence, p. 275).

MOORGREEN RESERVOIR, Nottinghamshire Situated at the back of **Haggs Farm**, which overlooks the reservoir to the hills of Annesley and High Park Wood.

NETHERMERE in D.H. Lawrence, *The White Peacock* (1911)

'Moorgreen Reservoir (Nethermere)' (Claude M. Sinzelle, 1964, *The Geographical Background of the Early Works of D.H. Lawrence* (Études Anglaises 1), Paris, p. 18; Pl. 8 is a photograph of Moorgreen Reservoir, 'the "Nethermere" of *The White Peacock*', reproduced from that in the Lawrence Collection at the University of Nottingham).

WILLEY WATER in D.H. Lawrence, *Women in Love* (1920)

'". . . the narrow little lake of Willey Water" – again Moorgreen' (H.T. Moore, 1960, *The Intelligent Heart: the story of D.H. Lawrence*, Harmondsworth: Penguin, p. 51; originally published 1955, London: Heinemann).

MORAN, Lois (1909–90) Film actress. From 1922 to 1924 she danced at the Paris Opera. She had her first great success in *Stella Dallas* in 1925, and she played The First Lady in *Of Thee I Sing* (Kaufman) in 1931. Scott Fitzgerald met her in 1931 on his first visit to Hollywood.

HELEN AVERY in F. Scott Fitzgerald, 'Magnetism' (1951)

'Just seventeen and unspoiled by her success as an actress. . . . Fitzgerald put his first emotion for her into . . . "Magnetism"' (Andrew Turnbull, 1962, *Scott Fitzgerald*, p. 158.

ROSEMARY HOYT in F. Scott Fitzgerald, *Tender is the Night* (1934)

'He did Rosemary once and for all as Rosemary Hoyt in *Tender is the Night*' (Turnbull, op. cit., p. 158). 'Although Fitzgerald would see Lois Moran only three or four times again [after returning east from Hollywood] she became a presence in his work and provided the model for Rosemary Hoyt' (M.J. Bruccoli, 1981, *Some Sort of Epic Grandeur: the life of F. Scott Fitzgerald*, London: Hodder & Stoughton, p. 259).

MORETON, Dorset A village situated east of Tincleton, in the Frome Valley.

MOREFORD in Thomas Hardy, 'The Fiddler of the Reels' (1894)

Identified in F.B. Pinion, 1968, *A Hardy Companion*, London: Macmillan.

MORGAN, Dr Charles (*fl.* 1822–50) Of 9 Bedford Row, Russell Square, London. In 1822 he became a Licentiate of the Apothecaries' Company, and in 1824 he became a Member of the Royal College of Surgeons.

DR CHILLIP in Charles Dickens, *David Copperfield* (1849–50)

'Down Yarmouth way . . . there were, not many years ago, plenty of people . . . who had a close acquaintance with Mr Chillip, the meek little doctor. And yet Mr Chillip was sketched from our family medical attendant in the old Devonshire Terrace days and never had anything to do with Suffolk' (Charles Dickens, the Younger, 1896, 'Notes on some Dickens places and people', *Pall Mall Magazine* (July): 349). '. . . in a copy . . . of *Copperfield* in the Forster collection [in the Victoria and Albert Museum] . . . (F.6.A.35–7) . . . with marginalia made by Forster . . . he . . . notes of Dr Chillip "actual person"' (Nina Burgis, 1980, Introd. to *David Copperfield*, p. xxvii). 'Of the Morgans in the Medical Directory for 1850 the most likely candidate, from his nearness to Devonshire Terrace, is Charles Morgan' (ibid., n. 2). In the number plan (i.e. draft for the instalment) in the Victoria and Albert, Dickens has written 'Morgan' for 'Chillip' (information from Professor Kathleen Tillotson). In 1849 Morgan was still the family doctor (see *Letters of Charles Dickens*, 1981, Vol. V, ed. Graham Storey and K.J. Fielding, Oxford: Oxford University Press, pp. 431 and 471).

MORGAN, Daniel (1828–65) The assumed name of Samuel Moran. He was a stock rider in New South Wales, Australia, and committed a series of highway robberies and hold-ups from 1863 until he was finally shot in 1865.

PATRICK in Ralph Boldrewood, *Robbery Under Arms* (1888)

'Said to be the original of Patrick in . . . *Robbery under Arms*' (Frederic Boase, 1892, *Modern English Biography*, Vol. II, col. 964).

MORGAN, Captain Elisha Ely (d. 1864) Of the American merchant service, from 1833 to 1850 he was in command of successive packet ships of the Black X Line, which at the time 'monopolised the cream of the passenger traffic between London and New York' (W.J. Carlton, 1957, 'Captain Morgan – alias Jorgan', *The Dickensian* 53: 75). He had a wide acquaintance in the literary and artistic world of London, his friends including Dickens, **Thackeray**, **Landseer** and Turner. Lady **Ritchie**, in *From the Porch* (1913), gives a charming account of a party on his ship that she attended as a child.

CAPTAIN SILAS JONAS JORGAN in Charles Dickens, 'A Message from the Sea' (1860)

'I hope you will have seen the Christmas number of "All Year Round". Here and there, in the description of the seagoing hero, I have given a touch or two of remembrance of somebody you know; very heartily desiring that thousands of people may have some faint reflection of the pleasure I have for many years desired from the contemplation of a ... most remarkable man' (to Morgan, December 1860, reproduced in *Letters of Charles Dickens*, 1938, ed. Walter Dexter, Vol. III, p. 198).

MORGAN, Evan, 2nd Viscount Tredegar (1893–1949) He succeeded to the title in 1934.

IVOR LOMBARD in Aldous Huxley, *Crome Yellow* (1921)

'The new friend is "the inimitable Evan Morgan ... the unique fairy prince of modern life" whom Aldous met at Garsington and made to re-appear at Crome. ("Nature and fortune had vied with one another in heaping on Ivor Lombard all their choicest gifts.")' (Sybille Bedford, 1973, *Aldous Huxley: a biography*, Vol. I, London: Chatto & Windus, p. 85).

EDDIE MONTEITH in Ronald Firbank, *The Flower Beneath the Foot* (1923)

'During the latter part of that period [1920–22] Firbank was writing. *The Flower Beneath the Foot*, in which he satirized Morgan in the person of the Honorable Eddie Monteith ...' (Miriam J. Benkovitz, 1969, *Ronald Firbank*, p. 191).

MORGAN, Sydney, Lady (1783?–1859) Irish novelist. Daughter of Robert Owenson, who after playing in London with Garrick, returned to Dublin where he opened the Fishamble Theatre. She made her reputation with *The Wild Irish Girl* (1806). In 1812 she married the surgeon Sir Thomas Charles Morgan (1783–1843), and in 1839 they moved to London where she devoted herself to Society.

MISS BATEMAN (THE 'ROSAMUNDA') in Maria Edgeworth, *Vivian* (1812)

'With some plausibility, the author-governess was assumed to be a caricature of Lady Morgan. ... Maria's letters do not deny this charge outright, and it is plausible to assume that she had been influenced by stories circulating about Lady Morgan. Still, she was pleased when [her brother] tried to put a stop to the rumours. "Thank you, my dear brother, for saying that I never saw Miss Owenson"' (Marilyn Butler, 1972, *Maria Edgeworth*, Oxford, p. 258).

LADY CALDERSFOOT in Lady Blessington, *Memoirs of a Femme de Chambre* (1846)

'I have been greatly entertained by the Femme de Chambre, who paints Society from a woman's eye. ... The spirit of our two sweet friends Morgan and Stepney, shining through their Representative. I would have identified the former, anywhere' (to Lady Blessington, 19 May 1846, reproduced in *Letters of Charles Dickens*, 1977, Vol. IV, ed. Kathleen Tillotson, Oxford: Oxford University Press, p. 548). The footnote reads: 'The "representative" of both ladies is Lady Caldersfoot (in III, chs. 11–16), a pretentious writer with "a thirst for celebrity"'. *See also* **Stepney**, Lady.

BECKY SHARP in W.M. Thackeray, *Vanity Fair* (1847–8)

'One can scarcely help feeling that Thackeray drew some of the most prominent traits of his heroine from the famous Irish writer' (Lionel Stevenson, 1933, *'Vanity Fair* and Lady Morgan', *Publications of the Modern Languages Association*: 551). *See also* **Reviss**, Theresa.

MORIARTY, George A criminal whose activities were described in the London papers of 1874.

PROFESSOR JAMES MORIARTY in Arthur Conan Doyle, the Sherlock Holmes stories (1890–1927)

'We have already seen the source of his surname in the reports about the criminal Moriarty in the London papers in 1874' (Charles Higham, 1976, 'The original Moriarty', *The Times* (20 November): 7). *See also* **Drayson**, Alfred Wilks; **Payn**, James; **Worth**, Adam.

MORPETH, George Howard, Lord (1773–1858) An MP from 1795 to 1820, he became the 9th Earl of Carlisle in 1825. In 1801 he married Georgiana Cavendish (**Morpeth**, below).

LORD TRELAWNEY in Lady Caroline Lamb, *Glenarvon* (1816)

Lord Trelawney is clearly an ill-natured caricature of Lord Morpeth.

MORPETH, Georgiana, Lady (1783–1858) Née Cavendish, she was the daughter of the 5th Duke of **Devonshire** and married Lord **Morpeth** in 1801. She was the sister of Lady **Granville**.

FRANCES SEYMOUR in Lady Caroline Lamb, **Glenarvon** (1816)

Identified in a key found among the papers of John Whishaw, a member of the Holland House circle, printed in *The 'Pope' of Holland House: selections from the correspondence of John Whishaw and his friends, 1813–1840*, ed. Lady Seymour, 1906, p. 151.

MORRELL, Harriet Anne (d. 1924) Daughter of Philip Wyater, President of St John's College, Oxford. In 1866 she married Frederick Parker Morrell, Steward of St John's; he was a solicitor to the university, sometime Mayor of Oxford, and the first MA to hold the office. He died in 1903 and she joined the Roman Catholic Church. She lived at **Black Hall** in Oxford and was the mother of Philip **Morrell**.

MRS ADELA GERETH in Henry James, *The Spoils of Poynton* (1897)

'Philip was devoted to his mother, who was a most gifted and unusually charming person . . . of immense artistic ability, especially in decoration and embroidery. She had been an important figure in Oxford, very much more remarkable in taste and entertaining than any other woman there. . . . Indeed, Henry James, it is said, took from her the inspiration for *The Spoils of Poynton'* (*Ottoline: the early memoirs of Lady Ottoline Morrell*, 1963, ed. R. Gathorne-Hardy, p. 125). '[A little history] was related to me last night at dinner. . . . Some young laird, in Scotland, inherited, by the death of his father, a large place filled with valuable things. . . . His mother was still living [there] . . . the son went down with his wife to take possession . . . he found that pictures and other treasures were absent – and had been taken by his mother . . . there is a hideous public scandal and quarrel' (*The Notebooks of Henry James*, 1947, ed. F.O. Matthiessen and K.B. Murdock, New York, pp. 136, 137).

MORRELL, Lady Ottoline (1873–1938) Sister of the 6th Duke of Portland. In 1902 she married Philip **Morrell**, and in 1905–15 they lived and entertained at 40 Bedford Square, London. From 1915 to 1927 they lived at **Garsington Manor**, and from 1927 to 1938 they lived at 10 Gower Street, London.

MRS LILIAN ALDWINKLE in Aldous Huxley, *Those Barren Leaves* (1925)

'Aldous guyed her . . . in *Those Barren Leaves*. . . . There was a grain or two of truth – Lady Ottoline, like Mrs Aldwinkle, had sometimes bought the stars' (Sybille Bedford, 1973, *Aldous Huxley: a biography*, Vol. I, London: Chatto & Windus, pp. 71, 72).

MRS CAROLINE BURY in Graham Greene, *It's a Battlefield* (1934)

'I was aware of Lady Ottoline Morrell's presence in the background of Lady Caroline' (Graham Greene, 1970, Introd. to *It's a Battlefield* (collected edn); in the edn of 1934 she is *Mrs* Bury).

LADY VIRGINIA CARAWAY in W.J. Turner, *The Aesthetes* (1927)

'I had hoped that you had not read "The Aesthetes" and so were unaware of the repulsive caricature that Turner had drawn of me in it – but obviously you knew all about it and you know that it was intended to be my portrait' (Ottoline Morrell to W.B. Yeats, 10 March 1937, draft letter in Humanities Centre, University of Texas, Austin; see S. Jobson Darroch, 1976, *Ottoline: the life of Lady Ottoline Morrell*, pp. 287–8).

MARY FOTHERINGHAM in J.A. Revermort, *Cuthbert Learmont* (1910)

'The parallel between Mary and Ottoline is striking – but not surprising when one learns that J.A. Revermort is the pseudonym of . . . John Adam Cramb, and amongst Ottoline's correspondence are ninety-four letters from Cramb, most of them dating from 1904' (Darroch, op. cit. p. 49).

LADY SEPTUAGESIMA GOODLEY in Osbert Sitwell, 'Triple Fugue' (1924)

'Osbert Sitwell portrayed her as Lady Septuagesima Goodley' (*The Diary of Virginia Woolf*, Vol. IV: *1931–1935*, 1982, ed. Anne Olivier Bell, London: Hogarth Press, p. 73 n. 18). The portrait in 'Triple Fugue' is unmistakable, one of the most vivid pictures of Lady Ottoline Morrell, voice and all, ever painted: 'She blossomed into a garish glory of clothes, such as was never seen in this world before. . . . Of impressive height . . . [she] had . . . deep-set flowerlike eyes . . . a long, definite nose, and clear-cut chin . . . and a mass of red-brown hair. . . . Her voice . . . was equally absurd, and in it mingled the peaceful lowing of cattle and the barbed drone of wasp and hornet. As she moved . . . through the London streets in her gaudy clothes, large hooped skirt and vast hat loaded with feathers . . . many who stopped to stare supposed that she was staggering-by under the weight of odd lots that had been bestowed upon her by a charitable theatrical costumier'.

HERMIONE RODDICE in D.H. Lawrence, *Women in Love* (1920)

'I think I shall have to give Ottoline Morrell the novel to read. Do you think it would really hurt her – the Hermione? Would you be hurt, if there was some of you in Hermione? You see it isn't really her at all – only suggested by her. It is probable she will think Hermione has nothing to do with her' (to Catherine Carswell, 2 December 1916, reproduced in *The Letters of D.H. Lawrence*, 1984, Vol. III, ed. J.T. Boulton and A. Robertson, Cambridge: Cambridge University Press, p. 44). *See also* **Chambers**, Jessie.

PRISCILLA WIMBUSH in Aldous Huxley, *Crome Yellow* (1921)

'Many of her friendships exploded into violent terminating quarrels, in the aftermath of which she could expect to see herself savagely caricatured in her friend's next novel – as Priscilla Wimbush in Aldous Huxley's *Crome Yellow*, for example' (Michael Holroyd, 1968, *Lytton Strachey*, Vol. II, London: Heinemann, p. 5). 'In fact, Ottoline does not appear in *Crome Yellow*' (*Ottoline at Garsington: memoirs of Lady Ottoline Morrell*, ed. R. Gathorne-Hardy, 1974, London: Faber, p. 24). Her daughter, Mrs Vinogradoff, absolutely denied that she was the original of Priscilla Wimbush (see W.G. Rogers, 1968, *Ladies Bountiful*, p. 93). *See also* **Sitwell**, Lady Ida.

MORRELL, Philip (1870–1943) Son of Harriet **Morrell**, he was a Liberal MP from 1906 to 1918. He married Lady Ottoline Cavendish-Bentinck (**Morrell**, above) in 1902.

ALEXANDER RODDICE in D.H. Lawrence, *Women in Love* (1920)

'Philip Morrell was depicted as he entered the gardens, "striding romantically like a Meredith hero who remembers Disraeli"' (Richard Aldington, 1950, *Portrait of a Genius, but . . . the life of D.H. Lawrence*, London: Heinemann, p. 186). 'I've been lent Lawrence's novel about Ottoline . . . Ott is there to the life and Pipsy [Philip Morrell] too' (to Vanessa Bell, June 1921, reproduced in *The Letters of Virginia Woolf*, 1976, ed. Nigel Nicolson, Vol. II, London: Hogarth Press, p. 475).

HENRY WIMBUSH in Aldous Huxley, *Antic Hay* (1923)

'If people . . . saw Henry Wimbush as Philip Morrell, was this not . . . [a] compliment as he is made the author of . . . the Dwarf's Story?' (Sybille Bedford, 1973, *Aldous Huxley: a biography*, Vol. I, London: Chatto & Windus, p. 123.) *See also* **Sitwell**, Sir George.

HUGH WHITBREAD in Virginia Woolf, *Mrs Dalloway* (1925)

'Although for a time Virginia toyed with the idea of incorporating Ottoline into one of her novels . . . she eventually decided not. . . . However she did portray Philip as Hugh Whitbread in *Mrs Dalloway*. (The name is something of a pun.)' (S. Jobson Darroch, 1976, *Ottoline: the life of Lady Ottoline Morrell*, p. 276).

MORRICE, James Wilson (1865–1924) Canadian painter. He studied and worked in Paris, where he was the friend of Somerset Maugham, Matisse, **Sickert**, Gerald **Kelly**, Clive Bell and Charles Conder.

J. CRONSHAW in W. Somerset Maugham, *Of Human Bondage* (1915)

'As for Morrice, there is no character to represent him exactly, but some of his traits, whether consciously or not, have been used by the author in his description of the poet Cronshaw' (D.W. Buchanan, 1936, *James Wilson Maurice: a biography*, Toronto, p. 68). *See also* **Crowley**, Aleister.

PRIAM FARLL in Arnold Bennett, *Buried Alive* (1908)

'When ... *Buried Alive* first appeared; those who knew Morrice ... were sure that more than a few *traits* of [his character] were portrayed in ... Priam Farll' (Buchanan, op. cit., p. 62). Bennett maintained that he drew Farll from no one but himself. Gerald Kelly, however, 'felt instinctively that a great many of the details of ... Farll had been filled in from Morrice', and Buchanan points out incidents recorded in Bennett's diary in which the parallel between Morrice and Farll is very close (ibid., pp. 63 ff.).

WARREN in W. Somerset Maugham, *The Magician* (1908)

'It is thirty years since I knew Morrice in France ... soon after I met him I wrote what I think was then an accurate portrait of him under the name of Warren in ... *The Magician*' (Maugham to D.W. Buchanan, 31 March 1935, quoted in Buchanan, op. cit., p. 51).

MORRIS, Jane (1839–1914) Daughter of Robert Burden, a groom in a livery stables in Holywell, Oxford. William Morris, **Rossetti** and **Burne-Jones** met her in the summer of 1857 when they were painting the frescoes in the Union. She was 'a tall large-boned girl with a pale ivory face, thick eyebrows, a neck like a tower and an abundance of black crinkly hair' (Philip Henderson, 1967, *William Morris*, p. 48). In 1859 she married William Morris; Rossetti was deeply attached to her and constantly painted her. They were particularly close in 1865–72 when the Morrises moved to London; they then moved to Kelmscot, Oxfordshire, and Rossetti went with them.

ANNE BROWN in Vernon Lee, *Miss Brown* (1884)

'*Miss Brown* was regarded from the first as a *roman à clef*. William Morris and Edmond Gurney had both educated girls to be their wives' (Peter Gunn, 1964, *Vernon Lee, 1856–1935*, London: Oxford University Press, p. 102). The description in ch. 1 of Anne Brown might be a description of Jane Morris. *See also* **Gurney**, Kate.

MOSLEY, Sir Oswald (1896–1980) Politician. He was a Conservative, Independent and Labour MP, successively, then resigned and founded and led the British Union of Fascists, the 'Blackshirt Movement'. In 1920 he married Cynthia, daughter of Earl Curzon. In 1936, three years after his first wife's death, he married Diana Mitford (Nancy **Mitford**'s sister), with whom he had a son, Oswald **Mosley**.

EVERARD WEBLEY in Aldous Huxley, *Point Counter Point* (1928)

'In *Point Counter Point* ... there could be no doubt that the fascist Everard Webley was Oswald Mosley' (Lionel Stevenson, 1967, *History of the English Novel*, Vol. XI, New York, p. 180).

MOSLEY, Oswald Alexander (b. 1938) Son of Sir Oswald **Mosley** and his second wife Diana, née Mitford, Nancy Mitford's sister.

BASIL WINCHAM in Nancy Mitford, *Don't Tell Alfred* (1960)

'Basil is my Diana's Ali' (Nancy Mitford to Handasyde Buchanan, 7 September 1960, quoted in Harold Acton, 1975, *Nancy Mitford: a memoir*, London: Hamilton, p. 141).

MOST, Johann (1846–1906) German anarchist. Born in Bavaria, he was active in the Social Democratic movement in Switzerland, Austria, Czechoslovakia and Germany between 1863 and 1880. In 1876 he was Editor of the Berlin *Freie Presse*, and in 1879 he was the founder of *Freiheit*. He moved to England in 1880 and in 1881 was sentenced to sixteen months' hard labour; he went to the USA in 1882. He was much influenced by **Bakunin** and the French communards, and from 1889 onwards was a close friend of Emma **Goldman**. Although he was constantly in and out of prison for advocating violence, he was never violent in action. His widow Helen maintained the publication of *Freiheit* until 1909.

THE PROFESSOR in Joseph Conrad, *The Secret Agent* (1907)

'The "perfect anarchist" is ... based upon certain psychological theories about criminal types, and is given a history derived from the personal background of at least two anarchists (Most and Creaghe) and one Fenian (Luke Dillon)' (Norman Sherry, 1971, *Conrad's Western World*, Cambridge, p. 285). *See also* **Creaghe**, Dr; **Dillon**, Luke; **Mezzeroff**, 'Professor'; **Rossetti**, Arthur.

KARL YUNDT in Joseph Conrad, *The Secret Agent* (1907)

'Conrad describes Yundt's character with some care ... [and] it seems most probable that [he] had in mind ... a well-known extremist ... who symbolised in himself all that terrified the ordinary and the rich citizen alike – the German anarchist, Johann Most' (Sherry, op. cit., p. 254). *See also* **Bakunin**, Michael.

MOTLEY, John Lothrop (1814–77) Historian and diplomat. Educated at Harvard and in Germany, he was the author of *The Rise of the Dutch Republic* (1856). He was the United States minister to Austria in 1861–7 and to Great Britain in 1869–70.

NATHAN GORE in Henry Adams, *Democracy* (1880)

'The identification of Nathan Gore as John Lothrop Motley ... posed no great puzzle. ... Gore explained his recall from Madrid in these words. "The President ... objects to the cut of my overcoat, which is unfortunately an English one. He also objects to the cut of my hair"' (Ernest Samuels, 1958, *Henry Adams: the middle years*, Cambridge, Mass., p. 92). According to Henry Adams, President Grant recalled Motley from London 'because he parted his hair in the middle' (*The Education of Henry Adams: an autobiography*, p. 276; see *The Letters of Mrs Henry Adams*, 1937, ed. Ward Thoron, London: Longman, p. 25 n. 1). *See also* **Lowell**, James Russell.

MOTTA, Signor An Italian music teacher.

SARTI in George Eliot, 'Mr Gilfil's Love Story', *Scenes of Clerical Life* (1857–8)

'Sir Roger [Newdigate's] second wife ... was very fond of music and took lessons in London of an Italian music master named Motta, the original of "Sarti"' (Charles S. Olcott, 1911, *George Eliot: scenes and people in her novels*, London: Cassell, p. 32; originally published 1910, New York: Thomas Y. Crowell). *See also under* **Anstruther**, Lady.

MOULE, Charles Son of Henry **Moule** and younger brother of Horace **Moule**. He became President of Corpus Christi College, Cambridge.

ANGEL CLARE in Thomas Hardy, *Tess of the d'Urbervilles* (1891)

'Hardy said that Angel Clare was drawn partly from Charles Moule' (F.B. Pinion, 1968, *A Hardy Companion*, London: Macmillan, p. 281).

MOULE, Revd Henry (1801–80) Educated in Marlborough and at St John's College, Cambridge, he was Vicar of Fordington, Dorset, from 1829 to 1880. In 1860, with James Bannelin, he invented and patented the dry-earth closet system that was subsequently used extensively in military camps and in India. He was the author of, *inter alia*, *Manure for the Million: to the cottage gardeners of England* (1861), and was the father of Horace and Charles **Moule**. Thomas Hardy became a close friend of the whole family.

REVD JAMES CLARE in Thomas Hardy, *Tess of the d'Urbervilles* (1891)

'I met a ... man on Friday (by the way, he is son of the old parson whose portrait I partially drew in Angel Clare's father)' (25 February 1900, reproduced in *One Rare Fair Woman: Thomas Hardy's letters to Florence Henniker, 1893–1922*, 1972, ed. Evelyn Hardy and F.B. Pinion, p. 92 n. 292).

CAPTAIN JOHN MAUMBRY in Thomas Hardy, 'A Changed Man' (1913)

'His work during the cholera epidemic was based on that of the vicar of Fordington' (F.B. Pinion, 1968, *A Hardy Companion*, London: Macmillan, p. 404). 'I well remember the cholera years in Fordington. ... For instance, every morning a man used to wheel the clothing and bed-linen of those who had died in the night out into the mead, where the Vicar had a large copper set. Some was boiled there, and some burnt. He also had large fires kindled in Mill Street to carry off infection' (Hardy to Handley Moule, Bishop of Durham, 29 June 1919, quoted in F.E. Hardy, 1972, *Life of Thomas Hardy, 1840–1928*, p. 391).

MOULE, Horace Mosley (1832–73) Son of Revd Henry **Moule** and elder brother of Charles **Moule**, he was educated at Trinity College, Cambridge, and at Queen's College, Oxford, but did not take a degree at either university until 1867. For some time he was a master at Marlborough College. He was a considerable Classical scholar, and contributed to the *Saturday Review*, including a notice of *Under the Greenwood Tree* and (probably) *A Pair of Blue Eyes*. In 1860 or 1861 he met Thomas Hardy, becoming his close friend and exerting a strong influence on the development of his thought. He fell prey to depression, took to drink and committed suicide.

HENRY KNIGHT in Thomas Hardy, *A Pair of Blue Eyes* (1873)

'In some respects the original of Henry Knight' (R.L. Purdy, 1954, *Thomas Hardy: a bibliographical study*, Oxford, p. 12 n. 2). *See also* **Hardy**, Thomas.

MOUNT EDGCUMBE, Richard Edgcumbe, Lord (1764–1839) 2nd Earl of Mount Edgcumbe. In 1808 he was a privy councillor and from 1808 to 1812 he was the Captain of a band of gentlemen-pensioners. He wrote, for private circulation, *Musical Reminiscences of an Old Amateur.*

LORD GULOSETON in Bulwer Lytton, *Pelham* (1828)

'There [is a portrait] ... of Lord Mount Edgcumbe' (Michael Sadleir, 1933, *Bulwer and His Wife*, London: Constable, p. 190). 'My father gave me to understand that Vincent and Guloseton had also their originals in real life, but he did not mention their names' (Owen Meredith, 1883, *Life, Letters and Literary Remains of Edward Bulwer, Lord Lytton*, p. 193). It would appear that the original of Guloseton was Lord Mount Edgcumbe.

MOUNTSIER, Robert (1888–1972) American journalist. In 1916 he visited Lawrence in Cornwall, and in 1920 he agreed to act as his agent in the USA. In 1910 he was Literary Editor for the *New York Sun*, and during the First World War he served with the Red Cross; subsequently, he was with the *Sun* until 1950.

MR MONSELL in D.H. Lawrence, *Kangaroo* (1923)

From Lawrence's letter to Mountsier (4 January 1917), it appears that after a visit to Cornwall, Mountsier had an encounter with the Special Branch at Scotland Yard: 'cf. *Kangaroo*, chap. XII where Monsell (Mountsier) was questioned at Scotland Yard' (*The Letters of D.H. Lawrence*, 1984, Vol. III, ed. J.T. Boulton and A. Robertson, Cambridge: Cambridge University Press, p. 65 n. 1).

MOYLES COURT, Hampshire A mid-seventeenth-century brick house located about three miles north-east of Ringwood, at Ellingham. It had two storeys with projecting wings and was a melancholy house.

BRAMHURST COURT in Thomas Hardy, *Tess of the d'Urbervilles* (1891)

Identified in F.B. Pinion, 1968, *A Hardy Companion*, London: Macmillan.

MULDOON, William (1852–1933) He retired at the age of 48, when he was the undefeated heavyweight wrestling champion of the world. He then opened a sanatorium, Olympia, at Purchase, near White Plains, New York, where he enforced a 'regimen of walking, running, wood-chopping ... plain diet and abstinence' (*The Dictionary of National Biography*, London: Oxford University Press). Theodore Dreiser sent his brother Paul **Dresser** there in 1903; another patient was Mr J. Reston Peters (of P.G. Wodehouse's *Something Fresh* (1915)), who recalled the place with shuddering horror. At the age of 82, Muldoon was Head of the Boxing Commission for the State of New York, ruling with a rod of iron: his nickname had been changed from the 'Professor' to the 'Duke'.

CULHANE in Theodore Dreiser, *Twelve Men* (1919)

'He included Muldoon as "Culhane, the solid man"' (F.O. Matthiessen, 1951, *Theodore Dreiser*, London: Methuen, p. 101).

MULVEY, Willie A young man whom Nora Joyce had known as a girl in Galway. 'Some time after this Nora met Willie Mulvey she just met him on the bridge he asked her would she meet him' (Mrs Mary O'Holleran (Nora's closest friend in Galway), quoted in Richard Ellmann, 1966, *James Joyce*, London: Oxford Paperbacks, p. 164).

LIEUTENANT HARRY MULVEY in James Joyce, *Ulysses* (1922)

'[Nora's] husband and her past lovers, among whom Mulvey of Galway makes an unexpected appearance, are speedily interchanged in the mind' (Ellmann, op. cit., p. 387).

MUNNINGS, Sir Alfred (1878–1959) Painter. An outstanding painter of horses, he was President of the Royal Academy from 1944 to 1949 and was deeply hostile to the whole movement of modern art.

JAMES LOVETT in John Prebble, *The Mather Story* (1953)

'The mere fact of you – in one page – speaking of *horses* and *horse quarters* spots me as Lovat [sic]' (Munnings to Prebble, 6 January 1953, quoted in Frederick Warburg, 1973, *All Authors Are Equal*, p. 268).

MUNTHE, Axel (1857–1949) Swedish physician and writer. He practised in Paris and Rome and for a long time had a house on Capri. He was variously regarded as a magical healer and an old fraud.

MELVILLE L. SMEAD in Norman Douglas, *Looking Back* (1933)

'[T]he remarks under the heading Melville L. Smead in *Looking Back*, referring to a certain collector on Capri as a fraud, refer to Munthe. ... Munthe's blindness was certainly exaggerated' (Mark Holloway, 1976, *Norman Douglas*, p. 501 n. 28). The identification comes from the copy of *Looking Back* in the Berg Collection, New York Public Library, which was annotated by Willie King under instruction from Douglas.

MURPHY, Anna She was George Moore's aunt and lived near Dublin with her two daughters.

MRS BARTON in George Moore, *Muslin* (1915)

'Mrs Barton was drawn in part from . . . Mrs Anna Murphy . . . she showed no resentment at the portrait and indeed returned good for evil by giving him the pretty Louis Seize clock that is mentioned in . . . *Conversations in Ebury Street*' (Joseph Hone, 1936, *The Life of George Moore*, London: Victor Gollancz, p. 103).

MURPHY, Esther Daughter of Gerald and Sara **Murphy**, in 1929 she married John Strachey, the English left-wing journalist and politician; they were divorced in 1933.

BOUNDING BESS in Djuna Barnes, *The Ladies Almanack* (1928)

Identified in Meryle Secrest, 1976, *Between Me and Life: a biography of Romaine Brooks*, London: MacDonald & Jane, p. 335; originally published 1974, Garden City, NY: Doubleday.

MURPHY, Gerald (1888–1964) Son of Patrick Murphy, who was the owner of the New York store Mark Cross. In 1915 he married Sara Wiborg (**Murphy,** below) and they moved to Europe, dividing their time between Paris and

Antibes; they returned to the United States in 1933. He possessed legendary charm and was well liked by many people. He had considerable talent as a painter, and his works (of which only six survive) uncannily foreshadowed the pop art of the 1970s.

RICHARD DIVER in F. Scott Fitzgerald, *Tender is the Night* (1934)

See under **Murphy**, Sara. *See also* **Fitzgerald**, F. Scott.

MURPHY, Sara (1883–1975) One of the three beautiful and gifted daughters of Frank Wiborg, a Cincinnati ink manufacturer. The sisters had a spectacular success in London Society in 1914, and in 1915 Sara married Gerald **Murphy**.

NICOLE DIVER in F. Scott Fitzgerald, *Tender is the Night* (1934)

'In my theory . . . about fiction, i.e. that it takes half a dozen people to make a synthesis to create a fiction character . . . I used you again and again in *Tender*. . . . I tried to evoke not you but the effect that you produce on men . . . an artist's . . . sincere attempt to preserve a true fragment rather than a "portrait" by Mr Sargent' (to Sara Murphy, 15 August 1935, reproduced in *The Letters of F. Scott Fitzgerald*, 1964, ed. Andrew Turnbull, London: Bodley Head, p. 423). *Tender is the Night* was dedicated to Sara and her husband Gerald. *See also* **Fitzgerald**, Zelda.

MURRAY, Basil (1902?–37) Son of Gilbert Murray, he was educated at Charterhouse and, from 1920 to 1923, at New College, Oxford. He was Private Secretary to Lloyd George, of whom he wrote a biography (1932), and was a war correspondent in Spain for the *Daily Express* during the Civil War. He died of pneumonia on a hospital ship between Alicante and Marseilles, and was buried at Marseilles.

JASPER ASPECT in Nancy Mitford, *Wigs on the Green* (1935)

'A satanic young man, strange offspring of puritan parents . . . there were times when he seemed possessed by a devil of mischief. There is a character derived from him in one of Nancy Mitford's early, out-of-print novels' (Evelyn Waugh, 1964, *A Little Learning . . . an autobiography*, London: Chapman and Hall, p. 204). A deduction, but almost certainly correct.

BASIL SEAL in Evelyn Waugh, *Black Mischief* (1932), *Scoop* (1938) and *Put Out More Flags* (1942)

'Some readers have professed to recognise . . . in the character "Basil Seal" . . . a combination of Basil and Peter [Rodd]' (ibid.). *See also* **Rodd**, Peter.

MURRAY, John[1] (1778–1843) Publisher. From 1803 to 1813 he was the London agent for the Edinburgh firm Constable, and in 1809 he started the High Tory *Quarterly Review*. In 1812 he moved his premises to Albermarle Street, where the firm remains. He published Jane Austen, **Byron**, Crabbe and many others, and the famous series of guidebooks. In 1826, at the suggestion of Disraeli, he embarked on a daily newspaper, *Representative*, but it failed after six months.

MARQUESS OF CARABAS in Benjamin Disraeli, *Vivian Grey* (1826-7)

'This prosy, politically disappointed and ... tipsy mediocrity ... despite all denials, must be Murray' (Robert Blake, 1966, *Disraeli*, London: Eyre & Spottiswoode, pp. 38–9). *See also* **Clanricarde**, 1st Marquess of; **Grenville**, Lord, 2nd Marquis of Chandos.

MURRAY, John[2] (d. 1910) James Joyce's uncle. He worked in the accounts department of the *Freeman's Journal.*

JOE DONNELLY in James Joyce, 'Clay', *Dubliners* (1914)

'Murray was a model for Joe Donnelly in "Clay"' (*Letters of James Joyce*, 1966, Vol. II, ed. Richard Ellmann, London: Faber & Faber, p. 186 n. 7).

MURRAY, William (1858–1912) The brother of Mrs John Stanislaus Joyce, he was James Joyce's uncle. He was employed as a billing clerk in a well-known firm of Dublin solicitors.

ALPHY DONNELLY in James Joyce, 'Clay', *Dubliners* (1914)

'William and John are the two brothers, Joe and Alphy, sketched in the story "Clay" in *Dubliners*' (Richard Ellmann, 1966, *James Joyce*, London: Oxford Paperbacks, p. 18).

RICHIE GOULDING in James Joyce, *Ulysses* (1922)

'William Murray appears transparently in *Ulysses* under the name of Richie Goulding' (ibid.).

MURROW, Edward R. (1908–65) Journalist and television commentator. His television programme 'See It Now' helped to finally swing opinion against **McCarthy** in February 1954.

ROBERT A. FLETCHER in William L. Shirer, *Stranger Come Home* (1954)

'The book's anti-hero, Robert A. Fletcher, a wartime radio broadcaster turned network executive, played an ambiguous, indeed shabby role in permitting the inquisition of the liberal-minded broadcaster clearly patterned on Shirer himself' (Alexander Kendrick, 1970, *Prime Time: the life of Edward R. Murrow*, p. 297). The plot of the novel bears some resemblance to the dispute between Murrow and Shirer in 1945 in what was known as the 'Freedom of the Air' controversy, the outcome of which was that Shirer lost his job with CBS News, with which Murrow was a corporation executive.

MURRY, John Middleton (1889–1957) Editor and critic. Born in Peckham, London, he met Katherine **Mansfield** in 1911 and married her in 1918. He edited the *Athenaeum* 1919–21, *The Adelphi* 1923–30 and *Peace News* 1940–6.

DENIS BURLAP in Aldous Huxley, *Point Counter Point* (1928)

'Murry remains in the novel as Burlap' (Jerome Meckier, 1969, *Aldous Huxley*, p. 87).

FRANCIS CHELIFER in Aldous Huxley, *Those Barren Leaves* (1925)

'... Chelifer (who, at times, is Murry) in *Those Barren Leaves*' (Meckier, op. cit., p. 82). 'In fact, Chelifer bears no resemblance to the real Murry ... and just as little to the fictional Murry . . . Burlap in *Point Counter Point* . . . but there are significant resemblances between him and Huxley' (George Woodcock, 1972, *Dawn and the Darkest Hour: a study of Aldous Huxley*, London: Faber & Faber, p. 122).

GERALD CRICH in D.H. Lawrence, *Women in Love* (1920)

'[Murry] didn't associate himself and Katherine Mansfield with *Women in Love* until Frieda [Lawrence] told him, years afterwards, that they were in it. Then Murry saw that the conversations between Gerald and Rupert paralleled those between Murry and Lawrence at Higher Tregerthen in 1916' (H.T. Moore, 1974, *The Priest of Love: a life of D.H. Lawrence*, rev. edn, London: Heinemann, pp. 259–60; originally published 1955 as *The Intelligent Heart: the story of D.H. Lawrence*, London: Heinemann). *See also* **Barber**, Sir Philip; **Neville**, G.H.

PHILIP FARQUHAR in D.H. Lawrence, 'The Border Line' (1928)

'"The Border Line"' is . . . the first of the short stories containing a portrait of Murry, who appears as the journalist whom . . . Anstruther reaches from beyond the grave to defeat' (Moore, op. cit., p. 387).

JIMMY FRITH in D.H. Lawrence, 'Jimmy and the Desperate Woman' (1928)

'Murry is Jimmy . . . the editor of a highbrow magazine who becomes comically entangled with a collier's wife' (Moore, op. cit., p. 393).

MARCHBANKS in D.H. Lawrence, 'The Last Laugh' (1928)

'. . . and [Murry] is Marchbanks' (Moore, op. cit., p. 393).

MATTHEW in D.H. Lawrence, 'Smile' (1928)

'"Smile" [is] obviously based on the death of Katherine Mansfield (with Murry . . . as Matthew)' (Moore, op. cit., p. 414).

PHILIP SURROGATE in Graham Greene, *It's a Battlefield* (1934)

'[M]y idea of Middleton Murry, whom I did not personally know, was responsible in small part for Mr Surrogate' (Graham Greene, 1970, Introd. to *It's a Battlefield*, p. x).

MUSHET, Robert (1782–1828) Officer of the Royal Mint. In 1819 he gave evidence to the parliamentary committee on currency questions.

MR MACQUEDY in Thomas Love Peacock, *Crotchet Castle* (1831)

'The best explanation of MacQuedy is that he is a creation of the imagination, a composite character formed from the ideas of several utilitarian economists. Three economists, Mill, McCullock and Mushet, can be identified as contributors to the literary image' (William F. Kennedy, 1966, 'Peacock's economists: some mistaken identities', *The Nineteenth Century* 21 (2): 188–90). *See also* **McCulloch**, John Ramsay; **Mill**, James.

N

NANKIVELL, Charles Benjamin He was a physician in Pisa in 1828 and moved to Coventry in 1831 to become the first physician at the new Provident Dispensary.

TERTIUS LYDGATE in George Eliot, *Middlemarch* (1871–2)

'I find a likelier prototype [than Sir Clifford Allbutt] in [Charles] Bray's friend Charles Benjamin Nankivell' (Gordon S. Haight, 1958, 'The George Eliot originals', *From Jane Austen to Joseph Conrad: essays collected in memory of James T. Hillhouse*, ed. R. Rathburn and M. Steinmann, Jun., Minneapolis, Minn.: University of Minnesota Press, p. 190). *See also* **Allbutt**, Sir Thomas Clifford; **Clarke** Edward.

NAPOLEON III, Charles Louis Napoléon Bonaparte, Emperor of France (1808–73) Born in Paris, the third son of Louis Bonaparte, he became head of the Napoleonic dynasty in 1832. After an abortive attempt to seize the French throne at Boulogne in 1840, he was imprisoned for life in Ham fortress. However, he escaped in 1846 and fled to England, but returned to Paris after the revolution of 1848 and took a seat in the Constituent Assembly. In 1851, after several years of power struggles with the National Assembly, he dissolved the Constitution and established imperial rule. He managed to preserve internal peace, but his foreign policy was marked by conflict, most notably with France's involvement in the Crimean War (1854–6) and the Franco-Prussian War (1870). It was after being defeated by Prussia that Napoleon was exiled to Kent in England, where he remained until his death. He married Eugénie de Montijo in 1853.

COLONEL ALBERT (PRINCE FLORESTAN) in Benjamin Disraeli, *Endymion* (1880)

Identified in 'Key to *Endymion*', *Notes and Queries* 83 (24 October 1942): 263; identifications attributed to G.E. Buckle.

PORPHYRO in Elizabeth Sara Sheppard, *Rumour* (1858)

'He is depicted under the name of Porphyro in . . . Rumour by the author of Charles Auchester . . . [Miss Elizabeth S. Sheppard]' (Frederic Boase, 1892, *Modern English Biography*, Vol. II, col. 1082).

MONSIEUR RIGAUD in Charles Dickens, *Little Dorrit* (1855–7)

'Both the descriptions of him in the text and the illustrations suggest that he was conceived as a caricature of Napoleon III' (Edgar Johnson, 1953, *Charles Dickens*, Vol. II, p. 886). *See also* **Laçenaire**, Pierre-François; **Wainewright**, Thomas Griffiths.

NASH, John (1752–1835) English architect. He was engaged by the Prince Regent (the future **George IV**) to plan the layout of the new Regent's Park and its environs of curved terraces. He recreated Buckingham Palace from the old Buckingham House, designed the Marble Arch which originally stood in front of it, and rebuilt Brighton Pavilion in oriental style. Although considered one the greatest town planners, 'His style lacks grandeur, and great monotony is produced by his persistent use of stucco' (*The Dictionary of National Biography*, London: Oxford University Press).

CUNNING NAT in Bulwer Lytton, *Paul Clifford* (1830)

Identification supplied by Sir John Summerson.

MR STUCCO in Benjamin Disraeli, *Vivian Grey* (1826-7)

Identified as Mr N—h in a key given in *The Star Chamber* (24 May 1826): p. 114; reprinted in *Vivian Grey*, 1904 (centenary edn), ed. Lucien Wolf, Vol. II, pp. 361–2. The full name appeared in a reprint of the key published in *Notes and Queries* 3 (29 April 1893). Lucien Wolf concludes that Disraeli was not responsible for the key.

NASH, Richard (Beau Nash) (1674–1762) 'King of Bath'. He went to Bath in 1705 and established the Assembly Rooms. In 1758, pensioned by the city corporation, he assisted in establishing the mineral water hospital.

BEAU BEAMISH in George Meredith, *A Tale of Chloe* (1879)

'Tell the Munich lady that Beau Beamish was modelled on the notorious Beau Nash, who was, by consent of the time, despot of Bath' (to W.M. Meredith, 24 June 1904, reproduced in *Letters of George Meredith*, 1970, ed. C.L. Cline, Oxford, p. 1501). Meredith's source was Goldsmith's biography of Nash.

NATHAN, George Jean (1882–1958) He was the most influential dramatic critic of his time in the United States. He joined the staff of the *New York Herald* in 1905 and discovered Eugene O'Neill.

MAURY NOBLE in F. Scott Fitzgerald, *The Beautiful and Damned* (1922)

'. . . George Jean Nathan (on whom he drew heavily for Maury Noble' (A. Mizener, 1951, *The Far Side of Paradise*, p. 138).

The *NATIONAL STANDARD* A literary journal edited by F.W.N. Bayley, from its inception on 1 January 1833 until 11 May. Thackeray became the proprietor of the paper towards the end of April and contributed to every issue until it ceased publication on 1 February 1834.

THE *MUSEUM* in W.M. Thackeray, *Lovel the Widower* (1860)

'It may be surmised that Thackeray's account . . . of how Mr Batchelor came to acquire the *Museum* derives from his own purchase of *The National Standard*' (*The Letters and Private Papers of W.M. Thackeray*, Vol. I: *1817–1840*, 1945, ed. Gordon N. Ray, London: Oxford University Press, p. 260 n. 2).

NEEDHAM, Ellice (*fl.* 1800) Of Highgate Wall, Buxton, Derbyshire. He was the owner of **Litton Mill**.

ELGOOD SHARPTON in Frances Trollope, *Michael Armstrong, the Factory Boy* (1840)

'In 1832 [the trade unionist John] Doherty had reprinted . . . John Brown's . . . *Memoir of Robert Blincoe*, originally published in 1828, which described the sufferings of a pauper apprentice, first in a cotton-mill at Lowdham near Nottingham, and then at Litton Mill. . . . This second mill was owned by Ellice Needham (i.e. "Elgood Sharpton")' (W.H. Chaloner, 1960, 'Mrs Trollope and the early factory system', *Victorian Studies* 4 (2): 164).

NELSON, Battling (1882–1954) An American boxer who became the world lightweight champion in 1908; he was famous for his capacity to fight back against almost inhuman punishment.

ADOLPH FRANCIS in Ernest Hemingway, 'The Battler', *In Our Time* (1925)

'The battler was . . . Ad Francis, whose personality was based on two real-life fighters . . . Ad Wolgast and Bat Nelson' (Carlos Baker, 1969, *Ernest Hemingway: a life story*, New York, p. 141). *See also* **Wolgast**, Ad.

NEUWIED, Germany A town on the Rhine, near Coblenz.

SARKELD in George Meredith, *The Adventures of Harry Richmond* (1871)

'The visits to Sarkeld are full of memories of the author's years at Neuwied' (A. Lionel Stevenson, 1954, *The Ordeal of George Meredith*, London: Peter Owen, p. 183).

de NÈVE, Edward (Jean Lenglet) He was the first husband of Jean **Rhys**, who helped him with the translation and publication of *Barred*, which was originally written in French.

JAN VAN LEEUWEN in Edward de Nève, *Barred* (1932)

'Another view of the Ford–Rhys relationship [from that in Jean Rhys's novel *Postures* or *Quartet*] is provided in a . . . novel . . . by de Nève. In its way de Nève's book is more directly personal than *Quartet*, and, as a reflection of actual events, seemingly more candid' (Thomas F. Staley, 1979, *Jean Rhys: a critical study*, p. 12.

NEVILLE, George Henry (1886–1959) He was a teacher from 1912 to 1916 and subsequently held a variety of jobs, until 1939 when his brother obtained employment for him as a regional disposals officer. He was a friend of D.H. Lawrence from their schooldays at Nottingham High School.

GERALD CRICH in D.H. Lawrence, *Women in Love* (1920)

See below under LESLIE TEMPEST. *See also* **Barber**, Sir Philip; **Murry**, J.M.

GEORGE SAXTON in D.H. Lawrence, *The White Peacock* (1911)

'. . . a character of which, without doubt, I happen to be the prototype' (George Neville, 1981, *A Memoir of D.H. Lawrence*, ed. Carl Baron, p. 160). *See also* **Chambers**, Alan. 'Lawrence based two works closely on Neville's life . . . the unfinished novel *Mr Noon* (1934) and the comic play *The Married Man* (1940)' (Carl Baron, 1981, introd. to Neville, op. cit., p. 23). The characters are Gilbert Noon and George Grainger. For a full discussion, see ibid., pp. 23–31.

LESLIE TEMPEST in D.H. Lawrence, *The White Peacock* (1911)

'In speaking of *Women in Love*, did I say that Gerald Crick is only a development of Leslie Tempest in *The White Peacock*, and that the character of the latter was founded in the first instance on D.H.L.'s schoolfriend, G.H. Neville?' (Jessie Chambers to Emile Delavenay, 5 March 1935, quoted in Delavenay, 1969, *D.H. Lawrence: l'homme et le génèse de son oeuvre*, Vol. II: *Documents*, Paris, p. 692).

NEVINSON, Christopher Richard Wynne (1889–1946) Painter. Son of M.W. and H.W. **Nevinson**, he was educated at Uppingham and at the Slade School of Fine Art, University College London. As a young man he was a leading Futurist and disciple of Marinetti. During both World Wars he was an artist of distinction.

HUMPHREY MITCHELL in Gilbert Cannan, *Mendel* (1916)

'Portraits of Edward Marsh, Brett, Carrington, Augustus John and C.R.W. Nevinson are also to be found in the book' (Diana Farr, 1978, *Gilbert Cannan: a Georgian prodigy*, London: Chatto & Windus, p. 40.

NEVINSON, Henry Woodd (1856–1941) Distinguished foreign and war correspondent, and writer. He was with the *Daily Chronicle* in 1897, the *Manchester Guardian* in 1907, and the *Daily News* in 1909. In 1915 he was a correspondent for the *Manchester Guardian* during the Gallipoli campaign, and from 1907 to 1923 he was on the staff of *The Nation*. He remained with the *Manchester Guardian* until 1929. In 1884 he married Margaret Wynne Jones (1857?–1932), suffragist and magistrate; she was the first woman to sit on the criminal bench in the County of London. Following her death, in 1933 he married Evelyn Sharp, the writer and suffragette.

CHARLES COURTIER in John Galsworthy, *The Patrician* (1911)

'[Courtier] is drawn from the adventurous figure of the great war correspondent, H.W. Nevinson' (David Garnett, 1979, *Great Friends*, p. 110).

NEW BRUNSWICK, New Jersey

NEW BOYNTON in Francis T. Field, *McDonough* (1951)

'New Boynton suggests New Brunswick' (Joseph Blotner, 1966, *The Modern American Political Novel*, Austin, Tex., p. 80 n. 45).

NEW COURT, Lincoln's Inn Fields, London

NEW SERJEANT'S INN in Arnold Bennett, *The Man from the North* (1898)

'New Court, Lincoln's Inn fields, has changed little since Arnold Bennett arrived in London in his twenty-first year to take up his junior post in . . . Le Brasseur and Oakley. . . . Bennett called it New Serjeant's Inn in his first novel' (Reginald Pound, 1959, *Arnold Bennett: a biography*, London: Heinemann, p. 74).

NEW FOREST, Hampshire

THE GREAT FOREST in Thomas Hardy, Wessex novels and tales (1871–95)

Identified on a map prepared by Thomas Hardy which hangs in the Dorset County Museum, Dorchester. *See under* **Abbotsbury**.

NEW PLAYWRIGHTS A group of writers that formed in New York in 1927 to write and produce left-wing, largely Marxist plays. The group was financed by Otto **Kahn** in 1927 and 1928, and the founder directors were John Howard **Lawson**, Mike Gold, John **Dos Passos**, E.J. Basshe and F.E. Faragoh. The group collapsed when Kahn withdrew his support.

THE CRAFTSMAN'S THEATRE in John Dos Passos, *Most Likely to Succeed* (1954)

'In *Most Likely to Succeed* Dos Passos fictionalizes the strife and disappointment of the theatre's hours of eclipse' (G.A. Knox and H.M. Stahl, 1964, *Dos Passos and 'The Revolting Playwrights'*, Lund, p. 85).

NEW YORK UNIVERSITY Thomas Wolfe taught in the English Department of the Washington Square branch from 1924 to 1930.

SCHOOL FOR UTILITY CULTURES in Thomas Wolfe, *Of Time and the River* (1935)

'[T]he school for Utility Cultures . . . was to be his satiric reflection on New York University' (*The Notebooks of Thomas Wolfe*, 1970, ed. Richard S. Kennedy and Paschal Reeves, Chapel Hill, NC: University of North Carolina Press, p. 440 n. 23).

NEWBURY, Berkshire A town on the River Kennet.

KENNETBRIDGE in Thomas Hardy, *Jude the Obscure* (1895)

Identified in Denys Kay-Robinson, 1972, *Hardy's Wessex Reappraised*, Newton Abbot, and in F.B. Pinion, 1968, *A Hardy Companion*, London: Macmillan.

NEWCASTLE, Henry Pelham Fiennes Pelham Clinton, 4th Duke of (1785–1851) An extreme Tory, he was one of the twenty-two stalwarts who voted against the Reform Bill on 4 June 1852. His speech with respect to some ejected tenants at Newark – 'Shall I not do what I like with my own?' – so inflamed the mob that they burnt down his mansion, Nottingham Castle, in 1830. 'For more than twenty years, it was assumed by the general public that the Duke's motives as a landlord and member of the House of Lords were most unworthy . . . and his appetite for jobbery was declared to be insatiable' (*The Dictionary of National Biography*, London: Oxford University Press).

LORD MOWBRAY in Robert Plumer Ward, *De Vere; or The Man of Independence* (1827)

'Mowbray was in part the Duke of Newcastle' (M.W. Rosa, 1936, *The Silver-Fork School: novels of fashion preceding 'Vanity Fair'*, New York, p. 68).

NEWCASTLE, Henry Pelham Pelham-Clinton, 6th Duke of (1811–64) He was Secretary of State for the Colonies from 1852 to 1854 and from 1859 to 1864, and Secretary for War from 1854 to 1855. He married William Beckford's granddaughter, Lady Susan Hamilton; they were divorced in 1850. 'He was a thoroughly upright, high-minded and patriotic gentleman . . . the fortitude with which he bore accumulated misfortune and torturing disease would have touched any heart' (Godwin Smith, 1910, *Reminiscences*, pp. 185–6).

PLANTAGENET PALLISER in Anthony Trollope, *Can You Forgive Her?* (1864)

'Plantagenet Palliser had already [November 1873] been decided on as the late Duke of Newcastle' (O.W. Hewett, 1956, *Strawberry Fair*, p. 236). *See also* **Parkinson-Fortescue**, Chichester; **Russell**, 1st Earl.

NEWCOMBE, John Reilly (1803–87) Actor-manager. He had the last stock company in Britain and was the lessee and Manager of the Theatre Royal, Plymouth, from 1845 to 1887, of the Devonport theatre until 1874, and of the Barnstaple theatre; the theatre in Plymouth was damaged or destroyed by fire three times. He engaged Taglioni to dance at £100 a night. He hunted for sixty years and rode at the Plymouth races.

OLDGO in Mortimer Collins, *Two Plunges for a Pearl* (1872)

'He is drawn . . . in *Two Plunges for a Pearl* . . . under name of Oldgo' (Frederic Boase, 1892, *Modern English Biography*, Vol. II, col. 1118).

NEWDEGATE, Rt. Hon. Charles N. (1816-87) Educated at Eton and at Christ Church, Oxford, he was the Conservative MP for North Warwickshire from 1834 to 1885. He was Privy Councillor in 1886.

MR OLDINPORT in George Eliot, 'The Sad Fortunes of the Revd Amos Barton', *Scenes of Clerical Life* (1857–8)

'Mr Oldinport, who loaned Amos Barton twenty pounds, was the Right Honourable Charles N. Newdegate' (Charles S. Olcott, 1911, *George Eliot: scenes and people in her novels*, London: Cassell, p. 24; originally published 1910, New York: Thomas Y. Crowell). It will be observed that at the time when the incident takes place (1835–6), Charles Newdegate was 19 or 20 years old, and had already been an MP (in the reformed parliament!) for a year.

NEWDEGATE ARMS, Nuneaton, Warwickshire

OLDINPORT ARMS in George Eliot, 'Mr Gilfil's Love Story', *Scenes of Clerical Life* (1857–8)

'The "Oldinport Arms" . . . stands in the market-place of Nuneaton. Its real name is the "Newdegate Arms"' (Charles S. Olcott, 1911, *George Eliot: scenes and people in her novels*, London: Cassell, p. 23; originally published 1910, New York: Thomas Y. Crowell).

NEWDIGATE, Francis (1774–1862) Eldest son of Francis Parker Newdigate of **Arbury Hall**, Warwickshire. He married Lady Barbara Legge in 1820, and in 1835 he inherited Kirk Hallam. In 1887 his son Edward inherited Arbury Hall and took the name Newdigate-Newdegate.

MR OLDINPORT in George Eliot, 'Mr Gilfil's Love Story', *Scenes of Clerical Life* (1857–8)

'[T]he somewhat shadowy Francis Newdigate . . . Robert Evans's boyhood friend, appears in the first chapter of the story as the unpopular Mr Oldinport'

(Marghanita Laski, 1973, *George Eliot and Her World*, London: Thames & Hudson, p. 58).

ANTHONY WYBROW in George Eliot, 'Mr Gilfil's Love Story', *Scenes of Clerical Life* (1857–8)

'It is the present writer's guess that Captain Wybrow is based not on Charles I [Charles Parker] but on Francis II [i.e. the subject of the present entry] and that it was the latter's behaviour to Sally Shilton that led to the estate's being left away from him' (Laski, op. cit., p. 118). *See also* **Parker**, Charles.

NEWDIGATE, Hester, Lady (1737–1801) Née Hester Margaretta Mundy, in 1776 she married Sir Roger **Newdigate**, becoming his second wife.

LADY CHEVEREL in George Eliot, 'Mr Gilfil's Love Story', *Scenes of Clerical Life* (1857–8)

See under **Newdigate**, Sir Roger.

NEWDIGATE, Sir Richard

SIR ANTHONY CHEVEREL in George Eliot, 'Mr Gilfil's Love Story', *Scenes of Clerical Life* (1857–8)

See under **Anstruther**, Lady.

NEWDIGATE, Sir Roger (1719–1806) Of **Arbury Hall**, Warwickshire. He was an MP for many years, and was the founder of the Newdigate Prize at Oxford. In 1776 he married Hester Margaretta Mundy (**Newdigate**, above), who became his second wife.

SIR CHRISTOPHER CHEVEREL in George Eliot, 'Mr Gilfil's Love Story', *Scenes of Clerical Life* (1857–8)

'Though Sir Roger Newdigate died long before her birth, Marian made convincing descriptions of him and his lady from her recollections of their full-length portraits by Romney (not Reynolds) which hang in the saloon [at Arbury]' (Gordon S. Haight, 1968, *George Eliot*, Oxford, p. 22). 'Certain vague traditions about Sir Robert Newdegate [sic] (him of "Newdegate-Prize" celebrity) which I heard when I was a child are woven into the character of Sir Christopher Cheverel, and the house which he improved into a charming Gothic place with beautiful ceilings, I know from actual vision – but the rest of "Mr Gilfil's Love Story" is spun out of the subtlest web of minute observation and inward experience, from my first childish recollections up to recent years. So it is with all the other stories. It would be very difficult for me to furnish a key to them myself' (to John Blackwood, 28 May 1858, reproduced in *The George Eliot Letters*, 1954, ed. Gordon S. Haight, Vol. II, London: Oxford University Press, pp. 459–60).

NEWMAN, John Henry (1801–90) English prelate and theologian. Born in London, the son of a banker, he was educated at Trinity College, Oxford. Elected a Fellow of Oriel College in 1822, and ordained in 1824, he became Vicar of St Mary's, Oxford, in 1828, but resigned in 1843. He became involved in the Tractarian movement (the 'Oxford Movement') and was received into the

Roman Catholic Church in 1845, afterwards spending a year in Rome and becoming a priest. He was Rector of Dublin Catholic University from 1851 until 1858, during which time he gave many of his famous lectures. He received the cardinal's hat from Pope Leo XIII in 1879.

THE 'FATHER' in Charles Kingsley, *Yeast* (1848)

'A clear portrait of Newman in the fourteenth chapter. Thus early began the antagonism that was to issue in the *Apologia*' (Kathleen Tillotson, 1965, *Writers and Readers in 1851: mid-Victorian studies*, p. 324).

DOCTOR OLDACRE in Elizabeth Jane Whately, *Maude; or The Anglican Sister of Mercy* (1869)

'He is described in *Maude, or the Anglican sister of mercy* . . . under the name of Dr Oldacre' (Frederic Boase, 1892, *Modern English Biography*, Vol. II, col. 1124).

CHARLES REDING in J.H. Newman, *Loss and Gain* (1848)

'Although the advertisement of 1848 states specifically that *Loss and Gain* is not the history of any individual mind among the recent converts, we now know enough of Newman's life to show that he has drawn largely upon his own experience, even to many details. . . . Like Newman [the hero] stood for honours and failed. . . . The "Father Dominic . . . who received Reding into the Church, was the same in name and antecedents as he who received Newman himself"' (J.E. Baker, 1932, *The Novel and the Oxford Movement*, Princeton, pp. 56, 57).

175 NEWPORT LANE, Burslem, Staffordshire

15 LESSWAYS STREET, TURNHILL, in Arnold Bennett, the *Clayhanger* trilogy (1910–16)

'As for 175 Newport Lane, Bennett made it Hilda Lessways' home' (Reginald Pound, 1952, *Arnold Bennett: a biography*, London: Heinemann, p. 52). 'The [Bennett] family] lived rent-free at one point in a house that belonged to Mr Longson [Mrs Bennett's father] in Newport Lane' (Margaret Drabble, 1975, *Arnold Bennett: a biography*, London: Weidenfeld & Nicolson, p. 27).

NEWTON, John Frank He was a naturist and vegetarian, and was a friend of William **Godwin**, through whom he met **Shelley** in 1812.

MR RAMSBOTTOM in Thomas Love Peacock, *Crotchet Castle* (1831)

'Mr Ramsbottom . . . [is] J.F. Newton. In his *Memoirs of Shelley* Peacock gives an amusing instance of Newton's obsession with the zodiac and an account of his mythological system' (*Nightmare Abbey*, 1969, ed. Raymond Wright, Harmondsworth: Penguin, p. 272 n. 5).

MR TOOBAD in Thomas Love Peacock, *Nightmare Abbey* (1818)

'A character based on J.F. Newton' (ibid., p. 262 n. 14).

NICHOLLS, Arthur Bell (1818–1906) Born in Antrim and educated at Trinity College, Dublin, in 1844 he became Curate to Revd Patrick Brontë at Haworth.

In 1854 he married Charlotte Brontë; after her death he remained at Haworth until Mr Brontë's death, and then returned to Ireland.

REVD MR MACARTHEY in Charlotte Brontë, *Shirley* (1849)

'I have looked for Mr Macarthey's character in Shirley, and I find it exactly corresponds with what you have told me of Mr Nicholls, and also with what she [Charlotte Brontë] herself said to me before now' (to John Greenwood (stationer at Haworth), after 5 May 1855, reproduced in *Letters of Mrs Gaskell*, 1966, ed. J.A.V. Chapple and A. Pollard, Manchester, p. 343, letter 239).

NICOLL, Sir William Robertson (1851–1923) Journalist and man of letters. Educated at Aberdeen University, he trained for the Free Church ministry, but in 1885 he abandoned the ministry and moved to London as a journalist. From 1886 to 1923 he was Editor of the *British Weekly*, and from 1891 to 1923 he was Editor of *The Bookman*.

THOMAS CARLYLE CRAW in John Buchan, *Castle Gay* (1930)

'Thomas Carlyle Craw ... Buchan told Beaverbrook, was a cross between Rothermere and Robertson Nicoll' (J. Adam Smith, 1965, *John Buchan*, p. 268). *See also* **Rothermere**, Lord.

TOMLINSON KEYHOLE in H.G. Wells, *Boon* (1915)

'H.G. Wells put him into *Boon* as "Dr Tomlinson Keyhole"' (John Gross, 1969, *The Rise and Fall of the Man of Letters*, p. 202).

NICOLSON, Benedict (1914–78) Art historian. Son of Harold **Nicolson** and Victoria **Sackville-West**. From 1947 to 1978 he was Editor of *Burlington Magazine*.

DAN JARROLD in Victoria Sackville-West, *Family History* (1932)

'Dan ... is an idealized portrait of Ben – as Vita had told him' (Victoria Glendinning, 1983, *Vita: the life of V. Sackville-West*, pp. 251–2).

NICOLSON, Sir Harold (1886–1968) Biographer and critic. Son of Sir Arthur Nicolson, Lord Carnock, and Mary Catherine **Nicolson**, he married Victoria **Sackville-West**: their son was Benedict **Nicolson**. In 1919 he served on the British delegation to the Paris Peace Conference, and was subsequently in the Diplomatic Service. He became a literary editor of London newspapers, and was the author of *Peacemaking* (1919), biographies of **Tennyson** and of his father, and of a novel, *Public Faces* (1932). He became an MP in 1935.

SIR RALPH BROMPTON in Evelyn Waugh, the *Sword of Honour* trilogy (1952–61)

'It would be untrue to say that Sir Ralph is a caricature of Harold Nicolson, but I think Evelyn had Nicolson occasionally in mind when he was contriving the picture' (Christopher Sykes, 1975, *Evelyn Waugh*, London: Collins, p. 426).

MARMADUKE BONTHROP SHELMERDINE in Virginia Woolf, *Orlando* (1928)

'In the things that happen to Orlando ... the ... reader will recognize all the significant events of [V. Sackville-West's] life, including her marriage to Harold

Nicolson – Marmaduke Bonthrop Shelmerdine Esq.' (Michael Stevens, 1973, *V. Sackville-West: a critical biography*, p. 47).

NICOLSON, Mary Catherine (1860?–1951) Daughter of A. Rowan Hamilton, in 1882 she married Sir Arthur Nicolson, later Lord Carnock, who was Ambassador at Madrid when Ronald Firbank visited Spain. She was the mother of Harold **Nicolson**, and her aunt was married to Lord Dufferin.

THE ENGLISH AMBASSADRESS in Ronald Firbank, *The Flower Beneath the Foot* (1923)

'The English Ambassadress is founded on Mrs Roscoe and Lady Nicolson' (Firbank to his mother, 14 January 1923, quoted in Miriam J. Benkovitz, 1969, *Ronald Firbank*, New York, p. 207). *See also* **Roscoe**, Flora.

NILES, Thomas (1825–94) Publisher. He was a member of the firm of Roberts Bros. of Boston, and it was he who in 1865 suggested to Louisa M. Alcott that she should write a story for girls.

MR TIBER in Louisa M. Alcott, *Jo's Boys* (1886)

'The generous and honourable Mr Niles would serve as an excellent employer for Demi, once his name was changed to Tiber' (M.B. Stern, 1950, *Louisa M. Alcott*, Norman, Okla., p. 319).

NIMROD A large deerhound given to Sir Walter Scott by **MacDonell of Glengarry** in 1825, to replace **Maida**.

BEVIS in Sir Walter Scott, *Woodstock* (1826)

'I hope you had the last novel which was sent as usual to Coutts. . . . I don't much like it except the picture of Bevis which is a large dog of my own his unpoetical name is Nimrod' (to Lady Abercorn, mid-August–late-September 1826, reproduced in *The Letters of Sir Walter Scott*, 1936, ed. H.J.C. Grierson, Vol. X, London: Constable, p. 90).

NIN, Andrés (1892–1937) Leader of the POUM (United Marxist Workers' Party) in Catalonia, during the Spanish Civil War, in 1836 and 1837. Originally a member of the Communist Party, he had spent almost ten years in Russia but left the Party over the persecution of Trotsky, whose secretary he had been. He broke with Trotsky in 1934. Upon returning to Spain, he formed a small group of his own. He was imprisoned in Barcelona by the Communists and died there, either through neglect, or, as his followers believed, murdered by a Russian agent.

EMMANUEL GOLDSTEIN in George Orwell, *Nineteen Eighty-four* (1949)

'Much of Goldstein's testimony . . . seems to derive from pamphlets by or about Nin, rather than – as has been supposed – directly from Trotsky' (Eileen Bernard Crick, 1980, *George Orwell: a life*, London: Secker & Warburg, p. 246).

NORBURY, Derbyshire A village on the Staffordshire border, about ten miles south of Ashbourne.

Norbourne in George Eliot, *Adam Bede* (1859)

'Norbury appears in the novel as Norbourne' (Charles S. Olcott, 1911, *George Eliot: scenes and people in her novels*, London: Cassell, p. 67; originally published 1910, New York: Thomas Y. Crowell).

NORFOLK, Bernard Edward Howard, 12th Duke of (1765–1842).

Duke of Juggernaut in Benjamin Disraeli, *Vivian Grey* (1826-7)

Identified as Duke of N—— in a key given in *The Star Chamber* (24 May 1826): 114; reprinted in *Vivian Grey*, 1904 (centenary edn), ed. Lucien Wolf, Vol. II, pp. 361–2. The full name appears on a copy of the key held in the British Museum. Lucien Wolf concludes that Disraeli was not responsible for the key.

NORIE, Mr Of the firm of Norie & Wilson at 157 Leadenhall Street, London, that was already established in 1812 as the Naval Academy and dealt in nautical instruments.

Solomon Gills in Charles Dickens, *Dombey and Son* (1846-8)

'The old nautical-instrument maker, Sol Gills, found his prototype in Mr Norrie [sic] . . . in front of whose small shop stood the little wooden Midshipman, since removed to the Minories' (F.G. Kitton, 1897, *The Novels of Charles Dickens: a bibliography and sketch*, London, p. 108).

NORTH WALK, Arbury Hall, Warwickshire

The Rookery, Cheverel Manor, in George Eliot, 'Mr Gilfil's Love Story', *Scenes of Clerical Life* (1857–8)

See under **Anstruther**, Lady.

NORTHCLIFFE, Alfred Charles William Harmsworth, Lord (1865–1922) 1st Viscount. Journalist and newspaper proprietor. He founded *Answers* (1888) and the *Daily Mail* (1896), and in 1908 became the chief proprietor of *The Times*. He was the elder brother of Lord **Rothermere**.

Richard Bulmer in W.L. George, *Caliban* (1920)

'More than thirty years [after the launching of *Answers*], when Alfred Harmsworth was rich, tired and not far from death, a writer who had worked for him and been dropped, W.L. George, took his revenge in a novel called "Caliban". Alfred is thinly disguised as Richard Bulmer, founder of *Zip*' (Paul Ferris, 1971, *The House of Northcliffe*, p. 7).

Fox in Joseph Conrad and Ford Madox Ford, *The Inheritors* (1901)

'Various people are satirised or portrayed in the book ... Northcliffe (the brilliant but unreliable Fox)' (Jocelyn Baines, 1969, *Joseph Conrad: a critical biography*, p. 239).

NORTHCOTE, Sir Stafford *See* **Iddesleigh**, 1st Earl of.

NORTHROP, John Howard (1891–1987) Biochemist. Born in New York and educated at Columbia University, he became an associate of Jacques **Loeb** at the Rockefeller Institute, New York, and was joint receiver of the Nobel Prize for Chemistry in 1946 for his work in crystallizing the enzymes pepsin and trypsin.

TERRY WICKETT in Sinclair Lewis, *Arrowsmith* (1925)

Identified in Mark Schorer, 1961, *Sinclair Lewis: an American life*, New York: McGraw-Hill, p. 418. *See also* **Le Blanc**, T.J.; **Lewis**, Sinclair.

NORTHUMBERLAND, Hugh Percy, 3rd Duke of (1785–1847) In 1817 he married Charlotte Florentina, daughter of Lord Powis, and succeeded to the title. He was Lord Lieutenant of Ireland in 1829 and 1830.

EARL OF NORBURY in M. Spencer Stanhope, *Almacks* (1826)

Identified in Michael Sadleir, 1951, *XIX Century Fiction*, 2 vols, London: Constable, and Los Angeles: California University Press, p. 331; reprinted from *Literary Gazette* (9 December 1826).

NORTON, Caroline (1808–77) Writer. One of the three beautiful daughters of Thomas Sheridan. Her sisters became the Duchess of Somerset and Lady Dufferin, while in 1836 she married the Hon. George Norton, who brought against Lord **Melbourne** the celebrated action for *Crim. Con.* (*see* **Norton v. Melbourne**. He lost the action, but the couple separated; she subsequently became a popular writer of novels and verse and had a long liaison with Sir William **Stirling-Maxwell** of Keir, marrying him shortly before her death.

LADY MONTFORT in Benjamin Disraeli, *Endymion* (1880)

Identified in 'Key to *Endymion*', *Notes and Queries* 83 (24 October 1942): 263. The identification is attributed to G.E. Buckle. It does not convince. *See also* **Bradford**, Countess of; **Palmerston**, Lady.

DIANA WARWICK in George Meredith, *Diana of the Crossways* (1884)

'I . . . am just finishing . . . a two-volume novel, to be called *Diana of the Crossways* – partly modelled upon Mrs Norton' (to R.L. Stevenson, 24 March 1884, reproduced in *Letters of George Meredith*, 1970, ed. C.L. Cline, Vol. II, Oxford, p. 840).

NORTON, Charles Eliot (1827–1908) Writer and scholar. Born in Cambridge, Massachusetts, he became Professor of the History of Fine Art at Harvard University in 1873, remaining as such until 1898. He became a close friend and correspondent of Mrs **Gaskell**, whom he met in Rome when a young man, and of Henry **James** and Edith Wharton, whose house at Lenox was within forty miles of his country house, Liliput, at Ashfield, Massachusetts. He regarded himself as a missionary for European culture in the United States: 'I propose this afternoon to make a few remarks on the hor-ri-ble vul-gar-ity of EVERYTHING' was a student's version of his lectures. He translated Dante and edited the letters of **Carlyle**. He married Susan Sedgewick in 1862.

LEWIS RAYCIE in Edith Warton, 'False Dawn', *Old New York* (1924)

'From young manhood on Norton drew to himself a host of European literary friends, in particular . . . John Ruskin, whom he met on a steamer crossing Lake Geneva. Edith Wharton put this encounter to good use in . . . *False Dawn*' (R.W.B. Lewis, 1975, *Edith Wharton: a biography*, London: Constable, p. 138). *See also* **Jones**, G.F.

NORTON, Richard (1872–1918) Archaeologist. Son of Charles Eliot **Norton**, he became Director of the American School of Classical Studies in Athens (1899–1907) and Director of the Archaeological Institute of America (1910–11). From 1914 to 1918 he was the organizer and head of the American Volunteer Ambulance Corps working with the French army (Norton–Hayes Brigade).

ELIOT STORY BRADFORD in John Dos Passos, *Chosen Country* (1951)

'The portrait of Eliot Story Bradford . . . is of course clearly inspired by Norton' (J.N. Westerhoven, 1976-7, 'Autobiographical elements in the camera eye [sections in *USA*]' (*American Literature* 48: 358).

NORTON CONYERS, Yorkshire Situated near Ripon, it was the home of the Grahams from the seventeenth century until it was bought in 1848 by Frederick Greenwood, brother of Mrs Benson Sidgwick of **Stone Gappe**.

THORNFIELD HALL in Charlotte Brontë, *Jane Eyre* (1847)

'The late Sir Reginald Graham . . . wrote: "I feel certain that at some time or other Charlotte Brontë must have had access to the house, as in *Jane Eyre* the interior of . . . Norton Conyers . . . from beginning to end is very precisely described even to the most minute details. "Charlotte Brontë visited Norton Conyers . . . as governess to the family of Mr J.B. Sidgwick [1839]' (Herbert Wroot, 1935, *Sources of Charlotte Brontë's Novels: persons and places*, Shipley, Yorks., pp. 19, 20). 'Charlotte told [Ellen Nussey] that she had visited [Norton Conyers] . . . she had been much impressed by the story of a madwoman confined there in an upper room in the eighteenth century' (Winifred Gérin, 1969, *Charlotte Brontë*, Oxford, p. 150). *See also* The **Rydings**.

NORTON V. MELBOURNE

BARDELL V. PICKWICK in Charles Dickens, *The Pickwick Papers* (1836-7)

'[In June 1836] the Hon. Charles Norton had brought an action against the Prime Minister, Lord Melbourne, accusing him of adultery with his wife [Caroline Norton]. . . . Norton's counsel, Sir W. Follett, laid much stress on three brief and particularly harmless notes – an aspect of the case of which [Dickens] is commonly believed to have made use in the Bardell v. Pickwick trial' (*Letters of Charles Dickens*, 1965, Vol. I, ed. Madeline House and Graham Storey, Oxford: Oxford University Press, p. 153 n. 3). 'Dickens himself reported the case in 26 columns of "The Morning Chronicle" (Percy T. Carden, 1936, 'Speculations on the source of Bardell v. Pickwick', *The Dickensian* 32: 105 ff.).

NOTTINGHAM

KNARBOROUGH in D.H. Lawrence, *The Lost Girl* (1920)

'Knarborough is, of course, Nottingham' (Ada Lawrence and G. Stuart Gelder, 1931, *Young Lorenzo: early life of D.H. Lawrence*, Florence, p. 54).

NOVY, Frederick (1864–1957) American microbiologist. He was head of the Department of Bacteriology at the University of Michigan. 'His influence in the growth of microbiology in the United States, extending over 50 years, was immense' (*Dictionary of American Biography*, London: Oxford University Press).

MAX GOTTLIEB in Sinclair Lewis, *Arrowsmith* (1925)

'Max Gottlieb was more than improbable. He was a muddy mélange of my revered chief, Professor Novy, and of Jacques Loeb' (Paul de Kruif, 1962, *The Sweeping Wind: a memoir*, London: Rupert Hart-Davis, p. 109). *See also* **Loeb**, Jacques.

NOYES, Nicholas Judge at the Salem witchcraft trials in 1692. At the execution of one Sarah **Good**, he urged her to confess, telling her he knew she was a witch, to which she replied, 'You are a liar – and if you take away my life God will give you blood to drink.' There was a tradition in Salem that 'a peculiar circumstance attended the death of this gentleman, he having choked with blood' (Thomas Hutchinson, 1795, *History of Massachusetts . . . 1628 . . . 1750*, Vol. II, Boston, p. 56).

COLONEL PYNCHEON in Nathaniel Hawthorne, *The House of the Seven Gables* (1851)

'We may be reasonably certain . . . that [Hawthorne] was . . . using the substance of [this] account [of the curse] with full knowledge of the Sarah Good and Nicholas Noyes incident' (Norman Farmer, Jun., 1964, 'Maule's curse and the Rev. Nicholas Noyes; a note on Hawthorne's source', *Notes and Queries* 209: 225). *See also* **Hathorne**, John.

NUGENT OF CARLANSTON, George Nugent Grenville, Lord (1789–1850) 2nd Baron, he was the second son of Mary Elizabeth, Marchioness of Buckingham, who in 1880 was created Baroness Nugent of Carlanston with special remainder to this son; he succeeded to the peerage in 1812. He was MP for Buckingham from 1810 to 1812, and for Aylesbury from 1812 to 1832 and from 1847 to 1850. From 1830 to 1832 he was a Lord of the Treasury, and from 1832 to 1835 he was Lord High Commissioner to the Ionian islands. A large, fat man, he was a Whig Radical in politics and a zealous partisan of Queen Caroline.

DUKE OF ALTAMONT in Benjamin Disraeli, *Vivian Grey* (1826-7)

'Lord Altamont is thought Lord Nugent' (letter of Robert Plumer Ward to Mrs Sarah Austen, 6 May 1826, reproduced in *Memoirs . . . of Robert Plumer Ward, Esq.*, 1850, ed. Edmund Phipps, Vol. II, p. 148).

NUNEATON, Warwickshire

MILBY in George Eliot, 'Janet's Repentance', *Scenes of Clerical Life* (1857–8)

'The Buchanans appear in all the "keys" to the originals of "Janet's Repentance" that were circulated in Warwickshire after its publication in 1857' (Gordon S.

Haight, 1968, *George Eliot*, Oxford, p. 10). As the Buchanans were resident in Nuneaton it was generally supposed that Nuneaton was the model for Milby.

NUNEHAM HOUSE, Oxfordshire Situated near Oxford. It was the home of Lord **Harcourt**.

MONK LAWRENCE in Mrs Humphry Ward, *Delia Blanchflower* (1915)

'The burning of Monk Lawrence, described as the ancient and beautiful house of an anti-suffragette political leader is based on the actual burning of Nuneham House, owned by the anti-suffragette cabinet minister Lewis Harcourt' (Georgia Dunbar, 1953, 'The faithful recorder: Mrs Humphry Ward and the background of her novels', unpublished Ph.D. dissertation, Columbia University, p. 250).

NUSSEY, Ellen (1817–97) A close friend of Charlotte Brontë, whom she met at Miss **Wooler**'s school at Roe Head in 1831; they remained friends until Charlotte's death.

CAROLINE HELSTONE in Charlotte Brontë, *Shirley* (1849)

'Are not you Caroline Helstone?' (to Ellen Nussey, 3 November 1855, reproduced in *Letters of Mrs Gaskell*, 1966, ed. J.A.V. Chapple and Arthur Pollard, Manchester, p. 875, letter 271a). *See also* **Brontë**, Anne.

NUSSEY, Revd Henry (1812–68?) Brother of Ellen **Nussey**. In 1832 he went to Cambridge, where he came under the influence of the Revd Charles Simeon, and in 1844 he became Vicar of Hathersage, Derbyshire, where he established a school. He left the active ministry in 1848, and thereafter lived much in the south of France. He proposed marriage to Charlotte Brontë in 1839.

ST JOHN EYRE RIVERS in Charlotte Brontë, *Jane Eyre* (1847)

'The Rev. Henry Nussey . . . is understood to have furnished the model of St John Rivers. Mrs Gaskell . . . alludes to Mr Nussey without naming him, and states that he had "a slight resemblance to the character of St John." The portrait drawn in the novel seems, however, to have been in reality more accurate than Mrs Gaskell found it convenient to acknowledge' (Herbert Wroot, 1935, *Sources of Charlotte Brontë's Novels: persons and places*, Shipley, Yorks., p. 60). *See also* **Martyn**, Henry.

NUTTALL, Zelia Maria Magdalena (1858–1933) American archaeologist. She was educated in Europe and studied antiquities and the history of Mexico. She was the author of *Fundamental Principles of Old and New World Civilisations*, one of Lawrence's main sources for the mythology of Mexican Indians. In 1923 Lawrence visited her several times at her home outside Mexico City. She married August Pinart in 1880, and they were divorced in 1887.

MRS NORRIS in D.H. Lawrence, *The Plumed Serpent* (1926)

'[T]he second chapter of *The Plumed Serpent* records with extraordinary fidelity the persons and interchange at a tea-party given us by Mrs Zelia Nuttall' (W. Bynner, 1953, *Journey with Genius*, London and New York: Peter Nevill, p. 22).

O

OAKWELL HALL, Birstall, Yorkshire Described as 'a sizeable house' (Nikolaus Pevsner, 1970, *Yorkshire: West Riding* (*Buildings of England* series), Harmondsworth: Penguin, p. 106), it is dated 1583 on the porch, but has clearly been remodelled since then.

FIELDHEAD in Charlotte Brontë, *Shirley* (1849)

'Fieldhead . . . has been identified with Oakwell Hall. . . . It is believed that while staying with her friend, Miss Nussey at Birstall, she visited the hall on more than one occasion, the tenants . . . at that time being friends of the Nussey family' (Herbert Wroot, 1935, *Sources of Charlotte Brontë's Novels: persons and places*, Shipley, Yorks., p. 79).

O'BEIRNE, Thomas Lewis (1748?–1823) Educated as a Roman Catholic at St Omer, although he later joined the Church of England. He was Chaplain and Secretary to the Duke of Portland, Viceroy of Ireland, in 1782, and to Lord Fitzwilliam in Ireland in 1794. In 1795 he was Bishop of Ossory, and in 1798 Bishop of Meath.

COMMISSIONER FALCONER in Maria Edgeworth, *Patronage* (1814)

'The bishop . . . who played the part which was taken in the novel by Commissioner Falconer, was none other than Thomas Lewis O'Beirne . . . now [Bishop] of Meath' (Marilyn Butler, 1972, *Maria Edgeworth*, Oxford, p. 256).

OBOLENSKY, Princess Zoë Sergeievna Née Soumarokov, in 1847 she married Prince Alexis Vassilievitch Obolensky, with whom she had five children. In the winter of 1855–6, she left her husband in Russia and settled at Naples with her children and household. She became the mistress of Valérien Ostroga-Mroczkowski, a Polish émigré and 'a photographer, of Menton' (R.I. Ermerin, 1892, *Annuaire de la noblesse de Russie*, 2me année, St Petersburg, p. 162 n. 157). She paraded extreme radical views and became the patron of **Bakunin**. In 1867 she moved to Vevey, and in 1869 her children were removed and returned to their father. In 1884, after the death of her husband, she married Mroczkowski.

PRINCESS CASAMASSIMA in Henry James, *The Princess Casamassima* (1886)

'[In *The Liberal Imagination*] Professor Trilling stresses James's reliability as an historian of the subterranean world. . . . In 1864 Michael Bakunin formed an international secret society with its headquarters in Naples. The nucleus of this secret society centered around a Princess Obolensky. In the summer of 1866 Princess Obolensky moved to Casamicciola on the island of Ischia. . . . There is a remarkable similarity between James's princess and this other princess. And is the closeness between the name "Princess Casamassima" and the location of the new home of Princess Obolensky entirely coincidental?' (M.S. Wilkins, 1957, 'A note on the Princess Casamassima', *The Nineteenth Century* 12 (1): 88). *See also* **Belgiojoso**, Principessa di.

O'BRIEN, Fitz-James (*c.*1828–62) Journalist. Born in Ireland, he went to the United States *c.*1852. He was a conspicuous figure in Bohemian circles, and was the author of short stories 'reminiscent of Poe' (James D. Hart (ed.), 1965, *The Oxford Companion to American Literature*, New York: Oxford University Press). He died as the result of a wound received in the Civil War.

BRANDNAGEE in Bayard Taylor, *John Godfrey's Fortunes* (1864)

'Brandnagee ... has been identified as Fitz-James O'Brien' (C.I. Glicksberg, 1937, 'Walt Whitman and Bayard Taylor', *Notes and Queries* 173 (3 July): 6).

OCKENDEN, Mr

MR CRICKLEDON in George Meredith, *The House on the Beach* (1877)

See under **Ockenden**, Mrs.

OCKENDEN, Mrs

MRS BERRY in George Meredith, *The Ordeal of Richard Feverel* (1859)

'Mrs Berry – like many of Meredith's most narrowly and symbolically controlled creations – had [a model] in life: . . . [she was based] on the Merediths' Seaford landlady, Mrs Ockenden' (Gillian Beer, 1970, *Meredith: a change of masks*, p. 203 n. 11).

MRS CRICKLEDON in George Meredith, *The House on the Beach* (1877)

'[Meredith's] Seaford friends the Ockendens were drawn to the life as Mr and Mrs Crickledon' (A. Lionel Stevenson, 1954, *The Ordeal of George Meredith*, London: Peter Owen, p. 210).

O'CONNELL, William James Joyce's great-uncle; he lived for a time with the Joyce family.

UNCLE CHARLES in James Joyce, *A Portrait of the Artist as a Young Man* (1916)

'[William O'Connell] . . . is a model for "Uncle Charles" who is described in detail at the beginning of Chapter II of *Portrait of the Artist*' (*Letters of James Joyce*, 1966, ed. Richard Ellmann, London: Faber & Faber, p. 151 n. 1).

O'CONNOR, Feargus Edward (1794–1855) Chartist leader. Educated at Trinity College, Dublin, he was later called to the Irish Bar. He took part in the reform agitation of 1831 and became associated with extreme English radicals and the English working class cause. His paper, the *Northern Star*, founded in 1837, was the official organ of Chartism, and in 1840 he was sentenced to imprisonment for seditious libel. He became MP for Nottingham in 1847, and in June 1852 he was pronounced insane.

O'FLYNN in Charles Kingsley, *Alton Locke* (1850)

'O'Flynn editor of the *Weekly Warhook*, is Feargus O'Connor, the Chartist leader' (Margaret Farrand Thorp, 1937, *Charles Kingsley, 1819–1875*, p. 75).

O'CONNOR, Monsignor John (1870–1952) Born at Clonmel, County Tipperary, Ireland, he studied at St Edmund's in Douai, France, and in Rome.

He was ordained in 1895 and became the Parish Priest of St Cuthbert's, Bradford. He wrote and translated a number of hymns for the *Amnoel Hymnal* (1901, ed. Charles Gatty), and was a well-known figure in Catholic literary circles. In 1904 he met G.K. Chesterton and they became lifelong friends. He published *Father Brown on Chesterton* in 1937 and translated Paul Claudel, *The Satin Slipper*.

FATHER BROWN in G.K. Chesterton, *The Innocence of Father Brown* (1911) and others

'O'Connor confessed ... that "his native talent for detection was of the slenderest." On the other hand, he admitted that he often carried brown paper parcels, that "the flat hat was true to life, but it perished in its prime," and that "the large and cheap umbrella was my defence against wearing an overcoat"' (Obituary, 1952, *The Times* (8 February)).

O'CONOR, Roderic (1860–1940) Born in Roscommon, Ireland, he studied in London, and in 1883 went to Paris. In 1892 he worked under **Gauguin** at Pont-Aven and he subsequently remained in Paris. He acquired a fine collection of paintings and was a friend of Roger Fry, who used to visit him in Paris and buy pictures from him.

CLUTTON in W. Somerset Maugham, *Of Human Bondage* (1915)

'. . . Clutton, a young painter clearly modelled after O'Conor' (R.L. Calder, 1972, *W. Somerset Maugham and the Quest for Freedom*, London: Heinemann, p. 131).

O'BRIEN in W. Somerset Maugham, *The Magician* (1908)

'O'Conor became O'Brien' (Calder, op. cit., p. 132).

ODLE, Alan (1888–1948) Artist. Son of a bank manager in Sittingbourne, Kent, he met Dorothy Richardson in 1915 when she lodged in the same house in St John's Wood, London; they were married in 1917. From 1917 onwards he signed himself Alan, but the name was originally Allan.

MR NOBLE in Dorothy Richardson, *Pilgrimage* (1915–67)

'Dorothy ... succeeded before dying ... in ... bringing [her work] ... to the point where Miriam ... meets the ... young man – whom we recognize as Alan Odle' (John Rosenberg, 1973, *Dorothy Richardson*, London, p. 178).

OGILVIE-GRANT, Mark (1905–69) He was one of Nancy Mitford's closest and oldest friends, and was a contemporary and friend at Oxford of Brian **Howard**, Harold **Acton**, Henry Yorke and Robert **Byron**. He had a house at Kew Green, London.

SIR IVOR KING in Nancy Mitford, *Pigeon Pie* (1940)

'Must tell you how the book is developing. Well you are called Mr Ivor King the King of Song' (Nancy Mitford to Mark Ogilvie-Grant, 13 November 1939, quoted in Harold Acton, 1975, *Nancy Mitford: a memoir*, London: Hamilton, p. 48).

O'HARA, Charles (1740?–1802) He entered the Coldstream Guards in 1756 and commanded a brigade of guards in America. In 1793, as Lieutenant-General, he was wounded and captured by the French at Toulon. From 1795 to 1802 he was Governor of Gibraltar. He was a friend of Horace **Walpole** and was for some time engaged to Mary **Berry**.

CYRIL THORNTON in Thomas Hamilton, *The Youth and Manhood of Cyril Thornton* (1827)

'We have in . . . "Cyril Thornton" . . . the portrait of him in his later years, vividly sketched by an eyewitness, and, it would seem, his personal friend' (Lord Houghton, 1873, 'The Berrys', *Monographs*, pp. 171–2). 'In *Cyril Thornton* the author gives his recollections of "The Old Cock of the Rock" as O'Hara was called' (*The Dictionary of National Biography*, London: Oxford University Press).

O'HARA, John (1905–70) American novelist. Born in Pottsville, Pennsylvania, he graduated from Niagara Preparatory School, New York, in 1924. He had a number of jobs, including evaluating engineer, ship steward, railway-freight clerk, gas-meter reader, guard in an amusement park, steel worker, soda-fountain assistant and press agent. He was a journalist for many papers, including the *Herald Tribune* and the *New Yorker*. He achieved phenomenal success with the publication of his first novel, *Appointment in Samarra* in 1934.

JAMES MALLOY in John O'Hara, *BUtterfield 8* (1935)

'The author put himself into [*BUtterfield 8*] as James Malloy of *The Doctor's Son*, now a young reporter in Manhattan' (Finis Farr, 1974, *O'Hara: a biography*, p. 115).

OLD CHUMLEY *See* **Chumley**, Old.

OLD KENTUCKY HOME, Asheville, North Carolina A boarding house kept by Julia **Wolfe**.

DIXIELAND in Thomas Wolfe, *Look Homeward, Angel* (1929)

'Dixieland is Julia Wolfe's boarding house, the Old Kentucky Home' (R.S. Kennedy, 1962, *The Window of Memory: the literary career of Thomas Wolfe*, Chapel Hill, NC, p. 30).

The OLD NICHOL, London A district in Bethnal Green comprising Old Nichol Street and the area of the Boundary Street Improvement Scheme (between Boundary Street and Arnold Circus), bordered to the south by Bethnal Green Road.

THE JAGO in Arthur Morrison, *A Child of the Jago* (1896)

'Early in 1895 the Reverend A. Osborne Jay, Vicar of Holy Trinity, Shoreditch, read *Tales of Mean Streets* and wrote a letter of appreciation to Morrison. . . . [He] pointed out that there were . . . areas of East London that did not conform with the *Mean Streets* image, and instanced . . . the Old Nichol, which he invited Morrison to visit. . . . [Morrison later wrote]: "I resolved to write *Child of the Jago*, in which I should tell the story of a boy who, but for his environment, would have become a good citizen; also the story of the horrible Nichol''' (P.J. Keating, 1971, biog. preface to *A Child of the Jago*, pp. 23, 24).

OLDFIELD, Sir Maurice (1915–81) Educated at Lady Manners School, Bakewell, and at Manchester University, he served in the Security Intelligence in the Middle East during the Second World War; he ended his career as the Director of the Secret Intelligence Service, retiring in 1978.

George Smiley in John Le Carré, *The Spy Who Came in from the Cold* (1963) and others

'Original of "George Smiley" in the Le Carré spy novels' ('Profile: Sir Maurice Oldfield, 1978, *New Statesman* (7 July): 12). 'Though he did not deliberately inspire Le Carré's fictional Smiley, he seems to have many shared characteristics' (ibid., p. 13).

OLIPHANT, Laurence[1] (1691–1767) Laird of Gask (1732–46) and distinguished Jacobite. In 1715 he fought at Sheriffmuir, and in 1745 he joined Prince Charles Edward at Perth, fighting in 1746 at Falkirk and Culloden; after the defeat he escaped with his son to Sweden and forfeited his estates. In 1753 the Gask estates were bought back for him, and he was allowed to return home in 1763.

Baron Bradwardine in Sir Walter Scott, *Waverley* (1814)

'It was largely from [William] Erskine's account of old Gask that Scott drew his Baron Bradwardine' (Florence MacCunn, 1909, *Sir Walter Scott's Friends*, p. 49). *See also* **Forbes**, Alexander; **Stuart of Invernahyle**, Alexander.

OLIPHANT, Laurence[2] (1829–88) Novelist, journalist and diplomat. Born in Cape Town, of Scottish descent, he was the son of the Attorney-General, and a cousin of the writer Margaret Oliphant. In 1852 he published *A Journey to Khatmandu* and in 1853 he became Secretary to Lord Elgin in Washington and in China; he became involved with **Garibaldi** in Italy and in Montenegro, and travelled in Japan, Korea, the Balkans and the Crimea. From 1865 to 1867 he was an MP, then from 1867 to 1870 he lived in the United States, in the religious community of Thomas Lake **Harris**, whom he had met in 1860. He was a correspondent with *The Times* during the Franco-Prussian war, and in 1883 he founded a community of Jewish immigrants at Haifa in Palestine, living there until 1886.

Reginald Clareville in Laurence Oliphant, *Masollam* (1886)

'Clareville is Oliphant's portrait of himself as he was when he first encountered Harris' (R.L. Wolff, 1971, *Strange Stories*, Boston, p. 104).

Cyril Gordon in Haskett Smith, *For God and Humanity, a Romance of Mount Carmel* (1891)

'. . . dedicated "to the Memoirs of My Beloved Friend Laurence Oliphant" and the preface declares that "An attempt has been made . . ." to portray in the following pages the salient points of his personal principles, and to embody in the character of Cyril Gordon a likeness of him who has gone' (Wolff, op. cit., pp. 131–2 n. 2).

HAROLD in Mary S. Emerson, *Among the Chosen* (1884)

'Oliphant also appears as "Harold" in . . . *Among the Chosen* . . . by an American girl who with her parents was for a time a member of Harris's community' (Wolff, ibid.).

OTHO LAURENCE in W.H. Mallock, *The New Republic* (1877)

'Otho Laurence is partly reminiscent of Laurence Oliphant, partly of Oliphant's fictional hero Lord Frank Vanecourt and is also based on aspects of Mallock himself' (John Lucas, 1975, Introd. to *The New Republic*, Leicester, p. 17).

LORD FRANK VANECOURT in Laurence Oliphant, *Piccadilly* (1870)

'Part novel, part *roman à clef*, part (thinly) disguised autobiography, *Piccadilly* . . . tells the story of . . . Lord Frank Vanecourt, an accomplished gentleman of leisure who gradually grows to detest London society and fashionable life, and who abandons it to go in search of his soul (as poor Oliphant did . . .)' (Lucas, op. cit., p. 15).

OLMEIJER, William Charles (1848–1900) Born in Sourabaya, Java, of a family of Dutch extraction, he was a gutta-percha and rubber trader in Berau when Conrad first met him in 1887–88 (see Conrad, 1912, *Some Reminiscences*, pp. 135 ff.; here, too, Conrad calls him Almayer). Olmeijer would seem to have settled in Berau in 1870.

KASPAR ALMAYER in Joseph Conrad, *Almayer's Folly* (1895)

'Kaspar Almayer . . . was drawn from William Charles Olmeijer of Berouw' (J.D. Gordon, 1941, *Joseph Conrad: the making of a novelist*, Cambridge, Mass., p. 36). '[I]f I had not got to know Almayer pretty well it is almost certain there would never have been a line of mine in print' (Joseph Conrad, 1916, *A Personal Record*, p. 186). 'Olmeijer . . . became the protagonist of Conrad's first novel and one of the heroes of the second; he also appears in *A Personal Record*. . . . In fact, Conrad did not get to know Olmeijer at all well for neither the . . . Almayer from *A Personal Record* nor the tragic Almayer from *Almayer's Folly* have much in common with the real Olmeijer. Married . . . he had eleven children . . . as a trader he was both successful and influential' (Z. Najder, 1983, *Joseph Conrad: a chronicle*, Cambridge: Cambridge University Press, p. 99).

OPIE, Mrs Amelia (1769–1853) Novelist and poet. Née Alderson, she married Thomas Opie the portrait painter (d. 1807), and saw much good society in London. She became a Quaker (under the influence of the **Gurneys**) in 1825, and was much occupied in philanthropic movements. She was a friend of Sydney **Smith**, **Sheridan**, and Lady **Corke**.

PHILOMELA POPPYSEED in Thomas Love Peacock, *Headlong Hall* (1816)

'[Character] based on Mrs Opie' (*The Novels of T.L. Peacock*, 1948, ed. David Garnett, London: Rupert Hart-Davis, p. 21 n. 3).

OPPENHEIMER, Robert (1904–67) Physicist. Born in New York City, in 1943 he became Director of Los Alamos Scientific Laboratory, being in charge of the project for the development of the atomic bomb, but resigned in 1945. From

1946 to 1952 he was Chairman of the General Advisory Committee to the United States Atomic Energy Commission. Under his chairmanship this committee advised against a major effort in developing thermonuclear weapons, but this advice was overruled and Oppenheimer was subsequently attacked for his opposition and barred from secret information on the grounds that his loyalty was in question. He insisted on submitting to a hearing by a three-man board, which decided (by a majority vote) that he was a security risk. From 1947 to 1966 he was Director of the Institute for Advanced Study at Princeton. In 1940 he married Katherine Harrison, whose first husband had been killed while fighting for the Republicans in Spain.

SEBASTIAN BLOCH in Haakon Chevalier, *The Man Who Would Be God* (1959)

'I had had the idea for this novel in 1948, and I had written an idea of the story, which was based on Oppenheimer and the [atom] bomb, and which was suggested in part by the stories that were going round about his complete reversal in views and character, but which was nevertheless almost wholly a flight into fantasy. . . . In the summer of 1954 . . . I pulled the six-year-old outline . . . out of my file and reread it. . . . To my amazement I found that my fiction now rang true' (Chevalier, 1966, *Oppenheimer*, pp. 113–114). 'The two characters [Bloch and Oppenheimer] are not . . . identical. It is the conflict that each of them is called upon to resolve within himself . . . that [is] more or less the same' (ibid., p. 178).

ORDÓÑEZ, Cayetano (1905–62) A young matador from Ronda, in 1925 he took part in the fiesta in Pamplona. Ernest Hemingway and his wife followed him to Madrid, where he dedicated a bull to Hadley, gave her his cape to hold and, after the kill, presented her with the ear (compare *The Sun Also Rises*, ch. xviii). This was his first year, but he was badly gored in the thigh later in the season, and according to Hemingway he lost his valour and never got it back. Nevertheless, he fought bulls for another twenty years. His son, Antonio Ordóñez, was a great matador in the 1950s.

PEDRO ROMERO in Ernest Hemingway, *The Sun Also Rises* (1926)

'"He [Hemingway] wrote about me in a book once," Cayetano said. "My bull fighting name was Niño de la Palma but in this book Ernesto called me Pedro Romero after Spain's greatest matador. Did you know that?"' (Sam Adams, 1930, 'The sun also sets', *Sports Illustrated* (29 June), reprinted in B.D. Sarason, 1972, *Hemingway and the Sun Set*, Washington, DC, pp. 212–13).

OREGLIA, Cardinal

CARDINAL OREZZA in F.W. Rolfe, *Hadrian VII* (1904)

'He describes Vatican officials like [Cardinal] . . . Oreglia (as Orezza)' (Shane Leslie, 1923, 'Frederick Baron Corvo', *The London Mercury* 8 (47): 514).

ORIOLI, Giuseppe ('Pino') (1884–1942) Antiquarian bookseller and publisher in Florence. He was the publisher and close friend of Norman **Douglas**, and also published *Lady Chatterley's Lover*. He died in Lisbon. Sitwell's description is affectionately exact.

GINO in Osbert Sitwell, 'Gino of the Bookshop' (1958)

'There were also portraits of his more famous friends – Orioli the bookseller . . .' (John Pearson, 1978, *Façades: Edith, Osbert, and Sacheverell Sitwell*, p. 458).

ORLEBAR, August (b. 1825?) Educated at Rugby School and at Wadham College, Oxford, he entered the church and in 1858 became Vicar of Willington, Bedfordshire.

GEORGE ARTHUR in Thomas Hughes, *Tom Brown's Schooldays* (1857)

'Arthur is supposedly a composite of Theodore Walrond, W.P. Adam, and August Orlebar' (Edward C. Mack and W.H.G. Armytage, 1952, *Thomas Hughes: the life of the author of Tom Brown's Schooldays*, London: Ernest Benn, p. 94). *See also* **Adam**, W.P.; **Walrond**, Theodore.

ORMISTON, Adam

CAPTAIN CLUTTERBUCK in Sir Walter Scott, *The Monastery* (1820) and *The Fortunes of Nigel* (1822)

'Captain Clutterbuck . . . finds a happy counterpart in Mr, *vulgo* Captain O[rmisto]n, a gentleman well known in Melrose as an amateur cicerone of "the Abbey". His peculiarities and pursuits very nearly resemble those of . . . Clutterbuck' (Robert Chambers, 1825, *Illustrations of the Author of Waverley*, p. 120). 'Captain Clutterbuck . . . has no real prototype in the village of Melrose or neighbourhood that ever I saw or heard of. . . . I was therefore a good deal surprised, when I found the antiquarian Captain identified with a neighbour and friend of my own. . . . This erroneous identification occurs in . . . "Illustrations of the Author of Waverley . . . by Robert Chambers"' (Walter Scott, 1830, Introd. to *The Monastery*, 1898 (Border edn), ed. Andrew Lang, p. xxvi). *See also* **Tait**, Walter.

ORTIZ Spanish matador.

PACO in Ernest Hemingway, 'The Mother of a Queen', *Winner Take Nothing* (1933)

'EH told Gingrich . . . that "The Mother of a Queen" was a true story about the bullfighter Ortiz' (Carlos Baker, 1969, *Ernest Hemingway: a life story*, New York, p. 606 n. 'Order of the Stories in "Winner Take Nothing"').

ORWELL, George (Eric Arthur Blair) (1903–50) English novelist, critic and political journalist. Born in Motihari, Bengal, he was educated at Eton. From 1922 to 1928 he served in the Indian Imperial Police in Burma. After his resignation he went to Paris, where he worked at various ill-paid jobs, and then moved to London two years later. He worked for a while as a schoolteacher, and later in a Hampstead bookshop. He fought, and was wounded, in the Spanish Civil War, and was a war correspondent for both the BBC and the *Observer* during the Second World War. His first wife, Eileen, died in 1945, and he married Sonia Mary Brownwell in 1949, the year before he died of tuberculosis.

BASIL in Stevie Smith, *The Holiday* (1949)

'Certainly Stevie Smith's portrait of Basil-cum Eric or George . . . shows she must have known him well, and included "two characters who divide between them", she wrote in a letter, "many of George's opinions and characteristics as I saw them". . . . One of the Orwells is clearly identifiable in "Basil"' (Bernard Crick, 1980, *George Orwell: a life*, London: Secker & Warburg, p. 289).

CHRISTOPHER DRAKE in Lettice Cooper, *Black Bethlehem* (1947)

The identification is based upon obvious parallels. *See under* **Blair**, Eileen.

J.G. QUIGGIN in Anthony Powell, *A Dance to the Music of Time* (1951–76)

'Quiggin in . . . *A Dance to the Music of Time* contains elements of Orwell' (Alan Franks, 1983, 'The road to Eric Blair', *The Times* (23 July): 8).

ALFRED, LORD WARMINSTER in Anthony Powell, *A Dance to the Music of Time* (1951–76)

'It argues a great restraint on Powell's part that there is only the merest whiff of Orwell, small but distinct, in . . . *A Dance to the Music of Time* – in the physical description of Alf . . . Earl of Warminster' (Crick, op. cit., p. 296 n.).

O'SHAUGHNESSY, Arthur William Edgar (1844–81) Poet. Born in London, he became an assistant in the British Library in 1861, and in 1863 he was promoted to the zoological department of the British Museum; he became an expert on herpetology. He published *An Epic of Woman and Other Poems* in 1870, *Lays of France* in 1872, and *Music and Moonlight* in 1874. In 1873 he married Eleanor, daughter of Westland Marston the English dramatic poet; she died in 1879.

COSMO CHOUGH in Vernon Lee, *Miss Brown* (1884)

'The poet Chough . . . could be identified with the late A.W. O'Shaughnessy' (Peter Gunn, 1964, *Vernon Lee, 1856–1935*, London: Oxford University Press, p. 102).

OSTERLEY PARK, Middlesex Redesigned in 1763 by Robert Adam for Robert Child, it later became the seat of the Earls of Jersey (see Nikolaus Pevsner, *Middlesex* (*Buildings of England* series), Harmondsworth: Penguin).

SUMMERSOFT in Henry James, 'The Lesson of the Master' (1888)

'"The Lesson of the Master" opens with an account of a Sunday under the cedar trees on the lawn at Osterley, but when he sent a copy to his hostess, admitting his debt for the background, he denied that he made use of what he called "the human furniture"' (Violet Powell, 1976, *Within the Family Circle*, pp. 21–2).

OTAGO A barque built in Glasgow in 1869 which became Conrad's first command, in 1888 and 1889. It was used as a trading vessel until 1903, then as a coal hulk; it was destroyed by fire in 1957.

THE SHIP in Joseph Conrad, *The Shadow-Line* (1917)

'At the moment when Conrad was preparing to return to Europe [from Singapore] in search of a ship, circumstances unexpectedly put him in the way of getting just what he wanted: the command of a sailing vessel. The circumstances are related with careful literalness in *The Shadow-Line*' (G. Jean-Aubry, 1927, *Joseph Conrad: life and letters*, London: Heinemann, p. 102).

OTTERY ST MARY, Devon Located about ten miles north-west of Exeter. It was the birthplace of S.T. **Coleridge.**

CLAVERING ST MARY in W.M. Thackeray, *The History of Pendennis* (1848–50)

'Ottery St Mary (which is Clavering)' (H.C. Minching, 1928, 'Thackeray in the Temple', *Cornhill Magazine* (NS) 65 (September): 291).

OUIDA (Marie Louise de la Ramée) (1839–1908) Popular novelist. Born in Bury St Edmunds, she was the daughter of an English mother and a French father, Louis **Ramé.** In 1874 she settled in Florence, where she lived lavishly. She wrote forty-five exuberantly romantic novels. After about 1890 her popularity waned, and she wrote mainly magazine articles. When her royalties eventually dried up, she fell into debt, moving in 1894 to Lucca and in 1904 to Viareggio, where she lived the rest of her life in poverty.

ETOILE, COMTESSE D'AVESNES in Ouida, *Friendship* (1878)

'The three principal characters were Prince Ioris (Stufa), the Lady Joan Challoner (Mrs Ros) and Etoile (Ouida)' (Eileen Bigland, 1951, *Ouida: the passionate Victorian*, p. 137). 'Some features of Ouida's own girlhood and upbringing are to be seen in those of Etoile' (Elizabeth Lee, 1914, *Ouida: a memoir*, p. 21).

OWEN, Robert (1771–1858) Socialist and philanthropist. He was born in and died at Newtown, Montgomeryshire. He was associated with William Allen and Bentham in the New Lanark Mills Company in Scotland, and in 1817 he put forward a plan for self-sufficient communities living around large quadrangles. He was described by Leslie Stephen in *The Dictionary of National Biography* (London: Oxford University Press) as one of those bores who are the salt of the earth.

MR TOOGOOD in Thomas Love Peacock, *Crotchet Castle* (1831)

'Mr Toogood: a character based on Robert Owen' (*Crotchet Castle*, 1969, ed. Raymond Wright, Harmondsworth: Penguin, p. 275 n. 3 (to ch. V)).

OWENS COLLEGE, Manchester Founded in 1852, it was later incorporated as the Victoria University of Manchester.

MOORHAMPTON COLLEGE in Morley Roberts, *The Private Life of Henry Maitland* (1912)

Identified in an 'Index of Recurring Pseudonyms' in the 1958 edition of *The Private Life of Henry Maitland*, ed. Morchard Bishop, p. 255.

OWERMOIGNE, Dorset A village located six miles south-east of Dorchester.

NETHER-MOYNTON in Thomas Hardy, Wessex novels and tales (1871–95)

Identified on a map prepared by Thomas Hardy which hangs in the Dorset County Museum, Dorchester. *See under* **Abbotsbury.**

OXFORD

CHRISTMINSTER in Thomas Hardy, *Jude the Obscure* (1895)

'By the way, [Christminster] is not meant to be exclusively Oxford, but any old-fashioned University about the date of the story, 1860–1870, before there were such chances for poor men as there are now' (Thomas Hardy to a friend, 1926, quoted in F.E. Hardy, 1972, *The Life of Thomas Hardy, 1840–1928*, p. 433). Also identified in Denys Kay-Robinson, 1972, *Hardy's Wessex Reappraised*, Newton Abbot, and in F.B. Pinion, 1968, *A Hardy Companion*, London: Macmillan.

OXFORD, Mississippi

JEFFERSON in William Faulkner, the Yoknapatawpha novels (1929–36)

'Modeled on his home town, Oxford' (James D. Hart (ed.), 1965, *The Oxford Companion to American Literature*, New York: Oxford University Press, p. 424).

OXFORD, Jane Elizabeth Harley, Lady (1773–1824) Née Scott. 'She, who was a very beautiful woman, had so indifferent a reputation that her children were referred to as "the Harleian Miscellany"' (G.E.C. (ed.), 1895, *The Complete Peerage of England, Scotland, Ireland, Great Britain and the United Kingdom*, Vol. VI, London: George Bell & Sons, p. 267 n.). She was married to the 5th Earl of Oxford.

LADY MANDEVILLE in Lady Caroline Lamb, *Glenarvon* (1816)

'Lady Mandeville is Ly. Oxford' (Lady Holland to Mrs Creevey, 21 May 1816, quoted in *The Creevey Papers*, 1903, ed. Sir Herbert Maxwell, Vol. I, p. 254.) Also identified in a key found among the papers of John Whishaw, a member of the Holland House circle, printed in *The 'Pope' of Holland House: selections from the correspondence of John Whishaw and his friends, 1813–1940*, 1906, ed. Lady Seymour, p. 151.

P

PABST, Lily Headmistress of the finishing school at Meterstrasse 13 in Hanover, to which Dorothy Richardson went in 1891 as a teacher of English.

LILY PFAFF in Dorothy Richardson, *Pilgrimage* (1915–67)

'Not until midway through the first draft [of *Pointed Roofs*] did it occur to her that the German names she had been using were the original ones and that she ought to make some changes, if only to protect herself. This she now apparently began to do. Fräulein Lily Pabst turned into Lily Pfaff' (Gloria G. Fromm, 1977, *Dorothy Richardson: a biography*, Urbana, Chicago and London, p. 69).

PAGDEN, John

EDWARD TULLIVER in George Eliot, *The Mill on the Floss* (1860)

'If our visitor drive through the town of Gainsborough, a mile or two north . . . he may see a large brick building on the right bank of the river with a conspicuous sign, "The Mill on the Floss". The owner is certain that it is the very mill that George Eliot describes . . . "The mill used [according to the present owner] to belong to an old fellow named . . . John Pagden, and it passed from him to the bank. They foreclosed a mortgage on it, and he lost this property and his house over there. . . . He was always gettin' into lawsuits, and that's the way he lost his money – just like Mr Tulliver in the book. Do you see that road runnin' from there to there? . . . Well, Pagden had trouble about the right of way of that very road – just like Mr Tulliver . . . in the book". The old man was only repeating what had been the talk of the neighbourhood for fifty years. George Eliot could see the old mill from . . . Morton Hall [where she stayed when she went to Gainsborough]; . . . no doubt, therefore, she knew well the misfortunes of the poor man and used them in the story of Mr Tulliver' (Charles S. Olcott, 1911, *George Eliot: scenes and people in her novels*, London: Cassell, pp. 77–9; originally published 1910, New York: Thomas Y. Crowell). *See also* **Evans, Robert**.

PAGET, Matilda (1815–96) Daughter of Edward Hamlin Adams of Middleton Hall, Carmarthenshire, who had business and banking interests in the West Indies. She married Captain Lee Hamilton, who died in 1852. She then married Henry Paget, her son's tutor, and their daughter Violet, born in 1856, was Vernon Lee.

MRS CLAUDIA MACGREGOR in Vernon Lee, *Miss Brown* (1884)

'The attractive Mrs MacGregor would seem to have many of the qualities of Mrs Paget' (Peter Gunn, 1964, *Vernon Lee, 1886–1935*, London: Oxford University Press, p. 102).

PAKEFIELD CHURCH, Suffolk Church of St Margaret's and All Saints. At the end of the 1800s Pakefield was a village about three miles south of Lowestoft; it is now a suburb. The churchyard still has cottages on three sides and the sea on the fourth. The crypt still existed in 1922, but it has now disappeared. The church was badly damaged in the Second World War, and was reconsecrated in 1950.

RAXTON CHURCH in Theodore Watts-Dunton, *Aylwin* (1899)

Identified in T. St E. Hake, 1902, 'Aylwin', *Notes and Queries* (9th series) 9 (7 June): 450–2, and 10 (2 August): 89–91; reprinted in *Aylwin*, 1914 (World's Classics), Oxford, App. II.

PAKENHAM, Admiral Sir Thomas (1757–1836) Brother of the 2nd Baron Longford and uncle of the 3rd Baron and 2nd Earl. He was also the uncle of Kitty Longford, who married the Duke of **Wellington**.

SIR ULICK O'SHANE in Maria Edgeworth, *Ormond* (1817)

'The early sketches to *Ormond* describe Sir Ulick as resembling two men, Sir John De Blaquiere and "T.P." ... [who] must have been Admiral Thomas Pakenham ... a neighbour of the Edgeworth family. [He] emerges from Maria's correspondence as a quick-witted, jovial, untrustworthy man, who had already been unflatteringly portrayed in one of her stories. He originally appeared in *Manoeuvring* as "a spirited profligate", but Edgeworth insisted that the character must be wholly changed before publication in case Pakenham was recognized' (Marilyn Butler, 1972, *Maria Edgeworth*, Oxford, pp. 249, 250). *See also* de **Blaquiere**, Baron.

PALESTINE The barque in which Conrad sailed as second mate in 1881–3, bound for Bangkok. On 17 September 1882, after being held up for a year for repairs, it finally sailed from Falmouth, Cornwall. On 15 March 1883, it went down off Sumatra, its cargo of coal having spontaneously ignited.

JUDEA in Joseph Conrad, 'Youth' (1902)

'The barque *Palestine* ... was none other than the barque he afterwards immortalized in *Youth* under the ... pseudonym *Judea*. ... [The] story [of the voyage] is precisely in every detail the story of the barque *Palestine*' (G. Jean-Aubry, 1927, *Joseph Conrad: life and letters*, Vol. I, London: Heinemann, p. 67).

PALEWSKI, Gaston (b. 1901) *Chef du cabinet* to Paul Reynaud. He reached London in 1940, after the fall of France, and in 1941 and 1942 he served in the Free French air squadron. From 1942 until 1946 he was *chef du cabinet* to General de Gaulle, and from 1957 to 1962 he was the French Ambassador in Italy. In 1969 he married Violette de Talleyrand Périgord, Duchesse de Sagan. He met Nancy Mitford in London in 1921 or 1942, and remained a close friend until her death.

FABRICE, DUC DE SAUVETERRE in Nancy Mitford, *The Pursuit of Love* (1945)

'There is nothing invented about Fabrice de Sauveterre ... except his name and his dukedom. He is Gaston Palewski' (Alastair Forbes, 1975, 'The Mitford Style', *Times Literary Supplement* (12 September): 1020).

CHARLES-EDOUARD, MARQUIS DE VALHUBERT in Nancy Mitford, *The Blessing* (1951)

'In a later book she turned him into Charles Edouard de Valhubert' (Forbes, op. cit., p. 1020).

PALFREY, Mary Ann (1796–1881) Daughter of Samuel Hammond of Boston, she married John Gorham Palfrey, the American Unitarian clergyman and historian, in 1823. They lived in Cambridge, Massachusetts.

MRS RIMMLE in Henry James, 'Europe' (1899)

'[James] recorded in the preface to *The Author of Beltraffio*, his distinct memory of [the] genesis of ["Europe"]: "I had preserved for long years an impression of a visit . . . to an ancient lady whose talk . . . bore upon a triumphant sojourn in Europe, long years before, in the hey-day of the high scholarly reputation of her husband, a dim displaced superseded celebrity at the time of my own observation." In such terms did he recall Mrs John Gorham Palfrey, the widow of the historian' (*The Notebooks of Henry James*, 1947, ed. F.O. Matthiessen and K.B. Murdock, New York, pp. 190, 191).

PALMERSTON, Emily Mary Temple, Lady (1787–1869) Née Lamb, she was the daughter of the 1st Viscount Melbourne, sister of Lord **Melbourne** the Prime Minister, and cousin of Lord **Byron**. In 1805 she married Lord Cowper, who died in 1837, and in 1839 she married Lord **Palmerston**; they had loved each other for many years and their intimacy did not escape ill-natured comment. Abraham Hayward described her when young as 'grace put into action' (H.A. Doubleday, Geoffrey H. White and Lord Howard de Walden (eds), *The Complete Peerage of England, Scotland, Ireland, Great Britain and the United Kingdom*, Vol. X, rev. edn, London: St Catherine Press, p. 297 n. c).

LADY MONTFORT in Benjamin Disraeli, *Endymion* (1880)

'I do not think that the lady your Majesty mentions [i.e. Duchess of Manchester] influenced me in the character of Lady Montfort. I would say . . . that I think there are features of Lady Palmerston in her youth in that representation' (Lord Beaconsfield to Queen Victoria, 10th February 1881, reproduced in *The Letters of Queen Victoria*, 1928 (2nd series), ed. G.E. Buckle, Vol. III, London: John Murray, p. 195). *See also* **Bradford**, Countess of; **Norton**, Caroline.

PALMERSTON, Henry John Temple, 3rd Viscount (1784–1865) English statesman. Born in Westminster, of the Irish branch of the ancient English family of Temple. Educated at Edinburgh and Cambridge Universities, he succeeded his father as viscount in 1802. He was MP for Newport (Isle of Wight) from 1807 to 1811, for Cambridge University from 1811 to 1830, losing his seat when he supported the Reform Bill, and later for South Hampshire and for Tiverton. He was Secretary at War under **Perceval**, the Earl of Liverpool, **Canning**, Ripon and the Duke of **Wellington**, and was Foreign Secretary from 1830 to 1841 under Earl Grey, and from 1846 to 1851 under Lord John **Russell**, during which time he earned the nickname 'Firebrand Palmerston'. He was Home Secretary in Aberdeen's coalition of 1852, winning the premiership from him in 1855, but losing it in 1858 over the Conspiracy Bill. He became Prime Minister again the following year, remaining in office until his death.

LORD BROCK in Anthony Trollope, *Framley Parsonage* (1861)

'... the identification of Lord Brock with Lord Palmerston may be added to those mentioned by Sadleir' (Frank E. Robbins, 1950, 'Chronology and history in Trollope's Barset and parliamentary novels', *The Nineteenth Century* 5 (4): 311).

LORD ROEHAMPTON in Benjamin Disraeli, *Endymion* (1880)

'"Roehampton" is Palmerston' (Walter Sichel, 1904, *Disraeli: a study in personality and ideas*, London: Methuen, p. 222 n. 1).

PALMES, Colonel Bryan (d. between 1927 and 1932) He was an Anglo-Indian and was described as 'close-fisted ... an entertaining talker, a good Russian scholar, and possessor of a noble erotic library' (Norman Douglas, 1933, *Looking Back*, pp. 98–9). He lived on Capri in a villa that he had built for himself.

MAJOR NATT in Compton Mackenzie, *Vestal Fire* (1927)

'He is the "Major Natt" of ... *Vestal Fire*' (ibid.).

PANKHURST, Christabel Harriette (1880–1958) Daughter of Richard Pankhurst (d. 1898), the radical Manchester barrister, and Emmeline Pankhurst, née Goulden (1857–1928), the suffragette. In 1906 she obtained first class honours in her LLB examination. She joined the Women's Social and Political Union (WSPU), the women's suffrage movement, when it was founded by her mother in 1903, and in 1907 she became its Organizing Secretary; she was imprisoned, and from 1908 she organized a militant campaign, which included arson. In 1912 she escaped to Paris, but returned to England in 1914 to support the First World War efforts. After 1920 she lived mostly in America, where she died.

GERTRUDE MARVELL in Mrs Humphry Ward, *Delia Blanchflower* (1915)

Gertrude Marvell resembles Christabel Pankhurst although she is given a different family background (information communicated by Georgia Dunbar from her unpublished Ph.D dissertation, 'The faithful recorder: Mrs Humphry Ward and the background of her novels', 1953, Columbia University.

von PAPPENHEIM, Jenny (1811–90) Daughter of Diana von Pappenheim and Prince Jérome Napoléon. She was living with her mother in Weimar at the time of Thackeray's visit in 1830, when she was a maid of honour at the court. In 1838 she married Baron Werner von Gustedt and retired to his estates in West Prussia.

OTTILIA VON SCHLIPPENSCHLOPP in W.M. Thackeray, *The Confessions of Fitz-Boodle* (1852)

'Ottilia ... is drawn in part from Fräulein von Pappenheim' (*The Letters and Private Papers of W.M. Thackeray*, 1945, ed. Gordon Ray, London: Oxford University Press, p. 129 n. 32).

PARK, Archibald (1770–1820) Originally of Lewinshope, Selkirk, where he was a neighbour of Scott's. He was a brother of Mungo Park, the Scottish explorer, and was 'a man of prodigious strength, in stature upwards of six feet' (Robert Chambers, 1884, *Illustrations of the Author of Waverley*, p. 57). In 1816, after suffering severe financial losses, he was obliged to give up his farm; he obtained, largely through Scott's influence and exertions, an appointment as Controller of Customs at Tobermory, but shortly afterwards he suffered a stroke, from which he never fully recovered.

DANDIE DINMONT in Sir Walter Scott, *Guy Mannering* (1815)

'Mr Archibald Park ... was the person always most strongly insisted on as being the original of Dandie. . . . On the appearance of the novel, his neighbours at once put him down as the Dandie Dinmont of real life, and he was generally addressed by the name of his supposed archetype ... as long as he remained in that part of the country. . . . [But Lewinshope] bore no similarity whatever to Charlieshope, excepting in the hospitality of the master and the Christian name of the mistress of the house. . . . [Mrs Park] ... bore, like Mrs Dinmont, the familiar abbreviated name of *Ailie*' (ibid.). *See also* **Davidson**, James; **Elliott**, Willie; **Laidlaw**, James; **Thorburn**, James.

PARK, James Alan (1763–1838) In 1816 he was appointed Justice of the Common Pleas and was knighted.

MR JUSTICE ST PROSE in Benjamin Disraeli, *Vivian Grey* (1826-7)

Identified as Mr Justice P— in a key given in *The Star Chamber* (24 May 1826): 114; reprinted in *Vivian Grey*, 1904 (centenary edn), ed. Lucien Wolf, Vol. II, pp. 361–2. The full name appeared in a reprint of the key published in *Notes and Queries* 3 (29 April 1893). Lucien Wolf concludes that Disraeli was not responsible for the key.

PARKER, Charles (1756-95) The favourite nephew of Sir Roger **Newdigate**, he married Miss **Anstruther**.

ANTHONY WYBROW in George Eliot, 'Mr Gilfil's Love Story', *Scenes of Clerical Life* (1857–8)

'Captain Wybrow is usually identified with Charles Parker. . . . This is accepted by Lady Newdigate-Newdegate [in the *Cheverels of Cheverel Hall*, 1898] (Marghanita Laski, 1973, *George Eliot and Her World*, London: Thames & Hudson, p. 58). *See also* **Newdigate**, Francis.

PARKER, Theodore (1810–60) American theologian and Unitarian clergyman. In 1837 he was a minister in West Roxbury, Massachusetts; he became an associate of **Emerson**, Bronson **Alcott** and the other Transcendentalists. In 1845 he resigned his pastorate and became the minister of a new Free Church in Boston. He was a dedicated abolitionist, and organized the Boston Vigilance Committee, which was established to protect runaway slaves from being returned to the South.

REVD THOMAS POWER in Louisa M. Alcott, *Work* (1873)

'[S]he used him as a model for the saintly Rev. Mr Power' (M. Saxton, 1978, *Louisa May: a modern biography of L.M. Alcott*, p. 193).

PARKINSON, Joe

PHINEAS FINN in Anthony Trollope, *Phineas Finn* (1869) and *Phineas Redux* (1874)

'Physically [Phineas] was Joe Parkinson, an English journalist who married a millionaire's daughter and became a wealthy director of companies' (Michael Sadleir, 1927, *Trollope: a commentary*, London: Constable, p. 416). *See also* **King-Harman**, Edward; **Parkinson-Fortescue**, Chichester; **Pope-Hennessy**, Sir John.

PARKINSON-FORTESCUE, Chichester Samuel, Baron Carlingford (1823–98) Politician. Originally Fortescue, he assumed the name of Parkinson in 1862. Liberal MP for Louth between 1847 and 1874, he was also Chief Secretary for Ireland from 1865 to 1866 and from 1868 to 1870, being responsible, along with **Gladstone**, for the Disestablishment of the Irish Church and Irish Land Act of 1870. From 1871 to 1874 he was President of the Board of Trade. He was admitted to the peerage in 1874, and was the fourth husband of Frances, Countess Waldegrave, and an uncle of F.F. **Urquhart**.

PHINEAS FINN in Anthony Trollope, *Phineas Finn* (1869) and *Phineas Redux* (1874)

'For some months Trollope's *Phineas Redux* had been appearing in the *Graphic* and everyone was trying to recognize the characters ... some ... now felt that possibly Madame Max Goesler was taken from [Frances Waldegrave], especially as there were points of resemblance between Phineas Finn and Chichester' (O.W. Hewett, 1956, *Strawberry Fair*, p. 236). *See also* **King-Harman**, Edward; **Parkinson**, Joe; **Pope-Hennessy**, Sir John.

PLANTAGENET PALLISER in Anthony Trollope, *Can You Forgive Her?* (1864)

'The Plantagenet Palliser who eventually becomes Duke of Omnium, recalls as the novelist intended that he should, the Mr Chichester Fortescue who died Lord Carlingford' (T.H. Escott, 1906, 'Anthony Trollope: an appreciation and reminiscence', *Fortnightly Review*: 1100). *See also* **Newcastle**, 6th Duke of; **Russell**, 1st Earl.

PASOLINI, Pier Desiderio, Count (1844–1920) A member of Vernon Lee's circle of close Italian friends in Rome in the 1890s and early 1900s.

COUNT SCIARRA in Maurice Baring, 'A Luncheon Party', *Half a Minute's Silence and Other Stories* (1925)

'There are many amusing stories told of Count Pasolini, of whom Maurice Baring has given a lifelike portrait as "Count Sciarra" (the Pasolinis lived in the Palazzo Sciarra)' (Peter Gunn, 1964, *Vernon Lee, 1856–1935*, London: Oxford University Press, p. 145).

PAST, Miss Lady's maid to Mrs Duncan **Stewart**.

BROOKSMITH in Henry James, 'Brooksmith' (1891)

'Another little thing was told me the other day by Mrs R[ogerson] about Mrs D[uncan] S[tewart]'s little maid ... Past, who was with her for years before her death. . . . She had to find a new place . . . on Mrs S's death, to relapse into ordinary service . . . "Ah yes, ma'am, and it's a great grief, but what is your loss to mine? . . . You continue to see good society, to live with clever, cultivated people: but I fall again into my own class, I shall never see such company – hear such talk – again . . . nothing will ever make up to me again for the loss of her conversation. Common, vulgar people now: that's my lot for the future'" (*The Notebooks of Henry James*, 1947, ed. F.O. Matthiessen and K.B. Murdock, New York, p. 64). 'Mrs Stewart's "lady's maid" was transmuted into the ineffable butler, Brooksmith' (ibid.).

PASTORET, Comtesse de She was married to Claude-Emmanuel-Joseph-Pierre, Comte (later Marquis) de Pastoret. In 1802, on her first visit to Paris, Maria Edgeworth met and formed a friendship with her.

MADAME DE FLEURY in Maria Edgeworth, 'Madame de Fleury', *Tales of Fashionable Life* (1809)

'Madame de Pastoret was the original of Madame de Fleury' (Marilyn Butler, 1972, *Maria Edgeworth*, Oxford, p. 190 n. 4).

PATER, Walter Horatio (1839–94) English critic and essayist. Born in London, he was educated at King's School, Canterbury, and Queen's College, Oxford, and in 1864 he became a Fellow of Brasenose College, Oxford. From 1869 he lived in London with his unmarried sisters Hester and Clara. He was associated with the Pre-Raphaelites and **Swinburne**. He was the author of *Studies in the History of the Renaissance* (1873) and *Marius the Epicurean* (1885).

MR ROSE in W.H. Mallock, *The New Republic* (1877)

'Mr Rose was Pater' (W.H. Mallock, 1920, *Memoirs of Life and Literature*, London: Chapman and Hall, p. 60). '[Pater] thought the portrait a little unscrupulous, and he was discomposed by the freedom of some of its details' (Edmund Gosse, 1933, *Critical Kit-Kats*, p. 258). Also identified in W.H. Mallock, 1920, *Memoirs of Life and Literature*, London: Chapman and Hall, pp. 65–6.

PATERSON, Robert (1716–1801) Stonemason. Known as 'Old Mortality', Scott first encountered him at Dunnottar Castle in 1793. He is believed to be buried at Balmaclellan. According to William Ranken his name was not Robert, but Walter or Wattie.

OLD MORTALITY in Sir Walter Scott, *Old Mortality* (1816)

'The real name of Old Mortality was Paterson. . . . He was a mason by trade, but from enthusiasm possibly something approaching to aberration of mind he forsook his family and wandered through Scotland repairing the tombs of the martyrs' (to the Revd John Carslaw of Airdrie, 2 May 1827, reproduced in *The Letters of Sir Walter Scott*, 1936, ed. H.J.C. Grierson, Vol. X, London: Constable, p. 200).

PATMORE, Brigit (1882–1964) She was married to J.D. Patmore, a grandson of the poet, and became a member of Violet *Hunt*'s circle in Kensington, London. After the breakup of her marriage in 1924, she lived for ten years with Richard **Aldington**.

CLARISS BROWNING in D.H. Lawrence, *Aaron's Rod* (1922)

In Brigit Patmore's memoirs, *My Friends When Young* (1968, pp. 73–75), there is an account of a conversation between Lawrence, Frieda Lawrence and Brigit Patmore, during the First World War, when the Lawrences were living in the Aldingtons' flat in London: 'Later, D.H. Lawrence used this conversation in his novel *Aaron's Rod*, in which Brigit Patmore appears as Clariss Browning' (ibid., p. 75 n.).

MORGAN LE FAY in H.D. (Hilda Doolittle), *Bid Me to Live* (1960)

Identified by Helen McNeil in the introduction to *Bid Me to Live*, 1984, pp. viii–ix, and by Perdita Schaffner in the afterword, p. 187.

PATTERSON, Captain

CAPTAIN GILES in Joseph Conrad, *The Shadow-Line* (1917)

'Giles is a Capt. Patterson, a very well known person there' (Conrad to Sir Sidney Colin, 27 February 1917, quoted in G. Jean-Aubry, 1927, *Joseph Conrad: life and letters*, Vol. II, London: Heinemann, p. 182).

PATTISON, Dorothy Wyndlow (1832–78) Known as Sister Dora. She was the youngest sister of Mark **Pattison** and was the tenth of the eleven children of the Revd Mark James Pattison. In 1864 she entered the Christ Church Sisterhood, Coatham (later Convent of the Holy Rood) as a novice, and in 1865 was sent to Walsall Cottage Hospital as a relief nurse; in 1868 she was Sister-in-Charge. The hospital dealt with surgical cases, mainly resulting from industrial accidents.

DOROTHEA CASAUBON (NÉE BROOKE) in George Eliot, *Middlemarch* (1871–2)

'Frances [sic] Pattison . . . described her remarkable sister-in-law to the Radical writer, Edith Simcox. There are arguable grounds for thinking that she also described her to George Eliot, and that certain strands of Dorothy Pattison's personality are woven through the character of Dorothea, into . . . *Middlemarch*' (Jo Manton, 1971, *Sister Dora*, p. 272). The arguments are set out in App. B, pp. 353 ff. *See also* **Eliot**, George; **Pattison**, Emilia Francis.

PATTISON, Emilia Francis (1840–1904) Née Strong. Privately educated in Oxford, she went on to study art in South Kensington, London, where, in 1859, she first met Charles **Dilke**. In 1861 she married Mark **Pattison**, but it was not a happy marriage. She published a number of works on French art of the Renaissance and eighteenth century, and stories and verses of a mystical sort. In 1884 she joined the Women's Trade Union League; she attended the Trades Union Congress until the year of her death, being passionately interested in improving the social and industrial lot of working women. In 1875 she met Dilke again; they began an affectionate correspondence, writing to each other two and three times a week. In July 1884, Mark Pattison died, and the following autumn Emilia became secretly engaged to Dilke. When the disaster of the Crawford divorce case broke upon him, she immediately announced the engagement, and they were married in October 1885, four months before the case opened.

DOROTHEA CASAUBON (NÉE BROOKE) in George Eliot, *Middlemarch* (1871–2)

'I have been out to a dinner-party where all the people were profoundly learned and clever; the chief guest . . . being the rector of Lincoln, a man who is supposed to be the Casaubon of "Middlemarch" – at least I believe his wife considers herself the model of Dorothea' (to Frank Wilson, from Oxford, 20 February 1879, reproduced in *Autobiography and Letters of Mrs M.O.W. Oliphant*, 1899, p. 235). This is the earliest allusion to this identification that Professor Haight was able to find (see Gordon S. Haight, 1968, *George Eliot*, Oxford, p. 563). 'To those who know, Emilia Strong was no more Dorothea Brooke than Pattison was Casaubon; but it is the case that the religious side of Dorothea Brooke was taken by George Eliot from the letters of Mrs Pattison' (Sir Charles Dilke, 1905, 'Memoir of E.F.S. Dilke', prefixed to Lady Dilke, 1905, *The Book of the Spiritual Life* (see ibid.). *See also* **Eliot**, George; **Pattison**, Dorothea Wyndlow.

BELINDA CHURCHILL in Rhoda Broughton, *Belinda* (1883)

'The rules for a novelist who uses a friend as model have never been defined. . . . If one rule is that the portrait must be pleasing, then . . . Rhoda Broughton erred in the treatment of [her friend] Emilia Francis Strong' (R.J. Harris, 1953, 'Emilia Francis Strong: portraits of a lady', *The Nineteenth Century* 8 (2): 93).

LADY GRACE in W.H. Mallock, *The New Republic* (1877)

'It seems to be traditionally accepted that . . . Lady Grace bears some resemblance to Mrs Mark Pattison. Certainly, her feminism and interest in social welfare suggest that Mallock may have had the wife of the Rector of Lincoln in mind. Yet the identification is far from complete. Lady Grace is made both older and less intelligent than Mrs Pattison, and I am not convinced that the identification can or ought to be made' (J. Lucas, 1975, Introd. to *The New Republic*, Leicester, p. 18).

ROSE LEYBURN in Mrs Humphry Ward, *Robert Elsmere* (1888)

'Rose is more like Francis Strong than Dorothea Brooke' (Betty Askwith, 1969, *Lady Dilke*, p. 18). *See also* **Asquith**, Margot.

PATTISON, Mark (1813–84) Rector of Lincoln College, Oxford. He was an ardent follower of **Newman**, and lived for a time in the latter's house in St Aldates, Oxford. He gradually severed his connection with the High Church party, and in 1831, in spite of brilliant success as a tutor, he failed to be elected Rector of Lincoln. He resigned his tutorship and devoted himself to writing, then in 1861 he was elected Rector. In 1875 he published *A Life of Isaac Casaubon*, in 1883 he dictated his *Memoirs*, and he contributed much to periodicals. In 1861 he married Emilia Francis Strong, later Lady Dilke (**Pattison**, above).

EDWARD CASAUBON in George Eliot, *Middlemarch* (1871–2)

'The most commonly accepted original was . . . Mark Pattison. . . . Sir Charles Dilke declared: "The grotesqueness of any attempt to find a likeness between a mere pedant like . . . Casaubon and a great scholar like Mark Pattison . . . was never made by any but a simpleton". . . . Mrs Humphry Ward wrote: "I do not believe she ever meant to describe the Rector in the dreary foolish pedant who overshadows *Middlemarch*." John Morley dismissed the identification as an "impertinent blunder"' (Gordon S. Haight, 1968, **George Eliot**, Oxford, pp. 448, 449). For a full discussion of this identification, see John Sparrow, 1967, *Mark*

Pattison and the Idea of a University; Haight, op. cit., pp. 563, 564; *Notes and Queries* 213 (May, November, December 1968); *Times Literary Supplement* (16 February 1973): 165 and subsequent correspondence. *See also* **Brabant**, R.H.; **Bryant**, Jacob; **Eliot**, George; **Mackay**, R.W; **Spencer**, Herbert.

PROFESSOR JAMES FORTH in Rhoda Broughton, *Belinda* (1883)

'[T]he Rector, calling upon the novelist, sent up his name as Professor Forth' (R.J. Harris, 1953, 'Emilia Francis Strong', *The Nineteenth Century* 8 (2): 91).

EDWARD LANGHAM in Mrs Humphry Ward, *Robert Elsmere* (1888)

'There is another don in the book named Langham who does not at all correspond to the Rector in personal appearance . . . but who seems to resemble him in his relationship to . . . Rose Leyburn' (Betty Askwith, 1969, *Lady Dilke*, p. 18). *See also* **Amiel**, Henri Frédéric.

ROGER WENDOVER in Mrs Humphry Ward, *Robert Elsmere* (1888)

'People say that in *Robert Elsmere* . . . the squire [is intended] for Mark Pattison' (Benjamin Jowett to Margot Tennant (afterwards Asquith), 28 November 1888, quoted in *The Autobiography of Margot Asquith*, 1920, pp. 120, 121). 'As to the relation between the Rector and the Squire of "Robert Elsmere" . . . it was confined . . . to a likeness in outward appearance . . . and . . . great learning and a general impatience of fools' (Mrs Humphry Ward, 1918, *A Writer's Recollections*, New York and London: Harper & Bros, pp. 110, 111).

MR WENLOCK in Mrs Humphry Ward, *Lady Connie* (1916)

'There [is an unmistakable portrait] of him in . . . *Lady Connie*' (Askwith, op. cit., p. 11).

PAUL, Clara (d. 1918) While a young woman engaged to be married, she visited Asheville, North Carolina, and formed a brief friendship with Thomas Wolfe. She died just two years after her marriage, in the influenza epidemic of 1918.

LAURA JAMES in Thomas Wolfe, *Look Homeward, Angel* (1929)

'"This girl Clara Paul was the Laura James in the book," Mrs Wolfe said' (Hayden Norwood, 1947, *The Marble Man's Wife: Thomas Wolfe's mother*, New York, p. 33).

PAULI, Charles Paine (1838–97) Barrister. Youngest son of Emilius Pauli of Lübeck, who had settled in England, he was educated in Winchester and Oxford. He first met Butler in 1863, in Christchurch, New Zealand, where he was employed on the local newspaper. In 1864, he being in bad health, Butler lent him £100 to return to England and undertook to lend him £200 a year until he should have recovered and established himself at the Bar: between 1864 and his death, Pauli received from Butler a total of between £6,000 and £7,000. For about a year, he shared Butler's flat in Clifford's Inn, London. At Pauli's funeral, Butler learned that he had for many years been living in comfort, on an income of between £700 and £1,000 a year, and that he had left an estate of £9,000: he left Butler nothing in his will. Pauli was one of those involved in bringing Cleopatra's Needle to London.

TOWNELEY in Samuel Butler, *The Way of All Flesh* (1903)

'Towneley was drawn more from Pauli, or rather from what Butler had persuaded himself that Pauli was, than from any one else' (H. Festing Jones, 1919, *Samuel Butler: the author of* Erewhon, Vol. II, London: Macmillan, p. 8). An account of the whole affair, by Butler, is to be found in *Butleriana* (1932, London).

PAYN, James (1830–98) Novelist. He contributed to *Household Words* and *Chambers's Journal*, editing the latter in 1859–74. In 1874 he was Reader to Smith, Elder & Company, and from 1883 to 1896 he was Editor of *Cornhill Magazine*.

JOHN GLASS in Morley Roberts, *The Private Life of Henry Maitland* (1912)

Identified in an 'Index of Recurring Pseudonyms' in the 1958 edition of *The Private Life of Henry Maitland*, ed. Morchard Bishop, p. 255.

PROFESSOR JAMES MORIARTY in Arthur Conan Doyle, the Sherlock Holmes stories (1890–1927)

'Moriarty's spidery figure, deathly complexion, and pallid brow suggest . . . James Payn. It is significant, therefore, that Conan Doyle gave him Payn's Christian name' (Charles Higham, 1976, 'The original Moriarty', *The Times* (20 November): 7). *See also* **Drayson**, Alfred Wilks; **Moriarty**, George; **Worth**, A.

PEABODY, Elizabeth Palmer (1804–94) From 1834 to 1836 she was an assistant to Bronson **Alcott** at Temple School, Boston. She studied the Froebel method of education, and in 1860 she opened the first American kindergarten. She was a sister-in-law to Nathaniel **Hawthorne**.

MISS BIRDSEYE in Henry James, *The Bostonians* (1884)

Immediately after the appearance of the early chapters, 'Henry James received word from his Aunt Kate, from James Russell Lowell and from his brother William that he had lampooned a much respected Boston reformer, Miss Elizabeth Peabody. . . . He pleaded not guilty. At best he had thought of Miss Peabody's spectacles on the bridge of her nose when he had described . . . Miss Birdseye – "the whole moral history of Boston was reflected in her displaced spectacles." Doubtless certain passages in the three full pages devoted to her could fit all reformers. . . . Henry replied to William that he had not seen Miss Peabody for twenty-five years, and that he had always had the most casual observation of her. "Miss Birdseye" he said, "was evolved entirely from my moral consciousness, like every person I have ever drawn . . .". In subsequent instalments he enlarged Miss Peabody's heroism. . . . Neither [William] nor anyone . . . noticed the close relationship between the names. . . . A "bird's eye" is indeed a "pea-body"' (Leon Edel, 1963, *Henry James: the middle years, 1884–1894*, pp. 79, 80).

PEABODY BUILDINGS, London A block of working-class flats (model dwellings) situated on Little Coram Street, now Herbrand Street, and built by the Peabody Trust in the nineteenth century. The Trust built similar blocks throughout London.

BROWN'S BUILDINGS, MAINE STREET, in Mrs Humphry Ward, *Marcella* (1894)

'Peabody's Buildings (called "Brown's Buildings") in Little Coram Street' (Enid Huws Jones, 1973, *Mrs Humphry Ward*, London: Heinmann, p. 102).

PEACOCK, Edward (1825?–67) Son of Thomas Love **Peacock**.

- EDWARD BLANCOVE in George Meredith, *Rhoda Fleming* (1865)

'It has been suggested that Meredith modelled Blancove upon his brother-in-law, Edward Peacock, who similarly fell out with his father over his infatuation with a girl of lower status' (A. Lionel Stevenson, 1954, *The Ordeal of George Meredith*, London: Peter Owen, p. 147).

PEACOCK, Thomas Love (1785–1866) English novelist and poet. He was born in Weymouth, the son of a London merchant. He wrote the most famous of his satirical romances, *Headlong Hall* (1816) and *Nightmare Abbey* (1818), before joining the East India Company in 1819. In the same year he married Jane **Gryffyddh**, daughter of 'Doctor' **Gryffyddh**; their daughter was Mary Ellen **Meredith**. Peacock was **Shelley's** literary executor.

MR ESCOT in Thomas Love Peacock, *Headlong Hall* (1816)

'Escot, who marries the beautiful Cephalis, is Peacock' (Martin Freeman, 1911, *Thomas Love Peacock*, London: Martin Secker, p. 96). *See also* **Shelley**, Percy Bysshe.

MR FOSTER in Thomas Love Peacock, *Headlong Hall* (1816)

'Mr Foster's views [are based] partly on Shelley's, partly on Peacock's libertarianism' (David Garnett (ed.), 1963, Introd. to *Headlong Hall*, in *The Novels of T.L. Peacock*, London: Rupert Hart-Davis, p. 8).

DR MIDDLETON in George Meredith, *The Egoist* (1879)

'Dr Middleton was drawn from T.L. Peacock' (Sir Paul Harvey (ed.), 1967, *Oxford Companion to English Literature*, Oxford: Oxford University Press, s.v. *The Egoist*).

PEARSON, 'Fatty' A bush pilot in Kenya. In January 1934 he flew Ernest Hemingway to Nairobi for treatment for the dysentery that he contracted while on safari in the Serengeti Plain. He was a friend of Philip **Percival**.

COMPTON in Ernest Hemingway, 'The Snows of Kilimanjaro', *The Fifth Column and the First Forty-nine Stories* (1938)

'The man who jumped down and came striding towards them in a tweed jacket, cord trousers and an experienced brown felt hat was Fatty Pearson . . . who was not fat at all' (Carlos Baker, 1969, *Ernest Hemingway: a life story*, New York, p. 251). In a note (ibid., p. 609), 'Identity of Fatty Pearson', Baker refers to the authority of Philip Percival and adds that Percival confirmed 'that the flight was substantially as described in "The Snows of Kilimanjaro"'.

PÉCHINET, Marie (1850?–1912) Head of the French department at Royal Holloway College from 1887 to 1909. Her assistant, when Ivy Compton-Burnett was a student there, was Pernel Strachey, sister of Lytton **Strachey**.

Miss LEMAÎTRE in I. Compton-Burnett, *Dolores* (1911)

'Miss Lemaître in *Dolores* (who was modelled on Marie Péchinet . . .) reappears in *More Women Than Men* as . . . Maria Rosetti' (Hilary Spurling, 1974, *Ivy When Young: the early life of I. Compton-Burnett, 1884–1919*, London: Gollancz, p. 152).

MARIA ROSETTI in I. Compton-Burnett, *More Women Than Men* (1933)

See above.

PEEL, Sir Robert (1788–1850) Son of a cotton manufacturer, he established the Irish police force in 1814, and the Metropolitan Police in London in 1829 (hence their nickname of 'Bobbies'). In 1828 he was Home Secretary under **Wellington**, and in 1829 he introduced a bill granting Catholic emancipation. He was Prime Minister in 1834–5 and 1841–6 and pursued a policy of free trade, culminating in the repeal of the corn laws in 1846.

MR FITZLOOM in Benjamin Disraeli, *Vivian Grey* (1826-7)

Identified as Sir R. P—l in a key given in a pamphlet published in 1827 by William Marsh. This key is discussed by Lucien Wolf in his notes to *Vivian Grey* (1904 (centenary edn), Vol. II, p. 364), who concludes that Disraeli was not responsible for the key.

PEMBROKE, George Robert Charles Herbert, 13th Earl of (1850–95) He succeeded his uncle to the title in 1862.

LORD ALLEN in W.H. Mallock, *The New Republic* (1877)

'Lord Pembroke has been suggested as the model for Lord Allen in *The New Republic* (ed. J.M. Patrick, Gainsville 1959, p. xiii)' (C.C. Nickerson, 1963, 'W.H. Mallock's pseudonyms', *Notes and Queries* 208: 460 n. 7).

PENN, Mrs (1757?–1864?) In 1849 she was still living at Innerleithen; in the summer of that year, 12-year-old James Murray, later the great lexicographer, was taken to see her.

LADY PENNEFEATHER in Sir Walter Scott, *St Ronan's Well* (1823)

'She had known Sir Walter Scott and was reputed to be the model for Lady Pennefeather' (K.M.E. Murray, 1977, *Caught in the Web of Words: James A.H. Murray and the 'Oxford English Dictionary'*, p. 19).

PENNELL, Theodore In the 1890s he used non-violent techniques in his dealings with American Indians.

JOSEPH MILLER in Aldous Huxley, *Eyeless in Gaza* (1936)

'Miller, who has learnt as an anthropologist that pacifist methods work admirably with primitive peoples, seems to have been based partly on Theodore Pennell' (George Woodcock, 1972, *Dawn and the Darkest Hour: a study of Aldous Huxley*, London: Faber & Faber, p. 202). *See also* **Alexander**, F. Matthias; **Heard**, Gerald.

PENNINGTON, Brigadier-General R.L.A. (1857–1920) He was a cousin of Anthony Powell on his mother's side. In 1876 he joined the Northumberland Fusiliers, in which his grandfather had served in Spain under **Wellington**; he became a colonel in 1901, and in 1917 he received the honorary rank of Brigadier-General.

GENERAL CONYERS in Anthony Powell, *A Dance to the Music of Time* (1951–76)

'So far as General Conyers had a model (he is in any case composite in his role of courtier), that was . . . Brigadier-General Pennington' (Anthony Powell, 1976, *To Keep the Ball Rolling: the memoirs of Anthony Powell*, Vol. I: *The Infants of Spring*, London: Heinemann, p. 53).

PENROSE, Mr and Miss (*fl.* 1907–8) Of Mount Pleasant Farm, Windmill Hill, Sussex. Dorothy Richardson lodged with them in 1907 and 1908.

RICHARD AND RACHEL ROSCORLA in Dorothy Richardson, *Pilgrimage* (1915–67)

'[Miriam] becomes a boarder at the . . . farm of the Quaker family, the Roscorlas, drawn from Dorothy's friends, the Penroses' (John Rosenberg, 1973, *Dorothy Richardson*, London, p. 142).

PENROSE, Francis Cranmer (1817–1903) Archaeologist and astronomer. Son of Elizabeth Penrose ('Mrs Markham'), he was a contemporary at Cambridge and lifelong friend of Charles Kingsley. In 1852 he was Surveyor of St Paul's Cathedral in London. He published archaeological and astronomical works, and from 1894 to 1896 he was President of the Royal Institute of British Architects; he became a Fellow of the Royal Society in 1894. His daughter, Dame Emily Penrose, was Principal of Bedford College, Royal Holloway College (where Ivy **Compton-Burnett** was one of her students) and Somerville College, Oxford, successively.

AMYAS LEIGH in Charles Kingsley, *Westward Ho!* (1855)

'Kingsley himself indicated that his model for . . . Amyas Leigh was his . . . old friend, Francis Penrose' (R.B. Martin, 1959, *The Dust of Combat: a life of Charles Kingsley*, London: Faber & Faber, p. 176).

PENTRIDGE, Dorset A village to the south-east of Cranborne Chase, not far from the border between Dorset and Hampshire.

TRANTRIDGE in Thomas Hardy, Wessex novels and tales (1871–95)

Identified in a map prepared by Thomas Hardy which hangs in the Dorset County Museum, Dorchester. *See under* **Abbotsbury**. *See also* **Tarrant Hinton**.

PENZANCE, Cornwall

PEN-ZEPHYR in Thomas Hardy, 'A Mere Interlude' (1913)

Identified in F.B. Pinion, 1968, *A Hardy Companion*, London: Macmillan.

PEPER HAROW, Surrey

MURESWELL RECTORY in Mrs Humphry Ward, *Robert Elsmere* (1888)

'It was in 1882 . . . when we took Peperharrow Rectory (the Murewell Vicarage of "Robert Elsmere") that we first came across Borough Farm' (Mrs Humphry Ward, 1918, *A Writer's Recollections*, New York and London: Harper & Bros, p. 191).

PERCEVAL, Spencer (1762–1812) English statesman. Educated at Harrow and at Trinity College, Cambridge, he was called to the Bar in 1786. He became an MP in 1796 and Prime Minister in 1809; he was shot dead in the lobby of the House of Commons by a bankrupt broker.

SPENCER NEWCOMB in Lady Charlotte Bury, *The Exclusives* (1830)

Identified in *Key to the Royal Novel 'The Exclusives'*, 1830, Marsh & Miller; reproduced in Michael Sadleir, 1951, *XIX Century Fiction*, 2 vols, London: Constable, and Los Angeles: California University Press, pp. 73–4.

PERCIVAL, Philip (b. 1893?) Born in Somerset, he went to Kenya in 1905 and settled in Limuru, where he raised ostriches, bred cattle and horses, and grew coffee and wheat. In 1930 he was Director for Kenya of Tanganyika Guides Ltd, and in 1933 he acted as white hunter on Ernest Hemingway's safari in Kenya.

JACKSON PHILLIPS in Ernest Hemingway, *The Green Hills of Africa* (1935)

'To give his story the air of fiction he had changed most of the names. . . . Philip Percival was Jackson Phillips or Pop' (Carlos Baker, 1969, *Ernest Hemingway: a life story*, New York, p. 260).

ROBERT WILSON in Ernest Hemingway, 'The Short Happy Life of Francis Macomber', *The Fifth Column and the First Forty-nine Stories* (1938)

'Robert Wilson . . . was based on Philip Percival, with his rubicund face, cool blue eyes, laconic speech habits, and his enviable combination of courage and judgement. Ernest later said that all he contributed to the invention of Wilson was to disguise Philip slightly for family and business reasons, and in order to keep him out of trouble with the Tanganyika Game Department' (Baker, op. cit., p. 284). Hemingway identified Percival as the model for Wilson in 'The Art of the short story', unpublished preface composed c. June 1959 (see ibid., p. 617 n. 'EH completes "The Short Happy Life, etc."').

PÉREZ TRIANA, Santiago Son of Santiago Pérez, President of Colombia from 1874 to 1876, he was Minister in London and Madrid in 1903 and 1904. He was a friend of R.B. **Cunninghame Graham**.

DON JOSÉ AVELLANOS in Joseph Conrad, *Nostromo* (1904)

'I am compunctious as to the use I've made of the impression produced upon me by the Ex. Sr. Don Pérez Triana's personality. Do you think I have committed an unforgivable fault there? He'll never see or hear of the book probably' (Joseph Conrad to R.B. Cunninghame Graham, 31 October 1904, reproduced in G. Jean-Aubry, 1927, *Joseph Conrad: life and letters*, London: Heinemann, p. 338).

Jocelyn Baines says this refers to the character of Avellanos Baines (*Joseph Conrad: a critical biography*, 1969, p. 294 n.).

PERKINS, Revd Mr He was Minister of the Baptist church in Dorchester, Dorset, when Thomas Hardy was a pupil in the office of the architect John Hicks, from 1856 to 1862. Through a fellow pupil, H.R. Baston, a Baptist, Hardy met the Perkins family, 'an austere and frugal household'. One of the sons became a close friend of Hardy.

REVD MR WOODWELL in Thomas Hardy, *A Laodicean* (1881)

'Among the few portraits of actual persons in Hardy's novels, that of the Baptist minister in *A Laodicean* is one – being a recognizable drawing of Perkins the father as he appeared to Hardy at this time, though the incidents are invented' (F.E. Hardy, 1962, *The Life of Thomas Hardy, 1840–1928*, p. 30).

PERKINS, Maxwell (1884–1947)   Editor at Scribner's, the New York publishing company; he edited the work of F. Scott **Fitzgerald**, **Hemingway** and Thomas Wolfe.

FOXHALL EDWARDS in Thomas Wolfe, *You Can't Go Home Again* (1940)

'Did you like the description of Max Perkins as "Foxhall"? I believe Max has mixed emotions' (F. Scott Fitzgerald to his daughter, 29 November 1940, reproduced in *The Letters of F. Scott Fitzgerald*, 1964, ed. Andrew Turnbull, London: Bodley Head, p. 98).

PERKINS, Stanhope

VERE PERKINS in F.W. Rolfe, *Nicholas Crabbe* (1958)

Identified by Cecil Woolf in his introduction to *Nicholas Crabbe*, 1958, pp. 5–7.

PERLMUTTER, Bronia and Tanya They arrived in Paris from Eastern Europe in the 1920s. In 1928 Bronia married René Clair, the film director. In the last months of his life, Bronia formed a close friendship with **Radiguet**.

MOYDIA AND KATYA in Djuna Barnes, 'The Grande Malade' (1962)

'"The Little Girl Continues" [the original title of 'The Grand Malade'] . . . is said to be based on Radiguet's acquaintance with the Perlmutter sisters' (F. Steegmuller, 1970, *Cocteau*, p. 535 n. 308).

PERRY, John George (1802–70)   Surgeon. He trained at St Bartholomew's Hospital, London, where he was a governor from 1834 until his death. From 1829 to 1843 he was Surgeon to the Foundling Hospital, after which he was a medical inspector of prisons until 1870. He was an amateur astronomer of some note and a Fellow of the Royal Astronomical Society. He took part in the Himalayan expedition and made some observations at Burgos.

MR LACY in Charles Reade, *It is Never Too Late to Mend* (1856)

'His representative in the novel, Mr Lacy, is the *Deus ex machinâ* who turns Mr Hawes out of the Gaol' ('The license of modern novelists', *Edinburgh Review* (July 1857): 144).

PERRY, Thomas Sergeant (1845–1928) Scholar, linguist and translator. He was the grandson of O.H. Perry, the victor of the Battle of Lake Erie, and on his mother's side was directly descended from Benjamin Franklin, whom he much resembled in looks. He was a close friend of Henry **James** from boyhood, and later became a friend of W.D. Howells. He was a Bostonian by marriage (to a Cabot) and by adoption.

Miles Arbuton in W.D. Howells, *A Chance Acquaintance* (1874)

'Howells had met ... Perry ... at Quebec, in 1869. ... Perry, who had just returned from Europe ... was bored with the St Lawrence, with the vulgarity of the passengers and the wonders of the Saguenay, and he said later, though Howells denied it, that his unseemly conduct had given rise to the portrait of Mr Arbuton' (Van Wyck Brooks, 1959, *Howells: his life and work*, pp. 61–2).

PERTH AMBOY, New Jersey Port and manufacturing city on the Raritan river.

Port Alby in Francis T. Field, *McDonough* (1951)

'Port Alby suggests Perth Amboy' (Joseph Blotner, 1966, *The Modern American Political Novel*, Austin, Tex., p. 80 n.).

PETO, Sir Samuel Morton (1809–89) He was a partner from 1830 to 1847 in the firm of Grissell & Peto, which built railways all over the world, including the Dorset section of the London and South-Western Railway, constructed Nelson's Column in London, and built the Balaclava railway during the Crimean War. He was a Liberal MP in 1847–54 and 1859–66, but he retired from public life when his company failed in 1866. A member of the Baptist Church, he had the Regent's Park Diorama reconditioned as a Baptist chapel. He married Miss Grissell.

Copperhead in Margaret Oliphant, *Phoebe Junior* (1876)

See below.

John Power in Thomas Hardy, *A Laodicean* (1881)

'Interestingly, Power and Copperhead, both railway-builders, seem to have been based on the same Baptist, Sir Samuel Morton Peto' (Valentine Cunningham, 1976, *Everywhere Spoken Against: dissent in the Victorian novel*, Oxford: Clarendon Press, p. 201).

PHILIPS, Mark (1800–73) Cotton merchant of Snitterfield and Welcombe, Warwickshire, he was MP for Manchester from 1832 to 1847. His daughter Caroline married George Otto, son of Sir Charles **Trevelyan**.

Mr Millbank in Benjamin Disraeli, *Coningsby* (1844)

Identified (as Phillips) in a key in *Notes and Queries* (8th series) 3 (13 May 1893): 363. *See also under* **Bright**, John.

PHILLIPS, Charles (1787–1859) Irish barrister. He was a member of Middle Temple in 1807, and was called to the Irish Bar in 1812 and to the English Bar in 1821; he was soon the leader at the Old Bailey. In 1840 he defended

Courvoisier, the valet who murdered Lord William Russell, and in 1849 he published a pamphlet against the death penalty.

MR SERJEANT BUZFUZ in Charles Dickens, *The Pickwick Papers* (1836-7)

'I have always believed that the speech of Serjeant Buzfuz was largely indebted to the eloquence of Charles Phillips on behalf of the plaintiff in Guthrie v. Sterne' (J.B. Atlay, 1908, *The Victorian Chancellors*, Vol. II, p. 163 n. 3). The speech, delivered in the Court of Common Pleas in Dublin, was much admired and published both in his collected speeches (1817) and separately as a pamphlet. *See also* **Bompas**, Mr Serjeant.

PHILLIPS, C.J. Steward of the sailor's home in Singapore in 1888.

THE STEWARD OF THE SAILORS' HOME in Joseph Conrad, *The Shadow-Line* (1917)

'The "Home" Steward's name . . . I don't remember. He was a meagre, wizened creature, always bemoaning his fate, and did try to do me an unfriendly turn' (letter from Joseph Conrad to St Clair'; see article in the *Malay Mail* (2 September 1924). 'The steward . . . was a retired sergeant of artillery. . . . His name was Phillips, really a very well meaning person, whose evangelical activities were mainly devoted to Malay missions' (W.G. St Clair, quoted in Norman Sherry, 1966, *Conrad's Eastern World*, Cambridge, App. E, p. 317).

PHILLIPS, Sir Percival (1877–1937) Journalist. Born in Brownsville, Pennsylvania. In 1898, as foreign correspondent, he covered the Spanish–American War, and in 1927 he covered the revolution in China. From 1901 to 1922 he was associated with the *Daily Express*, and from 1922 to 1934 he was a special correspondent on the *Daily Mail*.

SIR JOCELYN HITCHCOCK in Evelyn Waugh, *Scoop* (1938)

'Presumably the model for "Sir Jocelyn Hitchcock"' (*The Diaries of Evelyn Waugh*, 1976, ed. Michael Davie, London: Weidenfeld & Nicolson, p. 332 n. 3).

PHILLIPS, Sir Richard (1767–1840) Publisher. He began life as a schoolmaster, hosier, stationer and bookseller, and finally became a patent-medicine vendor in Leicester. In 1795 he moved to London, and in 1796 he established the *Monthly Magazine*. He was a friend of Priestley and a patron of Samuel Bamford and other radicals.

THE PUBLISHER in George Borrow, *Lavengro* (1851)

'The Publisher: Sir Richard Phillips' (*Lavengro*, 1907, ed. Prof. W.I. Knapp, p. 563 n. (to p. 185)).

PHILLIPS, Stephen (1864–1915) Poet and dramatist. Educated in Oundle, Northamptonshire, he was a member of Sir Frank Benson's theatrical company from 1888 to 1892. He took to letters as a profession *c.*1898 and was the author of dramas in verse, but sank into obscurity towards the end of his life.

JASPER GIBBONS in W. Somerset Maugham, *Cakes and Ale* (1930)

'Jasper Gibbons . . . is clearly the poet Stephen Phillips . . . promoted for a long time by Lady Colvin' (R.L. Calder, 1972, *W. Somerset Maugham and the Quest for Freedom*, London: Heinemann, p. 183). *See also* **Drinkwater**, John.

PICCOLI, Raffaello (*c*.1885–1933) In 1912 he was a lecturer in Italian at Cambridge University; *c*.1915 he returned to Naples and in 1921 he joined the Army. He was later appointed to the Serena Chair of Italian at Cambridge. He met Sinclair and Grace Hegger Lewis in Rome in 1929, and also became a friend of D.H. **Lawrence**: at the time of his death he was working on a study of Lawrence.

ANDREA VENGO in Grace Hegger Lewis, *Half a Loaf* (1931)

'Andrea Vengo . . . is apparently drawn after the man they saw most frequently in Rome, Raffaello Piccoli' (Mark Schorer, 1961, *Sinclair Lewis: an American life*, New York: McGraw-Hill, p. 325).

PICINISCO, Caserta, Italy A small town in the Abruzzi above Cassino; a hamlet some two miles away was the home of Orazio **Cervi**, and Frieda and D.H. Lawrence spent a few days there in December 1919.

PESCOCALASCIO in D.H. Lawrence, *The Lost Girl* (1920)

'The Lawrences' journey [to Picinisco from Rome] reappeared, in circumstantial detail, in *The Lost Girl*. . . . From Picinisco – Pescocalascio in *The Lost Girl* – Lawrence and Frieda had to scramble like goats for two miles along a steep mountain pathway, to the rude home of the Cervi family' (H.T. Moore, 1960, *The Intelligent Heart: the story of D.H. Lawrence*, Harmondsworth: Penguin, p. 325; originally published 1955, London: Heinemann).

PICKFORD, Thomas (1794–1865) He served in the Spanish army and in 1814 was Vice-Consul at Corunna; from 1820 he served in Paris, and from 1834 to 1865 he was Consul at Paris. In 1818 he fought a duel with a Frenchman at Caen.

MARMADUKE HEATH in James Payn, *Lost Sir Massingberd* (1864)

'. . . is drawn under name of Marmaduke Heath in Lost Sir Massingbird [sic]' (Frederic Boase, 1892, *Modern English Biography*, Vol. II, p. 1526).

PICKTHORN, Sir Kenneth (1892–1975) Historian. He was Dean of Corpus Christi College, Cambridge, from 1919 to 1927; Tutor from 1927 to 1935; and President from 1937 to 1944. He was MP for Cambridge from 1935 to 1950, and for the Carlton division of Nottinghamshire from 1950 to 1966. He was created Baronet in 1959. At Cambridge he was considered a formidable tutor.

MR GORSE in Christopher Isherwood, *Lions and Shadows* (1938)

'Christopher Isherwood's experiences with Kenneth Pickthorn were only marginally more unnerving . . . than those undergone by the pupils of the Reverend F.A. Simpson of Trinity' (T.E.B. Howarth, 1978, *Cambridge Between Two Wars*, p. 110).

PIDDLEHINTON, Dorset A village on the upper course of the long river called both the Piddle and the Trent, which runs from the chalk hills, through this village and Piddletrenthide, on to Puddletown and through Tolpuddle to Wareham.

LONGPUDDLE in Thomas Hardy, Wessex novels and tales (1871–95)

Identified on a map prepared by Thomas Hardy which hangs in the Dorset County Museum, Dorchester. *See under* **Abbotsbury**.

PIDDLETRENTHIDE, Dorset *See under* **Piddlehinton**.

LONGPUDDLE in Thomas Hardy, Wessex novels and tales (1871–95)

Identified on a map prepared by Thomas Hardy which hangs in the Dorset County Museum, Dorchester. *See under* **Abbotsbury**.

PIDSLEY, Miss Chief Assistant at the **London House** draper's shop in Eastwood when D.H. Lawrence was a boy and a young man.

MISS PINNEGAR in D.H. Lawrence, *The Lost Girl* (1920)

'Miss Wright kept the house together, with the somewhat sullen cooperation of Cullen's chief assistant at the shop, Miss Pidsley, whom Lawrence put into *The Lost Girl* as Miss Pinnegar' (H.T. Moore, 1960, *The Intelligent Heart: the story of D.H. Lawrence*, Harmondsworth: Penguin, p. 49; originally published 1955, London: Heinemann).

PIGOU, Arthur Cecil (1877–1959) Educated at Harrow and at King's College, Cambridge, he was the winner of the Chancellor's medal for English verse and took firsts in the History Tripos and Moral Sciences Tripos. From 1908 to 1943 he was Professor of Political Economy. He was the author of *The Economics of Welfare*.

MR GOW in Shane Leslie, *The Cantab* (1926)

Identified in a key in the hand of Dr Ivor Ramsay, a Kingsman of the year 1920, and later Dean, laid in a copy of *The Cantab*.

PINKER, James Brand (1863–1922) Literary agent. Born of a humble family, he began his working life as a clerk; in 1887 he was a journalist on the *Levant Herald* in Constantinople, and in 1891 he was Assistant Editor of *Black and White*, a London weekly. In 1896 he set himself up as a literary agent, and at one time or another he acted for Henry **James**, Joseph **Conrad**, Arnold **Bennett**, Stephen **Crane**, Ford Madox Ford, Somerset **Maugham** and D.H. **Lawrence**.

HORATIO GUBB in Ford Madox Ford, *The Simple Life Limited* (1911)

'[T]here are recognizable touches of Pinker about Mr Gubb' (Arthur Mizener, 1971, *The Saddest Story: a biography of Ford Madox Ford*, Cleveland: World Publishing, p. 558 n. 12). *See also* **Ford**, Ford Madox; **Wells**, H.G.

PITT, William, 1st Earl of Chatham (1708–78) English statesman and orator. Born in Westminster and educated at Eton and Trinity College, Oxford, he entered parliament in 1735 for Old Sarum. Paymaster-General from 1746 to 1755, by 1756 he was Secretary of State, but was actually prime minister in all but name. He resigned in 1761. In 1766 he formed a new ministry with himself as Privy Seal, taking a seat in the Upper House as Viscount Pitt, Earl of Chatham. Troubled by ill health, he resigned from office for the last time in 1768. In April 1778, after speaking against the motion to make peace with America on any terms, and securing a majority vote, he rose to respond to a question but fell back and died.

MR WENTWORTH in Robert Plumer Ward, *De Vere; or The Man of Independence* (1827)

'The principal character, identified, by the newspaper puffs of the day, with a great living statesman, is obviously a portrait, and upon the whole we consider it a just one, of Lord Chatham as he appeared in one of the most critical periods of his life' (*Quarterly Review* 36: 276). *See also* **Bolingbroke**, Lord; **Canning**, George; **Pitt**, William, the Younger.

PITT, William, the Younger (1759–1806) Second son of the Earl of Chatham (see **Pitt**), he was educated at home, because of ill health, before attending Pembroke, Cambridge, at the age of 14. He was called to the Bar in 1780 and became MP for Appleby, Cumbria, in 1781; he became Prime Minister at the age of 24.

MR WENTWORTH in Robert Plumer Ward, *De Vere; or The Man of Independence* (1827)

'We will . . . state our distinct belief . . . that much . . . of the admirable sketch of . . . Wentworth, is modelled from the joint characters of the late William Pitt and his present distinguished successor, Mr Canning' (*Literary Gazette* 532 (31 March 1827): 193). *See also* **Bolingbroke**, Lord; **Canning**, George; **Pitt**, William.

PLATOFF, Count Matvei Ivanovich (1757–1818) He became the Cossack Hetman in 1801 and gave distinguished service in attacks on the French rearguard during the French retreat from Russia in 1811, led the defeat of the French at Laon in 1813, and captured Nemours in 1814. Sir Walter Scott met him on his visit to Paris in 1815, and Platoff seemed to take a great fancy to him.

MR TOUCHWOOD in Sir Walter Scott, *St Ronan's Well* (1823)

'Scott acknowledges, in a note to *St Ronan's Well* [Border edn, ch. xv] . . . that he took from Platoff this portrait of Mr Touchwood: – "His face, which at the distance of a yard or two seemed hale and smooth, appeared, when closely examined, to be seamed with a million wrinkles, crossing each other in every direction possible, but as fine as if drawn with the point of a very fine needle." Thus did every little peculiarity remain, treasured in his memory, to be used in due time for giving the air of minute reality to some imagined personage' (*Memoirs of Sir Walter Scott*, ed. J.G. Lockhart, 1900, Vol. III, London: Macmillan, p. 21 n. 1 (to ch. 35)). 'This was a peculiarity of the celebrated Cossack leader Platoff' (*St Ronan's Well*, op. cit., ch. xv).

von PLEHVE, Wenzel (1846–1904) Russian lawyer and government administrator. He was Director of the Secret Police in 1881, Secretary of State for Finland in 1894 and Minister of the Interior in 1902. He was assassinated with a bomb.

Mr de P—— in Joseph Conrad, *Under Western Eyes* (1911)

'Listen to the theme. The student Razumov . . . gives up secretly to the police his fellow student, Haldin, who seeks refuge in his rooms after committing a political crime (supposed to be the murder of de Plehve)' (Conrad to John Galsworthy, 6 January 1908, quoted in G. Jean-Aubry, 1927, *Joseph Conrad: life and letters*, Vol. II, London: Heinemann, p. 64–5).

PLOMER, William (1903–74) Novelist and poet. Born in North Transvaal, he became a trader in Zululand before living for some time in Japan and then England.

Nigel Edge in William Plomer, *The Invaders* (1934)

'The character of Nigel is a recognisable portrait of William' (John Morris, 1974, 'William Plomer: a memoir', broadcast 13 January 1974, BBC Third Programme, London).

PLUM PUDDING STEPS, Clerkenwell, London

Riceyman Steps in Arnold Bennett, *Riceyman Steps* (1923)

'*Riceyman Steps*, a title that Bennett took from the name "Plum Pudding Steps" that local inhabitants applied to the steps leading to Granville Square in Clerkenwell. (The steps are so dark that if a young girl goes down them often with a young man she will soon be as fat as a plum pudding)' (*Letters of Arnold Bennett*, 1968, ed. James Hepburn, Vol. I, London: Oxford University Press, p. 319 n. 315).

POLLINGTON, Lady *See* **Mexborough**, Countess of.

POLLINGTON, Lord *See* **Mexborough**, 4th Earl of.

POLLITT, Herbert Charles (1871–1942) Educated at Trinity College, Cambridge. He was a book collector and formed a magnificent collection of books of the 'nineties'. He was a friend and patron of Aubrey Beardsley.

Arbuthnot ('The Babe') in E.F. Benson, *The Babe, B.A.* (1897)

'The most talked-about undergraduate, he was the central character in E.F. Benson's lightweight novel about the Cambridge of those days. . . . The undergraduate periodicals let themselves go on his theatrical performances, with the *Cambridge ABC* lyrical about his scarf dance, modelled on that of the American dancer Loie Fuller' (David Low, 1973, *With All Faults*, Tehran, p. 101).

POLLOCK, Sir John (1878–1963) Journalist and writer. Son of the jurist Sir Frederick Pollock, he was educated at Eton, at Trinity College, Cambridge, and at Harvard Law School.

Guy Dawlish in Edith Wharton, 'The Pretext' (1908)

'Among the stories written at this period one . . . was directly based upon a suggestion given to Edith Wharton by Henry James. He had related . . . some gossip about an English friend of his, and [she] had asked his permission to use the anecdote for a story. James replied: "Je vous le donne, je vous le donne indeed, one petite donnée . . . oddly enough I am more or less surrounded . . . by the English actors in the affair: that is the Sidney Waterlows . . . have taken a house here for the winter, & Jack himself, who is most charming and sympathetic, comes down sometimes to see them . . ." [7 January 1908]. The result was "The Pretext". . . . The chief actor, "Jack himself", seems to be the late Sir John Pollock' (Mildred Bell, 1966, *Edith Wharton and Henry James*, pp. 261–2).

PONDEN HALL, Yorkshire A Tudor manor house situated at Scar Top, five miles south-west of Keighley, above the reservoir, within two miles of Haworth and near Stanbury. It was owned by the Heaton family from 1513 onwards and was reconditioned in 1801.

THRUSHCROSS GRANGE in Emily Brontë, *Wuthering Heights* (1847)

'[Emily Brontë] knew it all so well that . . . she took Ponden House [sic] for the model of her Thrushcross Grange' (Winifred Gérin, 1971, *Emily Brontë*, Oxford, p. 32).

PONDEN KIRK, Yorkshire A jutting platform on the moors above Haworth.

PENISTONE CRAG in Emily Brontë, *Wuthering Heights* (1847)

'. . . Penistone Crag, as she calls it. . . whose local name is Ponden Kirk' (Winifred Gérin, 1971, *Emily Brontë*, Oxford, p. 149).

PONSONBY, Elizabeth (1900–40) Daughter of Arthur, 1st Baron Ponsonby of Shulbrede. In 1929 she married J.C.D. Pelly, but they were divorced in 1933. She was a leader of the Bright Young People of the 1920s, and was one of the first to have her hair shingled. When she died the popular press was full of her exploits in the 1920s, but a friend wrote in *The Times* (6 August 1940) that her two outstanding qualities were courage and loyalty. She showed, he said, fearless decision in any emergency or accident. 'It would', he quoted another friend as saying, 'be Elizabeth an unfortunate would be certain to find waiting for him when he came out of the prison gates.' Waugh met her in October 1925.

AGATHA RUNCIBLE in Evelyn Waugh, *Vile Bodies* (1930)

'Model for "Agatha Runcible"' (*The Diaries of Evelyn Waugh*, 1976, ed. Michael Davie, London: Weidenfeld & Nicolson, p. 804 (App. of Names)).

POOLE, Dorset A seaside town south-west of Bournemouth.

HAVENPOOL in Thomas Hardy, Wessex novels and tales (1871–95)

Identified on a map prepared by Thomas Hardy which hangs in the Dorset County Museum, Dorchester. *See under* **Abbotsbury**.

POOLE, Ernest (1880–1950) American novelist. He graduated from Princeton, and in 1902 was at the University Settlement, New York City, where a group of young men, who later became leading intellectuals in the American Socialist Party, were working. He spent his life writing in New York, and gradually his views moved to the right.

BILLY in Ernest Poole, *The Harbor* (1915)

'As his autobiography, *The Bridge*, reveals, Poole transmuted many of his own experiences and beliefs into those of his hero' (Walter Rideout, 1956, *The Radical Novel in the United States, 1900–1954*, Cambridge, Mass., p. 57).

POOLE, Henry George (1847–76) From 1832 to 1836 he was a tailor, in Savile Row, London, by appointment to most of the crowned heads of Europe, including **Napoleon III**.

VIGO in Benjamin Disraeli, *Endymion* (1880)

Identified in 'Key to *Endymion*', *Notes and Queries* 83 (24 October 1942): 263. The identification with both Poole and George Hudson is attributed to G.E. Buckle. It was said that Poole used to dress poor but promising young men for nothing, trusting that when they had made their fortunes they would pay his bill, exactly as Mr Vigo did (see *Notes and Queries* 172 (16 October 1937), p. 282). *See also* **Hudson**, George.

POPE-HENNESSY, Sir John (1834–91)

PHINEAS FINN in Anthony Trollope, *Phineas Finn* (1869) and *Phineas Redux* (1874)

'[I]ntellectually and politically (Phineas) was John Pope-Hennessy, a young Irish politician of brilliant parts who was a protégé of Disraeli and married the daughter of Sir Hugh Low' (Michael Sadleir, 1927, *Trollope: a commentary*, London: Constable, pp. 416, 417). 'John Pope-Hennessy was in fact [in 1859] undergoing the metamorphosis which so fascinated Trollope and which partly inspired him to write Phineas Finn. He was now becoming a man of the world' (James Pope-Hennessy, 1964, *Verandah*, p. 39). *See also* **King-Harman**, Edward; **Parkinson**, Joe; **Parkinson-Fortescue**, Chichester.

POPHAM, Arthur Frederick He married his cousin Florence Radford (**Popham, below**); they were connected with the long-established draper's business Popham & Radford in Plymouth, and in 1899 they were neighbours of H.G. Wells and his wife in Sandgate, Kent. His sister was the wife of Graham **Wallas**, through whom Wells first encountered the **Fabian Society**.

MR BUNTING in H.G. Wells, *The Sea Lady* (1902)

'The Pophams, the Wellses' next-door neighbours in Arnold House, if not the originals of the Buntings, must have been in on the joke and supplied, consciously or unconsciously, many of the features of this . . . household' (Lovat Dickson, 1972, *H.G. Wells*, Harmondsworth: Penguin, p. 132).

POPHAM, Florence Née Radford, she married her cousin A.F. **Popham**.

MRS BUNTING in H.G. Wells, *The Sea Lady* (1902)

See under **Popham**, A.F.

POPPER, Amalia Daughter of Leopoldo **Popper**, in 1913 and 1914 she was a pupil of James Joyce.

MARION ('MOLLY') BLOOM in James Joyce, *Ulysses* (1922)

'[Amalia Popper] was to serve as one of the models for the character and Southern European looks of Molly Bloom' (Richard Ellmann, 1966, *James Joyce*, London: Oxford Paperbacks, p. 353). *See also* **Chance**, Mrs Charles; **Dillon**, Mamie; **Joyce**, Nora; **Santos**, Signora.

POPPER, Leopoldo   A Jewish businessman. He was the father of Amalia **Popper**.

LEOPOLD BLOOM in James Joyce, *Ulysses* (1922)

'"Leopold Bloom" was named with due deliberation. Leopold was the first name of Signorina Popper's father in Trieste, Bloom was the name of two or three families who lived in Dublin when Joyce was young' (Richard Ellmann, 1966, *James Joyce*, London: Oxford Paperbacks, p. 386). *See also* **Bloom**, Joseph; **Byrne**, John Francis; **Chance**, Charles; **Hunter**, Alfred H.; **Jackson**, Holbrook; **Joyce**, James; **Joyce**, John Stanislaus; **Mayer**, Teodoro; **Schmitz**, Ettore.

PORCHESTER, Henry John George Herbert, Lord   (1800–49) He succeeded his father as the 8th Earl of Carnarvon in 1833. Sir Walter Scott described him as 'A young man who lies on the carpet and looks poetical and dandyish' (entry for 23 November 1825, in *Journal of Sir Walter Scott*, 1972, ed. W.E.K. Anderson, Oxford). He travelled in Spain, Portugal and Greece, and in 1825 published *The Moor*, a poem in six cantos; in the introduction to canto 5 he dilates on the indescribable fascination produced by the Alhambra on the traveller who beholds it for the first time. In 1838 he engaged Charles Barry to remodel Highclere, the family seat in Hampshire; the house emerged clothed in intricate lacy decoration strongly reminiscent of the decoration of the Alhambra.

LORD ALHAMBRA in Benjamin Disraeli, *Vivian Grey* (1826-7)

'Lord Alhambra . . . [is] without doubt [an] impressionist [caricature] of . . . Lord Porchester' (B.N. Langdon-Davies, 1904, Introd. to *Vivian Grey*, London: Alexander Moring, p. xxxiii; originally published 1826, London: Henry Colburn).

PORTLAND, Isle of   A rocky peninsula south of Weymouth, Dorset, with cliff quarries that were largely exploited by Sir Christopher Wren for St Paul's Cathedral in London. The most southerly point is known as the Bill.

ISLE OF SLINGERS in Thomas Hardy, Wessex novels and tales (1871–95)

Identified on a map prepared by Thomas Hardy which hangs in the Dorset County Museum, Dorchester. *See under* **Abbotsbury**.

PORTLAND, William John Cavendish Scott Bentinck, 5th Duke of (1800–79).

MR BADGER in Kenneth Grahame, *The Wind in the Willows* (1908)

'The most attractive feature about him from his creator's point of view . . . was undoubtedly his labyrinthine underground home. . . . This grandiose earthy catacomb . . . may have been suggested in part by the eccentricities of the fifth Duke of Portland, who "had been given to disappearing for weeks . . . and [had] built himself strange underground rooms and passages in his great park at Welbeck". These facts emerged during the hearing of the Druce case in 1907, about the time Mr Badger's residence was being invented' (Peter Green, 1959, *Kenneth Grahame, 1859–1932*, p. 282). Mrs Druce, widow of the owner of a store in Baker Street, London, claimed that her husband had in fact been the Duke of Portland. *See also* **Henley**, W.E.

LORD DERWENT in M. Spencer Stanhope, *Almacks* (1826)

Identified in Michael Sadleir, 1951, *XIX Century Fiction*, 2 vols, London: Constable, and Los Angeles: California University Press, p. 331; reprinted from *Literary Gazette* (9 December 1826).

PORTOFINO, Liguria, Italy

CASTEGNETO in 'Elizabeth', *The Enchanted April* (1922)

'Elizabeth Mary, Countess Russell, published in 1923 [sic] her immensely successful novel *An Enchanted April*, which had the Castello at Portofino as its setting' (Harold Nicolson, 1966, *Diaries and Letters, 1930–1939*, ed. Nigel Nicolson, London: Collins, p. 164 n. 2).

PORTSMOUTH, Hampshire

LYMPORT in George Meredith, *Evan Harrington* (1860)

'*Evan Harrington* depicted various scenes at the paternal and grand-paternal shop in Portsmouth, here thinly disguised as "Lymport", but . . . the book is no picture of Portsmouth' (S.M. Ellis, 1920, *George Meredith*, 2nd edn, London: Grant Richards, p. 17).

PORTSMOUTH, New Hampshire

RIVERMOUTH in T.B. Aldrich, *The Story of a Bad Boy* (1870)

'Rivermouth, which is actually Portsmouth' (Cornelia Meiggs, 1970, *Louisa M. Alcott and the American Family Story*, p. 115).

POTTER, Charles A salaried clerk 'who devoted the major part of his thirty shillings a week to his personal pleasure and adornment' (*The Pickwick Papers*, ch. 30). He was employed in the offices of Ellis & Blackmore, London solicitors, in 1827 and 1928, when Dickens was the office boy there.

ALFRED JINGLE in Charles Dickens, *The Pickwick Papers* (1836-7)

'According to George Lear, Potter figured . . . as Alfred Jingle in *Pickwick*' (W.J. Carlton, 1952, 'Mr Blackmore engages an office boy', *The Dickensian* 68 (September): 165). Lear was an articled clerk with Ellis and Blackmore at the time, and in 1828 Blackmore married his sister. W.J. Carlton apparently found his notes among the Blackmore family papers (including Blackmore's 'Reminiscences of Charles Dickens'), on which he based his article. It was Lear who identified Potter as the 'salaried clerk' (ibid., p. 20).

THOMAS POTTER in Charles Dickens, 'Making a Night of It', *Sketches by Boz* (1836)

'Dickens's partiality for the theatre was shared to the full by Charles Potter. . . . When the *Sketches by Boz* appeared, Blackmore at once recognised his one-time clerk thinly disguised as Thomas Potter' (Carlton, op. cit., p. 20).

AUGUSTUS SNODGRASS in Charles Dickens, *The Pickwick Papers* (1836-7)

'I well remember a convivial occasion when I invited all the clerks to dine with me. Potter was there and guilty of a little excess. He did not come to the office for a couple of days afterwards, and when he came Dickens chaffed him with having taken too much wine, but he insisted that his indisposition did not arise from the wine but "it was the salmon"' (Blackmore, see Carlton, op. cit., p. 166 (cf. *Pickwick*, ch. 8). This seems to be Potter's only contribution to the character of Mr Snodgrass.

POTTER, Thomas Bayley (1817–98) MP for Rochdale, Lancashire, from 1865 to 1895. He was the founder (1866) and Honorary Secretary of the Cobden Club, London, and the founder and President of the Union and Emancipation Society.

JOB THORNBERRY in Benjamin Disraeli, *Endymion* (1880)

Identified in 'Key to *Endymion*', *Notes and Queries* 83 (24 October 1942): 263; identifications attributed to G.E. Buckle. *See also* **Bright**, John; **Cobden**, Richard.

POTTSVILLE, Pennsylvania From 1850 to 1877 it was the centre of the secret society of immigrant Irish miners, known as the Molly Maguires.

GIBBSVILLE in John O'Hara, *Appointment in Samarra* (1934)

'The locale of the novel is Pottsville, called Gibbsville' (John O'Hara to his brother Tom, 12 February 1934, quoted in Finis Farr, 1974, *O'Hara: a biography*, p. 156).

VERMISSA in Arthur Conan Doyle, *The Valley of Fear* (1915)

'The Molly Maguires and their unmasking fascinated Conan Doyle, who gave Pottsville its first appearance in fiction when he wrote *The Valley of Fear*. . . . In Doyle's novel, Pottsville was called Vermissa' (Farr, op. cit., p. 55).

POUND, Ezra Weston Loomis (1885–1972) American poet and critic. Born in Hailey, Idaho, he was educated at Hamilton College, Pennsylvania, where he met Hilda Doolittle. After teaching for a time in Indiana, he travelled to Europe in 1908, and his first collection of poems, *A Lume Spento* (With Tapers Quenched) was published in Venice that year. He then moved to London, where he lectured for a while in medieval Romance literature at the Regent Street Polytechnic. He became Co-editor of the Vorticist magazine *Blast*, and London Editor of the Chicago-based *Little Review*. He founded the Imagist school of poetry with Hilda Doolittle and Richard **Aldington**. In 1924 he settled in Italy, but his involvement with the Fascist movement, culminating in his participation in an Italian radio broadcast in 1945, led to his extradition to the United States to face charges of treason. The trial was abandoned, however, on the grounds of insanity, and he was committed to an asylum, where he remained until he was certified sane in 1958 and returned to Italy.

LETT BARNES in H.D. (Hilda Doolittle), *Bid Me To Live* (1960)

Identified by Helen McNeil in the introduction to *Bid Me to Live*, 1984, pp. viii–ix, and by Perdita Schaffner in the afterword, p. 187.

RAOUL ROOT in Louis Wilkinson, *The Buffoon* (1916)

'Raoul Root ... who is Pound' (Barbara Guest, 1985, *Herself Defined: the poet H.D. and her world*, London: Collins, p. 45; originally published 1984, Garden City, NY: Doubleday).

POWELL, Major 'The Gallaher family was one Joyce knew well. ... Mrs Gallaher and [her sister] Mrs Clinch were two of four handsome girls whose father was an old soldier named Powell. He called himself Major Powell, although he was only a sergeant-major. ... [He] served many years in the army, took part in the Crimean War ... in the Aldershot Rifles in Australia. On retiring ... bought a farm in Cork ... came to Dublin ... married a woman with property' (Richard Ellmann, 1982, *James Joyce*, rev. edn, Oxford: Oxford University Press, p. 46 n.).

MAJOR TWEEDY in James Joyce, *Ulysses* (1922)

'I have been trying to collect my notes ... and find several names of people connected with the family who were of the older generation when I was a boy. I wonder if I sent you an exercise book with the names of these persons at the tops of the pages would you be kind enough ... to scribble down ... anything noteworthy ... just as you did for the questions I sent you about Major Powell – in my book Major Tweedy, Mrs Bloom's father (to Mrs William Murray, 21 December 1922, reproduced in *Letters of James Joyce*, 1957, Vol. I, ed. Stuart Gilbert, London: Faber & Faber, p. 198).

POWERS, Marcella (b. 1921) She met Sinclair Lewis in 1939 when she was with the Provincetown Players, remaining his close friend until her marriage in 1947 to Michael Amrine.

JINNY MARSHLAND in Sinclair Lewis, *Cass Timberlane* (1945)

'It is his own thinly veiled love story ... the picture of Jinny Marshland moving ambiguously into the society of Grand Republic is ... Lewis's impression of Miss Powers's reception in Duluth' (Mark Schorer, 1963, *Sinclair Lewis: an American life*, London: Heinemann, p. 738; originally published 1961, New York: McGraw-Hill).

POWLES, John Diston (1787–1867) Born at Helsingor, Denmark, he was the son of Richard Powles, an artist with Lowestoft pottery. He was the principal partner in J. & A. Powles, a leading firm of South American merchants, with whom Disraeli was concerned as a speculator in the mining share market.

MR MILLION in Benjamin Disraeli, *Vivian Grey* (1826-7)

'No impartial reader ... could fail to see ... Mr and Mrs Millions [sic] as Mr and Mrs Powles ... and some reviewers did, in fact, comment on these resemblances' (Robert Blake, 1969, *Disraeli*, 2nd edn, London: Oxford University Press, p. 43). 'Mrs Millions was a take-off of Mrs J.D. Powles' (ibid., p. 40). *See also* **Coutts**, Harriot.

POWYS, John Cowper (1872–1963) English novelist, poet and essayist. He was born in Shirley, Derbyshire, and educated at Sherborne and at Corpus Christi College, Cambridge, but he spent much of his adult life in America, although the countryside of his youth remained a major influence on his work. He published over fifty books.

JACK WELSH in Louis Wilkinson, *The Buffoon* (1916)

'The character unmistakably "drawn from" a recognizable original is ... Jack Welsh; and no student of John Cowper Powys can afford to miss that ... representation of John as he was in 1916' (Kenneth Hopkins, 1967, *The Powys Brothers*, p. 47). 'When we were both lecturing in America [Wilkinson] expressed most beautifully his mixed feelings towards me in that admirable book *The Buffoon*' (J.C. Powys, 1934, *Autobiography*, p. 268).

POWYS, Mrs Mary Friend of the Sneyd family, in particular of Honora, the second wife of Richard Lovell **Edgeworth** and stepmother of Maria. In 1791, after Honora's death, her son Lovell Edgeworth showed signs of tuberculosis; he was taken to England by his father, and Mrs Powys took charge of the children remaining at Edgeworthstown in Ireland. She remained a family friend.

MRS SOMERS in Maria Edgeworth, 'Madame de Fleury', *Tales of Fashionable Life* (1809)

'Mrs Somers is based on ... Mrs Powys' (Marilyn Butler, 1972, *Maria Edgeworth*, Oxford, p. 244).

POXWELL MANOR, Poxwell, Dorset Located five miles north-east of Weymouth.

OXWELL HALL, OXWELL, in Thomas Hardy, *The Trumpet Major* (1880)

Identified in F.B. Pinion, 1968, *A Hardy Companion*, London: Macmillan.

POYNTER, Sir Edward John (1836–1919) Painter. Born in Paris, he was educated at Westminster and at Ipswich, and in 1857 was a pupil in the atelier of **Gleyre**. He shared a studio with **Lamont** and du Maurier and exhibited in the Royal Academy from 1861 until his death. In 1871 he became Slade Professor, taking the newly founded Chair at University College London. In 1896 he became President of the Royal Academy and remained as such until 1918. He was a brother-in-law of **Burne-Jones** and the uncle of Rudyard **Kipling**.

LORRIMER in George Du Maurier, *Trilby* (1894)

'In *Trilby*, Poynter was Lorrimer, the "industrious apprentice"' (Gordon Fleming, 1978, *The Young Whistler*, p. 131).

PRATT, Herbert (1841–1915) After he qualified as a doctor at Harvard University in 1868, he spent a brief period in practice and then spent the next forty years travelling. He was a friend of William **James**, Henry James's brother.

GABRIEL NASH in Henry James, *The Tragic Muse* (1888–9)

'He was a most singular, most interesting type, and I shall certainly put him into a novel. I shall even make the portrait close and he won't mind' (*The Notebooks of Henry James*, 1961, ed. F.O. Matthiessen and K.B. Murdock, New York, p. 31). 'James embodied some of his characteristics and speeches in Gabriel Nash' (*Henry James Letters*, Vol. I: *1843–1875*, 1974, ed. Leon Edel, London: Macmillan, p. 293 n. 1).

PRATT, John Bridge (1833?–70) Son of Minot Pratt, of Concord, who had been one of the three directors of **Brook Farm** in 1844. He worked for an insurance firm, and in 1860 he married Anna **Alcott**.

JOHN BROOKE in Louisa M. Alcott, *Little Women* (1868) and sequels

'John would find a place as John Brooke, for the Pratts had come from Brook Farm' (M.B. Stern, 1952, *Louisa M. Alcott*, p. 175).

PRESTON, Dorset A village situated north of Weymouth Bay.

CRESTON in Thomas Hardy, *Desperate Remedies* (1871)

Identified in F.B. Pinion, 1968, *A Hardy Companion*, London: Macmillan.

PRESTON STRIKE In October 1853 the weavers of Preston went on strike for a 10 per cent increase in wages; the masters thereupon closed the mills, and the strike became a lock-out. The strikers were sustained by contributions from their comrades in other towns in Lancashire and from sympathizers all over the country, and in January 1854 Mark Lemon organized a benefit at Drury Lane for their funds. The subscriptions fell off, and the strike came to an end in April.

COKETOWN STRIKE in Charles Dickens, *Hard Times* (1854)

'There was one thing . . . which the choice of his subject made him anxious to verify . . . this was a strike in a manufacturing town. He had gone to Preston to see one at the end of January' (John Forster, 1928, *Life of Dickens*, ed. J.W.T. Ley, p. 567). When the *Illustrated London News* reported that 'the turn' of his new novel, to be called *Hard Times*, had been suggested by this visit, Dickens indignantly denied the connection (see D. Shusterman, 1957, 'Peter Cunningham, friend of Dickens', *The Dickensian* 53 (January): 30).

MILTON STRIKE in Elizabeth Gaskell, *North and South* (1855)

'*North and South* . . . certainly draws on newspaper accounts of the events in Preston' (H.I. Dutton and J.E. King, 1981, '*Ten Per Cent and No Surrender!*': *the Preston strike, 1853–4*, p. 199).

PRICE, Cornell (1835–1910) Educated at King Edward's School, Birmingham, where he formed a lifelong friendship with **Burne-Jones**. In 1860 he was a member of the Morris, **Rossetti** and **Swinburne** circle in London, and from 1860 to 1864 he was a private tutor in Russia. He was on the staff at Haileybury from 1864 until 1874, whereupon he became Headmaster of the United Services College, Westward Ho!, a position he held until 1895.

THE HEAD in Rudyard Kipling, *Stalky & Co.* (1899)

'He was known . . . as "Bates", and immortalized as the "Head" in *Stalky & Co.*' (H.A. Tapp, 1948, 'Rudyard Kipling and his old school', *The Kipling Journal* 15 (87): 15). Also identified in the caption to a photograph reproduced in the June 1981 issue of *The Kipling Journal*: 'Masters at the United Services College . . . in Kipling's day' (*The Kipling Journal* 48 (218): 21).

PRICE, Henry Blackwood An Ulsterman, he was Assistant Manager of the Eastern Telegraph Company in Trieste during the period 1905–15, when James Joyce lived there, and became one of Joyce's friends. 'Remember', he wrote to Joyce in 1912, 'that Sir John Blackwood died in the act of putting on his top boots in order to go to Dublin to vote against the Union.'

GARRETT DEASY in James Joyce, *Ulysses* (1922)

'[Francis Irwin's] personality is merged with that of . . . Henry Blackwood Price' (Richard Ellmann, 1966, *James Joyce*, London: Oxford Paperbacks, pp. 158, 159). Mr Deasy's letter is a parody of one by Price that Joyce forwarded to the *Evening Telegraph* on his behalf in 1912. The text is to be found in ibid., p. 337. *See also* **Irwin**, Francis.

PRICE, Stephen He was a member of the **Garrick Club** in London in the 1840s.

CAPTAIN SHINDY in W.M. Thackeray, *The Book of Snobs* (1848)

'[Thackeray] had . . . in his *Book of Snobs* . . . under the pseudonym of Captain Shindy, given an exact sketch of a former [club] member, Mr Stephen Price, reproducing Mr Price's frequent and well-known phrases' (Edmund Yates, 1884, *Edmund Yates: his recollections and experiences*, Vol. II, London: R. Bentley & Son, p. 16).

PRICE, Uvedale (1747–1829) Writer on the picturesque and the landscape garden. He was a close friend of Charles James Fox, with whom he travelled in Italy and Switzerland; they visited Voltaire at Ferney in 1768. His principal work was *An Essay on the Picturesque as Compared with the Sublime and Beautiful* (1794–8).

SIR PATRICK O'PRISM in Thomas Love Peacock, *Headlong Hall* (1816)

'. . . based on Sir Uvedale Price' (*The Novels of T.L. Peacock*, 1948, ed. David Garnett, London: Rupert Hart-Davis, p. 21 n. 2).

PRICE, William Samson (1817?–1912) At the time of his death he was the oldest lawyer in Philadelphia. In his youth he knew Edgar Allan Poe.

MR PIERCE in John Dos Passos, *U.S.A.* (1938)

'Quite clearly [Mr Price was the model for] the ancient Mr Pierce of Camera Eye 15' (J.N. Westerhoven, 1976-7, 'Autobiographical elements in the camera eye', *American Literature* 48: 347).

JUDGE JOSEPH THATCHER in John Dos Passos, *Chosen Country* (1951)

'When the elder Dos Passos was a young man he enlisted . . . in a Pennsylvania regiment during the Civil War. . . . On his return to Philadelphia he worked as an office boy for an attorney named Price, the model for Judge Thatcher' (Westerhoven, op. cit., p. 347).

PRICHARD, John Samuel A tailor of Gloucester. The story of the waistcoat was told to Beatrix Potter in 1894, while on a visit to her cousin Caroline Hutton in Gloucestershire. Miss Hutton 'had the [story] of Miss Lucy, of Gloucester, who had it of the tailor' (Leslie Linden, 1971, *A History of the Writings of Beatrix Potter*, p. 111).

THE TAILOR OF GLOUCESTER in Beatrix Potter, *The Tailor of Gloucester* (1902)

'What really happened was told . . . by Mrs Prichard, the tailor's wife' (ibid.). The tailor was commissioned to make a waistcoat for the new mayor of Gloucester for the annual procession of the Root, Fruit and Grain Society. He started work, but left the waistcoat unfinished on Saturday morning. His two assistants came to the shop secretly and worked until the waistcoat was finished but for one buttonhole; pinning a note – 'No more twist' – on the waistcoat, they crept away. The tailor, returning on Monday, put it in his window with a little sign, reading 'Come to Prichard where the waistcoats are made at night by the fairies.' 'When Beatrix Potter heard this story she was intrigued . . . at once she felt that she must make [it] into a story. She would change the fairies into . . . mice but the mayor and the tailor should remain true to life' (ibid., p. 112).

PRICHARD, Williams ap *See* **Williams ap Prichard**.

PRICKETT, Lancelot George Engineer and bridge builder. He was appointed Assistant Engineer in the Public Works Department in India in 1878. He died of cholera.

HITCHCOCK in Rudyard Kipling, 'The Bridge Builders' (1898)

'Hitchcock was . . . L.G. Prickett' (J.R. Bell to H.F. Storey of the Public Works Dept, India, 23 April 1903, reported in *The Kipling Journal* 16 (92): 15).

PRICKETT, Mary (1833?–1916?) Governess to the **Liddell** girls, daughters of H.G. Liddell, in 1871 she married Charles Foster, owner of the **Mitre Hotel** in Oxford.

THE RED QUEEN in Lewis Carroll, *Through the Looking-Glass* (1872)

'The Red Queen . . . is based on Miss Prickett (Dodgson described the Red Queen as "the concentrated essence of all governesses" and there was an obvious allusion . . . until the 1897 revision, when the Rose – Alice's small sister Rhoda – describes her as "one of the thorny kind": and Miss Prickett's nickname was "Pricks")' (R. Lancelyn Green, 1969, 'Alice's rail-journey', *Notes and Queries* 214: 218).

PRINGLE, Alexander (1791–1857) He was MP for Selkirkshire in 1830–32 and 1837–46.

TADPOLE in Benjamin Disraeli, *Coningsby* (1844)

Identified in a key in *Notes and Queries* (8th series) 3 (13 May 1893): 363. *See also under* **Bright**, John.

PRINSEP, Valentine Cameron ('Val') (1838–1904) Painter. Born in Calcutta, he was intimate from his youth with G.F. Watts, who lived in his parents' house, Little Holland House in Kensington, London. He was a pupil of **Gleyre** in Paris, and from 1862 exhibited at the Royal Academy, becoming a Royal Academician in 1894. He married Florence Leyland, daughter of F.R. **Leyland**, the owner of the Peacock Room.

TALBOT ('TAFFY') WYNNE in George Du Maurier, *Trilby* (1894)

'Du Maurier's "Taffy" in *Trilby*, a character inspired by Val Prinsep, R.A.' (Montague Weekley, 1959, 'A red-headed Bohemian', *Listener* 62 (November 19): 892). *See also* **Rowley**, Joe.

PRIOR, 'Donkey' He was a dwarf who hired out donkeys in Bath in the 1840s.

DANIEL QUILP in Charles Dickens, *The Old Curiosity Shop* (1840–1)

'Dickens loved to wander about the back streets of Bath, picking up the queer names which appear so often in his books. We [Mrs Paynter and her daughters] introduced him to the original of Quilp, a frightful little dwarf named Prior, who let donkeys on hire, and whose temper was as ugly as his person. He always carried with him a thick stick, with which he belaboured impartially his donkeys and his wife' (*Sketches from the Diaries of Rose, Lady Graves Sawle*, 1908, p. 55). Lady Graves Sawle was born Rose Paynter, and spent her early life in Bath; her mother was the half-sister of Landor's Rose Aylmer. *See also* **Dickens**, Charles; **Grimaldi**, Giuseppe.

PRIOR, James Michael Leathes (b. 1927) Politician. Educated at Charterhouse, where he was a contemporary of Simon Raven, and at Cambridge. He was an MP from 1959 onwards, and was Minister of Agriculture from 1970 to 1974.

PETER MORRISON in Simon Raven, *Alms for Oblivion* (1965–76)

'Raven now discloses that he has put Prior into several novels. . . . The novels are the ten *Alms for Oblivion* books. . . . The Prior character is Peter Morrison' (*Sunday Times* (22 May 1977): 13).

PRITCHETT, Walter (d. *c.*1964) Born in Kirbymoorside, Yorkshire, he was the son of a Congregational minister; in later life he became a Christian Scientist. He was V.S. Pritchett's father.

PHILIP BELUNCLE in V.S. Pritchett, *Mr Beluncle* (1951)

'I said that he [Walter Pritchett] knew that I did not believe in his religion. "I know that", he said. "And I know you've written that novel about it, *Mr Beluncle*, with me in it . . . I don't mind at all!"' (V.S. Pritchett, 1971, *Midnight Oil*, p. 247).

PÜCKLER-MUSKAU, Prince (1785–1871) German writer. He was the author of books on travel and of one work on landscape gardening; he laid out two splendid gardens on his estates at Muskau and Schloss Branitz, near Kottbus. In 1832 he published *A Tour in England*.

COUNT SMORLTORK in Charles Dickens, *The Pickwick Papers* (1836-7)

Identified in a manuscript list of characters inserted into the copy of E.W. Pugh, 1912, *The Charles Dickens Originals* held in the Dexter Collection in the British Library (Dex. 28) in London. *See also* von **Raumer**, Friedrich.

PUDDLETOWN, Dorset   A village situated about five miles north-east of Dorchester. Thomas Hardy's cousin, Tryphena **Sparks** lived there.

WEATHERBURY in Thomas Hardy, Wessex novels and tales (1871–95)

Identified on a map prepared by Thomas Hardy which hangs in the Dorset County Museum, Dorchester. *See under* **Abbotsbury**.

PUDDLETOWN HEATH, Dorset   A heath that extends eastwards for about fourteen miles, from Higher and Lower Bockhampton, to the area north of Wareham and Poole Harbour. It directly bordered the back of the Hardys' cottage south of Puddletown.

EGDON HEATH in Thomas Hardy, Wessex novels and tales (1871–95)

'Under the general name of "Egdon Heath" . . . are united or typified heaths of various real names, to the number of at least a dozen'('T.H.', 1895, preface to *The Return of the Native*, p. v). Identified on a map prepared by Thomas Hardy which hangs in the Dorset County Museum, Dorchester. *See under* **Abbotsbury**.

PUGH, Matthew Henry   (1852?–1914)   Educated at Rishworth Grammar School, Yorkshire, where his father was Head Master, and at St John's College, Cambridge. He was Assistant Master at the United Services College, Westward Ho!, from 1876 to 1893, and at Cranleigh School from 1893 until 1905. He died in Bristol.

MR PROUT in Rudyard Kipling, *Stalky & Co.* (1899)

'. . . their housemaster, Mr M.H. Pugh ("Prout" in *Stalky & Co.*). A suspicious, humourless, well-meaning man' (Charles Carrington, 1955, *Rudyard Kipling: his life and work*, p. 32). Also identified in the caption to a photograph reproduced in the June 1981 issue of *The Kipling Journal*: 'Masters at the United Services College . . . in Kipling's day' (*The Kipling Journal* 48 (218): 21).

PURDIE, Tom   (1777?–1829)   He entered Sir Walter Scott's service at Ashestiel in 1804, becoming the Manager of the farm and remaining with Scott to the end of his life; his brother-in-law, Peter Matheson, was Scott's coachman.

CRISTAL NIXON in Sir Walter Scott, *Redgauntlet* (1824)

'At starting we were joined by . . . Tom Purdie – and I may save myself the trouble of any attempt to describe his appearance, for his master has given us an inimitably true one in introducing a certain personage in his *Redgauntlet*:– "He was, perhaps, sixty years old; yet his brow was not much furrowed, and his jet black hair was only grizzled, not whitened. . . . All his motions spoke strength unabated. . . . A hard and harsh countenance; eyes far sunk under projecting eye-brows . . . a wide mouth, furnished from ear to ear with a range of unimpaired teeth of uncommon whiteness. . . ." Equip this figure in Scott's cast-off green jacket, white hat, and drab trousers . . . and Tom Purdie . . . stands before us' (*Memoirs of Sir Walter Scott*, 1900, ed. J.G. Lockhart, Vol. III, London: Macmillan, p. 363).

PURGSTALL, Jane Anne, Countess (1760?–1835) Sister of George Cranstoune, later Lord Corehouse, the friend of Sir Walter Scott, and sister of Helen, who was married to the philosopher Dugald Stewart. In 1797 she married Count Wenzel Gottfried Purgstall and lived in Austria until her death. Previous to her marriage, she kept house for her brother and was Scott's confidante during his attachment to Miss **Belsches**.

DIANA VERNON in Sir Walter Scott, *Rob Roy* (1817)

In the autumn of 1834 Captain Basil Hall, along with his wife and children on their way from Naples to England, paid a visit to the Countess Purgstall at her home at Schloss Hainfeld in Styria. They remained there until her death the following spring, and Captain Hall subsequently wrote an account of the visit, and of the Countess, who was old and totally bed-ridden although she had enjoyed undiminished intellectual vigour at least when they first arrived. '[W]e made out almost to demonstration, that one of the most original and spirited of all his female characters, no less a personage than Die [sic] Vernon, must have been sketched from this very lady' (Basil Hall, 1836, *Schloss Hainfeld*, Edinburgh, pp. 35–6). 'Captain Hall's conjecture of her having been the original of Diana Vernon, appeared to myself from the first chimerical; and I have since heard those who knew her best in the days of her intercourse with Sir Walter, express the same opinion in the most decided manner' (*Memoirs of Sir Walter Scott*, 1900, ed. J.G Lockhart, Vol. III, London: Macmillan, pp. 510–11).

PUSEY, Edward Bouverie (1800–82) Educated at Eton and at Christ Church, Oxford, he went on to study oriental languages and biblical criticism in Germany from 1825 to 1827. In 1822 he became a Fellow of Oriel College, Oxford, where he became the intimate friend of **Newman** and Keble. In 1828 he was Regius Professor of Hebrew at Oxford, and was later associated with Newman and Keble in the writing and publishing of *Tracts for the Times* (1833 ff.). From 1841, he was the leader of the Oxford Movement, and in later life he engaged in conflict with the spread of latitudinarian ideas. In 1862, before the Chancellor's court, he charged **Jowett** with teaching opinions that conflicted with the doctrines of the Church of England. He attempted to bring about the union of the Churches of Rome and of England, and of the Church of England with the Wesleyans and the Eastern Church.

DR SEYDON in W.H. Mallock, *The New Republic* (1877)

'Dr Seydon [is] a composite figure based on Pusey and Liddon. . . . And it is Pusey who is being glanced at in Laurence's remark that Seydon "prevented Dr Jenkinson being made a bishop"' (J. Lucas, 1975, Introd. to *The New Republic*, Leicester, p. 24). *See also* **Liddon**, H.P.

PYNE, Mary She married Harry **Kemp** in New York, and in 1917 became friendly with Theodore Dreiser and Hutchins **Hapgood**. She suffered from tuberculosis.

ESTHER NORN in Theodore Dreiser, 'Esther Norn', *A Gallery of Women* (1929)

' . . . a batch of stories about women in his life . . . Mary Pyne ("Esther Norn") among them' (W.A. Swanberg, 1965, *Dreiser*, New York, p. 244).

Q

The *QUARTERLY REVIEW* Founded in 1809 as a Tory counterblast to the Whig *Edinburgh Review*, it was published by John Murray and warmly supported by Sir Walter **Scott**. The first Editor was William **Gifford**, and J.G. **Lockhart** was the third.

THE *ATTACK-ALL REVIEW* in Benjamin Disraeli, *Vivian Grey* (1826-7)

Identified in a key given in a pamphlet published in 1827 by William Marsh. This key is discussed by Lucien Wolf in his notes to *Vivian Grey* (1904 (centenary edn), Vol. II, p. 364), with the conclusion that Disraeli was not responsible for the key. For Mr Vamp, Editor of the *Legitimate Review* in T.L. Peacock, 1817, *Melincourt, see* **Gifford**, William.

QUEENS HOUSE, Chelsea, London Located on Cheyne Walk, and formerly known as Tudor House, it was built by John Witt and was the home of Dante Gabriel **Rossetti** from 1862 until his death in 1882. Nikolaus Pevsner describes it as 'well preserved in its original appearance of 1717 with the exception of the painful bay window'.

COUNTESS OF CHELSEY'S HOUSE in W.M. Thackeray, *The History of Henry Esmond* (1852)

'Supposedly the model for the Countess of Chelsey's home in ... Henry Esmond' (G.H. Fleming, 1971, *That Ne'er Shall Meet Again: Rossetti, Millais, Hunt*, p. 233).

D'ARCY'S HOUSE in Theodore Watts-Dunton, *Aylwin* (1899)

'On page 204 of the illustrated edition [of *Aylwin*] an exact picture has been given by Rossetti's pupil, Dunn, of the famous studio at 16 Cheyne Walk' (*Aylwin*, 1911 (World's Classics), App. I, p. 497).

QUINTANA, Juanito (b. 1892?) He was the proprietor of the Hotel Quintana in Pamplona where Ernest Hemingway and his friends stayed in 1924 and 1925. He was forced to leave his hotel during the civil war and he lost everything; he spent eight years in exile in France before returning to Spain to a flat in San Sebastian. He returned every year to the fiesta at Pamplona, as 'an honoured guest' (see L.R. Kroontz, 1972, '"Montoya" remembers *The Sun Also Rises*', in B.D. Sarason, *Hemingway and The Sun Set*, Washington, DC, pp. 207–11). A passionate *aficionado*, Hemingway remained in touch with him and saw him in Spain in 1953 and 1954, and again in 1959, when Quintana helped Hemingway to cover all the bullfights in which Antonio Ordóñez and Domínguin took part, thus helping to supply material for 'The Dangerous Summer'.

JUANITO MONTOYA in Ernest Hemingway, *The Sun Also Rises* (1926)

'Here in San Sebastian I found Juanito Quintana, the Montoya of SAR' (Kroontz, op. cit., p. 209). The interview took place apparently in 1970.

QUINTANILLA, Luis (b. 1900?) French-born Mexican poet, academic and diplomat. He became friends with Lawrence during the latter's third stay in Mexico from November 1924 to March 1925.

MIRABAL in D.H. Lawrence, *The Plumed Serpent* (1926)

'This character is probably based, in part, on Luis Quintanilla' (*The Plumed Serpent*, 1983, ed. Ronald G. Walker, Harmondsworth: Penguin, p. 489 n. 15).

QUINTANILLA, Pepe He was the Chief Executioner of Madrid in 1937.

ANTONIO in Ernest Hemingway, 'The Fifth Column', *The Fifth Column and the First Forty-nine Stories* (1938)

'I was having lunch with Ernest Hemingway [in Madrid] when a bombardment started. . . . At the next table I noticed a fastidious-looking man dressed from head to toe in dove grey . . . "That", said Hemingway, "is the chief executioner of Madrid." Ernest invited him to join us and he accepted' (Virginia Cowles, 1941, *Looking for Trouble*, p. 34). In the conversation that followed, Hemingway pressed the man with questions, and as they left the restaurant said 'A *chic* type, eh? Now remember, he's mine.' Miss Cowles was not surprised when many months later she read *The Fifth Column*, to find the conversation reproduced almost verbatim with Quintanilla renamed Antonio.

QUORN, Leicestershire

BELDOVER in D.H. Lawrence, *The Rainbow* (1915)

'Beldover is the village of Quorn in Leicestershire' (Ada Lawrence and G. Stuart Calder, 1931, *Young Lorenzo: early life of D.H. Lawrence*, Florence, p. 274). *See also* **Eastwood**.

R

RACHEL, Éliza (Élisa Félix) (1821–58) Tragic actress. Born in Switzerland of poor Jewish parents, she was taken to Paris in 1830 and made her début in 1837 in *La Vendéenne*. She became famous in June 1938 when she appeared at the Théâtre-Français as Camille in *Horace*, and later appeared in London, where Charlotte Brontë saw her perform.

Vashti in Charlotte Brontë, *Villette* (1853)

'Apart from Thackeray's weekly lectures the high-light of Charlotte [Brontë's] London visit in 1851 was the performances of Rachel, the great French tragedienne. . . . Charlotte's comments . . . in the famous passage in *Villette* where she describes the performance of "Vashti", convey the fascination . . . that the great French artist awoke in her' (Winifred Gérin, 1969, *Charlotte Brontë*, Oxford, pp. 480–1).

RACOWITZ, Count

Prince Marco in George Meredith, *The Tragic Comedians* (1880)

'Count Racowitz was Prince Marko' (A. Lionel Stevenson, 1954, *The Ordeal of George Meredith*, London: Peter Owen, p. 239).

von RACOWITZA, Helene (1844–1911) Née von Dönniges, her father was in the service of Prince Max and Prince Louis of Bavaria. She married Yanko von **Racowitza**, who died within a year, and in 1877, after a long liaison, she married Sergei Schewitsch. She committed suicide.

Clotilde von Rüdiger in George Meredith, *The Tragic Comedians* (1880)

'In *The Tragic Comedians* [Meredith] shows the genuine and growing richness of love between a man and a woman (in history Ferdinand Lassalle and Helene von Dönniges). . . . Meredith's sources were Helene von Racowitza's *Meine Beziehungen zu Ferdinand Lassalle* and J.M. Ludlow's article "Ferdinand Lassalle, the German Social Democrat" in the "Fortnightly Review"' (Gillian Beer, 1970, *Meredith: a change of masks*, p. 137).

RADFORD, Dollie (1860–1920) Poet and essayist. Born Caroline Maitland, the daughter of an ironmonger in St Pancras, London, she became a member of the **Fabian Society** and knew Karl Marx and his family. In 1883 she married Ernest Radford, the poet, and in 1915 she became friends with D.H. and Frieda **Lawrence** accommodating them in London in 1917 after they were expelled from Cornwall; she lent them her cottage in Hermitage, Berkshire, in 1918–19.

Hattie Redburn in D.H. Lawrence, *Kangaroo* (1923)

'Dollie Radford was constantly at his beck and call, getting little thanks even when providing him with accommodation in London or in Berkshire. In *Kangaroo* she received shabby treatment in the person of Hattie Redburn' (E. Delavenay, 1972, *D.H. Lawrence: the man and his work, 1885–1919*, p. 285).

RADFORD, Margaret (b. 1890) Youngest daughter of Ernest and Dollie **Radford**.

JILL BANFORD in D.H. Lawrence, 'The Fox' (1923)

'Jill Banford may also be partly taken from Dollie Radford's daughter, Margaret, whom Lawrence disliked' (H.T. Moore, 1960, *The Intelligent Heart: the story of D.H. Lawrence*, Harmondsworth: Penguin, p. 304; originally published 1955, London: Heinemann). *See also* **Lambert**, Cecily.

RADIGUET, Raymond (1903–23) French poet and novelist. He was an intimate friend of Jean Cocteau from 1919 until his death from typhoid in 1923, although in the last days of his life he described himself as affianced to Bronia **Perlmutter**.

MONSIEUR X in Djuna Barnes, 'The Grande Malade' (1962)

'Djuna Barnes's short story, "The Little Girl Continues", describes Radiguet's death' (Robert McAlmon, 1970, *Being Geniuses Together*, rev. Kay Boyle, p. 115 n. 2). 'The Grande Malade' was first published as 'The Little Girl Continues' in *This Quarter* 2 (2); reprinted in *Spillway* (1962).

RAISBECK, Kenneth (1899?–1931) The ninth child in a middle-Western family of modest means, he went to Harvard on a scholarship and later became an assistant to G.P. **Baker**. He became a friend of Thomas Wolfe in 1920, and when the two met again in December 1924 they quarrelled after a month. His 1931 play, *Rock Me Julie*, failed and the talent he had shown earlier in his life came to nothing. He was homosexual and died in circumstances that suggested murder.

FRANCIS STARWICK in Thomas Wolfe, *Of Time and the River* (1935)

'Kenneth Raisbeck . . . was the model for . . . Francis Starwick' (R.S. Kennedy, 1962, *The Window of Memory: the literary career of Thomas Wolfe*, Chapel Hill, NC, p. 70 n. 18).

RALSTON, William (1828–89) Born in London, he was the son of a wealthy Calcutta merchant who dissipated the whole of his fortune in an attempt to prove himself heir to the Ralston estate in Ayrshire; when the family fortune was exhausted, the daughter of the house took up the pleadings, appearing on one occasion before a committee of the House of Lords. William Shedden was forced to abandon a career at the Bar; he changed his name to Ralston and in 1853 entered the Department of Printed Books in the British Museum library, London. He studied Russian and in 1869 published a translation of Turgenev's *Lisa* (later known as *A Nest of Gentlefolk*), becoming a close friend of the author. In 1873 he retired from the Museum and engaged in literary journalism.

GEORGE HEIMANN in Ford Madox Ford, *The Marsden Case* (1923)

'I am sending you a copy of the *Marsden Case* . . . the subject is not a very good one, though it's one that now haunted me certainly ever since I was eighteen on and off. It's the story of Ralston, the first translator of Turgenev – a man I liked very much' (to Edgar Jepson, 8 May 1923, reproduced in *Letters of Ford Madox Ford*, 1965, ed. R.M. Ludwig, Princeton, p. 149). Ralston's translation of

Lisa was in fact preceded by *A Sportsman's Sketches* (1855), *Fathers and Sons* (1867) and *Smoke* (1868), all by different translators and in two cases from the French versions.

RAMÉ, Louis Wine merchant. Resident in Bury St Edmunds, Suffolk, he was the father of Ouida. He was of French origin, but no other details of his life are known.

COUNT D'AVESNES in Ouida, *Friendship* (1878)

'[I]n 1878 he walked into . . . *Friendship* in which the heroine describes her father, the Count d'Avesnes' (Monica Stirling, 1957, *The Fine and the Wicked: the life and times of Ouida*, p. 24).

RAMPOLLA, Mariano, Marchese del Tindaro (1843–1913) Italian prelate. After entering the Diplomatic Service of the Roman Curia in 1869, he became a cardinal in 1887 and was Papal Secretary of State from 1887 until 1903. He was a champion of the temporal power of the Pope. 'A tall, common looking young priest; he was treated with immense distinction, candles being carried before him when he arrived and departed, which, seeing the palace was brilliantly illuminated, seemed to me somewhat unnecessary' (entry for 1890, in Lord Ronald Sutherland Gower, 1902, *My Old Diaries*).

CARDINAL RAGNA in F.W. Rolfe, *Hadrian VII* (1904)

'He describes Vatican officials like . . . Rampolla (as Ragna)' (Shane Leslie, 1923, 'Frederick Baron Corvo', *London Mercury* 8 (47): 514).

RAMSAY OF OCHTERTYRE, John (1736–1814) Born in Edinburgh, he was the son of a Writer to the Signet and qualified as an advocate. In 1760 he retired to manage Ochtertyre, which had been owned by his family since 1591. A liberal and improving landlord, he was much influenced by his neighbour Lord Kames, and when he died he left ten bulky volumes of notes of reading, recollections, and personal experiences. He was visited at Ochtertyre by Burns, of whom he wrote: 'I never witnessed such flashes of intellectual brightness as from him', and in 1793 by the young Walter Scott, with whom he maintained an acquaintanceship until he died.

JONATHAN OLDBUCK in Sir Walter Scott, *The Antiquary* (1816)

'He certainly stood with George Constable as the model from which the character of Monkbarns is painted. When I knew him he was an old man, and . . . had fallen, when alone, into slovenly habits of dress. When receiving company his appointments were those of a gentleman of the old school – a coat, usually blue, with bright metal buttons, a high collar, and lace frills at the wrist. I think he wore hair-powder, but I am not quite sure, though of his carefully tied queue or pigtail I have a clear remembrance. Breeches and blue stockings, with silver buckles in his shoes, were also worn on these occasions. At other times his legs would be encased in worsted stockings, to which it appeared as if he sometimes forgot to append garters' (G.R. Gleig, quoted in the Introd. to J. Ramsay of Ochtertyre, 1888, *Scotland and Scotsmen in the Eighteenth Century*, ed. Alexander Allardyce, Vol. I, p. xviii). Gleig, perhaps the only survivor at that date of those who had known Mr Ramsay, furnished these reminiscences to Allardyce. *See also* **Clerk of Eldin**, John; **Constable**, George, the Elder; **Gordon**, Alexander.

RASPE, Rudolf Eric (1737–1794) Born in Hanover and educated in Göttingen and Leipzig, he fled to England in 1775 after purloining the Landgrave of Hesse's antique gems and medals. He was the author of the original *Baron Munchausen* (1785), and in 1792 he became a storekeeper at a Cornish mine. He died at Mucross, County Kerry, Ireland.

HERMAN DOUSTERSWIVEL in Sir Walter Scott, *The Antiquary* (1816)

'Obtained money from Sir John Sinclair of Ulster by pretending to discover gold and silver on his estate, 1791, an incident commemorated by Sir Walter Scott in the "Antiquary"' (*Concise Dictionary of National Biography*, 1969, Oxford, p. 1088). The whole episode is discussed in Coleman O. Parsons, 1943, 'Sir John Sinclair's Raspe and Scott's Dousterswivel', *Notes and Queries* 184 (30 January): 62 ff.).

RASPUTIN, Grigori Efimovitch (1871?–1916) Born in Siberia, he left his family in 1904 and lived as a holy man, winning a reputation among the peasants. In 1907 he was in St Petersburg, where he gained an ascendency over the Tsar and Tsarina and interfered in political affairs. He was notoriously ignorant and debauched and was assassinated by a group of Russian noblemen.

BAZHAKULOFF in Norman Douglas, *South Wind* (1917)

'Father John of Cronstadt and Rasputin have subscribed their share of elements to the formation of the Russian "Messiah"' (Introd. to *South Wind*, 1942). *See also* **John of Cronstadt**, Father.

RATTIGAN, William He was a successful lawyer in Lahore in 1882 and was later a member of the Governor General's Legislative Council.

KIM in Rudyard Kipling, *Kim* (1901)

'It would be pleasing . . . if William Rattigan played some part [as Kipling's patron at the start of his career in Lahore]. Certainly, I believe Kipling owed another more important debt to Rattigan, for his grandson, Sir Terence Rattigan, tells me that his grandfather was the son of an illiterate private in the Indian Army who had to make his mark on his enlistment papers. By some means his son got to the High School in Agra in the eighteen-fifties and subsequently to King's College, London, and to Göttingen University. Surely here may be a factual foundation . . . for the Irish boy Kimball O'Hara's career' (Angus Wilson, 1977, *The Strange Ride of Rudyard Kipling*, p. 99). *See also* **Beatty**, Frank A.M.

von RAUMER, Friedrich (1781–1873) German historian. Professor of History at the University of Berlin from 1819 to 1847, he became a member of the German Parliament in 1848. He visited England in 1835 and 1836, and in March 1835 published *England in 1835*.

COUNT SMORLTORK in Charles Dickens, *The Pickwick Papers* (1836-7)

See K. Tillotson, 1957, 'Dickens's Count Smorltork', *Times Literary Supplement* (22 November): 712; Professor Tillotson puts forward arguments for accepting Professor Raumer as a possible part-original for Count Smorltork. *See also* **Pückler-Muskau**, Prince.

RAUSCHENBUSCH, Walter (1861–1918) American Baptist clergyman. The Leader of Reform Darwinism, he studied in Germany and England and in 1897–1918 was a leader of the Christian Socialist movement.

HENRY KUYKENDALL in Frederick Buecher, *The Return of Ansell Gibbs* (1958)

'Kuykendall suggests Walter Rauschenbusch' (Joseph Blotner, 1966, *The Modern American Political Novel*, Austin, Tex., p. 333 n. 44).

RAVELSTON HOUSE, Edinburgh Located in Corstorphine parish, it was the seat of the Keiths of Ravelston. Scott's maternal grandmother's sister was a Mrs Keith of Ravelston and he knew the place from childhood.

TULLY-VEOLAN in Sir Walter Scott, *Waverley* (1814)

'That picturesque old mansion, which furnished him in after-days with many of the features of his Tully-veolan, and whose venerable gardens, with their massive hedges of yew and holly, he always considered as the ideal of art' (*Memoirs of Sir Walter Scott*, 1900, ed. J.G. Lockhart, Vol. I, London: Macmillan, p. 72). *See also* **Craighall**.

RAWES, Robert Booth Owner of a small private school in Bromley, Kent, during the first half of the nineteenth century; after the school's collapse, one of the assistant masters founded the Bromley Academy, where H.G. **Wells** was a pupil in the 1870s.

SAMUEL PICKWICK in Charles Dickens, *The Pickwick Papers* (1836-7)

'There had originally been a school in Bromley owned by . . . Robert Booth Rawes, who is said to have provided Dickens with the original for Mr Pickwick' (N. Mackenzie and J. Mackenzie, 1973, *The Time Traveller: the life of H.G. Wells*, p. 25). *See also* **Foster**, John.

READING, Berkshire

ALDBRICKHAM in Thomas Hardy, Wessex novels and tales (1871–95)

Identified on a map prepared by Thomas Hardy which hangs in the Dorset County Museum, Dorchester. *See under* **Abbotsbury**.

BELFORD REGIS in Mary Russell Mitford, *Belford Regis* (1835)

'. . . *Belford Regis* (the name being an alias for Reading)' (P.F. Skottawe, 1969, 'Thomas Talfourd and David Copperfield', *The Dickensian* 65 (January): 30).

READING SCHOOL, Berkshire A grammar school founded in 1125; it was attended by the author T.N. **Talfourd** when it was under the headmastership of Richard **Valpy**.

DR STRONG'S SCHOOL in Charles Dickens, *David Copperfield* (1849–50)

'The present writer has no doubt whatever that Dr Strong's school was based upon Talfourd's old school, Reading' (P.F. Skottowe, 1969, 'Thomas Talfourd and David Copperfield', *The Dickensian* 65 (January): 29). 'If any school furnished hints for Dr Strong's, Reading has strong claims; but there need have been no original for that idealized institution' (N. Burgis, 1981, Introd. to *David Copperfield*, Oxford, p. xxxviii). *See also* **King's School**.

REASON, Robert (1763–1819) A shoemaker of Dorchester.

RObert Penny in Thomas Hardy, *Under the Greenwood Tree* (1872)

'Although Robert Reason had died twenty-one years before the birth of the author of *Under the Greenwood Tree*, he was faithfully described . . . as Mr Penny, the shoemaker, Hardy having heard so much of him from the inhabitants of Brockhampton' (F.E. Hardy, 1972, *The Life of Thomas Hardy, 1840–1928*, p. 429).

RED HOUSE, Gomersal, Yorkshire Nikolaus Pevsner gives a brief description of The Red House in *Yorkshire: West Riding* (*Buildings of England* series, Harmondsworth: Penguin, p. 223).

Briarmains in Charlotte Brontë, *Shirley* (1849)

'Briarmains, pictured as the dwelling of Mr Yorke . . . is based on a very close study of the actual house of Mr Joshua Taylor, the original of Mr Hiram Yorke' (Herbert Wroot, 1935, *The Sources of Charlotte Brontës Novels: persons and places*, Shipley, Yorks., p. 83).

REDESDALE, David Bertram Ogilvy Freeman-Mitford, Lord (1878–1958) 2nd Baron Redesdale, in 1904 he married Sidney Bowles (**Redesdale**, below); he was the father of Nancy, Jessica and Unity **Mitford**, Deborah, the Duchess of **Devonshire**, and Diana, who married Sir Oswald **Mosley**.

Uncle Matthew in Nancy Mitford, *The Pursuit of Love* (1945)

See below.

General Murgatroyd in Nancy Mitford, *Highland Fling* (1931)

'"You *can't* publish that [*Highland Fling*] under your own name", my mother insisted . . . for not only did thinly disguised aunts, uncles and family friends people the pages . . . but there, larger than life-size, felicitously named "General Murgatroyd" was Farve' (Jessica Mitford, 1960, *Hons and Rebels*, p. 30). 'As for Farve, he rather loved being General Murgatroyd' (ibid., p. 31). 'In subsequent years Nancy continued to perfect the process of capturing him and imprisoning him between the covers of novels, sometimes as General Murgatroyd, later as the terrifying Uncle Matthew of *The Pursuit of Love*' (ibid.).

REDESDALE, Sidney Freeman-Mitford, Lady (1880–1963) Daughter of Thomas Gibson Bowles, MP, in 1904 she married the 2nd Lord **Redesdale**. She was the mother of Jessica, Nancy and Unity **Mitford**, Deborah, Duchess of **Devonshire**, and Diana Mosley, who was married to Sir Oswald **Mosley**.

Lady Alconleigh ('Aunt Sadie') in Nancy Mitford, *The Pursuit of Love* (1945)

'Everybody knows that you are Aunt Sadie who is a character in the round and is you in middle life exactly as you were' (Nancy Mitford to her mother, after the publication of *The Water Beetle* (1962, London: Hamish Hamilton), reproduced in Harold Acton, 1975, *Nancy Mitford: a memoir*, London: Hamilton, p. 128). 'We used to call my mother Sadie. Her real name was Sidney' (Nancy Mitford to Laura Propper of the Oxford University Press, unpublished MS).

REDRUTH, Cornwall A town located nine miles west of Truro.

REDRUTIN in Thomas Hardy, 'A Mere Interlude' (1913)

Identified in F.B. Pinion, 1968, *A Hardy Companion*, London: Macmillan.

REED, Cecil A friend of Scott Fitzgerald's when he was a boy in St Paul.

RIPLY BUCKNER in F. Scott Fitzgerald, 'A Night at the Fair' (1957)

'. . . in addition to Fitzgerald himself, . . . the important characters in this story [include] Cecil Reed, the model for Riply Buckner' (F. Scott Fitzgerald, 1957, *Afternoon of an Author*, introd. and notes by Arthur Mizener, Princeton, p. 15).

REED, John (1887–1920) American journalist and poet. Born in Portland, Oregon, he was educated at Harvard and in 1913 was on the staff of *The Masses*. In 1914 he was a war correspondent during the Mexican revolt, from 1914 to 1916 he was in Europe with armies on the Eastern Front, and he was in Russia during the revolution in 1917. He organized and led the Communist Party in the United States; he was indicted for sedition and escaped to Russia, where he died of typhus and was buried in the Kremlin.

JO HANCOCK in Max Eastman, *Venture* (1927)

'Jo Hancock, whose prototype is clearly John Reed, comes . . . to the village in the early 1910s. . . . He has started to work out a scheme to distribute freshly roasted coffee with the morning milk, a scheme which in actual life had been the creation of Eugene Boissevain, the future husband of Edna Millay. But . . . [a] strike breaks out in Paterson, New Jersey . . . and Jo . . . is drawn into the struggle as John Reed was' (Walter B. Rideout, 1956, *The Radical Novel in the United States, 1900–1954*, Cambridge, Mass., pp. 119–20).

REES, Goronwy (1909–1979) Journalist and miscellaneous writer. In 1931 he was a Fellow of All Souls College, Oxford.

EDDIE in Elizabeth Bowen, *The Death of the Heart* (1938)

'A later romance had much more definite results – it assisted her to write a novel. . . . Again, she had loved a younger man; but Goronwy was an unusually accomplished young man, since 1931 a Fellow of All Souls. . . . Though Eddie is clearly a composite personage, many of her friends . . . thought they recognized a brilliant likeness; and her alleged victim . . . was inspired to threaten legal action' (Peter Quennell, 1982, *Customs and Characters*, pp. 90, 91).

REES, Sir Richard (1900–70) Writer and painter. He was the editor of *The Adelphi* from 1930 to 1936 and published essays and reviews by Orwell, whom he knew as a close friend at Eton.

PHILIP RAVELSTON in George Orwell, *Keep the Aspidistra Flying* (1936)

'Orwell, Rees asserted, "had an essentially simple mind". ... But perhaps Orwell's mind was neither so simple nor so uncritically friendly, if we assume that "Ravelston" ... is even in part modelled on Sir Richard Rees' (Bernard Crick, 1980, *George Orwell: a life*, London: Secker & Warburg, p. 160).

REES, Rowland (1816–1902) Beginning life as a clerk to the Royal Engineers and serving in Gibraltar and Hong Kong, he came under the influence of William Rule, a Methodist missionary. In the 1840s he retired to Dover and worked as an architect and surveyor, reforming the town's sewerage system. In 1861 he was an engineer and architect to the Harbour Board, and in 1883 he became Mayor of Dover. He was the father of Katharine **Compton-Burnett**, Ivy's mother.

ANDREW STACE THE ELDER in I. Compton-Burnett, *Brothers and Sisters* (1929)

'He was active in the cause of total abstinence, a leading member of the Dover Temperance Reformers and a fervent supporter in the 'seventies and 'eighties of the Social Purity Movement, resembling in this as in much else the elder Andrew Stace' (H. Spurling, 1974, *Ivy When Young: the early life of I. Compton-Burnett, 1884–1919*, London: Gollancz, p. 36).

REEVES, Amber *See* **Blanco White**, Amber.

REITLINGER, Gerald (1900–78) Historian of 'the economics of taste', painter, writer on contemporary history and collector of ceramics.

REINECKER in Robert Byron, *The Station* (1928)

'Reitlinger appears in *The Station* as Reinecker, a profile not wholly complimentary (there had been differences with Robert Byron on the Holy Mountain)' (Anthony Powell, 1978, *To Keep the Ball Rolling: the memoirs of Anthony Powell*, Vol. II: *Messengers of Day*, London: Heinemann, p. 171).

RENISHAW HALL, Derbyshire Built by George Sitwell in 1625, the original house survives as the core of a structure largely dating from 1800 and its gardens were laid out by George Sitwell in 1850. It is still the residence of the Sitwell family (see Nikolaus Pevsner, 1978, *Derbyshire (Buildings of England* series), Harmondsworth: Penguin, Pl. 57(b)).

WRAGBY HALL in D.H. Lawrence, *Lady Chatterley's Lover* (1928)

'An odd mixture of every period and style, full of beautiful things. ... Do you remember the house and park in Lawrence's improper book? And the light from all the works, at night? That is supposed to be a portrait of this house' (Ethel Sands to Anna Hope (Nan) Hudson, October 1929, quoted in Wendy Baron, 1977, *Miss Ethel Sands and Her Circle*, p. 204). Wragby is clearly in Nottinghamshire, but if one looks at John Piper's pictures of Renishaw one begins to think that perhaps Miss Sands (and presumably the Sitwells) were not so far out. *See also* **Lamb Close House**.

REPTON, Humphry (1752–1818) Landscape gardener. Born in Bury St Edmunds, he revolutionized the theory of garden design, moving away from the formality of the eighteenth century towards a more unstructured 'picturesque' style. He was employed by the chief noblemen of his day.

MARMADUKE MILESTONE in Thomas Love Peacock, *Headlong Hall* (1816)

'Many of [the ... guests at Headlong Hall] are already known to us: Mr Milestone (Humphry Repton), the landscape gardener ...' (Martin Freeman, 1911, *Thomas Love Peacock*, London: Martin Secker, p. 161).

RESTORATION HOUSE, Rochester, Kent Located on Maidstone Road, it is 'the most important town-house historically in Rochester; basically of the sixteenth century' (Nikolaus Pevsner, *West Kent (Buildings of England* series), Harmondsworth: Penguin, p. 476).

SATIS HOUSE in Charles Dickens, *Great Expectations* (1860–1)

'The Satis House of *Great Expectations*' (1935, *The Dickensian* 31: 2).

REUBELL, Henrietta (b. 1849) A wealthy American spinster who kept a salon in Paris during the 1880s. Will Rothenstein described her as having bright red hair, an expressive, ugly face, and reminding him of Queen Elizabeth, 'if one can imagine an Elizabeth with an American accent and a voice like a parrot's' (see *The Letters of Oscar Wilde*, 1962, ed. Rupert Hart-Davis, London: Rupert Hart-Davis, p. 157 n. 1).

MISS BARRACE in Henry James, *The Ambassadors* (1903)

'In a later letter ... to Howard Sturgis [James] actually refers to Miss Reubell as Etta Barrace, one of the rare instances in which he identified an original' (Leon Edel, 1963, *Henry James: the middle years, 1884–1894*, p. 329 n. *The Besotted Mandarins*).

REVELSTOKE, John Baring, Lord (1863–1929) Brother of Maurice Baring, he succeeded to the title of 2nd Baron in 1897. He was a partner in Baring Bros., the bankers, and was a director of the Bank of England. Although for many years he was devoted to Lady **Desborough**, he never married.

CARYL BRAMSLEY ('C') in Maurice Baring, *C* (1924)

'There is a novel by ... Maurice [Baring] written years later, but describing life in the 1890s, in which the heroine and hero are like Ettie [Desborough] and John Baring – or perhaps like Maurice himself, for he too was in love with Ettie. The novel is called, curiously or significantly, C ('C' being one of the code names in Ettie's and John Baring's letters)' (Nicholas Mosley, 1976, *Julian Grenfell*, London: Weidenfeld & Nicolson, p. 45). *See also* **Baring**, Maurice.

REVISS, Theresa (b. 1832) Known as 'Tizzy Reeves', she was the illegitimate daughter of Arthur (later Sir Arthur) Buller, whose mother, Isabella Barbara **Buller**, brought her up. 'Her history subsequent to 1847 affords a remarkable instance of life imitating art' ('Biographical memoranda', in *The Letters and Private Papers of W.M. Thackeray*, Vol. I: *1817–1840*, 1945, ed. Gordon N. Ray, London: Oxford University Press, p. clvii). Settled in an Italian villa by the then

Lord Chancellor, she married a Gateschi; on the death of the legal luminary, her benefactor, she gracefully surrendered everything to his heirs and disappeared, to reappear in London as the Countess de la Torre.

BLANCHE AMORY in W.M. Thackeray, *The History of Pendennis* (1848–50)

'Have you been reading Thackeray's "Pendennis"? If so, you have made acquaintance with Blanche Amory; and when I tell you that my young lady of last week is the original of that portrait, you will give me joy that she, lady's maid, and infinite baggage, are all gone! Not that the poor little [Theresa Reviss] is quite such a little devil as Thackeray, who has detested her from a child, has here represented; but the looks, the manners, the wiles, the *larmes*, and all that sort of thing, are a perfect likeness' (to John Welsh, 7 January 1851, reproduced in *Letters and Memorials of Jane Welsh Carlyle*, 1883, ed. J.A. Froude, Vol. II, London: Longman, pp. 144–5). *See also* **Thynne**, Cecilia Anne.

BECKY SHARP in W.M. Thackeray, *Vanity Fair* (1847–8)

'I may as well also state here, that one morning a hansom drove up to the door, and out of it emerged a most charming, dazzling little lady dressed in black, who greeted my father with great affection and brilliancy. . . . This was the only time I ever saw the fascinating little person who was . . . supposed to be the original of Becky' (Anne Thackeray Ritchie, 1898, biog. introd. to *The Works of W.M. Thackeray*, Vol. I: *Vanity Fair*, London: Smith, Elder, p. xxx). 'Last night I enjoyed myself immensely at the Richmonds – Henry James was there and the Andrew Langs who told me, of all people in the world that Becky Sharp is still alive, at least Miss Tizzy Reviss who was supposed to be Becky is, and she is now no less a person than the Countess de la Torre and her cats one reads of in the police courts' (to Mrs Gerald Ritchie, 1889, reproduced in *Letters of Anne Thackeray Ritchie*, 1924, ed. Hester Ritchie, London: John Murray, p. 208). *See also* **Morgan**, Lady.

REXROTH, Kenneth (1905–82) American poet. He settled in San Francisco in 1927 and became more generally known through his association with the 'Beat' poets in the 1950s.

REINHOLD CACOETHES in Jack Kerouac, *The Dharma Bums* (1958)

Identified in 'Character key to the Duluoz Legend', in Barry Gifford and Lawrence Lee, 1979, *Jack's Book*, pp. 322–32.

RHODES, Cecil John (1853–1902) Colonial administrator. In 1870 he was sent to Natal, where his brother was farming, and later returned to England to attend Oriel College, Oxford. He subsequently made a fortune in diamond mining in South Africa, and in 1881 he became a member of the Cape assembly. He was Prime Minister of Cape Colony from 1890 to 1896, and thereafter concentrated on the development of Rhodesia. He endowed the Rhodes scholarship.

FRANCIS CAREY in John Buchan, *A Lodge in the Wilderness* (1906)

Identified in a key dated January 1907 in a copy of *A Lodge in the Wilderness*, formerly the property of Grace Keily.

RHONDDA, David Alfred Thomas, 1st Viscount (1856–1918) Welsh statesman, colliery proprietor and financier. He was born in Ysgyborwen, Glamorganshire, and educated at Caius College, Cambridge. He was Liberal MP for Merthyr Tydfil from 1888 to 1910 and Food Minister between 1917 and 1918 at the time of war-time food rationing.

LORD RAINGO in Arnold Bennett, *Lord Raingo* (1926)

'Considerable detail about Lord Raingo's life was drawn from information that Beaverbrook gave to Bennett about Lord Rhondda' (*Letters of Arnold Bennett*, 1970, ed. James Hepburn, Vol. III, London: Oxford University Press, p. 276 n. 300). *See also* **Bennett**, Arnold; **Rickards**, Edwin Alfred.

RHYS, Jean (1894–1979) Novelist. Born Gwen Williams, in the West Indies, she was the daughter of a Welsh doctor and a Creole mother and grew up in Dominica. In 1910 she attended drama school in London and later became a chorus girl. She married Edward de Nève and lived for some years in Paris, and in 1924 she had an affair with Ford Madox **Ford**. Her first book, *The Left Bank*, a collection of short stories, was published in 1927 with an introduction by Ford, and four novels were published before the outbreak of the Second World War. She wrote nothing more until *The Wide Sargasso Sea* (1966), which received much critical acclaim and led to a revival of interest in her earlier works. Her second husband was Leslie Tilden **Smith** and her third was the Dutch poet Max Hamer.

STANIA VAN LEEUWEN in Edward de Nève, *Barred* (1932)

'Another view of the Ford–Rhys relationship [from that in Jean Rhys's novel *Postures* or *Quartet*] is provided in a . . . novel . . . by de Nève. In its way de Nève's book is more directly personal than *Quartet*, and, as a reflection of actual events, seemingly more candid' (Thomas F. Staley, 1979, *Jean Rhys: a critical study*, p. 12.

MARYA ZELLI in Jean Rhys, *Postures* (1928)

'*Postures* . . . the novel [Jean Rhys] wrote about her affair with Ford' (Arthur Mizener, 1971, *The Saddest Story: a biography of Ford Madox Ford*, Cleveland: World Publishing, p. 345). 'She originally sent [the novel] to Jonathan Cape . . . but she was told by the editors that they were afraid to publish [it] because of a possible libel action by Ford. They recognised immediately that the subject matter was too close to the actual circumstances of her life' (Thomas F. Staley, 1979, *Jean Rhys: a critical study*, p. 14).

RIBBENTROP A forester in the service of the Indian Government during the second half of the nineteenth century who rose to be Inspector-General of Forests. He claimed to have encountered Kipling in Lahore in 1883.

MULLER in Rudyard Kipling, 'In the Rukh' (1893)

'The gigantic German Muller of that tale . . . was a man called Ribbentrop. His house had a lurid reputation in Simla' (Lieutenant-Colonel J.K. Stanford, 1947, 'Some lesser-known aspects of Kipling in the East, II', *The Kipling Journal* 14 (83): 5).

RIBERA, Antonia

Antonia Avellanos in Joseph Conrad, *Nostromo* (1904)

'From Eastwick, Conrad took some ... names ... of geographical features ... and of people. ... The reigning beauty of Valencia is Antonia Ribera ... and although Conrad said that Antonia Avellanos was modelled on his first love there is very close correspondence between her character and appearance and that of Antonia Ribera' (Jocelyn Baines, 1969, *Joseph Conrad: a critical biography*, p. 295). The reference is to Edward B. Eastwick, 1868, *Venezuela; or Sketches of Life in a South American Republic*.

RICHARDS, Grant (1872–1948) Publisher of A.E. Housman and **Rolfe**. He described himself in *Who's Who* as having been educated in the office of W.T. Stead.

Barfleur in Theodore Dreiser, *A Traveler at Forty* (1913)

'Richards, the "Barfleur" of the chronicle' (W.A. Swanberg, 1965, *Dreiser*, New York, p. 168).

Doron Oldcastle in F.W. Rolfe, *Nicholas Crabbe* (1958)

'The two scheming villains – Slim Schelm and Doron Oldcastle ... are his publishers, John Lane and Grant Richards' (Cecil Woolf, 1958, Introd. to *Nicholas Crabbe*, pp. v–vi).

RICHARDS, Nigel (d. 1942) Killed in action. He was the husband of Betty, afterwards Batten.

Edgar Naylor in Cyril Connolly, *The Rock Pool* (1936)

'Betty was married to reputedly the best-looking man in England, Nigel Richards, who was the real-life inspiration for the anti-hero of ... *The Rock Pool*' (Henrietta Sharpe, 1981, *A Solitary Woman: a life of Violet Trefusis*, p. 131). 'Of the two young men from whose worst features ... Naylor was so competently welded, one has long lost all his arrogance and fire; the other, whose wit, generosity and sweetness, with his extraordinary beauty, had, for purposes of this narrative, to be ruthlessly suppressed, died in the black winter night above Germany' (Connolly, 1947, Postscript to *The Rock Pool*, p. xii).

RICHARDSON, Alice Mary (1868–1910) Second daughter of Charles **Richardson** and sister of Dorothy, for a time she was Governess to the **Harris** family (the bacon curers) in Calne, Wiltshire. She married a French citizen and moved to France.

Eve Henderson in Dorothy Richardson, *Pilgrimage* (1915–67)

'Her sisters she re-named Sarah, Eve & Harriett' (John Rosenberg, 1973, *Dorothy Richardson*, London, p. 70).

RICHARDSON, Charles (1836?–1915) Son of a family of non-conformist tradespeople settled for generations in Abingdon and district, Berkshire, he married Mary Miller Taylor (**Richardson**, below) in 1866; Dorothy Richardson was their daughter. In 1874 he inherited his father's property; he immediately sold the business, thenceforth attending the Anglican church and living the life of a gentleman in Abingdon (1866–80), Worthing (1880–83) and Putney (1883–93). In 1893 he went bankrupt and moved to a house in Chiswick, London, that was made over to him by his son-in-law, John **Batchelor**, and in 1904 he joined the Batchelors at Long Ditton.

MR HENDERSON in Dorothy Richardson, *Pilgrimage* (1915–67)

'[T]he Richardsons were now the Hendersons; incidents and impressions were set down exactly as she recalled them' (John Rosenberg, 1973, *Dorothy Richardson*, London, p. 70).

RICHARDSON, Dorothy Miller (1873–1957) English novelist. She was born in Abingdon, Berkshire, but moved to London in 1895 after her mother's suicide. She held a variety of jobs and had an affair with H.G. Wells which ended in a miscarriage and emotional breakdown in 1907. In 1917 she married a painter, Alan **Odle**. Her first novel, *Painted Roofs*, was published in 1915. She was the first to develop the 'stream of consciousness'.

MIRIAM HENDERSON in Dorothy Richardson, *Pilgrimage* (1915–67)

'The book . . . stayed close to its original, Dorothy became Miriam' (John Rosenberg, 1973, *Dorothy Richardson*, London, p. 70).

STELLA SUMMERSBY SATCHEL in H.G. Wells, *The Passionate Friends* (1913)

'Wells put her in his novel *The Passionate Friends* as a minor character called Stella Summersby Satchel, who is "blonde, erect, huffy-mannered"' (Tom Paulin, 1978, 'Fugitive spirits', *New Statesman* (21 July): 94; review of Gloria B. Fromm, *Dorothy Richardson*, University of Illinois).

RICHARDSON, Mary Miller (1843?–95) Née Taylor, she was the daughter of a manufacturer of canvas for sailing boats in East Coker, Somerset. In 1866 she married Charles **Richardson**, but she became a semi-invalid in 1880 and committed suicide in 1895. She was the mother of Dorothy Richardson.

MRS HENDERSON in Dorothy Richardson, *Pilgrimage* (1915–67)

'[D]escribing the decline and death of Miriam's mother, Dorothy is clearly harking back to her own mother's death in very similar circumstances' (John Rosenberg, 1973, *Dorothy Richardson*, London, p. 84).

RICHTHOFEN, Friedrich, Baron von (1845–1915) Army officer from East Prussia. He was compelled to leave the Army as a result of being wounded in the Franco-Prussian war, and became a member of the civil government of Metz. He was the father of Frieda **Lawrence**.

THE BARON in D.H. Lawrence, 'The Thorn in the Flesh' (1914)

'[Frieda's] father appears as one of the characters, the baron whose right hand had been shattered when he was a young man, in the Franco-Prussian war' (H.T. Moore, 1960, *The Intelligent Heart: the story of D.H. Lawrence*, Harmondsworth: Penguin, p. 196; originally published 1955, London: Heinemann).

RICKARDS, Edwin Alfred (1872–1920) Architect. He was a partner in the firm of Lanchester and Rickards, who in 1909 designed the Central Hall in Westminster, and the Town Hall in Cardiff. At one time he was an intimate friend of Bennett.

George Cannon in Arnold Bennett, *The Roll Call* (1917)

'You will appear in the following two novels of the "trilogy" (as the publishers and critics love to call it) and then you will be the hero of the fourth book, about London' (to E.A. Rickards, autumn 1910, reproduced in *Letters of Arnold Bennett*, 1968, ed. James Hepburn, Vol. II, London: Oxford University Press, p. 266). 'In the *Clayhanger* trilogy Rickards is Hilda's son, George Cannon. The fourth novel is *The Roll-Call*' (ibid., n. 207).

Lord Raingo in Arnold Bennett, *Lord Raingo* (1926)

'This experience [the last illness of Rickards] . . . must have provided the basis of the death-bed scene that occupies one-third of *Lord Raingo*' (*The Letters of Arnold Bennett*, 1968, ed. James Hepburn, Vol. I, London: Oxford University Press, p. 286 n. 279). *See also* **Bennett**, Arnold; **Rhondda**, 1st Viscount.

RIDGE, Lola (1873–1941) American poet. Born in Ireland, she moved to the United States, via Australia, in 1907. She achieved some critical success in the 1920s.

Dora in Robert McAlmon, *Post Adolescence* (1923)

Identified in Robert E. Knoll (ed.), 1962, *McAlmon and the Lost Generation: a self-portrait*, Lincoln, Nebr.: University of Nebraska Press, p. 108.

RIDGEWAY, Sir William (1853–1926) Educated at Trinity College, Dublin, and at Gonville and Caius College, Cambridge, he was Disney Professor of Archaeology at Cambridge from 1892 to 1926; he was opposed to the granting of degrees to women and the abolition of compulsory Greek. He was the author of, among other learned works, *The Origins and Influence of the Thoroughbred Horse* (1905).

Professor O'Rudgery in Shane Leslie, *The Cantab* (1926)

Identified in a key in the hand of Dr Ivor Ramsay, a Kingsman of the year 1920, and later Dean, laid in a copy of *The Cantab*.

RIMMER, William (1816–79) Sculptor. Born in Liverpool, in 1818 he was taken to the United States. He worked as a stonecutter, sculptor and painter in East Milton, Massachusetts, and was a man of considerable gifts. In 1863 May **Alcott** took anatomical drawing lessons from him in Boston; John **La Farge** was also among his pupils.

Friedrich Bhaer in Louisa M. Alcott, *Little Women* (1868) and sequels

'There can be little doubt that Dr Rimmer was the original of Professor Bhaer' (K. Anthony, 1939, *Louisa May Alcott*, p. 165). *See also* **Solger**, Reinhold.

RINGSTEAD BAY, Dorset Situated about four miles east of Weymouth.

RINGSWORTH in Thomas Hardy, Wessex novels and tales (1871–95)

Identified on a map prepared by Thomas Hardy which hangs in the Dorset County Museum, Dorchester. *See under* **Abbotsbury**.

RINGWOOD, Hampshire A small town on the Avon, fifteen miles south of Salisbury.

OOZEWOOD in Thomas Hardy, 'Master John Horseleigh, Knight' (1913)

Identified in F.B. Pinion, 1968, *A Hardy Companion*, London: Macmillan.

RIPON, Constance Gwladys, Lady de Grey, Marchioness of (1859–1917) Née Robinson, she was the daughter of Sidney **Herbert**, 1st Baron Herbert of Lea, and the sister of the 14th Earl of Pembroke. In 1878 she married Henry, 4th Earl of Lonsdale (d. 1882), but the marriage was very unhappy, and in 1885 she married Lord de Grey, who became Marquess of Ripon in 1909. She was a splendid Edwardian beauty, but Lady Augusta **Fane** said that she had one fault – 'an overwhelming curiosity to know everything and experience every sensation, and this inquisitiveness led her into dark places' (*Chit-Chat*, 1926, p. 98). For her role in the Londonderry scandal, *see* **Londonderry**, Lord and Lady. Oscar **Wilde** dedicated *A Woman of No Importance* to her.

LADY GROTE in E.F. Benson, *Robin Linnet* (1919)

Identification based upon private information.

RITCHIE, Anne Isabella, Lady (1837–1919) Elder daughter of W.M. Thackeray, in 1877 she married her cousin Richmond **Ritchie**. She was the sister of Leslie **Stephen**'s first wife, and thus Virginia Woolf's step-aunt.

MRS HILBERY in Virginia Woolf, *Night and Day* (1919)

'I think the most interesting character is evidently my mother [in the novel] who is made exactly like Lady Ritchie down to every detail apparently. Everyone will know who it is of course' (Vanessa Bell to Roger Fry, 14 April 1917, quoted in Quentin Bell, 1975, *Virginia Woolf*, Vol. II, p. 420). 'I think one's readers tend to identify one's characters more than one does oneself. Of course there are touches of Lady Ritchie in Mrs Hilbery; but in writing one gets more and more away from the reality, and Mrs Hilbery became to me quite different from any one in the flesh' (to C.P. Sanger, 2? December 1919, reproduced in *The Letters of Virginia Woolf*, 1976, ed. Nigel Nicolson, Vol. II, London: Hogarth Press, p. 406). '[T]he Ritchies are furious with me for Mrs Hilbery; and Hester [Ritchie] is writing a life of Aunt Anny to prove she was a shrewd, and silent, woman of business' (to Vanessa Bell, June 1921, ibid., p. 474).

HESTER LAMBERT in W.M. Thackeray, *The Virginians* (1857–9)

'If my young women set their hearts on anything they're pretty sure to get it. I am afraid the 2 Lambert girls in the Virginians are very like them but of course deny it if anyone accuses me' (to Mrs Baxter, 23 April 1858, reproduced in *The Letters and Private Papers of W.M. Thackeray*, 1946, ed. Gordon N. Ray, Vol. IV, London: Oxford University Press, p. 81).

RITCHIE, David (1740?–1811) A dwarf who lived as a recluse on the property of Sir James Naesmyth in Peebleshire. His cottage was still to be seen in 1912.

SIR EDWARD MANLEY in Sir Walter Scott, *The Black Dwarf* (1816)

'[I]n the summer of 1797 . . . Scott met . . . the archetype of his black Dwarf. Of all his characters, none has been more faithfully reproduced from the original. . . . The occasion was a visit to Hallyards . . . the home of . . . Adam Ferguson . . . his host took him to see David Ritchie. . . . *The Black Dwarf* was not published for nineteen years afterwards, but how true to the facts was the . . . reproduction of [the] scene in the cottage (chap. xvi)' (W.S. Crockett, 1912, *The Scott Originals: an account of notables and worthies, the originals of characters in the Waverley Novels*, Edinburgh and London: T.N. Foulis, pp. 146–9).

RITCHIE, Marion (d. 1822) Daughter of Walter Ritchie, Provost of Peebles, she became the Keeper of the Cross Keys Inn in Peebles.

MEG DODS in Sir Walter Scott, *St Ronan's Well* (1823)

'Before quitting the district [of Peebleshire, in 1797], Scott had an opportunity of visiting the old inn . . . of Miss Ritchie in Peebles. . . . Miss Ritchie . . . was somewhat of an original . . . and there can be little doubt that her peculiarities furnished such recollections as were afterwards matured in the character of "Meg Dods"' (R. Chambers, 1871, *Life of Sir Walter Scott*, p. 36).

RITCHIE, Sir Richmond (1854–1912) Brother of Blanche **Warre-Cornish**. In 1877 he married his cousin Anne Thackeray (**Ritchie**, above). He entered the India Office, and in 1909 became permanent Under-Secretary of State.

TREVOR HILBERY in Virginia Woolf, *Night and Day* (1919)

'Virginia Woolf . . . personified him as Mr Hilbery in . . . *Night and Day*' (Philip Leigh-Smith, 1961, *Record of an Ascent: a memoir of Sir Richmond Thackeray Ritchie*, p. 80). 'Certain traits would identify him immediately as Ritchie to those who knew him in real life: the love of music and the little green stone fingered like worrybeads' (E.F. Boyd, 1976, *Bloomsbury Heritage*, p. 92). *See also* **Stephen**, Sir Leslie.

ROBERSON, Revd Hammond (1757–1841) Curate of Dewsbury in 1779, he resigned the curacy in 1788 and took up teaching. He purchased Heald's Hall in Liversedge, Yorkshire, and became the incumbent of Hartshead-cum-Clifton; he ran a boy's school at Healds Hall and used the proceeds to build Christ Church, which was consecrated in 1812 and completed in 1816. In later life he was instrumental in getting churches built at Cleckheaton (1830–32) and Birkenshaw (1829–30). All three churches are still standing.

REVD MATTHEWSON HELSTONE in Charlotte Brontë, *Shirley* (1849)

'[Charlotte Brontë's] fictitious description of [Roberson] in *Shirley* is, according to some persons who knew him, very highly coloured: but the testimony of the natives is that his portraiture . . . is very true to life' (J.A. Erskine, 1886, *Yorkshire Weekly Post* (27 November); see Herbert Wroot, 1935, *The Sources of Charlotte Brontë's Novels: persons and places*, Shipley, Yorks., p. 108). Charlotte Brontë saw Revd Roberson only once, when she was 10 years old.

ROBERTS, J.M. He was married to Margaret **Roberts**.

JOHN DORSEY LEONARD in Thomas Wolfe, *Look Homeward, Angel* (1929)

See under **Roberts**, Margaret.

ROBERTS, Margaret She was married to J.M. **Roberts**, with whom she was founder and Principal of North State Filting School, Asheville, the private school attended by Wolfe in 1912–16.

MARGARET LEONARD in Thomas Wolfe, *Look Homeward, Angel* (1929)

'. . . the prototype[s] of Mrs Margaret Leonard . . . [and her husband]' (Floyd C. Watkins, 1957, *Thomas Wolfe's Characters: portraits from life*, Norman, Okla., p. 26).

ROBERTS, Morley (1857–1942) Novelist. Born in London, he was educated at Bedford Grammar School and at Owens College, Manchester, where he met George Gissing; they became close friends. In 1876–9 he worked in Australia as an able seaman, and in 1884–6, after a spell as a clerk in the civil service, he worked his way across the United States: this journey became the subject of his first book, *The Western Avernus*. He returned to London to write novels and, later, works on science.

J.H (OR J.C.H.) in Morley Roberts, *The Private Life of Henry Maitland* (1912)

Identified in an 'Index of Recurring Pseudonyms' in the 1958 edition of *The Private Life of Henry Maitland*, ed. Morchard Bishop, p. 255.

MALKIN in George Gissing, *Born in Exile* (1892)

'Many years before . . . Gissing had portrayed him in various of his novels. "Some of the sketches", as he observes, "are fairly complimentary, and many much the reverse." I think I know in which category he would have included the exuberant figure of Malkin' (Morchard Bishop, 1958, Introd. to *The Private Life of Henry Maitland*, p. 14).

ROSS MALLARD in George Gissing, *The Emancipated* (1890)

'It is a curious fact . . . that I stood as a model to him in many of these books, especially . . . for one particular character [Mallard] in . . . [*The Emancipated*]' (Morley Roberts, 1974, *The Private Life of Henry Maitland*, p. 195).

WHELPDALE in George Gissing, *New Grub Street* (1891)

'Roberts is the prototype of Whelpdale' (*The Letters of George Gissing to Eduard Bertz 1887–1903*, 1961, ed. Arthur C. Young, London: Constable, p. xxxiv).

ROBINS, Elizabeth (1862–1952) Novelist, playwright and actress. She appeared in early London productions of Ibsen's plays in the 1890s and was especially admired as his Hedda Gabler. She was a passionate adherent of the women's suffrage movement.

VIOLET GREY in Henry James, 'Nona Vincent' (1891)

'Miss Elizabeth is embodied in the ambiguous, faltering actress with the two-toned name of Violet Grey' (Leon Edel, 1969, *Henry James: the treacherous years, 1895–1901*, London: Rupert Hart-Davis, p. 28).

ROBINSON, Mrs She lived in the little house reached through an arched passage a few doors along from the **Buchanan's** house in Church Street, Nuneaton, Warwickshire.

MRS PETTIFER in George Eliot, 'Janet's Repentance', *Scenes of Clerical Life* (1857–8)

See under **Anstruther**, Lady.

ROBINSON, Agnes Frances Mary (1857–1944) Poet and writer. Daughter of George Robinson, a London banker with a wide literary acquaintance, she became the author of biographical works as well as works on French literature and sociology. She met Vernon Lee *c.*1880, remaining a close friend until 1887, when she married James Darmesteter. After the latter's death, she married Emile Duclaux, of the Pasteur Institute, in 1900.

MARY LEIGH in Vernon Lee, *Miss Brown* (1884)

'The sisters Mary and Marjorie Leigh . . . appear to have been based on Mary and Mabel Robinson' (Peter Gunn, 1964, *Vernon Lee 1856–1935*, London: Oxford University Press, p. 102).

ROBINSON, Margaret Hayes (1877?–1930) She became Head of the History Department at Royal Holloway College in 1898, directly after taking a first at Oxford; she was much younger than most of her colleagues. In 1916 she married an Oxford don.

MISS ADAM in I. Compton-Burnett, *Dolores* (1911)

Identified in a key given in the back of a copy of *Dolores*, signed 'H.M. Cam, 1912' in the front (Dr Helen Cam was a student at Holloway in Ivy Compton-Burnett's last two years there). The key was printed in Hilary Spurling, 1974, *Ivy When Young: the early life of I. Compton Burnett, 1884–1919*, London: Gollancz, App. II, p. 280.

ROBSON-SCOTT, William A friend of Isherwood, whom he met in Berlin in 1930.

PETER WILKINSON in Christopher Isherwood, *Goodbye to Berlin* (1939)

'Christopher borrowed some of William's mannerisms for . . . Peter Wilkinson, Otto Nowak's lover, in *Goodbye to Berlin*. In real life, William and Otto never even met' (Christopher Isherwood, 1977, *Christopher and His Kind*, London: Eyre Methuen, p. 185).

ROCESTER, Derbyshire

ROSSETER in George Eliot, *Adam Bede* (1859)

'"Rosseter" is Rocester' (Marghanita Laski, 1973, *George Eliot and Her World*, London: Thames & Hudson, p. 65).

ROCHESTER, Kent

CLOISTERHAM in Charles Dickens, *Edwin Drood* (1870)

'It is . . . unnecessary to state that Cloisterham is the ancient city of Rochester' (Walter Bertram, 1906, 'Cloisterham, the city of Edwin Drood', *The Dickensian* 2 (February): 63).

GREAT WINGLEBURY in Charles Dickens, 'The Great Winglebury Duel', *Sketches by Boz* (1836)

'[T]he description in the text is strongly suggestive of Rochester. It is evidently a composite picture' (T.W. Hill, 1951, 'Notes on *Sketches by Boz*', *The Dickensian* 47: 35).

ROCKEFELLER INSTITUTE, New York Set up in 1900 at the bequest of John D. Rockefeller to extend knowledge of fatal diseases.

McGURK INSTITUTE in Sinclair Lewis, *Arrowsmith* (1925)

'[De Kruif] had drawn further on his Rockefeller Institute experiences for the picture of the McGurk Institute' (Mark Schorer, 1961, *Sinclair Lewis: an American life*, New York: McGraw-Hill, p. 418).

ROCKINGHAM CASTLE, Northamptonshire It was restored in 1849–51 by Anthony Salvin, who also restored **Hafod House** in 1838–40.

CHESNEY WOLD in Charles Dickens, *Bleak House* (1852–3)

'In some of the descriptions of Chesney Wold, I have taken many bits, chiefly about trees and shadows, from observations made at Rockingham. I wonder whether you have ever thought so!' (to the Hon. Mrs Richard Watson, 27 August 1853, reproduced in *Letters of Charles Dickens*, 1938, ed. Walter Dexter, Vol. II, p. 484). 'I have always thought that, although the surroundings of the two houses are altogether different, and although there was, of course, not the faintest likeness between their occupants, Chesney Wold bears much more than an accident resemblance – especially in respect of the long drawing room and the terraced garden walk – to Rockingham Castle' (Charles Dickens, the Younger, 1896, Introd. to *Bleak House*, p. xxxiii).

RODD, Peter (1904–68) Third son of Lord Rennell of Rodd, the British Ambassador to Italy in 1908–19, he was educated in Wellington and at Balliol College, Oxford. In 1933 he married Nancy Mitford, but the marriage was dissolved in 1952. A man of considerable intellectual capacity, with a passion for acquiring information and passing it on, he could be a stupendous bore. He was totally devoid, by all accounts, of all sense of moral responsibility, and Harold **Acton** described him as a high-class con man.

RUDOLPH JOCELYN in Nancy Mitford, *Pigeon Pie* (1940)

'We glimpse [Peter] in the role of Rudolph Jocelyn' (Harold Acton, 1975, *Nancy Mitford: a memoir*, London: Hamilton, p. 49).

BASIL SEAL in Evelyn Waugh, *Black Mischief* (1932), *Scoop* (1938) and *Put Out More Flags* (1942)

'Mr Peter Rodd had the sulky, arrogant looks of the young Rimbaud. . . . Some readers have professed to recognize in . . . "Basil Seal" . . . a combination of Basil [Murray] and Peter [Rodd]' (Evelyn Waugh, 1964, *A Little Learning . . . an autobiography*, London: Chapman and Hall, p. 204). 'I was at dinner with Evelyn at Cyril Connolly's house . . . shortly after Basil Seal had been launched in *Black Mischief*. The model and the caricature were discussed, no doubts being expressed on either side that Peter and Basil were mutual reflections. "Haven't you had trouble with Peter?" asked Cyril. "None at all", replied Evelyn. "But don't you expect it?" went on Cyril. "No", said Evelyn. We all asked why. "Because" said Evelyn magisterially . . . "because you can draw any character as near to life as you want, and no offence will be taken provided you say that he is attractive to women' (Christopher Sykes, 1975, *Evelyn Waugh*, London: Collins, p. 41–2). *See also* **Murray**, Basil.

CHRISTIAN TALBOT in Nancy Mitford, *The Pursuit of Love* (1945)

'Christian is a thinly disguised version of Peter' (Acton, op. cit., p. 42).

ROEBUCK, John Arthur (1801–79) MP, with two short breaks, for Bath (1832–47) and Sheffield (1849–79), he was originally an independent Radical but became increasingly illiberal. He was a disciple of Bentham and a friend of John Stuart Mill.

G.O.A. HEAD in Benjamin Disraeli, *Coningsby* (1844)

Identified in a key in *Notes and Queries* (8th series) 3 (13 May 1893): 363. *See also under* **Bright**, John.

ROGERS, Mary Cecilia (1820–41) An assistant employed in 1837 and 1838 at John Anderson's tobacco shop at 319 Broadway, New York City; the shop was frequented by Poe, Fenimore Cooper, and other writers and journalists. She was murdered in August 1841.

MARIE ROGET in Edgar Allan Poe, *The Mystery of Marie Roget* (1842)

'The story is based upon the assassination of Mary Cecilia Rogers which created so vast an excitement . . . in New York' (Edgar Allan Poe to George Roberts, Editor of the *Boston Times*, 4 June 1842; see Irving Wallace, 1956, *The Fabulous Originals*, p. 161).

ROGERS, Samuel (1763–1855) English poet and man of letters. Born at Stoke Newington, London, he entered his father's bank and was taken into partnership in 1784, becoming head of the firm in 1793. He began his literary career in 1781, contributing essays to the *Gentleman's Magazine*, and he continued to write both during his time at the bank, which he left in 1803, and in his retirement. He was a great collector of art and a very generous man, though allegedly with a very unkind tongue. He is possibly better remembered now for his ill-natured sayings than for his poetry.

HORACE CHURCHILL in Maria Edgeworth, *Helen* (1834)

'The wit Horace Churchill was based on Samuel Rogers' (Marilyn Butler, 1972, *Maria Edgeworth*, Oxford, p. 465).

DEAD POET in Lady Caroline Lamb, *Glenarvon* (1816)

Identified in a key found among the papers of John Whishaw, a member of the Holland House circle, printed in *The 'Pope' of Holland House: selections from the correspondence of John Whishaw and his friends, 1813–1840*, ed. Lady Seymour, 1906, p. 151.

PARTHENOPEX PUFF in Benjamin Disraeli, *Vivian Grey* (1826–7)

Identified as Mr S—— R—— in a key given in *The Star Chamber* (24 May 1826): 114; reprinted in *Vivian Grey*, 1904 (centenary edn), ed. Lucien Wolf, Vol. II, pp. 361–2. The full name appears on a copy of the key held in the British Museum. Lucien Wolf concludes that Disraeli was not responsible for the key. *See also* **Rose**, William Stewart.

MR WHITMONBY in George Meredith, *Diana of the Crossways* (1884)

'Caroline [Norton]'s various admirers ... are also sketched in. There is Whitmonby (Samuel Rogers)' (Alice Acland, 1948, *Caroline Norton*, London: Constable, p. 179).

ROLFE, Frederick William Serafino Lewis Mary (1860–1913) Novelist and essayist. Known as 'Baron Corvo' and as Fr. Rolfe; in fact Fr. stood for Frederick, but was often supposed to mean Frater, an interpretation that did not displease Rolfe. He taught at a number of schools, including the Grammar School at Grantham under Dr Hardy, and in 1886 joined the Roman Catholic Church. He went to Oscott and the Scotch College in Rome, where he devoted his afternoons to aristocratic calls and developed gout. He failed to be accepted for the priesthood and later assumed the title of Baron Corvo, settling in Christchurch, Hampshire, where he lived on his wits and talents, among other things painting the walls of the local Catholic church. Politically, he was a 'medieval Tory' and a fanatical Jacobite. For 15 months he was housed and fed in Oxford by Dr Hardy, and he died in poverty and squalor in Venice. He contributed to the *Yellow Book*.

ENID BLESSINGTON in R.H. Benson, *Initiation* (1914)

'Benson draws Rolfe's portrait twice, once as Chris Dell ... once as Enid Blessington' (Betty Askwith, 1971, *Two Victorian Families*, p. 214).

NICHOLAS CRABBE in F.W. Rolfe, *Nicholas Crabbe* (1958)

'... Rolfe's own detailed account of the four dreadful years beginning with his arrival in London [in 1899] and ending in the early part of 1903' (Cecil Woolf, 1958, Introd. to *Nicholas Crabbe*, p. 4).

CHRIS DELL in R.H. Benson, *The Sentimentalists* (1906)

See above under ENID BLESSINGTON.

BARON FALCO in Shane Leslie, *The Cantab* (1926)

An unmistakable portrait; Leslie knew Rolfe well, greatly admired him, and dedicated his volume of short stories, *Masquerades* (1924), to him. Falco does not appear in the key in the hand of Dr Ivor Ramsay, a Kingsman of the year 1920, and later Dean, laid in a copy of *The Cantab*, being perhaps not sufficiently a Cambridge figure.

GEORGE ARTHUR ROSE in F.W. Rolfe, *Hadrian VII* (1904)

'His hero is himself, George Arthur Rose (who broods for years . . . wondering "why, O God, have you made me strange, uncommon, such a mystery to my fellow creatures?")' (Shane Leslie, 1923, 'Frederick Baron Corvo', *London Mercury* 8 (47): 514).

ROLLAND, Adam (1734–1819) After studying law at Edinburgh University, he was called to the Bar in 1757; he did not appear in Court but confined himself to written pleadings and giving of opinions. On retiring from the Bar he became Deputy Governor of the Bank of Scotland.

PAUL PLEYDELL in Sir Walter Scott, *Guy Mannering* (1815)

'At Luscar I saw with pleasure the painting by Raeburn of my old friend Samuel Roland [sic, a slip for Adam Rolland] Esq. who was in external circumstances but not in frolic or fancy my prototype for Paul Pleydell' (entry for 19 June 1830, *The Journal of Sir Walter Scott*, 1972, ed. W.E.K. Anderson, Oxford, p. 599). *See also* **Crosbie**, Andrew.

ROLLE, Lord (1756–1842) Of Stevenstone and Bicton, Devon. He was a Tory MP for Devon from 1780 to 1796 and was described by Greville (entry for 13 July 1834, *The Greville Memoirs, 1814–1860*, 1938, ed. Lytton Strachey and Roger Fulford, 8 vols, London: Macmillan) as 'a choleric hard-bitten old Tory'. In her diary, Queen Victoria described how at her coronation he, at the age of 82, stumbled and rolled down the steps in the endeavour to kiss her hand. He was created Baron in 1796.

SIR PITT CRAWLEY in W.M. Thackeray, *Vanity Fair* (1847–8)

'The original is sometimes said to have been Lord Rolle ... of whose eccentricities Thackeray may have heard in his Larkbeare days' (Introd. to *Vanity Fair*, 1908, ed. George Saintsbury, p. xvii). *See also* **Chaytor**, Sir William.

ROMÀN, Father

FATHER BERON in Joseph Conrad, *Nostromo* (1904)

'[G.F.] Masterman's torturer [in *Seven Eventful Years in Paraguay* (1869)] Father Romàn . . . is the model for Dr Monygham's torturer in *Nostromo*' (J.E. Saveson, 1963, 'Masterman as a source of "Nostromo"', *Notes and Queries* 208: 369).

ROOKSREST, Stevenage, Hertfordshire The house in which E.M. Forster lived as a child with his mother. A plan of the house and garden drawn by Forster at the age of 15 was reproduced on the dustjacket of the Abinger edition (1973) of the novel.

HOWARDS END in E.M. Forster, *Howards End* (1910)

'The garden, the overhanging wych-elm, the sloping meadow, the great view to the west, the cliff of fir trees to the north, the adjacent farm through the high tangled hedge of wild roses were all utilised by me in *Howards End*, and the interior is in the novel too' (E.M. Forster, 1956, *Marianne Thornton*, p. 269). 'To realize the wealth of detail which Howards End owed to Rooksrest it is necessary to read his account of the latter . . . published . . . as an appendix to this volume' (Oliver Stallybrass, 1973, Introd. to *Howards End*, p. viii).

ROOSEVELT, Franklin Delano (1882–1945) Thirty-second president of the USA. Born in Hyde Park, New York, to a wealthy family, he was a distant cousin of Theodore Roosevelt. He was educated in Europe and at Harvard and Columbia Law Schools, being admitted to the New York Bar in 1907. He was State Senator from 1909 to 1913, Assistant Secretary for the Navy from 1913 to 1920, and Democratic candidate for the vice-presidency in 1920. After a bout of paralysis (1921–3), he was Governor of New York from 1928 to 1932. In 1932 he became President, defeating Hoover. He launched his 'New Deal' programme in 1933 to combat the Great Depression, and this led to the passage of the Social Security Act in 1935. He was re-elected in 1936, securing an unprecedented third term in 1940 and a fourth in 1944. He died only three weeks before the Nazi surrender.

PAUL HAWLEY BARRACLOUGH in Stephen Longstreet and Ethel Longstreet, *The Politician* (1959)

'. . . he suffers an injury which produces partial paralysis and a limp, and he habitually uses a cigarette holder' (Joseph Blotner, 1966, *The Modern American Political Novel*, Austin, Tex., p. 51).

ROSCOE, Flora She was married to Henry Lincoln Roscoe, a partner in Field, Roscoe & Co., solicitors to the Firbank family. She was a friend of Constance **Collier**, with whom she visited Dieppe in August 1903 and who became briefly engaged to Max **Beerbohm**.

THE ENGLISH AMBASSADRESS in Ronald Firbank, *The Flower Beneath the Foot* (1923)

'The English Ambassadress is founded on Mrs Roscoe and Lady Nicolson' (Firbank to his mother, 14 January 1923, quoted in Miriam J. Benkovitz, 1969, *Ronald Firbank*, New York, p. 207). *See also* **Nicolson**, Mary Catherine.

ROSE, William Stewart (1775–1843) Poet. He was an MP from 1796 to 1800, and a reading clerk of the House of Lords and a clerk of private committees from 1800 to 1824. In 1803 he became a friend of Sir Walter **Scott**, and he published a translation of *Partenopex of Blois* in 1807 and a metrical version of Ariosto (1823–31).

PARTHENOPEX PUFF in Benjamin Disraeli, *Vivian Grey* (1826–7)

'Here, then, is the original of Parthenopex Puff, whose initials are W.S.R., and not the famous S.R.' (B.N. Langdon-Davies, 1904, Introd. to *Vivian Grey*, London: Alexander Moring, p. xxx; originally published 1826, London: Henry Colburn). *See also* **Rogers**, Samuel.

ROSEBERY, Archibald Philip Primrose, 5th Earl of (1847–1929) Liberal politician. He was Prime Minister in 1894–5 and in 1902 became leader of the imperialist wing of the Liberal Party; however, he left the Party in 1905. He won the Derby races three times.

LORD APPIN in John Buchan, *A Lodge in the Wilderness* (1906)

Identified in a key dated January 1907 in a copy of *A Lodge in the Wilderness*, formerly the property of Grace Keily. *See also* **Balfour**, A.J.

ROSS, **Charles** (1799–1860) Of St Germains, Hertfordshire. He was a West India proprietor and was a Conservative MP in 1826–32 for St Germains and in 1832–7 for Northampton.

MR TAPER in Benjamin Disraeli, *Coningsby* (1844)

Identified in a key in *Notes and Queries* (8th series) 3 (13 May 1893): 363. *See also under* **Bright**, John.

ROSS, **Henry James** (1820–1902) He was introduced to Janet Duff-Gordon (**Ross**, below) by Sir Henry Layard, and married her in 1860. He was a prosperous banker with Briggs & Co. of Alexandria, but the firm failed in 1866 and he moved to Florence. 'This modest, good and strong man . . . his amazing powers of story-telling . . . delighted people . . . "Every event" [wrote R.C. Trevelyan] "was presented with that vivid preciseness, which is the life of all great narrative"' (Lina Waterfield, 1961, *Castle in Italy*, p. 105). His *Letters from the East* was published in 1902.

ROBERT CHALLONER in Ouida, *Friendship* (1878)

'Henry Ross, the most upright and respected of men, was included in Ouida's slanders' (Waterfield, op. cit., p. 44).

ROSS, **Janet** (1842–1927) Daughter of Sir Alexander and Lady **Duff-Gordon** and granddaughter of John Austin, the jurist. She was a descendant, on her mother's side, of the Taylors of Norwich, and, on her father's side, of the Earls of Aberdeen and Dukes of Gordon.

LADY JOAN CHALLONER in Ouida, *Friendship* (1878)

'The three principal characters were Prince Louis (Stufa), the Lady Joan Challoner (Mrs Ross), and Etoile (Ouida)' (Eileen Bigland, 1951, *Ouida: the passionate Victorian*, p. 137).

JANET ILCESTER in George Meredith, *The Adventures of Harry Richmond* (1871)

'Janet Ilcester has always seemed to me a truer portrait of her [than Rose Jocelyn]' (Lina Waterfield, 1961, *Castle in Italy*, p. 34).

ROSE JOCELYN in George Meredith, *Evan Harrington* (1860)

'*Evan Harrington* . . . was *my* novel, because Rose Jocelyn was myself. . . . With the magnificent impertinence of sixteen I would interrupt Meredith, exclaiming: "No, I should never have said it like that", or, "I should not have done so"' (Janet Ross, 1912, *The Fourth Generation*, London: Constable, pp. 50–1).

ROSS, **Jean** (d. 1973?) She met Christopher Isherwood in Berlin in 1930 and remained his friend for life.

SALLY BOWLES in Christopher Isherwood, *Sally Bowles* (1937)

'I wish I could remember what impression Jean Ross – the real-life original of *Sally Bowles* ... made on Christopher when they first met. But I can't' (Christopher Isherwood, 1977, *Christopher and His Kind*, London: Eyre Methuen, p. 51).

ROSS, William Gribben (b. 1821?) A well-known comic singer in London taverns and music-halls; he was famous for his performance at the **Cider Cellars** of a song called 'Sam Hall', the chant of a murderous chimney-sweep of that name, just before his execution. '[T]he man, made up with a ghastly face, delivered it sitting across a chair, and there was a horrible anathematising *refrain*. The effect produced was tremendous, and for months and months, at the hour when it was known that "Sam Hall" would be sung, there was no standing-place in the Cider Cellars' (Edmund Yates, 1884, *Edmund Yates: his recollections and experiences*, Vol. I, London: R. Bentley & Son, pp. 167–8).

MR HODGEN in W.M. Thackeray, *The History of Pendennis* (1848–50)

'The singer from whom Hodgen was drawn was a man named Ross' (ibid.).

ROSSETTI, Arthur (1877–1932) Son of William Michael Rossetti, a clerk in the Excise Office. When Arthur and his sisters Helen (**Angeli**) and Olive were 16, 14 and 12 years old, respectively, they produced an anarchist periodical, the *Torch*, in the basement of their home at 3 St Edmund's Terrace, London.

THE PROFESSOR in Joseph Conrad, *The Secret Agent* (1907)

'The idea of the experimenter with explosives working in his laboratory at the top of his house was probably derived from Arthur Rossetti' (Norman Sherry, 1971, *Conrad's Western World*, Cambridge, p. 274); but the Professor in *The Secret Agent* derived nothing else from Arthur Rossetti. *See also* **Creaghe**, Dr; **Dillon**, Luke; **Mezzeroff**, 'Professor'; **Most**, Johann.

ROSSETTI, Christina Georgina (1830–94) Poet. Daughter of Gabriele **Rossetti** and sister of Dante Gabriel **Rossetti**, she was educated at home and had her first pamphlet published before she reached her teen years. She was a devout Anglican and spent much of her life as an invalid but continued to work; she was the author of *Goblin Market* (1862).

CHLOE MARTINWARD in George Meredith, *A Tale of Chloe* (1879)

'Violet Hunt states that [George Meredith] told her "The Tale of Chloe" was based on an episode in the life of Christina Rossetti. According to this report Christina's former fiancé, John Collinson, whom she had rejected when he joined the Church of Rome, re-entered her life after he had married another woman, and persuaded her to elope with him. Her devoted elder sister Maria suspected the scheme and thwarted it by lying on the mat inside the front door every night for a week. ... Chloe herself bears some resemblance to Christina Rossetti' (A. Lionel Stevenson, 1954, *The Ordeal of George Meredith*, London: Peter Owen, pp. 222–3).

ROSSETTI, Dante Gabriel (1828–82) Painter and poet. Born in London, he was the son of Gabriele **Rossetti** and brother of Christina **Rossetti**. He attended Cary's Art Academy and spent a short time at the Antique School of the Royal

Academy, and founded the Pre-Raphaelite Brotherhood with Holman **Hunt** and Sir John Everett **Millais**. In 1860, after a long liaison, he married Elizabeth Siddall, but she died in 1862. Rossetti insisted on placing in her coffin the manuscript of his poems, which at last were ready for publication. 'I have often', he declared, 'been writing at these poems when Lizzie was ill and suffering, and I might have been attending to her, and now they shall go.' In 1869 the manuscript was retrieved from Lizzie's grave and *Poems* was published in 1870. He lived from 1862 until his death at 16 Cheyne Walk (**Queens House**); the novelist Hall Caine, who became a close friend in the last year of his life, was present at his death.

T. D'ARCY in Theodore Watts-Dunton, *Aylwin* (1899)

Identified in T. St E. Hake, 1902, 'Aylwin', *Notes and Queries* (9th series) 9 (7 June): 450–2, and 10 (2 August): 89–91; reprinted in *Aylwin*, 1914 (World's Classics), Oxford, App. II.

WALTER HAMLIN in Vernon Lee, *Miss Brown* (1884)

'Although [Vernon Lee] incorporated elements of her own West Indian forebears in the character of Hamlin (his name was one of her maternal grandfather's), people would see in him a resemblance to Dante Gabriel Rossetti' (Peter Gunn, 1964, *Vernon Lee, 1885–1936*, London: Oxford University Press, p. 102).

OSCAR STEPHENSON in Hall Caine, *The Prodigal Son* (1904)

'The reviews of Hall Caine's latest – I cannot read the book – tell of a part of it concerning all who loved Rossetti and held the incident too sacred for allusion. The man has posed as Rossetti's friend. You will be feeling the same disgust as I' (to Theodore Watts-Dunton, 6 November 1904, reproduced in *Letters of George Meredith*, 1970, ed. C.L. Cline, Vol. III, Oxford, p. 1508). In this preposterous novel Oscar Stephenson, the central character, a composer of genius, places the manuscripts of his compositions in his wife's coffin, but later, to raise money with which to gamble, sells the manuscripts and allows them to be exhumed. Apart from this incident, Stephenson bears no resemblance to Rossetti, being a consummate charmless ass.

STEPHEN THORNICROFT in Mrs Alfred Hunt, *Thornicroft's Model* (1873)

'*Thornicroft's Model* . . . is just a romantic account of the career of Rossetti, and of the struggle against the Royal Academy which was in those days being carried on by many unacademic painters' (Ford Madox Ford, 1912, preface to Mrs Alfred Hunt and Violet Hunt, *The Governess*, p. xi). Thornicroft's meeting with Helen Morris in the novel corresponds very closely with Rossetti's method of picking up his models as described by William Bell Scott and A.C. Benson.

ROSSETTI, Gabriele (1783–1854) Italian poet. A political refugee from Naples, he was a member of the secret society of the Carbonari and took part in the revolution of 1820. He fled to London when King Ferdinand I returned to power, and in 1831 he became Professor of Italian at King's College, London. He was a commentator on Dante, considering the *Inferno* to be largely political and anti-papal. He was the father of Dante Gabriel, William (the English critic) and Christina **Rossetti**.

PROFESSOR PESCA in Wilkie Collins, *The Woman in White* (1860)

'It has been said that his character was suggested by Gabriele Rossetti' (Kenneth Robinson, 1951, *Wilkie Collins*, p. 152).

ROSSLYN, James Alexander St Clair-Erskine, 3rd Earl (1802–66) Known as Lord Loughborough from 1805 to 1837, whereupon he succeeded to the title of Earl. He was a Tory MP from 1830 to 1832 and Master of the Pytchley (a Northamptonshire hunt) in 1863.

LORD RAMBROOKE in Benjamin Disraeli, *Coningsby* (1844)

Identified in a key in *Notes and Queries* (8th series) 3 (13 May 1893): 363. *See also under* **Bright**, John.

ROSTON, Derbyshire A small village situated between Rocester and Norbury.

BROXTON in George Eliot, *Adam Bede* (1859)

'Broxton . . . is . . . Roston, a short distance up the hill from Norbury. Here . . . Robert Evans was born in a little cottage' (Charles S. Olcott, 1911, *George Eliot: scenes and places in her novels*, London: Cassell, p. 68; originally published 1910, New York: Thomas Y. Crowell).

ROTCH, Benjamin (1794–1854) A barrister at Lincoln's Inn, London, he became a magistrate in 1829 and was Visiting Magistrate for Coldbath Fields Prison between 1831 and 1849. He was MP for Knaresborough, Yorkshire, from 1832 to 1834 and in 1833 he was Chairman of the Middlesex general quarter session. He wrote *Suggestions for the Prevention of Juvenile Depravity* (1846).

MR CREAKLE in Charles Dickens, *David Copperfield* (1849–50)

'Mr Creakle [of the final instalment of *David Copperfield*] – who seems only nominally the same man as the brutal schoolmaster of fifty chapters earlier – is twice identified as a "Middlesex Magistrate". . . . I suggest that [Dickens] was here enjoying a private joke against one of [the Middlesex magistrates of the day], Mr Benjamin Rotch, JP. Dickens had come into contact with Rotch during his many visits to the Middlesex prisons, to recruit girls for Urania Cottage. This "Home for Fallen Women" was financed by Miss Burdett-Coutts, but planned and run by Dickens with the help chiefly of [the governor of Coldbath Fields Prison and the Governor of Tothill Fields House of Correction]' (P.W. Collins, 1961, 'The Middlesex Magistrate in *David Copperfield*', *Notes and Queries* 206: 87, 88). Dickens's animosity towards Rotch deepened steadily from his first mention of him in a letter to Miss Burdett Coutts (3 November 1847), and he mentioned him disrespectfully in November 1849 when Copperfield was well under way. *See also* **Jones**, William.

ROTHENSTEIN, Sir William (1872–1945) English artist. Born in Bradford, he studied in Paris and at the Slade School of Fine Art, London, and became Principal of the Royal College of Art. He was mainly a portrait painter, and was an official war artist in both world wars. He helped and encouraged young painters, including Mark **Gertler**.

EDGAR FROITZHEIM in Gilbert Cannan, *Mendel* (1916)

'[My brother] showed me a book dealing with your life and adventures. In it I read an account you gave Gilbert Cannan of your first meeting with me and of your impressions on that occasion' (letter from Sir William Rothenstein, 30 June 1918); Gertler's reply disclaimed any responsibility for 'that wretched book', to which Rothenstein replied 'I accept [your letter] unreservedly' (*Mark Gertler: selected letters*, 1965, ed. Noel Carrington, App., pp. 253–6.

ADOLPH GRIFFENBERG in Gilbert Cannan, *Mummery* (1916)

'. . . portraits of a number of the leading figures of the theatre appear, including Rothenstein, loosely disguised' (Diana Farr, 1978, *Gilbert Cannan: a Georgian prodigy*, London: Chatto & Windus, p. 164).

ROTHERMERE, Harold Sidney Harmsworth, Lord (1868–1940) Newspaper proprietor. 1st Viscount, he was the younger brother of Lord **Northcliffe**; in 1896 they founded the *Daily Mail*. In 1914 he took over the *Daily Mirror*, and in 1922–32 he controlled Associated Newspapers (*Daily Mail, Evening News* and *Sunday Dispatch*).

THOMAS CARLYLE CRAW in John Buchan, *Castle Gay* (1930)

'Buchan told Beaverbrook [that Craw] was a cross between Rothermere and Robertson Nicoll' (J. Adam Smith, 1965, *John Buchan*, p. 268). *See also* **Nicoll**, Sir William Robertson.

LORD YOUNGBROTHER in Hugh Kingsmill, *The Return of William Shakespeare* (1929)

'This fantasy . . . includes [a portrait] . . . of Lord Rothermere as Lord Youngbrother' (Michael Holroyd, 1964, *Hugh Kingsmill*, London: Unicorn Press, p. 107). There is no evidence that Kingsmill ever had any personal dealings with Rothermere.

de ROTHSCHILD, Adolph (1823–1900) Of Naples.

SIDONIA in Benjamin Disraeli, *Coningsby* (1844)

Identified in a key in *Notes and Queries* (8th series) 3 (13 May 1893): 363. A most implausible identification, Adolph de Rothschild being twenty-one years of age when *Coningsby* was published. He is described by Lady Battersea as 'a fair-haired, handsome, cheery youth' (*Reminiscences*, 1922, London, p. 67). *See also* **Disraeli**, Benjamin; de **Rothschild**, Baron James Mayer; de **Rothschild**, Lionel; **Urquhart**, David.

de ROTHSCHILD, Charlotte (1819–84) Daughter of Charles de Rothschild of Naples, she married her cousin Baron Lionel de **Rothschild**.

EVA BESSO in Benjamin Disraeli, *Tancred* (1847)

'Mr Disraeli was supposed in his character of "Eva" in *Tancred* to have portrayed my aunt, Baroness Lionel de Rothschild' (Constance Battersea, 1922, *Reminiscences*, p. 232).

de ROTHSCHILD, Baron James Mayer (1792–1868) Son of the German financier Meyer Amschel Rothschild (1743–1812). He was the founder of the Paris branch of the family.

BARON HAUSBERG in Oscar Wilde, 'The Model Millionaire' (1891)

'When Eugène Delacroix wanted to paint [Baron James de Rothschild] as a beggar, he agreed instantly. The following morning a pauper in rags rang the bell of Delacroix's studio. A disciple answered ... and sent [him] with a franc piece. ... Twenty-four hours later a liveried servant handed [the young man] the following letter: "Dear Sir, You will find enclosed the capital which you gave me at the door to M. Delacroix's studio, with the interest and compound interest on it – a sum of ten thousand francs. You can cash the cheque at my bank whenever you like. James de Rothschild"' (Frederick Morton, 1962, *The Rothschilds: a family portrait*, p. 73). The fact that Oscar Wilde's short story was founded on this anecdote was pointed out by A.R. Tintner in 1977 in 'A Rothschild anecdote as a source for "The Model Millionaire"', *Notes and Queries* 222 (1): 45).

SIDONIA in Benjamin Disraeli, *Coningsby* (1844) and *Tancred* (1847)

'In Paris [John Pope Hennessy] made friends with Montalambert and an impression of Baron James de Rothschild, the original of Disraeli's "Sidonia"' (James Pope Hennessy, 1964, *Verandah*, London, p. 39). *See also* **Disraeli**, Benjamin; de **Rothschild**, Adolph; de **Rothschild**, Lionel; **Urquhart**, David.

de ROTHSCHILD, Lionel Nathan (1808–79) Banker and philanthropist. Elder son of Nathan Meyer de Rothschild (1777–1836) and nephew of Baron James Mayer de **Rothschild**, he married his cousin Charlotte (de **Rothschild**, above). In 1850 he became the first practising Jew to be elected MP, but he was unable to take his seat until 1858. He was a close friend of Disraeli.

ADRIAN NEUCHATEL in Benjamin Disraeli, *Endymion* (1880)

Identified in 'Key to *Endymion*', *Notes and Queries* 83 (24 October 1942): 263; identifications attributed to G.E. Buckle.

SIDONIA in Benjamin Disraeli, *Coningsby* (1844)

'Sidonia in *Coningsby* is an idealised portrait of him' (*The Dictionary of National Biography*, Vol. XVII, London: Oxford University Press, p. 305). Also identified in a key in *Notes and Queries* (8th series) 3 (13 May 1893): 363. *See also under* **Bright**, John. *See also* **Disraeli**, Benjamin; de **Rothschild**, Adolph; de **Rothschild**, Baron James Mayer; **Urquhart**, David.

The ROTHSCHILDS

THE NEUCHATELS in Benjamin Disraeli, *Endymion* (1880)

Identified in 'Key to *Endymion*', *Notes and Queries* 83 (24 October 1942): 263; identifications attributed to G.E. Buckle.

ROTHSTEIN, Arnold (1882–1928) Gambler and racketeer. Known to millions as the man who fixed the 1919 World Series, he died after being shot by an unidentified assailant (see L. Katcher, 1959, *The Big Bankroll*).

MEYER WOLFSHIEM in F. Scott Fitzgerald, *The Great Gatsby* (1925)

'Wolfshiem . . . was based on Arnold Rothstein, and about him Fitzgerald knew only the ordinary rumours of the day' (A. Mizener, 1951, *The Far Side of Paradise*, p. 171). 'In *Gatsby* I selected the stuff . . . always starting from the *small* focal point that impressed me – my own meeting with Arnold Rothstein for instance' (to Corey Ford, July 1937, reproduced in *The Letters of F. Scott Fitzgerald*, 1964, ed. Andrew Turnbull, London: Bodley Head, p. 551).

ROUS, Peyton (1879–1970) Pathologist. A member of the Rockefeller Institute from 1909 to 1920, he carried out important research into cancer and in 1966 was awarded the Nobel Prize.

RIPPLETON HOLABIRD in Sinclair Lewis, *Arrowsmith* (1925)

Identified in Mark Schorer, 1961, *Sinclair Lewis: an American life*, New York: McGraw-Hill, p. 418. *See also* **Cole**, Rufus.

ROUTLEDGE, Henry (d. 1811) Legal grandson of a certain Mr Carruthers of Dormont, Dumfriesshire. Sometime in the mid-eighteenth century Mr Carruthers had reason to suspect his wife's fidelity and obtained a divorce, but his wife gave birth to a daughter before proceedings could be finished. Legally, Carruthers was the father, but he refused to have the child in his home and sent her to be brought up by a farmer in the Cheviot Hills. Somehow she learnt the facts of her birth, and when debts and poverty pressed her and her husband, a yeoman farmer called Routledge, they called on her legal father for a share in his estate. At length they agreed to sell their rights for £1,200, but by the time they died the money had all been spent. Their children, a boy and a girl, were left 'objects of charity to a distant relation. The boy was sent to the East Indies, "Before he went on board his benefactor put into his hands a packet and desired him to take charge of it. It referred he said to some claims of his mother on a Scotch estate and might one day be useful to him." In due course the boy returned to England, a successful man on leave. He took a shooting in Dumfriesshire, near Dormont . . . he lodged at a small inn hard by, and the landlady, struck by his name, began to gossip with him about his family history' (Andrew Lang, 1901, Introd. to *Guy Mannering* (Border edn), p. xiv). Upon his return to London, he examined the packet for the first time and took legal advice, then returned to India, having set in train a lawsuit laying claim to the Dormont estate. When he next returned on leave he learned that the decision of the first court had gone in his favour. He gave a dinner party to celebrate and next morning was found dead in his bed.

HENRY BERTRAM in Sir Walter Scott, *Guy Mannering* (1815)

In a letter to Lady Abercorn written on 21 May 1813 (reproduced in *Letters of Sir Walter Scott*, 1932, ed. H.J.C. Grierson, Vol. III, London: Constable, pp. 275–8), Scott recounts the facts of the Dormont Case, which had come before the last sitting of the court in which he was Clerk to the Sessions. Routledge's sister had taken his place as pursuer of the action after his death. Andrew Lang wrote:

'As [the case] occupied Scott's mind in 1813, and as he wrote *Guy Mannering* in 1814–15, it is not impossible that he may have borrowed his wandering heir from the Dormont case' (Lang, op. cit.). In 1820 the case finally reached the House of Lords: they decided against the Routledge claim. *See also* **Annesley**, James; **Maxwell**, Sir Robert.

ROWLEY, Joe (1831?–1908) The owner of collieries near Hawarden in Wales, he was a friend and neighbour of **Gladstone**. In 1857–8 he studied painting in Paris, where he knew **Whistler**.

TALBOT ('TAFFY') WYNNE in George Du Maurier, *Trilby* (1894)

'Rowley, the original of Taffy, died in 1908, a splendidly handsome old man' (Thomas Armstrong, 'Reminiscences of Du Maurier', in L.M. Lamont, 1912, *Thomas Armstrong, CB: a memoir, 1832–1911*, p. 112). Thomas Armstrong was one of the four original tenants of 53 rue Notre-Dame des Champs and his identification is undoubtedly correct. *See also* **Prinsep**, Valentine C.

ROYAL YORK HOTEL, Brighton Owned by Harry (later Sir Harry) Preston, Arnold Bennett stayed there while writing *Clayhanger* in January–March 1910.

ROYAL SUSSEX HOTEL in Arnold Bennett, the *Clayhanger* trilogy (1910–16)

'The "Royal Sussex" of [*Clayhanger*] is the Royal York' (Sir Harry Preston, 1936, *Leaves from My Unwritten Diary*, London: Hutchinson, p. 46).

ROYDE-SMITH, Naomi (d. 1964) Novelist. From 1912 to 1922 she was Literary Editor of the *Saturday Westminster*, and in 1926 she married the actor Ernest Milton. She became friends with Rose Macaulay in 1912.

EVELYN GRESHAM in Rose Macaulay, *Crewe Train* (1926)

'Rose had been swept off her feet, dazzled by Naomi's looks but even more by her mind and . . . conversation. Fair-haired, petite and attractive, with a liking for stylish clothes . . . Naomi was a sparkling talker' (C. Babington Smith, 1972, *Rose Macaulay*, p. 65). 'At some point during the first half of the 1920s . . . Rose and Naomi had a violent quarrel. It came about because Naomi had been spreading untrue and damaging gossip about Rose. . . . In *Crewe Train* . . . one of the central characters is a magnetic middle-aged woman, whose tongue inflicts pain and distress on all around her' (ibid., p. 102; the identification is made in the index).

ROYLANCE, Elizabeth (d. 1830)

MRS PIPCHIN in Charles Dickens, *Dombey and Son* (1846–8)

When Mrs Dickens and her younger children joined John Dickens in the Marshalsea prison in 1824, Dickens related (in an autobiographical fragment written for Forster many years later); 'I (small Cain that I was, except that I had never done any harm to anyone) was handed over as a lodger to a reduced old lady, long known to our family, in Little-College-Street, Camden-town, who took children in to board, and had once done so at Brighton, and who, with a few alterations and embellishments, unconsciously began to sit for Mrs Pipchin . . . when she took me in' (quoted in John Forster, 1928, *Life of Dickens*, ed. J.W.T.

Ley, Vol. I, ii, p. 27). 'When the family left the Marshalsea they all went to lodge with the lady in Little-College-Street, a Mrs Roylance' (ibid., p. 33). 'I hope you will like Mrs Pipchin's establishment. It is from the life, and I was there – I don't suppose I was eight years old; but I remember it all as well, and certainly understood it as well, as I do now. We should be devilish sharp in what we do to children' (to John Forster, 4 November 1846, ibid., Vol. VI, ii, p. 479). Forster (ibid.) writes in a footnote: 'I take, from his paper of notes for the number the various names, beginning with that of her real prototype, out of which the name selected came to him at last. "Mrs Roylance, House at the seaside. Mrs Wrychin, Mrs Tipchin, Mrs Elchin, Mrs Somching, Mrs Pipchin."'

RUBINSTEIN, Anton (1829–94) Russian Jewish pianist and composer. Born in Moldavia, he settled in St Petersburg and taught music, and later made concert tours in Europe and the United States.

JULIUS KLESMER in George Eliot, *Daniel Deronda* (1876)

'But [George Eliot] did meet at Weimar the musician from whom the conception of Klesmer grew. Anton Rubinstein ... fits precisely her description of "the German, the Sclave and the Semite" ... when Rubinstein came to London ... in ... 1876, Mrs Frederick Lehmann invited the Leweses to dine with him. ... "We shall so like to renew our acquaintance with Klesmer, whom we met in Weimar in '54!", Lewes wrote to Mrs Lehmann' (Gordon S. Haight, 1968, *George Eliot*, Oxford, p. 490). *See also* **Liszt**, Franz.

RUBY, George (b. *c.*1836) A crossing sweeper. On 8 January 1850 he was called to give evidence before Alderman Humphrey at the Mansion House Police Court in a case of assault. The case was reported in *The Times* on 9 January (p. 7), in the *Examiner* on 12 January, and in the January 1850 issue of *Household Narrative* (suppl. to *Household Words*). The boy, upon being handed the Testament, looked perfectly amazed. *The Times* recounted that, after examination, Alderman Humphrey refused to 'take the evidence of a creature who knew nothing whatever of the obligation to tell the truth'.

Jo in Charles Dickens, *Bleak House* (1852–3)

'One of the originals, for Jo was almost certainly George Ruby' (Humphry House, 1941, *Dickens' World*, p. 33). 'It is obvious that Dickens must have had George Ruby in mind in conceiving the whole situation and in making Jo a crossing-sweeper. But there is some reason for believing that this was not the only case he thought of as he wrote' (K.J. Fielding and Alec W. Brice, 1969, 'Charles Dickens on "The Exclusion of Evidence"', *The Dickensian* 65 (January): 39). Dickens began writing *Bleak House* in November 1851; Jo makes his first appearance in chapter XI (i.e. in the fourth of the monthly parts), published in June 1852. In March 1852 the *Monthly Narrative* reported another case in which the evidence of a child of eight was rejected. 'He was aware that something would be done to wicked people who told lies after they were dead, but did not know what it was.' 'References will show to what extent the cases quoted influenced the language and procedure which Dickens attached to his crossing sweeper' (John Suddaby, 1912, 'The crossing sweeper in *Bleak House*: Dickens and the original Jo', *The Dickensian* 8 (September): 249).

RUMLEY, Robert Parker A black preacher in Asheville, North Carolina, who was renowned for an oft-repeated sermon entitled 'De Dry Bones in De Valley'.

DICK PROSSER in Thomas Wolfe, *The Web and the Rock* (1939)

'Wolfe must have had in mind the stories he had heard about Rumley's sermon when he wrote of Prosser's preaching' (F.C. Watkins, 1957, *Thomas Wolfe's Characters: portraits from life*, Norman, Okla., p. 109). *See also* **Harris**, Will.

RUSKIN, John (1819–1900) Author and art critic. Son of a London wine merchant, he was tutored privately before receiving further education at Christ Church, Oxford, where he won the Newdigate Prize for Poetry. He became the art critic of his day, publishing works such as *The Seven Lamps of Architecture* (1848) and *The Stones of Venice* (1851–3). In 1869 he became the first Oxford Slade Professor of Fine Art, resigning in 1878; he filled the post again in 1883–4. In 1848 he married Euphemia Chalmers Gray, who later married John Everett **Millais**.

MR HERBERT in W.H. Mallock, *The New Republic* (1877)

'My characters in *The New Republic* were all portraits . . . the principal speakers drawn without any disguise . . . Mr Herbert was Ruskin' (W.H. Mallock, 1920, *Memoirs of Life and Literature*, London: Chapman and Hall, pp. 65–6). 'Ruskin . . . was delighted by the study of Mr Herbert and told friends and acquaintances that Mallock was the only man who really understood him' (J. Lucas, 1975, introd. to *The New Republic*, Leicester, p. 28).

JOHN WEMMICK in Charles Dickens, *Great Expectations* (1860–1)

'That both the then published work of Ruskin and some details of his private life not yet in print lie behind Dickens' creation of Wemmick – that Wemmick is a caricature of Ruskin – is but an engrossing possibility' (Lawrence Jay Dessner, 1975, '*Great Expectations*: the tragic comedy of John Wemmick', *Ariel* (Calgary) 6 (April): 67). Perhaps this was another of the private jokes that Dickens from time to time tucked in to his novels (cf. **Cole**, Sir Henry). As *Praeterita* was published in 1887, Dickens displayed considerable insight.

RUSSELL, Bertrand (1872–1969) 3rd Earl Russell. Mathematician and philosopher. Born in Gwent, Wales, he was the grandson of John, 1st Earl Russell, and was educated privately and at Trinity College, Cambridge. He became a Fellow of Trinity in 1895, and in 1896 he published his first book, *German Social Democracy*. During the First World War, he lost his Trinity fellowship in 1916 and was imprisoned in 1918 because of his active pacifism, but in 1939, when Fascism was on the rise, he renounced his pacifism and in 1944 his fellowship was restored. He received the Order of Merit when he returned to England after the Second World War, and the Nobel Prize for Literature in 1950. He was married four times: first to Alys Pearsall Smith; second, in 1921, to Dora Black, with whom he founded a progressive school near Petersfield in Hampshire; third, in 1936, to Patricia Spence; and fourth, to Edith Finch, with whom he was imprisoned in 1961 for taking part in a sit-down demonstration in Whitehall, London.

SIR JOSHUA MATTHESON in D.H. Lawrence, *Women in Love* (1920)

'Russell makes a brief but unmistakeable appearance as Sir Joshua Mattheson' (H.T. Moore, 1951, *Life and Letters of D.H. Lawrence*, p. 157).

MR SCOGAN in Aldous Huxley, *Crome Yellow* (1921)

'Almost half a century after the publication of *Crome Yellow*, Bertrand Russell still took a poor view of Mr Scogan' (Ronald W. Clark, 1968, *The Huxleys*, London: Heinemann, p. 224). *See also* **Douglas**, Norman.

MELIAN STOKES in Gilbert Cannan, *Pugs and Peacocks* (1921) and *Sembal* (1922)

'The speech Melian Stokes (Bertrand Russell) makes to the magistrate in . . . *Sembal* sums up some of Gilbert's feelings [about the Great War, which he saw as a crime against humanity]' (Diana Farr, 1978, *Gilbert Cannan: a Georgian prodigy*, London: Chatto & Windus, p. 134).

THORNTON TYRRELL in Siegfried Sassoon, *Memoirs of an Infantry Officer* (1930)

'It was Russell (Tyrrell in *Memoirs of an Infantry Officer*) who encouraged Sassoon to write his statement [to his commanding officer] of the reasons for which he . . . refused to serve further in the war' (Martin Seymour-Smith, 1982, *Robert Graves*, p. 56). Bertrand Russell was the inspiration for Mr Apollinax in T.S. Eliot's 'Prufrock' (1917) (see *Ottoline: the early memoirs of Lady Ottoline Morrell*, 1963, p. 257).

RUSSELL, Joe (d. 1941) A rum runner at Key West who for many years, during Prohibition, did the run between Florida and Cuba. He later ran a bar called **Sloppy Joe's** on Green Street in Key West. In 1932, Ernest Hemingway crossed to Havana with him and he spent two months fishing from his boat, the *Anita*; it was during this expedition that he first discovered the splendours of marlin fishing. It was in Joe's bar in 1936 that Hemingway first met Martha **Gellhorn**, who became his third wife.

HARRY MORGAN in Ernest Hemingway, *To Have and Have Not* (1937)

'Harry Morgan . . . was modelled after Josey' (Leicester Hemingway, 1962, *My Brother, Ernest Hemingway*, p. 118); but of course the identity was only partial, based on Russell's life as a rum-runner, which, like Harry Morgan's, came to an end with Prohibition.

FREDDY WALLACE in Ernest Hemingway, *To Have and Have Not* (1937)

'Joe Russell was the prototype for Freddy Wallace. . . . Ernest even made him complain, as Josie had done that spring, about the way his legs ached from standing up all day behind the bar waiting on customers' (Carlos Baker, 1969, *Ernest Hemingway: a life story*, New York, pp. 294–5).

RUSSELL, Dr John (1861?–1926) Of Waterloo Road, Burslem. He was Arnold Bennett's family doctor.

DR STERLING in Arnold Bennett, *The Old Wives' Tale* (1908)

'I suppose you've heard that Dr Russell went back to Scotland, bought a big house there, and immediately died in it. . . . According to the obituaries in all the London papers, his chief title to fame is that he is the original of Dr Sterling in "The Old Wives' Tale'" (17 August 1926, reproduced in *Arnold Bennett's Letters to His Nephew*, 1935, ed. R. Bennett, London: Heinemann, p. 168).

RUSSELL, John, 1st Earl (1792–1898) Liberal statesman. Born in London and educated at the University of Edinburgh, he was known as Lord John Russell until 1861. He was elected MP for Tavistock in 1813 and in 1835 he became leader of the House of Commons. He was Prime Minister from 1846 to 1852, and in 1866 his long political life came to an end. A tiny man, with a frail body and an enormous head, he was much caricatured. He was the grandfather of Bertrand and Frank **Russell**, who were brought up in his house after the early death of their parents.

LORD BULFINCH in Samuel Warren, *Ten Thousand a Year* (1841)

'He is the "Lord Bulfinch, MP" in Warren's once famous novel, *Ten Thousand a Year*' (Geoffrey H. White (ed.), 1949, *The Complete Peerage of England, Scotland, Ireland, Great Britain and the United Kingdom*, Vol. XI, rev. edn, London: St Catherine Press, p. 236 n. (b)).

LORD MICHIN MALICHO in Thomas Love Peacock, *Gryll Grange* (1860)

'Lord John Russell . . . [is] intended' (*The Novels of T.L. Peacock*, 1948, ed. David Garnett, London: Rupert Hart-Davis, p. 811 n. 2).

WILLIAM MILDMAY in Anthony Trollope, the Palliser novels (1864–79)

'[In] Trollope's letter of March 31st 1869 to the *Daily Telegraph*, which on that day had printed an article accusing him of "having drawn portraits of the leading politicians of the time" . . . [he denies depicting Bright as Mr Turnbull]. The letter contains also a general disclaimer, but this is not emphasized, and it is significant that Trollope makes no reference to the Telegraph's other identifications, viz; de Terier = Derby, Daubeny = Disraeli, Mildmay = Russell, Gresham = Gladstone (R.W. Chapman, 1948, 'Personal names in Trollope's political novels', *Essays Mainly on the Nineteenth Century Presented to Sir Humphrey Milford*, pp. 80–1).

PLANTAGENET PALLISER in Anthony Trollope, the Palliser novels (1864–79)

'I believe that, although Trollope misleads us, as he often does, by denying that the young Duke is based on any living man, he does base Palliser's portrait on the actual career and personality of Lord John Russell' (Blair G. Kenney, 1965, 'Trollope's ideal statesman: Plantagenet and Lord John Russell', *The Nineteenth Century* 20 (3): 281). *See also* **Parkinson-Fortescue**, Chichester; **Newcastle**, 6th Duke of.

RUSSELL, John Francis Stanley, 2nd Earl (1865–1931) Barrister and politician. Grandson of the 1st Earl **Russell** and elder brother of Bertrand **Russell**, he was Parliamentary Secretary to the Ministry of Transport in 1929 and to India during the first Labour government. He married M.E. Scott, but they were divorced in 1890; his second marriage, to Marion Cooke in 1890, also ended in divorce; and in 1916 he married the novelist 'Elizabeth', Mary Annette von Arnim (**Russell**, below), from whom he was separated in 1919. He was a Fabian and an agnostic.

JIM DARNLEY in George Santayana, *The Last Puritan* (1935)

'[George Santayana] wrote a novel in which my brother (for whom he had a considerable affection) appears as the villain' (Bertrand Russell, 1957, *Portraits from Memory*, p. 90).

EVERARD WEMYSS in 'Elizabeth', *Vera* (1921)

'Elizabeth, in her turn, left him and wrote an intolerably cruel novel about him, called *Vera*. In this novel, Vera is already dead; she had been his wife and he is supposed to be heartbroken at the loss of her. She died by falling out of one of the windows of the tower of Telegraph House. As the novel proceeds, the reader gradually gathers that her death was not an accident, but suicide brought on by my brother's cruelty. It was this that caused me to give my children an emphatic piece of advice: "Do not marry a novelist"' (Bertrand Russell, 1968, *Autobiography*, Vol. II, pp. 153, 154). It should perhaps be added that although Elizabeth's predecessor was married to Francis Russell for fifteen years, she resembled Vera in no other respect; she was fat and uncultivated and did not (intentionally or otherwise) fall out of a window at Telegraph House.

RUSSELL, Mary Annette, Countess ('Elizabeth') (1866–1941) Novelist under the pseudonym 'Elizabeth'. Born in Sydney, Australia, she was the daughter of a self-made businessman by the name of Beauchamp, and the cousin of Katherine **Mansfield**. In 1891 she married Count Henning von Arnim; she wrote *Elizabeth and Her German Garden* on his East Prussian estate, where E.M. Forster spent some months as tutor to her daughters in 1905. After Count von Arnim's death, she returned to England, and in 1916 she married John Francis Stanley, 2nd Earl **Russell**, becoming his third wife; they separated in 1919 and she resumed her novel writing.

MRS HARROWDEAN in H.G. Wells, *Mr Britling Sees It Through* (1916)

'[In 1912] Wells fell under her spell. . . . He was to have his revenge . . . in the part she was given to play in *Mr Britling Sees It Through*, where she appears as Mrs Harrowdean' (Lovat Dickson, 1972, *H.G. Wells*, Harmondsworth: Penguin, p. 248).

MRS EMILY FAILING in E.M. Forster, *The Longest Journey* (1907)

'I would guess that Mrs Failing . . . is drawn in part from "Elizabeth". The resemblance is very close' (P.N. Furbank, 1977, *E.M. Forster: a life*, Vol. I: *The Growth of the Novelist (1879–1914)*, London: Secker & Warburg, p. 125 n. 1). In 1930 Forster said to Virginia Woolf: 'No, I don't like her. I think she is unkind and selfish. But she has a wonderful way of making one wish to be nice to her' (reproduced in *The Letters of Virginia Woolf*, 1978, ed. Nigel Nicolson, Vol. IV, London: Hogarth Press, p. 218). *See also* **Forster**, W.H.

RUTHERFORD, Archibald, Lord (d. 1684/5) Fourth son of John Rutherford of Hunthill, he succeeded his brother Thomas as 3rd Baron in 1668. His nephew, David Dunbar, married Janet **Dalrymple**, who was said to have betrothed herself to Rutherford.

EDGAR, MASTER OF RAVENSWOOD in Sir Walter Scott, *The Bride of Lammermoor* (1819)

'He was betrothed, without the knowledge of her parents, to Janet, 1st d. of James Dalrymple, 1st Viscount Stair . . . but she was compelled by her mother to marry . . . David Dunbar of Baldoon. He was the original of the Master of Ravenswood' (Geoffrey H. White (ed.), 1949, *The Complete Peerage of England, Scotland, Ireland, Great Britain and the United Kingdom*, Vol. XI, rev. edn, London: St Catherine Press, p. 244 n. (a)).

RUTLAND, 7th Duke of *See* **Manners**, Lord John.

RUTLAND, Charles Cecil John Manners, 6th Duke of (1815–88) Styled Lord Granby until 1857, he was a Conservative MP in 1837–57, and was a strong protectionist and supporter of Lord George Bentinck. He was succeeded by his brother, Lord John **Manners**.

LORD BEAUMANOIR in Benjamin Disraeli, *Coningsby* (1844)

Identified in a key in *Notes and Queries* (8th series) 3 (13 May 1893): 363. *See also under* **Bright**, John.

RUTLAND, John Henry Manners, 5th Duke of (1778–1857)

THE DUKE in Benjamin Disraeli, *Coningsby* (1844)

Identified in a key in *Notes and Queries* (8th series) 3 (13 May 1893): 363. *See also under* **Bright**, John.

RYDER, Dudley, 2nd Earl of Harrowby (1798–1882) Previously known as Viscount Sandon, he succeeded to the title of Earl in 1847. A Tory MP from 1819 to 1847, he was a supporter of the Reform Bill and in 1845 followed **Peel** on free trade. He was Lord Privy Seal in 1835–8, and the first standing committee of Cabinet was established at his instance. He was also Chairman of the Maynooth committee and was a member of the Oxford University Commission.

LORD FITZBOOBY in Benjamin Disraeli, *Coningsby* (1844)

'Lord Fitzbooby is more likely to have been intended for Lord Harrowby, the leader of "The Waverers" at the time of the Reform Bill agitation' (*Coningsby*, 1904, ed. B.N. Langdon-Davies, p. 585). *See also* **Harrington**, Charles Stanhope.

The RYDINGS, Birstall, Yorkshire Charlotte Brontë visited the house in 1832, when she paid her first visit to Ellen **Nussey**, whose brother was the tenant at that time. 'A handsome house . . . standing in many acres of ground. The house has battlements, a rookery, and all that a country gentleman's seat might aspire to' (T.J. Wise and J.A. Symington, 1932, *The Brontës: their lives, friendships and correspondence*, Vol. I, p. 105).

THORNFIELD HALL in Charlotte Brontë, *Jane Eyre* (1847)

'It shares with Norton Conyers . . . the credit of having inspired the picture of "Thornfield Hall". . . . That The Rydings played some part in her word-picture is not . . . to be doubted, and she had much more intimate associations with the smaller house' (ibid.). *See also* **Norton Conyers**.

RYE, Sussex The small market town in which E.F. Benson lived at **Lamb House** in 1917–40.

TILLING in E.F. Benson, *Queen Lucia* (1920) and others

Benson described the conception of the novels: 'I vaguely began to meditate on some design. I outlined an elderly atrocious spinster and established her in Lamb House. . . . I knew that her name must be Elizabeth Mapp. Rye should furnish the topography, so that no one who knew Rye could possibly be in doubt where the scene was laid, and I would call it Tilling because Rye has its river the Tillingham' (E.F. Benson, 1940, *Final Edition: an informal autobiography*, London: Longman, p. 162).

S

SACKVILLE, Victoria Sackville-West, Lady (1862–1936) Illegitimate daughter of the 2nd Lord Sackville, she married the 3rd Lord Sackville; she separated from the latter in 1919. Of great charm in her youth, she became increasingly difficult and unbalanced in later life. She was Vita Sackville-West's mother.

LADY LE BRETON in Victoria Sackville-West, *The Dark Island* (1934)

'[T]his novel is interesting as showing . . . an idealized Grannyma in the person of old lady Le Breton' (Benedict Nicolson to Harold Nicolson, 1933, quoted in Victoria Glendinning, 1983, *Vita: the life of V. Sackville-West*, p. 274).

SACKVILLE-WEST, Edward (1901–65) Writer and music critic. He was a cousin of Victoria **Sackville-West**.

DAVID WARBECK in Nancy Mitford, *The Pursuit of Love* (1945)

Identification based upon private information.

SACKVILLE-WEST, Victoria ('Vita') (1892–1962) Poet and novelist. Daughter of the 3rd Lord Sackville and Lady **Sackville**. Until her father's death in 1928, her life centred around Knole House, Kent. In 1913 she married Harold **Nicolson**, who was, like herself, sexually ambivalent. She had a violent love affair between 1918 and 1921 with Violet **Trefusis** which culminated in their bolting together to France, pursued and captured by their respective husbands. An account of the Nicolsons' marriage is found in Nigel Nicolson's *Portrait of a Marriage* (1973). Apart from her marriage, the central event in her life was probably her relationship with Virginia Woolf, whom she met in 1923 and with whom friendship flowered into a brief love affair in 1925; their friendship survived the end of the affair.

MRS CHILLEYWATER in Ronald Firbank, *The Flower Beneath the Foot* (1923)

'Homage to Ronald Firbank from . . . Vita Sackville-West (. . . the Mrs Chilleywater of "the Flower")' (Miriam J. Benkovitz, 1969, *Ronald Firbank*, p. 249).

JULIAN DAVENANT in Victoria Sackville-West, *Challenge* (1924)

'While Vita was writing [the novel] she was living her life on two levels, the actual and the fictional, and as her love for Violet [Trefusis] intensified so did that between Julian and Eve in the novel, with incidents . . . lived . . . from reality' (Nicolson, op. cit., p. 151). During the affair, Violet Trefusis called her Julian.

ORLANDO in Virginia Woolf, *Orlando* (1928)

'But listen; suppose Orlando turns out to be Vita; and its all about you and the lusts of your flesh and the lure of your mind . . . – suppose there's the kind of shimmer of reality which sometimes attaches to my people, as the lustre on an oyster shell ... suppose, I say, that Sibyl [Colefax] next October says "There's Virginia gone and written a book about Vita".... Shall you mind? Say Yes or No: Your excellence as a subject arises largely from your noble birth ... and the opportunity thus given for florid descriptive passages in great abundance. Also, I admit, I should like to untwine and twist again some very odd, incongruous strands in you ... and so if agreeable to you I would like to toss this up in the air and see what happens' (to V. Sackville-West, 9 October 1927, reproduced in *The Letters of Virginia Woolf*, 1977, ed. Nigel Nicolson, Vol. III, London: Hogarth Press, pp. 28–9). Vita replied, on 11 October, 'You have my full permission. Only I think that having drawn and quartered me ... or whatever it is that you intend to do, you ought to dedicate it to your victim' (ibid., n.).

RUTH PENNISTAN in Victoria Sackville-West, *Heritage* (1919)

'In the character of ... Ruth, the heiress of her novel, she drew her self-portrait' (Nicolson, op. cit., p. 146).

CRISTINA RICH in Victoria Sackville-West, *The Dark Island* (1934)

'Cristina represents V. S.-W. herself' (Michael Stevens, 1973, *V. Sackville-West: a critical biography*, p. 62).

SADLEIR, John (1814–56) Solicitor in Dublin. He was the Director of the Tipperary joint-stock bank, and in 1847 and 1848 was an MP. In 1853 he was junior Lord of the Treasury. Upon the failure of the Tipperary Bank, he committed suicide on Hampstead Heath.

MR MERDLE in Charles Dickens, *Little Dorrit* (1855–7)

'I had the general idea ... of the Society business before the Sadleir affair, but I shaped Mr Merdle himself out of that precious rascality' (Dickens to Forster, 1857[?], quoted in John Forster, 1928, *Life of Charles Dickens*, ed. J.W.T. Ley, p. 625). 'If I might make so bold as to defend that extravagant conception Mr Merdle, I would hint that it originated after the Railroad-share epoch, in the times of a certain Irish bank, and of one or two equally laudable enterprises' (preface to *Little Dorrit*, 1859, p. v). 'Merdle resembles Sadleir physically, a contemporary description telling us that he was a sallow-faced man "wrinkled with multifarious intrigue, cold, callous, cunning"' (Grahame and Angela Smith, 1971, 'Dickens as a popular artist', *The Dickensian* 67 (September): 132). *See also* **Hudson**, George.

ST AUBYN, Gwendolen (b. 1896) Daughter of the 1st Baron Carnock and sister of Harold **Nicolson**. She married the 3rd Baron St Levan.

SHIRIN LE BRETON in Victoria Sackville-West, *The Dark Island* (1934)

'Shirin is a slightly romanticised version of Gwen St Aubyn (later Lady St Levan)' (Michael Stevens, 1973, *V. Sackville-West: a critical biography*, p. 62).

ST BARNABAS, Oxford A church that was designed by Arthur Blomfield, in whose drawing office, first in St Martin's Place and subsequently in the Adelphi, London, Hardy worked as an assistant architect from 1862 to 1867.

St Silas in Thomas Hardy, *Jude the Obscure* (1895)

Identified in Denys Kay-Robinson, 1972, *Hardy's Wessex Reappraised*, Newton Abbot, and in F.B. Pinion, 1968, *A Hardy Companion*, London: Macmillan.

ST CLAIR-MORFORD, Major-General Albert (1893–1945) Wounded four times in the First World War, he received the Military Cross. In 1940 and 1941 he was Brigade Commander at Kingsdown Royal Marine training camp in Kent. Evelyn Waugh was there in January 1940 and wrote, 'the Brigade Commander . . . looks like something escaped from Sing Sing . . . teeth like a stoat, ears like a fawn, eyes alight like a child playing pirates' (*The Diaries of Evelyn Waugh*, 1978, ed. Michael Davie, London: Weidenfeld & Nicolson, p. 461).

Ben Ritchie-Hook in Evelyn Waugh, the *Sword of Honour* trilogy (1952–61)

'The model for "Brigadier Ritchie-Hook" in *Men at Arms*' (ibid., n. 3). *See also* **Carton de Wiart**, Adrian.

ST CROSS HOSPITAL, Winchester

Hirams Hospital in Anthony Trollope, *The Warden* (1855)

'[T]he notion of Hiram's Hospital was taken from St Cross' (Trollope to E.A. Freeman, October 1882, quoted in Edward A. Freeman, 1883, 'Anthony Trollope', *Macmillan's Magazine* (January): 239).

SAINT-GAUDENS, Augustus (1848–1907) An Irish-born American, he trained as a cameo-cutter and studied sculpture in Paris and Rome. With Stanford White, he designed the Adams monument in Rock Creek Cemetery, Washington, DC.

Mr Wharton in Henry Adams, *Esther* (1884)

'He is the prototype of Mr Wharton in . . . *Esther*' (James D. Hart (ed.), 1965, *The Oxford Companion to American Literature*, New York: Oxford University Press, s.v. Saint-Gaudens. *See also* **Bigelow**, William Sturgis; **La Farge**, John.

ST GILES HOUSE, Wimborne St Giles, Dorset Located two miles south-west of Cranborne.

Knollingwood Hall in Thomas Hardy, 'Barbara of the House of Grebe' (1891)

Identified in F.B. Pinion, 1968, *A Hardy Companion*, London: Macmillan.

ST JOHN'S SQUARE, Burslem, Staffordshire

St Luke's Square in Arnold Bennett, the *Clayhanger* trilogy (1910–16)

'When Enoch Bennett married her, Sarah Ann Longson [Arnold Bennett's mother] . . . was living with her people over the draper's shop which Robert Longson . . . had opened in St John's Square, the St Luke's Square of the novels' (Reginald Pound, 1952, *Arnold Bennett: a biography*, London: Heinemann, p. 49).

ST JULIOT, Cornwall A village situated north-east of Boscastle. Thomas Hardy met his first wife, Emma Gifford, there in 1870 when he visited the church to undertake its restoration; she was staying with her sister, whose husband was Revd Caddell **Holder**, the Rector.

ENDELSTOW in Thomas Hardy, *A Pair of Blue Eyes* (1873)

'Based on the village of St Juliot, Cornwall' (F.B. Pinion, 1968, *A Hardy Companion*, London: Macmillan, p. 319). '[Hardy] revised the novel . . . in 1919 for the Mellstock Edition, "to correct the topography a little" he wrote to Sydney Cockerell, "the reasons that led me to disguise the spot when the book was written in 1872 no longer existing, the hand of death having taken care of that." The reference is to the first Mrs Hardy, who had died in 1912, the last of the little group Hardy found at St Juliot Rectory in 1870' (R.L. Purdy, 1954, *Thomas Hardy: a bibliographical study*, Oxford, pp. 12, 13).

ST LUCIA

PLAGUE CITY in Sinclair Lewis, *Arrowsmith* (1925)

'One hot, still Sunday afternoon our steamer touched for a couple of hours at the island of San Lucia. I wandered ashore . . . and came presently into a large square plunged into a deserted Sunday stillness, gloomy under the shade of giant mango trees. Here was our plague city! I hastened back to the ship, which was to leave in a half-hour, dragged Lewis from his work and hurried him to the square, where he proceeded to conjure up fantastic funeral processions of imaginary plague victims. . . . Then back to the ship to set down . . . the impression of that hot, dark-green, almost sinister twilight stillness' (Paul de Kruif, see Mark Schorer, 1963, *Sinclair Lewis: an American life*, London: Heinemann, pp. 367, 368; originally published 1961, New York: McGraw-Hill).

ST MARY'S COLLEGE, Oscott The Roman Catholic seminary that was made, by Cardinal **Vaughan**, the common seminary for the southern and midland group of dioceses of the Roman Church.

MARYVALE in F.W. Rolfe, *Hadrian VII* (1904)

'His hero is himself . . . who broods for years over his rejection from Maryvale (Oscott)' (Shane Leslie, 1923, 'Frederick Baron Corvo', *London Mercury* 7 (47): 514).

ST MICHAEL'S MOUNT, Cornwall The seat of Lord St Levan.

STORN in Victoria Sackville-West, *The Dark Island* (1934)

'Storn, the dark island, is directly modelled on the St Levans' home, St Michael's Mount in Cornwall' (Michael Stevens, 1973, *V. Sackville-West: a critical biography*, p. 62).

ST TROND, Belgium

LONGRES in Aldous Huxley, 'Uncle Spencer', *Little Mexican and Other Stories* (1924)

'[The story's] scene was St Trond in Belgium, the home town of my first wife's grandparents' (to James G. Kennedy, 28 May 1961, reproduced in *Letters of Aldous Huxley*, 1969, ed. Grover Smith, p. 913).

SALEM, Massachusetts In 1835 it was an almshouse on Salem Neck.

UNCLE VENNER'S 'FARM' in Nathaniel Hawthorne, *The House of the Seven Gables* (1851)

'It would later figure . . . as Uncle Venner's farm, where he expected to spend his last days' (Hawthorne, 1972, *The American Notebooks*, ed. Claude Simpson, Columbus, p. 562 n. 3.23).

SALISBURY, Wiltshire

BARCHESTER in Anthony Trollope, *The Warden* (1855)

'In the course of the job [of postal surveyor] I visited Salisbury [in 1852] and whilst wandering there one midsummer evening round the purlieus of the cathedral I conceived the story of *The Warden* . . . and on the 29th of July 1853 . . . I began *The Warden*. . . . It was then more than twelve months since I had stood for an hour on the little bridge in Salisbury, and had made out to my own satisfaction the spot on which Hiram's hospital should stand' (Anthony Trollope, 1883, *An Autobiography*, Vol. I, pp. 123, 127, 128). *See also* **Winchester**.

MELCHESTER in Thomas Hardy, Wessex novels and tales (1871–95)

Identified on a map prepared by Thomas Hardy which hangs in the Dorset County Museum, Dorchester. *See under* **Abbotsbury**.

SALISBURY, Robert Arthur Talbot Gascoyne, Lord (1830–1903) Born at Hatfield House and educated at Eton and Christ Church, Oxford, he (as Viscount Cranbourne) was Secretary for India in 1866. He succeeded to the title of 3rd Marquis of Salisbury in 1868 and became Chancellor of the University of Oxford in 1869. In 1874 he was again Secretary for India, and in 1878 he became Foreign Secretary. He was Prime Minister 1885–6, 1886–92 and 1895–1902. As a young man, he contributed regularly to the *Saturday Review*.

THE EARL OF AINSLIE in Lewis Carroll, *Sylvie and Bruno* (1889)

'[I]n an exchange between the Lord Chancellor and the Earl (supposedly modelled on Salisbury), [Lewis Carroll] exactly caught the deflating logic of his host' (Kenneth Rose, 1975, *The Later Cecils*, p. 31). From 1870 onwards, Dodgson was a frequent visitor at Hatfield.

WILLIAM PITT FERRARS in Benjamin Disraeli, *Endymion* (1880)

'[A] sketch of Lord Salisbury . . . may be seen in the last novel of Lord Beaconsfield. The mortified politician "who thought he would take 'India', but who only got a second-class clerkship for his son in Somerset House" (that son being Endymion Ferrars) . . . in his adversity largely supported his household by cheques from that periodical, "the organic law of which was payment to all contributors"' (T.H.S. Escott, 1898, *Personal Forces of the Period*, p. 25).

LORD WILTSHIRE in Sir Harry Johnston, *The Gay-Dombeys* (1919)

'Lord Wiltshire is a portrait of Lord Salisbury' (Sir Harry Johnston to John Gunther, quoted in J. Gunther, 1925, 'Multiple Sir Harry Johnston', *Bookman* 57 (November): 309). Johnston entered the service of the Foreign Office as Vice-Consul in the Cameroon and Niger Delta; he came to the notice of Lord Salisbury, who employed him in the (abortive) negotiations at Lisbon in 1889, aimed at settling the spheres of influence in Africa of Great Britain and Portugal.

SALISBURY PLAIN

THE GREAT PLAIN in Thomas Hardy, Wessex novels and tales (1871–95)

Identified on a map prepared by Thomas Hardy which hangs in the Dorset County Museum, Dorchester. *See under* **Abbotsbury**.

SALISBURY TRAINING COLLEGE For teachers. Hardy's sisters, Mary and Katherine, were trained there.

MELCHESTER NORMAL SCHOOL in Thomas Hardy, *Jude the Obscure* (1895)

'At Salisbury [in 1923] they stopped . . . to look at the Cathedral . . . and at various old buildings, including the Training College which he had visited more than fifty years before when his two sisters were students there, and which is faithfully described in *Jude the Obscure*' (F.E. Hardy, 1972, *The Life of Thomas Hardy, 1840–1928*, p. 420). Also identified in Denys Kay-Robinson, 1972, *Hardy's Wessex Reappraised*, Newton Abbot, and in F.B. Pinion, 1968, *A Hardy Companion*, London: Macmillan.

SALOMONS, Mrs She was married to the brother of Sir David Salomons (1797–1873), the first Jewish Lord Mayor of London (1855–6). In April 1856, Nathaniel Hawthorne was present at a dinner at the Mansion House, and Mrs Salomons sat opposite him. He was transfixed by her beauty: 'She was, I suppose, dark and yet not dark, but rather seemed to be of pure white marble . . . the purest and finest complexion . . . that I ever beheld. Her hair was a wonderful deep, raven black, black as night, black as death . . . hair never to be painted nor described – wonderful hair, Jewish hair. Her nose had a beautiful outline . . . and that, and all her features, were so fine that sculpture seemed a despicable art beside her; and certainly my pen is good for nothing' (Nathaniel Hawthorne, 1941, *English Notebooks*, 1941, ed. Randall Stewart, New York and London: Modern Languages Association of America, p. 321).

MIRIAM SCHAEFFER in Nathaniel Hawthorne, *The Marble Faun* (1860)

'The "miraculous Jewess" became the physical prototype of Miriam in *The Marble Faun*' (ibid., p. 646 n. 333). And 'less completely [her husband] whose description follows in the text [of the notebooks] suggested the physical appearance of Miriam's model'. His chief feature was 'an immense beard' – a 'density of beard'.

SALT, Mr Private tutor. He taught Classics to Guy and Noel **Compton-Burnett**, and in 1899 he prepared Ivy Compton-Burnett for the entrance examination to Royal Holloway College.

SIGISMUND CLAVERHOUSE in I. Compton-Burnett, *Dolores* (1911)

'Another possible model is Mr Salt ... who ... coached her alone at Addiscombe College. ... Ivy's sisters both agree that [the] description [of Claverhouse] fitted Mr Salt, whom Ivy evidently admired' (H. Spurling, 1974, *Ivy When Young: the early life of I. Compton-Burnett, 1899–1919*, London: Gollancz, p. 174). *See also* **Seccombe**, Thomas.

SAMUELS, Henry B. (1860–1933) Editor of the anarchist journal *Commonweal* at the time of the **Greenwich Bomb Outrage**. He was the brother-in-law of Martial **Bourdin**, the perpetrator.

JACOB MYERS in Isabel Meredith, *A Girl Among the Anarchists* (1903)

'[The novel] gave ... a thinly disguised account of the Greenwich explosion. The account is very close to Nicoll's as regards the role of Samuels (called Jacob Myers)' (Ian Watt (ed.), 1973, 'The political and social background of *The Secret Agent*', in *The Secret Agent: a casebook*, London: Macmillan, p. 237). David Nicoll (1859–1918), anarchist and also an editor of *Commonweal*, was the author of a pamphlet entitled *The Greenwich Mystery* (1907, Sheffield), reprinted in Norman Sherry, 1971, *Conrad's Western World*, Cambridge, App. I, pp. 379 ff.

ADOLF VERLOC in Joseph Conrad, *The Secret Agent* (1907)

'It is acceptable that Verloc's part in the fictional bomb outrage stems from the part played by Samuels in the actual event' (Sherry, op. cit., p. 314). *See also* **Coulon**, Auguste; **Krieger**, Adolf P.

SAN GIMIGNANO, Italy

MONTERIANO in E.M. Forster, *Where Angels Fear to Tread* (1905)

'Monteriano is in reality San Gimignano near Florence, the town of many towers' (Wilfred Stone, 1966, *The Cave and the Mountain: a study of E.M. Forster*, London: Oxford University Press, p. 163).

SAN TOMÉ, Portuguese Guinea Portuguese slave island north of the Equator, on the Gulf of Guinea.

SAN TOMÉ in Joseph Conrad, *Nostromo* (1904)

'[Conrad] ... probably ... [had] in mind the infamous Portuguese slave island of San Tomé. ... The San Tomé scandal, concerning the system of contract labour used on the island, did not become sensational in England until the Cadbury libel case of 1909, but conditions on the island had been notorious as early as 1865' (J.L. Winter, 1966, 'Conrad's San Tomé', *Notes and Queries* 211: 412).

SANBORN'S SCHOOL, Concord, Massachusetts The school attended in 1861 by **Emerson**'s son Edward, Julian **Hawthorne**, and by Wilkie and Robertson, the two younger brothers of Henry **James**.

PLUMFIELD in Louisa M. Alcott, *Little Men* (1871) and *Jo's Boys* (1886)

'Remembering the doctrines of the Temple School and Sanborn's academy [she combined] them in the pedagogy of Plumfield' (M.B. Stern, 1952, *Louisa M. Alcott*, p. 214). *See also* **Temple School**.

SANDFORD, Revd Mr

REVD MR BAIRD in George Eliot, 'The Sad Fortunes of the Revd Amos Barton', *Scenes of Clerical Life* (1857–8)

See under **Anstruther**, Lady.

SANDGATE, Kent The small seaside town where H.G. **Wells** was nursed back to health by his wife Jane (Dorothy Richardson's friend Amy Robbins (see **Wells**). In 1900 Wells built a house there.

BONNYCLIFF in Dorothy Richardson, *Pilgrimage* (1915–67)

'The details of the house [Bonnycliff] and the company . . . can be very closely identified with the Worcester Park and Sandgate houses of the Wells' (John Rosenberg, 1973, *Dorothy Richardson*, p. 105).

SANDS, Ethel (1873–1962) Painter. Born in Newport, Rhode Island, she was the daughter of Mahlon Sands and his wife Mary; she was a great beauty. In 1874 the family moved to England, where Mrs Sands's prodigious good looks won them the entrée to the Marlborough House set. They settled permanently in England, and their very wide circle included Henry James. After the death of Mahlon Sands as the result of a riding accident, his family remained in England. Ethel Sands studied painting in Paris, where she met Anna Hohe ('Nan') Hudson, with whom she lived until Miss Hudson's death in 1957. Both women were painters, much influenced by **Sickert**. Ethel, in her houses outside Dieppe, at Newington, Oxon, and The Vale in Chelsea, was one of the great hostesses of the years 1900–39; she was a link between Chelsea and Bloomsbury, a plain woman of immense charm, cultivation and perception, and a painter of considerable talent.

NANDA BROOKENHAM in Henry James, *The Awkward Age* (1899)

'The centenary of James's birth took place in 1943 and led the *Atlantic Monthly* to press Logan [Pearsall Smith] for reminiscences. In putting them together all sorts of questions occurred to Logan which Ethel was asked to answer . . . How many of James' characters were suggested by real people? A list of Logan's suggestions . . . followed, beginning with the idea that Margot Asquith and her set were reflected in *The Awkward Age*. It is indeed a pity that we have not got Ethel's answer to this particular query, because it was believed among many members of her circle that she herself had contributed to James's inspiration in portraying Nanda, a young girl ill-at-ease in the society in which she had been brought up' (Wendy Baron, 1977, *Miss Ethel Sands and Her Circle*, pp. 248–9).

SANGER, Margaret Louise (1883–1966) American social reformer and founder of the birth control movement. Née Higgins. Born in Corning, New York, she was educated at Claverack College, and became a nurse. She married William Sanger in 1902. In 1914 she published *The Woman Rebel*, a radical feminist magazine with advice on contraception. In 1916 she founded the first

American birth-control clinic in Brooklyn, and was imprisoned as a result. After her release she travelled abroad, returning to America to found the American Birth Control League in 1921. Divorced from Sanger in 1920, she married J. Noah H. Slee in 1922. She wrote a number of books, including *Motherhood and Bondage* (1928).

V.V. GRAMMONT in H.G. Wells, *The Secret Places of the Heart* (1922)

'I don't think that there is any room for doubt but that this is my father's portrait of Margaret Sanger as he first perceived her, and before he had come to know her properly' (Anthony West, 1984, *H.G. Wells: aspects of a life*, p. 87).

SANSON, James (d. 1795) Tutor to the children of Thomas Scott, Sir Walter Scott's uncle, and subsequently in the household of the Earl of Hopetown. He was 'of the greatest stature – near six feet high. . . . His person was coarse, his limbs large, and his manners awkward. . . . His soul was pure and untainted – the seat of many manly and amiable virtues' (Robert Chambers, 1884, *Illustrations of the Characters of Waverley*, p. 55).

DOMINIE SAMPSON in Sir Walter Scott, *Guy Mannering* (1815)

'There are few of our originals in whom we can exhibit such precise points of coincident resemblance between the real and fictitious character, as in him whom we now assign as the prototype of Dominie Sampson ... Mr James Sanson' (ibid., p. 53). 'Scott took from him the exclamation "Prodigious!" which he pronounced laconically, but without moving a muscle of his face. (*Guy Mannering*, chapt. iii)' (W.H.J., 1938, 'Dominie Sampson', *Notes and Queries* 174 (5 March): 175). 'It seems very unlike Sir Walter to mention this excellent man almost by his name' (Andrew Lang, 1901, Introd. to *Guy Mannering* (Border edn), p. xvi). *See also* **Thomson**, George.

SANTOS, Signora Wife of a fruit store owner, Nicolas Santos, whom Joyce knew in both Trieste and Zurich.

MARION ('MOLLY') BLOOM in James Joyce, *Ulysses* (1922)

'Signora Santos stayed indoors all day to preserve her complexion, for which she mixed her own creams. That Mrs Santos had a share in Mrs Bloom was an open secret in the Joyce family later' (Richard Ellmann, 1966, *James Joyce*, London: Oxford Paperbacks, pp. 386–7). *See also* **Chance**, Mrs Charles; **Dillon**, Mamie; **Joyce**, Nora; **Popper**, Amalia.

SARAH LAWRENCE COLLEGE, New York

BENTON in Randall Jarrell, *Pictures from an Institution* (1954)

This is a commonly received opinion, based on the fact that Randall Jarrell taught at Sarah Lawrence, as did Mary **McCarthy**. Any old student of Sarah Lawrence who picks the book up recognizes her Alma Mater within the first half-dozen pages. I have tried the experiment.

SASS, Henry (1788–1844)

MR GANDISH in W.M. Thackeray, *The Newcomes* (1854–5)

'The scenes in Mr Gandish's school of art in chapters 17 and 18 . . . appear to describe the establishment at the corner of Charlotte and Streatham Streets in Bloomsbury where Henry Sass offered training to young artists' (Gordon N. Ray, 1955, *Thackeray: a biography*, Vol. I: *The Uses of Adversity, 1811–1846*, London: Oxford University Press, p. 168). 'Lionel Aust writing in the DNB . . . is of the opinion that Gandish was not drawn from Sass, yet the resemblance between the two seems unmistakeable' (ibid., p. 464 n. 9).

SAUK CENTER, Minnesota The birthplace of Sinclair Lewis and his home when he was a boy.

GOPHER PRAIRIE in Sinclair Lewis, *Main Street* (1920)

'Sinclair Lewis [says] Sauk Center to a large extent played a part in his inspiration for *Main Street* according to a statement given out by the author before a club in Detroit, Mich. recently' (Sauk Center, 1963, *Herald* (31 March); see Mark Schorer, 1963, *Sinclair Lewis: an American life*, London: Heinemann, p. 273; originally published 1961, New York: McGraw-Hill).

JORALEMON in Sinclair Lewis, *The Trail of the Hawk* (1915)

'When the book opens, we meet . . . Carl Ericson . . . in a town called Joralemon, Minnesota, not to be distinguished from Sauk Center' (Schorer, op. cit., p. 222).

SAUNDERS, Eddie (1876–1949) Professional fishing guide at Key West, Florida. Ernest Hemingway met him there in 1928; they sailed together frequently until Hemingway left Key West.

SANTIAGO in Ernest Hemingway, *The Old Man and the Sea* (1952)

'Lorine Thompson [to C. Baker, 28 March 1965] held that Santiago was probably modeled in part on Bra Saunders, whose hands were often afflicted with fisherman's cramp like Santiago's in the story' (Carlos Baker, 1969, *Ernest Hemingway: a life story*, New York, p. 655 n. 'EH requests Baker not to mention the possible connection between Santiago and Carlos Gutiérrez'). *See also* **Gutiérrez**, Carlos.

SAUNDERS, Mrs Thomas (d. 1875) Daughter of Sir John Willcocks of Dublin. After 1815 she married Colonel Thomas Saunders, whose mother had been a member of an aristocratic French family; she emigrated with him to Guelph, Ontario, and there bore eight daughters and one son, who were brought up on the model of the French aristocracy of the eighteenth century. In 1865, her daughter (Elinor Glyn's mother), widowed after four years of marriage, brought her two young daughters back to Canada to live with their grandparents for six years: 'the young Elinor came under the influence of Mrs Saunders, with results that were to be lasting' (Anthony Glyn, 1968, *Elinor Glyn: a biography*, rev. edn, London: Hutchinson, p. 28; originally published 1955, London: Hutchinson).

MRS ATHELSTAN in Elinor Glyn, *The Reflections of Ambrosine* (1902)

'Ambrosine Athelstan . . . had been brought up in proud poverty by her grandmother (a ferocious portrait of Mrs Saunders)' (ibid., p. 97).

SAVAGE, Eliza M.A. (1836–85) Daughter of H.B. Savage, architect, and granddaughter of James Savage, the architect who designed St Luke's Church in Chelsea, London. From 1862 to 1866 she was Governess to the family of Revd John Summer, the son of Archbishop Summer. She studied at Heatherley's art school, where she met and became close friends with Samuel Butler. 'From [1871] until her death . . . Butler submitted to Miss Savage everything he wrote, and remodelled it in accordance with her criticisms and suggestions' (H. Festing Jones, 1919, *Samuel Butler: author of Erewhon*, Vol. I, London: Macmillan, p. 144).

ALETHEA PONTIFEX in Samuel Butler, *The Way of All Flesh* (1903)

'Alethea Pontifex . . . is drawn from Miss Savage – not as to her personal appearance, and in other respects not precisely as she actually was, but as Butler thought she might have been, had she been placed in Alethea's circumstances. Nearly all the things given to Alethea were said by Miss Savage' (ibid., p. 208).

SAVILE, John Charles George *See* **Mexborough**, 4th Earl of.

SAVILE, Rachel Katherine *See* **Mexborough**, Countess of.

SAVILLE, Victor (1897–1979) Film director. He entered films in 1916 after being wounded in action. In 1920 he joined Gaumont British, and from 1927 onwards he was a director. He lived in Hollywood from the late 1930s, returning to England in 1960.

MR CHATSWORTH in Christopher Isherwood, *Prater Violet* (1945)

'. . . came in useful by providing a few hints for the character of Chatsworth' (John Russell Taylor, 1983, *Strangers in Paradise: the Hollywood émigrés, 1933–50*, p. 139).

SAVOY HOTEL, London Founded by Richard D'Oyly Carte, it was designed by T.E. Collcutt and opened in 1889. It had seventy bathrooms, six hydraulic lifts, and electric light throughout.

THE IMPERIAL PALACE in Arnold Bennett, *The Imperial Palace* (1930)

'It is quite true that I have obtained a very large part of my material from the Savoy people, who were all told that I wanted the stuff for a novel. But the novel is not about the Savoy. It is about a larger and a different hotel, situated in Birdcage Walk, a hotel with a history of its own: The Imperial Palace' (Bennett to Hugh Walpole, 29 August 1930, quoted in Reginald Pound, 1952, *Arnold Bennett: a biography*, London: Heinemann, p. 353). 'The material which you so good-naturedly gave me, and enabled to get hold of, was enough for a dozen novels. . . . Much I have had to leave out . . . I do hope that none of your staff will take any character in the book as a portrait' (to George Reeves Smith (for forty years the manager of the Savoy group of hotels), 17 September 1930, reproduced in *Letters of Arnold Bennett*, 1970, ed. James Hepburn, Vol. III, London: Oxford University Press, p. 339).

SAXE-WEIMAR, Charles Augustus, Grand Duke of (1757–1828) Son of Duke Ernest, whom he succeeded in 1758. He entered the Prussian army in 1786, and in 1813 he joined the allies. He received the title of Grand Duke at the Congress of Vienna in 1815. He was a friend of Goethe.

GRAND DUKE OF REISENBERG in Benjamin Disraeli, *Vivian Grey* (1826–7)

Identified in a key given in a pamphlet published in 1827 by William Marsh. This key is discussed by Lucien Wolf in his notes to *Vivian Grey* (1904 (centenary edn), Vol. II, p. 364), with the conclusion that Disraeli was not responsible for the key.

SAYERS, Dorothy L. (Leigh) (1893–1957) Writer. Educated at Somerville College, Oxford, from 1915 to 1931 she was a member of the staff of S.H. **Benson Ltd**. In 1923 she published *Whose Body?*, and subsequently a dozen more detective stories. After 1937 she devoted herself to Christian apologetics.

MISS METEYARD in Dorothy L. Sayers, *Murder Must Advertise* (1933)

'Asked about the characters in this book, [R.A.] Bevan once said to me, "Miss Meteyard was Dorothy herself"' (R.D. Bloomfield, 1978, *The Times* (7 January): 14).

SAYN AND WITTGENSTEIN, Prince Gregory von (1873–1907) Lieutenant in the Imperial escort and Captain in the Cossack cavalry. In 1900, when in Cairo as a member of the suite of the Grand Duke Boris of Russia, he met Elinor Glyn. He was an immensely good-looking young daredevil of whom she wrote, 'I think that he was the most physically attractive creature that I have ever seen' (quoted in Anthony Glyn, 1968, *Elinor Glyn: a biography*, rev. edn, London: Hutchinson, p. 91; originally published 1955, London: Hutchinson). At the Khedive's ball that winter he danced with her, unintroduced, and embraced her passionately, but he could have done worse: allegedly he had stripped a defiant gypsy girl naked and dropped her over the balcony of the restaurant where they were dining into the soup tureen of the party below.

PRINCE GRITZKO MILASLAVSKI in Elinor Glyn, *His Hour* (1910)

'At tea one day . . . the Grand Duchess Hélène suggested that she might describe Prince Gritzko Wittgenstein, who had been killed in a duel recently. . . . At once [Eleanor] saw her way clearly. . . . She would put in all Gritzko's exploits, of which all the court were now busily reminding her, even the story of the gipsy girl' (ibid., p. 180).

SAZONOV, G. (d. 1904) A student at Moscow University who, in 1904, assassinated Wenzel von **Plehve** by throwing a bomb at his carriage.

VICTOR HALDIN in Joseph Conrad, *Under Western Eyes* (1911)

'Listen to the theme. The student Razumov . . . gives up secretly to the police his fellow student Haldin, who seeks refuge in his rooms after committing a political crime (supposed to be the murder of de Plehve)' (to John Galsworthy, 6 January 1908, reproduced in G. Jean-Aubry, 1927, *Joseph Conrad: life and letters*, Vol. II, London: Heinemann, pp. 64–5).

SCARLETT, Sir James (1769–1844) Born in Jamaica and educated at Trinity College, Cambridge, he was Whig MP for Peterborough in 1819, 1820–2 and

1823. He was Attorney-General in **Canning**'s ministry in 1827, and in **Wellington**'s from 1829 to 1831, and was opposed to the Reform Bill. In 1834 he was Chief Baron of the Exchequer, and in 1835 he was created Baron Abinger.

SCARLET JEM in Bulwer Lytton, *Paul Clifford* (1830)

Identified in a key set out by Rosina Bulwer Lytton, in a letter of 26 May 1830, reproduced in Michael Sadleir, 1968, *Bulwer and His Wife*, pp. 227–8.

SCHILLER, Ferdinand Canning Scott (1864–1937) Philosopher. Educated at Rugby and at Balliol College, Oxford, he was at Cornell University at Ithaca, New York, in 1893. From 1897 to 1926 he was a Fellow of Corpus Christi College, Oxford, and from 1929 to 1936 he was Professor at the University of Southern California. He was a pragmatist and published *Humanism: philosophical essays* (1903) and *Studies in Humanism* (1907).

PHILIP AUDUBON in G. Lowes Dickinson, *A Modern Symposium* (1905)

'Schiller is implicit in much that Dickinson wrote, particularly ... in the character of Philip Audubon' (E.M. Forster, 1934, *Goldsworthy Lowes Dickinson*, p. 76).

SCHINE, David (b. 1927) Born in New York State and educated at Phillips Academy, Harvard, from 1950 to 1963 he was President and General Manager of Schine Hotels, a luxury chain owned by his father. In 1952, he was Adviser and Special Assistant to the United States Attorney General, dealing with subversive activities. In 1954 he was drafted into the United States Army; it was Roy **Cohn**'s attempts to obtain his release, or special treatment, that led to the confrontation between the Army and the **McCarthy** Committee of Investigation, and ultimately to the collapse of the latter. He later moved to Los Angeles.

G. DUNCAN HARE in Warren Miller, *The Sleep of Reason* (1956)

'Peopling [the] *roman à clef* are ... McCarthy, Cohn and Schine figures' (Joseph Blotner, 1966, *The Modern American Political Novel*, Austin, Tex., p. 303).

SCHLEUSSNER, Ellie Known as Johnnie, she was of German birth and translated Strindberg. She shared a flat in Kenton Street, Bloomsbury, with Mabel **Heath**; both women became friends of Dorothy Richardson when she first lived in London in 1896.

JAN VON BOHLEN in Dorothy Richardson, *Pilgrimage* (1915–67)

'Dorothy's first two London friends, Ellie Schleussner and her flat-mate, become Jan and Mag' (John Rosenberg, 1973, *Dorothy Richardson*, p. 103).

SCHMITZ, Ettore (Italo Svevo) (1861–1928) Author of novels, including *La Cosciénza di Zeno*, under the pseudonym of Italo Svevo. With his wife Livia (**Schmitz**, below) he was a pupil of James Joyce from 1907 to 1909 in Trieste, where he was the manager of a company making paint for ships' hulls.

LEOPOLD BLOOM in James Joyce, *Ulysses* (1922)

'[Bloom] had at least one Triestine prototype, for, when Dr Daniel Brody asked Joyce later, "Mr Joyce, I can understand why the counterpart of your Stephen Dedalus should be a Jew, but why is he the son of a Hungarian?" Joyce, taking off his glasses and looking at him casually yet with an air of pronouncement, replied, "because he was". This prototype was almost certainly Ettore Schmitz' (Richard Ellmann, 1982, *James Joyce*, rev. edn, Oxford: Oxford University Press, p. 374). *See also* **Bloom**, Joseph; **Byrne**, John Francis; **Chance**, Charles; **Jackson**, Holbrook; **Hunter**, Alfred P.; **Joyce**, James; **Joyce**, John Stanislaus; **Mayer**, Teodoro; **Popper**, Leopoldo.

SCHMITZ, Livia She was married to Ettore **Schmitz**.

Anna Livia Plurabelle in James Joyce, *Finnegans Wake* (1939)

'Joyce wrote on February 20, 1924, that he was making use of Signora Livia Schmitz's name and hair for the heroine (Anna Livia Plurabelle) of his new book. . . . As [he] remarked to an Italian journalist, "They say I have immortalized Svevo, but I've also immortalized the tresses of Signora Svevo. These were long and reddish-blond. . . . The river at Dublin passes dye-houses and so has reddish water. So I have playfully compared these two things in the book I'm writing. A lady in it will have the hair which is really Signora Svevo's"' (Richard Ellmann, 1966, *James Joyce*, London: Oxford Paperbacks, p. 572).

SCHOFIELD, George (1839–1907) Sergeant Major. He enlisted in 1858, and was an army drill sergeant in England and India from 1869 to 1879, and at the United Services College at Westward Ho!, Harpenden and Windsor from 1879 to 1907. He was known in the school as the 'Weasel'.

Foxy in Rudyard Kipling, *Stalky & Co.* (1899)

'"Foxy" or George Schofield, to give him his real name, was one of the . . . very best sergeants any school ever possessed' (An O.U.S.C., 1930, 'Foxy, the school sergeant', *The Kipling Journal* 12 (January): 72). Also identified in the caption to a photograph reproduced in the June 1981 issue of *The Kipling Journal*: 'Masters at the United Services College . . . in Kipling's day' (*The Kipling Journal* 48 (218): 21).

SCHREIBERSHOFEN, Johanna ('Nusch') (1882–1971) Née von Richthofen. Younger sister of Frieda **Lawrence**, she married Max von **Schreibershofen** in 1900. She was divorced in 1923, and subsequently married Emil von Krug.

Anna-Maria von Prielau-Carolath ('Mitchka') in D.H. Lawrence, 'The Captain's Doll' (1923)

'[Frieda's] sister [was a] ready-made [original] for . . . the Baroness Mitchka' (H.T. Moore, 1980, *The Priest of Love: a life of D.H. Lawrence*, rev. edn, Harmondsworth: Penguin, p. 431; originally published 1955 as *The Intelligent Heart: the story of D.H. Lawrence*, London: Heinemann).

von SCHREIBERSHOFEN, Max (1864–1944) Officer on the German General Staff. He was married to Johanna (**Schreibershofen**, above) from 1900 to 1923.

Herr Regierungsrat Trepte in D.H. Lawrence, 'The Captain's Doll' (1923)

'He was probably the model for the Herr Regierungsrat Trepte' (H.T. Moore, 1980, *The Priest of Love: a life of D.H. Lawrence*, rev. edn, Harmondsworth: Penguin, p. 431; originally published 1955 as *The Intelligent Heart: the story of D.H. Lawrence*, London: Heinemann).

SCHUFFENECKER, Claude Emile (1851–1934) Painter. He was a friend and colleague of **Gauguin** and was one of the founders of the Salon des Indépendants.

DIRK STROEVE in W. Somerset Maugham, *The Moon and Sixpence* (1919)

'Stroeve was suggested by Gauguin's friend . . . Emile Schuffenecker' (Anthony Curtis, 1974, *The Pattern of Maugham: a critical portrait*, p. 104).

SCHULBERG, Budd (b. 1914) American novelist. Born in New York, he was the son of B.P. Schulberg, Head of Production for Paramount Film Company, and grew up in Hollywood.

CECILIA BRADY in F. Scott Fitzgerald, *The Last Tycoon* (1941)

'[Scott] said . . . "I sort of combined you with my daughter Scottie for Cecilia. . . . There'll be quite a few lines you'll recognise. I hope you won't mind?"' (Budd Schulberg, 1974, *The Four Seasons of Success*, p. 134). *See also* **Fitzgerald, Frances Scott**.

SCHWARTZ, Delmore (1914–66) American poet and writer of short stories. In 1937 he leapt into fame with the publication of his short story 'In dreams begin responsibilities' in the first number of *Partisan Review*. By the 1950s and 1960s he was writing almost nothing and was increasingly dependent upon alcohol and drugs. He died alone in a New York hotel.

VON HUMBOLDT FLEISCHER in Saul Bellow, *Humboldt's Gift* (1975)

'"Humboldt's Gift" . . . began . . . with an event, a feeling about an event. Bellow's old friend . . . Delmore Schwartz, had died in squalor. Bellow had seen him on the streets some weeks earlier and could not face him. He began a memoir . . . which, in a month, turned fictional, became a subject, a story' (Richard Stern, 1976, 'Bellow's gift', interview, *New York Times Magazine* (21 November): 48).

TOMMY WILHELM in Saul Bellow, *Seize the Day* (1957)

'Schwartz had loved *Seize the Day* though its loser hero Wilhelm was fitted out with Schwartz's eccentricities . . . his silent, panting laugh, his peculiar way of driving a car. . . . *Seize the Day* proved that Bellow had been observing him' (Jack Ludwig, 1979, 'Icarus grounded', review of James Atlas, *Delmore Schwartz*, *Partisan Review* 66 (4): 640).

SCILLY ISLES

ISLES OF LYONESSE in Thomas Hardy, 'A Mere Interlude' (1913)

Identified in F.B. Pinion, 1968, *A Hardy Companion*, London: Macmillan.

SCOTCH COLLEGE, Rome A Catholic seminary for the training of Scots for the secular clergy. It was founded by Clement VIII in 1600 and was directed by the Jesuits from 1615 to 1773. It was closed between 1798 and 1820, and from then on was directed by the secular clergy. The students attend the Gregorian University.

ST ANDREW'S COLLEGE in F.W. Rolfe, *Hadrian VII* (1904)

'His hero is himself ... who broods for years over his rejection from ... St Andrew's College (Scotch College, Rome)' (Shane Leslie, 1923, 'Frederick Baron Corvo', *London Mercury* 8 (47): 514).

The SCOTS NATION

PETER MACGRAWLER in Bulwer Lytton, *Paul Clifford* (1830)

Identified in a key set out by Rosina Bulwer Lytton, in a letter of 26 May 1830, reproduced in Michael Sadleir, 1968, *Bulwer and his wife*, pp. 227–8. 'The loathsome MacGrawler ... is no individual portrait, nor even ... a portrait at all. He represents partly Bulwer's dislike of his own Scotch critics, partly also the instinctive resentment felt by a clever Englishman at the more skilful *arrivisme* of his northern neighbours' (Michael Sadleir, 1933, *Bulwer and His Wife*, London: Constable, pp. 227–9).

SCOTT, Anne (1803–33) Youngest daughter of Sir Walter Scott. In 1820 Sophia, her elder sister, married J.G. **Lockhart**, in January 1826 Scott was bankrupted, and in May 1826 Lady **Scott** died. The care and support of her parents naturally fell largely on Anne; her death followed nine months after her father's.

ALICE LEE in Sir Walter Scott, *Woodstock* (1826)

'He was writing *Woodstock* in the early months of his bankruptcy while Lady Scott was dying, and the thought of his own dependence on Anne was plainly much in his mind. Lockhart refers to this, and ... speaks of the change which came over Anne's character and demeanour as "exactly similar to that painted in poor Alice Lee"' (Margaret H. Watt, 1932, 'Sophia and Anne: the daughters of Sir Walter Scott', *Cornhill Magazine* (NS) 73 (September): 367–8).

SCOTT, Charlotte, Lady (1770–1826) Daughter of Jean François Charpentier of Lyons, with whom Richard Lovell **Edgeworth** boarded in 1771. In 1797 she married Sir Walter Scott.

JULIA MANNERING in Sir Walter Scott, *Guy Mannering* (1815)

'[Julia Mannering] irresistibly recalls the lively dark-haired girl Sir Walter Scott married' (Edgar Johnson, 1979, *Sir Walter Scott*, p. 535).

SCOTT, Daniel (*c.*1774–1806) Younger brother of Sir Walter Scott. Having failed to make his way in England, he was found employment in Jamaica, where again he proved unsatisfactory, 'exhibiting a lamentable deficiency of spirit and conduct' (Scott – autobiographical fragment). He returned to Scotland and died soon after; Scott refused to attend his funeral or to wear mourning for him.

CONACHAR, CHIEF OF CLAN QUHELE, in Sir Walter Scott, *The Fair Maid of Perth* (1828)

'Talking over this character of Conachar just before the book appeared, [Scott] told me the unhappy fate of his brother Daniel. . . . He added – "My secret motive, in this attempt, was to perform a sort of expiation to my poor brother's *manes*. I have now learned to have more tolerance and compassion than I had in those days"' (Lockhart, 1900, *Life of Scott*, Vol. V, pp. 187–8). Compare: 'Suppose a man's nerves supported by feelings of honour . . . against constitutional timidity up to a certain point then suddenly giving way – I think something tragic might be produced' (entry for 4 December 1827, *Journal of Sir Walter Scott*, 1972, ed. W.E.K. Anderson, Oxford).

SCOTT, Sir Walter (1771–1832) Scottish novelist and poet. Born in Edinburgh, he was educated at Edinburgh High School and University. He contracted polio while young and was sent to recuperate at his grandfather's farm in Sandyknowe, where he acquired the knowledge of the Border country that features so frequently in his writing. He worked in his father's law office and became an advocate in 1792. He married Charlotte Charpentier (**Scott**, above) in 1797, and in 1799 was appointed Sheriff-Depute of Selkirkshire. He set up a publishing business in Canongate, Edinburgh, but went bankrupt in 1826. Although his last years were plagued by ill health, he continued writing until the end, and his last Waverley novels, *Castle Dangerous* and *Count Robert of Paris*, were published in 1832. He spent his last year touring the Mediterranean in a government frigate.

MR DERRYDOWN in Thomas Love Peacock, *Melincourt* (1817)

'[Character] based upon Sir Walter Scott' (*The Novels of T.L. Peacock*, 1948, ed. David Garnett, London: Rupert Hart-Davis, p. 145 n. 2).

ALAN FAIRFORD in Sir Walter Scott, *Redgauntlet* (1824)

'I have no sort of doubt that . . . Scott himself unquestionably sat for his own picture in . . . Alan Fairford' (J.G. Lockhart, 1900, *Memoirs of Sir Walter Scott*, Vol. I, London: Macmillan, p. 136).

GUY MANNERING in Sir Walter Scott, *Guy Mannering* (1815)

'When Guy Mannering was first published, the Ettrick Shepherd [James Hogg] said to Professor Wilson, "I have done wi' doubts now. Colonel Mannering is just Walter Scott, painted by himself." This was repeated to James Ballantyne, and he again mentioned it to Scott – who smiled in approbation of the Shepherd's shrewdness, and often afterwards, when [Ballantyne] expressed an opinion in which he could not concur, would cut him short with – "James – James – you'll find that Colonel Mannering has laid down the law on this point"' (Lockhart, op. cit., Vol. III, p. 495).

SCOTT, Walter, the Elder (1729–99) Writer to the Signet. He was the father of Sir Walter Scott.

ALEXANDER FAIRFORD (CALLED SAUNDERS) in Sir Walter Scott, *Redgauntlet* (1824)

'Mr [William] Clerk assures me that nothing could be more exact . . . than the resemblance of the Mr Saunders Fairford of *Redgauntlet* to his friend's father' (*Memoirs of Sir Walter Scott*, 1900, ed. J.G. Lockhart, Vol. I, London: Macmillan, p. 157).

SCOTT, Winfield An American who was married to a Mexican, he was Manager of the Arzapalo Hotel, Chapala, in 1923, when D.H. and Frieda **Lawrence** rented a house in the town.

Mr Bell in D.H. Lawrence, *The Plumed Serpent* (1926)

'Mr Scott . . . was to figure slightly in *The Plumed Serpent* as Mr Bell' (W. Bynner, 1953, *Journey with Genius*, London and New York: Peter Nevill, p. 124).

SCROPE, Henry (1862–1950) Of Danby Yorkshire, he was the head of a family that can be traced back to the twelfth century.

Gervase Crouchback in Evelyn Waugh, the *Sword of Honour* trilogy (1952–61)

'The probability is that [Waugh] was working closely from a model, and that his model was Harry Scrope, the head of an "Old Catholic" family which is one of the oldest in Europe. . . . Harry Scrope was a saintly man bearing a close resemblance to Mr Crouchback in almost every detail. That he was Evelyn's model cannot be proved. (They only met three or four times.) Remembering how profoundly (and rightly) Evelyn admired him, it seems to me a strong likelihood. More than that cannot be said' (Christopher Sykes, 1975, *Evelyn Waugh*, London: Collins, p. 417).

SEAMAN, Sir Owen (1861–1936) He was Editor of *Punch* from 1906 to 1932 and was a prolific parodist and writer of light verse.

Merton Densher in Henry James, *The Wings of the Dove* (1902)

'Henry James has sent me *The Wings of the Dove*. Clearly the man is meant to be Seaman. It is hard upon him. . . . I said, in acknowledging the book, "I know Densher. But he is far more child-like than you have made him." He (James) may take it that I mean "Densher" is an eternal type of the weak smug Englishman. All the same, the book was a bit too close to the facts' (Pearl Craigie [John Oliver Hobbes] to Father W.B. Brown, Bishop of Pella, 1902, quoted in M. Maison, 1976, *John Oliver Hobbes: her life and work*, p. 49). This would appear to be nonsense. *See also* **Ford**, Ford Madox; **Fullerton**, W. Morton.

SEAWARD, James For many years he was a chimney-sweep of Wokingham and the surrounding district of Hampshire. He swept the chimneys of the rectory at Eversley as a child when Kingsley was the Rector. Towards the end of his life he became Mayor of Wokingham.

Tom in Charles Kingsley, *The Water Babies* (1863)

'[A] lady, still living, who knew James Seaward when she was a child, has confirmed that he was . . . the original Tom. "When I was about seven or eight I ran into my neighbour's home to watch him at work. He asked me if I had read *The Water-Babies* and on hearing I had said, 'Well, I'm Tom.' I think I must have looked very sceptical, for his next remark was 'Mr Kingsley told a lie when he turned me into a water-baby'''' (Susan Chitty, 1974, *The Beast and the Monk: a life of Charles Kingsley*, p. 222).

SECCOMBE, Thomas (1866–1923) Educated at Felsted and at Balliol College, Oxford. From 1891 to 1900 he was an assistant to Sidney Lee on *The Dictionary of National Biography*. He was subsequently Professor of English at Morley College, Sandhurst, and at Queen's University, Kingston, Ontario. He wrote *The Age of Johnson* (1899), and was himself to some degree a Johnsonian figure: large, short-sighted, jolly, discursive and anecdotal, and every room he occupied was speedily filled with books, on the walls, chairs and floors.

SIGISMUND CLAVERHOUSE in I. Compton-Burnett, *Dolores* (1911)

'Of all the portraits in the book, Claverhouse is the hardest to identify. Helen Carr's key names him tentatively as: "?(looks only) T. Seccombe – visiting lecturer [at Royal Holloway College] in History 1905 –". . . . But Claverhouse . . . cannot have borne more than the most superficial resemblance to Seccombe' (Hilary Spurling, 1974, *Ivy when Young: the early life of I. Compton-Burnett, 1884–1919*, London: Gollancz, p. 173). *See also* **Salt**, Mr.

SELIVERSKOV, General A former Russian minister of police who was suspected of spying on Russian nihilists in Paris; in May 1890, some of the latter were arrested while making explosives in a village near Paris. Six months later Seliverskov was murdered in his hotel by a Pole, Padlewski, who was helped to escape by some revolutionary French socialists.

MR VLADIMIR in Joseph Conrad, *The Secret Agent* (1907)

'Mr Vladimir was suggested to me by that scoundrel Gen. Seliwertsov [sic] whom Padlewski shot (in Paris) in the nineties. Perhaps you will remember as there were peculiar circumstances in that case' (to R.B. Cunninghame Graham, 7 October 1907, reproduced in G. Jean-Aubry, 1927, *Joseph Conrad: life and letters*, Vol. II, London: Heinemann, p. 60).

SELKIRK, Alexander (1676–1721) Son of a shoemaker of Largo, Fife, he ran away to sea in 1695. In 1702 he joined a privateering expedition, under Captain William Dampier, to the South Seas. He was Sailing Master of the *Cinque Ports*, which was commanded by Thomas Stradling, with whom he quarrelled. In 1704 he was put ashore at his own request on the uninhabited island of Juan Fernandez; he was rescued by Woodes Rogers in 1709 and returned to London in 1711.

ROBINSON CRUSOE in Daniel Defoe, *The Life and Strange Surprising Adventures of Robinson Crusoe* (1719)

'Prototype of Robinson Crusoe' (*The Dictionary of National Biography*, London: Oxford University Press). 'Selkirk told the story . . . to Richard Steele who wrote an account of it. It was this account which . . . Defoe . . . used as the basis of his famous novel' (P.K. Kemp, 1976, *Oxford Companion to Ships and the Sea*, s.v. Selkirk).

SELLON, Priscilla Lydia (1821–76) Daughter of a Royal Navy commander, she learnt printing and advocated it as an industry for women. In 1848 she began work among the poor in Plymouth, Devonport and Stonehouse; she founded the Society of the Sisters of Mercy of the Holy Trinity Devonport and established schools and orphanages. In 1849 the Bishop of Exeter, as Visitor, instituted a public inquiry into her actions, but he resigned as Visitor in 1852 after considerable public controversy. She set up a missionary branch of the sisterhood which was to work in the Pacific.

Miss Melton in Elizabeth Jane Whately, *Maude; or The Anglican Sister of Mercy* (1869)

'Is described under the name of Miss Melton in *Maude, or the Anglican Sister of Mercy*' (Frederic Boase, 1901, *Modern English Biography*, Vol. III, col. 487).

SERENA, Enrico 'A blond North Italian with vehement manners and a patch over one of his eyes' (Carlos Baker, 1969, *Ernest Hemingway: a life story*, p. 72). In 1918 he befriended Ernest Hemingway, who was then in the American Red Cross hospital in Milan.

Rinaldo Rinaldi in Ernest Hemingway, *A Farewell to Arms* (1929)

'He had formed the habit of dropping in at the hospital, and had already befriended Ernest, whom he addressed as "Baby" – never imagining that he would one day serve as the prototype of Captain Rinaldi' (ibid.; in a note on p. 572, Baker says that the identification was suggested to him by Mrs Agnes Stanfield, i.e. Miss von Kurowsky.

SHAFTESBURY, Dorset Overlooking the Vale of Blackmoor.

Shaston in Thomas Hardy, Wessex novels and tales (1871–95)

Identified on a map prepared by Thomas Hardy which hangs in the Dorset County Museum, Dorchester. *See under* **Abbotsbury**.

SHAFTESBURY, Anthony Ashley Cooper, 5th Earl of (1761–1811) In 1786 he married Barbara Webb, daughter and heiress of Sir John Webb, 5th Baron, of Oldstock House, Wiltshire. '[H]e long resided in France and does not seem to have made any mark in the world' (*The Complete Peerage of England, Scotland, Ireland, Great Britain and the United Kingdom*, rev. edn, London: St Catherine Press, p. 649 n. (e)).

Lord Uplandtowers in Thomas Hardy, 'Barbara of the House of Grebe' (1891)

'Lord Uplandtowers (a fictional version, it seems, of the fifth Earl of Shaftesbury)' (J.I.M. Stewart, 1971, *Thomas Hardy: a critical biography*, p. 150).

SHAKERLEY, Sir Charles Peter (1792–1857) Of Somerford Park, Cheshire. He was High Sheriff of Cheshire in 1837.

Guy Flouncey in Benjamin Disraeli, *Coningsby* (1844) and *Tancred* (1847)

Identified in a key in *Notes and Queries* (8th series) 3 (13 May 1893): 363. *See also under* **Bright**, John.

SHAKESPEAR, George Trant (1809–44) Son of Emily Shakespear, née Thackeray, brother of Richmond **Shakespear**, and W.M. Thackeray's cousin.

He was with the latter at the same private school and at Charterhouse. In 1829 he went out to India in the service of the East India Company, returned to England on leave for the first time in 1843. By then he was a very rum character indeed, known in his family as 'the Polar Bear' because of his rotundity and rolling gait. He died suddenly in Geneva in 1844, having allegedly committed suicide, although no one knew of a reason that he should have done so.

JOSEPH SEDLEY in W.M. Thackeray, *Vanity Fair* (1847–8)

'There is a statement by Mr Henry Beveridge [father of Lord Beveridge] on record ... that he was informed by Mr Shawe ... (who was Thackeray's brother-in-law) that the character was an overcoloured picture of George Trant Shakespear ... who was Magistrate of Midnapore from 1839 to 1845. ... Mr Beveridge came out [to Bengal] in 1858: and ... Merrick ... Shawe was a writer of 1834 and retired in 1865' (Evan Cotton, 1927, 'The Editor's note book', *Bengal: past and present* 34 (October–December 1927): 144).

SHAKESPEAR, Sir Richmond (1812–61) Brother of George Trant **Shakespear**, he was educated at Charterhouse. In 1828 he was Second Lieutenant with the Bengal artillery; he had an immensely distinguished career as a soldier and civilian in India, and was knighted in 1841.

COLONEL THOMAS NEWCOME in W.M. Thackeray, *The Newcomes* (1854–5)

'I never heard my father say that, when he wrote Colonel Newcome, any special person was in his mind, but ... my step-grandfather had many of Colonel Newcome's characteristics, and ... General Charles Carmichael ... was very like Colonel Newcome in looks; a third family Colonel Newcome was Sir Richmond Shakespear' (Anne Thackeray Ritchie, 1911, Introd. to *The Newcomes* (biog. edn), p. li). See also **Carmichael**, C.M.; **Carmichael-Smyth**, Henry.

SHARP, Jack (d. before 1798) Nephew of John Walker of Walterclough Hall, Yorkshire, by whom he was adopted and taken into partnership in the wool trade. By 1758 Sharp had taken control of the house and the business and forced Mr Walker into retirement. In 1772, a cousin claimed the house upon marrying, and Sharp was obliged to leave Walterclough for Law Hill, which he built for himself less than a mile away, and to which he removed all the fixtures and heirlooms of Walterclough that he could carry away. He continued to direct the family business and to extract heavy payments of money from his cousin. However, when his business was ruined by the American War, he left Law Hill for London, never to return.

HEATHCLIFF in Emily Brontë, *Wuthering Heights* (1847)

'Prototype of Heathcliff' (Winifred Gérin, 1971, *Emily Brontë*, Oxford, p. 289, s.v. Sharp, Jack). Emily Brontë spent some time at Law Hill in 1837, teaching at the school kept there at that time by Miss Elizabeth Patchett. See also **Sutton**, Richard.

SHARPE, Charles Kirkpatrick (1781–1851) Of Hoddan in Annandale. Educated at Christ Church, Oxford, where he met **Shelley**, whom he entertained in Edinburgh in 1811. He lived in Princes Street, Edinburgh, and collected prints, engaged in antiquarian research, sketched, painted, and edited

James Knipton's *History of the Church in Scotland*. He met Sir Walter Scott in 1802, and they remained friends for life. A ballad collector from his earliest youth, it was he who sent Scott 'The Twa Corbies'. In 1814, James **Carlyle** became a tenant of the Sharpe family at Mainhill. The family had been High Tories for generations, and Mrs Sharpe was a descendant of the beautiful Susanna, Countess of Eglinton.

SIR MUNGO MALAGROWTHER in Sir Walter Scott, *The Fortunes of Nigel* (1822)

'Some of his characteristics are given to Sir Mungo Malagrowther' (*Journal of Sir Walter Scott*, 1972, ed. W.E.K. Anderson, Oxford, p. 2 n. 4).

SHAW, Charles (1832–1906) He spent his childhood working in the Potteries, and in later life entered the ministry of the Methodist New Connexion Church. He spent some years running a cotton-spinning business, but returned to the ministry and worked for the Methodist Church until 1904. He was the leading writer for the Radical *Oldham Express*, and was the author of *When I Was a Child, Recollections of an Old Potter* (1903).

DARIUS CLAYHANGER in Arnold Bennett, the *Clayhanger* trilogy (1910–16)

'Tuesday, September 14 [1909]. . . . Tonight I began to read again "When I was a Child" with a view to my next novel [*Clayhanger*], which I think must contain, near the beginning, a grimmish detailed sketch of industrial child life in 1840, about' (*The Journals of Arnold Bennett, 1896–1910*, 1932, ed. Sir Newman Flower, London: Cassell, p. 320). 'If anybody wishes to realise what the novelist's function is, and to understand the difference between history and fiction, let him read in its entirety the episode as related by Charles Shaw and then the episode in its entirety as related by me [in ch. 5 of *Clayhanger*]' (to the editor of *United Methodist*, 6 April 1916, reproduced in *Letters of Arnold Bennett*, 1970, ed. James Hepburn, Vol. III, London: Oxford University Press, p. 9). *See also* **Beardmore**, John; **Bennett**, Enoch.

SHAW, George Bernard (1856–1950) Irish playwright and polemicist. He was born in Dublin, the son of Irish Protestant parents. He left school at the age of 15, and worked briefly for an estate agent before leaving Ireland in 1876 to join his mother and sister in London. A devoted member of the **Fabian Society** (1884–1911), he was a socialist, free thinker, and supporter of women's rights. He was music critic on *The Star* from 1888 to 1890 and drama critic for the *Saturday Review* from 1895 to 1898. In 1898 he married Charlotte Payne-Townshend, with whom he lived until her death in 1948. He was awarded the Nobel Prize for Literature in 1925. He was a vegetarian, and never drank spirits, coffee or tea.

OSMOND HALL in Maurice Baring, 'A Luncheon Party', *Half a Minute's Silence and Other Stories* (1925)

'Most of the guests were people well known in London – Messrs Beerbohm Tree and Bernard Shaw . . . and others – all, of course, furnished with pseudonyms and . . . easy to identify' (Ethel Smyth, 1938, *Maurice Baring*, London and Toronto: Heinemann, p. 136). And so they are.

SHAW, William (1783?–1850) From 1822 he was the owner of Bowes Academy, Yorkshire; Dickens saw him while on his Yorkshire visit in February 1838.

WACKFORD SQUEERS in Charles Dickens, *Nicholas Nickleby* (1838–9)

'William Shaw, the prototype of Wackford Squeers, was unjustly made the victim . . . of an attack that should have been levelled at the whole tribe of pedagogues' (Arthur A. Adrian, 1949–50, 'Nicholas Nickleby and educational reform', *The Nineteenth Century* 4: 237). 'Although, in his 1839 preface to Nickleby, [Dickens] stated that Squeers was "the representative of a class, and not of an individual", Shaw was widely recognized as his original. . . . [He] was in fact the only local schoolmaster with one eye' (*Letters of Charles Dickens*, 1968, Vol. II, ed. Madeline House and Graham Storey, Oxford: Oxford University Press, p. 481 n. 5).

SHAWE, Isabella Née Creagh, she was born in Doneraile, County Cork, Ireland. She was the widow of Colonel Matthew Shawe, and in 1835 she was living in Paris on her small pension, although she later returned to Ireland. Her daughter Isabella married W.M. Thackeray.

MRS BAYNES in W.M. Thackeray, *The Adventures of Philip* (1861–2)

'Thackeray tells the story of Mrs Shawe's attempt to break off his engagement . . . in Chapters 24 to 28 of *Philip*. The attendant circumstances are no doubt rather different . . . but the situation in which Mrs Baynes, Charlotte, and Philip find themselves is essentially the same and their portraits are drawn from Thackeray's memories of Mrs Shawe, of Isabella, and of himself as a young man' (*The Letters and Private Papers of W.M. Thackeray*, Vol. I: *1817–1840*, 1945, ed. Gordon N. Ray, London: Oxford University Press, p. 315 n. 29).

MRS GAM in W.M. Thackeray, 'Dennis Haggarty's Wife', *Men's Wives* (1843)

'Mrs Gam is Thackeray's earliest portrait of his mother-in-law' (*Letters*, op. cit., Vol. I, p. 430 n. 42).

MRS MACKENZIE (THE 'CAMPAIGNER') in W.M. Thackeray, *The Newcomes* (1854–5)

'While reading one of the worst tirades of the "Campaigner" [Thackeray] interrupted himself to say, "That's my she-devil of a mother-in-law, you know, whom I have the good fortune to possess still"' (J.R. Lowell to Charles Eliot Norton, 11 August 1855, reproduced in *Letters*, op. cit., Vol. III, p. 465).

SHAWE, Jane Younger sister of Isabella **Thackeray**, wife of W.M. Thackeray.

JEMIMA GAM in W.M. Thackeray, 'Dennis Haggarty's Wife', *Men's Wives* (1843)

'Appears to have been suggested . . . by [Mr] Somerville's persistent wooing of Jane Shawe, although Jane Shawe, unlike Jemima Gam . . . did not marry her suitor' (*The Letters and Private Papers of W.M. Thackeray*, Vol. I: *1817–1840*, 1945, ed. Gordon N. Ray, London: Oxford University Press, p. 430 n. 42).

SHAWE, Merrick (*c.*1770–1843) Lieutenant-colonel. Uncle of Isabella **Thackeray**.

MAJOR PENDENNIS in W.M. Thackeray, *The History of Pendennis* (1848–50)

'Thackeray nowhere identifies Major Pendennis's "original", yet it may be readily demonstrated that the Major too was drawn from life. . . . Among Thackeray's associates in the later 1830s there was a man whose history was precisely that assigned to Major Pendennis in Thackeray's novel and who played much the same part in Thackeray's life as the Major does in Pen's. This was Lt. Colonel Merrick Shawe' (Gordon N. Ray, 1952, *The Buried Life*, p. 59).

SHEFFIELD

HILLSBOROUGH in Charles Reade, *Put Yourself in His Place* (1870)

'The scene of the novel [Sheffield] is thinly disguised under the name of Hillsborough' (M. Elwin, 1930, *Charles Reade*, p. 203).

SHELLEY, Harriet (d. 1816) Née Westbrook, she met **Shelley** and eloped with him to Scotland when she was 16. She became his first wife in 1811, and they had two children. She drowned herself in the Serpentine in London.

MARIONETTA CELESTINA O'CARROLL in Thomas Love Peacock, *Nightmare Abbey* (1818)

'A comparison of the description of this lady with Peacock's own account of Harriet Shelley will . . . show that the latter was his model for the sketch of Marionetta' (Martin Freeman, 1911, *Thomas Love Peacock*, London: Martin Secker, p. 202).

SHELLEY, Mary Wollstonecraft (1797–1851) Novelist, biographer and editor. Daughter of William **Godwin** and Mary (**Wollstonecraft**). When she was 16 years old, she eloped to France and Switzerland with Percy Bysshe **Shelley**. She gave birth to a daughter in 1815, but the baby died. The following year their son William was born, and they married immediately after the suicide of Shelley's first wife, Harriet (**Shelley**). She began her first novel, *Frankenstein* (1818), as her contribution to a ghost story competition in which Shelley, **Byron** and Polidori were participating. In 1818 the Shelleys left for Italy, where William died, and where their second son, Percy Florence, was born in 1819. After Shelley died in 1822, Mary returned to England with Percy in 1823, where she devoted herself to her son's welfare and to her writing career.

CELINDA ('STELLA') TOOBAD in Thomas Love Peacock, *Nightmare Abbey* (1818)

'[Marionetta and Celinda] in some ways reminiscent of Shelley's Harriet and Mary' (Carl Dawson, 1970, *His Fine Wit: a study of Thomas Love Peacock*, p. 213). '[Peacock] seems to have taken some trouble to insist, and perhaps too obviously, that she had no physical resemblance to Mary' (*Nightmare Abbey*, 1969, ed. Raymond Wright, p. 19). '["Stella" is] a character based on Mary Godwin, Shelley's second wife. Goethe's Stella, in his play of the same name, is the heroine in a three-cornered situation similar to that of Scythrop, Marionetta and "Stella"' (ibid., p. 268, n. (to ch. X)). *See also* **Clairmont**, Claire; **Hitchener**, Elizabeth.

SHELLEY, Percy Bysshe (1792–1822) English poet. Born in Sussex, and educated at Syon House Academy and Eton, he went to University College, Oxford, but was expelled in 1811 for his part in the publication of a pamphlet, *The Necessity of Atheism*. He then eloped to Scotland with 16-year-old Harriet Westbrook (**Shelley**, above). They moved to London in 1812, where Shelley befriended William **Godwin** and Thomas Love Peacock. After the failure of his first marriage in 1813, he eloped with Godwin's daughter, Mary (**Shelley**, above), marrying her in 1816 after Harriet's suicide, and they had a son, William. In 1818 the family left England for Italy, but the death of William the following year in Rome left Shelley devastated. The moved to Tuscany, living in Livorno, then Florence and finally settling in Pisa, where he enjoyed a period of exceptional creative energy. A second son, Percy, was born in 1819. In 1822, returning from a visit to **Byron** and Leigh **Hunt** in Livorno, Shelley was drowned when his schooner was hit by a squall in the Bay of Spezia. He was cremated on the beach at Viareggio.

JEFFREY ASPERN in Henry James, *The Aspern Papers* (1888)

See under **Clairmont**, Claire; **Silsbee**, Edward Augustus.

MR ESCOT in Thomas Love Peacock, *Headlong Hall* (1816)

'Mr Escot's views [are] partly based on Shelley's when he wrote *Queen Mab*' (David Garnett, 1948, Introd. to *Headlong Hall*, p. 8). All Mr Escot's arguments in ch. II about the disastrous consequences of carnivorousness are to be found in *Queen Mab*, n. to Canto VIII, ll. 211–12. *See also* **Peacock**, Thomas Love.

SYLVAN FORESTER in Thomas Love Peacock, *Melincourt* (1817)

'Peacock's characters are commonly mistaken for caricatures of well-known people, and it is usual to take Forester for a portrait of Shelley. But in reality Peacock . . . is much less interested in personalities than in systems of ideas. There is a connection between Forester and Shelley's conception of the poet, but there is also a connection between Forester and the oeuvre of Monboddo' (Marilyn Butler, 1977, letter, *Times Literary Supplement* (27 May): 653). *See also* **Monboddo**, Lord.

MR FOSTER in Thomas Love Peacock, *Headlong Hall* (1816)

'Mr Foster's views [are based] partly on Shelley's, partly on Peacock's libertarianism' (David Garnett (ed.), 1963, Introd. to *Headlong Hall*, in *The Novels of T.L. Peacock*, London: Rupert Hart-Davis, p. 8).

VICTOR FRANKENSTEIN in Mary Wollstonecraft Shelley, *Frankenstein; or The Modern Prometheus* (1818)

'Frankenstein himself is clearly, and to some extent must intentionally have been a portrayal of Shelley, and Shelley can scarcely have been unaware of it, if only on account of his name. Frankenstein's name is Victor . . . the same that Shelley took for himself on a number of occasions in boyhood and later. . . . But it is not only in name that Frankenstein resembles Shelley' (Christopher Small, 1972, *Ariel Like a Harpy: Shelley, Mary and Frankenstein*, London, pp. 101–2). 'One should not say that Frankenstein *is* Shelley, he is the Shelleyan ideal' (ibid., p. 121).

SCYTHROP GLOWRY in Thomas Love Peacock, *Nightmare Abbey* (1818)

'The Author of "Nightmare Abbey" seized on some points of his [Shelley's] character and some habits of his life when he painted Scythrop. He was not addicted to "port or Madeira", but in youth he had read of "Illuminati and Eleutherachs", and believed that he possessed the power of operating an immediate change in the minds of men and the state of society' (Mary Shelley (ed.), 1839, 'Note on poems of 1817', in *The Poetical Works of P.B. Shelley*, Vol. III, pp. 71–2).

PRINCE ALEXY HAIMATOFF in T.J. Hogg, *Memoirs of Prince Alexy Haimatoff* (1813)

'Some features of Haimatoff are plainly taken from Shelley' (Richard Garnett, 1891, in Leslie Stephen (ed.), *The Dictionary of National Biography*, London: Oxford University Press, s.v. Hogg). *See also* **Hogg**, T.J.

MARMION HERBERT in Benjamin Disraeli, *Venetia* (1837)

'Having ... to introduce Byron as Lord Cadurcis, and Shelley as Marmion Herbert, he cuts Byron's relations with Lady Byron and "Ada ..." off from ... Cadurcis, and superimposes them upon Herbert ... we find that Herbert is drawn ... precisely as Mr Shelley' (Richard Garnett, 1887, *Shelley and Lord Beaconsfield*, p. 11).

ELSLEY VAVASOUR (JOHN BRIGGS) in Charles Kingsley, *Two Years Ago* (1857)

'The absurdly improbable poet, Elsley Vavasour (born John Briggs), is probably modelled on Shelley and the poets Kingsley considered his successors, the Spasmodics; certainly, Vavasour is not a caricature of Tennyson' (R.B. Martin, 1959, *The Dust of Combat: a life of Charles Kingsley*, London: Faber & Faber, p. 203). *See also* **Tennyson**, Alfred.

EDWARD VILLIERS in Mary Wollstonecraft Shelley, *Lodore* (1835)

'Shelley turns up as a recognisable figure ... in the ... closely autobiographical *Lodore*' (Christopher Small, 1972, *Ariel Like a Harpy: Shelley, Mary and Frankenstein*, London, p. 120).

ADRIAN, EARL OF WINDSOR in Mary Wollstonecraft Shelley, *The Last Man* (1826)

'I have endeavoured, but how inadequately, to give some idea of him in my last published book – the sketch has pleased some of those who best loved him – I might have made more of it but there are feelings which one recoils from unveiling to the public eye' (to Sir John Bowring, 25 February 1826, reproduced in *The Letters of Mary Shelley*, 1944, ed. F.L. Jones, Vol. I, Norman, Okla., p. 260). Like Shelley, Adrian dies in a shipwreck.

SHEPPARD, Hugh Richard ('Dick') (1880–1937) Anglican clergyman. He was Rector of St Martins in the Fields in London from 1914 to 1927, Dean of Canterbury from 1929 to 1931, and Canon of St Paul's Cathedral from 1943 to 1937. A prominent pacifist in England in the 1930s, he founded the Peace Pledge Union in 1936.

PURCHAS in Aldous Huxley, *Eyeless in Gaza* (1936)

'[Anthony Beavis becomes] an active pacifist ... working for the movement headed by Purchas (a minor character modelled on the preacher and war-resister Dick Sheppard)' (George Woodcock, 1972, *Dawn and the Darkest Hour: a study of Aldous Huxley*, London: Faber & Faber, p. 203).

SHEPPARD, John Tressider (1881–1968) Provost of King's College, Cambridge, from 1933 to 1954.

MR SHERRARD in Shane Leslie, *The Cantab* (1926)

Identified in a key in the hand of Dr Ivor Ramsay, a Kingsman of the year 1920, and later Dean, laid in a copy of *The Cantab*.

SHERBORNE, Dorset

SHERTON ABBAS in Thomas Hardy, Wessex novels and tales (1871–95)

Identified on a map prepared by Thomas Hardy which hangs in the Dorset County Museum, Dorchester. *See under* **Abbotsbury**.

SHERBORNE SCHOOL, Dorset

FERNHURST in Alec Waugh, *The Loom of Youth* (1917)

'Thursday, April 12th [1917] . . . [T. Seccombe] said that the pupils at the Royal Military College were now the most extraordinary crowd. . . . He instanced Arthur Waugh's son, aged 18, who had written a remarkably realistic novel of school-life (Sherborne)' (*The Journals of Arnold Bennett*, 1932, ed. Sir Newman Flower, Vol. II, London: Cassell, p. 193).

GREYLANDS in John Cowper Powys, *Wolf Solent* (1929)

'Years later, in *Wolf Solent*, he gave an unflattering portrait of Sherborne as Greylands school' (R.P. Graves, 1983, *The Brothers Powys*, p. 26).

SHERIDAN, Richard Brinsley (1751–1816) Dramatist and parliamentary orator. Born in Dublin and educated at Harrow, in 1773 he married Elizabeth Linley and settled in London. He was the author of *The Rivals* (1775) and *The School for Scandal* (1777). He became MP for Stafford in 1780, and supported Charles James Fox. He was also confidential adviser to the Prince of Wales, later **George IV**. In 1783 he became Secretary to the Treasury and in 1794 he spoke against Warren Hastings. In 1806 he was appointed Treasurer to the Navy, and in 1806–7 he was MP for Westminster. He suffered from brain disease in his last years.

WILL SINGLETON in W. Massie, *Sydenham; or Memoirs of a Man of the World* (1830)

'In volume two . . . Sheridan (Singleton), [conducts] the destinies of the Whigs' (M.W. Rosa, 1936, *The Silver-Fork Schools: novels of fashion preceding 'Vanity Fair'*, New York, p. 81 n. 3).

SHILTON, Sally (d. 1823?) Daughter of a local collier, she was taken into **Arbury Hall** by Sir Roger **Newdigate** and his second wife, Hester Margaretta, and trained as a singer. In 1801 she married Revd **Ebdell**.

MIRAH COHEN (NÉE LAPIDOTH) in George Eliot, *Daniel Deronda* (1876)

'[T]he account of Mirah's drawing-room debut recalls that of Sally Shilton as told in Lady Newdigate's letters; the child Mary Ann [Evans] could have heard of it in the Arbury housekeeper's room, or indeed from Sally herself' (Marghanita Laski, 1973, *George Eliot and Her World*, London: Thames & Hudson, p. 106). *See also* **Ayrton**, Hertha.

CATERINA SARTI in George Eliot, 'Mr Gilfil's Love Story', *Scenes of Clerical Life* (1857–8)

'"Caterina" had her original in Sally Shilton' (Laski, op. cit., p. 57). *See also under* **Anstruther**, Lady.

SHINN, Everett (1876–1953) American painter. He was a member of the group known as 'The Eight', which was organized in 1910 by Robert Henri; the group was largely instrumental in organizing the Armory Show of 1913 in New York which introduced modern French painting to the American public. The group was also known, derisively, as the 'Ashcan School'.

EUGENE WITLA in Theodore Dreiser, *The 'Genius'* (1915)

'Originally drafted to concern a St Louis newspaperman, then changed to concern a painter whose work Dreiser modeled on that of . . . Everett Shinn' (Robert H. Elias, 1955, 'The survival of the fittest', in A. Kazin and C. Shapiro, *The Stature of Theodore Dreiser*, Bloomington, p. 190). 'It was probably Everett Shinn's show of New York pastels at the Boussard Vallodon Galleries which inspired Dreiser's account of Eugene Witla's Kellner Gallery show in the novel' (Ellen Moers, 1970, *Two Dreisers*, London: Thames & Hudson, p. 22; originally published 1969, New York: Viking). *See also* **Dreiser**, Theodore; **Sonntag**, William Louis.

SHIRER, William Lawrence (b. 1904) American journalist, author and broadcaster. He worked in Europe during the Second World War writing for the *New York Herald Tribune*. He also wrote *The Rise and Fall of the Third Reich* (1960).

RAYMOND WHITEHEAD in William L. Shirer, *Stranger Come Home* (1954)

Clearly a self-portrait.

SHIRLEY OF ETTINGTON, Evelyn Philip (1812–82) Of Ettington Park. He was Sheriff of Monaghan in 1837, and MP for Monaghan in 1841–7 and for South Warwickshire in 1853–65. He became a Fellow of the Society of Antiquaries in 1860, and Trustee of the National Portrait Gallery in 1876, and was the author of genealogical and topographical works.

MR ARDENNE in Benjamin Disraeli, *Lothair* (1870)

Identified in 'Key to *Lothair*', *Notes and Queries* 183 (12 September 1942): 173.

SHOAF, George A militant Socialist, he was Socialist reporter on the staff of the American weekly *The Appeal to Reason* and a colleague of Walter Hurt. He was also the author of *Fighting for Freedom* (1953), an autobiography.

SHOFORTH in Walter Hurt, *The Scarlet Shadow* (1907)

'George Shoaf . . . on whom Shoforth is based' (Walter Rideout, 1956, *The Radical Novel in the United States, 1900–1954*, Cambridge, Mass., p. 303 n. 14).

SHOPE, Pearl She was a friend of the Wolfe family in Asheville.

PEARL HINES in Thomas Wolfe, *Look Homeward, Angel* (1929)

'. . . the model for . . . Pearl Hines' (*The Notebooks of Thomas Wolfe*, 1970, ed. Richard S. Kennedy and Paschal Reeves, Chapel Hill, NC: University of North Carolina Press, p. 958 n. 9).

SHORTREED, Robert (1762–1829) Advocate. He became Sheriff-Substitute of Roxburghshire in 1792. His cousin Charles **Kerr** introduced him to Scott and, shortly after, he and Scott made their first 'raid' into Liddesdale (in the southern corner of Roxburghshire, just north of the Border), in search of ballads. On this expedition, Scott met Willie **Elliott** of Millburnham. The 'raids' were repeated annually for seven years, and Shortreed remained Scott's friend for life, Scott visiting him every year at the time of the Kelso assizes.

PROCURATOR FISCAL MACMORLAN in Sir Walter Scott, *Guy Mannering* (1815)

'The identification of Shortreed with Macmorlan requires a little special pleading . . . once a momentary shadow fell on Shortreed's proud satisfaction [at Scott's annual visits] when some officious fool pointed out to him that he had been portrayed in "Guy Mannering" as "the writer", and he had . . . concluded that his old friend had drawn him as Glossin! The misunderstanding was cleared away without coming to Scott's knowledge, and apparently without Shortreed's conjecturing that – the word "writer" being applicable to both – he had really been sketched as Macmorlan. There are points in that admirable figure . . . over which Scott lingers with more pleasure and affection than the story actually requires' (F. MacCunn, 1909, *Sir Walter Scott's Friends*, pp. 107–8).

SHREWSBURY SCHOOL English public school. Samuel Butler was educated there under Benjamin Hall **Kennedy** from 1848 to 1854.

ROUGHBOROUGH in Samuel Butler, *The Way of All Flesh* (1903)

The identification is based upon obvious parallels.

SIBREE, John Minister of Vicar Lane Independent Chapel, Coventry, from 1819 onwards, he was a political dissenting parson and published pamphlets advocating refusal to pay Church Rate (his property was distrained upon for refusal to pay Church Rate) and repeal of the Corn Laws. George Eliot knew the family well and gave German lessons to Mary Sibree, but Pastor Sibree 'came to disapprove of her as a baneful influence on his children' (Valentine Cunningham, 1975, *Everywhere Spoken Against: dissent in the Victorian novel*, Oxford: Clarendon Press, p. 146). He made an effort, wholly unsuccessful, to counter her unbelief and deputed an independent theologian to reason with her.

RUFUS LYON in George Eliot, *Felix Holt, the Radical* (1866)

'I would suggest that Rufus Lyon is . . . a disjunctive combination of two different kinds of Dissenting pastor, the old and the new. . . . Sibree has been disconcertingly grafted on to Franklin' (ibid., p. 188). *See also* **Franklin**, Francis.

SICKERT, Walter 1860–1942) Painter. He studied at the Slade School of Fine Art, London, and under J.M. **Whistler**. He settled at Dieppe and met the French Impressionists. He associated with the Camden Town Group, which later became the London Group.

RICHARD DRITTER in Wyndham Lewis, *The Roaring Queen* (1973)

'Dritter is plainly based on Sickert' (Walter Allen, 1973, Introd. to *The Roaring Queen*, p. 12).

SIDGWICK, John Benson (1835–1927) Younger son of J.B. Sidgwick of Stone Gappe, Yorkshire, who was a cousin of Archbishop Benson. He was educated at Trinity College, Cambridge, and was ordained in 1859. He was at his last parish, Ashby Parva, Leicestershire, from 1893 to 1916, and died at Worthing.

JOHN REED in Charlotte Brontë, *Jane Eyre* (1847)

'Charlotte Brontë acted as governess to my cousins at Stonegappe for a few months in 1839. . . . She was, according to her own account, very unkindly treated, but it is clear that she had no gifts for the management of children, and was also in a very morbid condition the whole time. My cousin Benson Sidgwick . . . certainly on one occasion threw a Bible at Miss Brontë. . . . Both Mr & Mrs Sidgwick were extraordinarily benevolent people, much beloved, and would not wittingly have given pain to anyone connected with them' (A.C. Benson, 1899, *Life of Edward White Benson: sometime Archbishop of Canterbury*, Vol. I, p. 12).

SILLIMAN, H.I. From 1914 he was the Editor of the *Pottsville Journal*, and in 1924 he engaged John O'Hara as a young reporter on his first newspaper job.

BOB HOOKER in John O'Hara, *Ten North Frederick* (1955)

'O'Hara took careful note of his older colleagues on the *Journal*, starting with Mr Silliman, from whom he took certain characteristics of Bob Hooker' (Finis Farr, 1974, *O'Hara: a biography*, p. 78).

SILSBEE, Edward Augustus (1813–1904) Born in Salem, Massachusetts, he became a captain in the American Merchant Marine. According to Sargent, who knew him as a boy, in 1869 he was lodging in Florence with Miss **Clairmont**. His great passion was **Shelley** and relics of the poet, and Sargent tells the same story as Henry James (see Evan Charteris, 1927, *Life of John S. Sargent*, pp. 14–15; *see under* **Clairmont**, Claire). In the library of Harvard University is a manuscript volume of Shelley's poems (including 'To a Skylark') 'given to the Library by Mr Edward A. Silsbee, who received it from a lady in Florence closely connected with the Shelleys' (G.E. Woodberry, 1889, 'Note on the MS volume of Shelley's poems in the library of Harvard College', *Harvard University Bulletin* 5 (5): 467).

THE NARRATOR in Henry James, *The Aspern Papers* (1888)

'This gentleman, an American of long ago, an ardent Shelleyite ... – I had known him a little, but there is not a reflected glint of him in "The Aspern Papers" – was named to me as having made interest with Miss Clairmont to be accepted as a lodger on the calculation that she would have Shelley documents' (Henry James, 1909, Introd. to *The Aspern Papers*, New York, p. viii). There is a charcoal portrait of Silsbee by Sargent, done in 1900, in the Bodleian Library, Oxford.

SILVERTON, Devon A village in the Exe valley, located about seven miles north of Exeter, just east of the road to Tiverton.

SILVERTHORN in Thomas Hardy, 'The Romantic Adventures of a Milkmaid' (1913)

Identified in F.B. Pinion, 1968, *A Hardy Companion*, London: Macmillan. The story was first published in a cheap edition in America (1883) and was widely pirated. Hardy was finally forced to collect it in 1913. In the original version the setting was Casterbridge and Stickleton, while in the later version the scene was shifted to Exonbury and the valley of the Exe, 'possibly to remove the story from the scene of Tess' (R.L. Purdy, 1954, *Thomas Hardy: a bibliographical study*, pp. 48, 49).

SIMI, Pension, Florence Located on the Lung'Arno delle Grazie.

PENSION BERTOLINI in E.M. Forster, *A Room with a View* (1908)

'The Bertolini = the Pension Simi ... where I stopped at the beginning of the century' (E.M. Forster, writing in a copy of *A Room with a View* belonging to the American artist Paul Cadmus; see Introd. to the Abinger edn, 1977, ed. Oliver Stallybrass, p. xi).

SIMMONS, Ronald (1885–1918) Born in Providence, Rhode Island, of a family that went to America in the *Mayflower*. He was educated at the Phillips Academy and at Yale, and studied architecture at the Massachusetts Institute of Technology and in Paris (1910–14). In 1914 he was engaged in war work, and in 1917 he enlisted in the Army as a private, moved into Intelligence, and was commissioned as an officer. During the last eighteen months of his life, he was a protégé and friend of Edith Wharton. He died in Marseilles.

BOYLSTON in Edith Wharton, *A Son at the Front* (1923)

'The novel contains ... the attractive portrait of Ronald Simmons, in the guise of ... Boylston' (R.W.B. Lewis, 1975, *Edith Wharton: a biography*, London: Constable, p. 457).

SINCLAIR, Harry Ford (1876–1956) American businessman. In 1923 and 1924 he was involved in the Teapot Dome scandal: in 1927 he served three months in prison for contempt of the United States Senate in refusing to testify on the Teapot Dome leases. He was acquitted of charges of conspiracy to defraud the government in 1928.

J. ARNOLD ROSS in Upton Sinclair, *Oil!* (1927)

'Although Ross is a composite character, there appears to be a particular indebtedness to certain events in the life of Harry F. Sinclair' (Joseph Blotner, 1966, *The Modern American Political Novel*, Austin, Tex., p. 115 n. 58).

SINCLAIR, Sir John (1754–1835) 1st Baronet. Scottish politician. He was MP for Caithness in 1780, and for Lostwithiel in 1784–1811. In 1796 he carried the Enclosure Bill in the House of Commons. He was an invigorating agriculturist and a busy pamphleteer, and was President of the Board of Agriculture 1793–8 and 1806–13. Scott, in his *Journal*, refers to him as Sir John Jackass. In 1791 R.E. **Raspe** obtained money from him by pretending to discover gold and silver on his land.

ASTERIAS in Thomas Love Peacock, *Nightmare Abbey* (1818)

'There is clear evidence that . . . the ichthyologist Asterias . . . is a caricature of . . . Sir John Sinclair' (Norma Leigh Rudinsky, 1977, 'Contemporary response to the caricature Asterias in Peacock's *Nightmare Abbey*', *Notes and Queries* 222 (July–August): 335). *See also* **Denys de Montfort**, Pierre.

SIR ARTHUR WARDOUR in Sir Walter Scott, *The Antiquary* (1816)

'A reader only had to imagine the plot of *The Antiquary* stripped of mixed diablerie . . . and his humorous-satirical deception of Sir John Sinclair (Sir Arthur Wardour), in order to appreciate the excellent narrative possibilities of the Raspe episodes' (Coleman O. Parsons, 1943, 'Sir John Sinclair's Raspe and Scott's Dousterswivel', *Notes and Queries* 43: 65). *See also* **Whitefoord**, Sir John.

SINCLAIR, Upton Beall (1878–1968) American novelist and social reformer. Born in Baltimore, Maryland, he wrote dime novels to pay his way through the College of the City of New York. His writing was constantly influenced by his strong socialist beliefs. For a long time he was prominent in Californian politics and in 1907 he attempted to found a utopian commune, the **Helicon Home Colony**, at Englewood, New Jersey. In 1934 he united large sections of the unemployed and progressive elements in the EPIC (End Poverty in California) league. In 1942 he won the Pulitzer Prize with *Dragon's Teeth*.

PENTON BAXTER in Harry Kemp, *More Miles* (1926)

The identification is based upon obvious parallels.

DOWNIE SINCERE in Dalton Trumbo, *Washington Jitters* (1936)

'Downie Sincere, deviser of the Millennium Plan. [An] obvious [caricature] of . . . Upton Sinclair' (Joseph Blotner, 1966, *The Modern American Political Novel*, Austin, Tex., p. 132).

de SISMONDI, Jean (1773–1842) Swiss historian and economist. He was of Italian descent and was the author of *Nouveaux principes d'economie politique* (1819), *Histoire des Français* (1821–44, 31 vols) and others.

MR VON CHRONICLE in Benjamin Disraeli, *Vivian Grey* (1826–7)

Identified in a key given in a pamphlet published in 1827 by William Marsh. This key is discussed by Lucien Wolf in his notes to *Vivian Grey* (1904 (centenary edn), Vol. II, p. 364), with the conclusion that Disraeli was not responsible for the key.

SITWELL, Dame Edith (1887–1964) English poet, critic and novelist. Born in Scarborough, she was the sister of Osbert and Sacheverell **Sitwell**. She was introduced to the poetry of **Swinburne** and the Symbolists by her governess and between 1916 and 1921 she edited *Wheels*, an anthology of new poetry. Her own *Façade* appeared in 1923. In the 1930s she began writing prose, but returned to poetry and during the late 1940s she began producing work with the rhythms of jazz and other dance music. She wrote an autobiography, *Taken Care Of*, which was published posthumously in 1965.

LADY HARRIET FINNIAN-SHAW in Wyndham Lewis, *The Apes of God* (1930)

See under **Sitwell**, Osbert.

LUCY LINDEN and ANNA MARTON in Edith Sitwell, *I Live Under a Black Sun* (1937)

'Edith casts herself in the dual role of the two women who are in love with [Jonathan Hare, clearly Tchelitchew]. The young and headstrong Ann is the Edith who went to live abroad to be near him; and the older disillusioned but still faithful Lucy is the Edith at Levanto as she wrote the book' (John Pearson, 1978, *Façades: Edith, Osbert and Sacheverell Sitwell*, London: Macmillan, p. 324).

SITWELL, Sir George (1860–1943) He inherited the title and **Renishaw Hall**, Derbyshire, in 1862 and grew up rich, owing to his long minority and the discovery of coal at Renishaw. He was an eccentric, with a passion for gardens, miscellaneous collecting (particularly antique beds), and antiquarian research. In 1886 he married Lady Ida Denison (**Sitwell**, above), and their children were Edith, Osbert and Sacheverell **Sitwell**. In 1909 he bought the Castello di **Montegufoni**, the restoration of which from that time obsessed him. In 1925 he left England and settled in Italy, carrying with him his tamed and ageing wife, and remained there after her death, until compelled in 1942 by age, ill-health and the Second World War to move to Switzerland. He waged a prolonged and unremitting war of his own with his children. He was known to his family as 'Ginger', and bore a striking resemblance to Kaiser Wilhelm II.

SIR HENRY ROTHERHAM in Edith Sitwell, *I Live Under a Black Sun* (1937)

'There is a marvellous portrait of Sir George as the retired politician, Sir Henry Rotherham, pacing his enormous house "like a procession of one person", worrying continually about his health, and being so obsessed with dodging all unnecessary risks, that although agnostic he said his prayers every night, on the chance of this proving to be a good investment' (John Pearson, 1978, *Façades: Edith, Osbert and Sacheverell Sitwell*, London: Macmillan, p. 324).

HENRY WIMBUSH in Aldous Huxley, *Crome Yellow* (1921)

'[T]here was even more of George in Henry Wimbush than of Ida in his wife – his dotty archaeological passions, the book . . . on the history of his family, and even his collection of expensive antique beds' (Pearson, op. cit., p. 169). *See also* **Morrell**, Philip.

SITWELL, Lady Ida (1869–1937) Daughter of the 1st Earl of Londesborough, she married Sir George **Sitwell** in 1886 and became the mother of Edith, Osbert and Sacheverell **Sitwell**. She was young, beautiful and wildly extravagant, and by 1912 she was some £12,000 in debt to a money-lender. In 1915, after the latter's death, she was accused by the heirs of the original guarantor of the loan of conspiring to cheat and defraud him. She was charged, found guilty and sentenced to three months' imprisonment. She seems never to have displayed any bitterness towards her husband for allowing her to go to prison.

DUCHESS OF TOWERS in George Du Maurier, *Peter Ibbetson* (1891)

'Much prettier, and truer likenesses of my mother [than those by Frank Miles], are . . . to be found in Du Maurier's illustrations to . . . *Peter Ibbetson*. He greatly admired her looks, and she figures in them, wearing a small fur cap on her head, as the Duchess of Towers' (Sir Osbert Sitwell, 1945, *Left Hand, Right Hand*, p. 209 n. 1).

PRISCILLA WIMBUSH in Aldous Huxley, *Crome Yellow* (1921)

'The Sitwells could not fail to notice that . . . Huxley had made use of some of their liveliest stories about Sir George and Lady Ida. . . . The outrageous "Old Priscilla" Wimbush . . . had once gone nearly bankrupt – through extravagance and gambling. "The number of thousands varied in different legends, but all put it high." Worse followed . . . her husband Henry had to sell some pictures to redeem her debts and had then asserted himself forcefully against his erring wife, just as Sir George had done' (John Pearson, 1978, *Façades: Edith, Osbert and Sacheverell Sitwell*, London: Macmillan, p. 169). *See also* **Morrell**, Lady Ottoline.

SITWELL, Sir Osbert (1892–1969) English poet, playwright and novelist. He was born in London, brother of Edith and Sacheverell **Sitwell**. After being educated at Eton, he served in the Brigade of Guards during the First World War, but was invalided home in 1916. His first collection of poems was published in 1919 and his first novel, *Before the Bombardment*, in 1927. His circle of friends included Ezra **Pound**, T.S. **Eliot** and Wyndham Lewis. He also wrote travel books and a five-volume autobiography (1944–50).

LORD BADGERY in Aldous Huxley, 'The Tillotson Banquet' (1924)

'Badgery is obviously drawn from Osbert, and so closely drawn that it would have taken the most thick-skinned of friends not to be mildly offended' (John Pearson, 1978, *Façades: Edith, Osbert and Sacheverell Sitwell*, London: Macmillan, p. 170). Sitwell took his revenge in 'The Machine Breaks Down', in which Huxley appears as William Erasmus.

SIR CLIFFORD CHATTERLEY in D.H. Lawrence, *Lady Chatterley's Lover* (1928)

'Edith believed that D.H. Lawrence had based the character of Chatterley on that of . . . Osbert – who, like Sir Clifford, was a baronet, a famous writer and a soldier from the war' (Pearson, op. cit., p. 223). Pearson goes on to discuss the relation between Osbert Sitwell and Chatterley, describes the one meeting between the Lawrences and the Sitwells, and analyses the traits in Chatterley which he concludes derived from Sitwell (pp. 223–32). *See also* **Asquith**, Herbert.

LORD OSMUND FINNIAN-SHAW in Wyndham Lewis, *The Apes of God* (1930)

'The Finnian-Shaws are transformed into hideous, sycophantic and moronic grotesques, with just enough information for the identification with the Sitwells to be made' (R.T. Chapman, 1973, *Wyndham Lewis: fictions and satires*, London: Vision Press, p. 37).

SITWELL, Sacheverell (1897–1988) English poet, writer and art critic, brother of Edith and Osbert **Sitwell**. He joined the Guards regiment as an officer. After the First World War he travelled extensively in Europe. He wrote a number of books on European art.

LORD PHOEBUS FINNIAN-SHAW in Wyndham Lewis, *The Apes of God* (1930)

See under **Sitwell**, Osbert.

SIZERGH CASTLE, Cumbria The seat of the Roman Catholic family of Strickland since the thirteenth century. It is described in Nikolaus Pevsner, 1967, *Westmorland (Buildings of England* series), Harmondsworth: Penguin, pp. 289–91.

BANNISDALE in Mrs Humphry Ward, *Helbeck of Bannisdale* (1898)

'Bannisdale . . . is compounded of Levens, and of Sizergh, that older, sterner house nearby, belonging to the Catholic family of which I have already spoken' (Introd. to *The Writings of Mrs Humphry Ward*, Vol. XI: *Helbeck of Bannisdale*, 1911 (Westmorland edn), London: Smith, Elder, p. xvi). *See also* **Levens Hall**.

SKEFFINGTON, Francis Sheehy (1878–1916) A contemporary and friend of James Joyce at University College, Dublin, he was, according to Joyce, the cleverest man there after himself. He was shot by the British during the Easter Rebellion.

McCANN in James Joyce, *A Portrait of the Artist as a Young Man* (1916)

'In *A Portrait* Skeffington appears as McCann' (Richard Ellmann, 1966, *James Joyce*, London: Oxford Paperbacks, p. 63).

SKEFFINGTON, Sir Lumley St George (1771–1850) A dandy and playwright, he was a friend of Shelley, whose contemporary he was at Eton. He was also a friend of the Prince Regent. He invented Skeffington brown. He was caricatured by Gillray and satirized by **Byron** and **Moore**.

HON. MR LISTLESS in Thomas Love Peacock, *Nightmare Abbey* (1818)

'A character based on Sir Lumley Skeffington' (*Nightmare Abbey*, 1969, ed. Raymond Wright, Harmondsworth: Penguin, p. 263 n. 2 (to ch. III)). *See also* **Brummell**, Beau.

SKELTON, John Henry Woollen draper and tailor in the neighbourhood of Regent Street, London. In 1855, at the age of about 70, he was an habitué of Saunders's coffee shop in Warwick Street. He was the author of *My Book; or the Anatomy of Conduct* (1837).

MR TURVEYDROP in Charles Dickens, *Bleak House* (1852–3)

'Strangely enough, neither Hotten [in *Thackeray the Humorist and Man of Letters* (1864)] nor Hollingshead [in his reminiscences] commented upon Skelton's resemblance to Turveydrop, but it is merely necessary to read their two descriptions in conjunction with chapter fourteen of *Bleak House* to recognize the fidelity of Dickens's portrait' (Lionel Stevenson, 1948, 'Who was Mr Turveydrop?', *The Dickensian* 44: 40).

CHARLES JEAMES YELLOWPLUSH in W.M. Thackeray, *The Yellowplush Correspondence* (1837) and later works

'[T]he first book [Thackeray] received for review [in *Fraser's Magazine*] was Skelton's. Ever since his school days, Thackeray had been . . . ridiculing . . . "snobbishness". Skelton was such a superlative example of the vice that Thackeray decided to hold him up to contempt in a devastating caricature . . . and so he created Charles Jeames Yellowplush. . . . The eccentric bankrupt tailor . . . appears therefore to have . . . sat as a model for the two greatest English novelists of the Victorian era' (Stevenson, op. cit., pp. 40–1).

SKENE, James (1775–1864) Of Rubislaw, Aberdeen. Educated in Germany, he was called to the Scottish Bar in 1797, and was in the Edinburgh Light Horse with Sir Walter Scott. He was probably Scott's closest friend, and when Scott heard the final news of his bankruptcy on the evening of 16 January 1826, Skene was with him at seven o'clock the next morning. He travelled much abroad, and lived in Greece from 1838 to 1844. He married the sister of Sir William Forbes (the husband of Williamina **Belsches**).

DUDLEY in Sir Walter Scott, *Guy Mannering* (1815)

'The description of that superfluous character, Dudley, the artist . . . is evidently suggested by Skene' (F. MacCunn, 1909, *The Friends of Sir Walter Scott*, p. 268).

SKENE, Martin (d. 1589) Otherwise Maarten Schenk or Skenk. General in command of the Dutch army at the siege of Namur in 1589, he was killed in forcing the passage of the river. The fort of Schenkenshans near Nijmegen is named after him.

DUGALD DALGETTY in Sir Walter Scott, *A Legend of Montrose* (1819)

'I was not aware till Sir Walter himself told me, that the amusing character of the old soldier Dugald Dalgetty was taken from the record of an ancestor of mine in the military annals of Holland . . . General Martin Skene' (James Skene, 1909, *Memories of Sir Walter Scott*, ed. Basil Thomson, p. 188). Skene gives the Dutch version of his ancestor's name as Skenk, and W.S. Crockett (*The Scott Originals: an account of notables and worthies, the originals for characters in the Waverley Novels*, Edinburgh and London: T.N. Foulis, p. 280) spells it Schenk. **See also Monro**, Robert; **Turner**, Sir James.

SKINNER, Jack (1870–1925) Brother of M.L. Skinner, whose novel *The House of Ellis* was revised by D.H. Lawrence and published as *The Boy in the Bush*. His father was an officer in the British army.

JACK GRANT in D.H. Lawrence and M.L. Skinner, *The Boy in the Bush* (1924)

'"Jack" in the "Boy" was her [M.L. Skinner's] brother' (D.H. Lawrence to Ada Clarke, 31 August 1924, quoted in Ada Clarke and G. Stuart Gelder, 1931, *Young Lorenzo: early life of D.H. Lawrence*, Florence, p. 128).

SKIPSEY, Joseph (1832–1903) Newcastle collier poet. Befriended and supported by **Burne-Jones**, Morris, **Browning** and others, he became the custodian of Shakespeare's birthplace at Stratford. A selection of his poems, edited by Basil Bunting, was published in 1976.

MORRIS GEDGE in Henry James, 'The Birthplace' (1903)

'The story follows closely the original idea given James in May 1901 during one of his visits to Welcombe. Lady Trevelyan had told him of a man and his wife who had been placed in charge of the Shakespeare house. They were "rather strenuous and superior people from Newcastle"' (Leon Edel, 1972, *Henry James: the master, 1901–1916*, p. 152). 'A late tale by Henry James, "The Birthplace" . . . is almost certainly founded on Skipsey's rather thankless Stratford post' (J.L. Bradley, 1978, 'Joseph Skipsey', *Notes and Queries* 203: 320). The article deals with a letter (in the Folger Shakespeare Library, Washington) addressed by Skipsey to an unidentified friend, describing the circumstances of his resignation from the post at Stratford. 'We had not', he writes, 'held our office more than a few months before we discovered that not a single one of the . . . relics on exhibition could be proved to be Shakespeare's.'

SLAUGHTER, E.J. Solicitor. In 1899 and 1900 he was a co-lodger with F.W. Rolfe at 69 Broadhurst Gardens, London. Rolfe had known the family since 1886.

NEDDY CARNAGE in F.W. Rolfe, *Nicholas Crabbe* (1958)

'E.J. Slaughter (the languid Neddy Carnage of the present book [Nicholas Crabbe]' (Cecil Woolf, 1968, Introd. to *Nicholas Crabbe*, p. iv).

SLIGO, Ireland A port on the north-west coast. For generations, it was the home of Mrs J.B. Yeats's family.

BALLAH in W.B. Yeats, *John Sherman* (1891)

'The novelette records that tension between Sligo (the "Ballah" of the novel) and the Babylon of London' (Ian Fletcher, 1971, 'Review: "William Butler Yeats: John Sherman and Dhoya"', *Notes and Queries* 216: 275).

SLOMAN, Charles (1808–70) He first appeared as an improvvisatore in 1824, performing at 'singing' taverns, including the **Coal Hole**, or supper rooms in London and in music halls. In 1857 he appeared as the clown at the pantomime at the Strand Theatre. He died in the Strand union workhouse.

LITTLE NADAB in W.M. Thackeray, *The Newcomes* (1854–5)

'It is certain that "little Nadab, the improvisatore", of whom Thackeray speaks, was a certain Mr Sloman, who called himself "the only English improvisatore", who used to sing at the Coal Hole, and the outpourings of whose improvisations were remarkably like the specimens given in *The Newcomes*'

(Edmund Yates, 1884, *Edmund Yates: his recollections and experiences*, Vol. I, London: R. Bentley & Son, p. 166).

SLOPPY JOE'S Joe **Russell**'s bar in Key West, Florida.

FREDDY'S BAR in Ernest Hemingway, *To Have and Have Not* (1937)

'Josie Russell's place, disguised as Freddy's Bar, could serve as a focal point for Harry's business dealings' (Carlos Baker, 1969, *Ernest Hemingway: a life story*, New York, p. 287).

SMEDLEY, Isaac Frank (1869?–1934) Educated at Shrewsbury and at Pembroke College, Cambridge. Master at Tonbridge School when Forster was there as a boy (1893–97), he was the only master who 'captured his imagination'. He was 'hopeless at keeping order, and . . . a militant agnostic . . . but boys who bothered to attend to him found him a brilliant teacher'. From 1898 to 1932 he was on the staff of Westminster School, and for the greater part of the time was in charge of the Classical Lower Sixth. He was a housemaster for many years.

MR JACKSON in E.M. Forster, *The Longest Journey* (1907)

'The original of "Mr Jackson" . . . he made one realize, said Forster, that Plato and Virgil were men who had actually lived and were writing for other living men' (P.N. Furbank, 1977, *E.M. Forster: a life*, Vol. I: *The Growth of the Novelist (1879–1914)*, London: Secker & Warburg, p. 43). *See also* **Wedd**, Nathaniel.

SMETHAM, James (1821–93) Born in Yorkshire, he studied at the Royal Academy School, London, in 1843 and exhibited there from 1851 to 1876. He formed a connection with Dante Gabriel **Rossetti** and his circle; when, in 1877, he had a mental breakdown, Rossetti gave unremitting help, doing all he could to promote the sale of his pictures.

WILDERSPIN in Theodore Watts-Dunton, *Aylwin* (1899)

Identified in T. St E. Hake, 1902, 'Aylwin', *Notes and Queries* (9th series) 9 (7 June): 450–2, and 10 (2 August): 89–91; reprinted in *Aylwin*, 1914 (World's Classics), Oxford, App. II.

SMITH, Abe He was one of Thomas Wolfe's students at Washington Square College, the branch of New York University where he taught in 1924 and 1925. The two men became friends and Smith typed the manuscript of the first version of *Look Homeward, Angel*.

ABE JONE in Thomas Wolfe, *Of Time and the River* (1935)

'The character of Abe Jones was modeled on Abe Smith' (Richard S. Kennedy, 1962, *The Window of Memory: the literary career of Thomas Wolfe*, Chapel Hill, NC, p. 88).

SMITH, Alfred Emanuel (1873–1944) He was Governor of New York in 1919 and 1920, and from 1923 to 1928, and was Democratic candidate for the United States presidency in 1928.

JIM WHITE in Stephen Endicott, *Mayor Harding of New York* (1931)

'Jim White . . . clearly suggests Alfred E. Smith' (Joseph Blotner, 1966, *The Modern American Political Novel*, Austin, Tex., p. 126).

SMITH, Ambrose *(fl.* 1820) A gypsy of Norfolk with whom George Borrow was acquainted as a young man.

PETULENGRO in George Borrow, *Lavengro* (1851)

'Jasper Petulengro . . . founded upon the Norfolk gipsy, Ambrose Smith' (Sir Paul Harvey (ed.), 1967, *The Oxford Companion to English Literature*, Oxford: Oxford University Press, p. 638).

SMITH, Sir Aubrey (1863–1948) Film actor. Educated at Charterhouse and at Cambridge, he later lived and worked in Hollywood for many years.

SIR AMBROSE ABERCROMBIE in Evelyn Waugh, *The Loved One* (1948)

'Sir Aubrey Smith was said to look with special suspicion on Evelyn, and I dare say that he is the original (with much variation) of the immensely successful Sir Ambrose Abercrombie' (Christopher Sykes, 1975, *Evelyn Waugh*, London: Collins, p. 309).

SMITH, Chard Powers (1894–1977) American writer. Educated at Yale, Harvard, Oxford and Columbia Universities, he later lectured on poetry and historical topics. In 1921 he married Olive Cary Macdonald, whom his first novel, *Along the Wind* (1925, Yale), was largely about. She died in 1924, and Smith subsequently married twice more.

HUBERT ELLIOT in Ernest Hemingway, 'Mr and Mrs Elliot', *In Our Time* (1925)

'He had also [1924] written a malicious gossip story called "Mr and Mrs Smith" making fun of the alleged sexual ineptitudes of Mr and Mrs Chard Smith' (Carlos Baker, 1969, *Ernest Hemingway: a life story*, New York, p. 133). The name 'Smith' survives in the original typescript, but was altered before publication in *The Little Review*. Smith naturally took exception to the story when he came across it in 1927, and an acrimonious correspondence ensued.

SMITH, Edith Delong (d. 1919) A Bohemian and active radical in Greenwich Village, she was a friend of Theodore Dreiser from 1917. In 1918 she divorced her first husband and married Edward H. **Smith**. Dreiser met A.A. Brill, the translator of Freud, at their home in 1918.

OLIVE BRAND in Theodore Dreiser, 'Olive Brand', *A Gallery of Women* (1929)

'Dreiser told Edith's story in "Olive Brand"' (Ellen Moers, 1970, *Two Dreisers*, London: Thames & Hudson, p. 272; originally published 1969, New York: Viking). 'His fictional appraisals of Ed and Edith Smith . . . and many others' (W.A. Swanberg, 1965, *Dreiser*, New York, p. 359). The story retails the course of the Smiths' marriage; like Olive, Edith De Long Smith died of a five-day illness after a year of marriage.

SMITH, Edward H. (1886?–1928?) From Kansas, he was educated at the University of Jena. He was the second husband of Edith **Smith**, whom he married in 1918 when he was a journalist on the New York *Sunday World*. He died of pneumonia, calling his wife's name.

JACK JETHRO in Theodore Dreiser, 'Olive Brand', *A Gallery of Women* (1929)

See under **Smith**, Edith.

SMITH, Elizabeth (1797–1878) Daughter of Alexander Murray of Edinburgh, she married George Smith the Elder in 1820, a year after the foundation of the publishing house of Smith and Elder. In 1851, while writing *Villette*, Charlotte Brontë stayed in London with her and her son George **Smith**.

MRS LOUISA LUCY BRETTON in Charlotte Brontë, *Villette* (1853)

'Mrs Smith was even more clearly drawn – sometimes to words and phrases which are still remembered in the Mrs Bretton of the book' (Mrs Humphry Ward, 1899, Introd. to *Villette* (Haworth edn), p. xii).

SMITH, Ellen ('Minnie') (b. 1860?) Daughter of Joseph Smith, a prosperous draper of St Matthews Street, Ipswich, she became nurse to the children of James **Compton-Burnett** upon the death of his first wife. She remained to bring up Ivy Compton-Burnett and the six children of James Compton-Burnett's second wife.

MISS PATMORE in I. Compton-Burnett, *Brothers and Sisters* (1929)

'Miss Patmore . . . bears, in character as much as in looks, an unmistakeable likeness to Minnie' (H. Spurling, 1974, *Ivy when Young: the early life of I. Compton-Burnett, 1884–1919*, London: Gollancz, p. 49).

SMITH, George (1824–1901) Publisher. Son of George and Elizabeth **Smith**, he succeeded his father in the firm of Smith and Elder. He published Charlotte Brontë, **Thackeray**, George **Eliot** and **Ruskin**, among others. He was the founder and publisher of *Cornhill Magazine* and the publisher of *The Dictionary of National Biography*.

DR JOHN GRAHAM BRETTON in Charlotte Brontë, *Villette* (1853)

'In November 1852 Miss Brontë sent to the firm her manuscript of "Villette", in which she drew her portrait of Smith in . . . Dr John, while his mother was the original of Mrs Bretton' (Sidney Lee (ed.), 1901, 'Memoir of George Smith', preface to *The Dictionary of National Biography* (Suppl. 1), London: Oxford University Press, p. xxii).

SMITH, Goldwin (1823–1910) From his youth, he entertained liberal political and religious views. He wrote for the *Saturday Review*, and in 1850 he was joint Secretary of the Oxford University commission. He left Oxford for Cornell University, Ithaca, New York, in 1868, and in 1871 he settled in Toronto.

THE OXFORD PROFESSOR in Benjamin Disraeli, *Lothair* (1870)

'In 1870 [Disraeli] published his *Lothair* and there he rancorously introduced an unnamed Oxford professor of advanced opinions . . . who was . . . about to settle in the New World. . . . The attack stung Smith, and he injudiciously replied in a letter to *The Times* (9 June 1870)' (Sidney Lee, 1976, *The Dictionary of National Biography* (Suppl.), 1901–11, Oxford: Oxford University Press, p. 334).

SMITH, Revd James William He was Curate to Mr Brontë at Haworth from 1842 to 1844, and then Curate at Keighley until 1846. He returned to Ireland, and is said to have disappeared after leaving for Canada.

PETER AUGUSTUS MALONE in Charlotte Brontë, *Shirley* (1849)

'Mr Peter Augustus Malone was the Rev. James William Smith' (Herbert Wroot, 1935, *Sources of Charlotte Brontë's Novels: persons and places*, Shipley, Yorks., p. 125). 'Mr Smith has not mentioned your name since you left, except once when papa said you were a nice girl, he said, "Yes, she is a nice girl – rather quiet. I suppose she has money," and that is all. I think the words speak volumes; they do not prejudice one in favour of Mr Smith' (Charlotte Brontë to Ellen Nussey, 16 July 1844, reproduced in T.J. Wise and J.A. Symington, 1935, *The Brontës: their lives, friendships and correspondence*, Vol. II, p. 7).

SMITH, Leslie Tilden (1885–1945) Educated at Merton College, Oxford, in 1906 he joined Curtis Brown, the London literary agents. He was married in 1909, and he served in the Royal Flying Corps during the First World War. He was later divorced, and by 1929 he was living with Jean Rhys, whom he subsequently married.

GEORGE HORSFIELD in Jean Rhys, *After Leaving Mr Mackenzie* (1931)

'The character was in large part drawn from Tilden Smith himself. The house where Horsfield lives in Holland Park . . . fits . . . the . . . house where Rhys and Tilden Smith lived at 1 Boyne Terrace Mews, Holland Park. . . . The point is not to identify absolutely these sources with the characters and places in the work, but to suggest that Rhys's own experience, from which she almost exclusively drew, had broadened her perceptions and insights, and that her life with Tilden Smith helped her to create a more rounded and complex male character' (Thomas F. Staley, 1979, *Jean Rhys: a critical study*, pp. 75–6).

SMITH, Madeleine (1836?–1928) Daughter of a prosperous Glasgow architect, in 1855 she met Pierre Emile l'Angelier, a clerk in a seedman's warehouse, and became his mistress. She met a more socially acceptable suitor, and in 1856 l'Angelier died of arsenical poisoning. In the summer of 1857 she was charged with his murder, her alleged object being to prevent his using the extremely compromising letters she had written him to impede her new attachment. She was tried in Edinburgh, but the prosecution failed to prove the case. According to Violet Hunt (see *The Wife of Rossetti*, 1932, p. 229 n. 3), in 1861 she was living very miserably in a London boarding house and working as a tapestry weaver for William Morris's firm. Certainly that year she married George Wardle, an employee of the firm who eventually rose to the position of manager. 'After the death of her husband, who had left Morris's employment in 1889, she lived for a time in Staffordshire, then in London again, and finally in the United States, where she was married to one Sheehy. She died . . . in great poverty . . . and was buried, as Lena Wardle Sheehy, in Mount Hope Cemetery, Hastings-on-Hudson, New York' (R.D. Altick, 1970, *Victorian Studies in Scarlet*, New York, pp. 185–6).

Madeleine Graham in Emma Robinson, *Madeleine Graham* (1864)

'Her three-volume *Madeleine Graham* is a thinly disguised fictionalization of the Madeleine Smith case' (ibid., p. 141 n.).

SMITH, Olive Cary (d. 1924) Née Macdonald. She married the author Chard Powers **Smith** in 1921, but died in Naples in the spring of 1924 during a pregnancy with twins. The friend in Hemingway's story was a woman called Janet Hurter, who was Mrs Smith's closest friend and visited her in Naples when her health was declining.

Cornelia Elliot in Ernest Hemingway, 'Mr and Mrs Elliot', *In Our Time* (1925)

See under **Smith**, Chard Powers.

SMITH, R.D. (**'Reggie'**) (1914–85) He was a British Council lecturer in Bucharest until driven out by the German invasion in 1939; he escaped with his wife Olivia Manning to Greece and the Middle East. From 1946 until 1973 he was a radio producer with the BBC.

Guy Pringle in Olivia Manning, *The Balkan Trilogy* (1960–5) and *The Levant Trilogy* (1977–80)

'... dispassionately portrayed ... as the bumbling, maddening Guy Pringle' (Douglas Cleverdon, 1985, obituary, *The Times* (9 May)).

SMITH, Rosalind (b. 1889?) Known in the family as 'Tootsie', she was the sister of Zelda **Fitzgerald**. She married Newman Smith.

Marion Peters in F. Scott Fitzgerald, 'Babylon Revisited' (1931)

'Wales's sister-in-law is obviously based on Rosalind Smith' (M.J. Bruccoli, 1981, *Some Sort of Epic Grandeur: the life of F. Scott Fitzgerald*, London: Hodder & Stoughton, p. 309).

SMITH, Sidney (1849–1922) Chief Mate of the clipper *Cutty Sark* in 1880, he struck a Negro sailor who had disobeyed an order; the man died but Smith was allowed by the Captain to escape by swimming to a neighbouring ship. He was apprehended in London two years later and sentenced to seven years' imprisonment for manslaughter. On coming out of prison he returned to sea and slowly worked his way up to a command.

Leggatt in Joseph Conrad, 'The Secret Sharer', *'Twixt Land and Sea* (1912)

'The Swimmer himself was suggested to me by a young fellow who was 2nd mate [sic] ... of the *Cutty Sark* and had the misfortune to kill a man on deck' (Joseph Conrad to A.T. Saunders, 14 June 1917, quoted in Norman Sherry, 1966, *Conrad's Eastern World*, Cambridge, p. 295). For an account of Smith's trial, see Basil Lubbock, 1924, *The Log of the Cutty Sark*, Glasgow, pp. 410–12, App. VII.

SMITH, Sydney (1771–1845) Educated at Winchester and at New College, Oxford, he took orders. As tutor to Michael Hicks Beach, he lived in Edinburgh, where he became intimate with **Jeffrey** and **Brougham** and associated with them in founding the *Edinburgh Review* in 1802. He moved to London, where he became resident wit at Holland House, and in 1831 he was Canon of St Paul's Cathedral.

BUCKHURST FALCONER in Maria Edgeworth, *Patronage* (1814)

'It was widely understood that Sydney Smith ... appeared in *Patronage* as Buckhurst Falconer. ... There is a clear indication in [his] letters that he had taken offence at *Patronage*. In reality Buckhurst Falconer could not have been based on Smith, or any character in *Patronage* on people the Edgeworths met in London in 1813, since the novel was completed ... before they left home in the spring' (Marilyn Butler, 1972, *Maria Edgeworth*, Oxford, p. 258).

SMITH, William Benjamin (1850–1934) Educated at the University of Kentucky and in Göttingen, he became Professor of Mathematics, and then of Philosophy (1906–15), at Tulane, University of Louisiana. He was the author of philosophical works and mathematical textbooks. In 1899 his wife Katherine died of tuberculosis; her sister, Mrs **Charles**, took over the care of his children. He was the father of Y.K. **Smith**, Bill **Smith** and Kate **Dos Passos**.

EZEKIEL HARRINGTON in John Dos Passos, *Chosen Country* (1951)

Identified in Carlos Baker, 1969, *Ernest Hemingway: a life story*, New York, p. 654 n. 'E.H. on Dos Passos's "Chosen Country"'.

SMITH, William ('Bill') Benjamin (1895–1972) Youngest child of W.B. **Smith**, and brother of Y.K. **Smith** and Katie **Dos Passos**. After their mother's death, they were brought up by their aunt, Mrs **Charles**, and spent their holidays at her farmhouse near the Hemingways' summer house. By 1916, Ernest Hemingway and Bill Smith were close friends, and Hemingway met his first wife, Hadley Richardson (*see* **Hemingway**), through the Smiths. Hemingway tried to find Smith a job in Paris in 1920, and Smith was one of a party at Pamplona in 1924 and 1925. He eventually entered the public service and wrote some speeches for President Truman.

BILL in Ernest Hemingway, 'The End of Something', *In Our Time* (1925), and 'The Three Day Blow' (1925)

'Smith is remembered ... also as the Bill of "The End of Something" and "The Three Day Blow"' (Donald St John, 1972, 'Interview with Hemingway's "Bill Gorton"', in B.D. Sarason (ed.), *Hemingway and the Sun Set*, Washington, DC, pp. 151–2).

BILL GORTON in Ernest Hemingway, *The Sun Also Rises* (1926)

'I guess everyone who cares knows that Bill Gorton ... was modelled after me, but then the character was really composite, as so many of Hemingway's characters were if people would just take time to examine them. Hem also used Don Ogden Stewart in creating this character. I explain it this way: I drank a lot in those days; I have a leg as hollow as Lady Brett Ashley's, but no one man could have drunk as much as Bill Gorton did ... it had to be composite' (W.B. Smith to D. St John, op. cit., p. 155). *See also* **Dos Passos**, John; **Stewart**, Donald Ogden.

BEN HARRINGTON in John Dos Passos, *Chosen Country* (1951)

Identified in Carlos Baker, 1969, *Ernest Hemingway: a life story*, New York, p. 654 n. 'E.H. on Dos Passos's "Chosen Country"'.

SMITH, Yeremya Kenley (1887–1969) Second son of W.B. **Smith**, and brother of Bill **Smith** and Kate **Dos Passos**, he was commonly known as Y.K. or Kenley, his first name being a corruption of Jeremiah. Hemingway lodged in his apartment in Chicago in 1920, and Y.K. introduced him to Sherwood **Anderson**; later, as so often happened with Hemingway, the two men quarrelled. Y.K. seems to have become an advertising executive in New York.

ZEKE HARRINGTON in John Dos Passos, *Chosen Country* (1951)

Identified in Carlos Baker, 1969, *Ernest Hemingway: a life story*, New York, p. 654 n. 'E.H. on Dos Passos's "Chosen Country"'.

SMITHSON, Charles (1805?–44) Solicitor. Son of Richard Smithson, Bailiff of Malton, he became a partner in Smithson, Dunn & Milton, of Southampton Buildings, who acted for Dickens from 1838. He was the 'professional friend' mentioned in the preface to the first Cheap edition of *Nicholas Nickleby* (1848) and who, on Dickens's visit to Yorkshire in 1838, gave him letters of introduction. In 1843 Dickens was godfather to his daughter Mary; Smith died the following year, leaving two young children and no will: "Every place has been searched that be thought of; and nothing has been found. He had even dropped a certain Life Insurance for £3,000 which in a man of business is extremely strange' (to Mrs Charles Dickens, 6 April 1844, reproduced in *Letters of Charles Dickens*, 1977, ed. Kathleen Tillotson, Vol. IV, Oxford: Oxford University Press, p. 97).

MR SPENLOW in Charles Dickens, *David Copperfield* (1849–50)

'[Dickens] perhaps recalled this in *David Copperfield*, ch. 38, where a lengthy search reveals that Mr Spenlow, the proctor, has made no will and: . . . "What was scarcely less astonishing to me, was, that his affairs were in a most disordered state"' (ibid., n. 4).

SMYTH, Edmund (1793–1853) Son of Revd William Smyth of Great Linford, Buckinghamshire, he was educated at Rugby School and at St John's College, Cambridge. He became Vicar of North Elkington, Lincolnshire, and East Haddon, Northamptonshire.

CRAB JONES in Thomas Hughes, *Tom Brown's Schooldays* (1857)

'Crab Jones is Edmund Smyth' (Edward C. Mack and W.H.G. Armytage, 1952, *Thomas Hughes: the life of the author of Tom Brown's Schooldays*, London: Ernest Benn, p. 94).

SMYTH, Dame Ethel (1858–1944) Composer of, amongst other works, an opera, *The Wreckers*, and an oratorio, *The Prisoner*, which was based on a book of the same title by Henry Brewster. The latter was a wealthy, half-American philosopher, who lived mainly in France and Italy: Ethel Smyth met him in Italy in 1858 and fell in love with him, their connection lasting until his death in 1908. She was a suffragette and was convinced that her works were not performed because she was a woman. She was a close friend of Maurice **Baring** and from

1930, as a result of the publication of *A Room of One's Own*, a friend of Virginia **Woolf**. She wrote a number of autobiographical volumes, and in later life she became deaf.

EDITH STAINES in E.F. Benson, *Dodo* (1893)

'Of the boys [the sons of Archbishop Benson] she knew Fred best – he puts her into *Dodo* as Edith Staines' (Betty Askwith, 1971, *Two Victorian Families*, 1971, p. 175).

SMYTHE, George A.F.P.S., 7th Viscount Strangford (1818–57) He was a member of the Young England party, and in 1852 he fought the last duel in England. He said of himself, 'I don't pretend to have any principle, but I have some heart, and I am a gentleman.' Disraeli recounts that he 'was very rich when he made up his mind to marry an heiress, gave his instructions to all the ladies who were, and who had been, in love with him to work for his benefit . . . he succeeded and married an heiress – but literally on his death-bed' (*Disraeli's Reminiscences*, 1975, ed. H. Swartz and M. Swartz, London: Hamilton, pp. 120–1). He died 'worn out by dissipation, brandy and water, and a delicate chest' (Sir William Gregory, 1894, *Autobiography*, p. 89).

HARRY CONINGSBY in Benjamin Disraeli, *Coningsby* (1844)

See Key to *Coningsby* given in Lord Lamington, 1906, *In the Days of the Dandies*, p. 148. *See also* **Lyttelton**, Lord.

GEORGE WALDERSHARE in Benjamin Disraeli, *Endymion* (1880)

Identified in 'Key to *Endymion*', *Notes and Queries* 83 (24 October 1942): 263; identifications attributed to G.E. Buckle. *See also* **Manners**, Lord John.

SNADDEN, Captain John (1837–87) Master of the *Otago*; he died on board, and Conrad succeeded him as Master.

THE FORMER CAPTAIN in Joseph Conrad, *The Shadow-Line* (1917)

'[T]he most unusual thing about Conrad's treatment of his source material lies in his transformation of the kindly, harmless Captain Snadden into the mad, malignant old man who was the narrator's predecessor' (Norman Sherry, 1966, *Conrad's Eastern World*, Cambridge, p. 286). For the facts about Captain Snadden, see ibid., pp. 218–27.

SNEYD GREEN, Staffordshire Situated near Burslem.

TOFT END in Arnold Bennett, *Anna of the Five Towns* (1902)

'Sneyd Green appears as Toft End in the Five Towns Stories' (*The Journals of Arnold Bennett*, 1932, ed. Sir Newman Flower, Vol. I, London: Cassell, p. 273 n.).

SNOW, Mrs She was an American who was long resident on Capri. In 1897, Lord Alfred **Douglas** dined with her when he and Oscar **Wilde** were living together at Posilipo. Norman Douglas knew her from 1904, when he first went to the island. She eventually returned to America.

DUCHESS OF SAN MARTINO in Norman Douglas, *South Wind* (1917)

'A vision of her helped me to portray the "Duchess" . . . other ladies contributed their share of suggestion; imagination also played its part. I have never tried to draw a figure from life. . . . My creed is that a human character, however engrossing, however convincing and true to itself, must be modelled anew before it became material for fiction' (Norman Douglas, 1934, *Looking Back*, p. 28).

SNOW, Charles Percy (1905–80) Novelist and physicist. Born in Leicester, the son of a church organist, he studied science at University College, Leicester, and at Christ's College, Cambridge, and became a fellow of Christ's College in 1930 and a tutor there from 1935 to 1945. During the Second World War he was Chief of Scientific Personnel for the Ministry of Labour, and was a civil service commissioner from 1945 to 1960. He was Lord Rector of St Andrews University from 1961 to 1953, was created a life peer in 1964, and was Parliamentary Secretary at the Ministry of Technology from 1964 to 1966. In 1950 he married Pamela Hansford Johnson, novelist, and daughter of Sir Henry Irving's manager.

Swan in William Cooper, *Young People* (1958)

'There is a particularly engaging representation of him as a very young man, illustrating both his power and his charm, in William Cooper's *Young People*' (obituary notice, 1980, *The Times* (2 July): 17). Swan's career exactly parallels Snow's up to the moment when he became a Fellow of Christ's and wrote his first novel.

SNYDER, Gary (b. 1930) American poet. Born in San Francisco and educated at the University of California, he was associated with the 'Beat' movement. Much of his writing is influenced by his interest in Asian religions and literature. He won the Pulitzer Prize in 1975 with *Turtle Island*.

Japhy Ryder in *The Dharma Bums* (1958), and Jarry Wagner in *Desolation Angels* (1965), both by Jack Kerouac

Identified in 'Character key to the Duluoz Legend', in Barry Gifford and Lawrence Lee, 1979, *Jack's Book*, pp. 322–32. He also appears under his own name in Kerouac's *Vanity of Duluoz* (1968).

SOCIETY FOR THE DIFFUSION OF USEFUL KNOWLEDGE Founded in 1825, largely as a result of the endeavours of Henry **Brougham**, who wrote the six-penny pamphlet on hydrostatics in the Society's 'Library of Useful Knowledge'.

Steam Intellect Society in Thomas Love Peacock, *Crotchet Castle* (1831)

'The Steam Intellect Society [is] the Society for the Diffusion of Useful Knowledge' (*Crotchet Castle*, 1969, ed. Raymond Wright, Harmondsworth: Penguin, p. 273 n. 3 (to ch. II).

SOCIETY OF THE DIVINE COMPASSION An Anglican order.

The Order of the Divine Blood in Shane Leslie, *The Cantab* (1926)

Identified in a key in the hand of Dr Ivor Ramsay, a Kingsman of the year 1920, and later Dean, laid in a copy of *The Cantab*.

SOLE END, Astley, Warwickshire The home of Mr George and Mrs Anne **Garner**.

GARUM FIRS in George Eliot, *The Mill on the Floss* (1860)

'Sole End, the Garum Firs of the novel' (Gordon S. Haight, 1958, 'The George Eliot Originals', in *From Jane Austen to Joseph Conrad: essays collected in memory of James T. Hillhouse*, ed. R. Rathburn and M. Steinmann, Jun., Minneapolis, Minn.: University of Minnesota Press, p. 189).

SOLGER, Reinhold (1817–66) Born in Stettin, Prussia, he was involved in the revolutionary movement in Germany in 1848. In 1853 he emigrated to Roxbury, Massachusetts, and became a lecturer at **Sanborn's School** in Concord. He was a strong supporter of the Abolitionists.

FRIEDRICH BHAER in Louisa M. Alcott, *Little Women* (1868) and sequels

'Professor Bhaer . . . whose traits she mined from her memories of Reinhold Solger' (M.B. Stern, 1952, *Louisa M. Alcott*, p. 184). *See also* **Rimmer**, William.

SOLOMONS, Isaac ('Ikey') (*c*.1785–1850) A notorious London receiver of the 1820s, in 1810 he was sentenced to fourteen years' transportation for picking pockets. He served six years in the hulks on the Thames and when he was released in 1816 he became a fence. He was again arrested in 1827, but he escaped to the United States, and in 1828 he joined his wife and family in Tasmania, where she was serving fourteen years' transportation for being a fence. He was rearrested in 1831 and again sentenced to transportation, but was pardoned in 1840. He died in poverty.

FAGIN in Charles Dickens, *Oliver Twist* (1837–8)

'Fagin was, I think, founded on the personality of . . . Ikey Solomons' (Edwin Pugh, 1913, *The Charles Dickens Originals*, London and Edinburgh: T.N. Foulis, p. 241). 'An examination of the evidence I think leads inescapably to the conclusion that Dickens did *not* model Fagin on Ikey Solomons' (J.J. Tobias, 1969, 'Ikey Solomons: a real-life Fagin', *The Dickensian* 65: 173).

SOLOWEITSCHIK, Gisa (*fl*. 1930) A young Jewish girl living in Berlin with her wealthy parents; Isherwood met her through Stephen **Spender** in 1930.

NATALIA LANDAUER in Christopher Isherwood, *Goodbye to Berlin* (1939)

'In *Goodbye to Berlin* Gisa is called Natalia Landauer. . . . [But] the Natalia character is a mere caricature of Gisa, as Stephen Spender pointed out' (Christopher Isherwood, 1977, *Christopher and His Kind*, London: Eyre Methuen, p. 54).

SOMERS, Virginia, Countess (1827–1910) The sixth of the seven daughters of James Pattle, in 1850 she married Charles Somers-Cocks, Viscount Eastnor, who became the 3rd Earl Somers in 1852. She was a ravishing beauty and was the great-aunt of Virginia **Woolf**.

ERMINIA in W.M. Thackeray, 'The Proser IV – On a Good-Looking Young Lady' (1850)

'Virginia is described under the name of Erminia. . . . Thackeray [writes] of Miss Pattle, "in every attitude of motion or repose her form moves or settles into beauty, so that a perpetual grace accompanies her"' (*The Letters and Private Papers of W.M. Thackeray*, 1945, ed. Gordon N. Ray, Vol. II, London: Oxford University Press, p. 695 n. 133).

SOMERSET County in the west of England; the county town is Bath, and the cathedral town is Wells.

BARSET in Anthony Trollope, *The Warden* (1855) and others

'He [Trollope] allowed Barset to be Somerset' (Edward A. Freeman, 1883, 'Anthony Trollope', *Macmillan's Magazine* (January): 239).

SOMERSET, Arthur (1816–45) Elder son of Lord Fitzroy Somerset (later first Baron Raglan). He quarrelled with his father over his marriage in July 1845 to Emilie Louise von Baumbach, and on 21 December 1845 he was mortally wounded in the battle of Ferozeshah, dying four days later.

GEORGE OSBORNE in W.M. Thackeray, *Vanity Fair* (1847–8)

'I saw Lord Fitzroy Somerset walking in St James's Park – with 2 girls in black, and absolutely crying. He had just quarrelled with his son about a marriage before receiving the news of the poor fellow's death, in that tremendous carnage' (to Mrs Carmichael-Smyth, 6 March 1846, reproduced in *The Letters and Private Papers of W.M. Thackeray*, 1945, ed. Gordon N. Ray, Vol. II, London: Oxford University Press, p. 232). 'This episode appears to have suggested to Thackeray George Osborne's quarrel with his father over his marriage to Amelia, shortly before Waterloo' (ibid., n. 17).

SONDLEY, Webster He was a rich and eccentric citizen of Asheville, North Carolina, who bequeathed his large library of North Carolina history to the Asheville Library.

JUDGE WEBSTER TAYLOE in Thomas Wolfe, *Look Homeward, Angel* (1929)

'The following entries [in *The Notebooks of Thomas Wolfe*] reflect Wolfe's work on the characterization of Judge Webster Tayloe, whom he fashioned after Webster Sondley' (*The Notebooks of Thomas Wolfe*, 1970, ed. Richard S. Kennedy and Paschal Reeves, Chapel Hill, NC: University of North Carolina, p. 102).

SONNTAG, William Louis (1822–1900) Painter. Born in Pittsburgh, in 1854 he moved to New York. He was largely self-taught, and from 1895 onwards Dreiser used his pictures as colour illustrations in *Ev'ry Month* when he was the Editor.

EUGENE WITLA in Theodore Dreiser, *The 'Genius'* (1915)

'Dreiser's interest in [William Louis Sonntag] – a member of the Ashcan School noted for street scenes – is demonstrated in [his] later drawing of Eugene Witla in . . . *The "Genius"*. The characterisation of [Witla] . . . derives as much from Sonntag as from . . . Everett Shinn' (Yoshinobu Hakutani, 1980, *Young Dreiser*, p. 111). *See also* **Dreiser**, Theodore; **Shinn**, Everett.

SOSKICE, David (1869–1943) A Russian refugee who had escaped from Siberia, in 1898 he presented himself at the Cearne (the **Garnetts'** house near Limpsfield). In 1899 he married Anna Sofia; they were divorced in February 1902 and in October of the same year he married Juliet Hueffer (**Soskice**, below).

CYRIL BRANDETSKI in Ford Madox Ford, *The Simple Life Limited* (1911)

Identified in Arthur Mizener, 1971, *The Saddest Story: a biography of Ford Madox Ford*, Clevelan: World Publishing, p. 558 n. 12. *See also* **Stepniak**, Sergius.

SOSKICE, Juliet (1881–1944) Sister of Ford Madox Ford, in 1902 she married David **Soskice**, becoming his second wife.

OPHELIA BRANSDON in Ford Madox Ford, *The Simple Life Limited* (1911)

Identified in Arthur Mizener, 1971, *The Saddest Story: a biography of Ford Madox Ford*, Cleveland: World Publishing, p. 558 n. 12.

The SOULS A group of friends in turn-of-the-century London society who were brought together by the death of Laura **Lyttelton**. They moved as a group from one great country house to another. Arthur **Balfour** was their high priest, but according to his sister-in-law, Lady Frances Balfour, the nucleus consisted of Laura Lyttelton's sisters, the Tennants (i.e. Margot **Asquith**, Lady Ribblesdale, and Mrs Graham Smith.

MRS BROOKENHAM'S CIRCLE in Henry James, *The Awkward Age* (1899)

'I suppose I must at any rate mention that I had in mind a certain special social (highly "modern" and actual) London group and type and tone, which seemed to me to *se prêter à merveille* to an ironic . . . treatment, and that clever people at least would know who, in general, and what, one meant. But here, at least, it appears there are very few clever people!' (to Miss Henrietta Reubell, 12 November 1899, reproduced in *The Letters of Henry James*, 1920, ed. Percy Lubbock, Vol. I, p. 341). '*The Awkward Age* is supposed to be about the Asquith set, but doesn't seem to be much like it' (to Cyril Connolly, 30 January 1930, reproduced in *A Portrait of Logan Pearsall Smith: from his letters and diaries*, 1950, introd. John Russell, p. 126).

SOUTH HARTING, Sussex The village in which H.G. Wells lived in the 1880s, when his mother was housekeeper to the owner of **Uppark** in the 1880s.

SIDDERMORTON in H.G. Wells, *The Wonderful Visit* (1895)

'The setting is South Harting' (Lovat Dickson, 1972, *H.G. Wells*, Harmondsworth: Penguin, p. 86).

SOUTH OTSELIC, New York

BLITZ in Theodore Dreiser, *An American Tragedy* (1925)

'Gillette seduced ... the daughter of poor but respectable farm people from nearby South Otselic (Blitz in the novel)' (Ellen Moers, 1970, *Two Dreisers*, London: Thames & Hudson, p. 200; originally published 1969, New York: Viking).

SOUTHEY, Robert (1774–1843) English poet. The son of a Bristol linen draper, he spent much of his childhood with an eccentric aunt. He was expelled from Westminster School for starting a radical magazine, and studied at Balliol College, Oxford, where he befriended S.T. **Coleridge**. In 1796 he married Elizabeth Fricker, whose sister, Sara, had married Coleridge the previous year. He began a long association with the *Quarterly Review* in 1809, and this provided almost his only regular income for the rest of his life. He was Poet Laureate in 1813. His wife died insane in 1837, and in 1939 he married Caroline Bowles. His last years were marked by an increasing mental decline.

MR FEATHERNEST in Thomas Love Peacock, *Melincourt* (1817)

'The Peacockian Southey is well known' (Martin Freeman, 1911, *Thomas Love Peacock*, London: Martin Secker, p. 142). 'Who once saw darkly through a glass of water, but now sees clearly through a glass of wine' (ibid., pp. 142–3).

HARPITON in Thomas Love Peacock, *Maid Marian* (1822)

'Harp-it-on, a corruption of *herpeton*, a creeping thing, "a phrase containing perhaps more compact virulence than any other writer could put into so many words – the minstrel in *Maid Marian*"' (Freeman, op. cit., p. 143).

MR NIGHTSHADE in Thomas Love Peacock, *Headlong Hall* (1816)

'Nightshade appears to be Southey' (*The Novels of T.L. Peacock*, 1948, ed. David Garnett, London: Rupert Hart-Davis, p. 21 n. 1).

THE PRINCIPAL WRITER FOR THE *ATTACK-ALL REVIEW* in Benjamin Disraeli, *Vivian Grey* (1826–7)

Identified as Mr R. S—y in a key given in a pamphlet published in 1827 by William Marsh. This key is discussed by Lucien Wolf in his notes to *Vivian Grey* (1904 (centenary edn), Vol. II, p. 364), with the conclusion that Disraeli was not responsible for the key.

RODERICK SACKBUT in Thomas Love Peacock, *Nightmare Abbey* (1818)

'Who reviews his own poems in the *Quarterly*' (Freeman, op. cit., p. 142).

RUMBLESACK SHANTSEE in Thomas Love Peacock, *Crotchet Castle* (1831)

'A turncoat whose company has brought Coleridge into bad repute' (Freeman, op. cit., p. 143).

SOUTHSEA, Hampshire Situated west of Portsmouth.

SOLENTSEA in Thomas Hardy, Wessex novels and tales (1871–95)

Identified on a map prepared by Thomas Hardy which hangs in the Dorset County Museum, Dorchester. *See under* **Abbotsbury**.

SOUVESTRE, Marie (1836?–1905) Daughter of the French Academician Emile Souvestre, she became Headmistress of Les Ruches, a celebrated and fashionable school for girls at Fontainebleau. She later conducted Allanswood School in Wimbledon, London, which was attended by Lytton **Strachey** and two of his sisters in 1887, and by Eleanor **Roosevelt**, afterwards the wife of Franklin D. Roosevelt.

MADEMOISELLE JULIE in Dorothy Bussy, *Olivia* (1949)

'In this memorable book, Marie Souvestre is portrayed tenderly and with realism under the name of Mlle Julie, the joint principal of a girls' boarding school in France, Les Avons' (Michael Holroyd, 1967, *Lytton Strachey*, Vol. I, London: Heinemann, p. 39).

SOYER, Alexis Benoit (1809–58) Born in Meaux en Brie, from 1837 to 1850 he was Cook to the Reform Club. In 1847 he was sent by the Government to Dublin, where he erected and conducted kitchens from which he issued rations of soup and meat at half the usual cost. In 1855 he was sent to Balaclava, where he reorganized the victualling of hospitals and cooking for the Army. He married Elizabeth Emma Jones, 'the English Murillo'.

MIROBOLANT in W.M. Thackeray, *The History of Pendennis* (1848–50)

'Once famous as the *chef* of the Reform Club and still alive as Mirobolant in Thackeray's *Pendennis*' (Sir Edward Cook, 1914, *The Life of Florence Nightingale*, Vol. I, p. 196).

SPAFFORD, Mrs Fortune-teller and reader of teacups. '[In 1917 Dreiser] occasionally consulted a tea-leaf reader named Mrs Spafford who he felt had amazing powers of divination' (W.A. Swanberg, 1965, *Dreiser*, New York, p. 221).

HONORIA GIFFORD in Theodore Dreiser, 'Giff', *A Gallery of Women* (1929)

'Now . . . in fictional form, appeared his appraisals of . . . a tea-leaf reader [he] had patronized, and many others' (ibid., p. 359).

SPARKS, Tryphena (1851–90) School teacher. In 1871 she was Headmistress of Plymouth Public Free School, and in 1877 she married Charles Gale, bookkeeper and publican of Topsham, near Exeter. She was Thomas Hardy's cousin, although it has been suggested that she was his niece and that she bore him an illegitimate son (see Lois Deacon and Terry Coleman, 1966, *Providence and Mr Hardy*).

SUE BRIDEHEAD in Thomas Hardy, *Jude the Obscure* (1895)

'In the 1895 preface to *Jude the Obscure*, Hardy wrote: "The scheme was jotted down in 1890, from notes made in 1887 and onwards, some of the circumstances being suggested by the death of a woman in the former year. This may well have been Tryphena. . . . The picture of Sue which Phillotson contemplates . . . is undoubtedly that of Tryphena in 1863 (see [Lois Deacon], *Tryphena and Thomas*

Hardy)' (F.P. Pinion, 1968, *A Hardy Companion*, London: Macmillan, p. 438). For a devastating attack on the elaborations of *Providence and Mr Hardy*, see Robert Gittings, 1973, 'Thomas Hardy and Tryphena Sparks', *Times Literary Supplement* (27 April): 477, and Gittings, 1973, letter to the Editor, *Times Literary Supplement* (6 June). *See also* **Henniker**, Hon. Florence.

SPENCER, Herbert (1820–1903) Philosopher. Employed as an engineer on Birmingham and Gloucester Railway in 1837–41, he was a sub-editor on *The Economist* in 1848–53. He published works on sociology and psychology, and became a friend of George Eliot, T.H. **Huxley** and **Tyndall**.

EDWARD CASAUBON in George Eliot, *Middlemarch* (1871–2)

'Ideally the [model] should combine avid learning with sexual insufficiency. This felicitous blend is unexpectedly hard to find. . . . For sexual low pressure, Herbert Spencer was probably the best example, and Beatrice Webb saw enough resemblance to refer to him as Casaubon. . . . But . . . Spencer came to regard [George Eliot] as the greatest woman who ever lived, an accolade she would not have so meagrely rewarded' (Richard Ellmann, 1973, 'Dorothea's husbands', in *Golden Codgers*, London: Oxford University Press, p. 20). *See also* **Brabant**, R.H.; **Bryant**, Jacob; **Eliot**, George; **Mackay**, R.W.; **Pattison**, Mark.

HUMBERT SPENDER in W.H. Mallock, *The Old Order Changes* (1886)

'"Humbert Spender", the scientist – Herbert Spencer, of course – whom Mallock hardly bothered to disguise' (R.L. Wolff, 1977, *Gains and Losses: novels of faith and doubt in Victorian England*, London: John Murray, p. 492).

SPENCER, John (d. 1944) A contemporary of Anthony Powell at Eton, he was killed in action during the Second World War.

PETER TEMPLER in Anthony Powell, *A Dance to the Music of Time* (1951–76)

'Templer (if such things must be established) – again [like Stringham] only at school – a trifle like John Spencer, a friend at another house, always dressed in the latest mode' (Anthony Powell, 1976, *To Keep the Ball Rolling: the memoirs of anthony Powell*, Vol. I: *The Infants of Spring*, London: Heinemann, p. 98).

SPENCER, Stanley (1891–59) Painter. Born in Cookham, Berkshire, where he lived most of his life, he was an Associate of the Royal Academy from 1932 to 1935 and a Royal Academician in 1950.

GULLEY JIMSON in Joyce Carey, *The Horse's Mouth* (1944)

'. . . popularly supposed to be based on Stanley Spencer' (Michael Holroyd, 1975, *Augustus John*, Vol. II, p. 225 n. 503). *See also* **John**, Augustus; **Thomas**, Dylan.

LIONEL MATHER in John Prebble, *The Mather Story* (1953)

'Prebble records . . . "When I was running the diary column for the *Sunday Express* an art dealer approached me. He had acquired some pencil drawings by Stanley Spencer of a pornographic nature and had shown them to Alfred Munnings who proposed to place them before Scotland Yard, Church House and the Athenaeum". This incident was the mainspring of the plot of *The Mather Story*' (Frederic Warburg, 1973, *All Authors Are Equal*, p. 268).

SPENDER, Emily (1841–1922) Novelist. Daughter of John Cottle Spender, a surgeon, she was born in and died in Bath. Her sister-in-law Lilian was a prolific novelist, and her brother Edward was the founder of the *Western Morning News*, a Plymouth newspaper that he edited until his death. She was the aunt of Stephen **Spender**. Forster met her in Italy in 1901.

MISS LAVISH in E.M. Forster, *A Room With a View* (1908)

'Miss Lavish was actually a Miss Spender' (E.M. Forster, interviewed in 1952, quoted in P.N. Furbank and F.J.H. Haskell, 1972, *Writers at Work: the Paris Review interviews*, selected by Kay Dick, Harmondsworth: Penguin, p. 13). In a letter to the *Times Literary Supplement* in 1971 (11 June), John Beer identified Miss Spender as Miss Lavish and pointed out the resemblances between the two writers' novels.

SPENDER, Stephen (b. 1909) English poet and critic. Born in London, son of the English authors Edward Harold Spender and Lilian Spender. He was educated at University College School, London, and at University College, Oxford, where he met W.H. **Auden**. Leaving Oxford without taking a degree, he went to Berlin in 1930, the year in which his first volume of poems was published. He was in Spain during the Civil War, and was a fireman in London during the Second World War. He was Professor of English at University College, London from 1970 to 1977.

STEPHEN SAVAGE in Christopher Isherwood, *Lions and Shadows* (1938)

'Stephen [Spender] at twenty-one still fitted pretty well the description of him at nineteen, as "Stephen Savage"' (Christopher Isherwood, 1977, *Christopher and His Kind*, London: Eyre Methuen, p. 48).

SPEYER, Sir Edgar (1862–1932) Born in New York, in 1887 he was Director of Speyer Bros., London, and in 1892 he was naturalized as a British citizen. He financed the Metropolitan District Railway Company, and was Chairman of the Underground Electric Railways Company. He was a friend of H.H. **Asquith**, and a great patron of music, financing the Queen's Hall promenade concerts. In 1915 he was accused of pro-German activities and returned to New York, where he continued to patronize the arts; his naturalization was revoked in 1921. He married Leonora (**Speyer**, above), daughter of Ferdinand, Count von Stosch of Mantze, Silesia.

SIR HERMANN GURTNER in E.F. Benson, *Robin Linnet* (1919)

Identification based upon private information.

SPEYER, Lady Leonara Daughter of Ferdinand, Count von Stosch of Mantze, Silesia, she married Sir Edgar **Speyer**. Deeply musical, 'she had a flair for parties, and would hire the whole London Symphony Orchestra for an evening to accompany one artist, and would ask twenty people to listen to it' (Muriel Draper, 1929, *Music at Midnight*, New York, p. 143). Osbert **Sitwell** shook hands with the French composer Debussy in her drawing room.

LADY GURTNER in E.F. Benson, *Robin Linnet* (1919)

Identification based upon private information.

von SPIEGEL, Melanie Later von Steckendorf. Daughter of Baron von Spiegel, who was Lord Marshall of the Court of Weimar when Thackeray first visited the town in 1830. She was a Maid of Honour and chief beauty at the Court, and Thackeray fell in love with her at first sight, describing her as 'the prettiest woman I ever saw in my life' (to Mrs Carmichael-Smyth, 20 October 1830, reproduced in *The Letters and Private Papers of W.M. Thackeray*, Vol. I: *1817–1840*, 1945, ed. Gordon N. Ray, London: Oxford University Press, p. 130). In 1852, when Thackeray was in Venice with his daughters, he saw her breakfasting in his hotel, a stout lady dressed in green and eating an egg; he was so much shaken that he was unable to bring himself to speak to her.

DOROTHEA VON SPECK in W.M. Thackeray, *The Confessions of Fitz-Boodle* (1852)

'She is the Dorothea of Fitz-Boodle's Confessions' (*Letters*, op. cit., p. 127 n. 30).

SQUIRE, Miss A mid-western American woman who arrived in Paris with her friend Miss **Mars** in the early 1900s: 'somewhat mousy, tailored and prim, within a year they were habitués of the local cafés ... and both appeared in public so heavily made up their faces had the appearance of masks' (James R. Mellow, 1974, *The Charmed Circle: Gertrude Stein and company*, London: Phaidon Press, p. 133). Miss Mars dyed her hair a flaming orange. They were taken to visit Gertrude Stein at the rue de Fleurus.

GEORGINA SKEENE in Gertrude Stein, 'Miss Furr and Miss Skeene', *Geography and Plays* (1922)

'The originals ... were Miss Mars and Miss Squire' (ibid.).

SQUIRE, Sir John Collings (1884–1958) Poet and man of letters. In 1913 he was Editor of the *New Statesman*, which had just been founded, and in 1919 he set up *London Mercury*, which he edited until 1934. He was a considerable parodist and edited a number of anthologies; he was also a passionate cricketer, and after the First World War he founded a cricket club, 'The Invalids', whose members were for the most part connected with literature. Until his death, he contributed weekly reviews to newspapers and periodicals. His last years were gravely disorganized, largely as a result of his addiction to alcohol.

WILLIAM HODGE in A.G. Macdonell, *England, Their England* (1933)

'It was into this atmosphere [the offices of the *London Mercury*] that ... the hero of A.G. Macdonell's *England Their England* was introduced. ... On meeting the editor, William Hodge, who is of course McDonell's [sic] representation of Squire, he was immediately asked whether he played cricket' (Patrick Howarth, 1963, *Squire, Most Generous of Men*, p. 154).

JACK SPIRE in Evelyn Waugh, *Decline and Fall* (1928)

'The headmaster, Dr Augustus Fagan, probably owed his surname to James Fagan ... of the Oxford Playhouse ... but there is no reason to suspect malice. It is otherwise with Evelyn's introduction into the story of a contemptibly ridiculous man of letters who he called Jack Spire of *The London Hercules*. Through Dudley Carew ... he had met Jack Squire [in 1924] ... and taken a great dislike to him' (Christopher Sykes, 1975, *Evelyn Waugh*, London: Collins, p. 86).

STAFFORD, Augustus, (Augustus Stafford O'Brien)   (1811–57) Son of Stafford O'Brien, he assumed the name of Stafford by royal license in 1847. He was MP for Northamptonshire North from 1841 to 1857, and in 1852 he was Secretary to the Admiralty.

Tom Chudleigh in Benjamin Disraeli, *Coningsby* (1844)

Identified in a key in *Notes and Queries* (8th series) 3 (13 May 1893): 363. *See also under* **Bright**, John.

STAFFORD HOUSE, Dorset   Formerly known as Froom-Everard, it is located on the southern side of the Frome River, opposite Lower Bockhampton.

Froom-Everard House in Thomas Hardy, 'The Waiting Supper' (1913)

'The house, plantation, and weir are very much as described by Hardy' (F.B. Pinion, 1968, *A Hardy Companion*, London: Macmillan, p. 336).

STAFFORDSHIRE

Loamshire in George Eliot, *Adam Bede* (1859)

'[Staffordshire] is Loamshire' (Charles S. Olcott, 1911, *George Eliot: scenes and people in her novels*, London: Cassell, p. 65; originally published 1910, New York: Thomas Y. Crowell).

The *STAFFORDSHIRE KNOT*   A local newspaper that was founded in 1882 as a weekly in Burslem by a group of friends of the Bennett family; Enoch Bennett was a shareholder. It became a daily in 1885, and in 1892 it was absorbed by the *Staffordshire Sentinel*.

The Chronicle in Arnold Bennett, the *Clayhanger* trilogy (1910–16)

'*The Chronicle*, clearly, [was the fictional counterpart] of the *Staffordshire Knot*' (Margaret Drabble, 1975, *Arnold Bennett: a biography*, London: Weidenfeld & Nicolson, p. 45 n.).

The *STAFFORDSHIRE SENTINEL*   The newspaper that took over the *Staffordshire Knot* in 1892.

The Signal in Arnold Bennett, the *Clayhanger* trilogy (1910–16)

'The *Signal* was the fictional counterpart of the *Staffordshire Sentinel*' (Margaret Drabble, 1975, *Arnold Bennett: a biography*, London: Weidenfeld & Nicolson, p. 45 n.).

STAIR, Margaret, Lady   (d. 1692) Daughter of James Ross, in 1643 she married James Dalrymple (1619–95), who was created 1st Viscount Stair in 1690; Janet **Dalrymple** was their daughter. She was the widow of Fergus Kennedy.

LADY ASHTON in Sir Walter Scott, *The Bride of Lammermoor* (1819)

'Scott is careful to disclaim any intention of "tracing the portrait of the first Lord Stair in . . . Sir William Ashton", but he virtually admits the close resemblance between Lady Ashton . . . and the wife of the Viscount' (W.S. Crockett, 1912, *The Scott Originals: an account of notables and worthies, the originals of characters in the Waverley Novels*, Edinburgh and London: T.N. Foulis, p. 263).

STALBRIDGE HOUSE, Dorset Situated about five miles east of Sherborne.

STAPLEFORD PARK in Thomas Hardy, 'Squire Petrick's Lady' (1891)

Identified in F.B. Pinion, 1968, *A Hardy Companion*, London: Macmilllan. 'Only the Park wall and gateway survive' (ibid., p. 480).

STAMFORD AND WARRINGTON, Katherine, Countess of (1827?–1905) Daughter of Henry Cocks, a farm labourer of gypsy origin, she, as Kitty Fleming, and her sisters Polly and Sukey created a great sensation as the three equestrienne sisters at Astley's Amphitheatre. In 1855 she married the Earl of Stamford and Warrington, becoming his second wife, and made a surprisingly successful Countess. Chichester **Parkinson-Fortescue**, who was previously the lover of her sister Polly, wrote of her, on seeing the announcement of the marriage, 'she was a nice creature'.

COUNTESS OF CAPERINGTON in R.S. Surtees, *Mr Facey Romford's Hounds* (1865)

'[She was] the original of the Countess of Caperington' ('. . . *and Mr Fortescue': a selection from the diaries of Chichester Fortescue, Lord Carlingford*, 1958, ed. O.W. Hewitt, London: John Murray, p. 55 n. 6).

STANLAWS, Penrhyn (1877–1957) American portrait painter and illustrator. Born as Adamson in Dundee, he went to the United States in 1891. He studied in Paris and London and was the author of two plays. He was in Hollywood in 1921 as a motion-picture director.

FLANAGAN in W. Somerset Maugham, *Of Human Bondage* (1915)

'Flanagan . . . has much in common with . . . Penrhyn Stanlaws' (D.W. Buchanan, 1936, *James Wilson Morrice*, Toronto, p. 68). Buchanan's identifications of originals were, he says, approved by Maugham.

STANLEY, Fabia, Lady (d. 1905) Supposedly the daughter of Santiago Federico San Roman of Seville, she was always known in England as Lady Stanley and went through four forms of marriage with the 3rd Lord Stanley: first, in 1862 in Algeria; second, in Constantinople according to Islamic rites, he having become a Muslim; third, in 1869 in the Registry Office in St George's, Hanover Square; and fourth, in 1874 in the Roman Catholic Church in Macclesfield. The Roman Catholic marriage was invalid because the Registrar was not present, and after the death of both parties it emerged that Lady Stanley was in fact Doña Serafina Fernandez y Funes of Alcandete in Jaen, Spain, who in 1851 married Don Ramon Peres y Abril (d. 1870). In between the four ceremonies, the couple are said to have led a tempestuous life.

MARCHIONESS OF BROTHERTON in Anthony Trollope, *Is He Popenjoy?* (1878)

'Henry, 3rd Baron Stanley of Alderley . . . became a Mohammedan. His "wife" – the marriage was invalid as she already had a husband living in Spain – was the original of the Marchioness in . . . *Is He Popenjoy?*' ('. . . *and Mr Fortescue': a selection from the diaries of Chichester Fortescue, Lord Carlingford*, 1958, ed. O.W. Hewitt, London: John Murray, p. 55 n. 6).

STANLEY, Sir Henry Morton (1841–1904) Journalist, explorer and administrator. Born John Rowlands of unmarried parents in Denby, Wales. In 1859 he became a cabin boy on a ship sailing to New Orleans, and was adopted by a merchant called Stanley. He served in the Confederate Army and US Navy, and in 1867 became a special correspondent for the *New York Herald*. In October 1869 he was instructed by his editor to 'find Livingstone'. He eventually found him in Ujiji, Tanganyika, in November 1871. He married the artist, Dorothy Tennant, in 1890, and was naturalized as a British subject in 1892.

MR KURTZ in Joseph Conrad, *Heart of Darkness* (1902)

'It is essential to the very nature of what Conrad was doing in *Heart of Darkness* that there should be not one but innumerable sources for Kurtz. Some of these have nothing to do with Africa or with Conrad's experiences there; but among those sources that do, Stanley is probably of central importance, though not so much as a basis for the character of Kurtz as for the moral atmosphere in which he was created' (Ian Watt, 1980, *Conrad in the Nineteenth Century*, p. 145). *See also* **Barttelot**, E.M.; **Hodister**, A.E.C.; **Klein**, G.A.

ALEC MACKENZIE in W. Somerset Maugham, *The Explorer* (1908)

'The chief character was suggested by H.M. Stanley' (W. Somerset Maugham, preface to *Liza of Lambeth*; see R.L. Calder, 1972, *W. Somerset Maugham and the Quest for Freedom*, London: Heinemann, p. 70).

THE MANAGING DIRECTOR in Joseph Conrad, 'An Outpost of Progress', *Tales of Unrest* (1898)

'Conrad could have found descriptions of the founding of such isolated stations and of the fortunes of the agents left at them in the writings of Stanley, and indeed I believe that the character of the managing director . . . is based upon Stanley himself – upon his activities, his character and his methods in establishing trading posts' (Norman Sherry, 1971, *Conrad's Western World*, Cambridge, p. 127).

STANLEY FALLS, Belgian Congo

INNER STATION in Joseph Conrad, *Heart of Darkness* (1902)

'[T]he Stanley Falls station . . . roughly corresponds to Marlow's Inner Station and is now called Kisangani' (Ian Watt, 1980, *Conrad in the Nineteenth Century*, p. 136).

STARR, James *See* **Achew**, James.

STEARNS, Harold (1891–1943) American journalist and man of letters. He was Associate Editor of the *Dial* from 1917 to 1919, when it was a political paper. In the 1920s he lived in Paris, and in 1928 he was a racing tipster ('Peter Pickem') for the Paris edition of the *Herald Tribune*. He returned to the United States in 1935. He was a very considerable drunk and died of throat cancer.

HARVEY STONE in Ernest Hemingway, *The Sun Also Rises* (1926)

'He appears as Harvey Stone in *The Sun Also Rises*. People used to look down on him sleeping on a café terrace and say "there lies civilization in the United States"' (Malcolm Cowley, 1961, *Exile's Return*, pp. 104–5).

WILTSHIRE TOBIN in Kay Boyle, *Monday Night* (1938)

'The collar of Harold's . . . shirt was frayed, and the ear that was turned towards me was dirty, and the side of his face was in need of a shave . . . but . . . once he began to talk you forgot the stubble-covered jowls packed hard from drink, and the stains of food on his jacket lapels, and the black-rimmed fingers holding his glass. As soon as he began to speak . . . I never questioned the truth of every word he said. . . . (I wrote a book about this man, and it is to me the most satisfying book I ever wrote)' (Robert McAlmon and Kay Boyle, 1968, *Being Geniuses Together, 1920–1930*, New York, p. 328; the book is identified in a footnote).

STEEVENS, Mrs George   Christine Rogerson, daughter of Mrs Duncan **Stewart**. In 1894 she married G.W. Steevens (1869–1900) of the *Pall Mall Gazette* and the *Daily Mail*; he died of enteric fever at Ladysmith. Somerset Maugham met Ethelwyn **Jones** at Mrs Steevens's house (where Horatio Nelson had lived with Lady Hamilton) in Merton Place, Wimbledon. *The Explorer* and *The Magician* were dedicated to Mrs Steevens.

MISS LEY in W. Somerset Maugham, *Mrs Craddock* (1902) and others

'A delightful minor character is Miss Ley. . . . Drawn from life, she reappears in a biographical sketch in Maugham's preface to *What a Life!* by Doris Arthur Jones. . . . Both Maugham and [Beerbohm] describe her, Mrs George Steevens, as generous, hospitable . . . and fond of shocking the prude. . . . Such a character as Miss Ley was made – ready for Maugham, who used her again in *The Merry-Go-Round* and *The Bishop's Apron*' (R.A. Cordell, 1969, *Somerset Maugham: a writer for all seasons*, Bloomington and London: Indiana University Press, p. 139–140).

STEIN, Amelia   (1842–88)   Née Keyser, she married Daniel **Stein**; Gertrude Stein was their daughter.

FANNY HERSLAND in Gertrude Stein, *The Making of Americans* (1925)

See under **Stein**, Daniel.

STEIN, Daniel   (1832?–91)   In 1841 he moved, with his parents and four brothers, from Bavaria, Germany, to Pennsylvania, and in 1884 he went to San Francisco, where he became Vice-Chairman of the Omnibus Cable Company. He married Amelia Keyser (**Stein**, above), whose family were German immigrants who had settled in Baltimore. He was Gertrude Stein's father.

DAVID HERSLAND in Gertrude Stein, *The Making of Americans* (1925)

'In the novel, David Hersland and his wife Fanny, whose fictional characters approximate those of Daniel and Milly Stein, have three children' (James R. Mellow, 1974, *The Charmed Circle: Gertrude Stein and company*, London: Phaidon Press, p. 116).

STEIN, Gertrude (1874–1946) American writer. Born in Allegheny, Pennsylvania, she lived for most of her life in France, first with her brother Leo **Stein**, then with her friend Alice B. Toklas from 1907 to her death. She was a friend and patron of Picasso, Matisse and Juan Gris, and was closely linked with the circle of expatriates living in Paris in the 1920s.

ADELE in *Things As They Are* (1950); JEFFERSON CAMPBELL in 'Melanctha', *Three Lives* (1909); MARTHA HERSLAND in *The Making of Americans* (1925); MISS MATHILDA in 'The Good Anna', *Three Lives* (1909); and NANCY REDFERN in *Fernhurst* (1971) – all by Gertrude Stein

For a justification and elaboration of these identifications, see James R. Mellow, 1974, *The Charmed Circle: Gertrude Stein and company*, London: Phaidon Press.

STEIN, Leo (1872–1947) He was the brother of Gertrude **Stein** and was an early patron of Picasso.

WALTER ROSEN in D.H. Lawrence, *Aaron's Rod* (1922)

'He was one of the Florentines who had figured in *Aaron's Rod*, as Walter Rosen' (Mark Holloway, 1976, *Norman Douglas*, p. 331).

STEIN, Pauline She was Gertrude Stein's aunt by marriage to Solomon **Stein**.

MRS HENRY DEHNING in Gertrude Stein, *The Making of Americans* (1925)

See under **Stein**, Solomon.

STEIN, Solomon (b. 1836?) Younger brother of Daniel **Stein**, he settled with his wife Pauline **Stein** in Pittsburgh, where he was in partnership with Daniel in a clothing store. They later moved to New York, where he went into banking. When Daniel returned to the United States in 1879, after five years in Europe, Solomon tried to persuade him to join him in his New York firm, but the effort failed because of the hostility that existed between their wives.

MR HENRY DEHNING in Gertrude Stein, *The Making of Americans* (1925)

'In the original version, it appears, Gertrude had intended to deal only with the Dehnings, a family based on the New York branch of the Stein family' (James R. Mellow, 1974, *The Charmed Circle: Gertrude Stein and company*, London: Phaidon Press, p. 116).

STEPHEN, Adrian (1883–1948) Younger brother of Virginia Woolf.

JAMES RAMSAY in Virginia Woolf, *To the Lighthouse* (1927)

'The voyage to the Lighthouse, although it is almost certainly recollected from an actual excursion, was not undertaken with Adrian Stephen (James Ramsay) as helmsman but with his elder brother, Thoby' (Quentin Bell, 1971, 'The biographer, the critic, and the lighthouse', *Ariel* 2 (1): 95).

STEPHEN, Sir Harry (1860–1945) 3rd Baronet. Son of Fitzjames Stephen, he was also the first cousin of Virginia Woolf. Until 1914 he was a judge of the High Court of Calcutta, and after his return to England he became an Alderman on London County Council.

PETER WALSH in Virginia Woolf, *Mrs Dalloway* (1925)

In her diary for 28 May 1918, Virginia Woolf describes a visit from Harry Stephen, who had proposed himself 'as if he'd been in the habit of dropping in after dinner once a week all these years'. 'He still takes out an enormous pocket knife, and slowly half opens the blade and shuts it.' Compare the description of Peter Walsh's way with his knife. Peter Walsh too has returned from India, 'an undoubted failure' (*The Diary of Virginia Woolf*, Vol. I: *1915–1919*, 1977, introd. Quentin Bell, London: Hogarth Press, p. 151 n. 17).

STEPHEN, Sir James (1789–1859) He was called to the Bar in 1811 and in 1813 he was Counsel to the Colonial Department; he gave up private practice in 1825 and devoted himself entirely to the service of the department. By 1829, Greville was writing of him: 'He does all the business of the Colonial Office and a great deal of that of the Board of Trade. In the former scarcely anybody knows anything, and nobody as much as Stephen' (*The Greville Memoirs, 1814–1860*, 1938, ed. Lytton Strachey and Roger Fulford, Vol. I, London: Macmillan, p. 337). He gave up his connection with the Board of Trade in 1836 and became Under-Secretary at the Colonial Office. His colleague Sir Henry Taylor said that for many years he literally ruled the colonial empire; he was known as Mr Over-Secretary Stephen. In 1847 he suffered a breakdown and retired, and in 1849 and 1850 he was Professor of Modern History at Cambridge. He was the father of Leslie **Stephen**, and his stepmother was the sister of William Wilberforce.

TITE BARNACLE in Charles Dickens, *Little Dorrit* (1855–7)

The Stephen family made the identification instantaneously. Sir James Fitzjames Stephen, his son, reviewed the novel ('The license of modern novelists', *Edinburgh Review* (July 1857): 124 ff.) in terms of deep personal affront. Nearly forty years later, his brother, Sir Leslie Stephen, wrote: 'The assault upon the "Circumlocution Office" was, I doubt not, especially offensive because Barnacle Tite [sic] and the effete aristocrats who are satirised in *Little Dorrit* stood for representatives of Sir James Stephen and his best friends' (*Life of Sir J.F. Stephen*, 1895, p. 159). Chapters VI and VII of Carlyle's pupil Charles Buller's *Responsible Government for the Colonies* (pub. anon. 1840) is an earlier attack on Stephen, there called 'Mr Mothercountry of the Colonial Office' and approached through 'The Sighing Rooms' (see E.M. Wrong, 1926, *Charles Buller and Responsible Government*, p. 137 n. 1). It was not in Dickens's library but was perhaps known to him through Carlyle: cf. Carlyle, 'Downing Street', 1850, *Latter-day Pamphlets*.

STEPHEN, Julia (1846–95) Daughter of John Jackson, physician, and Maria, who was the fourth of the beautiful Pattle sisters. In 1867 she married Herbert Duckworth, with whom she had a daughter, Stella **Duckworth**, and who died in 1870. In 1878 she married Sir Leslie **Stephen**, with whom she had four children, Thoby, Vanessa (**Bell**), Virginia (Woolf) and Adrian.

Mrs Ramsay in Virginia Woolf, *To the Lighthouse* (1927)

'It seemed to me in the first part of the book you have given a portrait of mother which is more like her to me than anything I could ever have conceived of as possible. It is almost painful to have her so raised from the dead. You have made one feel the extraordinary beauty of her character, which must be the most difficult thing in the world to do. It was like meeting her again with oneself grown up and on equal terms' (Vanessa Bell to Virginia Woolf, 11 May 1927, quoted in Quentin Bell, 1972, *Virginia Woolf*, Vol. II, p. 128; and reproduced in *The Letters of Virginia Woolf*, 1977, ed. Nigel Nicolson, Vol. III, London: Hogarth Press, p. 572).

STEPHEN, Sir Leslie (1832–1904) Man of letters. Son of Sir James **Stephen**, he was educated at Eton and Trinity Hall, Cambridge. He took Holy Orders in 1855 and became a Fellow of and Tutor at Trinity Hall in 1864, but in 1870 he lost his faith and resigned his college tutorship, and in 1875 he abandoned his cloth. From 1871 to 1882 he was Editor of *Cornhill Magazine*, and in 1882 he became the first Editor of *The Dictionary of National Biography*, remaining in that post until 1901. He was a dedicated mountaineer and great walker. In 1867 he married Harriet **Thackeray**, the daughter of W.M. **Thackeray**, but she died in childbirth in 1875. In 1878 he married Julia Duckworth (**Stephen** above), with whom he had four children, Vanessa (**Bell**), Thoby, Virginia (Woolf) and Adrian.

Ridley Ambrose in Virginia Woolf, *The Voyage Out* (1915)

'Ridley Ambrose has Leslie Stephen as his original in life' (B.K. Johnstone, 1954, *The Bloomsbury Group*, p. 350).

Trevor Hilbery in Virginia Woolf, *Night and Day* (1919)

'In an attempt to score a point against Bloomsbury, Q.D. Leavis [in *Scrutiny* 7 (March 1939): 405] has omitted to mention the complementary portrait of Stephen as Mr Hilberry in *Night and Day*' (Noel Annan, 1951, *Leslie Stephen*, p. 301 n. (to p. 105)). *See also* **Ritchie**, Sir Richmond.

Robert Leslie in W.H. Mallock, *The New Republic* (1877)

Identified in W.H. Mallock, 1920, *Memoirs of Life and Literature*, London: Chapman and Hall, pp. 65–6. *See also* **Hardinge**, Charles; **Hardinge**, William.

Mr Ramsay in Virginia Woolf, *To the Lighthouse* (1927)

'. . . the centre is father's character, sitting in a boat, reciting we perished, each alone, while he crushes a dying mackerel' (entry for 14 May 1925, reproduced in *The Diary of Virginia Woolf*, Vol. III: *1925–1930*, 1980, ed. Anne Olivier Bell, 2nd edn, London: Hogarth Press, pp. 18–19).

Vernon Whitford in George Meredith, *The Egoist* (1879)

'If you remember Vernon Whitford of *The Egoist*, it is a sketch of L. Stephen, but merely a sketch, not doing him full justice, though the strokes within and without are correct' (to André Raffalovich, 8 April 1872, reproduced in *Letters of George Meredith*, 1970, ed. C.L. Cline, Vol. II, Oxford, p. 658).

STEPHEN, Thoby (1881–1906) Son of Sir Leslie **Stephen**, and brother of Vanessa **Bell** and Virginia Woolf. With every promise of a brilliant career, he died of typhoid fever, which he contracted on a journey to Greece.

JACOB FLANDERS in Virginia Woolf, *Jacob's Room* (1922)

'Jacob himself I think is very successful. . . . Of course I see something of Thoby in him, as I suppose you intended' (Lytton Strachey to Virginia Woolf, 9 October 1922, reproduced in *Letters of Virginia Woolf and Lytton Strachey*, 1969, ed. Leonard Woolf and James Strachey, pp. 103–4).

TERENCE HEWET in Virginia Woolf, *The Voyage Out* (1915)

'Her friendships are echoed in certain characters . . . possibly Thoby in Terence' (*The Letters of Virginia Woolf*, 1975, ed. Nigel Nicolson, Vol. I, London: Hogarth Press, p. xxi).

PERCIVAL in Virginia Woolf, *The Waves* (1931)

'Of course there's the personal side – the feelings you describe on what I must take to be Thoby's death' (Vanessa Bell to Virginia Woolf, October 1931, reproduced in *The Letters of Virginia Woolf*, 1978, ed. Nigel Nicolson, Vol. IV, London: Hogarth Press, p. 390 n. 1). 'You didn't think it sentimental, did you, about Thoby? I had him so much in my mind – I have a dumb rage still at his not being with us always' (Virginia Woolf to Vanessa Bell, 15 October 1931, ibid., pp. 390–1).

STEPHENSON, Rowland A Lombard Street banker who, in December 1828, absconded from London and sailed for Savannah with his clerk James **Lloyd**.

TIMOTHY TOUCHANDGO in Thomas Love Peacock, *Crochet Castle* (1831)

'Timothy Touchandgo . . . [was] modelled on Rowland Stephenson' (*Crochet Castle*, 1969, ed. Raymond Wright, Harmondsworth: Penguin, p. 279 n. 3 (to ch. 40)).

STEPNEY, Catherine, Lady (d. 1845) Novelist and contributor to fashionable journals. She was first married to Russell Manners, and then in 1813 she married Sir Thomas Stepney.

LADY CALDERSFOOT in Lady Blessington, *Memoirs of a Femme de Chambre* (1846)

See under **Morgan**, Lady.

STEPNIAK, Sergius (1852–95) Pseudonym of Sergei Mikhailovich Kravchinsky, the Russian nihilist who in 1878 fled from Russia after assassinating the Chief of Police, General Mesentnev. He lived in Switzerland and Italy from 1879 to 1883, and in 1884 he settled in London. He was run over by a train.

CYRIL BRANDETSKI in Ford Madox Ford, *The Simple Life Limited* (1911)

'Olive (Garnett) would probably have been most angry about Ford's portrait, in Cyril Brandetski, of Sergius Stepniak' (Thomas C. Moser, 1980, *The Life in the Fiction of Ford Madox Ford*, Princeton, p. 307 n. 31). *See also* **Soskice**, David.

KIRYLO SIDOROVITCH RAZUMOV in Joseph Conrad, *Under Western Eyes* (1911)

'The Garnetts had also known well S.M. Kravchinsky, called Stepniak . . . [who] had . . . settled in England, but in 1895 was knocked down and killed when crossing a railway track; according to David Garnett he had not heard the engine approaching because he had the capacity to make himself deaf at will, and this may have given Conrad the idea for Razumov's accident' (Jocelyn Baines, 1967, *Joseph Conrad: a critical biography*, rev. edn, London: Weidenfeld & Nicolson, pp. 370, 371; originally published 1960).

STERLING, George (1869–1926) American poet. Born on Long Island, as a young man he joined his uncle's office in Oakland, California. He remained on the West Coast for the rest of his life and settled at Carmel in 1905. He committed suicide.

RUSS BRISSENDEN in Jack London, *Martin Eden* (1909)

'George Sterling . . . [figures] in it . . . as the poet Brissenden' (Kunitz and Haycraft, 1942, *Twentieth Century Authors*, New York, p. 844).

MARK HALL in Jack London, *The Valley of the Moon* (1913)

'An extended . . . account of life in the Carmel colony [in 1909] . . . is to be found in Chapters 6 through 10 of Book Three in . . . *The Valley of the Moon* . . . [London] included a reasonably accurate record of George Sterling's famous abalone feats' (Mark Schorer, 1963, *Sinclair Lewis: an American life*, London: Heinemann, p. 147; originally published 1961, New York: McGraw-Hill). The description of Hall is a fairly accurate description of Sterling, who was supposed to closely represent Dante.

STEVENS, Henry (d. 1933) From Asheville, he graduated from Yale Law School and was a friend of Thomas Wolfe. He was a turbulent alcoholic and committed suicide.

ROBERT WEAVER in Thomas Wolfe, *Of Time and the River* (1935)

'Robert Weaver was Henry Stevens' (Mrs Wolfe, quoted in Hayden Norwood, 1947, *The Marble Man's Wife: Thomas Wolfe's mother*, New York, p. 145).

STEVENSON, Robert ('Bob') Alan Mowbray (1847–1900) Landscape painter and art critic. He was a student in Antwerp and Paris in 1873, and from 1883 to 1893 he was Professor of Fine Arts at University College, Liverpool. Between 1893 and 1899, he was an art critic on the *Pall Mall Gazette*. He was a cousin of R.L. **Stevenson**, whose companion he was on *An Island Voyage*, and appeared as 'Spring-Heeled Jack' in Stevenson's *Talk and Talkers* (1910).

SIDNEY EWART in H.G. Wells, *Tono-Bungay* (1909)

'I have tried to give a faint impression of his style of . . . talking in Ewart's talk. . . . But Ewart is not even a caricature of Bob; only Bob's style of talk was grafted on to him' (H.G. Wells, 1934, *Experiment in Autobiography: discoveries and conclusions of a very ordinary brain since 1866*, London: Victor Gollancz, Cresset Press, p. 611).

STEVENSON, Robert Louis (1850–94) Scottish author. Born in Edinburgh, grandson of the engineer Robert Stevenson. As a child he was a constant invalid, and his ill health forced the family to move abroad. He returned to Edinburgh to study law and became an advocate in 1875. He travelled, chiefly in France, where he met Fanny Osborne, a divorcee, whom he followed to America and married in 1880. He suffered from tuberculosis, but continued to write and found fame with *Treasure Island* in 1833, the first of his successful adventure novels. He spent the last five years of his life in Samoa.

GOWER WOODSEER in George Meredith, *The Amazing Marriage* (1895)

'Robert Louis Stevenson did not live to read *The Amazing Marriage*, in which he was much interested from the fact that the character of Gower Woodseer, in its earlier stages, was drawn from him' (S.M. Ellis, 1920, *George Meredith*, 2nd edn, London: Grant Richards, p. 299). 'Now, in so far as you have adhered to your intention, Gower Woodseer will be a family portrait, age twenty-five, of the highly respectable and slightly influential and fairly aged "Tusitala"' (R.L.S. to Meredith, written from Samoa, 17 April 1894, reproduced in ibid., pp. 299, 300).

STEWART, Agnes Janet (1810–83) Daughter of John Wilson of Transy, Fife. She married Charles Augustus Stewart, a merchant of the Manchester firm of Robert Barbour Bros., in 1835. She was the mother of Mrs Mary Louisa Molesworth.

GRANDMOTHER DEAR in Mrs Molesworth, *'Grandmother Dear'* (1878)

'"Grandmother's Grandmother" tells incidents in the childhood of Louisa's mother, Agnes Janet Wilson. Here she is disguised as "Nellie" [sic]' (Roger Lancelyn Green, 1961, *Mrs Molesworth*, p. 17). '[In 1878 Mrs Molesworth] was more or less settled in and near Caen . . . accompanied by her widowed mother, the "Grandmother Dear" who gave her pet name to the . . . book' (ibid., p. 41).

STEWART, Donald Ogden (1894–1980) American actor and humorous writer. He was immensely successful as a script-writer in Hollywood. He moved to the Left with the rise of Nazism in Germany and in 1937 was President of the anti-fascist League of American Writers. In the 1950s he left Hollywood because he refused to 'name names' during the **McCarthy** inquisitions, and settled in England. He met Hemingway in Paris in 1932 and was with him in Pamplona in 1924 and 1925.

BILL GORTON in Ernest Hemingway, *The Sun Also Rises* (1926)

'Donald Ogden Stewart to author, Feb. 20, 1951, recognized himself in the figure of Bill Gorton' (Carlos Baker, 1969, *Ernest Hemingway: a life story*, New York, p. 594). *See also* **Dos Passos**, John; **Smith**, Bill.

STEWART, Dugald

DR CAMPBELL in Maria Edgeworth, 'Forester', *Moral Tales for Young People* (1801)

'[Maria Edgeworth] had already sketched the idea of Stewart she had received from her brothers [who had been his pupils] in the character of Dr Campbell' (Marilyn Butler, 1972, *Maria Edgeworth*, Oxford, p. 198 n. 1).

STEWART, Mrs Duncan (d. 1884) Harriet Everilda. She was the daughter of Major Antony Gore, but was left an orphan as an infant and was brought up in France, where her guardian was the Consul General in Haviede Grâce. In his house, she met Washington Irving and his brother, who were devoted to her. She married Duncan Stewart, a younger son of a family connected with the Stewarts of Appin, and a Baltic merchant in Liverpool. They later moved to London, where she remained, at 10 Sloane Street, after her husband's death in 1869. In the early part of their married life, they formed a close friendship with the **Disraelis** and with the Gore House set of Lady **Blessington**, and in later life she had a wide circle of friends who were mainly connected with literature and the stage. Her younger daughter was Christine Rogerson, later Mrs **Steevens**, and her son Charles Stewart was the solicitor who acted for Donald Crawford, the plaintiff in the notorious **Dilke** divorce case. 'Mrs Duncan Stewart is a good instance of how little money decides even in this money-loving land. Having a secure social position and a great love of society, she goes everywhere and knows everyone; poor as a rat and living in two wee rooms over a tailor's shop in an unfashionable street' (Mrs Henry Adams to her father, Dr Hooper, 10 August 1879, reproduced in *Letters of Mrs Henry Adams*, 1937, ed. Ward Thoron, p. 164). 'Mrs Duncan Stewart is dead . . . she was a charming old being . . . and I shall miss her much. Someday I shall put her into a book' (to Alice James, 29 February 1884, reproduced in *Henry James Letters*, 1981, ed. Leon Edel, Vol. III, London: Macmillan, p. 35). A study of Mrs Duncan Stewart is to be found in Augustus Hare, 1895, *Biographical Sketches*.

LADY DAVENANT in Henry James, 'A London Life' (1888)

'There must be an old lady – like Mrs Duncan S[tewart] – only of rank – a genial, clever, worldly, old-fashioned, half comforting, half shocking old lady' (Venice, 20 June 1887, in *The Notebooks of Henry James*, 1947, ed. F.O. Matthiessen and K.B. Murdock, New York, p. 78). 'Laura's remarkable old friend (Mrs D.S.)' (ibid., p. 80). Earlier (p. 77), James describes the milieu of the story as 'the Prince of Wales's set, etc.'. It is difficult not to find in the 'etc.' an oblique reference to the Dilke scandal of 1885 and 1886.

STIDGER, Revd William L. (d. 1949) A pastor in Detroit in 1922, he met Sinclair Lewis, whom he urged to write a novel about clergymen 'as they really are'. In 1926, in order to do this, Lewis lived with Stidger in Kansas City, where he was then Pastor of the Linwood Boulevard Episcopal Church. After the publication of *Elmer Gantry*, Stidger declared that the book contained fifty technical errors in its account of church practices and that the author had been drunk all the time he was working on the book. He moved to Boston in 1830.

ELMER GANTRY in Sinclair Lewis, *Elmer Gantry* (1927)

'Stidger was a flamboyant man who in many ways resembled Elmer Gantry . . . unaware of the kind of novel that *Elmer Gantry* was to be, he went about Kansas City . . . boasting that the central character was to be modelled on himself' (Mark Schorer, 1961, *Sinclair Lewis: an American life*, New York: McGraw-Hill, p. 441). *See also* **Straton**, J.R.

STINSFORD, Dorset Located two miles east of Dorchester.

MELLSTOCK in Thomas Hardy, Wessex novels and tales (1871–95)

Identified on a map prepared by Thomas Hardy which hangs in the Dorset County Museum, Dorchester. *See under* **Abbotsbury**.

TOLLAMORE in Thomas Hardy, 'An Indiscretion in the Life of an Heiress' (1878)

'Hardy's first presentation of Stinsford' (F.B. Pinion, 1968, *A Hardy Companion*, London: Macmillan, p. 440).

STINSFORD QUIRE A group of instrumentalists formed by Thomas Hardy's grandfather, who played the cello. Hardy's father and uncle took part, and from 1801 until 1841 or 1842, it provided the music in Stinsford Church.

MELLSTOCK QUIRE in Thomas Hardy, *Under the Greenwood Tree* (1872)

'Conducting the church choir all the year round involved carol-playing and singing at Christmas . . . the practice was kept up by Thomas Hardy the second, much as described in *Under the Greenwood Tree* . . . though the author . . . invented the personages, incidents, manners, etc., never having seen or heard the choir as such, they ending their office when he was about a year old' (F.E. Hardy, 1972, *The Life of Thomas Hardy, 1840–1928*, p. 12).

STIRLING-MAXWELL, Sir William (1818–78) Historian and bibliophile. Son of Archibald Stirling of Keir, he was an MP in 1852–68 and 1874–8, and succeeded to the baronetcy in 1865. In 1851 he married Elizabeth, daughter of Sir John Maxwell; in 1865 he married Lady Anna Melville (d. 1874); and in 1877 he married Caroline **Norton**, with whom he had had a long liaison, but she died three months later.

ALEXANDER HEPBURN in George Meredith, *Diana of the Crossways* (1884)

'Caroline's various admirers . . .. are also sketched in. There is . . . lastly Alexander Hepburn, the handsome Scot (probably William Stirling of Keir)' (Alice Acland, 1948, *Caroline Norton*, London: Constable, p. 179).

STOCKINGFORD, Warwickshire Located east of Nuneaton, it is now a suburb of the town.

PADDIFORD in 'Janet's Repentance' and WHITTLECOMBE in 'The Sad Fortunes of the Revd Amos Barton', both in George Eliot, *Scenes of Clerical Life* (1857–8)

See under **Anstruther**, Lady.

STOKE, Staffordshire

KNYPE in Arnold Bennett, *Anna of the Five Towns* (1902)

'Stoke became Knype' (Margaret Drabble, 1975, *Arnold Bennett: a biography*, London: Weidenfeld & Nicolson, p. 4).

Frederick A. STOKES COMPANY The New York publishing house in which Sinclair Lewis was employed from 1910 to 1912.

VANZILE MOTOR CORPORATION in Sinclair Lewis, *The Trail of the Hawk* (1915)

'[Carl Ericson] reappears . . . as the designer of the "Touricar" for the VanZile Motor Corporation, of New York City, which might just as well be called Stokes' (Mark Schorer, 1961, *Sinclair Lewis: an American life*, New York: McGraw-Hill, p. 223).

STONE GAPPE, Yorkshire Located near Skipton, it was the home of John Benson **Sidgwick**.

GATESHEAD HALL in Charlotte Brontë, *Jane Eyre* (1847)

'Gateshead Hall . . . has been identified with Stonegappe' (Herbert Wroot, 1935, *Sources of Charlotte Brontë's Novels: persons and places*, Shipley, Yorks., p. 9).

STONEY, Andrew Robinson (1745–1810) Irish adventurer. Afterwards Andrew Robinson Bowes. He married the Countess of **Strathmore** in 1777; she divorced him in 1789 after an unhappy and violent marriage.

BARRY LYNDON in W.M. Thackeray, *The Memoirs of Barry Lyndon Esq.* (1844)

See under **Strathmore**, Countess of.

STOPFORD, Hon. and Revd Mr

HON. AND REVD MR PRENDERGAST in George Eliot, 'Janet's Repentance', *Scenes of Clerical Life* (1857–8)

See under **Anstruther**, Lady.

STRACHAN, Lady She was the widow of Admiral Sir Richard Strachan, who in 1809 was Commander of the ill-fated Walcheren expedition, and the mistress of the 3rd Marquess of **Hertford**.

MADAME COLONNA in Benjamin Disraeli, *Coningsby* (1844)

Identified in a key in *Notes and Queries* (8th series) 3 (13 May 1893): 363. *See also under* **Bright**, John.

STRACHEY, Sir Edward (1812–1901) 3rd Baronet. Son of Julia **Strachey** and Edward Strachey, whose colleagues in the office of the East India Company included Peacock and James **Mill**. He would himself have entered the service of the East India Company had not ill health prevented him from doing so. In 1836 he was a friend and student of F.D. Maurice. In 1844 he married Elizabeth Wilkieson, and in 1857 he married Marivelle Mary Isabella, sister of John Addington **Symonds**. He was the author of *Talk at a Country House* (1895).

MR CHAINMAIL in Thomas Love Peacock, *Crochet Castle* (1831)

'Sir Edward Strachey was only eighteen years old when *Crotchet Castle* was written, nevertheless I think Peacock had him in mind, as the hero of *Cotswold Chace* (a fragment begun in 1860) seems obviously to be Sir Edward Strachey as a very young man and bears a considerable likeness to Mr Chainmail. . . . *Talk at a Country House* . . . bears every mark of Mr Chainmail's interests' (*The Novels of T.L. Peacock*, 1948, ed. David Garnett, London: Rupert Hart-Davis, p.

680 n.). In *Talk at a Country House*, Strachey refers to himself throughout as 'Foster', but in 1816 only a keenly prophetic eye could have used him as a model.

STRACHEY, Julia (1791–1846)   Daughter of Major-General William Kirkpatrick, she married Edward Strachey and was the mother of Sir Edward **Strachey**. She was also the sister of Isabella Barbara **Buller** and a cousin of Kitty **Kirkpatrick**. Carlyle met her in 1824 and felt for her a warm and affectionate admiration; they remained friends to the end of her life.

THE DUENNA COUSIN in Thomas Carlyle, *Sartor Resartus* (1833–4)

'"The story of the book," said Mrs Strachey to her son, "is as plain as a pikestaff. . . . The duenna cousin is myself."' (George Strachey, 1892, 'Carlyle and the "Rose-Goddess"', *The Nineteenth Century* 32 (September): 474).

STRACHEY, (Giles) Lytton (1880–1932)   English biographer and essayist. Born in London, the son of Sir Richard Strachey, a distinguished soldier and Indian administrator. He was educated at Leamington College and Liverpool University, and then went to Trinity College, Cambridge, where he befriended John Maynard Keynes, Leonard Woolf and E.M. **Forster**. He was elected to the Apostles in 1902, and was later a prominent member of the Bloomsbury Group. He was a book reviewer for the *Spectator* from 1904 to 1914, and was a conscientious objector during the First World War. In 1918 he published *Eminent Victorians*, which challenged smug Victorian self-assurance and turned biography into a literary genre. Strachey spent the last sixteen years of his life in a *ménage-a-trois* with Dora **Carrington** and her husband Ralph Partridge. He suffered from ill health throughout his life, but continued writing until his death, from cancer.

CEDRIC FURBER in Wyndham Lewis, *The Self-Condemned* (1954)

'There is no record . . . of Wyndham Lewis ever going down to Ham Spray but almost thirty years later . . . he published a novel, *Self-Condemned* . . . in which the character of Cedric Furber, a rich, lonely bachelor in his forties, strict and fussy and old-maidish, is founded on Lytton' (Michael Holroyd, 1968, *Lytton Strachey*, Vol. II, London: Heinemann, p. 484).

ST JOHN HIRST in Virginia Woolf, *The Voyage Out* (1915)

'At this time [1909, the time of Strachey's proposal of marriage] Virginia Stephen was already working at her first novel. *The Voyage Out* . . . which contains a portrait of Lytton under the name of St John Hirst' (Holroyd, 1967, op. cit., Vol. I, p. 433).

NEVILLE in Virginia Woolf, *The Waves* (1931)

'The characters in *The Waves* are not drawn from life, but there is something of Lytton in Neville' (Leonard Woolf, 1960, *Sowing*, p. 123).

MATTHEW PLUNKETT in Wyndham Lewis, *The Apes of God* (1930)

'. . . a maliciously distorted and hilarious caricature of Lytton under the name of Matthew Plunkett' (Holroyd, op. cit., Vol. II, pp. 194–5).

ROGER SIMON in Elizabeth Jenkins, *Virginia Water* (1930)

Identification based upon private information. This is a romantic but touching and oddly convincing picture drawn from the outside.

T.W. SOPLEY in Gilbert Cannan, *Pugs and Peacocks* (1921)

This ill-natured portrait is instantly recognizable. Cannan first met Strachey in 1913, through Lady Ottoline Morrell.

STRACHEY, Marjorie (1822–1964) Sister of Lytton and Pernel **Strachey**.

DEBORAH SIMON in Elizabeth Jenkins, *Virginia Water* (1930)

Identification based upon private information.

STRACHEY, Pernel (1876–1951) Sister of Lytton and Marjorie **Strachey**. She was Principal of Newnham College, Cambridge, from 1923 to 1941.

ATHENE SIMON in Elizabeth Jenkins, *Virginia Water* (1930)

Identification based upon private information.

KATHY WINTER in Elizabeth Jenkins, *The Winters* (1932)

'She's written a second novel, a variation on the theme of Strachey – you're Kathy Winter this time – but a theme so frail, so far, so impeccably well bred I can't recognise even the way you have of putting the accent all wrong, say on the word "donkey"' (to Pernel Strachey, 30 December 1931, reproduced in *The Letters of Virginia Woolf*, 1978, ed. Nigel Nicolson, Vol. IV, London: Hogarth Press, p. 424).

STRANGWAYS, Susanna (d. 1758) Daughter and heiress of Thomas Strangways of **Melbury House** at Melbury Sampford, Dorset, she married Thomas Horner of Mells Park, and her daughter became the Countess of **Ilchester**.

SUSAN DORNELL in Thomas Hardy, 'The First Countess of Wessex' (1891)

Identified in F.B. Pinion, 1968, *A Hardy Companion*, London: Macmillan.

STRATER, Henry A Princeton contemporary of F. Scott Fitzgerald.

BURNE HOLIDAY in F. Scott Fitzgerald, *This Side of Paradise* (1920)

'It was a time for idealism, and one of the sophomore ringleaders, Henry Strater, became the model for Burne Holiday, the rebel and pacifist in *This Side of Paradise*' (Andrew Turnbull, 1962, *Scott Fitzgerald*, p. 72).

STRATHMORE, Mary Eleanor, Countess of (1749–1800) Daughter and very rich heiress of G. Bowes of Streatlam Castle, County Durham, in 1767 she married John, 7th Earl of Strathmore. They had five children before he died in 1776. In 1777 she married Andrew Robinson **Stoney**, who took the name of Bowes, and they had one child in 1782. It was a very unhappy marriage (Walpole said her husband beat her for six days and nights), and in 1786 they separated. He 'contrived to abduct her', but with her family's help she escaped and in 1789 she divorced him. He was detained within the rules of the King's Bench until his death.

HONORIA, COUNTESS OF LYNDON in W.M. Thackeray, *The Memoirs of Barry Lyndon Esq.* (1844)

'Readers of *The Memoirs of Barry Lyndon* will recognize how closely the later chapters of that novel follow the history of Stoney-Bowes and his lady' (*The Letters and Private Papers of W.M. Thackeray*, Vol. I: *1817–1840*, 1945, ed. Gordon N. Ray, London: Oxford University Press, p. xcii).

STRATON, Revd John Roach (1875–1929) Pastor of Calvary Baptist Church in New York City from 1918 to 1929. He denounced cabaret life, liquor, dancing and prize-fighting.

ELMER GANTRY in Sinclair Lewis, *Elmer Gantry* (1927)

'Elmer himself [is] a composite made up in large part of traits observed in the Reverend Stidger and in the career and performance of Reverend John Roach Straton in New York (the very accents of his pulpit style come over into Elmer's rant)' (Mark Schorer, 1961, *Sinclair Lewis: an American life*, New York: McGraw-Hill, p. 481). *See also* **Stidger**, William L.

STREATLAM CASTLE, County Durham Situated near Gateshead, it was the family place of the Bowes family.

BRITTON HALL in W.M. Thackeray, 'Notes on the North What-d'ye-Callem Election' (1841)

Identified in *Letters and Private Papers of W.M. Thackeray*, 1945, ed. Gordon N. Ray, Vol. II, London: Oxford University Press, p. 27 n. 49.

STRINDBERG, Frida

MADAME in Ford Madox Ford, *The Marsden Case* (1923)

See under **Cave of the Golden Calf**.

STRONG, Emilia Francis *See* **Pattison**, Emilia Francis.

STRONG, Mary Pearson Of Broadstairs, Kent. Dickens and his family spent some time at Broadstairs every year during the 1840s, except for 1844 and 1846.

BETSEY TROTWOOD in Charles Dickens, *David Copperfield* (1849–50)

'The Trotwood donkey-fights did not take place at Dover at all, but at Broadstairs; where a certain Miss Strong ... lived in a little double fronted cottage in the middle of Nuckell's Place, on the seafront, firmly convinced of her right to stop the passage of donkeys along the road in front of her door' (Charles Dickens, the Younger, 1896, 'Notes on some Dickens places and people', *Pall Mall Magazine* (July): 350).

STROUGHILL, George Son of the Dickens family's next-door neighbours, who lived at 1 Ordnance Terrace, Chatham, Kent; the Dickenses lived at number 2 from 1817 to 1821.

JAMES STEERFORTH in Charles Dickens, *David Copperfield* (1849–50)

'The next door neighbours . . . were . . . the Stroughills, and George Stroughill the son, somewhat older than Charles Dickens, was his greatest friend during those happy years. Some characteristics of George, a frank, open and somewhat daring boy, are re-produced as Steerforth in *David Copperfield*' (Robert Langton, 1883, *The Childhood and Youth of Charles Dickens*, Manchester, p. 23).

STUART, William (1755–1822) Son of the 3rd Earl of Bute. From 1793 to 1800 he was Bishop of St Davids, and from 1800 to 1822 he was Archbishop of Armagh.

LORD OLDBOROUGH in Maria Edgeworth, *Patronage* (1814)

'Oldborough's personal attributes . . . belong to a man Maria knew personally, William Stuart, Archbishop of Armagh, the Irish Primate' (Marilyn Butler, 1972, *Maria Edgeworth*, Oxford, p. 255). *See also* **Ellenborough**, 1st Baron; **Walpole**, Sir Robert.

STUART OF INVERNAHYLE, Alexander (d. 1795) Chief of the Stewarts of Appin, Scotland. He was a Jacobite who took part in the uprisings of 1715 and 1745 and fought at Prestonpans and Culloden; he was pardoned under an act of indemnity. Scott described him (to Joseph Train, 22 February 1817, reproduced in *The Letters of Sir Walter Scott*, 1933, ed. H.J.C. Grierson, Vol. IV, London: Constable, p. 394) as his father's most intimate friend. 'One of our most constant visitors while I was a boy was old Stuart of Invernahyle. . . . He was an enthusiastic Highlander and had followed the standard of Charles Edward in 1745 and of his father in 1715. Hence his memory was stood [sic] with stories of these unfortunate campaigns as well as of older times. These he was as fond of telling as I was of listening to them' (to Mrs Clephane, 27 October 1809, reproduced in ibid., Vol. II, pp. 263–4).

BARON BRADWARDINE in Sir Walter Scott, *Waverley* (1814)

'[After Culloden] a small encampment of soldiers was formed on Invernahyle's property . . . searching in every direction for the leaders of the insurrection, and for Stuart in particular . . . hidden in a cave, (like the Baron of Bradwardine), he lay for many days within hearing of the sentinels, as they called their watch-word' (William Erskine, 1817, 'Tales of my landlord', *Quarterly Review* (January): 434). *See also* **Forbes**, Alexander; **Oliphant**, Laurence[1].

WAVERLEY in Sir Walter Scott, *Waverley* (1814)

'The mutual protection afforded by Waverley and Talbot to each other . . . is founded upon one of those anecdotes, which soften . . . even . . . civil war. . . . [At Preston] Alexander Stuart of Invernahyle was one of the foremost in the charge, and observed an officer of the King's forces, who scorning to join the flight of all around, remained with his sword in his hand. . . . [Stuart] commanded him to surrender, and received for answer a thrust which he caught in his target. The officer was thus now defenceless and the battle-axe of a gigantic Highlander . . . was uplifted to dash his brains out, when Mr Stuart with difficulty prevailed on him to surrender. He took charge of his enemy's property, protected his person and finally obtained him liberty on his parole.

The officer proved to be Colonel Alan Whiteford [sic]. . . . After the battle of Culloden it was Colonel Whiteford's turn to strain every nerve to obtain Mr Stuart's pardon' (*Letters*, op. cit, Vol. II, p. 433).

STUFA, Lotteringhi, Marchese della (d. 1889). 'Ouida had been introduced [in 1871] . . . to the Marchese Lotteringhi della Stufa, a gentleman-in-waiting to the then King of Italy, with whom she had fallen immediately and violently in love' (Eileen Bigland, 1951, *Ouida: the passionate pilgrim*, p. 79). An account of their relationship can be found on pp. 123 ff.

PRINCE IORIS in Ouida, *Friendship* (1878)

'The three principal characters [in *Friendship*] were Prince Ioris (Stufa), the Lady Joan Challoner (Mrs Ross) and Etoile (Ouida)' (ibid., p. 137).

STURGES, Jonathan (1864–1911) Essayist and translator. Born in Paris, he was the son of Frederick Sturges of New York and the nephew of the American financier J.P. Morgan, the Elder. He was educated at Princeton, and in Heidelberg and Berlin, and spent much time in Paris, although from 1899 he lived mainly in England. Towards the end of his life he lived in Eastbourne. He was a friend of **Whistler**, Henry James, Maurice **Baring**, Bertrand **Russell** and many others, and was a considerable wit. He was crippled by poliomyelitis as a child and was subject to bouts of acute ill health throughout his life.

JOHN BILHAM in Henry James, *The Ambassadors* (1903)

'John Little Bilham, who resembles Jonathan Sturges (the writer who had brought James the original idea for this novel)' (Leon Edel, 1972, *Henry James: the master, 1901–1916*, p. 71). For the part played by Jonathan Sturges in the genesis of *The Ambassadors*, see **Howells**, W.D.

CHADWICK NEWSOME in Henry James, *The Ambassadors* (1903)

'Jonathan Sturges was cut in two – into Chad and Little Bilham' (Logan Pearsall Smith to Ethel Sands, 29 March 1943, quoted in *A Portrait of Logan Pearsall Smith*, 1950, introd. John Russell, p. 157).

RALPH TOUCHETT in Henry James, *The Portrait of a Lady* (1880)

'How many characters [in Henry James], do you know, were suggested by real people? . . . The Sturgeses in *The Portrait of a Lady*?' (Pearsall Smith to Ethel Sands, op. cit., p. 157). Although Ralph Touchett and his father seem like portraits of Jonathan Sturges and (perhaps) his father, it is in fact impossible that they should be so. Sturges was 16 years old when the novel was published and did not become one of James's intimate friends until the 1890s. Ralph Touchett was a prophecy, not a portrait.

STURMINSTER NEWTON, Dorset Located on the river Stour. Thomas and Emma Hardy lived there, at Riverside Villa, from 1876 to 1878.

STOURCASTLE in Thomas Hardy, *Tess of the d'Urbervilles* (1891)

Identified in F.B. Pinion, 1968, *A Hardy Companion*, London: Macmillan.

DU SUALT, Léonice (*fl.* 1850–74) Née de Fontaine, she was the daughter of the Governor of Mauritius, who had retained his position when the island was transferred to Great Britain in 1814. She was the aunt of Flora Shaw, and after her marriage she lived at St Sever, in the Landes in France, where Flora Shaw visited her for long periods as a child and young girl.

MADAME LOUSTANOFF (GRANDMÈRE) in Flora Shaw, *Hector* (1883)

'The character of Grandmère is to some extent at least a portrait of Tante Léonice' (E. Moberley Bell, 1947, *Flora Shaw (Lady Lugard, DBE)*, London: Constable, p. 32).

SUDBURY, Suffolk

EATANSWILL in Charles Dickens, *The Pickwick Papers* (1836–7)

'For years it has been pretty generally assumed that Ipswich was the original of Eatanswill, but last February [1907] Mr C. Findon Waters . . . became interested, and was astonished to find that among residents of the two there seemed never to have existed the smallest doubt that the real honour belonged to the birthplace of Gainsborough. . . . [It] seems . . . perfectly fair to assume [on the evidence of Mr Pickwick's coach journeys, as described in the novel], . . . that Sudbury was the place Dickens had in mind' (J.W.T. Ley, 1907, 'Is Sudbury Eatanswill?', *The Dickensian* 3 (May): 117). Ley goes on to point out that Dickens sent a report to the *Morning Chronicle* from Sudbury on 14 January 1835, while the report in the paper of the events of the election in Ipswich was described as 'abridged from the *Suffolk Chronicle*'. Dickens was reporting the election from one of the most corrupt areas in the country. *See also* **Ipswich**.

SUHRAWARDY, Huseyn Shaheed (1893–1963) Pakistani politician. Son of Sir Zahid Suhrawardy, a judge of the Calcutta High Court, he was born in Bengal and educated at Oxford. He was called to the Bar from Grays Inn, and after his return to India he practised at the Calcutta Bar. In 1946 he was Chief Minister of Bengal, and in 1947, at the time of the troubles, he lived with Mahatma Gandhi in a Calcutta slum in order to demonstrate the need for and possibility of peace between Muslims and Hindus. He played a leading role in the creation of East Pakistan and was Prime Minister of Pakistan in 1956 and 1957. After the military *coup* he was imprisoned briefly and banned from political life, but in 1962 he formed the National Democratic League and stumped the country in opposition. He died of a heart attack.

HASAN in D.H. Lawrence, *Women in Love* (1920)

'The prototype for the character of "Hasan" seems to have been Suhrawardy, an Indian Lawrence met at a Garsington party at which Philip Heseltine was also present' (Vishnudat Singh, 1970, '*Women in Love*, a textual note', *Notes and Queries* (NS) 17 (12): 466). It is clear from the text of the article that Mr Singh had not fully identified Suhrawardy, and in fact believed him to be a Hindu. Alpers identifies Suhrawardy as a witness at the **Café Royal** of the Café Pompadour incident (see A. Alpers, 1980, *The Life of Katherine Mansfield*, London: Jonathan Cape, p. 217 n.).

SULLIVAN, Daniel (b. 1831) A seaman from County Kerry, Ireland.

SINGLETON in Joseph Conrad, *The Nigger of the 'Narcissus'* (1897)

'Most of the personages I have portrayed actually belonged to the crew of the real *Narcissus*, including the admirable Singleton (whose real name was Sullivan)' (to G. Jean-Aubry, reproduced in G. Jean-Aubry, 1927, *Joseph Conrad: life and letters*, Vol. I, London: Heinemann, p. 77). 'All through the manuscript he called ... Singleton by his real name, Sullivan' (J.D. Gordan, 1941, *Joseph Conrad: the making of a novelist*, Cambridge, Mass., p. 56). In fact there was no Sullivan in the crew of the *Narcissus*. 'The source for Singleton ... was Daniel Sullivan ... who served as an able seaman on the *Tilkhurst* and spent six months at sea with Conrad' (Jerry Allen, 1967, *The Sea Years of Joseph Conrad*, London: Methuen, p. 166).

SUMMERS, Edith She was Upton **Sinclair's** secretary at **Helicon Home Colony**, where she became engaged to Sinclair Lewis, then acting as furnace-man. In 1908 she married Allan **Updegraff**, but they were later divorced.

JESSIE in Harry Kemp, *More Miles* (1926)

'The character called Jessie is obviously meant to represent Edith Summers' (Mark Schorer, 1963, *Sinclair Lewis: an American life*, London: Heinemann, p. 190; originally published 1961, New York: McGraw-Hill).

JUDY in Edith Summers, *Weeds* (1923)

'It was rather acute of you to notice ... the fundamental resemblance between Judy and Leora. I was an early friend of Sinclair Lewis ... and I was his model for Leora. I put a good deal of myself into Judy; so you see the two girls are sisters' (Edith Summers to Louis Adamic, quoted in Schorer, op. cit., p. 420).

LEORA TOZER in Sinclair Lewis, *Arrowsmith* (1925)

See above. See also **De Kruif**, Rhea Elizabeth.

SUMNER, Charles Richard (1790–1874) The younger brother of John Bird Sumner, the English prelate, he was Bishop of Winchester from 1827 to 1869. He was appointed to the See of Winchester by **George IV**, with the King remarking that this time he had determined that the See should be filled by a gentleman. One of his first acts as Bishop was to purchase with the funds of the diocese a town house in St James's Square. He was an admirable administrator and church builder.

BISHOP SOLWAY in Frances Trollope, *Three Cousins* (1847)

'The world insisted on identifying Sumner with Bishop Solway ... but [Mrs Trollope] had no knowledge of him' (*The Dictionary of National Biography*, London: Oxford University Press, s.v. W.P. Courtenay).

SUN INN, Eastwood, Nottinghamshire

MOON AND STARS INN in D.H. Lawrence, *The Lost Girl* (1920)

'The "Moon and Stars Inn" is the "Sun Inn" at Eastwood' (Ada Lawrence and G. Stuart Gelder, 1931, *Young Lorenzo: early life of D.H. Lawrence*, Florence, pp. 54, 55).

SUTHERLAND, Millicent Fanny Leveson-Gower, Duchess of (1867–1955) Née St Clair, she was the daughter of the 4th Earl of Rosslyn; sister of the Countess of **Westmorland** and Lady Angela **Forbes**; half-sister of Frances, Lady **Warwick**; and aunt of Hamish **Erskine**. In 1884 she married Cromartie Leveson-Gower (1851–1931), known as the Marquess of Stafford until he succeeded to the dukedom in 1892; from 1874 to 1886 he was Liberal MP for County Sutherland, and he was a Unionist in the House of Lords. In 1914 she married Brigadier-General P.D. Fitzgerald, but the marriage was dissolved in 1919 and she married Lieutenant-Colonel G.E. Hawes. A famous beauty and leader of society, she was 'sometimes known as "Meddlesome Millie"' (*Letters of Arnold Bennett*, 1968, ed. James Hepburn, Vol. II, London: Oxford University Press, p. 278 n. 220).

Joscelind Bernardstone in Henry James, 'The Path of Duty' (1884)

'Jan. 29th, 1884. I heard the other day at Mrs Tennant's of a situation which struck me as a dramatic and a pretty subject. . . . It appears that [young Lord Stafford] has been for years in love with Lady Grosvenor whom he knew before her marriage. . . . Yielding to family pressure . . . he offered his hand to a young, charming, innocent girl, the daughter of Lord Rosslyn . . . the engagement was announced. Suddenly, a very short time after this . . . Lord Grosvenor dies, and his wife becomes free. The question came up – "what was Lord S. to do?"' (*The Notebooks of Henry James*, 1947, ed. F.O. Matthiessen and K.B. Murdock, New York, p. 54). James then discusses at length various possible courses of action referring to the actors as Lady G. and Miss R. ('or whatever her name is') and adds, 'I use these initials simply as convenient signs – knowing nothing of the people' (ibid.). Lord Grosvenor had in fact died only a week before the entry was made.

Countess of Chell in Arnold Bennett, *The Card* (1911)

'[A] leading character in *The Card*, the Countess of Chell, was identified in the minds of local readers with the Duchess of Sutherland' (Reginald Pound, 1952, *Arnold Bennett: a biography*, London: Heinemann, p. 219). Bennett sat next to the duchess at dinner shortly after the publication of *The Card* and she asked him, 'Why did you make fun of me in your book?' His letter of apology and explanation, dated 23 June 1911, is reproduced in *Letters of Arnold Bennett*, 1970, ed. James Hepburn, Vol. III, London: Oxford University Press, pp. 284–5. In part it runs: '. . . if there is a resemblance . . . it is simply because you are the sole representative of that particular class in the Five Towns. . . . I think you must admit that I am not the man to attempt the portrait of any person whatsoever in a novel, much less the portrait of one whom I had never seen. On the other hand, I willingly admit that certain qualities of the Countess were suggested by public knowledge of you. But that is all.'

SUTRO, Alfred (1863–1933) Playwright and translator of Maeterlinck. He had considerable success as a dramatist after 1904.

FELIX LEDGETT in Max Beerbohm, 'Walter Argallo and Felix Ledgett', *A Variety of Things* (1928)

'The futile little man of letters called Ledgett, possibly suggested by the dramatist Alfred Sutro' (David Cecil, 1964, *Max: a biography*, p. 418).

SUTTON, Richard (1782–1851)   Of Dent, West Riding, Yorkshire (now Cumbria). He was adopted as a foundling by Edmund and Elizabeth Sill of Rigg End, and in 1835 he inherited the property from their last surviving child, Ann.

HEATHCLIFF in Emily Brontë, *Wuthering Heights* (1847)

'The real-life model of Heathcliff . . . may have been uncovered thanks to the . . . research of an amateur historian [Mrs Kim Lyon]. If [her] theory is correct . . . [he] was based on . . . Richard Sutton . . . whose life . . . mirrors that of Heathcliff to an uncanny degree' (Robert Low and David Boulton, 1984, 'Real life story behind "Wuthering Heights"', *The Observer* (30 September): 3). The article identifies the Sills as the Earnshaws, and the family of Mason, also of Dent, as the Lintons. *See also* **Sharp**, Jack.

SUTTON SCARSDALE HALL, Derbyshire   The former residence of William Arkwright.

SHIPLEY HALL in D.H. Lawrence, *Lady Chatterley's Lover* (1928)

'The main Support for the "Arkwright theory" was Reresby Sitwells' conviction that the novel's Shipley Hall must be Sutton Scarsdale and that it must have been through hearing of Arkwright during talk of Osbert's interest in the hall that Lawrence came to visit Sutton Scarsdale' (Derek Britton, 1988, *Lady Chatterley: the making of the novel*, London: Unwin Hyman, p. 159).

SWAMI, Coomara   A Hindu barrister from Ceylon who was one of a house party at **Fryston Hall** in 1862.

JUGGONATH CHUNDANGO in Laurence Oliphant, *Piccadilly* (1870)

'[I]t is entirely plausible to assume that the appearance, and perhaps the behaviour, of Mr Coomar Swami at Fryston suggested to Oliphant the presence at Dickiefield of Juggonath Chundango' (James Pope-Hennessy, 1951, *Monckton Milnes: the flight of youth, 1851–1885*, p. 142).

The SWAN, West Malling, Kent

THE LION in Charles Dickens, *The Pickwick Papers* (1836–7)

See under **West Malling**.

SWAN BANK AND SWAN SQUARE

DUCK BANK AND DUCK SQUARE in Arnold Bennett, *Anna of the Five Towns* (1902)

'[Duck Square] exists under the name of Swan Square. . . . Duck Bank is really Swan Bank' (to J.C. Squire, 18 April 1915, reproduced in *Letters of Arnold Bennett*, 1968, ed. James Hepburn, Vol. II, London: Oxford University Press, p. 364).

SWANAGE, Dorset A seaside town south of Poole. Thomas Hardy and his wife lived there in 1875 and 1876.

KNOLLSEA in Thomas Hardy, Wessex novels and tales (1871–95)

Identified on a map prepared by Thomas Hardy which hangs in the Dorset County Museum, Dorchester. *See under* **Abbotsbury**.

SWEENY, Charles (1882–1963) Soldier of fortune. Ernest Hemingway first met him in Constantinople in 1922 when Hemingway was there as Correspondent for the Toronto *Star*. They became friends, and in 1925 Sweeny half persuaded Hemingway to accompany him to Morocco, to fight for the French against the Riff rebellion. Until 1940 his base was Paris, but by 1941 he was in Washington. The friendship continued until Sweeny suffered a stroke in 1959.

RICHARD CANTWELL in Ernest Hemingway, *Across the River and Into the Trees* (1950)

'[Hemingway wrote to Lanham] that his hero Cantwell was a composite portrait of . . . Charlie Sweeny; the former soldier of fortune; Lanham . . . and himself' (Carlos Baker, *Ernest Hemingway: a life story*, New York, p. 475). *See also* **Hemingway**, Ernest; **Lanham**, C.T.

SWIERCZIEWSKI, Karol (1897–1947) Born in Poland, he was educated largely in Russia, fought in the Russian army during the First World War and took part in the Russian Revolution and Civil War. He became a professor in the Moscow Military School, and in 1936 was Military Adviser in the recruiting office of the International Brigade of the Spanish Republican Army. Later in the same year, he was Commander of the XIVth International Brigade, and later of the 35th Division. In Spain he was known as 'General Walter'. He survived both Stalin's purges and the Second World War, to become Minister of Defence in Poland (1945–7), but was assassinated in 1947, allegedly by anti-Communist partisans.

GENERAL GOLZ in Ernest Hemingway, *For Whom the Bell Tolls* (1940)

'He appears in *For Whom the Bell Tolls* as General Golz' (Hugh Thomas, 1961, *The Spanish Civil War*, p. 299).

SWINBURNE, Algernon Charles (1837–1909) English poet and critic. He was educated in France, at Eton and at Balliol College, Oxford, but left without taking his degree. He travelled on the Continent and on his return became associated with Dante Gabriel **Rossetti** and William Morris. Intemperate living caused him to have a breakdown, after which he spent the rest of his life in semi-seclusion in the care of his friend Theodore **Watts-Dunton**. Apart from his poetry and criticism, he wrote one novel *Love's Cross Currents* published in 1877 under the pseudonym of Mrs H. Manners.

TRACY RUNNINGBROOK in George Meredith, *Sandra Belloni (Emilia in England)* (1864)

'He once told me that Swinburne was the original of Tracy Runningbrook' (Lady Butcher, 1919, *Memories of George Meredith O.M.*, London: Constable, p. 148 n. 1).

REGINALD SWYNFEN in Mortimer Collins, *Two Plunges for a Pearl* (1872)

'Mortimer Collins caricatured Swinburne as Swynfen' (Amy Cruse, 1962, *The Victorians and Their Books*, p. 381). The caricature was instantly recognized. 'If the repulsive sketch of an epicene poetaster, whose name we think it well to withhold, be really . . . intended as a personal onslaught on a living individual, so gross an offence against good feeling must destroy all the pleasure . . . in reading what, in other respects, we regard as a successful story' (review, 1871, *The Athenaeum* (11 November): 620).

SYDLING ST NICHOLAS, Dorset A village between Maiden Newton and Cerne Abbas, located seven miles north-north-east of Dorchester.

BROAD SIDLINCH in Thomas Hardy, 'The Grave by the Handpost' (1913)

Identified in F.B. Pinion, 1968, *A Hardy Companion*, London: Macmillan.

SYKES, Christopher[1] (1831–98) Of Brantingham. Second son of Sir Tatton Sykes, 4th Baronet of Sledmere Thorpe, he became an intimate friend of the Prince and Princess of Wales. He was MP for Beverley in 1865, for East Riding in 1868 and 1880, and for Buckrose from 1885 to 1892. During this time he made only six speeches and asked three questions.

MR BRANCEPETH in Benjamin Disraeli, *Lothair* (1870)

'Mr Brancepeth in *Lothair*, the young man who knew the art of giving dinners supremely well, has been widely recognised as a portrait of Mr Christopher Sykes' (obituary, 1898, *The Times* (17 December)). Also identified in 'Key to Lothair', *Notes and Queries* 183 (12 September 1942): 173.

SYKES, Christopher[2] (b. 1907) Author. He was a BBC radio producer from 1949 to 1969.

ROGER STILLINGFLEET in Evelyn Waugh, *The Ordeal of Gilbert Pinfold* (1957)

'I appear in the fiction under the name of Roger Stillingfleet' (Christopher Sykes, 1975, *Evelyn Waugh*, London: Collins, p. 361).

SYKES, Henrietta, Lady (1801?–46) Daughter of Henry Villebois, a partner in the brewing firm of Truman & Hanbury, in 1821 she married Sir Francis Sykes, 3rd Baronet, of Basildon, Berkshire. In 1833 she met Disraeli and became his mistress, probably conducting an affair with Lord **Lyndhurst** simultaneously. The affair with Disraeli ended in 1836, and she became the mistress of Daniel Maclise, the painter. Her husband instigated proceedings of criminal conduct against Maclise, but although he dropped the proceedings she was no longer able to move in Society. 'On 2 Feb. 1839 [the Queen] entered in her journal: "Talked of Maclise having run away with Lady Sykes; Lord M. said: 'They're a bad set; they're grand-daughters of Elmore, the horse dealer . . . old Elmore trafficked [sic] with his daughter as much as he did with his horses'"' (MS in The Royal Archives, Windsor Castle, quoted in *Letters of Charles Dickens*, 1968, ed. Madeline House and Graham Storey, Vol. II, Oxford: Oxford University Press, p. 79 n. 2).

HENRIETTA TEMPLE in Benjamin Disraeli, *Henrietta Temple* (1837)

'Henrietta ... bears little [resemblance] to the real Henrietta, except for her physical description, and her letters to Ferdinand. These are so like those of the real Henrietta that one is tempted to think that Disraeli transcribed them verbatim. But if the characters are fictitious, their experience is not. The account of love at first sight has an authentic ring of personal passion seldom found elsewhere among the novels' (Robert Blake, 1966, *Disraeli*, London: Eyre & Spottiswoode, p. 143).

SYMONDS, John Addington (1840–93) Historian and translator. Born in Bristol and educated at Harrow School and Balliol College, Oxford, he was obliged to live abroad, on account of his health, and settled at Davos Platz. He wrote *History of the Italian Renaissance* (1875–86) and *Walt Whitman* (1893), and translated Michelangelo's sonnets. He married Janet Catherine (1837–1913), daughter of Frederick Norton of Rougham, Norfolk, Liberal MP for Hastings, and was the father of Margaret ('Madge') **Vaughan**. He was a champion of male homosexual love, and in 1891 Roger Fry met him in Venice and described him as 'the most pornographic person I ever saw, but not in the least nasty' (*Letters*, Vol. I, p. 147).

MARK AMBIENT in Henry James, 'The Author of "Beltraffio"' (1884)

'March 26th, 1884. Edmund Gosse mentioned to me the other day a fact which struck me as a possible donnée. He was speaking of J.A.S. the writer ... of his extreme and somewhat hysterical aestheticism, etc.: the sad conditions of his life ... the illness of his daughter, etc. Then he said that, to crown his unhappiness, poor S's wife was in no sort of sympathy with what he wrote; disapproving its tone, thinking his books immoral. ... "I have never read any of John's works. I think them most *undesirable*." It seemed to me *qu'il y avait là un drame – un drame intime*' (*The Notebooks of Henry James*, 1947, ed. F.O. Matthiessen and K.B. Murdock, New York, p. 57). 'I am told, on all sides here, that my "Author of *Beltraffio*" is a living and scandalous portrait of J.A. Symonds and his wife, whom I have never seen' (Henry James to William James, 15 February 1885, quoted in Leon Edel, 1969, *Henry James: the treacherous years, 1895–1901*, London: Rupert Hart-Davis, pp. 117, 118). He appears under the name of Opalstein in R.L. Stevenson's *Memories and Portraits* (1887).

SYNGE, Robert Follett (1853–1920) Eldest son of W.W. Follett Synge, who was one of Thackeray's oldest friends, he obtained a nomination as a Foundation Boy at Charterhouse through Thackeray's good offices. He was created Knight Commander of the Most Distinguished Order of St Michael and St George in 1919, and was a Foreign Office official.

BOBBY MISTLETOE in W.M. Thackeray, 'Round About the Christmas Tree' (1899)

'The "Bobby Mistletoe" of "Round about the Christmas Tree"' (*The Letters and Private Papers of W.M. Thackeray*, 1946, ed. Gordon N. Ray, Vol. IV, London: Oxford University Press, p. 200).

T

TABART, Benjamin A small bookseller with a shop, Tabart's Juvenile Library, in Bond Street, London, publishing and selling juveniles. From the early 1800s he was associated with Richard **Phillips**: he acted as 'hack and principal amanuensis for Phillips' and 'supervised his juvenile publications' (A. Boyle, 1951, 'Portraiture in *Lavengro*', *Notes and Queries* 196 (15 September): 412).

TAGGART in George Borrow, *Lavengro* (1851)

'The real name of this individual was Tabart – Benjamin Tabart' (ibid., pp. 411–12).

TAFT, Robert Alphonso (1889–1953) Son of President William Howard Taft, the twenty-seventh president of the United States, he was born in Cincinnati, Ohio, and was educated at Yale and Harvard. He was a senator from 1939 to 1953 and was a member of the Republican party.

THEODORE BLAIR in James Reichley, *Hail to the Chief* (1960)

Identified in Joseph Blotner, 1966, *The Modern American Political Novel*, Austin, Tex., p. 129.

TAIT, Walter (d. 1836) He was a captain in the Royal Navy.

CAPTAIN CLUTTERBUCK in Sir Walter Scott, *The Monastery* (1820) and *The Fortunes of Nigel* (1822)

'The *Kelso Mail* of 21 Nov. 1836 recorded the death at Melrose of Capt. Walter Tait, R.N., "said to be the original of Capt. Clutterbuck"' (James C. Corson, 1979, *Notes and Index to Sir Herbert Grierson's . . . Letters of Sir Walter Scott*, Oxford, p. 257 (308 n. 1) n. 1). *See also* **Ormiston**, Adam.

TALFOURD, Thomas Noon (1795–1854) Lawyer and author. Educated at Mill Hill School and at **Reading School**, he became Justice of the Common Pleas in 1849 and was MP for Reading in 1835, 1837 and 1841. He vetted *Bardell v. Pickwick* for legal accuracy (in the case of *Norton v. Melbourne* he had held a brief for Mrs **Norton**); it was to him that Dickens dedicated *Pickwick Papers*. He was the author of the tragedy *Ion* (1835).

THOMAS TRADDLES in Charles Dickens, *David Copperfield* (1849–50)

'The similarity between "Thomas Traddles" and "Thomas Talfourd" cannot be denied' (P.F. Skottowe, 1969, 'Thomas Talfourd and *David Copperfield*', *The Dickensian* 65 (January): 290).

TANKERVILLE, Corisande Armandine Leonice Bennet, Lady (1782–1865) Daughter of Antoine, Duc de Gamont, in 1806 she married Charles, Lord Ossulton, who succeeded to the title of Tankerville in 1822.

LADY TENDERDEN in Lady Charlotte Bury, *The Exclusives* (1830)

Identified in *Key to the Royal Novel 'The Exclusives'*, 1830, Marsh & Miller; reproduced in Michael Sadleir, 1951, *XIX Century Fiction*, 2 vols, London: Constable, and Los Angeles: California University Press, pp. 73–4.

TAPLOW COURT, Buckinghamshire   The home of Lord and Lady **Desborough** before the First World War. 'Ghosts of the rich and great who stayed with Lord and Lady Desborough seem to haunt the mown walks and steep grass slopes to the river, once so fashionable. Taplow Court, the Desborough house, is a spired brick and stone Victorian Mansion, with a handsome, well-shaped hall inside, rising the whole height of the house, and in the Norman Revival style. The grounds are finely planted. There is an avenue of cedars of Lebanon, and a famous Saxon tumulus on the lawn' (John Betjeman and John Piper (eds), 1948, *Murray's Buckinghamshire Guide*, p. 125).

KEEB HALL in Max Beerbohm, 'Maltby and Braxton', *Seven Men* (1919)

'Keeb Hall is Taplow' (David Cecil, 1964, *Max: a biography*, p. 341).

TARRANT HINTON, Dorset   A village on the main road from Salisbury to Blandford.

TRANTRIDGE in Thomas Hardy, Wessex novels and tales (1871–95)

'There can be no doubt . . . that elsewhere [i.e. except in *Tess of the d'Urbervilles*] it is Tarrant Hinton' (F.B. Pinion, 1968, *A Hardy Companion*, London: Macmillan, p. 492). *See also* **Pentridge**.

TATUM, Mr   (d. 1914?) Of Philadelphia. He was a Quaker and the father of Anna **Tatum**.

SOLON BARNES in Theodore Dreiser, *The Bulwark* (1946)

'Anna Tatum [in 1912] told him . . . the story of [her] father, a singularly devout and gentle Quaker whose nobility of character, rather than bringing him happiness, plunged him and his family into deepest tragedy. . . . The story, which he later called *The Bulwark* made such an impression on him that . . . he began mentally to organize *The Bulwark*' (W.A. Swanberg, 1965, *Dreiser*, New York, p. 162).

TAUNTON, Somerset   County town located on the River Tone.

TONEBOROUGH in Thomas Hardy, Wessex novels and tales (1871–95)

Identified on a map prepared by Thomas Hardy which hangs in the Dorset County Museum, Dorchester. *See under* **Abbotsbury**.

TAYLOR   A prisoner in the Birmingham borough prison in 1853.

NAYLOR in Charles Reade, *It is Never Too Late to Mend* (1856)

'Taylor [is described] as Naylor' ('The license of modern novelists', *Edinburgh Review* (July 1857): 137).

TAYLOR, Mr He was an English master at **Wellington House Academy**.

CHARLES MELL in Charles Dickens, *David Copperfield* (1849–50)

'His prototype was Mr Taylor . . . poor soul, he found relief from his scholastic inferno by tuning a melancholy flute. . . . Taylor also figures as the usher in *Our School*, who was considered to know everything as opposed to the Chief, who was considered to know nothing' (Willoubly Matchett, 1911, 'Dickens at Wellington House Academy', *The Dickensian* 7 (July): 182). *See also* **Goldsmith**, Oliver.

TAYLOR, Ann Married to Joshua **Taylor**, her daughters were Martha and Mary **Taylor**. 'Mrs Taylor . . . was cordially disliked by Charlotte [Brontë] and not particularly loved by her daughters whose life she oppressed with her gloom and tyranny' (Winifred Gérin, 1969, *Charlotte Brontë*, Oxford, p. 71).

HESTHER YORKE in Charlotte Brontë, *Shirley* (1849)

See under **Taylor**, Joshua.

TAYLOR, Cecilia Delihant (b. 1880)

CLARA PAGE in F. Scott Fitzgerald, *This Side of Paradise* (1920)

'A first cousin on his father's side . . . sixteen years older than Scott. . . . Now she was an impoverished widow . . . Cousin "Ceci" was Fitzgerald's favourite relative; she would be the model for . . . Clara' (Andrew Turnbull, 1962, *Scott Fitzgerald*, p. 40). They remained friends and corresponded until his death.

TAYLOR, Dwight (b. 1903) Film-script writer. Son of the well-known American actress Laurette Taylor. He met Fitzgerald in 1931, when he was working in Hollywood.

JOEL COLES in F. Scott Fitzgerald, 'Crazy Sunday' (1935)

'[The story] was about two writers who had been asked to a big party at the beach house of a famous motion picture producer. One of them gets drunk and makes a jack-ass of himself by singing an unsolicited song. In a carefully delineated passage at the beginning of the story, giving a description of his appearance, and an oblique reference to his famous mother, there is no mistaking the fact that this famous drunk is supposed to be *me!*' (Dwight Taylor, 1959, *Joy Ride*, New York, p. 249). *See also* **Fitzgerald**, F. Scott.

TAYLOR, Edward Thompson (1793–1871) Sailor, peddler and Methodist clergyman. Known as 'Father Taylor', in 1830 he was Minister of the Boston (Massachusetts) Seamen's Bethel; he was one of the greatest preachers of his generation in the United States.

FATHER MAPPLE in Herman Melville, *Moby Dick* (1851)

'The sermon of Father Mapple in Herman Melville's *Moby Dick* is obviously a portrayal of Taylor's manner of preaching' (H.E. Stern, 1936, *Dictionary of American Biography*, Vol. XVIII, p. 321). When Dickens visited Boston in January 1842 he was taken by Charles Sumner and Longfellow to hear a sermon from Father Taylor – the only sermon he heard in America. He describes the chapel and the sermon in ch. 3 of *American Notes* (see *Letters of Charles Dickens*, 1974, ed. Madeline House, Graham Storey and Kathleen Tillotson, Vol. III, Oxford: Oxford University Press, p. 21 n. 2).

TAYLOR, George Ashton (1803?–22) He was buried in the churchyard at Bowes, Yorkshire: the inscription on his gravestone reads: 'Here lie I the remains of George Ashton Taylor, son of John Taylor of Trowbridge, Wiltshire, who died suddenly at Mr William Shaw's Academy, of this place, April 13th, 1822, aged 19 years. Young reader, thou must die, but after this the judgement.'

SMIKE in Charles Dickens, *Nicholas Nickleby* (1838–9)

'There is an old church near the school, and the first grave-stone I stumbled on that dreary winter afternoon was placed above the grave of a boy, eighteen long years old, who had died – suddenly, the inscription said; I suppose his heart broke – the Camel falls down "suddenly" when they heap the last load upon his back – died at that wretched place. I think his ghost put Smike into my head, upon the spot' (to Mrs S.C. Hall, 29 December 1838, reproduced in *The Letters of Charles Dickens*, 1965, ed. Madeline House and Graham Storey, Vol. I, Oxford: Oxford University Press, p. 482).

TAYLOR, Sir Henry (1800–86) Poet. Born in Durham, from 1824 until 1872 he held a small appointment in the colonial office. He was acquainted with Mill and Sir James **Stephen**. He contributed to periodicals and was the author of, amongst others, *Philip von Altevelde* (1834). He was knighted in 1869.

TIMOTHEUS in W.M. Thackeray, 'The Proser IV – On a Good-Looking Young Lady' (1850)

'Taylor ... appears as Timotheus' (*The Letters and Private Papers of W.M. Thackeray*, 1945, ed. Gordon N. Ray, Vol. II, London: Oxford University Press, p. 695 n. 133). This article gave great offence to the Taylors, and Thackeray felt obliged to write a letter of apology to Henry Taylor (see ibid., p. 694).

TAYLOR, Joseph (d. 1857) Son of Joshua **Taylor**. From 1831 his sister Mary **Taylor** was one of Charlotte Brontë's closest friends.

ROBERT MOORE in Charlotte Brontë, *Shirley* (1849)

'[There is] an unmistakeable evocation of Joe Taylor as the mill-owner hero, Robert Moore' (Winifred Gérin, 1969, *Charlotte Brontë*, Oxford, p. 389).

TAYLOR, Joshua (d. 1840) Cloth manufacturer. Of the Red House, Gomersal, Yorkshire. He was married to Ann **Taylor** and their children were Joseph, Martha and Mary **Taylor**.

YORKE HUNSDEN in Charlotte Brontë, *The Professor* (1857)

'The character of Hunsden is evidently a first sketch, for the more finished picture, we had in "Shirley", in Mr Hiram Yorke. This was admittedly ... studied upon ... Mr Joshua Taylor' (Herbert Wroot, 1935, *The Sources of Charlotte Brontë's Novels: persons and places*, Shipley, Yorks., p. 204).

HIRAM YORKE in Charlotte Brontë, *Shirley* (1849)

'As Hiram Yorke was a portrait of Mr Joshua Taylor . . . so the character of Mrs Yorke was studied from that of Mrs Taylor' (ibid., p. 138).

TAYLOR, Lewis He was a contemporary of Lawrence's at University College, Nottinghamshire.

WILL SELBY in D.H. Lawrence, 'Goose Fair' (1914)

'Do you recognize the people? – a glorified Lois Mee . . . a glorified (?) Taylor?' (early November 1909, reproduced in *Lawrence in Love: letters to Louie Burrows*, 1968, ed. James T. Boulton, Nottingham, p. 45). '"Taylor" was probably Lewis Taylor . . . he was most likely the original of Will Selby' (ibid., n. 2).

TAYLOR, Margaret Elizabeth Jane (1870–1964) She attended Girton College, Cambridge, from 1889 to 1893, and was Classical Lecturer there from 1895 to 1899. From 1899 to 1934 she was Classical Lecturer at Royal Holloway College.

MISS BUTLER in I. Compton-Burnett, *Dolores* (1911)

'Margaret Taylor . . . reappears in *Dolores* (1911) as "the lecturer in classics, Miss Butler"' (Hilary Spurling, 1974, *Ivy When Young: the early life of I. Compton-Burnett, 1884–1919*, London: Gollancz, pp. 155–6).

TAYLOR, Martha (1819?–42) Daughter of Joshua and Ann **Taylor** and sister of Mary **Taylor**, she died young, at the Château de Koekelberg near Brussels.

JESSY YORKE in Charlotte Brontë, *Shirley* (1849)

See under **Taylor**, Joshua.

TAYLOR, Mary (1817–93) Daughter of Joshua and Ann **Taylor** and sister of Martha **Taylor**, she was a pupil with Charlotte Brontë at Roe Head House School in Yorkshire, and they remained close friends until Charlotte's death. After leaving Roe Head, she went to school in Brussels, and in 1841 she emigrated to New Zealand, although she later returned to England. She was a woman of considerable intellectual capacity, and published a novel, *Miss Miles; or a Tale of Yorkshire Life 60 Years Ago* (1890), and a book of articles.

ROSE YORKE in Charlotte Brontë, *Shirley* (1849)

'Rose Yorke was an acknowledged portrait of Mary Taylor. . . . Mary Taylor herself, in a letter written to [Charlotte Brontë] soon after the publication of "Shirley", observes:– "You make us all talk much as I think we should have done if we'd ventured to speak at all. What a little lump of perfection you've made me! There is a strange feeling in reading it of hearing us all talking' (Herbert Wroot, 1935, *The Sources of Charlotte Brontë's Novels: persons and places*, Shipley, Yorks., p. 139).

TAYLOR, Zachary (1784–1850) Twelfth President of the United States (1849–50), nicknamed 'Old Rough-and-Ready'. Born in Orange County, Virginia, in 1808 he entered the US Army, and in 1845 he was Commander of the Army in Texas; in 1846–7 he led the war in northern Mexico to a victorious conclusion. He was elected as president in November 1848 but died after only a year and four months in office. During his administration, Hawthorne lost his position in the Salem custom house; in 1853, he arrived as the US Consul at Liverpool, and found his office adorned with 'a hideous colored lithograph of General Taylor, life-size'.

OLD BLOOD AND THUNDER in Nathaniel Hawthorne, 'The Great Stone Face' (1850)

'Zachary Taylor ... whom he had satirized as "Old Blood-and-Thunder" in "The Great Stone Face"' (Hawthorne, 1941, *English Notebooks*, ed. Randall Stewart, New York and London: Modern Languages Association of America, p. 625 n. 2).

TAYLOR OF NORWICH, William (1765–1836) Born in and largely resident in Norwich, he travelled abroad and in his travels met Goethe. He was an enthusiast for the French Revolution, and in 1791 he attended debates in the National Assembly in Paris. He translated Lessing and Goethe into English, and was the author of *Historic Survey of German Poetry (1828–30)*.

THE ANGLO-GERMANIST in George Borrow, *Lavengro* (1851)

'Chapter XXIII [describes an] interview between William Taylor (21 King Street, Norwich) and George Borrow' (*Lavengro*, 1900, p. 560 n. (to p. 146)).

TCHELITCHEW, Pavel (1898–1957) Born in Moscow, he moved to Paris as an émigré after the Russian Revolution. He became a painter, and was one of the Neo-Romantics who were in reaction against the abstractions of Picasso and Matisse. He was introduced to Gertrude **Stein**, who for a short while took him up and bought some of his paintings. In 1927, at her house in the rue de Fleurus, he met Edith Sitwell: 'If I present Pavlik to you', said Miss Stein, 'it's your responsibility because his character is not my affair.' Edith fell deeply in love with him; her relationship with him remained central to her life until his death, but he did not reciprocate her feelings. He was homosexual, and in 1934 he formed a permanent liaison with the American writer Charles Henri Ford. Furthermore, his need for Edith declined almost to nothing as his reputation increased. He achieved considerable success as a designer for Diaghilev and later for Massine, and in 1938 he established himself with an exhibition in London. He found himself acclaimed by such arbiters of taste as Edward James, Kenneth Clark, Lord **Berners** and Lady **Cunard**, but his reputation did not survive the war and he died in poverty. One of his many portraits of Edith Sitwell is in the Tate Gallery, London; another painting is in the New York Gallery of Modern Art; and a third, left to Edith in his will, hangs at **Renishaw Hall.**

JONATHAN HARE in Edith Sitwell, *I Live Under a Black Sun* (1937)

'Swift – or as she calls him, Jonathan Hare, is clearly Pavlik' (John Pearson, 1978, *Façades: Edith, Osbert and Sacheverell Sitwell*, London: Macmillan, p. 324).

TELEGRAPH HOUSE, Sussex Situated near Chichester, from 1895 it was the home of Francis **Russell**, and later of Bertrand **Russell**.

THE WILLOWS in 'Elizabeth', *Vera* (1921)

'In this novel, Vera is already dead ... she died by falling out of one of the windows of the tower of Telegraph House' (Bertrand Russell, 1968,

Autobiography, Vol. II, pp. 153, 154). Before 1894, Francis Russell lived at Broom Hall, on the Thames at Teddington. Elizabeth would seem to have used its situation for The Willows.

TEMKO, Allan Bernard (b. 1924) Art historian and architectural journalist. He became the art editor of the *San Francisco Chronicle* in 1961.

ROLAND MAJOR in *On the Road* (1957), ALLEN MINKO in *Visions of Gerard* (1963), and IRVING MINKO in *Book of Dreams* (1960), all by Jack Kerouac

Identified in 'Character key to the Duluoz Legend', in Barry Gifford and Lawrence Lee, 1979, *Jack's Book*, pp. 322–32.

TEMPLE, Mary ('Minny') (1845–70) She was a cousin of Henry James and died of tuberculosis.

ISABEL ARCHER in Henry James, *The Portrait of a Lady* (1880)

'Isabel Archer, avowedly modelled on Minny' (Leon Edel, 1953, *Henry James: the untried years 1843–1870*, pp. 238, 239).

MILLY THEALE in Henry James, *The Wings of the Dove* (1902)

'She began to figure in [his] short stories and novels long before the day when, a quarter of a century later, he made his first notebook entry of the theme that became *The Wings of the Dove*' (Edel, op. cit., p. 332; but see pp. 328–37 *passim*). *See also* **James**, Alice.

TEMPLE, Robert He was a cousin of Henry James and the elder brother of Minny **Temple**.

SCOTT HOMER in Henry James, 'Mrs Medwin' (1903)

'Finally I should like to suggest a source for Scott Homer. . . . He is based, almost certainly, on Robert Temple. . . . Curiously he does not appear in Edel's biography of James, and yet James devotes several pages of *Notes of a Son and Brother* to him' (Bernard Richards, 1980, 'The sources of Henry James's "Mrs Medwin"', *Notes and Queries* (NS) 27 (3): 228).

TEMPLE SCHOOL, Boston Founded in 1834 by Bronson **Alcott** with the assistance of Elizabeth **Peabody**. Alcott introduced gymnastics, organized play and the honour system, and he believed in beautiful school surroundings and a conversational method of instruction. The school failed in 1839 because the parents found his basic philosophical ideas dangerous and improper; the last pupils were withdrawn when Alcott admitted a black child.

PLUMFIELD in Louisa M. Alcott, *Little Women* (1868) and sequels

'Remembering the doctrines of the Temple School and Sanborne's Academy [she combined] them in the pedagogy of Plumfield' (M.B. Stern, 1952, *Louisa M. Alcott*, p. 214). 'The publication of *Little Men* seemed . . . an appropriate time . . . to reissue [Bronson] Alcott's *Record of a School*, on which Louisa said Plumfield was based' (M. Saxton, 1978, *Louisa May*, p. 312). *See also* **Sanborn's School**.

TENNYSON, Alfred, 1st Baron Tennyson (1809–92) English poet. Born in Lincolnshire, the fourth son of a rector. He was educated at Louth Grammar School and at Trinity College, Cambridge, but he left Cambridge without taking a degree when his father died. His early work was criticized for being too sentimental but in 1850 he published *In Memoriam* to great acclaim. In the same year he succeeded William **Wordsworth** as Poet Laureate and married Emily Sellwood. In 1865 he refused a baronetcy, though he eventually agreed to a title and took his seat in the House of Lords in 1883.

ELSLEY VAVASOUR (JOHN BRIGGS) in Charles Kingsley, *Two Years Ago* (1857)

'Tennyson was told and believed that Vavasour was a caricature of himself. . . . It is true that Vavasour is not unlike the . . . hero of "Maud". . . and Tennyson was morbidly sensitive about the opium addiction of one of his brothers and the alcoholism of his father and another brother. . . . On 16th October 1858 [F.D.] Maurice wrote . . . to [J.M.] Ludlow: "I should be grieved beyond expression if I thought that Kingsley had written anything against Tennyson, worst [of] all on the score of his private life. . . . If Kingsley . . . meant to strike at him in his Vavasour, he never made a greater blunder"' (R.B. Martin, 1959, *The Dust of Combat: a life of Charles Kingsley*, London: Faber & Faber, p. 163). 'Certainly, Vavasour is not a caricature of Tennyson' (ibid., p. 203). *See also* **Shelley**, Percy Bysshe.

TERNAN, Ellen Lawless (1839–1914) Youngest of the three daughters of Frances Eleanor **Ternan** and Thomas Lawless Ternan. Like her sisters, she followed her parents on to the stage, but she never achieved any outstanding distinction. In 1857, with her mother and sister, she appeared in the Manchester production of Wilkie Collins's play, *The Frozen Deep*, in which the leading male role was played by Charles Dickens himself. In August 1859 she made her last appearance on the professional stage, and in 1876 she married George Wharton Robinson, a schoolmaster, with whom she had two children. She died in London, having survived her husband by four years. It would seem that in 1857 Dickens became infatuated with her, that his feeling for her was the precipitating cause of his separation from his wife in 1858, and that after the separation she became his mistress.

HELENA LANDLESS in Charles Dickens, *Edwin Drood* (1870)

'He wrote her name into his last three novels as Estella Provis, Bella Wilfer and finally Helena Landless' (Edmund Wilson, 1952, *The Wound and the Bow*, p. 62). Certainly these three are very different from Dickens's previous heroines. It could, however, be argued that they were drawn from his daughters, at least one of whom, later Mrs Perugini, was a fairly strong-willed and flighty young woman. *See also* **Kent**, Constance.

ESTELLA PROVIS in Charles Dickens, *Great Expectations* (1860–1)

See above.

BELLA WILFER in Charles Dickens, *Our Mutual Friend* (1864–5)

See above.

TERNAN, Frances Eleanor (1803–73) Actress. She was the eldest of the six children of John Jarman, prompter at the Theatre Royal, York, and his actress wife. She made her début in 1815, and by 1827 she was playing Juliet at Covent Garden to Charles Kemble's Romeo; however, she was supplanted by Fanny **Kemble** in 1829. In 1834 she married the Irish actor Thomas Lawless Ternan; he committed suicide in 1846, leaving Mrs Ternan with three daughters – Maria, Frances (who married T.A. Trollope, brother of the novelist, becoming his second wife) and Ellen (above). During her long career, Mrs Ternan played alongside almost all the most celebrated managers and actors of the day, including Alfred Bunn, Kemble, Macready, Kean and, on 7 July 1857, Charles **Dickens**. She retired in June 1866.

EMILY FOTHERINGAY in W.M. Thackeray, *The History of Pendennis* (1848–50)

'[T]he fourth chapter of Pendennis ... tells how Pen and his young friend Harry Foker attended that ... performance of [Kotzeube's] *The Stranger* [in Exeter on 23 July 1828]. ... Thackeray gives us a very amusing account of the beginning of this preposterous work, and then, quite suddenly, the tempo of his writing changes completely as, "with a downcast look" Mrs Haller takes the stage. ... Whatever is fictitious in the early chapters of *Pendennis* ... this scene bears all the signs of having its basis in fact ... I think we may assume that among Miss Jarman's sparse audience on that July night ... was the young William Makepeace Thackeray' (Monchard Bishop, 1956, 'Emily Fotheringay and Ellen Ternan', *Times Literary Supplement* (27 January): 60).

TERRY, John Skally (d. 1953) He was a contemporary and friend of Thomas Wolfe at Chapel Hill, North Carolina, and graduated in 1918; he became Assistant Professor of English at New York University. In the 1930s he was a neighbour of Wolfe's in Brooklyn. He edited *Thomas Wolfe's Letters to His Mother* (1943) and was commissioned by Maxwell **Perkins** to write a biography of Wolfe, but he died, leaving no trace of it.

JERRY ALSOP in Thomas Wolfe, *The Web and the Rock* (1939)

'He changed ... John Skally Terry to Jerry Alsop' (F.C. Watkins, 1957, *Thomas Wolfe's Characters: portraits from life*, Norman, Okla., p. 91).

THACKERAY, Harriet Marian (1840–75) Known as 'Minnie', she was the younger daughter of W.M. and Isabella **Thackeray**. In 1867 she married Leslie **Stephen**. She died in childbirth.

LUCY LAMBERT in W.M. Thackeray, *The Virginians* (1857–9)

'If my young women set their hearts on anything they are pretty sure to get it. I am afraid the 2 Lambert girls in the Virginians are very like them, but of course deny it if anyone accuses me' (to Mrs Baxter, 23 April 1858, reproduced in *The Letters and Private Papers of W.M. Thackeray*, 1946, ed. Gordon N. Ray, Vol. IV, London: Oxford University Press, p. 81).

DOLLY VANBOROUGH in Lady Ritchie, *Old Kensington* (1873)

'See A. Thackeray, *Old Kensington* ... for a portrait of Minny Thackeray in the character of Dolly' (Noel Annan, 1984, *Leslie Stephen*, p. 363 n. (to p. 64)).

THACKERAY, Isabella (1818–93) Daughter of Isabella **Shawe**, in 1836 she married W.M. Thackeray in the face of violent opposition from her mother. She was the mother of Anne (later Lady **Ritchie**) and of 'Minnie' (Harriet **Thackeray**). Another daughter was born in 1838, but died when she was eight months old. Isabella was diagnosed as schizophrenic after Minnie was born, and in 1840, after two attempts at suicide, she was confined in a *Maison de santé* in Paris, while the children were also sent to Paris to live with their grandmother.

CHARLOTTE BAYNES in W.M. Thackeray, *The Adventures of Philip* (1861–2)

'We know only that Charlotte Baynes, her counterpart in Thackeray's rendering of this episode from his life in *Philip*, frets herself into a serious illness, until .. . her mother . . . abandons her opposition [to the marriage]' (Gordon N. Ray, 1952, *The Buried Life*, p. 19).

AMELIA SEDLEY in W.M. Thackeray, *Vanity Fair* (1847–8)

'You know you are only a piece of Amelia – My Mother is another half: my poor little wife *y est pour beaucoup*' (to Mrs Brookfield, 30 June 1848, reproduced in *The Letters and Private Papers of W.M. Thackeray*, 1945, ed. Gordon N. Ray, Vol. II, London: Oxford University Press, p. 394). '. . . and after all I see on reading over my books, that the woman I have been perpetually describing is not you nor my mother but that poor little wife of mine, who now does not care 2d for anything but her dinner and her glass of porter' (to the same, 14 October 1848, ibid., p. 440). *See also* **Brookfield**, Jane; **Carmichael-Smyth**, Anne.

THACKERAY, Mary Ann (1818–79) Daughter of George Thackeray, Provost of King's College, Cambridge: after his death in 1850, she lived in Portman Square, London, and entertained lavishly.

CATHERINE SLOPER in Henry James, *Washington Square* (1881)

The story of her engagement to Henry **Kemble** was told to Henry James by Fanny **Kemble** on the day of her death, 20 February 1879. *See under* **Kemble**, Henry.

THACKERAY, William Makepeace (1811–63) English novelist. Born in Calcutta, he was brought to England in 1816 and was educated at Charterhouse and at Trinity College, Cambridge, but left without taking his degree. He spent four years as an art student in Paris before marrying Isabella Shawe (**Thackeray**, above) and returning to England in 1836 to work as a journalist. His early work, written under various pseudonyms, was comparatively unsuccessful and it was with novels such as *Vanity Fair* (1847) – originally, like all his great novels, a monthly serial – that he found success and fame. He worked on *Punch* from 1942 until 1854, when he became Editor of the *Cornhill Magazine*.

HENRY ESMOND in W.M. Thackeray, *The History of Henry Esmond* (1852)

'I wish the new novel wasn't so grand and melancholy – the hero is as stately as Sir Charles Grandison . . . a handsome likeness of an ugly son of yours' (to Mrs Carmichael-Smyth, 17–18? November 1851, reproduced in *The Letters and Private Papers of W.M. Thackeray*, 1945, ed. Gordon N. Ray, Vol. II, London: Oxford University Press, p. 814). The parallels between Thackeray's boyhood, the boyhood of Esmond, and his relationship with Mr and Mrs **Brookfield** as reflected in Esmond's relationship with Lord and Lady Castlewood, are examined in ch. VI of Gordon Ray, 1952, *The Buried Life*.

PHILIP FIRMIN in W.M. Thackeray, *The Adventures of Philip* (1861–2)

'[The hero of Philip] so [Thackeray] told George Smith, follows "pretty much the career of WMT in the first year of his ruin and absurdly imprudent marriage"' (Gordon N. Ray, 1955, *Thackeray: a biography*, Vol. I: *The Uses of Adversity, 1811–1846*, London: Oxford University Press, p. 186).

HENRY GOWAN in Charles Dickens, *Little Dorrit* (1855–7)

'As Hesketh Pearson points out, Gowan is not a portrait of Thackeray, but he is a rendering of the attitude of Thackeray toward both life and art . . . which Dickens found distasteful' (Edgar Johnson, 1953, *Charles Dickens* Vol. II, p. 392).

ELIAS HOWE in Charles Lever, *Roland Cashel* (1850)

'When Lever described him in the person of Elias Howe of *Roland Cashel* as being "large and heavily built, but neither muscular nor athletic", Thackeray ruefully admitted that this was "*un portrait assez fidèle*"' (Gordon Ray, 1958, *Thackeray: the age of wisdom*, p. 77).

ARTHUR PENDENNIS in W.M. Thackeray, *The History of Pendennis* (1848–50)

'Turning over the leaves of "Pendennis" . . . he said, smiling, from time to time: "Yes, it is very like – it is certainly very like." "Like whom, Mr Thackeray?" said my mother. "Oh, like me, to be sure; Pendennis is very like me"' (Lucy Baxter, 1904, Introd. to *Thackeray's Letters to an American Family*, London, pp. 5–6). *See also* **Ellison**, Cuthbert; **Kenney**, C.L.

ST BARBE in Benjamin Disraeli, *Endymion* (1880)

'The parallel between St Barbe's behaviour and actual events forces one to conclude that Thomas Carlyle may have furnished a model for St Barbe's most repellent characteristic, ingratitude. Doubtless Disraeli had Thackeray in mind too, but it seems probable that when he finished the characterization of St Barbe he felt that he had done vengeance on both men' (James D. Merritt, 1968, 'The novelist St Barbe in Disraeli's *Endymion*. Revenge on whom', *The Nineteenth Century* (June): 88; the article discusses the whole question of the original of St Barbe). 'In 1845 Thackeray produced *Punch's Prize Novelists* (collected as *Novels by Eminent Hands*, 1856), his most exuberant burlesques . . . Lever and Disraeli were the authors most offended, and both retaliated with satirical portraits of Thackeray (in *Roland Cashel* and *Endymion*)' (Kathleen Tillotson, 1956, *Novels of the Eighteen-Forties*, pp. 226–7). *See also* **Carlyle**, Thomas; **Hayward**, Abraham.

THALBERG, Irving (1899–1936) Hollywood film producer. In 1927 he married the film actress Norma Shearer.

MILES CALMAN in F. Scott Fitzgerald, 'Crazy Sunday' (1935)

'Miles Calman is an easily recognizable portrait of Thalberg' (H.D. Piper, 1966, *F. Scott Fitzgerald*, p. 263).

THELWALL, John (1764–1834) He began life in his father's business as a mercer, and was later articled to an attorney. He took to writing and was caught up in the Radical and Revolutionary movement; in 1794 he was sent to the Tower with **Hardy** and Home Tooke, charged with High Treason, but he was acquitted. He was a friend of **Coleridge**, Lamb, **Southey** and **Godwin**, and with Richard **Phillips** he founded the *Monthly Magazine*, which he edited at its close. After his release from the Tower, he attempted farming in Brecon, but he failed and returned to London and set up a school for the 'cure of defects in speech' in the Brixton Road. He continued his connection with the *Monthly Magazine* until its sale in 1826.

T—— (THE TEACHER OF ORATORY) in George Borrow, *Lavengro* (1851)

'There is no one . . . whom [the] description can fit but John Thelwall' (A. Boyle, 1952, 'Portraiture in Lavengro, VI: the teacher of oratory – John Thelwall', *Notes and Queries* 197: 38).

THIRKELL, Angela (1890–1960) Novelist. She was the daughter of J.W. Mackail, granddaughter of Edward **Burne-Jones**, and her mother was the first cousin of Rudyard **Kipling**.

LAURA MORLAND in Angela Thirkell, *High Rising* (1933)

'"She is more or less myself", [Mrs Thirkell] wrote to Susan, Lady Tweedsmuir, "but much nicer than I am"' (M. Strickland, 1977, *Angela Thirkell: portrait of a lady novelist*, London: Duckworth, p. 79).

THIRKELL, Lance (b. 1921) Son of Angela Thirkell.

TONY MORLAND in Angela Thirkell, *High Rising* (1933)

'He was based on her own son, Lance' (M. Strickland, 1977, *Angela Thirkell: portrait of a lady novelist*, London: Duckworth, p. 80).

THIRROUL, New South Wales, Australia A small coastal town where D.H. and Frieda **Lawrence** rented a bungalow (**Wyewurk**) in 1922.

MULLUMBIMBY in D.H. Lawrence, *Kangaroo* (1923)

'A collection of Lawrence's letters, edited by . . . Aldous Huxley . . . supplied . . . the information that Lawrence's address had been Thirroul . . . not "Mullumbimby" as related in *Kangaroo*' (R.E. Robinson, 1953, *The Bulletin* (8 April), Sydney; see E. Nehls, 1959, *D.H. Lawrence: a composite biography*, Vol. III, Madison, p. 511).

THOMAS, Carey (1857–1935) Eldest of ten children in a Quaker family in Baltimore, she was educated at Cornell University, and in Leipzig and Zurich. At Leipzig, she met Mary **Gwinn** and became involved in a triangular situation with her and Alfred **Hodder**: the affair is described in Bertrand Russell, 1967, *Autobiography*, Vol. I, pp. 131, 132. In 1885 she was Dean and Professor of English at the newly founded **Bryn Mawr College**; she remained Dean until 1908, and from 1892 to 1922 she was President. In 1915 she inherited half a million dollars from Mary E. Garrett, and thenceforward travelled in Europe, India, and the Sahara, living luxuriously. She was a cousin of Alys Russell, the first wife of

Bertrand **Russell**, and of Mrs Bernard Berenson, and was an early champion of women's rights.

HANNAH CHARLES in Gertrude Stein, *The Making of Americans* (1925)

'[Gertrude Stein] embedded the *Fernhurst* story . . . into the . . . narrative of . . . *The Making of Americans*. At that point she changed the [name] of the headmistress . . . to Hannah Charles' (James R. Mellow, 1974, *The Charmed Circle: Gertrude Stein and company*, London: Phaidon Press, p. 67).

HELEN THORNTON in Gertrude Stein, *Fernhurst* (1971)

'The dean of [the] story is Carey Thomas' (Mellow, op. cit., p. 66).

THOMAS, David (d. 1916) Second Lieutenant, 3rd Battalion, Royal Welsh Fusiliers. Robert **Graves** says of him, 'David Thomas and Siegfried [Sassoon] were the closest friends I made while in France. David was a simple gentle fellow and fond of reading (Graves, 1929, *Goodbye to All That*, p. 229). He was killed on a wiring party.

DICK TILTWOOD in Siegfried Sassoon, *Memoirs of a Fox-Hunting Man* (1928)

'You ask about *The Last Meeting*. It was all experienced and written at Flixécourt – an elegy on my dear David Thomas, whom I called Dick Tiltwood' (Sassoon to Dame Felicitas Corrigan, 25 September 1964, reproduced in D. Felicitas Corrigan, 1973, *Siegfried Sassoon: poet's pilgrimage*, p. 79).

THOMAS, Dylan Marais (1914–53) Welsh poet. Born in Swansea, the son of a schoolmaster, he worked for a time as a reporter on the *South Wales Evening Post*. He published his first collection, *Eighteen Poems*, in 1934, and in 1936 he married Caitlin Macnamara. From 1944 he worked sporadically on a radio script about a Welsh village, which eventually became *Under Milk Wood*, published in 1954. He died from alcohol abuse on a lecture tour of the United States.

PINTO FREEMAN in Joyce Cary, *A House of Children* (1941)

See below.

GULLEY JIMSON in Joyce Cary, *The Horse's Mouth* (1944)

'One evening [in 1948] someone was relating a scrape of Dylan Thomas's. He had been lent a flat, it was said, and being broke had gradually pawned everything in the flat until only the silver was left. He had . . . begun to clean it before taking it to pawn also. His hosts unexpectedly returned. "How thoughtful of you to have cleaned the silver for us. You shouldn't have bothered". Trudy [Cary's wife] shot a mischievous glance at Joyce and he looked uncomfortable. We all thought of Pinto . . . similarly overtaken; and of Gulley's outrageous adventures in the Beeders' flat' (Dan Davin, 1957, *Closing Times*, p. 101). This famous incident happened before the war, and the victim was Lorna Wilmott. She and her newly married husband, the painter Rupert Shephard, spent 1940–2 at Shipston-on-Stour near Oxford. Although they did not then know Cary, they had many friends in common with him who would certainly have repeated the story to him. I owe this note to Rupert Shephard.

See also **John**, Augustus; **Spencer**, Stanley. Thomas appears as Gwilym in Louis MacNeice's *Autumn Sequel* (1954).

THOMPSON, Charles (b. 1898) Born and reared in Key West, Florida, where his family ran a succession of stores. Ernest Hemingway met him in April 1928, on his first visit to Key West; the two became fast friends. Thompson was as passionate a hunter and fisherman as Hemingway, and in 1934 he joined Hemingway on his safari in East Africa.

KARL in Ernest Hemingway, *The Green Hills of Africa* (1935)

'He had changed most of the names . . . Charles Thompson was Karl' (Carlos Baker, 1969, *Ernest Hemingway: a life story*, New York, p. 260). Thompson did indeed have the better luck on this expedition – or possibly he was simply the better shot.

THOMPSON, Jane A teacher of English, reading and poetry at the **Clergy Daughter's School**, Cowan Bridge, at the time when the Brontë sisters were there as pupils.

MISS TEMPLE in Charlotte Brontë, *Jane Eyre* (1847)

'I am . . . applying to Miss "Temple" of Jane Eyre, who is married to a clergyman holding a living on the estate of a friend of mine; I think she may give me some particulars of that terrible Cowan-Bridge time, and possibly some explanations which may modify that account of the school in Jane Eyre' (to George Smith, [July, 1855], *The Letters of Mrs Gaskell*, 1966, ed. J.A.V. Chapple and Arthur Pollard, Manchester, p. 360, letter 256). 'Based on Miss Jane Thompson' (ibid., n.). *See also* **Evans**, Anne.

THOMSON, George (1792–1838) Known as 'Dominie Thamson', he was the son of the minister at Melrose, Midlothian. In 1812 he was tutor to Sir Walter Scott's children; he had a wooden leg and 'an eccentricity about him that [defied] description' (entry for 8 December 1825, in *Journal of Sir Walter Scott*, 1972, ed. W.E.K. Anderson, Oxford). All Scott's efforts to find him a kirk failed.

DOMINIE SAMPSON in Sir Walter Scott, *Guy Mannering* (1815)

'Nor did Dominie Thomson at all quarrel in after-times with the universal credence of the neighbourhood that he had furnished many features for the inimitable personage whose designation so nearly resembled his own' (J.G. Lockhart, 1900, *Memoirs of Sir Walter Scott*, Vol. II, London: Macmillan, p. 226). *See also* **Sanson**, James.

THORBURN, Grant (1773–1863) Born in Midlothian, Scotland, he was the son of a nail maker and practised this trade himself at Dalkeith. In 1794 he emigrated to New York, and in 1796 he established a hardware business; in 1805 he started a seed business, which became one of the largest in the world.

LAWRIE TODD in John Galt, *Lawrie Todd* (1830)

'Well known as the original of John Galt's Lawrie Todd' (Frederic Boase, 1901, *Modern English Biography*, Vol. III, col. 956). In fact he published several books under the name of Lawrie Todd; for example, *Lawrie Todd's Notes on Virginia* (1848).

THORBURN, James A farmer of Juniper Bank, in Liddesdale, Scotland.

DANDIE DINMONT in Sir Walter Scott, *Guy Mannering* (1815)

'Mr John Thorburn . . . the person whom we consider to have stood in the next degree [after Archibald Park] of relationship to Dinmont, was a humorous good-natured farmer . . . the interior economy of Juniper Park is said to have more nearly resembled Charlieshope than did, that of Lewinshope' (Robert Chambers, 1884, *Illustrations of the Author of Waverley*, p. 51). *See also* **Davidson**, James; **Elliott**, Willie; **Laidlaw**, James; **Park**, Archibald.

THOREAU, Henry David (1817–62) American essayist and poet. Born in Concord and graduating from Harvard in 1837, he was briefly a teacher in Concord and then worked with his father, manufacturing lead pencils. In 1839 he began his studies of nature, which continued for the rest of his life. In 1845 he built himself a shanty in the woods by Walden Pond, living there for two years, and this experience formed the basis of his great work, *Walden*. He was a close friend of **Emerson** and associated with the Transcendentalists, including Bronson **Alcott**.

BARTLEBY in Herman Melville, 'Bartleby the Scrivener', *The Piazza Tales* (1856)

'I should like to suggest that the germ of the character . . . came not from Melville's searchings of his own relationship to society . . . but from an external contemporary source, namely Thoreau's withdrawal from society' (Egbert S. Oliver, 1945, 'A second look at "Bartleby"', *College English* 8 (May): 432 (Chicago)).

EGBERT in Herman Melville, *The Confidence Man* (1857)

'Melville introduces the mystic's disciple, Egbert, who is explicitly based on Henry David Thoreau . . . in appearance and in too many details for the resemblance to be accidental. . . . Egbert's discourse on friendship [is] an examination of the cold heartlessness of a section of *A Week on the Concord and Merrimack Rivers*' (Egbert S. Oliver, 1940, 'Melville's picture of Emerson and Thoreau in "The Confidence Man"', *College English* VIII (2): 68–9 (Chicago).

MR HYDE in Louisa M. Alcott, *Little Women* (1868) and sequels

'The naturalist [Mr Hyde] is very plainly . . . Thoreau' (Cornelia Meiggs, 1970, *Louisa M. Alcott and the American Family Story*, p. 69).

DAVID STERLING in Louisa M. Alcott, *Work* (1873)

'David . . . another version of Thoreau' (Martha Saxton, 1978, *Louisa May: a modern biography of L.M. Alcott*, p. 276).

ADAM WARWICK in Louisa M. Alcott, *Moods* (1865)

'The description [of Warwick] is of Thoreau' (Saxton, op. cit., p. 276). 'In the only adult novel of love she ever wrote [*Moods*], she described him as a man with "much alloy and many flaws; but beneath all defects the Master's eye saw the grand lines that were to serve as models for the perfect man"' (Saxton, op. cit., p. 116).

THORNTON, Charles He was an ex-subaltern in the Blues (Royal Horse Guards) in the 1880s, when the custom for officers in the Brigade of Guards was to wear coloured smoking jackets when messing in the Guards Club. One evening, he appeared in a black one; according to Compton Mackenzie, this was the first appearance of the dinner-jacket. By 1919, he had spent almost all his fortune; he lived in a cottage on Anacapri, where he spent his time playing the piano admirably (he was a former pupil of Clara Schumann). 'Almost the most remarkable figure of our Capri fauna [in 1919]' (Compton Mackenzie, 1966, *My Life and Times: Octave 5, 1915–1923*, p. 157).

ANTHONY BURLINGHAM in Compton Mackenzie, *Vestal Fire* (1927)

'Thornton, whom I painted in *Vestal Fire* as Anthony Burlingham' (ibid.). Described at length under the name of G.H. Townley in Norman Douglas, 1933, *Looking Back*, pp. 67–9).

THORNTON, Eveline Daughter of Ned **Thornton**.

EVELINE HILL in James Joyce, 'Eveline', *Dubliners* (1914)

'[Ned Thornton] was the father of Eveline for whom the story in *Dubliners* is named. . . . Eveline did fall in love with a sailor . . . but instead of leaving him at the pier . . . she settled down with him in Dublin and bore him a great many children' (Richard Ellmann, 1966, *James Joyce*, London: Oxford Paperbacks, p. 43).

THORNTON, Ned A tea taster. From 1894 to 1898 he was a neighbour of the Joyce family in North Richmond Street, Dublin. He was the father of Eveline *Thornton*.

TOM KERNAN in James Joyce, 'Grace', *Dubliners* (1914)

'In "Grace", Mr Kernan is mainly the Joyce's old neighbour, Ned Thornton' (Richard Ellmann, 1982, *James Joyce*, rev. edn, Oxford: Oxford University Press, p. 133 n.). Joyce gives him the initials 'R.J.' in a letter: 'My father's old friend R.J. Thornton ("Tom Kernan") used to tell me about Giuglini flying his big kite on Sandymount strand when he was a boy' (to Constantine P. Curran, 14 July 1937, reproduced in *The Letters of James Joyce*, 1957, Vol. I, ed. Stuart Gilbert, London: Faber & Faber, p. 393).

THORNYCROFT, Agatha (1864–1958) Daughter of Homersham Cox of Tonbridge, in 1884 she married Hamo Thornycroft, the sculptor.

TERESA ('TESS') DURBEYFIELD in Thomas Hardy, *Tess of the d'Urbervilles* (1891)

'Hardy regarded Mrs Thornycroft as the most beautiful of women; she was in some ways his model for Tess' (*One Rare Fair Woman: Thomas Hardy's letters to Florence Henniker, 1893–1922*, 1972, ed. Evelyn Hardy and F.B. Pinion, p. 95 n. 306). 'Uncle Hamo spoke of Hardy in a reserved and reverential way, but I learnt that he and my Aunt Agatha had stayed at Max Gate and had done quite a lot of bicycling in Dorset with Hardy. (Years afterwards, I discovered that he had my aunt's face in mind when describing Tess)' (Siegfried Sassoon, 1945, *Siegfried's Journey, 1916–1920*, p. 13). Sassoon is describing his visit to Hamo Thornycroft at Burford, while on leave in 1916.

THREE TUNS INN, Eastwood, Nottinghamshire A favourite pub of D.H. Lawrence's father, Arthur **Lawrence**.

MOON AND STARS INN in D.H. Lawrence, *Sons and Lovers* (1913)

'The Wakes ground was a cleared space before the Three Tuns Inn (the Moon and Stars of *Sons and Lovers*)' (H.T. Moore, 1960, *The Intelligent Heart: the story of D.H. Lawrence*, Harmondsworth: Penguin, p. 36; originally published 1955, London: Heinemann).

THURAU, Meta (*fl.* 1930) She was Isherwood's landlady in Berlin from December 1930 onwards.

LINA SCHROEDER in Christopher Isherwood, *Mr Norris Changes Trains* (1935) and *Goodbye to Berlin* (1939)

'Christopher's landlady . . . Meta Thurau, appears as Lina Schroeder in both *Mr Norris* and *Goodbye to Berlin*. Of all the chief characters in the two books, this one is least distorted from its original' (Christopher Isherwood, 1977, *Christopher and His Kind*, London: Eyre Methuen, p. 50). In John van Druten's dramatization, *I am a Camera* (1952), her name was changed to Schneider.

THURTELL, John (1794–1824) Son of a prosperous Norwich merchant, he was discharged from the Royal Marines at the end of the Napoleonic wars. He fell in with the London underworld, being especially involved in prize-fighting. In 1822–3 he was overwhelmed by business and gambling losses, and in October 1823 he attempted to solve his problems by murdering, with two accomplices, one William Weare, at Gill's Hill, near St Albans, in Hertfordshire. The murder was inadequately planned and incompetently carried out, and Weare proved to be carrying less than £20 instead of the expected £2,000. Five days after the crime, the perpetrators were arrested; Thurtell was convicted and executed.

THOMAS THORNTON in Bulwer Lytton, *Pelham* (1828)

'Bulwer adopted Thurtell as part model for . . . Tom Thornton' (R.D. Altick, 1970, *Victorian Studies in Scarlet*, New York, p. 28). Thurtell also appears in *Lavengro* (chapter XXIV) and *The Romany Rye* (chapter XLII), unnamed but instantly recognizable, in both.

THYNNE, Cecilia Anne (1826?–79) Known as Lady Edward Thynne. Daughter of Mrs Gore, the novelist, in 1853 she married Lord Edward Thynne, MP for Frome and son of the 2nd Marquess of Bath, becoming his second wife. Macaulay described the match as 'the noosing of a young – or rather a defiant young flirt to an old roué' (*Journal*, Vol. VI, p. 104).

BLANCHE AMORY in W.M. Thackeray, *The History of Pendennis* (1848–50)

'At the train whom do you think I found? Miss Gore who says she is Blanche Amory, amiable (at times), amusing, clever and depraved. She talked and persiflated all the way to London, and the idea of her will help me to a good chapter, in wh. I will make Pen and Blanche play at being in love' (to Mrs Brookfield, 21 August 1850, *The Letters and Private Papers of W.M. Thackeray*, 1946, ed. Gordon N. Ray, Vol. IV, London: Oxford University Press, p. 425). *See also* **Reviss**, Theresa.

THYNNE, John Alexander *See* **Bath**, 4th Marquis of.

TIME MAGAZINE A US periodical founded in 1923 by Henry Robinson **Luce** and Briton Hadden.

PRESENT DAY in John Nixon Brooks, *The Big Wheel* (1949)

'Whenever any of [Luce's employees] wrote a book, [Mrs Luce] would give him a ... copy. ... The collection grew to number several novels that caustically depicted a Luce-like publishing empire' (John Kobler, 1968, *Henry Luce*, p. 258; a footnote lists *The Big Wheel* among these novels).

THE TIMES

THE JUPITER in Anthony Trollope, *The Warden* (1855)

'I had introduced one Tom Towers as being potent among the contributors to the *Jupiter*, under which name I certainly did allude to the *Times*' (Anthony Trollope, 1843, *An Autobiography*, Vol. I, p. 133).

TINCLETON, Dorset A village four miles east of Stinsford.

STICKLEFORD in Thomas Hardy, Wessex novels and tales (1871–95)

Identified on a map prepared by Thomas Hardy which hangs in the Dorset County Museum, Dorchester. *See under* **Abbotsbury**.

TINTAGEL CASTLE, Cornwall A ruined medieval castle associated with the Arthurian legend.

DUNDAGEL in Thomas Hardy, *A Pair of Blue Eyes* (1873)

Identified in F.B. Pinion, 1968, *A Hardy Companion*, London: Macmillan.

TIT-BITS A London weekly paper founded in 1881 and closed in 1984. In December 1890, Arnold Bennett won a competition in it, the prize being 20 guineas.

THE TRIFLER in Arnold Bennett, *The Man from the North* (1898)

'He now began on what he describes as "the humiliating part of my literary career, the period of ... freelancing." He describes the miseries of this very vividly in *A Man from the North*, where Richard Larch also tries to write for *Tit-Bits* (disguised as *The Trifler*)' (Margaret Drabble, 1975, *Arnold Bennett: a biography*, London: Weidenfeld & Nicolson, p. 54).

TIVERTON, Devon A town located fifteen miles north of Exeter.

TIVWORTHY in Thomas Hardy, 'The Romantic Adventures of a Milkmaid' (1913)

Identified in F.B. Pinion, 1968, *A Hardy Companion*, London: Macmillan.

TOD, Willie

TOD GABBIE ('GABRIEL') in Sir Walter Scott, *Guy Mannering* (1815)

'It was in the course of one of these excursions [through Ettrick, in 1805 or thereabouts] that we encountered the ... personage introduced into ... *Guy Mannering* under the name of "Tod Gabbie", although the appellation by which the original passed in the country was "Tod Willie". He was one of those vermin-destroyers who gain a subsistence among the farmers in Scotland by relieving them of foxes, polecats, rats, and such like depredators' (James Skene, 1901, *Memories of Sir Walter Scott*, ed. B. Thomson, p. 34). There follows an account of a foxhunt very closely resembling that in *Guy Mannering*, although the 'huntsman' is a much less sinister, much more dilapidated figure than the Gabriel of the novel.

TODD, Thomas (1799?–1885) Of Frosterley, near Bowes, Yorkshire.

JOHN BROWDIE in Charles Dickens, *Nicholas Nickleby* (1838–9)

'The death is announced of Mr Thomas Todd, of Frosterley. . . . The deceased was by popular acceptation the John Browdie of . . . *Nicholas Nickleby*. Mr Todd was a man of the strictest integrity, [who] was held in esteem by numerous friends' (*Teesdale Mercury* (1 July 1885); see E. Hardy, 1911, 'Yorkshire schools', *The Dickensian* 7 (January): 11). *See also* **Barnes**, John and Richard.

TOLPUDDLE, Dorset A town located two miles east of Puddletown.

TOLCHURCH in Thomas Hardy, *Desperate Remedies* (1871)

Identified in F.B. Pinion, 1968, *A Hardy Companion*, London: Macmillan.

TOLSTOY, Count Leo Nicolaevich (1828–1910) Russian writer. Born on the family estate at Yasnaya Polyana in the Tula province, he was educated privately and studied oriental languages and law at the University of Kagan. In 1851 he joined an artillery regiment in the Caucasus, where his literary career began. He was commissioned in 1854 at the outbreak of the Crimean War and commanded a battery during the defence of Sebastopol (1854–5). He left the army after the war and wrote about his experiences in *Tales of Army Life* and *Sketches of Sebastopol*. In 1862 he married Sophie Andreyevna Behrs and they had thirteen children. In 1901 he was excommunicated by the Holy Synod and denounced worship of Jesus as blasphemy. He condemned everything sophisticated and stylized, including his own works, as worthless, handing over his fortune to his wife and living under her roof as a poor peasant. After a quarrel he left home with one of his daughters, caught a chill and died in a railway siding at Astapovo station, refusing to the last to see his wife.

PETER IVANOVICH in Joseph Conrad, *Under Western Eyes* (1911)

'Peter Ivanovich gives the impression of having been . . . modelled on an actual person, and it may be that Conrad was . . . having a dig at Tolstoy. . . . [A]n allusion in a cancelled passage to Peter Ivanovich as author of "The Resurrection of Yegor" and the "thrice famous Pfennig Cantata" suggests that Conrad at least had Tolstoy in mind' (Jocelyn Baines, 1969, *Joseph Conrad: a critical biography*, p. 372). *See also* **Kropotkin**, Prince.

TONBRIDGE, Kent A town on the upper Medway, now largely residential and in character almost suburban. E.M. Forster lived there and in the neighbouring Tunbridge Wells from 1893 to 1901.

SAWSTON in E.M. Forster, *Where Angels Fear to Tread* (1905) and *The Longest Journey* (1907)

'Tonbridge . . . appears as Sawston in *The Longest Journey* [and *Where Angels Fear to Tread*]' (Wilfred Stone, 1966, *The Cave and the Mountain: a study of E.M. Forster*, London: Oxford University Press, p. 43).

TONBRIDGE SCHOOL, Kent Founded as a free Grammar School in 1533, it became a public boarding school in the mid-nineteenth century under Dr Welldon. E.M. Forster was a pupil there from 1893 to 1897.

SAWSTON SCHOOL in E.M. Forster, *The Longest Journey* (1907)

'Forster's school was Tonbridge, which appears as Sawston in *The Longest Journey*' (Wilfred Stone, 1966, *The Cave and the Mountain: a study of E.M. Forster*, London: Oxford University Press, p. 43).

TOP WITHINS, Yorkshire An Elizabethan farmhouse on the high crest of the moors above Haworth and four miles above **Ponden Hall**, it was the home of the Midgley family. During Emily Brontë's childhood, Robert Heaton VII owned Pondens; his wife, Alice Heaton, was descended from the Midgley family.

WUTHERING HEIGHTS in Emily Brontë, *Wuthering Heights* (1847)

'Withins . . . which Emily made the site of Wuthering Heights' (Winifred Gérin, 1971, *Emily Brontë*, Oxford, p. 32). *See also* **High Sunderland Hall**.

TATUM, Anna She was a member of a Quaker family in Philadelphia and was a graduate of Wellesley College, Massachusetts. She first met Dreiser in 1912, when she was a young woman.

ETTA BARNES in Theodore Dreiser, *The Bulwark* (1946)

'Dreiser obviously used Anna Tatum as the model for Etta' (Richard Lehan, 1974, *Theodore Dreiser: his world and his novels*, Carbondale, Ill.: Arcturis Books, p. 232).

TORQUAY, Devon A large seaside town.

TOR-UPON-SEA in Thomas Hardy, 'A Mere Interlude' (1913)

Identified in F.B. Pinion, 1968, *A Hardy Companion*, London: Macmillan.

TOSTI, Sir Paolo (1847–1916) Composer. Born in Italy, he move to London in 1875, becoming a teacher of singing to the Royal Family in 1880. He was knighted in 1908 and returned to Rome in 1913. His best-known song was *Good-bye*.

SIR TITO LANDI in Ada Leverson, *Love at Second Sight* (1916)

'He was the original of . . . Sir Tito Landi' (Violet Wyndham, 1963, *The Sphinx and Her Circle: a biographical sketch of Ada Leverson, 1862–1933*, London: Deutsch, p. 33).

TOWLE, Mr

MR LOWME in George Eliot, 'Janet's Repentance', *Scenes of Clerical Life* (1857–8)

See under **Anstruther**, Lady.

TOWNE, Elizabeth
She was married to William E. Towne, with whom she was joint Editor of *Nautilus*, a magazine of New Thought published by Carmel. In 1909 the magazine published a short story by Sinclair Lewis called 'The Smile Lady'.

MRS EVANS RIDDLE in Sinclair Lewis, *Elmer Gantry* (1927)

On the publication of *Elmer Gantry*, 'his old editor, Mrs Elizabeth Towne, announced to the press that she was not disturbed by the probability that Lewis had modeled his New Thought female after her' (Mark Schorer, 1961, *Sinclair Lewis: an American life*, New York: McGraw-Hill, p. 477 n.).

TOWNSEND, Francis Everett
(1867–1900) Of California. He advocated old age pensions in the Townsend Plan, and was a supporter of William Lemke, whose presidential candidacy in 1936 was endorsed by Father **Coughlin**.

DR BURGHLIMIT in Dalton Trumbo, *Washington Jitters* (1936)

'Dr Burghlimit, dentist author of the Burghlimit Plan . . . [is an obvious caricature] of Dr Francis E. Townsend' (Joseph Blotner, 1966, *The Modern American Political Novel*, Austin, Tex., p. 132).

TOWNSHEND, Chauncey Hare
(1798–1868) Poet. He took holy orders but seceded from the Church of England. He was deeply interested in clairvoyance and mesmerism, and was a patron of the German clairvoyant, Alexis. Dickens dedicated *Great Expectations* to him ('I never, never was better loved by man than I was by him, I am sure', he said). Townshend appointed Dickens his literary executor, a task which involved preparing for publication *The Religious Opinions of Chauncey Hare Townshend*. He wrote *Facts in Mesmerism*.

COUSIN FEENIX in Charles Dickens, *Dombey and Son* (1846–8)

'I always fancy that I can recognise in "Cousin Feenix" a sketch of the ex-clergyman. . . . Chauncey Hare Townshend had all the gentle amiability and softness of "Cousin Feenix", with a sort of old-fashioned simplicity and aristocratic bearing' (Percy Fitzgerald, 1913, *Memories of Charles Dickens*, p. 317).

MELVIN TWEMLOW in Charles Dickens, *Our Mutual Friend* (1864–5)

'I have a sort of impression that . . . Twemlow was drawn from . . . Townshend' (Percy Fitzgerald, 1905, *The Life of Charles Dickens*, Vol. II, p. 135).

TOYNBEE HALL, Whitechapel, London

EAST END ELEVATION MISSION & PANSOPHICAL INSTITUTE in Arthur Morrison, *A Child of the Jago* (1896)

'The East End Elevation Mission . . . is based on Toynbee Hall' (P.J. Keating, 1971, biog. preface to *A Child of the Jago*, p. 17 n.).

TRAVERS, William A member of Old New York Society and something of a wit, he was one of the founders of the New York Racquet Club in 1873. His daughter Matilda and her husband Walter Gay were close friends of Edith Wharton's and, like her, lived largely in France.

SILLERTON JACKSON in Edith Wharton, *The Age of Innocence* (1920)

'There is, in short, [in the novel] a procession of lively and recognizable ghosts. . . . Egerton Winthrop reappears in the gossipy, snobbish and intelligent Sillerton Jackson, as does William Travers' (R.W.B. Lewis, 1975, *Edith Wharton: a biography*, London: Constable, pp. 430–1). *See also* **Winthrop**, Egerton.

TREBARWITH STRAND, Cornwall Located between Stout Point and Tintagel Head.

BARWITH STRAND in Thomas Hardy, *A Pair of Blue Eyes* (1873)

Identified in F.B. Pinion, 1968, *A Hardy Companion*, London: Macmillan.

TREE, Lady Beerbohm (1863–1937) Born Helen Maud Holt, she married Herbert **Tree** in 1883. She became a distinguished actress, excelling in comedy, and directed His Majesty's Theatre in London from 1902.

LADY BUTCHER in Gilbert Cannan, *Mummery* (1916)

'. . . portraits of a number of the leading figures of the theatre appear . . . loosely disguised' (Diana Farr, 1978, *Gilbert Cannan: a Georgian prodigy*, London: Chatto & Windus, p. 164).

TREE, Sir Herbert Beerbohm (1853–1917) Actor-manager. Educated in Germany, he was the half-brother of Max **Beerbohm** and in 1883 married his second wife, Helen Maud Holt (Lady **Tree**, above). In 1887, Beerbohm became Manager of the Haymarket Theatre in London, and in 1897 he completed the building of Her Majesty's Theatre. Between 1888 and 1914 he produced eighteen of Shakespeare's plays; his productions were lavish and his performances romantic.

SIR HENRY BUTCHER in Gilbert Cannan, *Mummery* (1916)

'. . . portraits of a number of the leading figures of the theatre appear . . . loosely disguised' (Diana Farr, 1978, *Gilbert Cannan: a Georgian prodigy*, London: Chatto & Windus, p. 164).

TREFUSIS, Violet (1894–1972) Daughter of Colonel George and Alice **Keppel**, it was her practice to suggest (misleadingly) that she was the fruit of her mother's long liaison with Edward VII. Between 1918 and 1921 she was engaged in a turbulent love affair with Victoria Sackville-West, whom she had known from childhood, although in 1919 she married Denys Trefusis. From 1929, after the death of her husband, she lived in Paris and was 'a focus of intellectual society and a distinguished novelist'. She wrote indifferently in

French and English. Asked to suggest a title for her memoirs, Nancy Mitford proposed *Here Lies Violet Trefusis*.

EVE DAVENANT in Victoria Sackville-West, *Challenge* (1924)

'Every evening Vita would read to Eve's model the pages which she had written during the day, and Violet loved the game ... suggesting extra touches ... to her own portrait' (Nigel Nicolson, 1973, *Portrait of a Marriage*, p. 151). The novel was printed in England, but never published; the English sheets were bound up and issued in New York in 1924.

LADY MONTDORE in Nancy Mitford, *Love in a Cold Climate* (1949)

'Many of her traits contributed to the character of Lady Montdore' (Harold Acton, 1975, *Nancy Mitford: a memoir*, London: Hamilton, p. 75). 'I've got a luncheon party today. Violet arrived for it yesterday ... I was eating a little bit of fish. I said you MUST go away but she tottered to the table, scooped up all the fish and all the potatoes, left half and threw cigarette ash all over it. I could have KILLED her. Lady Montdore exactly' (Nancy Mitford to Harold Acton, ibid., p. 96).

PRINCESS MAROUSHA ('SASHA') ROMANOVICH in Virginia Woolf, *Orlando* (1928)

'Violet, whom Virginia met once, comes into the book as Sasha, a Russian princess like a fox, or an olive tree' (Nicolson, op. cit., p. 206). 'Tomorrow I begin the chapter which describes Violet and you meeting on the ice' (to Vita Sackville-West, 14 October 1927, reproduced in *The Letters of Virginia Woolf*, 1977, ed. Nigel Nicolson, Vol. III, London: Hogarth Press, p. 430).

TRELAWNY, Edward John (1792–1881) Writer and adventurer. He was a friend of **Shelley** and of **Byron**. He eloped with Augusta, Lady Goring, who was married to Sir Henry Dent Goring of Highden, and later married her.

BORROMEO in William Godwin, *Cloudesley* (1830)

'Trelawny had called on Godwin on May 21, 1828, and he stalks through *Cloudesley* in the person of Borromeo' (*The Journals of Claire Clairmont*, 1968, ed. M.K. Stocking, Cambridge, Mass., p. 416).

HERNAN DE FARO in Mary Wollstonecraft Shelley, *Perkin Warbeck* (1830)

'[H]e appears as Hernan de Faro in *Perkin Warbeck*' (Clairmont, op. cit., p. 416 n. 5).

CAPTAIN JOHN PETER KIRBY in George Meredith, *The Amazing Marriage* (1895)

'[Meredith's] long description of the Old Buccaneer ... is Trelawny to the life' (Margaret Armstrong, 1941, *Trelawny*, London: Robert Hale, p. 338).

TRENT, River

THE FLOSS in George Eliot, *The Mill on the Floss* (1860)

'[On 26 September 1859 George Eliot and G.H. Lewes] were ... bound for Newark and Gainsborough. "Polly wanting to lay the scene of her novel on the Trent ... we took a boat from Gainsborough and rowed down to the Idle, which we ascended on foot some way, and walked back to Gainsborough." At last she had found a river that could provide a plausible flood for the catastrophe in her novel' (Gordon S. Haight, 1968, *George Eliot: a biography*, p. 308; quoting G.H. Lewes, journal entry for November 1969).

TRENTHAM PARK, Staffordshire Seat of the Dukes of Sutherland. H.G. **Wells**'s father was a gardener there at the time of his marriage in 1853.

BRENTHAM in Benjamin Disraeli, *Lothair* (1870)

'The greatest houses I have known are Blenheim, Trentham (the Brentham of Lord Beaconsfield's *Lothair*) and Cliveden' (W.H. Mallock, 1920, *Memoirs of Life and Literature*, London: Chapman and Hall, p. 112).

TREPOV, Dimitri Fedorovich (1855–1906) Russian general and government official. In 1896 he was Chief of the Imperial police in Moscow, and in 1905 he was in command of St Petersburg. The severity of his measures caused a number of strikes throughout Russia.

GENERAL T. in Joseph Conrad, *Under Western Eyes* (1911)

'It ... seems likely that General T—— was intended for General Trepov, a notorious Russian reactionary of that era' (Richard Curl, 1957, *Joseph Conrad and His Characters*, p. 23).

TREVELYAN, Sir Charles Edward (1807–86) 1st Baronet. English administrator. Educated at Charterhouse and at Haileybury, Hertfordshire, he became a writer in the Bengal Civil Service, introducing a new system of admission, by competitive examination, into the Civil Service in 1853. He became Governor of Madras in 1859, but was recalled in 1860 for publicly opposing the financial policy of Calcutta. In 1862 he returned to India as Finance Minister, and as such he carried out great social reforms. He married Hannah, sister of the author Thomas Macaulay, in 1834 and was created Baronet in 1874.

SIR GREGORY HARDLINES in Anthony Trollope, *The Three Clerks* (1857)

'Sir Gregory Hardlines was intended for Sir Charles Trevelyan – as anyone at the time would know who had taken an interest in the Civil Service. "We always call him Sir Gregory", Lady Trevelyan said to me afterwards, when I came to know her and her husband' (Trollope, 1883, *An Autobiography*, Vol. I, p. 149).

TREVELYAN, Sir Charles Philips (1870–1958) 3rd Baronet. Politician. Grandson of Sir Charles Edward **Trevelyan** and of Mark **Philips**, he was educated at Harrow and at Trinity College, Cambridge. He entered Parliament in 1899 and was President of the Board of Education in 1924 and 1929–31.

WILLIE CRAMPTON in H.G. Wells, *The New Machiavelli* (1911)

'In *The New Machiavelli* ... Wells wrote of Willie Crampton (Charles Trevelyan) ... having "no sense of self exposure, the gallant experiments in statement that are necessary for good conversation"' (A.J.A. Morris, 1977, *C.P. Trevelyan, 1870–1958*, Belfast, p. 10).

TRIMLESTON, Robert Barnewall, Lord (d. 1779) 12th Baron. Of Trimlestown, County Meath, Ireland.

COUNT O'HALLORAN in Maria Edgeworth, *The Absentee* (1812)

'O'Halloran probably derives at least in part from Lord Trimleston, a Roman Catholic who kept a similarly exotic household. This peer gave medical treatment to [Richard Lovell Edgeworth's] mother . . . about the year 1754' (Marilyn Butler, 1972, *Maria Edgeworth*, Oxford, p. 378 n. 2).

TRING, Hertfordshire

MAXWELL COURT in Mrs Humphry Ward, *Marcella* (1894)

See under **Ashridge Park.**

TRISTANY, Don Rafael (d. 1899) Aide to Don Carlos. In the 1870s he was a marshal in the Carlist army in Catalonia.

DON RAFFAEL DE VILLAREL in Joseph Conrad, *The Arrow of Gold* (1919)

'In an early draft of *The Arrow of Gold* [Conrad] wrote of Don Rafael Tristany – a name altered in the published version to Don Raffael de Villarel . . . as "a frail little man with a long yellow face . . . an inquisitor, an unfrocked monk"' (Jerry Allen, 1967, *The Sea Years of Joseph Conrad*, London: Methuen, p. 51).

TROLLOPE, Anthony (1815–82) English novelist. Born in London, the son of an unsuccessful lawyer, he was educated at Harrow and Winchester. After living for a time in Belgium, where his father died, he returned to England and was a junior clerk in the General Post Office in London from 1834 until 1841, when he was transferred to Ireland. There he married an English woman, Rose Heseltine, in 1844. He left the Post Office in 1867 after a distinguished career: his most notable achievement was the introduction of the pillar-box. From 1867 to 1870 he edited *St Paul's Magazine*, in which a number of his own books were serialized, and in 1868 he stood unsuccessfully as a Liberal parliamentary candidate for Beverley. In all he wrote forty-seven novels as well as travel books, biographies and various other works; he achieved this by adhering to a strict regime, which apparently involved rising at 5.30 a.m. and writing 3,000 words before breakfast.

JOHNNY EAMES in Anthony Trollope, *The Small House at Allington* (1864)

'To fill out the picture provided in the *Autobiography* [of Trollope's life in London from 1834 to 1841] students rely upon the two . . . characters generally regarded as at least partial self-portraits, Charley Tudor . . . and Johnny Eames' (N. John Hall, 1974, 'Trollope's "Hobbledehoyhood": a new letter', *Notes and Queries* 219: 446).

ARCHIBALD GREEN in Anthony Trollope, 'The O'Conors of Castle Conor' (1861) and 'Father Giles of Ballymoy' (1867)

'As has been said, the autobiographical element in [Trollope's] novels is surprisingly small; but the short stories give from time to time a recognisable glimpse of the author as he appeared to himself. Archibald Green in *The O'Conors of Castle Conor* is certainly the young Trollope, fresh to Ireland and to Irish hospitality . . . and when Green reappears in *Father Giles of Ballymoy* he is again Trollope, this time journeying on some Post Office business' (Michael Sadleir, 1927, *Trollope: a commentary*, London: Constable, pp. 176, 179).

CHARLEY TUDOR in Anthony Trollope, *The Three Clerks* (1857)

See above under JOHNNY EAMES.

SIR THOMAS UNDERWOOD in Anthony Trollope, *The New Heir* (1871)

'Wherever he appears as victim of political wire-pullers, as rebel against their lack of scruple, as waverer from their parroted idealism, Sir Thomas Underwood is Trollope himself. Sir Thomas receives the invitation to stand for Percycross as Trollope himself received the invitation to stand for Beverley.... In every one of these predicaments ... Underwood is Trollope aspiring foolishly to a seat in Parliament' (Sadleir, op. cit., p. 295).

TROLLOPE, Frances Eleanor (1780–1863) Mother of Anthony Trollope.

EMILY DUNSTABLE in Anthony Trollope, *Framley Parsonage* (1861)

'Mrs Trollope ... played a part in *Framley Parsonage* in the familiar figure of Emily Dunstable, of whose humour he managed to convince his readers, although they could not see the play of feature and the mimicry which had delighted Anthony in the old days' (Lily Skiffins and Richard Poate Skiffins, 1946, *The Trollopes*, London, p. 174).

TROUBRIDGE, Una, Lady (1887–1963) Granddaughter of the 1st Lord Monteagle, in 1908 she married Admiral Sir Ernest Troubridge; they separated in 1915 and she met Radclyffe **Hall**, with whom she lived until her death in 1943.

MARY LLEWELLYN in Radclyffe Hall, *The Well of Loneliness* (1928)

'... the purported prototype of the ingénue heroine of ... *The Well of Loneliness*' (Mark Schorer, 1961, *Sinclair Lewis*, New York: McGraw-Hill, p. 790).

TILLY TWEED-IN-BLOOD in Djuna Barnes, *The Ladies Almanack* (1928)

'Una is Tilly-Tweed-in-Blood' (Meryle Secrest, 1974, *Between Me and Life: a biography of Romaine Brooks*, Garden City, NY: Doubleday, p. 335).

TROWER, Harold (1853–1941) Consular Agent on Capri from 1900, he resigned in 1916. In 1906, he published a guide to the island, *Book of Capri*, and in early 1907 he was involved in Norman Douglas's dispute with his wife over the custody of their two sons. Trower, who must certainly have observed the goings-on that resulted from Douglas's sexual proclivities, supported Mrs Douglas, and it appears that he did his best to assemble evidence to support her case in the subsequent lawsuit. However, his efforts were to no avail, and Douglas obtained custody in a case that was heard by Lord Justice Warrington in chambers in March 1907.

FREDDY PARKER in Norman Douglas, *South Wind* (1917)

'He was on Elsa's side, and that in itself was probably enough to secure for him an immortality he could not have desired: a few years later he was to be ... transformed into that superb caricature of British expatriate seediness, Mr

Freddy Parker' (Mark Holloway, 1976, *Norman Douglas*, p. 161). 'From evidence . . . supplied by his niece, it seems that Trower was recognisable in Freddy Parker, and that ND's caricature was not as hugely exaggerated as might have been expected' (ibid., p. 503 n. 46).

TROY TOWN, Dorset A hamlet on the Dorchester Road, located a mile west of Puddletown. It formerly contained an important coaching inn, 'The Buck's Head', which was pulled down in the early 1900s.

Mistover Knap in Thomas Hardy, *The Return of the Native* (1878)

Identified in F.B. Pinion, 1968, *A Hardy Companion*, London: Macmillan.

Roy-Town in Thomas Hardy, Wessex novels and tales (1871–95)

Identified on a map prepared by Thomas Hardy which hangs in the Dorset County Museum, Dorchester. *See under* **Abbotsbury**.

TRUMPINGTON, Cambridgeshire A village on the southern outskirts of Cambridge.

Cherryumpton in Shane Leslie, *The Cantab* (1926)

Identified in a key in the hand of Dr Ivor Ramsay, a Kingsman of the year 1920, and later Dean, laid in a copy of *The Cantab*. *See also* **Cherry Hinton**.

TRURO, Cornwall A cathedral town.

Polchester in Hugh Walpole, *The Cathedral* (1922)

'Polchester was at first based almost wholly on Truro. . . . In later books the town developed characteristics of its own, so that in the end it was as much Hugh's creation as a transcription from life' (Rupert Hart-Davis, 1952, *Hugh Walpole*, p. 145).

Trufal in Thomas Hardy, 'A Mere Interlude' (1913)

Identified in F.B. Pinion, 1968, *A Hardy Companion*, London: Macmillan.

TUBMAN, Harriet (*c.*1821–1913) A fugitive slave from Maryland, she became a leading Abolitionist and a figure in the Underground Railway (the escape route to Canada and freedom).

Hepsey Johnson in Louisa M. Alcott, *Work* (1873)

'Unfortunately her rendition of [Harriet Tubman] in . . . *Work* is dismayingly sentimental' (Martha Saxton, 1978, *Louisa May: a modern biography of L.M. Alcott*, p. 240).

TUNSTALL, Lancashire Located two miles south-west of Cowan Bridge and three miles south of Kirkby Lonsdale. The church, rebuilt *c.*1415, is well spoken of by Nikolaus Pevsner (*North Lancashire*, 1969, (*Buildings of England* series), Harmondsworth: Penguin, p. 248).

Brocklebridge in Charlotte Brontë, *Jane Eyre* (1847)

'*Brocklebridge Church*: Tunstall Church, of which Carus Wilson was the vicar, was attended by the girls from Cowan Bridge' (Margaret Smith (ed.), 1976, *Jane Eyre*, p. 468 n. (to p. 60)).

TUNSTALL, Staffordshire One of the 'Five Towns'.

TURNHILL in Arnold Bennett, *Anna of the Five Towns* (1902)

'Tunstall became Turnhill' (Margaret Drabble, 1975, *Arnold Bennett: a biography*, London: Weidenfeld & Nicolson, p. 4).

TURGOT, Anne-Robert Jacques, Baron de L'Aulne (1727–81) French statesman and economist. From 1761 to 1774 he was Intendant of Limoges, and in 1774 he became Minister of Marine under Louis XVI. From 1774 to 1776 he was the Controller-General of Finance, and introduced wide reforms, but the privileged classes, whose comfort was threatened by the reforms, were successful in having him removed from office after only twenty months. He retired to devote himself to scientific and literary studies, and was a founder of the study of political economy.

MR MONTRESOR in Mrs Humphry Ward, *Lady Rose's Daughter* (1903)

'Turgot is represented by Montresor' (*Athenaeum* (4 April 1903): 430).

TURIN, Papa Proprietor of a roadhouse near Pottsville, Pennsylvania, in the 1920s.

FOXIE LEBRIX in John O'Hara, *Appointment in Samarra* (1934)

'Papa Turin ... had the exotic quality of a Frenchman in a region where Frenchmen were seldom seen ... and he served as physical model for Foxie Lebrix' (Finis Farr, 1974, *O'Hara: a biography*, p. 95).

TURNER, Sir James (1615–c.1686) Soldier and author. Enlisted under Gustavus Adolphus in 1632–4, he later joined the Scottish army, and in 1645 took part in the invasion of England. He accompanied Charles II to the Battle of Worcester in 1651, and he also joined Charles II in Paris. In 1666 he commanded forces in south-west Scotland to crush the Covenanters; he was granted a pension by James II.

DUGALD DALGETTY in Sir Walter Scott, *A Legend of Montrose* (1819)

'It was ... the memoirs of Sir James Turner to which Scott was most indebted for many touches of the portraiture of ... Dugald, and of the scenes in which he is made to figure' (W.S. Crockett, 1912, *The Scott Originals: an account of notables and worthies, the originals of characters in the Waverley Novels*, Edinburgh and London: T.N. Foulis, pp. 275–6). *See also* **Monro**, Robert; **Skene**, Martin.

TURNER, Reginald (1869–1938) Novelist. Illegitimate son of the 1st Lord Burnham, proprietor of the *Daily Telegraph*, he was educated at Hurstpierpoint College and at Merton College, Oxford, where he became the friend of Max **Beerbohm**. He was also a friend of Oscar **Wilde**. He was grotesquely ugly, but he possessed endearing charm and great wit, qualities that are only dimly reflected in his novels. He was resident in Florence for many years.

ALGY CONSTABLE in D.H. Lawrence, *Aaron's Rod* (1922)

'[Lawrence] neatly portrayed . . . Reggie Turner as Algy Constable' (H.T. Moore, 1960, *The Intelligent Heart: the story of D.H. Lawrence*, Harmondsworth: Penguin, p. 325; originally published 1955, London: Heinemann). 'Among the many portraits in *Aaron's Rod* immediately recognizable to those who knew the people is one of Reggie Turner' (Richard Aldington, 1941, *Life for Life's Sake*, p. 376). Max Beerbohm portrayed him as Comus in his essay on laughter in *And Even Now* (1921) and Osbert Sitwell as Algernon Braithwaite in the volume of verse entitled *On the Continent* (1958).

TURNER, William[1] (1749?–1829) Father of J.M.W. Turner (1775–1851), the painter. At the time of his son's birth, he was a barber in Maiden Lane in Covent Garden, London, and was well known in artistic and theatrical circles. He gave up his shop *c*.1800 and devoted himself to helping his son, who said he began and finished his paintings for him by stretching the canvases and varnishing the pictures. He lived with his son, who was devoted to him, until his death.

PAUL SWEEDLEPIPE in Charles Dickens, *Martin Chuzzlewit* (1843–4)

'[Dickens's] uncle [Thomas Barrow, who at that time (1822–3) was living in Gerrard Street, Soho] was shaved by a very odd old barber out of Dean Street, Soho' (John Forster, 1928, *Life of Dickens*, ed. J.W.T. Ley, p. 12). 'This barber may have been the original of Pol Sweedlepipes [sic]' (ibid., p. 22 n. 28). 'Whether William Turner was the prototype of Poll Sweedlepipe the reader must be left to decide for himself . . . he would seem to have strong claims to be considered as the identical barber who shaved Dickens's uncle' (W.J. Carlton, 1951, 'The barber of Dean Street', *The Dickensian* 48 (December): 12). Carlton points out that one of Turner's customers was allegedly Thomas Tomkison, the pianoforte maker of Dean Street, who was a friend of the Dickens family; although Turner had left Maiden Lane by 1822, it is possible that he returned to lodge in Soho at that time, when his son was touring on the European continent, and may well have taken up his trade again. There is just enough personal resemblance between old Turner and old Poll to make the identification plausible. It is certainly engaging.

TURNER, William[2] (1761–1859) Son of William Turner, dissenting minister at Wakefield, Yorkshire, he was educated at Warrington Academy and at Glasgow University. He was the Pastor of the Unitarian Chapel, Hanover Square, Newcastle, from 1782 to 1841, and in 1793 he was the founder of the Literary and Philosophical Society of Newcastle, staying as its Secretary until 1833. He was married twice, and both his wives had connections with Mrs Gaskell. When the latter's father died in 1829, Turner acted as her guardian and she spent the winters of 1829–30 and 1830–1 in his house. George Stephenson, the English railway engineer, was one of his pupils. Turner died in Manchester.

REVD THURSTAN BENSON in Elizabeth Gaskell, *Ruth* (1853)

'Mrs Gaskell [referred] to *Ruth* as her "Newcastle Story", in token of her basing the Rev. Thurstan Benson on her guardian William Turner' (Valentine

Cunningham, 1975, *Everywhere Spoken Against: dissent in the Victorian novel*, Oxford: Clarendon Press, p. 2).

DR TURNER'S SCHOOL, Chiswick Mall, London The school for boys kept by Thackeray's great-uncle and great-aunt, and which he attended in 1818–20.

MISS PINKERTON'S ACADEMY in W.M. Thackeray, *Vanity Fair* (1847–8)

'. . . the site of Miss Pinkerton's academy for young ladies' (*The Letters and Private Papers of W.M. Thackeray*, Vol. I: *1817–1840*, 1945, ed. Gordon N. Ray, London: Oxford University Press, p. 3 n. 4). 'Those filigree iron gates in Chiswick of which he writes when he describes Miss Pinkerton's establishment' (Lady Anne Ritchie, 1898, biog. introd. to *The Works of W.M. Thackeray*, Vol. I: *Vanity Fair*, London: Smith, Elder, p. xv).

TURNWORTH HOUSE, Dorset The house is no longer standing, but it was located near Blandford Forum.

HINTOCK HOUSE in Thomas Hardy, Wessex novels and tales (1871–95)

Identified on a map prepared by Thomas Hardy which hangs in the Dorset County Museum, Dorchester. *See under* **Abbotsbury**.

TURVILLE-PETRE, Francis (1901–42) Son of Oswald Turville-Petre of Bosworth Hall, Leicester, he was educated at Exeter College, Oxford, but left without taking a degree.

AMBROSE in Christopher Isherwood, *Down There on a Visit* (1962)

'In *Down There on a Visit*, Francis appears as a character called Ambrose' (Christopher Isherwood, 1976, *Christopher and His Kind*, New York, p. 23).

TWISS, Horace (1787–1849) Nephew of Mrs Siddons, cousin of Fanny **Kemble**. His mother kept a well-known girls' school at Bath, and in 1817 he married Anne Searle, who had previously been a pupil there. Their only child became the second wife of John Delane, Editor of *The Times* from 1841 to 1879. He was an MP in 1830 and 1831, and was 'one of the readiest and most amusing talkers in the world' (Frances Anne Kemble, 1878, *Record of a Girlhood*, Vol. I, p. 142).

VIVACITY DULL in Benjamin Disraeli, *Vivian Grey* (1826–7)

Identified as H. T—, Esq. in a key given in *The Star Chamber* (24 May 1826): 114; reprinted in *Vivian Grey*, 1904 (centenary edn), ed. Lucien Wolf, Vol. II, pp. 361–2. The full name appears on a copy of the key held in the British Museum. Lucien Wolf concludes that Disraeli was not responsible for the key.

TWYSDEN, Duff, Lady (1892–1938) Née Smurthwaite. Born in Yorkshire, her own account of her ancestry was highly romantic: she claimed to be descended from the Stuarts, and gave her maiden name as Stirling, as apparently did her mother and sister. It seems probable that her father was in fact a Yorkshire wine merchant. She was married briefly to Luttrell Byrom, and then in 1917 she married Sir Roger Twysden, 10th Baronet, with whom she had one son. She was divorced in 1926 and then married Clinton King, a painter from Texas. In

1924 she spent much time with Pat **Guthrie**, but she had a brief love affair with Harold **Loeb**. She was something of a painter and ran an art school in New York with Clinton King in 1934.

BRETT, LADY ASHLEY in Ernest Hemingway, *The Sun Also Rises* (1926)

'Harold Loeb's version of the events on which Hemingway drew for . . . *The Sun Also Rises* does not specifically identify any actual person with the fictional characters. Yet it is clear from his narrative that he associates Lady Duff Twysden with Brett Ashley' (Carlos Baker, 1972, *Hemingway: the writer as artist*, Princeton, p. 93 n. 28). This is one of the identifications about which there has never been a moment's doubt. Hemingway 'set down in one of his note-books seven fragments . . . obviously remembered from remarks that Duff had made' (Carlos Baker, 1969, *Ernest Hemingway: a life story*, New York) and one of them he used : 'We can't do it. You can't hurt people. It's what we believe in in place of God' (compare *The Sun Also Rises*, ch. XIX). Lady Twysden's main objection to the book was that in fact she had not slept with the bullfighter.

IRIS MARCH in Michael Arlen, *The Green Hat* (1924)

'There were evidently rumours that Duff was the model for Iris March. Duff told Loeb that she was not. He still believes that she was in part the model . . . (Loeb to Author). . . . Likewise [Malcolm] Cowley associated her with a green hat and mentioned the belief that she was the heroine of *The Green Hat* (quoted in White, *Studies in the Sun Also Rises*, 1969, p. 108)' (B.D. Sarason, 1972, *Hemingway and the Sun Set*, Washington, DC, p. 101 n. 223). Certainly Michael Arlen was in Paris at the relevant time and knew Lady Twysden, who he is sometimes said to have introduced to Loeb. Duff Twysden was the stuff of which myths are made, but this particular myth was most probably made from Nancy Cunard. *See also* **Cunard**, Nancy.

TYLER, Royall ('Peter') (1884–1953) Scholar and art historian. Educated at Yale, he married Elisina Palamadessi di Castelvecchio, who was previously married to Grant **Richards**. He was a friend of Bernard Berenson and Edith Wharton, and was in Paris during the First World War.

JOHN CRAMPTON in Edith Wharton, *A Son at the Front* (1923)

'Edith told Elisina Tyler . . . that . . . John Crampton . . . was based in part on Elisina's husband' (R.W.B. Lewis, 1975, *Edith Wharton: a biography*, London: Constable, p. 457).

TYNDALL, John (1820–93) Natural philosopher. Born in Ireland, he was a railway surveyor and teacher of mathematics in a girls' school, and then studied physics in England and Germany. He became Professor of Natural Philosophy at the Royal Institution in 1854, and his popular works on science were translated into many different languages and read throughout the world. He was a close friend of T.H. **Huxley**.

MR STOCKTON in W.H. Mallock, *The New Republic* (1877)

Identified in W.H. Mallock, 1920, *Memoirs of Life and Literature*, London: Chapman and Hall, pp. 65–6.

U

UNDERWOOD, Nottinghamshire

NUTTALL in D.H. Lawrence, *Sons and Lovers* (1913)

'Nuttall is Underwood and has nothing to do with the picturesque village . . . which lies on the Nottingham–Eastwood main road' (Ada Lawrence and G. Stuart Gelder, 1931, *Young Lorenzo: early life of D.H. Lawrence*, Florence, p. 274).

UNION FOR SOCIAL JUSTICE

THE LEAGUE OF FORGOTTEN MEN in Sinclair Lewis, *It Can't Happen Here* (1935)

Identified in Arthur M. Schlesinger, 1961, *The Politics of Upheaval (The Age of Roosevelt III)*, p. 89.

UNTERMANN, Ernest He translated *Das Capital* into English in three volumes (1906–9).

ERNEST EVERHARD in Jack London, *The Iron Heel* (1908)

'. . . a composite of Eugene Debs, Ernest Untermann and Jack London' (Joseph Blotner, 1966, *The Modern American Political Novel*, Austin, Tex., p. 151 n. 22). *See also* **Debs**, Eugene; **London**, Jack.

UNWIN, Thomas Fisher (1848–1935) Founder of the publishing house of his name.

POLEHAMPTON in Joseph Conrad and Ford Madox Ford, *The Inheritors* (1901)

'There is also . . . a merciless caricature of Fisher Unwin, Conrad and Hueffer's first publisher, in Polehampton who would seize any pretext to cheese-pare his payments to authors' (Jocelyn Baines, 1969, *Joseph Conrad*, p. 239).

UPDEGRAFF, Allan (1883–1965) Journalist and novelist. He was a friend and contemporary at Yale of Sinclair **Lewis**; they later shared a flat in the Bronx, and in 1906 they both spent a month at **Helicon Hall Colony**. In 1908 he married Edith **Summers**, but they were divorced in 1918; he then married Florence Maule, and later married Dora Miller.

JIM in Harry Kemp, *More Miles* (1926)

'Jim is Updegraff' (Mark Schorer, 1963, *Sinclair Lewis: an American life*, London: Heinemann, p. 190; originally published 1961, New York: McGraw-Hill).

UPDIKE, Wesley Father of John Updike.

GEORGE CALDWELL in John Updike, *The Centaur* (1963)

'I don't mind admitting that George Caldwell was assembled from certain gestures and plights characteristic of Wesley Updike' (John Updike interviewed by C.T. Samuels, quoted in 'The art of fiction, XLIII', 1968, *Paris Review* 12 (45): 91.

UPHAM, Charles Wentworth (1802–75) Unitarian clergyman, congressman, and historian of the Salem witchcraft 'delusion'. He was Associate Pastor of the First Church (Unitarian) in Salem from 1824 to 1844, and in 1848 he turned to politics. He was a member of Congress from 1853 to 1855, and when he retired from political life in 1860 he took to historical research.

JUDGE PYNCHEON in Nathaniel Hawthorne, *The House of the Seven Gables* (1851)

'It seems likely that Upham's reputation as a man will suffer as a result of his having incurred the enmity of Nathaniel Hawthorne. Because of Upham's activity in securing the removal of Hawthorne as surveyor of customs at Salem, the novelist is believed to have drawn, in the character of Judge Pyncheon, a satirical portrait of his opponent' (Randall Stewart, 1956, *Dictionary of American Biography*, Vol. XIX, London: Oxford University Press, s.v. Upham, C.W.).

UPPARK, South Harting, Sussex The residence of the Fetherstonhaugh family; Sarah **Wells**, H.G. Wells's mother, was housekeeper for Miss **Fetherstonhaugh** in the 1880s.

BLADESOVER in H.G. Wells, *Tono-Bungay* (1909)

'In a novel of mine . . . *Tono-Bungay*, I have made a little picture of Uppark as "Bladesover", and given a glimpse of its life below stairs' (H.G. Wells, 1934, *Experiment in Autobiography: discoveries and conclusions of a very ordinary brain since 1866*, London: Victor Gollancz, Cresset Press, p. 53).

UPRISING OF THE TWENTY THOUSAND The first full-scale battle of the five-year labour struggle in the garment industry of New York. In November 1909, a general strike of shirtwaist makers and dressmakers was declared; the strikers, nearly all women, held their picket lines throughout the ensuing winter against thugs hired by the employers. In spite of the hostility of police and magistrates, they won much public sympathy, and after nearly three months they 'won a limited but definite victory'.

UPRISING OF THE THIRTY THOUSAND in James Oppenheimer, *The Nine-tenths* (1911)

'The most nearly complete fictional account of the Uprising appears in . . . *The Nine-Tenths*' (Walter Rideout, 1956, *The American Radical Novel, 1900–1954*, Cambridge, Mass., p. 62).

UPWARD, Edward Falaise (b. 1903) Novelist. Born in Romford, Essex, and educated at Repton, where he was a contemporary of Isherwood, and at Corpus Christi College, Cambridge, where they remained friends. He worked closely with Isherwood when they both began to write. He was a member of the Communist Party during the 1930s, and contributed to *New Country* and *New Writing*. He became a schoolteacher.

CHALMERS in Christopher Isherwood, *Lions and Shadows* (1938)

'Edward Upward (who is called "Allen Chalmers" in *Lion and Shadows*) . . .' (Christopher Isherwood, 1977, *Christopher and His Kind*, London: Eyre Methuen, p. 42).

URQUHART, David (1805–77)   Politician. Educated on the European continent and at Oxford, in 1827 and 1828 he took part in the Greek war of independence. In 1835–8 he was Secretary at the Embassy at Constantinople and in 1847–52 he was MP for Stafford. He introduced the Turkish bath to England, and a description of his lavishly oriental establishment at Watford, complete with Turkish bath, will be found in Lord Lamington, 1906, *In the Days of the Dandies* (pp. 58–75).

SIDONIA in Benjamin Disraeli, *Coningsby* (1844)

'The eccentric Mr Urquhart, who furnished some of the traits for . . . "Sidonia"' (Walter Sichel, 1904, *Disraeli: a study in personality and ideas*, London: Methuen, p. 122). *See also* **Disraeli**, Benjamin; de **Rothschild**, Adolph; de **Rothschild**, Baron James Mayer; de **Rothschild**, Lionel.

URQUHART, Francis Fortescue (1868–1934)   Son of David **Urquhart**, from whom he inherited the chalet in the Haute Savoie where he entertained generations of undergraduates, and the nephew of Chichester **Parkinson-Fortescue**, Lord Carlingford. Known as 'Sligger', he was a Fellow of Balliol College, Oxford, and was a legendary figure.

EMERALD UTHWART in Walter Pater, 'Emerald Uthwart' (1892)

'It was said that Pater, who had met Urquhart as an undergraduate, modelled on him his description of "Emerald Uthwart"' (obituary notice, *The Times* (19 September 1934): 12).

V

VALE, Samuel (1797?–1848) Low comedy actor. He played in the provinces and at the Coburg Theatre, and later transferred to Covent Garden. He was recognized as an actor of very genuine ability: 'For the richness of his humour he had never been surpassed by recent comedians. . . . He had a mellowness of voice with an unctuousness of utterance which gave his drolleries of expression an unusual value' (E.L. Blanchard, 1882, *The Birmingham Daily Gazette* (9 May); see Cuthbert Bede, 1882, 'Sam Vale and Sam Weller', *Notes and Queries* (6th series) 5 (20 May): 388–9).

SAMUEL WELLER in Charles Dickens, *The Pickwick Papers* (1836–7)

'[Samuel Vale] had [in the 1820s] acquired a provincial reputation by impersonating Simon Spatterdash, a person who indulged in novel whimsical comparisons. . . . From Samivel Vale, as he was styled by his Surrey admirers, to Samivel Veller is not a very abrupt transition, and it may therefore, not be thought a perfectly unlikely supposition that [Dickens] found a suggestion for . . . Pickwick in the sayings of the droll actor' (Bede, op. cit.). Simon Spatterdash was a character in the operetta *The Boarding-House*, by Simon Beazley, first produced at the Lyceum Theatre, London, in March 1811. His humour consisted of such witticisms as '"Come on", as the man said to his tight boot'. *See also* **Frazier**, Richard.

VALENCIA, Venezuela

SULACO in Joseph Conrad, *Nostromo* (1904)

'We are, by the end of *Nostromo*, familiar . . . with the main features of the town of Sulaco, but it is Captain Mitchell's conducted tour of the city . . . at the end of the novel that draws the city together. . . . For most of the details given here, Conrad drew upon Eastwick's account of the city of Valencia. (See Edward Eastwick, *Venezuela: or Sketches of life in a south American Republic*, 1878, ch. IX, p. 176 ff.)' (Norman Sherry, 1971, *Conrad's Western World*, Cambridge, p. 199). 'Conrad made no use of his passing contact with Venezuela' (Jerry Allen, 1967, *The Sea Years of Joseph Conrad*, London: Methuen, p. 33).

VALPY, Richard (1754–1836) A native of Jersey, he was educated in both France and England, and from 1781 to 1830 he was a very successful as Headmaster of **Reading School**, where he introduced the performance of Greek plays, as described in Miss Mitford's *Belford Regis* (1832). Thomas **Talfourd** was his pupil.

DR STRONG in Charles Dickens, *David Copperfield* (1849–50)

'Talfourd dedicated his Greek tragedy *Ion* to Dr Valpy. . . . The dedication is almost a blueprint for Dr Strong' (P.F. Skottowe, 1969, 'Thomas Talfourd and *David Copperfield*', *The Dickensian* 65 (January): 30). *See also* **Birt**, John; **Wallace**, George.

VAN DER ELST, Mrs

ESMÉE STAINFORTH in John Prebble, *Brute Streets* (1954)

'[*Brute Streets*] too gave us a libel problem, since one of the central characters was based upon Mrs Van der Elst' (Frederick Warburg, 1973, *All Authors are Equal*, p. 269).

VAN VECHTEN, Carl (1880–1964) Journalist, novelist and photographer.

Born in Cedar Rapids, Iowa, he became a close friend of Alice B. Toklas and Gertrude **Stein**, whose most able interpreter he was. 'His writings were the *vade mecum* of sophisticated New Yorkers. He continued to edit an imaginary Yellow Book of his own' (Harold Acton, 1948, *Memoirs of an Aesthete*, p. 239).

PAUL VAN VLEECK in Thomas Wolfe, *The Web and the Rock* (1939)

'[In] the character Van Vleeck . . . he pilloried Carl Van Vechten as the author of "books about tattooed duchesses . . . and negro prize fighters who read Greek"' (R.S. Kennedy, 1962, *The Window of Memory: the literary career of Thomas Wolfe*, Chapel Hill, NC, p. 17 n. 17).

PETER WHIFFLE in Carl Van Vechten, *Peter Whiffle: His Life and Works* (1922)

'He had his doubts about the works of his contemporaries as expressed in his fictionalized autobiography, *Peter Whiffle*' (Linda Simon, 1978, *The Biography of Alice B. Toklas*, p. 90).

VANDEN BERG, Henry J. Distinguished surgeon at Grand Rapids, Michigan.

ANGUS DUER in Sinclair Lewis, *Arrowsmith* (1925)

Identified in Mark Schorer, 1961, *Sinclair Lewis: an American life*, New York: McGraw-Hill, p. 418.

VANDERBILT, Emily (d. 1935) She was the cousin of the Bradley Martin who

in 1897 gave a ball in New York costing $369,200. In 1923 she married William Henry Vanderbilt, but they were divorced in 1925; her second husband was Sigourney Thayer, the theatrical producer, and her third was Raoul Whitfield, the novelist. In June 1928 she met Aline **Bernstein** on a voyage to Europe, and they became friends. She also developed an affection for Wolfe. She committed suicide.

AMY CARLETON in Thomas Wolfe, *You Can't Go Home Again* (1940)

'The picture of "Amy Carleton" (Emily Davies Vanderbilt who used to come to our apartment in Paris – do you remember?), with the cracked grey eyes and the exactly reproduced speech, is just simply perfect. She tried hard to make Tom – *sans succès* – and finally ended by her own hand in Montana in 1934 in a lonely ranch house' (to his daughter, December 1940, reproduced in *The Letters of F. Scott Fitzgerald*, 1964, ed. Andrew Turnbull, London: Bodley Head, pp. 100–1).

VANE, Lord Harry George, 4th Duke of Cleveland (1803–91) Known as

Lord Harry Vane until his succession to the title in 1864, he was MP for South Durham and later for Hastings. He married Catherine Lucy Wilhelmina, widow of Archibald, Lord Dalmeny, in 1854. The Dukedom became extinct upon his death.

LORD GEORGE CRAMLEY in W.M. Thackeray, 'Notes on the North What-d'ye-Callem Election' (1841)

Identified in *Letters and Private Papers of W.M. Thackeray*, 1945, ed. Gordon N. Ray, Vol. II, London: Oxford University Press, p. 27 n. 49.

VASCONCELOS, José (1882–1959) Mexican educationalist and writer. He was Head of the National University of Mexico from 1920 to 1924, and was Minister of Education from 1920 to 1925. He was forced into exile by President Plutarco Calles, but returned and became Director of the Biblioteca Nacional. He was to have entertained D.H. Lawrence at a luncheon party in 1923, but it failed to come off; Lawrence left Mexico City the next day.

DON RAMÓN CARRASCO in D.H. Lawrence, *The Plumed Serpent* (1926)

'In Mexico [Lawrence] had found no true "leader", and for his Don Ramón he apparently had to borrow aspects of the career and personality of José Vasconcelos' (H.T. Moore, 1976, *The Priest of Love: a life of D.H. Lawrence*, rev. edn, Harmondsworth: Penguin, p. 503; originally published 1955 as *The Intelligent Heart: the story of D.H. Lawrence*, London: Heinemann). *See also* **Dibrell**, John.

VAUGHAN, Father Bernard (1847–1922) Social reformer. Brother of Cardinal **Vaughan**. He was well known for his preaching, organization and work among the poor. In 1883 he worked in Manchester, and in 1899 he worked at Jesuit House in Farm Street, London. He preached a series of sermons on the 'sins of society'.

FATHER PURDON in James Joyce, 'Grace', *Dubliners* (1914)

'Father Purdon . . . is based upon Father Bernard Vaughan, and as Stanislaus Joyce notes, the name was given him sarcastically because Purdon Street was in the brothel area' (Richard Ellmann, 1982, *James Joyce*, rev. edn, Oxford: Oxford University Press, p. 133 n.).

VAUGHAN, Cardinal Herbert Alfred (1832–1903) Elder brother of Father Bernard **Vaughan**. He was educated at Stonyhurst, Belgium, Downside and Rome, and was ordained in 1854: 'resolving to found missionary college in England, sailed for Caribbean Sea to collect funds, 1863' (*The Dictionary of National Biography*, London: Oxford University Press). In 1868 he bought the *Tablet*, which he edited until 1871. From 1872 until 1892, he was the Bishop of Salford, and in 1884 he started the Voluntary Schools Association. He was the Archbishop of Westminster from 1892 to 1903, and became Cardinal in 1893. He built Westminster Cathedral, the foundation stone of which was laid in 1895.

CARDINAL COURTLEIGH in F.W. Rolfe, *Hadrian VII* (1904)

'Cardinal Courtleigh (Vaughan)' (Shane Leslie, 1923, 'Frederick Baron Corvo', *The London Mercury* 8 (47): 514).

VAUGHAN, Margaret ('Madge') (1869–1925) Daughter of John Addington **Symonds**. Virginia Woolf, her first cousin, was infatuated with her during adolescence. In 1898 she married W.W. Vaughan, who was Headmaster of Giggleswick from 1904 to 1910, Wellington from 1919 to 1921, and Rugby from 1921 to 1931.

Sally Seton (Lady Rossiter) in Virginia Woolf, *Mrs Dalloway* (1925)

'V[irginia] told me the history of her early loves – Madge Symonds who is Sally in *Mrs Dalloway*' (V. Sackville-West, entry for 29 September 1928, in *Journal of Travel with Virginia Woolf*; see Quentin Bell, 1972, *Virginia Woolf*, Vol. I, p. 61 n.).

von VELTHEIM, Franz, Baron According to Norman Douglas, he 'turned up on Capri about the year 1903'; Douglas goes on to describe him as having shot one of the Joel brothers in South Africa, and later receiving 'a thundering sentence' for attempted blackmail of the surviving Joel (see Norman Douglas, 1933, *Looking Back*, p. 418).

Mühler (alias Retlow) in Norman Douglas, *South Wind* (1917)

'It was Veltheim whom I had in mind when . . . I invented the character of Mühler alias Retlow' (ibid., p. 420).

VENABLES, George Stovin (1810–88) Son of Richard Venables, Archdeacon of Carmarthen. He was a close friend of Thackeray, whose nose he broke during a fight at Charterhouse when they were contemporaries there. He was a Fellow of and Tutor at Jesus College, Cambridge. In 1836 he was called to the Bar and became Queen's Counsel in 1863. From 1855, he contributed anonymously almost every week to the *Saturday Review*. He was a friend of **Tennyson**.

Tom Towers in Anthony Trollope, *The Warden* (1855)

'[Venables] certainly sat for Tom Towers' (T.H. Escott, 1906, 'Anthony Trollope: an appreciation and reminiscence', *Fortnightly Review* (NS) 80 (December): 1097.

George Warrington in W.M. Thackeray, *The History of Pendennis* (1848–50)

'Morton McMichael, Jr. ("Thackeray's Visit", *Philadelphia Press*, June 12, 1887) notes that Thackeray, in discussing *Pendennis* at a dinner party in Philadelphia in 1856, "mentioned that Warrington . . . was drawn from an old school chum of his. . . . He spoke with great affection of the man, and said that it was he who at school had given him the broken nose"' (*The Letters and Private Papers of W.M. Thackeray*, Vol. I: *1817–1840*, 1945, ed. Gordon N. Ray, London: Oxford University Press, p. 207 n. 88). *See also* **Crawford**, G.M.

VENKATARAMAN, Maharshi A guru whom W. Somerset Maugham encountered during his travels in India in 1938.

Shri Ganesha in W. Somerset Maugham, *The Razor's Edge* (1944)

'In *A Writer's Notebook* Maugham describes "The Yogi", the holy man who in "The Saint" (*Points of View*) he identifies as the Maharshi Venkataraman. . . . [His] experience with the yogi provided the inspiration for Larry's guru, Shri Ganesha' (R.L. Calder, 1972, *W. Somerset Maugham and the Quest for Freedom*, London: Heinemann, p. 242).

VERNIÉ, Paul The doctor in Tahiti who attended **Gauguin** in his last illness and wrote an account of his last days.

DR COUTRAS in W. Somerset Maugham, *The Moon and Sixpence* (1919)

'Dr Paul Vernie ... appears in the novel as Dr Coutras' (Richard A. Cordell, 1969, *Somerset Maugham: a writer for all seasons*, Bloomington and London: Indiana University Press, p. 106).

VERRALL, Arthur Woollgar (1851–1912) Educated at Trinity College, Cambridge, he became a Fellow in 1874. In 1911 he was King Edward VII Professor of English Literature at Cambridge. He edited Aeschylus and Euripides.

DR VERUM in Shane Leslie, *The Cantab* (1926)

Identified in a key in the hand of Dr Ivor Ramsay, a Kingsman of the year 1920, and later Dean, laid in a copy of *The Cantab*.

VIARDOT, Pauline (1821–1910) Operatic singer. She was the daughter of Manuel **García**, and the sister of Maria **Malibran**. She married Louis Viardot, the French journalist; she maintained a *maison à trois* with him and Turgenev for many years.

JOSEPHINE CERINTHEA in Elizabeth Sara Sheppard, *Charles Auchester* (1853)

Identified in an anonymous typed key laid in a copy of the first edition of *Charles Auchester* which is now in the possession of the present author.

VIDAL, Gore (b. 1925) American novelist, essayist and playwright. Born Eugene Luther Vidal, Jun., at the US Military Academy at West Point, where his father was an aeronautics instructor, he was educated at Phillips Exeter Academy and the University of New Hampshire. In 1943 he joined the US Army Reserve Corps and served on army transports in the Aleutian Islands during the Second World War. He is the author of *Myra Breckenridge* (1968), *Burr* (1973) and others.

ARIAL LAVALINA in Jack Kerouac, *The Subterraneans* (1958)

Identified in 'Character key to the Duluoz Legend', in Barry Gifford and Lawrence Lee, 1979, *Jack's Book*, pp. 322–32.

SS VIDAR A steamship based in Singapore, commanded by Captain **Craig**. Conrad signed on as First Mate in August 1887, making five or six voyages before leaving in January 1888.

SOFALA in Joseph Conrad, 'The End of the Tether' (1902)

'An account of the voyages of the *Sofala* in "The End of the Tether" corresponds closely to the voyages of the *Vidar*' (Jocelyn Baines, 1967, *Joseph Conrad: a critical biography*, rev. edn, London: Weidenfeld & Nicolson, p. 91; originally published 1960).

VIDOCQ, François Eugène (1775–1857) French police officer. He was Chief of a small detective force in Paris from 1809 to 1827 and in 1832. He organized a daring robbery and was himself put in charge of the investigation; his part was discovered and he was dismissed from the police force. He died in poverty.

PREFECT G. in Edgar Allan Poe, *The Mystery of Marie Roget* (1842)

'The character of the blundering Prefect G. was undoubtedly drawn from . . . François Vidocq' (Irving Wallace, 1956, *The Fabulous Originals*, p. 166).

VIERTEL, Berthold (1885–1953) Film director. Born in Austria, in 1928 he moved to California, where he directed films for MGM in Hollywood. Isherwood worked with him in London in 1933 on a film called *Little Friend*.

FRIEDRICH BERGMANN in Christopher Isherwood, *Prater Violet* (1945)

'Berthold Viertel appears as "Friedrich Bergmann" in . . . *Prater Violet*"' (Christopher Isherwood, 1977, *Christopher and His Kind*, London: Eyre Methuen, p. 116).

de VILLENEUVE, Léontine (b. 1802) At the age of 25, after reading *La Genie du Christianisme*, she wrote to **Chateaubriand**, then Ambassador in Rome, and they exchanged letters; in the summer of 1829, he journeyed to Canterets, a spa in the Pyrenees where she was taking the waters with her family, to meet her; André Maurois (1938, *Chateaubriand*, Eng. trans., p. 301) suggests that the autobiographical fragment, *Amour et Vieillesse*, recalls this summer.

PAMELA TARN in Aldous Huxley, 'After the Fireworks' (1930)

'The story is an elaboration and emendation of an incident recorded in the letters of Chateaubriand. When he was sixty, a very young girl (Mlle de Villeneuve] at a watering place came and threw herself at his head. He wrote her a most exquisite letter, which is extant. And there the matter ended . . . with my usual sadism, I thought it would be amusing to give it the cruel ending. And as one couldn't use Chateaubriand himself . . . that emotional aridity would have been impracticable to handle – I made the hero one of those people . . . who know how to . . . get something for nothing' (to Mrs Flora Strousse, 14 June 1930, reproduced in *Letters of Aldous Huxley*, 1969, ed. Grover Smith, p. 338).

VILLIERS, Frederick, (afterwards Meynell) (b. 1801) Described by Bulwer Lytton as the natural son of a gentleman [Mr Meynell], he was educated at Eton, and in 1823 attended Trinity College, Cambridge, where he became a close friend of Bulwer Lytton. In 1829 he was MP for Saltash, and in 1835 and 1841 he was returned for Canterbury and Sudbury, respectively; both elections were declared void. He went to live in Italy, and in the latter part of his life he took his father's name of Meynell.

HENRY PELHAM in Bulwer Lytton, *Pelham* (1828)

'The least ambitious man of talent I ever met. Singularly fearless in youth. I have been his second in two duels; and he fought many more . . . much of my idea of Pelham was taken from him. He is now becoming rather a bore' (E. Bulwer Lytton, memorandum dated 1869 attached to a packet of letters from Villiers, reproduced in Edward Bulwer Lytton, Earl of Lytton, 1883, *The Life, Letters and Literary Remains of Edward Bulwer, Lord Lytton*, Vol. I, p. 332).

VINCENT, Sir Edgar (1857–1941) Brother of Sir Howard **Vincent**, in 1890 he married Lady Helen Duncombe (**Vincent**, below). In 1914 he was created 1st Baron D'Abernon. He was Ambassador to Germany from 1920 to 1926.

SIR HORACE SILVESTER in Maurice Baring, 'A Luncheon Party', *Half a Minute's Silence and Other Stories* (1925)

'Most of the guests were people well known in London . . . all, of course, furnished with pseudonyms and so presented that though they were easy to identify no one could have been hurt' (Ethyl Smyth, 1938, *Maurice Baring*, London and Toronto: Heinemann, p. 136).

VINCENT, Lady Helen (1866?–1954) Daughter of the 1st Earl of Feversham, she married Sir Edgar **Vincent**, younger brother of Sir Howard **Vincent**, in 1890. One of the **Souls**, she was the most celebrated hostess of her age and was 'by reason of her outstanding beauty, intelligence and charm, one of the most resplendent figures [in the later Victorian and Edwardian Social World]' (*The Times* (18 May 1954): 8).

LADY THISBE CROWBOROUGH in Max Beerbohm, 'Maltby and Braxton', *Seven Men* (1919)

'Lady Thisbe Crowborough is probably Lady Helen Vincent' (David Cecil, 1964, *Max: a biography*, p. 341).

LADY IRENE SILVESTER in Maurice Baring, 'A Luncheon Party', *Half a Minute's Silence and Other Stories* (1925)

See under **Vincent**, Sir Edgar.

VINCENT, Sir Howard (1849–1908) In the Army until 1873, in 1876 he represented the *Daily Telegraph* in the Russo-Turkish war. He devoted 1877 and 1878 to the examination of European police systems, and in 1878 to 1884 he was the first Director of the Criminal Investigation Department (CID) at Scotland Yard. He was an MP from 1885 to 1908; in 1905 he successfully advocated Acts concerning alien immigration, and in 1906, the appointment of a public trustee. In 1881 Lord Ronald Sutherland Gower met him at a dinner party: 'he works all day' he wrote 'and dances half the night'.

THE ASSISTANT COMMISSIONER in Joseph Conrad, *The Secret Agent* (1907)

'But the character of Howard Vincent comes out . . . in certain aspects of the reigning Assistant Commissioner in the novel' (Norman Sherry, 1971, *Conrad's Western World*, Cambridge, p. 298). *See also* **Anderson**, Sir Robert.

VIVIANI, Emilia Teresa (1801–36) Baptized Maria Teresa Anna Vincenzia Torella, she was the daughter of Niccolo Viviani, Governor of Pisa. In November 1820 she was introduced to Mary Shelley, being at that time confined by her parents in the convent school of St Anna until a marriage could be arranged for her. Of remarkable beauty, she was the inspiration of *Epipsychidion*. In 1821 she married Luigi Bondi, and thenceforth lived in Florence.

CLORINDA in Mary Wollstonecraft Shelley, *Lodore* (1835)

'[I]n the description of Clorinda, it is impossible not to recognise Emilia Viviani' (Mrs Julian Marshall, 1944, *The Life and Letters of Mary Wollstonecraft Shelley*, Vol. II, Norman, Okla., p. 109).

VLADIMIR OF RUSSIA, Marie-Alexander-Elizabeth-Eleanor, Grand Duchess (1854–1920) Daughter of Duke Frederic Francis II of Mecklenburg, in 1874 she married the Grand Duke Vladimir of Russia, son of Alexander II of Russia. She died at Contrexéville, France.

PRINCESS ARDACHEFF in Elinor Glyn, *His Hour* (1910)

'Tamara went to Russia to stay with . . . Princess Ardacheff (the Grand Duchess Vladimir)' (Anthony Glyn, 1968, *Elinor Glyn: a biography*, rev. edn, London: Hutchinson, p. 187: originally published, 1955, London: Hutchinson; the book is dedicated to the Grand Duchess).

VOCE, Mary (d. 1802)

HETTY SORREL in George Eliot, *Adam Bede* (1859)

'In 1839 [George Eliot's] aunt Elizabeth Evans was a visitor at Griff House. . . . [S]he related one of her early experiences. . . . An ignorant girl, named Mary Voce, was accused of poisoning her young child. She was . . . sentenced to be hanged [at Nottingham] . . . two [local Methodists] obtained permission to visit [her] . . . in . . . prison. One . . . was Elizabeth Evans. They remained all night praying and seeking to comfort the poor woman, who at last confessed her guilt. Mrs Evans rode with her in the cart to the gallows. . . . This anecdote . . . is woven into the career of Hetty Sorrel. . . . There is nothing else in common between . . . Mary Voce and . . . Hetty Sorrel' (Charles S. Olcott, 1911, *George Eliot: scenes and people in her novels*, London: Cassell, pp. 43–4; originally published 1910, New York: Thomas Y. Crowell).

VOELCKER, Thea (b. 1906) German artist. A divorcee, in 1936 she met Wolfe, who was in Berlin for the Olympic games; they fell violently in love and spent a stormy month together in the Austrian Tyrol. After his return to America his ardour cooled, and in 1937 they ceased to correspond and he never saw or heard from her again. She married a German who was later killed in the Second World War. She committed suicide.

ELSE VON KOHLER in Thomas Wolfe, *You Can't Go Home Again* (1940)

'. . . Thea Voelcker . . . who stood for the portrait of Else Von Kohler' (R.S. Kennedy, 1962, *The Window of Memory: the literary career of Thomas Wolfe*, Chapel Hill, NC, p. 332 n. 2).

VON KUROWSKY, Agnes (b. 1892) Born in Pennsylvania, her father was a naturalized American citizen of mixed Polish, Russian and German ancestry, while her mother was the daughter of Samuel Holabird, Quartermaster General to the United States Army during the Reconstruction period. She was educated in Washington, DC, and in 1914 trained as a nurse. She went to Europe in 1918 and was on the staff of the American Red Cross hospital in Milan when Ernest Hemingway was taken there in July after being seriously wounded at Fossalta.

He fell deeply in love with her and wanted to marry her, but she eventually refused him and returned to the United States, where she was twice married.

CATHERINE BARKLEY in Ernest Hemingway, *A Farewell to Arms* (1929)

'Ernest remembered Agnes in the creation of Catherine Barkley' (Leicester Hemingway, 1962, *My Brother Ernest Hemingway*, p. 52). 'I found [Bill Smith's] letters from Hemingway, going back to one sent from Milan . . . in Dec. of 1918 in which he spoke of his great love for Ag and how it was the real thing and how they were going to get married. Of course this was the original Catherine in *A Farewell to Arms*, at least partly' (Marion Smith to D. St John, quoted in 'Interview with Hemingway's "Bill Gorton"', in B.D. Sarason, 1972, *Hemingway and the Sun Set*, Washington, DC). By 1955, the house in which Hemingway had lived in the 1940s had become a privately owned museum, and before long the museum tour began making references to Agnes as the prototype of Catherine Barkley. In 1971, in an interview, Agnes von Kurowsky denied the identification, but the museum was still maintaining it a year later (see M.S. Reynolds, 1976, *Hemingway's First War: the making of* A Farewell to Arms, Princeton, NJ: Princeton University Press, pp. 182–3). 'Agnes Von Kurowsky contributes little to Catherine Barkley, other than her presence and her physical beauty' (ibid., p. 219). *See also* **Hemingway**, Hadley; **Hemingway**, Pauline; **Jessup**, Elsie.

LUZ in Ernest Hemingway, 'A Very Short Story', *In Our Time* (1925)

'"A Very Short Story" sketches the love affair and the breakup and summarizes . . . the letter of rejection. As first printed (. . . Paris, 1924) the story used the locale of Milan and the name of "Ag". Later . . . EH changed the locale to Padua and the name to Luz' (Carlos Baker, 1969, *Ernest Hemingway: a life story*, New York, p. 574 n. 'Agnes rejects EH').

VROOMAN, Walter Son of a Populist leader in Missouri, in 1894 he marched in Coxey's Army, comprised of bands of unemployed who marched on Washington, DC, to demonstrate in favour of public works to provide employment. He started a movement ostensibly directed toward expelling all Chinese from American soil, but in fact designed to recruit a secret army to capture the national government. He became insane and died in an institution.

HOOSTMAN in Walter Hurt, *The Scarlet Shadow* (1907)

'Hoostman appears to have as his prototype Walter Vrooman' (Walter Rideout, 1956, *The Radical Novel in the United States, 1900–1954*, Cambridge, Mass., p. 303 n. 15).

W

WAINEWRIGHT, Thomas Griffiths (1794–1847) Art critic, painter and forger. Grandson of Ralph Griffiths, the founder, proprietor and publisher of the *Monthly Review* who also published *Fanny Hill*. He was suspected of having poisoned three relatives who all died suddenly in 1828–30, and in 1837 was sentenced to transportation for life for committing forgery; he died a convict in Tasmania. In 1821 he married Frances Ward, who emigrated to the USA in 1851.

MONSIEUR RIGAUD in Charles Dickens, *Little Dorrit* (1855–7)

'In June 1837 Dickens visited Newgate, with John Forster, George Cattermole, the painter and W.C. Macready, the actor. Macready described the visit [*The Diaries of William Charles Macready, 1833–1851*, 1912, ed. William Toynbee, Vol. I, London: Chapman and Hall, pp. 401–2], mentioning in particular Thomas Griffiths Wainewright . . . "with large, heavy moustaches" . . . whom [Dickens] later drew upon for Julius Slinkton in *Hunted Down*, and Rigaud in *Little Dorrit'* (*Letters of Charles Dickens*, 1965, ed. Madeline House and Graham Storey, Vol. I, Oxford: Oxford University Press, p. 277 n. 2). *See also* **Laçenaire**, Pierre-François; **Napoleon III**.

JULIUS SLINKTON in Charles Dickens, *Hunted Down* (1870)

See above.

HONORÉ GABRIEL VARNEY in Bulwer Lytton, *Lucretia* (1847)

'The character of Varney . . . is based upon Thomas Wainewright, and that of Lucretia Clavering upon his wife' (Victor, Earl of Lytton, 1913, *Life of Edward Bulwer, First Lord Lytton*, Vol. II, p. 86 n. 1). 'I have just heard that Wainewright died recently in the hospital at Hobarton. His latter days in the sick ward were employed, I am told, in blaspheming to the pious patients and in terrifying the timid. I think that he never lived to know the everlasting fame to which he has been damned in "Lucretia"' (Henry P. Smith (of the Eagle Insurance Office) to Sir Edward Bulwer Lytton, 2 May 1849, quoted in ibid., p. 88 n.).

WAITE, Mr London dentist to Honora, Lady Beaufort, Maria Edgeworth's sister.

ST LEGER SWIFT in Maria Edgeworth, *Helen* (1834)

'St Leger Swift was Honora's dentist, Waite' (Marilyn Butler, 1972, *Maria Edgeworth*, Oxford, p. 465).

WAKEFIELD, Yorkshire An industrial town that is now almost a part of the conurbation of Leeds. It was the birthplace of George Gissing.

DUNFIELD in George Gissing, *A Life's Morning* (1888)

'"Dunfield" is Wakefield' (Gillian Tindall, 1974, *The Born Exile*, p. 30).

MIREFIELDS in Morley Roberts, *The Private Life of Henry Maitland* (1912)

Identified in an 'Index of Recurring Pseudonyms' in the 1958 edition of *The Private Life of Henry Maitland*, ed. Morchard Bishop, p. 255.

WALDIE, Ann (1755–1826) Daughter of Jonathan Ormiston of Spittals, Newcastle, who came from a well-known family of North Country Quakers. She was married to George **Waldie**.

RACHEL GEDDES in Sir Walter Scott, *Redgauntlet* (1824)

'[T]he Geddeses, Joshua and Rachel . . . [are] modelled from the Waldies of Hendersyde' (W.S. Crockett, 1912, *The Scott Originals: an account of notables and worthies, the originals of characters in the Waverley Novels*, Edinburgh and London: T.N. Foulis, p. 343). 'I had no occasion for your kind letter to put me in remembrance of my early . . . recollections of your family which began with your excellent and kind grandmother . . . when I was a boy' (to Mrs Charlotte Eaton, 8 June 1831, reproduced in *The Letters of Sir Walter Scott*, 1937, ed. H.J.C. Grierson, Vol. XII, London: Constable, p. 20).

WALDIE, George Of Hendersyde Park, Kelso, Scotland. He married Ann Ormiston (**Waldie**, above).

JOSHUA GEDDES in Sir Walter Scott, *Redgauntlet* (1824)

See under **Waldie**, Ann.

WALDRON, Sir John

EDMUND BRIDMAIN in George Eliot, 'The Sad Fortunes of the Revd Amos Barton', *Scenes of Clerical Life* (1857–8)

See under **Anstruther**, Lady.

WALKER, Edward Michael ('Mickey') (b. 1901) American boxer who challenged Jack **Britton** and won the title of American Welter-weight Champion at Madison Square Garden, New York, on 1 November 1922.

WALCOTT in Ernest Hemingway, 'Fifty Grand', *Men Without Women* (1927)

'Mickey Walker [appears in the story as] Walcott (no first name is given)' (Phillips G. Davies and Rosemary R. Davies, 1965, 'Hemingway's "Fifty Grand" and the Jack Britton–Mickey Walker Prize Fight', *American Literature* 37 (November): 251). The article sets out to prove that the story 'was based upon newspaper accounts of the . . . fight between . . . Jack Britton, and . . . Mickey Walker' (ibid.). *See also* **Leonard**, Benny.

WALKER, Frederick (1840–75) Painter, draughtsman and illustrator. He exhibited at the Royal Academy from 1863 to 1875 and became an Associate of the Royal Academy in 1871.

WILLIAM BAGOT ('LITTLE BILLEE') in George Du Maurier, *Trilby* (1894)

'The character of . . . "Little Billee" [was mainly drawn] from his friend Fred Walker' (J.G. Millais, 1899, *The Life and Letters of Sir John Everett Millais*, Vol. II, p. 281). *See also* **Armstrong**, Thomas.

WALKER, Frederick William (1830–1910) Schoolmaster. He was High Master of Manchester Grammar School from 1859 to 1876 and of St Paul's School, London, from 1876 to 1905.

SUNDAY in G.K. Chesterton, *The Man Who was Thursday* (1908)

'Some Paulines believed he had given Gilbert the first inspiration for the personality of "Sunday"' (Maisie Ward, 1944, *G.K. Chesterton*, London: Sheed & Ward, p. 40).

WALKER, Helen (1711?–91) Daughter of a small farmer of the parish of Irongray, Kirkcudbrightshire. In 1738 her sister Isobel **Walker** was tried for the murder of her illegitimate child. Helen refused to perjure herself on her sister's behalf at the trial and Isobel was condemned to death, whereupon Helen walked to London to present to the Duke of Argyle a petition for Isobel's reprieve, which was granted two days before the date fixed for her execution. In 1831 Scott had a stone raised to Helen's memory in the churchyard at Irongray; he composed the inscription.

JEANIE DEANS in Sir Walter Scott, *The Heart of Midlothian* (1818)

The story of Helen and Isobel Walker was recounted to Sir Walter Scott in a letter sent to him anonymously by Mrs Helen Goldie, of Craigmurie, Dumfries; Mrs Goldie had met Helen Walker, then an old woman, while on holiday at Lincluden, and had learned her story. Her letter was printed in the introduction to the novel: 'I learn from Mrs Gibson that it was from your Mother in law Mrs Goldie that I received the very interesting anonymous favour which enabled me to produce to the public the . . . character of Jeanie Deans as I have christened her most respectable friend Helen Walker' (to Walter Dickson, 27 October 1827, reproduced in *The Letters of Sir Walter Scott*, 1936, ed. H.J.C. Grierson, Vol. X, London: Constable, pp. 297–8). *See also* **Douglas**, Lady.

WALKER, Isobel Condemned to death for the murder of her illegitimate child, she was reprieved after her sister Helen **Walker** presented a petition to the Duke of Argyle. She later married the father of the child she had killed, and they lived at Whitehaven.

EFFIE DEANS in Sir Walter Scott, *The Heart of Midlothian* (1818)

See under **Walker**, Helen.

WALKER, Dr Mary (1832–1919) Physician and advocate of women's rights. She was born in Oswego, New York, and also died there. After training at Syracuse, New York, she practised in Ohio, New York State, and later in Washington.

DR MARY PRANCE in Henry James, *The Bostonians* (1884)

'There seem good grounds for believing that the character of Dr Mary Prance . . . was based on a contemporary of James's, Dr Mary Walker. . . . Like Dr Prance, Dr Walker practised medicine following the Civil War . . . she was best known as a suffragette . . . perhaps the first woman in America to wear men's clothing (special permission is supposed to have been given her by Congress)'

(Robert Emmett Long, 1964, 'A Source for Dr Mary Prance in *The Bostonians*', *The Nineteenth Century* 19 (1): 87).

WALKER, Patrick (b. *c.*1666) A member of the Cameronian Sect, he was the biographer of the Martyrs among the Scottish Covenanters. (He was not connected with Helen or Isobel **Walker**, except for any connection that might be traced by a passionate Scottish genealogist.)

DAVID DEANS in Sir Walter Scott, *The Heart of Midlothian* (1818)

'David Deans exhibits many of the traits of Patrick Walker, Cameronian. . . . Both avowedly and unavowedly, Scott borrowed incidents from him and has frequently appropriated his language and phraseology' (W.S. Crockett, 1932, *The Scott Originals: an account of notables and worthies, the originals of characters in the Waverley Novels*, Edinburgh and London: T.N. Foulis, p. 230).

WALLACE, Captain (1853–80) He became Master of the *Cutty Sark* in 1878. In 1880, the Chief Mate, Sidney **Smith**, killed one of the black seamen on board and Wallace appears to have assisted the murderer to escape to another ship; Wallace committed suicide four days later.

CAPTAIN MONTAGUE BRIERLY in Joseph Conrad, *Lord Jim* (1900)

'I think that Conrad . . . had in mind the story of the *Cutty Sark* . . . the suicide of her master . . . a very young and successful skipper . . .' (Norman Sherry, 1966, *Conrad's Eastern World*, Cambridge, p. 262).

WALLACE, Alfred Russel (1823–1913) Naturalist and traveller. His first journey, in 1848, was a collecting trip up the Amazon. In 1854–62, he voyaged in the Malay Archipelago, and on this expedition he conceived the idea of natural selection as a means of evolution; this resulted in the famous joint paper presented by Darwin to the Linnaean Society in July 1858. In 1862 he returned to England, and in 1869 he published his most important book, *The Malay Archipelago*.

STEIN in Joseph Conrad, *Lord Jim* (1900)

'Strongest of all is the strain of Wallace himself in Stein. It may be that Stein's very appearance was based on Wallace's, for Stein has certain striking physical characteristics which belong to Wallace. . . . It is as a naturalist . . . that Stein owes most to Wallace and *The Malay Archipelago*. . . . In that book is an exact description of the butterfly . . . which Stein was examining when Marlow called' (Florence Clemens, 1939, 'Conrad's favourite bedside book', *South Atlantic Quarterly* 38: 312–13). As far as physical resemblance goes, Norman Sherry points out that Wallace wore a beard, while Stein did not (see Norman Sherry, 1966, *Conrad's Eastern World*, Cambridge, p. 142). *See also* **Allen**, Charles; **Bernstein**, Dr; **Lingard**, Captain William; **Mesman**, Mr.

PETER WILLEMS in Joseph Conrad, *An Outcast of the Islands* (1896)

'In *An Outcast of the Islands* there is a scene in which the outcast, Willem, is greatly embarrassed simply because he is a white man. This scene was based firmly on Wallace's experience, and its use illustrates a peculiarly interesting method of borrowing, occasionally practised by Conrad' (Clemens, op. cit., p. 310). *See also* **De Veer**, Carel.

WALLACE, George (1808–71) He was Headmaster of King's School, Canterbury, from 1832 to 1859, after which he was Rector of Burghclere, Berkshire, until 1871.

DR STRONG in Charles Dickens, *David Copperfield* (1849–50)

'Dickens ... grafted Dr Birt's domestic unhappiness on to the genial temperament of Mr Wallace, Dr Birt's successor' (K.R. Cramp, 1952, 'Dr Strong of Canterbury', *The Dickensian* 48 (June): 119). *See also* **Birt**, John; **Valpy**, Richard.

WALLAS, Graham (1858–1932) Educated at Shrewsbury and at Corpus Christi College, Oxford, he was a member of the **Fabian Society** from 1886 until 1904 and was Professor of Political Science at the London School of Economics from 1914 to 1923. He wrote books on political psychology.

WILLERSLEY in H.G. Wells, *The New Machiavelli* (1911)

'In 1903 Wells and Wallas took a walking trip in the Alps . . . years later Wells incorporated that autumn vacation in *The New Machiavelli*, in which his discussions with Wallas were recorded in the arguments between Remington and Willersley' (N. Mackenzie and J. Mackenzie, 1973, *The Time Traveller: the life of H.G. Wells*, p. 169).

WALLINGTON, Nancy (1766–1838) The widow of John Wallington (d. 1805) of Charlcote, she managed the boarding school in Church Lane, Nuneaton, Warwickshire, that George Eliot attended *c*.1828–32. Her daughter Nancy married James **Buchanan**.

MRS RAYNOR in George Eliot, 'Janet's Repentance', *Scenes of Clerical Life* (1857–8)

See under **Anstruther**, Lady.

WALPOLE, Harriet Bettina Frances, Lady (1820–86) Daughter of Sir Fleetwood Pellew, her mother was the daughter of Lady **Holland** by her first marriage to Sir Godfrey **Webster**. In 1841 she married Horatio William, Lord Walpole (afterwards 4th Earl of Orford), who treated her with grotesquely violent cruelty; from 1846 she lived apart from him in Florence. Dickens described a dinner with her and her mother in 1846 where the other guests were by no means refined and Lady Walpole 'leaned against the mantelpiece . . . put out her stomach, folded her arms, and with her pretty face cocked up sideways and her cigarette smoking away like a Manchester cotton mill, laughed, and talked, and smoked, in the most gentlemanly manner I ever beheld . . . I never saw a woman – not a basket woman or a gipsy – smoke before!' (to John Forster, 11 October 1846, reproduced in *Letters of Charles Dickens*, 1977, ed. Kathleen Tillotson, Vol. IV, Oxford: Oxford University Press, pp. 634–5).

LADY CARDIFF in Ouida, *Friendship* (1878)

'Lady Walpole (by then Countess of Orford) appears under the guise of Lady Cardiff in . . . *Friendship*' (V. Surtees, 1977, *The Lady Lincoln Scandal*, p. 72 n.).

WALPOLE, Sir Hugh Seymour (1884–1941) Novelist. Born in Auckland, New Zealand, he was educated in England. He achieved enormous popularity although serious writers tended to speak of both his works and him with a kind of amused contempt. As a young man he inspired great affection in Henry **James**, and in the 1930s he had a warm, friendly relationship with Virginia **Woolf**. He was an avid collector of bibelots, pictures, books and people, and was a great encourager of young writers.

ALROY KEAR in W. Somerset Maugham, *Cakes and Ale* (1930)

'Also we had a tremendous visitation from Hugh Walpole. If you want a book from *The Times*, get Cakes and Ale. . . . All London is ringing with it. For there poor Hugh is most cruelly and maliciously at the same time unmistakable and amusingly caricatured [as Alroy Kear]. He was sitting on his bed with only one sock on when he opened it. There he sat with only one sock on till next morning reading it. Also, we gathered in tears. He almost wept . . . in telling us . . . "There are things in it that nobody knows but Willie and myself" he said. . . . "And that man has been my dearest friend for 20 years. And now I'm the laughing stock of London. And he writes to say he didn't mean it for me." "Oh but he undoubtedly did that" said Vita [Sackville-West] cheerfully' (to Vanessa Bell, 8 November 1930, reproduced in *The Letters of Virginia Woolf*, 1978, ed. Nigel Nicolson, Vol. IV, London: Hogarth Press, pp. 250–1; the matter in square brackets is Nicolson's addition).

MR POLEHUE in Elinor Mordaunt, *Gin and Bitters* (1931)

'. . . I figure as Mr Polehue' (Hugh Walpole, quoted in Rupert Hart-Davis, 1952, *Hugh Walpole*, p. 323).

WALPOLE, Sir Robert, 1st Earl of Orford (1676–1745) Statesman. Educated at Eton and at King's College, Cambridge, he became Whig MP for Castle Rising, Norfolk, in 1701 and for King's Lynn in 1702. Becoming First Lord of the Treasury and Chancellor of the Exchequer in 1715, he effectively became the first Prime Minister of England when George I withdrew from attending Parliament; he held the office from 1715 to 1717 and from 1721 to 1742. He was created Earl by George II, and was given the residence at 10 Downing Street, London, which has remained the home of each prime minister to the present day.

LORD OLDBOROUGH in Maria Edgeworth, *Patronage* (1814)

'Oldborough . . . is an amalgam of two real men. Some of the episodes in his political career . . . are based . . . on detail from Coxe's *Life of Walpole*' (Marilyn Butler, 1972, *Maria Edgeworth*, Oxford, p. 255). *See also* **Ellenborough**, 1st Baron; **Stuart**, William.

The WALPOLE SOCIETY

THE SIMEON SOCIETY in Shane Leslie, *The Cantab* (1926)

Identified in a key in the hand of Dr Ivor Ramsay, a Kingsman of the year 1920, and later Dean, laid in a copy of *The Cantab*.

WALROND, Theodore (1824–87) Educated at Rugby and at Balliol College, Oxford, he was a close friend of the poets A.H. Clough and Matthew **Arnold**.

In 1848 he was an assistant master at Rugby and from 1850 to 1857 he was a Fellow of Balliol. He was Civil Service Examiner, 1856–64; Secretary to the Board, 1863–75; and Civil Service Commissioner, 1875–87. In 1859 he married Charlotte Grenfell, daughter of R. Grenfell and niece of the author Charles Kingsley's wife, and in 1876 he married Henrietta Louisa Grenfell, daughter of C. Grenfell.

GEORGE ARTHUR in Thomas Hughes, *Tom Brown's Schooldays* (1857)

'Arthur is supposedly a composite of Theodore Walrond, W.P. Adam, and August Orlebar' (Edward C. Mack and W.H.G. Armytage, 1952, *Thomas Hughes: the life of the author of Tom Brown's Schooldays*, London: Ernest Benn, p. 94). Sydney Selfe, in *Chapters in the History of Rugby School* (1910, Rugby, p. 118), states that Arthur's original was in fact Hen Walrond, 'a very religious, lovable boy' who died soon after going to Oxford and was therefore unknown outside his family. *See also* **Adam**, W.P.; **Orlebar**, August.

WALTER, John (1818–94) Newspaper proprietor. Initially a barrister, he was proprietor of *The Times* from 1847 until the year of his death and was the third generation of his family to hold this position. He was an MP from 1847 to 1865 and from 1868 to 1885.

OSWALD MILLBANK in Benjamin Disraeli, *Coningsby* (1844)

'Oswald Millbank . . . as far as he is intended to suggest a real person, stands for John Walter, the heir-apparent of the ruling dynasty of *The Times*.' '[He] . . . was in close relations with Young England, had been a contemporary and friend of Smythe and Manners at Eton, and, like Millbank, had gone to Oxford when they had gone to Cambridge' (W.F. Monypenny, 1912, *Life of Disraeli*, Vol. II, London, p. 202 and n. 2). *See also* **Gladstone**, W.E.

WALTER, Peter[1] (*c*.1663–1746) Of Stalbridge, Dorset. A noted moneylender of unknown parentage, by 1694 he was Clerk to Richard Newman of Fifehead, Magdalen, Dorset, whose niece he married, and in 1695 was appointed his Executor. By 1707 he was Steward to John Holles, Duke of Newcastle, and was an MP 1715–27 and 1728–34. He built up a large fortune by taking up mortgages and then foreclosing on the estates, and was worth £300,000 when he died. He was portrayed by Henry Fielding as 'Peter Pounce' in *The Adventures of Joseph Andrews and his Friend, Mr Abraham Adams* (1742).

TIMOTHY PETRICK I in Thomas Hardy, 'Squire Petrick's Lady' (1891)

Identified in F.B. Pinion, 1968, *A Hardy Companion*, London: Macmillan.

WALTER, Peter[2] (1715–1753) Of Stalbridge, Dorset. Grandson of Peter **Walter**[1], he was Whig MP for Shaftesbury, Dorset, in 1741–7. On his death, he left his property to his brother, ignoring his wife and daughter.

TIMOTHY PETRICK II in Thomas Hardy, 'Squire Petrick's Lady' (1891)

Identified in F.B. Pinion, 1968, *A Hardy Companion*, London: Macmillan.

WALTERS, Catherine ('Skittles') (1839–1920) The most famous courtesan of her period. Probably born near Toxteth docks, Liverpool, she was the daughter of a minor customs official. Her nickname was said to come from early employment in a skittle alley. She may have later worked at a stable as she was a magnificent horsewoman. She arrived in London in 1859 and launched herself in Rotten Row. She became the mistress of the 8th Duke of **Devonshire**, who set her up in Mayfair and settled on her £2,000 a year for life. In 1863 she went to Paris, where she became the mistress of both Lord Hubert de Burgh and Wilfrid Scawen **Blunt**, both of whom were then serving in the British Embassy, and in 1872 she returned to London, settling in South Street, Mayfair, where she remained until 1920. She was visited, in friendship, by Lord Kitchener, **Gladstone**, the Prince of Wales (who continued to call after becoming Edward VII), and her old flames, Blunt and de Burgh (then Lord Clanricarde). She formed her last liaison in 1880, with Gerald de Saumarez, fourth son of the 3rd Baron de Saumarez; he called on her every day and they remained attached to each other until her death, at which he was present. Blunt arranged her burial in the graveyard of the Franciscan monastery at Crawley, Sussex; in later life she was known as Mrs Bailey, and on her tombstone are the letters CWB. Blunt's sonnet sequences, *Love Sonnets of Proteus* (1880) and *Esther* (1895), were addressed to her.

KATE MELLON in Edmund Yates, *Broken to Harness* (1864)

'There was living in those days a good-looking and very fascinating young woman, who rode much to hounds, and whom Landseer had painted as the "Pretty Horsebreaker" . . . and I thought out a plan by which I could utilise her [in a novel], placing her amidst the Mapesbury Stables . . . and . . . the surroundings with which I was familiar' (Edmond Yates, 1884, *Recollections and Experiences*, Vol. II, p. 84). 'The Pretty Horsebreaker' in the novel was Kate Mellon. Landseer's picture was in fact called 'The Shrew Tamed'; described as a portrait of Miss Gilbert, it was said to be a photographic likeness of Skittles. Mapesbury House, Willesden Lane was Yates's house, 'The Den' at Ealing in the novel.

RHODA TEMPEST in Charles Reade, *A Terrible Temptation* (1871)

'[I]n *A Terrible Temptation* . . . the courtesan Rhoda Somerset . . . Reade admitted was suggested by Skittles' (Cyril Pearl, 1955, *The Girl with the Swansdown Seat*, p. 137).

WALTON, Frederick Thomas Granville (1840–1925) Engineer.

FINDLAYSON in Rudyard Kipling, 'The Bridge Builders' (1898)

'I have information from . . . Colonel Granville Walton . . . and . . . his brother, Sir Cusack Walton . . . which make it conclusive that Findlayson was . . . "composite". Bell may have served as the type Kipling wanted, whilst the actual builder of the Kashi Bridge was the father of the Waltons, whose full name was Frederick Thomas Granville Walton' (A.F. Minchin, to the Editor, 1962, quoted in *The Reader's Guide to Rudyard Kipling's Work*, 1965, Sect. III, London: Kipling Society, p. 1333). 'About my father's bridges, Kipling stayed with him while he was building the . . . railway bridge at Benares and we always assumed that he was "Findlayson"' (Colonel Granville Walton, ibid.). *See also* **Bell**, J.R.; **Geddes**, Auckland.

WARD, Mrs Humphry (1851–1920) Mary Augusta. Novelist. Born in Tasmania, she was the daughter of Thomas **Arnold** and granddaughter of the Headmaster of Rugby School; her family returned to England in 1856 and she was educated privately there. She married Thomas Humphry Ward in 1872 and became a contributor to *Macmillan's* and various periodicals. Against women's suffrage, she was the first president of the Anti-Suffrage League and was the founder of the Passmore Edwards Settlement. She was the author of *Marcella* (1894), *Sir George Tressady* (1896) and *The Case of Richard Meynell* (1911). Aldous Huxley was her nephew.

MARCELLA BOYCE in Mrs Humphry Ward, *Marcella* (1894)

'[W]hen she was only nine and a half, she was transferred to a school . . . in Shropshire. . . . But . . . she fought blindly against the restrictions and rules of this new community. . . . In the first chapter of *Marcella* it is all described – the "sulks, quarrels and revolts" of Marcie Boyce (alias Mary Arnold)' (Janet Penrose Trevelyan, 1923, *The Life of Mrs Humphry Ward*, pp. 10–11). *See also* **Webb**, Beatrice.

RACHEL FOXE in Aldous Huxley, *Eyeless in Gaza* (1936)

'Mrs Foxe . . . is recognized by those who knew her as a portrait of his Aunt Marooe [Mrs Humphry Ward]' (Enid Huws Jones, 1973, *Mrs Humphrey Ward*, London: Heinemann, p. 123).

JANE HIGHMORE in Henry James, 'The Next Time' (1898)

'[Mrs Humphry Ward] had written *Bessie Costrell* in a sustained excitement which she took for prophetic afflatus. Henry James told her, fairly plainly, that it was not her best work. That summer [1895] . . . "The Next Time" came out in *The Yellow Book*. "She yearned", says James of Mrs Highmore . . . "to be . . . but of course, only once, an exquisite failure"; but "it was not given to her not to please"' (Huws Jones, op. cit., p. 113). *See also* **Braddon**, Mary Elizabeth.

WARD, John William, 1st Earl of Dudley (1781–1833) An MP from 1802 to 1823, he was created Earl of Dudley in 1827 and was Foreign Secretary in Canning's cabinet in 1827–8. He went mad in 1832.

LORD DALLAS in Lady Caroline Lamb, *Glenarvon* (1816)

Identified in a key found among the papers of John Whishaw, a member of the Holland House circle, printed in *The 'Pope' of Holland House: selections from the correspondence of John Whishaw and his friends, 1813–1840*, ed. Lady Seymour, 1906, p. 151.

LORD SALTREAM in Bulwer Lytton, *Godolphin* (1833)

'[A]ll mention of "Lord Saltream" was expunged from the later editions published over the author's name. . . . His appearance [in the 1st edition, Vol. III, ch. 8 ff.] was unmistakable. Alike his parentage, early circumstances, political opinions and extraordinary behaviour at dinner-tables were described . . . faithfully' (Michael Sadleir, 1933, *Bulwer and His Wife*, London: Constable, p. 318).

WARD, Robert Plumer (1765–1846) Novelist and politician. Known as Robert Ward until 1828, when he took the additional name of Plumer, he was a supporter of **Pitt** and was MP for Cockermouth (1802–6) and Haslemere (1807–23). He was Under-Secretary for Foreign Affairs from 1805 to 1806; Commissioner of the Admiralty from 1807 to 1811; and Clerk of the Ordnance from 1811 to 1823. He wrote three society novels.

MR FLOWERDALE and MR RIVERS in Robert Plumer Ward, *De Vere; or The Man of Independence* (1827)

'Ward drew portraits of himself as the man of imagination [Mr Rivers] and the man of content [Mr Flowerdale]' (M.W. Rosa, 1936, *The Silver-Fork School: novels of fashion preceding 'Vanity Fair'*, New York, p. 68). '[N]ot a little of the charming touches included in the episodes called "the Man of Imagination" and "the Man of Content", might be traced to the actual history of the author himself' (*Literary Gazette* 532 (31 March 1827): 193). Plumer Ward took Okeover, the name of the home of Flowerdale, the Man of Content, from a road book. In 1832 he met and married, as his third wife, Mrs Okeover of this same Okeover Hall.

WARD, Samuel (1814–84) Brother of Julia Ward Howe (the author of *The Battle Hymn of the Republic*) and uncle of F. Marion Crawford, during the period *c*.1865 to 1877 he was prominent as a lobbyist in Washington, DC, for financiers interested in congressional legislation. He is presumed to be author of 'The Diary of a Public Man' (1879), which is about Lincoln before he was president, and was well known as a bon vivant and raconteur in England and on the European continent. He is often referred to in English memoirs and letters of the period as 'Uncle Sam', and was sometimes called 'wicked Sam Ward' to distinguish him from a much more conventional contemporary, Samuel Gray Ward.

HORACE BELLINGHAM in Marion Crawford, *Claudius* (1883)

'F. Marion Crawford portrayed Ward in the character of Horace Bellingham, in *Dr Claudius* (1883)' (*Dictionary of American Biography*, 1956, Vol. XIX, London: Oxford University Press, p. 439).

WAREHAM, Dorset Located on the River Frome, near Poole Harbour.

ANGLEBURY in Thomas Hardy, Wessex novels and tales (1871–95)

Identified on a map prepared by Thomas Hardy which hangs in the Dorset County Museum, Dorchester. *See under* **Abbotsbury**.

WARLOCK, Peter *See* **Heseltine**, Philip.

WARNER, Reuben He was a friend of Scott Fitzgerald and was the leader of the set in which they moved when he was a boy in St Paul, Minnesota.

HUBERT BLAIR in F. Scott Fitzgerald, 'A Night at the Fair' (1957)

'All the Basil stories are based very immediately on Fitzgerald's boyhood experience in St Paul. . . . Their characters are modelled on Fitzgerald and his friends . . . in this story . . . Reuben Warner [is] the model for Hubert Blair' (F.

Scott Fitzgerald, 1958, *Afternoon of an Author*, introd. and notes by Arthur Mizener, p. 23).

WARRE-CORNISH, Blanche (1848–1922) Daughter of the Hon. William Ritchie, Advocate-General of Calcutta, and sister of Sir Richmond **Ritchie**, who was married to Ann **Thackeray**. In 1866 she married Francis Warre-Cornish, who was then a housemaster and was later a librarian before becoming Vice-Provost of Eton (1893–1916). She was remarkable for her inconsequential and frequently disconcerting conversation, often addressed more to herself than her company, and wrote two novels, *Alcestis* (1873) and *Northam Cloisters* (1882). She joined the Church of Rome in the early 1890s. Her daughter Mary married Desmond **MacCarthy**, and her memories of her parents are to be found in *A Nineteenth Century Childhood* (1924).

Mrs Cravister in Aldous Huxley, 'The Farcical History of Richard Greenow' (1920)

'Mrs Warre Cornish . . . was the original of Mrs Cravister' (*Letters of Aldous Huxley*, 1969, ed. Grover Smith, p. 132 n. 121). The portrait gave great offence and Mrs Cornish thought it constituted an abuse of hospitality.

WARREN'S BLACKING WAREHOUSE, London Situated on Hungerford Stairs (now Charing Cross), it was owned by George Lamert, Dickens's cousin, and in 1824 Dickens was employed there pasting and sticking labels on bottles.

Murdstone and Grinby in Charles Dickens, *David Copperfield* (1849–50)

'The wine store of this firm is known to be based on Warren's Blacking Warehouse . . . the labours of the little Dickens and those of the little David were similar – wrapping and labelling bottles' (T.W. Hill, 1943, 'Notes to *David Copperfield*', *The Dickensian* 39: 82).

WARWICK, Frances, Lady (1861–1938) Half-sister of Millicent, Duchess of **Sutherland**, Sybil, Countess **Westmorland**, and Lady Angela **Forbes**. For some years the lover of the Prince of Wales, she lived at Easton Lodge, Essex, which she made into a salon for writers, painters and left-wing politicians.

Countess of Frensham in H.G. Wells, *Mr Britling Sees It Through* (1916)

'[T]he background . . . is Easton, drawn in detail down to Lady Warwick. . . . The disguises are so transparent' (N. MacKenzie and J. MacKenzie, 1973, *The Time-Traveller: the life of H.G. Wells*, London: Wiedenfeld & Nicolson, p. 310).

Lady Tilchester in Elinor Glyn, *The Reflections of Ambrosine* (1902)

'The only comfort in her life was the company of Lady Tilchester (a charming character inspired by Lady Warwick)' (Anthony Glyn, 1968, *Elinor Glyn: a biography*, rev. edn, London: Hutchinson, p. 98; originally published 1955, London: Hutchinson).

WATERLOO ROAD, Burslem, Staffordshire Arnold Bennett's father, Enoch **Bennett**, was born off Waterloo Road, in Pitt Street.

Trafalgar Road in Arnold Bennett, the *Clayhanger* trilogy (1910–16)

'[Waterloo Road] is the Trafalgar Road of the . . . novels. . . . It is a dominant part of [the characters'] environment, as it was of Arnold Bennett's in his early youth' (Reginald Pound, 1952, *Arnold Bennett: a biography*, London: Heinemann, p. 45).

WATERLOW, Sydney (1878–1944) Diplomat. He entered the Diplomatic Service in 1900 and resigned in 1905, and then in 1919 he was employed at the Paris Peace Conference. In 1920 he rejoined the Foreign Office, and in 1926 he was British Minister at, successively, Bangkok, Addis Ababa, Sofia and Athens. He was on the fringe of the Bloomsbury group for many years and, while not yet divorced from his first wife, proposed marriage to Virginia Woolf.

MR S.W. in Virginia Woolf, *Orlando* (1928)

'Mr S.W. was, (if anybody), Sydney Waterlow. How could it have been you?' (to Edward Sackville-West, 21 November 1928, reproduced in *The Letters of Virginia Woolf*, 1977, ed. Nigel Nicolson, Vol. III, London: Hogarth Press, p. 559).

WATERSTON HOUSE, Puddletown, Dorset

WEATHERBURY UPPER FARM in Thomas Hardy, *Far from the Madding Crowd* (1874)

'Bathsheba's "bower" is drawn to some extent from Waterston House' (F.B. Pinion, 1968, *A Hardy Companion*, London: Macmillan, p. 504). '[The] description [of the great barn] is based on the medieval barn at Cerne Abbas' (*Far from the Madding Crowd*, 1978, ed. Ronald Blythe, Harmondsworth: Penguin, p. 483 n. 143). *See also* **Druce Farm**.

WATKINS, Ann She was an editorial assistant in 1909 on *Everybody's*, a magazine in the Butterick empire, when Dreiser was editor of the *Delineator*. Fritz **Krog** conceived a passion for her and then went out of his mind.

EMMANUELA in Theodore Dreiser, 'Emmanuela', *A Gallery of Women* (1929)

'Emmanuela is modelled on Ann Watkins' (Richard Lehan, 1969, *Theodore Dreiser: his world and his novels*, London and Amsterdam: Feffer & Simons, p. 264 n. 12). The short story describes Fritz Krog's attempts to force Ann Watkins to go away with him.

WATKINS, Emma (*fl.* 1852) A country girl from Kingston, Surrey, whose brother was a seller of groundsel. She was betrothed to a sailor. She met Holman **Hunt** when he and **Millais** were staying near Ewell, Surrey, to paint, and returned with them to Chelsea and lodged in the same house. In 1852 she sat for Hunt as the shepherdess in *The Hireling Shepherd* (Manchester Art Gallery); she left London to marry her betrothed.

CALMUCK in Robert Barnabas Brough, 'Calmuck', *Heads and Tails* (1859)

See under **Hunt**, W. Holman.

WATSON, Robert (1746–1838) Born in Elgin, Scotland, he was lamed for life while fighting with the rebels in the American Civil War; he was on friendly terms with George Washington. Upon his return to England he was involved in the Gordon Riots and with the London Corresponding Society (on his deathbed he described himself as Secretary to Lord George Gordon and President of the London Corresponding Society). He was imprisoned as a suspected agent of the revolutionaries in France, and after his release he went to Paris, where he became a tutor in English to the first consul, Napoleon Bonaparte (**Napoleon III**). In 1802–8 he was Principal of the revived Scots College, and after the fall of Napoleon he went to Rome, where in 1817 he achieved his greatest *coup*: for £22 he bought from the Attorney, who had been a confidential agent to the young Pretender's brother, Henry, Cardinal York, the great collection of Stuart papers left by the Cardinal upon his death in 1807. The Vatican seized the papers from him and they were eventually handed over to the Prince Regent and the Library at Windsor Castle. He left Rome and later died at the Blue Anchor Tavern in the Borough, London, penniless and stricken with paralysis, having strangled himself with a bizarre tourniquet contrived from a silk scarf and a steel poker. Colonel Maceroni, formerly aide-de-camp to Murat, attempted to raise a subscription to pay his funeral expenses, but the only contribution was two pounds from Lord **Brougham**.

GASHFORD in Charles Dickens, *Barnaby Rudge* (1841)

'[H]e is the prototype of Gashford' (W. Forbes Gray, 1933, 'The prototype of "Gashford" in *Barnaby Rudge*', *The Dickensian*: 175). Watson was the author of the *Life of Lord George Gordon* (1795), which Dickens consulted while writing the novel and he may well have remembered the report of the inquest on Watson which appeared in *The Times* (22 and 23 November 1838) and the obituary notice in the *Gentleman's Magazine* (February 1839): 327–8.

WATTS, Alan Wilson (1915–73) Philosopher and scholar of Eastern religion. Born in Britain, he settled in the United States in 1938 and was naturalized there in 1943. He is generally supposed to have introduced Zen Buddhism into the USA and was the author of *The Way of Zen* (1957). He was associated with the 'Beat' movement.

ALEX AUMS in *Desolation Angels* (1965), and ARTHUR WHANE in *Big Sur* (1962), both by Jack Kerouac

Identified in 'Character key to the Duluoz Legend', in Barry Gifford and Lawrence Lee, 1979, *Jack's Book*, pp. 322–32.

WATTS, Alfred Eugene (d. 1870 or 1871) The brother of Theodore Watts-Dunton. He lived at Park House in Sydenham, London.

CYRIL AYLWIN in Theodore Watts-Dunton, *Aylwin* (1899)

Identified in T. St E. Hake, 1902, 'Aylwin', *Notes and Queries* (9th series) 9 (7 June): 450–2, and 10 (2 August): 89–91; reprinted in *Aylwin*, 1914 (World's Classics), Oxford, App. II.

WATTS, James Orlando Theodore Watts-Duncan's uncle. 'He lived for many years [a] hermit life, surrounded by his books and old manuscripts. His two great passions were philology and occultism' (T. St E. Hake, 1902, 'Aylwin', *Notes and Queries* (9th series) 10: 90).

PHILIP AYLWIN in Theodore Watts-Dunton, *Aylwin* (1899)

Identified in T. St E. Hake, 1902, 'Aylwin', *Notes and Queries* (9th series) 9 (7 June): 450–2, and 10 (2 August): 89–91; reprinted in *Aylwin*, 1914 (World's Classics), Oxford, App. II.

WATTS-DUNTON, Theodore (1832–1914) Poet and man of letters. Born in St Ives, Cambridgeshire, he was the author of *The Coming of Love* (1897) and is best remembered as the protective friend of **Swinburne**, whom he cared for in his declining years.

HENRY AYLWIN in Theodore Watts-Dunton, *Aylwin* (1899)

'The hero . . . is to some degree an idealized self-portrait' (Lionel Stevenson, 1972, *The Pre-Raphaelite Poets*, Chapel Hill, NC, p. 290).

WAUGH, Alec (1898–1981) Novelist. Born in London, he was educated at Sherborne and was the author of *The Loom of Youth* (1917), which he wrote in less than two months. He subsequently wrote a large number of novels and books of travel. He was the brother of Evelyn **Waugh**, and when he was a prisoner of war during the First World War he was in the same camp as Hugh Kingsmill.

GLAYDE in Hugh Kingsmill, 'The End of the World', *The Dawn's Delay* (1924)

'. . . Glayde, who is Kingsmill's portrait of Alec Waugh' (Michael Holroyd, 1964, *Hugh Kingsmill*, London: Unicorn Press, p. 75).

WAUGH, Arthur (1866–1943) Chairman and Managing Director of the publishing firm of Chapman and Hall. He was the father of Evelyn and Alec **Waugh**.

MR RYDER in Evelyn Waugh, *Brideshead Revisited* (1945)

'The narrator's father is a very fine invention . . . drawn from Arthur Waugh, though . . . the original is much disguised. This is Arthur Waugh as he might have been if he had been selfish, without affection and markedly unpleasant' (Christopher Sykes, 1975, *Evelyn Waugh*, London: Collins, p. 252).

WAUGH, Evelyn Arthur St John (1903–66) English novelist. Born in Hampstead, London, son of Arthur **Waugh** and brother of Alec **Waugh**. He was educated at Lancing and Hertford College, Oxford. In 1925 he became a schoolmaster, beginning an unhappy period in his life, during which he attempted suicide. He gave up teaching in 1927, but the experience provided him with the material for his first novel *Decline and Fall* (1928). After a brief and unsuccessful marriage, he travelled extensively, contributing to various daily newspapers. In 1930 he converted to Roman Catholicism and in 1937 he married Laura Herbert, with whom he had six children, and settled in Gloucestershire. During the war he had a number of postings as a junior officer, out of which experience he produced the *Sword of Honour* trilogy (1952–61), the first of which, *Men at Arms*, won the James Tait Black Prize. At the time of his sudden death he was revered as a successful novelist and great wit. His diaries were published in 1976.

GILBERT PINFOLD in Evelyn Waugh, *The Ordeal of Gilbert Pinfold* (1957)

'Evelyn freely admitted that *The Ordeal of Gilbert Pinfold* was closely autobiographical. He could hardly do otherwise as he had described his experiences in detail to several of his friends. The events occurred between late January and early March 1954. It is significant that in his diaries he refers to the book as his "novel", in inverted commas' (Christopher Sykes, 1975, *Evelyn Waugh*, London: Collins, p. 359). 'The first chapter . . . is unashamedly a self-portrait' (ibid., p. 367).

WEBB, Beatrice (1858–1943) One of nine daughters of Richard Potter, whose fortune was founded on building huts for the armies in the Crimea. She became involved in social questions as the result of acting as rent collector for her father's properties in the East End of London, and in 1892 she married Sidney **Webb**; they worked together in writing, public service and the **Fabian Society**.

ALTIORA BAILEY in H.G. Wells, *The New Machiavelli* (1911)

'Macmillan would have been well aware of the identity of the Baileys. . . . They were only too clearly living portraits of Beatrice and Sidney Webb' (Lovat Dickson, 1969, *H.G. Wells: his turbulent life and times*, p. 187). Macmillan refused to publish the book.

MARCELLA BOYCE in Mrs Humphry Ward, *Marcella* (1894)

'Marcella . . . is similar to Beatrice Potter in her decision to live in the East End to familiarize herself with the living conditions of the workers' (Georgia Dunbar, 1953, 'The Faithful Recorder: Mrs Humphry Ward and the background of her novels', unpublished Ph.D. dissertation, Columbia University, NY, p. 204). *See also* **Ward**, Mrs Humphry.

'AUNT' PLESSINGTON in H.G. Wells, *Marriage* (1912)

'H.G. Wells . . . had guyed the Webbs in *The New Machiavelli*, and he had recently published another novel. I remember Beatrice Webb saying cheerfully: "I'm in it; I'm the woman whose voice is described as 'a strangulated contralto', but *you* are not, Sidney." "Oh yes, I am," said Webb . . . "I'm described as one of those supplementary males often found among the lower crustacea"' (Desmond MacCarthy, 1935, 'Dedication to Clifford Sharp', in *Experience*, p. xiii). George Bernard Shaw told William Archer that Vivie Warren in *Mrs Warren's Profession* (1898) was a portrait of Beatrice Webb.

WEBB, James Watson (1802–84) Journalist and diplomat. An officer in the United States Army since 1818, he resigned his commission in 1827 and acquired the New York *Morning Courier*, which he merged with the *Enquirer* in 1829 and edited until 1861; he then became US Minister to Brazil. He was a great duellist, narrowly escaped imprisonment in 1842, and was a personal friend of **Napoleon III**.

COLONEL DIVER in Charles Dickens, *Martin Chuzzlewit* (1843–4)

'[Colonel Webb is] perhaps recalled in Colonel Diver (. . . ch. 16)' (*Letters of Charles Dickens*, 1977, ed. Kathleen Tillotson, Vol. IV, Oxford: Oxford University Press, p. 13 n. 2).

WEBB, Sidney James (1859–1947) Social reformer and historian. Born in London, the son of an accountant, he graduated LLB at London University in 1885. He was one of the founders of the **Fabian Society** and of the London School of Economics, where he taught public administration from 1912 to 1927. He was a Labour MP from 1922 to 1929. In 1892 he married Beatrice Potter (**Webb**, above).

Oscar Bailey in H.G. Wells, *The New Machiavelli* (1911)

See under **Webb**, Beatrice.

Hubert Plessington in H.G. Wells, *Marriage* (1912)

See under **Webb**, Beatrice.

Paul Sheridan in Emma Brooke, *Transition* (1895)

'Emma Brooke ... daughter of a Cheshire cotton spinner ... served on the Fabian Executive Committee 1893–96, and was the author of several novels, published anonymously, including ... *Transition* ... which contained a fascinating portrait of Sidney Webb' (Bernard Shaw, 1965, *Collected Letters, 1874–1897*, ed. Dan H. Laurence, p. 265 n.).

WEBSTER, Sir Godfrey (1788–1836) He succeeded to the title of 5th Baronet in 1800 after his father's suicide. 'In 1810 [Lady Caroline Lamb's] name began to be mentioned in connection with Lady **Holland**'s son by her first marriage, Sir Godfrey Webster' (Lord David Cecil, 1939, *The Young Melbourne*, p. 144). In 1812 he was MP for Sussex.

William Buchanan in Lady Caroline Lamb, *Glenarvon* (1816)

Identified in a key found among the papers of John Whishaw, a member of the Holland House circle, printed in *The 'Pope' of Holland House: selections from the correspondence of John Whishaw and his friends, 1813–1840*, ed. Lady Seymour, 1906, p. 151.

WEDD, Nathaniel (1864–1940) Born in Tower Hill, London, and educated at City of London School and at King's College, Cambridge, he was a Fellow of King's from 1888 until his death, and in 1906 he married R.E. White, a lecturer at Newnham College, Cambridge. He began as a member of the **Fabian Society** but ended as a fanatical Tory, and remained anti-clerical throughout; he was also anti-aesthete and anti-coterie. He was passionately attached to Italy and its landscape, people and art, and became a friend of Forster during the latter's second year at Cambridge, exercising a strong influence on him.

Mr Jackson in E.M. Forster, *The Longest Journey* (1907)

'Mr Jackson, the enthusiast for the classics who "makes the past live" and knows the difference between "the golden mean and the pinchbeck mean", undoubtedly owes some of his qualities to Nathaniel Wedd' (Wilfred Stone, 1966, *The Cave and the Mountain: a study of E.M. Forster*, London: Oxford University Press, pp. 186–7). *See also* **Smedley**, I.F.

WEEKLEY, Ernest (1865–1954) English philologist. Educated in Berne, Cambridge, Paris and Freiburg im Breisgau, for forty years he was Professor of

French and Head of the Department of Foreign Languages at Nottingham University. In 1899 he married Frieda von Richthofen, later **Lawrence**.

JOHN BEAVIS in Aldous Huxley, *Eyeless in Gaza* (1936)

See below. See also **Huxley**, Leonard.

REVD ARTHUR SAYWELL in D.H. Lawrence, *The Virgin and the Gipsy* (1930)

'Following a principle which I have always used – that the only way of rendering simultaneously the subjective feeling of a person and the objective judgment of other people upon that person is to mingle tragedy with a certain element of extravagance – I introduced the element of philology. This was based upon descriptions given by Frieda Lawrence . . . of her first husband. . . . Treated in a different manner, the character yet has a strong resemblance to the parson in D.H. Lawrence's *Virgin and the Gipsy*, a figure who was actually derived from the same source' (to his stepmother Rosalind Huxley, 30 November 1936, reproduced in *Letters of Aldous Huxley*, 1969, ed. Grover Smith, p. 409).

WEIGHTMAN, William (1814–42) Curate at Haworth in 1839–42, he was known in the Brontë family as 'Celia Amelia'; he died of cholera.

EDWARD WESTON in Anne Brontë, *Agnes Grey* (1847)

'There was "a better side to his character" (the side which won Anne's love and that she portrayed in Edward Weston in *Agnes Grey*)' (Winifred Gérin, 1967, *Charlotte Brontë*, Oxford, p. 168).

WEIMAR, Germany

KALBSBRATEN in *The Confessions of Fitz-Boodle* (1852) and PUMPERNICKEL in *Vanity Fair* (1847–8), both by W.M. Thackeray

'The Pumpernickel of *Vanity Fair* and the Kalbsbraten of *Fitz-Boodle's Confessions*' (*The Letters and Private Papers of W.M. Thackeray*, Vol. I: *1817–1840*, 1945, ed. Gordon N. Ray, London: Oxford University Press, p. 123 n. 20).

WELDON, Thomas Dewar ('Harry') (1896–1958) Philosopher. He was a Fellow of and Tutor at Magdalen College, Oxford, in 1923–58.

LORD FEVERSTONE in C.S. Lewis, *That Hideous Strength* (1945)

'Lewis's old Magdalen foe Harry Weldon was in it, as Lord Feverstone' (Humphrey Carpenter, 1978, *The Inklings*, p. 198).

WELLER, Mary (1804–88) Of Chatham. She was Dickens's nurse from 1817 to 1822, and later married Tom Gibson, a shipwright.

NUPKINS'S MAID in Charles Dickens, *The Pickwick Papers* (1836–7)

Identified in a manuscript list of characters inserted into the copy of Edwin Pugh's *The Charles Dickens Originals* (1912) in the Dexter Collection in the British Library (Dex. 28).

CLARA PEGGOTTY in Charles Dickens, *David Copperfield* (1849–50)

'It was as a child that he saw Mary Weller, who became the Peggotty of *David Copperfield*' (Pugh, op. cit., p. 279).

WELLESLEY, Richard Colley Wellesley, Lord (1760–1842) Brother of the first Duke of **Wellington**. In 1797 he was Governor-General of India, and in 1821–8 and 1833–4 he was Lord Lieutenant of Ireland.

EARL OF MORNTON in Lord Brougham, *Albert Lunel* (1844)

Identified in Brougham's hand in the copy of *Albert Lunel* belonging to Michael Sadleir, formerly in the possession of Frederick Locker, and clearly originally Brougham's own copy.

WELLINGTON, Arthur Wellesley, Duke of (1769–1852) Irish soldier and statesman. Educated at Chelsea, Eton, Belgium and at a military school in Angers. In 1787 he was commissioned as an ensign in the 73rd Foot, rising to captain by transferring through a number of regiments, ending in the 58th Foot. He was Member for Trim in the Irish Parliament from 1790 to 1795. His brother, Lord **Wellesley**, bought him the command of the 33rd Foot and in 1797 the regiment was sent to India. He returned home in 1805, and in 1806 he married Lady Katherine Packenham, with whom he had two sons. From 1806 to 1809 he was MP for Rye, and he was Irish Secretary in 1807. After a number of successful military campaigns, he was created Duke of Wellington in 1814, and emerged the following year as the victor at Waterloo. He was Prime Minister in 1827, after the death of **Canning**, and in 1834 he was elected Chancellor of Oxford University. He retired from public life in 1846.

FIGHTING ATTIE in Bulwer Lytton, *Paul Clifford* (1830)

Identified in a key set out by Rosina Bulwer Lytton, in a letter of 26 May 1830, reproduced in Michael Sadleir, 1968, *Bulwer and His Wife*, pp. 227–8.

DUKE OF MERCINTON in Lady Charlotte Bury, *The Exclusives* (1830)

Identified in *Key to the Royal Novel 'The Exclusives'*, 1830, Marsh & Miller; reproduced in Michael Sadleir, 1951, *XIX Century Fiction*, 2 vols, London: Constable, and Los Angeles: California University Press, pp. 73–4.

COUNT VON SOHNSPEER in Benjamin Disraeli, *Vivian Grey* (1826–7)

Identified as the Duke of W——n in a key given in a pamphlet published in 1827 by William Marsh. This key is discussed by Lucien Wolf in his notes to *Vivian Grey* (1904 (centenary edn), Vol. II, p. 364), with the conclusion that Disraeli was not responsible for the key.

DUKE OF WATERLOO in Benjamin Disraeli, *Vivian Grey* (1826–7)

Identified as Duke of W—— in a key given in *The Star Chamber* (24 May 1826): 114; reprinted in *Vivian Grey*, 1904 (centenary edn), ed. Lucien Wolf, Vol. II, pp. 361–2. The full name appears on a copy of the key held in the British Museum. Lucien Wolf concludes that Disraeli was not responsible for the key.

WELLINGTON HOUSE ACADEMY, London A school situated in Mornington Crescent, on Hampstead Road; Dickens attended as a day boy in 1824–6. It was demolished in February 1964.

SALEM HOUSE in Charles Dickens, *David Copperfield* (1849–50)

'... Wellington House Academy ... drawn upon by [Charles Dickens] ... for Salem House' (*Letters of Charles Dickens*, 1965, ed. Madeline House and Graham Storey, Vol. I, Oxford: Oxford University Press, p. 1 n. 2).

WELLS, Somerset A cathedral town.

FOUNTALL in Thomas Hardy, Wessex novels and tales (1871–95)

Identified on a map prepared by Thomas Hardy which hangs in the Dorset County Museum, Dorchester. *See under* **Abbotsbury**.

WELLS, Mr An English resident of Florence in the 1870s.

SYLVERLEY BELL in Ouida, *Friendship* (1878)

'[E]ven Mr Wells appeared under the name of Mr Sylverley Bell' (Eileen Bigland, 1951, *Ouida: the passionate Victorian*, p. 137). For an account of Mr Wells's part in the drama that formed the basis of *Friendship*, see ibid., p. 135.

WELLS, Catherine Amy ('Jane') (1872–1927) Née Robbins. She was a close friend of Dorothy Richardson, with whom she went to school in Putney, London, and in 1895 she married H.G. Wells, becoming his second wife.

MARY BRITLING in H.G. Wells, *Mr Britling Sees It Through* (1916)

'Mrs Britling is unmistakeably Jane' (N. Mackenzie and J. Mackenzie, 1973, *The Time Traveller: the life of H.G. Wells*, p. 310).

MARGARET REMINGTON in H.G. Wells, *The New Machiavelli* (1911)

'Margaret is a prettification of Jane – a portrait with the patina of remorse over it' (Lovat Dickson, 1972, *H.G. Wells*, Harmondsworth: Penguin, p. 225).

ANN VERONICA STANLEY in H.G. Wells, *Ann Veronica* (1909)

'*Ann Veronica*, when it was written in 1908, was centred on the love-affair he was then having with Amber Reeves.... But ... to the story of Ann Veronica's bid for freedom and the man she wanted in 1908, H.G. attached for all to see the story of Catherine Robbins and himself in 1893' (Dickson, op. cit., pp. 70, 71). *See also* **Blanco White**, Amber.

ALMA WILSON in Dorothy Richardson, *Pilgrimage* (1915–67)

'Jane is Alma' (H.G. Wells, 1969, *Experiment in Autobiography*, p. 557).

WELLS, Frank (1856?–1933) Brother of H.G. Wells. He was apprenticed to a draper in Bromley, London, but gave up the struggle for success early on, finally settling with his parents in a cottage provided by Wells and wandering about the country repairing clocks and peddling watches.

ALFRED POLLY in H.G. Wells, *The History of Mr Polly* (1910)

'There is a touch of my brother about Mr Polly – the character I mean, not the story' (H.G. Wells, 1934, *Experiment in Autobiography: discoveries and conclusions of a very ordinary brain since 1866*, London: Victor Gollancz, Cresset Press, p. 197). *See also* **Wells**, H.G.; **Wells**, Joseph.

WELLS, Herbert George (1866–1946) English writer. Born in Bromley, Kent, the third son of an unsuccessful tradesman and professional cricketer, he worked as a draper's apprentice before becoming a pupil-teacher at Midhurst Grammar School at the age of 18. He won a scholarship to the Normal School of Science at South Kensington and studied biology under T.H. **Huxley**. In 1891 he married Isabel (**Wells**, below), leaving her in 1894 for Catherine ('Jane') Robbins (**Wells**, above), whom he married in 1895 after his divorce from Isabel. He also had numerous affairs, including one with the writer Rebecca **West**, with whom he had a son, Anthony **West**. In 1903 he joined the **Fabian Society**, but soon fell out with his sponsor George Bernard **Shaw**, and with Sidney and Beatrice **Webb**. He saw and warned against the rise of Fascism in *The Shape of Things to Come* (1933), his last novel.

GEORGE BOON in H.G. Wells, *Boon* (1915)

'Boon was what Wells longed to be . . . a thinker with a rigorously intellectual base' (Lovat Dickson, 1969, *H.G. Wells: his turbulent life and times*, p. 243).

HUGH BRITLING in H.G. Wells, *Mr Britling Sees It Through* (1916)

'Before the end of 1914, I had already set to work upon a record of my mental phases, elaborated in a novel, *Mr Britling Sees it Through*. It is only in the most general sense autobiographical . . . Mr Britling is not so much a representation of myself as of my type and class' (H.G. Wells, 1934, *Experiment in Autobiography: discoveries and conclusions of a very ordinary brain since 1866*, London: Victor Gollancz, Cresset Press, p. 670).

GODWIN CAPES in H.G. Wells, *Ann Veronica* (1909)

'. . . the self-portrait of Capes' (Dickson, op. cit., p. 51).

WILLIAM CLISSOLD in H.G. Wells, *The World of William Clissold* (1926)

'[A]t . . . Lou Bastidon . . . I dramatised myself as William Clissold' (Wells, *Autobiography*, op. cit., p. 740).

HORATIO GUBB in Ford Madox Ford, *The Simple Life Limited* (1911)

'His initials, his resemblance to a "Sunfish in outline" . . . his illegitimate child, his lack of a classical education, and his . . . socialist politics recall Wells' (Thomas C. Moser, 1980, *The Life in the Fiction of Ford Madox Ford*, Princeton, p. 95). *See also* **Ford**, Ford Madox; **Pinker**, J.B.

SIR RICHMOND HARDY in H.G. Wells, *The Secret Places of the Heart* (1922)

'. . . Sir Richmond Hardy – as my father is calling himself on this occasion' (Anthony West, 1984, *H.G. Wells: aspects of a life*, p. 87).

J.E. HOOPDRIVER in H.G. Wells, *The Wheels of Chance* (1896)

'In the extended series of Wells's fictional self-portraits, he divided his personality and early life into separate types. Kipps is what Wells would have been if he had possessed no talent whatsoever; Lewisham and George Ponderevo are equipped with his ability in science; Hoopdriver and Polly share the other side of his nature, his creative imagination' (Lionel Stevenson, 1967, *History of the English Novel*, Vol. XI, New York, p. 41).

ARTHUR KIPPS in H.G. Wells, *Kipps* (1905)

'Although ... Kipps's ignorance and the deformity of his accent and the deficiencies of his manner ... are exaggerated compared with those that marked Mr and Mrs Wells ... at Sandgate, there is no doubt that H.G.'s experiences in the drapery at Portsmouth are faithfully reflected in Kipps's at Folkestone, and the building of Spade House is reflected in Kipps's adventures in the same field' (Dickson, op. cit., p. 147).

GEORGE EDGAR LEWISHAM in H.G. Wells, *Love and Mr Lewisham* (1900)

'This ... was to be the first of the long string of novels in which he was to use his own recent experience ... as a quarry for material. ... The novel is not straight-forwardly autobiographical – none of my father's novels were to be that' (West, op. cit., p. 234). '... Well's own story of his student days at South Kensington and the failure of his first marriage' (Dickson, op. cit., p. 105). *See also* **Gregory**, Richard.

MR PARHAM in H.G. Wells, *The Autocracy of Mr Parham* (1930)

'In this ... work he caricatures himself as Mr Parham' (West, op. cit., p. 166).

HERBERT PETT in Ford Madox Ford, *The New Humpty-Dumpty* (1912)

'This is Ford's portrait of H.G. Wells. ... Wells's portrait of Ford as the Bulpington of Blup is mild in comparison with Ford's portrait of him' (Arthur Mizener, 1971, *The Saddest Story: a biography of Ford Madox Ford*, Cleveland: World Publishing, p. 226).

ALFRED POLLY in H.G. Wells, *The History of Mr Polly* (1910)

Mr Polly's experiences in the Port Burdock Drapery Bazaar are clearly based on Wells's memories of life at Rodgers and Denyer of Windsor and at the Southsea Drapery Emporium; but *see also* Frank **Wells**, whose earlier experiences were similar. *See also* **Wells**, Frank; **Wells**, Joseph.

GEORGE PONDEREVO in H.G. Wells, *Tono-Bungay* (1909)

'George Ponderevo is H.G. Wells not only in the incidental details of his life, but in the expression of his views' (Dickson, op. cit., p. 155).

RICHARD REMINGTON in H.G. Wells, *The New Machiavelli* (1911)

'The first third of the book is a magnificent recreation of Wells's own life in Bromley' (Dickson, op. cit., p. 188).

G.H. RIVERS in Morley Roberts, *The Private Life of Henry Maitland* (1912)

Identified in an 'Index of Recurring Pseudonyms' in the 1958 edition of *The Private Life of Henry Maitland*, ed. Morchard Bishop, p. 255.

THEODORE TASKOVER in Edwin Pugh, *The Quick and the Dead* (1914)

'Pugh ... put [Wells] into a novel entitled *The Quick and the Dead*. ... The novel is not a good one, but it does give a very clear picture of the way my father could plough into people's lives. ... Pugh describes the disintegration of a nice rather ordinary chap who is thrown off balance by the sexually reckless behaviour of a writer friend of his called Taskover. ... I think he has got at the essence of my father's style in these affairs' (Anthony West, 1978, 'The libertine and the lover', *Books and Bookmen* (July): 28); review of Gloria Fromm, *Dorothy Richardson*).

MAX TOWN in Anthony West, **Heritage** (1984)

'The open secret of *Heritage* is that Anthony West had for his own parents Rebecca West and H.G. Wells' (*Heritage*, 1984, blurb on dust jacket).

WILKINS in H.G. Wells, **Ann Veronica** (1909) and **Boon** (1915)

'Wilkins was Wells as he really was' (Dickson, op. cit., p. 243).

HYPO WILSON in Dorothy Richardson, **Pilgrimage** (1915–67)

'Among others who stayed with us was Dorothy Richardson, a schoolmate of Jane's . . . her *Pilgrimage* books are a very curious essay in autobiography . . . and in one of them, *The Tunnel*, she has described our Worcester Park life with astonishing accuracy. I figure as Hypo in that description' (Wells, *Autobiography*, op. cit., p. 557).

WELLS, Isabel Mary (1866–1931) Daughter of H.G. Wells's uncle William and his wife Jane, with whom Wells lodged at 181 Euston Road in 1885 when he was in his second year at the Normal School of Science, South Kensington, London. Isabel married Wells in 1891, but he left her for Catherine Robbins (**Wells**, above) in 1894 and they were divorced in 1895. In 1903 she married Fowler-Smith.

MARION PONDEREVO in H.G. Wells, **Tono-Bungay** (1909)

'There are ten pages in *Tono-Bungay* which describe George Ponderevo's separation from his wife Marion which cannot be far from a direct account of the way Wells parted from Isabel' (N. Mackenzie and J. Mackenzie, 1973, *The Time Traveller: the life of H.G. Wells*, p. 96 n.).

WELLS, Joseph (1827–1910) Shopkeeper. He married Sarah Neal (**Wells**, below) in 1853; they were the parents of H.G. Wells.

ALFRED POLLY in H.G. Wells, **The History of Mr Polly** (1910)

Both N. Mackenzie and J. Mackenzie (*The Time Traveller*, 1973, p. 266), and Anthony West (*H.G. Wells: aspects of a life*, 1983, p. 198) elaborate the idea that Joe Wells was the true prototype of Mr Polly. *See also* **Wells**, Frank; **Wells**, H.G.

ARTHUR REMINGTON in H.G. Wells, **The New Machiavelli** (1911)

'Remington's father is a beautifully observed portrait of Joe Wells' (Lovat Dickson, 1969, *H.G. Wells*, p. 188).

WELLS, Sarah (1822–1905) Née Neal. She married Joseph **Wells** in 1853 and was the mother of H.G. Wells.

MRS PONDEREVO in H.G. Wells, **Tono-Bungay** (1909)

The identification is based upon obvious parallels.

MRS REMINGTON in H.G. Wells, **The New Machiavelli** (1911)

'Remington's . . . mother is Mrs Wells, the one unretouched portrait of her that exists' (Lovat Dickson, 1969, *H.G. Wells*, p. 188).

WEMYSS, Anne Frederica, Countess of (1823–96) She married the 10th Earl, becoming his first wife.

LADY WINTERBOURNE in Mrs Humphry Ward, *Marcella* (1894)

'. . . Lady Wemyss, the deep-voiced, queerly-dressed *grande dame*, whom Mrs Ward loved for her heart's sake, and of whom she has recorded a suggestion, perhaps, in the Lady Winterbourne of *Marcella*' (Janet Penrose Trevelyan, 1923, *The Life of Mrs Humphrey Ward*, p. 189).

WEMYSS, Mary Constance, Lady (1864–1937) Born Mary Constance Wyndham, she was the daughter of the Hon. Percy Wyndham and the granddaughter of the 1st Lord Leconfield; the latter was the natural son of the 3rd Earl of Egremont, who reputedly was also the father of Lord **Melbourne**, the Prime Minister. In 1883 she married Hugo Charteris, Lord Elcho, later the 11th Earl of Wemyss, and their daughter became Lady Cynthia **Asquith**. One of the **Souls**, A.J. **Balfour** was devoted to her and she was a woman of immense, dotty charm. Kipling's sister gave a description of her in 'a purple velvet hat wreathed with daffodils . . . she wore it at church and looked lovely – but the sunny walk back wilted the flowers . . . she wore them triumphantly till tea time' (M. Strickland, 1977, *Angela Thirkell: portrait of a lady novelist*, London: Duckworth, pp. 86–7).

LADY BEVERIDGE in D.H. Lawrence, 'The Ladybird' (1923)

'Lady Cynthia and her mother are recognisable' (*The Diaries of Lady Cynthia Asquith, 1915–1918*, 1969, London, p. 510, Index s.v. Lawrence, D.H.).

LADY EMILY LESLIE in Angela Thirkell, *Wild Strawberries* (1934)

'It was said of Angela that she worshipped the Wemyss family . . . she transferred her entranced state to her readers. They all worshipped "Lady Emily Leslie", who was a portrait of Lady Wemyss' (Strickland, op. cit., p. 85). 'The identifiable portrait of Lady Wemyss did not amuse her family or friends' (ibid., p. 87).

WESCOTT, Glenway (b. 1901) American novelist. When he was a young man in Paris during the 1920s, he had an English accent. He was the author of *The Grandmothers*.

ROBERT PRENTISS in Ernest Hemingway, *The Sun Also Rises* (1926)

'[Maxwell] Perkins asked EH to change the name of a minor character, Roger Prescott, since it was too close to Glenway Wescott, EH's model. EH changed it to Roger [sic] Prentiss' (Carlos Baker, 1969, *Ernest Hemingway: a life story*, New York, p. 594 n. 'Identification of characters in "The Sun Also Rises"').

WESLEY, Samuel Sebastian (1810–76) Eminent organist and composer of church music. The natural son of the composer Samuel Wesley (1766–1837), he was the organist of Winchester Cathedral when Florence Mary Marryat visited the city in 1863. He conducted the Three Choirs Festival several times.

DR NESBITT in Florence Marryat, *Nellie Brooke, A Homely Story* (1868)

'[The] novel contains a thinly disguised portrait . . . of the leading members of the [Winchester] cathedral circle, including S.S. Wesley himself, who appears as "Dr Nesbitt"' (*Radio Times* (7 May 1976)).

WEST, Anthony (b. 1914) Novelist. Son of Rebecca **West** and H.G. **Wells**.

RICHARD SAVAGE in Anthony West, *Heritage* (1984)

'The open secret of *Heritage* is that Anthony West had for his own parents Rebecca West and H.G. Wells' (*Heritage*, 1984, blurb on dust jacket).

WEST, Rebecca (1892–1983) Critic and novelist. Born Cecily Isabel Fairfield, in County Kerry, Ireland, she was brought up in Edinburgh and trained for the stage in London. A suffragette, she wrote for *Freewoman* and *Clarion*, and from 1912 to 1924 she was the mistress of H.G. Wells, with whom she had a son, Anthony West. She moved to the United States, where she was a lecturer and was involved with the *New York Herald Tribune*, and in 1930 she married Henry Maxwell Andrews (d. 1968), with whom she lived in Buckinghamshire. She was the author of a number of novels and a critical study of Henry **James**.

HELEN in H.G. Wells, *The World of William Clissold* (1926)

'Glimpses of [rewards and periods of great happiness in the relationship between Rebecca West and Wells] are movingly recalled in William Clissold's . . . memories of his shared past with Helen' (Lovat Dickson, 1969, *H.G. Wells*, p. 289).

MARTIN LEEDS in H.G. Wells, *The Secret Places of the Heart* (1922)

Identification based upon obvious parallels.

STELLA SALT in Wyndham Lewis, *The Roaring Queen* (1973)

'He . . . portrayed her in *The Roaring Queen* as Stella Salt' (Jeffrey Meyers, 1980, *The Enemy: a biography of Wyndham Lewis*, London: Routledge & Kegan Paul, p. 31). Lewis painted her portrait in 1932.

NAOMI SAVAGE in Anthony West, *Heritage* (1984)

'The open secret of *Heritage* is that Anthony West had for his own parents Rebecca West and H.G. Wells' (*Heritage*, 1984, blurb on dust jacket).

WEST MALLING, Kent

MUGGLETON in Charles Dickens, *The Pickwick Papers* (1836–7)

'West Malling almost certainly "sat" for Muggleton and the real life Swan for the fictional Lion' (John Oliver, 1978, *Dickens' Rochester*, Rochester, p. 44). *See also* **Maidstone**.

WEST STAFFORD, Dorset A village situated about four miles east of Dorchester and due south of Stinsford.

LEW EVERARD in Thomas Hardy, *Tess of the d'Urbervilles* (1891)

Identified in F.B. Pinion, 1968, *A Hardy Companion*, London: Macmillan.

WESTALL, Henry A. Brother of Julia **Wolfe** and uncle of Thomas Wolfe. After many years as a Unitarian clergyman, he left the ministry and became a conveyancer in Boston. During his years at Harvard, Thomas Wolfe saw a great deal of him.

BASCOM PENTLAND in Thomas Wolfe, *Of Time and the River* (1935)

'Henry Westall was the model for Uncle Bascom in *Of Time and the River*' (*Beyond Love and Loyalty: the letters of Thomas Wolfe and Elizabeth Nowell*, 1983, ed. R.S. Kennedy, p. 22 n. 4). In an earlier version, *A Portrait of Bascom Hawke* (1932), Henry Westall was the model for the character Bascom Hawke.

WESTMACOTT, Charles Molloy (1787/8–1868) Journalist and publisher. He was the Editor and proprietor of *The Age*, a weekly newspaper that 'levied blackmail without mercy' (Frederic Boase, 1901, *Modern English Biography*, Vol. III). He lived in Paris from 1848.

SNEAK in Bulwer Lytton, *England and the English* (1833)

The identification is based upon obvious parallels.

WESTMORLAND, John Fane, 11th Earl of (1784–1859) Known as Lord Burghersh until 1841, he had a distinguished military career from 1803 to 1814, and in 1809 was aide-de-camp in Spain and Portugal to Sir Arthur Wellesley (later Duke of **Wellington**), whose niece he married in 1811. Between 1814 and 1825 he became equally distinguished as a diplomat. A gifted violinist and composer of seven operas, he founded the Royal Academy of Music in 1823.

LORD AMELIUS FITZFUDGE BOROUGHBY in Benjamin Disraeli, *Vivian Grey* (1826–7)

Identified as Lord B—g—h in a key given in a pamphlet published in 1827 by William Marsh. This key is discussed by Lucien Wolf in his notes to *Vivian Grey* (1904 (centenary edn), Vol. II, p. 364), with the conclusion that Disraeli was not responsible for the key.

WESTMORLAND, Sybil, Countess of (1871–1910) Second daughter of the 4th Earl of Rosslyn. She was the sister of Millicent, Duchess of **Sutherland**, and Lady Angela **Forbes**; the half-sister of Frances, Lady **Warwick**; and the aunt of Hamish **Erskine**. In 1892 she married the Earl of Westmorland.

LADY ROEHAMPTON in Victoria Sackville-West, *The Edwardians* (1930)

'And who's Lady Roehampton in the *Edwardians*? Please tell me' (to Victoria Sackville-West, 16 August 1933, reproduced in *The Letters of Virginia Woolf, 1932–1935*, 1975, ed. Nigel Nicolson, London: Hogarth Press, p. 214). '[Vita] replied . . . that the character . . . was based on the Countess of Westmorland . . . "a lovely sumptuous creature, who came to Knole when I was eight, and who first set my feet along the wrong path"' (ibid., n. 3).

WETHERELL, Sir Charles (1770–1846) Lawyer and politician. Educated at Magdalen College, Oxford, and an MP from 1812 to 1832, he was a High Tory and violently opposed Catholic emancipation and legal, municipal and parliamentary reform. He was Solicitor-General in 1824, Attorney-General in 1826 and 1828, and from 1826 he was the Recorder for Bristol. Described as 'that weird and unwashed Sibyl', his unpopularity led to the great Bristol riots of 1831.

C.J. STRYVER in Charles Dickens, *A Tale of Two Cities* (1859)

In 1817, with J.S. Copley (later Lord **Lyndhurst**) he appeared for James Watson and Arthur Thistlewood in the Spa Fields treason trial. 'The evidence of treasonable conspiracy rested solely on the testimony of one John Castle, who had turned King's evidence and was strongly suspected of having acted throughout as an *agent provocateur*. . . . Demolish Castle and the case for the Crown vanished into air . . . [Wetherell] attacked Castle in a cross-examination which furnished Dickens with the model of a famous scene in *A Tale of Two Cities*' (J.B. Atlay, 1906, *The Victorian Chancellors*, Vol. I, p. 18). Watson was acquitted, in part because of a brilliant speech for the defence by Copley. The scene is of course the cross-examination of Barsad (Solomon Pross) by Stryver, in Book II, ch. III. *See also* **James**, Edwin.

WETZEL (OR WEITZEL), Lewis (1764–1808?) A border scout and fighter against the American Indian, he was a famous frontier figure in West Virginia and Ohio who was captured by Indians as a young man; he became their dedicated opponent.

TIMOTHY WEASEL in J.K. Paulding, *The Dutchman's Fireside* (1831)

'He figures as Timothy Weasel in . . . *The Dutchman's Fireside*' (James D. Hart (ed.), 1965, *The Oxford Companion to American Literature*, New York: Oxford University Press, p. 907).

WEYHILL, Hampshire Situated west of Andover. For centuries it was the scene of a fair, held mainly for the selling of sheep and traditionally falling on 10 October, or as near as possible to that date.

WEYDON-PRIORS in Thomas Hardy, Wessex novels and tales (1871–95)

Identified on a map prepared by Thomas Hardy which hangs in the Dorset County Museum, Dorchester. *See under* **Abbotsbury**.

WEYMOUTH, Dorset A seaside town made fashionable by George III, who spent his summers there. Thomas Hardy worked there in an architect's office in 1869–70.

BUDMOUTH in Thomas Hardy, Wessex novels and tales (1871–95)

Identified on a map prepared by Thomas Hardy which hangs in the Dorset County Museum, Dorchester. *See under* **Abbotsbury**.

MELPORT in Thomas Hardy, 'An Indiscretion in the Life of an Heiress' (1878)

Identification given in map prepared by Thomas Hardy which hangs in the Dorset County Museum, Dorchester. *See under* **Abbotsbury**.

WHALEN, Philip (b. 1923) American poet. Active on the West Coast and associated with the 'Beat' movement. In 1973 he was ordained as a Zen Buddhist priest, and for some time he was resident in Japan.

WARREN COUGHLIN in *The Dharma Bums* (1958), and BEN FAGAN in *Big Sur* (1962), both by Jack Kerouac

Identified in 'Character key to the Duluoz Legend', in Barry Gifford and Lawrence Lee, 1979, *Jack's Book*, pp. 322–32.

WHARTON, Edith (1862–1937) American novelist. Born Edith Jones, into Old New York Society, she lived for many years in France and in 1855 married Edward Wharton; they were divorced in 1913. During the First World War she set up American hostels and started an employment agency and day nursery for refugees. She was appointed a Chevalier of the Legion of Honour in 1916 for her wartime relief work. She was a long-time friend of Henry James.

THE PRINCESS ('AMY EVANS') in Henry James, 'The Velvet Glove' (1910)

'The story harks back to James's visit to Paris in . . . 1908 and to the proposition put forward in the name of Edith Wharton that James devote an article to [her] writings. James was fully persuaded that Edith made no such suggestion, but he was characteristically intrigued by the thought that she might have done so. . . . The tale, as Leon Edel has demonstrated [*Henry James*, Vol. V, pp. 360–6], is packed with echoes of Edith Wharton and allusions to her work and manner of life' (R.W.B. Lewis, 1975, *Edith Wharton: a biography*, London: Constable, p. 254).

MRS WORTHINGHAM in Henry James, 'Crapey Cornelia' (1910)

'She is also Mrs Worthingham . . . and the resemblance is very strong' (*Henry James Letters*, Vol. IV: *1895–1916*, 1984, ed. Leon Edel, London: Macmillan, p. xxviii).

WHEATON, Mabel Sister of Thomas Wolfe, she was married to Ralph **Wheaton**.

HELEN GANT BARTON in Thomas Wolfe, *Look Homeward, Angel* (1929) and *Of Time and the River* (1935)

Identified in *My Other Loneliness: letters of Thomas Wolfe and Aline Bernstein*, 1983, ed. Suzanne Stutman, Chapel Hill, NC, and London: University of North Carolina Press, p. 44, n.3.

WHEATON, Ralph Married to Mabel **Wheaton**, he was Thomas Wolfe's brother-in-law. 'I think the way [Wheaton] was treated by the great corporation that employed him after he had given all his best energies since his fourteenth year, was simply damnable . . . he was kicked out ruthlessly, brutally, and without notice by the employers to whom he had given his life . . . for thirty years or more' (to Margaret Roberts, 20 May 1936, reproduced in *The Letters of Thomas Wolfe*, 1956, ed. Elizabeth Nowell, New York, p. 520).

HUGH BARTON in Thomas Wolfe, *Look Homeward, Angel* (1929) and *Of Time and the River* (1935)

Identified in *My Other Loneliness: letters of Thomas Wolfe and Aline Bernstein*, 1983, ed. Suzanne Stutman, Chapel Hill, NC, and London: University of North Carolina Press, p. 44, n.3.

RANDY SHEPPERTON in Thomas Wolfe, *The Web and the Rock* (1939) and *You Can't Go Home Again* (1940)

'Randy Shepperton is the new fictitious representation of . . . Ralph Wheaton . . . but Randy is much more of a composite character than Hugh [Barton] was' (Floyd Watkins, 1957, *Thomas Wolfe's Characters: portraits from life*, Norman, Okla., p. 88).

WHELPTON, Eric (1894–1981) Travel writer. He was born in France, where he received his early education. He joined the Army during the First World War but was invalided out, and during the 1920s he lived in Florence; he then returned to England as a schoolmaster, and during the Second World War he was in the Intelligence Service. He later devoted himself to writing travel books, a novel and two biographies.

LORD PETER WIMSEY in Dorothy L. Sayers, *Murder Must Advertise* (1933)

'Writing to me from Rye, Whelpton says that . . . he can neither support nor refute the suggestion that he is the original. But, he says, "during the year which we spent working six hours a day by ourselves in a small room she did discuss . . . her projects for writing crime books. . . . I have the impression that . . . Peter Wimsey was already beginning to take shape, based perhaps on me and on . . . Charles Crichton"' (Atticus, 1975, 'In the style of Wimsey', *Sunday Times* (30 March): 32). *See also* **Crichton**, Charles.

WHEWAY, Mr Parish Clerk at Nuneaton, Warwickshire, *c*.1830.

JONATHAN LAMB in George Eliot, 'Janet's Repentance', *Scenes of Clerical Life* (1857–8)

See under **Anstruther**, Lady.

WHICHELO, Louisa (1827–1911) Née Graham. She married Henry Mayle Whichelo, a drawing master at Stockwell Grammar School, but he died in 1866, leaving her with ten children: the third child and eldest daughter, Alice Clara ('Lily'), became the mother of E.M. Forster.

MRS HONEYCHURCH in E.M. Forster, *A Room with a View* (1908)

'Mrs Honeychurch was my grandmother' (E.M. Forster, interviewed in 1952, quoted in P.N. Furbank and F.J.H. Haskell, 1972, *Writers at Work: the Paris Review interviews*, selected by Kay Dick, Harmondsworth: Penguin, p. 13).

WHICHER, Jonathan (d. 1868?) Detective-Inspector at Scotland Yard. He was in charge of the Road Hill murder case in 1860, and as a result of his investigations Constance **Kent** was brought to trial. In 1866 he investigated the case of the Tichborne Claimant on behalf of the family.

SERGEANT RICHARD CUFF in Wilkie Collins, *The Moonstone* (1868)

'Wilkie Collins . . . found the model for Sergeant Richard Cuff in a . . . detective of Scotland Yard named Inspector Jonathan Whicher who was still alive and in retirement when *The Moonstone* first appeared' (Irving Wallace, 1956, *The Fabulous Originals*, p. 269). *See also* **Williamson**, A.F.

The WHIGS One of the two great parties that dominated English politics in the eighteenth and early nineteenth centuries.

AUGUSTUS TOMLINSON in Bulwer Lytton, *Paul Clifford* (1830)

Identified in a key set out by Rosina Bulwer Lytton, in a letter of 26 May 1830, reproduced in Michael Sadleir, 1968, *Bulwer and His Wife*, pp. 227–8.

WHIPP, Fanny (1832?–66) The niece of Mrs Hudson of Easton House, near Bridlington, Yorkshire, with whom Charlotte Brontë and Ellen **Nussey** stayed in the autumn of 1839. 'A sagacious and original child who completely captivated Charlotte and Ellen' (Winifred Gérin, 1969, *Charlotte Brontë*, Oxford, p. 156).

PAULINA MARY HOME in Charlotte Brontë, *Villette* (1853)

'[I]n seeking an original for [Paulina] . . . biographers and commentators have always harked back to . . . [Charlotte's] stay at Easton with the Hudsons in 1839, when her fancy was greatly taken by their little . . . niece, Fanny Whipp. . . . It was Ellen Nussey . . . who insisted on Fanny Whipp being the prototype for "Paulina". . . . But then Ellen Nussey was all too fond of finding originals for Charlotte's characters and incidents in which *she* had a part' (ibid., pp. 492, 493). *See also* **Gaskell**, Julia.

WHISTLER, James McNeill (1834–1903) Painter and etcher. Born in Massachusetts and educated at the Military Academy, West Point, he moved to Paris in 1855 and studied painting under **Gleyre**. He remained in Europe for the rest of his life and spent the period 1892–5 in Paris. In 1879 he decorated the Peacock Room for F.R. **Leyland**, and in the same year he was involved in a notorious libel case with **Ruskin**, as a result of which he went bankrupt. He married Beatrice, widow of the English architect E.W. Godwin, in 1888.

JOE SIBLEY in George Du Maurier, *Trilby* (1894)

'[The] serial issue [of *Trilby*, in *Harper's Magazine* for 1894] . . . contained a passage of nearly 1500 words, plus a drawing, introducing, describing and depicting a character "Joe Sibley".This passage and drawing . . . were suppressed after serial issue, as beyond a shadow of a doubt, they represented Whistler' (Michael Sadleir, 1951, *XIX Century Fiction*, Vol. I, London: Constable, and Los Angeles: California University Press, p. 256). In the original production of *Patience* (W.S. Gilbert, 1881), George Grossmith, playing 'Bunthorne', was made up to resemble Whistler, with eyeglass, moustache, imperial and streak of white hair.

WHITBY, Yorkshire

MONKSHAVEN in Elizabeth Gaskell, *Sylvia's Lovers* (1863)

'You are quite right in supposing that Whitby was the place I meant by Monkshaven' (to James Dixon, 14 November 1833, reproduced in *The Letters of Mrs Gaskell*, 1966, ed. J.A.V. Chapple and Arthur Pollard, Manchester, p. 717, letter 537).

WHITCOMBE PASS, New Zealand

EREWHON in Samuel Butler, *Erewhon* (1872)

'The section on Geography [in *The Cradle of Erewhon*] illuminates the opening narrative chapters of *Erewhon*, which give ... an account of Butler's own penetration into the Whitcombe Pass region. ... The "*Erewhon* journey" in January–February, 1861, was undertaken with J.H. Baker ... exploring the headwaters of the Rangitata and the Rakaia rivers in search of good sheep country' (Joan Stevens, 1961, review of *The Cradle of 'Erewhon'* by Joseph Jones (1959, Austin, Tex.), *Notes and Queries* 206: 38).

WHITE, George A member of the crew of the wool clipper *Duke of Sutherland* in which Conrad sailed as an ordinary seaman from Gravesend to Sydney in 1878–90.

JAMES WAIT (THE 'NIGGER') in Joseph Conrad, *The Nigger of the 'Narcissus'* (1897)

'One [member of the crew] was a negro of twenty-six, George White, from Barbados. Answering the roll call at the signing on . . . he spoke his name White in the clipped English accent of Barbados as "Wait" and so suggested to Conrad the name "James Wait" he was to use nineteen years later for the central character of *The Nigger of the Narcissus*' (Jerry Allen, 1967, *The Sea Years of Joseph Conrad*, London: Methuen, p. 101). 'As a matter of fact, the name of the Nigger of the Narcissus was not James Wait, which was the name of another nigger we had on board the *Duke of Sutherland*, and I was inspired with the first scene in the book by an episode in the embarkation of the crew at Gravesend on board the same *Duke of Sutherland*' (Conrad speaking to G. Jean-Aubry, quoted in Jean-Aubry, 1927, *Joseph Conrad: life and letters*, Vol. I, London: Heinemann, p. 77). *See also* **Barron**, Joseph.

WHITE, James Robert (1876–1946) Son of Field-Marshal Sir George White, who defended Ladysmith in the Boer War in 1899–1900. In 1913 he helped to organize the Irish Citizen Army at the time of the transport workers' strike in Dublin, and for a time he was forbidden to live in Ireland. In 1916 he served three months' imprisonment for attempting to organize a miners' strike in Wales in the hope of preventing the execution of James Connolly, the Irish Labour leader. He was the author the autobiographical *Misfit* (1930).

JIM BRICKNELL in D.H. Lawrence, *Aaron's Rod* (1922)

'The original of Jim Bricknell was . . . Captain James Robert White' (H.T. Moore, 1980, *The Priest of Love: a life of D.H. Lawrence*, rev. edn, Harmondsworth: Penguin, p. 364; originally published 1955 as *The Intelligent Heart: the story of D.H. Lawrence*, London: Heinemann).

WHITE, Lydia (d. 1827) A well-known London hostess of Irish birth, she was described by **Scott** as 'a lioness of the first order, with stockings nineteen times nine dyed blue, very lively, very good-humoured, and extremely absurd' (to Lady Louisa Stuart, 19 January 1808, reproduced in *The Letters of Sir Walter Scott*, 1932, ed. H.J.C. Grierson, Vol. II, London: Constable, p. 5). She was the 'Miss Diddle' of Byron's poem, 'The Blues'.

LADY ANGELICA HEADINGHAM in Maria Edgeworth, *Patronage* (1814)

'Lydia White suggested several details for the hostile vignette in *Patronage* of a fashionable patroness of the arts: Lady Angelica Headingham' (Marilyn Butler, 1972, *Maria Edgeworth*, Oxford, p. 254). *See also* **Davy**, Lady.

WHITE, William (1797–1882) Printer and bookseller in Bedford. A Trustee of the Old Meeting at Bedford (the Congregational church at which Bunyan was the first preacher), he was the Superintendent of the Sunday school work in 1842–50 and was an active lay preacher. Strong for the extension of the franchise, he had his windows smashed for being on Lord John **Russell**'s committee at the Bedford election during the time of the Reform Bill. He was Doorkeeper to the House of Commons from 1850 to 1880 and wrote *Inner Life of the House of Commons* (1897). He was the father of William Hale White (the author Mark **Rutherford**).

ZACHARIAH COLEMAN in Mark Rutherford, *The Revolution in Tanner's Lane* (1887)

'Zachariah Coleman is a tribute to William White . . . [his] love of Byron, and admiration for Cobbett, came from William White' (Valentine Cunningham, 1976, *Everywhere Spoken Against: dissent in the Victorian novel*, Oxford: Clarendon Press, pp. 272–3).

WHITE, William Hale (1831–1913) White. Born in Bedford, he was the son of William **White** and in 1854 became a civil servant. He wrote novels under the pseudonym of 'Mark Rutherford'.

MARK RUTHERFORD in Mark Rutherford, *The Autobiography of Mark Rutherford* (1881)

See under **Eliot**, George.

WHITE-MARIO, Jessie Meriton *See* **Mario**, Jessie Meriton.

The WHITE WOMAN OF BERNERS STREET A well-known figure about London in the 1820s, she was introduced by Charles Mathews in 1831 as 'Miss Mildew' in a sketch at the Adelphi Theatre, but the sketch was withdrawn after just one night owing to the hostility of the audience: this familiar, pathetic figure was not to be made a mockery of. In 1853 she appeared in *Household Words*: 'Another . . . person we associate with Berners Street. . . . The White Woman is her name. She is dressed entirely in white, with a ghastly white plaiting round her head and face, inside her white bonnet. . . . She is a conceited old creature, cold and formal in manner, and evidently went simpering mad . . . no doubt because a wealthy Quaker wouldn't marry her. This is her bridal dress' (Charles Dickens, 1853, 'When we stopped growing', *Household Words* 6 (1 January): 362–3).

MISS HAVISHAM in Charles Dickens, *Great Expectations* (1860–1)

'Here already are most of Miss Havisham's attributes: her externals ... her personality ... and her history' (Harry Stone, 1969, 'The genesis of a novel: *Great Expectations*', in E.F.W. Tomlin (ed.), *Charles Dickens, 1812–1870*, pp. 113–15). *See also* **Dick**, Margaret; **Joachim**, Martha.

WHITEFOORD, Charles (d. 1753) Lieutenant-Colonel. He joined the 5th marines in 1741, and in 1745 he fought against Scottish rebels; his life was saved at Prestonpans by Stuart of Invernahyle.

COLONEL TALBOT in Sir Walter Scott, *Waverley* (1814)

See under **Stuart of Invernahyle**, Alexander.

WHITEFOORD, Sir John (d. 1803) 3rd Baronet, he was the son of Sir John, 2nd Baronet, and was the nephew of Charles **Whitefoord**. Originally of Ballochmyle in Ayrshire, he fell into difficulties and moved to Edinburgh. Burns wrote 'The Braes of Ballochmyle' for his daughter Maria 'as a farewell to the family inheritance' (Allan Cunningham, 1834, *The Works of Robert Burns, With His Life*, Vol. IV, p. 157).

SIR ARTHUR WARDOUR in Sir Walter Scott, *The Antiquary* (1816)

'The ancestor of the Whitefoords [i.e. Sir John] supplied, it is said, the ground work of the character of Sir Arthur Wardour' (ibid.). *See also* **Sinclair**, Sir John.

WHITE'S CLUB, London Situated at 37–8 St James's Street, Piccadilly.

BELLAMY'S in Evelyn Waugh, the *Sword of Honour* trilogy (1952–61)

'16 March 1953 ... Lent began well. I wrote first pages of novel [*Officers and Gentlemen*], very good too. White's in an air raid' (*The Diaries of Evelyn Waugh*, 1976, ed. Michael Davie, London: Weidenfeld & Nicolson, p. 716).

WHITMAN, Alfred A pupil at **Sanborn's School**, Concord, in 1857–8, he was a close friend of Louisa Alcott. He later moved to Lawrence, Kansas.

THEODORE LAURENCE ('LAURIE') in Louisa M. Alcott, *Little Women* (1868) and sequels

'Why bless your heart I put you into my story as one of the best and dearest lads I ever knew! "Laurie" is you and my Polish boy "jintly" you are the sober half' (L.M. Alcott to Alfred Whitman, 6 January 1869, quoted in M.B. Stern, 1952, *Louisa M. Alcott*, p. 189). *See also* **Willis**, Frederick Llewellyn; **Wisniewski**, Ladislas.

WHITMAN, Walt (1819–91) American poet. Born on Long Island, New York, the son of a carpenter, he was brought up in Brooklyn from the age of 4. He worked first as an office boy, then as a printer's apprentice, and an itinerant teacher in country schools. He returned to Long Island in 1838 as a schoolteacher and printer, and then moved into journalism, starting a newspaper, the *Long Islander*, then editing the New York *Aurora* in 1842, the Brooklyn *Eagle* in 1846, and the New Orleans *Crescent* in 1848. He published the first edition of his major collection of poems, *Leaves of Grass*, in 1855, which through successive editions grew from 95 pages to over 400. In 1857 he became Editor of the Brooklyn *Times*, and during the Civil War he was a volunteer nurse for the Northern army. He obtained two government clerkships after the war, but in 1873 he suffered the first of a series of paralytic strokes, and he spent the remainder of his life in Camden, New Jersey.

SMITHERS in Bayard Taylor, *John Godfrey's Fortunes* (1864)

'. . . a character – or rather a caricature – who strikingly resembles the author of *Leaves of Grass*' (C.I. Glicksberg, 1937, 'Walt Whitman and Bayard Taylor', *Notes and Queries* 173 (3 July): 6).

WHITNEY, William Collins (1841–1904) Financier and politician. Born in Massachusetts, he was prominent in the affairs of the New York street-railway system between 1883 and 1902. In 1885–9 he was the United States Secretary of the Navy. He was a great racing man.

HOSMER HAND in Theodore Dreiser, *The Titan* (1914)

'. . . Whitney . . . (the Hand . . . of the novel)' (Richard Lehan, 1969, *Theodore Dreiser: his world and his novels*, London and Amsterdam: Feffer & Simons, p. 98).

WHITSTABLE, Kent

BLACKSTABLE in W. Somerset Maugham, *Of Human Bondage* (1915) and *Cakes and Ale* (1930)

'Whitstable – which Willie called Blackstable . . . has greatly changed in the past eighty years, but the High Street is still much as he described it . . . and the house now known as The Old Vicarage, where Willie lived with his guardian . . . lies at the bottom of the hill on the right-hand side. . . . The description in *Of Human Bondage* was completely accurate' (Robin Maugham, 1966, *Somerset and All the Maughams*, p. 145).

WIBORG, Mary Hoyt ('Hoytie') Born in Cincinnati, she was the sister of Sara **Murphy** and was 'a kind of Henry James heiress in London and Paris society and a rather amusing irritant to the Murphys' (Lillian Hellmann, 1969, *An Unfinished Woman*, p. 76).

BABY WARREN in F. Scott Fitzgerald, *Tender is the Night* (1934)

'Baby Warren was drawn from Sara Murphy's sister Hoyt' (M.J. Bruccoli, 1981, *Some Sort of Epic Grandeur: the life of F. Scott Fitzgerald*, London: Hodder & Stoughton, p. 342).

WICK HOUSE, Brighton The address of Dr Everard's School for Boys in 1830–7.

BLIMBER'S in Charles Dickens, *Dombey and Son* (1846–8)

See under **Everard**, E., **King**, J.C. *See also* **Chichester House**, Mr **King's School**.

WIDENER, Peter Arrell Brown (1834–1915) Financier and philanthropist. Born in Philadelphia, he made a modest fortune during the Civil War. During the 1880s, with William L. **Elkins**, he effected the consolidation of all the street railways in Philadelphia. He became one of the major figures in US industry and the richest man in Philadelphia.

NORMAN SCHRYHART in Theodore Dreiser, *The Titan* (1914)

'Widener . . . (the . . . Schryhart . . . of the novel)' (Richard Lehan, 1969, *Theodore Dreiser: his world and his novels*, London and Amsterdam: Feffer & Simons, p. 98).

WILBERFORCE, Samuel (1805–73) Born in London, he was the third son of William Wilberforce, the abolitionist, and was educated at Oriel College, Oxford. He was ordained in 1828 and became Bishop of Oxford in 1845 and of Winchester in 1869. Lewis Carroll first seems to have met him in 1859.

THE BISHOP in Benjamin Disraeli, *Lothair* (1870)

Identified in 'Key to *Lothair*', *Notes and Queries* 183 (12 September 1942): 173.

THE DUCHESS in Lewis Carroll, *Alice's Adventures in Wonderland* (1865)

'Shane Leslie's suggestions that the Bishop was the model for the Duchess in *Alice* and the Wilberforce–Huxley clash in 1860 the model for the battle between the white and red knights in *Looking Glass* are amusing, if far-fetched' ('Lewis Carroll and the Oxford Movement', in Robert Phillips (ed.), 1974, *Aspects of Alice*, Harmondsworth: Penguin, pp. 255–66). *See also* **Carinthia**, Duchess of.

WILDE, Oscar (1854–1900) Playwright, novelist and poet. Born in Dublin, he was educated at Trinity College, Dublin, and at Magdalen College, Oxford. He received the Newdigate Prize for Poetry in 1878, and his first volume of poetry, *Patience*, was published in 1881. In 1884 he married Constance Lloyd, with whom he had two sons, and in 1890 *The Picture of Dorian Gray*, based on his intimate John **Gray**[2] the poet, was published. He sued the Marquis of Queensberry, the father of his friend Lord Alfred **Douglas**, for libel, but lost the case and instead was imprisoned in 1895 for homosexuality. In 1897 he went to France and spent the rest of his life in Europe. He was the author of *A Woman of No Importance* (1893), *The Importance of Being Earnest* (1895) and *Salome*.

ESMÉ AMARINTH in Robert Hichens, *The Green Carnation* (1894)

'. . . a novel in which the two principal characters [Esmé Amarinth and Lord Reginald Hastings] are recognisable portraits of Oscar and Bosie [Lord Alfred Douglas]' (Violet Wyndham, 1968, *The Sphinx and Her Circle: a biographical sketch of Ada Leverson, 1862–1933*, London: Deutsch, p. 43). The novel was published on 15 September, and on 22 September Wilde sent a telegram to Ada **Leverson** which began, 'Esmé and Reggie are delighted to find that their sphinx is not a minx after all' (see *The Letters of Oscar Wilde*, 1962, ed. Rupert Hart-Davis, London: Rupert Hart-Davis, p. 373 n. 1).

CLAUDE DAVENANT in George Fleming, *Mirage* (1877)

'One of the characters may well have been based on Wilde, Claude Davenant, a young Oxford poet. . . . Here he is . . . on brothers-in-law: "I don't object to mine particularly . . . to be sure I don't see much of him. . . . Still I do go down there every autumn for a few days to shoot. Last year I shot the dog", he added mildly' (*Letters*, op. cit., p. 46 n.). George Du Maurier's Jeremy Postlethwaite, in his *Punch* cartoons of 1880 onwards, is clearly a portrait of Wilde.

WILKINSON, Louis (1881–1966) Novelist and biographer. He was a University extension lecturer from 1909 to 1949 and was a close friend of the **Powys** family. He published under the name of Louis Marlow.

EDWARD RAYNES in Louis Wilkinson, *The Buffoon* (1916)

'Edward (Wilkinson) . . .' (Barbara Guest, 1985, *Herself Defined: the poet H.D. and her world*, London: Collins, p. 44; originally published 1984, Garden City, NY: Doubleday).

WILLENHALL, Staffordshire During the 1840s it was the centre of small, home industries devoted to the manufacture of ironmongery such as keys, locks and currycombs.

WODGATE in Benjamin Disraeli, *Sybil* (1845)

'Les moeurs étranges de Willenhall frappèrent l'imagination de Disraeli; sous le nom de Wodgate . . . il mit en scène la "ville de serruriers". S'inspirant de texte officiel, il écrit deux des chapitres les plus curieux de la littérature social' (Louis Cazanian, 1934, *Le Roman sociale en Angleterre*, Vol. II, Paris, pp. 95–6). The 'texte officiel' was the *Appendix to the Second Report of the Commissioners* (*Trades and Manufactures*) Part II: *Reports and Evidence from Sub-Commissioners* (1842; report on the employment of children). The section of the appendix that deals with Staffordshire and contiguous counties was by Richard Henry Horne (poet, critic, dramatist and friend of Charles Dickens), and it was this section that Disraeli used to build his picture of Wodgate. '[C]ontrary to Cazanian's statement, Wodgate is not Willenhall' (Sheila Smith, 1961, 'Willenhall and Wodgate: Disraeli's use of Blue Book evidence', *RES* (NS) 13: 379). Smith shows that Disraeli amalgamates facts from Horne's accounts of several towns, including Wolverhampton and Sedgley.

WILLES, Revd George (b. 1844?) Educated at Christ Church, Oxford, he took Holy Orders and in 1879 was Chaplain and Assistant Master at Westward Ho!

REVD JOHN GILLETT in Rudyard Kipling, *Stalky & Co.* (1899)

'He seems to be a fairly accurate portrait of the Reverend George Willes' (R.L. Green (ed.), 1961, 'Preface and commentary to "The Complete Stalky & Co."', in *The Readers' Guide to Rudyard Kipling's Work*, Sect. I, London: Kipling Society, p. 400).

WILLIAMS, Augustine Podmore (1852–1916) Born in Cornwall, his father was Vicar of Porthleven. In August 1880 he was First Mate of the pilgrim-ship *Jeddah* when she sprang a leak on the voyage from Singapore to Jeddah; she was abandoned by her European master and officers off Cape Gardafui, and Williams subsequently joined **MacAlister & Co.** of Singapore as a ship's chandler's water-clerk.

JIM in Joseph Conrad, *Lord Jim* (1900)

'One problem from the beginning was Lord Jim. . . . I believed Conrad had known such a man . . . but it was to take six years before I secured the final proof – the . . . date . . . was February 15, 1960 – that Jim was primarily fashioned upon a former seaman named Augustine Podmore Williams' (Jerry Allen, 1967, *The Sea Years of Joseph Conrad*, London: Methuen, p. xi). 'While I was revising this book for publication . . . I received a letter from a Mrs Viola Allen of Surrey who . . . confirmed that my research was accurate, and that Williams was the source for Jim. She wrote: ". . . I think you are wrong when you say Conrad *met* Lord Jim in Singapore. We had many talks about people in *Jim* . . . and Conrad told me he *saw* Williams in Singapore and wondered why a man of that . . . *class* – should be a ship's chandler's clerk . . . and he was *told* Jim's story. . . . [He said] 'He was a fine looking man of about forty – his name was Williams – but I used that name somewhere else, so I called him Jim – I always wondered why a man like that was doing that sort of job. One day, I asked why. "Oh, don't you know his story?" Apparently everyone knew it in Singapore. I don't know the name of the ship – not *Patna*, but some name of that kind. Always, there was the shadow of that damn thing over him"' (letter of 20 February 1963, reproduced in Norman Sherry, 1966, *Conrad's Eastern World*, Cambridge, pp. 86–6). *See also* **Brooke**, Sir James; **Lingard**, William James.

WILLIAMS, Charles Walter Stansby (1886–1945) Author and scholar. The author of literary criticism, verse, and works that have been described as psychological thrillers, from 1908 to 1945 he was a reader for Oxford University Press.

CHARLES LUKE in Margery Allingham, *More Work for the Undertaker* (1948) and others

'I have my own theory, about the origin of Luke. To me, Margery Allingham's descriptions of him . . . recreate the poet Charles Williams' (Erik Routley, 1972, *The Puritan Pleasures of the Detective Story*, p. 151).

WILLIAMS, Florence She was married to William Carlos **Williams**.

NELLIE BOYLE in Robert McAlmon, *Post Adolescence* (1923)

Identified in Robert E. Knoll (ed.), 1962, *McAlmon and the Lost Generation: a self-portrait*, Lincoln, Nebr.: University of Nebraska Press, p. 108.

WILLIAMS, Horace (1858–1940) Professor of Philosophy at the University of North Carolina, in Chapel Hill.

PLATO GRANT in Thomas Wolfe, *You Can't Go Home Again* (1940)

'Wolfe knew Professor Horace Williams well, whom he called Plato Grant in fiction' (Floyd C. Watkins, 1957, *Thomas Wolfe's Characters: portraits from life*, Norman, Okla., pp. 131–2).

VERGIL WELDON in Thomas Wolfe, *Look Homeward, Angel* (1929)

'An address by Professor Horace Williams . . . "The Spirit of Truth" was delivered to the senior class of the University . . . in 1920 . . . Williams appears as Vergil Weldon in . . . *Look Homeward, Angel*; this address is satirized in the novel' (*National Union Catalogue*, 1980, Vol. 665, p. 47, s.v. Williams, Henry Horace).

WILLIAMS, William Carlos (1883–1963) American poet. In 1922, with Robert McAlmon, he founded the Contact Publishing Company, which published the periodical *Contact* and **Hemingway**'s first book, *Three Stories & Ten Poems*. He was married to Florence **Williams**.

JIM BOYLE in Robert McAlmon, *Post Adolescence* (1923)

Identified in Robert E. Knoll (ed.), 1962, *McAlmon and the Lost Generation: a self-portrait*, Lincoln, Nebr.: University of Nebraska Press, p. 108.

WILLIAMS AP PRICHARD (d. 1816) A native of the parish of Llandegai, Wales, he was a blind wandering minstrel who was killed in the fall of a gravel pit in Twynholm, Kirkcudbrightshire; he was buried in Twynholm Kirkyard, and in 1871 a tombstone marked 'a Welsh soldier' was erected.

WILLIE STEENSON (WANDERING WILLIE) in Sir Walter Scott, *Redgauntlet* (1824)

'Recently (1946) . . . members of the Galloway Association of Glasgow satisfied themselves that the 1871 tombstone marked the grave of Wandering Willie, and . . . decided to erect a . . . stone at the foot of the grave recording this fact' (J.C. Corson, 1946, *Notes and Queries* 190 (29 June): 281). The minstrel's real name was discovered later in a manuscript letter of 1830 from Joseph Train to Scott. *See also* **Metcalf**, John.

WILLIAMSON, Adolphus Frederick (1831–89) Detective. His father fought at Waterloo as a sergeant-major in the artillery and was a divisional superintendent of the Metropolitan police. In 1848 he was a clerk in the War Office, and in 1850 he was a constable in the Metropolitan police; in 1860 he assisted Inspector **Whicher** in the Constance **Kent** murder case, and in 1865 he recorded Constance Kent's confession. From 1869 to 1886 he was Superintendent of Whitehall (A) division, and from 1877 to 1886 he was also Chief Superintendent of the Criminal Investigation Department. In 1886–9 he was Chief Constable and was in charge of investigations into the Orsini conspiracy, the murder of Lord William Russell, and the Clerkenwell explosion and dynamite outrages.

SERGEANT RICHARD CUFF in Wilkie Collins, *The Moonstone* (1868)

'Cuff's famous passion for roses and rose-growing appears to have been suggested by the character of Adolphus Frederick Williamson . . . Major Arthur Griffiths, apparently a personal acquaintance . . . recorded [*Mysteries of Police and Crime*, 1898, Vol. I, p. 130]: "His talk, for choice, was about gardening, for which he had a perfect passion . . ."' (Ian V.K. Ousby, 1974, 'Wilkie Collins's *The Moonstone* and the Constance Kent case', *Notes and Queries* 219: 25). *See also* **Whicher**, Jonathan.

WILLIAMSON, Ida Laetitia Née Hibbert, she was married to Henry Williamson.

MARY OGILVIE in Henry Williamson, *The Pathway* (1928)

'Saturday, November 10th [1928] . . . Henry Williamson . . . came to dinner. . . . Seems to be very fond of his wife, and admires her. She is the original of "Mary" in *The Pathway*; so she must be fine' (*The Journals of Arnold Bennett*, 1933, ed. Sir Newman Flower, Vol. III, London: Cassell, p. 280).

WILLIS, Frederick Llewellyn (b. 1830?) At the age of 14, with his mother dead and his father in a debtor's prison, he was taken under Mrs Alcott's wing; from then on he often boarded with the Alcott family, to whom he was known as Fred Willis. He later went to Harvard.

THEODORE LAURENCE ('LAURIE') in Louisa M. Alcott, *Little Women* (1868) and sequels

'Both Bronson [Alcott] and Anna [Alcott] insisted that the model for Laurie was a certain Llewellyn Willis' (Cornelia Meigs, 1970, *Louisa M. Alcott and the American Family Story*, p. 69). *See also* **Whitman**, Alfred; **Wisniewski**, Ladislas.

WILSON, Charlotte Mary (1854–1944) Daughter of a Dr Martin in Tewkesbury, Gloucestershire, in 1873 she was a student at Merton Hall (later Newnham College), Cambridge, and in 1876 she married Arthur Wilson. In 1884 she became a member of the **Fabian Society**; she was a friend of **Stepniak** and of **Kropotkin**, and was Editor of the anarchist periodical *Freedom*. She was active in the fight for women's rights and divorce-law reform. She died in a nursing home in New York State.

GEMMA (JENNIFER) WARREN in Ethel Voynich, *The Gadfly* (1897)

'Voynich modelled the heroine of her successful novel, *The Gadfly*, on Mrs Wilson' (H. Oliver, 1983, *The International Anarchist Movement in Late Victorian London*, p. 37).

WILSON, John (1785–1854) 'Christopher North' of *Blackwood's Magazine*. Professor of Moral Philosophy at Edinburgh, he contributed to Coleridge's *Friend*. He joined *Blackwood's Magazine* in 1817 and, with J.G. **Lockhart**, was the principal contributor. In 1822–35 he contributed *Noctes Ambrosianae*.

MR MACLAUREL in Thomas Love Peacock, *Headlong Hall* (1816)

'M. Mayoux points out that . . . Gall is Jeffrey. . . . This fits in with the identification of Mac Laurel as John Wilson' (*The Novels of T.L. Peacock*, 1948, ed. David Garnett, London: Rupert Hart-Davis, p. 21 n.). *See also* **Campbell**, Thomas.

WILSON, Lestock Brother of Alicia Beaufort, the first wife of Francis Beaufort whose second wife was Honora **Edgeworth**. In 1829 Wilson married Frances ('Fanny') **Edgeworth**, Honora's half-sister.

GENERAL CLARENDON in Maria Edgeworth, *Helen* (1834)

'The respect that Maria had come . . . to feel for the sterling qualities of Lestock can be gauged from *Helen*, which was written in the first years of Fanny's marriage: . . . in that book, General Clarendon resembles Lestock in having every attribute that could be desired in a husband, except brilliance' (Marilyn Butler, 1972, *Maria Edgeworth*, Oxford, p. 424).

WILSON, William Carus *See* **Carus-Wilson**, William.

WILSON, William Thomas Francis Johnstone (1865–1938) Educated in Lancing, Sussex, he married Maude Ellen Caney (1869–1929) of Durban, whom he met during a stay in South Africa. He appears to have lived on dwindling family resources. He was the father of Angus Wilson.

ARTHUR CALVERT in Angus Wilson, *Late Call* (1964)

Identification based upon private information.

WINCHELL, Walter (1897–1972) American journalist. He was the writer of a widely syndicated, scandalous gossip column and later became a television commentator.

BERT WOODRUFF in William L. Shirer, *Stranger Come Home* (1954)

'A dozen of Shirer's major characters are clearly portraits from life; they include ... a syndicated columnist specializing in scandal [i.e. Walter Winchell]' (Joseph Blotner, 1966, *The Modern American Political Novel 1900–1960*, Austin, Tex., p. 295).

WINCHESTER, Hampshire

BARCHESTER in Anthony Trollope, *The Warden* (1855)

'Mr Trollope paid me a visit [in October 1882]. . . . [On 26 October] he was shown Wells and Glastonbury in due order . . . he denied that Barchester was Wells. Barchester was Winchester, where he was at school, and the notion of Hiram's Hospital was taken from St Cross' (Edward A. Freeman, 1883, 'Anthony Trollope', *Macmillan's Magazine* (January): 239). 'Nor will anyone familiar with Winchester fail to recognize Mr Harding's Church of St Cuthbert . . . as St Swithins-upon-King's Gate' (R.B. Martin, 1962, *Enter Rumour*, p. 180–1). *See also* **Salisbury**.

HILLSTONE in Florence Marryat, *Nellie Brooke, A Homely Story* (1868)

'Miss Marryat stayed in Winchester in 1863, and her novel contains a thinly disguised portrait of the city' (*Radio Times* (7 May 1976)).

WINTONCESTER in Thomas Hardy, Wessex novels and tales (1871–95)

Identified on a map prepared by Thomas Hardy which hangs in the Dorset County Museum, Dorchester. *See under* **Abbotsbury**.

WINDMILL HILL, Sussex Situated near Hurstmonceaux. Dorothy Richardson spent some months there in 1907 and 1908 at Mount Pleasant, a farm belonging to the **Penroses**, a Quaker family.

DIMPLE HILL in Dorothy Richardson, *Pilgrimage* (1915–67)

'The setting [Dimple Hill], we recognize from Dorothy's own life, to be Windmill Hill, on the East Sussex downs seven miles from the sea' (John Rosenberg, 1973, *Dorothy Richardson*, London, p. 135).

WINROD, Gerald B. The founder in the 1930s of a quasi-Fascist group in the USA known as the Defenders of the Christian Faith.

BERZELIUS ('BUZZ') WINDRIP in Sinclair Lewis, *It Can't Happen Here* (1935)

Identified in Arthur M. Schlesinger, Jun., 1961, *The Politics of Upheaval (The Age of Roosevelt, III)*, p. 89. *See also* **Long**, H.P.

WINTHROP, Egerton (d. 1916) A member of old New York Society, he had lived for many years in Paris and was a man of wide culture. He became a close friend of the young Whartons and accompanied them on their Italian journeys, and in 1880–90 he guided Edith Wharton's taste and her reading; he remained a close friend until his death.

SILLERTON JACKSON in Edith Wharton, *The Age of Innocence* (1920)

'Egerton Winthrop reappears in the gossipy, snobbish, and intelligent Sillerton Jackson' (R.W.B. Lewis, 1975, *Edith Wharton: a biography*, London: Constable, p. 430). *See also* **Travers**, William.

LAWRENCE SELDEN in Edith Wharton, *The House of Mirth* (1905)

'Fond as she was of her Walter Berrys, her Egerton Winthrops . . . and Selden has a little of each – she knew they had insufficient blood in their veins' (Lewis, op. cit., p. 155). *See also* **Berry**, Walter van Rensselaer; **Gregory**, Eliot.

WINTLE, Hector (b. 1903) He was a contemporary of Christopher Isherwood at Repton in 1916–22.

PHILIP LINDSAY in *All the Conspirators* (1928) and PHILIP LINSLEY in *Lions and Shadows* (1938), both by Christopher Isherwood.

'Hector is called Philip Lindsay in *All the Conspirators* and Philip Linsley in *Lions and Shadows* . . . because some libel-conscious lawyer feared that the repetition of the original surname might annoy the novelist Philip Lindsay' (Christopher Isherwood, 1977, *Christopher and His Kind*, London: Eyre Methuen, p. 77).

WISNIEWSKI, Ladislas (b. 1847?) A Polish refugee, Louisa M. Alcott met him in the Pension Victoria at Vevey in 1865. They remained friends, and in 1877 May Alcott visited him in Paris, where he was living with his mother.

THEODORE LAURENCE ('LAURIE') in Louisa M. Alcott, *Little Women* (1868) and sequels

'"Laurie" is you and my Polish boy "jintly" . . . my Ladislas (whom I met abroad) is the gay whirligig half' (L.M. Alcott to Alfred Whitman, 6 January 1869, quoted in M.B. Stern, 1952, *Louisa M. Alcott*, p. 189). *See also* **Whitman**, Alfred; **Willis**, Frederick Llewellyn.

WITHAM, Mr The friend of John **Bowes** who nominated him as a candidate for South Durham in the General Election of 1841.

Mr Hartington in W.M. Thackeray, 'Notes on the North What-d'ye-Callem Election' (1841)

Identified in *Letters and Private Papers of W.M. Thackeray*, 1945, ed. Gordon N. Ray, Vol. II, London: Oxford University Press, p. 27 n. 49.

WITTGENSTEIN, Prince Gregory von *See* **Sayn and Wittgenstein**, Prince Gregory von.

WOBURN BUILDINGS, Bloomsbury, London An alleyway now called Woburn Way, located off Upper Woburn Place. In 1906, Dorothy Richardson shared three rooms at number 2 with Miss **Moffatt**, while W.B. **Yeats** lived opposite at number 18.

Flaxman's Court in Dorothy Richardson, *Pilgrimage* (1915–67)

"The street name . . . she takes from Flaxman Terrace . . . leading on from Woburn Buildings . . . into the slums of St Pancras' (J. Rosenberg, 1973, *Dorothy Richardson*, London, p. 119). 'The details . . . of . . . the surroundings of Flaxman's very closely match those of . . . Woburn Buildings' (ibid., p. 121).

WOLCOTT-PERRY, Kate (1832?–1922) 'Miss Kate Wolcott and Miss Saidée Perry were Americans, and reputedly cousins, the former fifteen years older than the latter. When they were settled on Capri they joined and hyphenated their surnames' (Mark Holloway, 1976, *Norman Douglas*, p. 504 n. 65). They jointly conceived a passionate devotion to Baron **Fersen**, and both died on Capri.

Virginia Pepworth-Norton in Compton Mackenzie, *Vestal Fire* (1927)

'In *Vestal Fire* they are called the Misses Pepworth-Norton' (ibid.).

WOLCOTT-PERRY, Saidée (b. 1847?) Cousin of Kate **Wolcott-Perry**.

Maimie Pepworth-Norton in Compton Mackenzie, *Vestal Fire* (1927)

See under **Wolcott-Perry**, Kate.

WOLFE, Frank Thomas Wolfe's brother.

Stephen Gant in Thomas Wolfe, *Look Homeward, Angel* (1929) and *Of Time and the River* (1935)

'[T]he weaknesses of Little Stevie are taken from . . . Frank Wolfe' (Floyd Watkins, 1957, *Thomas Wolfe's Characters: portraits from life*, Norman, Okla., p. 15).

WOLFE, Fred Thomas Wolfe's brother.

Luke Gant in Thomas Wolfe, *Look Homeward, Angel* (1929) and *Of Time and the River* (1935)

Identified in *My Other Loneliness: letters of Thomas Wolfe and Aline Bernstein*, 1983, ed. Suzanne Stutman, Chapel Hill, NC, and London: University of North Carolina Press, p. 44 n. 5).

WOLFE, Julia (1860–1945) Née Westall, she married W.O. **Wolfe**. She was the mother of Thomas Wolfe.

ELIZA GANT in Thomas Wolfe, *Look Homeward, Angel* (1929) and *Of Time and the River* (1935)

See under **Wolfe**, W.O.

AUNT MAW in Thomas Wolfe, *The Web and the Rock* (1939)

'In addition to being a prototype of Amelia Joyner, Mrs Wolfe is also Aunt Maw [in the same novel]' (Floyd Watkins, 1957, *Thomas Wolfe's Characters: portraits from life*, Norman, Okla., p. 88).

AMELIA WEBBER in Thomas Wolfe, *The Web and the Rock* (1939)

See above.

WOLFE, Thomas (1900–38) Novelist. Born in Asheville, North Carolina, his parents were W.O. **Wolfe** and Julia **Wolfe** and he was educated at the University of North Carolina and at Harvard University. He began as a playwright and was encouraged in his work by Aline Bernstein, with whom he began an affair in 1925. He died of an infection following pneumonia.

EUGENE GANT in Thomas Wolfe, *Look Homeward, Angel* (1929) and *Of Time and the River* (1935)

See below under George Webber.

EUGENE LYONS in Aline Bernstein, *Three Blue Suits* (1933)

'The following letter . . . is evidently a first draft of the one he sent to Mrs Bernstein upon the publication of . . . *Three Blue Suits*, in which he is portrayed as "Eugene Lyons"' (*The Letters of Thomas Wolfe*, 1956, ed. Elizabeth Nowell, New York, p. 390). 'I think that what you did wrong in the story you wrote about me was to identify a living person so exactly . . . that no one who knew me could fail to identify me, and then . . . proceeded to create a situation and a conflict which was false' (Thomas Wolfe, draft letter to Aline Bernstein, 11 December 1933, ibid., p. 395).

GEORGE WEBBER in Thomas Wolfe, *The Web and the Rock* (1939) and *You Can't Go Home Again* (1940)

'One may at last freely and sadly say both George Webber and Eugene Gant are Thomas Wolfe' (Clifton Fadiman, 1953, 'The Web and the Rock', in Richard Walser (ed.), *The Enigma of Thomas Wolfe*, Cambridge, Mass., p. 150). Autobiographically, therefore, he [the protagonist] should bear perhaps about the same relation to the life of the author as Wilhelm Meister bears to the life of Goethe, or as Copperfield bears to the life of Dickens' (Thomas Wolfe, 'A Statement of Purpose', 14 February 1938, apropos of what became *The Web and the Rock* and *You Can't Go Home Again*, addressed to Edward Asdell (Wolfe's editor at Harper's) and found among his papers after his death, reproduced in *Letters*, op. cit., York, p. 714).

WOLFE, William Oliver (1851–1922) Stone-cutter. He married Julia Westall (**Wolfe**, above) and was the father of Thomas Wolfe.

W.O. GANT in Thomas Wolfe, *Look Homeward, Angel* (1929) and *Of Time and the River* (1935)

'We cannot avoid supposing that Wolfe drew these two characters after his own parents' (John Peale Bishop, 1939, 'The sorrows of Thomas Wolfe', *Kenyon Review* 1 (1): 9).

JOHN WEBBER in Thomas Wolfe, *The Web and the Rock* (1939)

'John Webber ... comes to Libya Hill ... just as W.O. Gant ... arrived in Altamont ... and as W.O. Wolfe ... had come to Asheville in life' (Floyd Watkins, 1957, *Thomas Wolfe's Characters: portraits from life*, Norman, Okla., p. 87).

WOLGAST, Ad A boxer known to Ernest Hemingway.

ADOLPH FRANCIS in Ernest Hemingway, 'The Battler', *In Our Time* (1925)

'The battler was ... Ad Francis, whose personality was based on two real-life fighters' (Carlos Baker, 1969, *Ernest Hemingway: a life story*, New York, p. 141). This identification was given to Baker by Hemingway on 1 February 1953, see ibid., p. 587 n.). 'On real-life originals of Ad Francis and Bugs.' 'Bugs was modeled on an actual Negro trainer who had looked after Wolgast in the period of his decline' (ibid., p. 141). *See also* **Nelson**, Battling.

WOLLSTONECRAFT, Mary (1759–97) Writer. Born in Spitalfields, London, she opened a school at Newington Green in 1784 with her sister Eliza and her friend Fanny Blood. After the school failed she began to write *Thoughts on the Education of Daughters* (published in 1797), and went to Ireland to be a governess to the daughters of Lord Kingsborough. She was dismissed in 1788, and returned to London, where she worked as a translator and reviewer for the radical publisher Joseph Johnson, who published her novel, *Mary* (1788), and her most famous work, *A Vindication of the Rights of Women* (1792). In 1792 she went to Paris, and met Gilbert Imlay, an American writer, with whom she had a daughter, Fanny Imlay (1794–1816). She returned to London in 1795, and twice attempted suicide. She married William **Godwin** in 1797, when she was pregnant, and died from septicaemia shortly after the birth of her second daughter, Mary (later **Shelley**).

ADELINE MOWBRAY in Mrs Amelia Opie, *Adeline Mowbray; or The Mother and Daughter* (1804)

'In 1804 [Amelia Opie] published *Adeline Mowbray* ... in part suggested by the history of Mary Wollstonecraft' (Elizabeth Lee, 1895, in *The Dictionary of National Biography*, London: Oxford University Press, s.v. Opie, Amelia). '*Adeline Mowbray* was a travesty of the story of Godwin and Mary, but there is no doubt that it used their experience and held them up to ridicule' (Claire Tomalin, 1977, *The Life and Death of Mary Wollstonecraft*, Harmondsworth: Penguin, p. 292).

MARGUERITE DE ST LEON in William Godwin, *St Leon* (1799)

'She is described as Marguerite in her husband's *St Leon*' (Leslie Stephen (ed.), 1890, *The Dictionary of National Biography*, London: Oxford University Press, s.v. Godwin, Mary Wollstonecraft).

WOLSTENHOLME, Joseph (1829–91) '[A] mathematician and a walker who had the gift of being able to spout thousands of lines of poetry by heart' (Noel Annan, 1984, *Leslie Stephen*, p. 54). A Cambridge friend of Sir Leslie Stephen, from 1852 to 1869 he was a Fellow of Christ's College, Cambridge, and from 1871 to 1889 he was Professor of Mathematics at the Royal Indian Engineering College, Cooper's Hill.

Augustus Carmichael in Virginia Woolf, *To the Lighthouse* (1927)

'Virginia Woolf drew the character of Mr Carmichael . . . from Wolstenholme. In old age he became something of a bore and Stephen irritated his family by asking the lonely old bachelor to stay in Cornwall with them for the holidays and then, finding his company tedious, leaving wife and daughters to entertain him. Wolstenholme was present on the summer holiday in Cornwall (see *To the Lighthouse*, Part III), of which Stephen wrote to C.E. Norton, 21 Sept. 1899: "I have lost the power of holiday making"' (ibid., p. 361 n.). Joseph Breitkopf (in *Mrs Dalloway*) resembles Carmichael so closely that it is difficult not to believe that he too is a portrait of Wolstenholme.

WOMBWELL, George (1792–1855) He succeeded as 3rd Baronet in 1846. He was well known in the fashionable world and on the turf, and his portrait was painted by Count **D'Orsay**.

Mr Cassilis in Benjamin Disraeli, *Coningsby* (1844) and *Tancred* (1847)

Identified in a key in *Notes and Queries* (8th series) 3 (13 May 1893): 363. *See also under* **Bright**, John.

WOOD, Absalom W. Architect. He was a friend and associate of Arnold Bennett's father.

Osmond Orgreave in Arnold Bennett, the *Clayhanger* trilogy (1910–16)

'Absalom Wood may be seen as the original of Osmond Orgreave' (Reginald Pound, 1952, *Arnold Bennett: a biography*, London: Heinemann, p. 69).

WOOD, Edmund Gough de Salis (1842–1932) Educated at King's School, Rochester, and at Emmanuel College, Cambridge, he became a deacon in 1865 and a priest in 1866. He was Curate from 1865 to 1885, and Vicar from 1885 to 1930, of St Clement's, Cambridge.

Father Goode in Shane Leslie, *The Cantab* (1926)

Identified in a key in the hand of Dr Ivor Ramsay, a Kingsman of the year 1920, and later Dean, laid in a copy of *The Cantab*.

WOOD, Thelma (1901–70?) Sculptor and silver-point artist. Born in St Louis, Missouri, she met Djuna Barnes in Paris in the early 1920s and became her lover.

Robin Vote in Djuna Barnes, *Nightwood* (1936)

'. . . prototype for the figure of Robin Vote' (Andrew Field, 1983, *The Formidable Miss Barnes*, London: Secker & Warburg, p. 16). In his *Memoirs of Montparnasse*, John Glassco calls her 'Emily Pine' (see ibid., p. 148).

WOODBURY HILL, Dorset Located east of Bere Regis. A great entertainment and sheep fair used to be held there annually in September.

GREENHILL in Thomas Hardy, Wessex novels and tales (1871–95)

Identified on a map prepared by Thomas Hardy which hangs in the Dorset County Museum, Dorchester. *See under* **Abbotsbury**.

WOOL, Dorset Located east of Dorchester on the road to Wareham, on the river Frome; the manor house of the Durberville family stands by the river.

WELLBRIDGE in Thomas Hardy, *Tess of the d'Urbervilles* (1891)

Identified in F.B. Pinion, 1968, *A Hardy Companion*, London: Macmillan.

WOOLER, Margaret (1792–1885) The eldest of the four sisters who founded Roe Head, the school near Mirfield, Yorkshire, that Charlotte Brontë attended in 1831–2 and at which she later taught. She and Charlotte formed a lifelong friendship, and she 'gave Charlotte away' at her marriage to Revd A.B. **Nicholls**. Sir Clifford **Allbutt** was her nephew.

ALICE FAIRFAX in Charlotte Brontë, *Jane Eyre* (1847)

'There is some reason to believe that the character of Mrs Fairfax . . . is sketched from Miss Wooler' (Herbert Wroot, 1935, *Sources of Charlotte Brontë's Novels: persons and places*, Shipley, Yorks., p. 49).

AGNES PRYOR in Charlotte Brontë, *Shirley* (1849)

'Mrs Pryor has been identified with Miss Margaret Wooler' (Wroot, op. cit., p. 130).

WOOLF, Virginia (1882–1941) Novelist. Daughter of Sir Leslie **Stephen** and sister of Vanessa **Bell**, she was born in London and educated at home. Her family was at the centre of the Bloomsbury group, from 1905 she contributed to the *Times Literary Supplement* and in 1915 she published her first novel. In 1917, she and Leonard Woolf, whom she had married in 1912, founded the Hogarth Press, and in the following years she continued to produce novels although she suffered from deep depression. She drowned herself by filling her pockets with stones and walking into the River Ouse.

MRS RHODA HYMAN in Wyndham Lewis, *The Roaring Queen* (1973)

'Who is . . . Mrs Hyman's original? I think there can be no doubt at all that she is, surprisingly, Mrs Virginia Woolf' (Walter Allen, 1973, Introd. to *The Roaring Queen*, pp. 12–13).

JANE ROSE in Hugh Walpole, *Hans Frost* (1929)

'Jane Rose looked like the wife of a Pre-Raphaelite painter, her dark hair brushed back in waves from her forehead, her grey dress cut in simple fashion, her thin pale face quiet and remote. She was, Hans thought, the best living novelist in England' (A.C. Ward, 1930, *The Nineteen-Twenties*, p. 105; the footnote reads 'If for "Jane Rose" we substitute Virginia Woolf, this passage may be read as a fine tribute to the living woman').

HELEN SCHLEGEL in E.M. Forster, *Howards End* (1910)

'[The] situation [of the Schlegel sisters] is like that of Virginia and Vanessa Stephen living at Gordon Square with their brother Thoby ("Tibby") in the early days of Bloomsbury. . . . They are thoroughly Bloomsbury. . . . Like Virginia and Vanessa Stephen, [they] have been strongly shaped by the example and teachings of a father' (Wilfred Stone, 1966, *The Cave and the Mountain: a study of E.M. Forster*, London: Oxford University Press, p. 239). 'There are discrepancies in plenty. Nevertheless . . . when I read Quentin Bell's account of Virginia Woolf's childhood tantrums I found myself involuntarily recalling "that tense wounding excitement that made [Helen Schlegel] a terror in their nursery days"' (Oliver Stallybrass, 1973, Introd. to *Howards End* (Abinger edn), p. x). *See also* **Dickinson**, The Misses.

RACHEL VINRACE in Virginia Woolf, *The Voyage Out* (1915)

'. . . Rachel Vinrace, the heroine based on Virginia Stephen herself' (Michael Holroyd, 1967, *Lytton Strachey*, Vol. I, London: Heinemann, p. 433).

WOOLLCOTT, Alexander (1887–1943) American journalist and writer. During the 1920s he was a member of the circle of writers that met at the Algonquin Hotel, New York.

THADDEUS HULBERT in Charles Brackett, *Entirely Surrounded* (1934)

'[Kaufman and Hart's play, *The Man Who Came to Dinner*] was not the first work conceived for the purpose of giving the public a close-up view of Woollcott. Brackett had aimed for verisimilitude. . . . His Thaddeus Hulbert is Woollcott at his worst' (M. Goldstein, 1979, *George S. Kaufman*, New York, p. 320). The novel is recognizably set on Neshole Island, Vermont, where Woollcott spent a large part of every year from 1923 onwards. In *The Man Who Came to Dinner* he appears as Sheridan Whiteside.

WALDO LYDECKER in Vera Caspary, *Laura* (1943)

The identification is based upon obvious parallels.

WOOLLEY, Katharine (1888?–1945) The widow of Lieutenant-Colonel Francis Keeling, she joined Leonard **Woolley** as an assistant in Ur in 1925; they were married in 1927 and she continued working at Ur until 1934.

LOUISE LEIDNER in Agatha Christie, *Murder in Mesopotamia* (1936)

See under **Woolley**, Leonard.

WOOLLEY, Leonard (1880–1960) Archaeologist. Educated at New College, Oxford, he began work in the Near East in 1907, excavating in Nulia, and in 1912 he worked with T.E. **Lawrence** on the dig at Carchemish in North Syria. In 1922–35 he was engaged in his major work at Ur, and in 1925 he was joined by an assistant, Mrs Katharine Keeling (**Woolley**, above), whom he married in 1927. In 1938, he became Archaeological Adviser to the government of India.

ERIC LEIDNER in Agatha Christie, *Murder in Mesopotamia* (1936)

'He has been characterized with all the enthusiastic warmth of the detective story-writer by Agatha Christie in her *Murder in Mesopotamia*' (Glyn Daniel, 1982, 'Remembrance of digs past' (notice of reprint of Woolley's *Ur of the*

Chaldees), The Times (22 July): 13). 'More closely related to our work [than the novels set in Egypt] is *Murder in Mesopotamia* . . . which would not have been written without a knowledge of Ur . . . and the parts of director played by . . . Leonard Woolley and his masterful wife Katharine. Here perhaps Agatha touched rather near the bone and for once was apprehensive about what this dramatis persona might say. Fortunately . . . Katharine did not recognise certain traits which might have been taken as applicable to herself' (Max Mallowan, 1977, *Mallowan's Memoirs*, p. 208).

WOOLSEY, Gamel (1899–1968) Born on a cotton plantation in South Carolina, she met Llewellyn Powys in 1927 and fell in love with him; she became pregnant but miscarried in 1929 and followed Powys and his wife to Dorset. In 1931 she married Gerald **Brenan**, but maintained a close relationship with Powys until his death. She was the author of a volume of verse and her half-brother was the judge who gave the decision that James **Joyce**'s *Ulysses* was not an obscene work.

Dittany Stone in Llewellyn Powys, *Love and Death* (1939)

'[She appears as Dittany Stone in] *Love and Death* [the novel] which he wrote about his love affair with Gamel' (Gerald Brenan, 1974, *Personal Record, 1920–1972*, p. 237).

WOOTTON HALL, Ellastone, Staffordshire In 1766 the Hall was let at a nominal rent to Rousseau and it was here that he began to write his *Confessions*. In 1822 it was inherited by Revd Walter Davenport Bromley, whose collection of paintings, mainly early Italian, was one of the finest of the period (three of the paintings are now in the National Gallery in London). In 1800–10, the house was let to Francis Parker (later **Newdigate**); Robert **Evans**'s first job was as Parker's bailiff. Only the entrance gates to the house now survive.

Donnithorne Chase in George Eliot, *Adam Bede* (1859)

'This beautiful estate is without doubt the original of Donnithorne Chase' (Charles S. Olcott, 1911, *George Eliot: scenes and people in her novels*, London: Cassell, p. 65; originally published 1910, New York: Thomas Y. Crowell).

WORDSWORTH, William (1770–1850) English poet. Born in Cockermouth, the son of an attorney, he was orphaned at an early age and sent by his guardian to St John's College, Cambridge. In 1791 he spent a year in Blois where he fell in love with Annette Valon, with whom he had a daughter, Ann Caroline. On receiving a legacy of £900, he was able to set up house with his sister Dorothy in 1795, and with her help, and that of **Coleridge**, realized his vocation as a poet. In 1802 he married Mary Hutchinson, with whom he had five children. They then had a fairly uneventful, contented life, clouded by the deaths of Wordsworth's brother John in 1805, and of two of their children in 1812. In 1829, Dorothy became seriously ill, developing arteriosclerosis, and her mental health deteriorated. Wordsworth became Poet Laureate in 1843, succeeding Robert **Southey**.

Mr Paperstamp in Thomas Love Peacock, *Melincourt* (1817)

'Gifford (Mr Vamp), Coleridge (Mr Mystic) and Wordsworth (Mr Paperstamp) come in for a share of the author's satire' (Sir Paul Harvey (ed.), 1967, *The Oxford*

Companion to English Literature, Oxford: Oxford University Press, p. 532, s.v. Melincourt).

WILFUL WONTSEE in Thomas Love Peacock, *Crotchet Castle* (1831)

'[Mr] Wontsee . . . Wordsworth' (*Crotchet Castle*, 1969, ed. Raymond Wright, Harmondsworth: Penguin, p. 275 n. 2. (to ch. V)).

THE WORLD New York newspaper.

THE *REVERBERATOR* in Henry James, *The Reverberator* (1888)

It was for *The World* that May Marcy **McClellan** wrote her article about the friends who had entertained her in Venice; there were of course other newspapers of the same sort, in London as well as New York.

WORTH, Adam A famous nineteenth-century criminal who was known, like Moriarty, as 'the Napoleon of crime'. He used the pseudonym of Harry Raymond and ran a vast criminal network.

PROFESSOR JAMES MORIARTY in Arthur Conan Doyle, the Sherlock Holmes stories (1890–1927)

'One of his most famous coups provided the plot of "The Red-Headed League".In 1869, he rented . . . a house next to the Boylestone Bank in Boston. He tunnelled through the cellars adjoining to rob the bank of $450,000 in cash and securities. Later he similarly robbed the vault of the Ocean Bank of New York' (Charles Higham, 1976, 'The original Moriarty', *The Times* (20 November): p. 7). Higham goes on to point out the connection between the plot of 'The Valley of Fear', in which Moriarty acquires a painting by Greuze entitled 'La Jeune fille a l'agneau', and Worth's theft of Gainsborough's portrait of the Duchess of Devonshire from Agnew's of Bond Street (the link being agneau/Agnew). *See also* **Drayson**, Alfred Wilks; **Moriarty**, George; **Payn**, James.

WRIGHT, Miss Fanny (1854–1904) She was Governess to George **Cullen's** family, of Eastwood, Nottinghamshire, when D.H. Lawrence was a boy at Nottingham High School. She and Lawrence became friends and she taught him French.

MISS FROST in D.H. Lawrence, *The Lost Girl* (1920)

'Miss Wright, the Miss Frost of the novel, was a splendid woman who stayed with the [Cullen] family until she died. She made a comfortable living by teaching music. She taught both my sister Emily and me [Ada Lawrence]' (Ada Lawrence and G. Stuart Gelder, 1931, *Young Lorenzo: early life of D.H. Lawrence*, Florence, p. 54).

WRIGHT, Whitaker (1845–1904) Company promoter. Born in Lancashire, he went to the United States in 1866 and settled in Philadelphia. In 1899 he lost his fortune and returned to England, and in 1904 he was charged with fraud in connection with the liquidation of the London and Globe Company; he committed suicide after he was tried and found guilty.

EDWARD PONDEREVO in H.G. Wells, *Tono-Bungay* (1909)

'[The novel's] planning may be dated from the suicide of Whitaker Wright in the London Law Courts early in 1904 . . . an incident which so impressed Wells that it appears in both *The Research Magnificent* and **Clissold**' (Geoffrey West, 1930, *H.G. Wells*, p. 180). 'Wells took some of the details of Ponderevo's business venture and later manner of life from the career of the notorious Whitaker Wright' (Gordon N. Ray, 1960, 'H.G. Wells', in Richard Ellmann (ed.) *Edwardians and the Late Victorians*, New York, p. 227 n. 89). His death was the model for that of Amanda Morris's father in *The Research Magnificent* (1915) and of William Clissold's in *The World of William Clissold* (1926). *See also* **Gissing**, George.

WYCOLLER HALL, Lancashire   Situated north-east of Burnley on the Yorkshire border of Lancashire. In the seventeenth century, Wycoller was a small weaving community; it lies just off the road from Colne to Haworth on the edge of the moors. In 1976 the County Council proposed restoring the house, which was then a ruin.

FERNDEAN MANOR in Charlotte Brontë, *Jane Eyre* (1847)

'It is believed now . . . that the original of Ferndean Manor . . . was Wycollar Hall, near Colne' (Herbert Wroot, 1935, *Sources of Charlotte Brontë's Novels: persons and places*, Shipley, Yorks., p. 23).

WYEWURK, Thirroul, Australia   A bungalow in a small mining village on the Pacific Ocean, situated in New South Wales about thirty miles south of Sydney; the Lawrence's rented it in May–July 1922 and it was here that Lawrence wrote *Kangaroo*.

COO-EE in D.H. Lawrence, *Kangaroo* (1923)

'But what a state the bungalow was in! A family of twelve children had stayed there before us . . . a sordid mess the whole thing. So we set to and cleaned, cleaned and cleaned. . . . But the paper in the garden was the worst; for days and days we kept gathering paper' (Frieda Lawrence, 1934, '*Not I But the Wind*, New York, p. 119). Compare *Kangaroo*, ch. V.

WYKOFF, Miss   Henry James's maternal grandmother.

JULIANA BORDEREAU in Henry James, *The Aspern Papers* (1888)

'. . . an image of living antiquity . . . that I was never to see surpassed' (Henry James, 1931, *A Small Boy and Others*, p. 132). 'The Great-Aunt probably sat for Juliana Bordereau . . . "throned, hooded and draped" as the small boy saw her' (Leon Edel, 1953, *Henry James: the untried years, 1843–1870*, p. 107). *See also* **Clairmont**, Claire.

WYLIE, Elinor (1885–1928)   American poet and novelist. Born in New Jersey, in 1905 she married Philip Hichborn. In 1910, however, she eloped with Horace Wylie, and they lived together in England from 1911 to 1915 as Mr and Mrs Waring. In 1915 they returned to the United States, marrying in 1916. In 1922 they moved to New York and in 1923 they were divorced. She later married William Rose Benét.

Rosalind Bailey in Thomas Wolfe, *The Web and the Rock* (1939)

'Thomas Wolfe describes an apparently typical exchange between Wylie and Van Vechten at a New York party. She is styled "the poetess, Rosalind Bailey"' (Judith Farr, 1983, *The Life and Art of Elinor Wylie*, p. 19). 'The most tiny hint that either her genius or its corporeal clothing in any most tiny feature fell short of perfection, would arouse straightaway, whether secludedly or in public, a storm of tears and beget an everlasting rancor' (James Branch Cabell, 1955, *As I Remember It*, New York, p. 179).

Y

YEATS, John Butler (1839–1922) Painter. He married Susan Pollexfen (**Yeats,** below) in 1863 and was the father of W.B. **Yeats**. In 1908 he went to New York on a two-week visit, but actually remained there until his death. In 1909 he met van Wyck **Brooks** and painted his portrait; they remained friends until Yeats's death.

BUTLER in Conrad Aiken, 'The Orange Moth' (1925)

'Aiken pictured Yeats as "Butler"' (J. Hooper, 1977, *Van Wyck Brooks*, Amherst, p. 72). Butler does not appear in person, but is referred to as 'the portrait painter at *Petitpas*', the boarding house where he lodged in New York.

YEATS, Susan (d. 1900) Née Pollexfen, in 1863 she married J.B. **Yeats**; W.B. Yeats was their son. She became a semi-invalid after suffering a stroke in 1887.

MRS SHERMAN in W.B. Yeats, *John Sherman* (1891)

'Mrs Sherman ... resembles Yeats's mother' (Ian Fletcher, 1971, 'Review: "William Butler Yeats: John Sherman and Dhoya"', *Notes and Queries* 216: 276).

YEATS, William Butler (1865–1939) Irish poet. He was born in Sandymount, Dublin, son of the painter John Butler **Yeats**. The family moved to London when he was 9 years old, but returned to Dublin in 1880, where he went to High School. His first volume of verse *Mosada: a dramatic poem* was published in book form in 1886 and in 1887 he returned to London with his family and contributed to anthologies of Irish poetry. In 1888 he became Editor of and a contributor to *Fairy Folk Tales of the Irish Peasantry*. He knew William Morris, Bernard **Shaw** and Oscar **Wilde**. In 1917 he married the 15-year-old Georgie Hyde-Lees, with whom he shared an interest in psychical research. He became a member of the Irish Senate in 1922, and in 1923 won the Nobel Prize for Literature. He moved to Italy in 1928 and died at Cap Martin, Alpes Maritime. His reputation became tainted by his interest in Fascism.

STEPHEN BRAXTON in Max Beerbohm, 'Maltby and Braxton', *Seven Men* (1919)

'Max is also reported to have said that Braxton ... was suggested by Yeats. He can only have been partly suggested by him' (David Cecil, 1964, *Max: a biography*, p. 341).

JOHN SHERMAN in W.B. Yeats, *John Sherman* (1891)

'The central figure ... is deeply autobiographical' (Ian Fletcher, 1971, 'Review: "William Butler Yeats: John Sherman and Dhoya"', *Notes and Queries* 216: 276). *See also* **Middleton**, Henry.

YELLOWHAM WOOD, Dorset Situated between Puddletown and Dorchester.

YALBURY WOOD in Thomas Hardy, Wessex novels and tales (1871–95)

Identified on a map prepared by Thomas Hardy which hangs in the Dorset County Museum, Dorchester. *See under* **Abbotsbury**.

YEOVIL, Somerset

IVELL (OR IVEL) in Thomas Hardy, Wessex novels and tales (1871–95)

Identified on a map prepared by Thomas Hardy which hangs in the Dorset County Museum, Dorchester. *See under* **Abbotsbury**.

YERKES, Charles Tyson (1837–1905) American financier. He started his career in Philadelphia, where in 1871 he was sentenced to a term of imprisonment for corrupt manipulation of municipal funds. In 1873 he recouped his fortunes in the financial panic of that year, then moved to Chicago where he gained control of the railway and street-car system (and presented an observatory to the University). In 1899 he was forced to sell his Chicago holdings and left Chicago, moving to London, where he headed the syndicate that built the London Underground railway. A philanderer, his last mistress was Emilie **Grigsby**, who was still moving in London society when *The Financier* and *The Titan* were written.

FRANK ALGERNON COWPERWOOD in Theodore Dreiser, *The Financier* (1912) and *The Titan* (1914)

'. . . based on the career of C.T. Yerkes' (James D. Hart (ed.), 1965, *The Oxford Companion to American Literature*, New York: Oxford University Press, p. 278, s.v. *Financier, The*). '[During] a meeting held at Philip D. Armour's house, Yerkes actually [said] the words Dreiser attributes to Cowperwood: "I must say I never saw so many straw hats at a funeral before"' (Richard Lehan, 1974, *Theodore Dreiser: his world and his novels*, Carbondale, Ill.: Arcturis Books, p. 102). See P.L. Gerber, 1973, 'The financier himself', *Publications of the Modern Language Association* 88 (1): 117–18, for an exposition of the exact parallels between the lives of Cowperwood and Yerkes.

YERKES, Mary Adelaide (1857–1911) Née Moore, she was one of nine children of a chemist employed by a pharmaceutical company, and she married Charles Tyson **Yerkes**, becoming his second wife. In 1907 she married Wilson **Mizner**.

AILEEN BUTLER in Theodore Dreiser, *The Financier* (1912)

'Aileen Butler . . . is modeled on Mary (Mollie) Adelaide Moore' (Richard Lehan, 1974, *Theodore Dreiser: his world and his novels*, Carbondale, Ill.: Arcturis Books, p. 104).

YONGE, Charlotte Mary (1823–1901) English novelist. Born in Otterbourne, Hampshire, she published over 100 novels, which were all pervaded by the same high church tone, beginning with *The Heir of Redclyffe* in 1853. She used part of the profits from this novel to aid Bishop George Selwyn in fitting out his missionary schooner *Southern Cross* and spent the entire profits of a later work, *Daisy Chain*, on building a missionary college in New Zealand. She also published some non-fiction works and edited a girls' magazine, *Monthly Packet*, from 1851 to 1890.

COUNTESS KATE in C.M. Yonge, *Countess Kate* (1862)

'[Charlotte Yonge] differs from the great majority of novelists because, in none of her many books, with two exceptions, did she ever project any version . . . of herself. The exceptions are *Countess Kate* and *Abbeychurch*. Countess Kate was quite certainly Charlotte as a child; the description that Charlotte gives of herself in the autobiographical fragment [written late in her life] is practically identical with the one she gives of Kate' (Georgina Battiscombe, 1943, *Charlotte Mary Yonge*, p. 9.).

ELIZABETH WOODBOURNE in C.M. Yonge, *Abbeychurch* (1844)

'The only other book in which it seems to me possible to detect Charlotte under another name is *Abbeychurch*. . . . There, the heroine, Elizabeth Woodbourne, is the embodiment of Charlotte's tastes, enthusiasms and aspirations, rather than of her personality' (ibid.).

YONGE, Dr James (1794–1870) Physician of Plymouth. He was an uncle of Charlotte Yonge.

DR MAY in C.M. Yonge, *The Daisy Chain* (1856)

'"A most eager, impulsive man, quick of speech, yet capable of great tenderness" , he is noteworthy as the possible original of the best-loved of all Charlotte's creations, Dr May of the *Daisy Chain*' (Georgina Battiscombe, 1943, *Charlotte Mary Yonge*, p. 21).

YORK, Sergeant Alvin Cullum (b. 1887) Of Tennessee. In October 1918 he captured 132 prisoners single-handed in the battle for the clearing of the Argonne.

SERGEANT MILL PORSUM in Robert Penn Warren, *At Heaven's Gate* (1943)

'The prototype for Private Porsum seems in some ways to have been Sergeant York' (Chester E. Eisinger, 1963, *Fiction of the Forties*, p. 213).

YORKE, Dorothy Known as 'Arabella', she was from Pennsylvania and had a lengthy involvement with John **Cournos**. In 1917 she arrived in London and embarked on an affair with Richard **Aldington** (who was married to Hilda Doolittle at the time) which lasted until 1928.

BELLA CARTER in H.D. (Hilda Doolittle), *Bid Me To Live* (1960)

Identified by Helen McNeil in the introduction to *Bid Me to Live*, 1984, pp. viii–ix, and by Perdita Schaffner in the afterword, p. 187.

JOSEPHINE FORD in D.H. Lawrence, *Aaron's Rod* (1922)

'This is Lawrence's Josephine Ford . . . "a cameo-like girl with neat black hair done tight and bright in the French mode"' (H.T. Moore, 1980, *The Priest of Love: a life of D.H. Lawrence*, rev. edn, Harmondsworth: Penguin, p. 361; originally published 1955 as *The Intelligent Heart: the story of D.H. Lawrence*, London: Heinemann).

WINIFRED GWYNNE in John Cournos, *Miranda Masters* (1926)

The identification is based upon obvious parallels.

YOUNG, William Richard Blackman (1894–1972) Educated at Wellington College and at Keble College, Oxford, he joined the staff of **Arnold House**, Llanddulas, in May 1925; at this time Evelyn Waugh was completing his last term as an assistant master at the school. Young confided to Waugh that he had been expelled from Wellington, sent down from Oxford, forced to resign his commission in the Army, and had left four schools precipitately: 'three in the middle of term through his being taken in sodomy and one through his being drunk six nights in succession' (entry for 3 July 1925, *The Diaries of Evelyn Waugh*, 1976, ed. Michael Davie, London: Weidenfeld & Nicolson, p. 213). According to the entry in the Keble College Centenary Register (perhaps composed by himself), he served with some distinction in the First World War, being mentioned in dispatches (in 1919!). In 1928 he abandoned schoolmastering and later qualified as a solicitor, practising until 1956. His last years were spent in the St Cross Almshouses at Winchester, owing to some unfortunate speculations, but he left £58,000 and a collection of German and Chelsea porcelain to the Ashmolean Museum in Oxford. In 1934, under the name of Richard MacNaughton, he published *The Preparatory School Murder*.

EDGAR GRIMES in Evelyn Waugh, *Decline and Fall* (1928)

'A very surprising man . . . had come . . . as second master; a dapper man of sunny disposition who spoke the idiom of the army. He later provided certain features for the character "Captain Grimes"' (Evelyn Waugh, 1964, *A Little Learning . . . an autobiography*, London: Chapman and Hall, p. 227). Identified as 'Young' in entry for 1 May 1925, Waugh, op. cit., p. 211 and n. 2).

YOUNG STREET, Kensington, London Thackeray lived at number 13 from 1846 to 1853.

WADDILOVE STREET in W.M. Thackeray, 'Our Street' (1848)

'[Thackeray] knew intimately the Kensington world of the 1840s . . . and he preserved it for posterity in . . . *Our Street* where . . . Young Street [is] faithfully presented under the [name] of Waddilove Street' (Gordon Ray, 1958, *Thackeray: the age of wisdom*, p. 4).

Z

ZAHN, Lois A stationery clerk at the Fair Store in Chicago. She met Theodore Dreiser at Christmas 1891, and they were close during the year before he left for St Louis.

ALICE KANE in Theodore Dreiser, *A Book About Myself* (1922)

'In the midst of his reporting duties he still tried to correspond with a Chicago girl called Lois (Alice in *A Book About Myself*)' (Yoshinobu Hakutani, 1980, *Young Dreiser*, p. 78).

ZANETTA, Isabella Daughter of the family who kept a hotel in Arona, Italy, where Samuel Butler stayed in 1871; Butler returned in 1878, accompanied by Festing Jones. In 1885 she moved to Florence, where she kept another hotel.

ELLEN in Samuel Butler, *The Way of All Flesh* (1903)

'The hotel was kept by a family, and one of the daughters, Isabella, was a magnificently beautiful woman of whom he had often spoken to me. . . . "Her lips were full and restful, with something of an Egyptian sphinx-like character about them." This is from the description of Ellen in *The Way of All Flesh* (chapter xxxviii), and I have no doubt that in writing it he was thinking of Isabella. . . . But Ellen's moral character was not taken from Isabella. . . . Butler made this note about – Isabella: "I have never seen any woman comparable to her, and kept out of her way on purpose after leaving Arona [in 1871] as the only thing to be done, for we had become thick. I kept away from Arona for years; but at last returned with Jones, for I wanted to show her to him and to see her again, which I might now safely do."' (H. Festing Jones, 1919, *Samuel Butler: author of Erewhon*, Vol. I, London: Macmillan, pp. 283–4).

ZELL-AM-SEE, Austria Located near Salzburg. Frieda **Lawrence**'s sister and brother-in law, Johanna and Max von **Schreibershofen**, owned the Villa Alpensee at Thumersbach, Zell-am-See, where the Lawrence's stayed from 20 July to 25 August 1921.

KAPRUN in D.H. Lawrence, 'The Captain's Doll' (1923)

'We were in Austria in 1921. "The Captain's Doll" ends in Zell-am-See' (to Gilbert Seldes, 25 February 1923, reproduced in *The D.H. Lawrence Letters*, 1987, Vol. IV, ed. W. Roberts, James T. Boulton and E. Mansfield, Cambridge: Cambridge University Press, p. 398).

ZELTER, Karl Friedrich (1758–1832) German conductor and composer. He corresponded with Goethe.

ARONACH in Elizabeth Sara Sheppard, *Charles Auchester* (1853)

Identified in Michael Sadleir, 1951, *XIX Century Fiction*, Vol. I, London: Constable, and Los Angeles: California University Press, p. 320; and in an anonymous typed key laid in a copy of the first edition of *Charles Auchester* which is now in the possession of the present author.

ZICHY-FERRARIS, Charlotte, Countess Youngest daughter of the mistress of Lord Hertford, Lady **Strachan**. In 1837 she married Count Emanuel Zichy-Ferraris, brother of Prince **Metternich**'s third wife and Chamberlain to the Austrian Emperor; Disraeli reports meeting the Count with Count **D'Orsay**. The Countess was reputed to have inherited £150,000 from Lord Hertford.

PRINCESS LUCRETIA COLONNA in Benjamin Disraeli, *Coningsby* (1844)

Identified in a key in *Notes and Queries* (8th series) 3 (13 May 1893): 363. *See also under* **Bright**, John.

3
Fictional Names

A

A., MR
The Adventures of Peregrine Pickle
(1751) (Chapter 98)
by Tobias Smollett
Annesley, James

ABBERVILLE, LADY
The Repealers (1833)
by Lady Blessington
Charleville, Lady

ABBERVILLE, LORD
The Repealers (1833)
by Lady Blessington
Charleville, Lord

ABBOTSCERNEL
Wessex novels and tales (1871–95)
by Thomas Hardy
Cerne Abbas, Dorset

ABBOTSEA
Wessex novels and tales (1871–95)
by Thomas Hardy
Abbotsbury, Dorset

ABBOTT, JERUSHA ('JUDY')
Daddy Long-Legs (1912)
by Jean Webster
Crapsey, Adelaide

ABERALVA
Two Years Ago (1857)
by Charles Kingsley
Clovelly, Devon

ABERCROMBIE, SIR AMBROSE
The Loved One (1948)
by Evelyn Waugh
Smith, Sir Aubrey

ADA
'Two Women' (1925)
by Gertrude Stein
Cone, Etta

ADAM, MISS
Dolores (1911)
by I. Compton-Burnett
Robinson, Margaret Hayes

ADAMS, HENRY (THE DOCTOR)
In Our Time (1925)
by Ernest Hemingway
Hemingway, C.E.

ADAMS, NICK
In Our Time (1925)
by Ernest Hemingway
Hemingway, Ernest

ADELE
Things As They Are (1950)
by Gertrude Stein
Stein, Gertrude

AGINCOURT, DUCHESS OF
Coningsby (1844)
by Benjamin Disraeli
Grenville, Lady

AGINCOURT, DUKE OF
Coningsby (1844)
by Benjamin Disraeli
**Grenville, Lord, 2nd Duke of
    Buckingham and Chandos**

AGNEAU, CHEVALIER ANDRÉ
Albert Lunel (1844)
by Lord Brougham
Agnew, Sir Andrew

AHEARN
The Young Lions (1948)
by Irwin Shaw
Hemingway, Ernest

AIDEN, LORD
The Old Order Changes (1886)
by W.H. Mallock
Lytton, Robert Bulwer, 1st Earl of

AINSLIE, The Earl of
Sylvie and Bruno (1889)
by Lewis Carroll
Salisbury, Lord

AINTREY, Larned
The Sleep of Reason (1956)
by Warren Miller
Alsop, Joseph

AINTREY, Procter
The Sleep of Reason (1956)
by Warren Miller
Alsop, Stewart

AKED, Mr
The Man from the North (1898)
by Arnold Bennett
Eland, John

ALBANY, Lord
The Repealers (1833)
by Lady Blessington
Alvanley, Lord

ALBERT
A Dance to the Music of Time
(1951–76)
by Anthony Powell
Gomme, James

ALBERT, Colonel (Prince
Florestan)
Endymion (1880)
by Benjamin Disraeli
Napoleon III, Emperor of France

ALCONLEIGH, Lady ('Aunt Sadie')
The Pursuit of Love (1945)
by Nancy Mitford
Redesdale, Lady

ALDBRICKHAM
Wessex novels and tales (1871–95)
by Thomas Hardy
Reading, Berkshire

ALDEN, Roberta ('Bert')
An American Tragedy (1925)
by Theodore Dreiser
Brown, Grace ('Billy')

ALDINGTON, Emily, Lady
The New Humpty-Dumpty (1912)
by Ford Madox Ford
Hunt, Violet

ALDWINKLE, Mrs Lilian
Those Barren Leaves (1925)
by Aldous Huxley
Morrell, Lady Ottoline

ALHAMBRA, Lord
Vivian Grey (1826–7)
by Benjamin Disraeli
Porchester, Lord

ALICE
Alice's Adventures in Wonderland
(1865) and *Through the
Looking-Glass* (1872)
by Lewis Carroll
Liddell, Alice

ALIX
Non-combatants and Others (1916)
by Rose Macaulay
Macaulay, Rose

ALLEN, Lord
The New Republic (1877)
by W.H. Mallock
Pembroke, 13th Earl of

ALLFAIR
Paul Clifford (1830)
by Bulwer Lytton
Alvanley, Lord

ALLPORT, Mr
The Trespasser (1912)
by D.H. Lawrence
Aylwin, R.H.

ALMACKS, Marchioness of
Vivian Grey (1826–7)
by Benjamin Disraeli
Londonderry, 3rd Marchioness of

ALMAYER, Kaspar
Almayer's Folly (1895)
by Joseph Conrad
Olmeijer, William Charles

ALSAGER, Mrs
'Nona Vincent' (1891)
by Henry James
Bell, Florence

ALSOP, Jerry
The Web and the Rock (1939)
by Thomas Wolfe
Terry, John Skally

ALTAMONT
Look Homeward, Angel (1929) and
Of Time and the River (1935)
by Thomas Wolfe
Asheville, North Carolina

ALTAMONT, Duke of
Vivian Grey (1826–7)
by Benjamin Disraeli
Nugent of Carlanston, Lord

ALTAMONTE, Duke of
Glenarvon (1816)
by Lady Caroline Lamb
Devonshire, 6th Duke of

ALVAN, Sigismund
The Tragic Comedians (1880)
by George Meredith
Lassalle, Ferdinand

AMARINTH, Esmé
The Green Carnation (1894)
by Robert Hichens
Wilde, Oscar

The AMBASSADOR
Eleanor (1899)
by Mrs Humphry Ward
Dufferin and Ava, 1st Marquis of

The —— AMBASSADOR
Alton Locke (1850)
by Charles Kingsley
Bunsen, Baron

AMBIENT, Mark
'The Author of "Beltraffio"' (1884)
by Henry James
Symonds, John Addington

AMBROSE
Down There on a Visit (1962)
by Christopher Isherwood
Turville-Petre, Francis

AMBROSE, Helen
The Voyage Out (1915)
by Virginia Woolf
Bell, Vanessa

AMBROSE, Ridley
The Voyage Out (1915)
by Virginia Woolf
Stephen, Sir Leslie

The AMERICAN AMBASSADOR
The Sense of the Past (1917)
by Henry James
Lowell, James Russell

AMES, Bob
Sister Carrie (1900)
by Theodore Dreiser
Gates, Elmer

AMORY, Blanche
The History of Pendennis (1848–50)
by W.M. Thackeray
Reviss, Theresa
Thynne, Cecilia Anne

AMY
Dawn (1931)
by Theodore Dreiser
Dreiser, Cecilia

AMYSFORT, Lady
A Lodge in the Wilderness (1906)
by John Buchan
Desborough, Lady

ANASTASE, Florimond
Charles Auchester (1853)
by Elizabeth Sara Sheppard
Berlioz, Hector

ANCHORAGE HOUSE
Vile Bodies (1930)
by Evelyn Waugh
Londonderry House, London

ANCRUM, Richard
The History of David Grieve (1891)
by Mrs Humphry Ward
Madge, Travers

DE ANGELIS, Villa
The Lost Stradivarius (1895)
by J. Meade Faulkner
Maya, Villa, Posilipo, Italy

ANGELO
Norman Leslie: A Tale of the Present Times (1835)
by Theodore S. Fay
Greenough, Horatio

ANGLEBURY
Wessex novels and tales (1871–95)
by Thomas Hardy
Wareham, Dorset

The ANGLO-GERMANIST
Lavengro (1851)
by George Borrow
Taylor of Norwich, William

ANN
Of Time and the River (1935)
by Thomas Wolfe
Harding, Helen

ANNA
'The Good Anna', *Three Lives* (1909)
by Gertrude Stein
Lebender, Lena

ANNA LIVIA PLURABELLE
See Plurabelle, Anna Livia

ANNESLEY, James
The Wandering Heir (1872)
by Charles Reade
Annesley, James

ANSELL, Stewart
The Longest Journey (1907)
by E.M. Forster
Ainsworth, A.R.
Meredith, H.O.

ANSELM'S INN
Pilgrimage (1915–67)
by Dorothy Richardson
Clifford's Inn, London

ANSTRUTHER, Vincent
Sydenham; or Memoirs of a Man of the World (1830)
by W. Massie
Canning, George

ANTICANT, Pessimus
The Warden (1855)
by Anthony Trollope
Carlyle, Thomas

ANTICHRIST
Keep the Aspidistra Flying (1936)
by George Orwell
The Adelphi

ANTIJACK, Mr Anyside
Melincourt (1817)
by Thomas Love Peacock
Canning, George

ANTILLES
Vivian Grey (1826–7)
by Benjamin Disraeli
Ellis, Charles Rose, 1st Baron Seaford

ANTONIO
'The Fifth Column', *The Fifth Column and the First Forty-nine Stories* (1938)
by Ernest Hemingway
Quintanilla, Pepe

APE, Mrs Melrose
Vile Bodies (1930)
by Evelyn Waugh
McPherson, Aimée Semple

APPIN, Lord
A Lodge in the Wilderness (1906)
by John Buchan
Balfour, A.J.
Rosebery, Lord

APSLEY, Major Basil
See Hepburn, Mr

APSLEY, Lady Daphne
See Hepburn, Lady

ARBUTHNOT ('The Babe')
The Babe, B.A. (1897)
by E.F. Benson
Pollitt, Herbert Charles

ARBUTHNOT, Sandy
Greenmantle (1916)
by John Buchan
Herbert, Aubrey

The Courts of the Morning (1929)
by John Buchan
Herbert, Aubrey
Lawrence, T.E.

ARBUTON, Miles
A Chance Acquaintance (1874)
by W.D. Howells
Perry, Thomas Sergeant

ARCHBOLD, Captain
'The Secret Sharer', *'Twixt Land and
    Sea* (1912)
by Joseph Conrad
Clark, Captain Joseph Lucas

ARCHER, Mr
The History of Pendennis (1848–50)
by W.M. Thackeray
Hill, Thomas

ARCHER, Frank
We Accept With Pleasure (1934)
by Bernard de Voto
Lewis, Sinclair

ARCHER, Isabel
The Portrait of a Lady (1880)
by Henry James
Temple, Mary ('Minny')

ARCHIESTOWN, Earl of ('Lord
    Archie')
Friendship (1878)
by Ouida
Duff-Gordon, Sir Alexander

ARDACHEFF, Princess
His Hour (1910)
by Elinor Glyn
Vladimir of Russia, Grand Duchess

ARDENNE, Mr
Lothair (1870)
by Benjamin Disraeli
Shirley of Ettington, Evelyn Philip

ARGALLO, Walter
'Walter Argallo and Felix Ledgett', *A
    Variety of Things* (1928)
by Max Beerbohm
Conrad, Joseph

ARGYLE, James
Aaron's Rod (1922)
by D.H. Lawrence
Douglas, Norman

ARLINGTON, Charles, Lord
The Two Friends (1835)
by Lady Blessington
Duncombe, Thomas Slingsby

ARMAND
'The Doldrums', *Forsytes, Pendyces
    and Others* (1935)
by John Galsworthy
Conrad, Joseph

ARNEEL, Timothy
The Titan (1914)
by Theodore Dreiser
Armour, Philip D.

ARONACH
Charles Auchester (1853)
by Elizabeth Sara Sheppard
Zelter, Karl Friedrich

ARROWSMITH, Martin
Arrowsmith (1925)
by Sinclair Lewis
Hussey, R.G.

ARTHUR, George
Tom Brown's Schooldays (1857)
by Thomas Hughes
Adam, W.P.

Orlebar, August
Walrond, Theodore

ARTIFONI, ALMIDANO
Ulysses (1922)
by James Joyce
Ghezzi, Father Charles, SJ

ASHBURNHAM, EDWARD
The Good Soldier (1915)
by Ford Madox Ford
Ford, Ford Madox

ASHBURNHAM, LEONORA
The Good Soldier (1915)
by Ford Madox Ford
Hueffer, Elsie

ASHE, WILLIAM
The Marriage of William Ashe (1905)
by Mrs Humphry Ward
Melbourne, Lord

ASHENDEN, WILLIAM
Ashenden; or The British Agent
(1928)
by W. Somerset Maugham
Maugham, W. Somerset

ASHLEY, BRETT, LADY
The Sun Also Rises (1926)
by Ernest Hemingway
Twysden, Duff, Lady

ASHTON, LADY
The Bride of Lammermoor (1819)
by Sir Walter Scott
Stair, Margaret, Lady

ASHTON, JULIA
Bid Me to Live (1960)
by H.D. (Hilda Doolittle)
Doolittle, Hilda

ASHTON, LUCY
The Bride of Lammermoor (1819)
by Sir Walter Scott
Dalrymple, Janet

ASHTON, RAFE
Bid Me To Live (1960)
by H.D. (Hilda Doolittle)
Aldington, Richard

ASPECT, JASPER
Wigs on the Green (1935)
by Nancy Mitford
Murray, Basil

ASPERN, JEFFREY
The Aspern Papers (1888)
by Henry James
Shelley, Percy Bysshe

ASSHER, LADY
'Mr Gilfil's Love Story', *Scenes of
    Clerical Life* (1857–8)
by George Eliot
Anstruther, Lady

ASSHER, BEATRICE
'Mr Gilfil's Love Story', *Scenes of
    Clerical Life* (1857–8)
by George Eliot
Anstruther, Miss

ASSHETON, ROBERT
Sooner or Later (1904)
by Violet Hunt
Crawfurd, Oswald

THE ASSISTANT COMMISSIONER
The Secret Agent (1907)
by Joseph Conrad
Anderson, Sir Robert
Vincent, Sir Howard

VON ASSLINGEN, JULIUS
Vivian Grey (1826–7)
by Benjamin Disraeli
Brummell, Beau

ASTBURY, LEWIS
A Lodge in the Wilderness (1906)
by John Buchan
Amery, L.S.

ASTERIAS
Nightmare Abbey (1818)
by Thomas Love Peacock
Denys de Montfort, Pierre
Sinclair, Sir John

ATHELHALL
Wessex novels and tales (1871–95)
by Thomas Hardy
Athelhampton Hall, Dorset

ATHELSTAN, Mrs
The Reflections of Ambrosine (1902)
by Elinor Glyn
Saunders, Mrs Thomas

The *ATTACK-ALL REVIEW*
Vivian Grey (1826–7)
by Benjamin Disraeli
The *Quarterly Review*

ATTIE, Fighting
See Fighting Attie

AUCHESTER, Charles
Charles Auchester (1853)
by Elizabeth Sara Sheppard
Horsley, Charles
Joachim, Joseph

AUDLEY COURT
Lady Audley's Secret (1862)
by M.E. Braddon
Ingatestone Hall, Essex

AUDUBON, Philip
A Modern Symposium (1905)
by G. Lowes Dickinson
Schiller, Ferdinand Canning Scott

AUGUSTUS, Lord Harold
Harold the Exile (1819)
by Anon.
Byron, Lord

AUMS, Alex
Desolation Angels (1965)
by Jack Kerouac
Watts, Alan Wilson

AVELLANOS, Antonia
Nostromo (1904)
by Joseph Conrad
Ribera, Antonia

AVELLANOS, Don José
Nostromo (1904)
by Joseph Conrad
Pérez Triana, Santiago

AVERY, Helen
'Magnetism' (1951)
by F. Scott Fitzgerald
Moran, Lois

D'AVESNES, Count
Friendship (1878)
by Ouida
Ramé, Louis

D'AVESNES, Etoile, Comtesse
Friendship (1878)
by Ouida
Ouida

AVONDALE, Lord
Glenarvon (1816)
by Lady Caroline Lamb
Melbourne, Lord

AXE
Anna of the Five Towns (1902) and
    others
by Arnold Bennett
Leek, Staffordshire

AYLWIN, Cyril
Aylwin (1899)
by Theodore Watts-Dunton
Watts, Alfred Eugene

AYLWIN, Henry
Aylwin (1899)
by Theodore Watts-Dunton
Watts-Dunton, Theodore

AYLWIN, Philip
Aylwin (1899)
by Theodore Watts-Dunton
Watts, James Orlando

AZANIA
Black Mischief (1932)
by Evelyn Waugh
Abyssinia

AZIZ, Dr
A Passage to India (1924)
by E.M. Forster
Masood, Syed Ross

B

B. (or W.S.B.)
The Enormous Room (1922)
by E.E. Cummings
Brown, William Slater

BABCOCK, Benjamin
The American (1876)
by Henry James
James, William

BABINGTON
Pilgrimage (1915–67)
by Dorothy Richardson
Abingdon, Berkshire

BACHELOR BILL
Paul Clifford (1830)
by Bulwer Lytton
Devonshire, 6th Duke of

The BACHELOR FRIEND
'The Nice Little Couple', *Sketches of
    Young Couples* (1840)
by Charles Dickens
Chapman, Edward

The BACK KITCHEN
The History of Pendennis (1848–50)
by W.M. Thackeray
The Cider Cellars, London

BACON, Mr
The History of Pendennis (1848–50)
by W.M. Thackeray
Bentley, Richard

BADGER, Mr
The Wind in the Willows (1908)
by Kenneth Grahame
Henley, W.E.
Portland, 5th Duke of

BADGERY, Lord
'The Tillotson Banquet' (1924)
by Aldous Huxley
Sitwell, Sir Osbert

BAGOT, William ('Little Billee')
Trilby (1894)
by George Du Maurier
Armstrong, Thomas
Walker, Frederick

BAGSHAW, Octavius
See Budden, Octavius

BAGSHOT
See Old Bags

BAILEY, Mrs
Pilgrimage (1915–67)
by Dorothy Richardson
Baker, Keziah

BAILEY, Altiora
The New Machiavelli (1911)
by H.G. Wells
Webb, Beatrice

BAILEY, Oscar
The New Machiavelli (1911)
by H.G. Wells
Webb, Sidney

BAILEY, Rosalind
The Web and the Rock (1939)
by Thomas Wolfe
Wylie, Elinor

BAILEY, Tom
The Story of a Bad Boy (1870)
by T.B. Aldrich
Aldrich, T.B.

BAILEY FARM
'The Fox' (1923)
by D.H. Lawrence
Grimsbury Farm, Berkshire

BAINBRIGGE
Nicholas Crabbe (1958)
by F.W. Rolfe
Bainbridge, Henry Charles

BAINES'S
The Old Wives' Tale (1908)
by Arnold Bennett
Longson's

BAIRD, REVD MR
'The Sad Fortunes of the Revd Amos
 Barton', *Scenes of Clerical Life*
 (1857–8)
by George Eliot
Sandford, Revd Mr

BAIRD, JENNIFER
Dusty Answer (1927)
by Rosamund Lehmann
Hartley, Grizel

BAKER, JORDAN
The Great Gatsby (1925)
by F. Scott Fitzgerald
Cummings, Edith

BALAYE, MONSIEUR
Albert Lunel (1844)
by Lord Brougham
Brougham, Lord

BALIOL, MARTHA BETHUNE
'The Highland Widow', *Chronicles
 of the Canongate* (1827) (1st
 series)
by Sir Walter Scott
Keith, Anne Murray

BALLAH
John Sherman (1891)
by W.B. Yeats
Sligo, Ireland

BANBRIGG
A Life's Morning (1888)
by George Gissing
Agbrigg, Yorkshire

BANBURY PARK
Pilgrimage (1915–67)
by Dorothy Richardson
Finsbury Park, North London

BANFORD, JILL
'The Fox' (1923)
by D.H. Lawrence
Lambert, Cecily
Radford, Margaret

BANKES, WILLIAM
To the Lighthouse (1927)
by Virginia Woolf
Headlam, Walter

BANNISDALE
Helbeck of Bannisdale (1898)
by Mrs Humphry Ward
Levens Hall, Cumbria
Sizergh Castle, Cumbria

BANNISTER, ALGY
The Conventionalists (1908)
by R.H. Benson
Firbank, Ronald

BAR
Little Dorrit (1855–7)
by Charles Dickens
Kelly, Sir Fitzroy

BARBAN, TOMMY
Tender is the Night (1934)
by F. Scott Fitzgerald
Braggiotti, Mario
Hitchcock, Thomas
Jozan, Edouard

BARBARA
The Will to Love (1919)
by Hugh Kingsmill
Bagnold, Enid

BARBECUE SMITH, MR
Crome Yellow (1921)
by Aldous Huxley
Bennett, Arnold

BARCHESTER
The Warden (1855)
by Anthony Trollope
Salisbury, Wiltshire
Winchester, Hampshire

BARDELL, Mrs
The Pickwick Papers (1836–7)
by Charles Dickens
Ellis, Ann

BARDELL V. PICKWICK
The Pickwick Papers (1836–7)
by Charles Dickens
Norton v. Melbourne

DE BARDI, Romola
Romola (1863)
by George Eliot
Bodichon, Barbara

BARFLEUR
A Traveler at Forty (1913)
by Theodore Dreiser
Richards, Grant

BARGÉ, Isabelle
This Side of Paradise (1920)
by F. Scott Fitzgerald
King, Ginevra

BARKLEY, Catherine
A Farewell to Arms (1929)
by Ernest Hemingway
Hemingway, Hadley
Hemingway, Pauline
Jessup, Elsie
Von Kurowsky, Agnes

BARMBY, Revd Mr
One of Our Conquerors (1891)
by George Meredith
Jessop, Augustus

BARNACLE, Tite
Little Dorrit (1855–7)
by Charles Dickens
Stephen, Sir James

BARNARD
Lions and Shadows (1938)
by Christopher Isherwood
Layard, John

BARNES, Etta
The Bulwark (1946)
by Theodore Dreiser
Tatum, Anna

BARNES, Jake
The Sun Also Rises (1926)
by Ernest Hemingway
Bird, William
Hemingway, Ernest

BARNES, Lett
Bid Me To Live (1960)
by H.D. (Hilda Doolittle)
Pound, Ezra

BARNES, Solon
The Bulwark (1946)
by Theodore Dreiser
Dreiser, John Paul
Tatum, Mr

BARNES, Stewart
The Bulwark (1946)
by Theodore Dreiser
Dreiser, Marcus Romanus

THE BARON
'The Thorn in the Flesh' (1914)
by D.H. Lawrence
Richthofen, Friedrich, Baron von

THE BARONESS
Vivian Grey (1826–7)
by Benjamin Disraeli
Amelia, Princess

BARONI, Francis, the Elder
Tancred (1847)
by Benjamin Disraeli
Belzoni, Giovanni Battista

BARRACE, Miss
The Ambassadors (1903)
by Henry James
Reubell, Henrietta

BARRACLOUGH, Paul Hawley
The Politician (1959)
by Stephen Longstreet and Ethel
    Longstreet
Roosevelt, Franklin D.

BARSET
The Warden (1855)
by Anthony Trollope
Somerset

BARTER, Timothy
Holy Deadlock (1934)
by A.P. Herbert
Haynes, E.S.P.

BARTLEBY
'Bartleby the Scrivener', *The Piazza
    Tales* (1856)
by Herman Melville
Thoreau, Henry David

BARTLETT, Charlotte
A Room with a View (1908)
by E.M. Forster
Forster, Emily

BARTON, Mr
Muslin (1915)
by George Moore
Browne, James

BARTON, Mrs
Muslin (1915)
by George Moore
Murphy, Anna

BARTON, Amelia ('Milly')
'The Sad Fortunes of the Revd Amos
    Barton', *Scenes of Clerical Life*
    (1857–8)
by George Eliot
Gwyther, Emma

BARTON, Revd Amos
'The Sad Fortunes of the Revd Amos
    Barton', *Scenes of Clerical Life*
    (1857–8)
by George Eliot
Gwyther, Revd John

BARTON, Helen Gant
Look Homeward, Angel (1929) and
    Of Time and the River (1935)
by Thomas Wolfe
Wheaton, Mabel

BARTON, Hugh
Look Homeward, Angel (1929) and
    Of Time and the River (1935)
by Thomas Wolfe
Wheaton, Ralph

BARTRAM, Ernita
'Ernita', *A Gallery of Women* (1929)
by Theodore Dreiser
Goldman, Emma

BARWITH STRAND
A Pair of Blue Eyes (1873)
by Thomas Hardy
Trebarwith Strand, Cornwall

BASIL
The Holiday (1949)
by Stevie Smith
Orwell, George

BASKE, Miriam
The Emancipated (1890)
by George Gissing
Gissing, Margaret

BATEMAN, Miss (the 'Rosamunda')
Vivian (1812)
by Maria Edgeworth
Morgan, Sydney, Lady

BATES (the gardener)
'Mr Gilfil's Love Story', *Scenes of
    Clerical Life* (1857–8)
by George Eliot
Baines

BATES, Elizabeth
'Odour of Chrysanthemums' (1914)
by D.H. Lawrence
Allam, Polly

BATTERSBY
The Way of All Flesh (1903)
by Samuel Butler
Langar, Nottinghamshire

BAUM, ADOLPH HERMAN
Most Likely to Succeed (1954)
by John Dos Passos
Kahn, Otto

BAXTER, PENTON
More Miles (1926)
by Harry Kemp
Sinclair, Upton

BAYHAM, FRED
The Newcomes (1854–5)
by W.M. Thackeray
Bolland, William Proctor

BAYNES, MRS
The Adventures of Philip (1861–2)
by W.M. Thackeray
Shawe, Isabella

BAYNES, CHARLOTTE
The Adventures of Philip (1861–2)
by W.M. Thackeray
Thackeray, Isabella

BAZHAKULOFF
South Wind (1917)
by Norman Douglas
John of Cronstadt, Father
Rasputin

BEAMISH, BEAU
A Tale of Chloe (1879)
by George Meredith
Nash, Richard (Beau Nash)

THE BEAR GARDEN
The Duke's Children (1879–80)
by Anthony Trollope
The Garrick Club, Covent Garden, London

BEARD, CAPTAIN ELIJAH
'Youth' (1902)
by Joseph Conrad
Beard, Captain John

BEARDSALL, CYRIL
The White Peacock (1911)
by D.H. Lawrence
Lawrence, D.H.

BEARDSALL, FRANK
The White Peacock (1911)
by D.H. Lawrence
Lawrence, John Arthur

BEARDSALL, LETTIE
The White Peacock (1911)
by D.H. Lawrence
Lawrence, Ada

BEAUCHAMP, HENRY
Arlington (1832)
by T.H. Lister
Brummell, Beau

BEAUCHAMP, NEVIL
Beauchamp's Career (1876)
by George Meredith
Maxse, Rear-Admiral Frederick Augustus

BEAUCLERC, GRANVILLE
Helen (1834)
by Maria Edgeworth
Edgeworth, Francis

BEAUFORT, JULIUS
The Age of Innocence (1920)
by Edith Wharton
Belmont, August
Jones, George Alfred

BEAUMANOIR
Coningsby (1844)
by Benjamin Disraeli
Belvoir Castle, Leicestershire

BEAUMANOIR, LORD
Coningsby (1844)
by Benjamin Disraeli
Rutland, 6th Duke of

BEAUMONT, Richard
Sydenham; or Memoirs of a Man of the World (1830)
by W. Massie
Brummell, Beau

BEAVER, Mrs
A Handful of Dust (1934)
by Evelyn Waugh
Maugham, Syrie

BEAVIS, John
Eyeless in Gaza (1936)
by Aldous Huxley
Huxley, Leonard
Weekley, Ernest

BEAVIS, Maisie
Eyeless in Gaza (1936)
by Aldous Huxley
Huxley, Julia

BECK, Madame Modeste Maria
Villette (1853)
by Charlotte Brontë
Héger, Madame Claire Zoë

BECKENDORFF
Vivian Grey (1826–7)
by Benjamin Disraeli
Metternich, Prince

BECKER, Geheimrat
The Web and the Rock (1939)
by Thomas Wolfe
Lexer, Erich

BEDE, Adam
Adam Bede (1859)
by George Eliot
Evans, Robert

BEDE, Dinah
See Morris, Dinah

BEDE, Seth
Adam Bede (1859)
by George Eliot
Evans, Samuel

BEDE, Thias
Adam Bede (1859)
by George Eliot
Evans, George[1]
Evans, George[2]

BEDFORD, Dick
Lovel the Widower (1860)
by W.M. Thackeray
James, Samuel

BEECH, Lady
Pigeon Pie (1940)
by Nancy Mitford
Hammersley, Violet

BEERSHEBA
Jude the Obscure (1895)
by Thomas Hardy
Jericho, Oxford

BEETLE
Stalky & Co. (1899)
by Rudyard Kipling
Kipling, Rudyard

BEGGS, Alabama
Save Me the Waltz (1932)
by Zelda Fitzgerald
Fitzgerald, Zelda

BEL, Aunt
See Current, Miss Isabella

BELDOVER
The Rainbow (1915)
by D.H. Lawrence
Eastwood, Nottinghamshire
Quorn, Leicestershire

BELFORD REGIS
Belford Regis (1835)
by Mary Russell Mitford
Reading, Berkshire

BELL, Mr
The Plumed Serpent (1926)
by D.H. Lawrence
Scott, Winfield

BELL, Parson (of Fairly)
Michael Armstrong, the Factory Boy
(1840)
by Frances Trollope
Bull, Revd G.S.

BELL, Geoffrey
The Roaring Queen (1973)
by Wyndham Lewis
Gould, Gerald

BELL, Laura
The History of Pendennis (1848–50)
by W.M. Thackeray
Brookfield, Jane

BELL, Sylverley
Friendship (1878)
by Ouida
Wells, Mr

BELLAIR, Lady
Henrietta Temple (1837)
by Benjamin Disraeli
Corke, Lady

BELLAMY'S
The *Sword of Honour* trilogy
(1952–61)
by Evelyn Waugh
White's Club, London

BELLANDARGUES, Château de
The Blessing (1951)
by Nancy Mitford
d'Ansouis, Château, Vaucluse

BELLARMINE, Rolfe
The Rebel Rose (1888)
by Justin McCarthy and Mrs
Campbell Praed
Churchill, Lord Randolph

BELLASIS, Mr
Eleanor (1899)
by Mrs Humphry Ward
James, Henry

BELLINGHAM, Geoffrey
Robin Linnet (1919)
by E.F. Benson
James, Henry

BELLINGHAM, Horace
Claudius (1883)
by Marion Crawford
Ward, Samuel

BELLONI, Emilia Sandra
Sandra Belloni (Emilia in England)
(1864)
by George Meredith
Macirone, Emilia

BELMONT CLUB
Pilgrimage (1915–67)
by Dorothy Richardson
Arachne Club, London

BELTON, Sir James
'The Tender Achilles' (1932)
by Rudyard Kipling
Bland-Sutton, Sir John

BELUNCLE, Philip
Mr Beluncle (1951)
by V.S. Pritchett
Pritchett, Walter

BEN NEVIS
See MacDonald of Ben Nevis

BENETTE, Clara
Charles Auchester (1853)
by Elizabeth Sara Sheppard
Lind, Jenny

BENNETT, Sergeant-Major
Ulysses (1922)
by James Joyce
Bennett, A. Percy

BENSON, Edward Pettigrew
('Buck')
Look Homeward, Angel (1929)
by Thomas Wolfe
Bernard, W.S.

BENSON, REVD THURSTAN
Ruth (1853)
by Elizabeth Gaskell
Turner, William²

BENSON'S CHAPEL
Ruth (1853)
by Elizabeth Gaskell
**Brook Street Unitarian Chapel,
  Knutsford, Cheshire**

BENTINCK HOTEL
A Generation Missing (1938)
by Carroll Carstairs
Cavendish Hotel, London

BENTON
Pictures from an Institution (1954)
by Randall Jarrell
Sarah Lawrence College, New York

BERGMANN, FRIEDRICH
Prater Violet (1945)
by Christopher Isherwood
Viertel, Berthold

BERNARD
The Waves (1931)
by Virginia Woolf
MacCarthy, Desmond

BERNARD, LADY
The Vicar's Daughter (1872)
by George MacDonald
Byron, Lady

BERNARDSTONE, JOSCELIND
'The Path of Duty' (1884)
by Henry James
Sutherland, Duchess of

BERNERS, ISOPEL
Lavengro (1851)
by George Borrow
Jarvis, Elizabeth

BERON, FATHER
Nostromo (1904)
by Joseph Conrad
Romàn, Father

BERRY, MRS
The Ordeal of Richard Feverel (1859)
by George Meredith
Ockenden, Mrs

BERTIE, AUGUSTUS TREMAINE
Endymion (1880)
by Benjamin Disraeli
**Bulwer, William Henry Lytton Earle
Milnes, Richard Monckton**

BERTOLINI, PENSION
A Room with a View (1908)
by E.M. Forster
Simi, Pension, Florence

BERTRAM, HENRY
Guy Mannering (1815)
by Sir Walter Scott
**Annesley, James
Maxwell, Sir Robert
Routledge, Henry**

BERTRAND, ARCHIE
*John Cornelius: His Life and
    Adventures* (1937)
by Hugh Walpole
Maugham, W. Somerset

BESSO, EVA
Tancred (1847)
by Benjamin Disraeli
de Rothschild, Charlotte

BESTWOOD
Sons and Lovers (1913)
by D.H. Lawrence
Eastwood, Nottinghamshire

BEVERIDGE, LADY
'The Ladybird' (1923)
by D.H. Lawrence
Wemyss, Lady

BEVIS
Woodstock (1826)
by Sir Walter Scott
Nimrod

BHAER, Friedrich
Little Women (1868) and sequels
by Louisa M. Alcott
Rimmer, William
Solger, Reinhold

BIDLAKE, John
Point Counter Point (1928)
by Aldous Huxley
John, Augustus

BIG BITTERN
An American Tragedy (1925)
by Theodore Dreiser
Big Moose Lake, New York

BILHAM, John
The Ambassadors (1903)
by Henry James
Sturges, Jonathan

BILL
'The End of Something', *In Our Time* (1925), and 'The Three Day Blow' (1925)
by Ernest Hemingway
Smith, Bill

BILLY
The Harbor (1915)
by Ernest Poole
Poole, Ernest

BIRCH, Harvey
The Spy (1821)
by James Fenimore Cooper
Crosby, Enoch

BIRCH END
Pugs and Peacocks (1921)
by Gilbert Cannan
Garsington Manor, Oxfordshire

BIRCHESTER
The Old Order Changes (1886)
by W.H. Mallock
Birmingham

BIRDSEYE, Miss
The Bostonians (1884)
by Henry James
Peabody, Elizabeth Palmer

BIRKIN, Rupert
Women in Love (1920)
by D.H. Lawrence
Lawrence, D.H.

The BISHOP
Lothair (1870)
by Benjamin Disraeli
Wilberforce, Samuel

BISSET, Imogene
'The Scandal Detectives' (1935)
by F. Scott Fitzgerald
Hersey, Marie

BITZER, George
Hard Times (1854)
by Charles Dickens
Bidder, George Parker

The BLACK DWARF
See MANLEY, Sir Edward

BLACKHOUSE, Tommy
The *Sword of Honour* trilogy (1952–61)
by Evelyn Waugh
Laycock, Sir Robert

BLACKSTABLE
Of Human Bondage (1915) and *Cakes and Ale* (1930)
by W. Somerset Maugham
Whitstable, Kent

BLACKSTONE
Of Time and the River (1935)
by Thomas Wolfe
Greenville, South Carolina

The BLACKWATER
Wessex novels and tales (1871–95)
by Thomas Hardy
Frome River

BLACKWATER, LADY KITTY
The Marriage of William Ashe (1905)
by Mrs Humphry Ward
Lamb, Lady Caroline

BLACKWOOD, HERBERT
Dolores (1911)
by I. Compton-Burnett
Blackie, Robert

BLADESOVER
Tono-Bungay (1909)
by H.G. Wells
Uppark, South Harting, Sussex

BLAIR, HUBERT
'A Night at the Fair' (1957)
by F. Scott Fitzgerald
Warner, Reuben

BLAIR, THEODORE
Hail to the Chief (1960)
by James Reichley
Taft, Robert A.

BLAKE, EDWARD
The Memorial (1932)
by Christopher Isherwood
Layard, John

BLAKE, WESLEY
Big Matt (1928)
by Brand Whitlock
Harding, Warren G.

BLANC, ADOLPHE
The Well of Loneliness (1928)
by Radclyffe Hall
Mirtil, Adrien

BLANCHE, ANTHONY
Brideshead Revisited (1945)
by Evelyn Waugh
Acton, Harold
Howard, Brian

BLANCOVE, EDWARD
Rhoda Fleming (1865)
by George Meredith
Peacock, Edward

BLANDINGS CASTLE
Something Fresh (1915) and others
by P.G. Wodehouse
Corsham Court, Wiltshire

BLEAK HOUSE
Bleak House (1852–3)
by Charles Dickens
Bleak Hall, St Albans,
Hertfordshire
Great Nast Hyde, Hertfordshire

BLEAKRIDGE
The *Clayhanger* trilogy (1910–16)
by Arnold Bennett
Cobridge, Burslem, Staffordshire

BLENHEIM, HEREWARD
'A Luncheon Party', *Half a Minute's*
Silence and Other Stories (1925)
by Maurice Baring
Churchill, Winston

BLESSINGTON, ENID
Initiation (1914)
by R.H. Benson
Rolfe, F.W.

BLIMBER, DR
Dombey and Son (1846–8)
by Charles Dickens
Everard, Revd E.
King, Joseph Charles

BLIMBER, CORNELIA
Dombey and Son (1846–8)
by Charles Dickens
King, Louisa

BLIMBER'S
Dombey and Son (1846–8)
by Charles Dickens
Chichester House, Brighton
Mr King's School, St John's Wood,
London
Wick House, Brighton

BLISS, REGINALD
Boon (1915)
by H.G. Wells
Bennett, Arnold

BLITHEDALE
The Blithedale Romance (1852)
by Nathaniel Hawthorne
Brook Farm, Massachusetts

BLITZ
An American Tragedy (1925)
by Theodore Dreiser
South Otselic, New York

BLOCH, SEBASTIAN
The Man Who Would Be God (1959)
by Haakon Chevalier
Oppenheimer, Robert

BLOOM, LEOPOLD
Ulysses (1922)
by James Joyce
Bloom, Joseph
Byrne, John Francis
Chance, Charles
Hunter, Alfred H.
Jackson, Holbrook
Joyce, James
Joyce, John
Mayer, Teodoro
Popper, Leopoldo
Schmitz, Ettore

BLOOM, MARION ('MOLLY')
Ulysses (1922)
by James Joyce
Chance, Mrs Charles
Dillon, Mamie
Joyce, Nora
Popper, Amalia
Santos, Signora

BLOOMFIELD, MARY ANN
Agnes Grey (1847)
by Anne Brontë
Ingham, Mary

BLOOMFIELD, TOM
Agnes Grey (1847)
by Anne Brontë
Ingham, Joshua

BLOUNDELL
The History of Pendennis (1848–50)
by W.M. Thackeray
Matthew, Henry

BLUE, ANGEL
The 'Genius' (1915)
by Theodore Dreiser
Dreiser, Sara Osborne White

BLUMINE
Sartor Resartus (1833–4)
by Thomas Carlyle
Carlyle, Jane
Gordon, Margaret
Kirkpatrick, Catherine Aurora
   ('Kitty')

BLUNDELL, RICHARD
A Son of Empire (1899)
by Morley Roberts
Burton, Sir Richard

BLUNDERSTONE
David Copperfield (1849–50)
by Charles Dickens
Blundeston, Suffolk

BLUNT, MRS
The Arrow of Gold (1919)
by Joseph Conrad
Blunt, Ellen

BLYTH, BETTY
The Apes of God (1930)
by Wyndham Lewis
Carrington, Dora

BOBBIN, SIR RODERICK ('BOBBY')
Christmas Pudding (1932)
by Nancy Mitford
Erskine, Hamish

BODIHAM, REVD MR
Crome Yellow (1921)
by Aldous Huxley
Horne, Revd Mr

BOGGART, Professor
The Cantab (1926)
by Shane Leslie
McTaggart, John McTaggart Ellis

von BOHLEN, Jan
Pilgrimage (1915–67)
by Dorothy Richardson
Schleussner, Ellie

BOHUN, Hugo
Lothair (1870)
by Benjamin Disraeli
Calcraft, Sir Henry

The BOMB OUTRAGE
The Secret Agent (1907)
by Joseph Conrad
Greenwich Bomb Outrage

BONNYCASTLE, Mrs
Pandora (1884)
by Henry James
Adams, Marian

BONNYCASTLE, Alfred
Pandora (1884)
by Henry James
Adams, Henry

BONNYCLIFF
Pilgrimage (1915–67)
by Dorothy Richardson
Sandgate, Kent

BONSON, Revd Bobugo
The Weird of the Wanderer (1912)
by F.W. Rolfe
Benson, R.H.

BOON, George
Boon (1915)
by H.G. Wells
Wells, H.G.

BOOTS AT CHRISTOPHERS HOTEL
Coningsby (1844)
by Benjamin Disraeli
Borthwick, Peter

BORCHARDT, Jacob
The Financier (1912)
by Theodore Dreiser
Fox, Daniel Miller

BORDEREAU, Juliana
The Aspern Papers (1888)
by Henry James
Clairmont, Claire
Wykoff, Miss

BORDEREAU, Tita ('Tina')
The Aspern Papers (1888)
by Henry James
Clairmont, Paula ('Pauline')

BOROUGHBY, Lord Amelius
   Fitzfudge
Vivian Grey (1826–7)
by Benjamin Disraeli
Westmorland, John Fane, 11th Earl
   of

BORROMEO
Cloudesley (1830)
by William Godwin
Trelawny, E.J.

BOSHERE, Jo
A Jew in Love (1930)
by Ben Hecht
Bodenheim, Maxwell

BOSINNEY, Philip
The Man of Property (1906)
by John Galsworthy
Garnett, Edward

The BOTTOMS
Sons and Lovers (1913)
by D.H. Lawrence
The Breach, Eastwood,
   Nottinghamshire

BOUNCER, Mr
'Notes on the North
   What-d'ye-Callem Election' (1841)
by W.M. Thackeray
Farrer, James

BOUNDERBY, Josiah
Hard Times (1854)
by Charles Dickens
Chambers, William

BOUNDING BESS
The Ladies Almanack (1928)
by Djuna Barnes
Murphy, Esther

BOWKER, William
Land at Last (1866)
by Edmund Yates
Bolland, William Proctor

BOWLES, Sally
Sally Bowles (1937)
by Christopher Isherwood
Ross, Jean

BOWLEY, Sir Joseph
The Chimes (1844)
by Charles Dickens
Brougham, Lord

BOXER, Tom
The History of Henry Esmond (1852)
by W.M. Thackeray
Forster, John

BOYCE, Marcella
Marcella (1894)
by Mrs Humphry Ward
Ward, Mrs Humphry
Webb, Beatrice

BOYLAN, Hugh ('Blazes')
Ulysses (1922)
by James Joyce
Boylan, Blazes
Kennedy, Hugh Boyle
Keogh, Ted

BOYLE, Jim
Post Adolescence (1923)
by Robert McAlmon
Williams, William Carlos

BOYLE, Nellie
Post Adolescence (1923)
by Robert McAlmon
Williams, Florence

BOYLSTON
A Son at the Front (1923)
by Edith Wharton
Simmons, Ronald

BOYTHORN, Lawrence
Bleak House (1852–3)
by Charles Dickens
Clarke, Charles Cowden
Landor, Walter Savage

BRACEGIRDLE, Mary
Crome Yellow (1921)
by Aldous Huxley
Carrington, Dora

BRADDOCKS, Mrs
The Sun Also Rises (1926)
by Ernest Hemingway
Bowen, Stella

BRADDOCKS, Henry
The Sun Also Rises (1926)
by Ernest Hemingway
Ford, Ford Madox

BRADFORD, Eliot Story
Chosen Country (1951)
by John Dos Passos
Norton, Richard

BRADLEY
The Blue Belles of England (1842)
by Frances Trollope
Landseer, Sir Edwin

BRADLEY, Tommy
To Have and Have Not (1937)
by Ernest Hemingway
Mason, George Grant

BRADSHAW, Thomas
The Revolution in Tanner's Lane
   (1887)
by Mark Rutherford
Binney, Revd Thomas

BRADWARDINE, BARON
Waverley (1814)
by Sir Walter Scott
Forbes, Alexander
Oliphant, Laurence[1]
Stuart of Invernahyle, Alexander

BRADY, CECILIA
The Last Tycoon (1941)
by F. Scott Fitzgerald
Fitzgerald, Frances Scott
Schulberg, Budd

BRAITHWAITE, MR
Sons and Lovers (1913)
by D.H. Lawrence
Brentnall, Alfred Woolston

BRAITHWAITE, LAURA
'The Witch à la Mode' (1934)
by D.H. Lawrence
Macartney, Laura

BRAMHURST COURT
Tess of the d'Urbervilles (1891)
by Thomas Hardy
Moyles Court, Hampshire

BRAMSLEY, CARYL ('C')
C (1924)
by Maurice Baring
Baring, Maurice
Revelstoke, Lord

BRANCEPETH, MR
Lothair (1870)
by Benjamin Disraeli
Sykes, Christopher[1]

BRAND, MR
'The Sad Fortunes of the Revd Amos
    Barton', *Scenes of Clerical Life*
    (1857–8)
by George Eliot
Harris, Mr

BRAND, OLIVE
'Olive Brand', *A Gallery of Women*
    (1929)
by Theodore Dreiser
Smith, Edith Delong

BRANDELL, RICHARD
The Web and the Rock (1939)
by Thomas Wolfe
Mansfield, Richard

BRANDERHAM, REVD JABES
Wuthering Heights (1847)
by Emily Brontë
Bunting, Revd Jabez

BRANDERS, HANS
Davray's Affairs (1906)
by Reginald Turner
Beerbohm, Max

BRANDETSKI, CYRIL
The Simple Life Limited (1911)
by Ford Madox Ford
Soskice, David
Stepniak, Sergius

BRANDNAGEE
John Godfrey's Fortunes (1864)
by Bayard Taylor
O'Brien, Fitz-James

BRANDON, CHRISTOPHER
The Journey of High Honour (1895)
by Olivia Shakespear
Garnett, Edward

BRANDON, GEORGE
A Shabby Genteel Story (1840)
by W.M. Thackeray
Matthew, Henry

BRANDON, LOUIS
The Death of Kings (1954)
by Charles Wertenbaker
Luce, Henry

BRANDT, HARRY F.
Between Day and Night (1959) and
    others
by Charles Angoff
Mencken, H.L.

BRANGWEN, GUDRUN
Women in Love (1920)
by D.H. Lawrence
Mansfield, Katherine

BRANGWEN, Lydia
See Lensky, Lydia

BRANGWEN, Ursula
The Rainbow (1915)
by D.H. Lawrence
Burrows, Louisa
Lawrence, Frieda

BRANGWEN, William
The Rainbow (1915)
by D.H. Lawrence
Burrows, Alfred

BRANSDON, Ophelia
The Simple Life Limited (1911)
by Ford Madox Ford
Soskice, Juliet

BRANSDON, Simon
The Simple Life Limited (1911)
by Ford Madox Ford
Conrad, Joseph

BRAXTON, Stephen
'Maltby and Braxton', *Seven Men*
   (1919)
by Max Beerbohm
Yeats, W.B.

BRAZIER, Mr
The Cantab (1926)
by Shane Leslie
Frazer, Sir James

BREADALBY
Women in Love (1920)
by D.H. Lawrence
Garsington Manor, Oxfordshire

BRENNAN, Jack
'Fifty Grand', *Men Without Women*
   (1927)
by Ernest Hemingway
Britton, Jack

BRENTHAM
Lothair (1870)
by Benjamin Disraeli
Trentham Park, Staffordshire

BRETHERTON, Isabel
Miss Bretherton (1884)
by Mrs Humphry Ward
Anderson, Mary

BRETTON
Villette (1853)
by Charlotte Brontë
Bridlington, Yorkshire

BRETTON, Dr John Graham
Villette (1853)
by Charlotte Brontë
Smith, George

BRETTON, Mrs Louisa Lucy
Villette (1853)
by Charlotte Brontë
Smith, Elizabeth

BRIARFIELD
Shirley (1849)
by Charlotte Brontë
Birstall, Yorkshire

BRIARMAINS
Shirley (1849)
by Charlotte Brontë
Red House, Gomersal, Yorkshire

BRICKNELL, Alfred
Aaron's Rod (1922)
by D.H. Lawrence
Brentnall, Alfred Woolston

BRICKNELL, Jim
Aaron's Rod (1922)
by D.H. Lawrence
White, James Robert

BRIDEHEAD, Sue
Jude the Obscure (1895)
by Thomas Hardy
Henniker, Florence
Sparks, Tryphena

BRIDESHEAD
Brideshead Revisited (1945)
by Evelyn Waugh
**Castle Howard, North Riding,
   Yorkshire**

Madresfield Court, Malvern, Worcestershire

BRIDGEPOINT
'The Good Anna', *Three Lives* (1909)
by Gertrude Stein
Baltimore, Maryland

BRIDGES, Dorothy
'The Fifth Column', *The Fifth Column and the First Forty-nine Stories* (1938)
by Ernest Hemingway
Gellhorn, Martha

BRIDMAIN, Edmund
'The Sad Fortunes of the Revd Amos Barton', *Scenes of Clerical Life* (1857–8)
by George Eliot
Waldron, Sir John

BRIERLY, Captain Montague
Lord Jim (1900)
by Joseph Conrad
Wallace, Captain

BRIG PLACE
Dombey and Son (1846–8)
by Charles Dickens
Montague Place, London

BRIGGS, Adolphus
The Cantab (1926)
by Shane Leslie
Brooke, Rupert

BRIGGS, John
See Vavasour, Elsley

BRINDELL, Dr
Women in Love (1920)
by D.H. Lawrence
Bingham, Tom Herring

BRISCOE, Lily
To the Lighthouse (1927)
by Virginia Woolf
Bell, Vanessa

BRISSENDEN, Russ
Martin Eden (1909)
by Jack London
Sterling, George

BRITLING, Hugh
Mr Britling Sees It Through (1916)
by H.G. Wells
Wells, H.G.

BRITLING, Mary
Mr Britling Sees It Through (1916)
by H.G. Wells
Wells, Catherine ('Jane')

BRITTON, Francis
'Notes on the North What-d'ye-Callem Election' (1841)
by W.M. Thackeray
Bowes, John

BRITTON HALL
'Notes on the North What-d'ye-Callem Election' (1841)
by W.M. Thackeray
Streatlam Castle, County Durham

BROAD, John
The Revolution in Tanner's Lane (1887)
by Mark Rutherford
Jukes, John

BROAD SIDLINCH
'The Grave by the Handpost' (1913)
by Thomas Hardy
Sydling St Nicholas, Dorset

BROCK, Lord
Framley Parsonage (1861)
by Anthony Trollope
Palmerston, Lord

BROCKLEBRIDGE
Jane Eyre (1847)
by Charlotte Brontë
Tunstall, Lancashire

BROCKLEHURST, MR
Jane Eyre (1847)
by Charlotte Brontë
Carus-Wilson, William

BROCKWAY, BARNEY
Oil! (1927)
by Upton Sinclair
Daugherty, Harry M.

BRODIE, BENNETT
Pilgrimage (1915–67)
by Dorothy Richardson
Batchelor, John Arthur

BROMPTON, SIR RALPH
The *Sword of Honour* trilogy
  (1952–61)
by Evelyn Waugh
Nicolson, Sir Harold

BROMSTEAD
The New Machiavelli (1911)
by H.G. Wells
Bromley, Kent

BRONSON, DEWEY
Washington Jitters (1936)
by Dalton Trumbo
Johnson, Hugh S.

BROOKE, MR
Middlemarch (1871–2)
by George Eliot
Bracebridge, Charles Holt

BROOKE, CATHERINE
Esther (1884)
by Henry Adams
Cameron, Elizabeth

BROOKE, CELIA
Middlemarch (1871–2)
by George Eliot
Clarke, Christiana

BROOKE, DOROTHEA
See CASAUBON, Dorothea

BROOKE, ELLIS
Neutral Ground (1933)
by Helen Corke
Corke, Helen

BROOKE, JOHN
Little Women (1868) and sequels
by Louisa M. Alcott
Pratt, John Bridge

BROOKENHAM, NANDA
The Awkward Age (1899)
by Henry James
Sands, Ethel

MRS BROOKENHAM'S CIRCLE
The Awkward Age (1899)
by Henry James
The Souls

BROOKES, WINSOME
Vainglory (1915)
by Ronald Firbank
Brooke, Rupert

BROOKSMITH
'Brooksmith' (1891)
by Henry James
Past, Miss

BROTHERTON, MARCHIONESS OF
Is He Popenjoy? (1878)
by Anthony Trollope
Stanley, Fabia, Lady

BROUGHTON, GEORGE
*Sydenham; or Memoirs of a Man of
  the World* (1830)
by W. Massie
Brougham, Lord

BROWDIE, JOHN
Nicholas Nickleby (1838–9)
by Charles Dickens
Barnes, John and Richard
Todd, Thomas

BROWN, FATHER
The Innocence of Father Brown
(1911) and others
by G.K. Chesterton
O'Connor, Monsignor John

BROWN, ANNE
Miss Brown (1884)
by Vernon Lee
Gurney, Kate
Morris, Jane

BROWN, GENTLEMAN
Lord Jim (1900)
by Joseph Conrad
Brownrigg, Captain

BROWN, GINGERLY
Coningsby (1844)
by Benjamin Disraeli
Layard, Brownlow Villiers

BROWN, THOMAS
Tom Brown's Schooldays (1857)
by Thomas Hughes
Hughes, Thomas

BROWNING, CLARISS
Aaron's Rod (1922)
by D.H. Lawrence
Patmore, Brigit

BROWNLOW, OLIVER
The Cantab (1926)
by Shane Leslie
Browning, Oscar

BROWN'S BUILDINGS, Maine
   Street
Marcella (1894)
by Mrs Humphry Ward
Peabody Buildings, London

BROXTON
Adam Bede (1859)
by George Eliot
Roston, Derbyshire

BRUCE, JANET
Fernhurst (1971)
by Gertrude Stein
Gwinn, Mary

BRUGA, COUNT
Count Bruga (1926)
by Ben Hecht
Bodenheim, Maxwell

BRUGES, CAPTAIN
Lothair (1870)
by Benjamin Disraeli
Cluseret, G.P.

BRUME, LADY FLORA
A Lodge in the Wilderness (1906)
by John Buchan
Grosvenor, Susan

BUCHANAN, LADY MARGARET
Glenarvon (1816)
by Lady Caroline Lamb
Bessborough, Lady
Devonshire, Elizabeth, Duchess of
Kinnaird, Mrs Maria

BUCHANAN, WILLIAM
Glenarvon (1816)
by Lady Caroline Lamb
Webster, Sir Godfrey

BUCK-AND-BALK, LADY
The Ladies Almanack (1928)
by Djuna Barnes
Hall, Radclyffe

BUCKET, INSPECTOR
Bleak House (1852–3)
by Charles Dickens
Field, Charles Frederick

BUCKHURST, SIR CHARLES
Coningsby (1844)
by Benjamin Disraeli
Lamington, Lord

BUCKNELL, LEILA
C (1924)
by Maurice Baring
Desborough, Lady

Lytton, Countess of

BUCKNER, Riply
'A Night at the Fair' (1957)
by F. Scott Fitzgerald
Reed, Cecil

BUCKTROUT, Baby
The Roaring Queen (1973)
by Wyndham Lewis
Cunard, Nancy

BUDD, Mr
'Janet's Repentance', *Scenes of Clerical Life* (1857–8)
by George Eliot
Burton, Mr

BUDDEN (formerly Bagshaw), Octavius
'Mr Minns and His Cousin', *Sketches by Boz* (1836)
by Charles Dickens
Leigh, John Porter

BUDMOUTH
Wessex novels and tales (1871–95)
by Thomas Hardy
Weymouth, Dorset

von BUGLE, Baron
The Cantab (1926)
by Shane Leslie
von Hügel, Anatole, Baron

BULFINCH, Lord
Ten Thousand a Year (1841)
by Samuel Warren
Russell, John, 1st Earl

BULLER
The Loom of Youth (1917)
by Alec Waugh
Carey, G.M.

BULMER, Richard
Caliban (1920)
by W.L. George
Northcliffe, Lord

BULPINGTON, Theodore
The Bulpington of Blup (1933)
by H.G. Wells
Ford, Ford Madox

BULSTRODE
Eyeless in Gaza (1936)
by Aldous Huxley
Hillside, Surrey

BUNGAY, Mr
The History of Pendennis (1848–50)
by W.M. Thackeray
Colburn, Henry

BUNION, Miss
Mrs Perkins's Ball (1847)
by W.M. Thackeray
Landon, Letitia Elizabeth

BUNTING, Miss
Marling Hall (1942) and *Miss Bunting* (1945)
by Angela Thirkell
Bennet, Miss

BUNTING, Mr
The Sea Lady (1902)
by H.G. Wells
Popham, Arthur Frederick

BUNTING, Mrs
The Sea Lady (1902)
by H.G. Wells
Popham, Florence

BURGHLIMIT, Dr
Washington Jitters (1936)
by Dalton Trumbo
Townsend, Francis E.

BURGOYNE, Eleanor
Eleanor (1899)
by Mrs Humphry Ward
de Beaumont, Pauline

BURKE, O'Madden
'A Mother', *Dubliners* (1914) and *Ulysses* (1922)
by James Joyce
Curtis, O'Leary

BURKE, R. JOHN
The Sleep of Reason (1956)
by Warren Miller
Cohn, Roy M.

BURLAP, DENIS
Point Counter Point (1928)
by Aldous Huxley
Murry, John Middleton

BURLINGHAM, ANTHONY
Vestal Fire (1927)
by Compton Mackenzie
Thornton, Charles

BURNELL, LINDA
'Prelude' (1918) and 'At the Bay'
　(1921)
by Katherine Mansfield
Beauchamp, Annie

BURNEY, CANON
The Master of Marton (1864) and
　Diary of a Novelist (1870)
by Eliza Tabor
Binney, Revd Thomas

BURNEY, STARWOOD
Charles Auchester (1853)
by Elizabeth Sara Sheppard
Bennett, Sir William Sterndale

BURNLEY, LORD EDWARD
Mystery at Geneva (1922)
by Rose Macaulay
Balfour, A.J.

BURNS, MONSIGNOR
The Cantab (1926)
by Shane Leslie
Barnes, Monsignor

BURNS, MR
The Shadow-Line (1917)
by Joseph Conrad
Born, Charles

BURNS, HELEN
Jane Eyre (1847)
by Charlotte Brontë
Brontë, Maria

BURTON, MISS CONSUELO
The Old Order Changes (1886)
by W.H. Mallock
von Hügel, Baroness

BURY, MRS CAROLINE
It's a Battlefield (1934)
by Graham Greene
Morrell, Lady Ottoline

BURYAN, JOHN THOMAS
Kangaroo (1923)
by D.H. Lawrence
Hocking, William Henry

BUTCHER, LADY
Mummery (1916)
by Gilbert Cannan
Tree, Lady Beerbohm

BUTCHER, GUY
Tarr (1918)
by Wyndham Lewis
Baker, Guy

BUTCHER, SIR HENRY
Mummery (1916)
by Gilbert Cannan
Tree, Sir Herbert Beerbohm

BUTLER
'The Orange Moth' (1925)
by Conrad Aiken
Yeats, J.B.

BUTLER, FATHER
'An Encounter', *Dubliners* (1914)
by James Joyce
Henry, Father William, SJ

BUTLER, MISS
Dolores (1911)
by I. Compton-Burnett
Taylor, Margaret

BUTLER, MRS
Beany-Eye (1935)
by David Garnett
Garnett, Constance

BUTLER, AILEEN
The Financier (1912)
by Theodore Dreiser
Yerkes, Mary Adelaide

BUTLER, EDWARD
The Financier (1912)
by Theodore Dreiser
Butler, Edward R.

BUTLER, JAMES
Beany-Eye (1935)
by David Garnett
Garnett, Edward

BUTTERBOY, DONALD
The Roaring Queen (1973)
by Wyndham Lewis
Howard, Brian

BUZFUZ, MR SERJEANT
The Pickwick Papers (1836–7)
by Charles Dickens
Bompas, Mr Serjeant
Phillips, Charles

BYRNE, CECIL
The Trespasser (1912)
by D.H. Lawrence
Lawrence, D.H.

BYRON, CASHEL
Cashel Byron's Profession (1886)
by George Bernard Shaw
Beatty, Pakenham Thomas
Burke, Jack

C

C
See BRAMSLEY, Caryl

CACOETHES, REINHOLD
The Dharma Bums (1958)
by Jack Kerouac
Rexroth, Kenneth

CADBURY RINGS
The Longest Journey (1907)
by E.M. Forster
Figsbury Rings, Wiltshire

CADOVER
The Longest Journey (1907)
by E.M. Forster
Acton House, Felton,
** Northumberland**

CADURCIS, LORD
Venetia (1837)
by Benjamin Disraeli
Byron, Lord

CAFÉ POMPADOUR
Women in Love (1920)
by D.H. Lawrence
Café Royal, London

CAIRN
Postures (1928)
by Jean Rhys
Hemingway, Ernest

CALAMY, MR
Crome Yellow (1921)
by Aldous Huxley
Asquith, H.H.

CALDERON, TULLIA
Elders and Betters (1944)
by I. Compton-Burnett
Kidd, Dorothy

CALDERSFOOT, LADY
Memoirs of a Femme de Chambre
  (1846)
by Lady Blessington
Morgan, Sydney, Lady
Stepney, Lady

CALDWELL, GEORGE
The Centaur (1963)
by John Updike
Updike, Wesley

CALHOUN, Webster
The Sleep of Reason (1956)
by Warren Miller
Chambers, Whittaker

CALIFANO, Pancrazio
The Lost Girl (1920)
by D.H. Lawrence
Cervi, Orazio

CALLAN
The Inheritors (1901)
by Joseph Conrad and Ford Madox
   Ford
Crockett, Samuel Rutherford

CALLCOTT, Victoria
Kangaroo (1923)
by D.H. Lawrence
Jenkins, Mrs A.L.

CALMAN, Miles
'Crazy Sunday' (1935)
by F. Scott Fitzgerald
Thalberg, Irving

CALMUCK
'Calmuck', *Heads and Tails* (1859)
by Robert Barnabas Brough
Watkins, Emma

CALTHROP
Mendel (1916)
by Gilbert Cannan
John, Augustus

CALVERT, Arthur
Late Call (1964)
by Angus Wilson
Wilson, William Johnstone

CAMBRAI, Dr
Ormond (1817)
by Maria Edgeworth
Beaufort, Daniel Augustus

CAMELTON
A Pair of Blue Eyes (1873)
by Thomas Hardy
Camelford, Cornwall

CAMILLE
On the Road (1957)
by Jack Kerouac
Cassady, Carolyn

CAMPBELL, Dr
'Forester', *Moral Tales for Young
   People* (1801)
by Maria Edgeworth
Stewart, Dugald

CAMPBELL, Jefferson
'Melanctha', *Three Lives* (1909)
by Gertrude Stein
Stein, Gertrude

CAMPBELL, Michael
The Sun Also Rises (1926)
by Ernest Hemingway
Guthrie, Pat

CAMPION, Luis
Tender is the Night (1934)
by F. Scott Fitzgerald
Mendl, Sir Charles

CAMPION, Theodora
Lothair (1870)
by Benjamin Disraeli
Mario, Jessie Meriton

CANE, Ethel
'None of That' (1928)
by D.H. Lawrence
Carrington, Dora

CANNON, George
The Roll Call (1917)
by Arnold Bennett
Rickards, Edwin Alfred

CANTWELL, Richard
Across the River and into the Trees
   (1950)
by Ernest Hemingway
Hemingway, Ernest
Lanham, C.T.
Sweeny, Charles

CAPERINGTON, Countess of
Mr Facey Romford's Hounds (1865)
by R.S. Surtees
**Stamford and Warrington,
    Katherine, Countess of**

CAPES, Godwin
Ann Veronica (1909)
by H.G. Wells
Wells, H.G.

CAPTAIN OF THE *MAUD MARY*
Tono-Bungay (1909)
by H.G. Wells
Conrad, Joseph

CARABAS, Marquess of
Vivian Grey (1826–7)
by Benjamin Disraeli
**Clanricarde, 1st Marquess of
Grenville, Lord, 2nd Marquis of
    Chandos
Murray, John**[1]

CARAWAY, Lady Virginia
The Aesthetes (1927)
by W.J. Turner
Morrell, Lady Ottoline

CARDEW, Revd Theophilus
Catharine Furze (1893)
by Mark Rutherford
Lewis, Revd W. Reuben

CARDIFF, Lady
Friendship (1878)
by Ouida
Walpole, Lady

CARDINAL COLLEGE,
    Christminster
Jude the Obscure (1895)
by Thomas Hardy
Christ Church, Oxford

CAREY, Mrs
Of Human Bondage (1915)
by W. Somerset Maugham
Maugham, Edith Mary

CAREY, Francis
A Lodge in the Wilderness (1906)
by John Buchan
Rhodes, Cecil

CAREY, Louise
Of Human Bondage (1915)
by W. Somerset Maugham
Maugham, Barbara Sophia

CAREY, Philip
Of Human Bondage (1915)
by W. Somerset Maugham
Maugham, W. Somerset

CAREY, Revd William
Of Human Bondage (1915)
by W. Somerset Maugham
Maugham, Revd Henry Macdonald

CARGILL, Josiah
St Ronan's Well (1823)
by Sir Walter Scott
**Duncan, Alexander
Lawson, George**

CARISBROOKE, Lord
Lothair (1870)
by Benjamin Disraeli
Bath, 4th Marquis of

CARLETON, Amy
You Can't Go Home Again (1940)
by Thomas Wolfe
Vanderbilt, Emily

CARLTON, Archdeacon
Almacks (1826)
by M. Spencer Stanhope
Bury, Revd Edward John

CARLTON, Lady Margaret
Almacks (1826)
by M. Spencer Stanhope
Bury, Lady Charlotte

CARLYLE, Gretchen
Sartor Resartus (1833–4)
by Thomas Carlyle
Carlyle, Margaret

CARLYON, Arnold
Halcyone (1912)
by Elinor Glyn
Bradley, F.H.

CARMICHAEL, Augustus
To the Lighthouse (1927)
by Virginia Woolf
Wolstenholme, Joseph

CARMODY, Dodie
On the Road (1957)
by Jack Kerouac
Burroughs, Julie

CARMODY, Frank
On the Road (1957)
by Jack Kerouac
Burroughs, William S.

CARMODY, Jane
On the Road (1957)
by Jack Kerouac
Burroughs, Joan Vollmer

CARMODY, Ray
On the Road (1957)
by Jack Kerouac
Burroughs, William, Junior

CARNAGE, Neddy
Nicholas Crabbe (1958)
by F.W. Rolfe
Slaughter, E.J.

CAROLINA, Madame
Vivian Grey (1826–7)
by Benjamin Disraeli
Holland, Lady

CARPE, Revd Mr
'The Sad Fortunes of the Revd Amos
    Barton', *Scenes of Clerical Life*
    (1857–8)
by George Eliot
Hake, Revd George

CARR, Private
Ulysses (1922)
by James Joyce
Carr, Henry

CARRASCO, Don Ramón
The Plumed Serpent (1926)
by D.H. Lawrence
Dibrell, John
Vasconcelos, José

CARRINGTON, John
Esther (1884)
by Henry Adams
Lowndes, James

CARRINGTON, Louise
'St Mawr' (1925)
by D.H. Lawrence
Humes, Elizabeth

CARROL, Sally
'The Ice Palace' (1921)
by F. Scott Fitzgerald
Fitzgerald, Zelda

CARROTS
See Desart, Fabian

CARSON, Harry
Mary Barton (1843)
by Elizabeth Gaskell
Ashton, Thomas

CARSON WAITE & CO.
Sons and Lovers (1913)
by D.H. Lawrence
Barber Walker & Co.

CARTER
It is Never Too Late to Mend (1856)
by Charles Reade
Hunt

CARTER, Bella
Bid Me To Live (1960)
by H.D. (Hilda Doolittle)
Yorke, Dorothy

CARTON, Sydney
A Tale of Two Cities (1859)
by Charles Dickens
Allan, James Gordon

CARTWRIGHT, Mr
'St Mawr' (1925)
by D.H. Lawrence
Carter, Frederick

CARTWRIGHT, Revd William Jacob
The Vicar of Wrexhill (1840)
by Frances Trollope
Cunningham, Revd J.W.

CARYLL, Julian ('Hoodie')
Hoodie (1882)
by Mrs Molesworth
Ainslie, Juliet

CASAMASSIMA, Princess
The Princess Casamassima (1886)
by Henry James
Belgiojoso, Principessa di
Obolensky, Princess Zoë Sergeievna

CASANOVA'S CHINESE
  RESTAURANT
A Dance to the Music of Time
  (1951–76)
by Anthony Powell
Maxim's Chinese Restaurant, Soho,
  London

CASAUBON (née Brooke),
  Dorothea
Middlemarch (1871–2)
by George Eliot
Eliot, George
Pattison, Dorothy Wyndlow
Pattison, Emilia Francis

CASAUBON, Edward
Middlemarch (1871–2)
by George Eliot
Brabant, R.H.
Bryant, Jacob
Eliot, George
Mackay, R.W.
Pattison, Mark
Spencer, Herbert

CASEY, John
A Portrait of the Artist as a Young
  Man (1916)
by James Joyce
Kelly, John

CASSELL, Dr
Dolores (1911)
by I. Compton-Burnett
Molson, Dr

CASSIDY, Maggie
Maggie Cassidy (1959) and *Vanity*
  of Duluoz (1968)
by Jack Kerouac
Carney, Mary

CASSILIS, Mr
Coningsby (1844) and *Tancred* (1847)
by Benjamin Disraeli
Wombwell, George

CASTEGNETO
The Enchanted April (1922)
by 'Elizabeth'
Portofino, Italy

CASTERBRIDGE
Wessex novels and tales (1871–95)
by Thomas Hardy
Dorchester, Dorset

CASTI, Julian
The Unclassed (1884)
by George Gissing
Bertz, Eduard

CASTLE BOTEREL
A Pair of Blue Eyes (1873)
by Thomas Hardy
Boscastle, Cornwall

CASTLEMAINE, Cecil
Sans Merci; or Kestrels and Falcons
  (1866)
by G.A. Lawrence
Clay, James

CASTLEWOOD
The History of Henry Esmond (1852)
by W.M. Thackeray
Clevedon Court, Somerset

CASTLEWOOD, Lady
The History of Henry Esmond (1852)
by W.M. Thackeray
Brookfield, Jane

CASTLEWOOD, Lord
The History of Henry Esmond (1852)
by W.M. Thackeray
Brookfield, William Henry

CATARAQUI COUNTY
An American Tragedy (1925)
by Theodore Dreiser
Herkimer County, New York

CATESBY, Monsignor
Lothair (1870)
by Benjamin Disraeli
Capel, Monsignor Thomas John

CATHCART, Mr
'The Man Who Loved Islands' (1928)
by D.H. Lawrence
Mackenzie, Compton

CATHERICK, Anne
The Woman in White (1860)
by Wilkie Collins
Graves, Caroline

CAVAN, Edward
Faithful are the Wounds (1955)
by May Sarton
Matthiessen, F.O.

The CAVE OF HARMONY
The Newcomes (1854–5)
by W.M. Thackeray
The Cider Cellars, London
The Coal Hole, London

CAW, William
The Honourable Schoolboy (1977)
by John Le Carré
Hughes, Richard

The CENTRAL STATION
Heart of Darkness (1902)
by Joseph Conrad
Kinshasa, Zaire

CERINTHEA, Joseph
Charles Auchester (1853)
by Elizabeth Sara Sheppard
García, Manuel

CERINTHEA, Josephine
Charles Auchester (1853)
by Elizabeth Sara Sheppard
Viardot, Pauline

CERINTHEA, Maria
Charles Auchester (1853)
by Elizabeth Sara Sheppard
Hensel, Fanny
Malibran, Maria

CHAFFANBRASS, Mr
Orley Farm (1861–2)
by Anthony Trollope
Ballantine, William

CHAINMAIL, Mr
Crotchet Castle (1831)
by Thomas Love Peacock
Strachey, Sir Edward

The CHAIRMAN OF THE
    NATIONAL CONVENTION
Hail to the Chief (1960)
by James Reichley
Martin, Joseph

CHALDON
'The Distracted Preacher' (1888)
by Thomas Hardy
East Chaldon (or Chaldon Herring),
    Dorset

CHALK NEWTON
Wessex novels and tales (1871–95)
by Thomas Hardy
Maiden Newton, Dorset

CHALLONER, Lady Joan
Friendship (1878)
by Ouida
Ross, Janet

CHALLONER, Robert
Friendship (1878)
by Ouida
Ross, Henry James

CHALMERS
Lions and Shadows (1938)
by Christopher Isherwood
Upward, Edward

CHANCELLOR, Olive
The Bostonians (1884)
by Henry James
Loring, Katharine Peabody

CHANDRAPORE
A Passage to India (1924)
by E.M. Forster
Bankipore, Patna

CHANNON, John
The Region Cloud (1925)
by Percy Lubbock
James, Henry

DE CHAPELEY, Monsieur
Albert Lunel (1844)
by Lord Brougham
Lyndhurst, Lord

CHARLES, Uncle
*A Portrait of the Artist as a Young
   Man* (1916)
by James Joyce
O'Connell, William

CHARLES, Hannah
The Making of Americans (1925)
by Gertrude Stein
Thomas, Carey

CHARLES, Nora
The Thin Man (1932)
by Dashiel Hammett
Hellmann, Lillian

CHARMLEY
Under the Greenwood Tree (1872)
by Thomas Hardy
Charminster, Dorset

CHASEBOROUGH
Wessex novels and tales (1871–95)
by Thomas Hardy
Cranborne, Dorset

CHATSWORTH, Mr
Prater Violet (1945)
by Christopher Isherwood
Saville, Victor

CHATTERIS
The History of Pendennis (1848–50)
by W.M. Thackeray
Exeter, Devon

CHATTERIS, Harry
The Sea Lady (1902)
by H.G. Wells
Cust, Henry J.C. ('Harry')

CHATTERLEY, Sir Clifford
Lady Chatterley's Lover (1928)
by D.H. Lawrence
Asquith, Herbert
Sitwell, Sir Osbert

CHATTERLEY, Constance
Lady Chatterley's Lover (1928)
by D.H. Lawrence
Asquith, Lady Cynthia

CHEERYBLE BROTHERS
Nicholas Nickleby (1838–9)
by Charles Dickens
Grant, Daniel and William

CHELIFER, Francis
Those Barren Leaves (1925)
by Aldous Huxley
Murry, John Middleton

CHELL, Countess of
The Card (1911)
by Arnold Bennett
Sutherland, Duchess of

CHENE MANOR
Wessex novels and tales (1871–95)
by Thomas Hardy
Canford Manor, Dorset

CHERRY-MARVEL, Mr
The Green Hat (1924)
by Michael Arlen
Melvill, Harry

CHERRYUMPTON
The Cantab (1926)
by Shane Leslie
Cherry Hinton, Cambridgeshire
Trumpington, Cambridgeshire

CHESNEY WOLD
Bleak House (1852–3)
by Charles Dickens
Rockingham Castle,
  Northamptonshire

CHESTER, Sir John
Barnaby Rudge (1841)
by Charles Dickens
Chesterfield, Lord

CHESTER, Kate
Not Wisely, But Too Well (1867)
by Rhoda Broughton
Broughton, Rhoda

CHESTERFIELD, Lady
See Vane, Dodo

CHESTERFIELD, Mr
St Albans; or The Prisoners of Hope
  (1853)
by Felicia Skene
Chamberlain, Revd Thomas

CHETWODE, Felicity, Lady
The Twelfth Hour (1907)
by Ada Leverson
Martineau, Kitty

CHEURET, Madame
Lions and Shadows (1938)
by Christopher Isherwood
Mangeot, Olive

CHEURET, Monsieur
Lions and Shadows (1938)
by Christopher Isherwood
Mangeot, André

CHEVEREL, Lady
'Mr Gilfil's Love Story', *Scenes of*
  Clerical Life (1857–8)
by George Eliot
Newdigate, Hester, Lady

CHEVEREL, Sir Anthony
'Mr Gilfil's Love Story', *Scenes of*
  Clerical Life (1857–8)
by George Eliot
Newdigate, Sir Richard

CHEVEREL, Sir Christopher
'Mr Gilfil's Love Story', *Scenes of*
  Clerical Life (1857–8)
by George Eliot
Newdigate, Sir Roger

CHEVEREL MANOR
'Mr Gilfil's Love Story', *Scenes of*
  Clerical Life (1857–8)
by George Eliot
Arbury Hall, Warwickshire

CHEVRE-FEUILLE, Jacques
Save Me the Waltz (1932)
by Zelda Fitzgerald
Jozan, Edouard

CHEVRON
The Edwardians (1930)
by Victoria Sackville-West
Knole, Kent

CHEYNE, Romola
The Edwardians (1930)
by Victoria Sackville-West
Keppel, Alice

CHEZ CARREL
Trilby (1894)
by George Du Maurier
Atelier Gleyre, Paris

CHHOKRAPUR, Maharajah of
Hindoo Holiday (1932)
by J.R. Ackerley
Chhatarpur, Maharajah of

CHICKEREL, Ethelberta
The Hand of Ethelberta (1876)
by Thomas Hardy
Hardy, Jemima

CHIEF STREET, Christminster
Jude the Obscure (1895)
by Thomas Hardy
High Street, Oxford

Le CHIEN NOIR
The Magician (1908)
by W. Somerset Maugham
Le Chat Blanc, Paris

CHILLEYWATER, Mrs
The Flower Beneath the Foot (1923)
by Ronald Firbank
Sackville-West, Victoria

CHILLIP, Dr
David Copperfield (1849–50)
by Charles Dickens
Morgan, Dr Charles

CHILTERN, Lord
Phineas Finn (1869)
by Anthony Trollope
Camelford, Lord
Devonshire, 8th Duke of

CHIRRUP, Mr
'The Nice Little Couple', *Sketches of
 Young Couples* (1840)
by Charles Dickens
Hall, William

CHISELHURST, Lady
The Old Order Changes (1886)
by W.H. Mallock
Herbert, Elizabeth, Lady

CHITTERLOW, Harry
Kipps (1905)
by H.G. Wells
Bowkett, Sidney

CHITTY, Muriel
'That Flesh is Heir to . . .' (1930)
by Osbert Sitwell
Hammersley, Violet

CHIVAS, Las
See Las Chivas

CHOSELWIT, Jos.
The Gay-Dombeys (1919)
by Sir Harry Johnston
Chamberlain, Joseph

CHOUGH, Cosmo
Miss Brown (1884)
by Vernon Lee
O'Shaughnessy, Arthur

CHOWNE, Parson
The Maid of Sker (1872)
by R.D. Blackmore
Froude, Revd John

CHRISTIAN, Charlie
*John Cornelius: His Life and
 Adventures* (1937)
by Hugh Walpole
Cheevers, Harold

CHRISTMINSTER
Jude the Obscure (1895)
by Thomas Hardy
Oxford

CHRISTOPHER, Roy
Miranda Masters (1926)
by John Cournos
Fletcher, John Gould

The *CHRONICLE*
The *Clayhanger* trilogy (1910–16)
by Arnold Bennett
The *Staffordshire Knot*

CHUDLEIGH, Tom
Coningsby (1844)
by Benjamin Disraeli
Stafford, Augustus

CHUNDANGO, Juggonath
Piccadilly (1870)
by Laurence Oliphant
Swami, Coomara

CHURCHILL, Belinda
Belinda (1883)
by Rhoda Broughton
Pattison, Emilia Francis

CHURCHILL, Edward
The Inheritors (1901)
by Joseph Conrad and Ford Madox
  Ford
Balfour, A.J.

CHURCHILL, Florence
The Constant Nymph (1924)
by Margaret Kennedy
Kennedy, Lucy

CHURCHILL, Horace
Helen (1834)
by Maria Edgeworth
Rogers, Samuel

CIBBER, Jeremy Pratt
Stepping Heavenward (1931)
by Richard Aldington
Eliot, T.S.

CIRCUMFERENCE, Lady
Decline and Fall (1928)
by Evelyn Waugh
Graham, Jessie

The CIRCUMLOCUTION OFFICE
Little Dorrit (1855–7)
by Charles Dickens
The Colonial Office

The CITIZEN
Ulysses (1922)
by James Joyce
Cusack, Michael

CLANELLAN, Lady
*De Vere; or The Man of
  Independence* (1827)
by Robert Plumer Ward
Grenville, Lady

CLARE, Angel
Tess of the d'Urbervilles (1891)
by Thomas Hardy
Moule, Charles

CLARE, Fabian
The Present and the Past (1953)
by I. Compton-Burnett
Compton-Burnett, Guy

CLARE, Guy
The Present and the Past (1953)
by I. Compton-Burnett
Compton-Burnett, Noel

CLARE, Revd James
Tess of the d'Urbervilles (1891)
by Thomas Hardy
Moule, Revd Henry

CLAREMONT
The Loom of Youth (1917)
by Alec Waugh
King, Henry Robinson

CLARENDON, General
Helen (1834)
by Maria Edgeworth
Wilson, Lestock

CLAREVILLE, Reginald
Masollam (1886)
by Laurence Oliphant
Oliphant, Laurence[2]

CLAVERHOUSE, Sigismund
Dolores (1911)
by I. Compton-Burnett
**Salt, Mr
Seccombe, Thomas**

CLAVERING ST MARY
The History of Pendennis (1848–50)
by W.M. Thackeray
Ottery St Mary, Devon

CLAVERTON, Duke of
*Sydenham; or Memoirs of a Man of
  the world* (1830)
by W. Massie
Devonshire, 5th Duke of

CLAVERTON HOUSE
Sydenham; or Memoirs of a Man of the World (1830)
by W. Massie
Devonshire House, London

CLAYFOOT, Captain Theophanes
Nicholas Crabbe (1958)
by F.W. Rolfe
Graham, Arthur Smith

CLAYHANGER, Darius
The *Clayhanger* trilogy (1910)
by Arnold Bennett
Beardmore, John
Bennett, Enoch
Shaw, Charles

CLAYHANGER, Edwin
The *Clayhanger* trilogy (1910–16)
by Arnold Bennett
Beardmore, Edward Harry
Bennett, Arnold

CLAYSON
The Magician (1908)
by W. Somerset Maugham
Bartlett, Paul

CLEEVE COLLEGE
The Constant Nymph (1924)
by Margaret Kennedy
Cheltenham Ladies' College

CLEMENTINA
The World of William Clissold
(1926)
by H.G. Wells
Keun, Odette

CLEVELAND, Captain Clement
The Pirate (1821)
by Sir Walter Scott
Gow, John

CLEVELAND, Frederick
Vivian Grey (1826–7)
by Benjamin Disraeli
Lockhart, J.G.

CLEVES, Revd Martin
'The Sad Fortunes of the Revd Amos Barton', *Scenes of Clerical Life*
(1857–8)
by George Eliot
Fisher, Revd John

CLIFF, Miss
Dolores (1911)
by I. Compton-Burnett
Block, Katharine S.

CLIFFORD, Martha
Ulysses (1922)
by James Joyce
Fleischmann, Marthe

CLISSOLD, William
The World of William Clissold
(1926)
by H.G. Wells
Wells, H.G.

CLOISTERHAM
Edwin Drood (1870)
by Charles Dickens
Rochester, Kent

CLORINDA
Lodore (1835)
by Mary Wollstonecraft Shelley
Viviani, Emilia Teresa

CLOUDESLEY, Julian
Cloudesley (1830)
by William Godwin
Annesley, James

CLOWES, Edith
Mendel (1916)
by Gilbert Cannan
Brett, Dorothy

CLUTTERBUCK
Pelham (1828)
by Bulwer Lytton
Lytton, Richard Warburton

CLUTTERBUCK, Captain
The Monastery (1820) and *The
 Fortunes of Nigel* (1822)
by Sir Walter Scott
Ormiston, Adam
Tait, Walter

CLUTTON
Of Human Bondage (1915)
by W. Somerset Maugham
O'Conor, Roderic

CLYNE, Frances
The Sun Also Rises (1926)
by Ernest Hemingway
Cannell, Kitty

CLYTH, Andy
Lord Raingo (1926)
by Arnold Bennett
Lloyd George, David

COCKLETON
'Notes on the North
 What-d'ye-Callem Election' (1841)
by W.M. Thackeray
Hartlepool, County Durham

COELEBS
Coelebs in Search of a Wife (1809)
by Hannah More
Harford, John Scandrett

COGGLESBY, Mr and Mrs Andrew
Evan Harrington (1860)
by George Meredith
Hellyer, John and Harriet Eustace

COHEN (née Lapidoth), Mirah
Daniel Deronda (1876)
by George Eliot
Ayrton, Hertha
Shilton, Sally

COHEN, Mordecai
Daniel Deronda (1876)
by George Eliot
Cohn (or Kohn)
Deutsch, Emanuel
Louis, Alfred Hyman

COHN, Robert
The Sun Also Rises (1926)
by Ernest Hemingway
Loeb, Harold

COKETOWN
Hard Times (1854)
by Charles Dickens
Hanley, Staffordshire

COKETOWN STRIKE
Hard Times (1854)
by Charles Dickens
Preston Strike

COLCHICUM, Lord
The History of Pendennis (1848–50)
by W.M. Thackeray
Lonsdale, 2nd Earl of

COLCORD, Mr
Dr Grimshawe's Secret (1883)
by Nathaniel Hawthorne
Alcott, Bronson
Bradford, George Partridge

COLD LAIRS
The Jungle Books (1894–5)
by Rudyard Kipling
Chitor, Rajasthan, India

COLEMAN
Antic Hay (1923)
by Aldous Huxley
Heseltine, Philip

COLEMAN, Zachariah
The Revolution in Tanner's Lane
 (1887)
by Mark Rutherford
White, William

COLES, Joel
'Crazy Sunday' (1935)
by F. Scott Fitzgerald
Fitzgerald, F. Scott
Taylor, Dwight

THE COLLEGE
The Masters (1951)
by C.P. Snow
Christ's College, Cambridge

COLONNA, MADAME
Coningsby (1844)
by Benjamin Disraeli
Strachan, Lady

COLONNA, PRINCESS LUCRETIA
Coningsby (1844)
by Benjamin Disraeli
Zichy-Ferraris, Charlotte, Countess

THE COMMISSIONER
It's a Battlefield (1934)
by Graham Greene
Greene, Sir William Graham

THE COMPANY DIRECTOR
Heart of Darkness (1902)
by Joseph Conrad
Hope, G.F.W.

THE COMPANY STATION
Heart of Darkness (1902)
by Joseph Conrad
Matadi, Congo

COMPTON
'The Snows of Kilimanjaro', *The
    Fifth Column and the First
    Forty-nine Stories* (1938)
by Ernest Hemingway
Pearson, 'Fatty'

CONACHAR, CHIEF OF CLAN QUHELE
The Fair Maid of Perth (1828)
by Sir Walter Scott
Scott, Daniel

CONINGSBY, HARRY
Coningsby (1844)
by Benjamin Disraeli
**Lyttelton, Lord
Smythe, George**

Tancred (1847)
by Benjamin Disraeli
Lyttelton, Lord

CONNAGE, ROSALIND
This Side of Paradise (1920)
by F. Scott Fitzgerald
Fitzgerald, Zelda

CONROY, GABRIEL
'The Dead', *Dubliners* (1914)
by James Joyce
**Curran, Constantine P.
Joyce, John**

CONROY, HUNT
You Can't Go Home Again (1940)
by Thomas Wolfe
Fitzgerald, F. Scott

CONSTABLE, ALGY
Aaron's Rod (1922)
by D.H. Lawrence
Turner, Reginald

CONYERS, GENERAL
A Dance to the Music of Time
    (1951–76)
by Anthony Powell
**Pennington, Brigadier-General
    R.L.A.**

CONYERS, EGLINTON
The Club and the Drawing Room
    (1870)
by Cecil Hay
Hannay, James

COO-EE
Kangaroo (1923)
by D.H. Lawrence
Wyewurk, Thirroul, Australia

COOKE
'The Orange Moth' (1925)
by Conrad Aiken
Brooks, Van Wyck

COOLEY, BENJAMIN
Kangaroo (1923)
by D.H. Lawrence
**Eder, David
Koteliansky, S.S.
Monash, Sir John**

COPPARD, George
Sons and Lovers (1913)
by D.H. Lawrence
Beardsall, George

COPPER, Lord
Scoop (1938)
by Evelyn Waugh
Beaverbrook, Lord

COPPERFIELD, David
David Copperfield (1849–50)
by Charles Dickens
Dickens, Charles

COPPERHEAD
Phoebe Junior (1876)
by Margaret Oliphant
Peto, Sir Samuel Morton

CORKRAN, Arthur ('Stalky')
Stalky & Co. (1899)
by Rudyard Kipling
Dunsterville, Lionel Charles

CORNELIAN, Edward
The Power of the Dead (1963)
by Henry Williamson
Garnett, Edward

CORNIGAN
God's Man (1915)
by George Bronson Howard
Corrigan, Joseph

CORRIE, Felix
Pilgrimage (1915–67)
by Dorothy Richardson
Avory, Sir Horace

CORRIE, Rollo
Pilgrimage (1915–67)
by Dorothy Richardson
Avory, Lady

CORVSGATE CASTLE
Wessex novels and tales (1871–95)
by Thomas Hardy
Corfe Castle, Dorset

CORY, Roderick
The Will to Love (1919)
by Hugh Kingsmill
Kingsmill, Hugh

COSSETHAY
The Rainbow (1915)
by D.H. Lawrence
Cossall, Nottinghamshire

COUGHLIN, Warren
The Dharma Bums (1958)
by Jack Kerouac
Whalen, Philip

COUNTESS OF CHELSEY'S HOUSE
The History of Henry Esmond (1852)
by W.M. Thackeray
Queens House, Chelsea, London

COURTENAY, Mr
Lady Rose's Daughter (1903)
by Mrs Humphry Ward
Abbott, Evelyn

COURTENEY, Sir Samson
Black Mischief (1932)
by Evelyn Waugh
Barton, Sir Sidney

COURTIER, Charles
The Patrician (1911)
by John Galsworthy
Nevinson, H.W.

COURTLEIGH, Cardinal
Hadrian VII (1904)
by F.W. Rolfe
Vaughan, Cardinal Herbert Alfred

COURTNEY, Ida
Samson Unshorn (1909)
by Reginald Turner
Frankau, Julia

COUTRAS, Dr
The Moon and Sixpence (1919)
by W. Somerset Maugham
Vernié, Paul

COVERDALE, Miles
The Blithedale Romance (1852)
by Nathaniel Hawthorne
Hawthorne, Nathaniel

COWPERWOOD, Frank Algernon
The Financier (1912) and *The Titan*
(1914)
by Theodore Dreiser
Yerkes, C.T.

COYLE, Boss
McDonough (1951)
by Francis T. Field
Hague, Frank

COYLE, Ed
McDonough (1951)
by Francis T. Field
Eggers, Frank Hague

CRABBE, Nicholas
Nicholas Crabbe (1958)
by F.W. Rolfe
Rolfe, F.W.

CRABTREE, Joel
But Gentlemen Marry Brunettes
(1927)
by Anita Loos
Adams, Franklin P.

CRACKYE, Reginald
Post Adolescence (1923)
by Robert McAlmon
Kreymborg, Alfred

The CRAFTSMAN'S THEATRE
Most Likely to Succeed (1954)
by John Dos Passos
New Playwrights

CRAMLEY, Lord George
'Notes on the North
What-d'ye-Callem Election' (1841)
by W.M. Thackeray
Vane, Lord Harry

CRAMPSFORD
The Way of All Flesh (1903)
by Samuel Butler
Langar, Nottinghamshire

CRAMPTON, John
A Son at the Front (1923)
by Edith Wharton
Tyler, Royall ('Peter')

CRAMPTON, Willie
The New Machiavelli (1911)
by H.G. Wells
Trevelyan, Sir Charles Philips

CRANE, Ichabod
'The Legend of Sleepy Hollow', *The
Sketch Books of Geoffrey Crayon,
Gent* (1820)
by Washington Irving
Lockie Longlegs

CRANFORD
Cranford (1853)
by Elizabeth Gaskell
Knutsford, Cheshire

CRANIUM, Mr
Headlong Hall (1816)
by Thomas Love Peacock
Gryffydh, John

CRANLY
*A Portrait of the Artist as a Young
Man* (1916)
by James Joyce
Byrne, John Francis

CRAVISTER, Mrs
'The Farcical History of Richard
Greenow' (1920)
by Aldous Huxley
Warre-Cornish, Blanche

CRAW, Thomas Carlyle
Castle Gay (1930)
by John Buchan
**Nicoll, Sir William Robertson
Rothermere, Lord**

CRAWFORD, Homer T. 'Chuck'
Number One (1943)
by John Dos Passos
Long, Huey P.

CRAWFORD, Mary
Mansfield Park (1814)
by Jane Austen
Austen, Eliza

CRAWFORD, Myles
Ulysses (1922)
by James Joyce
Mead, Patrick J.

CRAWLEY, Conway Townsend
Florence Macarthy (1818)
by Lady Sydney Morgan
Croker, John Wilson

CRAWLEY, Harriet
Vanity Fair (1847–8)
by W.M. Thackeray
Butler, Harriet

CRAWLEY, Sir Pitt
Vanity Fair (1847–8)
by W.M. Thackeray
Chaytor, Sir William
Rolle, Lord

CREAKLE, Mr
David Copperfield (1849–50)
by Charles Dickens
Jones, William
Rotch, Benjamin

von CREFELDT, Baroness Lucie
The Tragic Comedians (1880)
by George Meredith
von Hatzfeldt, Countess Sophie

CREIGHTON, Colonel
Kim (1901)
by Rudyard Kipling
Mason, A.H.

CRESSCOMBE
Jude the Obscure (1895)
by Thomas Hardy
Letcombe Bassett, Oxfordshire

CRESTON
Desperate Remedies (1871)
by Thomas Hardy
Preston, Dorset

CREWE, Revd Mr
'Janet's Repentance', *Scenes of
    Clerical Life* (1857–8)
by George Eliot
Hughes, Revd Hugh

CRICH, Diana
Women in Love (1920)
by D.H. Lawrence
Barber, Cicely

CRICH, Gerald
Women in Love (1920)
by D.H. Lawrence
Barber, Thomas Philip
Murry, John Middleton
Neville, George Henry

CRICH, Thomas
Women in Love (1920)
by D.H. Lawrence
Barber, Thomas

CRICKLEDON, Mr
The House on the Beach (1877)
by George Meredith
Ockenden, Mr

CRICKLEDON, Mrs
The House on the Beach (1877)
by George Meredith
Ockenden, Mrs

CRISCROSS, Professor James
'Triple Fugue' (1924)
by Osbert Sitwell
Gosse, Edmund

CROCKHAM
'England, My England' (1915)
by D.H. Lawrence
Greatham, Sussex

CROCUS, Dr
American Notes (1842)
by Charles Dickens
Melrose, Angus

CROFT, Elisha
Chosen Country (1951)
by John Dos Passos
Darrow, Clarence Seward

CROFTON, Mary ('Aunt William')
The Twelfth Hour (1907)
by Ada Leverson
Leverson, Henrietta

CROME
Crome Yellow (1921)
by Aldous Huxley
Beckley Park, Oxfordshire
Garsington Manor, Oxfordshire

CROMLECH, David
Memoirs of an Infantry Officer
(1930)
by Siegfried Sassoon
Graves, Robert

CRONSHAW, J.
Of Human Bondage (1915)
by W. Somerset Maugham
Crowley, Aleister
Morrice, James Wilson

CROUCHBACK, Gervase
The *Sword of Honour* trilogy
(1952–61)
by Evelyn Waugh
Scrope, Henry

CROWBOROUGH, Lady Thisbe
'Maltby and Braxton', *Seven Men*
(1919)
by Max Beerbohm
Vincent, Lady Helen

The CROZIER
Edwin Drood (1870)
by Charles Dickens
The Mitre Inn, Chatham, Kent

The CROZIER HOTEL,
Christminster
Jude the Obscure (1895)
by Thomas Hardy
The Mitre Hotel, Oxford

CRUMMLES, Ninetta (the 'Infant
Phenomenon')
Nicholas Nickleby (1838–9)
by Charles Dickens
Lander, Jean Margaret

CRUMMLES, Vincent
Nicholas Nickleby (1838–9)
by Charles Dickens
Davenport, Thomas Donald

CRUMP, Dr
The Wonderful Visit (1895)
by H.G. Wells
Collins, William

CRUMP, Lottie
Vile Bodies (1930)
by Evelyn Waugh
Lewis, Rosa

CRUSOE, Robinson
The Life and Strange Surprising
Adventures of Robinson Crusoe
(1719)
by Daniel Defoe
Selkirk, Alexander

CUFF, Sergeant Richard
The Moonstone (1868)
by Wilkie Collins
Whicher, Jonathan
Williamson, Adolphus Frederick

CULHANE
Twelve Men (1919)
by Theodore Dreiser
Muldoon, William

CULWIN, Andrew
'The Eyes', *Tales of Men and Ghosts*
(1910)
by Edith Wharton
Berry, Walter
Fullerton, Morton

CUMBERLAND MANSIONS
(FORMERLY RESIDENCES)
The Private Life of Henry Maitland
(1912)
by Morley Roberts
Cornwall Mansions

CUNNING NAT
Paul Clifford (1830)
by Bulwer Lytton
Nash, John

CUNNINGHAM, JULIA
Aaron's Rod (1922)
by D.H. Lawrence
Doolittle, Hilda

CUNNINGHAM, MARTIN
'Grace', *Dubliners* (1914) and
Ulysses (1922)
by James Joyce
Kane, Matthew

CUNNINGHAM, ROBERT
Aaron's Rod (1922)
by D.H. Lawrence
Aldington, Richard

CURGENVEN, WILL
The Degradation of Geoffrey Alwith
(1895)
by Morley Roberts
Gissing, George

CURPET & SMYTHE
The Man from the North (1898)
by Arnold Bennett
Le Brasseur & Oakley

CURRENT, MISS ISABELLA ('AUNT
BEL')
Evan Harrington (1860)
by George Meredith
Courtenay, Louisa

CUTE, ALDERMAN
The Chimes (1844)
by Charles Dickens
Laurie, Sir Peter

CUTTER, MAMIE
'Mrs Medwin' (1903)
by Henry James
Balch, Elizabeth

CUTTLE, CAPTAIN
Dombey and Son (1846–8)
by Charles Dickens
Mainland, David

CYPRESS, MR
Nightmare Abbey (1818)
by Thomas Love Peacock
Byron, Lord

D

DACIER, PERCY
Diana of the Crossways (1884)
by George Meredith
Herbert, Sidney

DAEDALUS, MAURICE
Stephen Hero (1944)
by James Joyce
Joyce, Stanislaus

DALE, EDITH
Peter Whiffle: His Life and Works
(1922)
by Carl Van Vechten
Luhan, Mabel Dodge

DALE, EMILY
The 'Genius' (1915)
by Theodore Dreiser
Cudlipp, Annie Ericsson

DALE, SUZANNE
The 'Genius' (1915)
by Theodore Dreiser
Cudlipp, Thelma

DALGETTY, DUGALD
A Legend of Montrose (1819)
by Sir Walter Scott
Monro, Robert
Skene, Martin

Turner, Sir James

DALLAS, LORD
Glenarvon (1816)
by Lady Caroline Lamb
**Ward, John William, 1st Earl of
    Dudley**

DALLOWAY, CLARISSA
The Voyage Out (1915) and *Mrs
    Dalloway* (1925)
by Virginia Woolf
Maxse, Katharine ('Kitty')

DALLOWAY, RICHARD
The Voyage Out (1915)
by Virginia Woolf
Hills, J.W.

DAMER'S WOOD
The Trumpet Major (1880)
by Thomas Hardy
Came Wood, Dorset

DAN
Puck of Pook's Hill (1906) and
    Rewards and Fairies (1910)
by Rudyard Kipling
Kipling, John

DAN
The Green Hills of Africa (1935)
by Ernest Hemingway
Fourie, Ben

D'ANGELI, DAVID
Desolation Angels (1965)
by Jack Kerouac
Lamantia, Philip

DANIELSTOWN
The Last September (1929)
by Elizabeth Bowen
**Bowen's Court, Kildorsey, County
    Cork, Ireland**

DANNISBURGH, LORD
Diana of the Crossways (1884)
by George Meredith
Melbourne, Lord

DA PAVIA, FRANCIS
The Dharma Bums (1958)
by Jack Kerouac
Lamantia, Philip

DARCY, MONSIGNOR
This Side of Paradise (1920)
by F. Scott Fitzgerald
Fay, Monsignor Sigourney

D'ARCY, BARTELL
'The Dead', *Dubliners* (1914)
by James Joyce
M'Guckin, Barton

DARCY, LAETITIA
Robert Elsmere (1888)
by Mrs Humphry Ward
Cradock, Harriet

D'ARCY, T.
Aylwin (1899)
by Theodore Watts-Dunton
Rossetti, Dante Gabriel

D'ARCY'S HOUSE
Aylwin (1899)
by Theodore Watts-Dunton
Queens House, Chelsea, London

DARE, VICTORIA
Democracy (1880)
by Henry Adams
Beale, Emily

DARLING
'The Spirit's Trials', *Shadows of the
    Clouds* (1847)
by James Anthony Froude
Dartington, Devon

DARNLEY, JIM
The Last Puritan (1935)
by George Santayana
Russell, Francis, 2nd Earl

DARRELL, LAURENCE
The Razor's Edge (1944)
by W. Somerset Maugham
Isherwood, Christopher

DARRINGTON, Minette
Women in Love (1920)
by D.H. Lawrence
Carrington, Dora
Channing, Minnie

DARTLE, Rosa
David Copperfield (1849–50)
by Charles Dickens
Brown, Hannah

DAUBENY, Mr
Phineas Finn (1869)
by Anthony Trollope
Disraeli, Benjamin

DAUNCEY, Margaret
The Magician (1908)
by W. Somerset Maugham
Crowley, Rose

DAVENANT, Lady
Helen (1834)
by Maria Edgeworth
Edgeworth, R.L.

'A London Life' (1888)
Stewart, Mrs Duncan

DAVENANT, Claude
Mirage (1877)
by George Fleming
Wilde, Oscar

DAVENANT, Eve
Challenge (1924)
by Victoria Sackville-West
Trefusis, Violet

DAVENANT, Julian
Challenge (1924)
by Victoria Sackville-West
Sackville-West, Victoria

DAVID
'A Meeting South', *Death in the Woods* (1933)
by Sherwood Anderson
Faulkner, William

DAVIN
A Portrait of the Artist as a Young Man (1916)
by James Joyce
Clancy, George

DAVY, Lenhart
Charles Auchester (1853)
by Elizabeth Sara Sheppard
Hullah, John Pyke

DAWES, Clara
Sons and Lovers (1913)
by D.H. Lawrence
Dax, Alice

DAWLISH, Guy
'The Pretext' (1908)
by Edith Wharton
Pollock, Sir John

DAWSON, Nigel
Vestal Fire (1927)
by Compton Mackenzie
Andrews, Vernon

DEACON, Edgar
A Dance to the Music of Time (1951–76)
by Anthony Powell
Millard, Christopher

DEAD POET
Glenarvon (1816)
by Lady Caroline Lamb
Rogers, Samuel

DE ALTAMONT, James
Memoirs of an Unfortunate Young Nobleman (1743–7)
by Anon.
Annesley, James

DEAN, Matthew
'Triple Fugue' (1924)
by Osbert Sitwell
Marsh, Sir Edward

DEAN OF STUDIES
A Portrait of the Artist as a Young Man (1916)
by James Joyce
Darlington, Father Joseph, SJ

DEANE, Lucy
The Mill on the Floss (1860)
by George Eliot
Clarke, Christiana
Garner, Bessie

DEANE (née Dodson), Susan
The Mill on the Floss (1860)
by George Eliot
Garner, Anne

De ANGELIS, George
Mayor Harding of New York (1931)
by Stephen Endicott
La Guardia, Fiorello Henry

DEANS, David
The Heart of Midlothian (1818)
by Sir Walter Scott
Walker, Patrick

DEANS, Effie
The Heart of Midlothian (1818)
by Sir Walter Scott
Walker, Isobel

DEANS, Jeanie
The Heart of Midlothian (1818)
by Sir Walter Scott
Douglas, Frances, Lady
Walker, Helen

DEANSLEIGH PARK
'Lady Mottisfont' (1891)
by Thomas Hardy
Broadlands, Romsey, Hampshire

DEARBORN, Hugh
'The Machine Breaks Down' (1924)
by Osbert Sitwell
Melvill, Harry

DEASY, Garrett
Ulysses (1922)
by James Joyce
Irwin, Francis
Price, Henry Blackwood

DE BARRAL
Chance (1914)
by Joseph Conrad
Humbert, Frédéric

DEBINGHAM, Henry
I Live Under a Black Sun (1937)
by Edith Sitwell
Lewis, Wyndham

DE CASTRO
Aylwin (1899)
by Theodore Watts-Dunton
Howell, Charles Augustus

DE CLIFFORD, Lady
Cheveley; or The Man of Honour (1839)
by Lady Lytton
Lytton, Rosina Bulwer, Lady

DE CLIFFORD, Lord
Cheveley; or The Man of Honour (1839)
by Lady Lytton
Lytton, Bulwer

DEDALUS, Simon
A Portrait of the Artist as a Young Man (1916)
by James Joyce
Joyce, John

DEEP VALLEY MILL
Michael Armstrong, the Factory Boy (1840)
by Frances Trollope
Litton Mill, Derby

DEERBROOK
Deerbrook (1839)
by Harriet Martineau
Diss, Norfolk

DEERING, Vincent
'The Letters', *Tales of Men and Ghosts* (1910)
by Edith Wharton
Fullerton, Morton

DE FARO, Hernan
Perkin Warbeck (1830)
by Mary Wollstonecraft Shelley
Trelawny, E.J.

DEFREYNE, Harry
The Limit (1911)
by Ada Leverson
Gordon-Lennox, Cosmo

DEHNING, Mr Henry
The Making of Americans (1925)
by Gertrude Stein
Stein, Solomon

DEHNING, Mrs Henry
The Making of Americans (1925)
by Gertrude Stein
Stein, Pauline

DEHNING, Julia
The Making of Americans (1925)
by Gertrude Stein
Gans, Bird

DE JONES, Lord
Jazz and Jasper (1928)
by William Gerhardi
Castlerosse, Lord

DE JONGH, Ernestine
'Ernestine', *A Gallery of Women* (1929)
by Theodore Dreiser
Deshon, Florence

DELACOUR, Lady
Belinda (1801)
by Maria Edgeworth
Delaval, Sir Francis

DELAFIELD, Lady Henry
Lady Rose's Daughter (1903)
by Mrs Humphry Ward
Deffand, Marquise du

DELANEY, Mrs
Caroline Mordaunt; or The Governess (1853)
by Mary Martha Sherwood
Hamilton, Elizabeth

DELAUNAY, Elise
The History of David Grieve (1891)
by Mrs Humphry Ward
Bashkirtseff, Marie

DELAVAL, Lady Calantha
Glenarvon (1816)
by Lady Caroline Lamb
Lamb, Lady Caroline

DELAVAL, Castle
Glenarvon (1816)
by Lady Caroline Lamb
Devonshire House, London

DELISLEVILLE
In Connection with the De Willoughby Claim (1899)
by Frances Hodgson Burnett
Knoxville, Tennessee

DELL, Chris
The Sentimentalists (1906)
by R.H. Benson
Rolfe, F.W.

DEMPSEY, Miss
Delia Blanchflower (1915)
by Mrs Humphry Ward
Butler, Josephine

DEMPSTER, Janet
'Janet's Repentance', *Scenes of Clerical Life* (1857–8)
by George Eliot
Buchanan, Nancy

DEMPSTER, Robert
'Janet's Repentance', *Scenes of Clerical Life* (1857–8)
by George Eliot
Buchanan, J.W.

DENBIGH, Sir Gerald
Arlington (1832)
by T.H. Lister
D'Orsay, Count

DENKA
'I Can't Get Drunk' (1933)
by Kay Boyle
McAlmon, Robert

DENNIS
Barnaby Rudge (1841)
by Charles Dickens
Calcraft, William

DENNISON, Will
The Town and the City (1950)
by Jack Kerouac
Burroughs, William S.

DENSHER, Merton
The Wings of the Dove (1902)
by Henry James
Ford, Ford Madox
Fullerton, Morton
Seaman, Sir Owen

DEODATA, Santa
Where Angels Fear to Tread (1905)
by E.M. Forster
Fina, Santa

DERONDA, Daniel
Daniel Deronda (1876)
by George Eliot
Bond, Sir Edward
Goldsmid, Colonel Albert
Gurney, Edmund
Lewes, G.H.
Louis, Alfred Hyman

DERRINGHAM, John
Halcyone (1912)
by Elinor Glyn
Curzon, Lord

DERRYDOWN, Mr
Melincourt (1817)
by Thomas Love Peacock
Scott, Sir Walter

DERWENT, Lord
Almacks (1826)
by M. Spencer Stanhope
Portland, 5th Duke of

DE SALDAR, Countess
Evan Harrington (1860)
by George Meredith
Meredith, Louise Mitchell

DESART, Fabian ('Carrots')
'Carrots': Just a Little Boy (1878)
by Mrs Molesworth
Molesworth, Lionel Charles
Molesworth, Richard Bevil

DESART, Captain Frank
'Carrots': Just a Little Boy (1878)
by Mrs Molesworth
Molesworth, Richard

DESBROW
The Two Friends (1835)
by Lady Blessington
Lytton, Bulwer

DE TERRIER, Lord
Framley Parsonage (1861)
by Anthony Trollope
Derby, Lord

DE VERE
Florence Macarthy (1818)
by Lady Sydney Morgan
Byron, Lord

DEXTER, Benjamin
'The Third Man' (1958)
by Graham Greene
Forster, E.M.

DICKIEFIELD
Piccadilly (1870)
by Laurence Oliphant
Fryston Hall, Ferrybridge, Yorkshire

DICKIEFIELD, Lord
Piccadilly (1870)
by Laurence Oliphant
Milnes, Richard Monckton

DIMPLE HILL
Pilgrimage (1915–67)
by Dorothy Richardson
Windmill Hill, Sussex

DINMONT, AILIE
Guy Mannering (1815)
by Sir Walter Scott
Laidlaw, Catherine

DINMONT, DANDIE
Guy Mannering (1815)
by Sir Walter Scott
Davidson, James
Elliott, Willie
Laidlaw, James
Park, Archibald
Thorburn, James

D'INVILLIERS, THOMAS P.
This Side of Paradise (1920)
by F. Scott Fitzgerald
Bishop, John Peale

DINWIDDIE, EUNICE
The Buffoon (1916)
by Louis Wilkinson
Doolittle, Hilda

HMS DIOMÈDE
Peter Simple (1834)
by Frederick Marryat
HMS Impérieuse

DIRKES, PRISM
Tarr (1918)
by Wyndham Lewis
Barry, Iris

DIVER, COLONEL
Martin Chuzzlewit (1843–4)
by Charles Dickens
Webb, James Watson

DIVER, NICOLE
Tender is the Night (1934)
by F. Scott Fitzgerald
Fitzgerald, Zelda
Murphy, Sara

DIVER, RICHARD
Tender is the Night (1934)
by F. Scott Fitzgerald
Fitzgerald, F. Scott
Murphy, Gerald

DIXIELAND
Look Homeward, Angel (1929)
by Thomas Wolfe
Old Kentucky Home, Asheville,
    North Carolina

DOANE
'Esther Norn', *A Gallery of Women*
    (1929)
by Theodore Dreiser
Kemp, Harry

DOBBIN, WILLIAM
Vanity Fair (1847–8)
by W.M. Thackeray
Allen, John[2]

DOBSON, ZULEIKA
Zuleika Dobson (1911)
by Max Beerbohm
Collier, Constance

DODD, LEWIS
The Constant Nymph (1924)
by Margaret Kennedy
Lamb, Henry

DODDERINGHAM OLD HALL
'Triple Fugue' (1924)
by Osbert Sitwell
Garsington Manor, Oxfordshire

DODS, MEG
St Ronan's Well (1823)
by Sir Walter Scott
Ritchie, Marion

DODSWORTH, FRAN
Dodsworth (1929)
by Sinclair Lewis
Lewis, Grace Hegger

DOLAN, FATHER
A Portrait of the Artist as a Young Man (1916)
by James Joyce
Daly, Father James, SJ

DOLPHIN, MR
The History of Pendennis (1848–50)
by W.M. Thackeray
Bunn, Alfred

DOMBEY, MR
Dombey and Son (1846–8)
by Charles Dickens
Chapman, Thomas

DOMBEY, PAUL
Dombey and Son (1846–8)
by Charles Dickens
Burnett, Henry Augustus

DOMINIC
The Arrow of Gold (1919)
by Joseph Conrad
Cervoni, Dominic

DONALD, GEOFFREY
Desolation Angels (1965)
by Jack Kerouac
Duncan, Robert

DONKIN
The Nigger of the 'Narcissus' (1897)
by Joseph Conrad
Dutton, Charles

DONN, ARABELLA
Jude the Obscure (1895)
by Thomas Hardy
H——, Rachel

DONNE, GRIFFITH
Dolly (1877)
by Frances Hodgson Burnett
Burnett, Swan

DONNE, JOSEPH
Shirley (1849)
by Charlotte Brontë
Grant, Revd Joseph Brett

DONNELLY, ALPHY
'Clay', *Dubliners* (1914)
by James Joyce
Murray, William

DONNELLY, HUGHIE
Ward Eight (1936)
by Joseph Dineen
Lomasney, 'Czar' Martin

DONNELLY, JOE
'Clay', *Dubliners* (1914)
by James Joyce
Murray, John^2

DONNITHORNE ARMS, HAYSLOPE
Adam Bede (1859)
by George Eliot
Bromley-Davenport Arms, Ellastone, Staffordshire

DONNITHORNE CHASE
Adam Bede (1859)
by George Eliot
Wootton Hall, Ellastone, Staffordshire

DONOVAN
A Portrait of the Artist as a Young Man (1916)
by James Joyce
Curran, Constantine P.

DORA
Post Adolescence (1923)
by Robert McAlmon
Ridge, Lola

DORLCOTE MILL
The Mill on the Floss (1860)
by George Eliot
Arbury Mill, Warwickshire

DORNELL, BETTY
'The First Countess of Wessex' (1891)
by Thomas Hardy
Ilchester, Elizabeth, Countess of

DORNELL, Susan
'The First Countess of Wessex' (1891)
by Thomas Hardy
Strangways, Susanna

DORNELL, Thomas
'The First Countess of Wessex' (1891)
by Thomas Hardy
Horner, Thomas

DORRIFORTH (afterwards Lord
 Elmwood)
A Simple Story (1791)
by Elizabeth Inchbald
Kemble, John Philip

DORRINGTON, Miss
Dolores (1911)
by I. Compton-Burnett
Cunningham, Marjorie

DORRIT, William
Little Dorrit (1855–7)
by Charles Dickens
Dickens, John

DOSSON, Francina
The Reverberator (1888)
by Henry James
McClellan, May Marcy

DOUBTFUL, Lady
Vivian Grey (1826–7)
by Benjamin Disraeli
Blessington, Lady

DOUGLAS, Ellen
The Lady of the Lake (1810)
by Sir Walter Scott
Hood, Lady

DOUNOR, Cora
The Making of Americans (1925)
by Gertrude Stein
Gwinn, Mary

DOUSTERSWIVEL, Herman
The Antiquary (1816)
by Sir Walter Scott
Raspe, Rudolf Eric

DOWELL, Florence
The Good Soldier (1915)
by Ford Madox Ford
Hunt, Violet

DOWELL, John
The Good Soldier (1915)
by Ford Madox Ford
Ford, Ford Madox

DOWELL, Mary
Bid Me to Live (1960)
by H.D. (Hilda Doolittle)
Lowell, Amy

DOWNE LODGE
'Baa, Baa, Black Sheep' (1888)
by Rudyard Kipling
**4 Campbell Rd, Havelock Park,
 Southsea**

DOWNSTABLE
'The Honourable Laura' (1891)
by Thomas Hardy
Barnstaple, Devon

DOYE, Basil
Non-combatants and Others (1916)
by Rose Macaulay
Brooke, Rupert

DRAKE, Ann
Black Bethlehem (1947)
by Lettice Cooper
Blair, Eileen

DRAKE, Christopher
Black Bethlehem (1947)
by Lettice Cooper
Orwell, George

DRESSLER, Pension
Scoop (1938)
by Evelyn Waugh
Hefts, Ethiopia

DRIFFIELD, Amy
Cakes and Ale (1930)
by W. Somerset Maugham
Hardy, Florence

DRIFFIELD, EDWARD
Cakes and Ale (1930)
by W. Somerset Maugham
Hardy, Thomas

DRIFFIELD, ROSE
Cakes and Ale (1930)
by W. Somerset Maugham
Jones, Ethelwyn Sylvia

DRITTER, RICHARD
The Roaring Queen (1973)
by Wyndham Lewis
Sickert, Walter

DROLLIN, FELIX
Lothair (1870)
by Benjamin Disraeli
Ledru-Rollin, Alexandre Auguste

DRUMMOND, HUGH ('BULL-DOG')
Bull-dog Drummond (1920) and
    others
by Sapper (H.C. McNeile)
Fairlie, Gerard

DUCAYNE, GERALD
Pilgrimage (1915–67)
by Dorothy Richardson
Hale, Jack

THE DUCHESS
Alice's Adventures in Wonderland
    (1865)
by Lewis Carroll
Carinthia, Margaret, Duchess of
Wilberforce, Samuel

THE DUCK
Alice's Adventures in Wonderland
    (1865)
by Lewis Carroll
Duckworth, Robinson

DUCK BANK AND DUCK SQUARE
Anna of the Five Towns (1902) and
    others
by Arnold Bennett
Swan Bank and Swan Square

DUCROS, STANISLAUS RICHARD
Friday's Business (1932)
by Maurice Baring
Bourchier, J.D.

DUDLEY
Guy Mannering (1815)
by Sir Walter Scott
Skene, James

DUDLEY, ESTHER
Esther (1884)
by Henry Adams
Adams, Marian

DUDLEY, WILLIAM
Esther (1884)
by Henry Adams
Hooper, Robert William

THE DUENNA COUSIN
Sartor Resartus (1833–4)
by Thomas Carlyle
Strachey, Julia

DUER, ANGUS
Arrowsmith (1925)
by Sinclair Lewis
Vanden Berg, Henry J.

DUFFY, JAMES
'A Painful Case', *Dubliners* (1914)
by James Joyce
Joyce, Stanislaus

DUFRÉNOIS, PAUL
Fountains in the Sand (1912)
by Norman Douglas
Duterme, Robert

THE DUKE
Coningsby (1844)
by Benjamin Disraeli
Rutland, 5th Duke of

DUKE, REVD ARCHIBALD
'The Sad Fortunes of the Revd Amos
    Barton', *Scenes of Clerical Life*
    (1857–8)
by George Eliot
Hoke, Revd Mr

DULL, Vivacity
Vivian Grey (1826–7)
by Benjamin Disraeli
Twiss, Horace

DULUOZ, Jack
Maggie Cassidy (1959)
by Jack Kerouac
Kerouac, Jack

DUNCAN, Lady Harriet
Granby (1826)
by T.H. Lister
Lamb, Lady Caroline

DUNDAGEL
A Pair of Blue Eyes (1873)
by Thomas Hardy
Tintagel Castle, Cornwall

DUNFIELD
A Life's Morning (1888)
by George Gissing
Wakefield, Yorkshire

DUNSTABLE, Emily
Framley Parsonage (1861)
by Anthony Trollope
Trollope, Frances Eleanor

DUNSTANE, Lady
Diana of the Crossways (1884)
by George Meredith
Duff-Gordon, Lucie, Lady

DUPONT
Still Life (1916)
by J.M. Murry
Carco, Francis

DUQUETTE, Raoul
'Je ne parle pas français' (1920)
by Katherine Mansfield
Carco, Francis

DURBEYFIELD, Teresa ('Tess')
Tess of the d'Urbervilles (1891)
by Thomas Hardy
Thornycroft, Agatha

DURNOVER
Wessex novels and tales (1871–95)
by Thomas Hardy
Fordington, Dorset

DURNWOOD, Russett
Nigger Heaven (1926)
by Carl Van Vechten
Mencken, H.L.

E

EAGLEDALE
Adam Bede (1859)
by George Eliot
Dovedale, Staffordshire

EAMES, Ernest
South Wind (1917)
by Norman Douglas
Brooks, John Ellingham

EAMES, Johnny
The Small House at Allington (1864)
by Anthony Trollope
Trollope, Anthony

The EARL
The Provost (1822)
by John Galt
Eglinton, 12th Earl of

EARWICKER, Humphrey Chimpden
Finnegans Wake (1939)
by James Joyce
Joyce, John

EARWIG, Mr
Coningsby (1844)
by Benjamin Disraeli
Clerk, Sir George

EAST EGDON
The Return of the Native (1878)
by Thomas Hardy
Affpuddle, Dorset

EAST END ELEVATION MISSION
& PANSOPHICAL INSTITUTE
A Child of the Jago (1896)
by Arthur Morrison
Toynbee Hall, Whitechapel, London

EAST QUARRIERS
The Well-Beloved (1897)
by Thomas Hardy
Easton, Portland, Dorset

EATANSWILL
The Pickwick Papers (1836–7)
by Charles Dickens
Ipswich, Suffolk
Sudbury, Suffolk

EBERWICH
The White Peacock (1911)
by D.H. Lawrence
Eastwood, Nottinghamshire

EDDIE
The Death of the Heart (1938)
by Elizabeth Bowen
Rees, Goronwy

EDEN
Martin Chuzzlewit (1843–4)
by Charles Dickens
Cairo, Illinois

EDEN, MARTIN
Martin Eden (1909)
by Jack London
London, Jack

EDGE
The Cantab (1926)
by Shane Leslie
Edghill, E.A.

EDGE, NIGEL
The Invaders (1934)
by William Plomer
Plomer, William

EDGEWORTH, HAROLD
The Private Life of Henry Maitland
(1912)
by Morley Roberts
Harrison, Frederic

THE EDITOR OF THE *UNIVERSAL
REVIEW* (OXFORD)
Lavengro (1851)
by George Borrow
Busby, Thomas
Carey, John
Gifford, William

EDWARDS, FOXHALL
You Can't Go Home Again (1940)
by Thomas Wolfe
Perkins, Maxwell

EDWARDS, REVD SLINGSBY
Hostages to Fortune (1875)
by M.E. Braddon
Jones, James Rhys ('Kilsby')

EGAN, KEVIN
Ulysses (1922)
by James Joyce
Casey, Joseph

EGBERT
'England, My England' (1915)
by D.H. Lawrence
Lucas, Perceval Drewett

EGBERT
The Confidence Man (1857)
by Herman Melville
Thoreau, Henry David

EGDON HEATH
Wessex novels and tales (1871–95)
by Thomas Hardy
Puddletown Heath, Dorset

EGLETT, LADY CHARLOTTE
Lord Ormont and His Aminta (1894)
by George Meredith
Maxse, Lady Caroline

EGSTRÖM & BLAKE
Lord Jim (1900)
by Joseph Conrad
MacAlister & Co.

ELDORADO EXPLORING
  EXPEDITION
Heart of Darkness (1902)
by Joseph Conrad
Katanga Expedition

ELEANOR
Dawn (1931)
by Theodore Dreiser
Dreiser, Mary Frances

ELINOR
Of Time and the River (1935)
by Thomas Wolfe
Fairbanks, Marjorie

ELIZABETH
The Visits of Elizabeth (1900)
by Elinor Glyn
Forbes, Lady Angela

ELLEN
The Way of All Flesh (1903)
by Samuel Butler
Zanetta, Isabella

ELLIOT, CAPTAIN
Lord Jim (1900) and 'The End of the
  Tether' (1902)
by Joseph Conrad
Ellis, Captain Henry

ELLIOT, CORNELIA
'Mr and Mrs Elliot', *In Our Time*
  (1925)
by Ernest Hemingway
Smith, Olive Cary

ELLIOT, FREDERICK ('RICKIE')
The Longest Journey (1907)
by E.M. Forster
Forster, E.M.

ELLIOT, HUBERT
'Mr and Mrs Elliot', *In Our Time*
  (1925)
by Ernest Hemingway
Smith, Chard Powers

ELLIS, CAPTAIN
'The Shadow Line' (1917)
by Joseph Conrad
Ellis, Captain Henry

ELM-CRANLYNCH
'The First Countess of Wessex' (1891)
by Thomas Hardy
Corfe Mullen, Dorset

ELMWOOD, LORD
See DORRIFORTH

ELSENFORD
'The Waiting Supper' (1913)
by Thomas Hardy
Ilsington Farm, Dorset

ELSIE
Alice's Adventures in Wonderland
  (1865)
by Lewis Carroll
Liddell, Louisa

ELSMERE, CATHERINE
See LEYBURN, Catherine

ELY, REVD MR
'The Sad Fortunes of the Revd Amos
  Barton', *Scenes of Clerical Life*
  (1857–8)
by George Eliot
King, Revd William Hutchinson

EMANUEL, PAUL
Villette (1853)
by Charlotte Brontë
Héger, Constantin

EMERSON, MR
A Room with a View (1908)
by E.M. Forster
Butler, Samuel

EMMANUEL, Mr
Jadoo (1898)
by Newnham Davis
Jacob, Alexander M.

EMMANUELA
'Emmanuela', *A Gallery of Women*
(1929)
by Theodore Dreiser
Watkins, Ann

EMMINSTER
Wessex novels and tales (1871–95)
by Thomas Hardy
Beaminster, Dorset

EMMOTT, David
Murder in Mesopotamia (1936)
by Agatha Christie
Mallowan, Max

ENDELSTOW
A Pair of Blue Eyes (1873)
by Thomas Hardy
St Juliot, Cornwall

ENDELSTOW HOUSE
A Pair of Blue Eyes (1873)
by Thomas Hardy
Lanhydrock House, Cornwall

The ENGLISH AMBASSADRESS
The Flower Beneath the Foot (1923)
by Ronald Firbank
Nicolson, Mary Catherine
Roscoe, Flora

ENTEPFUHL
Sartor Resartus (1833–4)
by Thomas Carlyle
Ecclefechan, Dumfriesshire

EREWHON
Erewhon (1872)
by Samuel Butler
Whitcombe Pass, New Zealand

ERICSON, Carl
The Trail of the Hawk (1915)
by Sinclair Lewis
Lewis, Sinclair

ERMINIA
'The Proser IV – On a Good-Looking
Young Lady' (1850)
by W.M. Thackeray
Somers, Virginia, Countess

ERPINGHAM, Constance, Countess
of
Godolphin (1833)
by Bulwer Lytton
Blessington, Lady

ERRICE, Mr
The Repealers (1833) and *The Belle
of a Season* (1840)
by Lady Blessington
Ellice, Edward

ERROLL, Cedric
See Fauntleroy, Lord

ERSKINE, Chichester
An Unsocial Socialist (1887)
by George Bernard Shaw
Beatty, Pakenham Thomas

ESCOT, Mr
Headlong Hall (1816)
by Thomas Love Peacock
Peacock, Thomas Love
Shelley, Percy Bysshe

ESKDALE, Lord
Tancred (1847) and *Coningsby* (1844)
by Benjamin Disraeli
Lonsdale, 2nd Earl of

ESMOND, Henry
The History of Henry Esmond (1852)
by W.M. Thackeray
Thackeray, W.M.

ESSLING-STERLINGHOVEN,
Gräfin
Heritage (1984)
by Anthony West
Keun, Odette

ETHELRED, Sir
The Secret Agent (1907)
by Joseph Conrad
Harcourt, Sir William

ETOILE
See d'Avesnes, Etoile, Comtesse

EVANS, Amy
See The Princess

E.V.C.
Blindness (1926)
by Henry Green
Anderson, Colin

EVERARD, George
The Simple Life Limited (1911)
by Ford Madox Ford
Harris, Frank

EVERHARD, Ernest
The Iron Heel (1908)
by Jack London
Debs, Eugene
London, Jack
Untermann, Ernest

EVERINGHAM, Lady
Coningsby (1844)
by Benjamin Disraeli
Clarendon, Catherine, Countess of

EVERINGHAM, Lord
Coningsby (1844)
by Benjamin Disraeli
Cardigan, 7th Earl of
Clarendon, 4th Earl of

EVERSHEAD
Wessex novels and tales (1871–95)
by Thomas Hardy
Evershot, Dorset

EVESHAM, Mr
The New Machiavelli (1911)
by H.G. Wells
Balfour, A.J.

EWART, Sidney
Tono-Bungay (1909)
by H.G. Wells
Low, Walter
Stevenson, R.A.M. ('Bob')

EXONBURY
Wessex novels and tales (1871–95)
by Thomas Hardy
Exeter, Devon

EZRA, Raphael Aben
Hypatia (1853)
by Charles Kingsley
Louis, Alfred Hyman

F

FACING-BOTH-WAYS, Lord
Gryll Grange (1860)
by Thomas Love Peacock
Brougham, Lord

FAGAN, Ben
Big Sur (1962)
by Jack Kerouac
Whalen, Philip

FAGIN
Oliver Twist (1837–8)
by Charles Dickens
Solomons, Ikey

FAILING, Mrs Emily
The Longest Journey (1907)
by E.M. Forster
Forster, W.H.
Russell, Countess

FAIRCHILD, Dawson
Mosquitoes (1927)
by William Faulkner
Anderson, Sherwood

FAIRFAX, Alice
Jane Eyre (1847)
by Charlotte Brontë
Wooler, Margaret

FAIRFORD, Alan
Redgauntlet (1824)
by Sir Walter Scott
Scott, Sir Walter

FAIRFORD (called Saunders),
  Alexander
Redgauntlet (1824)
by Sir Walter Scott
Scott, Walter, the Elder

FAIRLADIES
Redgauntlet (1824)
by Sir Walter Scott
Mereworth Castle, Kent

FAIRLAND
'An Indiscretion in the Life of an
  Heiress' (1878)
by Thomas Hardy
Higher Bockhampton, Dorset

FAIRLIE, Laura
The Woman in White (1860)
by Wilkie Collins
Douhault, Marquise de

FAIROAKS
The History of Pendennis (1848–50)
by W.M. Thackeray
**Larkbeare House, Ottery St Mary,
  Devon**

FAIRPORT
The Antiquary (1816)
by Sir Walter Scott
Arbroath, Tayside, Scotland

FAIRPORT
Denis Duval (1864)
by W.M. Thackeray
Fareham, Hampshire

FALCO, Baron
The Cantab (1926)
by Shane Leslie
Rolfe, F.W.

FALCONER, Commissioner
Patronage (1814)
by Maria Edgeworth
O'Beirne, Thomas Lewis

FALCONER, Buckhurst
Patronage (1814)
by Maria Edgeworth
Smith, Sydney

FALLS-PARK
'The First Countess of Wessex' (1891)
by Thomas Hardy
Mells, Somerset

FANE, Walter
The Painted Veil (1925)
by W. Somerset Maugham
**Maugham, Frederic Herbert, 1st
  Viscount**

FANG, Mr
Oliver Twist (1837–8)
by Charles Dickens
Laing, Allan Stewart

FANNING, Long John
Ulysses (1922)
by James Joyce
Clancy, John

FANNING, Miles
'After the Fireworks' (1930)
by Aldous Huxley
Chateaubriand, François René de

FANSHAWE, Ginevra
Villette (1853)
by Charlotte Brontë
Miller, Maria

FARINTOSH, Marquis of
The Newcomes (1854–5)
by W.M. Thackeray
Bath, 4th Marquis of

FARLL, Priam
Buried Alive (1908)
by Arnold Bennett
Morrice, James Wilson

FARQUHAR, Mr
'The Sad Fortunes of the Revd Amos
    Barton', *Scenes of Clerical Life*
    (1857–8)
by George Eliot
Harper (or Harpur), Henry Richard

FARQUHAR, Katherine
'The Border Line' (1928)
by D.H. Lawrence
Lawrence, Frieda

FARQUHAR, Philip
'The Border Line' (1928)
by D.H. Lawrence
Murry, John Middleton

FARRADAY, Nigel
Entirely Surrounded (1934)
by Charles Brackett
Coward, Noël

The 'FATHER'
Yeast (1848)
by Charles Kingsley
Newman, J.H.

FAUBOURG, Monsieur
'A Luncheon Party', *Half a Minute's
    Silence and Other Stories* (1925)
by Maurice Baring
Bourget, Paul

FAUNTLEROY, Cedric Erroll, Lord
Little Lord Fauntleroy (1886)
by Frances Hodgson Burnett
Burnett, Vivian

FAX, Mr
Melincourt (1817)
by Thomas Love Peacock
Malthus, Thomas

FAY, Ted
'The Freshest Boy' (1935)
by F. Scott Fitzgerald
Coy, Edward Harris

FEATHERNEST, Mr
Melincourt (1817)
by Thomas Love Peacock
Southey, Robert

FEENIX, Cousin
Dombey and Son (1846–8)
by Charles Dickens
Townshend, Chauncey Hare

FELL, Carlotta (afterwards Lady
    Lathkill)
'Glad Ghosts' (1928)
by D.H. Lawrence
Asquith, Lady Cynthia
Brett, Dorothy

FELL, Dr Gideon
The Mad Hatter Mystery (1933) and
    others
by John Dickson Carr
Chesterton, G.K.

FELLOWES, Revd Mr
'The Sad Fortunes of the Revd Amos
    Barton', *Scenes of Clerical Life*
    (1857–8)
by George Eliot
Bellairs, Revd Mr

FENSWORTH
Jude the Obscure (1895)
by Thomas Hardy
Letcombe Regis, Oxfordshire

FENTIMAN, General Arthur
*The Unpleasantness at the Bellona
    Club* (1928)
by Dorothy L. Sayers
Crockford, William

FERNANDEZ, Beryl
The Case is Altered (1932)
by William Plomer
Da Costa, Sybil

FERNANDEZ, Paul
The Case is Altered (1932)
by William Plomer
Achew, James

FERNDEAN MANOR
Jane Eyre (1847)
by Charlotte Brontë
Wycoller Hall, Lancashire

FERNELL HALL
'Lady Mottisfont' (1891)
by Thomas Hardy
Embley House, Romsey, Hampshire

FERNHURST
Fernhurst (1971)
by Gertrude Stein
Bryn Mawr College, Pennsylvania

FERNHURST
The Loom of Youth (1917)
by Alec Waugh
Sherborne School, Dorset

FERRARS, ENDYMION
Endymion (1880)
by Benjamin Disraeli
Dilke, Sir Charles Wentworth

FERRARS, WILLIAM PITT
Endymion (1880)
by Benjamin Disraeli
Salisbury, Lord

FERROL, COUNT
Endymion (1880)
by Benjamin Disraeli
von Bismarck, Otto

FEVEREL, HIPPIAS
The Ordeal of Richard Feverel (1859)
by George Meredith
Charnock, Richard Stephen

FEVERSTONE, LORD
That Hideous Strength (1945)
by C.S. Lewis
Weldon, T.D. ('Harry')

FIELD, JULIAN
Both Sides of the Blanket (1945)
by Halcott Glover
Hunt, Leigh

FIELDHEAD
Shirley (1849)
by Charlotte Brontë
Oakwell Hall, Birstall, Yorkshire

FIGHTING ATTIE
Paul Clifford (1830)
by Bulwer Lytton
Wellington, Duke of

FINCHING, FLORA
Little Dorrit (1855–7)
by Charles Dickens
Beadnell, Maria

FINDLAYSON
'The Bridge Builders' (1898)
by Rudyard Kipling
Bell, J.R.
Geddes, Auckland
Walton, F.T.G.

FINESPIN, MR
Can You Forgive Her? (1864)
by Anthony Trollope
Gladstone, William

FINISH, HARRY
Paul Clifford (1830)
by Bulwer Lytton
de Ros, Henry

FINN, PHINEAS
Phineas Finn (1869) and *Phineas Redux* (1874)
by Anthony Trollope
King-Harman, Edward Robert
Parkinson, Joe
Parkinson-Fortescue, Chichester
Pope-Hennessy, Sir John

FINNIAN-SHAW, LADY HARRIET
The Apes of God (1930)
by Wyndham Lewis
Sitwell, Edith

FINNIAN-SHAW, LORD OSMUND
The Apes of God (1930)
by Wyndham Lewis
Sitwell, Sir Osbert

FINNIAN-SHAW, LORD PHOEBUS
The Apes of God (1930)
by Wyndham Lewis
Sitwell, Sacheverell

FINSBURY, MICHAEL
The Wrong Box (1889)
by R.L. Stevenson and Lloyd
  Osbourne
Baxter, Charles

FINSTER-AR-HORN, ARCHDUCHESS
  HARRIET AND ARCHDUKE HARRY OF
Orlando (1928)
by Virginia Woolf
**Lascelles, Henry G.C., 6th Earl of
  Harewood**

FIREBRACE, SIR VAVASOUR
Sybil (1845)
by Benjamin Disraeli
Broun, Sir Richard

FIRMIN, DR GEORGE
The Adventures of Philip (1861–2)
by W.M. Thackeray
James, E.J.

FIRMIN, PHILIP
The Adventures of Philip (1861–2)
by W.M. Thackeray
Thackeray, W.M.

FISHER, HORNE
The Man Who Knew Too Much
  (1922)
by G.K. Chesterton
Baring, Maurice

FISHER, MAX
Pending Heaven (1930)
by William Gerhardi
Kingsmill, Hugh

FITCH, ANDREA
A Shabby Genteel Story (1840)
by W.M. Thackeray
Brine, John

FITCHETT, MR
'The Sad Fortunes of the Revd Amos
  Barton', *Scenes of Clerical Life*
  (1857–8)
by George Eliot
Baker, Mr

FITZBOOBY, LORD
Coningsby (1844)
by Benjamin Disraeli
Harrington, Lord
Ryder, Dudley

FITZGERALD, M.
A Pier and a Band (1918)
by Mary MacCarthy
MacCarthy, Desmond

FITZGERALD & MOY
Sister Carrie (1900)
by Theodore Dreiser
Chapin & Gore, Chicago

FITZLOOM, MR
Vivian Grey (1826–7)
by Benjamin Disraeli
Peel, Sir Robert

FITZPATRICK, BENNETT
The Subterraneans (1958)
by Jack Kerouac
Burnett, Whit

FITZPATRICK, WALT
The Subterraneans (1958)
by Jack Kerouac
Burnett, David

121 FITZROY SQUARE
The Newcomes (1854–5)
by W.M. Thackeray
37 Fitzroy Square, London

FIZKIN, HORATIO
The Pickwick Papers (1836–7)
by Charles Dickens
Kelly, Sir Fitzroy

FLACK, George
The Reverberator (1888)
by Henry James
Hawthorne, Julian

FLANAGAN
Of Human Bondage (1915)
by W. Somerset Maugham
Stanlaws, Penrhyn

FLANDERS, Jacob
Jacob's Room (1922)
by Virginia Woolf
Stephen, Thoby

FLATMAN, Julius 'Red'
More Miles (1926)
by Harry Kemp
Lewis, Sinclair

FLAXMAN'S COURT
Pilgrimage (1915–67)
by Dorothy Richardson
**Woburn Buildings, Bloomsbury,
London**

FLEET, Nigel
Death to Slow Music (1956)
by Beverley Nichols
Coward, Noël

FLEISCHER, Von Humboldt
Humboldt's Gift (1975)
by Saul Bellow
Schwartz, Delmore

FLEMING, Baron
Contarini Fleming (1832)
by Benjamin Disraeli
Israeli, Benjamin

FLEMING, Berenice
The Titan (1914)
by Theodore Dreiser
Grigsby, Emilie

FLEMING, Contarini
Contarini Fleming (1832)
by Benjamin Disraeli
Disraeli, Benjamin

FLETCHER, Robert A.
Stranger Come Home (1954)
by William L. Shirer
Murrow, Edward R.

de FLEURY, Madame
'Madame de Fleury', *Tales of
Fashionable Life* (1809)
by Maria Edgeworth
Pastoret, Comtesse de

FLORESTAN, Prince
See ALBERT, Colonel

FLOSKY, Ferdinando
Nightmare Abbey (1818)
by Thomas Love Peacock
Coleridge, Samuel Taylor

The FLOSS
The Mill on the Floss (1860)
by George Eliot
Trent, River

FLOUNCEY, Guy
Coningsby (1844) and *Tancred* (1847)
by Benjamin Disraeli
Shakerley, Sir Charles Peter

FLOWER-DE-LUCE
Tess of the d'Urbervilles (1891)
by Thomas Hardy
**Fleur-de-Lis Inn, Cranbourne,
Dorset**

FLOWERDALE, Mr
*De Vere; or The Man of
Independence* (1827)
by Robert Plumer Ward
Ward, Robert Plumer

FLYCHETT
The Hand of Ethelberta (1876)
by Thomas Hardy
Lytchett Minster, Dorset

FLYTE, Sebastian
Brideshead Revisited (1945)
by Evelyn Waugh
Graham, Alastair
Lygon, Hugh

FOINET
Of Human Bondage (1915)
by W. Somerset Maugham
Binet, G.-J.-E.

FOKER, HARRY
The History of Pendennis (1848–50)
by W.M. Thackeray
Arcedeckne, Andrew

FOLIO, COUNTESS FLOR DI
Serena Blandish (1924)
by Enid Bagnold
d'Erlanger, Catherine, Baroness

FONTAN AND MADAME FONTAN
'Wine of Wyoming', *Winner Take
    Nothing* (1933)
by Ernest Hemingway
Moncini, Charles and Alice

FONTENOY, LORD
Sir George Tressady (1896)
by Mrs Humphry Ward
Churchill, Lord Randolph

FOPPA
A Dance to the Music of Time
    (1951–76)
by Anthony Powell
Castano, Pietro

FOPPA'S RESTAURANT
A Dance to the Music of Time
    (1951–76)
by Anthony Powell
Castano's Restaurant, Soho, London

FORBES, DUNCAN
Lady Chatterley's Lover (1928)
by D.H. Lawrence
Grant, Duncan

FORD, CAPTAIN
Almayer's Folly (1895)
by Joseph Conrad
Craig, Captain James

FORD, JOSEPHINE
Aaron's Rod (1922)
by D.H. Lawrence
Yorke, Dorothy

FOREMAN, JOSIAH
The Old Order Changes (1886)
by W.H. Mallock
Hyndman, H.M.

FORESTER
'Forester', *Moral Tales for Young
    People* (1801)
by Maria Edgeworth
Ashburton, Lord
Day, Thomas

FORESTER, SYLVAN
Melincourt (1817)
by Thomas Love Peacock
Monboddo, Lord
Shelley, Percy Bysshe

THE FORMER CAPTAIN
The Shadow-Line (1917)
by Joseph Conrad
Snadden, Captain John

FORSTER, TOM
One of Two (1871)
by Hain Friswell
Field, Charles Frederick

FORSYTE, IRENE
The Man of Property (1906)
by John Galsworthy
Galsworthy, Ada

FORT PENN
A Rage to Live (1949)
by John O'Hara
Harrisburg, Pennsylvania

FORTH, PROFESSOR JAMES
Belinda (1883)
by Rhoda Broughton
Pattison, Mark

FOSTER, Mr
Headlong Hall (1816)
by Thomas Love Peacock
Peacock, Thomas Love
Shelley, Percy Bysshe

FOTHERINGAY, Emily
The History of Pendennis (1848–50)
by W.M. Thackeray
Ternan, Frances Eleanor

FOTHERINGAY, Paul
Christmas Pudding (1932)
by Nancy Mitford
Betjeman, John

FOTHERINGHAM, Mary
Cuthbert Learmont (1910)
by J.A. Revermort
Morrell, Lady Ottoline

FOUNTALL
Wessex novels and tales (1871–95)
by Thomas Hardy
Wells, Somerset

The FOURWAYS, Christminster
Jude the Obscure (1895)
by Thomas Hardy
Carfax, Oxford

FOWLER, Canon
'The Spirit's Trials', *Shadows of the
    Clouds* (1847)
by James Anthony Froude
Froude, Robert Hurrell

FOWLER, Edward
'The Spirit's Trials', *Shadows of the
    Clouds* (1847)
by James Anthony Froude
Froude, James Anthony

FOX
The Inheritors (1901)
by Joseph Conrad and Ford Madox
    Ford
Northcliffe, Lord

FOX, Madeline
Arrowsmith (1925)
by Sinclair Lewis
Lewis, Grace Hegger

FOXE, Brian
Eyeless in Gaza (1936)
by Aldous Huxley
Huxley, Noel Trevenen

FOXE, Rachel
Eyeless in Gaza (1936)
by Aldous Huxley
Ward, Mrs Humphry

FOXY
Stalky & Co. (1899)
by Rudyard Kipling
Schofield, George

FRANCIS, Adolph
'The Battler', *In Our Time* (1925)
by Ernest Hemingway
Nelson, Battling
Wolgast, Ad

FRANCIS, Mobbing
See MOBBING FRANCIS

FRANKENSTEIN, Alphonse
*Frankenstein; or The Modern
    Prometheus* (1818)
by Mary Wollstonecraft Shelley
Godwin, William
Lind, James

FRANKENSTEIN, Victor
*Frankenstein; or The Modern
    Prometheus* (1818)
by Mary Wollstonecraft Shelley
Shelley, Percy Bysshe

FRANKS, Sir William
Aaron's Rod (1922)
by D.H. Lawrence
Becker, Sir Walter

FREDDY'S BAR
To Have and Have Not (1937)
by Ernest Hemingway
Sloppy Joe's

FREDERICK ('FREDERICO')
Bid Me to Live (1960)
by H.D. (Hilda Doolittle)
Lawrence, D.H.

FREDERICK, ELSE
Bid Me to Live (1960)
by H.D. (Hilda Doolittle)
Lawrence, Frieda

FREEMAN, PINTO
A House of Children (1941)
by Joyce Cary
Thomas, Dylan

FREEMANTLE, RORY
Extraordinary Women (1928)
by Compton Mackenzie
Hall, Radclyffe

FRENSHAM, COUNTESS OF
Mr Britling Sees It Through (1916)
by H.G. Wells
Warwick, Frances, Lady

FRESLEVEN, CAPTAIN
Heart of Darkness (1902)
by Joseph Conrad
Freiesleben, Captain

THE FRIEND IN PARIS
'The Informer', *A Set of Six* (1908)
by Joseph Conrad
Ford, Ford Madox

FRITH, JIMMY
'Jimmy and the Desperate Woman'
 (1928)
by D.H. Lawrence
Murry, John Middleton

FROITZHEIM, EDGAR
Mendel (1916)
by Gilbert Cannan
Rothenstein, Sir William

FROOM-EVERARD HOUSE
'The Waiting Supper' (1913)
by Thomas Hardy
Stafford House, Dorset

FROST, MISS
The Lost Girl (1920)
by D.H. Lawrence
Wright, Miss Fanny

FRY
It is Never Too Late to Mend (1856)
by Charles Reade
Freer

FUDGE, MR FOAMING
Vivian Grey (1826–7)
by Benjamin Disraeli
Brougham, Lord

FULKERSON
A Hazard of New Fortunes (1890)
by W.D. Howells
McClure, Samuel Sidney

FURBER, CEDRIC
The Self-Condemned (1954)
by Wyndham Lewis
Strachey, Lytton

FUREY, MICHAEL
'The Dead', *Dubliners* (1914)
by James Joyce
Bodkin, Michael 'Sonny'

FUTTERAL, ANDREAS
Sartor Resartus (1833–4)
by Thomas Carlyle
Carlyle, James

FUZBOZ
Cheveley; or The Man of Honour
 (1839)
by Lady Lytton
Forster, John

G

G. , PREFECT
The Mystery of Marie Roget (1842)
by Edgar Allan Poe
Vidocq, François Eugène

G——T, Duchesse de
Coningsby (1844)
by Benjamin Disraeli
Gramont, Ida, Duchesse de

GABBIE, Tod ('Gabriel')
Guy Mannering (1815)
by Sir Walter Scott
Tod, Willie

GALL, Alice
The White Peacock (1911)
by D.H. Lawrence
Hall, Alice

GALL, Geoffrey
Headlong Hall (1816)
by Thomas Love Peacock
Jeffrey, Francis, Lord

GALLAHER, Ignatius
'A Little Cloud', *Dubliners* (1914)
    and *Ulysses* (1922)
by James Joyce
Gallaher, Fred
Gogarty, Oliver St John

GALLEON, Henry
Fortitude (1913)
by Hugh Walpole
James, Henry

GAM, Mrs
'Dennis Haggarty's Wife', *Men's
    Wives* (1843)
by W.M. Thackeray
Shawe, Isabella

GAM, Jemima
'Dennis Haggarty's Wife', *Men's
    Wives* (1843)
by W.M. Thackeray
Shawe, Jane

GANDISH, Mr
The Newcomes (1854–5)
by W.M. Thackeray
Sass, Henry

GANESHA, Shri
The Razor's Edge (1944)
by W. Somerset Maugham
Venkataraman, Maharshi

GANT, Eliza
Look Homeward, Angel (1929) and
    Of Time and the River (1935)
by Thomas Wolfe
Wolfe, Julia

GANT, Eugene
Look Homeward, Angel (1929) and
    Of Time and the River (1935)
by Thomas Wolfe
Wolfe, Thomas

GANT, Luke
Look Homeward, Angel (1929) and
    Of Time and the River (1935)
by Thomas Wolfe
Wolfe, Fred

GANT, Stephen
Look Homeward, Angel (1929) and
    Of Time and the River (1935)
by Thomas Wolfe
Wolfe, Frank

GANT, W.O.
Look Homeward, Angel (1929) and
    Of Time and the River (1935)
by Thomas Wolfe
Wolfe, William Oliver

GANTRY, Elmer
Elmer Gantry (1927)
by Sinclair Lewis
Stidger, Revd William L.
Straton, Revd John Roach

GARCÍA, Señor
The Plumed Serpent (1926)
by D.H. Lawrence
Covarrubias, Miguel

GARDEN, Aubrey
A Tale Told by an Idiot (1923)
by Rose Macaulay
Arnold, Thomas

GARDEN, IRWIN
Big Sur (1962)
by Jack Kerouac
Ginsberg, Allen

GARDEN, MAURICE
A Tale Told by an Idiot (1923)
by Rose Macaulay
Arnold, W.T.

GARNER, JOE
'Ten Indians', *Men Without Women*
  (1927)
by Ernest Hemingway
Bacon, Joseph

GARRIBARDINE, LADY
The Career of Katherine Bush (1917)
by Elinor Glyn
Londonderry, Lady

GARTH, CALEB
Middlemarch (1871–2)
by George Eliot
Evans, Robert

GARUM FIRS
The Mill on the Floss (1860)
by George Eliot
Sole End, Astley, Warwickshire

GAS, MR CHARLATAN
Vivian Grey (1826–7)
by Benjamin Disraeli
Canning, George

GASCOIGNE, LORD
The Exclusives (1830)
by Lady Charlotte Bury
Alvanley, Lord

GASHFORD
Barnaby Rudge (1841)
by Charles Dickens
Watson, Robert

GATES, ALBERT
Highland Fling (1931)
by Nancy Mitford
Byron, Robert
Lees-Milne, James

GATESHEAD HALL
Jane Eyre (1847)
by Charlotte Brontë
Stone Gappe, Yorkshire

GATSBY, JAY
The Great Gatsby (1925)
by F. Scott Fitzgerald
Fitzgerald, F. Scott

GAUNT SQUARE
Vanity Fair (1847–8)
by W.M. Thackeray
Berkeley Square, London
Cavendish Square, London
Manchester Square, London

GAVERSTOCK, LADY
Coningsby (1844)
by Benjamin Disraeli
Mexborough, Countess of

GAVERSTOCK, LORD
Coningsby (1844)
by Benjamin Disraeli
Mexborough, 4th Earl of

GAVESTON, DUDLEY
A Family and a Fortune (1939)
by I. Compton-Burnett
Compton-Burnett, Ivy

GAY, LUCIAN
Coningsby (1844)
by Benjamin Disraeli
Hook, Theodore

GAZAY, CLÉO
Extraordinary Women (1928)
by Compton Mackenzie
Borgatti, Renata

GEAKE, ROSCOE
Arrowsmith (1925)
by Sinclair Lewis
Canfield, R. Bishop

GEDDES, JOSHUA
Redgauntlet (1824)
by Sir Walter Scott
Waldie, George

GEDDES, RACHEL
Redgauntlet (1824)
by Sir Walter Scott
Waldie, Ann

GEDGE, MORRIS
'The Birthplace' (1903)
by Henry James
Skipsey, Joseph

GEE, MRS
'The Man Who Loved Islands' (1928)
by D.H. Lawrence
Mackenzie, Faith Compton

GEE, CAMERON
'Two Blue Birds' (1928)
by D.H. Lawrence
Mackenzie, Compton

GELLATLEY, DAVIE
Waverley (1814)
by Sir Walter Scott
Gray, John[1]
Hinves, David

GENTLEMAN BROWN
See BROWN, Gentleman

GENTLEMAN GEORGE
Paul Clifford (1830)
by Bulwer Lytton
George IV

GEORGE, UNCLE
'Indian Camp', *In Our Time* (1925)
by Ernest Hemingway
Hemingway, George R.

GERETH, MRS ADELA
The Spoils of Poynton (1897)
by Henry James
Morrell, Harriet Anne

GERHARDT, MR
Jennie Gerhardt (1911)
by Theodore Dreiser
Dreiser, John Paul

GERHARDT, MRS
Jennie Gerhardt (1911)
by Theodore Dreiser
Dreiser, Sarah Schönäb

GERHARDT, JENNIE
Jennie Gerhardt (1911)
by Theodore Dreiser
Dreiser, Cecilia
Dreiser, Mary Frances

GERHARDT, SEBASTIAN ('BASS')
Jennie Gerhardt (1911)
by Theodore Dreiser
Dreiser, Marcus Romanus
Dresser, Paul

GIANNI, GIOVANNI
Erewhon (1872)
by Samuel Butler
Gianni, Giovanni

GIBBONS, JASPER
Cakes and Ale (1930)
by W. Somerset Maugham
Drinkwater, John
Phillips, Stephen

GIBBSVILLE
Appointment in Samarra (1934)
by John O'Hara
Pottsville, Pennsylvania

GIFFARD, RUTH
More Women Than Men (1933)
by I. Compton-Burnett
Compton-Burnett, Tertia

GIFFORD, HONORIA
'Giff', *A Gallery of Women* (1929)
by Theodore Dreiser
Spafford, Mrs

GILES, CAPTAIN
The Shadow-Line (1917)
by Joseph Conrad
Patterson, Captain

GILES, APOLLONIA
Lothair (1870)
by Benjamin Disraeli
**Cavendish-Bentinck, Prudentia
Penelope**

GILES, PUTNEY
Lothair (1870)
by Benjamin Disraeli
Israeli, Benjamin

GILES, RICHARD
'A Luncheon Party', *Half a Minute's
Silence and Other Stories* (1925)
by Maurice Baring
Gosse, Edmund

GILFIL, REVD MAYNARD
'Mr Gilfil's Love Story' and 'The Sad
Fortunes of the Revd Amos
Barton', *Scenes of Clerical Life*
(1857–8)
by George Eliot
Ebdell, Revd Bernard Gilpin

GILHOOLEY, MARY
The Town and the City (1950)
by Jack Kerouac
Carney, Mary

GILLETT, REVD JOHN
Stalky & Co. (1899)
by Rudyard Kipling
Willes, Revd George

GILLS, SOLOMON
Dombey and Son (1846–8)
by Charles Dickens
Norie, Mr

GIMMITCH, MRS
It Can't Happen Here (1935)
by Sinclair Lewis
Dilling, Elizabeth

GINGERLY BROWN
See BROWN, Gingerly

GINO
'Gino of the Bookshop' (1958)
by Osbert Sitwell
Orioli, Giuseppe ('Pino')

GIROUETTE, EMILY
Nightmare Abbey (1818)
by Thomas Love Peacock
Grove, Harriet

GISBURN, JACK
'The Verdict', *The Hermit and the
Wild Woman* (1908)
by Edith Wharton
Curtis, Jack

GLASS, JOHN
The Private Life of Henry Maitland
(1912)
by Morley Roberts
Payn, James

GLAYDE
'The End of the World', *The Dawn's
Delay* (1924)
by Hugh Kingsmill
Waugh, Alec

GLEGG (NÉE DODSON), JANE
The Mill on the Floss (1860)
by George Eliot
Everard, Mary

GLENARVON, LORD
Glenarvon (1816)
by Lady Caroline Lamb
Byron, Lord

GLENMORE, LADY
Almacks (1826)
by M. Spencer Stanhope
**Coke, Lady Anne
Digby, Jane**

GLENMORE, LADY
The Exclusives (1830)
by Lady Charlotte Bury
Digby, Jane

GLENMORE, LORD
Almacks (1826)
by M. Spencer Stanhope
**Coke, Thomas William, 1st Earl of
Leicester**

GLENMORE, LORD
The Exclusives (1830)
by Lady Charlotte Bury
Ellenborough, 1st Earl of

GLENMURRAY, FREDERIC
*Adeline Mowbray; or The Mother
and Daughter* (1804)
by Mrs Amelia Opie
Godwin, William

GLIGORIC, YURI
The Subterraneans (1958)
by Jack Kerouac
Corso, Gregory

GLOWRY, SCYTHROP
Nightmare Abbey (1818)
by Thomas Love Peacock
Shelley, Percy Bysshe

GODBOLE, NARAYAN
A Passage to India (1924)
by E.M. Forster
Chhatarpur, Maharajah of

GODOLPHIN, PERCY
Godolphin (1833)
by Bulwer Lytton
D'Orsay, Count

GOLDBROOK, ALVAH
The Dharma Bums (1958)
by Jack Kerouac
Ginsberg, Allen

GOLDSTEIN, EMMANUEL
Nineteen Eighty-four (1949)
by George Orwell
Nin, Andrés

GOLDSTEIN, SOPHIA
By Bread Alone (1901)
by I.K. Friedman
Goldman, Emma

GOLZ, GENERAL
For Whom the Bell Tolls (1940)
by Ernest Hemingway
Swiercziewski, Karol

GOMBAROV, JOHN
Miranda Masters (1926)
by John Cournos
Cournos, John

GOMBAULD
Crome Yellow (1921)
by Aldous Huxley
Gertler, Mark

GONERIL
The Confidence Man (1857)
by Herman Melville
Kemble, Fanny

GOODE, FATHER
The Cantab (1926)
by Shane Leslie
Wood, E.G.

GOODENOUGH, DR
The History of Pendennis (1848–50)
by W.M. Thackeray
Elliotson, John

GOODLEY, LADY SEPTUAGESIMA
'Triple Fugue' (1924)
by Osbert Sitwell
Morrell, Lady Ottoline

GOPHER PRAIRIE
Main Street (1920)
by Sinclair Lewis
Sauk Center, Minnesota

GORDON, CYRIL
*For God and Humanity, a Romance
of Mount Carmel* (1891)
by Haskett Smith
Oliphant, Laurence[2]

GORDON, DONALD
The New Republic (1877)
by W.H. Mallock
Carlyle, Thomas
MacDonald, George

GORDON, Richard
To Have and Have Not (1937)
by Ernest Hemingway
Dos Passos, John
Fisher, Edward

GORDON, Stephen
The Well of Loneliness (1928)
by Radclyffe Hall
Hall, Radclyffe

GORE, Ben
Blindness (1926)
by Henry Green
Byron, Robert

GORE, Nathan
Democracy (1880)
by Henry Adams
Lowell, James Russell
Motley, John Lothrop

GORSE, Mr
Lions and Shadows (1938)
by Christopher Isherwood
Pickthorn, Sir Kenneth

GORTON, Bill
The Sun Also Rises (1926)
by Ernest Hemingway
Dos Passos, John
Smith, Bill
Stewart, Donald Ogden

GOSSOLS
The Making of Americans (1925)
by Gertrude Stein
East Oakland, California

GOTHA, Monsieur
Memoirs of Prince Alexy Haimatoff
  (1813)
by T.J. Hogg
Lind, James

GOTTLIEB, Max
Arrowsmith (1925)
by Sinclair Lewis
Loeb, Jacques
Novy, Frederick

GOULD, Charles
Nostromo (1904)
by Joseph Conrad
Cunninghame Graham, Robert

GOULDING, Richie
Ulysses (1922)
by James Joyce
Murray, William

The GOVERNOR
Midshipman Easy (1836)
by Frederick Marryat
Maitland, Sir Thomas

The GOVERNOR OF NEW YORK
Hail to the Chief (1960)
by James Reichley
Dewey, Thomas Edward

GOW, Mr
The Cantab (1926)
by Shane Leslie
Pigou, A.C.

GOWAN, Henry
Little Dorrit (1855–7)
by Charles Dickens
Thackeray, W.M.

GRACE, Lady
The New Republic (1877)
by W.H. Mallock
Pattison, Emilia Francis

GRADGRIND SCHOOL
Hard Times (1854)
by Charles Dickens
Birkbeck Schools

GRAHAM, Madeleine
Madeleine Graham (1864)
by Emma Robinson
Smith, Madeleine

GRAMMONT, V.V.
The Secret Places of the Heart (1922)
by H.G. Wells
Sanger, Margaret

GRAND, Digby
Captain Digby Grand: An Autobiography (1851)
by G.J. Whyte-Melville
Maxse, Sir Henry

GRANDCOURT, Henleigh Mallinger
Daniel Deronda (1876)
by George Eliot
Labouchère, Henry du Pré

GRANDGOUT, Marquess of
Vivian Grey (1826–7)
by Benjamin Disraeli
Hertford, 3rd Marquess of

GRANDISON, Cardinal
Lothair (1870)
by Benjamin Disraeli
Manning, Henry Edward

GRANDMOTHER DEAR
'Grandmother Dear' (1878)
by Mrs Molesworth
Stewart, Agnes Janet

GRANHAM, Dan
The Sound of the Trumpet (1953)
by Leicester Hemingway
Hemingway, Leicester

GRANHAM, Rando
The Sound of the Trumpet (1953)
by Leicester Hemingway
Hemingway, Ernest

GRANT, Jack
The Boy in the Bush (1924)
by D.H. Lawrence and M.L. Skinner
Skinner, Jack

GRANT, Plato
You Can't Go Home Again (1940)
by Thomas Wolfe
Williams, Horace

GRAY, Dorian
The Picture of Dorian Gray (1891)
by Oscar Wilde
Gray, John²

THE GREAT FOREST
Wessex novels and tales (1871–95)
by Thomas Hardy
New Forest, Hampshire

THE GREAT PLAIN
Wessex novels and tales (1871–95)
by Thomas Hardy
Salisbury Plain

GREAT WINGLEBURY
'The Great Winglebury Duel',
Sketches by Boz (1836)
by Charles Dickens
Rochester, Kent

GREEN, Mr and Mrs
Pilgrimage (1915–67)
by Dorothy Richardson
Harris, Mr and Mrs

GREEN, Archibald
'The O'Conors of Castle Conor'
(1861) and 'Father Giles of
Ballymoy' (1867)
by Anthony Trollope
Trollope, Anthony

GREENE, Nicholas
Orlando (1928)
by Virginia Woolf
Gosse, Edmund

GREENHILL
Wessex novels and tales (1871–95)
by Thomas Hardy
Woodbury Hill, Dorset

GREENLOW, Miss
Dolores (1911)
by I. Compton-Burnett
Frost, Catherine

GREFFI, Count
A Farewell to Arms (1929)
by Ernest Hemingway
Greppi, Count Giuseppe

GREGG, Lou
'The Love Nest' (1926)
by Ring Lardner
Buck, E.E. ('Gene')

GRENFEL, Henry
'The Fox' (1923)
by D.H. Lawrence
Lambert, Mr

GRESHAM, Mr
Phineas Finn (1869)
by Anthony Trollope
Gladstone, William

GRESHAM, Evelyn
Crewe Train (1926)
by Rose Macaulay
Royde-Smith, Naomi

GREY, Hargrave
Vivian Grey (1826–7)
by Benjamin Disraeli
Basevi, Nathaniel

GREY, Henry
Robert Elsmere (1888)
by Mrs Humphry Ward
Green, T.H.

GREY, Horace
Vivian Grey (1826–7)
by Benjamin Disraeli
D'Israeli, Isaac

GREY, Violet
'Nona Vincent' (1891)
by Henry James
Robins, Elizabeth

GREY, Vivian
Vivian Grey (1826–7)
by Benjamin Disraeli
Disraeli, Benjamin

GREYFRIARS
The Newcomes (1854–5)
by W.M. Thackeray
Charterhouse

GREYLANDS
Wolf Solent (1929)
by John Cowper Powys
Sherborne School, Dorset

THE GRIDLEY CASE
Bleak House (1852–3)
by Charles Dickens
Cooke v. Fynney **(1844) c.59**

GRIEVE, Sandy
The History of David Grieve (1891)
by Mrs Humphry Ward
Huxley, Julian

GRIFFENBERG, Adolph
Mummery (1916)
by Gilbert Cannan
Rothenstein, Sir William

GRIFFITHS
Of Human Bondage (1915)
by W. Somerset Maugham
Kelly, Sir Gerald

GRIFFITHS, Asa
An American Tragedy (1925)
by Theodore Dreiser
Conklin, Asa
Dreiser, John Paul

GRIFFITHS, Clyde
An American Tragedy (1925)
by Theodore Dreiser
Gillette, Chester

GRIFFITHS, Elvira
An American Tragedy (1925)
by Theodore Dreiser
Dreiser, Sarah Schönäb

GRIFFITHS, Esta
An American Tragedy (1925)
by Theodore Dreiser
Dreiser, Mary Frances

GRIMES, Edgar
Decline and Fall (1928)
by Evelyn Waugh
Young, W.R.B.

GROBY
Parade's End (1924–8)
by Ford Madox Ford
Busby Hall, Carlton-in-Cleveland, North Yorkshire

GROTAIT, George
Put Yourself in His Place (1870)
by Charles Reade
Broadhead, William

GROTE, Lady
Robin Linnet (1919)
by E.F. Benson
Ripon, Lady

GROVE, Mr
Pilgrimage (1915–67)
by Dorothy Richardson
Fenton, Frederick

GUBB, Horatio
The Simple Life Limited (1911)
by Ford Madox Ford
Ford, Ford Madox
Pinker, J.B.
Wells, H.G.

GUDETOWN
The Provost (1822)
by John Galt
Irvine, Ayrshire

GUERNSEY, Countess of
The Repealers (1833)
by Lady Blessington
Jersey, Countess of

GULLSON, Dr
It is Never Too Late to Mend (1856)
by Charles Reade
Gully, James Manby

GULOSETON, Lord
Pelham (1828)
by Bulwer Lytton
Mount Edgcumbe, Lord

GUMBRIL, Mrs
Antic Hay (1923)
by Aldous Huxley
Huxley, Julia

GURNARD, Charles
The Inheritors (1901)
by Joseph Conrad and Ford Madox Ford
Chamberlain, Joseph

GURTNER, Lady
Robin Linnet (1919)
by E.F. Benson
Speyer, Lady Leonara

GURTNER, Sir Hermann
Robin Linnet (1919)
by E.F. Benson
Speyer, Sir Edgar

GUSHY, Mr
Endymion (1880)
by Benjamin Disraeli
Dickens, Charles

GWYNNE, Francis
Her Title of Honour (1871)
by Holme Lee
Martyn, Henry

GWYNNE, Winifred
Miranda Masters (1926)
by John Cournos
Yorke, Dorothy

H

HACKIT, Mr
'The Sad Fortunes of the Revd Amos Barton', *Scenes of Clerical Life* (1857–8)
by George Eliot
Evans, Robert

HACKIT, Mrs
'The Sad Fortunes of the Revd Amos
   Barton', *Scenes of Clerical Life*
   (1857–8)
by George Eliot
Evans, Christiana

HADDO, Oliver
The Magician (1908)
by W. Somerset Maugham
Crowley, Aleister

HAGGARDON
The Trumpet Major (1880)
by Thomas Hardy
Eggardon Hill, Dorset

HAIK, Dewey
It Can't Happen Here (1935)
by Sinclair Lewis
MacArthur, Douglas

HAIMATOFF, Prince Alexy
Memoirs of Prince Alexy Haimatoff
   (1813)
by T.J. Hogg
Hogg, T.J.
Shelley, Percy Bysshe

HAJJI BABA
*The Adventures of Haji Baba of
   Ispahan* (1824)
by James Morier
Hajji Baba

HALCYON HALL
More Miles (1926)
by Harry Kemp
Helicon Home Colony, New Jersey

HALDIN, Victor
Under Western Eyes (1911)
by Joseph Conrad
Sazonov, G.

HALE, Susan
Half a Loaf (1931)
by Grace Hegger Lewis
Lewis, Grace Hegger

HALE, Timothy
Half a Loaf (1931)
by Grace Hegger Lewis
Lewis, Sinclair

HALKETT, Cecilia
Beauchamp's Career (1876)
by George Meredith
Brandreth, Alice Mary

HALL, Cyril
Shirley (1849)
by Charlotte Brontë
Heald, Revd William Margetson

HALL, Mark
The Valley of the Moon (1913)
by Jack London
Sterling, George

HALL, Osmond
'A Luncheon Party', *Half a Minute's
   Silence and Other Stories* (1925)
by Maurice Baring
Shaw, George Bernard

HALLIDAY, Julius
Women in Love (1920)
by D.H. Lawrence
Heseltine, Philip

HALLIDAY, Manley
The Disenchanted (1950)
by Budd Schulberg
Fitzgerald, F. Scott

HAMILTON, Derrick
Neutral Ground (1933)
by Helen Corke
Lawrence, D.H.

HAMLIN, Walter
Miss Brown (1884)
by Vernon Lee
Rossetti, Dante Gabriel

HAMMERGLOW, Lady
The Wonderful Visit (1895)
by H.G. Wells
Fetherstonhaugh, Miss

HAMMOND, Mrs
'The Stranger' (1922)
by Katherine Mansfield
Beauchamp, Annie

HAMMOND, Judson Cumming
Gabriel Over the White House (1933)
by Thomas Frederic Tweed
Harding, Warren G.

HAMPS, Mrs Clara
The *Clayhanger* trilogy (1910–16)
by Arnold Bennett
Bennett, Sarah
Bourne, Frances

HANCOCK, Mr
Pilgrimage (1915–67)
by Dorothy Richardson
Badcock, John Henry

HANCOCK, Jo
Venture (1927)
by Max Eastman
Reed, John

HANCOCK, Thornton
This Side of Paradise (1920)
by F. Scott Fitzgerald
Adams, Henry

HAND, Hosmer
The Titan (1914)
by Theodore Dreiser
Whitney, William Collins

HANGBIRD, Mr
The Simple Life Limited (1911)
by Ford Madox Ford
Crane, Stephen

HANNAH
Jane Eyre (1847)
by Charlotte Brontë
Aykeroyd, Tabitha

HANNAY, Richard
The Thirty-nine Steps (1915) and
 others
by John Buchan
Ironside, William Edmund, 1st
 Baron

HANNELE
See Rassentlow, Countess Johanna
zu

HARBY, Mr
The Rainbow (1915)
by D.H. Lawrence
Beacroft, Thomas

HARDEN, James
The Revolution in Tanner's Lane
 (1887)
by Mark Rutherford
Hillyard, Samuel

HARDER, Max
Glass Mountain (1930)
by J.W. Beach
Hemingway, Ernest

HARDER, Norma
Glass Mountain (1930)
by J.W. Beach
Hemingway, Hadley

HARDINGE, Emma
'The Spirit's Trials', *Shadows of the*
 Clouds (1847)
by James Anthony Froude
Bush, Harriet

HARDLINES, Sir Gregory
The Three Clerks (1857)
by Anthony Trollope
Trevelyan, Sir Charles Edward

HARDY, Sir Richmond
The Secret Places of the Heart (1922)
by H.G. Wells
Wells, H.G.

HARE, G. Duncan
The Sleep of Reason (1956)
by Warren Miller
Schine, David

HARE, Jonathan
I Live Under a Black Sun (1937)
by Edith Sitwell
Tchelitchew, Pavel

HARLETH, Gwendolen
Daniel Deronda (1876)
by George Eliot
Leigh, Geraldine

HARLEY, Adrian
The Ordeal of Richard Feverel (1859)
by George Meredith
Fitzgerald, Maurice

HARNETT, Dartnell
The Sleep of Reason (1956)
by Warren Miller
Hammett, Dashiel

HAROLD
Among the Chosen (1884)
by Mary S. Emerson
Oliphant, Laurence[2]

HARPITON
Maid Marian (1822)
by Thomas Love Peacock
Southey, Robert

HARRINGTON, Ben
Chosen Country (1951)
by John Dos Passos
Smith, Bill

HARRINGTON, Evan
Evan Harrington (1860)
by George Meredith
Meredith, Augustus Urmiston
Meredith, George

HARRINGTON, Ezekiel
Chosen Country (1951)
by John Dos Passos
Smith, W.B.

HARRINGTON, Lulie
Chosen Country (1951)
by John Dos Passos
Dos Passos, Katharine Foster

HARRINGTON, Melchisedek
Evan Harrington (1860)
by George Meredith
Meredith, Melchisedek

HARRINGTON, Zeke
Chosen Country (1951)
by John Dos Passos
Smith, Y.K.

HARRIS, Larry
The Dust Which is God (1941)
by William Rose Benét
Lewis, Sinclair

HARROWDEAN, Mrs
Mr Britling Sees It Through (1916)
by H.G. Wells
Russell, Countess

HARRY, Uncle
'Baa, Baa, Black Sheep' (1888)
by Rudyard Kipling
Holloway, Pryse Agar

HARTHOVER PLACE
The Water Babies (1863)
by Charles Kingsley
Malham Tarn House, Yorkshire

HARTINGTON, Mr
'Notes on the North
    What-d'ye-Callem Election' (1841)
by W.M. Thackeray
Witham, Mr

HARTOPP, Mr
Stalky & Co. (1899)
by Rudyard Kipling
Evans, Herbert Arthur

HARVEY, Mrs
'Broken Wings' (1903)
by Henry James
Fletcher, Constance

HARVILLE, CAPTAIN
Persuasion (1818)
by Jane Austen
Austen, Sir Francis

HASAN
Women in Love (1920)
by D.H. Lawrence
Suhrawardy, Huseyn Shaheed

HASLAM, SIR GODFREY
Men and Wives (1931)
by I. Compton-Burnett
Blackie, Robert

HASTINGS, LORD REGINALD
The Green Carnation (1894)
by Robert Hichens
Douglas, Lord Alfred

HATCHER, PROFESSOR
Of Time and the River (1935)
by Thomas Wolfe
Baker, George Pierce

HAUKSBEE, LUCY
Plain Tales from the Hills (1888)
by Rudyard Kipling
Burton, Mrs F.C.

HAUSBERG, BARON
'The Model Millionaire' (1891)
by Oscar Wilde
de Rothschild, Baron James Mayer

HAUTON, LADY
Almacks (1826)
by M. Spencer Stanhope
Jersey, Countess of

HAVENPOOL
Wessex novels and tales (1871–95)
by Thomas Hardy
Poole, Dorset

HAVILAND, COLONEL
The Trail of the Hawk (1915)
by Sinclair Lewis
Benét, James Walker

HAVISHAM, MISS
Great Expectations (1860–1)
by Charles Dickens
Dick, Margaret Catherine
Joachim, Martha
The White Woman of Berners Street

HAWES, MR
It is Never Too Late to Mend (1856)
by Charles Reade
Austin, William

HAWKER, WILLIAM
The Third Violet (1897)
by Stephen Crane
Crane, Stephen

HAWTHORNE, PHILIP
The Vicar of Langthwaite (1893)
by Lily Watson
Green, S.G.

HAYE, JOHN
Blindness (1926)
by Henry Green
Green, Henry

HAYSLOPE
Adam Bede (1859)
by George Eliot
Ellastone, Staffordshire

HAYWARD, G. ETHERIDGE
Of Human Bondage (1915)
by W. Somerset Maugham
Brooks, John Ellingham

HAZARD, STEPHEN
Esther (1884)
by Henry Adams
Brooks, Phillips

THE HEAD
Stalky & Co. (1899)
by Rudyard Kipling
Price, Cornell

HEAD, G.O.A.
Coningsby (1844)
by Benjamin Disraeli
Roebuck, John Arthur

HEADINGHAM, LADY ANGELICA
Patronage (1814)
by Maria Edgeworth
Davy, Jane, Lady
White, Lydia

HEADLONG, HARRY
Headlong Hall (1816)
by Thomas Love Peacock
Johnes, Thomas
Madocks, W.A.

HEADLONG HALL
Headlong Hall (1816)
by Thomas Love Peacock
Hafod House, Cardiganshire
High Elms, Bracknell, Berkshire

HEAT, CHIEF INSPECTOR
The Secret Agent (1907)
by Joseph Conrad
Melville, William

HEATH, MARMADUKE
Lost Sir Massingberd (1864)
by James Payn
Pickford, Thomas

HEATHCLIFF
Wuthering Heights (1847)
by Emily Brontë
Sharp, Jack
Sutton, Richard

HECHT, SHANE
A Murder of Quality (1962)
by John Le Carré
Hartley, Grizel

HEIDLER, H.J.
Postures (1928)
by Jean Rhys
Ford, Ford Madox

HEIDLER, LOIS
Postures (1928)
by Jean Rhys
Bowen, Stella

HEILDIG, FRANZ
You Can't Go Home Again (1940)
by Thomas Wolfe
Ledig-Rowohlt, Heinrich

HEIMANN, GEORGE
The Marsden Case (1923)
by Ford Madox Ford
Ralston, William

HELEN
The World of William Clissold
(1926)
by H.G. Wells
West, Rebecca

HELENA, SAINT
Helena (1950)
by Evelyn Waugh
Betjeman, Penelope

HELGIN, BEN
Ninth Avenue (1926)
by Maxwell Bodenheim
Hecht, Ben

HELSTONE, CAROLINE
Shirley (1849)
by Charlotte Brontë
Brontë, Anne
Nussey, Ellen

HELSTONE, REVD MATTHEWSON
Shirley (1849)
by Charlotte Brontë
Roberson, Revd Hammond

HENDERSON, MR
Pilgrimage (1915–67)
by Dorothy Richardson
Richardson, Charles

HENDERSON, MRS
Pilgrimage (1915–67)
by Dorothy Richardson
Richardson, Mary Miller

HENDERSON, EVE
Pilgrimage (1915–67)
by Dorothy Richardson
Richardson, Alice Mary

HENDERSON, Harriett
Pilgrimage (1915–67)
by Dorothy Richardson
Hale, Jessie Abbott

HENDERSON, Miriam
Pilgrimage (1915–67)
by Dorothy Richardson
Richardson, Dorothy

HENDERSON, Sarah
Pilgrimage (1915–67)
by Dorothy Richardson
Batchelor, Frances Kate

HENRY, Frederic
A Farewell to Arms (1929)
by Ernest Hemingway
Hemingway, Ernest
McKey, Edward

HEPBURN, Lady
'The Thimble' (1917)
by D.H. Lawrence
Asquith, Lady Cynthia

HEPBURN, Mr
'The Thimble' (1917)
by D.H. Lawrence
Asquith, Herbert

HEPBURN, Alexander
Diana of the Crossways (1884)
by George Meredith
Stirling-Maxwell, Sir William

HEPBURN, Alexander
'The Captain's Doll' (1923)
by D.H. Lawrence
Carswell, Donald
Lawrence, D.H.

HERBERT, Dr
De Vere; or The Man of
*   Independence* (1827)
by Robert Plumer Ward
Jackson, Cyril

HERBERT, Mr
The New Republic (1877)
by W.H. Mallock
Ruskin, John

HERBERT, Marmion
Venetia (1837)
by Benjamin Disraeli
Shelley, Percy Bysshe

HERBERT, Melanctha
'Melanctha', *Three Lives* (1909)
by Gertrude Stein
Bookstaver, May

HERIOT, Eliza
The Last and the First (1970)
by I. Compton-Burnett
Compton-Burnett, Katharine

HERMISTON, Lord
See Weir, Adam

HERON, Vincent
A Portrait of the Artist as a Young
*   Man* (1916)
by James Joyce
Connolly, Albrecht
Connolly, Vincent

HERRITON, Philip
Where Angels Fear to Tread (1905)
by E.M. Forster
Dent, E.J.
Forster, E.M.

HERSLAND, David
The Making of Americans (1925)
by Gertrude Stein
Stein, Daniel

HERSLAND, Fanny
The Making of Americans (1925)
by Gertrude Stein
Stein, Amelia

HERSLAND, Martha
The Making of Americans (1925)
by Gertrude Stein
Stein, Gertrude

HERTFORDSHIRE, Duchess of
'Maltby and Braxton', *Seven Men*
   (1919)
by Max Beerbohm
Desborough, Lady

HERVEY, Clarence
Belinda (1801)
by Maria Edgeworth
Day, Thomas

HEWET, Terence
The Voyage Out (1915)
by Virginia Woolf
Stephen, Thoby

HIGGINS, Nicholas
North and South (1855)
by Elizabeth Gaskell
Cowell, George

HIGGS, Mr
The Head of Kay's (1905) and others
by P.G. Wodehouse
Hicks, Seymour

HIGH-PLACE HALL
The Mayor of Casterbridge (1886)
by Thomas Hardy
Colliton House, Dorchester, Dorset

HIGHCLOSE
The White Peacock (1911)
by D.H. Lawrence
Lamb Close House, Eastwood,
   Nottinghamshire

HIGHMORE, Jane
'The Next Time' (1898)
by Henry James
Braddon, Mary Elizabeth
Ward, Mrs Humphry

HILARY
Dangerous Ages (1921)
by Rose Macaulay
Macaulay, Grace

HILBERY, Mrs
Night and Day (1919)
by Virginia Woolf
Ritchie, Anne Isabella, Lady

HILBERY, Katherine
Night and Day (1919)
by Virginia Woolf
Bell, Vanessa

HILBERY, Trevor
Night and Day (1919)
by Virginia Woolf
Ritchie, Sir Richmond
Stephen, Sir Leslie

HILL, Alwyn
'The Duchess of Hamptonshire'
   (1891)
by Thomas Hardy
Holder, Revd Caddell

HILL, Eveline
'Eveline', *Dubliners* (1914)
by James Joyce
Thornton, Eveline

HILLIER, Lionel
Cakes and Ale (1930)
by W. Somerset Maugham
Kelly, Sir Gerald

HILLSBOROUGH
Put Yourself in His Place (1870)
by Charles Reade
Sheffield

HILLSTONE
Nellie Brooke, A Homely Story
   (1868)
by Florence Marryat
Winchester, Hampshire

HILTON, Marian
The Private Life of Henry Maitland
   (1912)
by Morley Roberts
Gissing, Nell

HINES, Pearl
Look Homeward, Angel (1929)
by Thomas Wolfe
Shope, Pearl

HINTERSCHLAG
Sartor Resartus (1833–4)
by Thomas Carlyle
Annan, Dumfriesshire

HINTERSCHLAG GYMNASIUM
Sartor Resartus (1833–4)
by Thomas Carlyle
Annan Academy

HINTOCK HOUSE
Wessex novels and tales (1871–95)
by Thomas Hardy
Turnworth House, Dorset

HIPPY, Humphrey
Melincourt (1817)
by Thomas Love Peacock
Hogg, T.J.

HIRAMS HOSPITAL
The Warden (1855)
by Anthony Trollope
St Cross Hospital, Winchester

HIRSCH, Mr
A Sovereign Remedy (1906)
by Flora Annie Steel
Heinemann, William

HIRST, St John
The Voyage Out (1915)
by Virginia Woolf
Strachey, Lytton

HITCHCOCK
'The Bridge Builders' (1898)
by Rudyard Kipling
Prickett, L.G.

HITCHCOCK, Sir Jocelyn
Scoop (1938)
by Evelyn Waugh
Phillips, Sir Percival

HOAX, Mr Stanislaus
Vivian Grey (1826–7)
by Benjamin Disraeli
Hook, Theodore

HODGE, William
England, Their England (1933)
by A.G. Macdonell
Squire, Sir J.C.

HODGEN, Mr
The History of Pendennis (1848–50)
by W.M. Thackeray
Ross, William Gribben

HOGARTH, Tom
Lord Raingo (1926)
by Arnold Bennett
Churchill, Winston

HOIAONSKIM
Glenarvon (1816)
by Lady Caroline Lamb
Allen, John[1]

HOLABIRD, Rippleton
Arrowsmith (1925)
by Sinclair Lewis
Cole, Rufus
Rous, Peyton

HOLIDAY, Mr
The Trespasser (1912)
by D.H. Lawrence
Humphreys, Ernest

HOLIDAY, Burne
This Side of Paradise (1920)
by F. Scott Fitzgerald
Strater, Henry

HOLLAND, Selina
Pilgrimage (1915–67)
by Dorothy Richardson
Moffatt, Miss

HOLLOWS MILL
Shirley (1849)
by Charlotte Brontë
Hunsworth Mill, Yorkshire

HOLMAN, Ebenezer
Cousin Phillis (1864)
by Elizabeth Gaskell
Holland, Samuel

HOLMES, Sherlock
The Sherlock Holmes stories
    (1890–1927)
by Arthur Conan Doyle
Bell, Joseph

HOLT, Felix
Felix Holt, the Radical (1866)
by George Eliot
Massey, Gerald

HOME, Paulina Mary
Villette (1853)
by Charlotte Brontë
Gaskell, Julia
Whipp, Fanny

HOMER, Scott
'Mrs Medwin' (1903)
by Henry James
Temple, Robert

HONEYCHURCH, Mrs
A Room with a View (1908)
by E.M. Forster
Whichelo, Louisa

HONEYMAN, Martha
The Newcomes (1854–5)
by W.M. Thackeray
Becher, Anne

HOOK, Stephen
The Web and the Rock (1939)
by Thomas Wolfe
Beer, Thomas

HOOKER, Bob
Ten North Frederick (1955)
by John O'Hara
Silliman, H.I.

HOOPDRIVER, J.E.
The Wheels of Chance (1896)
by H.G. Wells
Wells, H.G.

HOOPER, Lady Artemis
Aaron's Rod (1922)
by D.H. Lawrence
Cooper, Lady Diana

HOOSTMAN
The Scarlet Shadow (1907)
by Walter Hurt
Vrooman, Walter

HOPINGTON, H.M.
The Cantab (1926)
by Shane Leslie
Hope-Jones, William

HORSFIELD, George
After Leaving Mr Mackenzie (1931)
by Jean Rhys
Smith, Leslie Tilden

HORTENSE
Bleak House (1852–3)
by Charles Dickens
Manning, Maria

HOUGHTON, Alvina
The Lost Girl (1920)
by D.H. Lawrence
Cullen, Florence ('Flossie')

HOUGHTON, Clariss
The Lost Girl (1920)
by D.H. Lawrence
Cullen, Lucy

HOUGHTON, James
The Lost Girl (1920)
by D.H. Lawrence
Cullen, George

HOUGHTON, Willie
Touch and Go (1919)
by D.H. Lawrence
Hopkin, William

THE HOUSE
Orlando (1928)
by Virginia Woolf
Knole, Kent

HOUSE OF THE SEVEN GABLES
The House of the Seven Gables (1851)
by Nathaniel Hawthorne
Montpelier, Maine

THE HOUSEKEEPER
The *Clayhanger* trilogy (1910–16)
by Arnold Bennett
Collings, Beatrice

HOWARD, REVD WILLIAM
John Sherman (1891)
by W.B. Yeats
Johnson, Lionel

HOWARDS END
Howards End (1910)
by E.M. Forster
Rooksrest, Stevenage, Hertfordshire

HOWE, ELIAS
Roland Cashel (1850)
by Charles Lever
Thackeray, W.M.

HOYT, ROSEMARY
Tender is the Night (1934)
by F. Scott Fitzgerald
Moran, Lois

HUBBARD, BULL
Book of Dreams (1960) and
    Desolation Angels (1965)
by Jack Kerouac
Burroughs, William S.

HUBBARD, WILL
Vanity of Duluoz (1968)
by Jack Kerouac
Burroughs, William S.

HÜBNER
Barred (1932)
by Edward de Nève
Ford, Ford Madox

HUDSON, MRS
Cakes and Ale (1930)
by W. Somerset Maugham
Foreman, Mrs

HULBERT, THADDEUS
Entirely Surrounded (1934)
by Charles Brackett
Woollcott, Alexander

HULL, MR
Gilbert Gurney (1836)
by Theodore Hook
Hill, Thomas

HUME, MRS SYDNEY
Probation and Other Tales (1832)
by Anon.
Keith, Mrs Anne Murray

HUMSON, MR
The Gold-Worshippers (1851)
by Emma Robinson
Hudson, George

HUNGARY, PRINCE
Vivian Grey (1826–7)
by Benjamin Disraeli
Esterházy, Prince Paul Anton

HUNSDEN, YORKE
The Professor (1857)
by Charlotte Brontë
Taylor, Joshua

HUNTER, ANSON
'The Rich Boy' (1926)
by F. Scott Fitzgerald
Fowler, Ludlow Sebring

HURLE, LAURENCE
Gin and Bitters (1931)
by Elinor Mordaunt
Maugham, W. Somerset

HURSTCOTE MANOR
Aylwin (1899)
by Theodore Watts-Dunton
Kelmscot Manor, Oxfordshire

HURSTLEY
Endymion (1880)
by Benjamin Disraeli
Bradenham, Buckinghamshire

HURSTWOOD, George
Sister Carrie (1900)
by Theodore Dreiser
Hopkins, L.A.

HUTCHINSON, Joseph
T. Tembaron (1913)
by Frances Hodgson Burnett
Fahnestock, Ernest

HUTTON, Dolores
Dolores (1911)
by I. Compton-Burnett
Compton-Burnett, Ivy

HUTTON, Henry
'The Gioconda Smile' (1922)
by Aldous Huxley
Greenwood, Harold

HUTTON, Sophia
Dolores (1911)
by I. Compton-Burnett
Compton-Burnett, Katharine

HYDE, Mr
Little Women (1868) and sequels
by Louisa M. Alcott
Thoreau, Henry David

HYDE, Edward
See Jekyll, Dr Henry/Hyde, Edward

HYMAN, Mrs Rhoda
The Roaring Queen (1973)
by Wyndham Lewis
Woolf, Virginia

I

ICENWAY HOUSE
'The Lady Icenway' (1891)
by Thomas Hardy
Herriard House, Hampshire

ILCESTER, Janet
The Adventures of Harry Richmond
   (1871)
by George Meredith
Ross, Janet

ILEX, Miss
Gryll Grange (1860)
by Thomas Love Peacock
Courtenay, Louisa

IMBERT, Ralph
'The Next Time' (1898)
by Henry James
James, Henry

The IMPERIAL PALACE
The Imperial Palace (1930)
by Arnold Bennett
Savoy Hotel, London

The INFANT PHENOMENON
See Crummles, Ninetta

INGLEBY, Mr
Murder Must Advertise (1933)
by Dorothy L. Sayers
Bevan, R.A.

INNER STATION
Heart of Darkness (1902)
by Joseph Conrad
Stanley Falls, Belgian Congo

IORIS, Prince
Friendship (1878)
by Ouida
Stufa, Lotteringhi, Marchese della

IRAIS
Elizabeth and Her German Garden
   (1898)
by 'Elizabeth'
Forbes-Mosse, Irene

IRELA, Madame
Evensong (1932)
by Beverley Nichols
Melba, Nellie

IRELAND, Ross
Dodsworth (1929)
by Sinclair Lewis
Hunt, Frazier

ISAACS, Mr
Mr Isaacs (1882)
by Marion Crawford
Jacob, Alexander M.

ISAACS, Max
Look Homeward, Angel (1929)
by Thomas Wolfe
Israel, Max

ISELIN, John
The Manchurian Candidate (1959)
by Richard Condon
McCarthy, Joseph

ISHMAELIA
Scoop (1938)
by Evelyn Waugh
Abyssinia

ISLE OF SLINGERS
Wessex novels and tales (1871–95)
by Thomas Hardy
Portland, Isle of

IVELL (OR IVEL)
Wessex novels and tales (1871–95)
by Thomas Hardy
Yeovil, Somerset

J

JABLONOWSKY, Paula
'Love Among the Haystacks' (1930)
by D.H. Lawrence
Lawrence, Frieda

JACK
Book of Dreams (1960)
by Jack Kerouac
Kerouac, Jack

JACK, Alma
The Web and the Rock (1939) and
    You Can't Go Home Again (1940)
by Thomas Wolfe
Bernstein, Edla

JACK, Esther
The Web and the Rock (1939)
by Thomas Wolfe
Bernstein, Aline

JACK, Frederick
The Web and the Rock (1939)
by Thomas Wolfe
Bernstein, Theodore

JACKSON, Mr
The Longest Journey (1907)
by E.M. Forster
Smedley, I.F.
Wedd, Nathaniel

JACKSON, Sillerton
The Age of Innocence (1920)
by Edith Wharton
Travers, William
Winthrop, Egerton

JACOBI, Baron
Democracy (1880)
by Henry Adams
Aristarchi Bey, Grégoire

The JAGO
A Child of the Jago (1896)
by Arthur Morrison
The Old Nichol

JAMES, Miss
'The Last Laugh' (1928)
by D.H. Lawrence
Brett, Dorothy

JAMES, Laura
Look Homeward, Angel (1929)
by Thomas Wolfe
Paul, Clara

JANET
Dawn (1931)
by Theodore Dreiser
Dreiser, Emma

JARNDYCE V. JARNDYCE
Bleak House (1852–3)
by Charles Dickens
Jennings v. Jennings

JARROLD, DAN
Family History (1932)
by Victoria Sackville-West
Nicolson, Benedict

JASPAR, EVELINA
'After Holbein', *Certain People*
(1930)
by Edith Wharton
Astor, Caroline Webster

JEFFERSON
The Yoknapatawpha novels
(1929–36)
by William Faulkner
Oxford, Mississippi

JEKYLL, DR HENRY/HYDE, EDWARD
The Strange Case of Dr Jekyll and
Mr Hyde (1886)
by R.L. Stevenson
Brodie, William

JELLYBY, MRS
Bleak House (1852–3)
by Charles Dickens
Chisholm, Caroline

JENKINSON, DR
The New Republic (1877)
by W.H. Mallock
Jowett, Benjamin

JENKISON, MR
Headlong Hall (1816)
by Thomas Love Peacock
Hogg, T.J.

JENNINGS, EZRA
The Moonstone (1868)
by Wilkie Collins
Jennings, Hargrave

JEROME, THOMAS
'Janet's Repentance', *Scenes of*
Clerical Life (1857–8)
by George Eliot
Everhard, Mr

JESSIE
More Miles (1926)
by Harry Kemp
Summers, Edith

JETHRO, JACK
'Olive Brand', *A Gallery of Women*
(1929)
by Theodore Dreiser
Smith, Edward H.

J.H. (or J.C.H.)
The Private Life of Henry Maitland
(1912)
by Morley Roberts
Roberts, Morley

JIM
Lord Jim (1900)
by Joseph Conrad
Brooke, Sir James
Lingard, William James ('Jim')
Williams, Augustine Podmore

JIM
More Miles (1926)
by Harry Kemp
Updegraff, Allan

JIM
The Judgment of Paris (1952)
by Gore Vidal
Fouts, Denham

JIMSON, GULLEY
The Horse's Mouth (1944)
by Joyce Cary
John, Augustus
Spencer, Stanley
Thomas, Dylan

JINGLE, Alfred
The Pickwick Papers (1836–7)
by Charles Dickens
Potter, Charles

JINIWIN, Mrs
The Old Curiosity Shop (1840–1)
by Charles Dickens
Hogarth, Georgina[1]

J.J.
'Esther Norn', *A Gallery of Women*
    (1929)
by Theodore Dreiser
Hapgood, Hutchins

JO
Bleak House (1852–3)
by Charles Dickens
Ruby, George

JOCELYN, Lady
Evan Harrington (1860)
by George Meredith
Duff-Gordon, Lucie, Lady

JOCELYN, Sir Frank
Evan Harrington (1860)
by George Meredith
Duff-Gordon, Sir Alexander

JOCELYN, Rose
Evan Harrington (1860)
by George Meredith
Ross, Janet

JOCELYN, Rudolph
Pigeon Pie (1940)
by Nancy Mitford
Rodd, Peter

JOHN, Sir
Nostromo (1904)
by Joseph Conrad
Eastwick, Edward B.

JOHNS, John
The Adventures of John Johns (1897)
by Frederic Carrel
Harris, Frank

JOHNSON, Gertrude
Pictures from an Institution (1954)
by Randall Jarrell
McCarthy, Mary

JOHNSON, Henry
The Cantab (1926)
by Shane Leslie
Jackson, Henry

JOHNSON, Hepsey
Work (1873)
by Louisa M. Alcott
Tubman, Harriet

JOHNSON, Tiaré
The Moon and Sixpence (1919)
by W. Somerset Maugham
Chapman, Lovina

JONES, Professor
Finnegans Wake (1939)
by James Joyce
Lewis, Wyndham

JONES, Abe
Of Time and the River (1935)
by Thomas Wolfe
Smith, Abe

JONES, Crab
Tom Brown's Schooldays (1857)
by Thomas Hughes
Smyth, Edmund

JONES, Gallipot
Lavengro (1851)
by George Borrow
Hunt, Henry 'Orator'

JONES, Tasker
Tasker Jones: The Real Story (1916)
by May Sinclair
Bennett, Arnold

JONES, Tenby
The Golden Virgin (1957) and *The
    Innocent Moon* (1961)
by Henry Williamson
John, Augustus

JONSEN, Sophus
The Journalist (1898)
by C.F. Keary
Delius, Frederick

JORALEMON
The Trail of the Hawk (1915)
by Sinclair Lewis
Sauk Center, Minnesota

JORDAN, Robert
For Whom the Bell Tolls (1940)
by Ernest Hemingway
Merriman, Robert

JORDAN, Thomas
Sons and Lovers (1913)
by D.H. Lawrence
Haywood, John Harrington

JORGAN, Captain Silas Jonas
'A Message from the Sea' (1860)
by Charles Dickens
Morgan, Captain Elisha Ely

JOSEPH, Father
Among the Chosen (1884)
by Mary S. Emerson
Harris, Thomas Lake

JOSEPHS, Edward
It is Never Too Late to Mend (1856)
by Charles Reade
Andrews, Edward

JOYCE
'England, My England' (1915)
by D.H. Lawrence
Lucas, Sylvia

JUDEA
'Youth' (1902)
by Joseph Conrad
Palestine

JUDY
'Baa, Baa, Black Sheep' (1888)
by Rudyard Kipling
Kipling, Alice Macdonald

JUDY
Weeds (1923)
by Edith Summers
Summers, Edith

JUGGERNAUT, Duke of
Vivian Grey (1826–7)
by Benjamin Disraeli
Norfolk, 12th Duke of

JUGGINS, Mr
Coningsby (1844)
by Benjamin Disraeli
Booth, Sir Felix

JULIAN
'The Snows of Kilimanjaro', *The*
    Fifth Column and the First
    Forty-nine Stories (1938)
by Ernest Hemingway
Fitzgerald, F. Scott

JULIE, Mademoiselle
Olivia (1949)
by Dorothy Bussy
Souvestre, Marie

JUNGFLEISCH, Mildred
Don't Tell Alfred (1960)
by Nancy Mitford
Alsop, Susan Mary

The *JUPITER*
The Warden (1855)
by Anthony Trollope
The Times

JUPP, Mrs
The Way of All Flesh (1903)
by Samuel Butler
Boss, Mrs

K

KATYA
See MOYDIA and KATYA

KALBSBRATEN
The Confessions of Fitz-Boodle
   (1852)
by W.M. Thackeray
Weimar, Germany

KAMI
The Light that Failed (1890)
by Rudyard Kipling
Gleyre, Charles

KANDISKY
The Green Hills of Africa (1935)
by Ernest Hemingway
Koritschoner, Hans

KANE, ALICE
A Book About Myself (1922)
by Theodore Dreiser
Zahn, Lois

KANE, LESTER
Jennie Gerhardt (1911)
by Theodore Dreiser
Ashley, Don

KANE, WILLARD
The Bulwark (1946)
by Theodore Dreiser
Dreiser, Theodore

KAPRUN
'The Captain's Doll' (1923)
by D.H. Lawrence
Zell-am-See, Austria

KARKOV
For Whom the Bell Tolls (1940)
by Ernest Hemingway
Koltsov, Mihail

KARL
The Green Hills of Africa (1935)
by Ernest Hemingway
Thompson, Charles

KATE, COUNTESS
Countess Kate (1862)
by C.M. Yonge
Yonge, Charlotte

KATHLEEN
The Last Tycoon (1941)
by F. Scott Fitzgerald
Graham, Sheila

KAWA DOL
A Passage to India (1924)
by E.M. Forster
Kauwādol, Bihar, India

KEANE, LEROY
The Young Lions (1948)
by Irwin Shaw
Hemingway, Leicester

KEAR, ALROY
Cakes and Ale (1930)
by W. Somerset Maugham
Walpole, Hugh

KEEB HALL
'Maltby and Braxton', *Seven Men*
   (1919)
by Max Beerbohm
Taplow Court, Buckinghamshire

KEELDAR, SHIRLEY
Shirley (1849)
by Charlotte Brontë
Brontë, Emily

KELLY, IVOR
The Boy Who Made Good (1955)
by Mary Deasy
Fitzgerald, F. Scott

KELLY, STELLA
The Boy Who Made Good (1955)
by Mary Deasy
Fitzgerald, Zelda

KELLYNCH, LADY
Bird of Paradise (1914)
by Ada Leverson
Leverson, Mrs George
Leverson, Henrietta

KELLYNCH, Bertha
Bird of Paradise (1914)
by Ada Leverson
Martineau, Kitty

KEMP, 'Lord' George
Cakes and Ale (1930)
by W. Somerset Maugham
Holden, George

KEMP, Robert
Nicholas Crabbe (1958)
by F.W. Rolfe
Douglas, Sholto

KENNETBRIDGE
Jude the Obscure (1895)
by Thomas Hardy
Newbury, Berkshire

KENNETT STREET
Pilgrimage (1915–67)
by Dorothy Richardson
Kenton Street, Bloomsbury, London

KENNICOTT, Carol
Main Street (1920)
by Sinclair Lewis
Lewis, Sinclair

KERNAN, Tom
'Grace', *Dubliners* (1914)
by James Joyce
Thornton, Ned

KERRIGAN, Patrick
The Titan (1914)
by Theodore Dreiser
Kenna, Michael

KEYHOLE, Tomlinson
Boon (1915)
by H.G. Wells
Nicoll, Sir William Robertson

KILLIAN, Cedric
'The Intimate Strangers' (1935)
by F. Scott Fitzgerald
Flynn, Lefty

KILLIAN, Sara
'The Intimate Strangers' (1935)
by F. Scott Fitzgerald
Flynn, Nora

KILLTHEDEAD, Mr
Melincourt (1817)
by Thomas Love Peacock
Barrow, Sir John
Croker, John Wilson

KIM (Kimball O'Hara)
Kim (1901)
by Rudyard Kipling
Beatty, Frank A.M.
Rattigan, William

KING, Mr
Stalky & Co. (1899)
by Rudyard Kipling
Crofts, William Carr
Haslam, F.W.

KING, Sir Ivor
Pigeon Pie (1940)
by Nancy Mitford
Ogilvie-Grant, Mark

KINGHAM
Two or Three Graces (1926)
by Aldous Huxley
Lawrence, D.H.

KING'S HINTOCK
Wessex novels and tales (1871–95)
by Thomas Hardy
Melbury Osmond, Dorset

KING'S HINTOCK COURT
Wessex novels and tales (1871–95)
by Thomas Hardy
Melbury House, Dorset

KINGSBERE
Wessex novels and tales (1871–95)
by Thomas Hardy
Bere Regis, Dorset

KINGSCREECH
Old Mrs Chundle (1929)
by Thomas Hardy
Kingston, Dorset

KINGSFORD, PERDITA
Dolores (1911)
by I. Compton-Burnett
Harvey, Daisy Elizabeth

KINTYRE, THE DUKE OF
The New Humpty-Dumpty (1912)
by Ford Madox Ford
Marwood, Arthur

KIOWSKI, MONSIEUR
A Week in a French Country-House
   (1867)
by Adelaide Kemble
Leighton, Frederic, Lord

KIPPS, ARTHUR
Kipps (1905)
by H.G. Wells
Wells, H.G.

KIRBY, CAPTAIN JOHN PETER
The Amazing Marriage (1895)
by George Meredith
Trelawny, E.J.

KITTRIDGE, MARY
Venture (1927)
by Max Eastman
Luhan, Mabel Dodge

KLESMER, JULIUS
Daniel Deronda (1876)
by George Eliot
Liszt, Franz
Rubinstein, Anton

KNAPWATER HOUSE
Desperate Remedies (1871)
by Thomas Hardy
Kingston Maurward House,
   Stinsford, Dorset

KNARBOROUGH
The Lost Girl (1920)
by D.H. Lawrence
Nottingham

KNEBLEY
'The Sad Fortunes of the Revd Amos
   Barton', *Scenes of Clerical Life*
   (1857–8)
by George Eliot
Astley, Warwickshire

KNIGHT, DAVID
Save Me the Waltz (1932)
by Zelda Fitzgerald
Fitzgerald, F. Scott

KNIGHT, HENRY
A Pair of Blue Eyes (1873)
by Thomas Hardy
Hardy, Thomas
Moule, Horace Mosley

KNOLLINGWOOD HALL
'Barbara of the House of Grebe'
   (1891)
by Thomas Hardy
St Giles House, Wimborne St
   Giles, Dorset

KNOLLSEA
Wessex novels and tales (1871–95)
by Thomas Hardy
Swanage, Dorset

KNOX, GEORGE
High Rising (1933)
by Angela Thirkell
Lucas, E.V.

KNYPE
Anna of the Five Towns (1902) and
   others
by Arnold Bennett
Stoke, Staffordshire

VON KOHLER, ELSE
You Can't Go Home Again (1940)
by Thomas Wolfe
Voelcker, Thea

KÜHLER, MENDEL
Mendel (1916)
by Gilbert Cannan
Gertler, Mark

KURTZ, MR
Heart of Darkness (1902)
by Joseph Conrad
Barttelot, Major Edmund Musgrave
Hodister, Arthur Eugene Constant
Klein, Georges Antoine
Stanley, H.M.

KUYKENDALL, HENRY
The Return of Ansell Gibbs (1958)
by Frederick Buecher
Rauschenbusch, Walter

KYAUKTADA
Burmese Days (1934)
by George Orwell
Katha, Upper Burma

L

LABASSECOEUR, THE KING OF
Villette (1853)
by Charlotte Brontë
Leopold I, King of the Belgians

LACIE
Alice's Adventures in Wonderland
(1865)
by Lewis Carroll
Liddell, Alice

LA CREEVY, MISS
Nicholas Nickleby (1838–9)
by Charles Dickens
Drummond, Rose Emma
Mannin, Mary Anne

LA CROASSE, MONSIEUR
Albert Lunel (1844)
by Lord Brougham
Croker, John Wilson

LACY, MR
It is Never Too Late to Mend (1856)
by Charles Reade
Perry, John George

LADISLAW, WILL
Middlemarch (1871–2)
by George Eliot
Cross, John Walter

LAFCADIO, JOHN
Death of a Ghost (1934)
by Margery Allingham
John, Augustus

LÄGERSTROM, COUNT MARSAC
Vestal Fire (1927)
by Compton Mackenzie
Fersen, Count

THE LAIRD
See MCALLISTER, Sandy

LAKE, DR
The Private Life of Henry Maitland
(1912)
by Morley Roberts
Hick, Henry

THE LAMA
Kim (1901)
by Rudyard Kipling
Burne-Jones, Edward

LAMB, JONATHAN
'Janet's Repentance', *Scenes of*
Clerical Life (1857–8)
by George Eliot
Wheway, Mr

LAMBERT, HESTER
The Virginians (1857–9)
by W.M. Thackeray
Ritchie, Anne Isabella, Lady

LAMBERT, LUCY
The Virginians (1857–9)
by W.M. Thackeray
Thackeray, Harriet

LANDAUER, Bernhard
Goodbye to Berlin (1939)
by Christopher Isherwood
Israel, Wilfrid

LANDAUER, Natalia
Goodbye to Berlin (1939)
by Christopher Isherwood
Soloweitschik, Gisa

LANDI, Sir Tito
Love at Second Sight (1916)
by Ada Leverson
Tosti, Sir Paolo

LANDLESS, Helena
Edwin Drood (1870)
by Charles Dickens
Kent, Constance Emily
Ternan, Ellen

LANDOR, Mr
'The Sad Fortunes of the Revd Amos
   Barton', *Scenes of Clerical Life*
   (1857–8)
by George Eliot
Greenway, Mr

LANDOR, Benjamin
'Janet's Repentance', *Scenes of
   Clerical Life* (1857–8)
by George Eliot
Craddock, Mr

LANG, Sir Wilfrid
Delia Blanchflower (1915)
by Mrs Humphry Ward
Harcourt, Lewis, 1st Viscount

LANGHAM
All Our Yesterdays (1930)
by H.M. Tomlinson
Masterman, C.F.

LANGHAM, Edward
Robert Elsmere (1888)
by Mrs Humphry Ward
Amiel, H.F.
Pattison, Mark

LANGHAM, Liz
His Own Man (1961)
by Martha Gellhorn
Montagu, Judith Venetia

LANKIN, Serjeant
The Kickleburys on the Rhine (1850)
by W.M. Thackeray
Gale, Frederick

LANTENENGO STREET, Gibbsville
Appointment in Samarra (1934)
by John O'Hara
Mahantongo Street, Pottsville,
   Pennsylvania

LANWIN, Margaret
The Memorial (1932)
by Christopher Isherwood
Mangeot, Olive

LANYON, Joyce
Arrowsmith (1925)
by Sinclair Lewis
Lewis, Grace Hegger

LAPIDOTH, Mirah
See COHEN, Mirah

LARCH, Richard
The Man from the North (1898)
by Arnold Bennett
Bennett, Arnold

LA SARTHE, Halcyone
Halcyone (1912)
by Elinor Glyn
Glyn, Elinor

LAS CHIVAS
'St Mawr' (1925)
by D.H. Lawrence
Kiowa Ranch, San Cristobal, New
   Mexico

LATHAM, Lady
Suspense (1925)
by Joseph Conrad
Legard, Jane, Lady

LATHAM, SIR CHARLES
Suspense (1925)
by Joseph Conrad
Legard, Sir John

LATHKILL, LADY
See FELL, Carlotta

LATHKILL, LUKE, LORD
'Glad Ghosts' (1928)
by D.H. Lawrence
Asquith, Herbert

LATIMER, DARSIE
See REDGAUNTLET, Sir Arthur

LAUGHLIN, REVD DR
Washington Jitters (1936)
by Dalton Trumbo
Coughlin, Father Charles

LAUGHTON, JAMES
To Have and Have Not (1937)
by Ernest Hemingway
Coles, Jack

LAUGHTON, MRS JAMES
To Have and Have Not (1937)
by Ernest Hemingway
Coles, Mrs Jack

LAUNCE, MRS
Fortitude (1913)
by Hugh Walpole
Belloc Lowndes, Marie

LAUNCESTON, LORD
A Lodge in the Wilderness (1906)
by John Buchan
Milner, Alfred, 1st Viscount

LAURENCE, MR
Little Women (1868) and sequels
by Louisa M. Alcott
May, Colonel Joseph

LAURENCE, OTHO
The New Republic (1877)
by W.H. Mallock
Oliphant, Laurence[2]

LAURENCE, THEODORE ('LAURIE')
Little Women (1868) and sequels
by Louisa M. Alcott
Whitman, Alfred
Willis, Frederick Llewellyn
Wisniewski, Ladislas

LAVALINA, ARIAL
The Subterraneans (1958)
by Jack Kerouac
Vidal, Gore

LAVINGTON, SQUIRE
Yeast (1848)
by Charles Kingsley
Cope, Sir John

LAVINGTON, ARGEMONE
Yeast (1848)
by Charles Kingsley
Froude, Charlotte
Kingsley, Frances
Mansfield, Caulia

LAVINGTON, HONORIA
Yeast (1848)
by Charles Kingsley
Gifford, Anna
Kingsley, Frances

LAVISH, MISS
A Room With a View (1908)
by E.M. Forster
Spender, Emily

LAWRENCE, MISS
Charles Auchester (1853)
by Elizabeth Sara Sheppard
Hutchins, Sophia

LAWRENCE, MRS
This Side of Paradise (1920)
by F. Scott Fitzgerald
Chanler, Mrs Winthrop

LAWSON, FREDERICK
Of Human Bondage (1915)
by W. Somerset Maugham
Kelly, Sir Gerald

LAZARD, Milton
'The Parasite' (1912)
by George Bronson Howard
Mizner, Wilson

LEA
The Inheritors (1901)
by Joseph Conrad and Ford Madox
    Ford
Garnett, Edward

The LEAGUE OF FORGOTTEN
    MEN
It Can't Happen Here (1935)
by Sinclair Lewis
Union for Social Justice

The LEARNED FRIEND
Crotchet Castle (1831)
by Thomas Love Peacock
Brougham, Lord

LE BRETON, Lady
The Dark Island (1934)
by Victoria Sackville-West
Sackville, Lady

LE BRETON, Julie
Lady Rose's Daughter (1903)
by Mrs Humphry Ward
de Lespinasse, Julie

LE BRETON, Shirin
The Dark Island (1934)
by Victoria Sackville-West
St Aubyn, Gwendolen

LEBRIX, Foxie
Appointment in Samarra (1934)
by John O'Hara
Turin, Papa

LEDDENTON
Jude the Obscure (1895)
by Thomas Hardy
Gillingham, Dorset

LEDERMAN, Mrs
'The Woman Who Rode Away'
    (1928)
by D.H. Lawrence
Luhan, Mabel Dodge

LEDGETT, Felix
'Walter Argallo and Felix Ledgett', *A
    Variety of Things* (1928)
by Max Beerbohm
Sutro, Alfred

LEE
Lions and Shadows (1938)
by Christopher Isherwood
Moody, Robert

LEE, Miss
Silcote of Silcotes (1867)
by Henry Kingsley
Kingsley, Sarah Maria

LEE, Alice
Woodstock (1826)
by Sir Walter Scott
Scott, Anne

LEE, Basil Duke
'A Night at the Fair' (1957)
by F. Scott Fitzgerald
Fitzgerald, F. Scott

LEE, Madeleine
Democracy (1880)
by Henry Adams
Adams, Henry
Adams, Marian
Lawrence, Mrs Bigelow

LEE, Old Bull
On the Road (1957)
by Jack Kerouac
Burroughs, William S.

LEEDS, Martin
The Secret Places of the Heart (1922)
by H.G. Wells
West, Rebecca

LE FAY, Morgan
Bid Me to Live (1960)
by H.D. (Hilda Doolittle)
Patmore, Brigit

LEFSKY, Ivan
Bid Me To Live (1960)
by H.D. (Hilda Doolittle)
Cournos, John

LEGGATT
'The Secret Sharer', *'Twixt Land and Sea* (1912)
by Joseph Conrad
Smith, Sidney

LEIDNER, Eric
Murder in Mesopotamia (1936)
by Agatha Christie
Woolley, Leonard

LEIDNER, Louise
Murder in Mesopotamia (1936)
by Agatha Christie
Woolley, Katharine

LEIGH, Amyas
Westward Ho! (1855)
by Charles Kingsley
Penrose, Francis Cranmer

LEIGH, Frank
Westward Ho! (1855)
by Charles Kingsley
Mansfield, Charles Blackford

LEIGH, Mary
Miss Brown (1884)
by Vernon Lee
Robinson, Agnes Frances Mary

LEIGH, Olimpia
Extraordinary Women (1928)
by Compton Mackenzie
Brooks, Romaine

LEINSENGEN, Comtesse
The Exclusives (1830)
by Lady Charlotte Bury
Lieven, Princess

LEIVERS, Mr
Sons and Lovers (1913)
by D.H. Lawrence
Chambers, Edmund

LEIVERS, Edgar
Sons and Lovers (1913)
by D.H. Lawrence
Chambers, Alan

LEIVERS, Miriam
Sons and Lovers (1913)
by D.H. Lawrence
Chambers, Jessie

LEMAÎTRE, Miss
Dolores (1911)
by I. Compton-Burnett
Péchinet, Marie

LENAPE COUNTY
McDonough (1951)
by Francis T. Field
Middlesex County, New Jersey

LENEHAN, T.
'Two Gallants', *Dubliners* (1914) and *Ulysses* (1922)
by James Joyce
Hart, Michael

LENNOX, David
Decline and Fall (1928)
by Evelyn Waugh
Beaton, Cecil

LENSKY (afterwards Brangwen), Lydia
The Rainbow (1915)
by D.H. Lawrence
Lawrence, Frieda

LEONARD, John Dorsey
Look Homeward, Angel (1929)
by Thomas Wolfe
Roberts, J.M.

LEONARD, Margaret
Look Homeward, Angel (1929)
by Thomas Wolfe
Roberts, Margaret

LEONE, Lady
Don't Tell Alfred (1960)
by Nancy Mitford
Cooper, Lady Diana

LEONIDOV, Anastasia
Alexandrovna
'Love and Russian Literature',
Ashenden; or The British Agent
(1928)
by W. Somerset Maugham
Kropotkin, Alexandra

LEPORELLI, Palazzo
The Wings of the Dove (1902)
by Henry James
Barbaro, Palazzo, Venice

LEROY
The Subterraneans (1958)
by Jack Kerouac
Cassady, Neal

LESLIE, Lady Emily
Wild Strawberries (1934)
by Angela Thirkell
Wemyss, Lady

LESLIE, Robert
The New Republic (1877)
by W.H. Mallock
Hardinge, Charles, 1st Baron
Hardinge of Penshurst
Hardinge, W.M.
Stephen, Sir Leslie

15 LESSWAYS STREET, Turnhill
The *Clayhanger* trilogy (1910–16)
by Arnold Bennett
175 Newport Lane, Burslem,
Staffordshire

LE STRANGE, Ellinor
Cometh Up as a Flower (1867)
by Rhoda Broughton
Broughton, Rhoda

LETOILE, Baba
Evensong (1932)
by Beverley Nichols
Dal Monte, Toti

LEVINSKY, Leon
The Town and the City (1950)
by Jack Kerouac
Ginsberg, Allen

LEW EVERARD
Tess of the d'Urbervilles (1891)
by Thomas Hardy
West Stafford, Dorset

LEWISHAM, George Edgar
Love and Mr Lewisham (1900)
by H.G. Wells
Gregory, Sir Richard
Wells, H.G.

LEY, Miss
Mrs Craddock (1902) and others
by W. Somerset Maugham
Steevens, Mrs George

LEYBURN, Catherine
Robert Elsmere (1888)
by Mrs Humphry Ward
Lyttelton, Laura

LEYBURN, Rose
Robert Elsmere (1888)
by Mrs Humphry Ward
Asquith, Margot
Pattison, Emilia Francis

LIBERAL PRINCIPLES, Mr
Vivian Grey (1826–7)
by Benjamin Disraeli
Huskisson, William

LIBERAL SNAKE
Vivian Grey (1826–7)
by Benjamin Disraeli
McCulloch, John Ramsay

LIBIDNIKOV, Maxim
Women in Love (1920)
by D.H. Lawrence
Koteliansky, S.S.
Litvinov, Maxim

LIBYA HILL
The Web and the Rock (1939) and
You Can't Go Home Again (1940)
by Thomas Wolfe
Asheville, North Carolina

LIGHT, CHRISTINA
Roderick Hudson (1875)
by Henry James
Low, Elena

THE LIGHTHOUSE
To the Lighthouse (1927)
by Virginia Woolf
Godrevy Lighthouse, Cornwall

LILLEY CLOSE
Touch and Go (1919)
by D.H. Lawrence
**Lamb Close House, Eastwood,
Nottinghamshire**

LILLY, RAWDON
Aaron's Rod (1922)
by D.H. Lawrence
Lawrence, D.H.

LILLY, TANNY
Aaron's Rod (1922)
by D.H. Lawrence
Lawrence, Frieda

LINDEN, LUCY
I Live Under a Black Sun (1937)
by Edith Sitwell
Sitwell, Edith

LINDER, JOE
The Web and the Rock (1939)
by Thomas Wolfe
Frankau, Joseph

LINDSAY, PHILIP
All the Conspirators (1928)
by Christopher Isherwood
Wintle, Hector

LINGARD, TOM
Almayer's Folly (1895)
by Joseph Conrad
Lingard, Captain William

The Rescue (1920)
by Joseph Conrad
Brooke, Sir James

LINNET, MARY AND REBECCA
'Janet's Repentance', *Scenes of
Clerical Life* (1857–8)
by George Eliot
Hill, The Misses

LINSLEY, PHILIP
Lions and Shadows (1938)
by Christopher Isherwood
Wintle, Hector

THE LION
The Pickwick Papers (1836–7)
by Charles Dickens
The Swan, West Malling, Kent

LISTER, ANTONY
My Next Bride (1934)
by Kay Boyle
Crosby, Harry

LISTLESS, HON. MR
Nightmare Abbey (1818)
by Thomas Love Peacock
Brummell, Beau
Skeffington, Sir Lumley St George

LITTLE, PROFESSOR
The Private Life of Henry Maitland
(1912)
by Morley Roberts
Greenwood, Joseph Goudge

LITTLE BILLEE
See BAGOT, William

LITTLE NADAB
The Newcomes (1854–5)
by W.M. Thackeray
Sloman, Charles

LITTLE NELL
See TRENT, Nell

LITTLEJOHN, HUGH
Tales of a Grandfather (1827–9)
by Sir Walter Scott
Lockhart, John Hugh

LLANABBA CASTLE
Decline and Fall (1928)
by Evelyn Waugh
**Arnold House, Llanddulas,
   Denbighshire**

LLEWELLYN, Mary
The Well of Loneliness (1928)
by Radclyffe Hall
Troubridge, Una, Lady

LOAMSHIRE
Adam Bede (1859)
by George Eliot
Staffordshire

LOCKE, Alton
Alton Locke (1850)
by Charles Kingsley
Cooper, Thomas[1]
Cooper, Walter

LOCKSON, Mr
The Cantab (1926)
by Shane Leslie
Dickinson, Lowes

LODORE
Lodore (1835)
by Mary Wollstonecraft Shelley
Byron, Lord

LOERKE
Women in Love (1920)
by D.H. Lawrence
Gertler, Mark

LOGAN, James
Mendel (1916)
by Gilbert Cannan
Currie, John
Lawrence, D.H.

LOGAN, Piggy
You Can't Go Home Again (1940)
by Thomas Wolfe
Calder, Alexander

LOIS
'Goose Fair' (1914)
by D.H. Lawrence
Mee, Lois

LOMBARD, Ivor
Crome Yellow (1921)
by Aldous Huxley
Morgan, Evan

LONG JOHN SILVER
Treasure Island (1883)
by R.L. Stevenson
Henley, W.E.

LONG NED
Paul Clifford (1830)
by Bulwer Lytton
Ellenborough, 1st Earl of

LONGPUDDLE
Wessex novels and tales (1871–95)
by Thomas Hardy
Piddlehinton, Dorset
Piddletrenthide, Dorset

LONGRES
'Uncle Spencer', *Little Mexican and
   Other Stories* (1924)
by Aldous Huxley
St Trond, Belgium

LONGSHAW
Anna of the Five Towns (1902) and
   others
by Arnold Bennett
Longton, Staffordshire

LOOKING-GLASS HOUSE
Through the Looking-Glass (1872)
by Lewis Carroll
Hetton Lawn, Gloucestershire

The LORD CHANCELLOR
Bleak House (1852–3)
by Charles Dickens
Lyndhurst, Lord

LORD CHIEF JUSTICE
Patronage (1814)
by Maria Edgeworth
Bushe, Charles Kendal

LORNTON INN
'Barbara of the House of Grebe'
 (1891)
by Thomas Hardy
Horton Inn, Dorset

LORRAINE, Mrs Felix (Amalia)
Vivian Grey (1826–7)
by Benjamin Disraeli
Lamb, Lady Caroline

LORRIMER
Trilby (1894)
by George Du Maurier
Poynter, Sir Edward

The LORY
Alice's Adventures in Wonderland
 (1865)
by Lewis Carroll
Liddell, Louisa

LOTHAIR
Lothair (1870)
by Benjamin Disraeli
Bute, Lord

LOTHAIR, Duchess of
Lothair (1870)
by Benjamin Disraeli
Abercorn, Louisa Jane

LOTHAIR, Duke of
Lothair (1870)
by Benjamin Disraeli
Abercorn, James Hamilton

LOTTIE
'To Meet Jesus Christ', *Four O'Clock*
 (1926)
by Mary Borden
Colefax, Sybil, Lady

LOUISA
The Trespasser (1912)
by D.H. Lawrence
Mason, Agnes

LOUSTANOFF, Madame
 (grandmère)
Hector (1883)
by Flora Shaw
du Sualt, Léonice

LOVELL, Delia
Of Flowers and a Village (1963)
by Wilfrid Blunt
Hartley, Grizel

LOVELL, Margaret
Rhoda Fleming (1865)
by George Meredith
Meredith, Mary Ellen

LOVETT, James
The Mather Story (1953)
by John Prebble
Munnings, Sir Alfred

LOWER BINFIELD
Coming up for Air (1939)
by George Orwell
Henley, Oxfordshire

LOWER MELLSTOCK
Wessex novels and tales (1871–95)
by Thomas Hardy
Lower Bockhampton, Dorset

LOWERSDALE, Lord
Vivian Grey (1826–7)
by Benjamin Disraeli
Lonsdale, 1st Earl of

LOWME, Mr
'Janet's Repentance', *Scenes of
 Clerical Life* (1857–8)
by George Eliot
Towle, Mr

LOWOOD SCHOOL
Jane Eyre (1847)
by Charlotte Brontë
Clergy Daughters' School, Cowan Bridge, Lancashire

LOWTON
Jane Eyre (1847)
by Charlotte Brontë
Kirkby Lonsdale, Westmorland

THE LOYALTY CLUB
The Green Hat (1924)
by Michael Arlen
The Embassy Club, Soho, London

LUBOW, LILY
The Way It Was (1959)
by Harold Loeb
Cannell, Kitty

LUCAS, EMMELINE ('LUCIA')
Queen Lucia (1920) and others
by E.F. Benson
Anderson, Mary
Colefax, Sybil, Lady

LUCAS, WALDEN
The Titan (1914)
by Theodore Dreiser
Harrison, Carter H.

LUDLOW, LADY
My Lady Ludlow (1858)
by Elizabeth Gaskell
Hereford, Viscountess

LUDOVIC, CORPORAL-MAJOR
The *Sword of Honour* trilogy
(1952–61)
by Evelyn Waugh
Connolly, Cyril

LUKE, MR
The New Republic (1877)
by W.H. Mallock
Arnold, Matthew

LUKE, CHARLES
More Work for the Undertaker
(1948) and others
by Margery Allingham
Williams, Charles

LULWIND COVE
Wessex novels and tales (1871–95)
by Thomas Hardy
Lulworth Cove, Dorset

LUMLEY
The Lost Girl (1920)
by D.H. Lawrence
Langley Mill, Nottinghamshire

LUMSDON
Jude the Obscure (1895)
by Thomas Hardy
Cumnor, Oxfordshire

LURCOCK, DAN
Revelry (1926)
by Samuel Hopkins Adams
Daugherty, Harry M.

LURGAN SAHIB
Kim (1901)
by Rudyard Kipling
Jacob, Alexander M.

LUSCOMBE, EVANGELINE
The Simple Life Limited (1911)
by Ford Madox Ford
Marwood, Caroline

LUSCOMBE, FLORA
The Limit (1911)
by Ada Leverson
Beardsley, Mabel

LUSCOMBE, GERALD
The Simple Life Limited (1911)
by Ford Madox Ford
Marwood, Arthur

LUZ
'A Very Short Story', *In Our Time*
(1925)
by Ernest Hemingway
Von Kurowsky, Agnes

THE LYCURGANS
Pilgrimage (1915–67)
by Dorothy Richardson
Fabian Society

LYCURGUS
An American Tragedy (1925)
by Theodore Dreiser
Cortland, New York

LYDE, AUNT
See RUMFORD, Lydia

LYDECKER, WALDO
Laura (1943)
by Vera Caspary
Woollcott, Alexander

LYDGATE, TERTIUS
Middlemarch (1871–2)
by George Eliot
Allbutt, Sir Thomas Clifford
Clarke, Edward
Nankivell, Charles Benjamin

LYLE, EUSTACE
Coningsby (1844)
by Benjamin Disraeli
de Lisle, Ambrose

LYMPORT
Evan Harrington (1860)
by George Meredith
Portsmouth, Hampshire

LYNCH, VINCENT
A Portrait of the Artist as a Young Man (1916) and *Ulysses* (1922)
by James Joyce
Cosgrave, Vincent

LYNDON, BARRY
The Memoirs of Barry Lyndon Esq. (1844)
by W.M. Thackeray
Stoney, Andrew Robinson

LYNDON, HONORIA, COUNTESS OF
The Memoirs of Barry Lyndon Esq. (1844)
by W.M. Thackeray
Strathmore, Mary Eleanor, Countess of

LYNE, ANGELA
Black Mischief (1932) and *Put Out More Flags* (1942)
by Evelyn Waugh
Dunn, Irene Clarice, Lady

LYON, RUFUS
Felix Holt, the Radical (1866)
by George Eliot
Franklin, Francis
Sibree, John

LYONESSE, ISLES OF
'A Mere Interlude' (1913)
by Thomas Hardy
Scilly Isles

LYONS
A Family Party (1956) and other stories
by John O'Hara
Lykens, Pennsylvania

LYONS, EUGENE
Three Blue Suits (1933)
by Aline Bernstein
Wolfe, Thomas

M

M—É, COUNT
Coningsby (1844)
by Benjamin Disraeli
Molé, Louis Mathieu, Comte

MAARTENS, KATY
The Genius and the Goddess (1955)
by Aldous Huxley
Lawrence, Frieda

MACADAM, Effie
Vestal Fire (1927)
by Compton Mackenzie
Grahame, Sophie

McALLISTER, Sandy ('the Laird')
Trilby (1894)
by George Du Maurier
Lamont, Thomas Reynolds
Millais, Sir John Everett

McCANN
*A Portrait of the Artist as a Young
Man* (1916)
by James Joyce
Skeffington, Francis Sheehy

MACARTHEY, Revd Mr
Shirley (1849)
by Charlotte Brontë
Nicholls, Arthur Bell

McCOY, C.P.
'Grace', *Dubliners* (1914) and
Ulysses (1922)
by James Joyce
Chance, Charles

McCOY, Hunter Griswold
The Web and the Rock (1939)
by Thomas Wolfe
Graham, Edward Kidder

MACDONALD, Countess
The New Humpty-Dumpty (1912)
by Ford Madox Ford
Hueffer, Elsie

MACDONALD, Count Sergius
Mihailovich
The New Humpty-Dumpty (1912)
by Ford Madox Ford
Ford, Ford Madox

MACDONALD, Sophie
The Razor's Edge (1944)
by W. Somerset Maugham
Fouts, Denham

MacDONALD OF BEN NEVIS,
Donald
The Monarch of the Glen (1941)
by Compton Mackenzie
**Cameron of Lochiel, Sir Donald
Walter**

McDOUGALL, Donald
Donald McDougall (1958)
by Osbert Sitwell
Douglas, Norman

MacDOWELL, Gertie
Ulysses (1922)
by James Joyce
Fleischmann, Marthe

MacGRAWLER, Peter
Paul Clifford (1830)
by Bulwer Lytton
The Scots Nation

MacGREGOR, Mrs Claudia
Miss Brown (1884)
by Vernon Lee
Paget, Matilda

Mr McGREGOR'S GARDEN
The Tale of Peter Rabbit (1902) and
others
by Beatrix Potter
**Camfield Place, Essendon,
Hertfordshire**
Fawe Park, Cumbria

The Tale of the Flopsy Bunnies (1909)
by Beatrix Potter
Gwaynynog, Denbighshire

McGURK INSTITUTE
Arrowsmith (1925)
by Sinclair Lewis
Rockefeller Institute, New York

McHAIG, Lloyd
You Can't Go Home Again (1940)
by Thomas Wolfe
Lewis, Sinclair

MACHIN, EDWARD HENRY ('DENRY')
The Card (1911)
by Arnold Bennett
Hales, H.K.

MacHUGH, PROFESSOR
Ulysses (1922)
by James Joyce
MacNeill, Hugh

MacIVOR, FERGUS
Waverley (1814)
by Sir Walter Scott
MacDonell of Glengarry, Alexander

MacJONES, BALLIOL
The Subterraneans (1958)
by Jack Kerouac
Holmes, John Clellon

MACKAYE, SANDY
Alton Locke (1850)
by Charles Kingsley
Carlyle, Thomas

MACKENZIE, MRS (THE
   'CAMPAIGNER')
The Newcomes (1854–5)
by W.M. Thackeray
Shawe, Isabella

MACKENZIE, ALEC
The Explorer (1908)
by W. Somerset Maugham
Stanley, H.M.

MACKINTOSH, NORTHEY
Don't Tell Alfred (1960)
by Nancy Mitford
Brandolini, Contessa Cristiana
Devonshire, Deborah, Duchess of

MACKWORTH, LORD
Lilian (1922)
by Arnold Bennett
Castlerosse, Lord

MacLAUREL, MR
Headlong Hall (1816)
by Thomas Love Peacock
Campbell, Thomas

Wilson, John

MACLEAN, RUBY, LADY
The Loved and Envied (1951)
by Enid Bagnold
Cooper, Lady Diana

MACMORLAN, PROCURATOR FISCAL
Guy Mannering (1815)
by Sir Walter Scott
Shortreed, Robert

MacNAIR, SIEGMUND
The Trespasser (1912)
by D.H. Lawrence
Macartney, H.B.

MACOMBER, MARGOT
'The Short Happy Life of Francis
   Macomber', *The Fifth Column
   and the First Forty-nine Stories*
   (1938)
by Ernest Hemingway
Mason, Jane

MACPHERSON, HUGH
See MARRIOTT, John Hugh William
   Macpherson

McPHERSON, SAM
Windy McPherson's Son (1916)
by Sherwood Anderson
Anderson, Sherwood

McPHERSON, WINDY
Windy McPherson's Son (1916)
by Sherwood Anderson
Anderson, Irwin

MacQUEDY, MR
Crotchet Castle (1831)
by Thomas Love Peacock
McCulloch, John Ramsay
Mill, James
Mushet, Robert

MacWALSEY, JOHN
To Have and Have Not (1937)
by Ernest Hemingway
Burns, Harry H.
Gingrich, Arnold

MacWHIRTER, Mr
The Trespasser (1912)
by D.H. Lawrence
McLeod, A.W.

MADAGASCAR, Princess of
Glenarvon (1816)
by Lady Caroline Lamb
Holland, Lady

MADAME
The Marsden Case (1923)
by Ford Madox Ford
Strindberg, Frida

MAG
Pilgrimage (1915–67)
by Dorothy Richardson
Heath, Mabel

MAI DUN
The Mayor of Casterbridge (1886)
by Thomas Hardy
Maiden Castle, Dorset

MAINE, Wentworth
Prisoners (1906)
by Mary Cholmondeley
Benson, A.C.

MAINWROTH, Robert
'The Love-Bird' (1930)
by Osbert Sitwell
Berners, Lord

MAISIE
The Light that Failed (1890)
by Rudyard Kipling
Garrard, Violet Florence

MAITLAND, Henry
The Private Life of Henry Maitland
   (1912)
by Morley Roberts
Gissing, George

MAJOR, Mr
The Simple Life Limited (1911)
by Ford Madox Ford
Cowlishaw, William Harrison

MAJOR, Roland
On the Road (1957)
by Jack Kerouac
Temko, Allan Bernard

MALAGROWTHER, Sir Mungo
The Fortunes of Nigel (1822)
by Sir Walter Scott
Sharpe, Charles Kirkpatrick

MALASPINA, Palazzo
Those Barren Leaves (1925)
by Aldous Huxley
Montegufoni, Castello di, Italy

MALINS, Freddy
'The Dead', *Dubliners* (1914)
by James Joyce
Lyons, Freddy

MALIPIZZO, Signor
South Wind (1917)
by Norman Douglas
Capolozzi, Signor

MALKIN
Born in Exile (1892)
by George Gissing
Roberts, Morley

MALLARD, Ross
The Emancipated (1890)
by George Gissing
Roberts, Morley

MALLARDS
Queen Lucia (1920) and others
by E.F. Benson
Lamb House, Rye, East Sussex

MALLINGFORD
Lover and Husband (1870)
by Mrs Molesworth
Knutsford, Cheshire

MALLOCK, Castle
The Valley of Bones (1964)
by Anthony Powell
**Gosford Castle, County Armagh,
   Ireland**

MALLOWS, Henry
You Can't Go Home Again (1940)
by Thomas Wolfe
Bellows, George

MALLOY, James
BUtterfield 8 (1935)
by John O'Hara
O'Hara, John

MALMAINS, Eugenia
Wigs on the Green (1935)
by Nancy Mitford
Mitford, Unity

MALONE, Peter Augustus
Shirley (1849)
by Charlotte Brontë
Smith, Revd James William

MALONE, Seamus
The Web and the Rock (1939)
by Thomas Wolfe
Boyd, Ernest

MALPRACTICE, Miles
Decline and Fall (1928)
by Evelyn Waugh
Gathorne-Hardy, Robert

The MANAGER
Heart of Darkness (1902)
by Joseph Conrad
Delcommune, Camille

The MANAGER'S UNCLE
Heart of Darkness (1902)
by Joseph Conrad
Delcommune, Alexandre

The MANAGING DIRECTOR
'An Outpost of Progress', *Tales of
Unrest* (1898)
by Joseph Conrad
Stanley, H.M.

MANCHESTER HOUSE
The Lost Girl (1920)
by D.H. Lawrence
**London House, Eastwood,
Nottinghamshire**

MANDELL, Lily
You Can't Go Home Again (1940)
by Thomas Wolfe
Curtiss, Mina Kirstein

MANDEVILLE, Lady
Glenarvon (1816)
by Lady Caroline Lamb
Oxford, Lady

MANEFOLD
Anna of the Five Towns (1902) and
others
by Arnold Bennett
Leek, Staffordshire

Dr MANETTE'S HOUSE
A Tale of Two Cities (1859)
by Charles Dickens
**Carlisle House, Soho, London
1 Greek Street, Soho, London**

MANISTY, Edward
Eleanor (1899)
by Mrs Humphry Ward
**Chateaubriand, François René,
Vicomte de**

MANLEY, Sir Edward ('the Black
Dwarf')
The Black Dwarf (1816)
by Sir Walter Scott
Ritchie, David

MANN, Charles
Mummery (1916)
by Gilbert Cannan
Craig, Edward Gordon

MANNERING, Guy
Guy Mannering (1815)
by Sir Walter Scott
Scott, Sir Walter

MANNERING, Julia
Guy Mannering (1815)
by Sir Walter Scott
Scott, Charlotte, Lady

MANOR FARM, Dingley Dell
The Pickwick Papers (1836–7)
by Charles Dickens
Birling Place, Kent
Cob Tree Manor, Sandling, Kent

MANSFIELD PARK
Mansfield Park (1814)
by Jane Austen
Cottesbrooke Hall,
   Northamptonshire
Godmersham Park, Kent

MANTON, Steve
The Dust Which is God (1941)
by William Rose Benét
Mooney, Tom

MAPPLE, Father
Moby Dick (1851)
by Herman Melville
Taylor, Edward Thompson

MARABAR CAVES
A Passage to India (1924)
by E.M. Forster
Barabar Caves

MARASCA, Francesco
The Lost Girl (1920)
by D.H. Lawrence
Cacopardo, Francesco

MARCH, Mr
Little Women (1868) and sequels
by Louisa M. Alcott
Alcott, Bronson

MARCH, Mrs ('Marmee')
Little Women (1868) and sequels
by Louisa M. Alcott
Alcott, Abigail

MARCH, Amy
Little Women (1868) and sequels
by Louisa M. Alcott
Alcott, May

MARCH, Beth
Little Women (1868) and sequels
by Louisa M. Alcott
Alcott, Elizabeth

MARCH, Iris
The Green Hat (1924)
by Michael Arlen
Cunard, Nancy
Twysden, Duff, Lady

MARCH, Jo
Little Women (1868) and sequels
by Louisa M. Alcott
Alcott, Louisa May

MARCH, Meg
Little Women (1868) and sequels
by Louisa M. Alcott
Alcott, Anna

MARCH, Nellie
'The Fox' (1923)
by D.H. Lawrence
Monk, Violet

MARCHBANKS
'The Last Laugh' (1928)
by D.H. Lawrence
Murry, John Middleton

MARCHMAIN, Lord
Brideshead Revisited (1945)
by Evelyn Waugh
Beauchamp, William, 6th Earl
Duggan, Hubert

MARCHMILL, Ella
'An Imaginative Woman' (1896)
by Thomas Hardy
Henniker, Florence

MARCO, Prince
The Tragic Comedians (1880)
by George Meredith
Racowitz, Count

MARION, Jervase
'Lady Tal', *Vanitas* (1892)
by Vernon Lee
James, Henry

MARIUS
Marius the Epicurean (1885)
by Walter Pater
Jackson, Richard Charles

MARJORIE
'The End of Something', *In Our Time* (1925)
by Ernest Hemingway
Bump, Marjorie

MARKER, HARVEY
Desolation Angels (1965)
by Jack Kerouac
Mailer, Norman

MARKHAM, WILLIS
Revelry (1926)
by Samuel Hopkins Adams
Harding, Warren G.

MARKTON
A Laodicean (1881)
by Thomas Hardy
Dunster, Somerset

MARL, DIANTHA
Kingsblood Royal (1947)
by Sinclair Lewis
Banning, Margaret

MARLBURY DOWNS
'What the Shepherd Saw' (1913)
by Thomas Hardy
Marlborough Downs, Wiltshire

MARLOTT
Wessex novels and tales (1871–95)
by Thomas Hardy
Marnhull, Dorset

MARMION
The Bostonians (1884)
by Henry James
Marion, Cape Cod, Massachusetts

MARRIOTT, HUGH MACPHERSON
The Web and the Rock (1939) and
    You Can't Go Home Again (1940)
by Thomas Wolfe
Cecil, John Francis Amherst

MARRIOTT, JOHN HUGH WILLIAM
    MACPHERSON
Of Time and the River (1935)
by Thomas Wolfe
Cecil, John Francis Amherst

MARSH, DAVID
Male and Female (1933)
by James L. Grant
Lawrence, D.H.

MARSH, JIM
The Harbor (1915)
by Ernest Poole
Haywood, W.D.

MARSHALL, MR
'England, My England' (1915)
by D.H. Lawrence
Meynell, Wilfrid

MARSHALL, EDDY
To Have and Have Not (1937)
by Ernest Hemingway
Lowe, Joe

MARSHALL, HENRY
Confessions of a Young Man (1888)
    and others
by George Moore
Hawkins, Lewis Weldon

MARSHLAND, JINNY
Cass Timberlane (1945)
by Sinclair Lewis
Powers, Marcella

MARTEL
Vestal Fire (1927)
by Compton Mackenzie
Clavel, Gilbert

MARTEL, DR
Suspense (1925)
by Joseph Conrad
Marshall, Dr

MARTHA
'Two Women' (1925)
by Gertrude Stein
Cone, Claribel

MARTIN, PETER
The Town and the City (1950)
by Jack Kerouac
Kerouac, Jack

MARTINDALE CASTLE
Peveril of the Peak (1823)
by Sir Walter Scott
Haddon Hall, Derbyshire

MARTINWARD, CHLOE
A Tale of Chloe (1879)
by George Meredith
Braddock, Frances
Rossetti, Christina

MARTON, ANNA
I Live Under a Black Sun (1937)
by Edith Sitwell
Sitwell, Edith

MARVELL, GERTRUDE
Delia Blanchflower (1915)
by Mrs Humphry Ward
Pankhurst, Christabel

MARVIN, HENRY
By Bread Alone (1901)
by I.K. Friedman
Frick, Henry Clay

MARVIN STEEL MILL
By Bread Alone (1901)
by I.K. Friedman
Homestead Steel Mill,
Pennsylvania

MARX, CARLO
On the Road (1957)
by Jack Kerouac
Ginsberg, Allen

MARY JANE
'The Dead', *Dubliners* (1914)
by James Joyce
Callanan, Mary Ellen

MARYGREEN
Jude the Obscure (1895)
by Thomas Hardy
Fawley, Berkshire

MARYVALE
Hadrian VII (1904)
by F.W. Rolfe
St Mary's College, Oscott

MÄRZ, FRÄULEIN
Women in Love (1920)
by D.H. Lawrence
Huxley, Juliette

MASOLLAM, DAVID
Masollam (1886)
by Laurence Oliphant
Harris, Thomas Lake

MASON
Stalky & Co. (1899)
by Rudyard Kipling
Beste, C.W.L.

MASSON, WILLIAM
Pastors and Masters (1925)
by I. Compton-Burnett
Macaulay, W.H.

MASTERMAN
Kipps (1905)
by H.G. Wells
Gissing, George

MASTERS, ARNOLD
Miranda Masters (1926)
by John Cournos
Aldington, Richard

MASTERS, MIRANDA
Miranda Masters (1926)
by John Cournos
Doolittle, Hilda

MASTERSON, EDWARD
The Big Wheel (1949)
by John Nixon Brooks
Luce, Henry

MATCHINGS EASY
Mr Britling Sees It Through (1916)
by H.G. Wells
Little Easton, Essex

MATHER, Lionel
The Mather Story (1953)
by John Prebble
Spencer, Stanley

MATHILDA, Miss
'The Good Anna', *Three Lives* (1909)
by Gertrude Stein
Stein, Gertrude

MATILDA OF ROKEBY
Rokeby (1813)
by Sir Walter Scott
Belsches, Williamina

MATTHESON, Sir Joshua
Women in Love (1920)
by D.H. Lawrence
Russell, Bertrand

MATTHEW
'Smile' (1928)
by D.H. Lawrence
Murry, John Middleton

MATTHEW, Uncle
The Pursuit of Love (1945)
by Nancy Mitford
Lord, Redesdale

MAU
A Passage to India (1924)
by E.M. Forster
Chhatarpur, India
Dewas, Central India

MAULE, Mathew
The House of the Seven Gables (1851)
by Nathaniel Hawthorne
Good, Sarah

MAUMBRY, Captain John
'A Changed Man' (1913)
by Thomas Hardy
Moule, Revd Henry

MAUNCIPLE, Virginia
After Many a Summer (1939)
by Aldous Huxley
Davis, Marion
Goddard, Paulette

MAW, Aunt
The Web and the Rock (1939)
by Thomas Wolfe
Wolfe, Julia

MAXIM, Gifford
The Middle of the Journey (1947)
by Lionel Trilling
Chambers, Whittaker

MAXWELL, Duncan
Vestal Fire (1927)
by Compton Mackenzie
Douglas, Norman

MAXWELL COURT
Marcella (1894)
by Mrs Humphry Ward
Ashridge Park, Hertfordshire
Tring, Hertfordshire

MAY, Dr
The Daisy Chain (1856)
by C.M. Yonge
Yonge, Dr James

MAY, Mr
The Lost Girl (1920)
by D.H. Lawrence
Magnus, Maurice

MAY, Ethel
The Daisy Chain (1856)
by C.M. Yonge
Moberly, Charlotte

MAYLIE, Rose
Oliver Twist (1837–8)
by Charles Dickens
Hogarth, Mary Scott

The MAYPOLE INN
Barnaby Rudge (1841)
by Charles Dickens
The King's Head, Chigwell, Essex

MEARS, Cyril
The Will to Love (1919)
by Hugh Kingsmill
Kingsmill, Hugh

MEDWIN, Mrs
'Mrs Medwin' (1903)
by Henry James
Grantley, Lady

MEEBER, Caroline
Sister Carrie (1900)
by Theodore Dreiser
Dreiser, Emma

MEHAFFERTY, Ed
Washington Jitters (1936)
by Dalton Trumbo
Farley, James A.

MELCHESTER
Wessex novels and tales (1871–95)
by Thomas Hardy
Salisbury, Wiltshire

MELCHESTER NORMAL SCHOOL
Jude the Obscure (1895)
by Thomas Hardy
Salisbury Training College

MELEAGER, Dr
The Cantab (1926)
by Shane Leslie
Headlam, Walter

MELINCOURT, Anthelia
Melincourt (1817)
by Thomas Love Peacock
Falkner, Fanny
Gryffydh, Jane

MELL, Charles
David Copperfield (1849–50)
by Charles Dickens
Goldsmith, Oliver
Taylor, Mr

MELLIFONT, Lord
'The Private Life' (1891)
by Henry James
Leighton, Frederic, Lord

MELLON, Kate
Broken to Harness (1864)
by Edmund Yates
Walters, Catherine ('Skittles')

MELLOR PARK
Marcella (1894)
by Mrs Humphry Ward
Hampden House, Buckinghamshire

MELLSTOCK
Wessex novels and tales (1871–95)
by Thomas Hardy
Stinsford, Dorset

MELLSTOCK QUIRE
Under the Greenwood Tree (1872)
by Thomas Hardy
Stinsford Quire

MELMOTTE, Augustus
The Way We Live Now (1875)
by Anthony Trollope
Grant, Albert
Hudson, George

MELNOTTE, Daniel
The Scarlet Shadow (1907)
by Walter Hurt
Moffat, David Halliday

MELPORT
'An Indiscretion in the Life of an
  Heiress' (1878)
by Thomas Hardy
Weymouth, Dorset

MELTON, Miss
*Maude; or The Anglican Sister of
  Mercy* (1869)
by Elizabeth Jane Whateley
Sellon, Priscilla Lydia

MELTON, Mr
Coningsby (1844)
by Benjamin Disraeli
Macdonald, James William Bosville

MELVILLE, Erasmus
'Things' (1933)
by D.H. Lawrence
Brewster, Earl Henry

MELVILLE, Valerie
'Things' (1933)
by D.H. Lawrence
Brewster, Achsah

MENTEITH HOUSE
Glenarvon (1816)
by Lady Caroline Lamb
Melbourne House, London

MERCER, Lady
The Vampyre: A Tale (1819)
by J.W. Polidori
Lamb, Lady Caroline

MERCINTON, Duke of
The Exclusives (1830)
by Lady Charlotte Bury
Wellington, Duke of

MERDLE, Mr
Little Dorrit (1855–7)
by Charles Dickens
Hudson, George
Sadleir, John

MERE, Jenny
The Happy Hypocrite (1897)
by Max Beerbohm
Loftus, Marie Cecilia ('Cissy')

MERLIN, Lord
The Pursuit of Love (1945) and *Love
in a Cold Climate* (1949)
by Nancy Mitford
Berners, Lord

MERRILIES, Meg
Guy Mannering (1815)
by Sir Walter Scott
Euston, Margaret
Gordon, Jean

MERRILL, Anson
The Titan (1914)
by Theodore Dreiser
Elkins, William L.

MERRIVALE, Sir Henry
The Plague Court Murders (1934)
and others
by Carter Dickson
Churchill, Winston

MERSCH, Duc de
The Inheritors (1901)
by Joseph Conrad and Ford Madox
Ford
Leopold II, King of the Belgians

MERSHAM, Cyril
'A Modern Lover' (1934)
by D.H. Lawrence
Lawrence, D.H.

MERTON, Miss
The New Republic (1877)
by W.H. Mallock
von Hügel, Baroness

METEYARD, Miss
Murder Must Advertise (1933)
by Dorothy L. Sayers
Sayers, Dorothy L.

MICAWBER, Mrs
Nicholas Nickleby (1838–9)
by Charles Dickens
Dickens, Elizabeth[2]

MICAWBER, Wilkins
David Copperfield (1849–50)
by Charles Dickens
Dickens, John

MICHAEL
The Secret River (1909)
by Rose Macaulay
Brooke, Rupert

MICHAELIS
The Secret Agent (1907)
by Joseph Conrad
Bakunin, Michael
Condon, Edward O'Meara
Davitt, Michael

MICHAELIS
Lady Chatterley's Lover (1928)
by D.H. Lawrence
Arlen, Michael

MICHIN MALICHO, Lord
Gryll Grange (1860)
by Thomas Love Peacock
Russell, John, 1st Earl

MIDDLEMARCH
Middlemarch (1871–2)
by George Eliot
Coventry, Warwickshire

MIDDLETON, Dr
The Egoist (1879)
by George Meredith
Peacock, Thomas Love

MIDDLETON ABBEY
The Woodlanders (1887)
by Thomas Hardy
Milton Abbas, Dorset

THE MIGHTY ROURKE
See ROURKE, the Mighty

MIKULIN, Councillor
Under Western Eyes (1911)
by Joseph Conrad
Lopukhin, Aleksey Aleksandrovich

MILASLAVSKI, Prince Gritzko
His Hour (1910)
by Elinor Glyn
**Sayn and Wittgenstein, Prince
    Gregory von**

MILBY
'Janet's Repentance', *Scenes of
    Clerical Life* (1857–8)
by George Eliot
Nuneaton, Warwickshire

MILDMAY, William
The Palliser novels (1864–79)
by Anthony Trollope
Russell, John, 1st Earl

MILESTONE, Marmaduke
Headlong Hall (1816)
by Thomas Love Peacock
Repton, Humphry

MILL POOL
'Squire Petrick's Lady' (1891)
by Thomas Hardy
Milborne Port, Somerset

MILLBANK, Mr
Coningsby (1844)
by Benjamin Disraeli
**Ashworth, Edmund
Philips, Mark**

MILLBANK, Oswald
Coningsby (1844)
by Benjamin Disraeli
**Gladstone, William
Walter, John**

MILLER, Joseph
Eyeless in Gaza (1936)
by Aldous Huxley
**Alexander, F. Matthias
Heard, Gerald
Pennell, Theodore**

MILLFIELD
Dolores (1911)
by I. Compton-Burnett
**Dent, Yorkshire
Great Clacton, Essex**

MILLION, Mr
Vivian Grey (1826–7)
by Benjamin Disraeli
Powles, John Diston

MILLION, Mrs
Vivian Grey (1826–7)
by Benjamin Disraeli
Coutts, Harriot

MILTON
North and South (1855)
by Elizabeth Gaskell
Manchester

MILTON STRIKE
North and South (1855)
by Elizabeth Gaskell
Preston Strike

MINGOTT, Catherine Manson
The Age of Innocence (1920)
by Edith Wharton
Jones, Mary Mason

MINISTRY OF TRUTH
Nineteen Eighty-four (1949)
by George Orwell
Broadcasting House, London

MINKO, Allen
Visions of Gerard (1963)
by Jack Kerouac
Temko, Allan Bernard

MINKO, Irving
Book of Dreams (1960)
by Jack Kerouac
Temko, Allan Bernard

MINTON
Sons and Lovers (1913)
by D.H. Lawrence
Moorgreen, Nottinghamshire

M'INTYRE, Hector
The Antiquary (1816)
by Sir Walter Scott
Constable, George, the Younger

MINUS, Mr
The Man of Sorrow (1809)
by Theodore Hook
Moore, Thomas

MIRABAL
The Plumed Serpent (1926)
by D.H. Lawrence
Quintanilla, Luis

MIRABEL, Count Alcibiades de
Henrietta Temple (1837)
by Benjamin Disraeli
D'Orsay, Count

MIREFIELDS
The Private Life of Henry Maitland
   (1912)
by Morley Roberts
Wakefield, Yorkshire

MIROBOLANT
The History of Pendennis (1848–50)
by W.M. Thackeray
Soyer, Alexis Benoit

MISSELTHWAITE MANOR
The Secret Garden (1911)
by Frances Hodgson Burnett
Maytham Hall, Rolverden, Kent

MISTLETOE, Bobby
'Round About the Christmas Tree'
   (1899)
by W.M. Thackeray
Synge, Robert Follett

MISTOVER KNAP
The Return of the Native (1878)
by Thomas Hardy
Troy Town, Dorset

MITCHELL, Carrie
Workers in the Dawn (1880)
by George Gissing
Gissing, Nell

MITCHELL, Humphrey
Mendel (1916)
by Gilbert Cannan
Nevinson, C.R.W.

MIXEN LANE, Durnover
The Mayor of Casterbridge (1886)
by Thomas Hardy
Mill Street, Fordington

M'KIMBER, Louise
The Young Lions (1948)
by Irwin Shaw
Hemingway, Mary

MOBBING FRANCIS
Paul Clifford (1830)
by Bulwer Lytton
Burdett, Sir Francis

MOEST, PAULA
'New Eve and Old Adam' (1934)
by D.H. Lawrence
Lawrence, Frieda

MOFFATTS
Mr Perrin and Mr Traill (1911)
by Hugh Walpole
Epsom College, Surrey

MOLINA, TORO
The Harder They Fall (1947)
by Budd Schulberg
Carnera, Primo

MOLLENHAUER, HENRY A.
The Financier (1912)
by Theodore Dreiser
McManes, James

MOLYNEUX, COUNCILLOR
'Rosanna', *Popular Tales* (1804)
by Maria Edgeworth
Edgeworth, R.L.

MONK LAWRENCE
Delia Blanchflower (1915)
by Mrs Humphry Ward
Nuneham House, Oxfordshire

MONKSHAVEN
Sylvia's Lovers (1863)
by Elizabeth Gaskell
Whitby, Yorkshire

MONMOUTH, LORD
Coningsby (1844)
by Benjamin Disraeli
Hertford, 3rd Marquess of

MONMOUTH, MISS
Glenarvon (1816)
by Lady Caroline Lamb
Byron, Lady

MONSANTO, LORENZO
Big Sur (1962)
by Jack Kerouac
Ferlinghetti, Lawrence

MONSELL, MR
Kangaroo (1923)
by D.H. Lawrence
Mountsier, Robert

MONTDORE, LADY
Love in a Cold Climate (1949)
by Nancy Mitford
Trefusis, Violet

MONTE BENI, VILLA
The Marble Faun (1860)
by Nathaniel Hawthorne
Montauto, Villa, Florence

MONTEAGLE, LADY
Venetia (1837)
by Benjamin Disraeli
Lamb, Lady Caroline

MONTEITH, EDDIE
The Flower Beneath the Foot (1923)
by Ronald Firbank
Morgan, Evan

MONTERESSO, COMTESSE DE
Suspense (1925)
by Joseph Conrad
de Boigne, Adèle, Comtesse

MONTERESSO, COUNT DE
Suspense (1925)
by Joseph Conrad
de Boigne, Benoit, Comte

MONTERIANO
Where Angels Fear to Tread (1905)
by E.M. Forster
San Gimignano, Italy

MONTES, SOCRATES TOMÁS
The Plumed Serpent (1926)
by D.H. Lawrence
Calles, Plutarco Elias

MONTFORT, LADY
Endymion (1880)
by Benjamin Disraeli
Bradford, Selina, Countess of
Norton, Caroline
Palmerston, Lady

MONTFORT TOURNAMENT
Endymion (1880)
by Benjamin Disraeli
Eglinton Tournament

MONTGOMERY
A Mummer's Wife (1885)
by George Moore
Glover, James

MONTISLOPE HOUSE
'Master John Horseleigh, Knight'
    (1913)
by Thomas Hardy
Montacute House, Somerset

MONTOYA, Juanito
The Sun Also Rises (1926)
by Ernest Hemingway
Quintana, Juanito

MONTRESOR, Mr
Lady Rose's Daughter (1903)
by Mrs Humphry Ward
Turgot, Anne-Robert Jacques

MONYGHAM, Dr
Nostromo (1904)
by Joseph Conrad
Masterman, George Frederick

MOOKERJEE, Hurree Chander
Kim (1901)
by Rudyard Kipling
Das, Sarat Chandra

MOON AND STARS INN
Sons and Lovers (1913)
by D.H. Lawrence
Three Tuns Inn, Eastwood,
    Nottinghamshire

The Lost Girl (1920)
by D.H. Lawrence
Sun Inn, Eastwood,
    Nottinghamshire

MOONEY
Bleak House (1852–3)
by Charles Dickens
Looney

MOORAD, Adam
The Subterraneans (1958)
by Jack Kerouac
Ginsberg, Allen

MOORE, Donal
Doreen (1904)
by Edna Lyall
Davitt, Michael

MOORE, Hortense
Shirley (1849)
by Charlotte Brontë
Haussé, Mademoiselle

MOORE, Robert
Shirley (1849)
by Charlotte Brontë
Taylor, Joseph

MOOREHOUSE, J. Ward
U.S.A. (1938)
by John Dos Passos
Lee, Ivy Ledbetter

MOORHAMPTON
The Private Life of Henry Maitland
    (1912)
by Morley Roberts
Manchester

MOORHAMPTON COLLEGE
The Private Life of Henry Maitland
    (1912)
by Morley Roberts
Owens College, Manchester

MOPES, Tom
'Tom Tiddler's Ground' (1861)
by Charles Dickens
Lucas, James

MOREAU, Hortense-Pauline
Anne (1883)
by Constance Fenimore Woolson
Chagaray, Madame

MOREFORD
'The Fiddler of the Reels' (1894)
by Thomas Hardy
Moreton, Dorset

MOREL, Gertrude
Sons and Lovers (1913)
by D.H. Lawrence
Lawrence, Lydia

MOREL, Walter
Sons and Lovers (1913)
by D.H. Lawrence
Lawrence, John Arthur

MOREL, William
Sons and Lovers (1913)
by D.H. Lawrence
Lawrence, William Ernest

MORELAND, Hugh
A Dance to the Music of Time
(1951–76)
by Anthony Powell
Lambert, Constant

MORGAN, Harry
To Have and Have Not (1937)
by Ernest Hemingway
Russell, Joe

MORGAN, Trafford
'A Florentine Experiment' (1880)
by Constance Fenimore Woolson
James, Henry

MORIARTY, Dean
On the Road (1957)
by Jack Kerouac
Cassady, Neal

MORIARTY, Professor James
The Sherlock Holmes stories
(1890–1927)
by Arthur Conan Doyle
Drayson, Alfred Wilks
Moriarty, George
Payn, James
Worth, Adam

MORIER, Mark
'Glad Ghosts' (1928)
by D.H. Lawrence
Lawrence, D.H.

MORKAN, Miss Julia
'The Dead', *Dubliners* (1914) and
Ulysses (1922)
by James Joyce
Lyons, Mrs

MORKAN, Miss Kate
'The Dead', *Dubliners* (1914)
by James Joyce
Callanan, Mrs

MORLAND, Laura
High Rising (1933)
by Angela Thirkell
Thirkell, Angela

MORLAND, Thomas
The Power of the Dead (1963)
by Henry Williamson
Galsworthy, John

MORLAND, Tony
High Rising (1933)
by Angela Thirkell
Thirkell, Lance

MORNTON, Earl of
Albert Lunel (1844)
by Lord Brougham
Wellesley, Richard, Lord

MORRIS, Dinah
Adam Bede (1859)
by George Eliot
Evans, Elizabeth

MORRIS, J.E.D.
Most Likely to Succeed (1954)
by John Dos Passos
Lawson, John Howard

MORRISON, Greta
Mendel (1916)
by Gilbert Cannan
Carrington, Dora

MORRISON, Peter
Alms for Oblivion (1965–76)
by Simon Raven
Prior, James

MORTON
Jane Eyre (1847)
by Charlotte Brontë
Hathersage, Derbyshire

MORTON, CECILY
Neutral Ground (1933)
by Helen Corke
Mason, Agnes

MOSS, GRITTY
The Mill on the Floss (1860)
by George Eliot
Clarke, Christiana

MOTTRAM, REX
Brideshead Revisited (1945)
by Evelyn Waugh
Bracken, Brendan

DE MOULIN, EMMELINE
Albert Lunel (1844)
by Lord Brougham
Brougham, Eleanor

MOUNT, BELLA
The Ordeal of Richard Feverel (1859)
by George Meredith
Meredith, Mary Ellen

MOUNT WYROC, REGINALD, 11TH
EARL OF
Young Men in Love (1927)
by Michael Arlen
Castlerosse, Lord

MOWBRAY, LORD
*De Vere; or The Man of
Independence* (1827)
by Robert Plumer Ward
Newcastle, 4th Duke of

MOWBRAY, ADELINE
*Adeline Mowbray; or The Mother
and Daughter* (1804)
by Mrs Amelia Opie
Wollstonecraft, Mary

MOWBRAY, ELIZA
A Father and His Fate (1957)
by I. Compton-Burnett
Compton-Burnett, Katharine

MOWCHER, MISS
David Copperfield (1849–50)
by Charles Dickens
Hill, Mrs Jane Seymour

MOYDIA AND KATYA
'The Grande Malade' (1962)
by Djuna Barnes
Perlmutter, Bronia and Tanya

M'QUIRK, THADY
Castle Rackrent (1800)
by Maria Edgeworth
Langan, John

M'TURK, WILLIAM
Stalky & Co. (1899)
by Rudyard Kipling
Beresford, G.C.

MUDFOG ASSOCIATION FOR
THE ADVANCEMENT OF
EVERYTHING
The Mudfog Papers (1837–8)
by Charles Dickens
**British Association for the
Advancement of Science**

VON MÜFFE, HERR
'The Bachelor Bedroom' (1859)
by Wilkie Collins
Andersen, Hans Christian

MUGGLETON
The Pickwick Papers (1836–7)
by Charles Dickens
**Maidstone, Kent
West Malling, Kent**

MUGONNIGLE, SENATOR
The Sleep of Reason (1956)
by Warren Miller
McCarthy, Joseph

MÜHLER (ALIAS RETLOW)
South Wind (1917)
by Norman Douglas
von Veltheim, Baron

MULLER
'In the Rukh' (1893)
by Rudyard Kipling
Ribbentrop

MULLIGAN, BUCK
Ulysses (1922)
by James Joyce
Gogarty, Oliver St John

MULLION, JENNY
Crome Yellow (1921)
by Aldous Huxley
Brett, Dorothy

MULLUMBIMBY
Kangaroo (1923)
by D.H. Lawrence
**Thirroul, New South Wales,
    Australia**

MULVEY, LIEUTENANT HARRY
Ulysses (1922)
by James Joyce
Mulvey, Willie

MURDOCK, BOGAN
At Heaven's Gate (1943)
by Robert Penn Warren
Lea, Luke

MURDSTONE & GRINBY
David Copperfield (1849–50)
by Charles Dickens
**Warren's Blacking Warehouse,
    London**

MURESWELL RECTORY
Robert Elsmere (1888)
by Mrs Humphry Ward
Peper Harow, Surrey

MURGATROYD, GENERAL
Highland Fling (1931)
by Nancy Mitford
Redesdale, Lord

MURIEL
'A Modern Lover' (1934)
by D.H. Lawrence
Chambers, Jessie

MURPHY, W.B.
Ulysses (1922)
by James Joyce
Budgen, Frank

MURPHY FAMILY
Of Time and the River (1935)
by Thomas Wolfe
Casey Family

MURRAY, FELICIA
Dolores (1911)
by I. Compton-Burnett
Bremner, Isabel

MURTHA, RONA
'Rona Murtha', *A Gallery of Women*
    (1929)
by Theodore Dreiser
Mallon, Anna T.

THE *MUSEUM*
Lovel the Widower (1860)
by W.M. Thackeray
The *National Standard*

MUSSET, EVANGELINE
The Ladies Almanack (1928)
by Djuna Barnes
Barney, Natalie Clifford

MYERS, AUGUSTIN
A Girl Among the Anarchists (1903)
by Isabel Meredith
Bourdin, Martial

MYERS, JACOB
A Girl Among the Anarchists (1903)
by Isabel Meredith
Samuels, Henry B.

MYSTIC, MOLEY
Melincourt (1817)
by Thomas Love Peacock
Coleridge, Samuel Taylor

N

NADAB, LITTLE
See LITTLE NADAB

NAN
Dangerous Ages (1921)
by Rose Macaulay
Macaulay, Rose

NANCY
An Island Cabin (1902)
by Arthur Henry
Mallon, Anna T.

NANNY
The Blessing (1951)
by Nancy Mitford
Dicks, Laura

NARCISSA
A Christmas Child (1880)
by Mrs Molesworth
Hutton, Mary Josephine

THE NARRATOR
The Aspern Papers (1888)
by Henry James
Silsbee, Edward Augustus

NASH, GABRIEL
The Tragic Muse (1888–9)
by Henry James
Pratt, Herbert

NASSE HOUSE
Dead Man's Folly (1956)
by Agatha Christie
Greenway, Devon

NATESCOURT, CLITORESSA, DUCHESS
OF
The Ladies Almanack (1928)
by Djuna Barnes
**Clermont-Tonnerre, Elisabeth,
Duchesse de**

NATT, MAJOR
Vestal Fire (1927)
by Compton Mackenzie
Palmes, Colonel Bryan

NATTATORINI, COUNTESS ELLA
The Tattooed Countess (1926)
by Carl Van Vechten
Douglas, Mahala Dutton Benedict

NAYLOR
It is Never Too Late to Mend (1856)
by Charles Reade
Taylor

NAYLOR, EDGAR
The Rock Pool (1936)
by Cyril Connolly
Richards, Nigel

NEAL, FRED
The New Machiavelli (1911)
by H.G. Wells
Garvin, J.L.

NEATHE, SOPHIE
Things As They Are (1950)
by Gertrude Stein
Haynes, Mabel

NELL, LITTLE
See TRENT, Nell

NELLO
Romola (1863)
by George Eliot
Burchiello, Domenico

NEPENTHE
South Wind (1917)
by Norman Douglas
Capri

NESBITT, DR
Nellie Brooke, A Homely Story
 (1868)
by Florence Marryat
Wesley, Samuel Sebastian

NETHER-MOYNTON
Wessex novels and tales (1871–95)
by Thomas Hardy
Owermoigne, Dorset

NETHERMERE
The White Peacock (1911)
by D.H. Lawrence
**Moorgreen Reservoir,
   Nottinghamshire**

NEUCHATEL, ADRIAN
Endymion (1880)
by Benjamin Disraeli
de Rothschild, Lionel Nathan

THE NEUCHATELS
Endymion (1880)
by Benjamin Disraeli
The Rothschilds

NEVILLE
The Waves (1931)
by Virginia Woolf
Strachey, Lytton

NEW BOYNTON
McDonough (1951)
by Francis T. Field
New Brunswick, New Jersey

NEW SERJEANT'S INN
The Man from the North (1898)
by Arnold Bennett
**New Court, Lincoln's Inn Fields,
   London**

NEWALL, ROSE
Sooner or Later (1904)
by Violet Hunt
Hunt, Violet

NEWCOMB, SPENCER
The Exclusives (1830)
by Lady Charlotte Bury
Perceval, Spencer

NEWCOME, ETHEL
The Newcomes (1854–5)
by W.M. Thackeray
**Airlie, Countess of
Baxter, Sarah ('Sally')**

NEWCOME, COLONEL THOMAS
The Newcomes (1854–5)
by W.M. Thackeray
**Carmichael, Charles Montaubon
Carmichael-Smyth, Henry
Shakespear, Sir Richmond**

NEWSOME, CHADWICK
The Ambassadors (1903)
by Henry James
Sturges, Jonathan

NEWTON, ALLGOOD
Cakes and Ale (1930)
by W. Somerset Maugham
Gosse, Edmund

NICHOLSON, RICHARD
Mary Olivier (1919)
by May Sinclair
Aldington, Richard

NICK'S FATHER
'Fathers and Sons', *Winner Take
   Nothing* (1933)
by Ernest Hemingway
Hemingway, C.E.

NICKLEBY, MRS
Nicholas Nickleby (1838–9)
by Charles Dickens
Dickens, Elizabeth[2]

NICKLEBY, NICHOLAS
Nicholas Nickleby (1838–9)
by Charles Dickens
Burnett, Henry

THE NIGHTCLUB
The Marsden Case (1923)
by Ford Madox Ford
**The Cave of the Golden Calf,
   London**

NIGHTMARE ABBEY
Nightmare Abbey (1818)
by Thomas Love Peacock
**Albion House, Marlow,
   Buckinghamshire**

NIGHTSHADE, Mr
Headlong Hall (1816)
by Thomas Love Peacock
Southey, Robert

NIXON, Cristal
Redgauntlet (1824)
by Sir Walter Scott
Purdie, Tom

NOAT
Blindness (1926)
by Henry Green
Eton College, Berkshire

NOAT ART SOCIETY
Blindness (1926)
by Henry Green
**Eton Society of Arts, Eton College,
    Berkshire**

NOBLE, Mr
Pilgrimage (1915–67)
by Dorothy Richardson
Odle, Alan

NOBLE, Maury
The Beautiful and Damned (1922)
by F. Scott Fitzgerald
Nathan, George Jean

NOGGS, Newman
Nicholas Nickleby (1838–9)
by Charles Dickens
Knott, Newman

NORBOURNE
Adam Bede (1859)
by George Eliot
Norbury, Derbyshire

NORBURY, Earl of
Almacks (1826)
by M. Spencer Stanhope
Northumberland, 3rd Duke of

NORMANBY, The Hon. Beatrice
Tono-Bungay (1909)
by H.G. Wells
Hunt, Violet

NORN, Esther
'Esther Norn', *A Gallery of Women*
    (1929)
by Theodore Dreiser
Pyne, Mary

NORNA OF THE FITFUL HEAD
    (Ulla Troil)
The Pirate (1821)
by Sir Walter Scott
Bessie Millie

NORRIS, Mrs
The Plumed Serpent (1926)
by D.H. Lawrence
Nuttall, Zelia

NORRIS, Arthur
Mr Norris Changes Trains (1935)
by Christopher Isherwood
Hamilton, Gerald

NORTH, Abe
Tender is the Night (1934)
by F. Scott Fitzgerald
Fitzgerald, F. Scott
Lardner, Ring

NORTHBRIDGE
Northbridge Rectory (1941)
by Angela Thirkell
Chipping Camden, Gloucestershire

NORTON, John
A Mere Accident (1887)
by George Moore
Martyn, Edward

NOSTROMO
Nostromo (1904)
by Joseph Conrad
Cervoni, Dominic

NUNNELLY
Shirley (1849)
by Charlotte Brontë
Hartshead, Yorkshire

NUN'S HOUSE, CLOISTERHAM
Edwin Drood (1870)
by Charles Dickens
Eastgate House, Rochester, Kent

NUPKINS
The Pickwick Papers (1836–7)
by Charles Dickens
Laing, Allan Stewart

NUPKINS'S MAID
The Pickwick Papers (1836–7)
by Charles Dickens
Weller, Mary

NUTTALL
Sons and Lovers (1913)
by D.H. Lawrence
Underwood, Nottinghamshire

NUTTLEBURY
Tess of the d'Urbervilles (1891)
by Thomas Hardy
Hazelbury Bryan, Dorset

O

OAKBOURNE
Adam Bede (1859)
by George Eliot
Ashbourne, Derbyshire

OAKSHOTT, LORD
Oakshott Castle (1873)
by Henry Kingsley
Kingsley, Henry

OBERLAND
Pilgrimage (1915–67)
by Dorothy Richardson
Adelboden, Switzerland

O'BRIAN
Post Adolescence (1923)
by Robert McAlmon
Burke, Kenneth

O'BRIEN
The Magician (1908)
by W. Somerset Maugham
O'Conor, Roderic

O'BRIEN, SENATOR
Stranger Come Home (1954)
by William L. Shirer
McCarthy, Joseph

O'BRIEN, TERENCE
Peter Simple (1834)
by Frederick Marryat
Jackson, George Vernon

THE *OBSERVATOR*
The History of Henry Esmond (1852)
by W.M. Thackeray
The *Examiner*

O'CARROLL, MARIONETTA CELESTINA
Nightmare Abbey (1818)
by Thomas Love Peacock
Shelley, Harriet

OCHILTREE, EDIE
The Antiquary (1816)
by Sir Walter Scott
Gemmells, Andrew

O'CONNOR, MR
It is Never Too Late to Mend (1856)
by Charles Reade
Maconochie, Alexander

O'CONNOR, KANE
Tongue of Fire (1960)
by Ernest Frankel
McCarthy, Joseph

O'CONNOR, MATTHEW
Ryder (1928) and *Nightwood* (1936)
by Djuna Barnes
Mahoney, Daniel A.

O'DONOVAN, MRS
The Blessing (1951)
by Nancy Mitford
Hammersley, Violet

O'FLYNN
Alton Locke (1850)
by Charles Kingsley
O'Connor, Feargus

OGDEN, BRANDER
Post Adolescence (1923)
by Robert McAlmon
Hartley, Marsden

OGILVIE, MARY
The Pathway (1928)
by Henry Williamson
Williamson, Ida Laetitia

O'HALLORAN, COUNT
The Absentee (1812)
by Maria Edgeworth
Trimleston, Lord

O'HARA, KIMBALL
See KIM

O'HARA, LARRY
The Subterraneans (1958)
by Jack Kerouac
Ferlinghetti, Lawrence

OKE, ALICE
'Oke of Okehurst' (1890)
by Vernon Lee
Campbell, Janey Sevilla

OKEHURST
'Oke of Okehurst' (1890)
by Vernon Lee
Godinton, Kent

OLD BAGS
Paul Clifford (1830)
by Bulwer Lytton
Eldon, Lord

OLD BLOOD AND THUNDER
'The Great Stone Face' (1850)
by Nathaniel Hawthorne
Taylor, Zachary

OLD GRANITE
Democracy (1880)
by Henry Adams
Hayes, Rutherford Birchard

OLD MORTALITY
Old Mortality (1816)
by Sir Walter Scott
Paterson, Robert

THE OLD RADICAL
The Romany Rye (1857)
by George Borrow
Bowring, Sir John

OLDACRE, DOCTOR
*Maude; or The Anglican Sister of
   Mercy* (1869)
by Elizabeth Jane Whately
Newman, J.H.

OLDBOROUGH, LORD
Patronage (1814)
by Maria Edgeworth
Ellenborough, 1st Baron
Stuart, William
Walpole, Robert

OLDBUCK, GRISELDA
The Antiquary (1816)
by Sir Walter Scott
Constable, Matilda

OLDBUCK, JONATHAN
The Antiquary (1816)
by Sir Walter Scott
Clerk of Eldin, John
Constable, George, the Elder
Gordon, Alexander
Ramsay of Ochtertyre, John

OLDCASTLE, DORON
Nicholas Crabbe (1958)
by F.W. Rolfe
Richards, Grant

OLDGO
Two Plunges for a Pearl (1872)
by Mortimer Collins
Newcombe, John Reilly

OLDHAM, HON. AND REVD MR
'The Grave by the Handpost' (1913)
by Thomas Hardy
Fox-Strangways, Charles Redlynch

OLDHOUSEN, Georgius
His Excellency The Ambassador
   Extraordinary (1879)
by Robert Kerr
Burges, William

OLDINPORT, Mr
'The Sad Fortunes of the Revd Amos
   Barton', *Scenes of Clerical Life*
   (1857–8)
by George Eliot
Newdegate, Rt. Hon. Charles N.

'Mr Gilfil's Love Story', *Scenes of*
   Clerical Life (1857–8)
by George Eliot
Newdigate, Francis

OLDINPORT ARMS
'Mr Gilfil's Love Story', *Scenes of*
   Clerical Life (1857–8)
by George Eliot
Newdegate Arms, Nuneaton,
   Warwickshire

OLIVER, Mrs
A Generation Missing (1938)
by Carroll Carstairs
Lewis, Rosa

OLIVER, Edmund
Edmund Oliver (1798)
by Charles Lloyd
Coleridge, Samuel Taylor

OLIVER, Eugene
The Torches Flare (1928)
by Stark Young
Faulkner, William

OLIVER, Nelly
Mendel (1916)
by Gilbert Cannan
Henry, Dolly
Lawrence, Frieda

OLIVIA
The Trespasser (1912)
by D.H. Lawrence
Babbage, Violet Mary

O'LYMPOS, Kenneth
Nicholas Crabbe (1958)
by F.W. Rolfe
Grahame, Kenneth

O'MALLEY
'His Excellency', *Ashenden; or The*
   British Agent (1928)
by W. Somerset Maugham
Kelly, Sir Gerald

The ONDT
Finnegans Wake (1939)
by James Joyce
Lewis, Wyndham

O'NEILL, Danny
A World I Never Made (1936) and
   others
by James T. Farrell
Farrell, James T.

ONITON
Howards End (1910)
by E.M. Forster
Clun, Shropshire

OOZEWOOD
'Master John Horseleigh, Knight'
   (1913)
by Thomas Hardy
Ringwood, Hampshire

OPHELIA
'Smile' (1928)
by D.H. Lawrence
Mansfield, Katherine

O'PRISM, Sir Patrick
Headlong Hall (1816)
by Thomas Love Peacock
Price, Uvedale

ORANGE, Robert
The School for Saints (1897) and
   Robert Orange (1900)
by John Oliver Hobbes
Disraeli, Benjamin

ORCHARD STREET, MILBY
'Janet's Repentance', *Scenes of Clerical Life* (1857–8)
by George Eliot
Church Street, Nuneaton, Warwickshire

THE ORDER OF THE DIVINE BLOOD
The Cantab (1926)
by Shane Leslie
Society of the Divine Compassion

OREZZA, CARDINAL
Hadrian VII (1904)
by F.W. Rolfe
Oreglia, Cardinal

ORGREAVE, OSMOND
The *Clayhanger* trilogy (1910–16)
by Arnold Bennett
Wood, Absalom W.

ORILLA
The Plumed Serpent (1926)
by D.H. Lawrence
El Fuerte

ORLANDO
Orlando (1928)
by Virginia Woolf
Sackville-West, Victoria

ORLEY FARM
Orley Farm (1861–2)
by Anthony Trollope
Julian's Hill, Middlesex

ORLY, LEYTON, AND FAMILY
Pilgrimage (1915–67)
by Dorothy Richardson
Baly, Charles Francis Peyton, and family

ORME, LAMBERT
Some People (1927)
by Harold Nicolson
Firbank, Ronald

ORMONT, LORD
Lord Ormont and His Aminta (1894)
by George Meredith
Cardigan, 7th Earl of

ORMSBY, MR
Coningsby (1844) and *Tancred* (1847)
by Benjamin Disraeli
Dick, Quentin
Irving, John

ORMSKIRK, DR
Dr Grimshawes Secret (1883)
by Nathaniel Hawthorne
Kirkup, Seymour Stocker

ORTH, RALPH
'The Bell in the Fog' (1905)
by Gertrude Atherton
James, Henry

O'RUDGERY, PROFESSOR
The Cantab (1926)
by Shane Leslie
Ridgeway, Sir William

OSBORNE, GEORGE
Vanity Fair (1847–8)
by W.M. Thackeray
Somerset, Arthur

O'SHANE, CORNELIUS
Ormond (1817)
by Maria Edgeworth
Corry, James

O'SHANE, SIR ULICK
Ormond (1817)
by Maria Edgeworth
de Blaquiere, John, Baron
Pakenham, Admiral Sir Thomas

OSMOND, GILBERT
The Portrait of a Lady (1880)
by Henry James
Boott, Francis

OSMOND, PANSY
The Portrait of a Lady (1880)
by Henry James
Duveneck, Elizabeth

OSSORY, Charles
England, Their England (1933)
by A.G. Macdonell
MacCarthy, Desmond

OTRANTO, The Misses
Vivian Grey (1826–7)
by Benjamin Disraeli
Berry, The Misses

OTTERCOVE, Lord
Jazz and Jasper (1928)
by William Gerhardi
Beaverbrook, Lord

OTTLEY, Edith
Love's Shadow (1908) and others
by Ada Leverson
Leverson, Ada

OVERTON, Edward
The Way of All Flesh (1903)
by Samuel Butler
Butler, Samuel

OWEN
The Diary of a Drug Fiend (1922)
by Aleister Crowley
John, Augustus

OWEN, Mrs
The Fair Haven (1873)
by Samuel Butler
Butler, Fanny

OWEN, John Pickard
The Fair Haven (1873)
by Samuel Butler
Butler, Samuel

THE OXFORD PROFESSOR
Lothair (1870)
by Benjamin Disraeli
Smith, Goldwin

OXWELL HALL, Oxwell
The Trumpet Major (1880)
by Thomas Hardy
Poxwell Manor, Poxwell, Dorset

DE P——, Mr
Under Western Eyes (1911)
by Joseph Conrad
von Plehve, Wenzel

P

PACKER CITY
McDonough (1951)
by Francis T. Shield
Jersey City, New Jersey

PACO
'The Mother of a Queen', *Winner
    Take Nothing* (1933)
by Ernest Hemingway
Ortiz

PADDIFORD
'Janet's Repentance', *Scenes of
    Clerical Life* (1857–8)
by George Eliot
Stockingford, Warwickshire

PAGE, Clara
This Side of Paradise (1920)
by F. Scott Fitzgerald
Taylor, Cecilia Delihant

THE PAGEBOY AT THE ROYAL
    SUSSEX HOTEL
The *Clayhanger* trilogy (1910–16)
by Arnold Bennett
Hardy

THE PAINTER OF THE HEROIC
Lavengro (1851)
by George Borrow
Haydon, Benjamin Robert

THE PALAZZINO
The Aspern Papers (1888)
by Henry James
Capello, Palazzo, Venice

PALEY, Susan
Point Counter Point (1928)
by Aldous Huxley
Mansfield, Katherine

PALLISER, Plantagenet
Can You Forgive Her? (1864)
by Anthony Trollope
**Newcastle, 6th Duke of
Parkinson-Fortescue, Chichester
Russell, John, 1st Earl**

PAN
The Wind in the Willows (1908)
by Kenneth Grahame
Furnivall, F.J.

THE PANJANDRUM OF
  PHILANTHROPY
A Child of the Jago (1896)
by Arthur Morrison
Booth, General William

PANSCOPE, Mr
Headlong Hall (1816)
by Thomas Love Peacock
Coleridge, Samuel Taylor

PANTAI RIVER
Almayer's Folly (1895)
by Joseph Conrad
Berau River, Borneo

PANTOPRAGMATIC SOCIETY
Gryll Grange (1860)
by Thomas Love Peacock
**Association for the Promotion of
  Social Science**

PAPERSTAMP, Mr
Melincourt (1817)
by Thomas Love Peacock
Wordsworth, William

PARADISE, Sal
On the Road (1957)
by Jack Kerouac
Kerouac, Jack

PARHAM, Mr
The Autocracy of Mr Parham (1930)
by H.G. Wells
Wells, H.G.

PARKER, Freddy
South Wind (1917)
by Norman Douglas
Trower, Harold

PARKER, Ralph
The Will to Love (1919)
by Hugh Kingsmill
Harris, Frank

PARKER, Robert
The Pursuit of Love (1945)
by Nancy Mitford
Darling, Donald

PARLOAD
In the Days of the Comet (1906)
by H.G. Wells
Gregory, Sir Richard

PARMONT, Mr
The Simple Life Limited (1911)
by Ford Madox Ford
Garnett, Edward

PARR, Augustus
Down There on a Visit (1962)
by Christopher Isherwood
Heard, Gerald

PARSNIP
Put Out More Flags (1942) and *Love
  Among the Ruins* (1953)
by Evelyn Waugh
Auden, W.H.

PAST CENTURY, Lord
Vivian Grey (1826–7)
by Benjamin Disraeli
Eldon, Lord

PASTON, Hunter
Of Time and the River (1935)
by Thomas Wolfe
Astor, Vincent

PATCH, ANTHONY
The Beautiful and Damned (1922)
by F. Scott Fitzgerald
Fitzgerald, F. Scott

PATCH, GLORIA
The Beautiful and Damned (1922)
by F. Scott Fitzgerald
Fitzgerald, Zelda

PATMORE, MISS
Brothers and Sisters (1929)
by I. Compton-Burnett
Smith, Ellen

SS PATNA
Lord Jim (1900)
by Joseph Conrad
SS Jeddah

PATRICK
Robbery Under Arms (1888)
by Ralph Boldrewood
Morgan, Daniel

PATTEN, MRS
'The Sad Fortunes of the Revd Amos
    Barton', *Scenes of Clerical Life*
    (1857–8)
by George Eliot
Hutchins, Mrs

PATTERNE, CROSSJAY
The Egoist (1879)
by George Meredith
Ellis, George Hasted

PATTERNE, SIR WILLOUGHBY
The Egoist (1879)
by George Meredith
Kay-Shuttleworth, Ughtred James

PATUSAN, PATUSAN RIVER
Lord Jim (1900)
by Joseph Conrad
Berau, Borneo

PAUL
Down There on a Visit (1962)
by Christopher Isherwood
Fouts, Denham

PAULET
*Sydenham; or Memoirs of a Man of
    the World* (1830)
by W. Massie
D'Orsay, Count

PAULLE, LADY QUEENIE
The Pretty Lady (1918)
by Arnold Bennett
Cooper, Lady Diana

PAWKIE, JAMES
The Provost (1822)
by John Galt
Fullerton, Bailie

PEAK, GOODWIN
Born in Exile (1892)
by George Gissing
Gissing, George

PEARL
The Scarlett Letter (1850)
by Nathaniel Hawthorne
Hawthorne, Una

PEARL, JENNY
Carnival (1912)
by Compton Mackenzie
Maude, Christine

PECKSNIFF, SETH
Martin Chuzzlewit (1843–4)
by Charles Dickens
Hall, Samuel Carter

PEGGOTTY, CLARA
David Copperfield (1849–50)
by Charles Dickens
Weller, Mary

PELET, MONSIEUR
The Professor (1857)
by Charlotte Brontë
Lebel, Joachim-Joseph

PELHAM, HENRY
Pelham (1828)
by Bulwer Lytton
Villiers, Frederick

PEN-ZEPHYR
'A Mere Interlude' (1913)
by Thomas Hardy
Penzance, Cornwall

PENDENNIS, MAJOR
The History of Pendennis (1848–50)
by W.M. Thackeray
Shawe, Merrick

PENDENNIS, ARTHUR
The History of Pendennis (1848–50)
by W.M. Thackeray
Ellison, Cuthbert Edward
Kenney, Charles Lamb
Thackeray, W.M.

PENDENNIS, HELEN
The History of Pendennis (1848–50)
by W.M. Thackeray
Carmichael-Smyth, Anne

PENISTONE CRAG
Wuthering Heights (1847)
by Emily Brontë
Ponden Kirk, Yorkshire

PENNEFEATHER, LADY
St Ronan's Well (1823)
by Sir Walter Scott
Penn, Mrs

PENNISTAN, RUTH
Heritage (1919)
by Victoria Sackville-West
Sackville-West, Victoria

PENNY, ROBERT
Under the Greenwood Tree (1872)
by Thomas Hardy
Reason, Robert

PENROSE, HARRY
The Secret Battle (1919)
by A.P. Herbert
Dyett, Edwin

PENRUDDOCK, NIGEL
Endymion (1880)
by Benjamin Disraeli
Manning, Henry Edward

THE PENTAGRAM CLUB
The New Machiavelli (1911)
by H.G. Wells
The Coefficients

PENTLAND, BASCOM
Of Time and the River (1935)
by Thomas Wolfe
Westall, Henry A.

PEPPER, WILLIAM
The Voyage Out (1915)
by Virginia Woolf
Gibbs, Frederick Waymouth

PEPWORTH-NORTON, MAIMIE
Vestal Fire (1927)
by Compton Mackenzie
Wolcott-Perry, Saidée

PEPWORTH-NORTON, VIRGINIA
Vestal Fire (1927)
by Compton Mackenzie
Wolcott-Perry, Kate

PERCEPIED, LEO
The Subterraneans (1958)
by Jack Kerouac
Kerouac, Jack

PERCIVAL
The Waves (1931)
by Virginia Woolf
Stephen, Thoby

PERCIVAL, MR
Belinda (1801)
by Maria Edgeworth
Edgeworth, R.L.

PERCY, MR
Patronage (1814)
by Maria Edgeworth
Edgeworth, R.L.

PERCY, CAROLINE
Patronage (1814)
by Maria Edgeworth
Edgeworth, Honora

PERCY, GODFREY
Patronage (1814)
by Maria Edgeworth
Edgeworth, Richard

PERCY, ROSAMOND
Patronage (1814)
by Maria Edgeworth
Edgeworth, Maria

PERKER, MR
The Pickwick Papers (1836–7)
by Charles Dickens
Ellis, Edward

PERKINS, VERE
Nicholas Crabbe (1958)
by F.W. Rolfe
Perkins, Stanhope

PERNE, DEBORAH
Pilgrimage (1915–67)
by Dorothy Richardson
Ayre, Miss

PERRANCE, MR
Pilgrimage (1915–67)
by Dorothy Richardson
Cook, Francis

PERRY, JOSEPHINE
'First Blood' (1930) and others
by F. Scott Fitzgerald
King, Ginevra

PERVIN, ISABEL
'The Blind Man' (1922)
by D.H. Lawrence
Carswell, Catherine

PESCA, PROFESSOR
The Woman in White (1860)
by Wilkie Collins
Rossetti, Gabriele

PESCOCALASCIO
The Lost Girl (1920)
by D.H. Lawrence
Picinisco, Caserta, Italy

PETER
Twelve Men (1919)
by Theodore Dreiser
McCord, Peter B.

PETER
Post Adolescence (1923)
by Robert McAlmon
McAlmon, Robert

PETER IVANOVICH
Under Western Eyes (1911)
by Joseph Conrad
Kropotkin, Peter
Tolstoy, Leo

PETERPORT
*The Story of the New Priest in
    Conception Bay* (1858)
by R.T.S. Lowell
Bay Roberts, Newfoundland

PETERS, MARION
'Babylon Revisited' (1935)
by F. Scott Fitzgerald
Smith, Rosalind

PETHEL, JAMES
'James Pethel', *Seven Men* (1919)
by Max Beerbohm
Hannay, Arthur

PETHERTON, REVD ROGER
'Happily Ever After' (1920)
by Aldous Huxley
Bevan, C.O.

PETRICK, TIMOTHY, I
'Squire Petrick's Lady' (1891)
by Thomas Hardy
Walter, Peter[1]

PETRICK, TIMOTHY, II
'Squire Petrick's Lady' (1891)
by Thomas Hardy
Walter, Peter[2]

PETT, HERBERT
The New Humpty-Dumpty (1912)
by Ford Madox Ford
Wells, H.G.

PETTIFER, Mrs
'Janet's Repentance', *Scenes of
    Clerical Life* (1857–8)
by George Eliot
Robinson, Mrs

PETULENGRO
Lavengro (1851)
by George Borrow
Smith, Ambrose

PEYROL, Jean
The Rover (1923)
by Joseph Conrad
Cervoni, Dominic

PFAFF, Father
Arrowsmith (1925)
by Sinclair Lewis
Adams, Theodore

PFAFF, Lily
Pilgrimage (1915–67)
by Dorothy Richardson
Pabst, Lily

PHILBRICK, Mercy
Mercy Philbrick's Choice (1876)
by Helen Hunt Jackson
Dickinson, Emily

PHILISTINE
Sartor Resartus (1833–4)
by Thomas Carlyle
Irving, Edward

PHILLIPS, Howard
Neutral Ground (1933)
by Helen Corke
McLeod, A.W.

PHILLIPS, Jackson
The Green Hills of Africa (1935)
by Ernest Hemingway
Percival, Philip

The PHILOSOPHER OF THE VILLA
    PLINIANA
Vivian Grey (1826–7)
by Benjamin Disraeli
Gell, Sir William

PHIPPS, Mr
'Janet's Repentance', *Scenes of
    Clerical Life* (1857–8)
by George Eliot
Bull, Mr

'The Sad Fortunes of the Revd Amos
    Barton', *Scenes of Clerical Life*
    (1857–8)
by George Eliot
**Bull, Mr
Craddock, Mr**

PHOEBUS, Gaston
Lothair (1870)
by Benjamin Disraeli
Leighton, Frederic, Lord

PICHERBOUGH, Alnus
Arrowsmith (1925)
by Sinclair Lewis
De Kleine, William

PICKWICK, Samuel
The Pickwick Papers (1836–7)
by Charles Dickens
**Foster, John
Rawes, Robert Booth**

PICKWICK CLUB
The Pickwick Papers (1836–7)
by Charles Dickens
**British Association for the
    Advancement of Science**

PIERCE, Mr
U.S.A. (1938)
by John Dos Passos
Price, William Samson

PIERCE, Joel
Of Time and the River (1935)
by Thomas Wolfe
Dows, Olin

PIESCHI, Attilio
Suspense (1925)
by Joseph Conrad
Cervoni, Dominic

PIGNATELLI, James Knox Polk
Chosen Country (1951)
by John Dos Passos
Dos Passos, John R.

PIGNATELLI, Jay
Chosen Country (1951)
by John Dos Passos
Dos Passos, John

PILGRIM, Mr
'The Sad Fortunes of the Revd Amos
  Barton', *Scenes of Clerical Life*
  (1857–8)
by George Eliot
Bucknill, William

PINE, Randolph
The Pursuit of Love (1945)
by Nancy Mitford
Hare, Humphrey

PINE ROCK COLLEGE
The Web and the Rock (1939)
by Thomas Wolfe
Chapel Hill, North Carolina

PINFOLD, Gilbert
The Ordeal of Gilbert Pinfold (1957)
by Evelyn Waugh
Waugh, Evelyn

PINKERTON, Jim
The Wrecker (1892)
by R.L. Stevenson and Lloyd
  Osbourne
McClure, Samuel Sidney

Miss PINKERTON'S ACADEMY
Vanity Fair (1847–8)
by W.M. Thackeray
**Dr Turner's School, Chiswick Mall,
  London**

PINNEGAR, Miss
The Lost Girl (1920)
by D.H. Lawrence
Pidsley, Miss

PINTO, Mr
Lothair (1870)
by Benjamin Disraeli
Calcraft, Sir Henry

PIPCHIN, Mrs
Dombey and Son (1846–8)
by Charles Dickens
Roylance, Elizabeth

PITTMAN, Mr
'Janet's Repentance', *Scenes of
  Clerical Life* (1857–8)
by George Eliot
Greenway, Mr

PIXLEY, Randal
Love and Death (1939)
by Llewellyn Powys
Brenan, Gerald

PLACID, Sir Baptist
Coningsby (1844)
by Benjamin Disraeli
Eardley-Wilmot, Sir John

PLAGUE CITY
Arrowsmith (1925)
by Sinclair Lewis
St Lucia

PLESSINGTON, 'Aunt'
Marriage (1912)
by H.G. Wells
Webb, Beatrice

PLESSINGTON, Hubert
Marriage (1912)
by H.G. Wells
Webb, Sidney

PLEYDELL, Paul
Guy Mannering (1815)
by Sir Walter Scott
Crosbie, Andrew
Rolland, Adam

PLUMFIELD
Little Women (1868) and sequels
by Louisa M. Alcott
Temple School, Boston

Little Men (1871) and *Jo's Boys* (1886)
by Louisa M. Alcott
Sanborn's School, Concord, Massachusetts

PLUNKETT, MATTHEW
The Apes of God (1930)
by Wyndham Lewis
Strachey, Lytton

PLURABELLE, ANNA LIVIA
Finnegans Wake (1939)
by James Joyce
Joyce, Nora
Schmitz, Livia

POCKLINGTON SQUARE
'Our Street' (1848)
by W.M. Thackeray
Kensington Square, London

PODSNAP, MR
Our Mutual Friend (1864–5)
by Charles Dickens
Forster, John

POLCHESTER
The Cathedral (1922)
by Hugh Walpole
Truro, Cornwall

POLEHAMPTON
The Inheritors (1901)
by Joseph Conrad and Ford Madox Ford
Unwin, T. Fisher

POLEHUE, MR
Gin and Bitters (1931)
by Elinor Mordaunt
Walpole, Hugh

POLLOCK, GUY
Main Street (1920)
by Sinclair Lewis
Dorion, Charles T.

POLLY, ALFRED
The History of Mr Polly (1910)
by H.G. Wells
Wells, Frank
Wells, H.G.
Wells, Joseph

POLMONT, BENJAMIN
'The End of the World', *The Dawn's Delay* (1924)
by Hugh Kingsmill
Kingsmill, Hugh

P.O.M.
The Green Hills of Africa (1935)
by Ernest Hemingway
Hemingway, Pauline

POMERAY, CODY
Cassady, Neal
Visions of Cody (1960), *Big Sur* (1962) and *Desolation Angels* (1965)
by Jack Kerouac
Cassady, Neal

PONDEREVO, MR
Tono-Bungay (1909)
by H.G. Wells
Cowap, Mr

PONDEREVO, MRS
Tono-Bungay (1909)
by H.G. Wells
Cowap, Mrs
Wells, Sarah

PONDEREVO, EDWARD
Tono-Bungay (1909)
by H.G. Wells
Gissing, George
Wright, Whitaker

PONDEREVO, GEORGE
Tono-Bungay (1909)
by H.G. Wells
Wells, H.G.

PONDEREVO, MARION
Tono-Bungay (1909)
by H.G. Wells
Wells, Isabel

PONTIFEX, ALETHEA
The Way of All Flesh (1903)
by Samuel Butler
Savage, Eliza

PONTIFEX, CHRISTINA
The Way of All Flesh (1903)
by Samuel Butler
Butler, Fanny

PONTIFEX, ERNEST
The Way of All Flesh (1903)
by Samuel Butler
Butler, Samuel

PONTIFEX, GEORGE
The Way of All Flesh (1903)
by Samuel Butler
Butler, Dr Samuel

PONTIFEX, JOHN
The Way of All Flesh (1903)
by Samuel Butler
Butler, William

PONTIFEX, THEOBALD
The Way of All Flesh (1903)
by Samuel Butler
Butler, Thomas

POPPYSEED, PHILOMELA
Headlong Hall (1816)
by Thomas Love Peacock
Opie, Mrs Amelia

POPULAR SENTIMENT, MR
The Warden (1855)
by Anthony Trollope
Dickens, Charles

PORPHYRO
Rumour (1858)
by Elizabeth Sara Sheppard
Napoleon III, Emperor of France

PORSUM, SERGEANT MILL
At Heaven's Gate (1943)
by Robert Penn Warren
York, Sergeant Alvin Cullum

PORT ALBY
McDonough (1951)
by Francis T. Field
Perth Amboy, New Jersey

PORT-BREDY
Wessex novels and tales (1871–95)
by Thomas Hardy
Bridport, Dorset

PORTER, MRS JOSEPH
'Mrs Joseph Porter', *Sketches by Boz* (1836)
by Charles Dickens
Leigh, Mrs J.P.

PORTMAN, REVD DR
The History of Pendennis (1848–50)
by W.M. Thackeray
Cornish, Revd Sidney
Huysh, Revd Francis

POTT, MR
The Pickwick Papers (1836–7)
by Charles Dickens
Brougham, Lord

POTTER, THOMAS
'Making a Night of It', *Sketches by Boz* (1836)
by Charles Dickens
Potter, Charles

POVEY, CYRIL
The Old Wives' Tale (1908)
by Arnold Bennett
Bennett, Septimus

POVEY, RICHARD
The Old Wives' Tale (1908)
by Arnold Bennett
Hales, H.K.

POWER, Jack
'Grace', *Dubliners* (1914) and
    Ulysses (1922)
by James Joyce
Devin, Thomas

POWER, John
A Laodicean (1881)
by Thomas Hardy
Peto, Sir Samuel Morton

POWER, Revd Thomas
Work (1873)
by Louisa M. Alcott
Parker, Theodore

POYNTON
The Spoils of Poynton (1897)
by Henry James
Black Hall, St Giles, Oxford

The *PRAISE-ALL REVIEW*
Vivian Grey (1826–7)
by Benjamin Disraeli
The *Edinburgh Review*

PRANCE, Dr Mary
The Bostonians (1884)
by Henry James
Walker, Dr Mary

PRANG, Bishop Paul
It Can't Happen Here (1935)
by Sinclair Lewis
Coughlin, Father Charles

PRATT, Richard
'Janet's Repentance', *Scenes of
    Clerical Life* (1857–8)
by George Eliot
Bond, Mr

PRAX
The Arrow of Gold (1919)
by Joseph Conrad
Frétigny

The PREACHER AT THE RETREAT
*A Portrait of the Artist as a Young
    Man* (1916)
by James Joyce
Cullen, Father James A.

PRENDERGAST, Hon. and Revd Mr
'Janet's Repentance', *Scenes of
    Clerical Life* (1857–8)
by George Eliot
Stopford, Hon. and Revd Mr

PRENTISS, Robert
The Sun Also Rises (1926)
by Ernest Hemingway
Wescott, Glenway

PRESENT DAY
The Big Wheel (1949)
by John Nixon Brooks
Time Magazine

The PRESIDENT OF THE
    NATIONAL LABOUR
    PROTECTION LEAGUE
The Great Bread Riots (1890)
by J. St Loe Strachey
Churchill, Lord Randolph

PREST, Mrs
The Aspern Papers (1888)
by Henry James
Bronson, Katherine De Kay

PREWITT, Jim
'1939' (1960)
by Peter Taylor
Lowell, Robert

PRICE, Matthew
The Old Men at the Zoo (1961)
by Angus Wilson
King, William

PRICE, William
Mansfield Park (1814)
by Jane Austen
Austen, Charles John

VON PRIELAU-CAROLATH,
ANNA-MARIA ('MITCHKA')
'The Captain's Doll' (1923)
by D.H. Lawrence
Schreibershofen, 'Nusch'

PRIMA DONNA, LORD
Vivian Grey (1826–7)
by Benjamin Disraeli
Lennox, Lord William

PRINCE, MR
Doctor Birch and His Young Friends
(1849)
by W.M. Thackeray
Churton, Revd Edward

THE PRINCESS ('AMY EVANS')
'The Velvet Glove' (1910)
by Henry James
Wharton, Edith

PRINCESS PUFFER
Edwin Drood (1870)
by Charles Dickens
Lascar Sal

THE PRINCIPAL WRITER FOR THE
ATTACK-ALL REVIEW
Vivian Grey (1826–7)
by Benjamin Disraeli
Southey, Robert

PRINCIPLES, MR LIBERAL
See LIBERAL PRINCIPLES, Mr

PRINGLE, GUY
The Balkan Trilogy (1960–5) and *The
Levant Trilogy* (1977–80)
by Olivia Manning
Smith, R.D.

THE PRIORY
Yeast (1848)
by Charles Kingsley
Formosa Place, Cookham, Berkshire

THE PROFESSOR
The Secret Agent (1907)
by Joseph Conrad
Creaghe, Dr

Dillon, Luke
Mezzeroff, 'Professor'
Most, Johann
Rossetti, Arthur

PROPTER, WILLIAM
After Many a Summer (1939)
by Aldous Huxley
Heard, Gerald

PROSSER, DICK
The Web and the Rock (1939)
by Thomas Wolfe
Harris, Will
Rumley, Robert Parker

PROUT, MR
Stalky & Co. (1899)
by Rudyard Kipling
Pugh, Matthew Henry

PROVIS, ESTELLA
Great Expectations (1860–1)
by Charles Dickens
Ternan, Ellen

THE PROVOST
Robert Elsmere (1888)
by Mrs Humphry Ward
Jowett, Benjamin

THE PROVOST
The Cantab (1926)
by Shane Leslie
James, M.R.

PRYOR, AGNES
Shirley (1849)
by Charlotte Brontë
Wooler, Margaret

PSMITH, RUPERT
Mike (1909) and others
by P.G. Wodehouse
D'Oyly Carte, Rupert

THE PUBLISHER
Lavengro (1851)
by George Borrow
Phillips, Sir Richard

PUFF, PARTHENOPEX
Vivian Grey (1826–7)
by Benjamin Disraeli
Rogers, Samuel
Rose, William Stewart

PULLETT (NÉE DODSON), SOPHY
The Mill on the Floss (1860)
by George Eliot
Johnson, Elizabeth

PULLMAN ('Pulley')
The Childermass (1928)
by Wyndham Lewis
Joyce, James

PULPIT HILL
Look Homeward, Angel (1929)
by Thomas Wolfe
Chapel Hill, North Carolina

PUMPERNICKEL
Vanity Fair (1847–8)
by W.M. Thackeray
Weimar, Germany

PUNCH
'Baa, Baa, Black Sheep' (1888)
by Rudyard Kipling
Kipling, Rudyard

PURCHAS
Eyeless in Gaza (1936)
by Aldous Huxley
Sheppard, Hugh Richard

PURDON, FATHER
'Grace', *Dubliners* (1914)
by James Joyce
Vaughan, Father Bernard

THE PURE DROP INN, MARLOTT
Wessex novels and tales (1871–95)
by Thomas Hardy
Crown Inn, Marnhull, Dorset

PURVIS, DAISY
You Can't Go Home Again (1940)
by Thomas Wolfe
Lavis, Daisy

PYM'S PUBLICITY LTD
Murder Must Advertise (1933)
by Dorothy L. Sayers
S.H. Benson Ltd

PYNCHEON, COLONEL
The House of the Seven Gables (1851)
by Nathaniel Hawthorne
Hathorne, John
Noyes, Nicholas

PYNCHEON, JUDGE
The House of the Seven Gables (1851)
by Nathaniel Hawthorne
Upham, C.W.

Q

QUAIN, MAURICE
Maurice Quain (1897)
by Morley Roberts
Gissing, George

QUARLES, ELINOR
Point Counter Point (1928)
by Aldous Huxley
Huxley, Maria

QUARLES, PHILIP, THE YOUNGER
Point Counter Point (1928)
by Aldous Huxley
Huxley, Matthew
Mitchison, Geoffrey

QUARTERSHOT
Jude the Obscure (1895)
by Thomas Hardy
Aldershot, Hampshire

QUICKSILVER, MR
Ten Thousand a Year (1841)
by Samuel Warren
Brougham, Lord

QUIGGIN, J.G.
A Dance to the Music of Time
    (1951–76)
by Anthony Powell
Orwell, George

QUILP, DANIEL
The Old Curiosity Shop (1840–1)
by Charles Dickens
Dickens, Charles
Grimaldi, Giuseppe
Prior, 'Donkey'

QUINN, AUBERON
The Napoleon of Notting Hill (1904)
by G.K. Chesterton
Beerbohm, Max
Chesterton, G.K.

R

RACKRENT, LADY
Castle Rackrent (1800)
by Maria Edgeworth
Cathcart, Elizabeth, Lady

RACKRENT, SIR CONNOLLY ('CONDY')
Castle Rackrent (1800)
by Maria Edgeworth
Elers, Paul

RACKRENT, SIR KIT
Castle Rackrent (1800)
by Maria Edgeworth
MacGuire, Colonel Hugh

RADLETT, JASSY
The Pursuit of Love (1945) and *Love
    in a Cold Climate* (1949)
by Nancy Mitford
Mitford, Jessica

RADLETT, LINDA
The Pursuit of Love (1945) *Love in a
    Cold Climate* (1949)
by Nancy Mitford
Devonshire, Deborah, Duchess of

RAEBURN
Mr Britling Sees It Through (1916)
by H.G. Wells
Masterman, C.F.

RAEBURN, LUKE
Donovan (1882) and *We Two* (1884)
by Edna Lyall
Bradlaugh, Charles

RAFFERTY, NORA
The Dust Which is God (1941)
by William Rose Benét
Benét, Theresa Frances

RAGNA, CARDINAL
Hadrian VII (1904)
by F.W. Rolfe
Rampolla, Mariano

RAINGO, LORD
Lord Raingo (1926)
by Arnold Bennett
Bennett, Arnold
Rhondda, 1st Viscount
Rickards, Edwin Alfred

RAMBROOKE, LORD
Coningsby (1844)
by Benjamin Disraeli
Rosslyn, Lord

RAMPION, MARK
Point Counter Point (1928)
by Aldous Huxley
Lawrence, D.H.

RAMPION, MARY
Point Counter Point (1928)
by Aldous Huxley
Lawrence, Frieda

RAMSAY, MR
To the Lighthouse (1927)
by Virginia Woolf
Stephen, Sir Leslie

RAMSAY, MRS
To the Lighthouse (1927)
by Virginia Woolf
Stephen, Julia

RAMSAY, JAMES
To the Lighthouse (1927)
by Virginia Woolf
Stephen, Adrian

RAMSAY, PRUE
To the Lighthouse (1927)
by Virginia Woolf
Duckworth, Stella

RAMSBOTTOM, MR
Crotchet Castle (1831)
by Thomas Love Peacock
Newton, John Frank

RANDAL, JOHN ('MR LEOPOLD')
Esther Waters (1894)
by George Moore
Appleby, Joseph

RANDALL, MERRILL
Desolation Angels (1965)
by Jack Kerouac
Merrill, James Ingram

RANDALL, WILLIS, I
Washington Jitters (1936)
by Dalton Trumbo
Hearst, William Randolph

RANDOLPH, JAMES HEYWARD ('JIM')
The Web and the Rock (1939)
by Thomas Wolfe
Folger, Bill

RANDOM, VARNUM
Desolation Angels (1965)
by Jack Kerouac
Jarrell, Randall

RANSOM, BASIL
The Bostonians (1884)
by Henry James
Lamar, Lucius Q.C.

RASSENTLOW, COUNTESS JOHANNA
('HANNELE') ZU
'The Captain's Doll' (1923)
by D.H. Lawrence
Lawrence, Frieda

RAT
The Wind in the Willows (1908)
by Kenneth Grahame
Atkinson, Edward
Furnivall, F.J.
Henley, W.E.

RATCLIFFE, SILAS P.
Democracy (1880)
by Henry Adams
Blaine, James G.

RATNER, JAMES JULIUS
The Apes of God (1930)
by Wyndham Lewis
Joyce, James

RAVELSTON, PHILIP
Keep the Aspidistra Flying (1936)
by George Orwell
Rees, Sir Richard

RAVENSWOOD, EDGAR, MASTER OF
The Bride of Lammermoor (1819)
by Sir Walter Scott
Rutherford, Archibald, Lord

RAWLINGS, RICHARD
*The Ladder of Gold: An English
    Story* (1850)
by Robert Bell
Hudson, George

RAWNG, HYMAN
The Web and the Rock (1939)
by Thomas Wolfe
Liveright, Horace

RAXTON CHURCH
Aylwin (1899)
by Theodore Watts-Dunton
Pakefield Church, Suffolk

RAYCIE, LEWIS
'False Dawn', *Old New York* (1924)
by Edith Wharton
Jones, George Frederic
Norton, Charles Eliot

RAYMOND, Lord
The Last Man (1826)
by Mary Wollstonecraft Shelley
Byron, Lord

RAYNER, David
The Four Winds of Love: The South Wind (1937)
by Compton Mackenzie
Lawrence, D.H.

RAYNER, Hildegarde
The Four Winds of Love: The South Wind (1937)
by Compton Mackenzie
Lawrence, Frieda

RAYNES, Edward
The Buffoon (1916)
by Louis Wilkinson
Wilkinson, Louis

RAYNOR, Mrs
'Janet's Repentance', *Scenes of Clerical Life* (1857–8)
by George Eliot
Wallington, Nancy

RAZUMOV, Kirylo Sidorovitch
Under Western Eyes (1911)
by Joseph Conrad
Stepniak, Sergius

THE READER
The Mather Story (1953)
by John Prebble
Beaverbrook, Lord

REBECCA
Ivanhoe (1819)
by Sir Walter Scott
Gratz, Rebecca

THE RED LION
A Passionate Pilgrim (1875)
by Henry James
The Albany, Piccadilly, London

THE RED LION
'Janet's Repentance', *Scenes of Clerical Life* (1857–8)
by George Eliot
The Bull Hotel, Nuneaton, Warwickshire

THE RED QUEEN
Through the Looking-Glass (1872)
by Lewis Carroll
Prickett, Mary

REDBURN, Hattie
Kangaroo (1923)
by D.H. Lawrence
Radford, Dollie

REDFERN, Nancy
Fernhurst (1971)
by Gertrude Stein
Stein, Gertrude

REDFERN, Philip
Fernhurst (1971)
by Gertrude Stein
Hodder, Alfred

REDGAUNTLET, Sir Arthur
(Darsie Latimer)
Redgauntlet (1824)
by Sir Walter Scott
Clerk, William
Kerr, Charles

REDGAUNTLET, Lilias
Redgauntlet (1824)
by Sir Walter Scott
Belsches, Williamina

REDGAUNTLET, Sir Robert
Redgauntlet (1824)
by Sir Walter Scott
Grierson, Sir Robert

REDGOLD, Mrs
The Gold-Worshippers (1851)
by Emma Robinson
Manning, Maria

REDING, Charles
Loss and Gain (1848)
by J.H. Newman
Newman, J.H.

REDRUTIN
'A Mere Interlude' (1913)
by Thomas Hardy
Redruth, Cornwall

REED, John
Jane Eyre (1847)
by Charlotte Brontë
Sidgwick, John Benson

REINECKER
The Station (1928)
by Robert Byron
Reitlinger, Gerald

REISENBERG, Grand Duke of
Vivian Grey (1826–7)
by Benjamin Disraeli
Saxe-Weimar, Charles Augustus, Grand Duke of

REMINGTON, Mrs
The New Machiavelli (1911)
by H.G. Wells
Wells, Sarah

REMINGTON, Arthur
The New Machiavelli (1911)
by H.G. Wells
Wells, Joseph

REMINGTON, Margaret
The New Machiavelli (1911)
by H.G. Wells
Wells, Catherine ('Jane')

REMINGTON, Richard
The New Machiavelli (1911)
by H.G. Wells
Wells, H.G.

RENATA
Across the River and into the Trees (1950)
by Ernest Hemingway
Ivancich, Adriana

RENNELL, Wilfred
Miranda Masters (1926)
by John Cournos
Gray, Cecil

RETLOW
See Mühler

THE *REVERBERATOR*
The Reverberator (1888)
by Henry James
The World

REYNARD, Stephen (afterwards Earl of Wessex)
'The First Countess of Wessex' (1891)
by Thomas Hardy
Ilchester, Stephen Fox, 1st Earl of

RHEINHARDT, 'Pap'
Look Homeward, Angel (1929)
by Thomas Wolfe
Hildebrand, 'Daddy'

RHODES, Arthur
Diana of the Crossways (1884)
by George Meredith
Meredith, George

RHODES, Maurice
A Domestic Animal (1970)
by Francis King
Grant, Duncan

RHYS, Owen
The Plumed Serpent (1926)
by D.H. Lawrence
Bynner, Witter

T.T. RICEYMAN, Bookshop
Riceyman Steps (1923)
by Arnold Bennett
T. James & Co.

RICEYMAN SQUARE
Riceyman Steps (1923)
by Arnold Bennett
Granville Square, London

RICEYMAN STEPS
Riceyman Steps (1923)
by Arnold Bennett
**Plum Pudding Steps, Clerkenwell,
London**

RICH, Cristina
The Dark Island (1934)
by Victoria Sackville-West
Sackville-West, Victoria

RICHARDSON, Solon
Half a Loaf (1931)
by Grace Hegger Lewis
Hunt, Frazier

RICHMAN, Danny
Book of Dreams (1960) and *Visions
of Gerard* (1963)
by Jack Kerouac
Ferlinghetti, Lawrence

RICHMOND, Augustus
The Adventures of Harry Richmond
(1871)
by George Meredith
**Allen, John and Charles
Meredith, Augustus Urmiston
Meredith, Melchisedek**

RIDDLE, Mrs Evans
Elmer Gantry (1927)
by Sinclair Lewis
Towne, Elizabeth

RIDLEY, Laura
'St Mawr' (1925)
by D.H. Lawrence
Brett, Dorothy

RIGAUD, Monsieur
Little Dorrit (1855–7)
by Charles Dickens
**Laçenaire, Pierre-François
Napoleon III, Emperor of France
Wainewright, Thomas Griffiths**

RIGBY, Nicholas
Coningsby (1844)
by Benjamin Disraeli
Croker, John Wilson

RIMMLE, Mrs
'Europe' (1899)
by Henry James
Palfrey, Mary Ann

RINALDI, Rinaldo
A Farewell to Arms (1929)
by Ernest.Hemingway
Serena, Enrico

RINGSWORTH
Wessex novels and tales (1871–95)
by Thomas Hardy
Ringstead Bay, Dorset

RINGWOOD, Lord
The Adventures of Philip (1861–2)
by W.M. Thackeray
Fitzhardinge, Lord

RIORDAN, Mrs Dante
*A Portrait of the Artist as a Young
Man* (1916) and *Ulysses* (1922)
by James Joyce
Conway, Mrs Hearn

RITCHIE-HOOK, Ben
The *Sword of Honour* trilogy
(1952–61)
by Evelyn Waugh
**Carton de Wiart, General Adrian
St Clair-Morford, Major-General
Albert**

RIVERMOUTH
The Story of a Bad Boy (1870)
by T.B. Aldrich
Portsmouth, New Hampshire

RIVERS, Mr
*De Vere; or The Man of
Independence* (1827)
by Robert Plumer Ward
Ward, Robert Plumer

RIVERS, Diana
Jane Eyre (1847)
by Charlotte Brontë
Brontë, Emily

RIVERS, G.H.
The Private Life of Henry Maitland
(1912)
by Morley Roberts
Wells, H.G.

RIVERS, HELEN
The Genius and the Goddess (1955)
by Aldous Huxley
Huxley, Maria

RIVERS, MARY
Jane Eyre (1847)
by Charlotte Brontë
Brontë, Anne

RIVERS, MORDAUNT
A Babe in Bohemia (1889)
by Frank Danby
Brooks, Reginald Shirley

RIVERS, ST JOHN EYRE
Jane Eyre (1847)
by Charlotte Brontë
Martyn, Henry
Nussey, Revd Henry

ROBERTSHAW, JOHN A.
Arrowsmith (1925)
by Sinclair Lewis
Lombard, Warren P.

ROBIN HILL
The Man of Property (1906)
by John Galsworthy
Coombe Warren, Surrey

ROBTHETILL, RODERICK
Crotchet Castle (1831)
by Thomas Love Peacock
Lloyd, James

ROCHESTER, EDWARD FAIRFAX
Jane Eyre (1847)
by Charlotte Brontë
Greg, William Rathbone

RODDICE, ALEXANDER
Women in Love (1920)
by D.H. Lawrence
Morrell, Philip

RODDICE, HERMIONE
Women in Love (1920)
by D.H. Lawrence
Chambers, Jessie
Morrell, Lady Ottoline

RODEN, EDMUND
The Private Life of Henry Maitland
(1912)
by Morley Roberts
Clodd, Edward

RODFITTEN, LADY
'Maltby and Braxton', *Seven Men*
(1919)
by Max Beerbohm
Londonderry, Lady

RODNEY, FREDERICK
The Four Winds of Love: The South
Wind (1937)
by Compton Mackenzie
Cannan, Gilbert

RODNEY, WILLIAM
Night and Day (1919)
by Virginia Woolf
Headlam, Walter

ROEHAMPTON, LADY
The Edwardians (1930)
by Victoria Sackville-West
Westmorland, Sybil, Countess of

ROEHAMPTON, LORD
Endymion (1880)
by Benjamin Disraeli
Palmerston, Lord

ROGET, MARIE
The Mystery of Marie Roget (1842)
by Edgar Allan Poe
Rogers, Mary Cecilia

ROKEBY, MATILDA
See MATILDA OF ROKEBY

ROLFE
The Blue Belles of England (1842)
by Frances Trollope
Mathias, Thomas James

ROLFE, Hughie
In the Year of the Jubilee (1894) and
    The Whirlpool (1897)
by George Gissing
Gissing, Walter Leonard

ROLLE, Father Robert
The Cantab (1926)
by Shane Leslie
Benson, R.H.

ROLLIN, Michel
Of Human Bondage (1915)
by W. Somerset Maugham
Collin, Raphaël

ROMANOVICH, Princess
    Marousha ('Sasha')
Orlando (1928)
by Virginia Woolf
Trefusis, Violet

ROMERO, Pedro
The Sun Also Rises (1926)
by Ernest Hemingway
Ordóñez, Cayetano

ROMFREY, Everard
Beauchamp's Career (1876)
by George Meredith
Berkeley, Grantley

RONNY
Down There on a Visit (1962)
by Christopher Isherwood
Bower, Tony

RONTINI, Bruno
Time Must Have a Stop (1944)
by Aldous Huxley
Heard, Gerald

THE ROOKERY, Cheverel Manor
'Mr Gilfil's Love Story', *Scenes of
    Clerical Life* (1857–8)
by George Eliot
**North Walk, Arbury Hall,
    Warwickshire**

ROOKINGTON PARK
The Hand of Ethelberta (1876)
by Thomas Hardy
Hurn Court, Bournemouth, Dorset

ROOKWOOD HALL
Rookwood: A Romance (1834)
by W. Harrison Ainsworth
Cuckfield Place, Sussex

ROOT, Raoul
The Buffoon (1916)
by Louis Wilkinson
Pound, Ezra

ROSA, Aunty
'Baa, Baa, Black Sheep' (1888)
by Rudyard Kipling
Holloway, Sarah

ROSALBA
Extraordinary Women (1928)
by Compton Mackenzie
Franchetti, Mimi

THE ROSAMUNDA
See Bateman, Miss

ROSBRIN, Lord
Florence Macarthy (1818)
by Lady Sydney Morgan
Blessington, Lord

ROSCORLA, Richard and Rachel
Pilgrimage (1915–67)
by Dorothy Richardson
Penrose, Mr and Miss

THE ROSE
Through the Looking-Glass (1872)
by Lewis Carroll
Liddell, Rhoda

ROSE, Mr
The New Republic (1877)
by W.H. Mallock
Pater, Walter

ROSE, George Arthur
Hadrian VII (1904)
by F.W. Rolfe
Rolfe, F.W.

ROSE, Jane
Hans Frost (1929)
by Hugh Walpole
Woolf, Virginia

ROSE, Louisa
The Anglo-Catholic (1929)
by Shane Leslie
Lewis, Rosa

ROSEN, Mr
The Web and the Rock (1939)
by Thomas Wolfe
Goodman, Edwin

ROSEN, Walter
Aaron's Rod (1922)
by D.H. Lawrence
Stein, Leo

ROSETTI, Maria
More Women Than Men (1933)
by I. Compton-Burnett
Péchinet, Marie

ROSS, J. Arnold
Oil! (1927)
by Upton Sinclair
Sinclair, Harry Ford

ROSS, Sybil
Democracy (1880)
by Henry Adams
Chapman, Fanny

ROSSETER
Adam Bede (1859)
by George Eliot
Rocester, Derbyshire

ROSSITER, Lady
See Seton, Sally

ROSWAL
The Talisman (1825)
by Sir Walter Scott
Maida

ROTHERHAM, Sir Henry
I Live Under a Black Sun (1937)
by Edith Sitwell
Sitwell, Sir George

ROUGETNOIRBOURG
The Kickleburys on the Rhine (1850)
by W.M. Thackeray
Homburg, Hesse, Germany

ROUGHBOROUGH
The Way of All Flesh (1903)
by Samuel Butler
Shrewsbury School

ROUNCEWELL, Mrs
Bleak House (1852–3)
by Charles Dickens
Dickens, Elizabeth[1]

ROURKE, The Mighty
Twelve Men (1919)
by Theodore Dreiser
Burke, Mike

ROY-TOWN
Wessex novels and tales (1871–95)
by Thomas Hardy
Troy Town, Dorset

ROYAL SUSSEX HOTEL
The *Clayhanger* trilogy (1910–16)
by Arnold Bennett
Royal York Hotel, Brighton

VON RÜDIGER, Clotilde
The Tragic Comedians (1880)
by George Meredith
von Racowitza, Helene

RUIZ, Gaspar
'Gaspar Ruiz', *A Set of Six* (1908)
by Joseph Conrad
Benavides

RUMFORD, Lydia (Aunt Lyde)
Chosen Country (1951)
by John Dos Passos
Charles, Mrs J.W.

RUNCIBLE, Agatha
Vile Bodies (1930)
by Evelyn Waugh
Ponsonby, Elizabeth

RUNNINGBROOK, TRACY
Sandra Belloni (Emilia in England)
   (1864)
by George Meredith
Swinburne, Algernon Charles

RUSSELTON, JOHN
Pelham (1828)
by Bulwer Lytton
Brummell, Beau

THE RUSSIAN AMBASSADOR
Coningsby (1844)
by Benjamin Disraeli
Lieven, Prince

THE RUSSIAN AMBASSADRESS
Coningsby (1844)
by Benjamin Disraeli
Lieven, Princess

THE RUSSIAN ARCHDUKE
Vivian Grey (1826–7)
by Benjamin Disraeli
Esterházy, Prince Paul Anton

RUTH
An Island Cabin (1902)
by Arthur Henry
Dreiser, Sara Osborne White

RUTH
Dawn (1931)
by Theodore Dreiser
Dreiser, Theresa

RUTHERFORD, MARK
*The Autobiography of Mark
   Rutherford* (1881)
by Mark Rutherford
White, William Hale

RUTHIE
Down There on a Visit (1962)
by Christopher Isherwood
Connolly, Jean

RUTHVEN, LORD
The Vampyre: A Tale (1819)
by J.W. Polidori
Byron, Lord

RYDER, MR
Brideshead Revisited (1945)
by Evelyn Waugh
Waugh, Arthur

RYDER, JAPHY
The Dharma Bums (1958)
by Jack Kerouac
Snyder, Gary

S

SACKBUT, RODERICK
Nightmare Abbey (1818)
by Thomas Love Peacock
Southey, Robert

SACKVILLE HOTEL
The Anglo-Catholic (1929)
by Shane Leslie
Cavendish Hotel, London

THE SACRED GROVE
Tono-Bungay (1909)
by H.G. Wells
The Academy

ST ANDREW'S COLLEGE
Hadrian VII (1904)
by F.W. Rolfe
Scotch College, Rome

ST ANTHONY'S
The Preparatory School Murder
   (1934)
by Richard Macnaughtan
**Arnold House, Llanddulas,
   Denbighshire**

ST BARBE
Endymion (1880)
by Benjamin Disraeli
**Carlyle, Thomas
Hayward, Abraham
Thackeray, W.M.**

ST BUNGAY, Duke of
Can You Forgive Her? (1864)
by Anthony Trollope
Lansdowne, Lord

ST GENEVIÈVE (seat of Eustace
    Lyle)
Coningsby (1844)
by Benjamin Disraeli
Garendon Park, Leicestershire

ST JEROME, Lady
Lothair (1870)
by Benjamin Disraeli
Herbert, Elizabeth, Lady

ST JEROME, Lord
Lothair (1870)
by Benjamin Disraeli
Howard, Lord

ST JULIANS, Lady
Coningsby (1844) and *Sybil* (1845)
by Benjamin Disraeli
Jersey, Countess of

ST LAUNCE'S
A Pair of Blue Eyes (1873)
by Thomas Hardy
Launceston, Cornwall

DE ST LEON, Marguerite
St Leon (1799)
by William Godwin
Wollstonecraft, Mary

ST LUKE'S SQUARE
The *Clayhanger* trilogy (1910–16)
by Arnold Bennett
**St John's Square, Burslem,
    Staffordshire**

ST LYS, Aubrey
Sybil (1845)
by Benjamin Disraeli
Faber, Frederick William

ST MICHEL
Charles Auchester (1853)
by Elizabeth Sara Sheppard
Costa, Sir Michael

ST OGG'S
The Mill on the Floss (1860)
by George Eliot
Gainsborough, Lincolnshire

ST PHILIP'S
The Rainbow (1915)
by D.H. Lawrence
**Eastwood British School,
    Nottinghamshire**

DE ST PIERRE, Zélie
Villette (1853)
by Charlotte Brontë
Blanche, Mademoiselle

ST PROSE, Mr Justice
Vivian Grey (1826–7)
by Benjamin Disraeli
Park, James Alan

ST SILAS
Jude the Obscure (1895)
by Thomas Hardy
St Barnabas, Oxford

ST VITUS, Vere
Post Adolescence (1923)
by Robert McAlmon
Millay, Edna St Vincent

SALEM HOUSE
David Copperfield (1849–50)
by Charles Dickens
**Wellington House Academy,
    London**

The SALLOW GENTLEMAN
Paul Clifford (1830)
by Bulwer Lytton
Huskisson, William

SALT, Stella
The Roaring Queen (1973)
by Wyndham Lewis
West, Rebecca

SALTRAM, Frank
'The Coxon Fund' (1894)
by Henry James
Coleridge, Samuel Taylor

SALTREAM, Lord
Godolphin (1833)
by Bulwer Lytton
**Ward, John William, 1st Earl of
  Dudley**

SAMBIR
Almayer's Folly (1895)
by Joseph Conrad
Berau, Borneo

SAMGRASS, Mr
Brideshead Revisited (1945)
by Evelyn Waugh
Bowra, Maurice

SAMPSON, Dominie
Guy Mannering (1815)
by Sir Walter Scott
Sanson, James
Thomson, George

SAN MARTINO, Duchess of
South Wind (1917)
by Norman Douglas
Snow, Mrs

SAN REMO, Hotel
The Plumed Serpent (1926)
by D.H. Lawrence
Hotel Monte Carlo, Mexico City

SAN SALVATORE
The Enchanted April (1922)
by 'Elizabeth'
The Castello, Portofino, Italy

SAN SPIRITO
The Trail of the Hawk (1915)
by Sinclair Lewis
Benicia, California

SAN TOMÉ
Nostromo (1904)
by Joseph Conrad
San Tomé, Portuguese Guinea

SANDBOURNE
Wessex novels and tales (1871–95)
by Thomas Hardy
Bournemouth, Dorset

SANDYFORD, Lord
Sir Andrew Wylie (1822)
by John Galt
Blessington, Lord

SANDYSHORE
'Carrots': Just a Little Boy (1878)
by Mrs Molesworth
Fleetwood, Lancashire

SANGER, Albert
The Constant Nymph (1924)
by Margaret Kennedy
John, Augustus

SANTIAGO
The Old Man and the Sea (1952)
by Ernest Hemingway
Gutiérrez, Carlos
Saunders, Eddie

SARASON, Lee
It Can't Happen Here (1935)
by Sinclair Lewis
Clements, Robert E.

SARKELD
The Adventures of Harry Richmond
  (1871)
by George Meredith
Neuwied, Germany

SARTI
'Mr Gilfil's Love Story', *Scenes of
  Clerical Life* (1857–8)
by George Eliot
Motta, Signor

SARTI, Caterina
'Mr Gilfil's Love Story', *Scenes of
  Clerical Life* (1857–8)
by George Eliot
Shilton, Sally

SARTORIS, Colonel John
The Unvanquished (1938)
by William Faulkner
Falkner, William Cuthbert

SATCHEL, Stella Summersby
The Passionate Friends (1913)
by H.G. Wells
Richardson, Dorothy

SATIS HOUSE
Great Expectations (1860–1)
by Charles Dickens
Restoration House, Rochester, Kent

SAUNDERS, Mr
The New Republic (1877)
by W.H. Mallock
Clifford, W.K.

SAUNDERS, Alexander
See FAIRFORD, Alexander

SAUVETERRE, Fabrice, Duc de
The Pursuit of Love (1945)
by Nancy Mitford
Palewski, Gaston

SAVAGE, Captain
Peter Simple (1834)
by Frederick Marryat
Cochrane, Admiral Thomas

SAVAGE, Naomi
Heritage (1984)
by Anthony West
West, Rebecca

SAVAGE, Richard
Heritage (1984)
by Anthony West
West, Anthony

SAVAGE, Stephen
Lions and Shadows (1938)
by Christopher Isherwood
Spender, Stephen

SAWSTON
Where Angels Fear to Tread (1905)
    and *The Longest Journey* (1907)
by E.M. Forster
Tonbridge, Kent

SAWSTON SCHOOL
The Longest Journey (1907)
by E.M. Forster
Tonbridge School, Kent

SAXTON, Mr
The White Peacock (1911)
by D.H. Lawrence
Chambers, Edmund

SAXTON, Emily
The White Peacock (1911)
by D.H. Lawrence
Chambers, Jessie

SAXTON, George
The White Peacock (1911)
by D.H. Lawrence
Chambers, Alan
Neville, G.H.

SAYBROOK, Tom
On the Road (1957)
by Jack Kerouac
Holmes, John Clellon

SAYULA
The Plumed Serpent (1926)
by D.H. Lawrence
Chapala, Mexico

SAYWELL, Revd Arthur
The Virgin and the Gipsy (1930)
by D.H. Lawrence
Weekley, Ernest

SCAMPERDALE, Lord
Mr Sponge's Sporting Tour (1853)
by R.S. Surtees
Chaytor, Sir William

SCARLET JEM
Paul Clifford (1830)
by Bulwer Lytton
Scarlett, Sir James

SCARVE, John
The Miser's Daughter (1842)
by W. Harrison Ainsworth
Elwes, John

SCATCHERD, Miss
Jane Eyre (1847)
by Charlotte Brontë
Andrews, Miss

SCHAEFFER, Miriam
The Marble Faun (1860)
by Nathaniel Hawthorne
Salomons, Mrs

SCHÄFER, Wilbur
'Behind the Scenes', *Ashenden; or
    The British Agent* (1928)
by W. Somerset Maugham
Francis, David Rowland

SCHEIB, Ernest
'Emmanuela', *A Gallery of Women*
    (1929)
by Theodore Dreiser
Krog, Fritz

SCHELM, Slim
Nicholas Crabbe (1958)
by F.W. Rolfe
Lane, John

SCHLEGEL, Helen
Howards End (1910)
by E.M. Forster
Dickinson, The Misses
Woolf, Virginia

SCHLEGEL, Margaret
Howards End (1910)
by E.M. Forster
Bell, Vanessa
Dickinson, The Misses

von SCHLIPPENSCHLOPP, Ottilia
The Confessions of Fitz-Boodle
    (1852)
by W.M. Thackeray
von Pappenheim, Jenny

SCHMIDT
The Private Life of Henry Maitland
    (1912)
by Morley Roberts
Bertz, Eduard

SCHOMBERG'S HOTEL
Lord Jim (1900) and *Victory* (1915)
by Joseph Conrad
Hotel du Louvre, Singapore

SCHOOL FOR UTILITY CULTURES
Of Time and the River (1935)
by Thomas Wolfe
New York University

SCHROEDER, Lina
Mr Norris Changes Trains (1935)
    and *Goodbye to Berlin* (1939)
by Christopher Isherwood
Thurau, Meta

SCHRYHART, Norman
The Titan (1914)
by Theodore Dreiser
Widener, Peter A.B.

SCIARRA, Count
'A Luncheon Party', *Half a Minute's
    Silence and Other Stories* (1925)
by Maurice Baring
Pasolini, Count

SCOGAN, Mr
Crome Yellow (1921)
by Aldous Huxley
Douglas, Norman
Russell, Bertrand

SCOTT, Cyril
Aaron's Rod (1922)
by D.H. Lawrence
Gray, Cecil

SCOTT, Cyril
Immaturity (1930)
by George Bernard Shaw
Lawson, Cecil

SCRIMPTON
'Audrey Satchel and the Parson'
    (1894)
by Thomas Hardy
Frampton, Dorset

SCRIVEN, MARY
The Memorial (1932)
by Christopher Isherwood
Mangeot, Olive

SCROPE, HENRY
All Men are Enemies (1933)
by Richard Aldington
Blunt, Wilfrid Scawen

SCUDAMORE
Vestal Fire (1927)
by Compton Mackenzie
Jerome, Thomas Spencer

SEAL, BASIL
Black Mischief (1932), *Scoop* (1938)
and *Put Out More Flags* (1942)
by Evelyn Waugh
Murray, Basil
Rodd, Peter

SEDLEY, AMELIA
Vanity Fair (1847–8)
by W.M. Thackeray
Brookfield, Jane
Carmichael-Smyth, Anne
Thackeray, Isabella

SEDLEY, JOHN
Vanity Fair (1847–8)
by W.M. Thackeray
Langslow, Robert

SEDLEY, JOSEPH
Vanity Fair (1847–8)
by W.M. Thackeray
Shakespear, George Trant

SELBY
Sons and Lovers (1913)
by D.H. Lawrence
Brinsley Colliery

SELBY, WILL
'Goose Fair' (1914)
by D.H. Lawrence
Taylor, Lewis

SELDEN, LAWRENCE
The House of Mirth (1905)
by Edith Wharton
Berry, Walter
Gregory, Eliot
Winthrop, Egerton

SELWYN, LADY AUGUSTA
Glenarvon (1816)
by Lady Caroline Lamb
Collier, Lady
Jersey, Countess of

SEMPLE, LILLIAN
The Financier (1912)
by Theodore Dreiser
Gamble, Susan Guttridge

SEPHORA
'The Secret Sharer', *'Twixt Land and
Sea* (1912)
by Joseph Conrad
Cutty Sark

SERAPHAEL
Charles Auchester (1853)
by Elizabeth Sara Sheppard
Mendelssohn, Felix

SETON, SALLY (LADY ROSSITER)
Mrs Dalloway (1925)
by Virginia Woolf
Vaughan, Madge

SEVERN, EDWARD
'The Old Adam' (1934)
by D.H. Lawrence
Lawrence, D.H.

SEYDON, DR
The New Republic (1877)
by W.H. Mallock
Liddon, H.P.
Pusey, E.B.

SEYMOUR, MRS
Glenarvon (1816)
by Lady Caroline Lamb
Bessborough, Lady
Kinnaird, Mrs Maria
Melbourne, Lady

SEYMOUR, FRANCES (AFTERWARDS
  LADY TRELAWNEY)
Glenarvon (1816)
by Lady Caroline Lamb
Morpeth, Georgiana, Lady

SEYMOUR, LEWIS
A Modern Lover (1883)
by George Moore
Hawkins, Lewis Weldon

SEYMOUR, SOPHIA
Glenarvon (1816)
by Lady Caroline Lamb
Granville, Lady

SEYMOUR, VALÉRIE
The Well of Loneliness (1928)
by Radclyffe Hall
Barney, Natalie Clifford

SHAKEFOREST TOWERS
'What the Shepherd Saw' (1913)
by Thomas Hardy
Clatford Hall, Wiltshire

SHALFORD, EDWIN
Kipps (1905)
by H.G. Wells
Hyde, Edwin

SHAMEFOOT, MRS
Vainglory (1915)
by Ronald Firbank
Forbes, Lady Angela

SHANDON, CAPTAIN
The History of Pendennis (1848–50)
by W.M. Thackeray
Maginn, William

SHANTSEE, RUMBLESACK
Crotchet Castle (1831)
by Thomas Love Peacock
Southey, Robert

SHARP, BECKY
Vanity Fair (1847–8)
by W.M. Thackeray
Morgan, Sydney, Lady
Reviss, Theresa

SHARP, JAWSTER
Coningsby (1844)
by Benjamin Disraeli
Bright, John

SHARPE, BOND
Henrietta Temple (1837)
by Benjamin Disraeli
Crockford, William

SHARPTON, ELGOOD
Michael Armstrong, the Factory Boy
  (1840)
by Frances Trollope
Needham, Ellice

SHASTON
Wessex novels and tales (1871–95)
by Thomas Hardy
Shaftesbury, Dorset

SHATOV, AMABEL
Pilgrimage (1915–67)
by Dorothy Richardson
Grad, Avice Veronica

SHATOV, MICHAEL
Pilgrimage (1915–67)
by Dorothy Richardson
Grad, Benjamin

SHAUN
Finnegans Wake (1939)
by James Joyce
De Valera, Éamon
Ford, John
Joyce, Stanislaus

SHAWCROSS, HAMER
Fame is the Spur (1940)
by Howard Spring
Macdonald, Ramsay

SHEARWATER, JAMES
Antic Hay (1923)
by Aldous Huxley
Haldane, J.B.S.

SHELMERDINE, Marmaduke
   Bonthrop
Orlando (1928)
by Virginia Woolf
Nicolson, Sir Harold

SHEM
Finnegans Wake (1939)
by James Joyce
Ford, James
Joyce, James

SHENE, Mr
The Heir of Redclyffe (1853)
by C.M. Yonge
Dyce, William

SHEPHEARD'S HOTEL
Vile Bodies (1930)
by Evelyn Waugh
Cavendish Hotel, London

SHEPPERTON
'The Sad Fortunes of the Revd Amos
   Barton', *Scenes of Clerical Life*
   (1857–8)
by George Eliot
Chilvers Coton, Warwickshire

SHEPPERTON, Randy
The Web and the Rock (1939) and
   You Can't Go Home Again (1940)
by Thomas Wolfe
Wheaton, Ralph

SHERARDY, Dr
Aaron's Rod (1922)
by D.H. Lawrence
Feroze, Dr Dhunjabhi Mullan

SHERBORNE, Mr
Vivian Grey (1826–7)
by Benjamin Disraeli
D'Israeli, Isaac

SHERIDAN, Mrs
'The Garden Party' (1922)
by Katherine Mansfield
Beauchamp, Annie

SHERIDAN, Paul
Transition (1895)
by Emma Brooke
Webb, Sidney

SHERMAN, Mrs
John Sherman (1891)
by W.B. Yeats
Yeats, Susan

SHERMAN, John
John Sherman (1891)
by W.B. Yeats
Middleton, Henry
Yeats, W.B.

SHERRARD, Mr
The Cantab (1926)
by Shane Leslie
Sheppard, J.T.

SHERTON ABBAS
Wessex novels and tales (1871–95)
by Thomas Hardy
Sherborne, Dorset

SHINDY, Captain
The Book of Snobs (1848)
by W.M. Thackeray
Price, Stephen

The SHIP
The Shadow-Line (1917)
by Joseph Conrad
Otago

SHIPLEY HALL
Lady Chatterley's Lover (1928)
by D.H. Lawrence
Sutton Scarsdale Hall, Derbyshire

SHOBBE, Mr
Death of a Hero (1929)
by Richard Aldington
Ford, Ford Madox

SHODBUTT, Samuel
The Roaring Queen (1973)
by Wyndham Lewis
Bennett, Arnold

SHOFORTH
The Scarlet Shadow (1907)
by Walter Hurt
Shoaf, George

SHORTLANDS
Women in Love (1920)
by D.H. Lawrence
**Lamb Close House, Eastwood,
  Nottinghamshire**

SHOTTSFORD FORUM
Wessex novels and tales (1871–95)
by Thomas Hardy
Blandford Forum, Dorset

SHRAPNEL, DR
Beauchamp's Career (1876)
by George Meredith
Hearne, Dr Edwin

SHRIKE
The Day of the Locust (1933)
by Nathanael West
Mencken, H.L.

THE SIB
The Apes of God (1930)
by Wyndham Lewis
Leverson, Ada

SIBLEY, JOE
Trilby (1894)
by George Du Maurier
Whistler, James McNeill

SIDDERMORTON
The Wonderful Visit (1895)
by H.G. Wells
South Harting, Sussex

SIDONIA
Coningsby (1844)
by Benjamin Disraeli
**de Rothschild, Adolph
de Rothschild, Baron James Mayer
de Rothschild, Lionel Nathan
Disraeli, Benjamin
Urquhart, David**

Tancred (1847)
by Benjamin Disraeli
de Rothschild, Baron James Mayer

Framley Parsonage (1861)
by Anthony Trollope
Disraeli, Benjamin

THE *SIGNAL*
The *Clayhanger* trilogy (1910–16)
by Arnold Bennett
The *Staffordshire Sentinel*

SILK, AMBROSE
Put Out More Flags (1942)
by Evelyn Waugh
Howard, Brian

SILVA, T.J.H.
Arrowsmith (1925)
by Sinclair Lewis
Hinzinger, T.G.

SILVER, LONG JOHN
See LONG JOHN SILVER

THE SILVER APPLE
The Cantab (1926)
by Shane Leslie
The Golden Bough

SILVERTHORN
'The Romantic Adventures of a
  Milkmaid' (1913)
by Thomas Hardy
Silverton, Devon

SILVESTER, SIR HORACE
'A Luncheon Party', *Half a Minute's
  Silence and Other Stories* (1925)
by Maurice Baring
Vincent, Sir Edgar

SILVESTER, LADY IRENE
'A Luncheon Party', *Half a Minute's
  Silence and Other Stories* (1925)
by Maurice Baring
Vincent, Lady Helen

THE SIMEON SOCIETY
The Cantab (1926)
by Shane Leslie
The Walpole Society

SIMMONS, ROBERT ('BEE-LIPS')
To Have and Have Not (1937)
by Ernest Hemingway
Brooks, Georgie

SIMON, ATHENE
Virginia Water (1930)
by Elizabeth Jenkins
Strachey, Pernel

SIMON, DEBORAH
Virginia Water (1930)
by Elizabeth Jenkins
Strachey, Marjorie

SIMON, ROGER
Virginia Water (1930)
by Elizabeth Jenkins
Strachey, Lytton

SINCERE, DOWNIE
Washington Jitters (1936)
by Dalton Trumbo
Sinclair, Upton

SINCLAIR, MRS
The New Republic (1877)
by W.H. Mallock
Currie, Mary, Lady

SINGLETON
The Nigger of the 'Narcissus' (1897)
by Joseph Conrad
Sullivan, Daniel

SINGLETON, SAM
Roderick Hudson (1875)
by Henry James
Benson, Eugene

SINGLETON, WILL
*Sydenham; or Memoirs of a Man of
    the World* (1830)
by W. Massie
Sheridan, Richard Brinsley

SIRENE
Vestal Fire (1927)
by Compton Mackenzie
Capri

SISSON, AARON
Aaron's Rod (1922)
by D.H. Lawrence
Cooper, Thomas[2]

SKEENE, GEORGINA
'Miss Furr and Miss Skeene',
    Geography and Plays (1922)
by Gertrude Stein
Squire, Miss

SKEFFINGTON, FRANCIS
The Last Hurrah (1956)
by Edwin O'Connor
Curley, James Michael

SKENE, NED
Cashel Byron's Profession (1886)
by George Bernard Shaw
Donnelly, Ned

SKIMPOLE, HAROLD
Bleak House (1852–3)
by Charles Dickens
Hunt, Leigh

SKINNER, MISS
The Way of All Flesh (1903)
by Samuel Butler
Kennedy, Miss

SKINNER, DR SAMUEL
The Way of All Flesh (1903)
by Samuel Butler
Kennedy, Benjamin Hall

SKIONAR, MR
Crotchet Castle (1831)
by Thomas Love Peacock
Coleridge, Samuel Taylor

SLACKBRIDGE
Hard Times (1854)
by Charles Dickens
Grimshaw, Mortimer

SLAMMER, DR
The Pickwick Papers (1836–7)
by Charles Dickens
Lamert, Dr Matthew

SLEARY
Hard Times (1854)
by Charles Dickens
Clarke, John

SLINKTON, JULIUS
Hunted Down (1870)
by Charles Dickens
Wainewright, Thomas Griffiths

SLOPER, CATHERINE
Washington Square (1881)
by Henry James
Thackeray, Mary Ann

SLUM, MR
The Old Curiosity Shop (1840–1)
by Charles Dickens
Kemp, Alexander

SMEAD, MELVILLE L.
Looking Back (1933)
by Norman Douglas
Munthe, Axel

SMIKE
Nicholas Nickleby (1838–9)
by Charles Dickens
Taylor, George Ashton

SMILEY, GEORGE
The Spy Who Came in from the Cold
(1963) and others
by John Le Carré
Oldfield, Sir Maurice

SMIRKE, REVD MR
The History of Pendennis (1848–50)
by W.M. Thackeray
Cornish, Revd Sidney

SMITH, LANCELOT
Yeast (1848)
by Charles Kingsley
Kingsley, Charles

SMITH, LUCREZIA ('REZIA') WARREN
Mrs Dalloway (1925)
by Virginia Woolf
Lopokova, Lydia

SMITH, RAY
The Dharma Bums (1958)
by Jack Kerouac
Kerouac, Jack

SMITHERS
John Godfrey's Fortunes (1864)
by Bayard Taylor
Whitman, Walt

SMITHERS, ROBERT
'Making a Night of It', *Sketches by
Boz* (1836)
by Charles Dickens
Dickens, Charles

SMORLTORK, COUNT
The Pickwick Papers (1836–7)
by Charles Dickens
**Pückler-Muskau, Prince
von Raumer, Friedrich**

SNAKE, LIBERAL
See LIBERAL SNAKE

SNAPPER, JAPHET
The Old Order Changes (1886)
by W.H. Mallock
Chamberlain, Joseph

SNEAK
England and the English (1833)
by Bulwer Lytton
Westmacott, Charles Molloy

SNODGRASS, AUGUSTUS
The Pickwick Papers (1836–7)
by Charles Dickens
Potter, Charles

SNOWDON, MARQUIS OF
*Sydenham; or Memoirs of a Man of
the World* (1830)
by W. Massie
George IV

SNOWE, Lucy
Villette (1853)
by Charlotte Brontë
Brontë, Charlotte

SOFALA
'The End of the Tether' (1902)
by Joseph Conrad
SS Vidar

SOHNSPEER, Count von
Vivian Grey (1826–7)
by Benjamin Disraeli
Wellington, Duke of

SOLENTSEA
Wessex novels and tales (1871–95)
by Thomas Hardy
Southsea, Hampshire

SOLWAY, Bishop
Three Cousins (1847)
by Frances Trollope
Sumner, Charles Richard

SOMERS, Mrs
'Madame de Fleury', *Tales of
    Fashionable Life* (1809)
by Maria Edgeworth
Powys, Mrs Mary

SOMERS, Harriet
Kangaroo (1923)
by D.H. Lawrence
Lawrence, Frieda

SOMERS, Richard Lovat
Kangaroo (1923)
by D.H. Lawrence
Lawrence, D.H.

SOMERVILLE, Hugh
A Lodge in the Wilderness (1906)
by John Buchan
Buchan, John

SOPLEY, T.W.
Pugs and Peacocks (1921)
by Gilbert Cannan
Strachey, Lytton

SORREL, Hetty
Adam Bede (1859)
by George Eliot
Voce, Mary

SPAIN, Ed
The Blessing (1951)
by Nancy Mitford
Connolly, Cyril

SPANDREL
Point Counter Point (1928)
by Aldous Huxley
Baudelaire, Charles

SPANIEL ROW
Sons and Lovers (1913)
by D.H. Lawrence
Castle Gate, Nottingham

SPARKLE, Reginald
The Tuft-Hunter (1843)
by Lord William Lennox
Hook, Theodore

VON SPECK, Dorothea
The Confessions of Fitz-Boodle
    (1852)
by W.M. Thackeray
von Spiegel, Melanie

SPENDER, Humbert
The Old Order Changes (1886)
by W.H. Mallock
Spencer, Herbert

SPENLOW, Mr
David Copperfield (1849–50)
by Charles Dickens
Smithson, Charles

SPENLOW, Dora
David Copperfield (1849–50)
by Charles Dickens
Beadnell, Maria

SPIRE, Jack
Decline and Fall (1928)
by Evelyn Waugh
Squire, Sir J.C.

VON SPITTERGEN, DR
Vivian Grey (1826–7)
by Benjamin Disraeli
Abernethy, John

SPRATT, MR
'The Sad Fortunes of the Revd Amos
   Barton', *Scenes of Clerical Life*
   (1857–8)
by George Eliot
Hackett, Mr

SPRINGROVE, EDWARD
Desperate Remedies (1871)
by Thomas Hardy
Hardy, Thomas

SPROTT, VERNON
Jazz and Jasper (1928)
by William Gerhardi
Bennett, Arnold

SPRUCE, EVERARD
The *Sword of Honour* trilogy
   (1952–61)
by Evelyn Waugh
Connolly, Cyril

SQUEERS, WACKFORD
Nicholas Nickleby (1838–9)
by Charles Dickens
Shaw, William

THE SQUIRE
The Scouring of the White Horse
   (1859)
by Thomas Hughes
Atkins, Edwin Martin

STACE, ANDREW, THE ELDER
Brothers and Sisters (1929)
by I. Compton-Burnett
Rees, Rowland

STACE, CHRISTIAN
Brothers and Sisters (1929)
by I. Compton-Burnett
Compton-Burnett, James

STACE, ROBIN
Brothers and Sisters (1929)
by I. Compton-Burnett
Compton-Burnett, Noel

STACE, SOPHIA
Brothers and Sisters (1929)
by I. Compton-Burnett
Compton-Burnett, Katharine

STAGFOOT LANE
Wessex novels and tales (1871–95)
by Thomas Hardy
Hartfoot Lane, Dorset

STAHR, MINNA
The Last Tycoon (1941)
by F. Scott Fitzgerald
Fitzgerald, Zelda

STAINES, EDITH
Dodo (1893)
by E.F. Benson
Smyth, Dame Ethel

STAINFORTH, ESMÉE
Brute Streets (1954)
by John Prebble
Van der Elst, Mrs

STALKY
See CORKRAN, Arthur

STANBURY, MISS
He Knew He was Right (1869)
by Anthony Trollope
Bent, Fanny

STANCY CASTLE
A Laodicean (1881)
by Thomas Hardy
Dunster Castle, Somerset

STANHOPE, ALISON
Alison's House (1930)
by Susan Glaspell
Dickinson, Emily

STANLAKE
Two Years Ago (1857)
by Charles Kingsley
Hurlbert, W.H.

STANLEY, Ann Veronica
Ann Veronica (1909)
by H.G. Wells
Blanco White, Amber
Wells, Catherine ('Jane')

STANLEY, Peter
Ann Veronica (1909)
by H.G. Wells
Bland, Hubert

STAPLEFORD PARK
'Squire Petrick's Lady' (1891)
by Thomas Hardy
Stalbridge House, Dorset

STARBUCK, Lucas P.
Hail to the Chief (1960)
by James Reichley
Eisenhower, Dwight D.

STARELEIGH, Mr Justice
The Pickwick Papers (1836–7)
by Charles Dickens
Gaselee, Sir Stephen

STARK, Willie
All the King's Men (1946)
by Robert Penn Warren
Long, Huey P.

STARLING, Joe
Beany-Eye (1935)
by David Garnett
Hedgecock, Bill

STARWICK, Francis
Of Time and the River (1935)
by Thomas Wolfe
Raisbeck, Kenneth

STEAM INTELLECT SOCIETY
Crotchet Castle (1831)
by Thomas Love Peacock
Society for the Diffusion of Useful
 Knowledge

STEENSON, Willie (Wandering
 Willie)
Redgauntlet (1824)
by Sir Walter Scott
Metcalf, John
Williams ap Prichard

STEERFORTH, James
David Copperfield (1849–50)
by Charles Dickens
Stroughill, George

STEIN
Lord Jim (1900)
by Joseph Conrad
Allen, Charles
Bernstein, Dr
Lingard, Captain William
Mesman, Mr
Wallace, Alfred Russel

STEIN & ROSEN
The Web and the Rock (1939)
by Thomas Wolfe
Bergdorf-Goodman Company, New
 York

STELLA
See Toobad, Celinda

STENER, George W.
The Financier (1912)
by Theodore Dreiser
Marcer, Joseph F.

STEPHENSON, Oscar
The Prodigal Son (1904)
by Hall Caine
Rossetti, Dante Gabriel

STERLING, Dr
The Old Wives' Tale (1908)
by Arnold Bennett
Russell, Dr John

STERLING, Bob
Look Homeward, Angel (1929)
by Thomas Wolfe
Burdick, Edmund

STERLING, David
Work (1873)
by Louisa M. Alcott
Thoreau, Henry David

STEVIE
The Secret Agent (1907)
by Joseph Conrad
Bourdin, Martial

The STEWARD OF THE SAILORS'
    HOME
The Shadow-Line (1917)
by Joseph Conrad
Phillips, C.J.

STEYNE, Marquis of
Vanity Fair (1847–8)
by W.M. Thackeray
Fitzhardinge, Lord
Hertford, 3rd Marquess of

STEYNLIN, Madame
South Wind (1917)
by Norman Douglas
Grein, Clara

STICKLEFORD
Wessex novels and tales (1871–95)
by Thomas Hardy
Tincleton, Dorset

STILLINGFLEET, Roger
The Ordeal of Gilbert Pinfold (1957)
by Evelyn Waugh
Sykes, Christopher[2]

STITCH, Algernon
Scoop (1938) and the *Sword of
    Honour* trilogy (1952–61)
by Evelyn Waugh
Cooper, Alfred Duff

STITCH, Julia
Scoop (1938) and the *Sword of
    Honour* trilogy (1952–61)
by Evelyn Waugh
Cooper, Lady Diana

STOBHALL, Miss
The Simple Life Limited (1911)
by Ford Madox Ford
Garnett, Constance
Garnett, Olive

STOCKTON, Mr
The New Republic (1877)
by W.H. Mallock
Tyndall, John

STODDARD, Cynthia
Gin and Bitters (1931)
by Elinor Mordaunt
Maugham, Syrie

STOKE-BAREHILLS
Jude the Obscure (1895)
by Thomas Hardy
Basingstoke, Hampshire

STOKES, Melian
Pugs and Peacocks (1921) and
    Sembal (1922)
by Gilbert Cannan
Russell, Bertrand

STONE, Dittany
Love and Death (1939)
by Llewellyn Powys
Woolsey, Gamel

STONE, Harvey
The Sun Also Rises (1926)
by Ernest Hemingway
Stearns, Harold

STONYSHIRE
Adam Bede (1859)
by George Eliot
Derbyshire

STORKS, Mr
The New Republic (1877)
by W.H. Mallock
Huxley, T.H.

STORN
The Dark Island (1934)
by Victoria Sackville-West
St Michael's Mount, Cornwall

STOURCASTLE
Tess of the d'Urbervilles (1891)
by Thomas Hardy
Sturminster Newton, Dorset

STOYTE, JOSEPH PAUL
After Many a Summer (1939)
by Aldous Huxley
Hearst, William Randolph

STRANGEWAYS, NIGEL
A Question of Proof (1935) and
 others
by Nicholas Blake
Auden, W.H.

STRATLEIGH
A Pair of Blue Eyes (1873)
by Thomas Hardy
Bude, Cornwall

STREET OF WELLS
Wessex novels and tales (1871–95)
by Thomas Hardy
Fortune's Well, Portland, Dorset

STRELLEY MILL
The White Peacock (1911)
by D.H. Lawrence
Felley Mill, Nottinghamshire
Haggs Farm, Nottinghamshire

STRETHER, LEWIS LAMBERT
The Ambassadors (1903)
by Henry James
Howells, William Dean

STRETT, SIR LUKE
The Wings of the Dove (1902)
by Henry James
Baldwin, William Wilberforce
Clark, Sir Andrew

STRICKLAND
Plain Tales from the Hills (1888)
by Rudyard Kipling
Christie, Mr[1]
Goad, Horace B.

STRICKLAND, AMY
The Moon and Sixpence (1919)
by W. Somerset Maugham
Colefax, Sybil, Lady

STRICKLAND, CHARLES
The Moon and Sixpence (1919)
by W. Somerset Maugham
Gauguin, Paul
John, Augustus

STRIKE, MAJOR
Evan Harrington (1860)
by George Meredith
Ellis, Sir Samuel Burdon

STRIKE, MRS
Evan Harrington (1860)
by George Meredith
Ellis, Catherine Matilda, Lady

STRINGHAM, CHARLES
A Dance to the Music of Time
 (1951–76)
by Anthony Powell
Duggan, Hubert

STROEVE, DIRK
The Moon and Sixpence (1919)
by W. Somerset Maugham
Schuffenecker, Claude Emile

STRONG, DR
David Copperfield (1849–50)
by Charles Dickens
Birt, John
Valpy, Richard
Wallace, George

STRONG, EDWARD
The History of Pendennis (1848–50)
by W.M. Thackeray
Glynn, Henry

STRONG, GEORGE
Esther (1884)
by Henry Adams
King, Clarence

STRONG, Mildmay
'Calmuck', *Heads and Tails* (1859)
by Robert Barnabas Brough
Hunt, Holman

Dr STRONG'S SCHOOL
David Copperfield (1849–50)
by Charles Dickens
King's School, Canterbury
Reading School, Berkshire

STRUTHERS
Aaron's Rod (1922)
by D.H. Lawrence
John, Augustus

STRUTHERS, Willie
Kangaroo (1923)
by D.H. Lawrence
Holman, James
Hopkin, William

STRYVER, C.J.
A Tale of Two Cities (1859)
by Charles Dickens
James, E.J.
Wetherell, Sir Charles

STUBBS, Victor
'Disintegration of a Politician', *The Dawn's Delay* (1924)
by Hugh Kingsmill
Asquith, H.H.

STUCCO, Mr
Vivian Grey (1826–7)
by Benjamin Disraeli
Nash, John

STUFFINGTON
'Notes on the North What-d'ye-Callem Election' (1841)
by W.M. Thackeray
Darlington, County Durham

STURT, The Revd Henry (Father Sturt)
A Child of the Jago (1896)
by Arthur Morrison
Jay, Revd Austin Osborne

SULACO
Nostromo (1904)
by Joseph Conrad
Valencia, Venezuela

SUMMER STREET
A Room with a View (1908)
by E.M. Forster
Holmbury St Mary, Surrey

SUMMERSOFT
'The Lesson of the Master' (1888)
by Henry James
Osterley Park, Middlesex

SUMMERSON, Esther
Bleak House (1852–3)
by Charles Dickens
Hogarth, Georgina[2]

SUMMERTUNE, Essex
The Four Winds of Love: The South Wind (1937)
by Compton Mackenzie
Chesham, Buckinghamshire

SUNDAY
The Man Who was Thursday (1908)
by G.K. Chesterton
Walker, F.W.

SURBITON, Lord
A Romance of the Nineteenth Century (1881)
by W.H. Mallock
Lytton, Bulwer
Milnes, Richard Monckton

SURROGATE, Philip
It's a Battlefield (1934)
by Graham Greene
Murry, John Middleton

SURVIVAL
The *Sword of Honour* trilogy (1952–61)
by Evelyn Waugh
Horizon

SUTHERLAND, Markham
The Nemesis of Faith (1849)
by James Anthony Froude
Froude, James Anthony

SUTTON, Daniel
'The Primrose Path' (1922)
by D.H. Lawrence
Beardsall, Herbert

S.W., Mr
Orlando (1928)
by Virginia Woolf
Waterlow, Sydney

SWAN
Young People (1958)
by William Cooper
Snow, C.P.

SWANCOURT, Elfride
A Pair of Blue Eyes (1873)
by Thomas Hardy
Hardy, Emma

SWANSON, Governor
The Titan (1914)
by Theodore Dreiser
Altgeld, John Peter

SWEEDLEPIPE, Paul
Martin Chuzzlewit (1843–4)
by Charles Dickens
Turner, William[1]

SWEETING, David
Shirley (1849)
by Charlotte Brontë
Bradley, Revd James Chesterton

SWIFT, Jonathan
More Women than Men (1933)
by I. Compton-Burnett
Butler, Samuel

SWIFT, St Leger
Helen (1834)
by Maria Edgeworth
Waite, Mr

SWIVELLER, Dick
The Old Curiosity Shop (1840–1)
by Charles Dickens
D'Orsay, Count

SWYNFEN, Reginald
Two Plunges for a Pearl (1872)
by Mortimer Collins
Swinburne, Algernon Charles

SYBIL
'Carrots': Just a Little Boy (1878)
by Mrs Molesworth
Höhler, Agnes Venetia

SYDENHAM, Oswald
Joan and Peter (1918)
by H.G. Wells
Johnston, Sir Harry

SYDNEY, Lord Henry
Coningsby (1844) and *Tancred* (1847)
by Benjamin Disraeli
Manners, Lord John

SYMONDS
Aylwin (1899)
by Theodore Watts-Dunton
Leyland, Frederick Richards

SYNESIUS, Bishop
Hypatia (1853)
by Charles Kingsley
Kingsley, Charles

SYNTHESIS OF ART STUDIES
The Coast of Bohemia (1893)
by W.D. Howells
The Art Students' League

T

T—— (the Teacher of Oratory)
Lavengro (1851)
by George Borrow
Thelwall, John

T. , GENERAL
Under Western Eyes (1911)
by Joseph Conrad
Trepov, Dimitri Fedorovich

TADPOLE
Coningsby (1844)
by Benjamin Disraeli
Pringle, Alexander

TAFFY
See WYNNE, Talbot

TAGGART
Lavengro (1851)
by George Borrow
Tabart, Benjamin

THE TAILOR OF GLOUCESTER
The Tailor of Gloucester (1902)
by Beatrix Potter
Prichard, John Samuel

TALBOT, COLONEL
Waverley (1814)
by Sir Walter Scott
Whitefoord, Charles

TALBOT, CHRISTIAN
The Pursuit of Love (1945)
by Nancy Mitford
Rodd, Peter

TALBOT, FLORRY
Ulysses (1922)
by James Joyce
Crawford, Fleury

TANTAMOUNT, LORD EDWARD
Point Counter Point (1928)
by Aldous Huxley
Haldane, J.S.

TANTAMOUNT, LUCY
Point Counter Point (1928)
by Aldous Huxley
Cunard, Nancy

TAPER, MR
Coningsby (1844)
by Benjamin Disraeli
Ross, Charles

TARN, PAMELA
'After the Fireworks' (1930)
by Aldous Huxley
de Villeneuve, Léontine

TARTAR
Shirley (1849)
by Charlotte Brontë
Keeper

TASKOVER, THEODORE
The Quick and the Dead (1914)
by Edwin Pugh
Wells, H.G.

TATE, MR
*A Portrait of the Artist as a Young
   Man* (1916)
by James Joyce
Dempsey, George Stanislaus

TAYLOE, JUDGE WEBSTER
Look Homeward, Angel (1929)
by Thomas Wolfe
Sondley, Webster

TAYLOR, MR
National Velvet (1935)
by Enid Bagnold
McHardy

TAYLOR, GEORGE
Pilgrimage (1915–67)
by Dorothy Richardson
Daniel, Charles

TED
A Christmas Child (1880)
by Mrs Molesworth
Hutton, Thomas Grindal

TELLSON'S BANK
A Tale of Two Cities (1859)
by Charles Dickens
Child's Bank, Strand, London

TEMPEST, LESLIE
The White Peacock (1911)
by D.H. Lawrence
Neville, G.H.

TEMPEST, Rhoda
A Terrible Temptation (1871)
by Charles Reade
Walters, Catherine ('Skittles')

TEMPEST WARRALL & CO.
The White Peacock (1911)
by D.H. Lawrence
Barber Walker & Co.

TEMPLE
*A Portrait of the Artist as a Young
    Man* (1916)
by James Joyce
Elwood, John Rudolph

TEMPLE, Miss
Jane Eyre (1847)
by Charlotte Brontë
Evans, Anne
Thompson, Jane

TEMPLE, Claire
There Were No Windows (1946)
by Norah Hoult
Hunt, Violet

TEMPLE, Henrietta
Henrietta Temple (1837)
by Benjamin Disraeli
Sykes, Henrietta, Lady

TEMPLECOMBE, Lady
The Edwardians (1930)
by Victoria Sackville-West
Londonderry, Lady

TEMPLECOMBE, Lord
The Edwardians (1930)
by Victoria Sackville-West
Londonderry, Lord

TEMPLER, Peter
A Dance to the Music of Time
    (1951–76)
by Anthony Powell
Spencer, John

TEMPLETON, Elliott
The Razor's Edge (1944)
by W. Somerset Maugham
Channon, Sir Henry ('Chips')
May, Henry

TENDERDEN, Lady
The Exclusives (1830)
by Lady Charlotte Bury
Tankerville, Lady

TERCANBURY
Of Human Bondage (1915)
by W. Somerset Maugham
Canterbury

TEUFELSDRÖCKH, Diogenes
Sartor Resartus (1833–4)
by Thomas Carlyle
Carlyle, Thomas

TEVERSHALL
Lady Chatterley's Lover (1928)
by D.H. Lawrence
Eastwood, Nottinghamshire

THATCHER, Judge Joseph
Chosen Country (1951)
by John Dos Passos
Price, William Samson

THEALE, Milly
The Wings of the Dove (1902)
by Henry James
James, Alice
Temple, Mary ('Minny')

THERESA
*The Autobiography of Mark
    Rutherford* (1881)
by Mark Rutherford
Eliot, George

THE THIRD GENTLEMAN
Hard Times (1854)
by Charles Dickens
Cole, Sir Henry

THOMAS, Mr
'The Old Adam' (1934)
by D.H. Lawrence
Jones, John William

THOMAS, Mrs
'The Old Adam' (1934)
by D.H. Lawrence
Jones, Marie

THOMAS, Helen
Things As They Are (1950)
by Gertrude Stein
Bookstaver, May

THORAH, Sydney
Nicholas Crabbe (1958)
by F.W. Rolfe
Harland, Henry

THORLEY, Henry, Lord
Robin Linnet (1919)
by E.F. Benson
Balfour, A.J.

THORNBERRY, Job
Endymion (1880)
by Benjamin Disraeli
Bright, John
Cobden, Richard
Potter, Thomas Bayley

THORNFIELD HALL
Jane Eyre (1847)
by Charlotte Brontë
Norton Conyers, Yorkshire
The Rydings, Birstall, Yorkshire

THORNHIRST, Sir Anthony
The Reflections of Ambrosine (1902)
by Elinor Glyn
Finch, Seymour Wynne

THORNICROFT, Stephen
Thornicroft's Model (1873)
by Mrs Alfred Hunt
Rossetti, Dante Gabriel

THORNTON, Cyril
The Youth and Manhood of Cyril Thornton (1827)
by Thomas Hamilton
O'Hara, Charles

THORNTON, Helen
Fernhurst (1971)
by Gertrude Stein
Thomas, Carey

THORNTON, Thomas
Pelham (1828)
by Bulwer Lytton
Thurtell, John

THORNWELL, Cornelia
Boston (1928)
by Upton Sinclair
Burton, Mrs

The THREE MARINERS
The Mayor of Casterbridge (1886)
by Thomas Hardy
The King of Prussia, Dorchester, Dorset

THRUSHCROSS GRANGE
Wuthering Heights (1847)
by Emily Brontë
Ponden Hall, Yorkshire

THURLOE, Roger
The Great Days (1958)
by John Dos Passos
Forrestal, James

THURNALL, Tom
Two Years Ago (1857)
by Charles Kingsley
Kingsley, George Henry

TIBER, Mr
Jo's Boys (1886)
by Louisa M. Alcott
Niles, Thomas

TIERNAN, Michael
The Titan (1914)
by Theodore Dreiser
Coughlin, John

TIETJENS, Christopher
Parade's End (1924–8)
by Ford Madox Ford
Marwood, Arthur

TILCHESTER, Lady
The Reflections of Ambrosine (1902)
by Elinor Glyn
Warwick, Frances, Lady

TILLIE
Alice's Adventures in Wonderland
(1865)
by Lewis Carroll
Liddell, Edith

TILLING
Queen Lucia (1920) and others
by E.F. Benson
Rye, Sussex

TILLOTSON, Walter
'The Tillotson Banquet' (1924)
by Aldous Huxley
Melvill, Harry

TILNEY, Lady
The Exclusives (1830)
by Lady Charlotte Bury
Jersey, Countess of

TILTWOOD, Dick
Memoirs of a Fox-Hunting Man
(1928)
by Siegfried Sassoon
Thomas, David

TIMBERLANE, Cass
Cass Timberlane (1945)
by Sinclair Lewis
Lewis, Sinclair

TIMOTHEUS
'The Proser IV – On a Good-Looking
Young Lady' (1850)
by W.M. Thackeray
Taylor, Sir Henry

TINMAN, Martin
The House on the Beach (1877)
by George Meredith
Busby, Mr

TIPTOFF, Captain Granby
The History of Pendennis (1848–50)
by W.M. Thackeray
Calcraft, Granby Hales

TISDALE, Walter
Dawn (1931)
by Theodore Dreiser
Brennan, Austin

TIVWORTHY
'The Romantic Adventures of a
Milkmaid' (1913)
by Thomas Hardy
Tiverton, Devon

TLACOLULA
The Plumed Serpent (1926)
by D.H. Lawrence
Coyoacán, Mexico

TOAD, Mr
The Wind in the Willows (1908)
by Kenneth Grahame
Grahame, Alistair

TOAD HALL
The Wind in the Willows (1908)
by Kenneth Grahame
Cliveden, Buckinghamshire
Harleyford Manor,
Buckinghamshire
Mapledurham House, Oxfordshire

TOBIN, Wiltshire
Monday Night (1938)
by Kay Boyle
Stearns, Harold

TODD, Miss
The Bertrams (1859)
by Anthony Trollope
Cobbe, Frances Power

TODD, JAMES
A Handful of Dust (1934)
by Evelyn Waugh
Christie, Mr[2]

TODD, LAWRIE
Lawrie Todd (1830)
by John Galt
Thorburn, Grant

TOFT END
Anna of the Five Towns (1902) and
    others
by Arnold Bennett
Sneyd Green, Staffordshire

TOLCHURCH
Desperate Remedies (1871)
by Thomas Hardy
Tolpuddle, Dorset

TOLLAMORE
'An Indiscretion in the Life of an
    Heiress' (1878)
by Thomas Hardy
Stinsford, Dorset

TOLLAMORE HOUSE
'An Indiscretion in the Life of an
    Heiress' (1878)
by Thomas Hardy
**Kingston Maurward House,
    Stinsford, Dorset**

TOM
The Water Babies (1863)
by Charles Kingsley
Seaward, James

TOM
An Island Cabin (1902)
by Arthur Henry
Dreiser, Theodore

TOM, UNCLE
Uncle Tom's Cabin (1851–2)
by Harriet Becher Stowe
Henson, Josiah

TOMLINSON, MR
'Janet's Repentance', *Scenes of
    Clerical Life* (1857–8)
by George Eliot
Hinks, Mr

TOMLINSON, AUGUSTUS
Paul Clifford (1830)
by Bulwer Lytton
The Whigs

TONEBOROUGH
Wessex novels and tales (1871–95)
by Thomas Hardy
Taunton, Somerset

TONER, ADRIENNE
Adrienne Toner (1921)
by Anne Douglas Sedgwick
Childers, Mary Alden

TOOBAD, MR
Nightmare Abbey (1818)
by Thomas Love Peacock
Newton, John Frank

TOOBAD, CELINDA ('STELLA')
Nightmare Abbey (1818)
by Thomas Love Peacock
Clairmont, Claire
Hitchener, Elizabeth
Shelley, Mary Wollstonecraft

TOODLE, POLLY
Dombey and Son (1846–8)
by Charles Dickens
Hayes, Mrs

TOOGOOD, MR
Crotchet Castle (1831)
by Thomas Love Peacock
Owen, Robert

TOOGOOD, REVD BILLY
'Audrey Satchel and the Parson'
    (1894)
by Thomas Hardy
Butler, Revd William

TOPE, Mr
Edwin Drood (1870)
by Charles Dickens
Miles, Mr

TOPPING ABBEY
Daniel Deronda (1876)
by George Eliot
Lacock Abbey, Wiltshire
Maxstoke Priory, Warwickshire

TOR-UPON-SEA
'A Mere Interlude' (1913)
by Thomas Hardy
Torquay, Devon

TOUCHANDGO, Timothy
Crotchet Castle (1831)
by Thomas Love Peacock
Stephenson, Rowland

TOUCHETT, Ralph
The Portrait of a Lady (1880)
by Henry James
Sturges, Jonathan

TOUCHWOOD, Mr
St Ronan's Well (1823)
by Sir Walter Scott
Platoff, Count

TOUGHGUT
See Towgood ('Toughgut')

TOURNEUR, Stephen
The Story of Elizabeth (1863)
by Lady Ritchie
Monod, Adolphe

TOWERS, Duchess of
Peter Ibbetson (1891)
by George Du Maurier
Sitwell, Lady Ida

TOWERS, Tom
The Warden (1855)
by Anthony Trollope
Venables, George Stovin

TOWGOOD
Sartor Resartus (1833–4)
by Thomas Carlyle
Irving, Edward

TOWGOOD ('TOUGHGUT')
Sartor Resartus (1833–4)
by Thomas Carlyle
Buller, Charles, the Younger

TOWN, Max
Heritage (1984)
by Anthony West
Wells, H.G.

TOWNELEY
The Way of All Flesh (1903)
by Samuel Butler
Pauli, Charles Paine

TOWNSEND, Constance
'Now Lies She There', *Soft Answers*
    (1932)
by Richard Aldington
Cunard, Nancy

TOWNSEND, Morris
Washington Square (1881)
by Henry James
Kemble, Henry

TOZER, Leora
Arrowsmith (1925)
by Sinclair Lewis
De Kruif, Rhea E.
Summers, Edith

TRADDLES, Thomas
David Copperfield (1849–50)
by Charles Dickens
Talfourd, Thomas Noon

TRAFALGAR ROAD
The *Clayhanger* trilogy (1910–16)
by Arnold Bennett
Waterloo Road, Burslem,
    Staffordshire

TRAFFORD, Barton
Cakes and Ale (1930)
by W. Somerset Maugham
Colvin, Sir Sidney

TRAFFORD, Mrs Barton
Cakes and Ale (1930)
by W. Somerset Maugham
Colvin, Lady

TRANTRIDGE
Wessex novels and tales (1871–95)
by Thomas Hardy
Pentridge, Dorset
Tarrant Hinton, Dorset

TRAPNEL, Xavier Francis
A Dance to the Music of Time
(1951–76)
by Anthony Powell
Maclaren-Ross, Julian

TREBECK, Mr
Granby (1826)
by T.H. Lister
Brummell, Beau

TREBY MAGNA
Felix Holt, the Radical (1866)
by George Eliot
Coventry, Warwickshire

TREGARVA
Yeast (1848)
by Charles Kingsley
Carlyle, Thomas

TRELAWNEY, Dr
A Dance to the Music of Time
(1951–76)
by Anthony Powell
Crowley, Aleister

TRELAWNEY, Lady
See Seymour, Frances

TRELAWNEY, Lord
Glenarvon (1816)
by Lady Caroline Lamb
Morpeth, Lord

TREMAINE, Canon
Sweet and Twenty (1875)
by Mortimer Collins
Hawker, Revd Robert Stephen

TREMAINE, Bertie
Endymion (1880)
by Benjamin Disraeli
Lytton, Bulwer

TRENT, Nell ('Little Nell')
The Old Curiosity Shop (1840–1)
by Charles Dickens
Hogarth, Mary Scott

TREPTE, Herr Regierungsrat
'The Captain's Doll' (1923)
by D.H. Lawrence
von Schreibershofen, Max

TRESSADY, Sir George
Sir George Tressady (1896)
by Mrs Humphry Ward
Dugdale, William Stratford

TRESSEL, Tommy
The Rebel Rose (1888)
by Justin McCarthy and Mrs
Campbell Praed
Labouchère, Henry du Pré

TREVOR, Alan
'The Model Millionaire' (1891)
by Oscar Wilde
Delacroix, Eugène

TREWHELLA, Jaz
Kangaroo (1923)
by D.H. Lawrence
Hawken, Mr

The *TRIFLER*
The Man from the North (1898)
by Arnold Bennett
Tit-Bits

TRILLO, Mr
Crotchet Castle (1831)
by Thomas Love Peacock
Moore, Thomas

TRIMMER
The *Sword of Honour* trilogy
 (1952–61)
by Evelyn Waugh
Lovat, Simon Fraser, Lord

TRIPPLEGATE
'The Sad Fortunes of the Revd Amos
 Barton', *Scenes of Clerical Life*
 (1857–8)
by George Eliot
Higham on the Hill, Leicestershire

TROIL, ULLA
See NORNA OF THE FITFUL HEAD

TROTWOOD, BETSEY
David Copperfield (1849–50)
by Charles Dickens
Strong, Mary Pearson

TRUFAL
'A Mere Interlude' (1913)
by Thomas Hardy
Truro, Cornwall

TRYAN, REVD EDGAR
'Janet's Repentance', *Scenes of
 Clerical Life* (1857–8)
by George Eliot
Jones, Revd John Edmund

TRYERS, REGGIE
The Buffoon (1916)
by Louis Wilkinson
Lyon, Thomas Henry

TUBBS, A. DEWITT
Arrowsmith (1925)
by Sinclair Lewis
Flexner, Simon

TUCKMAN, BLACKBURN
Beauchamp's Career (1876)
by George Meredith
Hardman, Sir William

TUDOR, CHARLEY
The Three Clerks (1857)
by Anthony Trollope
Trollope, Anthony

TUFT, VENOM
Ten Thousand a Year (1841)
by Samuel Warren
Hayward, Abraham

TULKINGHORN, MR
Bleak House (1852–3)
by Charles Dickens
Blackmore, Edward

TULLIVER, EDWARD
The Mill on the Floss (1860)
by George Eliot
Evans, Robert
Pagden, John

TULLIVER, MAGGIE
The Mill on the Floss (1860)
by George Eliot
Eliot, George

TULLIVER, TOM
The Mill on the Floss (1860)
by George Eliot
Evans, Isaac

TULLY-VEOLAN
Waverley (1814)
by Sir Walter Scott
Craighall, Perthshire
Ravelston House, Edinburgh

TURNBULL, MP, MR
Can You Forgive Her? (1864)
by Anthony Trollope
Bright, John

TURNHILL
Anna of the Five Towns (1902) and
 others
by Arnold Bennett
Tunstall, Staffordshire

TURTLES CLUB
The *Sword of Honour* trilogy
 (1952–61)
by Evelyn Waugh
Boodles Club, London

TURVEYDROP, Mr
Bleak House (1852–3)
by Charles Dickens
Skelton, John Henry

TWEED-IN-BLOOD, Tilly
The Ladies Almanack (1928)
by Djuna Barnes
Troubridge, Una, Lady

TWEEDY, Major
Ulysses (1922)
by James Joyce
Powell, Major

TWEMLOW, Melvin
Our Mutual Friend (1864–5)
by Charles Dickens
Townshend, Chauncey Hare

TWO-HEARTED RIVER
'Big Two-Hearted River', *In Our
Time* (1925)
by Ernest Hemingway
Fox River, Michigan

TYRRELL, Thornton
Memoirs of an Infantry Officer
(1930)
by Siegfried Sassoon
Russell, Bertrand

TYSOE, Tylney
Mendel (1916)
by Gilbert Cannan
Marsh, Sir Edward

U

UNA
Puck of Pook's Hill (1906) and
Rewards and Fairies (1910)
by Rudyard Kipling
Kipling, Elsie

The UNCLE
A Christmas Child (1880)
by Mrs Molesworth
Jevons, William Stanley

UNDERWOOD, Sir Thomas
The New Heir (1871)
by Anthony Trollope
Trollope, Anthony

The UNIVERSE
Can You Forgive Her? (1864)
by Anthony Trollope
The Cosmopolitan Club, London

UPLANDTOWERS, Lord
'Barbara of the House of Grebe'
(1891)
by Thomas Hardy
Shaftesbury, 5th Earl of

UPPER MELLSTOCK
Wessex novels and tales (1871–95)
by Thomas Hardy
Higher Bockhampton, Dorset

UPRISING OF THE THIRTY
THOUSAND
The Nine-tenths (1911)
by James Oppenheimer
Uprising of the Twenty Thousand

URQUHART, Mary Henrietta
'The Princess' (1925)
by D.H. Lawrence
Brett, Dorothy

URSO, Raphael
Book of Dreams (1960) and
Desolation Angels (1965)
by Jack Kerouac
Corso, Gregory

UTHWART, Emerald
'Emerald Uthwart' (1892)
by Walter Pater
Urquhart, Francis Fortescue

V

VALHUBERT, Charles-Edouard,
Marquis de
The Blessing (1951)
by Nancy Mitford
Palewski, Gaston

VALHUBERT, Grace, Marquise de
Don't Tell Alfred (1960)
by Nancy Mitford
Mitford, Nancy

VAMP, Mr
Melincourt (1817)
by Thomas Love Peacock
Gifford, William

VAN LEEUWEN, Jan
Barred (1932)
by Edward de Nève
de Nève, Edward

VAN LEEUWEN, Stania
Barred (1932)
by Edward de Nève
Rhys, Jean

VAN VLEECK, Paul
The Web and the Rock (1939)
by Thomas Wolfe
Van Vechten, Carl

VANBOROUGH, Dolly
Old Kensington (1873)
by Lady Ritchie
Thackeray, Harriet

VANDELEUR, Margaret, Lady
'The Path of Duty' (1884)
by Henry James
Grosvenor, Sibell Mary, Lady

VANE
Bid Me to Live (1960)
by H.D. (Hilda Doolittle)
Gray, Cecil

VANE, Dodo (Lady Chesterfield)
Dodo (1893)
by E.F. Benson
Asquith, Margot

VANE, Lady Isabel
East Lynne (1861)
by Mrs Henry Wood
Fane, Lady Augusta

VANECOURT, Lord Frank
Piccadilly (1870)
by Laurence Oliphant
Oliphant, Laurence[2]

VANZILE MOTOR CORPORATION
The Trail of the Hawk (1915)
by Sinclair Lewis
Frederick A. Stokes Company

VARNEY, Honoré Gabriel
Lucretia (1847)
by Bulwer Lytton
Wainewright, Thomas Griffiths

VASHTI
Villette (1853)
by Charlotte Brontë
Rachel, Éliza

VAUGHAN, Gilbert Hereford
The Limit (1911)
by Ada Leverson
Maugham, W. Somerset

VAVASOUR, Mr
Tancred (1847)
by Benjamin Disraeli
Milnes, Richard Monckton

VAVASOUR, Elsley (John Briggs)
Two Years Ago (1857)
by Charles Kingsley
Shelley, Percy Bysshe
Tennyson, Alfred, Lord

VAWDREY, Clare
'The Private Life' (1891)
by Henry James
Browning, Robert

VECK, Margaret ('Meg')
The Chimes (1844)
by Charles Dickens
Furley, Mary

VELOUR, Monsieur
Albert Lunel (1844)
by Lord Brougham
Leach, Sir John

VENGO, Andrea
Half a Loaf (1931)
by Grace Hegger Lewis
Piccoli, Raffaello

Uncle VENNER'S 'FARM'
The House of the Seven Gables (1851)
by Nathaniel Hawthorne
Salem, Massachusetts

VENTURIST SOCIETY
Marcella (1894)
by Mrs Humphry Ward
Fabian Society

VERDEN, Helena
The Trespasser (1912)
by D.H. Lawrence
Corke, Helen

VERE, Lord
Coningsby (1844)
by Benjamin Disraeli
Howard, Lord
Lyttelton, Lord

VERLOC, Adolf
The Secret Agent (1907)
by Joseph Conrad
Coulon, Auguste
Krieger, Adolf P.
Samuels, Henry B.

VERLOC, Winnie
The Secret Agent (1907)
by Joseph Conrad
Conrad, Jessie

VERMISSA
The Valley of Fear (1915)
by Arthur Conan Doyle
Pottsville, Pennsylvania

VERNON, Diana
Rob Roy (1817)
by Sir Walter Scott
Purgstall, Countess

VERUM, Dr
The Cantab (1926)
by Shane Leslie
Verrall, A.W.

The VIA
The Mayor of Casterbridge (1886)
by Thomas Hardy
Icening Way, Dorchester, Dorset

VIGO
Endymion (1880)
by Benjamin Disraeli
Hudson, George
Poole, Henry George

VILLAREL, Don Raffael de
The Arrow of Gold (1919)
by Joseph Conrad
Tristany, Don Rafael

VILLETTE
Villette (1853)
by Charlotte Brontë
Brussels

VILLIERS, Bud
The Plumed Serpent (1926)
by D.H. Lawrence
Johnson, Willard

VILLIERS, Edward
Lodore (1835)
by Mary Wollstonecraft Shelley
Shelley, Percy Bysshe

VILLIERS, Perdita
A Pier and a Band (1918)
by Mary MacCarthy
MacCarthy, Mary

VINCENT, LORD
Pelham (1828)
by Bulwer Lytton
Hook, Theodore

VINCENT, ARTHUR
Salem Chapel (1873)
by Margaret Oliphant
Irving, Edward

VINRACE, RACHEL
The Voyage Out (1915)
by Virginia Woolf
Woolf, Virginia

VIOLA, GIORGIO
Nostromo (1904)
by Joseph Conrad
Clerici, Enrico
Garibaldi, Giuseppe
Giuliolo, Giovanni ('Leggero')

THE VIOLET
Through the Looking-Glass (1872)
by Lewis Carroll
Liddell, Violet

VIS, VIVIDA
Vivian Grey (1826–7)
by Benjamin Disraeli
Croker, John Wilson

VITAL
The Fun House (1961)
by William Brinkley
Life **magazine**

VIVEASH, MYRA
Antic Hay (1923)
by Aldous Huxley
Cunard, Nancy

VIVIAN, COUNT
Glenarvon (1816)
by Lady Caroline Lamb
Byron, Lord

VIVIAN, GEOFFREY
A Modern Symposium (1905)
by G. Lowes Dickinson
Meredith, George

VLADIMIR, MR
The Secret Agent (1907)
by Joseph Conrad
Seliverskov, General

VLASTO, WINFIELD
'Rona Murtha', *A Gallery of Women*
(1929)
by Theodore Dreiser
Henry, Arthur

VOISIN, MADEMOISELLE
The Tragic Muse (1888–9)
by Henry James
Bartet, Jeanne Julia

VOLKBEIN, FELIX
Nightwood (1936)
by Djuna Barnes
Bruno, Guido

VON CHRONICLE, MR
Vivian Grey (1826–7)
by Benjamin Disraeli
de Sismondi, Jean

VON TRUMPETSON, COLONEL
Vivian Grey (1826–7)
by Benjamin Disraeli
Londonderry, 3rd Marquis of

VOTE, ROBIN
Nightwood (1936)
by Djuna Barnes
Wood, Thelma

VYSE, CECIL
A Room with a View (1908)
by E.M. Forster
Forster, E.M.

W

WADDILOVE STREET
'Our Street' (1848)
by W.M. Thackeray
Young Street, Kensington, London

WAGG, Mr
Vanity Fair (1847–8)
by W.M. Thackeray
Hook, Theodore

WAGNER, Jarry
Desolation Angels (1965)
by Jack Kerouac
Snyder, Gary

WAIT, James (the 'nigger')
The Nigger of the 'Narcissus' (1897)
by Joseph Conrad
Barron, Joseph
White, George

WAKEM, Philip
The Mill on the Floss (1860)
by George Eliot
D'Albert-Durade, François

WALCOTT
'Fifty Grand', *Men Without Women*
(1927)
by Ernest Hemingway
Leonard, Benny
Walker, Edward Michael

WALDERSHARE, George
Endymion (1880)
by Benjamin Disraeli
Manners, Lord John
Smythe, George

WALDMAN
*Frankenstein; or The Modern
Prometheus* (1818)
by Mary Wollstonecraft Shelley
Lind, James

WALES, Honoria
'Babylon Revisited' (1935)
by F. Scott Fitzgerald
Fitzgerald, Frances Scott

WALKENSHAW, Lady Atalanta
'Lady Tal', *Vanitas* (1892)
by Vernon Lee
Callander, Mrs Alice

WALKER, Mick
David Copperfield (1849–50)
by Charles Dickens
Fagin, Bob

WALLACE, Freddy
To Have and Have Not (1937)
by Ernest Hemingway
Russell, Joe

WALLINGER, Sir Joseph
Coningsby (1844)
by Benjamin Disraeli
Clay, Sir William

WALMER, Lady
The Two Friends (1835)
by Lady Blessington
Digby, Jane

WALSH, Peter
Mrs Dalloway (1925)
by Virginia Woolf
Stephen, Sir Harry

WANDERING WILLIE
See Steenson, Willie

WANDROUS, Gloria
BUtterfield 8 (1935)
by John O'Hara
Faithfull, Starr

WANNOP, Mrs
Parade's End (1924–8)
by Ford Madox Ford
Hunt, Margaret

WARBECK, David
The Pursuit of Love (1945)
by Nancy Mitford
Sackville-West, Edward

WARDOUR, Sir Arthur
The Antiquary (1816)
by Sir Walter Scott
Sinclair, Sir John
Whitefoord, Sir John

WARE, Randolph
The Web and the Rock (1939)
by Thomas Wolfe
Greenlaw, Edwin

WARKWORTH, Captain Henry
Lady Rose's Daughter (1903)
by Mrs Humphry Ward
Guibert, Jacques, Comte de

WARMINSTER, Alfred, Lord
A Dance to the Music of Time
  (1951–76)
by Anthony Powell
Orwell, George

WARNER, Dr
Chosen Country (1951)
by John Dos Passos
Hemingway, C.E.

WARNER, George Elbert
Chosen Country (1951)
by John Dos Passos
Hemingway, Ernest

WARREN
The Magician (1908)
by W. Somerset Maugham
Morrice, James Wilson

WARREN, Baby
Tender is the Night (1934)
by F. Scott Fitzgerald
Wiborg, Mary Hoyt

WARREN, Gemma (Jennifer)
The Gadfly (1897)
by Ethel Voynich
Wilson, Charlotte Mary

WARRINGTON, George
The History of Pendennis (1848–50)
by W.M. Thackeray
Crawford, George Malcolm
Venables, George Stovin

WARWICK, Adam
Moods (1865)
by Louisa M. Alcott
Thoreau, Henry David

WARWICK, Diana
Diana of the Crossways (1884)
by George Meredith
Norton, Caroline

WATERBATH
The Spoils of Poynton (1897)
by Henry James
Foxwarren Park, Surrey

WATERFORD, Rose
The Moon and Sixpence (1919)
by W. Somerset Maugham
Hunt, Violet

WATERHOUSE, Stephen Fenwick
Parade's End (1924–8)
by Ford Madox Ford
Masterman, C.F.

WATERLOO, Duke of
Vivian Grey (1826–7)
by Benjamin Disraeli
Wellington, Duke of

WATSON, James
Book of Dreams (1960)
by Jack Kerouac
Holmes, John Clellon

WAVERLEY
Waverley (1814)
by Sir Walter Scott
Stuart of Invernahyle, Alexander

WAYMARK, Osmund
The Unclassed (1884)
by George Gissing
Gissing, George

WEASEL, Timothy
The Dutchman's Fireside (1831)
by J.K. Paulding
Wetzel (or Weitzel), Lewis

WEATHERBURY
Wessex novels and tales (1871–95)
by Thomas Hardy
Puddletown, Dorset

WEATHERBURY UPPER FARM
Far from the Madding Crowd (1874)
by Thomas Hardy
Druce Farm, Puddletown, Dorset
Waterston House, Puddletown,
  Dorset

WEAVER, ROBERT
Of Time and the River (1935)
by Thomas Wolfe
Stevens, Henry

WEBBER, AMELIA
The Web and the Rock (1939)
by Thomas Wolfe
Wolfe, Julia

WEBBER, GEORGE
The Web and the Rock (1939) and
  You Can't Go Home Again (1940)
by Thomas Wolfe
Wolfe, Thomas

WEBBER, JOHN
The Web and the Rock (1939)
by Thomas Wolfe
Wolfe, William Oliver

WEBLEY, EVERARD
Point Counter Point (1928)
by Aldous Huxley
Mosley, Sir Oswald

WEEKS, ELMER
Adventures of a Young Man (1939)
by John Dos Passos
Browder, Earl

WEENER, FRITZ
Washington Jitters (1936)
by Dalton Trumbo
Frankfurter, Felix

WEIR, ADAM (LORD HERMISTON)
Weir of Hermiston (1896)
by R.L. Stevenson
Braxfield, Robert Macqueen, Lord

WELDON, VERGIL
Look Homeward, Angel (1929)
by Thomas Wolfe
Williams, Horace

WELLAND, AUGUSTA
The Age of Innocence (1920)
by Edith Wharton
Jones, Lucretia

WELLBRIDGE
Tess of the d'Urbervilles (1891)
by Thomas Hardy
Wool, Dorset

WELLER, SAMUEL
The Pickwick Papers (1836–7)
by Charles Dickens
Frazier, Richard
Vale, Samuel

WELLER, TONY
The Pickwick Papers (1836–7)
by Charles Dickens
Chumley, Old

WELLESLEY-CROOK, MRS MAISIE
The Roaring Queen (1973)
by Wyndham Lewis
Cunard, Maud ('Emerald'), Lady

WELLING, SENATOR
Revelry (1926)
by S.H. Hopkins
La Follette, Robert

WELLWOOD HOUSE
Agnes Grey (1847)
by Anne Brontë
Blake Hall, Mirfield, Yorkshire

WELSH, JACK
The Buffoon (1916)
by Louis Wilkinson
Powys, John Cowper

WEMMICK, JOHN
Great Expectations (1860–1)
by Charles Dickens
Ruskin, John

WEMYSS, Everard
Vera (1921)
by 'Elizabeth'
Russell, Francis, 2nd Earl

WENDOVER, Roger
Robert Elsmere (1888)
by Mrs Humphry Ward
Pattison, Mark

WENHAM, Mr
Vanity Fair (1847–8) and *The
   History of Pendennis* (1848–50)
by W.M. Thackeray
Croker, John Wilson

WENLOCK, Mr
Lady Connie (1916)
by Mrs Humphry Ward
Pattison, Mark

WENTWORTH, Mr
*De Vere; or The Man of
   Independence* (1827)
by Robert Plumer Ward
**Bolingbroke, Lord
Canning, George
Pitt, William, 1st Earl of Chatham
Pitt, William, the Younger**

WENTWORTH, Mr
The Europeans (1878)
by Henry James
Loring, Frank

WERNER, Frank
The Web and the Rock (1939)
by Thomas Wolfe
Moeller, Philip

WESSEX, Earl of
See Reynard, Stephen

WEST END, Sir Warwick
The Three Clerks (1857)
by Anthony Trollope
**Iddesleigh, Stafford Northcote, 1st
   Earl of**

WESTERLEIGH, Lord
The Return of William Shakespeare
   (1929)
by Hugh Kingsmill
Beaverbrook, Lord

WESTERN, Louisa Lily Denys
Sons and Lovers (1913)
by D.H. Lawrence
Dennis, Gypsy

WESTGATE HOUSE
The Pickwick Papers (1836–7)
by Charles Dickens
Eastgate House, Rochester, Kent

WESTLAKE
Diana of the Crossways (1884)
by George Meredith
Kinglake, A.W.

WESTLAKE, David
Parties (1930)
by Carl Van Vechten
Fitzgerald, F. Scott

WESTLAKE, Rilda
Parties (1930)
by Carl Van Vechten
Fitzgerald, Zelda

WESTON, Edward
Agnes Grey (1847)
by Anne Brontë
Weightman, William

WESTON, Hugh
Lions and Shadows (1938)
by Christopher Isherwood
Auden, W.H.

WEYDON-PRIORS
Wessex novels and tales (1871–95)
by Thomas Hardy
Weyhill, Hampshire

WHANE, Arthur
Big Sur (1962)
by Jack Kerouac
Watts, Alan Wilson

WHARTON, Mr
Esther (1884)
by Henry Adams
Bigelow, William Sturgis
La Farge, John
Saint-Gaudens, Augustus

WHELPDALE
New Grub Street (1891)
by George Gissing
Roberts, Morley

WHIFFLE, Peter
Peter Whiffle: His Life and Works (1922)
by Carl Van Vechten
Van Vechten, Carl

WHIPPLE, Nathan 'Shagpoke'
A Cool Million (1934)
by Nathanael West
Coolidge, Calvin

WHISPERING GLADES
The Loved One (1948)
by Evelyn Waugh
Forest Lawn, Glendale, California

WHITBREAD, Hugh
Mrs Dalloway (1925)
by Virginia Woolf
Morrell, Philip

WHITE, Jim
Mayor Harding of New York (1931)
by Stephen Endicott
Smith, Alfred Emanuel

The WHITE KNIGHT
Through the Looking-Glass (1872)
by Lewis Carroll
Dodgson, Charles (Lewis Carroll)

WHITEHEAD, Raymond
Stranger Come Home (1954)
by William L. Shirer
Shirer, William L.

WHITESTOCKE, Revd Frank
'The Curate's Walk', *Punch's Prize Novelists* (1853)
by W.M. Thackeray
Brookfield, William Henry

WHITFORD, Vernon
The Egoist (1879)
by George Meredith
Stephen, Sir Leslie

WHITMONBY, Mr
Diana of the Crossways (1884)
by George Meredith
Rogers, Samuel

WHITTLECOMBE
'The Sad Fortunes of the Revd Amos Barton', *Scenes of Clerical Life* (1857–8)
by George Eliot
Stockingford, Warwickshire

WICKETT, Terry
Arrowsmith (1925)
by Sinclair Lewis
Le Blanc, T.J.
Lewis, Sinclair
Northrop, J.H.

WICKFIELD, Agnes
David Copperfield (1849–50)
by Charles Dickens
Hogarth, Georgina[2]

WIDMERPOOL, Kenneth
A Dance to the Music of Time (1951–76)
by Anthony Powell
Manningham-Buller, Reginald

WILBECK, Dolores
Apropos of Dolores (1938)
by H.G. Wells
Keun, Odette

WILDERSPIN
Aylwin (1899)
by Theodore Watts-Dunton
Smetham, James

WILDFIRE, Madge
The Heart of Midlothian (1818)
by Sir Walter Scott
Feckless Fannie

WILFER, Bella
Our Mutual Friend (1864–5)
by Charles Dickens
Ternan, Ellen

WILHELM, Tommy
Seize the Day (1957)
by Saul Bellow
Schwartz, Delmore

WILKINS
Ann Veronica (1909)
by H.G. Wells
Wells, H.G.

Boon (1915)
by H.G. Wells
Wells, H.G.

WILKINSON, Peter
Goodbye to Berlin (1939)
by Christopher Isherwood
Robson-Scott, William

WILLEMS, Peter
An Outcast of the Islands (1896)
by Joseph Conrad
De Veer, Carel
Wallace, Alfred Russel

WILLERSLEY
The New Machiavelli (1911)
by H.G. Wells
Wallas, Graham

WILLEY FARM
Sons and Lovers (1913)
by D.H. Lawrence
Haggs Farm, Nottinghamshire

WILLEY WATER
Women in Love (1920)
by D.H. Lawrence
**Moorgreen Reservoir,
    Nottinghamshire**

WILLIAM, Aunt
See CROFTON, Mary

WILLIAMS, Eric
Eric; or Little by Little (1858)
by F.W. Farrar
Battersea, Cyril Flower, 1st Baron

WILLIAMS, 'Slogger'
Tom Brown's Schooldays (1857)
by Thomas Hughes
Jones, Bulkeley Owen

WILLIE, Wandering
See STEENSON, Willie

THE WILLOWS
Vera (1921)
by 'Elizabeth'
Telegraph House, Sussex

WILMERS, Dorset
Diana of the Crossways (1884)
by George Meredith
Greville, Charles

WILMERS, Henry
Diana of the Crossways (1884)
by George Meredith
Greville, Henry

WILSON, Alma
Pilgrimage (1915–67)
by Dorothy Richardson
Wells, Catherine ('Jane')

WILSON, Hypo
Pilgrimage (1915–67)
by Dorothy Richardson
Wells, H.G.

WILSON, Reine
'Your Obituary, Well Written' (1928)
by Conrad Aiken
Mansfield, Katherine

WILSON, Robert
'The Short Happy Life of Francis
    Macomber', *The Fifth Column*

and the First Forty-nine Stories
(1938)
by Ernest Hemingway
Percival, Philip

WILSON, TOM
Vanity of Duluoz (1968)
by Jack Kerouac
Holmes, John Clellon

WILSON-HARRIS
The Sun Also Rises (1926)
by Ernest Hemingway
Dorman-Smith, E.E.

WILTON, SIDNEY
Endymion (1880)
by Benjamin Disraeli
Herbert, Sidney

WILTSHIRE, LORD
The Gay-Dombeys (1919)
by Sir Harry Johnston
Salisbury, Lord

WIMBLEHURST
Tono-Bungay (1909)
by H.G. Wells
Midhurst, Sussex

WIMBUSH, ANNE
Crome Yellow (1921)
by Aldous Huxley
Huxley, Maria

WIMBUSH, HENRY
Crome Yellow (1921)
by Aldous Huxley
Sitwell, Sir George

Antic Hay (1923)
by Aldous Huxley
Morrell, Philip

WIMBUSH, PRISCILLA
Crome Yellow (1921)
by Aldous Huxley
Morrell, Lady Ottoline
Sitwell, Lady Ida

WIMSEY, LORD PETER
Murder Must Advertise (1933)
by Dorothy L. Sayers
Crichton, Charles
Whelpton, Eric

WINCHAM, BASIL
Don't Tell Alfred (1960)
by Nancy Mitford
Mosley, Oswald Alexander

WINDRIP, BERZELIUS ('BUZZ')
It Can't Happen Here (1935)
by Sinclair Lewis
Long, Huey P.
Winrod, Gerald B.

WINDSOR, ADRIAN, EARL OF
The Last Man (1826)
by Mary Wollstonecraft Shelley
Shelley, Percy Bysshe

WINIFRED
'England, My England' (1915)
by D.H. Lawrence
Lucas, Madeline

WINSLOW, RUTH
The Trail of the Hawk (1915)
by Sinclair Lewis
Lewis, Grace Hegger

WINSOME, MARK
The Confidence Man (1857)
by Herman Melville
Emerson, Ralph Waldo

WINTER, KATHY
The Winters (1932)
by Elizabeth Jenkins
Strachey, Pernel

WINTERBOURNE, LADY
Marcella (1894)
by Mrs Humphry Ward
Wemyss, Anne Frederica, Countess of

WINTONCESTER
Wessex novels and tales (1871–95)
by Thomas Hardy
Winchester, Hampshire

WITHERSPOON, Sɪʀ Hᴇʀʙᴇʀᴛ
'His Excellency', *Ashenden; or The
    British Agent* (1928)
by W. Somerset Maugham
Buchanan, Sir George

WITLA, Eᴜɢᴇɴᴇ
The 'Genius' (1915)
by Theodore Dreiser
Dreiser, Theodore
Shinn, Everett
Sonntag, William Louis

WITT, Rᴀᴄʜᴇʟ
'St Mawr' (1925)
by D.H. Lawrence
Humes, Mrs

WODGATE
Sybil (1845)
by Benjamin Disraeli
Willenhall, Staffordshire

WOLFSHIEM, Mᴇʏᴇʀ
The Great Gatsby (1925)
by F. Scott Fitzgerald
Rothstein, Arnold

WOLLASTON, Mʀ
*The Autobiography of Mark
    Rutherford* (1881)
by Mark Rutherford
Chapman, John

WOLSTENHOLME, Sɪʀ Cʜᴀʀʟᴇs
Ten Thousand a Year (1841)
by Samuel Warren
Lyndhurst, Lord

WOLSTENHOLME, Hᴇɴʀʏ
*William Langshawe, the Cotton
    Lord* (1842)
by Elizabeth Stone
Ashton, Thomas

WONTSEE, Wɪʟғᴜʟ
Crotchet Castle (1831)
by Thomas Love Peacock
Wordsworth, William

WOODBOURNE, Eʟɪᴢᴀʙᴇᴛʜ
Abbeychurch (1844)
by C.M. Yonge
Yonge, Charlotte

WOODCOCK, Mʀ
It is Never Too Late to Mend (1856)
by Charles Reade
Luckcock, Mr

WOODCOCK, Mʀs
'The Sad Fortunes of the Revd Amos
    Barton', *Scenes of Clerical Life*
    (1857–8)
by George Eliot
Craddock, Mrs

WOODCOCK, Sɪʀ Bᴜssʏ
The Autocracy of Mr Parham (1930)
by H.G. Wells
Beaverbrook, Lord

WOODHOUSE
The Lost Girl (1920)
by D.H. Lawrence
Eastwood, Nottinghamshire

WOODRUFF, Bᴇʀᴛ
Stranger Come Home (1954)
by William L. Shirer
Winchell, Walter

WOODSEER, Gᴏᴡᴇʀ
The Amazing Marriage (1895)
by George Meredith
Stevenson, Robert Louis

WOODSTOCK, Lᴏʀᴅ Rᴇɢɪɴᴀʟᴅ
The American Duchess (1890–1)
by W.F. Rae
Churchill, Lord Randolph

WOODVIEW
Esther Waters (1894)
by George Moore
**Buckingham House, Old
Shoreham, Sussex**

WOODWELL, Revd Mr
A Laodicean (1881)
by Thomas Hardy
Perkins, Revd Mr

WOOSTER, Bertram ('Bertie')
My Man Jeeves (1919) and others
by P.G. Wodehouse
**Kimberley, John Wodehouse, 3rd
Earl of**

WOOTTON, Lord Henry
The Picture of Dorian Gray (1891)
by Oscar Wilde
Leveson-Gower, Lord Ronald

WORDSWORTH HOUSE
Pilgrimage (1915–67)
by Dorothy Richardson
**Edgeworth House, Finsbury Park,
London**

WORDY, Mr
Coningsby (1844)
by Benjamin Disraeli
Alison, Sir Archibald

WORTHINGHAM, Mrs
'Crapey Cornelia' (1910)
by Henry James
Wharton, Edith

WRAGBY HALL
Lady Chatterley's Lover (1928)
by D.H. Lawrence
**Lamb Close House, Eastwood,
Nottinghamshire
Renishaw Hall, Derbyshire**

WRYKYN
The Gold Bat (1904)
by P.G. Wodehouse
Dulwich College, London

W.S.B.
See B.

WULLUS, Marta
Post Adolescence (1923)
by Robert McAlmon
Moore, Marianne

WUTHERING HEIGHTS
Wuthering Heights (1847)
by Emily Brontë
**High Sunderland Hall, Yorkshire
Top Withins, Yorkshire**

WYBROW, Anthony
'Mr Gilfil's Love Story', *Scenes of
Clerical Life* (1857–8)
by George Eliot
**Newdigate, Francis
Parker, Charles**

WYLD, Beatrice
Sons and Lovers (1913)
by D.H. Lawrence
Hall, Alice

WYNNE, Talbot ('Taffy')
Trilby (1894)
by George Du Maurier
**Prinsep, Val
Rowley, Joe**

X

X., Dr
Belinda (1801)
by Maria Edgeworth
Moore, John

X, Monsieur
'The Grande Malade' (1962)
by Djuna Barnes
Radiguet, Raymond

XTMNPQRTOSKLW, Prince
Vivian Grey (1826–7)
by Benjamin Disraeli
Gortchakoff, Prince

Y

Y., LORD
'Ennui', *Tales of Fashionable Life*
  (1809)
by Maria Edgeworth
Charlemont, Lord

YALBURY WOOD
Wessex novels and tales (1871–95)
by Thomas Hardy
Yellowham Wood, Dorset

YELLOWPLUSH, CHARLES JEAMES
The Yellowplush Correspondence
  (1837) and later works
by W.M. Thackeray
Skelton, John Henry

YEOBRIGHT, MR
The Return of the Native (1878)
by Thomas Hardy
Hardy, Thomas, the First

YEWSHOLT LODGE
'Barbara of the House of Grebe'
  (1891)
by Thomas Hardy
Farr House, Dorset

YOKNAPATAWPHA COUNTY
The Yoknapatawpha novels
  (1929–36)
by William Faulkner
Lafayette County, Mississippi

YORKE, DR
The Vicar of Langthwaite (1893)
by Lily Watson
Acworth, James

YORKE, HESTHER
Shirley (1849)
by Charlotte Brontë
Taylor, Ann

YORKE, HIRAM
Shirley (1849)
by Charlotte Brontë
Taylor, Joshua

YORKE, JESSY
Shirley (1849)
by Charlotte Brontë
Taylor, Martha

YORKE, ROSE
Shirley (1849)
by Charlotte Brontë
Taylor, Mary

YOUNG LADY ANARCHIST
'The Informer', *A Set of Six* (1908)
by Joseph Conrad
Angeli, Helen Rossetti

THE YOUNG MASTER
Tom Brown's Schooldays (1857)
by Thomas Hughes
Cotton, George Edward Lynch

THE YOUNG SECRETARY
Aylwin (1899)
by Theodore Watts-Dunton
Hake, George

YOUNGBROTHER, LORD
The Return of William Shakespeare
  (1929)
by Hugh Kingsmill
Rothermere, Lord

YUNDT, KARL
The Secret Agent (1907)
by Joseph Conrad
Bakunin, Michael
Most, Johann

Z

ZÄHDARM, GRAF
Sartor Resartus (1833–4)
by Thomas Carlyle
Buller, Charles, the Elder

ZÄHDARM, GRÄFIN
Sartor Resartus (1833–4)
by Thomas Carlyle
Buller, Isabella

ZALENSKA, Madame ('the Lady')
Three Weeks (1907)
by Elinor Glyn
**Alexandra Feodorovna, Empress of
  Russia**

ZELLI, Marya
Postures (1928)
by Jean Rhys
Rhys, Jean

ZENITH
Babbit (1922)
by Sinclair Lewis
Minneapolis, Minnesota

ZENOBIA
The Blithedale Romance (1852)
by Nathaniel Hawthorne
Fuller, Margaret

ZENOBIA
Endymion (1880)
by Benjamin Disraeli
Jersey, Countess of

ZIZI, 'Duke'
The Sun Also Rises (1926)
by Ernest Hemingway
Mitzicus, Demetrius

ZOSIM, Father
Under Western Eyes (1911)
by Joseph Conrad
Gapon, G.A.

Title Index